International Investments

The Addison-Wesley Series in Finance

Chambers/Lacey
Modern Corporate Finance:
Theory and Practice

Copeland/Weston
Financial Theory
and Corporate Policy

Dufey/Giddy
Cases in International Finance

Eakins
Finance: Investments,
Institutions, and Management

Eiteman/Stonehill/Moffett
Multinational Business Finance

Gitman
Principles of Managerial Finance

Gitman
Principles of Managerial Finance
—Brief Edition

Gitman/Joehnk
Fundamentals of Investing

Gitman/Madura
Introduction to Finance

Hughes/MacDonald
International Banking:
Text and Cases

Madura
Personal Finance

McDonald
Derivatives Markets

Megginson
Corporate Finance Theory

Melvin
International Money and Finance

Mishkin/Eakins
Financial Markets and Institutions

Moffett
Cases in International Finance

Moffett/Stonehill/Eiteman
Fundamentals of
Multinational Finance

Rejda
Principles of Risk Management
and Insurance

Solnik/McLeavey
International Investments

International Investments

FIFTH EDITION

Bruno Solnik
H.E.C. SCHOOL of MANAGEMENT

&

Dennis McLeavey
ASSOCIATION for INVESTMENT MANAGEMENT and RESEARCH

PEARSON

Addison
Wesley

Boston San Francisco New York
London Toronto Sydney Tokyo Singapore Madrid
Mexico City Munich Paris Cape Town Hong Kong Montreal

Editor in Chief: Denise Clinton
Sponsoring Editor: Donna Battista
Production Supervisor: Meredith Gertz
Production Services: Nesbitt Graphics, Inc.
Marketing Manager: Barbara LeBuhn
Cover and Interior Designer: Joyce Cosentino Wells
Senior Print Buyer: Hugh Crawford
Media Producer: Jennifer Pelland

Cover Image © 2003 EyeWire

Library of Congress Cataloging-in-Publication Data

Solnik, Bruno H., 1946–
       International investments / Bruno Solnik, Dennis McLeavey,—5th ed.
            p. cm. — (The Addison-Wesley series in finance)
       Includes bibliographical references and index.
       ISBN 0-201-78568-4
          1. Investments, Foreign. I. McLeavey, Dennis W. II. Title. III. Series.

    HG4538.S52 2003
    332.673'3—dc21

                                                                                    2003045954

    6 7 8 9 10—HT—06 05

Preface

Almost thirty years ago, Bruno Solnik published an article entitled "Why not diversify internationally rather than domestically?" in the *Financial Analysts Journal* (July/August 1974). At the time, U.S. pension funds had never invested outside of the United States. The situation was not very different in most other countries (except Britain) in which international investment by pension funds and other institutional investors was legally prohibited or regarded as exotic. Although European banks and private investors have long been international investors by cultural heritage as well as necessity (given the small size of most countries), institutional investors' guidelines often limited or prohibited international investments. Because institutional investors are large and sophisticated investors, their absence on the international scene was significant. Various forms of capital and currency controls constrained international investing. Few brokers or asset managers offered global services. Most corporations only reported annual accounts in their local language, and publicly available information was scarce and often unreliable. The combination of poor information, low expertise, stringent regulations, and high costs inhibited global investing. Thirty years later, the investment scene has changed dramatically.

Back in 1974, the world stock market capitalization stood below $1 trillion. Since the publication of the first edition of this book in 1988, the world stock market capitalization has passed the $25 trillion mark. Global debt markets have developed and opened up to foreign investors. Derivatives markets on financial instruments were in their infancy in 1974, but now provide major risk management instruments in all countries. It is now common to see U.S. pension funds with 10 percent or 20 percent of their assets invested internationally; individual investors have followed the trend, and the number of international mutual funds offered to American investors is astonishing. Non-U.S. investors hold extensive international investments. For example, ABP, the pension fund of Dutch civil servants and one of the largest in the world with total assets well over $100 billion, decided in 1989 to move from a purely domestic strategy to invest a growing percentage of its assets abroad. Dutch institutional investors now have more than 30 percent of their assets abroad.

The rapid pace of international investing is due to a change in mentality based on many factors. First, the benefits of international diversification in terms of risk and return have increasingly been recognized, as detailed in this book. This has led to a push toward guidelines and legislation more favorable to foreign investment. A second factor is the deregulation and internationalization of financial markets throughout the world. This global integration of financial markets has led to reduced costs, easier access to information, and the development of worldwide expertise by major financial institutions. In 1986, foreign organizations and banks were allowed to become members of the Tokyo and London stock exchanges. A similar step was taken in France in 1988 and is now the rule in all major countries. Computerized quotation and trading systems that allow global round-the-clock trading have been developed. At the start of 1990, restrictions to capital flows were removed within the countries of the European Union (EU); European-based investment management firms can freely market their products to residents of any EU member state. Hence, American or Japanese asset managers established in London can easily provide their services to any European client. This globalization of investment management has led to increased competition among money managers of all nationalities. It has also led to a wave of alliances, mergers, and acquisitions among financial institutions seeking to extend their international management expertise and the geographic coverage of their client base. A third factor is the general acceptance of a common set of standards and ethical principles by investment professionals. Debt issues are rated by the same rating agencies worldwide. Listed corporations are progressively adopting common or related international accounting standards. The Chartered Financial Analyst® (CFA®) designation of the Association for Investment Management and Research (AIMR®) has progressively been adopted as a standard by the worldwide investment profession. A majority of the CFA candidates are non-U.S. The AIMR Global Investment Performance Standards (AIMR-GIPS®) are adopted by institutional asset managers worldwide and are recognized as the leading global industry standard for ethical presentation of investment performance results.

Target Audience

This book is designed for CFA candidates, MBA students, and professionals working in the investment area. In some cases, it has been used for senior-level undergraduates majoring in finance. It is also used for students in master's programs in fields such as engineering or economics. To a large extent, the book is self-contained and does not take a specific national viewpoint (e.g., American); hence, it has been successfully used in courses and professional seminars throughout the world.

Structure of This Book

The international investor is faced with a complex task. The financial markets throughout the world are quite different from one another, and information on them is sometimes difficult to obtain. Trading in different time zones and languages further complicates the task. But the most important aspect of international investment is the use of multiple currencies. An American investing in France must do so in euros; therefore, the performance (and risk) of the investment will depend in part on changes in the euro/U.S. dollar exchange rate. Because of the importance of exchange rates in international investment, this book begins with a description of foreign exchange transactions.

In this text, we develop the analysis needed for the international investment and portfolio management process. The first three chapters lay the foundation of exchange rates, which link the economies of different countries and regions. In Chapter 1, we introduce the basic facts of foreign exchange quotation, their interpretation, and arbitrage implications. In Chapter 2, we develop the theory of international parity conditions. The theory helps in defining real foreign currency risk, an important factor to be managed in international investing and portfolio management. Chapter 3 then discusses the empirical validation of the theories introduced in Chapter 2 and explores the techniques and empirical results in the difficult task of exchange rate forecasting.

The next five chapters explore the various assets available for international investing. Chapter 4 is the lead chapter in a series of chapters on international assets. In it we develop international asset pricing in general with attention to foreign currency risk. Chapter 5 places a particular focus on the transaction costs involved in various equity markets and instruments allowing entry into international investments. Following this general introduction to international asset pricing, Chapters 6, 7, and 8 focus on the available international assets and investments themselves: equities, bonds, and alternative investments, respectively.

The final five chapters develop the techniques and perspective of international investment and portfolio management. After building the case for and against international diversification in Chapter 9, we move into the foreign currency risk and return analysis needed for international portfolio management. We develop the risk control techniques available with derivatives in Chapter 10 and then apply these techniques in currency risk management in Chapter 11. In Chapter 12, we examine the performance measures to judge the risk and return contributions of global diversification. Finally, we summarize the global investment and portfolio management process in Chapter 13. Throughout the text, we attempt to isolate those elements of the process that have unique international aspects.

Pedagogical Approach

To operate in a complex, multicurrency, multimarket, multicultural environment, you need a strong conceptual framework as well as a working knowledge of institutional aspects. Presenting concepts without resorting to lengthy theoretical expositions full of equations is a challenge. We have attempted to present all the major concepts and theories by illustrating their applications with numerous examples. Our guiding principle has been that rigor and intuition are equally necessary for a good understanding of the subject.

New to this edition, the "model-in-action" approach is used to integrate the chapter content. In the model-in-action approach, each chapter is motivated with questions of how to solve a valuation or portfolio management problem. These questions reflect the chapter's learning outcome statements found on the first page of each chapter. Examples are provided throughout the chapter to demonstrate answers to the questions and also to preview end-of-chapter problems. Thus the end-of-chapter problems should be familiar reinforcements for those students who have followed the learning outcome statements and worked through the examples of the chapter. The first twelve chapters end with a large number of problems and their solutions. Chapter 13, entitled "Structuring the Global Investment Process," ends with two case studies and proposed solutions.

A basic investment course is a useful prerequisite to this text. Some knowledge of international economics may also help in the early chapters. Familiarity with discounting techniques and basic statistics (e.g., standard deviation, correlation, and regression) will make some of the chapters easier to read. However, this book is intended to be accessible to students and portfolio managers without recent training in portfolio theory.

New to the Fifth Edition

As with the previous editions, this new edition provides students and practitioners with comprehensive yet accessible coverage of international investments. The authors have revised the book in a way that meets the needs of CFA candidates and prepares them for the CFA exams, while continuing to provide the coverage and accuracy our higher education adopters have come to expect. The fifth edition is a major revision in terms of both content and presentation. Major changes in terms of presentation have already been discussed. Besides the new model-in-action approach, the chapters have been reordered and some of them merged. In terms of content, this revision of the book focuses more on international applications. First, those aspects unique to international investments are key to the revision. Thus background material on bonds, swaps, futures, and options have been condensed. Second, more emphasis is placed on what is known from theory meeting the test of time rather than from empirical results that may be time-bound. For example, the chapter on the international asset-pricing model seeks to put the model into action and develops the valuation implications of the theory along with examples and illustrations. Empirical discussion has been shortened and a balance is sought between empirical results supporting and those not supporting theories under consideration.

- The material on foreign exchange presented in the first three chapters of the fourth edition has been rearranged. **Chapter 1** presents foreign exchange quotation and arbitrage relations with more precision. The coverage of the economic determinants of the exchange rate presented in **Chapter 2** has been strengthened. In **Chapter 3,** the empirical material from the original three chapters is gathered in one place so that the first two chapters can emphasize what is known from the theory in the original three chapters.

- **Chapter 4** (International Asset Pricing) replaces the old Chapter 5. We give more attention to foreign currency risk, valuation, and portfolio management.

- **Chapter 5** (Equity: Markets and Instruments) replaces the old Chapter 6. It places a particular focus on transaction costs.

- **Chapter 6** (Equity: Concepts and Techniques) is a new version of the old Chapter 7. It provides a new focus on global industry analysis and goes much deeper into equity valuation.

- **Chapter 7** (Global Bond Investing) merges the old Chapters 9 and 10. It also includes a section on structured notes, which were partly covered in the old Chapter 13. The coverage of institutional details and of basic bond valuation principles has been shortened. But it remains sufficient to make the chapter self-contained and is consistent with the presentation in other CFA readings.

- **Chapter 8** (Alternative Investments) is a more comprehensive version of the old Chapter 15. It now covers most forms of alternative investments and their valuation methods.

- **Chapter 9** (The Case for International Diversification) is a completely new version of the old Chapter 5. It presents arguments in favor and against international diversification in light of recent trends. It also discusses the case for investing in emerging markets.

- **Chapter 10** (Derivatives) introduces the basics of derivatives: principles, valuation, and usage. The chapter deals with forward, futures, options, and swap contracts that were previously covered in the old Chapters 11, 12, and 13. Most readers would have been introduced to derivatives before. This chapter is present for those who need a refresher and to make the book self-contained. It is used in Chapter 11.

- **Chapter 11** (Currency Risk Management) corresponds to the old Chapter 14. But the presentation has been improved and focused on implementation. A section on currency overlay has been added.

- **Chapter 12** (Global Performance Evaluation) is an extensively revised version of the old Chapter 16. It clearly differentiates the three steps of global performance evaluation: measurement, attribution, and appraisal.

- **Chapter 13** (Structuring the Global Investment Process) is an extensively revised version of the old Chapter 17. After a brief tour of the global investing industry, it reviews the various global investment philosophies that can be chosen. The chapter focuses on the various steps of the global portfolio management process: the formulation of an investment policy statement, the formulation of capital market expectations, the derivation of a strategic and tactical asset allocation as well as of a currency hedging policy, and performance evaluation. Two case studies serve as a review and application of the principles outlined in the chapter.

No specific chapter is devoted to emerging stock markets. But the material contained in the old Chapter 8 is now covered in Chapter 5 (Equity: Markets and Instruments), Chapter 6 (Equity: Concepts and Techniques), and Chapter 9 (The Case for International Diversification).

Significant changes also have been made to pedagogy. The number of end-of-chapter problems has been expanded; most of them are new and targeted to test all important topics covered in the chapter. In addition, we have added the following pedagogical features.

Learning Outcome Statements: Each chapter begins with Learning Outcome Statements (LOS). The LOS serve to guide the reader to all the major points of the chapter and follow the order of the topics that are covered.

Concepts in Action: These high-interest boxed features are drawn from published press articles and provide recent illustrations of the concepts in the chapter.

Solutions to End-of-Chapter Problems: In the fifth edition, solutions to all end-of-chapter problems are included at the end of each chapter so that readers can check their own work and work at their own pace.

Capstone Cases: In lieu of end-of-chapter problems, Chapter 13, "Structuring the Global Investment Process," ends with two capstone cases and proposed solutions. These cases allow readers to apply many of the concepts from Chapter 13 and the preceding chapters.

Web Site

A web site for this book is available at www.aw.com/solnik_mcleavey. It has two main features. It contains a database that can be used by the instructor to assign various projects related to some of the chapters. This database includes monthly stock indexes, bond indexes, interest rates, exchange rates, and inflation rates for major countries and a sample of emerging countries. This allows students to conduct tests of various theories presented in the text. A test bank is also available on a password-protected part of the site; it contains problems and solutions as well as a list of cases that can be used for various chapters of the book. The test bank will be progressively enriched.

Acknowledgments

We owe a debt to many colleagues and friends.

Bruno Solnik is indebted to his former teachers at MIT: Fischer Black, Robert Merton, Franco Modigliani, Stewart Myers, Gerald Pogue, and Myron Scholes; and to Blaise Allaz, Dean of the Faculty at H.E.C. Thierry Lombard and Patrick Odier were a constant source of ideas and inspiration for earlier versions of this book. Jeff Diermeier, and all his colleagues at UBS Global Asset Management, provided challenges and inspiration for many of the new concepts and approaches discussed in this fifth edition.

Dennis McLeavey is indebted to former teachers, and friends, especially John Muth, Richard Farmer, Ronald Wonnacott, Victor Cabot, and Donald Tuttle, CFA. Special thanks go to Robert R. Johnson, CFA, Senior Vice President in Curriculum and Exams at AIMR, who encouraged and supported this project.

An AIMR Visiting Scholar, Gerald E. Pinto, CFA, provided assistance on various aspects of the text, including some examples and the glossary, as well as a quality control review of the completed manuscript; Jan R. Squires, CFA, made many, many helpful suggestions and his influence on the project went far beyond his role as co-author of the last chapter in the text. Philip J. Young, CFA, provided a review of the markets and instruments chapter and made suggestions for improvement. Mary K. Erickson, CFA, provided feedback and suggestions on particular chapters and gave advice on the testability of some of the material. Victoria J. Rati, CFA, did a remarkable job of creating the scenario for the integrative case in the book's final chapter. Thomas B. Welch, CFA, provided very intensive reviews and revision recommendations for the case. Sanjiv Sabherwal and Murli Rajan, CFA, showed great care in developing many of the end-of-chapter problems and solutions. Sanjiv Sabherwal also provided a quality control review of the completed manuscript. AIMR associates, Wanda Lauziere and Helen Weaver, cheerfully assisted us with innumerable details. Lois Lombardo, of Nesbitt Graphics, steered the project through the editing and production stages with great skill. Several Addison Wesley reviewers contributed valuable reviews: Bulent Aybar, Southern New Hampshire University; John F.O. Bilson, Illinois Institute of Technology; Joel Carton, Texas Tech University; Louis K. C. Chan, University of Illinois, Urbana-Champaign; Kevin Chiang, University of Alaska, Fairbanks; Joseph Daniels, Marquette University; Jennifer Foo, Stetson University; Yee-Tien Fu, Stanford University; Debra Glassman, University of Washington; Ameeta Jaiswal-Dale, University of St. Thomas; Henry Kim, Tufts University; Andrew Naranjo, University of Florida; Gregory Noronha, CFA, Arizona State University; Harri Ramcharran, University of Akron; Sanjiv Sabherwal, University of Rhode Island; Jaeyoung Sung, University of Illinois, Chicago; Raul Susmel, University of Houston; and Lawrence Tai, Loyola Marymount University. Bonnie Buchanan of University of Georgia did a very careful and detailed accuracy check of several chapters. In addition to the Addison Wesley reviewers, several others provided valuable reviews: William A. Barker, CFA, Lee Kha Loon, CFA, Thomas R. Robinson, CFA, Jot K. Yau, CFA, Dean Takahashi, Daniel Pritchard, Mark Kritzman, CFA, James Jones, CFA, and Frank Fabozzi, CFA.

Bruno Solnik
Dennis McLeavey

Contents

Chapter 1   Foreign Exchange   1

Learning Outcomes   1
Foreign Exchange Quotations   3
    Basic Principles and the Forex Quotation Convention   3
    More on Quotation Conventions   4
    Bid-Ask (Offer) Quotes and Spreads   5
Arbitrage   7
    Cross-Rate Calculations with Bid-Ask Spreads   7
    Bilateral Arbitrage   10
    Triangular Arbitrage   12
Forward Quotes   14
    Interest Rate Parity: The Forward Discount and the Interest Rate Differential   16
Summary   21
Problems   23
Solutions   25

Chapter 2   Foreign Exchange Parity Relations   31

Learning Outcomes   31
Foreign Exchange Fundamentals   33
    Supply and Demand for Foreign Exchange   33
    Balance of Payments   34
    Current Account Deficits and Financial Account Surpluses   35
    Factors That Cause a Nation's Currency to Appreciate or Depreciate   38
    Government Policies: Monetary and Fiscal   40
    Exchange Rate Regimes   42
International Parity Relations   44
    Some Definitions   44
    Interest Rate Parity   45
    Purchasing Power Parity: The Exchange Rate and the Inflation Differential   46
    International Fisher Relation: The Interest Rate and Expected Inflation Rate Differentials   48
    Uncovered Interest Rate Parity   50
    Foreign Exchange Expectations: The Forward Premium (Discount) and the Expected
       Exchange Rate Movement   52
    Combining the Relations   53
    International Parity Relations and Global Asset Management   55

Exchange Rate Determination   56
    Purchasing Power Parity Revisited   56
    Fundamental Value Based on Absolute PPP   59
    Fundamental Value Based on Relative PPP   59
    The Balance of Payments Approach   62
    The Asset Market Approach   70
Summary   77
Problems   79
Solutions   83
Bibliography   89

Chapter 3   Foreign Exchange Determination and Forecasting   91

Learning Outcomes   91
International Monetary Arrangements   92
    A Historical Perspective   92
The Empirical Evidence   100
    Interest Rate Parity   100
    International Fisher Relation   100
    Purchasing Power Parity   101
    Foreign Exchange Expectations   105
    Practical Implications   106
Exchange Rate Forecasting   107
    Is the Market Efficient and Rational?   108
    The Econometric Approach   111
    Technical Analysis   112
    Central Bank Intervention   114
    The Use and Performance of Forecasts   115
Summary   119
Problems   119
Solutions   122
Bibliography   127

Chapter 3   Appendix: Statistical Supplements on Forecasting and Asset Returns   130

Some Notations   130
Traditional Statistical Models with Constant Moments   131
Traditional Statistical Models with Time-Varying Moments   132
Nontraditional Models   134
Data Mining, Data Snooping, and Model Mining   136

Chapter 4   International Asset Pricing   139

Learning Outcomes   139
International Market Efficiency   140
Asset-Pricing Theory   143
    The Domestic Capital Asset-Pricing Model   143
    Asset Returns and Exchange Rate Movements   146
    The Domestic CAPM Extended to the International Context   147
    International CAPM   150
    Market Imperfections and Segmentation   157
Practical Implications   158
    A Global Approach to Equilibrium Pricing   158
    Estimating Currency Exposures   161
    Tests of the ICAPM   169
Summary   171
Problems   173
Solutions   177
Bibliography   181

Chapter 5   Equity: Markets and Instruments   185

Learning Outcomes   185
Market Differences: A Historical Perspective   186
    Historical Differences in Market Organization   187
    Historical Differences in Trading Procedures   188
    Automation on the Major Stock Exchanges   189
Some Statistics   195
    Market Size   195
    Liquidity   197
    Concentration   198
Some Practical Aspects   199
    Tax Aspects   199
    Stock Market Indexes   202
    Information   205
Execution Costs   206
    Components of Execution Costs   206
    Estimation and Uses of Execution Costs   208
    Some Approaches to Reducing Execution Costs   211
Investing in Foreign Shares Listed at Home   214
    Global Shares and American Depositary Receipts   214
    Closed-End Country Funds   211
    Open-End Funds   221
    Exchange Traded Funds   222

Summary   225
Problems   226
Solutions   230
Bibliography   234

Chapter 6   Equity: Concepts and Techniques   237

Learning Outcomes   237
Approaching International Analysis   238
   The Information Problem   240
   A Vision of the World   241
Differences in National Accounting Standards   242
   Historical Setting   243
   International Harmonization of Accounting Practices   244
   Differences in Global Standards   247
   The Effects of Accounting Principles on Earnings and Stock Prices   254
   The Information Content of International Differences in GAAP   255
Global Industry Analysis   256
   Country Analysis   256
   Industry Analysis: Return Expectation Elements   262
   Industry Analysis: Risk Elements   268
   Global Industry Analysis in Practice: An Example   273
Equity Analysis   277
Global Risk Factors in Security Returns   292
   Risk-Factor Model: Industry and Country Factors   292
   Other Risk Factors: Styles   293
   Other Risk Factors: Macroeconomic   294
   Practical Use of Factor Models   296
Summary   296
Problems   297
Solutions   302
Bibliography   309

Chapter 7   Global Bond Investing   311

Learning Outcomes   311
The Global Bond Market   312
   The Various Segments   312
   World Market Size   314
   Bond Indexes   315
   The Eurobond Market   316
   Emerging Markets and Brady Bonds   320

Major Differences Among Bond Markets   323
  Types of Instruments   323
  Quotations, Day Count, and Frequency of Coupons   324
  Legal and Fiscal Aspects   326
A Refresher on Bond Valuation   327
  Zero-Coupon Bonds   328
  Bond with Coupons   330
  Duration and Interest Rate Sensitivity   332
  Credit Spreads   334
Multicurrency Approach   335
  International Yield Curve Comparisons   335
  The Return and Risk on Foreign Bond Investments   338
  Currency-Hedging Strategies   339
  International Portfolio Strategies   340
Floating-Rate Notes and Structured Notes   344
  Floating-Rate Notes (FRNs)   345
  Bull FRN   351
  Bear FRN   352
  Dual-Currency Bonds   353
  Currency-Option Bonds   356
Summary   359
Problems   361
Solutions   365
Bibliography   370

Chapter 8   Alternative Investments   371

Learning Outcomes   371
Investment Companies   373
  Valuing Investment Company Shares   373
  Fund Management Fees   374
  Investment Strategies   374
  Exchange Traded Funds   377
Real Estate   386
  Forms of Real Estate Investment   387
  Valuation Approaches   388
  Real Estate in a Portfolio Context   396
Private Equity: Venture Capital   398
  Stages of Venture Capital Investing   400
  Investment Characteristics   401
  Types of Liquidation/Divestment   403
  Valuation and Performance Measurement   404
Hedge Funds and Absolute Return Strategies   406

Definition   409
Classification   410
Funds of Funds   414
Leverage and Unique Risks of Hedge Funds   416
The Case for Hedge Funds   417
Caveats   421
Closely Held Companies and Inactively Traded Securities   424
Legal Environment   424
Valuation Alternatives   424
Bases for Discounts/Premiums   425
Distressed Securities/Bankruptcies   425
Commodity Markets and Commodity Derivatives   426
Commodity Futures   428
Motivation and Investment Vehicles   428
Active Investment   429
The Example of Gold   430
Commodity-Linked Securities   432
Summary   433
Problems   436
Solutions   441
Bibliography   447

Chapter 9   The Case for International Diversification   451

Learning Outcomes   451
The Traditional Case for International Diversification   454
Risk Reduction Through Attractive Correlations   454
Portfolio Return Performance   464
Currency Risk Not a Barrier to International Investment   471
The Case Against International Diversification   472
Increase in Correlations   473
Past Performance Is a Good Indicator of Future Performance   476
Barriers to International Investments   477
The Case for International Diversification Revisited   481
Pitfalls in Estimating Correlation During Volatile Periods   481
Expanded Investment Universe and Performance Opportunities   483
Global Investing Rather Than International Diversification   483
The Case for Emerging Markets   486
The Basic Case   486
Volatility, Correlations, and Currency Risk   488
Portfolio Return Performance   489
Investability of Emerging Markets   490
Segmentation versus Integration Issue   491

Summary   491
Problems   493
Solutions   496
Bibliography   505

Chapter 10   Derivatives   507

Learning Outcomes   507
Forward and Futures   508
  The Principles of a Forward and a Futures Contract   508
  The Different Instruments   511
  Forward and Futures Valuation   517
  Use of Forward and Futures   522
Swaps   528
  The Principles of a Swap   528
  The Different Instruments   529
  Swaps Valuation   533
  Use of Swaps   537
Options   542
  Introduction to Options   542
  The Different Instruments   543
  Option Valuation   546
  Use of Options   549
Summary   555
Problems   556
Solutions   562
Bibliography   570

Chapter 11   Currency Risk Management   571

Learning Outcomes   571
Hedging with Futures or Forward Currency Contracts   573
  The Basic Approach: Hedging the Principal   573
  Minimum-Variance Hedge Ratio   576
  Optimal Hedge Ratio   580
  Hedging Strategies   582
  Hedging Multiple Currencies   582
Insuring and Hedging with Options   584
  Insuring with Options   584
  Dynamic Hedging with Options   587
  Hedging Strategies   589
Other Methods for Managing Currency Exposure   590
Currency Overlay   592
Summary   595

Problems   597
Solutions   602
Bibliography   613

Chapter 12   Global Performance Evaluation   615

Learning Outcomes   615
The Basics   616
   Principles and Objectives   616
   Calculating a Rate of Return   619
Performance Attribution in Global Performance Evaluation   626
   The Mathematics of Multicurrency Returns   627
   Total Return Decomposition   629
   Performance Attribution   631
   An Example of Output   634
   More on Currency Management   636
   From Quarterly to Multi-Year Performance   637
Performance Appraisal in Global Performance Evaluation   637
   Risk   638
   Risk-Adjusted Performance   639
   Risk Allocation and Budgeting   642
   Some Potential Biases in Return and Risk   644
Implementation   645
   More on Global Benchmarks   646
   *Global Investment Performance Standards and Other Performance Presentation
      Standards   648*
Summary   650
Problems   651
Solutions   659
Bibliography   674

Chapter 13   Structuring the Global
                Investment Process   677

Learning Outcomes   677
A Tour of the Global Investment Industry   679
   Investors   679
   Investment Managers   684
   Brokers   685
   Consultants and Advisers   686
   Custodians   687
Global Investment Philosophies   688
   The Passive Approach   688
   The Active Approach   689

Balanced or Specialized 691
Industry or Country Approach 692
Top-Down or Bottom-Up 692
Style Management 693
Currency 694
Quantitative or Subjective 695

The Investment Policy Statement 695
Capital Market Expectations 698
Defining Asset Classes 698
Long-Term Capital Market Expectations: Historical Returns 699
Long-Term Capital Market Expectations: Forward-Looking Returns 701
Short-Term Capital Market Expectations 705

Global Asset Allocation: From Strategic to Tactical 706
Strategic Asset Allocation 706
Tactical Asset Allocation 711

Global Asset Allocation: Structuring and Quantifying the Process 712
Research and Market Analysis 713
Asset Allocation Optimization 715
Portfolio Construction 717
Performance and Risk Control 718

Summary 719
John Bouderi: Case Study A 720
Leigh Brennan: Solution A 730
John Bouderi: Case Study B 731
Leigh Brennan: Solution B 735
Bibliography 736

Glossary 738
Index 751

About the Authors

Bruno Solnik is professor of finance at the H.E.C. School of Management in France. He holds an engineering degree from Polytechnique in Paris and a Ph.D. from Massachusetts Institute of Technology. Before joining H.E.C., he was on the faculty of the Graduate School of Business of Stanford University.

Professor Solnik has been a visiting professor at the University of California at Berkeley, U.C.L.A., Strathclyde University, and the Université de Genève. He was the founding president of the European Finance Association. He has written seven books, five in France and two in the United States, including *International Investments*. He has published some fifty articles in leading finance journals such as the *Journal of Finance,* the *Financial Analysts Journal,* the *Journal of Financial and Quantitative Analysis,* and the *Journal of Portfolio Management.* He serves on the board of editors of several major finance journals in America, Europe, and Asia. Professor Solnik has served as a trustee of the Research Foundation of AIMR. He has received many prizes, including two Graham & Dodd Awards of Excellence by the *Financial Analysts Journal,* the "Finance Award of the Year" at the 1998 Interlaken Finance Symposium, and the Nicholas Molodovsky Award, presented by the AIMR Board of Governors on May 22, 1999. "This award is given periodically only to those individuals who have made outstanding contributions of such significance as to change the direction of the profession and to raise it to higher standards of accomplishment."

Professor Solnik's work focuses on international financial markets, from exchange risk to international portfolio diversification. His expertise has been called upon by many pension funds and banks in Europe, the United States, and Asia. He sits on the Investment Advisory Board of Zurich Financial Services, a global insurance company with investments of some \$190 billion.

Dennis McLeavey, CFA, is vice president, Curriculum and Examinations, at the Association for Investment Management and Research. He earned his CFA charter in 1990. During the early 1990s, he taught in the Boston University and the Boston Security Analysts Society's CFA review programs. Prior to joining AIMR in 2000, he served on various AIMR committees. He is a co-author of AIMR's texts, *Quantitative Methods for Investment Analysis* and *Analysis of Equity Investments: Valuation,* as well as two college texts, *Production Planning and Inventory Control* and *Operations Research for Management Decisions.* His research has been published in *Management Science* and in the *Journal of Operations Research.* In his twenty-five year academic career, he taught at the University of Western Ontario, the University of Connecticut, the University of Rhode Island where he founded a student managed fund, and Babson College. He serves as chairperson of the AIMR Retirement Investment Policy Committee and as a New York Stock Exchange Arbitrator. After studying economics for his bachelor's degree at the University of Western Ontario in 1968, he completed a doctorate in production management and industrial engineering at Indiana University in 1972.

To Catherine, who remains, after three decades of marriage and medical practice, the heart of my life. She has now enjoyed all the exciting aspects of the leading financial cities of the world. She has also shared numerous sleepless, interminable airplane hauls and middle-of-the-night phone calls from Hong Kong, Tokyo, or Chicago. Let this book add to the long list of pleasures and suffering we happily share.

To Alexandra Solnik and Vincent Solnik, CFA, my former students, who have learned to suffer through and enjoy the previous editions of this book.

Bruno Solnik

To Janet, my wife and best friend. Her teaching preparation and awards as a mathematics professor have constantly inspired me with the knowledge that even the most difficult concept is intelligible if enough effort and care are put into the presentation. She has been remarkably tolerant of book deadlines.

To Christine McLeavey and Andy McLeavey, who continue to refine their wonderful talents in physics, music, political science, and theater. They fill our lives with joy.

Dennis McLeavey

Foreign Exchange

After completing this chapter, you will be able to do the following:

- Define direct and indirect methods of foreign exchange quotations

- Define and calculate the spread on a foreign currency quotation

- Explain how spreads on foreign currency quotations can differ as a result of market conditions, bank/dealer positions, and trading volume

- Convert direct (indirect) foreign exchange quotations into indirect (direct) foreign exchange quotations

- Calculate currency cross-rates, given either two spot mid-point exchange rates or two spot bid-ask quotations involving three currencies

- Calculate the widest interval within which the midpoint of the bid–ask spread in the domestic country must remain to allow no arbitrage between the currencies of two countries, given the direct exchange rate quote for the midpoint of the bid–ask spread in the foreign country, and a transaction cost expressed as a percentage of the direct quote in the foreign country

- Calculate the profit on a triangular arbitrage opportunity, given the bid–ask quotations for the currencies of three countries

- Distinguish between the spot and forward markets for foreign exchange

- Define and calculate the spread on a forward foreign currency quotation

- Explain how spreads on forward foreign currency quotations can differ as a result of market conditions, bank/dealer positions, trading volume, and maturity/length of contract

- Define forward discount and forward premium

- Calculate a forward discount or premium and express either as an annualized rate

- Explain interest rate parity, sometimes called covered interest rate parity

- Define and illustrate covered interest arbitrage

The international investor is faced with a complex task. The financial markets throughout the world are quite different from one another, and information on them is sometimes difficult to obtain. Trading in different time zones and languages further complicates the task. But the most important aspect of international investment is the use of multiple currencies. An American investing in France must do so in euros; therefore, the performance (and risk) of the investment will depend in part on changes in the euro/U.S. dollar exchange rate. Because of the importance of exchange rates in international investment, this book begins with a chapter describing foreign exchange transactions.

In this text, we develop the analysis needed for the international investment and portfolio management process. The first three chapters lay the foundation of exchange rates, which link the economies of different countries and regions. The next five chapters explore the various assets available for international investing. The final five chapters develop the techniques and perspective of international investment and portfolio management.

In Chapter 2, we develop the theory of international parity conditions. This theory helps in defining real foreign currency risk, an important factor to be managed in global investing and portfolio management. Chapter 3 then explores the techniques and empirical results in the difficult task of exchange rate forecasting.

Chapter 4 is the lead chapter in a series of chapters on international assets. In that chapter, we develop international asset pricing in general, with attention to foreign currency risk. Then, Chapter 5 places a particular focus on the transaction costs involved in various equity markets and instruments allowing entry into international equity investments. Following this general introduction to international asset pricing, Chapters 6, 7, and 8 focus on the available international assets themselves: equities, bonds, and alternative investments, respectively.

After building cases for and against international diversification in Chapter 9, we move into the foreign currency risk-and-return analysis needed for international portfolio management. We develop the risk-control techniques available with derivatives in Chapter 10 and then apply these techniques to currency risk management in Chapter 11. Then, in Chapter 12, we examine the performance measures to judge the risk–return contributions of international diversification. Finally, we summarize the global investment and portfolio management process in Chapter 13. Throughout the text, we attempt to isolate those elements of the process that have unique international aspects.

Chapter 1 begins with foreign exchange quotes and the relationships between different types of quotes, as well as the nature of bid–ask spreads in the foreign exchange market. Then, the implications of no-arbitrage conditions appear in three exchange rate applications. First, the quotes of the domestic currency versus a foreign currency must be aligned when given in the two countries for which the exchange rates are being quoted. Second, the exchange rates quoted between two foreign currencies must be aligned with the exchange rate quotes between the domestic currency and each of the foreign currencies. Finally, the exchange rate quotes for current and future delivery must be aligned with the risk-free interest rates in the two countries for which the quotes are given. Chapter 1 presents the basic facts of foreign exchange involving quotation interpretation and arbitrage. Foreign exchange theories are saved for subsequent chapters.

Foreign Exchange Quotations

Before we can discuss exchange rates, which relate to price levels in two countries, we need to know something about the price level in a single country, and this depends on the supply and demand for money within the country. The domestic money supply is a policy variable set by the domestic central bank. The demand for money comes from the need to buy goods and services, as well as from other motives. The price level in the country is determined by the intersection of the demand and supply curve for money in the economy. Just as the value of money is determined by supply and demand in the domestic economy, its value in relation to foreign currencies is also determined by supply and demand. In Chapters 2 and 3, we explore exchange rate determination in detail. Here, we point out that the demand for domestic currency comes mainly from exports and financial inflows (foreigners' purchases of domestic securities) and that the supply comes from imports and financial outflows (purchases of foreign securities). A higher price for the domestic currency is termed a *strengthening* of the currency and a lower price, a *weakening*.

Basic Principles and the Forex Quotation Convention

For most currencies in worldwide foreign exchange (Forex) markets, all trades take place using one convention. The U.S. dollar is still the major currency so that the interbank market is still mostly dollar. All currencies are still quoted against the U.S. dollar, although there are such regional exceptions as the yen in Asia and the euro in Europe. Over time, exchange rates change, so we will sometimes use assumed values for the current exchange rate. For example, we might assume that the value of the euro is quoted as 0.8 euros per U.S. dollar. In other words, one dollar ($) can be exchanged in the foreign exchange market for 0.8 euros. Conversely, the value of one euro (€) in terms of U.S. dollars is given by the reciprocal of 0.8, which is 1.25 dollars. We will define €/$ as the number of euros per dollar and $/€ as the number of dollars per euro:

$$€/\$ = 0.80 \quad \text{and}$$

$$\$/€ = 1.25$$

Similarly, the Japanese yen (¥) may be quoted as 120 yen per dollar, so that 100 yen is worth 0.8333 dollars. Quotations for the yen are usually indicated for 100 yen rather than for one yen.

The Forex convention specifies rates for all currencies per dollar (as in ¥/$), except for the pound ($/£) and the euro ($/€). From the quotation of two currencies against the U.S. dollar, one can derive the cross-exchange rate between the two currencies:

$/€ = 1.25   and

¥/$ = 120   implies that

¥/€ = 120 × 1.25 = 150

In this example, one euro is worth 150 yen, or 100 yen are worth 0.6667 euros.

Abbreviations are used to refer to the various currencies. These could be commonly used symbols or "official" three-letter codes. For example, the yen is JPY; the pound, GBP; the U.S. dollar, USD; and the euro, EUR.

More on Quotation Conventions

Worldwide, quotations are generally made in terms of the amount of local or domestic currency (DC) required to purchase one unit of foreign currency (FC), and this is called the *direct* exchange rate. For example, the Japanese quote the dollar exchange rate as 120 ¥/$ (120 yen per dollar), a direct rate in Japan. However, the U.S. convention, adapted from the British, is the opposite. In New York and London, traders quote the amount of foreign currency required to purchase one unit of home currency, a rate called an *indirect* rate. In New York, therefore, the yen is also quoted as 120 ¥/$. Because of the central role played by the U. S. dollar, it is important to remember that in countries other than the United States, all exchange rates with the dollar are usually given as direct rates, the domestic currency value of one dollar. However, there are two exceptions that give the indirect rates in countries other than the United States. The British pound played a historical role on the international scene, and it has always been quoted as the dollar price of one pound. When the euro was introduced in 1999, the decision was made to adopt the convention to quote the foreign currency value of one euro. This convention applies for the exchange rate of the euro against any currency, including the dollar. So the exchange rate between the dollar and the euro would appear on trading screens as 1.25 dollars per euro, an indirect quote from the European perspective.

When quotations involve the U.S. dollar, the dollar price of one unit of the second currency is referred to as *American terms,* a direct quote from the U.S. perspective. The amount of the second currency per U.S. dollar is called *European terms,* an indirect quote from the U.S. perspective.

In the foreign exchange market, quotations are generally given with five digits. For example, the ¥/$ could appear as 120.10, the $/€ as 1.2515, and the £/€ as 0.7015.[1]

---

[1] For exchange rates that are below one, quotes often include five decimal places.

Because a number is usually quoted without any indication of the role played by each currency, it is important to keep track of which is the domestic currency and what quote convention is being used in order to connect an appreciation or depreciation with an increase or decrease in the exchange rate. For example, the exchange rate between the euro and the U.S. dollar may be quoted in terms of either euros per dollar or dollars per euro. If the domestic country is the United States and the direct quote is given, a depreciation of the quoted euro would mean a decline in its price in dollars. For an indirect quote, an increase in the exchange rate would mean an appreciation of the quoted euro. An appreciation of the foreign currency coincides with a depreciation of the domestic currency.

Domestic Currency	Foreign Currency	Indirect Exchange Rate	Direct Exchange Rate
Appreciates	Depreciates	Increases	Decreases
Depreciates	Appreciates	Decreases	Increases

Bid-Ask (Offer) Quotes and Spreads

The foreign exchange market is a worldwide interbank market. Only the major banks and specialized brokers who act as middlemen for some local markets are admitted to this club, which is linked by telephone. The market is organized like an international over-the-counter market. A customer wanting to buy a specified amount of a currency calls several banks to get the best price. The foreign exchange dealer quotes not one price, but two. The *bid* price is the exchange rate at which the dealer is willing to buy a currency; the *ask* (or *offer*) price is the exchange rate at which the dealer is willing to sell a currency. The midpoint price is the average of the bid and ask price: (ask + bid)/2.

Suppose a dealer provides the following quotes:

Quote in the United States	Bid	Ask
Direct ($/€)	$0.9836	$0.9839
Indirect (€/$)	€1.0164	€1.0167

Paying a $0.9839/euro ask rate is equivalent to a counter-party bidding $1/0.9839 = €1.0164$ per dollar.

Two principles apply to cross-rates:

- The DC/FC direct ask exchange rate is the reciprocal of the indirect bid exchange rate.

- The DC/FC direct bid exchange rate is the reciprocal of the indirect ask exchange rate.

For both direct and indirect quotes, the bid–ask spread can be given as a percentage defined as 100 times (ask price − bid price)/ask price.[2] The direct rate bid–ask spread is $100 \times (0.9839 - 0.9836)/0.9839 = 0.0305\%$, or approximately 3 bps. For the indirect rate, the bid–ask spread is $100 \times (1.0167 - 1.0164)/1.0167 = 0.0295\%$.

Spreads differ as a result of market conditions, bank/dealer positions, and trading volume. The size of the bid–ask spread increases with exchange rate uncertainty (volatility) because of bank/dealer risk aversion. In contrast to its relation to market conditions, the size of the bid–ask spread does not depend on bank/dealer positions. Rather, the midpoint of the spread moves in response to dealer positions. For example, a dealer with excess supply of a foreign currency would move the midpoint of his direct quote down rather than adjust the size of his spread. A dealer quoting a large spread relative to other dealers will basically not trade. Neither will the dealer want to quote a smaller spread because that would mean raising his bid price, when he does not want to buy. With excess supply a dealer will make a favorable quote on the ask price or on the bid price, depending on his position. For example, with excess euros, a U.S. dealer will try to sell them and therefore lower his ask price of $0.9839 to, say, $0.9837 and probably also lower his bid to avoid having to buy more euros. Finally, spreads are larger for currencies that have a low trading volume (thinly traded currencies).

Investors need to understand how quotations will be presented. In the following example, we illustrate a likely exchange between a bond portfolio manager and a bank. An example may help to show how a transaction is initiated and completed.

EXAMPLE 1.1 EXCHANGE RATE QUOTES AND FRENCH BONDS

A U.S. portfolio manager wants to buy $10 million worth of French bonds. The manager wants to know how many euros can be obtained to invest using the $10 million. The manager calls several banks to get their €/$ quotation, without indicating whether a sale or a purchase of euros is desired. Bank A gives the following quotation:

€/$ = 0.80000–0.80020

In other words, Bank A is willing to buy a dollar for 0.80000 euro or to sell a dollar for 0.80020 euros. These quotes are consistent with the following quotes for the $/€:

$/€ = 1.2497–1.2500

To make the quotation faster, only the last digits, called the *points,* are sometimes quoted. The preceding quotation would often be given as follows:

€/$ = 0.80000–20

or even

€/$ = 000–20

---

[2] Sometimes the spread is expressed as a percentage of the midpoint price, instead of the ask price. The difference is miniscule. Spreads are often quoted in basis points (bps) where 0.01% equals 1 bp.

Let's assume that the portfolio manager gets the following quotations from three different banks:

	Bank A	Bank B	Bank C
€/$	0.80000–20	0.79985–05	0.79995–15

Note that the ask for all three quotations add 0.00020 to the bid. How many euros will the portfolio manager get to invest?

SOLUTION

The manager will immediately choose Bank A and indicate that she will buy 8 million euros for $10 million. Both parties indicate where each sum should be transferred. The portfolio manager indicates that the euros should be transferred to an account with the Société Générale, the manager's business bank in Paris, whereas Bank A indicates that it will receive the dollars at its account with Citibank in New York. Faxes, telexes, or other electronic messages are exchanged to confirm the oral agreement. The settlement of the transaction takes place simultaneously in Paris and in New York two days later.

Arbitrage

Arbitrage keeps exchange rates in line with each other and with risk-free interest rates. We will see that triangular arbitrage and interest rate parity are thus reflections of the same principle. Triangular arbitrage and cross-rates involve exchange rates between three currencies and the riskless profit-seeking motive that pushes exchange rates into alignment with each other. Before examining triangular arbitrage, we need to develop the concepts of cross-rate calculations.

Cross-Rate Calculations with Bid-Ask Spreads

Recall that a cross rate is the exchange rate between two countries inferred from each country's exchange rate with a third country. Suppose the dollar per euro exchange rate is 0.9836 and the dollar per pound rate is 1.5231. The euro pound cross-rate can be calculated by multiplying the euro per dollar rate (1/0.9836) by the dollar per pound rate: $(1/0.9836) \times 1.5231 = 1.5485$, or €1.5485 per pound.

In the case of bid and ask (offer) prices, the calculations are only slightly more complex. To calculate a currency cross-rate, we can use the following two equations:

$$(FC_1/FC_2)_{ask} = (FC_1/DC)_{ask} \times (DC/FC_2)_{ask} \qquad (1.1)$$

$$(FC_1/FC_2)_{bid} = (FC_1/DC)_{bid} \times (DC/FC_2)_{bid} \qquad (1.2)$$

where FC_1, FC_2, and DC are the two foreign currencies and the domestic currency, respectively.

Similarly,

$$(FC_2/FC_1)_{ask} = (DC/FC_1)_{ask} \times (FC_2/DC)_{ask} \tag{1.3}$$

$$(FC_2/FC_1)_{bid} = (DC/FC_1)_{bid} \times (FC_2/DC)_{bid} \tag{1.4}$$

And we must verify that $(FC_2/FC_1)_{ask} = 1/(FC_1/FC_2)_{bid}$ and $(FC_2/FC_1)_{bid} = 1/(FC_1/FC_2)_{ask}$.[3]

EXAMPLE 1.2   CROSS-RATES WITH THE DOLLAR, POUND, AND EURO

Consider the following quotes involving the dollar, the pound, and the euro.

	$ and €		€ and £	
	Bid in Eurozone	**Ask in Eurozone**	**Bid in London**	**Ask in London**
Indirect	$0.9836	$0.9839	€1.5473	€1.5480
Direct	€1.0164	€1.0167	£0.6460	£0.6463

Compute the effective $/£ ask and bid cross-rates, as well as the £/$ ask and bid cross-rates. Assume the euro is the domestic currency.

SOLUTION

The effective $/£ ask cross-rate can be calculated from using dollars to buy euros first, and then using the euros to buy pounds:

$/£ = $/€ × €/£ = 0.9839 × 1.5480 = 1.5231 dollars per pound ask rate.

The effective £/$ bid cross-rate can be calculated by selling dollars for euros first and then selling the euros for pounds.

£/$ = €/$ × £/€ = 1.0164 × 0.6460 = 0.6566 pounds per dollar bid rate.

	$ and €		€ and £		$ and £	
	Bid in Eurozone	**Ask in Eurozone**	**Bid in London**	**Ask in London**	**Effective Bid in London**	**Effective Ask in London**
Indirect	$0.9836	$0.9839	€1.5473	€1.5480		$1.5231
Direct	€1.0164	€1.0167	£0.6460	£0.6463	£0.6566	

In the same fashion, we find the $/£ bid is equal to:

$/£ = $/€ × €/£ = 0.9836 × 1.5473 = 1.5219 dollars per pound bid rate.

---

[3] Because of rounding of the quotes to five digits, the cross-rates computed using direct and indirect quotes could yield slightly different results (in the last digit). As mentioned, foreign exchange markets trade and quote using one convention (all exchange rates are the foreign currency value of one dollar, except for the pound and euro), so the cross-rates are best computed using this convention.

And the £/$ ask rate is equal to:

$$£/\$ = €/\$ \times £/€ = 1.0167 \times 0.6463 = 0.6571 \text{ pounds per dollar ask rate, or}$$

simply the reciprocal of the dollar per pound bid rate ($1/1.5219 = 0.6571$).

	$ and €		€ and £		$ and £	
	Bid in Eurozone	**Ask in Eurozone**	**Bid in London**	**Ask in London**	**Effective Bid in London**	**Effective Ask in London**
Indirect	$0.9836	$0.9839	€1.5473	€1.5480	$1.5219	$1.5231
Direct	€1.0164	€1.0167	£0.6460	£0.6463	£0.6566	£0.6571

Other rates can be calculated from dollar or euro quotations and the following example develops familiarity with how to calculate cross-rates from bank quotes. For example, the ¥/€ rate can be calculated using the ¥/$ and €/$ rates. This calculation usually implies a larger bid–ask spread on cross-exchange rates.

EXAMPLE 1.3 *EXCHANGE RATE QUOTES AND CROSS-RATES*

Following are the quotations given by Bank A:

$$€/\$ = 0.80000\text{–}0.80020$$

$$¥/\$ = 120.00\text{–}120.01$$

What should be the ¥/€ bid and ask quotations?
The ¥/€ quotation is obtained as follows:

- The ¥/€ bid price is the price at which Bank A is willing to buy euros against yen, that is, the number of yen it is willing to pay to buy one euro. This transaction (buy euros—sell yen) is equivalent to selling yen to buy dollars (at a bid rate of 120.00) and simultaneously reselling those dollars to buy euros (at an ask rate of 0.80020). Mathematically, the transaction is as follows:

$$\text{Bid } ¥/€ = 120.00/0.80020 = 149.96$$

- The ¥/€ ask price is the price at which Bank A is willing to sell euros for yen, that is, the number of yen it wants to get for selling one euro. This transaction (sell euros—buy yen) is equivalent to buying yen with dollars (at an ask rate of 120.01) and simultaneously purchasing these dollars with euros (at a bid rate of 0.80000). This may be expressed as follows:

$$\text{Ask } ¥/€ = 120.01/0.80000 = 150.01$$

The resulting quotation by the bank is

$$¥/€ = 149.96\text{ –}150.01$$

To verify that the calculations have been made correctly, there are two checks. A *first check* to make sure that you measure the cross-rate in the right direction is to look at the symbols. To get the ¥/€ rate, we divide the ¥/$ rate by the €/$ rate. Observe that the $ symbol disappears:

$$¥/€ = ¥/\$ / €/\$$$

Similarly, if the euro quotation were given as the number of dollars per euro ($/€), we would have:

$$¥/€ = ¥/\$ × \$/€$$

A *second check* on the result is to make sure that you maximize the bid–ask spread. To get the bid cross-rate, which is the smaller rate, put the smaller figure (the bid—¥/$) in the numerator and the larger figure (the ask—€/$) in the denominator. To get the ask cross-rate, do the reverse.

Arbitrage aligns exchange rate quotations throughout the world. The quotation for the €/$ rate must be the same, at a given instant, in Frankfurt, Paris, and New York. If quotations were to deviate by more than the spread, a simple phone call would allow a trader to make enormous profits. There are enough professionals in the world watching continuous quote fluctuations to rule out such riskless profit opportunities.

Quotations are directly available online from many financial institutions which have their own computer services. International database services, such as Reuters, provide continuously revised quotations from several banks. Portfolio managers armed with this information on market prices can rapidly arbitrage or hedge their portfolios of foreign assets.

With exchange rates, there are two types of arbitrage opportunities to consider. As with any asset, the law of one price indicates that the exchange rate quotes in two countries should be the same within a transaction cost band. With respect to the exchange rate between two countries, the bid–ask spread in one country should be aligned with the bid–ask spread in the other, or a bilateral arbitrage opportunity would be present. In addition to bid–ask spread alignment, there is also a question of cross-rate alignment. A triangular arbitrage opportunity occurs if the quoted cross-rate between two currencies is higher or lower than the cross-rate implied by the exchange rates of the two currencies against a third currency. We will examine bilateral and triangular arbitrage opportunities in turn.

Bilateral Arbitrage

To detect a bilateral arbitrage opportunity, it is useful to understand the conditions under which no bilateral arbitrage can occur. Suppose that transaction costs are given as 0.015 percent ($t_c = 0.015\%$) of the direct quote midpoint in a foreign country (FC). The direct quote midpoint *in the foreign country* is $S_f = 2$ (i.e., 2 FC units for 1 DC unit). The FC bid–ask spread will be $2 × (1 ± 0.00015)$, giving a bid–ask spread of [1.9997, 2.0003]. The equivalent direct bid–ask spread *in the domestic country* must then be given by [1/2.0003, 1/1.9997], or [0.49993, 0.50008].

In examining the possibility of an arbitrage opportunity, we delineate the widest interval within which a bid–ask midpoint in the domestic country would allow no arbitrage profits. Clearly, an arbitrageur would not want to invest 1 DC to buy FC units at the direct bid price in the foreign country, 1.9997 FC, simply to sell those FC units at the direct bid price in the domestic county, 0.49993 DC, to lose money by incurring transaction costs of 0.0003 DC, on every 1 DC unit invested.

A way of expressing this is to develop a formula for the widest interval within which the midpoint of the bid–ask spread in the domestic country must remain in order to allow no arbitrage between the currencies of two countries. With one unit of domestic currency, one could obtain $(1 - t_c) \times S_f = (0.99985 \times 2)$ units of the foreign currency in the foreign country. Then, using the foreign currency in the domestic country, an investor ought to be able to purchase no more than the one unit of domestic currency that the investor started with in the first place. Letting x be the largest no-arbitrage deviation in the domestic midpoint from the reciprocal of the foreign direct midpoint, this implies that $(1 - t_c) \times S_f \times (1 - t_c) \times (1/S_f + x) \leq 1$ unit of domestic currency; for example, $0.99985 \times 2 \times 0.99985 \times (0.5 + x) \leq 1$, or $x = -0.5 + 1/(0.99985 \times 2 \times 0.99985) = 0.00015$. Given the equivalent direct quote midpoint of $1/S_f = 0.5$, this means that the largest deviation in the no-arbitrage domestic midpoint would be $0.5 \pm 0.00015 = [0.49985, 0.50015]$. If the midpoint quote is below 0.49985 or above 0.50015, there exists a profitable arbitrage. In general,

$$x = -(1/S_f) + 1/(k^2 \times S_f)$$

where:

S_f is the direct exchange rate quote in the foreign country,

k is 1 minus the transaction cost percentage, t_c, given against the direct quote midpoint (e.g., $k = 0.99985$ if $t_c = 0.015\%$),

and the no-arbitrage range of domestic midpoints is $(1/S_f) \pm x$.

EXAMPLE 1.4   BILATERAL ARBITRAGE POSSIBILITY DETECTION

Suppose that an arbitrageur in a domestic country faces an indirect exchange rate midpoint of approximately 1.25 FC units for 1 DC unit. The domestic and foreign currency transaction costs are 0.02 percent of the direct quote midpoint in each country. The direct bid–ask spread on the foreign currency in the domestic country is (0.80025 bid, 0.80041 ask). In the foreign country, the direct bid–ask spread is (1.2498 bid, 1.2503 ask). Is there an arbitrage opportunity? What is the widest interval within which the midpoint of the bid–ask spread in the domestic country must remain to allow no arbitrage between the currencies of two countries?

SOLUTION

Multiplying the foreign country direct bid price by the domestic country direct bid price, we get a value $1.2498 \times 0.80025 = 1.00015$ that is greater than one, an indication of an arbitrage opportunity. The transaction cost is $t_c = 0.02\%$, and the direct exchange rate midpoint in the foreign country is $S_f = 1.25$. Hence, $x = -(1/1.25) + 1/(0.9998^2 \times 1.25) = -0.8 + 0.80032 = 0.00032$, and the no-arbitrage range of midpoint exchange rate quotes in the domestic country is [0.79968, 0.80032]. Notice that the midpoint of the domestic bid–ask spread is $0.80033 = (0.80025 + 0.80041)/2$, a midpoint outside the no-arbitrage range.

Triangular Arbitrage

Turning now to triangular arbitrage, we look for a quoted cross-rate between two foreign currencies, FC_1 and FC_2, that is different from the cross-rate implied by the domestic country exchange rate against the two foreign currencies.

EXAMPLE 1.5   *TRIANGULAR ARBITRAGE PROFIT WITHOUT BID–ASK SPREAD CONSIDERATIONS*

The direct exchange rate is 2 DC units for 1 FC_1 unit, and 3 DC units for 1 FC_2 unit. The quoted cross-rate is 1.48 FC_1 for 1 FC_2 unit. Is there an arbitrage opportunity?

SOLUTION

Ignoring transaction costs, we can find the cross-rates with Equation 1.1:

$$FC_1/FC_2 = (FC_1/DC) \times (DC/FC_2)$$
$$= (1/2) \times (3/1)$$
$$= 1.5$$

The quoted cross-rate is less than the cross-rate implied by the domestic country exchange rate against the two foreign currencies. An arbitrage sequence would be: with 1 DC unit, buy 0.5 FC_1 units; convert to $0.5/1.48 = 0.33784$ FC_2 units; and then convert to $0.33784 \times 3 = 1.0135$ DC units. Notice that this opportunity would not be present if the quoted cross-rate matched the implied cross-rate of 1.5: with 1 DC unit, buy 0.5 FC_1 units; convert to $0.5/1.5 = 1/3$ FC_2 units; and then convert back to $(1/3) \times 3 = 1$ DC unit.

In the realistic case, triangular arbitrage must be examined with bid–ask spreads. There are several steps in calculating the profit from a triangular arbitrage opportunity:

1. Pick the cross-rate currency.

2. Determine whether the cross-rate bid–ask quotes are in line with the direct quotes by determining whether it is cheaper to buy foreign currency directly or indirectly (through the cross-quoted currency).

3. If the actual cross-rate quote is not in line with the quoted cross-rate quote, an arbitrage opportunity exists.

EXAMPLE 1.6   *TRIANGULAR ARBITRAGE PROFIT WITH BID–ASK SPREAD CONSIDERATIONS*

Consider the following quotes involving the dollar, the euro, and the pound. Because these are major currencies, an arbitrage opportunity would not arise. Arbitrage aligns exchange rate quotations throughout the world. As mentioned earlier, the quotation for the €/$ rate, for example, cannot deviate by more than the spread in Frankfurt, Paris, and New York at a given instant. Nevertheless, a hypothetical opportunity will help the reader gain familiarity with the cross-rate concepts already introduced.

Recall the data given in Example 1.2, showing consistent cross-rates.

	$ and €		€ and £		$ and £	
	Bid in Eurozone	**Ask in Eurozone**	**Bid in London**	**Ask in London**	**Effective Bid in London**	**Effective Ask in London**
Indirect	$0.9836	$0.9839	€1.5473	€1.5480	$1.5219	$1.5231
Direct	€1.0164	€1.0167	£0.6460	£0.6463	£0.6566	£0.6571

Now consider a hypothetical set of rates that might allow an arbitrage opportunity. In gray screens, we show the rates that are out of line with Example 1.2.

	$ and €		€ and £		£ and $	
	Bid in Eurozone	**Ask**	**Bid in London**	**Ask**	**Bid in New York**	**Ask**
Indirect	$0.9836	$0.9839	€1.5373	€1.5380	£0.6566	£0.6571
Direct	€1.0164	€1.0167	£0.6502	£0.65049	$1.5219	$1.5231

Is there a hypothetical arbitrage opportunity involving the euro/pound cross-rate? If so, what transactions would permit a U.S. arbitrageur to capture an arbitrage profit? The strategy is to compare two alternatives:

1. Buy pounds directly in New York.

2. Buy pounds indirectly through euros.

SOLUTION

Here the cross-rate quote is €/£.

1. Buy pounds directly in New York for $1.5231.

2. Buy pounds indirectly through euros for 0.9839 × 1.5380 = 1.5132.

Because the indirect rate is cheaper, we conclude that there may be an arbitrage opportunity.

To examine the strategy of buying the pound more cheaply and then selling it in New York, we trace the steps, starting with $1 in New York.

1. With $1, buy 1.0164 euros in Europe; convert these to 0.66086 pounds in London (1.0164×0.6502).

2. Sell the 0.66086 pounds in New York for 1.0058 dollars in New York (0.66086×1.5219).

We start with $1 and end up with $1.0058, an arbitrage profit of $0.0058. If the cross-rate quote had been in line, it would have been a London indirect ask quote of €1.5480 for one pound. Paying the ask price in Europe ($0.9839) and in London (€1.5480), we would face a $/pound ask price of $1.5231, the same rate as the direct ask rate in New York. Using the "true" London quotes given in Example 1.2, we can verify that the arbitrage constructed above would result in a loss of $0.0007.

Having examined two consequences of arbitrage, alignment of quotes in two countries and alignment of cross-rates, we next examine how the currency exchange quotes for immediate or future delivery are aligned with the risk-free interest rates in the two countries. In order to do this, we need to explain the nature of forward quotes.

Forward Quotes

Spot exchange rates are quoted for immediate currency transactions, although in practice the settlement takes place 48 hours later. Spot transactions are used extensively to settle commercial purchases of goods, as well as for investments.

Foreign exchange dealers also quote forward exchange rates in the interbank market. These are rates contracted today but with delivery and settlement in the future, usually 30 or 90 days hence. For example, a bank may quote the one-month €/$ exchange rate as 0.80200–0.80250. This means that the bank is willing to commit itself today to buy dollars for 0.80200 euro or to sell them for 0.80250 euro in one month. In a forward, or futures, contract (described in detail in Chapter 10), a commitment is irrevocably made on the transaction date, but delivery, that is, the exchange of currency, takes place later, on a date set in the contract. The origins of the forward currency market may be traced back to the Middle Ages, when merchants from all over Europe met at major trade fairs and made forward contracts for the next fair.

As with spot rates, bid–ask spreads differ as a result of market conditions, bank/dealer positions, and trading volume. Unique to forward transactions is the feature that liquidity decreases with the increasing maturity of the forward contract. Consequently, bid–ask spreads increase with the increasing maturity of the contract.

Forward exchange rates are often quoted as a *premium,* or *discount,* to the spot exchange rate. With a quote showing the currency price of one dollar, there is a premium on the dollar when the forward exchange rate is higher than the spot rate and a discount otherwise. Clearly, a negative premium is a discount. If the one-month forward exchange rate is €/$ = 0.80200 and the spot rate is €/$ = 0.80000, the dollar quotes with a premium of 0.0020 euro per dollar. In the language of currency traders, the dollar is "strong" relative to the euro, as its forward value is higher than its spot value. Conversely, the euro is traded at a discount, as the forward value of one euro ($/€ = 1/0.80200 = 1.24688) is less than its spot value ($/€ = 1.2500). Consequently, when a trader announces that a currency quotes at a premium, the premium should be added to the spot exchange rate to obtain the value of the forward exchange rate. If a currency quotes at a discount, the discount should be subtracted from the spot exchange rate to obtain the value of the forward rate.

The forward discount, or premium, is often calculated as an annualized percentage deviation from the spot rate as given by the following formula:

Given an exchange rate of x/y, the annualized forward premium on y

$$= \left(\frac{\text{Forward rate} - \text{Spot rate}}{\text{Spot rate}} \right) \left(\frac{12}{\text{No. months forward}} \right) 100\%$$

Of course, the annualized forward premium on x can be found by taking the spot rate *minus* the forward rate in this equation.

The percentage premium (discount) is annualized by multiplying by 12 and dividing by the length of the forward contract in months.

Annualized forward premium on the dollar

$$= \left(\frac{0.802 - 0.800}{0.800} \right) \left(\frac{12}{1} \right) 100\% = 3.0\%$$

Interbank quotations are often done in the form of an annualized premium (discount) for reasons that will become obvious in the next section. However, forward rates quoted to customers are usually outright (e.g., €/$ = 0.80200–0.80250).

Spot and forward dollar exchange rates can be found in newspapers around the world, such as the London-based *Financial Times.* For example, the spot SFr/$ exchange rate could be SFr/$ = 1.3593–1.3603. The midpoint is equal to 1.3598. At the same time, the SFr/$ for delivery three months later could be quoted at a midpoint of 1.3471. The dollar quotes at a discount and the Swiss franc at a premium. The dollar's discount is the Swiss franc's premium and the annualized percentage premium of the Swiss franc would then be equal to 3.7 percent per annum; this is obtained by taking the difference between the spot and the forward rate and dividing it by the spot rate:

$$\text{Annualized three-month forward premium} = \left(\frac{0.0127}{1.3598} \right) \left(\frac{12}{3} \right) 100\% = 3.7\%$$

CONCEPTS IN ACTION   *STRONG CURRENCIES*

The sign of the premium as reported in newspapers such as the *Financial Times* must be considered carefully. This is because the convention for quotation of the dollar exchange rate differs across currencies. For all currencies except the euro and British pound, a positive premium indicates that the currency on the line is "strong" relative to the dollar because the rates quoted are the currency price of one dollar, e.g. SFr/$. Because the euro and the pound are quoted as the dollar value of one euro or one pound, a premium for these two lines indicates that the currency is "weak" relative to the dollar, while a discount (a negative premium) indicates that the currency is "strong." In the quotations here, positive premiums for the Swiss franc and Japanese yen indicate strength relative to the U.S. dollar but the Canadian dollar's negative discount indicates that it is weak relative to the U.S. dollar. The positive premiums for the euro and the pound indicate that they are both weak relative to the U.S. dollar.

Foreign Exchange Quotations
Dollar Spot Forward Against the Dollar

		Closing		Three Months	
Aug. 30		**Midpoint**	**Bid/Offer[1]**	**Rate**	**%PA[2]**
Euro	(€)	0.9841	839–842	0.9802	1.6
UK	(£)	1.5492	490–494	1.541	2.1
Switzerland	(SFr)	1.4926	922–929	1.4887	1.1
Canada	(C$)	1.5612	610–614	1.566	−1.2
Japan	(¥)	118.185	160–210	117.655	1.8

[1]Bid/offer spreads show only the last three decimal places. UK £ and euro are quoted in U.S. currency.

[2]Means % per annum.

Source: Data from the *Financial Times* and WM/REUTERS.

Interest Rate Parity: The Forward Discount and the Interest Rate Differential

As mentioned earlier, arbitrage aligns exchange rates and risk-free interest rates. Spot exchange rates, forward exchange rates, and interest rates are technically linked for all currencies that are part of the free international market. In the following discussion, we define the exchange rate as the units of foreign currency (FC) for one unit of domestic currency (DC), an indirect rate.

Interest rate parity (IRP) is a relationship linking spot exchange rates, forward exchange rates, and interest rates. For two currencies, DC and FC, the interest rate parity relationship is that the forward discount (premium) equals the discounted interest rate differential between the two currencies. Stated more simply, the product of the forward rate and one plus the domestic risk-free rate equals the product of the spot rate multiplied by one plus the foreign risk-free rate. The relation is driven by arbitrage as illustrated here.

Assume that the following data exist for the FC and DC currencies:

Spot exchange rate	FC/DC = 0.8
One-year forward exchange rate	FC/DC = 0.808
One-year interest rates	
FC	14%
DC	10%

To take advantage of the interest rate differential, a speculator could borrow DC currency units (at 10 percent), convert them immediately into FC units (at the indirect rate of FC/DC = 0.8), and invest the FC currency (at 14 percent). This action is summarized in Exhibit 1.1. (In this exhibit, the U.S. dollar is DC and the euro is FC.) The speculator makes a profit of 4 percent on the borrowing/lending position but runs the risk of a large depreciation of the FC currency.

In Exhibit 1.1, borrowing DC currency means bringing money from the future to the present. Lending DC currency means the reverse. At the end of the period, at time 1, the speculator must convert foreign currency into domestic currency at an unknown rate to honor the claim in DC currency borrowed.

This position may be transformed into a covered (riskless) interest rate arbitrage by simultaneously buying a forward exchange rate contract to repatriate the FC currency into DC currency in one year at a known forward exchange rate of FC/DC = 0.808. In the process shown in Exhibit 1.2, the investor still benefits on the interest rate differential (a gain of 4 percent), but loses on the repatriation of the FC currency into DC currency on the forward contract. In one year, the exchange rate loss will be equal to

$$\frac{0.800 - 0.808}{0.800} = -1\%$$

EXHIBIT 1.1
_____

Currency Speculation

EXHIBIT 1.2
Covered Interest Rate Arbitrage

Per DC currency unit borrowed, the net gain on the position is 3 percent. This gain is certain at time 0, because all interest rates and exchange rates are fixed at that time.

No capital is invested in the position, which is a pure swap with simultaneous borrowing and lending. If such rates were quoted in reality, banks would arbitrage to exploit this riskless profit opportunity. Enormous swaps could occur, because no capital needs to be invested. To prevent this obviously riskless arbitrage, the forward discount must exactly equal the interest rate differential. In other words, the various rates must adjust so that interest rate parity holds. Note that if the forward discount were larger than the interest rate differential, the arbitrage would simply go the other way. Arbitrageurs would borrow FC currency units and swap them for DC currency units.

The exact mathematical relationship is slightly more complicated, because one must buy a forward contract covering both the principal and the accrued interest in order to achieve a perfect arbitrage. In the previous example, for every dollar borrowed, the forward hedge should cover 0.8 FC currency units plus the interest rate of 14 percent, that is, $0.80 (1.14) = 0.912$. For two currencies, DC and FC, the interest rate parity relationship is that the forward discount (premium) equals the discounted interest rate differential between the two currencies,

$$\text{(Forward rate} - \text{Spot rate)}/\text{Spot rate} = (r_{FC} - r_{DC})/(1 + r_{DC})$$

$$\text{or } (F - S)/S = (r_{FC} - r_{DC})/(1 + r_{DC}) \tag{1.5}$$

where:

r_{DC} is the interest rate of currency DC (the domestic currency)

r_{FC} is the interest rate of currency FC (the foreign currency)

the exchange rates are indirect quotes as the number of units of foreign currency FC for one unit of domestic currency DC

Equivalently, we have the relation

$$F(1 + r_{DC}) = S(1 + r_{FC}), \quad \text{or} \quad F/S = (1 + r_{FC})/(1 + r_{DC}) \tag{1.6}$$

EXAMPLE 1.7　INTEREST RATE PARITY

If the United States is the domestic country and an indirect quote is provided (rates are quoted as the number of euros per one U.S. dollar), arbitrage ensures that

$$F(1 + r_\$) = S(1 + r_\text{€})$$

where S and F are the spot and forward exchange rates (euro price of one U.S. dollar) and $r_\text{€}$ and $r_\$$ are the interest rates in euros and U.S. dollars, respectively. This relation implies that

$$\frac{F - S}{S} = \frac{r_\text{€} - r_\$}{1 + r_\$}$$

If the spot exchange rate is €/$ = 1.05 and the dollar and euro one-year interest rates are 1.76 percent and 3.39 percent, respectively, what is the one-year forward exchange rate?

SOLUTION

Using Equation 1.6, we have

$$F = S(1 + r_\text{€})/(1 + r_\$) = 1.05(1.0339/1.0176) = 1.0668$$

Hence, the one-year forward exchange rate is €1.0668 per dollar.

When the U.S. dollar trades with a forward premium relative to the euro, for example, in a case in which the forward rate is €1.0721 and the spot rate is €1.05, the euro trades with a forward discount relative to the U.S. dollar. Recall that we have defined *strength* by the existence of a premium. The forward premium on the U.S. dollar reflects its strength in this example. Notice that a forward premium is associated with a lower interest rate. A currency with a high risk-free interest rate is considered weak because this rate is needed to compensate for its expected depreciation. A depreciation of the domestic currency coincides with a decrease in the indirect exchange rate. In general, the following table summarizes these relationships:

Domestic Country	Currency Strength	Currency	Indirect Exchange Rate	Direct Exchange Rate	Forward Premium or Discount
Lower risk-free interest rate	Stronger currency	Appreciates	Increases	Decreases	Premium
Higher risk-free interest rate	Weaker currency	Depreciates	Decreases	Increases	Discount

A similar arbitrage relation holds for maturities of less than a year, provided that the right interest rates are used. Annual interest must be converted into rates over the investment period. For a contract with n months maturity, the quoted interest rate must be divided by 12 and multiplied by n.

EXAMPLE 1.8 INTEREST RATE PARITY WITH MATURITIES OF LESS THAN ONE YEAR

Consider the following data:

Spot exchange rate €/$ = 1.058

Annual risk-free interest rates for currency investments:

euro	3.39%
U.S. dollar	1.76%

What is the three-month forward exchange rate?

SOLUTION

Three-month interest rates

euro	3.39%(3/12) = 0.8475%
U.S. dollar	1.76%(3/12) = 0.44%

The three-month forward exchange rate is equal to

$$\text{Forward exchange rate} = \text{Spot exchange rate} \frac{1 + r_€}{1 + r_\$}$$

$$= 1.058(1.008475/1.0044) = 1.0623$$

Thus, the three-month forward rate is €1.0623 per dollar.

In working with interest rate parity, one should know which type of rate is being quoted before proceeding any further. The equation for IRP is different for direct exchange rates. With direct exchange rates, the direct spot rate times one plus the domestic risk-free rate (investing domestically the amount of DC units required to purchase one FC unit) equals the forward rate times one plus the foreign risk-free rate (exchanging for one FC unit now, investing in the foreign country, and repatriating later). This means that Equations 1.5 and 1.6 must be rewritten with an interchange of the domestic and foreign currency. With indirect rates, the domestic risk-free rate is in the denominator of both Equations 1.5 and 1.6. The domestic risk-free rate is subtracted from the foreign risk-free rate in the numerator of Equation 1.5 and the foreign risk-free rate appears in the numerator of Equation 1.6. With direct rates, the foreign risk-free rate is in the denominator of both equations. The foreign risk-free rate is subtracted from the domestic risk-free rate in the numerator of Equation 1.7 and the domestic risk-free rate is in the numerator of Equation 1.8.

The forward premium (discount) can be expressed as

$$\text{(Forward rate} - \text{Spot rate)}/\text{(Spot rate)} = (r_{DC} - r_{FC})/(1 + r_{FC})$$

$$\text{or } (F - S)/S = (r_{DC} - r_{FC})/(1 + r_{FC}) \tag{1.7}$$

or, equivalently,

$$\text{(Forward rate/Spot rate)}$$

$$= (1 + \text{Domestic risk-free rate})/(1 + \text{Foreign risk-free rate}) \tag{1.8}$$

$$\text{or } F/S = (1 + r_{DC})/(1 + r_{FC}).$$

where r_{FC} is the risk-free interest rate of the foreign currency, and r_{DC} is the risk-free interest rate of the domestic currency, and the exchange rates are direct quotes as the number of units of domestic currency DC for one unit of foreign currency FC.

Finally, we note that interest rate parity is sometimes called covered interest rate parity (covered by a forward contract) to distinguish it from uncovered interest rate parity. Uncovered interest rate parity is based on economic theory rather than on arbitrage and involves expected exchange rates rather than forward rates. Uncovered interest rate parity is a theory that links interest rate differentials and the difference between the spot and expected exchange rate. We leave it and other parity theories for Chapter 2.

Summary

- A direct exchange rate is the domestic price of foreign currency.

- An indirect exchange rate is the amount of foreign currency equivalent to one unit of the domestic currency.

- The spread on a foreign currency transaction is the difference between the rate at which the bank is willing to commit itself today to buy (bid) foreign currency and to sell (ask). When given as a percentage, this spread is given as $100 \times (\text{ask} - \text{bid})/\text{ask}$.

- Spreads differ as a result of market conditions and trading volume but not dealer positions. The size of the bid–ask spread increases with exchange rate uncertainty (volatility) because of bank/dealer risk aversion. Spreads are larger for currencies that have a low trading volume (thinly traded currencies).

- To work with currency cross-rates and bid–ask spreads, we can use two principles: the DC/FC direct ask exchange rate is the reciprocal of the FC/DC indirect bid exchange rate, and the DC/FC direct bid exchange rate is the reciprocal of the FC/DC indirect ask exchange rate.

- The largest no-arbitrage deviation in the domestic midpoint from the reciprocal of the direct midpoint of the foreign bid–ask spread that allows no arbitrage between the currencies of two countries is given by

$$x = -(1/S_f) + 1/(k^2 \times S_f)$$

  where S_f is the direct exchange rate quote in the foreign country, and k is 1 minus the transaction cost t_c, which is given as a percentage of the direct quote midpoint (e.g., $k = 0.9997$ if $t_c = 0.03\%$), and the no arbitrage bid–ask spread is $(1/S_f) \pm x$.

- To calculate the profit on a triangular arbitrage opportunity, the basic step is to determine whether the quoted cross-rate is different from the implied cross-rate.

- Spot exchange rates are quoted for immediate currency transactions, but forward change rates are rates contracted today for delivery and settlement in the future.

- As with spot rates, forward contract bid–ask spreads differ as a result of market conditions and trading volume but not bank/dealer positions. Bid–ask spreads increase with increasing maturity of the contract.

- The forward discount (negative) or premium (positive) is defined as the difference between the forward rate and spot rate expressed as a percentage of the spot rate.

- The forward discount, or premium, is often calculated as an annualized percentage deviation from the spot rate as given by the following formula:

  Annualized forward premium

$$= \left(\frac{\text{Forward rate} - \text{Spot rate}}{\text{Spot rate}}\right)\left(\frac{12}{\text{No. months forward}}\right)100\%$$

- For two currencies, A and B, the interest rate parity relationship is that the forward discount (premium) equals the interest rate differential between the two currencies. With the exchange rate quoted as the number of units of B for one unit of A,

$$\frac{\text{Forward rate} - \text{Spot rate}}{\text{Spot rate}} = \frac{r_B - r_A}{1 + r_A}$$

  Note that an equivalent relation is

$$\text{forward rate} = \text{spot rate} \times \frac{1 + r_B}{1 + r_A}$$

- Covered interest arbitrage is the process of simultaneously borrowing the domestic currency, transferring it into foreign currency at the spot exchange rate, lending it, and buying a forward exchange rate contract to repatriate the foreign currency into domestic currency at a known forward exchange rate. The net result of such an arbitrage should be nil.

Problems

1. If the exchange rate value of the British pound goes from US$1.80 to US$1.60, then:
   a. The pound has appreciated, and the British will find U.S. goods cheaper.
   b. The pound has appreciated, and the British will find U.S. goods more expensive.
   c. The pound has depreciated, and the British will find U.S. goods more expensive.
   d. The pound has depreciated, and the British will find U.S. goods cheaper.

2. If the exchange rate between Australian dollar and U.S. dollar, A$/$, changes from 1.60 to 1.50, then:
   a. The Australian dollar has appreciated, and the Australians will find U.S. goods cheaper.
   b. The Australian dollar has appreciated, and the Australians will find U.S. goods more expensive.
   c. The Australian dollar has depreciated, and the Australians will find U.S. goods more expensive.
   d. The Australian dollar has depreciated, and the Australians will find U.S. goods cheaper.

3. Over the past six years, the exchange rate between Swiss franc and U.S. dollar, SFr/$, has changed from about 1.20 to about 1.60. Would you agree that over this six-year period, the Swiss goods have become cheaper for buyers in the United States?

4. You noticed that the exchange rate between the Thai baht and the dollar has changed considerably. In particular, the baht/$ exchange rate has increased from 25 to 30.
   a. Has the Thai baht appreciated or depreciated with respect to the dollar? By what percentage?
   b. By what percentage has the value of the dollar changed with respect to the Thai baht?

5. A foreign exchange trader with a U.S. bank took a short position of £5,000,000 when the $/£ exchange rate was 1.45. Subsequently, the exchange rate has changed to 1.51. Is this movement in the exchange rate good from the point of view of the position taken by the trader? By how much has the bank's liability changed because of the change in exchange rate?

6. A financial newspaper provided the following midpoint spot exchange rates. Compute all the cross-exchange rates based on these quotes.

$/€	0.9119
SFr/$	1.5971
¥/$	128.17

7. You visit the foreign exchange trading room of a major U.S. bank. A trader asks for quotations of the euro from various correspondents and hears the following quotes:

From Bank A	1.1210–15
From Bank B	12–17

   What do these quotes mean?

8. Do you think the dollar exchange rate of the British pound or the Polish zloty, has a higher percentage bid–ask spread? Why?

9. Here are some quotes of the Japanese yen/U.S. dollar spot exchange rate given simultaneously on the phone by three banks:

Bank A	121.15–121.25
Bank B	121.30–121.35
Bank C	121.15–121.35

   Are these quotes reasonable? Is there an arbitrage opportunity?

10. The euro is quoted as $/€ = 1.1610–1.1615, and the Swiss franc is quoted as SFr/$ = 1.4100–1.4120. What is the implicit SFr/€ quotation?

11. A bank is quoting the following exchange rates against the dollar for the Swiss franc and the Australian dollar:

    SFr/$ = 1.5960–70

    A$/$ = 1.8225–35

    An Australian firm asks the bank for a SFr/A$ quote. What cross-rate would the bank quote?

12. A bank is quoting the following exchange rates against the dollar for the Swiss franc and the Australian dollar:

    SFr/$ = 1.5960–1.5970

    A$/$ = 1.8225–1.8235

    A Swiss firm asks the bank for an A$/SFr quote. What cross-rate would the bank quote?

13. Based on the Japanese yen and Canadian dollar direct quotes by a bank, the implicit yen per Canadian dollar cross-rate quotation is ¥/C$ = 82.515–82.575. What would be the implicit Canadian dollar per yen cross-rate, C$/¥, quotation?

14. The dollar spot exchange rate of the Danish kroner is DKr8.25/$, and the dollar spot exchange rate of the Swiss franc is SFr1.65/$.
    a. What should the DKr/SFr cross-rate be so that there are no arbitrage opportunities (ignore transaction costs)?
    b. Suppose a bank is offering DKr5.20/SFr. At this exchange rate, which currency is overvalued with respect to the other?

15. Barclays bank is quoting a dollar/pound exchange rate of $1.4570/£, Industrial bank is quoting a Japanese yen/dollar exchange rate of ¥128.17/$, and Midland bank is quoting a Japanese yen/pound cross rate of ¥183/£. Ignoring bid–ask spreads, is there an arbitrage opportunity here? If there is an arbitrage opportunity, what steps would you take to make an arbitrage profit, and how much would you profit if you have $1,000,000 available for this purpose?

16. Jim Waugh specializes in cross-rate arbitrage. He notices the following quotes:

    Swiss franc/dollar = SFr1.5971/$

    Australian dollar/U.S. dollar = A$1.8215/$

    Australian dollar/Swiss franc = A$1.1450/SFr

Ignoring transaction costs, does Jim Waugh have an arbitrage opportunity based on these quotes? If there is an arbitrage opportunity, what steps would he take to make an arbitrage profit, and how much would he profit if he has $1,000,000 available for this purpose?

17. Paf is a small country that wishes to control international capital flows. The currency of Paf is the pif. Paf put in place an exchange control whereby all current account transactions can be transferred using the normal exchange rate, but financial account transactions must be transferred at a financial pif rate. In other words, foreigners wishing to invest in the assets of Paf must buy them at the financial pif rate, whereas dividends are repatriated at the normal pif rate. The current financial pif rate is 0.8 pifs per dollar or 1.25 dollars per financial pif. The financial rate in dollars/pif quotes at a premium of 25 percent over the normal rate.
    a. Assume that the premium of the financial rate stays constant over time. Will a U.S. investor make the same return on investment as will a resident of Paf, once the asset is resold?
    b. You hear that the exchange controls may be lifted and that the financial rate may disappear. Would this be good news to an existing foreign investor?
    c. Would the lifting of exchange controls and removal of the financial rate be good news to a new foreign investor?

18. You notice the following exchange rates in the newspaper:

    $/£ spot: 1.46

    $/£ three months forward: 1.42

    SFr/$ spot: 1.60

    SFr/$ three months forward: 1.65

    In the language of currency traders, would the pound be considered "strong" or "weak" relative to the dollar? What about the Swiss franc?

19. The spot dollar to pound exchange rate is $/£ = 1.4570–1.4576. The six-month forward dollar to pound exchange rate is $/£ = 1.4408–1.4434.
    a. Is the pound trading at a discount or at a premium relative to the dollar in the forward market?
    b. Compute the annualized forward discount or premium on the pound relative to the dollar?

20. The spot Swiss franc to dollar exchange rate is SFr/$ = 1.5960–70. The three-month forward Swiss franc to dollar exchange rate is SFr/$ = 1.5932–62.
    a. Is the Swiss franc trading at a discount or at a premium relative to the dollar in the forward market?
    b. Compute the annualized forward discount or premium on the Swiss franc relative to the dollar?

Solutions

1. Since the value of the British pound in U.S. dollars has gone down, it has depreciated with respect to the U.S. dollar. Therefore, the British will have to spend more British pounds to purchase U.S. goods. Accordingly, the correct answer is (c).

2. Since the number of Australian dollars needed to purchase one U.S. dollar has decreased from 1.60 to 1.50, the Australian dollar has appreciated with respect to the U.S. dollar. Therefore, the Australians will have to spend fewer Australian dollars to purchase U.S. goods. Accordingly, the correct answer is (a).

3. The value of the dollar in Swiss francs has gone up from about 1.20 to about 1.60. Therefore, the dollar has appreciated relative to the Swiss franc, and the dollars needed by Americans to purchase Swiss goods have decreased. Thus, the statement is correct.

4. a. One baht was worth 1/25 or 0.04 dollars earlier. It is worth 1/30 or 0.0333 dollars now. Thus, the baht has depreciated with respect to the dollar. Percentage change in the dollar value of baht $= ((0.0333 - 0.04)/0.04)100\% = -16.7\%$.
   b. One dollar was worth 25 bahts earlier and is worth 30 bahts now. Percentage change in the value of dollar $= ((30 - 25)/25)100\% = 20.0\%$.

5. The increase in $/£ exchange rate implies that the pound has appreciated with respect to the dollar. This is unfavorable to the trader since the trader has a short position in pounds.

   Bank's liability in dollars initially was $5,000,0000 \times 1.45 = \$7,250,000$

   Bank's liability in dollars now is $5,000,0000 \times 1.51 = \$7,550,000$

   Thus, the bank's liability has increased by $300,000

6. Three cross-exchange rates need to be computed: SFr/€, ¥/€, SFr/¥.
   a. SFr/€ = SFr/$ × $/€ = SFr 1.5971/$ × $ 0.9119/€ = 1.4564
   b. ¥/€ = ¥/$ × $/€ = ¥ 128.17/$ × $ 0.9119/€ = 116.88
   c. SFr/¥ = SFr/$ × $/¥ = (SFr/$)/(¥/$) = (SFr 1.5971/$)/(¥ 128.17/$) = 0.0125

7. These quotations mean that Bank A is willing to buy a euro for 1.1210 dollars (bid rate) or to sell one for 1.1215 dollars (ask rate). Bank B's $/€ bid rate is 1.1212; its ask rate is 1.1217. That is, Bank B is willing to buy a euro for 1.1212 dollars or to sell one for 1.1217 dollars.

8. The percentage spread is considerably higher for the Polish zloty than for the British pound. The market for the Polish zloty is much less liquid than the market for the British pound. There is a lot more competition between market makers for the British pound than for the Polish zloty. Consequently, the percentage spread is considerably higher for the Polish zloty than for the British pound.

9. These quotes are unreasonable because they deviate from Bank A to Bank B by more than the spread; for example, Bank A's ask rate (121.25) is smaller than Bank B's bid rate (121.30). There is, therefore, an arbitrage opportunity. One can buy Bank A's dollars for 121.25 yen per dollar, sell these dollars to Bank B for 121.30 yen per dollar, and thereby make a profit of 0.05 yen per dollar traded. This is a riskless, instantaneous operation that requires no initial investment.

10. The SFr/€ quotation is obtained as follows. In obtaining this quotation, we keep in mind that SFr/€ = SFr/$ × $/€, and that the price for each transaction (bid or ask) is the one that is more advantageous to the trader.

    The SFr/€ bid price is the number of Swiss francs that a trader is willing to pay for one euro. This transaction (buy euro—sell Swiss francs) is equivalent to selling Swiss francs to buy dollars (at a bid rate of 1.4100), and then selling those dollars to buy euros (at a bid rate of 1.1610). Mathematically, the transaction is as follows:

$$(\text{bid SFr/\$}) \times (\text{bid \$/€}) = 1.4100 \times 1.1610 = 1.6370$$

The SFr/€ ask price is the number of Swiss francs that a trader is asking for one euro. This transaction (sell euros—buy Swiss francs) is equivalent to buying Swiss francs with dollars (at an ask rate of 1.4120) and simultaneously purchasing these dollars against euros (at an ask rate of 1.1615). Mathematically, this can be expressed as follows:

$$(\text{ask SFr/\$}) \times (\text{ask \$/€}) = 1.4120 \times 1.1615 = 1.6400$$

So the resulting quotation by the trader is

$$\text{SFr/€} = 1.6370 - 1.6400$$

11. The SFr/A$ quotation is obtained as follows. In obtaining this quotation, we keep in mind that SFr/A$ = SFr/$ /A$/$, and that the price (bid or ask) for each transaction is the one that is more advantageous to the bank.

The SFr/A$ bid price is the number of SFr the bank is willing to pay to buy one A$. This transaction (buy A$—sell SFr) is equivalent to selling SFr to buy dollars (at a bid rate of 1.5960) and then selling those dollars to buy A$ (at an ask rate of 1.8235). Mathematically, the transaction is as follows:

$$\text{bid SFr/A\$} = (\text{bid SFr/\$})/(\text{ask A\$/\$}) = 1.5960/1.8235 = 0.8752$$

The SFr/A$ ask price is the number of SFr that the bank is asking for one A$. This transaction (sell A$—buy SFr) is equivalent to buying SFr with dollars (at an ask rate of 1.5970) and simultaneously purchasing these dollars against A$ (at a bid rate of 1.8225). This may be expressed as follows:

$$\text{ask SFr/A\$} = (\text{ask SFr/\$})/(\text{bid A\$/\$}) = 1.5970/1.8225 = 0.8763$$

The resulting quotation by the bank is

$$\text{SFr/A\$} = 0.8752\text{–}0.8763$$

12. The A$/SFr quotation is obtained as follows. In obtaining this quotation, we keep in mind that A$/SFr = A$/$ / SFr/$, and that the price (bid or ask) for each transaction is the one that is more advantageous to the bank.

The A$/SFr bid price is the number of A$ the bank is willing to pay to buy one SFr. This transaction (buy SFr—sell A$) is equivalent to selling A$ to buy dollars (at a bid rate of 1.8225) and then selling those dollars to buy SFr (at an ask rate of 1.5970). Mathematically, the transaction is as follows:

$$\text{bid A\$/SFr} = (\text{bid A\$/\$})/(\text{ask SFr/\$}) = 1.8225/1.5970 = 1.1412$$

The A$/SFr ask price is the number of A$ that the bank is asking for one SFr. This transaction (sell SFr—buy A$) is equivalent to buying A$ with dollars (at an ask rate of 1.8235) and simultaneously purchasing these dollars against SFr (at a bid rate of 1.5960). This may be expressed as follows:

$$\text{ask A\$/SFr} = (\text{ask A\$/\$})/(\text{bid SFr/\$}) = 1.8235/1.5960 = 1.1425$$

The resulting quotation by the bank is

A\$/SFr = 1.1412 − 1.1425

13. The bid C\$/¥ rate would be the inverse of the ask ¥/C\$ rate, and the ask C\$/¥ rate would be the inverse of the bid ¥/C\$ rate. Therefore,

bid C\$/¥ = 1 / ask(¥/C\$) = 1/82.5750 = 0.01211
ask C\$/¥ = 1 / bid(¥/C\$) = 1/82.5150 = 0.01212

Thus, the quote is C\$/¥ = 0.01211–0.01212.

14. a. There would be no arbitrage opportunities if cross-rate DKr/SFr = DKr/\$ × \$/SFr.

Because SFr/\$ =1.65, \$/SFr = 1/1.65 = 0.6061.

So, there would be no arbitrage opportunities if the cross-rate DKr/SFr = DKr 8.25/\$ × \$ 0.6061/SFr = DKr 5/SFr.

b. In the DKr 5.20/SFr cross-rate, one SFr is worth DKr5.20. The implicit rate computed in part (a) above indicates that one SFr should be worth DKr5. Therefore, the SFr is overvalued with respect to the DKr at the exchange rate of DKr 5.20/SFr.

15. The implicit cross-rate between yen and pound is ¥/£= ¥/\$ × \$/£ = 128.17 × 1.4570 = 186.74. However, Midland bank is quoting a lower rate of ¥183/£. So, triangular arbitrage is possible.

   In the cross-rate of ¥183/£ quoted by Midland, one pound is worth 183 yen, whereas the cross-rate based on the direct rates implies that one pound is worth 186.74 yen. Thus, pound is undervalued relative to the yen in the cross-rate quoted by Midland, and your strategy for triangular arbitrage should be based on using yen to buy pounds from Midland. Accordingly, the steps you would take for an arbitrage profit are as follows.
   i. Sell dollars to get yen: Sell \$1,000,000 to get \$1,000,000 × ¥128.17/\$ = ¥128,170,000.
   ii. Use yen to buy pounds: Sell ¥128,170,000 to buy ¥128,170,000 / ¥183/£ = £700,382.51
   iii. Sell pounds for dollars: Sell £700,382.51 for £700,382.51 × \$1.4570/£ = \$1,020,457.32.

Thus, your arbitrage profit is \$1,020,457.32 − \$1,000,000 = \$20,457.32.

16. a. The implicit cross-rate between Australian dollars and Swiss francs is A\$/SFr = A\$/\$ × \$/SFr = (A\$/\$)/(SFr/\$) = 1.8215/1.5971 = 1.1405. However, the quoted cross-rate is higher at A\$1.1450/SFr. So, triangular arbitrage is possible.
   b. In the quoted cross-rate of A\$1.1450/SFr, one Swiss franc is worth A\$1.1450, whereas the cross-rate based on the direct rates implies that one Swiss franc is worth A\$1.1405. Thus, the Swiss franc is overvalued relative to the A\$ in the quoted cross-rate, and Jim Waugh's strategy for triangular arbitrage should be based on selling Swiss francs to buy A\$ as per the quoted cross-rate. Accordingly, the steps Jim Waugh would take for an arbitrage profit are as follows.
   i. Sell dollars to get Swiss francs: Sell \$1,000,000 to get \$1,000,000 × SFr1.5971/\$ = SFr1,597,100.

    ii. Sell Swiss francs to buy Australian dollars: Sell SFr1,597,100 to buy SFr1,597,100 × A$1.1450/SFr = A$1,828,679.50

    iii. Sell Australian dollars for dollars: Sell A$1,828,679.50 for A$1,828,679.50/ A$1.8215/$ = $1,003,941.53.

Thus, your arbitrage profit is $1,003,941.53 − $1,000,000 = $3,941.53.

17. a. The American investor has paid a 25 percent premium over the price paid by a domestic investor. Yet, he receives the same dividends as the domestic investor. Therefore, his investment bears a smaller yield than it would for a domestic investor.

    b. Lifting of the exchange controls would be bad news to an existing foreign investor in Paf, since her asset could only be repatriated at the normal pif rate (1.00), while she had bought it at the financial rate (1.25)

    c. Lifting of the exchange controls would be good news to foreign investors planning to invest in Paf in the future, because they would no longer have to pay the 25 percent premium when buying assets in Paf.

18. The value of the £ in $ is worth less three months forward than it is now. Thus, the £ is trading at a forward discount relative to the $. Therefore, the £ is "weak" relative to the $. Because a $ is worth SFr1.60 now but worth SFr1.65 three months forward, the $ is "strong" relative to the SFr. That is, the SFr is "weak" relative to the $.

19. The midpoint of the spot dollar to pound exchange rate is $/£ = 1.4573. The midpoint of the six-month forward dollar to pound exchange rate is $/£ = 1.4421.

    a. Based on the midpoints, the dollar value of a pound is 1.4573 now and only 1.4421 six months forward. Thus, the pound is worth less six months forward than now. That is, the pound is trading at a discount relative to the dollar in the forward market.

    b. Difference between midpoints of the forward and spot rates = 0.0152.

Annualized discount

$$= \left(\frac{\text{Difference between forward and spot rates}}{\text{Spot rate}} \right) \left(\frac{12}{\text{No. months forward}} \right) 100\%$$

$$= \left(\frac{0.0152}{1.4573} \right) \left(\frac{12}{6} \right) 100\% = 2.09\%$$

20. The midpoint of the spot Swiss franc to dollar exchange rate is SFr/$ = 1.5965. The midpoint of the three-month forward Swiss franc to dollar exchange rate is SFr/$ = 1.5947.

    a. Based on the midpoints, a dollar is worth SFr1.5965 now and only 1.5947 three months forward. So, the dollar is trading at a discount relative to the SFr in the forward market. That is, the SFr is trading at a premium relative to the dollar in the forward market.

    b. Difference between midpoints of the forward and spot rates = 0.0018.

Annualized premium

$$= \left(\frac{\text{Difference between forward and spot rates}}{\text{Spot rate}} \right) \left(\frac{12}{\text{No. months forward}} \right) 100\%$$

$$= \left(\frac{0.0018}{1.5965} \right) \left(\frac{12}{3} \right) 100\% = 0.45\%$$

2

Foreign Exchange Parity Relations

- Explain how exchange rates are determined in a flexible or floating exchange rate system

- Explain the role of each component of the balance of payments accounts

- Explain how current account deficits or surpluses and financial account deficits or surpluses affect an economy

- Describe the factors that cause a nation's currency to appreciate or depreciate

- Explain how monetary and fiscal policies affect the exchange rate and balance of payments components

- Describe a fixed exchange rate and a pegged exchange rate system

- Define and discuss absolute purchasing power parity and relative purchasing power parity

- Calculate the end-of-period exchange rate implied by purchasing power parity, given the beginning-of-period exchange rate and the inflation rates

- Define and discuss the international Fisher relation

- Calculate the real interest rate, given interest rates and inflation rates and the assumption that the international Fisher relation holds

- Calculate the international Fisher relation, and its linear approximation, between interest rates and expected inflation rates

- Define and discuss the theory of uncovered interest rate parity and explain the theory's relationship to other exchange rate parity theories

- Calculate the expected change in the exchange rate, given interest rates and the assumption that uncovered interest rate parity holds

- Discuss the foreign exchange expectation relation between the forward exchange rate and the expected exchange rate

- Calculate the expected change in the exchange rate, given the forward exchange rate discount or premium, and discuss the implications of a foreign currency risk premium

- Calculate the forward exchange rate given the spot exchange rate and risk-free interest rates, using interest rate parity or its linear approximation

- Discuss the implications of the parity relationships combined

- Explain the role of absolute purchasing power parity and relative purchasing power parity in exchange rate determination

- Discuss the elements of balance of payments and their role in exchange rate determination

- Discuss the asset markets approach to pricing exchange rate expectations

- Calculate the short-term and the long-run exchange rate effects of a sudden and unexpected increase in the money supply

Fluctuations in exchange rates seem to be generated by a large variety of economic and political events. Exchange rate uncertainty adds an important dimension to the economics of capital markets. Chapter 2 starts with a review of foreign exchange fundamentals. In the flexible (or floating) exchange rate system of all major currencies, the foreign exchange rate is freely determined by supply and demand. Many international transactions affect foreign exchange demand and supply and these are detailed in the country's balance of payments. After a brief review of the interaction between the two major components of the balance of payments (current account and financial account), we list the major factors that cause a currency to appreciate or depreciate.

Nevertheless, a detailed analysis of exchange rates and their importance in asset management requires a strong conceptual framework. Many domestic and foreign monetary variables interact with exchange rates. Before presenting the basic models of exchange rate determination, it is useful to recall well-known international parity conditions linking domestic and foreign monetary variables: inflation rates, interest rates, and foreign exchange rates. The relations among these are the basis for a simple model of the international monetary environment and are discussed in the second part of this chapter. Given the complexity of a multi-currency environment, it is most useful to start by building a simplified model linking the various domestic and foreign monetary variables. The third part of this chapter then discusses exchange rate determination theories and their practical implications.

Foreign Exchange Fundamentals

Supply and Demand for Foreign Exchange

Just as the value of money is determined by supply and demand in the domestic economy, its value in relation to foreign currencies is also determined by supply and demand. Major currencies, such as the dollar, euro, yen, British pound, or Swiss franc, belong to a *flexible* or *floating exchange rate system*. These currencies are freely exchanged on the foreign exchange market, and their exchange rate depends on supply and demand.

Let's assume that the equilibrium exchange rate between the euro and the U.S. dollar is $1.25 = 1 euro. So one needs 1.25 dollars to buy one euro. The dollar price of one euro results from the supply and demand for euros. American investors wishing to buy European goods or assets need to sell dollars to buy euros. Conversely, Europeans wishing to buy American goods or assets need to sell euros to buy dollars. If the exchange rate were artificially higher, say $1.50 = 1 euro, European goods would look more expensive to Americans, as more dollars would be needed to spend the same amount of euros to buy European goods. Americans would decrease their purchase of European goods: The demand for euros from Americans would decrease. Conversely, American goods would look cheaper to Europeans, who would increase their purchase of American goods: The supply of euros from Europeans would increase.

In this two-country example, Exhibit 2.1 illustrates the demand and supply curves for euros. In the marketplace, the current exchange rate of $1.25 per euro is

---

EXHIBIT 2.1

Foreign Exchange Market Equilibrium

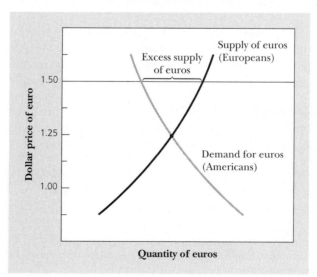

the price that equilibrates demand and supply. If the exchange rate were set higher, say $1.50 per euro, there would be excess supply of euros, which would lead to a market disequilibrium.

The illustration presented in Exhibit 2.1 is simple, as we referred only to transactions motivated by trading demand between two countries. In general, there are many types of transactions that affect the demand and supply of one national currency. From an accounting viewpoint, each country keeps track of the payments on all international transactions in its *balance of payments*.

Balance of Payments

The balance of payments tracks all financial flows crossing a country's borders during a given period (a quarter or a year). It is an accounting of all cash flows between residents and nonresidents of a country (called "home country" in the discussion that follows). For example, an export creates a financial inflow for the home country, whereas an import creates an outflow (a negative inflow). A resident's purchase of a foreign security creates a negative financial inflow, whereas a loan made by a foreign bank to a resident bank creates a positive financial inflow. The convention is to treat all inflows (e.g., exports or sale of domestic assets) as a credit to the balance of payments.

For example, assume that a resident imports 100 worth of goods from a foreign country and uses trade credit from the foreign exporter. There will be two accounting entries:

- 100 debit for the goods (imports)

- 100 credit for the loan obtained

International transactions, such as these, are further grouped into two main categories[1]: current account and financial account.

Current Account   The *current account* covers all current transactions that take place in the normal business of residents of a country. It is dominated by the *trade balance,* the balance of all exports and imports. It also includes various other current transactions. To summarize, the current account is made up of

- exports and imports (the trade balance)

- services (such as services in transportation, communication, insurance, and finance)

- income (interest, dividends, and various investment income from cross-border investments)

---

[1] We follow the 1993 IMF (International Monetary Fund) presentation and terminology, which is currently used by the IMF and most countries. A more detailed description of the balance of payments is given later in this chapter.

- current transfers (transfers are gifts and other flows without quid pro quo compensation)

The current account balance represents the net value of all these flows associated with current transactions by residents abroad or by nonresidents in the home country.

Financial Account   The *financial account* covers investments by residents abroad and investments by nonresidents in the home country. It includes

- direct investment made by companies

- portfolio investments in equity, bonds, and other securities of any maturity

- other investments and liabilities (such as deposits or borrowing with foreign banks and vice versa)

The financial account balance represents the net value of all these flows associated with investments and liabilities by residents abroad or by nonresidents in the home country.

The sum of these two accounts, called the *overall balance,*[2] should be zero. If it is not zero, the monetary authority must use reserve assets to fill the gap. If the overall balance is negative, the central bank can use up part of its reserves to restore a zero balance. The *official reserve* account tracks all reserve transactions by the monetary authorities. By accounting definition, the sum of all the balance of payments accounts must be zero.

Current Account Deficits and Financial Account Surpluses

The trade balance, the primary component of the current account, receives major attention in the media of all countries. Monthly trade figures are widely discussed when they are released. The usual undertone is that a current account deficit is "bad." This simple value judgment is based on some economic arguments that are often incorrect. We now address some of the issues.

A Current Account Deficit Is Offset by a Financial Account Surplus   The current account is only one component of a country's balance of payments. A current account deficit should not be confused with an overall balance deficit. A current account deficit has to be offset by a financial account surplus. Of course, official reserves can be used to offset a current account deficit, in a given quarter or year, but this can be only a temporary measure, as the country's reserves will quickly be depleted. To be sustained, a current account deficit must be financed by a financial

---

[2] Two other small accounts also exist in the balance of payments terminology. They are the *capital account* (which tracks capital transfers, i.e., capital gifts to other countries such as debt forgiveness) and *net errors and omissions* (to adjust for statistical discrepancies). These accounts are small in magnitude and usually added to the financial account balance for analysis purposes. We follow this convention. A more detailed presentation of the balance of payments is proposed in the third part of this chapter.

EXHIBIT 2.2

Summary 2001 Balance of Payments of the United States, Japan, the United Kingdom, and France
(in billions of U.S. dollars)

Balance	USA	Japan	UK	France
Current account	−417	89	−29	21
Financial account	422	−49	25	−27
Overall balance	5	40	−4	−6

Source: IMF Financial Statistics, September 2002.

account surplus. This has been the case for the United States since the mid-nineties. Exhibit 2.2 reports the two major components of the 2001 balance of payments of the United States, Japan, the United Kingdom, and France, as calculated by the IMF.[3]

The large current account deficit of the United States ($417 billion) is mostly caused by its trade deficit ($424 billion). But foreigners are large investors in the U.S. economy. They are attracted by a stable country with good investment opportunities and a major currency. Investment flows are largely directed at Treasury bonds and other debt securities (around $400 billion), while the balance of direct and equity portfolio investment is almost zero. The overall balance of the United States is close to equilibrium ($5 billion), leading to a small increase in official reserves. If a nation runs a current account deficit, it must also run a financial account surplus and vice versa.

Is a Current Account Deficit a Bad Economic Signal?   A country faces a trade deficit when its imports exceed its exports. As long as foreign investors are willing to finance this difference by net capital flows into the country, the situation poses no economic problem. Actually, U.S. residents consume more than they produce (current account deficit), and the difference is paid by financial inflows from abroad. In terms of the exchange rate, a current account deficit puts depreciation pressures on the home currency (excess demand for foreign currencies to purchase imports), but the financial account surplus puts appreciation pressures on the home currency (excess supply of foreign currencies to buy home securities). If the overall balance is close to zero, the two effects cancel each other.

A current account deficit is sometimes caused by economic growth. When a country grows faster than its trading partners, it tends to need more imports to sustain its output growth. Because other countries do not have the same growth rate, demand for exports does not grow as fast as that for imports. Higher economic growth also yields attractive returns on invested capital and attracts foreign investment. This capital inflow provides natural financing for the current account deficit. Economic growth differentials with other major countries can explain part of the

---

[3] The capital account and net errors and omissions have been added to the financial account.

U.S. trade deficit in the nineties. It can also explain part of the Japanese trade surplus in the nineties, as the Japanese economy went into a severe recession that reduced the need for imports. In this case, an excessive current account surplus could be a bad signal, rather than a good one.

Large current account imbalances can have social implications. American unions have repeatedly pointed to the U.S. current account deficit to show that free trade has penalized U.S. labor: U.S. jobs are lost to foreign countries. Periodically, U.S. tariffs have been imposed on some foreign goods for political reasons. Similarly, countries with large current account surpluses can be singled out and become the target of tariffs and other protectionist measures by countries with large current account deficits.

To summarize, a current account deficit is not a bad economic signal as long as nonresidents are willing to offset it by investment flows. But large current account imbalances, positive or negative, can be deemed as "bad" politically.

Is a Large Current Account Deficit Sustainable?   First, we need to judge the size of a deficit relative to some benchmark. This deficit can be compared with total imports or gross domestic product (GDP). For example, the U.S. trade (or current account) deficit was almost 40 percent of total imports in 2001. This is a very large number. It represented around 4 percent of U.S. GDP, a more reasonable number but still large compared with that of most economies. For example, the current account balances of Japan, the United Kingdom, and France represent around 2 percent of their GDP. It is not unusual to see emerging countries sometimes running current account deficits on the order of 5 to 8 percent of their GDP.

CONCEPTS IN ACTION   *BALANCE OF PAYMENTS ANALYSIS*

Let's briefly analyze the 2001 balance of payments of Japan, the United Kingdom, and France using Exhibit 2.2.

Japan: Japan runs a large current account surplus of $89 billion. This is partly offset by a deficit in the financial account balance ($49 billion). Part of this financial account deficit consists of direct investment of Japanese companies to produce abroad (e.g., manufacturing Japanese cars in the United States, or transferring production of electronic equipment to low-cost developing neighbors). Part of it consists in the purchase of U.S. Treasury bonds. But the large current account surplus led to a large increase in official reserves ($40 billion). The case of Japan is unique.

The United Kingdom: The United Kingdom had a current account deficit of $29 billion. This is mostly offset by a financial account surplus of $25 billion. London attracts extensive foreign investments, especially in the banking and financial services industry. Official reserves decreased by a small amount ($4 billion).

France: France had a current account surplus of $21 billion and a financial account deficit of $27 billion. This financial account deficit is mostly explained by extensive foreign direct investments made by French corporations.

A large current account deficit can be sustained as long as nonresidents are willing to finance it continuously. As long as a country offers attractive investment opportunities and a stable "investment climate," it can keep attracting additional financial flows.[4] The situation is no different for a corporation that relies on debt and equity financing to generate more activity. External financing is a normal recourse for a growing corporation. But as with corporations, external financing of a country also increases the risk of a crisis. As soon as foreign investors reduce their financial flows, or seek to repatriate their invested capital, the financing of the trade deficit will disappear and adjustments will need to take place.

In the early nineties, all developing East Asian countries had a large and sustained current account deficit, offset by large investment flows from America, Japan, and Europe. As illustrated in Exhibit 2.3, Thailand's current account deficit reached $14.7 billion in 1996, some 10 percent of its GDP. This was offset by large capital inflows that induced a positive overall balance. During 1996, the Thai baht had a stable exchange rate around 25 bahts per dollar. But in 1997, foreign investors started to worry that capital was not invested in productive activities, that Thai banks were overextended without proper risk control, and that the local regulatory and legal framework was not progressing quickly enough. This deterioration in the investment climate led to a rapid withdrawal of foreign capital and a negative financial flow balance. The overall balance became a huge deficit in 1997, and the baht was forced to be devalued to a level above 40 bahts per dollar. The financial crisis also affected the local real estate and stock markets, and a severe recession took place. Imports were cut back because of the economic recession and because of their increased price due to the baht depreciation. Exports increased as they became very competitive internationally with the large depreciation of the currency. By 1998, the current account had moved back to a $14 billion surplus, which helped absorb a continuing deficit in the financial account. But the adjustment shock was very painful for the country.

Factors That Cause a Nation's Currency to Appreciate or Depreciate

As discussed in Chapter 1, a currency appreciates if its price measured in foreign currency units goes up. For example, the euro appreciates if its exchange rate moves from 1.25 dollars per euro to 1.50 dollars per euro. Conversely, the euro depreciates if its exchange rate moves from 1.25 dollars per euro to 1 dollar per euro. In a flexible exchange rate system, the value of a currency is driven by changes in fundamental economic factors. The major factors that move an exchange rate can be associated with the transaction motives on the foreign exchange market, namely, current account transactions and financial account transactions.

Differences in National Inflation Rates   A country's imports and exports depend on the relative prices of foreign-produced and domestically produced goods.

---

[4] But note that cumulative investment flows will require the payment of dividend and interest income, which will tend to increase the current account deficit.

EXHIBIT 2.3

Selected Balance of Payments Data for Thailand: 1996–1998 (in billions of U.S. dollars)

Balance	1996	1997	1998
Current account	−14.7	−3.0	14.2
Financial account	16.9	−15.2	−16.9
Overall balance	2.2	−18.2	−2.7

Source: IMF Financial Statistics, September 2002.

A rise in the prices of domestically produced goods (domestic inflation) that is not matched abroad leads to a depreciation of the domestic currency.

For example, suppose that the price of a good-quality golf club is $150 in the United States and £100 in the United Kingdom. Although the clubs are different brands produced locally, they are regarded as equivalent by golfers. The exchange rate is $1.5 = £1. In the coming year, there is no inflation in the United Kingdom, but a 10 percent inflation rate in the United States, so that U.S. clubs now cost $165. If the exchange rate remained at $1.5 = £1, American clubs would not be competitive in the marketplace. Americans would buy more British clubs, and the British would buy fewer American clubs. The current account would deteriorate and the exchange rate would be pushed upward (the pound would appreciate). The pound would need to appreciate against the dollar by 10 percent to restore an equal price between American and British golf clubs.

The currency of a country with high inflation tends to depreciate. The currency of a country with low inflation tends to appreciate. In theory, the movement in the exchange rate between two currencies should exactly offset the difference in inflation rate between the two countries. For example, if there is an annual inflation rate of 5 percent in the United States and 1 percent in the United Kingdom, one would expect the dollar to depreciate by 4 percent against the pound during the course of the year. Conversely, the pound will appreciate by 4 percent against the dollar. This theory is known as "purchasing power parity" and is discussed in detail later in the chapter.

Changes in Real Interest Rates   Financial flows are attracted by high expected return. For debt securities, investors search for high real interest rates. The real interest rate is the difference between the interest rate and expected inflation. If exchange rates do indeed adjust to inflation differentials, the country offering the highest real interest rate will provide the highest expected return after an exchange rate adjustment and will attract international loanable funds.

If a country's real interest rate increases, it will lead to an appreciation of its currency. If a country's real interest rate decreases, it will lead to a depreciation of its currency. Of course, if the real interest rate movement of one country is matched by a similar real interest rate movement in another country, their exchange rates should stay unchanged. It is the relative movement in the real interest rate that is of importance for the exchange rate change.

Differences in Economic Performance   Financial flows are attracted by high expected return. For equity securities, investors search for high performance of individual firms and of the economy as a whole. So, good news on the prospect for growth of a nation should attract more international equity capital. The nation's currency should appreciate.

Although growth should boost the financial account of a nation, there is also an opposite effect on the current account. As mentioned, a fast-growing economy has a fast-growing demand for imports. But demand for exports does not grow at the same rate because other countries do not grow as fast. This will put a downward pressure on the current account, which could lead to a depreciation of the nation's currency.

The direction of the cumulative effect is unclear. In the early 1990s, Asian emerging countries grew at a very fast rate with stable currencies. Their imports grew rapidly to sustain the growth in production and to satisfy the consumption needs of their wealthier residents. But this deficit was offset by foreign financial flows. The net result was a stable exchange rate.

It is important to stress that capital flows are motivated by *expected* returns. So, it is the expected future long-run economic growth that affects investment flows. As indicated by its name, the *current* account reflects the influence of current economic growth on imports and exports. Current economic growth affects the current account; future economic growth affects the financial account.

Changes in Investment Climate   Financial flows are attracted by high expected return, but also by low risk. Investors favor countries with a good investment climate and dislike uncertainty. Among desired attributes, one can list

- a stable political system;

- a rigorous but fair legal system, protecting the rights of all investors;

- a tax system that is fair to foreign investors;

- free movements of capital; and

- monetary authorities that favor price stability.

An improvement in a country's investment climate will lead to increased financial inflows and a currency appreciation. Negative news will worsen investment risk perception and tend to lead to capital outflows and a depreciation of the currency.

Government Policies: Monetary and Fiscal

Many of the previously mentioned factors are affected by government policies, such as monetary and fiscal policies. In this section, we sketch the reaction of the exchange rate and components of the balance of payments to an unanticipated change in monetary or fiscal policy. This is a complex issue, and we have to assume that everything else remains the same, including policies of other governments.

Monetary Policy and the Foreign Exchange Rate   Suppose that a country decides to shift to a more expansionary monetary policy. This is a shift that was not anticipated. Most economists would agree that this monetary shock would have, at least, two effects on the domestic economy:

- The real interest rate will temporarily drop.

- There will be an upward pressure on the domestic price level, and inflation will accelerate.

As discussed, both factors would lead to a depreciation of the domestic currency relative to other currencies. Otherwise, both the current account (because of inflation) and the financial account (because of the low real interest rate) would be in deficit.

Whether an expansionary monetary policy creates economic growth in the short and long run is a matter of debate among economists. Many would argue that an unanticipated monetary expansion would induce a short run boost in economic growth, but no long-run stimulation. Because this boost is not likely to be long-lived, it will hardly motivate additional foreign financial flows, but it will put additional pressures on the current account (imports will grow faster than exports).

For all these reasons, an expansionary monetary policy will lead to a depreciation of the home currency, while a restrictive monetary policy will lead to an appreciation of the home currency.[5]

Fiscal Policy and the Foreign Exchange Rate Suppose that a country decides to use a budget/fiscal policy mix to finance government expenditures. *Everything else equal,* a more restrictive fiscal policy means that a government increases the share of taxes and reduces the share of borrowing to finance government spending. A more expansionary fiscal policy means that a government reduces taxes while increasing the budget deficit.

A more restrictive fiscal policy implies less government borrowing, which should induce a reduction in the domestic real interest rate. In turn, this drop in the domestic real interest rate should lead to a depreciation of the home currency (investment outflows). However, a more restrictive fiscal policy should also slow down economic activity and inflation. These two factors should lead to an appreciation of the home currency (current account improvement).

These influences are conflicting, and it is hard to draw general conclusions on the link between fiscal policy and exchange rates. Many economists believe that the interest rate factor will dominate and that the net result of a more restrictive policy will be a depreciation of the home currency.

A more expansionary fiscal policy has the reverse effect. It will induce a higher domestic real interest rate, which should lead to an appreciation of the currency. However, this expansionary fiscal policy should also induce a rise in output and inflationary pressures, which tend to put depreciation pressure on the home currency. The net result is usually expected to be an appreciation of the home currency. The reaction will be somewhat stronger if the shift in fiscal policy is expected to be permanent rather than temporary.

---

[5] A detailed analysis of the dynamics of the exchange rate response to a monetary shock is given in the last part of this chapter (Asset Market Approach).

Exchange Rate Regimes

The previous discussion was conducted assuming that exchange rates were flexible. Historically, exchange rates have operated under three different types of regimes:

- Flexible (or floating) exchange rates
- Fixed exchange rates
- Pegged exchange rates

Flexible (or Floating) Exchange Rates   A *flexible exchange rate regime* is one in which the exchange rate between two currencies fluctuates freely in the foreign exchange market. Today, all major currencies are freely traded, and their pairwise exchange rates fluctuate in the foreign exchange market in a flexible manner. A central bank can intervene on the foreign exchange market, but it is only one of the many players that contribute to total currency supply and demand, albeit an important one. A government can announce what it believes to be the "normal" exchange rate of its currency, and this announcement will be taken into account by the marketplace.[6] But governments have neither the power nor the will to set official exchange rates (usually called *parities*). In a "pure" floating exchange rate system, governments intervene in the foreign exchange market only to smooth temporary imbalances. If a government has some exchange rate target, it will try to achieve it by adopting the proper macroeconomic policies.

The *advantage* of a flexible exchange rate system is that the exchange rate is a market-determined price that reflects economic fundamentals at each point in time. Governments do not intervene to defend some exchange rate level, so there is no incentive to speculate "against" them. Because exchange rates are flexible, governments are free to adopt independent domestic monetary and fiscal policies.

The *disadvantage* is that flexible exchange rates can be quite volatile. This volatility is unpleasant for agents engaged in trade and investment, but currency risk-hedging strategies are available.

Fixed Exchange Rates   A *fixed exchange rate regime* is one in which the exchange rate between two currencies remains fixed at a preset level, known as *official parity*. In a truly fixed system, the exchange rate is expected to remain at its fixed parity forever. It is not sufficient for a country to announce that it will keep a fixed exchange rate with other currencies. To be credible, it must put in place some disciplined system to maintain the official parity at all times.

Historically, the first international exchange rate regime was one of fixed exchange rates, in which all currencies had a value fixed in terms of gold content ("gold standard"). In such a gold standard, the domestic money supply is fully backed by an equivalent of gold reserves. This was a system that worked well in the

---

[6] There is some similarity with a CEO announcing that the corporation's share price is undervalued. The company could decide to use cash reserves to buy back shares.

1800s and up to the conclusion of World War I, but progressively disappeared thereafter. Today, some countries still attempt to maintain a fixed exchange rate against the dollar or the euro. This is usually done by adopting a *currency board*. In a currency board, a country (say, Argentina) commits to keep a fixed exchange rate (say, 1 peso per dollar) with a major currency (the U.S. dollar), and the supply of home currency is fully backed by an equivalent amount of that major currency.

Suppose there is a deficit in the balance of payments of the home country. It must be financed out of reserves: The amount of dollars held as reserves will be reduced and so will the domestic money supply (100 percent dollar backing). As the country's money supply is reduced, prices of goods must drop and interest rates must rise. In turn, these adjustments make domestic goods more competitive internationally, and the balance of payments equilibrium is restored.

The *advantage* of a fixed exchange rate is that it eliminates exchange rate risk, at least in the short run. It also brings discipline to government policies; this is particularly useful for emerging countries, which are prone to running inflationary policies.

The *disadvantage* of a fixed exchange rate is that it deprives the country of any monetary independence: Its monetary policy is dictated by the "defense" of its parity. It also constrains the country's fiscal policy. A major problem with a fixed exchange rate is its long-term credibility. As soon as a country runs into economic problems, there will be strong speculatory and political pressures to remove the fixed rate system and a push toward a sizable devaluation, with major economic disruption (as happened in Argentina).

Pegged Exchange Rates   A *pegged exchange rate regime* is one characterized as a compromise between a flexible and a fixed exchange rate. A country decides to peg its currency to another major currency (dollar or euro) or to a basket of currencies. A target exchange rate is set (the peg), but this is not a fixed exchange rate to be defended at all costs. First, the exchange rate is allowed to fluctuate within a (small) band around this target exchange rate. Second, periodic changes in the target exchange rate can take place to reflect trends in economic fundamentals (mostly higher inflation in the home country).[7]

Smaller countries, especially emerging countries, frequently use a pegged exchange rate. To defend a target exchange rate against speculation pressures, a country can resort to a variety of measures. Central bank intervention, possibly coordinated with other countries, is the first possibility. The demand and supply for its currency can also be constrained by imposing various restrictions on trade flows (tariffs and quotas) and on capital flows (capital and currency repatriation restrictions, taxes). In the end, aid from international agencies could be requested. But artificially defending a pegged exchange rate could be a costly process for a central bank if devaluation ultimately happens. Speculators will benefit, and this chain of events will also deter foreign investments in the future.

---

[7] For example, Brazil had a "crawling peg" with the U.S. dollar for many years, whereby the target exchange rate (peg) was automatically adjusted for inflation differential between Brazil and the United States.

The *advantage* of a pegged exchange rate is that it reduces exchange rate volatility, at least in the short run. This is beneficial to international trade. Setting a fixed exchange rate target also encourages monetary discipline for the home country.

The *disadvantage* of a pegged exchange rate system is that it can induce destabilizing speculation. The more rigid the application of a pegged exchange rate system, the more likely speculation will try to take advantage of the lack of adjustment in the exchange rate.

International Parity Relations

We now introduce a simple theoretical framework that is useful to understand the interplay between exchange rates, interest rates, and inflation rates. Traditionally, different nations use different currencies, which allows each nation some independence in setting its national interest rate and monetary policy. Thus, inflation rates and interest rates can differ markedly among countries, which implies that the currencies' exchange rates will not stay constant over time. Consider first how these variables would be linked in a simple and perfect world.

Some Definitions

First, we need to recall some notation introduced in Chapter 1 and introduce notation for the inflation rate.

- The *spot exchange rate, S.* The rate of exchange of two currencies tells us the amount of one currency that one unit of another currency can buy. *Spot* means that we refer to the exchange rate for immediate delivery. For example, the U.S. dollar/euro spot exchange rate might be $S = \$1.25$, indicating that one euro is worth 1.25 dollars (one U.S. dollar is worth 0.8 euros).

- The *forward exchange rate, F.* The rate of exchange of two currencies set on one date for delivery at a future specified date, the *forward* rate is quoted today for future delivery. For example, the U.S. dollar/euro forward exchange rate for delivery in one year might be $F = \$1.2061$ per euro.

- The *interest rate, r.* The rate of interest for a given time period is a function of the length of the time period and the denomination of the currency. Interest rates are usually quoted in the marketplace as an annualized rate. With the euro as the domestic currency and the U.S. dollar as the foreign currency, for example, the one-year rate in the domestic country (DC) might be $r_{DC} = 14\%$, and the one-year rate in the foreign country (FC) might be $r_{FC} = 10\%$. In this case, the *interest rate differential* is equal to -4 percent ($r_{FC} - r_{DC} = 10 - 14$).

- The *inflation rate, I.* This is equal to the rate of consumer price increase over the period specified. The *inflation differential* is equal to the difference of inflation rates between two countries. For example, if the inflation in the FC is $I_{FC} = 8.91\%$ and the inflation in the DC is $I_{DC} = 12.87\%$, the inflation differential over the period is approximately -4 percent ($I_{FC} - I_{DC} = 8.91 - 12.87 = -3.96\%$).

The parity relations of international finance are as follows:

1. The *interest rate parity relation,* linking spot exchange rates, forward exchange rates, and interest rates by the no arbitrage condition

2. The *purchasing power parity relation,* linking spot exchange rates and inflation

3. The *international Fisher relation,* linking interest rates and expected inflation

4. The *uncovered interest rate parity relation,* linking spot exchange rates, expected exchange rates, and interest rates

5. The *foreign exchange expectation relation,* linking forward exchange rates and expected spot exchange rates

The last four relations are all theoretical.

Interest Rate Parity

As discussed in Chapter 1, spot exchange rates, forward exchange rates, and interest rates are linked by the interest rate parity relation:

$$F/S = (1 + r_{FC})/(1 + r_{DC}) \quad \text{or} \quad (F - S)/S = (r_{FC} - r_{DC})/(1 + r_{DC}) \tag{2.1}$$

where S and F are indirect quotations (the amount of foreign currency that one unit of domestic currency can buy), and r_{DC} and r_{FC} are the domestic and foreign risk-free interest rates, respectively.

Defining $f = (F - S)/S = (r_{FC} - r_{DC})/(1 + r_{DC})$, we have a linear approximation for interest rate parity:[8]

$$f \cong r_{FC} - r_{DC} \tag{2.1'}$$

which states that the percentage difference between the forward and the spot exchange rates is equal to the interest rate differential. This parity relation results from riskless arbitrage and must be true at any point of time (within a transaction cost band).

EXAMPLE 2.1   *THE INTEREST RATE PARITY RELATION*

Suppose that the Eurozone is the domestic country and the United States is the foreign country. The spot exchange rate quote is $S = \$1.25$. Suppose[9] further that the U.S. risk-free interest rate is 10 percent and the Eurozone risk-free interest rate is 14 percent. Calculate the exact forward rate and the approximate forward rate.

---

[8] All parity equations numbered with a prime are expressed in percentage rather than level. This presentation helps to gain an intuitive understanding of the various parity relations.

[9] Although these rates are unrealistic for the United States and the Eurozone, given today's low inflation policy targets and interest rates, such large rates help illustrate the needed principles and relations.

> **SOLUTION**
>
> Using Equation 2.1, we have $F/S = (1 + r_{FC})/(1 + r_{DC})$, and $F/1.25 = (1.10)/(1.14)$ gives $F = 1.2061$, $1.2061 per euro. For a linear approximation with Equation 2.1', we have $f \cong r_{FC} - r_{DC} = 10\% - 14\% = -4\%$. Then we have $F = (1 + f) \times S = (1 - 0.04) \times 1.25 = 1.20$, $1.20 per euro.

Purchasing Power Parity: The Exchange Rate and the Inflation Differential

Purchasing power parity (PPP) is a well-known relation in international finance.[10] It states that the spot exchange rate adjusts perfectly to inflation differentials between two countries. There are two versions of PPP: absolute PPP and relative PPP.

Absolute PPP   This version of PPP is inspired by a basic idea known as the law of one price, states that the real price of a good must be the same in all countries. If goods prices rise in one country relative to another, the country's exchange rate must depreciate to maintain a similar real price for the goods in the two countries. This argument is obvious for traded goods with no trade restrictions. Consider the following scenario: Suppose the price of wheat in the Eurozone is 2.68 euros per bushel, and the U.S. price is 2.55 dollars per bushel; the exchange rate is 1.05 euros per dollar. In the next year, suppose the euro price of wheat rises by 3.03 percent, whereas the U.S. dollar price of wheat rises by only 1.4 percent. If the euro depreciation does not offset this hypothetical 1.63 percent inflation differential, Eurozone wheat will be less competitive in the international market and trade flows from the United States to Europe will increase to take advantage of this price differential. If trade could take place instantaneously, at no cost and with no impediments, we would expect the law of one price to hold exactly for all traded goods.

If we take a weighted average of the prices of all goods in the economy, absolute PPP claims that the exchange rate should be equal to the ratio of the average price levels in the two economies. So absolute PPP is some "average" version of the law of one price. If the weights differ among countries, absolute PPP could be violated even if the law of one price held for each individual good. In practice, determining an average national price level is a daunting task that is never undertaken. Rather than calculating average price levels, expressed in euros in Europe and dollars in the United States, countries calculate movements in price indexes. A price index can be based on a representative sample of produced goods (GDP deflator) or a representative basket of consumed goods (consumer price index). A price index is a pure number, without meaning in itself. Its purpose is to calculate price increases, or inflation rates, from one period to the next.

---

[10]This theory was originally presented by Cassel (1916). A review of purchasing power parity may be found in Rogoff (1996).

Relative PPP   Most economists are concerned with relative PPP when they talk about purchasing power parity. Because of domestic inflation, a currency loses some of its purchasing power. For example, a 6 percent annual inflation rate in South Africa implies that one South African rand loses 6 percent of its purchasing power over a year. Relative PPP focuses on the general, across-the-board inflation rates in two countries and claims that the exchange rate movements should exactly offset any inflation differential between the two countries.

The purchasing power parity relation might be written as follows:

$$S_1/S_0 = (1 + I_{FC})/(1 + I_{DC}) \tag{2.2}$$

where

S_0 is the spot exchange rate at the start of the period (the foreign price of one unit of the domestic currency);

S_1 is the spot exchange rate at the end of the period;

I_{FC} is the inflation rate, over the period, in the foreign country (e.g., Canada); and

I_{DC} is the inflation rate, over the period, in the domestic country (e.g., Britain).

Suppose the indirect exchange rate is 2.235 Canadian dollars for one pound and inflation rates are $I_{FC} = 1.3\%$ in Canada and $I_{DC} = 2.1\%$ in Britain. Then the end-of-period spot exchange rate "should" be equal to S_1, such that

$$S_1 = S_0(1 + I_{FC})/(1 + I_{DC})$$

$$S_1 = 2.235(1 + 0.013)/(1 + 0.021) = 2.2175, \text{ C\$ per pound}$$

Here, the higher British inflation rate means that the pound depreciates against the Canadian dollar as seen by a decline in the indirect exchange rate. Define s to represent the exchange rate movement:

$$s = (S_1 - S_0)/S_0 = S_1/S_0 - 1$$

The PPP relation is often presented as the linear approximation stating that the exchange rate variation is equal to the inflation rate differential:

$$s = S_1/S_0 - 1 \cong I_{FC} - I_{DC} \tag{2.2'}$$

For the preceding example, we would have $I_{FC} - I_{DC} = 1.3 - 2.1 = -0.8$, and expect the indirect exchange rate to decline by 0.8 percent to give $S_1 = (1 - 0.008) \times 2.235 \cong 2.2171$, C\$2.2171 per pound. Compared with the C\$2.2175 per pound calculated with the exact formula, this is close to the exact figure, even though Equation 2.2′ gives us only a first-order approximation of the exact relation (Equation 2.2).

This PPP relation is of major importance in international portfolio management. If it holds, PPP implies that the real return on an asset is identical for investors from any country. For example, consider an Australian asset with an annual rate of return equal to 20 percent in Australian dollars. Assume that the inflation rate is 2.5

percent in Australia and 1.3 percent in Canada and that PPP is verified so that the Australian dollar depreciates against the Canadian dollar by about 1.2 percent. With the linear approximation, the Canadian dollar rate of return on this Australian asset is roughly 18.8 percent (20% − 1.2%). The real rate of return is approximately 17.5 percent for both an Australian investor (20% − 2.5%) and a Canadian investor (18.8% − 1.3%). Because investors should care about real returns, they all agree, whatever their nationality, on the return and risk of a specific asset. Exchange rate movements have no influence, because they only mirror inflation differentials and equalize real return across countries. Of course, PPP is only an economic theory and the relation does not necessarily hold, especially in the short run.

EXAMPLE 2.2   THE PURCHASING POWER PARITY RELATION

Suppose that the Eurozone is the domestic country and the United States is the foreign country. The spot exchange rate quote is $S = \$1.25$ per euro. Suppose further that the expected annual U.S. inflation rate is 8.91 percent and the expected Eurozone annual inflation rate is 12.87 percent. Calculate the expected spot rate and the approximate expected spot rate one year away.

SOLUTION

Using Equation 2.2, we have $S_1/S_0 = (1 + I_{FC})/(1 + I_{DC})$ and $S_1/1.25 = (1.0891)/(1.1287)$ gives $S_1 = 1.20614$, or \$1.20614 per euro. For a linear approximation with Equation 2.2′, we have $s \cong I_{FC} - I_{DC} = 8.91\% - 12.87\% = -3.96\%$. This indicates that the indirect exchange rate should decline by approximately 3.96 percent to $(1 - 0.0396) \times 1.25 = 1.2005$, or \$1.2005 per euro.

International Fisher Relation: The Interest Rate and Expected Inflation Rate Differentials

Inspired by the *domestic* relation postulated by Irving Fisher (1930), the *international Fisher relation* states that the interest rate differential between two countries should be equal to the expected inflation rate differential over the term of the interest rate. In the *domestic* relation, the nominal interest rate, r, is the sum (or rather, the compounding) of the real interest rate, ρ, and of expected inflation over the term of the interest rate, $E(I)$:

$$(1 + r) = (1 + \rho)(1 + E(I)) \tag{2.3}$$

The nominal interest rate is observed in the marketplace and is usually referred to as *the interest rate*, while the real interest rate is calculated from the observed interest rate and the forecasted inflation. For example, consider a nominal FC interest rate of 10 percent and an expected inflation rate of 8.91 percent. The real interest rate is equal to 1 percent, because

$$1 + 0.10 = (1 + 0.01)(1 + 0.0891)$$

This relation is often presented with the linear approximation stating that the interest rate is equal to a real interest rate *plus* expected inflation:

$$r \cong \rho + E(I) \tag{2.3'}$$

The economic theory proposed by Fisher is that real interest rates are stable over time. Hence, fluctuations in interest rates are caused by revisions in inflationary expectations, not by movements in real interest rates.[11] The international counterpart of this domestic relation is that the interest rate differential between two countries is linked to the difference in expected inflation:

$$(1 + r_{FC})/(1 + r_{DC}) = ((1 + \rho_{FC})/(1 + \rho_{DC})) \times (1 + E(I_{FC}))/(1 + E(I_{DC}))$$

The international Fisher relation claims that real interest rates are equal across the world; hence, differences in nominal interest rates are caused only by differences in national inflationary expectations. The international Fisher relation can be written as

$$(1 + r_{FC})/(1 + r_{DC}) = (1 + E(I_{FC}))/(1 + E(I_{DC})) \tag{2.4}$$

or, with the linear approximation,

$$r_{FC} - r_{DC} \cong E(I_{FC}) - E(I_{DC}) \tag{2.4'}$$

Suppose that Thailand is the domestic country and that the expected South Korean inflation rate is 2.3 percent, the expected Thai inflation rate is 0 percent, and the interest rates are 4.74 percent in South Korea and 2.39 percent in Thailand. The real interest rate will then be equal to 2.39 percent in both countries, because

$$(1 + r) = (1 + \rho)(1 + E(I))$$

In South Korea,

$$1 + 0.0474 = (1 + 0.0239)(1 + 0.023)$$

and in Thailand

$$1 + 0.0239 = (1 + 0.0239)(1 + 0)$$

With these equal real rates, the ratio of the nominal interest rates is the same as the ratio of the expected inflation rates:

$$(1 + r_{FC})/(1 + r_{DC}) = 1.0474/1.0239 = 1.023$$

and

$$(1 + E(I_{FC}))/(1 + E(I_{DC})) = 1.023/1 = 1.023$$

---

[11]Many economists would disagree with this simple approach. They claim that real interest rates vary with liquidity conditions and with the business cycle. Real interest rates would be higher in periods of strong economic growth than in recession periods: High economic growth sustains high real interest rates. See Dornbusch, Fischer, and Startz (2001).

EXAMPLE 2.3   *THE INTERNATIONAL FISHER RELATION*

Suppose that the Eurozone is the domestic country and the United States is the foreign country. The spot exchange rate quote is $S = \$1.25$ per euro. Suppose further that the expected annual U.S. inflation rate is 8.91 percent and the expected Eurozone annual inflation rate is 12.87 percent. Interest rates are 10 percent in the U.S. and 14 percent in the Eurozone. Demonstrate how interest rates are related to expected inflation rates exactly and by approximation, and calculate the real risk-free interest rate for each country.

SOLUTION

Using Equation 2.4, $(1 + r_{FC})/(1 + r_{DC}) = (1 + E(I_{FC}))/(1 + E(I_{DC}))$, we have

$(1 + 0.10)/(1 + 0.14) = 0.96491$ and $(1 + 0.0891)/(1 + 0.1287) = 0.96492$

With Equation 2.4′, $r_{FC} - r_{DC} = E(I_{FC}) - E(I_{DC})$, we have

$10 - 14 = -4\%$ and $8.91 - 12.87 = -3.96\%$

To calculate the real rate of interest for each country, we take either country and use Equation 2.3. $(1 + r) = (1 + \rho)(1 + E(I))$ and solve for ρ. Using the Eurozone, then, we have $\rho = (1 + r)/(1 + E(I)) - 1 = 1.0\%$. The real rates are the same in both countries by the international Fisher assumption.

Again, many economists would not agree that real interest rates should be equalized worldwide, simply because national business cycles are not fully synchronized. Countries with different levels of economic growth could sustain different real interest rates.

Uncovered Interest Rate Parity

Purchasing power parity combined with the international Fisher relation implies that the expected currency depreciation should offset the interest differential between the two countries over the term of the interest rate. To see this, take the expected values of the future exchange rate and the inflation in PPP equation (2.2). PPP applied to expected values implies

$$E(S_1)/S_0 = (1 + E(I_{FC}))/(1 + E(I_{DC}))$$

Combining with Equation (2.4), we get the theory of uncovered interest rate parity:

$$E(S_1)/S_0 = (1 + r_{FC})/(1 + r_{DC}) \tag{2.5}$$

or, with the linear approximation,

$$E(s) \cong r_{FC} - r_{DC} \tag{2.5'}$$

Uncovered interest rate parity refers to the idea that the exchange rate exposure is not covered or protected by a forward contract. Although the relation looks similar to covered interest rate parity, the difference is dramatic. Covered interest rate parity must hold by arbitrage. Uncovered interest rate parity is an economic theory whose empirical validity can be questioned.

From the linear approximation to Equation 2.5, the expected movement in the exchange rate should offset the interest rate differential. The basic idea behind the international Fisher relation is that differences in real interest rates among countries would motivate capital flows between countries to take advantage of these real interest rate differentials. These capital flows would lead to an equalization of real interest rates across the world.

Consider for a moment a simple world in which goods and financial markets are perfect. Throughout the world, costless arbitrage can take place instantaneously for physical goods and financial assets. Further assume that all nationals consume the same goods and that there is *no uncertainty*. Hence we know *exactly* what the inflation and the exchange rates will be in the future. In this simple world, arbitrage guarantees that the previous parity relations hold exactly. If the exchange rate does not adjust to the inflation differential as claimed by PPP, one would simply have to buy the goods in the country with the lower real price and ship them for sale in the country with the higher real price to make a certain profit. In a perfect world with costless and instantaneous shipping, such attractive situations cannot exist for long; arbitrage will make the exchange rate movement adjust exactly to inflation in both countries. In the same spirit, if the interest rate differential does not reflect the anticipated and certain exchange rate movement exactly, an arbitrageur would simply borrow in one currency, transfer the amount to the other currency, and lend it at that currency interest rate. By doing so, the arbitrageur would make a certain profit with no capital investment. This riskless profit opportunity would attract huge arbitrage capital, and market rates would adjust to "prevent" such an arbitrage.

In reality, the future exchange rate is uncertain, and arbitrage in the goods market cannot be instantaneous and costless. So, the parity relations developed here are only *theories* claiming that real prices and interest rates should be equalized across the world. The empirical evidence on the validity of these relations is presented in Chapter 3.

EXAMPLE 2.4 THE UNCOVERED INTEREST RATE PARITY RELATION

Suppose that the Eurozone is the domestic country and the United States is the foreign country. The spot exchange rate quote is $S = \$1.25$ per euro, the one-year rate in the domestic country (DC) is $r_{DC} = 14\%$, and the one-year rate in the foreign country (FC) is $r_{FC} = 10\%$. Calculate the exact expected spot rate and the approximate expected spot rate one year forward.

SOLUTION

$E(S_1) = 1.25 \times 1.1/1.14 = 1.2061$, using Equation 2.5. By linear approximation, $s = r_{FC} - r_{DC} = 10\% - 14\% = -4\%$. This means that the spot rate is expected to decline by 4% to $(1 - 0.04) \times 1.25 = \$1.20$ per euro.

Foreign Exchange Expectations: The Forward Premium (Discount) and the Expected Exchange Rate Movement

The *foreign exchange expectation* relation states that the forward exchange rate, quoted at time 0 for delivery at time 1, is equal to the expected value of the spot exchange rate at time 1. This can be written as

$$F = E(S_1) \tag{2.6}$$

This relation would certainly hold if the future values of exchange rates were known with certainty. If one were sure at time 0 that the exchange rate would be worth S_1 at time 1, the current forward rate for delivery at time 1 would have to be S_1; otherwise, a riskless arbitrage opportunity would exist.

Assume, for example, that we know for sure that the spot exchange rate will be 1.2061 \$/€ in a year but, surprisingly, the one-year forward rate is 1.25 \$/€. We could then do the following arbitrage:

- Sell euros forward at 1.25 dollars per euro and hold the contract until maturity.

- At maturity, simultaneously receive delivery of the forward contract and take an offsetting position in the spot exchange rate market.

On the forward contract, the arbitrageur receives 1.25 dollars per euro but pays 1.2061 dollars on the spot market, leading to a profit of 0.0439 dollars per euro. If the expected spot exchange rate is certain, this is a riskless arbitrage that requires no invested capital on the forward commitment. Banks would keep doing this arbitrage until the buying pressure pushed the forward exchange rate to 1.2061 \$/€.

Of course, this parity relation depends strongly on the certainty assumption. Some economists claim, however, that the forward exchange rate should be an unbiased predictor of the future spot exchange rate in the presence of uncertainty, thereby leading to Equation 2.6. Others claim the existence of a risk premium appended to this relation.[12]

The foreign exchange expectation relation is often stated relative to the current spot exchange rate. If we subtract S_0 on both sides of Equation 2.6 (remember that the current spot exchange rate is known with certainty) and divide by S_0, we get

$$(F - S_0)/S_0 = E((S_1 - S_0)/S_0) = E(s) \tag{2.7}$$

As mentioned in Chapter 1, the left-hand side is usually referred to as the forward discount, or premium, and is denoted f. It is the percentage deviation of the forward rate from the current spot rate. This relation states that the forward discount (or premium) is equal to the expected exchange rate movement and can be written as

$$f = E(s) \tag{2.7'}$$

---

[12]See Chapter 4.

The practical relevance of this foreign exchange expectation relation is obvious. If verified, it means that there is, on the average, no reward for bearing foreign exchange uncertainty. If a risk premium were to be added to the relation, the symmetry of the exchange rate means the risk premium will be paid by some investors (e.g., those selling forward euros for dollars) and received by other investors (e.g., those buying forward euros for dollars). A zero-risk premium means that a forward hedge, that is, the use of forward currency contracts to hedge the exchange risk of a portfolio of foreign assets, will be "costless" in terms of expected returns (except for commissions on the forward contracts).

EXAMPLE 2.5   THE FOREIGN EXCHANGE EXPECTATION RELATION

Suppose that the Eurozone is the domestic country and the United States is the foreign country. The spot exchange rate quote is $S = \$1.25$. Suppose further that the U.S. risk-free interest rate is 10 percent and the Eurozone risk-free interest rate is 14 percent. Calculate the exact expected spot rate and the approximate expected spot rate one year away.

SOLUTION

Using Equation 2.1, we have $F/S = (1 + r_{FC})/(1 + r_{DC})$ and $F/1.25 = (1.10)/(1.14)$ gives $F = 1.2061$, or \$1.2061 per euro. The expected spot rate is \$1.2061 per euro. Using the linear approximation in Equation 2.1', $f \cong r_{FC} - r_{DC} = -4\%$. Hence, the exchange rate is expected to depreciate by 4% to $(1 - 0.4) \times 1.25 = \$1.20$ per euro.

Combining the Relations

The relations link the forward discount to the interest rate differential, the exchange rate movement to the inflation differential, the expected inflation differential to the interest rate differential, and the interest rate differential to the expected currency depreciation, and back to the forward discount:

- *Interest rate differential:* The forward discount (premium) equals the interest rate differential.

- *Inflation differential:* The exchange rate movement should exactly offset any inflation differential.

- *Expected inflation rate differential:* The expected inflation rate differential should be matched by the interest rate differential, assuming (Fisher) real interest rates are equal.

- *The interest rate differential:* The interest rate differential is expected to be offset by the currency depreciation.

- *The expected exchange rate movement:* The forward discount (or premium) is equal to the expected exchange rate movement.

These relations can also be organized in the following manner to show linkages discussed.

Factor	Related to	By
Forward discount	Interest rates	Interest rate parity
Exchange rate movement	Inflation rates	Purchasing power parity
Interest rates	Expected inflation rates	Fisher relation
Expected exchange rate movement	Interest rates	Uncovered interest rate parity (PPP plus Fisher)
Forward discount	Expected exchange rate movement	Foreign exchange expectation

Recall that the *interest rate parity* relation states that the interest rate differential must equal the forward discount (or premium). This is a financial arbitrage condition that does not involve any economic theory. It must hold. Purchasing power parity also relies on some international arbitrage, but in the physical goods markets. Given the heterogeneity in goods and transaction costs, we cannot expect it to hold precisely. All other relations involve expectations on exchange rates and prices; they are based on simple economic theories about agent behavior. The various parity relations are illustrated in Exhibit 2.4, using the linear approximation.

EXHIBIT 2.4

International Parity Relations
Linear Approximation

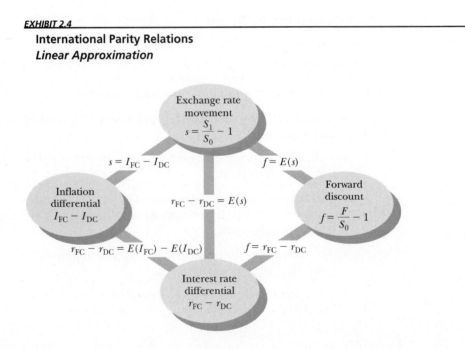

International Parity Relations and Global Asset Management

The multicurrency dimension adds great complexity to global asset management. Interest rates differ among currencies. A foreign investment carries currency risk in addition to market risks. Because of exchange rate fluctuations, an investment could have a positive return when measured in one currency, but a negative one when measured in another currency. International parity relations provide the simplest framework to gain a better understanding of global investing in the presence of various exchange rates. From this basic framework, various complexities can be incorporated as done later.

International parity relations provide a useful base for the relationship among exchange rates, inflation, and interest rates. Using this simple framework as a starting point, an international investor can draw several practical implications:

- Interest rate differentials reflect expectations about currency movements. In other words, the expected return on default-free bills should be equal among countries. This is true whether we measure return in a common currency or in real terms.

- Investing in a country with a high interest rate is not a particularly attractive option. The high interest rate is expected to be offset by a matching currency depreciation.

- Investors from different countries expect the same real return on a given asset, once currency is taken into account. For example, consider an investment in a Swiss stock. U.S., French, and Japanese investors will all realize the same real rate of return in their home currency (dollar, euro, and yen).

- Exchange risk reduces to inflation uncertainty if all these relationships hold perfectly. In this instance, an investor concerned with real returns would not be affected by exchange rate uncertainty.

- Currency hedging allows investors to eliminate currency risk without sacrificing expected return, because the forward exchange rate is equal to the expected spot exchange rate.

In this simplified world, currency risk is basically of little real importance; however, deviations from parity relations can introduce complexities. Of primary importance is the observation that currency fluctuations can have real effects if the exchange rate deviates from its PPP value, as illustrated in Example 2.6.

It could also be that real interest rates differ between two countries that are at different stages of the business cycle. Similarly, investors are not risk neutral and could append a risk premium to the foreign exchange expectations relation (see Chapter 4).

We now go one step further and give a brief review of the simple economic models of the exchange rate that could induce deviations from the international parity relations.[13] The empirical validity of these relations is discussed in Chapter 3.

---

[13]These models are detailed in standard international economics textbooks. See, for example, Dornbusch, Fischer, and Startz (2001).

EXAMPLE 2.6   ARE FOREIGN RISK-FREE INVESTMENTS RISK-FREE TO A DOMESTIC INVESTOR?

During June 2002, the U.S. dollar depreciated by 7 percent against the euro. One-month bills in euro and in dollar had the same interest rate of 3 percent (annualized), and annual inflation rates were about 2 percent in both regions. Would a European investor holding U.S. Treasury bills have the same return as U.S. investors?

SOLUTION

A U.S. investor has a rate of return of 0.25 percent over the month (3%/12), and a real return of approximately 0.08 percent (1%/12). However, a European investor made a loss of 6.75 percent (7 percent currency loss minus 0.25 percent dollar interest rate) when measured in euro. The real return for European investors is −6.92 percent (−6.75 percent return in euro minus 0.17 percent monthly European inflation rate). The exchange rate movement has a dramatic real impact.

Exchange Rate Determination

In this chapter so far, the traditional view indicates that exchange rates should adjust the purchasing power of the two currencies. It is worth looking at this relation again. Other economic variables affecting the exchange rate will then be introduced.

Purchasing Power Parity Revisited

The short-run behavior of exchange rates does not conveniently conform to PPP. The empirical evidence to be introduced in Chapter 3 demonstrates that yearly exchange rates can deviate significantly from the inflation differentials between countries. The real exchange rate is the observed exchange rate adjusted for inflation. Hence, movements in the real exchange rate are equal to movements in the exchange rate minus the actual inflation differential between the two countries. These movements in the real exchange rate are not explained by PPP. However, the theory, supported by extensive empirical evidence, claims that such real exchange rate movements (deviations from PPP) will be corrected in the long run. So, one approach to understanding the path of the exchange rate is to compute its long-run "fundamental" (or "equilibrium") value based on PPP, and to assume that any observed deviation of the current exchange rate from this fundamental value will be progressively corrected. To provide a forecast of the future short-run movement in exchange rates, one must first estimate the *fundamental PPP value* of a currency.

CONCEPTS IN ACTION BIG MAC CURRENCIES (2002)

Currency forecasters have had it hard in recent years. Most expected the euro to rise after its launch in 1999, yet it fell. When America went into recession last year, the dollar was tipped to decline; it rose. So to help forecasters really get their teeth into exchange rates, *The Economist* has updated its Big Mac index.

Devised 16 years ago as a light-hearted guide to whether currencies are at their "correct" level, the index is based on the theory of purchasing-power parity (PPP). In the long run, countries' exchange rates should move towards rates that would equalize the prices of an identical basket of goods and services. Our basket is a McDonald's Big Mac, produced in 120 countries. The Big Mac PPP is the exchange rate that would leave hamburgers costing the same in America as elsewhere. Comparing these with actual rates signals if a currency is under- or overvalued.

The first column of the table shows the local-currency prices of a Big Mac. The second converts these into dollars. The average American price has fallen slightly over the past year, to $2.49. The cheapest Big Mac is in Argentina (78 cents), after its massive devaluation; the most expensive ($3.81) is in Switzerland. (More countries are listed on our website.) By this measure, the Argentine peso is the most undervalued currency and the Swiss franc the most overvalued.

The third column calculates Big Mac PPPs. Dividing the Japanese price by the American price, for instance, gives a dollar PPP of ¥105, against an actual exchange rate of ¥130. This implies that the yen is 19% undervalued. The euro is only 5% undervalued relative to its Big Mac PPP, far less than many economists claim. The euro area may have a single currency, but the price of a Big Mac varies widely, from €2.15 in Greece to €2.95 in France. However, that range has narrowed from a year ago. And prices vary just as much within America, which is why we use the average price in four cities.

The Australian dollar is the most undervalued rich-world currency, 35% below McParity. No wonder the Australian economy was so strong last year. Sterling, by contrast, is one of the few currencies that is overvalued against the dollar, by 16%; it is 21% too strong against the euro.

Overall, the dollar now looks more overvalued against the average of the other big currencies than at any time in the life of the Big Mac index. Most emerging-market currencies also look cheap against the dollar. Over half the emerging-market currencies are more than 30% undervalued. That implies that any currency close to McParity (e.g., the Argentine peso last year, or the Mexican peso today) will be overvalued against other emerging-market rivals.

Adjustment back towards PPP does not always come through a shift in exchange rates. It can also come about partly through price changes. In 1995 the yen was 100% overvalued. It has since fallen by 35%; but the price of a Japanese burger has also dropped by one-third.

Every time we update our Big Mac index, readers complain that burgernomics does not cut the mustard. The Big Mac is an imperfect basket. Hamburgers cannot be traded across borders; prices may be distorted by taxes, different profit margins or differences in the cost of non-tradable goods and services, such as rents. Yet it seems to pay to follow burgernomics.

In 1999, for instance, the Big Mac index suggested that the euro was already overvalued at its launch, when nearly every economist predicted it would rise. Several studies confirm that, over the long run, purchasing power parity—including the Big Mac PPP—is a fairly good guide to exchange-rate movements.

Still, currencies can deviate from PPP for long periods. In the early 1990s the Big Mac index repeatedly signaled that the dollar was undervalued, yet it continued to slide for several years until it flipped around. Our latest figures suggest that, sooner or later, the mighty dollar will tumble: relish for fans of burgernomics.

The hamburger standard:

	Big Mac Prices		Implied	Actual Dollar	Under(−)/over(+)
	In Local Currency	In Dollars	PPP* of the Dollar	Exchange Rate 23/04/02	Valuation against the Dollar, %
United States†	$2.49	2.49	—	—	—
Argentina	Peso 2.50	0.78	1.00	3.13	−68
Australia	A$3.00	1.62	1.20	1.86	−35
Brazil	Real 3.60	1.55	1.45	2.34	−38
Britain	£1.99	2.88	1.25‡	1.45‡	+16
Canada	C$3.33	2.12	1.34	1.57	−15
Chile	Peso 1,400	2.16	562	655	−14
China	Yuan 10.50	1.27	4.22	8.28	−49
Czech Rep	Koruna 56.28	1.66	22.6	34.0	−33
Denmark	DKr24.75	2.96	9.94	8.38	+19
Euro area	€2.67	2.37	0.93§	0.89§	−5
Hong Kong	HK$11.20	1.40	4.50	7.80	−42
Hungary	Forint 459	1.69	184	272	−32
Indonesia	Rupiah 16,000	1.71	6,426	9,430	−32
Israel	Shekel 12.00	2.51	4.82	4.79	+1
Japan	¥262	2.01	105	130	−19
Malaysia	M$5.04	1.33	2.02	3.8	−47
Mexico	Peso 21.90	2.37	8.80	9.28	−5
New Zealand	NZ$3.95	1.77	1.59	2.24	−29
Peru	New Sol 8.50	2.48	3.41	3.43	−1
Philippines	Peso 65.00	1.28	26.1	51.0	−49
Poland	Zloty 5.90	1.46	2.37	4.04	−41
Russia	Ruble 39.00	1.25	15.7	31.2	−50
Singapore	S$3.30	1.81	1.33	1.82	−27

South Africa	Rand 9.70	0.87	3.90	10.9	−64
South Korea	Won 3,100	2.36	1,245	1,304	−5
Sweden	SKr26.00	2.52	10.4	10.3	+1
Switzerland	SFr6.30	3.81	2.53	1.66	+53
Taiwan	NT$70.00	2.01	28.1	34.8	−19
Thailand	Baht 55.00	1.27	22.1	43.3	−49
Turkey	Lira 4,000,000	3.06	1,606,426	1,324,500	+21
Venezuela	Bolivar 2,500	2.92	1,004	857	+17

*Purchasing-power parity: local price divided by price in United States
†Average of New York, Chicago, San Francisco, and Atlanta
‡Dollars per pound
§Dollars per euro
Source:"Big Mac Currencies," *The Economist,* April 27, 2002, p. 76. © 2002 The Economist Newspaper Ltd. All rights reserved. Reprinted with permission. Further reproduction prohibited. www.economist.com.

Fundamental Value Based on Absolute PPP

Ideally, one would like to compare directly the price of goods in two countries to see if an exchange rate conforms to absolute PPP, or whether it is overvalued or undervalued in real terms. This can only be done for some individual goods that are clearly comparable ("law of one price"), and the estimation for different goods can lead to opposing conclusions.

There is a wide dispersion in the dollar prices of the Big Mac throughout the world. Differences in taxes, rents, and labor costs partly contribute to these differences. But several studies have shown that Big Mac PPP is a useful predictor of future exchange rate movements because deviations tend to be corrected over the long run.[14] This adjustment takes place either by a change in the exchange rate or by a change in the local-currency price of a Big Mac. For example, Cumby (1996) states that, after correcting for currency-specific constants, "a 10 percent undervaluation according to the hamburger standard in one year is associated with a 3.5 percent appreciation over the following year" (p. 13).

In practice, no one would estimate the fundamental value of a currency by applying absolute PPP to a single good, especially a nontraded one, and the preceding discussion is only anecdotal. Some attempts have been made to compare the prices of baskets of goods, but goods consumed in different countries are seldom identical, so a direct comparison of their prices is not realistic. How, for example, can one directly compare the value of a 19th-century Parisian house and that of a Dallas suburban home?

Fundamental Value Based on Relative PPP

Instead, *relative PPP* is most commonly used to explain and forecast currency movements. Remember that relative PPP considers across-the-board movements in

---

[14]See Cumby (1996) and Annaert and De Ceuster (1997).

prices over time, rather than absolute price levels. Several steps are required to implement this approach:

- Select an inflation index for each country.

- Select a historical period for which to compute long-run PPP.

- Determine the fundamental PPP value of the exchange rate, and hence, the current amount of over/undervaluation of the currency.

The definition of a proper inflation index is open to question. The estimation of the inflation rate depends on the basket of goods chosen for the index. Different baskets of goods will exhibit different price increases, as the relative prices of the goods change over time. An inflation rate measured from an index of consumed goods (CPI) will be different from an inflation rate measured from an index of produced goods (wholesale price index, WPI), because of differences in imported and exported goods. Differences in price movements between tradable and nontradable goods can also make a difference as illustrated in the case of Japan below.

CONCEPTS IN ACTION   THE CASE OF JAPAN

The strength of the yen since World War II is a puzzle for many investors. From 1950 to 2002, the yen has appreciated against the dollar from ¥360 per dollar to some ¥120 per dollar. This yen appreciation exceeds the consumer price index (CPI) inflation differential between the two countries. How can such a real appreciation of the yen be sustained?

Several studies, including one by McKinsey et al. (1993), show that Japan has experienced remarkable growth in productivity in many manufacturing industries whose products trade internationally. However, productivity gains for nontradables, such as services and locally consumed agricultural products, have lagged considerably. Locally produced nontradables are a significant share of the Japanese consumption basket (CPI).

The growth in productivity in the tradables sector has allowed wage increases that spread through the economy. Because of the low productivity gains in the nontradables sector, this increase in wages has forced a rapid rise in prices of nontradables. So, the prices of nontradables have risen much faster than the prices of tradables. Calculating the PPP value of the yen based on the CPI results in an apparent real appreciation of the currency. But there is no market pressure to correct such a deviation from PPP, because Japanese traded goods are competitive internationally at that exchange rate.

Because of cultural and regulatory restrictions on imports of competing goods and services (including agricultural products), prices of Japanese nontradables can remain high in the long run. The relative price of nontradables versus tradables has also risen in other countries, but to a much smaller extent.

The historical period selected to compute the fundamental PPP exchange rate value is important. For example, assume that the year is 2002 and you wish to determine the fundamental PPP value of the yen/dollar exchange rate. You can select December 31, 1972, as the base year. Then, the current 2002 fundamental value will be equal to the December 1972 exchange rate, adjusted by the inflation differential over the period 1973–2001. As of the end of 2001, the fundamental PPP value would have been equal to the December 1972 spot exchange rate, $S_{1972} = 302$ ¥/\$, multiplied by the ratio of Japanese price indexes at the end of 2001 and at the end of 1972 ($CPI¥_{2001}/CPI¥_{1972}$), and divided by the ratio of U.S. price indexes at the end of 2001 and at the end of 1972 ($CPI\$_{2001}/CPI\$_{1972}$).

This yields a fundamental value of 199 ¥/\$ for year-end 2001, compared with an actual spot rate of 131 ¥/\$. This is shown in Exhibit 2.5, in which the solid line is the actual spot exchange rate at year-end, and the top dotted line is the PPP value using 1972 as base year. When the dotted line (PPP value) is above the solid line (actual value), the yen is overvalued (or the dollar is undervalued). Conversely, the yen is undervalued when the dotted line is below the solid line. The yen seemed strongly overvalued at the end of 2001. Based on PPP, you can only conclude that the yen should depreciate relative to the dollar.

If a different base year had been selected, however—for example, 1978—the conclusion would have been markedly different. The bottom dotted line in Exhibit

---

EXHIBIT 2.5

Fundamental Value for the Japanese Yen

2.5 plots the PPP value using 1978 as base year: 1978 is a year in which the yen was strong relative to 1972. Hence, calculations using 1978 as a base year lead to a fundamental PPP value equal to only 106 ¥/$ at the end of 2001, a value below the actual spot rate of 131 ¥/$ at the end of 2001. The conclusion would have been that the yen was undervalued in 2001. (Note that the December 31, 2002, exchange rate was ¥120 per dollar, meaning an appreciation of the yen in 2002). Clearly, the choice of base year can make a significant difference. One pragmatic idea implemented by Arnott (1999) is to estimate the fundamental PPP value using a wide range of starting dates. In this smoothing process, the fundamental PPP value is then taken as the average of all the estimates derived with different base years.

To summarize, estimating a currency's fundamental PPP value should help explain future short-term movements in the exchange rate. Such estimation is not an easy task, however, and exchange rates can become grossly misaligned and remain so for several years without a correction. This correction will take place, but it may take several years, and its timing is unclear. Additional models are needed to provide a better understanding of exchange rate movements.

The Balance of Payments Approach

Historically, an analysis of the balance of payments provided the first approach to the economic modeling of the exchange rate. The balance of payments tracks all financial flows crossing a country's borders during a given period (a quarter or a year). For example, an export creates a positive financial inflow for the country, whereas an import creates a financial outflow (a negative financial inflow). A resident's purchase of a foreign security creates a negative financial inflow, whereas a loan made by a foreign bank to a resident bank creates a positive financial inflow. The balance of payments compiles all financial flows. The convention is to treat all financial inflows as a credit to the balance of payments, and all financial outflows as debits.

A balance of payments is not an income statement or a balance sheet, but a cash balance of the country relative to the rest of the world. The balance of all financial flows must be equilibrated, because the foreign exchange market always clears. In other words, the final balance *must* be zero.

This concept can best be confirmed by a simple example. Consider a small country whose only international transactions consist of exports and imports of goods. Its central bank has a large reserve of foreign currencies accumulated over the years. Assume that in the year 2000, this country runs a trade deficit of $1 million (imports greater than exports). Then the central bank will need to use $1 million of reserves to offset this deficit. The net balance will then be zero. Of course, the importers could instead borrow $1 million abroad to finance the payment of the trade balance; this will create a financial inflow that will be recorded in the balance of payments as a positive inflow offsetting the trade deficit. Again, the balance of payments will be equilibrated.

A parallel can be drawn with an individual's cash balance. If expenses exceed receipts at the end of the month, an individual must use his reserves to cover the deficit, borrow money from the outside world, or sell some assets to the outside world. The net balance must be zero. Hence, what is interesting is to analyze and interpret the various components of the balance of payments, because we know that the final balance must be zero.

The tradition is to separate the balance according to the type of transaction involved. There are many types of international transactions, including the following:

- International trade, leading to payment for goods imported and exported

- Payment for services, such as tourism and consulting contracts

- Income received (and paid) on loans and existing investments

- Direct investments made by domestic corporations abroad and by foreign corporations at home

- Portfolio investments, such as purchase of foreign securities by domestic investors and purchase of domestic securities by foreign investors

- All types of short-term and long-term capital flows

- Sale of foreign currency reserves by the central bank

Several chapters could be devoted to the accounting details of the balance of payments and to the controversy surrounding the various accounting conventions. The establishment of a balance of payments requires the collection of statistics from many sources, such as customs data, central bank statistics, and bank reports of transactions. Some countries, such as the United States, construct their balance of payments from a sampling of transactions. Most other countries attempt to trace every single international transaction. It is common to see the balance of payments figures revised periodically after a few months or years to reflect corrected data or changes in accounting conventions.

To simplify the presentation of a balance of payments, it is useful to consider four component groups of lines:

- Current account

- Capital account

- Financial account

- Official reserve account

The *current account* includes the balance of goods and services, and income received or paid on existing investments. Exports, or income received from abroad, appear as credits to the balance. It must be stressed that the current account does not include the amounts paid for investments abroad, but only the income received on current holding of foreign assets, usually in the form of dividends or interest payments. Actual investments are reflected in the financial account section. The current account also includes current *transfers,* which are transactions without compensation, such as gifts to relatives living abroad, grants to foreign students, or government aid to developing countries.

An important component of the current account, often mentioned by the news media, is the *trade balance,* which is simply the balance of merchandise exports minus merchandise imports. Many economists believe that the merchandise trade balance is given too much importance and that services should be added to the trade balance. Altogether, the current account gives a more global view of all current (i.e., noninvestment) transactions. Introducing straightforward notation, the current account (*CA*) is the sum of the following:

Trade balance	*TB*
Balance of services	*BS*
Net income received	*NI*
Current transfers	*CT*
Current account	***CA***

The *capital account* (*KA*) section reflects unrequited (or unilateral) transfers corresponding to capital flows entailing no compensation (in the form of goods, services, or assets). These capital transfers are different from current transfers and cover, for example, investment capital given (without future repayment) in favor of poor countries, debt forgiveness, and expropriation losses. It is generally a very small account, whose title is a bit misleading.

The *financial account*[15] (*FA*) includes all short-term and long-term capital transactions. The definition in this textbook excludes transactions made by the central bank, which will be assigned to the official reserve account. The financial account includes direct investment, portfolio investment, other investment flows (especially short-term capital). Direct investment is the net amount of direct purchases of companies or real estate made by a resident abroad and by foreigners at home. "Direct" means that the purchase did not go through the capital market and involves some form of control in the foreign company, as opposed to portfolio investment. The purchase (sale) of a foreign company by a resident is treated as a debit (credit), because it corresponds to a financial outflow (inflow). The purchase (sale) of a domestic company by a foreign resident is treated as a credit (debit), because it corresponds to a financial inflow (outflow). Portfolio investments correspond to the balance of investments made on financial markets by domestic and foreign investors.[16] "Other investment flows" captures many types of private and official capital flows, including short-term deposits made by foreigners at domestic banks and vice versa. Introducing straightforward notation, the financial account (*FA*) is the sum of these three items:

---

[15]Although the term *current account* is standard in the balance of payments literature, many terms have been used to refer to the sum of all capital flows, defined here as "financial account." Hence, the reader should be careful in applying the concept of "financial account" to published balance of payments data. Here we use the IMF terminology adopted in 1993 and applied since 1995 by most countries (see IMF, 1995).

[16]The balance of payments tracks investment flows. It does not take into account changes in value of foreign investments or liabilities caused by changes in market prices of securities.

Direct investment	*DI*
Portfolio investment	*PI*
Other investment flows	*OI*
Financial account	***FA***

"Net errors and omissions" is very embarrassing for balance-of-payments accountants. At the end of the day, when all statistics are collected from many different sources, the balance of payments must balance, like any cash balance. "Net errors and omissions" includes a few unaffected transactions, but consists mostly of whatever is needed to equilibrate the final balance to zero. Apparently disliking this terminology, the United States in 1976 changed it to "statistical discrepancy." This line is often assigned to the financial account, because transactions in the current account are more reliably tracked than are capital transactions. Aggregating all these items in the *capital and financial account* (*KFA*), we get

Capital account	*KA*
Financial account	*FA*
Net errors and omissions	*NE*
Capital and Financial account	***KFA***

The sum of the current account, the capital account, and the financial account is generally called the *overall balance* (IMF terminology). Denoting *OB,* the overall balance, we have

$$OB = CA + KFA$$

The *official reserve account* reflects net changes in the government's international reserves.[17] These reserves can take the form of foreign currency holdings and loans to foreign governments. Conversely, liabilities that constitute foreign governments' reserves come in the deduction of the domestic reserves. When the U.S. Federal Reserve Bank sells foreign currencies to equilibrate a deficit in the current and financial accounts, it will receive dollars in exchange. This inflow of dollars is treated as a credit to the balance of payments. This means that a *reduction* in the official reserves has a *positive* sign in the balance of payments accounting. This is often a source of confusion, because most of us tend to regard a drop in reserves as "bad" or "negative." However, this convention is quite logical. If a country sells goods or services, it receives a financial inflow in exchange for these goods or services. If its government sells foreign currencies, it also receives a financial inflow. Similarly, if a government is forced to borrow abroad to finance a deficit, the loan will induce a financial inflow and, hence, create a credit to the balance of payments. This credit is treated as an increase in official liabilities and, hence, as a reduction in official reserves.

By definition of a balance of payments, the sum of the current account (*CA*), the capital and the financial account (*KFA*), and the change in official reserves (*OR*) must be equal to zero:

$$CA + KFA + OR = 0$$

---

[17]The official reserve account is sometimes included as a subcategory of the financial account.

In other words, the change in official reserves simply mirrors the overall balance:

$$OR = -OB$$

The traditional approach to foreign exchange rate determination is to focus on the influence of balance of payments flows. Let's consider a country in which capital flows are restricted, as is often the case with developing nations. A trade deficit would lead to a reduction in the country's reserves and, ultimately, to a depreciation of the home currency. In turn, this depreciation would improve the terms of trade. National exports would become cheaper abroad and more competitive: Exports should increase. Imported goods would become more expensive: Imports should drop. This should lead to an improvement in the trade balance, and the currency should stabilize.

For example, the drop in oil prices in 1985 and 1986 led to a Mexican trade balance deficit; the value of the oil that Mexico exported suddenly dropped, without a corresponding reduction in imports. This deficit forced the Mexican government to borrow abroad to offset the imbalance; it also led to a depreciation of the peso. This devaluation helped restore the terms of trade.

This analysis requires us to estimate the trade flow elasticities in response to a movement in the exchange rate: How will imports and exports react to an exchange rate adjustment? The answers have to be built on often complex models of the economy. For example, oil imports by an emerging country are necessary for the domestic production process, as well as other domestic needs. A devaluation of the home currency is unlikely to strongly affect the demand for oil. Conversely, the demand for some imported goods, such as liquor or luxury items, is going to decrease if such goods become more expensive in home-currency terms.

Furthermore, the model must be dynamic, because the improvement in the trade balance will only be progressive. The immediate technical effect is not a quantity adjustment (more exports and less imports), but a price adjustment. Because imports are more expensive in terms of the home currency, as soon as the devaluation takes place, the trade deficit will immediately increase, given the new exchange rate. This is known as the *J-curve effect:* The trade balance will first deteriorate following a devaluation, before improving following the amelioration in the terms of trade. Of course, this scenario is not always rosy: The rise in import prices can feed higher inflation at home, leading to further depreciation of the currency. The monetary authorities will have to adjust their monetary/fiscal policy to control this "imported" inflation.

The analysis becomes even more complex when we consider capital flows, which is necessary to analyze the various components of the balance of payments. We must draw the line between flows that are autonomous—caused by current economic or political conditions—and those that are created to compensate for a potential imbalance.

The United States has run systematic, large trade deficits from the 1970s through 2002 without a structural depreciation of its currency, because of a financial account surplus. Foreign investors were happy to hold an increasing amount of dollar assets. The 1980s marked an important period for the United States as the dollar developed into the major international reserve currency: The U.S. dollar value

┌───┐
│ *CONCEPTS IN ACTION*   *THE DOLLAR: A CLIFF-HANGER* │
└───┘

How Might a Weak Dollar Affect the Global Economy?

Currency forecasters who have long predicted its decline have seen the dollar climb inexorably for years. At last it seems to be turning. Since February the dollar has fallen by 9% against the euro, to a 17-month low of $0.94. It has also hit a six-month low against the yen, of ¥123. It may well fall further over the coming year.

Two factors weigh against the dollar. First, it is by most yardsticks overvalued. Its trade-weighted level, adjusted for inflation differentials, remains well above its average over the past couple of decades. And second, America's large current-account deficit, at more than 4% of GDP and growing, looks unsustainable. If the dollar stays roughly where it is as the economy rebounds, then the deficit will grow. As a rule, once a country's external deficit approaches 5% of GDP, its currency tends to fall.

To trigger a slide, foreign investors do not have to become net sellers of American assets. The dollar will fall if they merely reduce the pace at which they add to their holdings. It will fall even more if American investors continue or expand this year's buying of foreign assets, notably European equities.

Until recently, net capital inflows more than covered America's current-account deficit. Yet investors are now reassessing their expectations about future relative returns. Recent data appear to confirm that America's recovery is on track. Indeed, The Economist's latest poll of forecasters suggests that the American economy is again expected to outpace Western Europe and Japan this year.

Still, the part of this growth that finds its way into company profits is in greater doubt. America's productivity growth may have risen, but the fruits have so far gone mainly to workers and consumers, rather than to profits. And a growing band of investors guesses that higher potential returns now lie in Europe and Japan—so long as governments carry out reforms and firms continue to restructure.

Currency Complacency?

Most forecasters predict another fall in the dollar, but they generally expect it to be gradual and relatively painless—except, of course, for foreigners with large dollar holdings. For example, UBS Warburg expects the dollar to fall to $1.05 to the euro and to ¥115 by the end of 2003—a drop of around one-sixth from its peak earlier this year. George Magnus, the banker's chief economist, argues that a gradual fall in the dollar would benefit the world economy. It would underpin America's recovery, by helping to bolster exports, profits and investment. A stronger euro and yen would also intensify the pressure for structural reform and corporate restructuring in the euro area and Japan.

By helping to hold down inflation in Europe, a strong euro would also reduce the pressure on the European Central Bank (ECB) to raise interest rates.

For Japan, however, a weaker dollar would be bad news, threatening to choke a nascent recovery. With interest rates already close to zero, the exchange rate is one of the few policy tools left for the Bank of Japan. GDP figures for the first quarter, due to be published on June 7th, are widely expected to show strong annualized growth of around 5%. However, Japan's GDP figures are notoriously volatile; many economists reckon that output will stumble again in the second quarter.

The Bank of Japan has intervened four times in the past two weeks in a bid to hold down the yen. Yet intervention rarely has much effect unless it is carried out jointly with other central banks. A new paper by Takatoshi Ito, an economist at the University of Tokyo, finds that joint intervention in the 1990s was 20–50 times more effective than intervention by the Bank of Japan alone. This time round, the Federal Reserve and the ECB are unlikely to join in, as both would be reasonably happy with a weaker dollar.

America's economy would certainly benefit from a moderate fall in the dollar. Some economists fret that this would push up inflation and thus force the Federal Reserve to raise interest rates. Yet the Fed would probably be happy to see some increase in inflation. America's GDP deflator, the broadest measure of inflation, rose by less than 0.5% at an annual rate over the past two quarters, its lowest for almost 50 years. This is getting close to deflation.

While a moderate decline of the dollar might be benign for the world, a sudden plunge would be another story altogether. It would probably trigger a slump in American share prices, and a rise in bond yields, as foreigners pulled out their money. Foreigners own fully two-fifths of American Treasury bonds, a quarter of corporate bonds and 13% of American equities. Share prices around the world would probably be hit.

A further drop in share prices would erode consumer and business confidence, and harm world growth. There is also a question over whether the ECB would react fast enough to a dollar crash by cutting interest rates to offset the deflationary impact on the euro-area economies. Stephen Roach, at Morgan Stanley, estimates that a 20% fall in the dollar over six months could knock up to one percentage point off global growth over the following year.

For now, most economists are sanguine, expecting a moderate fall in the dollar towards its "fair value," rather than a plunge. These are the same forecasters who in 2000 failed to predict a bear market in shares (the S&P 500 is now one-third below its peak) and who last year ruled out a recession. Currencies almost always overshoot, downwards as well as up. From its 1985 peak, the dollar fell by half against the D-mark within two years. A repeat performance is possible.

swung widely and the U.S. overall balance (OB) moved into a large deficit during the second half of the 1980s. The events from the late 1970s to the early 1990s led

EXHIBIT 2.6

Balance of Payments and the Dollar Exchange Rate

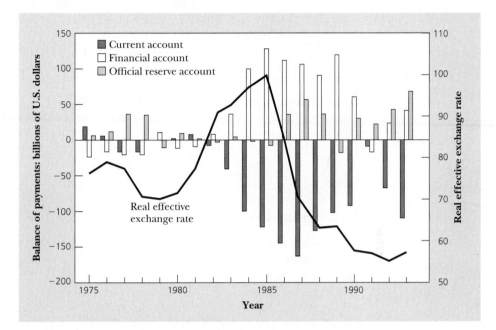

to a better understanding of the current situation. The story is told in Exhibit 2.6, which gives the three major components of the U.S. balance of payments, as well as the real effective exchange rate index, as calculated by the IMF. The real effective exchange rate index is the weighted average of the currencies of selected U.S. trading partners, adjusted for relative inflation differentials. It is more representative of the value of the U.S. dollar than any single exchange rate. A real appreciation of the dollar would lead to an increase in the effective exchange rate index. To analyze Exhibit 2.6, remember that a positive official reserve account means a drop in reserves. In 1977 and 1978, the combined deficits of the current and capital accounts led to a drop in official reserves, as well as a depreciation of the dollar. The improvement in the balance of payments (stable reserves, no trade deficit) from 1979 to 1982 led to an appreciation of the dollar. From 1983 to 1985, the United States started to run a huge trade and current account deficit. However, this current deficit was offset by fast-growing foreign investments, and the reserves did not deteriorate: The dollar kept rising. By 1986, the capital flows became insufficient to cover the current account deficit, the official reserve position deteriorated,[18] and

---

[18]Remember that the IMF changed its accounting convention for official reserves in 1997, and back-calculated all its balance of payments statistics. "Liabilities constituting foreign authorities reserves" were moved from official reserves to the financial flows account. This move has been questioned, because its main implication is to drastically reduce the apparent overall balance deficit of the United States. Here, we use data under the old convention, because it is better suited for our analysis.

the dollar started to slide. In 1990, the financial account began to deteriorate; it recovered in the mid 1990s. The big surge in capital investment in the 1980s came partly from Japanese investors who engaged in real estate and business acquisitions in the United States. The Japanese were running huge surpluses in their trade and current account balances, which allowed them to invest extensively in the United States and other countries (a Japanese deficit of the financial account). This situation of a huge U.S. trade deficit offset by foreign capital flows still prevailed in the late 1990s.

Although this story sounds reasonable, it is difficult to understand the huge swings in the value of the dollar. The timing of these swings is also difficult to forecast. Small changes in current account flows cannot justify such dramatic turning points and volatility in the exchange rate. In particular, we might ask what drives the behavior of investors and their willingness (or unwillingness) to hold U.S. dollars.

The Asset Market Approach

The General Idea   Many economists reject the view that the short-term behavior of exchange rates is determined in flow markets. Exchange rates are financial prices traded in an efficient asset market. Indeed, an exchange rate is the relative price of two currencies and, therefore, is determined by the willingness to hold each currency. Like other asset prices, the exchange rate is determined by expectations about the future, not by current trade flows.[19]

A parallel with other asset prices may illustrate the approach. Consider the stock price of a winery traded on the Paris Bourse. A frost in late spring results in a poor harvest, in terms of both quantity and quality. After harvesting and a year of wine making, the wine is finally sold, and the income is much less than in the previous year. On the day of the final sale, there is no reason for the stock price to be influenced by this low cash flow. First, the unusually low level of income has already been discounted in the winery stock price since the previous spring. Second, the stock price is affected by future, in addition to current, prospects. The stock price is based on expectations of future earnings, and the major cause for a change in stock price is a revision of these expectations.

A similar reasoning applies to exchange rates: Contemporaneous international flows should have little effect on exchange rates to the extent that they are expected. Only news about future economic prospects will affect exchange rates. The mere announcement of some unexpected news is sufficient to trigger an immediate adjustment in market value, even if it will take several months or years to be fully reflected in economic data. Because economic expectations are potentially volatile and influenced by many variables, including those of a political nature, the short-run behavior of exchange rates is volatile.

---

[19]A review of this approach can be found in Dornbusch, Fischer, and Startz (2001) or Krugman and Obstfeld (2000).

Several types of news influence exchange rates, but many of them have to do with inflationary expectations and interest rates. The relationship between interest rates and exchange rates is often presented in a confusing fashion in the media. Hence, we will introduce some simple models to help explain this relationship. In particular, we need to distinguish between interest rate movements caused by changes in inflationary expectations and those caused by changes in the real interest rate. We also need to distinguish between short-run and long-run effects.

More on Interest Rates   As mentioned, the interest rate can be separated into an "expected inflation" component and a "real interest rate" component, as in Equation 2.3′:

$$r \cong \rho + E(I)$$

The relation introduced by Irving Fisher is a *long-run* equilibrium relation. It states that an increase in expected inflation causes a proportional increase in money rates. Over the long run, the real interest rate is assumed constant.

But monetary policy affects the real interest rate in the *short run*. To illustrate this point, it is useful to introduce a simple domestic monetary model.

Equilibrium in the money market requires that money supply, M^S, equals money demand, M^D. The money supply is provided by the central bank. Money demand by all agents can be written as the product of the price level, P, and real money demand. Real money demand, M^D/P, can be a function of many variables, but it is generally supposed to be an inverse function of the interest rate.[20] So we can write

$$M^D/P = L(r)$$

This inverse relation between money demand and interest rate is intuitive. Higher interest rates mean that it becomes more costly to hold money balances than to invest in interest-bearing assets. This opportunity cost reduces the demand for money. Equilibrium implies that money supply equals real money demand times the price level:[21]

$$M^S = P \times L(r) \qquad (2.8)$$

The interest rate will adjust so that the quantity of money demanded by agents will equal the money supply. For example, assume that the central bank decides to provide more liquidity (unexpected increase in money supply). Agents will have additional cash balances to invest. The supply of loanable funds will increase and the interest rate will drop.

It must be stressed that the money equilibrium equation (2.8) is commonly used in two very different contexts:

---

[20]Demand for real cash balances is also a function of economic activity. To simplify the analysis, we do not explicitly introduce the real sector here, but real output (real GDP) is implicit in L.

[21]M^S/P is called the real money supply.

- In the *long run,* monetarists use Equation 2.8 as an equilibrium relation between the money supply and the price level. Everything else equal, an increase in the money supply will cause a proportional increase in the price level. For example, if the money supply doubles, without any change in real output, the price level must also double. In the long run, goods prices adjust to a change in money supply, and real interest rates revert back to their normal equilibrium level.

- In the *short run,* goods prices are inelastic. They react only slowly to monetary shocks and changes in interest rates. An unexpected increase in money supply will not immediately translate into a proportional price increase for physical goods. Goods prices are generally slow to adjust ("sticky prices") and the price level will only increase progressively. This is quite different for financial prices, such as interest rates, which react immediately to new information that affect expectations. So, Equation 2.8 is used, assuming that the price level, *P,* remains unchanged in the short run. An increase in money supply translates immediately into a drop in the interest rate. This is a drop in the *real* interest rate because expected inflation has clearly not decreased (but rather increased).

This difference between short-run and long-run effects is equally important for the exchange rate.

Exchange Rate Dynamics: Asset Market Approach   The asset market approach is generally used to estimate the impact of some disturbance on the current value of a currency. Typically, a monetary shock (disturbance) such as a central bank intervention on the interest rate will take time to propagate through the economy, but its expected impact will be immediately reflected in current exchange rates. The asset market approach first determines the new equilibrium value of the exchange rate once the influence of the monetary shock has been fully reflected in the economy (long run). Then, knowing that this equilibrium exchange rate is expected to prevail in the long run, one can infer the current exchange rate using uncovered interest parity.

The typical asset market approach to the exchange rate assumes that the parity relations described previously will apply in the long run. The equilibrium value of the exchange rate is driven by PPP, but goods prices are sticky and PPP will not hold in the short run. Because exchange rates are financial prices, however, they will immediately reflect expected changes in this long-run equilibrium value. So, we must clearly differentiate between the long-run and the short-run effects. Thus, the asset market approach studies the dynamics of the exchange rate and proceeds in two steps:

1. Determine the *long run* expected value of the exchange rate based on PPP, *E(S).* This is its fundamental PPP value expected to prevail in the long run.

2. Infer the *short-run* value of the exchange rate, S_0, assuming that the uncovered interest rate parity relation holds. Using Eq. 2.5, we get

$$S_0 = E(S) \times (1 + r_{DC})/(1 + r_{FC}) \qquad (2.9)$$

If the expected long-run exchange rate $E(S)$ were known with certainty, Equation 2.9 could be viewed as an arbitrage condition. S_0 would have to be equal to the expected exchange rate adjusted by the interest rate differential[22]; otherwise arbitrage would occur.

Exchange Rate Dynamics: A Simple Model   A simple model reflects the economic reasoning behind the asset market approach. Assume that the foreign currency is the U.S. dollar and the domestic currency is the euro. $M_{\$}$ and $M_{€}$ are the money supplies, and $P_{\$}$ and $P_{€}$ are the price levels in both countries. S is the $\$/€$ spot exchange rate. For the sake of simplicity, assume that there is no inflation in either country and that the money supplies have been constant over time and are expected to remain so in the future. Further, assume that the yield curves are flat in both countries, with $r_{\$} = r_{€}$.

An unexpected increase in money supply takes place in the United States, at time t_0, from $M_{\$}$ to $M_{\$}^*$. This is a one-time but permanent money expansion. In other words, the U.S. money supply is now expected to remain at $M_{\$}^*$ for the foreseeable future. Nothing has changed in Europe: the money supply, interest rate, and price level remain constant at $M_{€}$, $r_{€}$, and $P_{€}$. How should the exchange rate react to this money supply shock?

The time path of the various variables is described on Exhibit 2.7.

- The money supply jumps *permanently* from $M_{\$}$ to $M_{\$}^*$ at time t_0 (Exhibit 2.7a).

- The *long-run* equilibrium price level in the United States must increase proportionally to the increase in money supply. In the long run, it will reach a level $P_{\$}^* = P_{\$} \times M_{\$}^*/M_{\$}$, as implied by Equation 2.8. Once the price level reaches $P_{\$}^*$, it will remain at that level because there is no expected monetary expansion beyond the one-time shock. The real money supply will get back to its equilibrium level: $M_{\$}^*/P_{\$}^* = M_{\$}/P_{\$}$. But goods prices are sticky in the short run, so it will take time for the price to reach the level $P_{\$}^*$. The increase in price level will be progressive (Exhibit 2.7b).

- Once the monetary shock is fully absorbed, the U.S. interest rate will revert, in the *long run,* to its normal level of $r_{\$}$. But, in the *short run,* the price level does not move, so the real money supply increases to $M_{\$}^*/P_{\$}$. This increase in money supply will lead to a drop in the U.S. interest rate (say, to a level $r_{\$}'$),

---

[22]Note Equation 2.9 does not specify the time period necessary for the long-run adjustment. So, the interest rates r_{DC} and r_{FC} are compounded over the whole time period; they are not annualized. For example, assume that it takes two years for the exchange rate to reach its new fundamental value; then the interest rates should be equal to the annualized rates compounded over two years.

EXHIBIT 2.7

Exchange Rate Dynamics

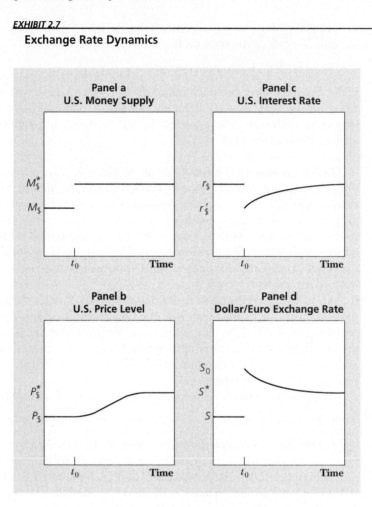

which will progressively get back to its long-run equilibrium value in line with the increase in price level (Exhibit 2.7c).

- The exchange rate started at its PPP value of $S = P_\$/P_€$. In the long run it is expected to rise to its new equilibrium PPP value of $E(S) = S^* = P_\$^*/P_€$. The long-run exchange rate of the euro (number of dollars per euro) will appreciate in proportion to the increase in U.S. money supply, which is also the percentage increase in U.S. price level. Knowing what the exchange rate will be in the long run, we can infer its short-run value using uncovered interest parity. The short-run value (S_0) should be equal to the expected long-run value adjusted by the interest rate differential. Because the U.S. interest rate has dropped, the exchange rate will be higher than its new long-run expected value. The exchange rate will progressively move to its long-run PPP value (Exhibit 2.7d).

EXAMPLE 2.9   *EXCHANGE RATE DYNAMICS*

The United States and Europe have no inflation, a constant money supply, and (annualized) interest rates equal to 3% for all maturities. The exchange rate is equal to one dollar per euro; this is its PPP value, and the price indexes can be assumed to be equal to one in both countries.

Suddenly and unexpectedly, the United States increases its money supply by 2 percent. This is a one-time but permanent shock. Immediately on the announcement, the U.S. interest rate drops from 3 percent to 2 percent for all maturities. It is expected that it will take two years for the shock in money supply to translate fully into a price increase. There is no effect on the real sector, nor any effect on Europe. Assume that the Eurozone is the domestic country. What will be the exchange rate dynamics?

SOLUTION

First, determine the long-run exchange rate. After two years, the U.S. price level will rise by 2 percent to 1.02. The exchange rate expected to prevail at that time, $E(S)$, is the new fundamental PPP value of the exchange rate:

$$S^* = 1 \times \frac{1.02}{1.000} = 1.02 \text{ dollars per euro}$$

After two years, the U.S. interest rate will be back to 3 percent. In the short run (immediately after the announcement), the exchange rate will move to

$$S_0 = E(S) \times (1 + r_{DC})/(1 + r_{FC}) = 1.02 \times \frac{(1 + 3\%)^2}{(1 + 2\%)^2} = 1.04 \text{ dollars per euro}$$

Following the money supply shock, the short-run effect on the dollar is a depreciation of 4 percent. This is caused by two phenomena:

- The fundamental PPP value depreciates by 2 percent because of the 2 percent long-run increase in the U.S. price level.

- The drop in the U.S. interest rate leads to an additional 2 percent dollar depreciation (a total of 4 percent).

This second phenomenon is caused by the drop in U.S. interest rates. If the exchange rate S_0 had settled at its long-run value of 1.02 $/€, an arbitrage could be constructed. Rather than investing dollars at a 2 percent interest rate, it is much more attractive to exchange dollars for euros spot at 1/1.02 euros, to invest those euros at 3 percent and to repatriate the euros into dollars two years from now at the exchange rate of $S^* = 1.02$ $/€. This would enable a speculator to "pocket" the interest rate differential and put pressure on the spot exchange rate until it reaches $S_0 = 1.04$ $/€. Of course, such reasoning relies on the assumption that the future exchange rate S^* is known with certainty.

The immediate result of this U.S. monetary shock is a depreciation of the U.S. dollar (appreciation of the euro) beyond its new fundamental PPP value. This phenomenon, caused by the U.S. interest drop, is known as "overshooting": The short-run reaction to a shock is larger than its long-run reaction. Here we see two phenomena at play:

- The dollar depreciates from S to S^* because of the long-run increase in the U.S. price level (*expected inflation*).

- The dollar depreciates even more in the short run (from S to S_0) because of the drop in the U.S. interest rate (drop in the *real interest rate*). As shown in Eq. 2.9, the exchange rate S_0 is equal to the long-run expected exchange rate S^*, compounded by the domestic interest rate (euro) and discounted at the foreign interest rate (dollar). A drop in the dollar interest rate implies that S_0 is higher than S^*.

To summarize:

- An increase in expected inflation in the foreign country leads to a depreciation of the foreign currency.

- A drop in the real interest rate in the foreign country leads to a depreciation of the foreign currency.

This simple example illustrates how an exchange rate reacts immediately, and in a volatile fashion, to monetary news. More complex monetary expansion scenarios could be modeled. For example, one could consider an unexpected, but permanent, increase in the *rate of growth* in money supply rather than a quantity shock in its level. Then the long-run interest rate would rise because of the permanent increase in expected inflation, but there would also be short-run effects.

Difficulties   The challenge of the asset market approach is to specify the news that should affect the exchange rate and quantify its *a priori* influence in the short run and the long run. One of the important components of such an approach is modeling the behavior of monetary authorities, because investors will try to guess their reactions. Another important component is risk perception. Investors discount expected events, and a change in risk perception affects the pricing of the exchange rate, as in any forward-looking pricing model. The influence of uncertainty is particularly important for the currencies of weaker economies.

Central banks usually convey their attitude by interest rate announcements. One has to evaluate the content and credibility of interest rate announcements carefully. If the rise in interest rates simply reflects an increase in home inflation, not a rise in the real interest rate, it should not have a positive effect on the currency. Even worse, it could carry some negative information. For example, during currency crises, a rise in interest rates is often interpreted as evidence that the currency is under speculative attack, that the central bank has had serious problems defending the exchange rate, and that its foreign exchange reserves are being exhausted. It prompts other speculators to join the attack and basically sends a negative signal for the home currency.

Summary

- In a flexible exchange rate regime, exchange rates are determined by supply and demand.

- In the balance of payments accounts, the current account includes the balance of goods and services, the income received or paid on existing investments, and current transfers. The financial account includes short-term and long-term capital transactions.

- Current account deficits can be balanced by financial account surpluses, and these deficits have a negative effect on the economy only if the country cannot attract financial inflows.

- Factors causing a country's currency to appreciate include lower inflation rates and higher real interest rates, but the effect of differences in economic performance is indeterminate.

- Expansionary monetary policy will generally lead to a depreciation of the home currency.

- Expansionary fiscal policy will generally lead to an appreciation of the home currency.

- A fixed exchange rate system is one in which the exchange rate between two currencies remains fixed at a preset level, known as "official parity."

- A pegged exchange rate system is one in which a target exchange rate (the peg) is set against a major currency, the exchange rate is allowed to fluctuate in a narrow band around the peg, and the peg is adjusted periodically to take account of economic fundamentals.

- Interest rate parity is the relation that the forward discount (premium) equals the interest rate differential between two currencies.

- Absolute purchasing power parity claims that the exchange rate should be equal to the ratio of the average price levels in the two economies.

- Relative purchasing power parity claims that the percentage movement of the exchange rate should be equal to the inflation differential between the two economies.

- Purchasing power parity implies that the ratio of the end-of-period exchange rate to the beginning-of-period exchange rate (in indirect quotes) equals the ratio of one plus the foreign inflation rate to one plus the domestic inflation rate.

- The real interest rate can be approximated for all countries by subtracting the expected inflation rate from the nominal interest rate.

- The international Fisher relation claims that real interest rates are equal across the world and hence, differences in nominal interest rates are caused by differences in national inflationary expectations. Interest rate differences approximately equal expected inflation rate differences if the international Fisher relation holds.

- One plus the real interest rate for any country equals one plus the nominal rate divided by one plus the expected inflation rate for that country.

- Uncovered interest rate parity claims that the expected change in the indirect exchange rate approximately equals the foreign minus the domestic interest rate.

- Uncovered interest rate parity is a theory combining purchasing power parity and the international Fisher relation.

- The forward exchange rate equals the expected exchange rate under the condition of no foreign currency risk premium.

- The forward exchange rate discount or premium equals the expected change in the exchange rate under the condition of no foreign currency risk premium.

- Combining all the parity relations indicates that the expected return on default-free bills should be the same in all countries, and exchange risk reduces to inflation uncertainty because there is no real foreign currency risk.

- Deviations from purchasing power parity should be corrected in the long run.

- The elements in the balance of payments are the current account, the capital account, the financial account, and the official reserves account; without central bank intervention, a current account deficit must be balanced by a financial account surplus. Exchange rate adjustments can be needed to restore balance of payments equilibrium.

- The asset market approach to pricing exchange rate expectations claims that the exchange rate is the relative price of two currencies, determined by investors' expectations about these currencies.

- The long-run exchange rate effect of a sudden and unexpected increase in the money supply is a depreciation of the currency so that purchasing power parity is maintained as the percentage increase in the price level matches the percentage increase in the money supply. Given sticky-goods prices, the short-run exchange rate effect is an immediate drop in the real interest rate and more depreciation of the currency than the depreciation implied by purchasing power parity.

Problems

1. Consider two countries, A and B, whose currencies are α and β, respectively. The interest rate in A is greater than the interest rate in B. Which of the following is true?
   a. α is expected to appreciate relative to β, and α should trade with a forward discount.
   b. α is expected to appreciate relative to β, and α should trade with a forward premium.
   c. α is expected to depreciate relative to β, and α should trade with a forward discount.
   d. α is expected to depreciate relative to β, and α should trade with a forward premium.

2. The spot \$/€ is equal to 1.1795. The annual one-year interest rates on the Eurocurrency market are 4 percent in euros and 5 percent in U.S. dollars. The annualized one-month interest rates are 3 percent in euros and 4 percent in U.S. dollars.
   a. What is the one-year forward exchange rate?
   b. What is the one-month forward exchange rate?

3. You are given the following quotes.
   Spot exchange rates:

\$/€	1.1865–1.1870
¥/\$	108.10–108.20

   Three-month interest rates (percent per year):

in \$	5–5¼
in €	3¼–3½
in ¥	1¼–1½

   What should the quotes be for the
   a. ¥/€ spot exchange rate?
   b. \$/€ three-month forward ask exchange rate? *Hint:* Buying euros forward is equivalent to borrowing dollars to buy euros spot and investing the euros.
   c. €/\$ three-month forward bid exchange rate?
   d. ¥/\$ three-month forward bid and ask exchange rate?

4. Jason Smith is a foreign exchange trader with Citibank. He notices the following quotes.

Spot exchange rate:	SFr1.6627/\$
Six-month forward exchange rate:	SFr1.6558/\$
Six-month \$ interest rate:	3.5% per year
Six-month SFr interest rate:	3.0% per year

   a. Ignoring transaction costs, is the interest rate parity holding?
   b. Is there an arbitrage possibility? If yes, what steps would be needed to make an arbitrage profit? Assuming that Jason Smith is authorized to work with \$1,000,000 for this purpose, how much would the arbitrage profit be in dollars?

5. A foreign exchange arbitrageur notices that the Japanese yen to U.S. dollar spot exchange rate is ¥108/\$ and the three-month forward exchange rate is ¥107.30/\$. The three-month \$ interest rate is 5.20 percent per annum and the three-month ¥ interest rate is 1.20 percent per annum.
   a. Is the interest rate parity holding?

b. Is there an arbitrage possibility? If yes, what steps would be needed to make an arbitrage profit? Assuming that the arbitrageur is authorized to work with $1,000,000 for this purpose, how much would the arbitrage profit be in dollars?

6. The following chart illustrates the domestic prices of three items (shoes, watches, and electric motors) of similar quality in the United States and Mexico.

Items	United States (dollars)	Mexico (peso)
Shoes	20	80
Watches	40	180
Electric motors	80	600

If one dollar exchanges for five Mexican pesos and transportation costs are zero, Mexico will import
a. shoes and watches, and the United States will import electric motors.
b. shoes, and the United States will import watches and electric motors.
c. all three goods from the United States.
d. electric motors, and the United States will import shoes and watches.

7. A group of countries decides to introduce a common currency. What do you think would happen to the inflation rates of these countries after the introduction of the common currency?

8. The current Swiss franc to U.S. dollar spot exchange rate is SFr1.60/$. The expected inflation over the coming year is 2 percent in Switzerland and 5 percent in the United States. According to purchasing power parity, what is the expected value of the Swiss franc to U.S. dollar spot exchange rate a year from now?

9. Let us consider a utopian world in which there are only three goods: sake, beer, and TV sets.
   - Japanese consume only a locally produced food, called sake, and an industrially produced and traded good, called TV sets.
   - Americans consume only a locally produced food, called beer, and an industrially produced and traded good, called TV sets.

   TV sets are produced in both countries and actively traded; their local prices follow the law of one price. Foods are produced only locally and are not traded. The consumption basket of a Japanese consists of two-thirds sake and one-third TV sets. The consumption basket of an American consists of one-half beer and one-half TV sets. Prices of beer and TV sets in the United States are constant over time, in U.S. dollars. Japanese are very competitive and export a lot of TV sets. Japanese farmers want to share in the increased national wealth, and the price of sake is rising at a rate of 10 percent per year, in yen. Assume that the yen/dollar exchange rate stays constant.
   a. What is the consumer price index inflation in Japan?
   b. Does relative PPP hold between Japan and the United States?

10. a. Explain the following three concepts of purchasing power parity:
     i. The law of one price
     ii. Absolute PPP
     iii. Relative PPP
    b. Evaluate the usefulness of relative PPP in predicting movements in foreign exchange rates on a
     i. short-term basis (e.g., three months).
     ii. long-term basis (e.g., six years).

11. A French company is importing some equipment from Switzerland and will need to pay 10 million Swiss francs three months from now. The current spot exchange rate is SFr1.5543/€. The treasurer of the company expects the franc to appreciate in the next few weeks, and is concerned about it. The three-month forward rate is SFr1.5320/€.
    a. Given the treasurer's expectation, what action can he take using the forward contract?
    b. Three months later, the spot exchange rate turns out to be SFr1.5101/€. Did the company benefit because of the treasurer's action?

12. Suppose the international parity conditions hold. Does that mean that the nominal interest rates would be equal among countries? Why or why not?

13. You are given the following information about Australia, Switzerland, and the United States. The Australian dollar is expected to depreciate relative to the United States dollar. The nominal interest rate in the United States is greater than that in Switzerland. Can you say whether the Australian dollar is expected to depreciate or appreciate relative to the Swiss Franc?

14. Following are some statistics about the Swedish Krona and the dollar:

	SKr	$
Inflation (annual rate)	6%	?%
One-year interest rate	8%	7%
Spot exchange rate (SKr/$)	?	
Expected exchange rate in one year (SKr/$)	6	
One-year forward exchange rate (SKr/$)	?	

Based on the linear approximations of the international parity conditions, replace the question marks with appropriate answers.

15. Assume that the one-year interest rate is 12 percent in the United Kingdom. The expected annual rate of inflation for the coming year is 10 percent for the United Kingdom and 4 percent for Switzerland. The current spot exchange rate is SFr3/£. Using the precise form of the international parity relations, compute the one-year interest rate in Switzerland, the expected Swiss franc to pound exchange rate in one year, and the one-year forward exchange rate.

16. Following are some statistics for Malaysia, the Philippines, and the United States.

Inflation Rates: Annual Rates in Percent per Year

	1991	1992	1993	1994	1995	1996
Malaysia	4.40	4.69	3.57	3.71	5.28	3.56
Philippines	18.70	8.93	7.58	9.06	8.11	8.41
United States	4.23	3.03	3.00	2.61	2.81	2.34

Exchange Rate per U.S. Dollar: Annual Average

	1991	1992	1993	1994	1995	1996
Malaysia	2.75	2.55	2.57	2.62	2.50	2.52
Philippines	27.48	25.51	27.12	26.42	25.71	26.22

In 1997, Malaysia and the Philippines suffered a severe currency crisis. Use the numbers in the preceding table to provide a partial explanation.

17. Paf is a small country whose currency is the pif. Twenty years ago, the exchange rate with the United States dollar was two pifs per dollar, and the inflation indexes were equal to 100 in both the United States and Paf. Now, the exchange rate is 0.9 pifs per dollar, and the inflation indexes are equal to 400 in the United States and 200 in Paf.
    a. What should the current exchange rate be if PPP prevailed?
    b. Is the pif over- or undervalued according to PPP?

18. Paf is a small country. Its currency is the pif, and the exchange rate with the United States dollar is 0.9 pifs per dollar. Following are some of the transactions affecting Paf's balance of payments during the quarter:
    - Paf exports 10 million pifs of local products.
    - Paf investors buy foreign companies for a total cost of $3 million.
    - Paf investors receive $0.1 million of dividends on their foreign shares.
    - Many tourists visit Paf and spend $0.5 million.
    - Paf pays 1 million pifs as interest on Paf bonds currently held by foreigners.
    - Paf imports $7 million of foreign goods.
    - Paf receives $0.3 million as foreign aid.

    Illustrate how the preceding transactions would affect Paf's balance of payments for the quarter, including the current account, the financial account, and the official reserves account.

19. The domestic economy seems to be overheating, with rapid economic growth and low unemployment. News has just been released that the monthly activity level is even higher than expected (as measured by new orders to factories and unemployment figures). This news leads to renewed fears of inflationary pressures and likely action by the monetary authorities to raise interest rates to slow the economy down.
    a. Based on the traditional flow market approach, discuss whether this news is good or bad for the exchange rate?
    b. Based on the asset market approach, discuss whether this news is good or bad for the exchange rate?

20. Even though the investment community generally believes that Country M's recent budget deficit reduction is "credible, sustainable, and large," analysts disagree about how it will affect Country M's foreign exchange rate. Juan DaSilva, CFA, states, "The reduced budget deficit will lower interest rates, which will immediately weaken Country M's foreign exchange rate."
    a. Discuss the direct (short-term) effects of a reduction in Country M's budget deficit on
        i. demand for loanable funds.
        ii. nominal interest rates.
        iii. exchange rates.
    b. Helga Wu, CFA, states, "Country M's foreign exchange rate will strengthen over time as a result of changes in expectations in the private sector in country M." Support Wu's position that Country M's foreign exchange rate will strengthen because of the changes a budget deficit reduction will cause in
        i. expected inflation rates.
        ii. expected rates of return on domestic securities.

Solutions

1. Because the interest rate in A is greater than the interest rate in B, α is expected to depreciate relative to β, and should trade with a forward discount. Accordingly, the correct answer is (c).

2. Because the exchange rate is given in $\$/\euro$ terms, the appropriate expression for the interest rate parity relation is

$$\frac{F}{S} = \frac{1 + r_\$}{1 + r_\euro}$$

($r_\$$ is a part of the numerator and $r_\euro$ is a part of the denominator).

a. The one-year $\$/\euro$ forward rate is given by

$$\$/\euro = 1.1795 \, \frac{1.05}{1.04} = 1.1908$$

b. The one-month $\$/\euro$ forward rate is given by

$$\$/\euro = 1.1795 \, \frac{1 + (0.04/12)}{1 + (0.03/12)} = 1.1805$$

Of course, these are central rates, and bid–ask rates could also be determined on the basis of bid–ask rates for the spot exchange and interest rates.

3. a. bid $\yen/\euro$ = (bid $\yen/\$$) $\times$ (bid $\$/\euro$) = 108.10 $\times$ 1.1865 = 128.2607.
   ask $\yen/\euro$ = (ask $\yen/\$$) $\times$ (ask $\$/\euro$) = 108.20 $\times$ 1.1870 = 128.4334.

   b. Because the exchange rate is in $\$/\euro$ terms, the appropriate expression for the interest rate parity relation is $F/S = (1 + r_\$)/(1 + r_\euro)$.

$$\$/\euro \text{ 3-month ask} = (\text{spot ask } \$/\euro)\frac{1 + (\text{ask } r_\$)}{1 + (\text{bid } r_\euro)} = 1.1870 \, \frac{1 + (0.0525/4)}{1 + (0.0325/4)}$$
$$= 1.1929$$

   Thus, the $\$/\euro$ 3-month forward ask exchange rate is: 1.1929.

   c. bid $\euro/\$$= 1/ask $\$/\euro$ = 1/1.1929 = 0.8383.
   Thus, the 3- month forward bid exchange rate is $\euro/\$$ = 0.8383.

   d. Because the exchange rate is in $\yen/\$$ terms, the appropriate expression for the interest rate parity relation is $F/S = 1 + r_\yen/1 + r_\$$.

$$\yen/\$ \text{ 3-month bid} = (\text{spot bid } \yen/\$)\frac{1 + (\text{bid } r_\yen)}{1 + (\text{ask } r_\$)} = 108.10 \, \frac{1 + (0.0125/4)}{1 + (0.0525/4)} = 107.03$$

$$\yen/\$ \text{ 3-month ask} = (\text{spot ask } \yen/\$)\frac{1 + (\text{ask } r_\yen)}{1 + (\text{bid } r_\$)} = 108.20 \, \frac{1 + (0.0150/4)}{1 + (0.0500/4)} = 107.26$$

Thus, the $\yen/\$$ 3-month forward exchange rate is: 107.03–107.26. *Note:* The interest rates one uses in all such computations are those that result in a lower forward bid (so, bid interest rates in the numerator and ask rates in the denominator) and a higher forward ask (so, ask interest rates in the numerator and bid rates in the denominator).

4. a. For six months, $r_{SFr} = 1.50$ percent and $r_\$ = 1.75$ percent. Because the exchange rate is in SFr/$ terms, the appropriate expression for the interest rate parity relation is

$$\frac{F}{S} = \frac{1 + r_{SFr}}{1 + r_\$}, \text{ or } \frac{F}{S}(1 + r_\$) = (1 + r_{SFr})$$

The left side of this expression is

$$\frac{F}{S}(1 + r_\$) = \frac{1.6558}{1.6627}(1 + 0.0175) = 1.0133$$

The right side of the expression is: $1 + r_{SFr} = 1.0150$. Because the left and right sides are not equal, IRP is not holding.

b. Because IRP is not holding, there is an arbitrage possibility: Because $1.0133 < 1.0150$, we can say that the SFr interest rate quote is more than what it should be as per the quotes for the other three variables. Equivalently, we can also say that the $ interest rate quote is less than what it should be as per the quotes for the other three variables. Therefore, the arbitrage strategy should be based on borrowing in the $ market and lending in the SFr market. The steps would be as follows:

   - Borrow $1,000,000 for six months at 3.5 percent per year. Need to pay back $1,000,000 × (1 + 0.0175) = $1,017,500 six months later.
   - Convert $1,000,000 to SFr at the spot rate to get SFr1,662,700.
   - Lend SFr1,662,700 for six months at 3 percent per year. Will get back SFr1,662,700 × (1 + 0.0150) = SFr1,687,641 six months later.
   - Sell SFr1,687,641 six months forward. The transaction will be contracted as of the current date but delivery and settlement will only take place six months later. So, six months later, exchange SFr1,687,641 for SFr1,687,641/SFr1.6558/$ = $1,019,230.

   The arbitrage profit six months later is $1,019,230 - 1,017,500 = \$1,730$.

5. a. For three months, $r_\$ = 1.30$ percent and $r_¥ = 0.30$ percent. Because the exchange rate is in ¥/$ terms, the appropriate expression for the interest rate parity relation is

$$\frac{F}{S} = \frac{1 + r_¥}{1 + r_\$}, \text{ or } \frac{F}{S}(1 + r_\$) = (1 + r_¥)$$

The left side of this expression is

$$\frac{F}{S}(1 + r_\$) = \frac{107.30}{108.00}(1 + 0.0130) = 1.0064$$

The right side of this expression is: $1 + r_¥ = 1.0030$. Because the left and right sides are not equal, IRP is not holding.

b. Because IRP is not holding, there is an arbitrage possibility. Because $1.0064 > 1.0030$, we can say that the $ interest rate quote is more than what it should be as per the quotes for the other three variables. Equivalently, we can also say that the ¥ interest rate quote is less than what it should be as per the quotes for the other three variables. Therefore, the arbitrage strategy should be based on lending in the $ market and borrowing in the ¥ market. The steps would be as follows:

   - Borrow the yen equivalent of $1,000,000. Because the spot rate is ¥108/$, borrow $1,000,000 × ¥108/$ = ¥108,000,000. Need to pay back ¥108,000,000 × (1 + 0.0030) = ¥108,324,000 three months later.
   - Exchange ¥108,000,000 for $1,000,000 at the spot exchange rate.

- Lend $1,000,000 for three months at 5.20 percent per year. Will get back $1,000,000 $\times$ (1 + 0.0130) = $1,013,000 three months later.
- Buy ¥108,324,000 three months forward. The transaction will be contracted as of the current date, but delivery and settlement will only take place three months later. So, three months later, get ¥108,324,000 for ¥108,324,000/¥107.30/$ = $1,009,543.

The arbitrage profit three months later is 1,013,000 − 1,009,543 = $3,457.

6. At the given exchange rate of 5 pesos/$, the cost in Mexico in dollar terms is $16 for shoes, $36 for watches, and $120 for electric motors. Thus, compared with the United States, shoes and watches are cheaper in Mexico, and electric motors are more expensive in Mexico. Therefore, Mexico will import electric motors from the United States, and the United States will import shoes and watches from Mexico. Accordingly, the correct answer is (d).

7. Consider two countries, A and B. Based on relative PPP,

$$\frac{S_1}{S_0} = \frac{1 + I_A}{1 + I_B}$$

where S_1 and S_0 are the expected and the current exchange rates between the currencies of A and B, and I_A and I_B are the inflation rates in A and B. If A and B belong to the group of countries that introduces the same currency, then one could think of both S_1 and S_0 being one. Then, I_A and I_B should both be equal for relative PPP to hold. Thus, introduction of a common currency by a group of countries would result in the convergence of the inflation rates among these countries. A similar argument could be applied to inflation among the various states of the United States.

8. Based on relative PPP,

$$\frac{S_1}{S_0} = \frac{1 + I_{Switzerland}}{1 + I_{US}}$$

where S_1 is the expected SFr/$ exchange rate one year from now, S_0 is the current SFr/$ exchange rate, and $I_{Switzerland}$ and I_{US} are the expected annual inflation rates in Switzerland and the United States, respectively. So,

$$\frac{S_1}{1.60} = \frac{1 + 0.02}{1 + 0.05} \quad \text{and} \quad S_1 = 1.60 \, (1.02/1.05) = SFr1.55/\$$$

9. a. A Japanese consumption basket consists of two-thirds sake and one-third TV sets. The price of sake in yen is rising at a rate of 10 percent per year. The price of TV sets is constant. The Japanese consumer price index inflation is therefore equal to

$$\frac{2}{3}(10\%) + \frac{1}{3}(0\%) = 6.67\%$$

b. Relative PPP states that

$$\frac{S_1}{S_0} = \frac{1 + I_{FC}}{1 + I_{DC}}$$

Because the exchange rate is given to be constant, we have $S_0 = S_1$, which implies $S_1/S_0 = 1$. As a result, in our example, PPP would hold if $1 + I_{FC} = 1 + I_{DC}$ (i.e., $I_{FC} = I_{DC}$). Because the Japanese inflation rate is 6.67 percent and the American inflation rate is 0 percent, we do not have $I_{FC} = I_{DC}$, and PPP does not hold.

10. a.

    i. The law of one price is that, assuming competitive markets and no transportation costs or tariffs, the same goods should have the same real prices in all countries after converting prices to a common currency.

    ii. Absolute PPP, focusing on baskets of goods and services, states that the same basket of goods should have the same price in all countries after conversion to a common currency. Under absolute PPP, the equilibrium exchange rate between two currencies would be the rate that equalizes the prices of a basket of goods between the two countries. This rate would correspond to the ratio of average price levels in the countries. Absolute PPP assumes no impediments to trade and identical price indexes that do not create measurement problems.

    iii. Relative PPP holds that exchange rate movements reflect differences in price changes (inflation rates) between countries. A country with a relatively high inflation rate will experience a proportionate depreciation of its currency's value vis-à-vis that of a country with a lower rate of inflation. Movements in currencies provide a means for maintaining equivalent purchasing power levels among currencies in the presence of differing inflation rates.

        Relative PPP assumes that prices adjust quickly and price indexes properly measure inflation rates. Because relative PPP focuses on changes and not absolute levels, relative PPP is more likely to be satisfied than the law of one price or absolute PPP.

b.

    i. Relative PPP is not consistently useful in the short run because of the following: (1) Relationships between month-to-month movements in market exchange rates and PPP are not consistently strong, according to empirical research. Deviations between the rates can persist for extended periods. (2) Exchange rates fluctuate minute by minute because they are set in the financial markets. Price levels, in contrast, are sticky and adjust slowly. (3) Many other factors can influence exchange rate movements rather than just inflation.

    ii. Research suggests that over the long term, a tendency exists for market and PPP rates to move together, with market rates eventually moving toward levels implied by PPP.

11. a. If the treasurer is worried that the franc might appreciate in the next three months, she could hedge her foreign exchange exposure by trading this risk against the premium included in the forward exchange rate. She could buy 10 million Swiss francs on the three-month forward market at the rate of SFr1.5320/€. The transaction will be contracted as of the current date, but delivery and settlement will only take place three months later.

b. Three months later, the company received the 10 million Swiss francs at the forward rate of SFr1.5320/€ agreed on earlier. Thus, the company needed (SFr10,000,000)/ (SFr1.5320/€), or €6,527,415. If the company had not entered into a forward contract, the company would have received the 10 million Swiss francs at the spot rate of SFr1.5101/€. Thus, the company would have needed (SFr10,000,000)/ (SFr1.5101/€), or €6,622,078. Therefore, the company benefited by the treasurer's action, because €6,622,078 − €6,527,415 = €94,663 were saved.

12. The nominal interest rate is approximately the sum of the real interest rate and the expected inflation rate over the term of the interest rate. Even if the international Fisher relation holds, and the real interest rates are equal among countries, the expected inflation can be very different from one country to another. Therefore, there is no reason why nominal interest rates should be equal among countries.

13. Because the Australian dollar is expected to depreciate relative to the dollar, we know from the combination of international Fisher relation and relative PPP that the nominal interest rate in Australia is greater than the nominal interest rate in the United States. Further, the nominal interest rate in the United States is greater than that in Switzerland. Thus, the nominal interest rate in Australia has to be greater than the nominal interest rate in Switzerland. Therefore, we can say from the combination of international Fisher relation and relative PPP that the Australian dollar is expected to depreciate relative to the Swiss franc.

14. According to the approximate version of the international Fisher relation, $r_{\text{Sweden}} - r_{\text{US}} = I_{\text{Sweden}} - I_{\text{US}}$. So, $8 - 7 = 6 - I_{\text{US}}$, which means that $I_{\text{US}} = 5\%$.

    According to the approximate version of relative PPP,

    $$\frac{S_1 - S_0}{S_0} = I_{\text{Sweden}} - I_{\text{US}}$$

    where, S_1 and S_0 are in SKr/$ terms. $I_{\text{Sweden}} - I_{\text{US}} = 6 - 5 = 1\%$, or 0.01. So, $(6 - S_0)/S_0 = 0.01$. Solving for S_0, we get $S_0 = \text{SKr } 5.94/\$$.

    According to the approximate version of IRP,

    $$\frac{F - S_0}{S_0} = r_{\text{Sweden}} - r_{\text{US}}$$

    where, F and S_0 are in SKr/$ terms. $r_{\text{Sweden}} - r_{\text{US}} = 8 - 7 = 1\%$, or 0.01. So, $(F - 5.94)/5.94 = 0.01$. Solving for F, we get $F = \text{SKr } 6/\$$.

    Because we are given the expected exchange rate, we could also have arrived at this answer by using the foreign exchange expectations relation.

15. According to the international Fisher relation,

    $$\frac{1 + r_{\text{Switzerland}}}{1 + r_{\text{UK}}} = \frac{1 + I_{\text{Switzerland}}}{1 + I_{\text{UK}}}$$

    So,

    $$\frac{1 + r_{\text{Switzerland}}}{1 + 0.12} = \frac{1 + 0.04}{1 + 0.10}$$

    Therefore, $r_{\text{Switzerland}} = 0.0589$, or 5.89%.

    According to relative PPP,

    $$\frac{S_1}{S_0} = \frac{1 + I_{\text{Switzerland}}}{1 + I_{\text{UK}}}$$

    where, S_1 and S_0 are in SFr/£ terms. So,

    $$\frac{S_1}{3} = \frac{1 + 0.04}{1 + 0.10}$$

    Solving for S_1, we get $S_1 = \text{SFr } 2.8364/£$.

According to IRP,

$$\frac{F}{S_0} = \frac{1 + r_{\text{Switzerland}}}{1 + r_{\text{UK}}}$$

where, F and S_0 are in SFr/£ terms. So,

$$\frac{F}{3} = \frac{1 + 0.0589}{1 + 0.12}$$

Solving for F, we get $F = $ SFr 2.8363/£. This is the same as the expected exchange rate in one year, with the slight difference due to rounding.

16. During the 1991–1996 period, the cumulative inflation rates were about 25 percent in Malaysia, 61 percent in the Philippines, and 18 percent in the United States. Over this period, based on relative PPP, one would have expected the Malaysian ringgit to depreciate by about 7 percent relative to the United States dollar (the inflation differential). In reality, the Malaysian ringgit *appreciated* by about 8 percent. Similarly, in view of the very high inflation differential between the Philippines and the United States, one would have expected the Philippine peso to depreciate considerably relative to the dollar. But it did not. Thus, according to PPP, both currencies had become strongly overvalued.

17. a. According to PPP, the current exchange rate should be

    $$S_1 = S_0 \frac{PI_1^{\text{Pif}}/PI_0^{\text{Pif}}}{PI_1^{\$}/PI_0^{\$}}$$

    where subscript 1 refers to the value now, subscript 0 refers to the value 20 years ago, PI refers to price index, and S is the pif/\$ exchange rate. Thus, the current exchange rate based on PPP should be $S_1 = 2\left(\dfrac{200/100}{400/100}\right) = $ pif 1/\$

    b. As per PPP, the pif is overvalued at the prevailing exchange rate of pif 0.9/\$.

18. Exports equal 10 million pifs and imports equal \$7 million (6.3 million pifs). Accordingly, the trade balance is $10 - 6.3 = 3.7$ million pifs.
    - Balance of services includes the \$0.5 million spent by tourists (0.45 million pifs).
    - Net income includes \$0.1 million or 0.09 million pifs received by Paf investors as dividends, minus 1 million pifs paid out by Paf as interest on Paf bonds (-0.91 million pifs).
    - Unrequited transfers include \$0.3 million (0.27 million pifs) received by Paf as foreign aid.
    - Portfolio investment includes the \$3 million or 2.7 million pifs spent by Paf investors to buy foreign firms. So, portfolio investment $= -2.7$ million pifs.

    Based on the preceding,
    - Current account $= 3.24$ ($= 3.70 + 0.45 - 0.91$)
    - Capital account $= 0.27$
    - Financial account $= -2.7$

    The sum of current account, capital account, and financial account is 0.81. By definition of balance of payments, the sum of the current account, the capital account, the financial account, and the change in official reserves must be equal to zero. Therefore, official reserve account $= -0.81$.

The following summarizes the effect of the transactions on the balance of payments.

Current account		*3.24*
Trade balance	3.70	
Balance of services	0.45	
Net income	−0.91	
Capital account		*0.27*
Unrequited transfers	0.27	
Financial account		*− 2.70*
Portfolio investment	−2.70	
Official reserve account		*− 0.81*

19. a. A traditional flow market approach would suggest that the home currency should depreciate because of increased inflation. An increase in domestic consumption could also lead to increased imports and a deficit in the balance of trade. This deficit should lead to a weakening of the home currency in the short run.

    b. The asset market approach claims that this scenario is good for the home currency. Foreign capital investment is attracted by the high returns caused by economic growth and high interest rates. This capital inflow leads to an appreciation of the home currency.

20. a. i. The immediate effect of reducing the budget deficit is to reduce the demand for loanable funds because the government needs to borrow less to bridge the gap between spending and taxes.

    ii. The reduced public-sector demand for loanable funds has the direct effect of lowering nominal interest rates, because lower demand leads to lower cost of borrowing.

    iii. The direct effect of the budget deficit reduction is a depreciation of the domestic currency and the exchange rate. As investors sell lower yielding Country M securities to buy the securities of other countries, Country M's currency will come under pressure and Country M's currency will depreciate.

    b. i. In the case of a credible, sustainable, and large reduction in the budget deficit, reduced inflationary expectations are likely because the central bank is less likely to monetize the debt by increasing the money supply. Purchasing power parity and international Fisher relationships suggest that a currency should strengthen against other currencies when expected inflation declines.

    ii. A reduction in government spending would tend to shift resources into private-sector investments, in which productivity is higher. The effect would be to increase the expected return on domestic securities.

Bibliography

Annaert, J., and De Ceuster, M. "The Big Mac: More Than a Junk Asset Allocator?" *International Review of Financial Analysis,* 6(3), 1997, pp. 179–192.

Arnott, R. "Tactical Currency Allocation," in Managing Currency Risks in Investment Portfolios, AIMR Proceedings, 1999.

Cassel, G. "The Present Situation on the Foreign Exchanges," *Economic Journal,* 1916, pp. 62–65.

Cumby, R. E. "Forecasting Exchange Rates and Relative Prices with the Hamburger Standard: Is What You Want What You Get with McParity?" NBER Working Paper No. 5675, 1996.

Dornbusch, R., Fischer, S., and Startz, R. *Macroeconomics,* 8th edition, New York: McGraw-Hill, 2001.

Fisher, I. *The Theory of Interest,* New York: Macmillan, 1930.

IMF, *Balance of Payments Textbook,* International Monetary Fund, Washington, D.C., 1995.

Krugman, P., and Obstfeld, M. *International Economics: Theory and Policy,* 5th edition, New York: Addison-Wesley, 2000.

McKinsey Global Institute, Manufacturing Productivity, Washington D.C., McKinsey & Co., 1993.

Rogoff, K. "The Purchasing Power Parity Puzzle," *Journal of Economic Literature,* 34, June 1996, pp. 647–668.

3

Foreign Exchange Determination and Forecasting

LEARNING OUTCOMES

After completing this chapter, you will be able to do the following:

- Discuss the evolution of international monetary arrangements

- Discuss the empirical evidence on the various parity conditions

- Contrast the findings for purchasing power parity in the short run and in the long run

- Draw the implications for international management in terms of risk and return

- Discuss the various methods used in exchange rate forecasting

- State why possible central bank intervention should be considered when forecasting exchange rates

- Discuss the use of forecasts for different types of investors

- Define how you would measure the performance of foreign exchange forecasters

In previous chapters, we presented a theoretical framework that helps to analyze the international monetary environment and the contribution of currencies to international investment returns. *Parity relations* combine inflation rates, interest rates, and foreign exchange rates in a simple manner to guide investing in a global environment. In real life, exchange rates deviate from their parity values. This creates exchange rate uncertainty to be managed, as well as profit opportunities, if exchange rate forecasting can be implemented.

The behavior of exchange rate is constrained by some international institutional arrangements, so we first briefly review these international monetary arrangements. The next section discusses the empirical evidence on the parity relations introduced in Chapter 2. Although there appears to be a lot of exchange rate volatility in the short run, currencies tend to revert to their fundamental value over the very long run. This result suggests that currency forecasting could be a fruitful exercise. Two methods are actively used to forecast exchange rates: economic analysis and technical analysis. Central banks are active players on the foreign exchange market; because their motivations differ from the usual risk–return paradigm, it is important to take into account their interventions in any forecasting model. This chapter concludes with a presentation of the use and performance of exchange rate forecasting.

International Monetary Arrangements

A Historical Perspective

Countries use different currencies, which means that an exchange rate (i.e., a spot exchange rate) must be set in order for trade in goods and assets to occur between countries. The traditional method has been to use a common standard for assessing the value of each currency. Over the centuries, various commodities have served as the international standard, including small sea shells, salt, and such metals as bronze, silver, and gold (the best known and most recent). Silver played an important role until the middle of the 19th century, when gold was found in Transvaal and in California. Thereafter, an international monetary system started to prevail.

Gold Standard   In the 19th century, most countries had decided that their currency would be exchangeable into gold bullion at a fixed parity. This system, known as the *gold standard*, prevailed quite informally and was not sanctioned by an official international treaty. During the era of the gold standard, gold was the international means of payment, and each currency was assessed according to its gold value. At the time, one could exchange French francs for British pounds in exact proportion to their gold value. For example, if one ounce of gold bullion was worth ten francs in France and two pounds in the United Kingdom, the exchange rate was five French francs per British pound, or 0.2 British pounds per French franc. The domestic monetary authorities set the domestic purchasing power of a currency, by establishing its gold content, and they thereby controlled the exchange rate.

To maintain equilibrium in the system, gold bullion was used to settle international transactions. Gold made up all the international reserves of a country. National bank notes and coins were backed by the gold reserves of the country. The balance of all monetary flows in and out of a country is referred to as the *balance of payments*. These flows were linked to either trade (payments of imports and exports) or financial flows (borrowing and lending abroad). Under the gold standard, a deficit in the balance of payments resulted in an outflow of gold and a reduction in the domestic reserves; this was equivalent to a reduction in the domestic money supply, because the gold stock of a country was its real money supply. As a country's money supply was reduced, prices of goods had to drop and interest rates had to rise. In turn, this adjustment made domestic goods more competitive internationally. Similarly, higher interest rates attracted foreign capital. Both phenomena served to replenish the country's national gold reserves. Hence, the adjustment in the balance of payments was automatic. *Purchasing power parity* (PPP) held by construction. Inflation was basically absent, and the last three decades of the 19th century witnessed negative inflation in all major countries.

One problem with this gold standard system was that the world money supply could grow only at the rate of new gold mining. The economic growth rate in the early 1900s became much larger than the physical growth in gold reserves. Another major problem was that national economic policies were totally subordinated to the fixed exchange rate objective. A country could not have a flexible monetary policy. While exchange rates remained stable, any sudden disequilibrium in the balance of payments led to severe shocks in domestic economies. With the industrial revolution at the start of the 20th century, the gold standard system became too rigid.

CONCEPTS IN ACTION   ECONOMICS FOCUS PLUS ÇA CHANGE

The Lessons of Sound Money from One Thousand Years' Experience

This month has seen progress in one bold monetary experiment, the issuance of euro notes and coins, and the failure of another, Argentina's currency board. In the history of money, this is all par for the course. Currencies, and systems for managing them, have come and gone with striking frequency ever since Croesus, king of Lydia, first minted coins in the sixth century BC.

Might the euro also fail? A new book, "The Big Problem of Small Change,"* underscores how little has been learnt from more than a millennium of monetary experiment. This fascinating new history of money shows that the key ingredients of a sound currency were identified in Europe hundreds of years ago. The mystery is why, even today, so many governments fail to put this knowledge to work.

The authors, Thomas Sargent of the Hoover Institution and François Velde of the Federal Reserve Bank of Chicago, argue that today's monetary orthodoxy has its origins in an ancient puzzle. For several centuries after 1200, when Charlemagne's famous silver penny was supplemented throughout Europe with coins of other denominations, there were inexplicable shortages of small change, which curiously coincided with a fall in their value, apparently defying the laws of supply and demand. Why?

Most of the value of a coin derived from the amount of precious metal in it. The amount by which the value of a coin could vary had an upper and lower limit. One reflected the cost of turning, say, an ounce of silver into a coin (this included minting costs plus a government coinage tax known as seigniorage). The other was what could be bought if the coin were melted down and the metal it contained used as payment. The supply of each denomination depended on how much silver people took to the mint.

A shortage might occur because of an unexpected rise in national income or its distribution, causing ordinary people to increase their purchases of bread, beer and so on. Small coins, not big ones, were needed for these transactions, which would often be for far less than the denomination of a high-value coin. At the same time, the value of small coins relative to big coins would often fall.

The authors explain this using modern monetary theory—which, alas, is somewhat counterintuitive. Broadly, instead of using simple supply and demand, it explains changes in the demand for one asset (a small silver coin, say) relative to another (a large coin) in terms of changes in the rate of return that the holder of the assets can expect from each. Depreciating smaller-denomination coins—which lowered the expected return from holding them—was the market's way to encourage holders of money to ease the shortage by getting rid of their small coins, the authors reckon. But this often made things worse, because the depreciation took the value of small coins below the point at which it paid to melt them down.

For centuries governments responded to a shortage of small coins by debasing them, i.e., reducing the amount of silver required to make a penny. This provided an incentive for people to turn silver into pennies, but it generated inflation.

Eventually an ingenious way was found out of the mess. Instead of each denomination containing precious metal, only one higher-denomination coin would do so. All other denominations would be tokens, made of a metal too cheap to be worth melting down, that could be exchanged for higher-denomination ones (or for a set amount of the precious metal) at a rate fixed and guaranteed by the government.

Following the invention of the Boulton steam press in 1787—which raised the cost of forgery—a British token currency flourished, initially issued by private firms before being nationalized in 1816. By the late 19th century, most other leading countries had token currencies, mostly pegged to the value of gold. Hence the rise of the gold standard.

A question is left unanswered. If the problem of small change led economists to understand how to run a system of token money, did some of the greatest economists of the early 20th century learn the wrong lesson from the system's success? John Maynard Keynes and Irving Fisher, among others, opposed the gold standard as a waste of valuable resources. They argued for a currency based entirely on tokens, with no link to an underlying physical commodity. Governments, greedy to spend their gold reserves, warmed to this idea, particularly during the 1930s depression. When America belatedly and finally abandoned the gold standard in 1971, it was history.

Abandoning the link to gold meant that it was entirely up to governments to ensure that their token-based currencies kept their value. In the event, for most of the 20th century they failed. They presided over levels of inflation that were seldom seen when money was backed by precious metal, debasement notwithstanding. Does history teach that a token-based currency works only if it is anchored to some unambiguous real store of value that a government cannot inflate away? Ironically, this was the logic behind Argentina's currency board, anchored to the American dollar rather than to gold. In the end, Mr. Sargent says, that failed in part because even anchored systems cannot co-exist with unsustainable government debts, as in Argentina; the temptation to reduce debts by tampering with the value of money is too great. Even economic insights developed over hundreds of years cannot work their magic without the requisite political will.

---

* *The Big Problem of Small Change,* by Thomas Sargent and François Velde. Princeton University Press, 2002.

Source: "Economics Focus Plus ça Change," *The Economist,* January 26, 2002, p. 66. © 2002 The Economist Newspaper Ltd. All rights reserved. Reprinted with permission. Further reproduction prohibited. www.economist.com.

Pegged Exchange Rates The 20th century saw many attempts to establish international currency regimes under the global coordination of the International Monetary Fund (IMF). In 1944, the *Bretton Woods* agreement created the IMF and a system of *pegged* exchange rates. The objective was to create a stable system in which countries would have more autonomy in setting their domestic economic policies. This Bretton Woods system, also called the *gold exchange standard,* was distinguished by two characteristics: an enlargement of international reserves and the design of stable but adjustable exchange rates or pegged exchange rates.

- In order to soften the impact of balance of payments deficits or surpluses on domestic economies, hard currencies were introduced to increase international reserves. These currencies—the U.S. dollar, later followed by the British pound and the Deutsche mark—were freely convertible into gold.

- This Bretton Woods system, also allowed exchange rates to fluctuate within a band around fixed parities. It further allowed infrequent devaluation or revaluation of the fixed parities, requiring the IMF's agreement.

Hence, exchange rates, were semifixed, or *pegged,* around official parities set in global cooperation. To understand how the system worked, consider the example of a country facing a sudden balance of payments deficit. First, it could use its international reserves of gold and convertible currencies to cover this balance of payments deficit. It could also let its exchange rate drop within the assigned band (typically 1 percent) around the fixed parity. Both options gave a nation more time to implement policies to restore equilibrium in the balance of payments. For example, a country could tighten its monetary policy and raise interest rates. It could also introduce various forms of capital controls to limit currency speculation. If the deficit turned out to be structural and permanent, the country had to ask the IMF's permission to devalue its currency (i.e., adjust the parity). This devaluation made its goods more competitive in the international markets, improving the trade balance and removing the motivation for speculative capital flows.

This international system did not work for long. National economic policies and inflation rates quickly became so diverse that it was difficult to maintain these pegged exchange rates. The internationalization of financial markets led to an increase in the amount of capital trying to take advantage of currency swings. A fixed exchange rate, defended by central banks, offered great profit opportunities for speculation. Gold stopped playing a role and the U.S. dollar became de facto *the* international currency. After several failed attempts at an improved system of global coordination, a system of floating exchange rates became the rule, with each currency's value determined in the marketplace.

The Current Situation: Floating Exchange Rates and Pegged Exchange Rates
The international monetary system progressively evolved toward a system of *floating* exchange rates. Under the current system, the price of each currency is freely determined by market forces. Exchange rates are not fixed by governments, but fluctuate according to supply and demand. Of course, governments attempt to "manage" their exchange rates through central bank intervention in the foreign exchange market and various policy and regulatory measures. However, the exchange rate is determined at each instant in the marketplace without reference to an "official" parity. All major currencies, including the U.S. dollar, the British pound, the yen, and the euro are floating.

In this world of flexible exchange rates, some governments have linked their currency to others. Sometimes the link is rigid. For example, a *currency board* was adopted by Argentina in 1991. In a currency board, the exchange rate is fixed (one Argentinean peso per U.S. dollar) and the supply of domestic currency is fully backed by an equivalent amount of U.S. dollars. This system is comparable to the gold standard, with the dollar replacing gold. De facto, Argentina abandoned an independent monetary policy. Indeed, the peso remained equal to one dollar for several years following the introduction of the currency board, and Argentinean inflation dropped down from more than 100 percent per year to a figure comparable to that of the United States. However, even a slight annual inflation differential can lead to deterioration in competitive position if it is accumulated over several years with a fixed exchange rate. To be operational, a currency board requires a full and credible commitment of present and future governments; otherwise, speculative pressure will build on the domestic currency. This happened in Argentina, which ran large budget deficits in the late nineties and was forced to abandon the currency board with a severe devaluation in 2002. Argentina's dollar currency board also suffered strong pressures in the early 2000s when Brazil, a major trading partner, devalued its currency against the dollar. Currency boards have also been implemented in Lithuania (backed by U.S. dollars), Bulgaria, and Estonia (backed by euros).

On the other hand, Hong Kong presents an interesting case in that it did not formally put a currency board in place, but announced a total commitment to maintain a parity of 7.80 H.K. dollars per U.S. dollar, with the Central Bank standing ready to use its reserve to defend the fixed rate.

Many other currencies are linked, tightly or loosely, to the U.S. dollar. Many emerging countries attempt to maintain a link between their currencies and the U.S. dollar; but maintaining a fixed exchange rate, when not justified by economic fundamentals, inevitably leads to currency speculation. Other pegged currencies are linked to a basket of currencies. By far the most important linkage affecting major investment currencies is the original system put into place by the European Union, which led to the euro.

The Euro   The European Union (EU) is the name given to the former European Economic Community. Fifteen countries belonged to the EU in 1999, but twelve of those abandoned their national currency on January 1, 1999, to replace it with the euro, denoted as €, or more formally, EUR. The other countries, including new entrants[1] to the EU, are considering joining the euro at a later stage:

Euro Countries

Austria	Ireland
Belgium	Italy
Finland	Luxembourg
France	Netherlands
Germany	Portugal
Greece	Spain

Other Possible Euro Countries

Denmark
Sweden
United Kingdom
New entrants to the EU

As of January 1, 1999, the euro was introduced for all official and interbank transactions, as well as for securities quotations and transactions. The exchange rate between each of the 12 national currencies (e.g., the French franc or the Deutsche mark) and the euro was set on January 1, 1999, and remained fixed until the disappearance of the national currencies in 2002. These fixed exchange rates were called "legacy rates." On January 1, 2002, euro bank notes were introduced and all former legacy currencies ceased to exist. The euro is now the sole currency of the Eurozone countries.

Established in Frankfurt, the European Central Bank (ECB) is an independent central bank. Board members are appointed by the various EU governments with an eight-year term of office. The ECB sets the monetary policy for the Eurozone. The ECB's primary objective is to maintain price stability in the Eurozone. Without prejudice to the objective of price stability, the ECB will support the general eco-

---

[1] As of 2002, several Central European countries were considered as candidates for the EU. Turkey has also been a candidate for many years.

nomic policies of the EU. The euro has a floating exchange rate against the other currencies, such as the U.S. dollar, the Japanese yen, and the British pound (at least in these early years).

Although these countries have adopted a common currency, their national budgets and fiscal and socioeconomic policies differ, so tensions within the European monetary system could easily develop until full harmonization of policies is reached.

CONCEPTS IN ACTION   THE CASE FOR COOPERATING

Europe's Stability and Growth Pact Is Producing Perverse Results

As the River Elbe burst its banks this month, the German government's budget deficit threatened to breach the limits of the euro area's "stability and growth pact." The pact prohibits fiscal deficits above 3% of GDP. Except in severe recessions, they can attract a fine of up to 0.5% of GDP. Germany now has a deficit of 2.8%. This week, Gerhard Schröder, Germany's chancellor delayed popular tax cuts in order to be able to dispense flood aid without violating the pact. With an election coming up, this is a political embarrassment. Portugal, which admits to a fiscal deficit in 2001 of over 4%, already faces the prospect of punishment. Conceivably, France and Italy may also test the limits of the pact before long.

A decade ago, the pact's architects, most of them German, feared that the euro's credibility might be undermined by fiscal laxity among its members. If a government's borrowing becomes unsustainable, its central bank might be forced to bail it out, inflating away the real value of its debts. Such bail-outs are expressly forbidden in the euro area, while the European Central Bank (ECB) enjoys a forbiddingly strong position relative to national-level fiscal authorities.

Prudent or not, the euro area's 12 finance ministers remain accountable for their fiscal choices. If they court insolvency, financial markets will apply a risk premium to the government's bonds, or refuse to lend to them altogether. Why should the European Commission try to police sovereign borrowing when the markets already do so? If anything, monetary union calls for granting more fiscal discretion to national governments, not less. Having ceded monetary policy to the centre, member nations have greater need of fiscal flexibility to cope with problems that afflict them at home.

Germany is a case in point. If it were still in a position to conduct its own monetary policy, interest rates would now almost certainly be lower. Meanwhile, a weak German economy probably needs precisely the kind of tax cuts that Mr. Schröder was forced to shelve this week. In other words, the pact's "excessive deficit procedure" looms large at precisely the moment it will do most harm. Germany may yet escape fines, by invoking a special exemption for events beyond its control—observing the letter, if not the spirit of the pact.

The Pain of Solitary Punishment

The pact may be flawed, but the euro area still has fiscal problems which its members need to address. Between 1990 and 1996, the future euro-area members ran an average deficit of well over 4% of GDP. Stronger economic growth, along with the tough rules of the stability pact, have since forced that figure down, to 1.5% on average. But now that "Maastricht fatigue" may be setting in, those deficits may widen again. Euro-area government debt stands at 72% of GDP, a deal higher than the 60% figure the Maastricht treaty deemed sustainable. Many European governments face hefty pension liabilities in the near future. If Europeans are serious about putting their budgets in order, they will need to undertake long-term fiscal reforms. Is it better that they do so singly, as and when the pact forces them to, or together, as part of a collective effort?

Christopher Allsopp and David Vines of Oxford University, together with Warwick McKibbin of the Australian National University, argue against going it alone. Budget cuts are never painless, but within a monetary union individual cuts can be excruciating. A country with an autonomous monetary policy can offset tighter fiscal policy by expanding credit and devaluing the exchange rate. But in a monetary union, where an individual country can no longer cut interest rates, nothing cushions the blow.

The authors asked what would happen if France were to cut its budget deficit unilaterally, by 2% of GDP. According to their simulation, French output would fall by more than 2%. Prices would fall a bit in France, but across the euro area as a whole they would barely change. So the ECB would have little cause to cut nominal interest rates. As a result, the real rate of interest—nominal rates adjusted for inflation—would actually rise in France. Output would eventually recover, but not before a recession of up to three years.

What if France agreed with the other member states to cut deficits together? Surely, a synchronized contraction would be even more damaging, as each country's recession spilled over into its neighbors' economies. Possibly, the authors acknowledge. Yet, while the ECB might not respond to a slowdown in one country, fiscal austerity in all 12 euro countries would probably force it to cut rates, so bolstering private spending even as government spending falls. A rate cut would also weaken the euro, boosting exports.

Investors might provide another cushion. Collectively, the euro area accounts for a big share of the demand for global savings. As they reduced their claims on these savings, Europe's governments would take pressure off the world's long-term real interest rates, boosting share prices and "crowding in" private-sector investment.

If fiscal reforms are undertaken jointly, the short-term sacrifices may be surprisingly light, and the long-term benefits may arrive surprisingly early. Such a happy outcome hangs upon pursuing reforms that are both credible and cooperative. It is a pity, then, that Europe's stability and growth pact, as it stands, is neither.

The Empirical Evidence

The international parity relations presented in Chapter 2 provide a useful framework for analyzing the international interplay of monetary variables. As a theory, it relies on restrictive assumptions about uncertainty, as well as about the perfection of trade and money markets. In the real world, future inflation and exchange rates are uncertain and physical arbitrage cannot take place instantly. In developing a forecasting methodology, the next step is to evaluate the extent that each parity condition holds true and to examine the causes of any deviations. A better understanding of parity condition deviations can help in forecasting exchange rates and in estimating currency risks.

Interest Rate Parity

As demonstrated in Chapter 1, the interest rate parity (IRP) relation is derived from riskless financial arbitrage among the various money markets. If these markets are free and deregulated, interest rate parity must hold, within a transaction cost band: The interest rate differential must be equal to the forward discount/premium. Because the bid–ask spreads are minuscule on the Eurocurrency market, interest parity is always verified within a few basis points. By arbitrage, IRP *must hold* for all major investment currencies. However, some countries, especially developing ones, still impose various forms of capital controls and taxes that impede arbitrage. Furthermore, some smaller currencies can be borrowed and lent only domestically; the domestic money markets are often subject to political risk and various types of costly regulations and controls.[2] The continuing deregulation and international integration of financial markets throughout the world are certain to reduce these deviations in the future, even for emerging markets.

International Fisher Relation

Although it has exchange rate implications, the international Fisher relation does not directly involve the exchange rate. The question raised is whether real interest rates are equal among countries. This question is illustrated in Exhibit 3.1, which plots the real interest rate for three-month bills for the three major international currencies over the period 1973–2001. Because it requires a measure of expected inflation, the calculation of the real interest rate is somewhat difficult. In Exhibit 3.1, expected inflation is simply replaced by the realized inflation over the life of the three-month bill; real rates observed each quarter have been averaged over the year. Real rates differed markedly during the first oil shock of 1973–74. Real rates were very high in the 1980s and became lower on the U.S. dollar than on other currencies in the early 1990s. Japan witnessed a period of economic slowdown in the

---

[2] Frankel and MacArthur (1988) have confirmed that deviations from interest rate parity can be quite large for what they call "closed less-developed countries."

EXHIBIT 3.1

Real Interest Rates
USA, Japan, and Germany, 1973–2001

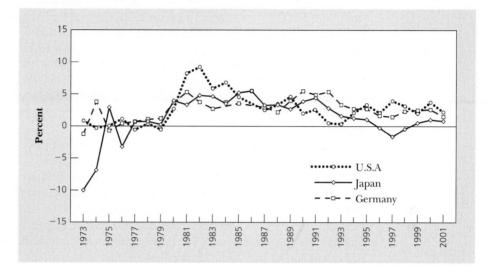

1990s, with dropping real interest rates, while the United States witnessed a period of sustained economic growth, which could accommodate much higher real rates. Averaged over the 1973–2001 period, the real interest rates in the United States and Germany are almost identical (a few basis points difference), as is the case with other European countries. However, Japan had lower real rates.

A casual observation of Exhibit 3.1, confirmed by more sophisticated econometric tests, suggests that real interest rates tend to move up and down together worldwide as a function of the world business cycle. Because national business cycles are not fully synchronized, however, significant differences in real rates can exist in any time period.

An investment strategy that takes advantage of such deviations from parity would be to invest in high-interest-rate currencies. In terms of risk and return, the results of this strategy would depend on the evolution of the exchange rate. We now turn to the empirical evidence on parity relations involving the exchange rate.

Purchasing Power Parity

Purchasing power parity is one of the economic subjects that has attracted the largest number of empirical articles. The empirical findings on the validity of PPP in the short run can be characterized as disappointing in the sense that they are unsupportive.[3] Regressions of monthly or quarterly exchange rate movements on

---

[3] For surveys of the empirical literatures, see Grossman and Rogoff (1995), Rogoff (1996), Lothian and Taylor (1996), and Lothian (1998).

inflation differentials yield low explanatory power (R^2) for the recent period of floating exchange rates. Typically, inflation differentials explain less than 5 percent of monthly exchange rate movements in major currencies. This means that 95 percent of currency movements were not caused by current inflation. Some researchers have even suggested that short-term movements in the real exchange rate tend to follow a random pattern. Deviations from PPP may not be corrected unless by chance. More encouraging recent research shows that exchange rates revert to their PPP values, but it seems to take many years for this correction to take place. Purchasing power parity is a poor explanation for *short-term* exchange rate movements, and hence for exchange rate volatility, but it holds quite well over the *long run*.[4] This phenomenon, in which exchange rates revert to their fundamental (PPP) value over the long run, is known as "mean reversion" of the real exchange rate.

Going beyond a summary of research results, we provide a quick look at the international monetary environment of the past 26 years (1976 through 2001). Exhibit 3.2 indicates the simple relationships among inflation rates, interest rates, and exchange rates. Two pairs of countries and their exchange rates are presented: the United States and Japan, and Germany and the United Kingdom. For each year, the figure indicates the inflation differential in percentage terms, the exchange rate movement, and the short-term interest rate differential. Differentials are calculated as the value for the first country minus that of the second one. For example, Exhibit 3.2 shows that in 1998, the United States had about 2 percent more inflation than Japan and a higher short-term interest rate (a differential of approximately 5 percent). The exchange rate used is the value of the second country's currency in units of the first country's currency. For example, in Exhibit 3.2, we can track the dollar value of the Japanese yen ($/¥). In 1998, the yen appreciated by some 15 percent relative to the U.S. dollar. In theory, we would expect all three measures to be of the same sign and magnitude: For each year, the three bars should be at the same level, but they typically are not.

If PPP were to hold, exchange rate movements and inflation differentials should be identical. Although the interest rate and inflation differentials tend to be of the same sign and magnitude each year, this is not the case for exchange rate movements and inflation differentials. For many years, the exchange rate has moved in the opposite direction from the inflation differential. Note that this effect is not dollar-specific because it also applies to the euro/British pound exchange rate. For example, Exhibit 3.2 shows that the British pound appreciated strongly relative to the euro in 1999, although inflation was lower in Germany than in the United Kingdom.

PPP is more tenable over the long run, as can be seen from the last bars in Exhibit 3.2 giving the annualized means over the period 1976–2001. The means of

[4] The econometric methodology has moved from the traditional regression techniques to a cointegration approach. The latter approach states that the exchange rate and the price level series should be cointegrated if the PPP holds as a long-term equilibrium relation. Tests performed in the 1990s provide supportive evidence in favor of long-run PPP. See, among others, Grossman and Rogoff (1995), Mark (1995), Lothian and Taylor (1996), and Cheung and Lai (1998).

EXHIBIT 3.2

Annual Comparison of Exchange Rate Movements, Inflation Differentials, and Interest Rate Differentials, 1976–2001

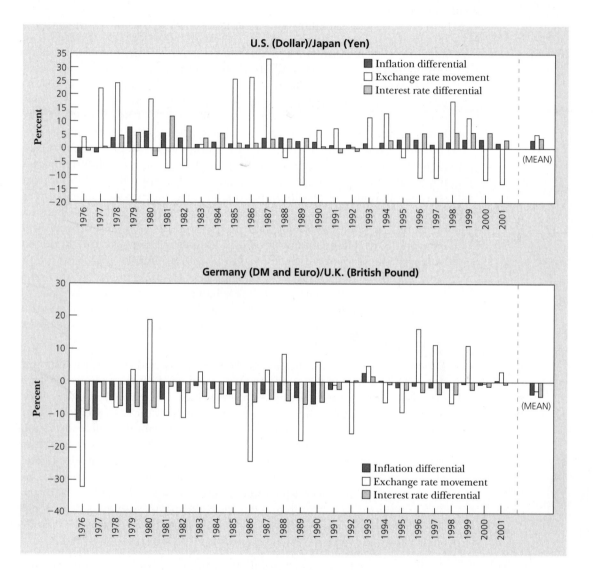

the exchange rate movements, the inflation differentials, and the interest rate differentials are fairly similar. Over the whole period, there was more inflation in the United States than in Japan, and more in the U.K. than in Germany; and this should have had exchange rate depreciation implications. In keeping with PPP theory, the dollar depreciated against the yen and the British pound depreciated against the euro (formerly the Deutsche mark). Although the long-run exchange rate movement does not exactly match the inflation differential, this could be caused by measurement error in the inflation rate or by some structural real exchange rate movement.

There are several explanations of why PPP is not verified in the short run:

- *First,* the very measurement of an inflation rate is questionable. Investors throughout the world have different consumption preferences, and a common basket of consumption goods does not exist. In the short run, relative prices of different consumption goods vary extensively with specific influences on specific consumption baskets. Different baskets of goods will exhibit different price increases, as the relative prices of the goods change over time. For example, price changes for a haircut or bread in Uruguay do not closely track changes in imported computer prices. Because of differences in imported and exported goods, an inflation rate measured from an index of consumed goods will be different from an inflation rate measured from an index of produced goods. Similarly, non-traded goods enter the national consumption price index, but their prices should have little short-run influence on the exchange rate. As an illustration, the price of sake might double in Japan (thereby affecting the local price index), but the price rise should have little influence on the yen exchange rate; few foreigners consume sake, so its price is not very relevant to the exchange rate, even though it would be included in a domestic price index. In the long run, consumption substitution will take place in Japan to reflect the higher price of sake, and Japanese people may consume more beer or wine.

- *Second,* transfer costs, import taxes and restrictions, and export subsidies may not allow arbitrage in the goods markets to restore PPP. In the long run, however, industries from countries with overvalued currencies will make direct investments in undervalued countries. For example, the U.S. dollar was overvalued in terms of PPP in the early 1980s, which meant that the real price of U.S. goods was high compared with the goods of other countries. Because the U.S. dollar was strong, wages were lower in Europe than in the United States when converted into dollars. U.S. exports were not competitive because of their high prices, which were a result of the exchange rate; similarly, foreign imports to the United States were cheap. Because the situation persisted, many U.S. companies built plants abroad to take advantage of this deviation from PPP. In time, such behavior leads to a restoration of PPP.

- *Third,* many factors other than inflation influence exchange rates. Because physical goods arbitrage is constrained, PPP plays only a small role in the short run; other variables have a major impact on the short-run behavior of exchange rates. Over the long run, economic fundamentals, such as PPP, are restored.

The practical implications of these deviations from PPP are very important. The real returns of one asset as measured by investors from different countries are different.

In Chapter 2, we saw that an exchange rate movement can have a dramatic real impact on an investor holding even a foreign risk-free instrument. During June 2002, the U.S. dollar depreciated by 7 percent against the euro. One-month bills in euro and in dollar had the same interest rate of 3 percent (annualized) and annual inflation rates were about 2 percent in both regions. Consider a European investor holding U.S. Treasury bills. Such an investor would have had a real return of minus 6.92 percent (−6.75% return in euro minus 0.17 percent monthly European inflation rate).

Furthermore, uncertainty about the real exchange rate adds uncertainty to a foreign investment. Consider, for example, an investment in an emerging country. Many emerging countries have attempted to maintain a fixed or stable exchange rate with the U.S. dollar despite a much higher inflation rate. This tactic leads to a real appreciation of their currencies. Such overvaluation can persist for a few years, but at some point in time, the bubble will burst and the currency will be forced to devalue. Many examples can be found in the past few years: the Mexican peso devaluation in 1994, the East Asian crisis of 1997, the Russian ruble devaluation of 1998, and the Argentinean peso devaluation of 2002. Over the long run, exchange rates tend to revert to fundamentals.

Foreign Exchange Expectations

The foreign exchange expectations relation links the expected future exchange rate to the forward rate. In a risk-neutral world, the expected exchange rate movement should be equal to the forward discount/premium, and hence to the interest rate differential between the two currencies.

Exchange rate expectations are not directly observable, so the *ex post* movements are used instead, assuming that the realized exchange rate movement is equal to its expectation plus a random unpredictable element. Tests of this parity relation focus on two aspects:

- Is the interest rate differential a good predictor of future spot exchange rate movements?

- Is there a currency risk premium in the form of a systematic difference between the spot exchange rate movement and the interest rate differential?

Although complex econometric procedures are often used,[5] an examination of Exhibit 3.2 allows a summary of the main conclusions. The exchange rate is very volatile, so the interest rate differential is a poor forecaster of the exchange rate in the short run. Over the long run (here, 26 years), the foreign exchange expectation relation is reasonably well verified. The mean realized exchange rate movement and interest rate differentials are of the same direction and magnitude. For the dollar/yen and euro/pound, there appears to exist a 1 percent currency risk

---

[5] See Hodrick (1987), Kaminsky and Peruga (1990), Bekaert and Hodrick (1993), Baillie and Bollerslev (2000). Other researchers have tested this relation by drawing exchange rate expectations from survey data; see Liu and Maddala (1992) and Cavaglia, Verschoor, and Wolff (1993).

premium. Of course, the question is whether this risk premium is statistically significant and could have been expected *ex ante*. Furthermore, it is unlikely that an *ex ante* currency risk premium stays constant.[6]

In making foreign investments, one should not expect foreign exchange rates to deviate strongly from fundamentals forever. Again, this reversion to fundamentals is most apparent with currencies from emerging countries. In trying to maintain a stable exchange rate with the U.S. dollar, many could achieve this only with high domestic interest rates to induce capital flows to support their currency. At some point, the emerging country cannot defend the fixed exchange rate and a large devaluation takes place. This situation is illustrated for the Korean won in Exhibit 3.3, which gives the annual depreciation of the won relative to the U.S. dollar, as well as the short-term interest rate differential between the two countries. From 1991 to 1996, the won had a much higher interest rate than the dollar (an annual differential of several percent), but the exchange rate with the dollar remained stable. In 1997, the Asian crisis hit many currencies in the region and the won was devalued by some 50 percent. Averaging over the 1991–97 period, we find that the interest rate differential roughly matches the currency depreciation. So, any investor applying the strategy to invest in this high-interest-rate currency would have made a profit for several years and lost all of it in 1997.

The current variability of exchange rates is very large compared with that of interest rates and inflation rates. So, risk must be an important factor in all parity relations involving the expected exchange rate. Any strategy designed to take advantage of real interest rate differentials or of expected exchange rate movements has a very uncertain outcome.

Practical Implications

To summarize the experience of the past decades, exchange rates have been quite volatile year to year. International investors have been faced with currency risk in the short run. Over the long run, this impact becomes smaller because of mean reversion toward fundamentals, but it does not fully disappear. Parity conditions are very useful because they help frame the approach to investing in an international context. The complexity brought by multiple interest rates and currencies requires a simplifying theoretical base. Investors can then take into account empirical evidence to adopt currency-risk hedging strategies and/or formulate expectations about future currency movements.

The empirical findings are both perplexing and exciting. Exchange rates are a matter of concern for all international investors because evidence shows that they do not simply neutralize inflation differentials in real terms. Furthermore, movements do not generally correct interest rate differences between two currencies. Basically, one cannot rely on money markets to correctly assess and neutralize future exchange rate movements, at least in the short run. Exchange rates have a

---

[6] For example, Dumas and Solnik (1995) found evidence of time-varying currency risk premiums.

EXHIBIT 3.3

Korean Won
Depreciation vs. Interest Rate Differential (in % per year)

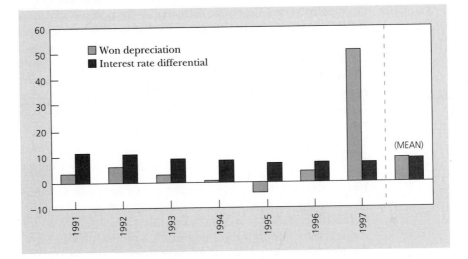

significant influence on returns and risks in a global setting. In the longer run, fundamentals start to prevail. But the horizon to obtain "mean reversion" might be considered too long for an investment manager.

The empirical evidence gives analysts a chance to improve the performance of a portfolio significantly by forecasting exchange rates correctly, as discussed in the next section. Even over a period of 26 years, exchange rate movements are not fully offset by interest rate differentials, so the currency-hedging decision is meaningful and the question of a currency risk premium needs to be addressed. Exchange rates add a dimension to international investments not encountered in the domestic situation, which makes it all the more important to gain an understanding of the influence of international monetary variables on equity and bond prices and to develop international asset pricing models that explicitly incorporate exchange risk (see Chapter 4).

Exchange Rate Forecasting

Exchange rate forecasting is novel to traditional portfolio investors. Rather than examining companies or industrial sectors, financial analysts must study the relative social, political, and economic situations of several countries. Two methods are actively used to forecast exchange rates: Economic analysis is the usual approach for assessing the fair value, present and future, of foreign exchange rates. However, it is often argued that technical analysis may better explain short-run exchange rate fluctuations. This brings us back to the traditional segmentation of financial analysts into fundamentalists and technicians. Both methods often use quantitative models that make extensive use of computers, as well as qualitative (or judgmental) analysis.

Before proceeding any further, it is important to determine what our naive forecast would be in the absence of any specific model or information. In other words, assuming efficient foreign exchange markets, what is the exchange rate prediction implicit in market quotations? As discussed previously, the forward exchange rate (or spot exchange rate plus the interest rate differential) is the rational, expected value of the future spot exchange rate in a *risk-neutral* world. Suppose the spot exchange rate is €/$ = 1.05 and the dollar and euro annual interest rates are 1.76 percent and 3.39 percent, respectively. The one-year forward exchange rate would then be

$$F = S(1 + r_{€})/(1 + r_{\$}) = 1.05(1.0339/1.0176) = 1.0668.$$

Hence, the one-year forward exchange rate would be €1.0668 per dollar.

Arbitrageurs would buy (or sell) currency forward and arbitrage away profit opportunities if this forward exchange rate did not reflect all information available to the market. Note that the international money market does in fact meet most of the technical criteria of an efficient market, at least for the major currencies. A huge volume of quick and almost costless transactions is performed by numerous informed and competent traders. The only restriction on the market might be central bank intervention. On the other hand, central banks may simply be regarded as transactors like any others, although having somewhat different motives. The main upshot of this scenario is that investors should average the same returns on their deposits in every currency because short-term interest rate differentials are expected to offset exchange rate movements.

In a *risk-averse* world, forward exchange rates deviate from the pure expectation value by a risk premium. If the direction and magnitude of this risk premium are hard to estimate and volatile over time, the best market estimate of the future spot exchange rate is still the forward rate.

As mentioned, forward exchange rates are poor indicators of future spot rates because of exchange rate volatility. This does not necessarily mean that a better forecasting model can be found. It may be that frequent unanticipated news have a strong influence on spot exchange rates, making them inherently volatile and unpredictable. Before reviewing the various approaches to foreign exchange forecasting, it is useful to ask whether the foreign exchange market treats information efficiently and whether market participants are rational. These questions seem reasonable in view of the negative comments often made by the press and government officials.

Is the Market Efficient and Rational?

In an efficient market, all information should be immediately reflected in the exchange rates. Rational market traders should base their forecasts on all available information. Consider an information set ϕ_t known at time t; the spot exchange rate for time $t + 1$ forecasted, or expected, at time t and based on this information set is usually denoted

$$E(S_{t+1}|\phi_t) \tag{3.1}$$

Finance tends to focus on rates of returns and percentage variations. Using the notations introduced in previous chapters, we have

$$s_{t+1} = (S_{t+1} - S_t)/S_t$$

$$E(s_{t+1}|\phi_t) = [E(S_{t+1}|\phi_t) - S_t]/S_t$$

The percentage forecast error is defined as the percentage deviation of the realized rate at time $t + 1$ from the expected rate:

$$e_{t+1} = s_{t+1} - E(s_{t+1}|\phi_t) \tag{3.2}$$

If market participants are rational, the forecast error should be uncorrelated with the information previously available at time t. Deviations from the expected value should be caused only by unpredictable news. Any information already available at time t should be reflected in the forecast and should not explain subsequent deviations from the forecast.

In a *risk-neutral* world, the forward exchange rate should be the best predictor of the future spot rate. It should already incorporate all relevant information available at the time of quotation. Let's denote F_t the forward rate quoted at time t for maturity $t + 1$ and f_t its percentage deviation from the spot exchange rate:

$$f_t = (F_t - S_t)/S_t$$

Remember that f_t is also called the forward premium (discount) and is equal, by arbitrage, to the interest differential. We should get

$$F_t = E(S_{t+1}|\phi_t)$$

$$f_t = (F_t - S_t)/S_t = E(s_{t+1}|\phi_t)$$

The forecast error of the exchange rate movement is given by

$$e_{t+1} = s_{t+1} - f_t \tag{3.3}$$

One simple way to test that the foreign exchange market is efficient in processing information, and therefore that the forecast error is uncorrelated with f_t, is to run a regression between the realized exchange rate movement and the forward premium/discount:

$$s_{t+1} = \alpha + \beta f_t + \varepsilon_{t+1} \tag{3.4}$$

We should find that α is equal to 0 and that β is equal to 1.

Numerous studies have tested this relation on many currencies and for various time periods.[7] They tend to find that the slope coefficient β is significantly smaller

---

[7] See Hodrick (1987), Froot and Thaler (1990), Bekaert and Hodrick (1992), and Baillie and Bollerslev (2000).

than 1, and sometimes negative. This negative sign is surprising. It means that a successful strategy would be to bet against the forward exchange rate. When a currency quotes with a forward premium, it should depreciate rather than appreciate. Because the forward premium (discount) is equal to the interest rate differential, the currency with the higher interest rate should appreciate. But as shown by Baillie and Bollerslev (2000), the power of these tests is very limited given the volatility in exchange rates and the difficulty in measuring expectations. The return on such investment strategies is highly uncertain.

Another common finding is that the forecast errors appear to be positively correlated over successive periods. In other words, exchange rates follow trends. Again, this is inconsistent with market rationality. It seems that exchange rate movements (or forecast errors) are positively correlated over time for short horizons (one or two years) and start to exhibit negative autocorrelation for long horizons (several years). A possible justification for this finding is that exchange rates tend to exhibit *jumps*. Over short periods that exclude the jump, exchange rates appear to trend, and forecast errors exhibit positive autocorrelation. This phenomenon disappears when the jump is included in the data. Market traders expect this jump but do not know when it will take place. The exchange rate drifts away from its fundamental, or equilibrium, value, and the correction can take several years to materialize but in a brutal fashion. This is sometimes referred to as the "peso problem." The Mexican peso used to see its real exchange rate against the U.S. dollar appreciate progressively until the Mexican government finally devalued the peso (generally after an election). Such problems are more likely to appear on foreign exchange markets, in which participants try to forecast the policy and timing of monetary authorities, than on other capital markets, such as stock markets. Surveys of foreign exchange expectations formulated by various market participants conducted in New York, London, and Tokyo suggest that expectations extrapolate the recent trend for short horizons and predict a reversal for long horizons.[8]

Another possible explanation for the autocorrelation of forecast errors is the existence of a time-varying risk premium. The forward exchange rate could deviate from the future expected value of the spot exchange rate by a risk premium rp_t, which can change over time:

$$f_t = E(s_{t+1}|\phi_t) + rp_t$$

The percentage forecast error becomes

$$e_{t+1} = s_{t+1} - f_t + rp_t$$

and autocorrelation in forecast errors could come from the time-series properties of the required risk premium. However, the magnitude and volatility of this risk premium would have to be very large to justify the observed phenomenon.[9]

Any test of market efficiency/rationality confronts serious econometric problems. Clearly, exchange rates are not stationary, in the sense that exchange rate

---

[8] See Dominguez (1986), Frankel and Froot (1987), and Liu and Maddala (1992).
[9] See Fama (1984).

movements are not identically independently distributed. Expected returns vary over time in a somewhat predictable fashion, but more work is needed to attempt to model these time-varying expectations (see the appendix to this chapter). The volatility of an exchange rate is not constant, and researchers have found evidence of GARCH effects (see the appendix to this chapter). Modeling variance is quite difficult, given the existence of infrequent jumps whose timing and magnitude are unknown. Many studies illustrate the econometric difficulties in estimating the foreign exchange risk premium.[10]

It seems fair to say that current empirical research has not solved the exchange rate puzzle. More work is needed to establish rationality and to understand the behavior of exchange rates over time. Hence, attempts to forecast exchange rates seem potentially rewarding.

The Econometric Approach

Advisory services and institutional investors that have developed foreign exchange forecasting tools may use a *subjective* approach, an *econometric* model, or both. An econometric approach implies that a quantitative model of the exchange rate is estimated on past data and used to make predictions. A subjective approach implies that a large number of parameters are taken into account in a subjective, not a quantitative, way. One set of models attempts to deduce theoretical values for current exchange rates. If the values deviate from going market rates, the models assume that the deviation will quickly be corrected by the market. Another set of models assumes that current exchange rates are correctly priced, or in equilibrium, and attempts to forecast rates in the future based on the present and predicted values of other variables.

Econometric models, which are statistical estimations of the economic theories, make it feasible to take complex correlations between variables into account explicitly. Parameters for the models are drawn from historical data. Then, current and expected values for causative variables are entered into the model, producing forecasts for exchange rates. Econometric models clearly suffer from two drawbacks. First, most of them rely on predictions for certain key variables (money supply, interest rates) that are not easy to forecast. Second, the structural correlation estimated by the parameters of the equation can change over time, so that even if all causative variables are correctly forecasted, the model can still yield poor exchange rate predictions. In periods when structural changes are rapid compared with the amount of time-series data required to estimate parameters, econometric models are of little help.[11] In these instances, subjective analysis is generally more reliable.

Many econometric forecasts rely on a single equation founded on PPP and equated to an expression containing variables for interest rates, trade balances, and

---

[10]See Bekaert and Hodrick (1993) and Evans and Lewis (1995).

[11]The failure of econometric models to satisfactorily depict the behavior of the exchange rates is illustrated in Meese and Rogoff (1983) and Huizinga (1987).

money supply. Other models rely on a large number of simultaneous equations, which no doubt provide a more satisfactory description of international correlations than simplistic, single-equation models. But at the same time, complex models cannot be revised frequently. Moreover, it is time-consuming to simulate each scenario, as the amount of input required is very large.

The recent models developed for exchange rate forecasting take the view that an exchange rate is the price of an asset (the currency). This asset market approach implies that the short-term behavior of exchange rates is influenced mostly by news. News appears when economic data or a political statement differs from its predicted value. The time-series properties of the exchange rate are specifically modeled with a focus on time variations in expected returns and volatility. These models seem to fare better than the traditional economic approach.

Several banks and advisory services make their models available worldwide on time-sharing systems. Using terminals with simple telephone modems, subscribers may input their own forecasts for the causative variables and even change parameters in the model equations. In fact, portfolio managers commonly use home or hotel telephones to connect laptops to any one of several wire services that provide information ranging from up-to-date economic forecasts to quoted prices to investment management packages. In periodic reports, econometric forecasts are generally combined with more subjective discussions of the international scene.

Technical Analysis

Technical analysis of exchange rates bases predictions solely on price information. The analysis is technical in the sense that it does not rely on fundamental analysis of the underlying economic determinants of exchange rates, but only on extrapolations of past price trends.[12] Technical analysis looks for the repetition of specific price patterns. Once the start of such a pattern has been detected, it automatically suggests what the short-run behavior of an exchange rate will be.

Technical analysis has long been applied to commodity and stock markets. Its application to the foreign exchange market is a more recent phenomenon, but has attracted a wide and rapidly growing audience. One difference that sets the currency market apart from other markets is that data for trading volume are not available for currencies, so price history is the only source of information. As for economic analysis, technical analysts often use quantitative computer models or subjective analysis based on the study of charts *(chartism)*.

Computer models attempt to detect both major trends and critical, or turning, points. These models are often simple and rely on *moving averages, filters,* or *momentum.* The objective of all computer models is to detect when a sustainable trend has begun.

In moving-average models, buy and sell signals are usually triggered when a short-run moving average (SRMA) of past rates crosses a long-run moving average

---

[12]For a general description of technical analysis, see Murphy (1999) and Pring (1991); see also Rosenberg (1996).

EXHIBIT 3.4

Computer Methods in Technical Analysis

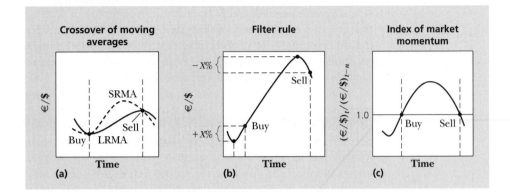

(LRMA). The aim of a moving average is to smooth erratic daily swings of exchange rates in order to signal major trends. An LRMA will always lag behind an SRMA because the LRMA gives a smaller weight to recent movements of exchange rates than an SRMA does. If a currency is moving downward, its SRMA will be below its LRMA. When it starts rising again, as in Exhibit 3.4a, it soon crosses its LRMA, generating a buy signal/(buy dollar). The opposite is true for sell signals.

Filter methods generate buy signals when an exchange rate rises X percent (the filter) above its most recent trough and sell signals when it falls X percent below the previous peak. Again, the idea is to smooth (filter) daily fluctuations in order to detect lasting trends (see Exhibit 3.4b). Momentum models determine the strength of a currency by examining the change in velocity of currency movements. If an exchange rate climbs at increasing speed, a buy signal is issued (see Exhibit 3.4c).

In a sense, these models monitor the derivative (slope) of a time-series graph. Signals are generated when the slope varies significantly.

Note that there is a good deal of discretionary judgment inherent in these models. Signals are sensitive to alterations in the filters used, the period lengths used to compute moving averages, and the methods used to compute rates of change in momentum models. More sophisticated statistical models have evolved, some of which are direct applications of statistical models developed for other disciplines, such as physics and seismology. Among them are wave-and-cycle models, chaos theory, and autoregressive integrated moving average (ARIMA) estimations à la Box-Jenkins. Some powerful quantitative methods have been applied to forecast the short-term behavior of foreign exchange rates, such as multivariate vector autoregressive methods, multivariate spectral methods, ARCH models, and nonlinear autoregressive methods. Some of these methods are described in the appendix to this chapter.

Chartism (technical) analysis relies on the interpretation of exchange rate charts. Analysts usually attempt to detect recurrent price formations on bar charts that plot daily price ranges as vertical bars. They also use line charts connecting daily closing

prices, or point-and-figure charts, which take into account a series of price movements in the same direction.

Chartists consider numerous price patterns significant. Each pattern is representative of a typical market situation, the outcome of which is usually predictable,
thereby giving clear sell or buy signals. The various patterns are interpreted as
logical sequences, in various market phases (accumulation, resistance, breakaway,
reaction). Colorful terminology is generally used to describe the various patterns,
including *flag, pennant, head and shoulder,* and *camel.*

Obviously, chartism is more an art than a science. Its main tenet is that market
participants tend to behave in the same way over time when confronted with a similar market environment. This repetition of response is ascribed partly to emotional factors and partly to the regulatory and other constraints imposed on major
market participants, such as multinational companies' treasurers, bankers, and
central bankers. In other words, guidelines, regulations, and central bank intervention help create repeated and predictable currency market patterns.

Charts are sometimes used to time purchases and sales of currencies when
large actors, such as central banks, intervene in the market. With the development
of graphics software on microcomputers, many more people now engage in technical analysis. One should be aware that technical models, such as moving averages,
are constantly calculated by thousands of investors. As a result, those who use this
method rarely beat the market, because so many others use similar models.

Central Bank Intervention

It might seem strange to discuss central bank intervention in a section devoted to
foreign exchange forecasting, but the behavior of central bankers is somewhat
predictable, and forecasters attempt to factor their market intervention into the
forecasts. The central banks are major players in the foreign exchange markets,
although their motives are somewhat different from those of most other market
participants.[13] Some central banks are renowned for the active management of
their foreign currency reserves, but most do not attempt to profit from trading.
They try to implement the monetary policy and exchange rate targets defined by
their monetary authorities.

In the early 1970s, the Bretton Woods system of pegged exchange rates ex-
ploded due to the magnitude of speculative flows and the unreasonable attitude of
some governments attempting to defend unrealistic exchange rates. In a semifixed
exchange rate system, exchange rates must stay within a narrow band of a fixed
central parity. When a currency is under too much pressure, the monetary authorities must de(re)value its central parity. Let's assume that because of political and
economic fundamentals, the British pound is "weak," as was the case in 1967.
Speculators can speculate against the pound with little risk. They sell pound forward against dollar. If the Bank of England is successful in defending the parity of
the pound, the exchange rate will stay constant, and the speculators will lose noth-

---

[13]See Lewis (1995), Baillie and Osterberg (1997), Dominguez (1998), Bekaert and Gray (1998), and
Neely and Weller (2001).

ing, or very little. If the Bank of England exhausts its foreign currency reserves in defending the pound and is forced to devalue, the speculators will pocket the amount of devaluation by buying back the pound at a cheaper price. It is a game in which there can be only one loser: the central bank. Of course, monetary authorities and market forces will lift the interest rates of the weak currencies, but this is a small cost to speculation, given the speed at which it can succeed in forcing a de(re)valuation. In the late 1960s, the amount of capital available for currency speculation became large compared with the amount of official reserves of central banks, and the number of currencies forced to de(re)value became large, leading to large losses for central banks. Within two months, the Dutch guilder was forced to devalue by almost 10 percent and then forced to revalue by a similar amount.

The move to floating exchange rates made this type of speculation against the central banks much more problematic. Unfortunately, monetary authorities tend to forget lessons from the past fairly quickly.[14] Before the introduction of the euro, the European Monetary System relied on a collective defense of the central parities by all its members, thereby increasing the amount of reserves usable to defend the parities. Unfortunately for the central banks, the amount of private speculative capital also increased. In 1992 and 1993, several European central banks lost many billions of dollars unsuccessfully defending their currencies against a devaluation relative to the Deutsche mark. Conversely, hedge funds and George Soros became notorious for their profit in currency speculation.

However, speculation against central banks is not an easy game, as illustrated by big losses taken by these same currency hedge funds in early 1994. But it is clear that a lucid analysis of the policy and objectives of a country's monetary authorities can, in some cases, help forecast the short-term behavior of speculation and of the exchange rate. In the face of an uncertain social, political, and even electoral environment, monetary authorities are inclined to defend a currency beyond dangerous levels. More generally, the various aspects of central banks' policies should be incorporated in a forecasting model for the exchange rate.

An illustration of the importance of news about official intervention is given in Exhibit 3.5, which tracks the DM/$ exchange rate around October 20, 1994. On October 20, United States Treasury Secretary Lloyd Bentsen made a surprise, and imprudent, announcement that the United States had no plans to intervene in the foreign exchange market to defend the dollar, sending the market into a frenzy when the statement appeared on the traders' Reuters screens. The next morning, Treasury Undersecretary Lawrence Summers corrected the statement and suggested that there were times when an intervention was appropriate. The dollar immediately rebounded.

The Use and Performance of Forecasts

Technical analysts closely follow the market and forecast the very near future. Detecting a pattern is beneficial if the market continues to follow that pattern faithfully. But no pattern can be expected to last for more than a few days, possibly

---

[14]See Goodhart (1993), Leahy (1995), and Szakmary and Mathur (1997).

EXHIBIT 3.5

An Example of the Impact of News about Central Bank Intervention

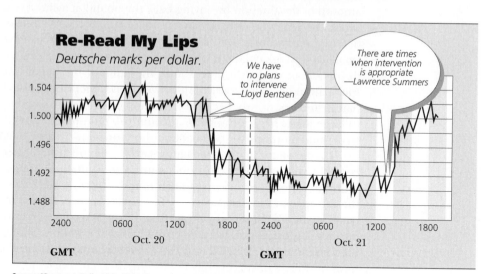

Source: "Bentsen's Dollar Talk. 6 Very Expensive Words," from an article by Alan Friedman, *International Herald Tribune,* October 22, 1994 © International Herald Tribune. Reprinted by permission.

weeks; market inefficiencies are corrected too quickly. Indeed, if a technical analyst persuades enough clients to act on her recommendations, prices will move rapidly to a level that rules out additional profits. The more publicity a successful analyst gets, the more quickly the market corrects the inefficiencies she reports. As a result, all systematic black-box models must be continually modified to counter this self-correcting process. A client must react very quickly to a technical recommendation. Unfortunately, there are often time lags between the moment a technical service issues a recommendation, the time it takes to reach the money manager, and the moment it is finally implemented. For this reason, immediate transmission via telephone, fax, or computer terminal of buy and sell signals is essential in order to make a profit.

The corporate treasurer who manages a complex international position with daily cash flows and adjustments in his foreign exchange exposure can respond readily to technical analysis recommendations. This is not the case for portfolio managers; they cannot continually adjust their long-term asset allocations on the basis of technical signals on currencies. In practice, therefore, technical foreign exchange models are used mainly by money managers for timing their investment sales and purchases or for currency-hedging decisions using derivatives. Transaction costs on equity are just too high to make an active trading strategy based on short-term currency forecasts worthwhile. Part of an institutional portfolio is sometimes entrusted to a currency-overlay money manager. The objective of a currency-overlay strategy is, in part, to benefit from currency forecasts. Such managers often resort to short-term currency trading strategies that make use of technical analysis and interpret interventions by central banks. Currency hedge funds have also developed. These are leveraged funds that take bets on currencies and engage in active trading. Banks also trade extensively in currencies for their proprietary accounts. All these traders make use of all the available short-term forecasting techniques described here.

By contrast, long-term economic forecasts for currencies and interest rates are a basic component of the international asset allocation decision. In fact, currency analysis is one of several economic analyses of the international environment that a manager must undertake. Briefly, economic models of exchange rates are commonly used for long-term asset allocation, whereas technical models are more helpful for timing transactions. When the Bank of England conducted a survey among chief foreign exchange dealers based in London, it found that 90 percent of the respondents place some weight on technical analysis when forming views at one or more time horizons.[15] Although technical analysis is used extensively for very short-term forecasts, fundamental economic analysis becomes dominant for longer-term forecasts.

Two questions that remain for the user of foreign exchange forecasts are: How do we measure the performance of these forecasts, and what is their track record? All methods compare a particular forecast to the forward exchange rate, which is both the implied market forecast and the price at which an investor may contract to try to make a profit based on his or her specific forecast. In order to study the performance of a given forecasting model over a specific time period, we must collect the values for the following series:

forecasts formulated in t for time $t + n$, $E(S_{t+n}|\phi_t)$

forward rates quoted in t for time $t + n$, F_t, and

spot rates realized in t, S_t and $t + n$, S_{t+n}

With this set of data in hand, several methods may be used to evaluate the performance of a forecast relative to the forward rate.

A common statistical approach is to compare the forecast errors of the two models (the forecasting model versus the forward rate). The percentage forecast errors (ε and e) for each forecast are computed as

$$\varepsilon_{t+n} = [S_{t+n} - E(S_{t+n}|\phi_t)]/S_t$$

$$e_{t+n} = [S_{t+n} - F_t]/S_t$$

Average forecasting accuracy is usually measured by the root mean squared error, or RMSE. The error is squared because a positive error is no better than a negative one; the squared errors are averaged over all forecasts, and we take the square root of this average to get a number that has the same units as the forecasting errors themselves. A forecasting model is more accurate than the forward rate if it has a smaller RMSE.

This commonly used statistical measure of forecasting accuracy does not satisfy those managers for whom the generation of correct buy and sell signals is an

---

[15]See Taylor and Allen (1992).

important part of the forecast, even if the magnitude of the expected move is inaccurate. In other words, those managers want to know the number of times the forecast turns out to be on the correct side of the forward exchange rate. The fraction P = correct forecast/total forecasts estimates the probability of making correct forecasts during a given period. If the model has no forecasting ability, P is close to 0.5. If it is unusually accurate, P should be larger than 0.5, and its statistical significance may be measured.

A final method for evaluating forecasting performance is to assume that the money manager systematically buys forward contracts if the forecast is above the forward rate and sells them if the forecast is below the forward rate. The *ex post* financial return on this strategy is then computed, and the forecasting ability is judged on the basis of the manager's return on the capital invested.

In the 1980s, *Euromoney* provided an annual performance review of major foreign exchange advisory services, using the three methods mentioned previously. Although results vary every year, there is no doubt that exchange rate forecasting is difficult. In some years, advisory services have consistently underperformed the forward exchange rate. As one might expect, the reward for active exchange rate forecasting strategies is potentially large, but so are the risks. Technical models seem to have a slightly better track record, at least in the short run. But those models are too short-term oriented to benefit the international portfolio manager to use systematically.

An illustration of the rather poor performance of forecasters is given in the following summary of the 1984 *Euromoney* survey. The average return is very poor (4.5%), and no single service was able to beat the Treasury bill rate over 1983.

> *Euromoney*'s sixth annual survey of foreign exchange forecasters finds that technical services were once again profitable. But their performance declined in terms of return on capital at risk, from 10.8% in 1982 to 4.5% in 1983. In addition their percentage of correct signals was only 44.9%, worse than the toss of a coin.[16]

As a group, forecasters tend to look at the same variables, use similar methodologies, and come up with forecasts that are often mostly in the same direction. Given the high volatility of exchange rates, it is not surprising to find that they do quite badly as a group in a given year.

However, the long-term record is not that bad. For example, several studies indicate that technical analysis has been able to take advantage of exchange rate trending behavior to generate large returns.[17] Because central banks seem to be consistent losers in the foreign exchange market, with a somewhat predictable trading strategy, one should not be surprised to find that active currency strategies could lead to profits,[18] despite the high risks involved. It also seems possible to model the time variation of expected exchange rate movements in a fashion that can lead, in the long run, to profitable returns on an active asset allocation strategy.

---

[16] *Euromoney*, August 1984.

[17] Several studies found that technical trading rules can be profitable. See Levich and Thomas (1993a and 1993b), Bilson (1993), Szakmary and Mathur (1997), Lyons (1998), and Neely and Weller (2001).

[18] See Solnik (1993), Glen and Jorion (1993), and Arnott (1999). Strange (1998) shows that currency overlay managers add value.

Summary

- The international monetary system evolved from the gold standard to a system of freely floating exchange rate.

- Nevertheless, some currencies of emerging countries are pegged to the dollar, the euro or to the value of a basket of major currencies. The euro is the new common currency of a dozen of European countries.

- Parity conditions provide a useful guide to global international investing. But foreign exchange rates are very volatile in the short run. In the longer run they tend to revert to fundamental values.

- Empirical evidence suggests that foreign exchange risk is large and that currency hedging should be seriously considered. It also suggests that currency forecasting could be a fruitful exercise.

- Forecasters resort to technical or economic analysis methods. Technical analysis focuses on the short-run behavior of exchange rates, whereas the economic approach is, by nature, better designed for long-run forecasts. A modeling of central bank intervention sometimes helps to understand the short-term behavior of foreign exchange rates.

- Foreign exchange forecasting is a difficult exercise, and no theory of exchange rate determination can claim to be consistently successful. Some observations have been repeatedly made by forecasters:
  - Exchange rates revert to PPP (real exchange rates are "mean reverting").
  - Exchange rates tend to trend (positive autocorrelation).

- Different measures of forecasting ability can be used. The track record of forecasters shows the difficulty of the task.

- The type of method used to forecast exchange rates depends on the user's motivation. A currency hedge fund focuses on short-term movements, while an international asset allocator cares about long-term prospects.

Problems

1. Under a system of exchange rates pegged around official parities, each of the following is a possible remedy for a country facing a balance of payments deficit *except:*
   a. Using its international reserves of gold and convertible currencies.
   b. Adopting tariffs on imports and introducing capital controls.
   c. Applying expansionary macroeconomic policy that drives prices up and interest rates down.
   d. Letting its exchange rate drop within the allowable band around the central parity.

2. In the European Monetary System, a member country was allowed to fluctuate its exchange rates within a band around the fixed parities with other members. In 1993, this system came under severe speculative pressures. Several currencies were pushed down to the limit of their allowed fluctuation margin against the DM; for example, the French

franc could not stay within 2.25 percent of its central parity with the DM. One solution would have been to keep the same fluctuation band around the central parity but devalue the parity of the franc against the DM. Instead, the European Union decided to keep the same bilateral parities but widen the allowed fluctuation band to 15 percent on each side of the parity.

  a. What do you think are the advantages and disadvantages of each solution?

  b. Which solution is more likely to prevent currency speculation?

3. Which of the following statements about the euro is false?

  I. The euro is the sole currency of the Eurozone countries.

  II. The countries in the Eurozone have been limited to the ones that are already in it, and no more countries would be allowed to join it in the future.

  III. The euro has a floating rate against other currencies, such as the U.S. dollar and the Japanese yen.

4. Interest rate parity between two currencies is more likely to be violated when one of the currencies is from a developing market than when both the currencies are from developed markets. Discuss whether or not you agree with this statement.

5. A U.S. institutional investor has invested in a portfolio of stocks in India. The annual inflation rate is 6 percent in India and 2.5 percent in the United States.

  a. If the purchasing power parity holds between the United States and India, by how much should the Indian rupee appreciate or depreciate with respect to the dollar over a year?

  b. Suppose that the annual return on the portfolio is 12 percent in Indian rupees, and the Indian rupee depreciated with respect to the dollar by 5 percent. Also suppose that an Indian institutional investor also held a portfolio with the same composition. Compare the real returns for both investors, and discuss why they do or do not differ from one another.

6. Consider a country whose currency is undervalued as compared to what the PPP relationship indicates. Discuss what is likely to happen in terms of foreign investment and trade, which may help restore PPP in the long run.

7. The spot SFr/$ is equal to 1.4723. The three-month interest rates are 1.80 percent for the U.S. dollar (7.2% annualized) and 0.95 percent for the Swiss franc (3.8% annualized). Assuming that the foreign exchange market participants are risk-neutral, what is the implied market prediction for the three-month ahead SFr/$ exchange rate?

8. The six-month forward $/€ exchange rate is $0.9976/€. A major commercial bank has made public a model that it uses to forecast future $/€ spot exchange rates. This model forecasts the spot exchange rate six months later to be $0.9781/€. Suppose that the market participants believe that this model is quite good, and they all start using this model. What do you think would happen to the spot and forward exchange rates and the six-month interest rates in dollars and euros?

9. Dustin Green likes to invest in the foreign exchange market. After an analysis of the last 10 years of U.S. dollar to British pound exchange rate data, he has come up with his own model to forecast the $/£ exchange rate one year ahead. Based on this model, the forecast for the one-year ahead exchange rate is $1.5315/£. The spot $/£ is equal to 1.5620. The annual one-year interest rates on the Eurocurrency market are 2 percent in dollars and 4.25 percent in pounds.

    a. What is the one-year forward exchange rate?

    b. If Dustin Green invests based on his model, which currency would he buy forward?

    c. If everyone were to start using Dustin Green's model and follow his transaction, what would happen to the exchange and interest rates?

10. Suppose that the participants in the foreign exchange market know the interest rates for all maturities and have reliable forecasts for inflation rates. If the foreign exchange market is efficient, discuss what is the expected future spot exchange rate if the

    a. market participants are risk-neutral.

    b. market participants are risk-averse.

11. Discuss the dangers of forecasting future spot exchange rates using methods based on trends.

12. Each of the following statements about central banks of countries and foreign exchange markets is true *except:*

    a. The central banks are generally major players in the foreign exchange market.

    b. Most central banks actively manage their foreign exchange reserves with the purpose of generating trading profits from favorable exchange rate movements.

    c. A modeling of central bank intervention in the foreign exchange market sometimes helps to understand the short-term behavior of exchange rates.

    d. Central banks may intervene in the foreign exchange market for the implementation of monetary policy and exchange rate targets.

13. Define what is meant by a "mean reverting" time series. What does the empirical evidence indicate about exchange rates being mean reverting?

14. What are the problems associated with using econometric models for forecasting exchange rates?

15. For each of the following, indicate whether the individual is more likely to use the econometric approach or technical analysis for foreign exchange forecasting.

    a. Manager of a currency hedge fund

    b. Manager of an international stock portfolio

    c. Currency trader

    d. Long-term strategic planner of a corporation

16. Suppose that the three-month forward Swiss franc to dollar rate is SFr1.440/$. The forecast for the three-month ahead spot exchange rate by Analyst A is SFr1.410/$ and the forecast by Analyst B is SFr1.580/$. The actual spot rate realized three months later is SFr1.308/$.

    a. Which of the three forecasts, including the forward rate, is the most accurate?

    b. If the spot rate at the time of prediction was SFr1.420/$, which analyst(s) correctly predicted the appreciation of Swiss franc relative to the dollar?

17. During the early 1990s, *Risk* magazine published exchange rate forecasts provided by 10 of the world's major commercial banks. In one such set of forecasts, Commerzbank and Harris Bank predicted the six-month ahead spot exchange rate to be ¥142/$ and ¥156/$, respectively. At the time of prediction, the Japanese yen to dollar spot rate was 145.41. The six-month forward rate was ¥144.697/$. The actual spot exchange rate realized six months later was ¥148.148/$.

    a. Rank the three forecasts, including the forward rate, based on the forecast error.

    b. Which forecast(s) correctly predicted the depreciation of Japanese yen relative to the dollar?

    c. David Brock and Brian Lee are speculators who buy and sell currencies forward. David Brock took a position based on Commerzbank's forecast for the yen to dollar exchange rate while Brian Lee took a position based on Harris Bank's forecast. Who turned out to be better off?

    d. Discuss if there is any conflict in your answers to parts (a) and (c).

18. The following table contains Japanese yen to dollar exchange rate data that were published in issues of the *Risk* magazine. Each period is three months. *Spot rate* is the actual spot exchange rate prevailing at the start of a period. *Forward rate* is the three-month forward exchange rate prevailing at the start of a period. *Forecast rate* is the forecast made by the Industrial Bank of Japan at the start of a period for the spot exchange rate at the start of the next period (that is, the forecast for three months later). To illustrate, at the beginning of the third period, the actual spot exchange rate was 152.750, the three-month ahead forward rate was 153.600, and the rate forecast by the Industrial Bank for the start of the fourth period was 151. The actual spot exchange rate that was realized at the start of the fourth period was 149.400. Based on the root mean squared error, was the Industrial Bank of Japan able to outperform the forward rate (do the calculations for the percentage forecast error)? You are also given that the spot rate realized three months after the last forecast given in the table was 139.25.

Period	Spot Rate	Forward Rate	Forecast Rate
1	143.164	142.511	140
2	144.300	143.968	141
3	152.750	153.600	151
4	149.400	149.400	143
5	129.600	129.700	130
6	129.500	129.800	131

Solutions

1. Applying expansionary macroeconomic policy, which results in higher goods prices and lower real interest rates, will not reduce the balance of payments deficit. Higher prices will make the country's goods less competitive internationally, and lower interest rates will discourage foreign capital. Thus, the balance of payments deficit will worsen instead of improve. On the other hand, (a), (b), and (d) will help in remedying the balance of payments deficit. Accordingly, the answer is (c).

2. a. One advantage of a wider band is "emotional." France could claim that it did not devalue its currency. Another advantage is flexibility. If there were no long-term fundamental reasons (inflation, balance of payments deficit, etc.) for a devaluation, the temporary pressure on the franc could ease and the franc could later revert to its previous level. The disadvantage of a wider band is exchange rate uncertainty for all firms. A "credible" small band is preferable for firms conducting international trade.

    b. A wider band makes speculation less attractive, because there is no guarantee that a central bank will defend its currency until the wide fluctuation margin is reached.

3. Remember that the Eurozone is made up of those countries in the EU that have adopted the euro as common currency. Statements I and III are clearly correct. Statement II is clearly not correct, because there is a possibility that more countries may join the Eurozone in future. For example, the British are debating whether to join the Eurozone.

4. The statement is true. Because of riskless arbitrage, interest rate parity between two currencies would hold if the markets for both are free and deregulated. Developed financial markets tend to be more free and deregulated. A developing country is more likely to impose various forms of capital controls and taxes that impede arbitrage. A developing country is economically not as well integrated with the world financial markets as the developed markets are. Also, some smaller currencies can only be borrowed and lent domestically, and the domestic money markets of developing countries are more likely to be subjected to political risk.

5. a Using the first-order approximation of PPP relationship, the variation in rupee to dollar exchange rate should equal the inflation differential between rupee and dollar. So, the rupee to dollar exchange rate should increase by $6 - 2.5 = 3.5\%$. That is, rupee should depreciate by 3.5 percent relative to the dollar.

   b. The nominal dollar return for the U.S. institutional investor is approximately $12 - 5 = 7\%$. The real return for the U.S. investor is approximately $7 - 2.5 = 4.5\%$. The real return for the Indian investor is approximately $12 - 6 = 6\%$. Thus, the U.S. investor has a lower real return than the Indian investor. This is so because the rupee depreciated with respect to the dollar by more than what the PPP relationship would indicate. Indeed, the difference between the real returns is $6 - 4.5 = 1.5\%$, which is the same as the difference between the actual depreciation of the rupee and the depreciation that should have occurred as per PPP ($5 - 3.5 = 1.5\%$).

6. If a country's currency is undervalued, it means that the real prices of assets in this country are low compared with other countries. Also, the wages are lower in real terms than in other countries. Thus, investors from other countries would invest in this country to take advantage of low prices and wages. This action would help in the appreciation of the undervalued currency and restoration of the PPP in the long run. In terms of foreign trade, an undervalued currency implies that exports from this country would get a boost while imports would become less attractive. This would also help in the appreciation of the undervalued currency and restoration of the PPP in the long run.

7. In risk-neutral efficient foreign exchange markets, the forward rate is the expected value of the future spot rate. The forward rate can be computed using the interest rate parity relation. Because the exchange rate is given in SFr/$ terms, the appropriate expression for the interest rate parity relation is

$$\frac{F}{S} = \frac{1 + r_{SFr}}{1 + r_\$}$$

(that is, r_{SFr} is a part of the numerator and $r_\$$ is a part of the denominator). Accordingly, the three-month forward rate is

$$F = 1.4723 \frac{1 + 0.0095}{1 + 0.0180} = 1.4600$$

Thus, the implied market prediction for the three-month ahead exchange rate is SFr1.4600/$.

8. As per the model, one € would be worth $0.9781 six months later. Based on the forward rate, one € would be worth $0.9976 six months later. Therefore, the market participants, who believe that the model is quite good, would buy the dollar in the forward market (sell euros). Consequently, the price of euro forward would decrease (the dollar forward would increase) and the forward rate would become equal to $0.9781/€. The spot exchange rate and the dollar and euro interest rates would change so as to be consistent with this forward rate. A look at the interest rate parity relationship—written in the form

$$\frac{F}{S} = \frac{1 + r_\$}{1 + r_€}$$

as F and S are in $/€ terms—suggests that with the decrease in forward rate from $0.9976/€ to $0.9781/€, the spot rate and interest rate in dollars are likely to go down and interest rate in euros is likely to go up.

9. a. The forward rate can be computed using the interest rate parity relation. Because the exchange rate is given in $/£ terms, the appropriate expression for the interest rate parity relation is

$$\frac{F}{S} = \frac{1 + r_\$}{1 + r_£}$$

(that is, $r_\$$ is a part of the numerator, and $r_£$ is a part of the denominator). Accordingly, the one-year forward rate is

$$F = 1.5620 \, \frac{1.0200}{1.0425} = \$ 1.5283/£$$

b. Based on the forward rate, one pound would be worth $1.5283 one year later. The model predicts that one pound would be worth $1.5315 one year later. Thus, as per the model, the pound is underpriced in the forward market. Accordingly, Dustin Green would buy pounds forward at $1.5283/£.

c. If everyone were to buy pounds forward, the price of pounds forward would increase and become equal to $1.5315/£. The spot exchange rate and the dollar and pound interest rates would change so as to be consistent with this forward rate. A look at the interest rate parity relationship suggests that the spot rate and the interest rate in dollars are likely to go up and the interest rate in pounds is likely to go down, to be consistent with the increase in the forward rate.

10. a. If the market participants are risk-neutral, the expected future spot exchange rate would be the same as the current forward rate. The forward rate is determined based on the current spot exchange rate and the interest rate differential between the two currencies. Thus, the expected future spot exchange rate would depend on the current spot exchange rate and the interest rate differential.

b. If the market participants are risk-averse, the forward rate would differ from the expected future spot exchange rate by the risk premium. The risk premium, based on the extent of risk aversion of the market participants, could be positive or negative. So, the expected future spot exchange rate is the forward rate less the risk premium. Since the forward rate is based on the current spot exchange rate and the interest rate differential between the two currencies, the expected future spot exchange rate would depend on the current spot exchange rate, the interest rate differential, and the risk premium.

11. There is some evidence of positive serial correlation in exchange rate movements (real and nominal). Hence, when a currency is going up, a reasonable forecast is that it will continue going up. Similarly, when a currency is going down, a reasonable forecast is that it will continue going down. However, at some point in time, the trend would reverse, and the problem is that a trend-based forecasting model cannot forecast when this turning point would occur. Although these turning points may be infrequent, they can be the occasion of a huge swing. The Mexican peso is a good example. For a few years until the end of 1994, the real value of the peso appreciated steadily. So, forecasters using trend models for the real exchange rates were quite successful for many months. However, in December 1994, the peso suddenly crashed and lost around half of its value.

12. Statements (a), (c), and (d) are true. Statement (b) is not true, because the objective of central bank activity in the foreign exchange market is not to profit from trading activities, but to implement monetary policy and exchange rate targets.

13. A mean reverting time series is one that may diverge from its fundamental value in the short run but reverts to its fundamental value in the long run. Empirical evidence suggests that exchange rates are mean reverting. The real exchange rates (observed exchange rate minus inflation) do deviate from the fundamental value implied by PPP in the short run, but tend to revert to the fundamental value in the long run.

14. Most econometric models are unsuitable for short-term exchange rate forecasts, as they model long-term structural economic relationships. For long-term exchange rate forecasts, the use of econometric models has some problems. First, most of them rely on predictions for certain key variables, such as money supply and interest rates. It is not easy to forecast these variables. Second, the structural correlation estimated by the parameters of the equation can change over time, so that even if all causative variables are correctly forecasted, the model can still yield poor exchange rate predictions. In periods when structural changes are rapid compared with the amount of time-series data required to estimate parameters, econometric models are of little help.

15. Technical analysis is more likely to be used for short-term exchange rate movements, while the econometric approach is more likely to be used for long-term exchange rate movements. The manager of a currency hedge fund and currency traders change their foreign exchange positions quite quickly, and are interested in short-term changes in exchange rates. On the other hand, the manager of an international stock portfolio is unlikely to change his foreign exchange positions quickly, because the transaction costs of buying and selling stocks are quite high. Therefore, the manager of an international stock portfolio is more interested in the long-term movements in exchange rates. Similarly, the long-term strategic planner of a corporation is interested in the long-term movements. Accordingly, the answers are:
    a. Technical analysis
    b. Econometric approach
    c. Technical analysis
    d. Econometric approach

16. a. The absolute values of prediction errors are as follows. Forward rate: 1.440 − 1.308 = 0.132; Analyst A: 1.410 − 1.308 = 0.102; and Analyst B: 1.580 − 1.308 = 0.272. Thus, the forecast by Analyst A was the most accurate.

    b. The forward rate and Analyst B erroneously predicted that the SFr to $ exchange rate would go up from the then spot rate of SFr1.420/$; that is, the SFr would depreciate. Only Analyst A correctly predicted that the Swiss franc would appreciate.

17. a. The absolute values of forecast errors are as follows. Forward rate: 148.148 − 144.697 = 3.451; Commerzbank: 148.148 − 142 = 6.148; and Harris Bank: 156 − 148.148 = 7.852. Thus, the forecast as per the forward rate was the most accurate, followed by Commerzbank, and then by Harris Bank.

    b. Although the forward rate and Commerzbank were more accurate than Harris Bank, both of them erroneously predicted that the yen would appreciate relative to the dollar. Only Harris Bank correctly predicted that the yen would depreciate.

    c. Commerzbank's forecast was ¥142/$, which was less than the forward rate. Therefore, David Brock bought yen forward (sold dollars) at the rate of ¥144.697/$. Because the actual rate turned out to be ¥148.148/$, buying yen forward did not turn out to be the right strategy. On the other hand, Harris Bank's forecast was ¥156/$, which was more than the forward rate. Therefore, Brian Lee sold yen forward (bought dollars) at the rate of ¥144.697/$. Because the actual rate turned out to be ¥148.148/$, selling yen forward turned out to be the right strategy.

    d. Commerzbank's forecast had a lower forecast error than Harris Bank's in part (a). However, in part (c), it was right to buy and sell based on Harris Bank's forecast and not Commerzbank's. The reason is that Harris Bank's forecast turned out to be on the right side of the forward rate, while Commerzbank's did not.

18. Let the forecasts made by the Industrial Bank of Japan at the beginning of period t for the beginning of period $t + 1$ be $E(S_{t+1}|\phi_t)$. Let the forward rates quoted at the beginning of period t for the beginning of period $t + 1$ be F_t, and the actual spot rates at the beginning of periods t and $t + 1$ be S_t and S_{t+1}, respectively. The percentage forecast errors (ϵ and e) for each forecast made by the Industrial Bank of Japan and the forward rate are computed as $\epsilon_{t+1} = [S_{t+1} - E(S_{t+1}|\phi_t)]/S_t$ and $e_{t+1} = [S_{t+1} - F_t]/S_t$, respectively. The following table details the computations.

Pd.	S_t	F_t	$E(S_{t+1}|\phi_t)$	S_{t+1}	ϵ_{t+1}	e_{t+1}	ϵ^2_{t+1}	e^2_{t+1}
1	143.164	142.511	140	144.300	0.0300	0.0125	0.0009	0.0002
2	144.300	143.968	141	152.750	0.0814	0.0609	0.0066	0.0037
3	152.750	153.600	151	149.400	−0.0105	−0.0275	0.0001	0.0008
4	149.400	149.400	143	129.600	−0.0897	−0.1325	0.0080	0.0176
5	129.600	129.700	130	129.500	−0.0039	−0.0015	0.0000	0.0000
6	129.500	129.800	131	139.250	0.0637	0.0730	0.0041	0.0053
						MSE	0.0033	0.0046
						RMSE	0.0573	0.0678

The RMSE for the Industrial Bank of Japan is lower than that for the forward rate. Thus, as per the limited data set in this problem, the Industrial Bank outperformed the forward rate in terms of accuracy of the forecasts, as measured by the RMSE. We have not tested whether the difference in forecast performances is statistically significant.

Bibliography

Angel, J. J. "Implications of Chaos for Portfolio Management," *Journal of Investing,* Summer 1994.

Arnott, R. "Tactical Currency Allocation," *Managing Currency Risks in Investment Portfolios,* AIMR Proceedings, 1999.

Baillie, R. T., and Osterberg, W. P. "Why Do Central Banks Intervene?" *Journal of International Money and Finance,* 16(6), December 1997, pp. 909–920.

Baillie, R. T., and Bollerslev, T. "The Forward Premium Anomaly Is Not as Bad as You Think," *Journal of International Money and Finance,* 19(4), August 2000, pp. 471–488.

Bekaert, G., and Gray, S. "Target Zones and Exchange Rates: An Empirical Investigation," *Journal of International Economics,* 1998.

Bekaert, G., and Hodrick, R. J. "Characterizing Predictable Components in Excess Returns on Equity and Foreign Exchange," *Journal of Finance,* June 1992.

————. "On Biases in the Measurement of Foreign Exchange Risk Premiums," *Journal of International Money and Finance,* 12, April 1993, pp. 115–138.

Bilson, I. "Value, Yield and Trend: A Composite Forecasting Approach to Foreign Exchange Trading," in A. Gritlin, ed., *Strategic Currency Investing,* Chicago: Probus, 1993.

Bollerslev, T., Chou, R. Y., and Kroner, K. F. "ARCH Modelling in Finance: A Review of the Theory and Empirical Evidence," *Journal of Econometrics,* 52, 1992.

Box, G. E., and Jenkins, G. M. *Time Series Analysis, Forecasting and Control,* San Francisco: Holden Day, 1994.

Cavaglia, S., Verschoor, W. F., and Wolff, C. P., "Further Evidence on Exchange Rate Expectations," *Journal of International Money and Finance,* 12, February 1993.

Cheung, Y-W., and Lai, K. S. "Parity Reversion in Real Exchange Rates during the Post-Bretton Woods Period," *Journal of International Money and Finance,* 17(4), August 1998, pp. 597–614.

Dominguez, K. M. "Are Foreign Exchange Forecasts Rational? New Evidence from Survey Data," *Economic Letters,* 21, 1986, pp. 277–281.

————. "Central Bank Intervention and Exchange Rate Volatility," *Journal of International Money and Finance,* 17(1), February 1998, pp. 161–190.

Dumas, B., and Solnik, B. "The World Price of Foreign Exchange Risk," *Journal of Finance,* 50(2), June 1995, pp. 445–479.

Engle, R. "Statistical Models for Financial Volatility," *Financial Analysts Journal,* January/February 1993.

Evans, M. D., and Lewis, K. K. "Do Long-Term Swings in the Dollar Affect Estimates of the Risk Premium?" *Review of Financial Studies,* 8(3), Fall 1995, pp. 709–742.

Fama, E. "Forward and Spot Exchange Rates," *Journal of Monetary Economics,* November 1984.

Frankel, J. A., and Froot, K. A. "Using Survey Data to Test Standard Propositions Regarding Exchange Rate Expectations," *American Economic Review,* March 1987.

Frankel, J., and MacArthur, M. A. "Political vs Currency Premia in International Real Interest Differentials: A Study of Forward Rates for 24 Countries," *European Economic Review,* 32, June 1988.

Froot, K. A., and Thaler, R. H. "Anomalies: Foreign Exchange," *Journal of Economic Perspectives,* 4(3), 1990.

Glen, J., and Jorion, P. "Currency Hedging for International Portfolios," *Journal of Finance,* December 1993.

Goodhart, C. A. E. "Central Bank Forex Intervention Assessed in Continuous Time," *Journal of International Money and Finance,* August 1993.

Grossman, G., and Rogoff, K., eds. *Handbook of International Economics,* Volume 3, Amsterdam: North-Holland, 1995.

Hodrick, R. J. *The Empirical Evidence on the Efficiency of Forward Futures Foreign Exchange Market,* Chur, Switzerland: Harwood Academic, 1987.

Huizinga, J. "An Empirical Investigation of the Long-Run Behavior of Real Exchange Rates," in K. Brunner and A. Meltzer, eds., *Carnegie-Rochester Series on Public Policy,* 27, Amsterdam: North-Holland, 1987.

Jorion, P. "On Jump Processes in the Foreign Exchange and Stock Markets," *Review of Financial Studies,* 1, 1989.

Kaminsky, G., and Peruga, R. "Can a Time-Varying Risk Premium Explain Excess Returns in the Forward Market for Foreign Exchange?" *Journal of International Economics,* 28 February, 1990.

Kryzanowski, L., Galler, M., and Wright, D. W. "Using Artificial Network to Pick Stocks," *Financial Analysts Journal,* July/August 1993.

Leahy, M. P. "The Profitability of U.S. Intervention in the Foreign Exchange Market," *Journal of International Money and Finance,* 14(6), December 1995, pp. 823–844.

Levich, R. M., and Thomas, L. "The Merits of Active Currency Risk Management: Evidence from International Bond Portfolios," *Financial Analysts Journal,* 49(5), September/October 1993a, pp. 63–70.

———. "The Significance of Technical Trading-Rule Profits in the Foreign Exchange Market: A Bootstrap Approach," *Journal of International Money and Finance,* 12(5), October 1993b, pp. 451–474.

Lewis, K. L. "Occasional Interventions to Target Rates," *American Economic Review,* September 1995.

Liu, P. C., and Maddala, G. S. "Rationality of Survey Data and Tests for Market Efficiency in the Foreign Exchange Markets," *Journal of International Money and Finance,* August 1992.

Lothian, J. "Some New Stylized Facts of Floating Exchange Rates," *Journal of International Money and Finance,* 17(1), February 1998, pp. 29–40.

Lothian, J., and Taylor, M. "Real Exchange Rate Behavior: The Recent Float from the Perspective of the Past Two Centuries," *Journal of Political Economy,* June 1996, pp. 488–509.

Lyons, R. K. "Profits and Position Control: A Week of FX Dealing," *Journal of International Money and Finance,* 17(1), February 1998, pp. 97–116.

Mark, N. "Exchange Rates and Fundamentals: Evidence on Long-Horizon Predictability," *American Economic Review,* March 1995, pp. 201–218.

Medsker, L., Turban, E., and Trippi, R. "Neural Network Fundamentals for Financial Analysts," *Journal of Investing,* Spring 1993.

Meese, R., and Rogoff, K. "Empirical Exchange Rate Models of the Seventies: Do They Fit Out-of-Sample?" *Journal of International Economics,* February 1983.

Murphy, J. J. *Technical Analysis of the Financial Markets: A Comprehensive Guide to Trading Methods and Applications,* New York: Prentice Hall, 1999.

Neely C. J., and Weller, P. A., "Technical Analysis and Central Bank Intervention," *Journal of International Money and Finance,* 20(7), December 2001, pp. 949–970.

Peters, E. *Fractal Market Analysis,* New York: Wiley, 1994.

Pring, M. J. *Technical Analysis Explained: The Successful Investor's Guide to Spotting Investment Trends and Turning Points,* New York: McGraw-Hill, 1991.

Rogoff, K. "The Purchasing Power Parity Puzzle," *Journal of Economic Literature,* 34, June 1996, pp. 647–668.

Rosenberg, M. *Currency Forecasting: A Guide to Fundamental and Technical Models of Exchange Rate Determination,* Chicago: Irwin, 1996.

Solnik, B. *Predictable Time-Varying Components of International Asset Returns,* Charlottesville, VA: The Research Foundation of Chartered Financial Analysts, 1993.

Strange, B. "Do Currency Overlay Managers Add Value?" *Pension and Investments,* June 15, 1998.

Szakmary, A. C., and Mathur, I. "Central Bank Intervention and Trading Rule Profits in Foreign Exchange Markets," *Journal of International Money and Finance,* 16(4), August 1997, pp. 513–536.

Taylor, M. P., and Allen, H. "The Use of Technical Analysis in the Foreign Exchange Market," *Journal of International Money and Finance,* June 1992.

Chapter 3: Appendix

Statistical Supplements on Forecasting Asset Returns

The reader is assumed to have some familiarity with standard statistics. This appendix is intended as a brief but somewhat technical introduction to less conventional statistical models used in forecasting. The basic question is: How can we describe the time behavior of a random variable in a tractable way, that is, in a model whose statistical properties are such that it can easily be estimated from past data and used to forecast the future value of the variable?

Some Notations

Prices move over time in a somewhat random fashion. It is common in finance to focus on the stochastic process followed by the rate of return of an asset, that is, its percentage price movement. Let's introduce some mathematical notations:

r_{t+1}	the rate of return observed at time $t + 1$
$E_t(r_{t+1})$	the rate of return *expected* in period t for period $t + 1$
e_{t+1}	the deviation of the rate realized in period $t + 1$ from its expected value in period t: $e_{t+1} = r_{t+1} - E_t(r_{t+1})$; sometimes called *forecast error* or *shock* or *innovation*
σ^2_{t+1}	the *variance* of the rate of return r_{t+1}; also the variance of e_{t+1}; its square root, σ_{t+1}, is the standard deviation of returns

The process for the rate of return can be written as

$$r_{t+1} = E_t(r_{t+1}) + e_{t+1} \tag{3.5}$$

where the forecast error e_{t+1} has a zero expected return and a variance σ^2_{t+1}. The variance is equal to

$$\sigma^2_{t+1} = E_t(e^2_{t+1})$$

The variance and expected returns are called *moments* of the probability distribution of the rates of return. The variance is a measure of the *volatility* of the asset.

The notations may seem a bit complicated but are necessary. They stress that the expectation and variance estimates are taken at time t, for a return to be realized at time $t + 1$. At this point, we do not assume that expected returns and variances are constant over time. They are assumed to be *conditional* on some set of information available at time t. A more descriptive notation would be

$$E_t(r_{t+1}) = E_t(r_{t+1} | \phi_t)$$

$$\sigma_{t+1}^2 = E_t(e_{t+1}^2 | \phi_t)$$

where the notation $| \phi_t$ means that the expectation is conditional on an information set ϕ_t known at time t.

Traditional Statistical Models with Constant Moments

The traditional approach to statistical modeling uses models with constant expected returns and variances.

Normal Distribution   The most simple and common statistical model describing the process followed by an asset rate of return is the *normal* distribution, with constant expected return and variance. A normal, or Gaussian, distribution is completely summarized by its mean and variance. The distribution takes the famous bell shape. At each time period $t + 1$, rates of return are assumed to be drawn independently from the same distribution; they are identically independently distributed (i.i.d.). In other words, the rate of return for each time period $t + 1$ is independent from what happened in the past and always has the same expected return and variance. We have

$$E_t(r_{t+1}) = E(r) = \text{constant}$$

$$\sigma_{t+1}^2 = \sigma^2 = \text{constant}$$

and

$$r_{t+1} = E(r) + e_{t+1} \tag{3.6}$$

This distribution is *unconditional* in the sense that its expected return and variance are constant through time and not conditional on time or current information.

Let's now see how one would empirically estimate the parameters of such a model and use it to forecast. One would look at past data; the expected return is simply estimated as the mean return over the sample. Hence, the best empirical estimate of the future return is the mean return estimated over past data. In the foreign exchange market, the best forecast for a future movement in the exchange rate is its past trend.

Jumps   Some asset prices are likely to exhibit infrequent big *jumps*. For example, exchange rates are periodically devalued or revalued under speculative pressures. The date of the jump is uncertain.

The statistical distribution of daily exchange rate movements could be thought of as a combination of daily normal movements and infrequent jumps.[19] The simplest jump process is a binomial approach, whereby a jump of size J has a probability p to take place at time $t + 1$ and a probability $1 - p$ not to take place. Hence, the return on date $t + 1$ is a random variable λ_{t+1} such that

$$\lambda_{t+1} = \begin{vmatrix} J \text{ with probability } p \\ 0 \text{ with probability } 1 - p \end{vmatrix} \tag{3.7}$$

This can lead to so-called *Poisson* distributions.

Note that both types of distributions—normal and Poisson—are i.i.d. In the simple jump process described, the probability of occurrence of a jump is independent of what happened in the previous periods or independent of current information. Hence, the expected return and the variance are the same for each period. Such a simple statistical jump process is not satisfactory for describing the behavior of exchange rate movements. The probability of a jump in exchange rate is clearly a function of past jumps. If a big jump (e.g., a devaluation) has just taken place, it is unlikely to take place again in the very near future. Also the magnitude of the jump is uncertain. Unfortunately, complex time-dependent jump processes are untractable from a practical viewpoint.

Traditional Statistical Models with Time-Varying Moments

No theory claims that the expected return on an asset should always stay the same. The assumption that the expected return is constant through time can be relaxed in a number of ways. One way is to assume that past returns influence future returns in a specified manner. Another is to model the influence of a change in the economic environment by stating a linear relation between current observed economic variables and future returns. Another is to assume that a change in market volatility affects the expected return.

Time-Varying Expected Return: ARIMA   The first approach is to assume that future returns are a function of past returns. A powerful model of time dependence in returns is the ARIMA (AutoRegressive Integrated Moving Average) process. This theory was developed by Box and Jenkins.[20] The basic idea is that the return at time $t + 1$ will be affected by past returns in a specified and predictable way. A general ARIMA process can be written as

$$r_{t+1} = a_0 + b_0 r_t + b_1 r_{t-1} + b_2 r_{t-2} + \ldots + c_0 e_t + c_1 e_{t-1} + c_2 e_{t-2} + \ldots + e_{t+1} \tag{3.8}$$

The variance of the innovations e_{t+1} is assumed to be constant.

The terms with the b coefficients are the autoregressive terms. The terms with the c coefficients are the moving-average terms. The *order* of the ARIMA process is

---

[19]See, for example, Jorion (1989) and Bekaert and Gray (1998).
[20]See Box and Jenkins (1994).

the number of lags included on the right-hand side. The number of lags for the moving-average terms and for the autoregressive terms can be different. In Equation 3.8, we stopped detailing the terms at order 3 for both.

One must clearly understand what is known at time t. All past returns, including r_t have been observed at time t. All innovation terms, including e_t have also been observed at time t. Hence, and assuming an ARIMA process of order 3, the expectation formulated at time t for the return at time $t + 1$ is equal to

$$E_t(r_{t+1}) = a_0 + b_0 r_t + b_1 r_{t-1} + b_2 r_{t-2} + c_0 e_t + c_1 e_{t-1} + c_2 e_{t-2} \qquad (3.9)$$

To use this model in forecasting, one would first estimate the c and b coefficients over past data, using standard ARIMA econometric software. The forecast for $t + 1$ would then be derived using Equation 3.9.

Expected returns can depend on past returns in ways other than those specified by ARIMA processes. Technical analysis uses a variety of methods, such as filter rules or charts, described in this chapter.

Time-Varying Expected Return: Information Variables   The economic environment changes over time. Clearly, the level of interest rates or the business cycle could affect expectations for future asset returns. A wide body of literature[21] has modeled a linear relation between time-varying expected returns and a set of n observed economic variables Z_t. This can be written as

$$E_t(r_{t+1}) = d_0 + d_1 Z_{1t} + d_2 Z_{2t} + \ldots + d_n Z_{nt} \qquad (3.10)$$

The process followed by r_{t+1} can then be written as

$$r_{t+1} = d_0 + d_1 Z_{1t} + d_2 Z_{2t} + \ldots + d_n Z_{nt} + e_{t+1} \qquad (3.11)$$

where the variance of innovation e_{t+1} is assumed constant.

It must be stressed that the information variables are known at time t when the forecast of the return for $t + 1$ is formulated. The information variables commonly used are the level of interest rates, the spread between short- and long-term interest rates, the interest rate differential between two currencies, and so on.

To use this model in forecasting, one would first estimate the coefficients d's over past data, using a regression technique. The forecast for $t + 1$ is obtained by observing the current value Z_t of the information variables and inputting them in Equation 3.10.

Time-Varying Variances: GARCH
Financial market volatility changes over time in a somewhat predictable fashion. This implies that the variance of the returns changes over time in a predictable fashion, conditional on a set of information. To be more precise, the *conditional* variance for period $t + 1$ estimated in t, σ_{t+1}^2, depends on the information set available at time t.

---

[21]A review of the literature can be found in Solnik (1993).

The simplest specification of the conditional variance is the ARCH(p) model, in which the conditional variance is simply a weighted average of p past squared forecast errors:

$$\sigma_{t+1}^2 = \alpha + \beta_1 e_t^2 + \beta_2 e_{t-1}^2 + \ldots + \beta_p e_{t-p+1}^2 \qquad (3.12)$$

The order of the ARCH process is the number p of lags included in the equation. A natural generalization is to allow past conditional variance to enter the equation. This is known as Generalized ARCH, or GARCH.[22] The GARCH(p,q) model is written as

$$\sigma_{t+1}^2 = \alpha + \beta_1 e_t^2 + \ldots + \beta_p e_{t-p+1}^2 + \gamma_1 \sigma_t^2 + \ldots + \gamma_q \sigma_{t-q+1}^2 \qquad (3.13)$$

The orders of the GARCH process are the number of lags for the squared error terms (p) and for the past variances (q). Most researchers have found that a GARCH(1,1) is generally appropriate for modeling and forecasting the volatility of asset returns. The GARCH(1,1) is written as

$$\sigma_{t+1}^2 = \alpha + \beta_1 e_t^2 + \gamma_1 \sigma_t^2 \qquad (3.14)$$

This model means that the current volatility estimate can be deducted from the volatility estimated in the previous period, σ_t^2, modified by the innovation, or shock, e_t^2, just observed. The observation of large shocks leads to an increase in forecasted volatility.

Estimation of the GARCH coefficients requires some specialized econometric software using a so-called maximum-likelihood algorithm. One is sometimes faced with convergence problems in such an algorithm. Once the parameters β's and γ's have been estimated, Equation 3.14 can be used to forecast the next period volatility, using the past period volatility and observed shocks.

It is possible to simultaneously model the time variation in expected return and in volatility. For example, the variance of the forecast error in Equation 3.11 could be modeled as a GARCH process, and the conditional variance could be added as an explanatory variable in the conditional expected return. This is known as a GARCH-M process. Numerous variants of GARCH models have been developed.

Nontraditional Models

Numerous models developed in other fields, such as physics and artificial intelligence, have also been applied to forecasting financial returns. Only the most widely quoted of these nonlinear models are briefly described here.

Chaos Theory   Scientists have observed that some mathematical and physical systems that exhibit enormously complicated behavior that appears random are actually generated by some simple nonlinear deterministic models. A *deterministic* model

---

[22]A review of GARCH models can be found in Engle (1993) and Bollerslev, Chou, and Kroner (1992).

is governed by some mathematical rules that involve no random elements, so that its outcome can be fully described and explained once the rules are known. However, the future behavior is extremely difficult to predict, because of the high dependence of these systems on the initial conditions. Such nonlinear deterministic systems, which are highly sensitive to initial conditions, are called *chaotic* systems.[23]

A classic example of chaos is the weather system. The famous "butterfly problem" in weather forecasting is that the wing flapping of a butterfly in a specific spot at a specific time may cause a hurricane several months later in another place. Although weather systems appear to be random, they follow very precise models but are very sensitive to small changes in initial conditions. A reasonable weather forecast for tomorrow can be the same weather as today, but precise forecasts for the weather in 30 days are not possible. Another example of a chaotic system is a random-number generator used on computers. These random numbers are indeed generated by a deterministic system, but they look random for all practical purposes.

Chaos is caused by exact nonlinear mathematical functions but appears to be virtually random, and the next state of the system appears virtually unpredictable. Chaotic systems periodically settle into regular cycles, which leads the observer to believe that the systems are predictable, but they suddenly explode in wild movements. A simple definition of a chaotic system could be a system generated by nonlinear dynamics whereby small differences in starting values can have a very large influence on the time-series dynamics of the variable.

Similarly, financial markets could be chaotic in the sense that financial prices appear to follow random movements, although they follow a set of exact rules. Forecasting returns is extremely difficult, because a minor change in initial conditions can lead to major changes in forecasts. At best, chaos theory could help detect "pockets" of stability that could help the astute forecaster. The estimation of a chaotic system is a difficult empirical exercise that will not be discussed here. It is very difficult, if not impossible, to differentiate between a stochastic process, whereby random shocks affect the financial variable studied, and a deterministic chaotic process whose underlying model is unknown.

Chaotic systems are one class of *nonlinear dynamic* systems. They are related to *fractal* models and other nonlinear dynamic models that will not be discussed here.[24]

Artificial Intelligence, Expert Systems, and Neural Networks   *Artificial intelligence* attempts to computerize human reasoning. An *expert system* is a simple class of artificial model that attempts to learn from the behavior of market participants and that translates this learning into a set of program rules. In the 1980s, expert systems became quite fashionable in financial markets. They can be used in risk management,

---

[23]Most references on chaos theory are very technical. A good introduction to chaos theory and its implications for portfolio management can be found in Angel (1994). See also Peters (1994).
[24]Ibid.

trading, and forecasting. The computer program attempts to replicate the *sequential* decision process of interviewed "experts" in the field. An expert system is a computer program that uses a set of rules, procedures, and facts to make inferences to simulate the problem-solving ability of human experts. Although these systems are well adapted to replicate the classic behavior of a portfolio manager or a trader, they have not been very successfully applied to forecasting financial prices. One of the problems with expert systems is that they are sequential processes based on fixed decision rules that need to be adapted continuously. In other words, the market learns more quickly than the expert system designed to mimic the behavior of market participants.

Another approach to artificial intelligence, favored in the 1990s, is constructing programs that mimic the architecture and processing capabilities of the brain. These are known as *artificial neural networks* (ANN), or, more simply, *neural networks*.[25] Conventional computer programs (like earlier expert systems) process information *sequentially*; the innovation in neural networks is massive *parallel* processing of information, in the sense that, as in a brain, all information is processed simultaneously. A human brain is composed of interconnected neurons. An artificial neural network consists of a set of layers of neurons. Each neuron receives inputs, processes them, and delivers a single output. This output can be an input to another neuron or a final output. The network structures can have different shapes. A typical neural network used in finance would have three layers of 10 to 1,000 neurons.

The development of a neural network requires a vast amount of data, because little *a priori* theoretical structure is assumed. The data are separated into a *training* set and a *test* set. The training set is used to determine the parameters of the neural network system, and the test set is used to validate, or test, the network. Once the neural network has been validated, it can be used in forecasting. The observed values of the relevant variables are entered as inputs, and the neural network generates a forecast.

Data Mining, Data Snooping, and Model Mining

A word of caution is required after this review of models used in forecasting. All these models used for forecasting are estimated over some past data. Although the models may look attractive over the data sample on which they are estimated, their out-of-sample forecasting performance can be quite poor. The problems come from the fact that researchers report and use only the models that best fit the past data, although they search ("mine") a huge number of possible models.

Data Mining   *Data mining* refers to the fact that when researchers study a given database long enough, they are likely to find some strong, but spurious, association

---

[25]A good nontechnical description of neural networks can be found in Medsker, Turban, and Trippi (1993). See also Kryzanowski, Galler, and Wright (1993).

between some sets of variables. This relation happened by chance over the specific period covered by the data set and is not likely to repeat over the future. A statistician would say that the relation is not stable. There is an obvious selection bias in trying a large number of models and reporting only the one that yields the best explanatory power in-sample.

For example, let's assume that a regression is performed, over the past 10 years, between the French stock index return and a large number of economic and financial variables from many countries. The researchers attempt to find a combination of any five variables observed at time t that have a good explanatory power for French stock return in the next month (time $t + 1$). By chance, a good explanatory power will be found if they mine across a large number of variables. For example, it could be that the French stock market went up, by chance, on the very months when it rained in Australia or when there was a full moon in South China. Such a relation found over a past data set would be of little practical help for the future, because it is only a statistical artifact of the studied data sample, not a reasonable economic model.

Data Snooping   *Data snooping* can be defined as using the data mining of other researchers on a similar database. For example, a bank could estimate only one forecasting model, which is quite close to the one published by another researcher after extensive data mining. Data mining is like cheating at an exam by bringing unauthorized notes, whereas data snooping is like looking over your neighbor's shoulder to read his unauthorized notes.

In data snooping you can genuinely claim that you did not personally engage in any data mining and that, hence, your model cannot be guilty of the statistical biases just reported. However, it should be clear that your model is no more likely to work well out-of-sample.

Model Mining   In traditional statistical models, as described earlier, a theoretical model is postulated, and its parameters are estimated over a set of data. The problem of data mining is already present for these traditional econometric models, which clearly expose their underlying theoretical logic. It is more acute for complex systems whose underlying structure is primarily empirical and that need a long data history to be estimated and revised. In artificial intelligence systems, the estimation procedure searches through a huge number of possible model classes. This means that the researcher can also be guilty of *model mining*. It is even less likely that a model that fits well over some past data will do so in the future.

4

International Asset Pricing

- Explain international market integration and international market segmentation

- Discuss the impediments to international capital mobility

- Discuss the factors that favor international market integration

- Explain the extension of the domestic capital asset pricing model (CAPM) to an international context (the extended CAPM)

- Describe the assumptions needed to justify the extended CAPM

- Determine whether the real exchange rate changes in a period, given the beginning-of-period (nominal) exchange rate, the inflation rates in the period, and the end-of-period (nominal) exchange rate

- Calculate the expected exchange rate and the expected domestic-currency holding period return on

a foreign bond (security), given expected and predictable inflation rates for the period, the beginning-of-period nominal exchange rate, and the real exchange rate (assumed to be constant)

- Calculate the end-of-period real exchange rate and the domestic-currency *ex post* return on a foreign bond (security), given the end-of-period exchange rate, the beginning-of-period real exchange rate, and the inflation rates during the period

- Explain a foreign currency risk premium in terms of interest rate differentials and in terms of forward rates

- Calculate a foreign currency risk premium

- State the risk-pricing relation and the formula for the international capital asset pricing model (ICAPM)

- Calculate the expected returns on a stock, given its world market beta and currency exposure, as well as the appropriate risk-free rates and risk premiums

- Define currency exposure and explain exposures in terms of correlations

- Explain the effect of market segmentation on the ICAPM

- Discuss the likely exchange rate exposure of a company based on a description of its activities and explain the impact of both real and nominal exchange rate changes on the valuation of the company

- Discuss the currency exposures of national economies, equity markets, and bond markets

- Explain the models that relate real exchange rate changes to domestic economic activity

In this chapter, we explore the valuation and portfolio implications of international asset pricing. Several asset-pricing questions arise: What would happen if all investors diversified their portfolios internationally? What asset prices would result from such a market equilibrium? What type of risks would be priced in the marketplace? Would taking foreign currency risk be rewarded, and what would be the optimal currency-hedging policy?

Answers to these questions require some theoretical market equilibrium framework. In this chapter, we review international asset pricing. All asset-pricing theories start from the assumption that markets are efficient, so the first section is devoted to this concept. The second section reviews international asset pricing models. The last section presents some discussion of the relation between exchange rates and asset prices, a central issue in international asset pricing.

Throughout this chapter, we use direct currency quotes expressed as X units of domestic currency per 1 unit of foreign currency.

International Market Efficiency

The notion of an efficient market is central to finance theory. In an *efficient market, any new information would be immediately and fully reflected in prices*. Because all current information is already impounded in the asset price, only news—that is, unanticipated information—could cause a change in price in the future.

Consider why a financial market *quickly*, if not instantaneously, discounts all available information. Any new information will immediately be used by some privileged investors, who will take positions to capitalize on it, thereby making the asset price adjust (almost) instantaneously to this piece of information. For example, a new balance of payments statistic would immediately be used by foreign exchange traders to buy or sell a currency until the foreign exchange rate reached a level considered consistent with the new information. Similarly, investors might use surprise information about a company, such as a new contract or changes in forecasted income, to reap a profit until the stock price reached a level consistent with the news. The adjustment in price would be so rapid that it would not pay to buy information that has already been available to other investors. Hundreds of thousands of expert financial analysts and professional investors throughout the world search for information and make the world markets *close* to fully efficient.

In an efficient market, the typical investor could consider an asset price to reflect its true *fundamental value* at all times. The notion of fundamental value is somewhat philosophical; it means that at each point in time, each asset has an intrinsic value that all investors try to discover. Because the true fundamental value is unknown, the only way to test for market efficiency is to detect whether some specific news is not yet impounded in the asset price and could therefore be used to make some abnormal profit in the future.

All in all, the general consensus is that individual markets across the world are quite efficient, probably due to the intense competition among professional security analysts and managers in each national market. In addition, the number of foreign investors and securities firms using their own financial analysis techniques has increased, helping to make each national market more efficient. Of course, the degree of efficiency is likely to vary among countries, depending on the maturity, liquidity, and degree of regulation of the market. However, investors must be aware that it is not easy to "beat" the market in any developed stock market. This observation also suggests that theoretical asset pricing models, based on the premise that markets are efficient, are useful guides to investment policy.

Although many national markets may be quite efficient, making it difficult to consistently outperform the local index, the question of international market efficiency still remains. Could active asset allocation among countries consistently outperform the world market index? There is less analyst competition among countries than within a single market. The fundamental issue of international market efficiency is often viewed in terms of international market *integration* or *segmentation*. An integrated world financial market would achieve international efficiency, in the sense that capital flows across markets would instantaneously take advantage of any new information throughout the world. For example, an international investor would not hesitate to move money from Germany to France if the investor forecasted an election result in France that would improve the competitiveness of French firms against German firms. Similarly, a portfolio manager would arbitrage an Italian chemical stock against a U.S. chemical stock, based on new information on their prospective earnings and market shares. In an efficient, integrated, international market, prices of all assets would be in line with their relative investment values. For example, the market consensus expectation of a prolonged period of outstanding economic growth in one country would be immediately discounted in higher current equity prices and not translate into higher future stock returns once the widely expected superior growth materializes.

The debate over integration versus segmentation involves two somewhat different concepts:

- The first concept has to do with impediments to capital mobility. Are there legal restrictions or other forms of constraints that segment one national market from others?

- The second concept has to do with international asset pricing. Are "similar" securities priced in the same manner on different national markets?

It is sometimes claimed that international markets are not integrated but segmented because of various *impediments to capital mobility.* Although each national market might be efficient, numerous factors might prevent international capital flows from taking advantage of relative mispricing among countries:

- *Psychological barriers.* Unfamiliarity with foreign markets, language, sources of information, and so on, might curtail foreign investment.

- *Legal restrictions.* Institutional investors are often constrained in their foreign investments. Also, some national markets regulate foreign investment flowing into or out of the market. Foreign ownership is sometimes constrained to avoid loss of national control.

- *Transaction costs.* The costs of foreign investment can be high and greater than for domestic investment. Access to sources of information throughout the world is costly, as are international transaction costs, management fees, and custodial services.

- *Discriminatory taxation.* Foreign investment might be more heavily taxed than domestic investment. Withholding taxes might lead to double taxation.

- *Political risks.* The political risks of foreign investment might dampen enthusiasm for international diversification. This political transfer risk might take the form of a prohibition on repatriation of profits or capital investment from a foreign country. Although the risk is extremely small in the major markets, the associated potential loss is large.

- *Foreign currency risks.* Foreign investments bear the risk of local market movements and unexpected changes in the foreign exchange rate. Foreign currency risk is the risk that the foreign currency *in real terms,* will depreciate or the domestic currency will appreciate during the time an investor holds an investment denominated in foreign currency.

All these factors tend to reduce international capital flows and lead to somewhat segmented national markets. This result is most apparent in emerging markets, in which foreign investment restrictions are often severe.

However, international integration requires only a sufficient flow of capital to make the world market efficient and to eliminate relative mispricing among countries. In many countries, private and institutional investors are extensively invested abroad. All major corporations have truly multinational operations; their shares are often listed on several stock exchanges. Large corporations, as well as governments, borrow internationally and quickly take advantage of relative bond mispricing between countries, thereby making the markets more efficient. The flow of foreign investment has grown rapidly over the years; thus, it does not seem that the international markets are fully segmented. What is really important for investors is whether two firms that they regard as similar are priced identically in their respective national markets. To have a meaningful discussion of market segmentation, we must first introduce asset-pricing models.

Asset-Pricing Theory

The Domestic Capital Asset-Pricing Model

The value of an asset depends on its discounted anticipated cash flows adjusted for risk. For example, the value of a risk-free bill is equal to the repayment value of the bill discounted at the risk-free interest rate. There is an inverse relation between the price of an asset and its expected return and risk. Modern portfolio theory has proposed models of asset pricing in *fully efficient markets*. All of these models attempt to determine what the expected return should be on an asset in an efficient market given the risk borne by the investor. Market equilibrium requires that the expected return be equal to the risk-free rate plus risk premiums to reward the various sources of risk borne by the investor. The major challenge is to determine the relevant measures of risk, as well as the size of the associated premiums.[1] The capital asset-pricing model (CAPM) is the first well-known model of market equilibrium. Because the reality of the international market is extremely complex, entailing a huge number of securities and sources of uncertainties, the objective of the model is to provide a simplified view of the world, capturing the major aspects of reality. This simplification is required to allow the formation of operational concepts.

The domestic (standard) CAPM is therefore built on fairly restrictive assumptions regarding investors' preferences. Many of these assumptions can be somewhat relaxed, leading to more complex (and less operational) versions. The assumptions of the standard CAPM are as follows:

- Investors care about risk and return. They are risk-averse and prefer less risk and more expected return.

- A consensus among all investors holds, and everyone agrees about the expected return and risk of all assets.

- Investors care about nominal returns in their domestic currency; for example, U.S. investors care about U.S. dollar returns.

- A risk-free interest rate exists, with unlimited borrowing or lending capacity at this rate.

- There are no transaction costs or taxes.

---

[1] See Elton and Gruber (1995), Reilly and Brown (2003), and Sharpe, Alexander, and Bailey (1999).

In the CAPM, all investors determine their demand for each asset by a mean–variance optimization (expected-utility maximization). They optimize a portfolio, P, made up of a set of assets, i. They do so by minimizing the variance of the portfolio, σ_p^2, for a selected level of expected return, $E(R_p)$. The selected level of expected return depends on the investor's risk aversion.

The demands from each investor are aggregated and set equal to the supply of assets, their market capitalization. The net supply of borrowing and lending (the risk-free asset) is assumed to be zero.

Two conclusions emerge from the domestic CAPM.

Separation Theorem   The *normative* conclusion of the domestic CAPM is that everyone should hold the same portfolio of risky assets, and the optimal combination of risky assets can be separated from the investor's preferences toward risk and return. This portfolio of risky assets must therefore be the *domestic market portfolio*, made up of all assets traded in proportion to their market capitalization. All investors should hold a combination of

- the risk-free asset, and

- the market portfolio.

Investors adjust their risk preference by putting some of their money in the risk-free asset (more risk-oriented investors will borrow, instead of lend, at the risk-free interest rate). In other words, investors need only two portfolios to design their investment strategies: a market index fund and the risk-free asset.

Risk-Pricing Relation   The *descriptive* conclusion of the CAPM is that the equilibrium expected return of an asset should be equal to the risk-free rate plus a risk premium proportional to the covariance of the asset return with the return on the market portfolio. The notation beta, β_i, is used to represent the ratio of the covariance between the asset and the market returns to the variance of the market return; it is the measure of the *sensitivity* of the asset return to market movements. It is sometimes called *market exposure*. The risk-pricing relation of the CAPM for asset i can be written as

$$E(R_i) = R_0 + \beta_i \times RP_m \tag{4.1}$$

where

$E(R_i)$ is the expected return on asset i

$E(R_m)$ is the expected return on the market portfolio

R_0 is the risk-free interest rate

β_i is the sensitivity of asset i to market movements (i.e., market exposure)

RP_m is the market risk premium equal to $E(R_m) - R_0$

Equation 4.1 describes the risk-pricing relation for all assets i. So RP_m and R_0 are constant, whereas $E(R_i)$ and β_i vary, depending on the asset i considered. There is a linear relation between the expected return on all assets and their sensitivity to market movements. This straight line is usually called the *security market line.*

Intuition   The type of risk that is relevant to pricing an asset is its sensitivity to market movements, β_i, not its total risk, σ_i^2. To understand the intuitive reason for this result, let's decompose the return on asset i into two components: the market influence and a specific component.

$$R_i = \alpha_i + \beta_i \times R_m + \varepsilon_i \tag{4.2}$$

where α_i and β_i are constants and R_i, R_m, and ε_i are stochastic, which means that they vary over time in a somewhat unpredictable fashion. The term ε_i is specific to asset i and independent of the market return R_m. This equation can easily be estimated as a simple regression of the asset return on the market return; β_i is the slope of the regression. Then the total risk of asset i can be decomposed into its *market* (or *systematic*) *risk* and its *specific* (or *residual*) *risk:*

$$\sigma_i^2 = \beta_i^2 \times \sigma_m^2 + \sigma_\varepsilon^2 \tag{4.3}$$

A similar relation applies to any portfolio P. The beta of a portfolio, β_p, is simply the weighted average of the betas of all securities included in the portfolio. As the number of securities included in the portfolio increases, its specific risk decreases. This is because the specific risks of individual securities tend to be independent of each other and tend to cancel each other out. In a well-diversified portfolio, specific risks vanish and the total risk of the portfolio reduces to its market risk σ_m^2:

$$\sigma_p^2 = \beta_p^2 \times \sigma_m^2 \tag{4.4}$$

So the only risk that counts for any investor holding a well-diversified portfolio is market risk.

The average beta of all securities is equal to one (the beta of the market portfolio). Securities with a high beta are more sensitive to the market environment and should provide a higher expected return than securities with a low beta given a positive market risk premium. Investors should care only about the beta of a security, not about its total risk. In an international context, the domestic CAPM implies that all domestic securities would be priced in line with their risk relative to the domestic market. Even if a company has extensive foreign operations, its international risks would not be taken into account specifically.

The simplifying assumptions of any theory, including the CAPM, are never verified exactly in the real world. The empirical question is whether the results are robust. A major problem mentioned by Roll (1977) is that the CAPM requires an exact identification of the market portfolio, including all investable assets. Hence, a proper CAPM should include all world assets in the market portfolio, but this would require a model that accounts for a multicurrency environment.

Asset Returns and Exchange Rate Movements

As we expand the investment universe to include international assets, the currency used to measure returns becomes an issue. For example, a Swiss investor holding the Swiss company Novartis measures value and return in Swiss francs. A U.S. investor would translate Novartis' value and return into dollars. Consider an investor who uses his domestic currency (DC) to measure return on some securities of a foreign country with a foreign currency (FC). The direct exchange rate between the two currencies is S units of DC for one FC unit. For example, we could have a U.S. investor holding shares of Novartis. The value of Novartis in domestic currency (dollar), V, is equal to its foreign currency (Swiss franc) value, V^{FC}, multiplied by the spot exchange rate, S, expressed in dollars per Swiss franc:[2]

$$V = V^{FC} \times S \tag{4.5}$$

Using Equation 4.5, a simple calculation of return from time 0 to time 1 shows that the DC (dollar) rate of return on an investment in Novartis, $R = (V_1 - V_0)/V_0$, is equal to the FC (Swiss franc) rate of return on Novartis, $R^{FC} = (V_1^{FC} - V_0^{FC})/V_0^{FC}$, plus the percentage exchange rate movement, $s = (S_1 - S_0)/S_0$, plus the cross-product of R^{FC} and s. This cross-product comes from the fact that the exchange rate movement applies to the original Swiss franc value of Novartis and also to the Swiss franc capital gain (loss), R^{FC}:

$$R = R^{FC} + s + (s \times R^{FC}) \tag{4.6}$$

The last term is of second order and assumed to be very small for short time periods, giving the first order approximation

$$R = R^{FC} + s \tag{4.7}$$

Alternatively, investors can hedge currency risk in the forward exchange market. The forward exchange rate quoted today for the period-end is F units of DC for 1 unit of FC. A 100 percent hedge would imply selling forward an amount V_1^{FC} of foreign currency. In turn, the investor knows with certainty at the start of the period what exchange rate will be used at the end of the period. So F replaces S_1, and the *hedged* return on the foreign share becomes

$$R = R^{FC} + (F - S_0)/S_0 \tag{4.8}$$

Note that the forward discount/premium $(F - S_0)/S_0$ is fully known at the start of the period.[3]

---

[2] We use the superscript FC when we measure return or value in the foreign currency, but no superscript when we measure return or value in the investor's domestic currency.

[3] Again, Equation 4.8 is a first-order approximation. We can hedge the start-of-period value V_0, but the exact end-of-period value is not known, so the unexpected capital gain (loss) cannot be hedged.

In terms of expected returns, the DC return on an *unhedged* investment is given by

$$E(R) = E(R^{FC}) + E(s) = E(R^{FC}) + [E(S_1) - S_0]/S_0$$

and the DC expected return on a *hedged* investment is given by

$$E(R) = E(R^{FC}) + (F - S_0)/S_0$$

The Domestic CAPM Extended to the International Context

Attempts have been made to justify the use of the domestic CAPM in an international context, in which investors in different countries use different currencies and have different consumption preferences.[4] Such a domestic CAPM extension would involve the domestic rate for the risk-free rate and the market capitalization weighted portfolio of all risky assets in the world for the market portfolio. This domestic CAPM extension can be justified only with the addition of two unreasonable assumptions:

- Investors throughout the world have identical consumption baskets.

- Real prices of consumption goods are identical in every country. In other words, purchasing power parity holds exactly at any point in time.

In this type of perfect world, exchange rates would simply mirror inflation differentials between two countries. Exchange rate uncertainty would be money illusion; it would not matter whether investors used euros or dollars. The exchange rate would be a pure translation-accounting device, and real FC risk would not exist. The real exchange rate is defined as the actual exchange rate multiplied by the ratio of the price levels of the consumption baskets in the two countries. Recall that with direct exchange rates, the relation between the real and nominal exchange rates is

$$X = S \times (P_{FC}/P_{DC}) \tag{4.9}$$

where

X is the real exchange rate   (direct quote DC/FC)

S is the nominal exchange rate   (direct quote DC/FC)

P_{FC} is the foreign country price level

P_{DC} is the domestic country price level

Real exchange rate movements are defined as movements in the exchange rates that are not explained by the inflation differential between the two countries. We can rewrite Equation 4.9 in terms of percentage changes over a time period (say a year):

$$x = s + I_{FC} - I_{DC} = s - (I_{DC} - I_{FC}) \tag{4.10}$$

---

[4] See Grauer, Litzenberger, and Stehle (1976).

where

x and s are the percentage movement in the real and nominal exchange rates
I_{DC} and I_{FC} are the inflation rates in the domestic and foreign countries.

If purchasing power parity holds (see Chapter 2), the real exchange rate is constant
($x = 0\%$), and the nominal exchange rate movement (DC/FC) is equal to the
inflation rate differential (domestic minus foreign inflation). For example, assume
that there is a one-month inflation rate of 1 percent in the USA (DC) and 0 percent
in Switzerland (FC). For the real exchange rate (dollar value of one Swiss franc) to
stay constant over the month, the franc has to appreciate by 1 percent against the
dollar ($x = 0\%, s = 1\%$). If the franc turned out to appreciate by 5 percent ($s = 5\%$)
during that month, then there would be a real appreciation of 4 percent of the
franc ($x = 4\%$). Any such real exchange rate movement would violate the
assumptions supporting the domestic CAPM extension. To summarize, in the
absence of real foreign currency risk, however, the extended CAPM would hold.

EXAMPLE 4.1   CONSTANT REAL EXCHANGE RATE

An investor in his home (domestic) country considers investing in the securities of a foreign country. The direct exchange rate between the two countries is
currently two domestic currency (DC) units for one foreign currency (FC)
unit. The price level of the typical consumption basket in domestic country relative to the price level of the typical consumption basket in foreign country is
also 2 to 1, which means that the real exchange rate is 1 to 1. A year later the inflation rate has been 3 percent in domestic country and 1 percent in foreign
country. The foreign currency has appreciated and the exchange rate is now
2.04. What is the new real exchange rate?

SOLUTION

The new real exchange rate is equal to the new nominal exchange rate adjusted by the ratio of the new price levels: $S \times (P_{FC}/P_{DC}) = X$, or $2.04 \times$
$(1.01/2.06) = 1$. The real exchange rate remains constant because the foreign
exchange appreciation of 2 percent is equal to the inflation differential between the two countries. As the real exchange rate is fixed, the currencies have
fully retained their purchasing power. The appreciation of the nominal exchange rate has no real impact.

Because the real exchange rate is constant in Example 4.1, there is no real foreign currency risk. Note that exchange rate uncertainty due to inflation is generally
very small, because inflation rates are highly predictable in the short run, especially
relative to equity returns. Predictable inflation rates mean predictable exchange
rates if purchasing power parity holds. Even with predictable inflation in the next
example, real foreign currency risk arises.

EXAMPLE 4.2   *FOREIGN CURRENCY RISK*

An investor in her home (domestic) country would like to expand her portfolio to include one-year bonds in foreign countries. The expected inflation rate in domestic country is 3 percent and the expected inflation rate in one of the foreign countries is 1 percent. Inflation rates are totally predictable over the next year. The exchange rate between the two countries is currently two DC units for one FC unit. The price level of the typical consumption basket in domestic country relative to the price level of the typical consumption basket in foreign country is also 2 to 1. The real exchange rate is 1 to 1. The one-year interest rate is 5 percent in domestic country and 3 percent in foreign country. The investor expects the real exchange rate to remain constant over time.

1. What are the expected exchange rate and the expected return on the foreign bond in domestic currency?

A year later the inflation rates have indeed been 3 percent in DC and 1 percent in FC. The foreign exchange rate has been very volatile over the year, and the foreign currency has depreciated with an end-of-the-year exchange rate of 1.80.

2. What is the real exchange rate at the end of the year and the *ex post* return on the foreign bond?

3. How would you qualify the risk-return characteristics of this investment?

SOLUTIONS

1. The future exchange rate should be equal to 2.04 DC units per FC unit if the real exchange rate remained constant, corresponding to a 2 percent appreciation of the foreign currency. The expected return on the foreign bond should therefore be approximately 5 percent, the sum of the foreign interest rate and of the currency appreciation, or more precisely $1.03 \times (2.04/2.00) - 1 = 5.06\%$.

2. Unfortunately, the *ex post* exchange rate is equal to 1.80 and the real exchange rate has become $S \times (P_{FC}/P_{DC}) = X$, or $1.80 \times (1.01/2.06) = 0.88$. The actual exchange rate movement is not equal to the inflation differential between the two countries, and there is a severe real depreciation of the foreign currency. The *ex post* return on the foreign bond is negative and equal to $1.03 \times (1.80/2.00) - 1 = -7.3\%$.

3. This investment had an expected return similar to that of the domestic risk-free rate, but it carried a lot of foreign currency risk. All of the foreign currency risk is real risk, as inflation rates here were predictable. Of course, this foreign currency risk could be hedged.

International CAPM

Deviations from purchasing power parity can be a major source of exchange rate variation, and consumption preferences can differ among countries. In these cases, the risk that real prices of consumption goods might not be identical in every country is called *real foreign currency risk, real exchange rate risk,* or *purchasing power risk.*

In real life, daily exchange rate movements are volatile and cannot be simply explained by an adjustment to daily inflation. Because inflation rates are very stable compared with asset returns and exchange rate movements, most if not all of the short-term variability in exchange rates can be referred to as real foreign currency risk. Investors will want to hedge against real foreign currency risk. An international CAPM (or ICAPM) can be developed under the assumption that nationals of a country care about returns and risks measured in their *domestic currency* (e.g., the U.S. dollar for U.S. investors and the Swiss franc for Swiss investors).[5] All the assumptions of the CAPM still hold. In particular, investors can freely borrow or lend in any currency. Using interest rate parity, investors can therefore freely replicate forward currency contracts to hedge foreign currency risk. It must be stressed that a dollar short-term bill that is risk-free for U.S. investors becomes risky for foreign investors who are concerned with returns in their domestic currency because of foreign currency risk.

Interest Rate Parity   It is important here to recall the concept of interest rate parity (IRP). Interest rate parity lies behind the ability to replicate forward currency contracts. In the world of foreign currency risk and the international CAPM, we will encounter foreign currency risk premiums. These premiums will be defined in reference to the movement in the exchange rate implied by parity conditions. In review of IRP, the direct spot exchange rate times one plus the domestic risk-free rate (investing domestically the amount of DC units required to purchase 1 FC unit) equals the direct forward exchange rate times one plus the foreign risk-free rate (exchanging for 1 FC unit now, investing in the foreign country, and repatriating later). Recall that IRP with direct exchange rates is given by

$$F = S(1 + r_{DC})/(1 + r_{FC}) \tag{4.11}$$

where

F is the direct forward rate

S is the direct spot rate

r_{DC} is the domestic risk-free rate

r_{FC} is the foreign risk-free rate

As a first-order linear approximation, the percentage forward premium on the exchange rate must equal the domestic risk-free rate minus the foreign risk-free rate, given as

$$(F - S)/S \cong r_{DC} - r_{FC} \tag{4.12}$$

---

[5] See Solnik (1974), Sercu (1980), and Adler and Dumas (1983).

EXAMPLE 4.3   *INTEREST RATE PARITY*

The one-year domestic country risk-free rate of return is 5 percent, and the one-year foreign country rate is 3 percent. The current exchange rate is 2 DC units for 1 FC unit. What is the current level of the forward exchange rate that is implied by these data?

SOLUTION

The investor could invest 2 DC units at the local risk-free rate of $r_{DC} = 5$ percent and would get $2 \times (1 + r_{DC})$ or 2.1 DC units in a year. Alternately, the investor could combine three operations:

- Exchange those 2 DC units at the spot exchange rate S for $2/S = 1$ FC unit.

- Invest this FC unit at the foreign country rate of $r_{FC} = 3$ percent and get 1.03 FC units in a year.

- Sell forward today the proceeds of $1 + r_{FC} = 1.03$ units of FC received in a year at the forward exchange rate of F.

In a year, the investor will therefore receive, with certainty, an amount of DC units equal to

$$(2/S) \times F \times (1 + r_{FC}) \text{ or } F \times 1.03$$

This combination should yield an identical result as the first alternative, as they are both riskless in domestic currency and involve the same investment. Otherwise, an arbitrage will take place. Hence, $F \times 1.03 = 2.1$ and $F = 2.039$, giving our answer that the forward exchange rate is 2.039 DC units per 1 FC unit.

The forward premium can be approximated as the interest rate differential, or a 2 percent premium on the foreign currency. In general, with direct exchange rates, we have

$$F = S \times \frac{1 + r_{DC}}{1 + r_{FC}}$$

Foreign Currency Risk Premiums   As a background for the international CAPM, it is also useful to recall the definition of a foreign currency risk premium. The risk premium on any investment is simply equal to its expected return in excess of the domestic risk-free rate:

$$RP = E(R) - R_0$$

Someone investing in a foreign currency will exchange the domestic currency (e.g. U.S. dollar) for the foreign currency (e.g. Swiss franc) and invest it at the foreign risk-free interest rate. So the expected domestic currency return on the foreign currency investment is equal to the foreign risk-free rate plus the expected percentage movement in the exchange rate. The foreign currency risk premium (SRP) is defined as the expected return on an investment minus the domestic currency risk-free rate. Thus, the foreign currency risk premium is equal to the expected movement in the exchange rate *minus* the interest rate differential (domestic risk-free rate minus foreign risk-free rate):

$$SRP = E[(S_1 - S_0)/S_0] - (r_{DC} - r_{FC}) = E(s) - (r_{DC} - r_{FC}) \qquad (4.13)$$

Substituting for $r_{DC} - r_{FC}$ using the interest rate parity approximation, the risk premium can also be expressed as the difference between the expected exchange rate and the forward rate, in percentage of the current exchange rate: $[E(S_1) - F]/S_0$.

EXAMPLE 4.4   FOREIGN CURRENCY RISK PREMIUM

The one-year risk-free interest rates are 5 percent in DC and 3 percent in FC. The exchange rate between the two countries is currently 2 DC units for 1 FC unit. The expected exchange rate appreciation of FC is 3 percent. What is the foreign currency risk premium?

SOLUTION

Because the interest differential is 2 percent (domestic minus foreign), interest rate parity implies that the forward exchange rate quotes at a premium of approximately 2 percent over the current exchange rate while the expected exchange rate appreciation of FC currency is 3 percent. Therefore, the foreign exchange risk premium is equal to +1 percent (3% − 2%). The expected DC return on the foreign investment is the 3 percent FC risk-free rate plus the 3 percent expected currency appreciation. It is also equal to the 5 percent domestic risk-free rate plus the 1 percent foreign currency risk premium. Note that the hedged investment return is the foreign risk-free rate plus the forward premium, a return of approximately 5 percent. Thus, the expected return on an unhedged foreign investment is 1 percent higher than if hedged against real foreign currency risk. However, hedging removes foreign currency risk.

In the international CAPM, as in the domestic CAPM, all investors determine their demand for each asset by a mean–variance optimization (expected-utility maximization), using their *domestic currency as base currency*. The demand from each investor is aggregated and set equal to the supply of assets, their market capitalization. The net supply of borrowing and lending (the risk-free asset) *in each currency* is assumed to be zero. Two conclusions emerge from this international CAPM.

Separation Theorem   The *normative* conclusion is that the optimal investment strategy for any investor is a combination of two portfolios: a risky portfolio common to all investors, and a personalized hedge portfolio used to reduce purchasing-power risks. If there is no uncertainty about future inflation rates in any country, the personalized hedge portfolio reduces to the national risk-free asset, and a simpler separation theorem can be demonstrated.[6] All investors should hold a combination of

---

[6] It has been observed repeatedly that the variability of inflation rates is very small compared with that of exchange rates or asset returns. Therefore, using nominal returns to measure returns is quite reasonable from a practical viewpoint.

- the risk-free asset in their own currency, and

- the world market portfolio optimally hedged against foreign currency risk.

This world market portfolio is the same for each investor and is the only portfolio of risky assets that should be held, partly hedged against foreign currency risk, by any investor. However, it must be stressed that the optimal currency hedge ratio need not be unitary and will generally be different for different assets and currencies.[7] The optimal hedge ratios depend on variables such as differences among countries in relative wealth, foreign investment position, and risk aversion. Unfortunately, these variables cannot be observed or inferred from market data. The international CAPM does not provide simple, clear-cut, operational conclusions about the optimal currency-hedge ratios.

Risk-Pricing Relation   The *descriptive* conclusion of the international CAPM is an international equilibrium risk-pricing relation that is more complex than in the domestic CAPM, in which the expected return on any asset is simply a function of its covariance with the domestic market portfolio. In the presence of exchange rate risk, additional risk premiums must be added to the risk-pricing relation to reflect the covariance of the asset with the various exchange rates (the currencies' betas). If there are $k + 1$ countries, there will be k additional currency risk premiums. Hence, the expected return on an asset depends on the market risk premium plus various foreign currency risk premiums:

$$E(R_i) = R_0 + \beta_{iw} \times RP_w + \gamma_{i1} \times SRP_1 + \gamma_{i2}SRP_2 + \ldots + \gamma_{ik}SRP_k \qquad (4.14)$$

where

R_0 is the domestic currency risk-free interest rate,

β_{iw} is the sensitivity of asset i domestic currency returns to market movements (market exposure),

RP_w is the world market risk premium equal to $E(R_w) - R_0$,

γ_{i1} to γ_{ik} are the currency exposures, the sensitivities of asset i domestic currency returns to the exchange rate on currencies 1 to k, and

SRP_1 to SRP_k are the foreign currency risk premiums on currencies 1 to k.

In Equation 4.14, all returns are measured in the investor's domestic currency.[8] Equation 4.14 indicates that the foreign investment return in domestic currency equals (a) the domestic risk-free rate, plus (b) a world market risk premium, times

---

[7] The hedge ratio is the proportion of the value of the portfolio (or component of a portfolio) that is currency hedged.

[8] As stressed by Adler and Dumas (1983), Equation 4.14 applies to returns measured in any base currency. For example, one could choose arbitrarily to measure all returns in U.S. dollars; then Equation 4.14 would apply for dollar returns, and R_0 would be the U.S. risk-free rate. Or one could choose to measure all returns in euros; then Equation 4.14 would apply for euro returns, and R_0 would be the euro risk-free rate.

the asset's sensitivity to the world market, plus (c) foreign currency risk premiums times the investment's currency exposures.

For an asset that is uncorrelated with the various exchange rates or that is optimally hedged against currency risk, the traditional CAPM still applies with its single-market risk premium given as a function of the covariance of the asset with the world market portfolio. So the traditional CAPM applies only to securities or portfolios perfectly hedged against currency risk.[9]

The ICAPM differs from a domestic CAPM in two respects. First, the relevant market risk is world (global) market risk, not domestic market risk. This is not surprising. Second, additional risk premiums are linked to an asset's sensitivity to currency movements. The different currency exposures of individual securities would be reflected in different expected returns.

Intuition on Foreign Currency Risk Premiums in the ICAPM   Again, the basic idea is that a risk premium should be earned for taking those risks that cannot be trivially eliminated by a naive diversification of the portfolio. Currency risks will remain in a diversified portfolio because currency movements affect all securities to some extent. One could argue that currency risks could be hedged with forward contracts and, therefore, portfolios need not bear this type of risk.[10] However, a similar argument could be developed for market risk, because futures contracts exist on stock indexes. The basic point is that the world market portfolio has to be held in aggregate, so world market risk has to be borne by investors. Similarly, because the world market portfolio is sensitive to currency risks, these currency risks have to be borne in aggregate.

A question often raised is: Why is there a non-zero currency risk premium? The theoretical answer is that investors from different countries have different net foreign investment positions and different risk aversions. In equilibrium, this will result in positive or negative currency risk premiums. Assume, for example, that Americans invest a lot abroad so that their net foreign investment position is positive while that of foreigners is negative. In other words, Americans have more wealth invested abroad than foreigners have invested in America. Also assume that Americans are more risk-averse than foreigners. Then Americans have a larger demand to hedge their foreign currency position (sell foreign currency forward) than foreigners have to hedge their dollar position (sell dollar forward). This im-

---

[9] Note, however, that optimal currency hedging does not mean 100 percent hedging. This is because the value of a foreign asset could be affected by an exchange rate movement. This is detailed in the section on currency exposures. The gammas (γ_{ik}) are sometimes called regression hedge ratios because they can be estimated from a multiple regression of the asset return on the various exchange rate movements.

[10] It is sometimes argued that on a forward or futures currency contract there is one seller for each buyer so that the expected return should be zero. This is a flawed argument. If it were true, it would apply to any forward contract. For example, there is one seller for every buyer of an S&P 500 futures contract. Still, the buyer is expected to receive the U.S. equity risk premium, while the seller is expected to lose it.

EXAMPLE 4.5   *PAYING/RECEIVING THE FOREIGN CURRENCY RISK PREMIUM*

Suppose Americans are big net investors in a hypothetical country, Arland, and the Arlanders invest little abroad. The Americans have a vast net foreign wealth and are worried about currency risk; hence, they have a strong demand for hedging Arlandian francs into American dollars. The Arlanders have little demand for hedging American dollars, because they do not invest much in America. The Americans are long in Arlandian stocks, and they can hedge their exposure to the Arlandian franc by selling forward Arlandian francs (buy dollars forward). Arlandians and other speculators buy Arlandian francs forward (sell dollars forward), induced by a positive risk premium on the franc. The one-year risk-free interest rates are 5 percent in America and 3 percent in Arland. The exchange rate between the two countries is currently two dollars for one franc. The expected exchange rate appreciation of the Arlandian franc is 3 percent. The expected return on Arlandian stocks is 6 percent in francs.

1. What is the expected return on Arlandian stocks in dollars if there is no currency hedging?

2. What is the expected return on Arlandian stocks in dollars with full currency hedging?

3. What is the foreign currency risk premium on the Arlandian franc and who pays/receives it?

SOLUTION

1. The expected return on Arlandian stocks in dollars is equal to the expected return in francs, 6 percent, plus the expected currency appreciation of 3 percent, a total expected return of 9 percent.

2. With currency hedging, the forward premium is equal to the interest rate differential of 2 percent. Hence, the expected return on Arlandian stocks, hedged against currency risk is 8 percent (6 percent plus 2 percent). The expected return is less than for an unhedged investment, but the risk is also less.

3. There is a 1 percent foreign currency risk premium, that is, the difference between the expected currency appreciation of the franc and the forward premium on the franc. This risk premium is "paid" by Americans and "received" by Arlandians. In equilibrium, Americans are willing to pay this currency risk premium to remove currency risks on their net foreign position in Arlandian stocks. Arlandians (and other speculators) are willing to provide that hedge because of the expected return due to the currency risk premium.

balance will create, in equilibrium, a currency risk premium on the foreign currency. Americans will have to pay a currency risk premium on their currency hedge, while foreigners will receive a currency risk premium. This is because the selling pressure on the forward exchange rate will reduce it relative to the expected spot exchange rate. While Americans sell foreign currency forward for hedging motives, foreigners will buy forward to accommodate American needs if induced by a positive expected return, the currency risk premium. Using the dollar as the base currency, the expected exchange rate (in $ per FC units) for the foreign currency will be larger than the forward rate, and this difference as a percentage of the current exchange rate is a risk premium by definition.

Individual assets have different exposures to currencies, and these exposures affect their equilibrium pricing. Foreign currency risk premiums arise from the risk exposures of the average investor. If the average investor is sensitive to the real foreign currency risk of a particular country, he will bid up the price of those stocks that have a low or negative currency exposure (γ). Those are the stocks that are negatively correlated with real foreign currency risk. He is actually paying to hedge and thus accepts a lower expected return as a trade-off for the benefit of reducing real foreign currency risk.

EXAMPLE 4.6   INTERNATIONAL ASSET PRICING

You are a European investor considering investing in a foreign country. The world market risk premium is estimated at 5 percent, the foreign currency offers a 1 percent risk premium, and the current risk-free rates are equal to 5 percent in euros and 3 percent in FC units. In other words, you expect the FC unit to appreciate against the euro by an amount equal to the interest rate differential (which is also equal to the expected inflation differential) plus the foreign currency risk premium, or a total of 3 percent. Your broker provides you with some statistics:

	Stock A	Stock B	Stock C	Stock D
World beta	1.0	1.0	1.2	1.4
Currency exposure (γ)	1.0	0.0	0.5	−0.5

1. According to the International CAPM, what should be the expected returns on the four stocks, in euros?

2. Stocks A and B have the same world beta, but different expected returns. Give an intuitive explanation for this difference.

SOLUTIONS

1. With one foreign currency and the euro as the base currency, the asset pricing equation of the International CAPM simplifies to

$$E(R_i) = R_0 + \beta_{iw} \times RP_w + \gamma_i \times SRP_{FC}$$

where all returns are measured in euros, RP_w is the risk premium on the world index, and SRP_{FC} is the risk premium on the foreign currency unit, assumed to be the only other currency. If the euro is used as the base currency, then all β's and γ's should be measured using euro returns. Using the exposures (or "sensitivities") given, we get the theoretical expected returns given in the following table. For example, the expected return of Stock A is equal to the euro risk-free rate of 5 percent, plus a world equity risk premium of 5 percent ($1 \times 5\%$), plus a foreign currency risk premium of 1 percent ($1 \times 1\%$).

	Stock A	Stock B	Stock C	Stock D
Theoretical expected return (€)	11.0%	10.0%	11.5%	11.5%

2. Stock A has an expected return of 11 percent, compared with 10 percent for Stock B. The difference is explained by their different exposures to currency movements. The euro value of Stock B is insensitive to unexpected movements in the FC/euro exchange rate. As far as foreign currency risk is concerned, Stock B is less risky than Stock A (currency risk exposure of +1), so its expected return should be different from that of Stock A. Because the currency risk premium is equal to +1 percent, the difference in expected return between Stock A and Stock B should be 1 percent.

Market Imperfections and Segmentation

The international asset pricing relation described applies to all securities only in an integrated world capital market. Financial markets are segmented if securities that have the same risk characteristics, but are listed in two different markets, have different expected returns.

In many countries, various types of institutional investors face severe legal constraints on their international investments. This is often the case with public pension funds or insurance companies that have liabilities denominated in their national currencies and are required to invest in assets denominated in the same currency. The psychological aspects are also important. Investors are much more familiar with their local financial market than with foreign markets. Hence, they feel somewhat uneasy about investing their money in a remote country or an unfamiliar currency.

If currency hedging is not available, either physically or legally, the simple pricing relation breaks down. Furthermore, official restrictions, fear of expropriation, discriminatory taxes, and higher investment costs push domestic investors to underinvest in foreign assets compared with the world market portfolio. The argument for international comparative advantage in imperfect markets might be firm-specific; investors might prefer foreign companies that are not found in other parts of the world (e.g., Club Méditérranée) and avoid companies that are deemed sensitive to national interests (e.g., armament companies) or are located in countries in which foreign interests might be expropriated on short notice.

If all these impediments to international investments are of significant magnitude, buying the market is not a reasonable first-cut strategy. Although it certainly does not mean that investors should avoid foreign investments, the additional costs and risks of foreign investments may cause market segmentation and affect asset pricing.

International asset pricing under various forms of market segmentation, including differential taxes, has been studied, and more complex asset pricing relations have been found.[11] The risk premium has a more complex form than in the traditional international capital asset pricing model. It generally depends on the form of market imperfection, the relative wealth of investors, and parameters of their utility function. However, most forms of market imperfections and constraints to foreign investments cannot be easily incorporated in an equilibrium asset pricing framework. Hence, their precise influence on the resulting optimal portfolio holdings cannot be easily modeled.

Practical Implications

A Global Approach to Equilibrium Pricing

The ICAPM gives useful insights on asset pricing in an efficient world capital market and in the absence of privileged information. It tells us what should be the return on assets if we do not formulate specific forecasts for them; therefore, the ICAPM offers default values from which to start. It also proposes a simplified structure to global asset management—in other words, a benchmark or passive investment strategy. It basically tells us "buy the market" optimally hedged against currency risk. The conclusion to buy the market is not truly original, but the recommendations in terms of currency hedging are. We will now study the practical implications of this optimal hedging conclusion and then turn to potential usage of the international asset pricing relation.

More on Currency Hedging   The ICAPM concludes that everyone should hold the same risky portfolio, with the same amount of currency hedging. Hence, French and U.S. investors should use the same hedge ratio for their Japanese investments.[12]

Black (1989, 1990) uses this result, derived by Solnik (1974), Sercu (1980), and Adler and Dumas (1983), to suggest the existence of a "universal hedging formula"

---

[11]See Black (1974), Subrahmanyam (1975), Stapleton and Subrahmanyam (1977), Stulz (1981), Errunza and Losq (1985, 1989), Eun and Janakiramanan (1986), and Hietla (1989).

[12]It appears that a Japanese investor should also hedge her domestic assets in the same proportion, but hedging yen into yen is totally neutral.

that every investor should use, independent of nationality and fairly easily estimated. Indeed, everyone hedges the world market portfolio with forward currency contracts, in the same way, because everyone holds the same risky portfolio. The aggregate hedge ratio need not be unity, and Black provides a historical estimate around 0.7. Unfortunately, this universal hedging formula gives only the aggregate dollar amount used to hedge as a proportion of the total dollar value of the world market portfolio of equity. Optimal hedge ratios vary across markets and assets. We also know that these individual currency hedge ratios are complex, because they depend on such parameters as the covariance structure of assets and currency, the risk aversion of investors from various countries, and investors' relative wealth. Because individual preferences and relative wealth are not observable, the optimal currency hedging policy cannot be deduced from market-observable data. Holding the market portfolio is a practical passive recommendation because we observe market capitalizations and can derive some proxy for the "market." This is not the case for the optimal passive currency hedging policy. To summarize, the ICAPM does not provide simple, clear-cut, operational conclusions about the optimal currency hedge ratios. It is not likely that any reasonable theory could ever produce simple hedging rules.

Equally important, this nice result of a unique aggregate hedge ratio breaks down if, for theoretical or practical purposes, investors do not hold the world market portfolio. For all kinds of reasons, investors tend to underweight foreign assets relative to the world market weights. If a U.S. pension fund puts its 10 percent of foreign assets in a rest-of-the-world index fund, there is no theoretical basis to suggest using the same hedge ratio that should be used if the fund were invested 70 percent in rest-of-the-world assets. Intuitively the risk diversification benefits brought to the U.S. portfolio by the foreign assets are different in the two cases. A foreign currency risk component may actually lower the total risk of a portfolio with only a small investment in foreign assets (say, 5 percent) because it provides some diversification of the U.S. monetary policy risk. For example, Jorion (1989) conducted an empirical study of optimal asset allocations for a U.S. investor. He concluded that the importance of currency hedging depends on the proportion of foreign assets held in the portfolio, and states that "this question of hedging may not matter so much if the amounts invested in the foreign assets are small, in which case overall portfolio volatility is not appreciably influenced by hedging. Hedging therefore brings no particular benefits in terms of risk reduction . . ." (p. 54). The difference between the risk diversification benefits from small versus large foreign allocations should be even more pronounced if the portfolio of foreign assets is actively managed with country weights that differ markedly from the rest-of-the-world market index.

Hence, currency hedging becomes an individual empirical decision—a function of the portfolio to be hedged—and risk preferences matter. Optimal currency hedging requires the estimation of the currency risk exposure of each asset (as we discuss later).

In the absence of simple, widely accepted recommendations for a benchmark, simple hedging policy rules with a fixed hedge ratio are commonly adopted. The international benchmark typically used is either fully hedged or unhedged. But several plan sponsors, especially in Canada, have a 50 percent-hedged benchmark.

Expected Returns   Equation 4.14 describes equilibrium asset pricing in fully efficient global markets. It quantifies the risk premiums for each asset. To use this equation, one needs to estimate two types of variables:

- The market and currency exposures of each asset;

- The risk premiums on the (global) market and on currencies.

Estimating a market risk premium is a usual task in asset management. Everyone would agree that it should be positive over the long run. Historical estimates give us an order of magnitude for the future that can be refined by some conceptual forward-looking reasoning.

The task is more difficult for foreign currency risk premiums, which could be positive or negative and unstable over time. For example, a positive foreign currency risk premium on the dollar against the euro implies a negative foreign currency risk premium for the euro against the dollar. Furthermore, the demand for currency hedging is likely to change over time, affecting the risk premiums. For example, individuals and corporations of one country could progressively become large international investors, or conversely reduce their holdings in another country because of political risk or other considerations. These developments would change the magnitude and even the signs of foreign currency risk premiums. Although investors can formulate expectations about currencies over short horizons (say a year), it is harder to do so over the very long run. Hence, asset managers often assume that the risk premiums of all currencies are zero over the very long run, and use equilibrium pricing relations that only include a market risk premium. A zero long-term foreign currency risk premium assumes that the best predictor of exchange rates is the interest rate differential.[13] This leads to a linear relation between the expected return on assets and the market exposure (β), the *global market line*.

Applications of the ICAPM depend on the investment horizon. An assessment of the *long-term* risk premiums according to the ICAPM is usually only undertaken for asset classes or national markets, not for individual securities, because securities within the same asset class tend to be priced relative to each other and richer risk models are developed for each asset class. The ICAPM is used to anchor expected returns as default values.

An investor who believes that markets are not fully efficient could deviate from the global market line. An illustration of this is Exhibit 4.1 where GIM (Global Investable Market) stands for the world market portfolio of all investable assets. (In the exhibit, risk premium is the expected return in excess of the risk-free return.) Deviations can be explained by several factors:

- The corresponding market or asset class could be felt to be undervalued.

- Its lack of liquidity could justify an additional risk premium.

---

[13]It is also consistent with an assumption that exchange rates revert to fundamentals in the long run and that foreign currency risk is much smaller in the long run than in the short run, thereby justifying no risk premium.

EXHIBIT 4.1
_____

Example of Relation between Beta and Risk Premiums of Various Asset Classes

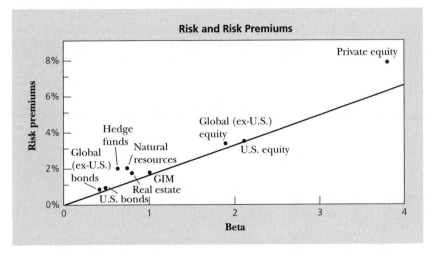

Source: B. Singer, R. Staub, and K. Terhaar, "Asset Allocation: The Alternatives Approach," *Quarterly Focus*, UBS Asset Management, June 30, 2001.

- Foreign currency risk premiums could be added that translate into a deviation from the global market line.

The determination of the risk premiums will drive the strategic global asset allocation. In the shorter run, the portfolio composition could be revised to reflect changes in the risk premiums and the risk coefficients. This is often called a *tactical revision* or *tactical asset allocation*. (see Chapter 13). In tactical asset allocation, a good appreciation of the risk elements becomes quite important.

Estimating Currency Exposures

The relation between asset returns and exchange rate movements is central to international asset pricing. To benefit from the insights of the ICAPM and knowledge of exchange rate determination, it now seems appropriate to investigate the link between security prices and exchange rates, in theory and in practice. We need to understand what determines the currency exposures of securities, the γ's of Equation 4.14. From a practical standpoint, any investor should be concerned about the reaction of the domestic capital market to international monetary disturbances, such as exchange rate movements. The international investor measures total return as the sum of returns on the assets, in local currencies, plus any currency movements: The investor bears both market and foreign currency risks. Setting aside considerations of portfolio diversification, the reaction of asset prices to fluctuations in currency values is a matter of prime concern for international investors. A major question is whether stocks and bonds provide a hedge against exchange rate movements. We want to get a better economic intuition for the sign and magnitude of the currency exposure γ mentioned in Equation 4.14.

Defining Currency Exposure The currency used to measure the currency exposure of an asset is of great importance. An investor cares about the currency exposure measured in his domestic currency. The *currency exposure* of an asset can be defined as the sensitivity of the asset return, measured in the investor's domestic currency, to a movement in the exchange rate. Just like market β's, currency γ's can be estimated by a regression, namely a time-series regression of domestic currency asset returns on foreign exchange rate movements.

It is also possible to refer to the *local-currency (FC) exposure* of a non-domestic asset asset, γ^{FC}, which is defined as the sensitivity of the asset return, measured in the asset's local currency (the foreign currency) to a movement in the exchange rate. The relation between the two exposures follows from the relation between DC returns and FC returns given by Equation 4.7:

$$R = R^{FC} + s$$

The currency exposure of the currency itself is equal to 1. So, the currency exposure of a foreign asset is equal to its local-currency exposure plus one:

$$\gamma = \gamma^{FC} + 1. \tag{4.15}$$

Perhaps an illustration will contribute to a better understanding of the concept of currency exposure. Consider a U.S. investor holding shares of the Swiss company Novartis, a leading pharmaceutical firm. We shall study various scenarios of the correlation[14] of the price of Novartis stock with the U.S. dollar/Swiss franc exchange rate. Assume a sudden depreciation of the Swiss franc (FC), giving a 1.25 percent loss on the Swiss currency for the U.S. investor (one Swiss franc loses 1.25 percent of its dollar value). The price of Novartis shares may react in different fashions to this exchange rate movement:

- A *zero* correlation between local-currency stock returns and exchange rate movements would mean no systematic reaction to exchange rate adjustments. The immediate rate of return on Novartis shares would tend to be zero for Swiss investors (the Swiss franc price of Novartis does not move) and -1.25 percent for U.S. investors because of the currency translation into U.S. dollars: The dollar value of one share of Novartis drops by 1.25 percent. The local-currency exposure of the Swiss franc price of Novartis is zero ($\gamma^{FC} = 0$), and the investor has a currency exposure of $\gamma = 1$: When the Swiss franc loses 1.25 percent, the investor tends to lose the same amount of 1.25 percent on Novartis in domestic (in this case U.S. dollar) currency.

- A *negative* correlation would mean that the local stock price benefits from a depreciation of the local currency. In other words, the loss on the Swiss cur-

---

[14]In this text, we use the convention that "negative" means a correlation in which the local stock price goes up when the local currency depreciates. Also, in this illustration, we assume that the volatility of the stock's local currency return and the volatility of the exchange rate are equal.

rency would be partly offset by a Swiss franc capital gain on the stock price. A perfect currency hedge would be attained if the Swiss franc price of Novartis moved up 1.25 percent. Then the return to a U.S. investor would be zero, because the final dollar price of Novartis would be unchanged. In that case, the local-currency exposure of the Swiss franc price of Novartis is $\gamma^{FC} = -1$, and the investor has a currency exposure of $\gamma = 0$: When the Swiss franc loses 1.25 percent, the investor tends to have a zero return on Novartis in domestic currency.

- A *positive* correlation would mean that the local stock price drops in reaction to a depreciation of the local currency. With a perfect positive correlation, for example, Novartis might drop by 1.25 percent with news of the franc depreciation (or go up, following a franc appreciation). The dollar return to a U.S. investor would be -2.5 percent. In this case, foreign asset prices would compound the currency effect and might be considered a bad hedge against currency movement. Here, the currency exposure of the Swiss franc price of Novartis is $\gamma^{FC} = 1$, and the investor has a currency exposure of $\gamma = 2$; when the Swiss franc loses 1.25 percent, the investor tends to lose twice that much on Novartis in domestic currency.

The local-currency exposure simply describes the sensitivity of the stock price (measured in local currency) to a change in the value of the local currency. A statistical estimate of the currency exposure can be obtained by a regression between Swiss franc (FC) returns on Novartis and the percentage movements in the \$/SFr exchange rate. If we limit ourselves to one period, the local-currency exposure is simply equal to the return on the Swiss franc price of Novartis during this period divided by percentage movements in the \$/SFr exchange rate:

$$\gamma^{FC} = \frac{R^{FC}}{s}$$

where R^{FC} is the return on the foreign investment in local (foreign) currency and s is the percentage change in the direct exchange rate, $s = (S_1 - S_0)/S_0$.

The currency exposure is equal to

$$\gamma = \frac{R}{s} = \frac{R^{FC} + s}{s} = \gamma^{FC} + 1$$

For example, if the Swiss franc loses 1.25 percent against the dollar (a drop in the dollar value of one Swiss franc, or a negative s) and the Swiss franc price of Novartis goes up by 1.25 percent, the local-currency exposure is $\gamma^{FC} = 1.25/(-1.25) = -1$. In this case, the currency exposure is $\gamma = 0$. If the stock price only goes up by 0.625 percent, the local-currency exposure is $\gamma^{FC} = 0.625/(-1.25) = -0.5$. Hence, the currency exposure is $\gamma = 0.5$.

We now discuss what causes the local-currency exposure to be positive or negative.

Currency Exposure of Individual Companies   To the extent that purchasing power parity holds—that is, if exchange rates exactly adjust to inflation differentials—exchange rate movements simply mirror relative inflation and do not add another dimension to the analysis. They have no specific influence on the economy or equity prices beyond that of domestic inflation. But virtually all studies indicate that purchasing power parity does not hold, especially since the advent of floating exchange rates. Short-term shocks to the exchange rate, and hence foreign exchange rate volatility, cannot be explained by an existing inflation differential. This means that real exchange rate movements (deviations from purchasing power parity) are the relevant variable to study, and the actual effect of real exchange rate movements is large compared with inflation-induced variations. As such, real currency movements may have a significant influence on domestic economies and corporations, and hence, on stock markets.

It might be useful to look at an *individual firm* to examine the influence of a *real exchange appreciation.* Consider a strong real appreciation of the U.S. dollar relative to all currencies, including the Swiss franc, as was the case from 1984 to 1985. Typically, a U.S. tourist had great incentive to spend a skiing vacation in the Swiss Alps, because the dollar purchased much more in terms of accommodations and food. Conversely, Novartis drugs manufactured in Switzerland became highly price-competitive when exported to the United States. The 50 percent *real* appreciation of the U.S. dollar in the early 1980s meant that Novartis could lower its U.S. selling price without reducing its Swiss franc profit margin. The story is only partially true, because the real dollar appreciation raises the cost of some imported goods.

The effect of this real dollar appreciation is the opposite for Merck & Co., an American pharmaceutical company; it gives them incentives for establishing plants in countries such as Switzerland, where they can benefit from lower production costs. Note, however, that the importance of the exchange rate for an individual firm depends on the currency structure of its exports, imports, and financing. For example, a French firm importing U.S. computers financed in U.S. dollars is badly hurt by the real dollar appreciation. An interesting analysis of the influence of a currency movement on the value of the firm is provided in Heckman (1985, 1986).

Another argument that would suggest that the local stock market should react favorably to a depreciation of its currency is based on the rapid internationalization of many corporations. Many corporations are now heavy foreign investors. They have operations abroad and directly own foreign companies. As such, these firms should be valued as global portfolios. For example, Novartis derives over 95 percent of its revenue outside of Switzerland. A Swiss franc depreciation should not greatly influence the "real" value of Novartis. If the Swiss franc depreciates, the Swiss franc price of Novartis should increase. Novartis can be seen as a diversified portfolio of assets in foreign currencies. As those currencies appreciate against the franc, the foreign assets should be worth more Swiss francs.

Currency exposures of individual companies could be estimated historically by regressing the company's stock returns on market returns and currency returns.[15] This estimate can be refined by a detailed analysis of the activities and financing of the company, the geographical distribution of its sales and investments, the currency origin of its profits and costs, the currency structure of its debt, and so on.

---

[15]See Diermeier and Solnik (2001).

EXAMPLE 4.7   INDIVIDUAL COMPANY RISK EXPOSURE

Two Canadian firms are in quite different businesses:

- *Enga* manufactures engine parts in Canada for export, and prices are set and paid in U.S. dollars. Production costs are mostly domestic (the labor force) and considered to follow the Canadian inflation rate.

- *Klub* imports computers from the United States and sells them in Canada to compete with Canadian products.

The market values both at a price–earnings ratio of 10, so that the stock price in Canadian currency is equal to 10 times next year's expected earnings. What will happen to the earnings and valuations of the two companies if there is a sudden *real* depreciation of the Canadian dollar? What is likely to happen in the long-run? Would your findings be the same if the Canadian dollar depreciation only matched the Canadian–U.S. inflation differential?

SOLUTION

Enga's earnings and stock price, measured in Canadian dollars, should increase because its revenues come from the United States and are worth more in Canadian dollars at the same time that its costs are in Canadian dollars. Enga's revenues in real terms are rising, while its costs are not. Klub faces the opposite situation. Its costs in real terms are rising, while its revenues are not. In the long run, Enga will meet competition from U.S. competitors who will be motivated to build plants in Canada. Klub will be motivated to find Canadian sources for its computers. If the Canadian dollar depreciation only matched the Canadian–U.S. interest rate differential, then the findings would be different. The effects would only be nominal and not real. Real revenues and costs would remain the same.

EXAMPLE 4.8   OIL AND MINING RISK EXPOSURE

In 2001, the South African rand depreciated. South African oil and mining companies sell in dollars but have costs in rand. According to these currency sensitivity factors and given that this was a real depreciation, what should have happened to South African oil and mining company revenues and valuations as a result?

SOLUTION

According to an *Economist* (May 18, 2002, p. 71) article about the Johannesburg Stock Exchange, "for the past few months the local index has roared. The rand's slump last year helped exporters, and gave a shine to oil and mining companies, which sell in dollars but have costs in rand."

Currency Exposure of National Economies and Equity Markets   In the *macroeconomic* approach, it is widely recognized that economic activity is a major determinant of stock market returns, so the influence of exchange rate movements on domestic economic activity may explain the relation between exchange rate movements and stock returns. Various economic theories have been proposed to explain the influence of real exchange rate movements on domestic economies. The traditional approach can be sketched as follows: A decline in a currency's real exchange rate tends to improve competitiveness, whereas the concomitant deterioration in terms of trade increases the cost of imports, which creates additional domestic inflation and reduces real income and, hence, domestic demand and production. The initial reduction in real gross national product (GNP) caused by a deterioration in the terms of trade should eventually be offset by improved international competitiveness and export demand until purchasing power parity is restored.

A simple example may help to illustrate this phenomenon. Let's assume a sudden 10 percent depreciation of the Swiss franc. Let's also assume that the Swiss trade balance (Swiss exports minus imports) is in deficit. The immediate effect of a 10 percent depreciation of the franc is to make current imports more expensive in terms of francs—if all imports were denominated in foreign currency, the cost of imports would immediately increase by 10 percent. This increase in cost has two major effects. First, the Swiss trade balance deficit measured in francs widens. Although the franc value of exports increases somewhat because part of the export sales are contracted in foreign currency, the percentage of exports denominated in foreign currency is usually smaller than that of imports. Second, the rise in imported goods prices leads to an increase in the domestic price index and imports inflation. Both of these effects are bad for the Swiss economy, and, in a sense, the real wealth is reduced. However, this currency depreciation makes Swiss firms more competitive; they can lower the price of their products by 10 percent in terms of foreign currency without lowering their Swiss franc income. In the long run, this should help increase foreign sales and stimulate the Swiss economy. The reaction of the deficit to the depreciation is often called the J-curve effect because of the J-shape of the trade balance curve as a function of time (Exhibit 4.2). However, if the economy is slow to improve, this chain of events threatens to become a vicious cycle: The immediate economic activity and trade balance worsens, leading to a further currency depreciation, which in turn may worsen domestic economic conditions, and so on.

The stock market, which immediately discounts the overall influence of an exchange rate movement on the economy, may be positively or negatively affected, depending on whether the short-term or long-term effect dominates. In late 1985, the U.S. dollar was at its highest point, well above its purchasing power parity value. The Group of Five, leading industrialized nations (United States, Japan, United Kingdom, Germany, and France), met at the Plaza Hotel in New York and made the surprising announcement that they would coordinate their intervention policies to lower the value of the dollar on the foreign exchange market. The reaction to this news was immediate; the dollar fell by 5 percent, and the U.S. stock market rose by

<u>EXHIBIT 4.2</u>
The J-Curve Effect

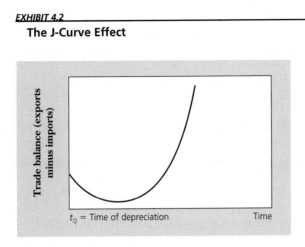

<u>EXHIBIT 4.2</u>
The J-Curve Effect

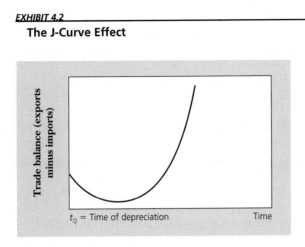

more than 1 percent, anticipating that the dollar depreciation would have an overall positive effect on the U.S. economy. In many cases, however, a currency depreciation is not followed by this type of stock market reaction.

A money-demand model has also been proposed.[16] In this model, real growth in the domestic economy leads to increased demand for the domestic currency through a traditional money-demand equation. This increase in currency demand induces a rise in the relative value of the domestic currency. Because domestic stock prices are strongly influenced by real growth, this model justifies a positive association between real stock returns and domestic currency appreciation. Although the traditional trade approach suggests that a real exchange rate appreciation tends to reduce the competitiveness of the domestic economy and, therefore, to reduce domestic activity, the money-demand approach leads to the opposite effect: An increase in domestic economic growth leads to a real currency appreciation.

Finally, it is important to stress that the situation of emerging markets is somewhat different from that of developed countries. The economies of emerging countries are usually not very diversified. They rely heavily on foreign investment. A drop in the value of an emerging country's currency is often a signal that the country is running into severe problems. The fate of the currency and of the stock markets is closely linked to the country's economic and political situation. Their correlation is strongly positive. Hence, foreign investors are doubly affected by a drop in the value of the emerging currency: Investors lose not only in the currency translation to their domestic currency, but also in the drop in the local currency value of the emerging stock market.

---

[16]See, for example, Lucas (1982).

Currency Exposure of Bonds   Because bond prices are directly linked to long-term interest rates, the story for bonds is told by the relation between changes in long-term interest rates and exchange rates. Bond returns are negative when bond yields rise.

There are at least two competing theories about the correlation between bond returns and currency movements:

- It is often stated that a rise in the national real interest rate leads to the appreciation of the home currency, because of international investment flows attracted by the higher real interest rate. This would induce a negative local-currency exposure for bonds (bond prices go down, because of the rise in yields, when the local currency goes up, and vice versa). However, it is important to be careful in differentiating between an interest rate movement caused by a rise in the real rate of interest, as mentioned, and an interest rate movement caused by changes in inflationary expectations (the Fisher effect). Increased inflationary fears in a foreign country could lead to a simultaneous rise in local interest rates (hence, a drop in bond prices) and a drop in the currency. So, investors from abroad will lose doubly.

- Some governments adopt monetary policies that contain foreign exchange rate targets. They attempt to stabilize their home currency's exchange rate. A fall in the domestic currency induces the monetary authorities to raise real interest rates to defend the currency, and a strong domestic currency induces the authorities to ease the interest rate policy. Branson (1984) calls this exchange rate policy reaction a "leaning-against-the-wind" policy, whereby foreign monetary authorities use interest rates to stabilize the exchange rate of their home currency. This policy would induce a positive local-currency exposure for domestic bonds.

Economic Versus Accounting Currency Exposure   This chapter focuses on economic exposure—the impact of a currency movement on the total return on a foreign investment. Accounting-wise investors often separate the return in local currency and the return on the currency itself. For example, most portfolio accounting systems first value an asset in its local currency and then translate it at the proper exchange rate. So, the local-currency asset return and the currency return will appear as two distinct elements. From an accounting standpoint, currency risk will only be measured by looking at the currency return. For example, consider a U.S. investor holding a foreign stock with little dollar currency exposure, so that the local-currency price tends to offset any depreciation of the foreign currency ($\gamma = 0$). From an economic standpoint, there is little foreign currency exposure: If the foreign currency depreciates by 10 percent, the local-currency stock price will rise by 10 percent, offsetting the depreciation. But from an accounting standpoint, the two returns are treated separately so that a 10 percent currency loss will be reported. If an investor only focuses on this accounting or translation measure of currency risk, then all foreign assets are fully exposed to currency risk.

Tests of the ICAPM

A brief look at investors' portfolio holdings would suggest that a major conclusion of the ICAPM is violated often. Portfolios are strongly biased toward domestic investments. U.S. investors devote almost all of their equity portfolios to U.S. securities, although the theory would have them hold the world market portfolio. French and Poterba (1991), Cooper and Kaplanis (1994), and Tesar and Werner (1995) present evidence of a home preference in portfolio investment and fail to find satisfactory explanations for such a large bias. This does not mean that financial markets are necessarily segmented and that the theory does not provide useful and robust implications regarding the pricing of securities. International capital flows, which are indeed large, could be sufficient to make the markets efficient. The international capital market would be integrated if all securities followed the same international risk-pricing relation outlined here.

Few tests of international market integration and asset pricing models have been performed so far. One problem has been the limited amount of long-term historical data available on international capital markets. Other problems are methodological and affect the testing of any CAPM, whether domestic or international. They have to do with the difficulty of exactly identifying the market portfolio and with the time-varying nature of the expected return and risk measures. The major problem is that any CAPM deals with expected returns, and those are simply not observable. Using past realized returns to proxy expected returns can be very misleading.

A test of the ICAPM investigates whether cross-sectional differences in expected returns among securities are explained by the various risk exposures, β and γ's, as described in Equation 4.14. Empirical researchers have explored several questions:

- Is currency risk priced?

- Is domestic market risk priced beyond global market risk (segmentation)?

- Are other firms' attributes priced beyond global market risk?

Is Currency Risk Priced?   In *unconditional* tests, researchers assume that expected returns and risk measures are constant over time. This approach will not be detailed here. In *conditional* tests, expected returns and risk measures are allowed to vary in some specified way. Dumas and Solnik (1995) modeled the time variation in expected return and risk. They found that significant currency risk premiums exist, and they rejected a model that would exclude currency risk factors. De Santis and Gérard (1998) found strong support for a specification of the ICAPM that includes both market risk and currency risk. They stress the importance of a conditional approach allowing variation in market and currency risk premiums. In terms of asset management, this conclusion would encourage tactical revisions in the global asset allocation.

Segmentation   Other researchers focus on market segmentation, but exclude currency risk from their analysis. The approach is to test an alternative model, including both global risk factors and country-specific factors. If the ICAPM holds, those country-specific factors should not be priced. Bekaert and Harvey (1995) allowed conditionally expected returns in any country to be affected by their exposure to the world market portfolio (beta) *and* by the variance of the country's returns. In a perfectly integrated market, only the beta counts. In segmented markets, the country's variance is a more relevant measure of risk. Bekaert and Harvey looked at emerging markets and allowed the degree of market integration to change over time. They found evidence that many emerging markets were segmented in their early years but have become more integrated to the global market. However, several markets show signs of segmentation, which is not too surprising for most of the emerging markets. De Santis and Gérard (1997) focused on the major equity markets and introduced as country-specific factors the country's variance plus a constant to accommodate other forms of segmentation, such as differences in taxation. They concluded: "To summarize, we find that expected excess returns are positively related to their conditional covariance with a world-wide portfolio, whereas country specific risk is not priced" (p. 1901). These studies, however, suffer from the deficiency that currency factors are not introduced in the test.

Other Attributes   In a domestic or international CAPM, attributes of a firm that are not linked to the risk factors outlined here should not be priced. In a domestic framework, Fama and French (1992, 1996) find that some attributes of a firm provide a much better explanation of the differences in return among U.S. firms than their beta. For example, "value" stocks (as measured by ratios such as book-to-market value or earnings-to-price) outperform "growth" stocks. This leads to a rejection of the CAPM. Numerous criticisms have been leveled at this conclusion (see Kothari, Shanken, and Sloan, 1995). Fama and French (1998) extend their analysis to international data. They find that value stocks outperform growth stocks in 12 out of 13 major markets. Value stocks are more likely to go bankrupt than are growth stocks, and they interpret their results in terms of financial distress. They claim that financial distress is a risk that is not well captured by the standard ICAPM, and that it should be added as a factor to explain stock pricing. On the other hand, Ferson and Harvey (1998) find that the book-to-market value ratio of a firm is strongly related to its world market risk exposure. A fruitful direction of research is to refine the analysis of risk by looking at the underlying economic risk factors, rather than by summarizing all the risk information in a single beta.

Current empirical evidence is still fragmentary, and the results are likely to evolve as the world financial markets are increasingly liberalized and transaction costs are driven down. A summary of current research tends to support the conclusion that assets are priced in an integrated global financial market. The evidence is sufficiently strong to justify using the ICAPM as an anchor in structuring global portfolios. However, the evidence can be somewhat different for emerging and smaller markets, in which constraints are still serious.

Summary

- International markets are integrated if they are efficient in the sense that securities with the same risk characteristics have the same expected return wherever in the world they are traded.

- International markets are segmented if they are inefficient in the sense that securities with the same risk characteristics sell at different exchange-rate-adjusted prices in different countries, thus violating the law of one price.

- Six impediments to international capital mobility are psychological barriers, legal restrictions, transaction costs, discriminatory taxation, political risks, and foreign exchange risks.

- International integration requires only a sufficient flow of capital to make the world market efficient and to eliminate relative mispricing among countries. Investment and borrowing actions of private and institutional investors, major corporations, and governments quickly take advantage of relative mispricing, thereby making the markets more efficient.

- The expected return on an unhedged foreign investment is

$$E(R) = E(R^{FC}) + E(s)$$

where $E(R)$ is the expected domestic-currency return on the investment, $E(R^{FC})$ is the expected foreign investment return, and $E(s)$ is the expected percentage currency movement.

- The expected return on a hedged foreign investment is

$$E(R) = E(R^{FC}) + (F - S)/S$$

where $E(R)$ is the expected domestic-currency return on the hedged investment, $E(R^{FC})$ is the expected foreign investment return, F is the forward rate, and S is the spot exchange rate. Both F and S are direct quotes.

- The extended CAPM is the domestic CAPM with the domestic rate for the risk-free rate and the market capitalization weighted portfolio of all risky assets in the world for the market portfolio.

- The domestic CAPM extension can be justified only with the usual domestic CAPM assumptions and the addition of two assumptions: Investors throughout the world have identical consumption baskets, and real prices of consumption goods are identical in every country (purchasing power parity holds exactly at any point in time).

- With direct rates, the real exchange rate is the nominal exchange rate times the ratio of the foreign price level to the domestic price level: $X = S \times (P_{FC}/P_{DC})$.

- The real exchange rate changes in a period if the foreign exchange appreciation during the period does not equal the inflation differential between the two countries during the period.

- The expected foreign currency appreciation or depreciation should be approximately equal to the interest rate differential: $E(s) = r_{DC} - r_{FC}$, where s is the percentage change in the price of foreign currency (direct exchange rate).

- A foreign currency risk premium (*SRP*) is equal to the expected movement in the exchange rate *minus* the interest rate differential (domestic risk-free rate minus foreign risk-free rate): $SRP = E[(S_1 - S_0)/S_0] - (r_{DC} - r_{FC})$.

- A foreign currency risk premium is equal to the difference between the expected exchange rate and the forward rate, in percentage of the current exchange rate: $SRP = [E(S_1) - F]/S_0$.

- The risk-pricing expression for the international CAPM (ICAPM) is that the expected return on an asset i is the sum of the market risk premium plus various currency risk premiums:

$$E(R_i) = R_0 + \beta_{iw} \times RP_w + \gamma_{i1} \times SRP_1 + \gamma_{i2} \times SRP_2 + \ldots + \gamma_{ik} \times SRP_k$$

  where β is the world market exposure of the asset and the γ's are the currency exposures, sensitivities of the asset returns to the various exchange rates.

- With one foreign currency, for example, the asset pricing equation of the ICAPM simplifies to

$$E(R_i) = R_0 + \beta_{iw} \times RP_w + \gamma_i \times SRP_{FC}$$

- The international asset pricing relation applies to all securities only in an integrated world capital market with currency hedging available.

- Most forms of market imperfections and constraints to foreign investments cannot be easily incorporated in an equilibrium asset pricing framework.

- A local-currency exposure is the sensitivity of a stock price (measured in local currency) to a change in the value of the local currency. A zero correlation between stock returns and exchange rate movements would mean no systematic reaction to exchange rate adjustments. A negative correlation would mean that the local stock price would benefit from a depreciation of the local currency. A positive correlation would mean that the local stock price would drop in reaction to a depreciation of the local currency.

- For an investor, the currency exposure of a foreign investment is the sensitivity of the stock price (measured in the investor's domestic currency) to a change in the value of the foreign currency. It is equal to one plus the local-currency exposure of the asset.

- The exchange rate exposure for an individual firm depends on the currency structure of its exports, imports, and financing. Generally, for example, an importer is hurt by foreign currency appreciation and an exporter helped. If exchange rate movements only reflect inflation rate differentials, they have no specific influence on the economy or equity prices beyond that of domestic inflation. Real exchange rate movements, however, have an effect on equity prices, depending on currency exposures.

- In the macroeconomic approach, it is widely recognized that economic activity is a major determinant of stock market returns, so the influence of exchange rate movements on domestic economic activity may explain the relation between exchange rate movements and stock returns. On the bond side, a rise in the national real interest rate leads to an appreciation of the domestic currency, because of international investment flows attracted by the higher real interest rate. Domestic bond price declines would accompany domestic currency appreciation.

- The two models of how real exchange rate changes affect domestic economic activity give opposite conclusions. The traditional approach can be sketched as follows: A decline in a currency's real exchange rate tends to improve competitiveness, whereas the concomitant deterioration in terms of trade increases the cost of imports, which creates additional domestic inflation and reduces real income and, hence, domestic demand and production. The initial reduction in real GNP caused by a deterioration in the terms of trade should eventually be offset by improved international competitiveness and export demand until purchasing power parity is restored. In the money-demand model, on the other hand, real growth in the domestic economy leads to increased demand for the domestic currency through a traditional money-demand equation. This increase in currency demand induces a rise in the relative value of the domestic currency. Because domestic stock prices are strongly influenced by real growth, this model justifies a positive association between real stock returns and domestic currency appreciation.

Problems

1. Consider an asset that has a beta of 1.25. If the risk-free rate is 3.25 percent and the market risk premium is 5.5 percent, calculate the expected return on the asset.

2. An asset has a beta of 0.9. The variance of returns on a market index, σ_m^2, is 90. If the variance of returns for the asset is 120, what proportion of the asset's total risk is systematic, and what proportion is residual risk?

3. A portfolio consists of three assets. Asset 1 has a beta of 0.85, Asset 2 has a beta of 1.3, and Asset 3 has a beta of 0.9. Asset 1 has an allocation of 50 percent, while Assets 2 and 3 each have an allocation of 25 percent. The variance of returns on a market index, σ_m^2, is 120. Calculate the variance of portfolio returns, assuming that the specific risk of the portfolio is negligible.

4. A Canadian investor is considering the purchase of U.K. securities. The current exchange rate is Can$1.46 per pound. Assume that the price level of a typical consumption basket in Canada is 1.46 times the price level of a typical consumption basket in the United Kingdom.
   a. Calculate the real exchange rate.
   b. One year later, price levels in Canada have risen 2 percent, while price levels in the United Kingdom have risen 4 percent. The new exchange rate is Can$1.4308 per pound. What is the new real exchange rate?
   c. Did the Canadian investor experience a change in the real exchange rate?

5. Consider a U.S. investor who wishes to purchase U.K. securities. The current exchange rate is $1.80 per pound. Assume that the price level of a typical consumption basket in the United States is three times the price level of a typical consumption basket in the United Kingdom.
   a. Calculate the real exchange rate.
   b. One year later, price levels in the United States have risen 5 percent, while price levels in the United Kingdom have risen 2 percent. The new exchange rate is $1.854 per pound. What is the new real exchange rate?
   c. Did the U.S. investor experience a change in the real exchange rate?

6. An investor based in the United States wishes to invest in Swiss bonds with a maturity of one year. Suppose that the ratio of the price levels of a typical consumption basket in the United States versus Switzerland is 1 to 1.5 and the current exchange rate is $0.62 per Swiss franc. The one-year interest rate is 2 percent in the United States and 4.5 percent in Switzerland. Assume that inflation rates are fully predictable, and expected inflation over the next year is 1.5 percent in the United States and 4 percent in Switzerland.
   a. Assuming that real exchange rates remain constant, calculate the real exchange rate, the expected exchange rate in one year, and the expected return over one year on the Swiss bond in U.S. dollar terms.
   b. Now assume that the inflation rate over the one-year period has been 1.5 percent in the United States and 4 percent in Switzerland. Further, assume that the exchange rate at the end of one year is $0.63 per Swiss franc. Calculate the real exchange rate at the end of one year. What is the return on the Swiss bond investment now? Is the return on the Swiss bond the same as in Part (a)? Explain.

7. A portfolio manager based in the United Kingdom is planning to invest in U.S. bonds with a maturity of one year. Assume that the ratio of the price levels of a typical consumption basket in the United Kingdom versus the United States is 1.2 to 1. The current exchange rate is £0.69 per dollar. The one-year interest rate is 1.76 percent in the United States and 4.13 percent in the United Kingdom. Assume that inflation rates are fully predictable, and expected inflation over the next year is 1.5 percent in the United States and 3.75 percent in the United Kingdom.
   a. Assuming that real exchange rates remain constant, calculate the real exchange rate, the expected exchange rate in one year, and the expected return over one year on the U.S. bonds in pounds.
   b. Now assume that the inflation rate over the one-year period has been 1.5 percent in the United States and 3.75 percent in the United Kingdom. Further, assume that the exchange rate at the end of one year is £0.67 per dollar. Calculate the real exchange rate at the end of one year. What is the return on the U.S. bond investment now? Is the return on the U.S. bond the same as in Part A? Explain.

8. Assume that the Eurozone risk-free interest rate on bonds with one year to maturity is 4.78 percent and the U.S. risk-free interest rate on one-year bonds is 3.15 percent. The current exchange rate is $0.90 per euro. Assume that the United States is the domestic country.
   a. Calculate the one-year forward exchange rate.
   b. Is the euro trading at forward premium or discount?
   c. Is your answer to Part (b) consistent with interest rate parity? Explain.

9. Take the case of a U.S. firm that wishes to invest some funds (U.S. dollars) for a period of one year. The choice is between investing in a U.S. bond with one year to maturity,

paying an interest rate of 2.75 percent, and a U.K. bond with one year to maturity, paying an interest rate of 4.25 percent. The current exchange rate is $1.46 per pound, and the one-year forward exchange rate is $1.25 per pound. Should the U.S. firm invest in U.S. bonds or in U.K. bonds?

10. Consider a German firm that wishes to invest euro funds for a period of one year. The firm has a choice of investing in a euro bond with one year to maturity, paying an interest rate of 3.35 percent, and a U.S. dollar bond with one year to maturity, paying an interest rate of 2.25 percent. The current exchange rate is €1.12 per U.S. dollar, and the one-year forward exchange rate is €1.25 per U.S dollar. Should the German firm invest in euro bonds or in U.S. dollar bonds?

11. The interest rate on one-year risk-free bonds is 4.25 percent in the United States and 3.75 percent in Switzerland. The current exchange rate is $0.65 per Swiss franc. Suppose that you are a U.S. investor and you expect the Swiss franc to appreciate by 2.75 percent over the next year.
   a. Calculate the foreign currency risk premium.
   b. Calculate the domestic currency return on the foreign bond, assuming that your currency appreciation expectations are met.

12. Suppose that you are an investor based in Switzerland, and you expect the U.S. dollar to depreciate by 2.75 percent over the next year. The interest rate on one-year risk-free bonds is 5.25 percent in the United States and 2.75 percent in Switzerland. The current exchange rate is SFr1.62 per U.S. dollar.
   a. Calculate the foreign currency risk premium from the Swiss investor's viewpoint.
   b. Calculate the return on the U.S bond from the Swiss investor's viewpoint, assuming that the Swiss investor's expectations are met.

13. Assume you are a U.S. investor who is considering investments in the French (Stocks A and B) and Swiss (Stocks C and D) stock markets. The world market risk premium is 6 percent. The currency risk premium on the Swiss franc is 1.25 percent, and the currency risk premium on the euro is 2 percent. The interest rate on one-year risk-free bonds is 3.75 percent in the United States. In addition, you are provided with the following information:

Stock	A	B	C	D
Country	France	France	Switzerland	Switzerland
β_w	1	0.90	1	1.5
γ_ϵ	1	0.80	−0.25	−1.0
γ_{SFr}	−0.25	0.75	1.0	−0.5

   a. Calculate the expected return for each of the stocks. The U.S. dollar is the base currency.
   b. Explain the differences in the expected returns of the four stocks in terms of β_w, γ_ϵ, and γ_{SFr}.

14. a. List reasons that an international extension of the CAPM is problematic.
    b. In an international extension of the CAPM, why would the optimal portfolio differ from the world market portfolio, as suggested by the traditional CAPM, even if the markets are fully efficient?

15. You are a U.S. investor who is considering investments in the Australian stock market, but you worry about currency risk. You run a regression of the returns on the Australian

stock index (in A$) on movements in the Australian dollar exchange rate (U.S.$ per A$), and find a slope of -0.5.

a. What is your currency exposure if you invest in a diversified portfolio of Australian stocks?

b. You invest 10 million U.S. dollars in the diversified portfolio, but fear that the Australian dollar will depreciate by 10 percent relative to the U.S. dollar. How much do you expect to lose because of the currency movement?

16. Consider two French firms listed on the Paris stock market:
   - *Mega* manufactures engine parts in France for export, and the prices are set and paid in dollars. Production costs are mostly domestic (the labor force) and considered to follow the French inflation rate.
   - *Club* imports computers from the United States and sells them in France to compete with French products.

   a. What will happen to the earnings of the two companies in the short run if there is a sudden depreciation of the euro (say, 20 percent)?

   b. What is the difference between the short-run effect and the long-run adjustments?

   c. Would your findings be the same if the euro depreciation were only a progressive adjustment to the United States–Europe inflation differential that reflected the higher European inflation rate?

17. Consider two Australian firms listed on the Sydney stock exchange:
   - *Company I*. Its stock return shows a consistent negative correlation with the euro per A$ exchaange rate. The stock price of Company I (in Australian dollars) tends to go up when the Australian dollar depreciates relative to the euro.
   - *Company II*. Its stock return shows a consistent positive correlation with the euro per A$ exchange rate. The stock price of Company II (in Australian dollars) tends to go down when the Australian dollar depreciates relative to the euro.

   A European investor wishes to buy Australian stocks but is unsure about whether to invest in Company I or Company II. She is afraid of a depreciation of the Australian dollar. Which of the two investments would offer some protection against a weakening Australian dollar?

18. KoreaCo, a South Korean company, is a worldwide leader in widget (a hypothetical manufactured product) production. Europe is KoreaCo's single largest market.

   Assumptions:
   - KoreaCo's production capacity is located in South Korea and all of its costs are incurred in Korean won.
   - Additions to capacity require a lead time of more than one year.
   - KoreaCo borrows only in South Korean won.

   a. Describe the effect of a short-term appreciation of the won versus the euro on the profitability of KoreaCo's sales in Europe. Address *only* the effects on KoreaCo unit sales and profit margins.

   b. KoreaCo expects the appreciation of the won versus the euro to continue for the long term and is considering two business strategies:
      - Continue to operate production plants solely in South Korea.
      - Shift production equal to current European sales to Europe.
        Explain the effect of each of these strategies on the long-run profitability of KoreaCo's European sales.

19. In 2002, a strong depreciation of the U.S. dollar is expected by some observers over the next two years. Are nondollar bonds a good investment for U.S. investors? Why or why not?

20. As a money manager based in the Netherlands, you are asked to advise a domestic client about investing in foreign bonds to diversify domestic inflation risk. You fear that the strong economic recovery observed in the Netherlands and elsewhere in the Eurozone—but not yet in the Far East and North America—will feed inflationary expectations in Europe. Try to build a "marketing" case for international bond diversification.

Solutions

1. According to the CAPM, expected return = $3.25 + 1.25(5.5) = 10.125\%$.

2. The total risk of the asset is 120 percent. The systematic risk = $0.9^2(90) = 72.9$. Thus, the portion of total risk that can be attributed to market risk is $72.9/120 = 60.75\%$. The balance, 39.25 percent, can be attributed to asset-specific risk.

3. The portfolio beta, $\beta_p = 0.5(0.85) + 0.25(1.3) + 0.25(0.90) = 0.975$.
   Total portfolio risk, $\sigma_p^2 = 0.975^2(120) = 114.1$. So, $\sigma_p = 10.7\%$.

4. a. Current real exchange rate = Can$1.46(1/1.46) = Can$1 per pound.
   b. Real exchange rate one year later = Can$1.4308(1.04/1.4892) = Can$1 per pound.
   c. The Canadian investor did not experience a change in the real exchange rate. While inflation in the United Kingdom is greater than inflation in Canada by two percentage points, the pound has depreciated relative to the Canadian dollar by 2 percent. Thus, the real exchange rate is unchanged.

5. a. Current real exchange rate = $1.80(1/3) = $0.60 per pound.
   b. Real exchange rate one year later = $1.854(1.02/3.15) = $0.60 per pound.
   c. The U.S. investor did not experience a change in the real exchange rate. This is because while inflation in the United Kingdom is less than inflation in the United States by three percentage points, the pound has appreciated relative to the dollar by 3 percent. Thus, the real exchange rate is unchanged.

6. a. The current real exchange rate = $0.62(1.5/1) = $0.93 per Swiss franc.
   The inflation differential between the United States and Switzerland is 2.5%. That is, U.S. inflation minus Swiss inflation is −2.5%. Thus, for real exchange rates to remain the same, the Swiss franc would have to depreciate by 2.5 percent.
   The expected exchange rate = $0.62(1 − 0.025) = $0.6045 per Swiss franc.
   The real exchange rate would then be = $0.6045(1.56/1.015) = $0.93 per Swiss franc.
   The expected return on the Swiss bond = $(1 + 0.045)(1 − 0.025) − 1 = 0.0189$, or 1.9 percent.
   b. If the exchange rate at the end of one year is $0.63 per Swiss franc, the Swiss franc has appreciated by 1.61 percent.
   The real exchange rate is = $0.63(1.56/1.015) = $0.9683 per Swiss franc.
   The return on the Swiss bond = $(1 + 0.045)(1 + 0.0161) − 1 = 0.0618$, or 6.18 percent.
   The return on the Swiss bond is higher than in Part A because the Swiss franc has appreciated by 1.61%, whereas in Part A, the Swiss Franc depreciated by 2.5 percent.

7. a. The current real exchange rate = 0.69(1/1.2) = £0.575 per U.S. dollar.

   The inflation differential between the United Kingdom and the United States is 2.25 percent. That is, U.K. inflation minus U.S. inflation is 2.25 percent. Thus, for real exchange rates to remain the same, the U.S. dollar would have to appreciate by 2.25 percent.

   The expected exchange rate = 0.69(1 + 0.0225) = £0.7055 per U.S. dollar.

   The real exchange rate would then be = 0.7055(1.015/1.245) = £0.575 per U.S. dollar.

   The expected return on the U.S. bond = (1 + 0.0176)(1 + 0.0225) − 1 = 0.0405, or 4.05 percent. This is close to the U.K. one-year interest rate of 4.13 percent.

   b. If the exchange rate at the end of one year is £0.67 per U.S. dollar, the U.S. dollar has depreciated by approximately 2.9 percent.

   The real exchange rate is = 0.67(1.015/1.245) = £0.5462 per dollar.

   The return on the U.S. bond is = (1 + 0.0176)(1 − 0.029) − 1 = −0.0119, or −1.19 percent.

   The return on the U.S. bond is lower than in Part A because the U.S. dollar has depreciated by 2.9 percent, whereas in Part (a), the U.S dollar appreciated by 2.25 percent.

8. a. The forward rate = 0.90(1.0315/1.0478) = $0.886 per euro.

   b. The euro is trading at a forward discount = (0.886 − 0.90)/0.90 = −0.0156, or −1.56 percent.

   c. The interest rate differential between the domestic interest rate and the foreign interest rate (U.S minus Eurozone) is 3.15 − 4.78 = −1.63%. This is in line with the forward discount on the foreign currency (euro) of 1.56 percent. This result is consistent with interest rate parity.

9. If the U.S. firm invests funds (say, $1) in one-year U.S. bonds, at the end of one year it will have 1(1 + 0.0275) = $1.0275.

   Alternatively the U.S. firm could convert $1 into £(1/1.46) = £0.6849. This amount would be invested in one-year U.K. bonds, and at the end of one year it will have 0.6849(1 + 0.0425) = £0.714.

   This can be converted back to U.S. dollars at the forward exchange rate = 0.714(1.25) = $0.8925.

   The firm is better off investing domestically in U.S. bonds.

10. If the German firm invests funds (say, €1) in one-year euro bonds, at the end of one year it will have 1(1 + 0.0335) = €1.0335.

    Alternatively the German firm could convert €1 into $(1/1.12) = $0.8929. This amount would be invested in one-year U.S. bonds, and at the end of one year it will have 0.8929(1 + 0.0225) = $0.913.

    This can be converted back to euros = 0.913(1.25) = €1.1412.

    The firm is better off investing in U.S. bonds.

11. a. The interest rate differential (U.S. minus Swiss) = 0.0425 − 0.0375 = 0.005, or 0.50 percent. This implies that the Swiss Franc trades at a forward premium of 0.50 percent. That is, the forward exchange rate is quoted at a premium of 0.50 percent over the spot exchange rate of $0.65 per Swiss franc.

    The foreign currency risk premium = 0.0275 − 0.005 = 0.0225, or 2.25 percent.

    b. The domestic currency (U.S.$) return on the foreign bond is 6.5%. This can be calculated in one of two ways:

- Domestic risk-free rate + Foreign currency risk premium = 4.25% + 2.25% = 6.5%.
- Foreign risk-free rate + Expected exchange rate movement = 3.75% + 2.75% = 6.5%.

12. a. The interest rate differential (Swiss minus U.S.) = 0.0275 − 0.0525 = −0.025, or −2.50 percent. This implies that the U.S. dollar trades at a forward discount of 2.50 percent. That is, the forward exchange rate is quoted at a discount of 2.50 percent over the spot exchange rate, SFr 1.62 per dollar.

    The foreign currency risk premium = −0.0275 − (−0.025) = −0.0025 = −0.25%.

   b. The domestic currency (Swiss franc) return on the foreign (U.S.) bond is 2.5 percent. This can be calculated in one of two ways:
   - Domestic risk-free rate + Foreign currency risk premium = 2.75% + (−0.25%) = 2.5%.
   - Foreign risk-free rate + Expected exchange rate movement = 5.25% + (−2.75%) = 2.5%.

13. a. The expected return for each of the stocks is calculated using the following version of the ICAPM:

$$E(R_i) = R_0 + \beta_{iw}\,(RP_w) + \gamma_{i\euro}\,(SRP_\euro) + \gamma_{iSF}\,(SRP_{SF})$$

Thus, the expected returns for Stocks A, B, C, and D are

$E(R_A) = 0.0375 + 1(0.06) + 1(0.02) - 0.25(0.0125) = 0.1144$, or 11.44%
$E(R_B) = 0.0375 + 0.90(0.06) + 0.80(0.02) + 0.75(0.0125) = 0.1169$, or 11.69%
$E(R_C) = 0.0375 + 1(0.06) - 0.25(0.02) + 1(0.0125) = 0.1050$, or 10.50%
$E(R_D) = 0.0375 + 1.5(0.06) - 1(0.02) - 0.50(0.0125) = 0.1013$, or 10.13%

   b. Stock B has the lowest world beta but the highest expected return, whereas Stock D has the highest world beta and the lowest expected return. The reason lies with differences in currency exposures of the stocks. The negative currency exposures of Stock D result in a lower expected return. Stock B, on the other hand, has positive currency exposures, which increase expected returns in this example.

14. a. The derivation of the traditional CAPM relies on assumptions about investors' expectations and market perfection.

    In the international context, tax differentials, high transaction costs, regulations, capital, and exchange controls are obvious market imperfections. Their magnitude is greater than in a domestic context and is more likely to create problems in the model.

    Because of deviations from purchasing power parity (real exchange rate movements), investors from different countries have a different measure of the real return of a given asset. For example, if the euro depreciates by 20 percent, a U.S. investor may obtain a negative (real dollar) return on his Club Med investment, while a French investor could obtain a positive (real euro) return on Club Med.

   b. Even if markets were fully efficient and integrated, deviations from purchasing power parity alone could explain why, in theory, optimal portfolios differ from the world market portfolio.

15. a. From a U.S. dollar viewpoint, the currency exposure of a diversified Australian portfolio (similar to the index) is equal to +0.5. The regression coefficient $\gamma^{A\$}$ measures

the sensitivity of the Australian dollar value of the portfolio to changes in the value of the Australian dollar—this coefficient is -0.50. Thus, the currency exposure of the Australian portfolio is $= \gamma = 1 + \gamma^{A\$} = 1 - 0.5 = 0.5$.

  b. Because the currency exposure is 0.5, if the Australian dollar declined by 10 percent against the U.S. dollar, you can expect to lose approximately 5 percent of U.S.$10 million, i.e.; $500,000.

16. a. For *Mega:* Assume a sudden and unanticipated depreciation of the euro. Production costs are unaffected in the short run; they stay constant in euros. Product prices stay constant in dollars and therefore increase by 20 percent in euros. The earnings are vastly increased in the short run.
     For *Club:* The short-run effect is opposite to that of *Mega.* The import costs rise while the product prices must stay constant to match French competition.
  b. For *Mega:* In the longer run, this unanticipated depreciation of the euro could have several effects. *Mega* could use it to lower the dollar price of its products and increase its sales (and earnings) as it becomes more competitive. On the other hand, this euro depreciation could "import" inflation into Europe. The price of imported goods and inflation rise. Wages consequently adjust. In the long run, *Mega*'s production costs in euros will rise.
     For *Club:* In the long run, the importer will still be in a difficult position. However, French and European competitors may seize this opportunity to raise the price of their products.
  c. For *Mega:* Assume now that the euro depreciation is simply an adjustment to the existing inflation differential (high inflation rate in Europe). This purchasing power parity movement has no real effect on *Mega.* It will simply make the euro price of its products rise at the same rate as the inflated production costs.
     For *Club:* Again, the effect should be neutral as on *Mega.*

17. Because you want an asset whose price will go up if the Australian dollar depreciates, you would choose Company I. However, this is only one factor of the investment choice. For example, it may be more interesting to buy the most attractive assets (even if they exhibit a positive correlation with the euro per A$ exchange rate) and hedge the currency risk using currency futures.

18. a. In general, the short-term appreciation of the won versus the euro would make South Korean goods more expensive to European buyers and would make European goods cheaper for South Korean citizens.
     The likely effect of a short-term appreciation of the won versus the euro on KoreaCo's unit sales in Europe would be a decline in KoreaCo's sales resulting from the increased cost of the imported KoreaCo widgets relative to domestic alternatives (or other imports). European widgets or other imports would become more attractive, and purchases would shift to them.
     A decline in unit sales as a result of the appreciation, and an assumption that variable costs are not subjected to change, implies a higher cost per unit *because of* the lower number of units over which the fixed costs can be spread. Profit margins would contract.
     In the short run, KoreaCo could absorb the currency impact by lowering the won price in an effort to maintain the euro price of widgets and unit sales/market share in Europe. The lower price would cause a decline in profit margins on European sales unless KoreaCo could stabilize margins through manipulation of such variable costs as labor and materials.

b. The traditional trade approach suggests that real exchange rate appreciation tends to reduce the competitiveness of a domestic economy and, therefore, reduce domestic activity over time. Worsening economic conditions resulting from reduced competitiveness would be expected to lead to a depreciation of the currency at some point, restoring competitiveness and foreign sales.

In the long run, industries from countries with overvalued currencies will make direct investments in countries with undervalued currencies. In time, such activity will contribute to restoration of purchasing power parity.

- If KoreaCo elects to maintain all production facilities in South Korea based on its expectation of a long-term currency appreciation, such a strategy would be expected to have a *negative effect* on its competitive position in the European market, and thus on the long-run profitability of its European sales. Such a decision would result in downward pressure on unit European sales. Because all costs are variable in the long run, KoreaCo may be able to adjust capacity utilization and other factors of production to maintain margins in the face of declining sales.

- KoreaCo's shift of production facilities to Europe would be expected to have a beneficial or positive effect on its long-run competitive position in Europe. The proposed strategy would lower average total costs on KoreaCo's European sales as it establishes production facilities in the cheaper currency. KoreaCo's lower cost structure and improved competitiveness would be expected to have a positive effect on the profitability of KoreaCo's European sales.

19. The dollar value of the foreign bonds would rise because the foreign currency appreciates relative to the dollar. Furthermore, many countries practice a "leaning against the wind" exchange rate policy. Foreign bond yields are likely to drop to stabilize the exchange rate against the dollar. The local currency price of foreign bonds tends to go up when the dollar depreciates relative to the local currency. Hence, the dollar value of the foreign bonds would rise both because the foreign currency appreciates relative to the dollar and because the foreign bond prices rise.

20. The following are some arguments in favor of international bond diversification:
- A rise in European inflationary anticipations is bad for European bond prices (increasing nominal yields), but should not affect foreign bond prices. Because foreign economies are lagging the European economy, inflationary pressures are not yet felt abroad.
- Increased European inflation would lead to a depreciation of the euro, which would be good for the euro return of assets denominated in foreign currencies.
- An inflation-induced depreciation of the euro (appreciation of the foreign currency) is good for investing in foreign bond markets, if foreign governments lower their interest rates to avoid too strong an appreciation of their domestic currency ("leaning against the wind").

Bibliography

Adler, M., and Dumas, B. "International Portfolio Choice and Corporation Finance: A Synthesis," *Journal of Finance,* June 1983.

Bekaert, G., and Harvey, C. R. "Time-Varying World Market Integration," *Journal of Finance,* 50(2), June 1995, pp. 403–444.

Black, F. "International Capital Market Equilibrium with Investment Barriers," *Journal of Financial Economics,* December 1974.

———. "Universal Hedging: Optimizing Currency Risk and Reward in International Equity Portfolios," *Financial Analysts Journal,* July/August 1989.

———. "Equilibrium Exchange Rate Hedging," *Journal of Finance,* July 1990.

Branson, W. H. "Exchange Rate Policy after a Decade of Floating," in J. Bilson and R. Marston, eds., *Exchange Rate Theory and Practice,* Chicago: University of Chicago Press, 1984.

Cooper, I., and Kaplanis, E. "Home Bias in Equity Portfolios, Inflation Hedging and International Capital Market Equilibrium," *Review of Financial Studies,* Spring 1994.

De Santis, G., and Gérard, B. "International Asset Pricing and Portfolio Diversification with Time-Varying Risk," *Journal of Finance,* 52(5), December 1997, pp. 1881–1912.

———. "How Big Is the Premium for Currency Risk?" *Journal of Financial Economics,* 49(3), September 1998, pp. 375–412.

Diermeier, J. J., and Solnik, B. "Global Pricing of Equity," *Financial Analysts Journal,* July/August 2001.

Dumas, B., and Solnik, B. "The World Price of Foreign Exchange Risk," *Journal of Finance,* June 1995.

Elton, E., and Gruber, M. *Modern Portfolio Theory and Investment Analysis,* New York: Wiley, 1995.

Errunza, V., and Losq, E. "International Asset Pricing under Mild Segmentation: Theory and Test," *Journal of Finance,* 40(1), March 1985.

———. "Capital Flow Controls, International Asset Pricing and Investor's Welfare: A Multi-Country Framework," *Journal of Finance,* September 1989.

Eun, C., and Janakiramanan, S. "A Model of International Asset Pricing with a Constraint on the Foreign Equity Ownership," *Journal of Finance,* September 1986.

Fama, E., and French, K. "The Cross-Section of Expected Stock Returns," *Journal of Finance,* June 1992.

———. "Multifactor Explanations of Asset Pricing Anomalies," *Journal of Finance,* 51(1), March 1996, pp. 54–84.

———. "Value versus Growth: The International Evidence," *Journal of Finance,* 52(6), December 1998, pp. 1975–99.

Ferson, W. E., and Harvey, C. R. "Fundamental Determinants of National Equity Returns: A Perspective on Conditional Asset Pricing," *Journal of Banking and Finance,* 21, October 1998, pp. 1625–65.

French, K., and Poterba, J. "Investor Diversification and International Equity Markets," *American Economic Review,* March 1991.

Grauer, F., Litzenberger, R., and Stehle, R. "Sharing Rules and Equilibrium in an International Capital Market under Uncertainty," *Journal of Financial Economics,* June 1976.

Heckman, C. R. "A Financial Model of Foreign Exchange Exposure," *Journal of International Business Studies,* Summer 1985.

————. "Don't Blame Currency Values for Strategic Errors: Protecting Competitive Position by Correctly Assessing Foreign Exchange Exposure," *Midland Corporate Finance Journal,* Fall 1986.

Hietla, P. T. "Asset Pricing in Partially Segmented Markets: Evidence from the Finnish Market," *Journal of Finance,* July 1989.

Jorion, P. "Asset Allocation with Hedged and Unhedged Foreign Stocks and Bonds," *Journal of Portfolio Management,* Summer 1989.

Kothari, S. P., Shanken, J., and Sloan, R. G. "Another Look at the Cross-Section of Expected Stock Returns," *Journal of Finance,* 50(1), March 1995, pp. 185–224.

Lucas, R. "Interest Rates and Currency Prices in a Two-Country World," *Journal of Monetary Economics,* November 1982.

Reilly, F. K., and Brown, K., *Investment Analysis and Portfolio Management,* 7th ed., South-Western, 2003.

Roll, R. "A Critique of the Asset Pricing Theory's Test: On Past and Potential Testability of the Theory," *Journal of Financial Economics,* 4, March 1977.

Sercu, P. "A Generalization of the International Asset Pricing Model," *Revue de l'Association Française de Finance,* June 1980.

Sharpe, W. F., Alexander, G. J., and Bailey, J. V., *Investments,* 6th ed., Englewood Cliffs, NJ: Prentice Hall, 1999.

Solnik, B. "An Equilibrium Model of the International Capital Market," *Journal of Economic Theory,* July/August 1974.

Stapleton, R. C., and Subrahmanyam, M. G. "Market Imperfections, Capital Asset Equilibrium and Corporation Finance," *Journal of Finance,* 32, May 1977.

Stulz, R. "A Model of International Asset Pricing," *Journal of Financial Economics,* 9, December 1981.

Subrahmanyam, M. G. "On the Optimality of International Capital Market Integration," *Journal of Financial Economics,* August 1975.

Tesar, L., and Werner, I. "Home Bias and High Turnover," *Journal of International Money and Finance,* August 1995.

5

Equity: Markets and Instruments

- Explain the origins of different national market organizations

- Differentiate between an order-driven market and a price-driven market, and discuss the risk and advantages of each

- Discuss the evolution of stock markets worldwide and their differences in terms of size, transaction volumes, and concentration

- Calculate the impact of different national taxes on the return of an international investment

- Explain the relative advantages of various stock indexes

- Explain how indexes are adjusted for free float

- Describe the components of execution costs: commissions and fees, market impact, and opportunity cost

- Explain ways to reduce execution costs, and discuss the advantages and disadvantages of each

- Describe an American Depositary Receipt (ADR) and differentiate the various forms of ADRs in terms of trading and information supplied by the company listed

- Explain why firms choose to be listed abroad

- Calculate the cost trade-off between buying shares listed abroad and buying ADRs

- State the determinants of the value of a closed-end country fund

- Discuss the advantages of exchange traded funds (ETFs) and explain the pricing of international ETFs in relation to their net asset value

- Discuss the advantages and disadvantages of the various alternatives to direct international investing

This chapter discusses equity markets worldwide, and also presents facts and concepts relevant to executing trades in those markets.[1] The financial specialist is often struck by the differences among stock market organizations across the world. Traditionally, national stock markets have not only different legal and physical organizations but also different transaction methodologies. The international investor must have a minimal familiarity with these technical differences because they influence the execution costs of every transaction. After reviewing some statistics on the market size, liquidity, and concentration, we discuss some practical aspects of international investing. These include taxes, market indexes, and the availability of information. A major practical aspect of international investing is the estimation of execution costs in each market. Understanding the determinants and magnitude of overall transaction costs is very important when implementing a global investment strategy. Getting best execution does not reduce to minimizing commissions and fees; market impact must also be estimated. Investment performance depends on the overall execution costs incurred in implementing a strategy. This chapter concludes with a review of alternatives to direct international investing, which involve the purchase of foreign shares listed at home. These alternatives include American Depositary Receipts (ADRs), closed-end country funds, and open-end funds, especially exchange traded funds (ETFs). Each of these investment vehicles has advantages and disadvantages relative to directly investing on foreign markets.

Market Differences: A Historical Perspective

Financial paper, in the form of debt obligations, has long been traded in Europe, whereas trading in company shares is relatively recent. The Amsterdam Bourse is usually considered the oldest stock market. The first common stock to be publicly traded in the Netherlands was the famous East Indies Trading Company (Verenigde Oost-Indische Compagnie) in the 17th century. But organized stock markets really started in the mid to late 18th century. In Paris, a stock market was started on a bridge (Pont au Change). In London, the stock market originated in a tavern; churches and open-air markets were also used as stock markets on the Continent. For example, the Amsterdam Bourse spent some time in the Oude-Kerk (Old Church) and later in the Nieuwe-Kerk (New Church). Most of these European exchanges became recognized as separate markets and were regulated around 1800. The same holds for the United States. However, stock exchanges in Japan and other countries in Asia and most of the Americas are more recent creations.

Historical and cultural differences explain most of the significant differences in stock-trading practices around the world. Rather than engage in a detailed analy-

---

[1] Jan R. Squires, CFA, and Philip J. Young, CFA, provided important suggestions for this chapter.

sis of each national market, this section looks at the major differences in terms of market structures and trading procedures. Many of these differences are being eliminated, but some historical perspective helps gain a better understanding of the current working of those stock markets.

Historical Differences in Market Organization

Each stock exchange (bourse) has its own unique characteristics and legal organization, but broadly speaking, all exchanges have evolved from one of three market organization types.

Private Bourses   Private stock exchange corporations are founded by private individuals and entities for the purpose of securities trading. Several private stock exchanges may compete within the same country, as in the United States, Japan, and Canada. In other countries, one leading exchange has emerged through either attrition or absorption of its competitors. Although these bourses are private, they are not free of public regulation, but the mix of self-regulation and government supervision is oriented more toward self-regulation than in the public bourses. Historically, these private bourses developed in the British sphere of influence.

Public Bourses   The public bourse market structure has its origin in the legislative work of Napoleon I, the French emperor. He designed the bourse to be a public institution, with brokers appointed by the government and enjoying a monopoly over all transactions. Commissions are fixed by the state. Brokerage firms are private, but their number is fixed and new brokers are proposed to the state for nomination by the brokers' association. The Paris Bourse followed this model until 1990. Stock exchanges organized under the authority of the state were found in the sphere of influence of Napoleon I: Belgium, France, Spain, Italy, Greece, and some Latin American countries. Most have moved toward a private bourse model.

Bankers' Bourses   In some countries, banks are the major, or even the only, securities traders. In Germany, the Banking Act granted a brokerage monopoly to banks. Bankers' bourses were found in the German sphere of influence: Austria, Switzerland, Scandinavia, and the Netherlands. Bankers' bourses may be either private or semipublic organizations, but their chief function is to provide a convenient place for banks to meet. Sometimes trading takes place directly between banks without involving the official bourse at all. Government regulation is imposed both on the bourse itself and directly on the banks. Bankers' bourses suffered from potential conflicts of interests, and more trading transparency was required by international investors. Most bankers' bourses moved to a private bourse model in the 1990s to allow foreign financial intermediaries to become brokers.

Historical Differences in Trading Procedures

Apart from legal structure, numerous other historical differences are found in the operation of national stock markets. The most important differences are in the trading procedures.

Cash versus Forward Markets   In most markets, stocks are traded on a cash basis, and transactions must be settled within a few days (typically three business days after the transaction). To allow more leveraged investment, margin trading is available on most cash markets. In margin trading, the investor borrows money (or shares) from a broker to finance a transaction. This is still a cash market transaction, and trade settlement takes place in three days; however, a third party steps in to lend money (shares) to the buyer (seller) to honor a cash transaction commitment.

In contrast, some stock markets were organized as a forward market. This was the case for London and Paris, as well as some markets in Latin America and Asia. In Paris, the settlement date was the end of the month for all transactions made during the month (London settled accounts every two weeks). To simplify the clearing operations, all transactions were settled at the end of the month on the settlement day. This is a periodic settlement system. Of course, a deposit is required to guarantee a position, as on most forward markets. Moreover, the transaction price is fixed at the time of the transaction and remains at this value even if the market price has changed substantially by the settlement time. Settling all accounts once a month greatly simplifies the security clearing system, but it also opens the door to short-term speculation and to frequent misconceptions on the part of foreign investors who are unfamiliar with the technique. Although most forward markets have moved to a cash market, they usually have institutionalized procedures to allow investors to trade forward, if desired.

Price-Driven versus Order-Driven Markets   U.S. investors are accustomed to a *continuous* market, whereby transactions take place all day and *market makers* (also called *dealers*) ensure market liquidity at virtually any point in time. The market maker quotes both a *bid* price (the price at which the dealer offers to buy the security) and an *ask* price (the price at which the dealer offers to sell the security). The ask price is sometimes called the *offer* price. These quotes are firm commitments by the market maker to transact at those prices for a specified transaction size. The customer will turn to the market maker who provides the best quote. Of course, market makers adjust their quotes continuously to reflect supply and demand for the security as well as their own inventory. This type of market is often referred to as a *dealer market*. It is also known as a *price-driven* market (or *quote-driven* market), because market makers publicly post their bid–ask prices to induce orders. For example, Nasdaq is a dealer market.[2]

---

[2] The New York Stock Exchange (NYSE) has a unique system where each stock is allocated to one specialist who acts both as a dealer and as an auctioneer. As a dealer, a specialist posts bid and ask quotes and uses its own capital to buy or sell securities (under strict regulations). As an auctioneer, a specialist maintains the order book of all orders that are submitted.

In many other markets and countries, however, active market makers do not exist, and the supply and demand for securities are matched directly in an *auction market*. Because the quantities demanded and supplied are a function of the transaction price, a price will exist that equilibrates demand and supply. In a traditional auction market, liquidity requires that an asset be traded only once or a few times per day. This is known as a *call* or *fixing* procedure, whereby orders are batched together in an order book until the auction when they are executed at a single price that equilibrates demand and supply. This auction price maximizes trade volume. In the past, many stock markets used an open *criée* (outcry) system in which brokers would negotiate loudly until a price was found that would equilibrate buy and sell orders (quietness is restored). All these stock markets have moved to computerized trading systems in which buy-and-sell orders are entered on the computer trading system, which matches them directly. An auction market is also known as an *order-driven* market because all traders publicly post their orders, and the transaction price is the result of the equilibrium of supply and demand. Although a single call auction provides excellent liquidity at one point in time, it makes trading at other times difficult. Hence, the market-making function is being developed on all call auction markets, (e.g., Paris, Tokyo, or Frankfurt) to allow the possibility of trading throughout the day.

Automation on the Major Stock Exchanges

Trading on a floor where participants noisily meet is increasingly being replaced by computerized trading. Automation allows more efficient handling of orders, especially a large number of small orders. Competition across national stock exchanges and the increased volume of trading hastened the adoption of computerized systems, including price quotation, order routing, and automatic order matching. The design of the automated systems reflects the historical and cultural heritage of the national market. Automated trading systems have followed two different paths, depending on whether the traditional market organization was dominated by dealers making the market or by brokers acting as agents in an auction system.

Price-Driven and Order-Driven Systems   The U.S. Nasdaq is a typical *price-driven* system. The automated system posts firm quotes by market makers. There is no centralized book of limit orders. When posting a quote, the market maker does not know what trades it will generate. In a price-driven system, a market maker is placing the equivalent of limit orders: a buy limit order representing his bid and a sell limit order representing his ask.

At the other extreme, *auction markets,* such as Paris, Frankfurt, or Tokyo (and most other markets), have put in place electronic order-driven systems. The computer stores all orders, which become public knowledge. All limit orders that have not been executed are stored in a central *order book*. A new order is immediately matched with the book of orders previously submitted. The central limit order book is the hub of these automated systems. Viewing all standing orders, a trader knows exactly what trades will be executed if she enters a new order. Market makers provide liquidity by entering limit buy-and-sell orders in the order book. The highest limit bid and the lowest limit offer act as the bid and ask prices in a price-driven market.

EXAMPLE 5.1   ORDER-DRIVEN MARKET

LVMH (Moët Hennesy Louis Vuitton) is a French firm listed on the Paris Bourse. You can access the central limit order book directly on the Internet and find the following information (the limit prices for sell orders are ask prices and those for buy orders are bid prices:

Sell Orders		Buy Orders	
Quantity	Limit	Limit	Quantity
1,000	58	49	2,000
3,000	54	48	500
1,000	52	47	1,000
1,000	51	46	2,000
500	50	44	10,000

You wish to buy 1,000 shares and enter a market order to buy those shares. A market order will be executed against the best matching order. At what price will you buy the shares?

SOLUTION

Unless a new sell order is entered at a price below 51 before your order is executed, you will buy 500 shares at 50 and 500 shares at 51.

To improve liquidity, most order-driven markets have retained periodic call auctions. There is a fixing at the opening of the market, where all orders that arrived before opening are stored and the opening price is set through a call auction.[3] In Frankfurt, call auctions take place periodically throughout the day, at prespecified times other than opening and closing. At the time of the call auction, the continuous trading of the stock on XETRA is interrupted. (XETRA is a trading platform that includes all stocks on the Deutsche Boerse.)In a *pretrading* phase, traders can submit limit and market orders, which are accumulated in the order book. At auction time, orders are automatically crossed (matched) at a price that maximizes the volume of trading. In Tokyo, a call auction system, called *itayose*, is used to establish prices at the start of the morning and afternoon sessions (the market closes for lunch). During the sessions, a continuous auction is used for new orders. This auction system, called *zaraba*, is an order-matching method and does not require the intervention of a market maker.

---

[3] On the New York Stock Exchange, the opening price is determined through a call auction.

The NYSE combines price-driven and order-driven systems. Specialists maintain limit order books and shares may also trade in auctions.

Advantages and Risks of Each System   Automation brings many improvements in the speed and costs of trading. An order-driven system requires little human intervention and is therefore less costly to run. Cost considerations have pushed all markets in this direction. Only American stock markets have retained a price-driven model. Markets with lesser transaction volumes have found it more efficient to adopt order-driven electronic trading systems. For example, London had a price-driven market with competitive market makers. Cost-efficiency considerations caused it to move to an automated order-driven system called SETS (*Stock Exchange Electronic Trading Service*) at the end of the 20th century.[4] Market makers enter their bid-and-ask quotes directly in the order book in the form of limit orders. Most emerging stock markets have adopted an order-driven electronic trading system.

The cost of running the trading system, however, is only one component of the transaction cost borne by investors. Investors try to get the best execution price for each trade. This raises the question: Which market structure provides the best liquidity and lowest execution costs? Theoretical and experimental research suggests that the market design affects trader behavior, transaction prices, and market efficiency. In real life, the answer depends on the market environment, and there is no clear-cut conclusion. An electronic auction market is cheaper to operate, but that could be at the expense of liquidity—hence, trading could be more costly because of overall execution costs, including price impact.[5] Domowitz (2001) suggests that the public dissemination of the electronic order book in order-driven markets allows traders to monitor liquidity and provide liquidity at a lower cost than in price-driven markets.

A drawback of electronic order-driven systems is their inability to execute large trades. In the absence of active market makers, trading a block (a large transaction) on an automated order-driven system is difficult. Because of the lack of depth in the market, it may take a long time before the block is traded. This will leave the trader who discloses the block on the system fully exposed to the risk that new information might hurt him unless he continuously updates the limit on the block order. This is the risk of being "picked off"; that is, having an order accepted at a price no longer desired by the trader at the time of the transaction. Blocks are generally traded away from the automated system. This is often called *upstairs* trading. Order-driven systems have developed in part because they are much cheaper to operate than traditional dealers' markets. However, market makers are still needed for trading large blocks.

---

[4] Smaller companies and foreign companies, however, are still traded in a traditional nonautomated price-driven model (SEAQ and SEAQ International).

[5] Conrad, Johnson and Wahal (forthcoming) find some evidence that realized execution costs are lower on electronic trading systems for U.S. stocks. Using data up to 2000, Huang (2002) finds that electronic communication network quoted spreads are smaller than dealer spreads for Nasdaq stocks. However, the period of study was prior to the U.S. adoption of decimal quotations, which reduced spreads markedly.

Another drawback of a continuous order-driven system, in the absence of developed market making, is the danger in placing market orders (i.e., orders with no price limits). In the absence of competitive market makers providing liquidity, a sell market order will be immediately crossed with the highest "buy" limit order, which could be very far from the lowest "sell" limit order. The Tokyo Stock Exchange has a special procedure to limit this risk. Other markets are trying to implement rules protecting market orders. This is typically true for less active stocks, in which market making would help provide liquidity.

Any automated trading system exposes one party to transparency risk. It forces one side of the transaction to expose itself first and, therefore, run the risk of being "picked off." In all cases, a limit order gives a free trading option to other market participants. In an order-driven market, the trader who submits the order implicitly

---

EXAMPLE 5.2   EXPOSITION RISK IN TWO TYPES OF MARKETS

LVMH is traded on the Paris Bourse, and the last transaction was at 50 euros per share. An investor entered on the French electronic trading system NSC *(Nouveau Système Cotation)* a limit order to sell LVMH shares at 51 euros while the market price was 50.

LVMH is also traded as an ADR on Nasdaq. One ADR represents one-fifth of an LVMH French share (so 5 ADRs equal one LVMH share). The exchange rate is one dollar per euro, and the ADR price is quoted by a market maker at 10–10.20. Assume that the exchange rate remains constant over time.

Suppose that favorable information suddenly arrives that justifies a higher price for LVMH—say, 55 euros. Who are the parties exposed to losses on the Paris Bourse and on Nasdaq if they do not react immediately?

SOLUTION

- On the Paris Bourse, informed market participants have an option worth four euros per share, and the investor who has a standing order in the electronic order book gets "picked off" (the informed participant can buy at 51 euros a share now worth 55 euros).

- On Nasdaq, the market maker posts a firm bid–ask quote for LVMH of 10–10.20 for the dollar ADR, which is equivalent for the French share of LVMH quoted in euros to a quote of 50–51. Under the same scenario, informed market participants suddenly get a free option worth 0.8 dollar per ADR or four euros per French share (they can buy at 10.2 dollars from the market maker a share now worth 11 dollars). In a price-driven market, dealers run the risk of being "picked off."

  The danger of automation is that market liquidity may be reduced, because dealers (in a price-driven system) or public investors (in an order-driven system) may be less willing to publicly place limit orders.

gives the free option to the rest of the market. In a price-driven market, it is the dealer posting a firm quote who gives this free option, as shown in Example 5.2. Of course, the option holder depends on the dealer to deliver in a non-automated system, and "backing away" (reneging) can be a problem.

Electronic Communication Networks and Electronic Crossing Networks (ECNs)
Some electronic trading systems have developed alongside official exchanges. They tend to be privately owned and offer trading on stocks of one market or of a region. Electronic communication networks and electronic crossing networks are both often called ECNs, although they are quite different.

Electronic communication networks are order-driven systems, in which the limit order book plays a central role as previously described. Many of them coexist in the United States. (Instinet-Island, Tradebook, Archipelago, Nasdaq SuperMontage, and others). Virt-x is a pan-European ECN specialized in blue chips.

Electronic crossing networks are different systems. These crossing systems anonymously match the buy and sell orders of a pool of participants, generally institutional investors and broker-dealers. Participants enter market orders,[6] which are

---

EXAMPLE 5.3   CROSSING

Market orders for LVMH have been entered on a crossing network for European shares. There is one order from Participant A to buy 100,000 shares, one order from Participant B to sell 50,000 shares, and one order from Participant C to sell 70,000 shares. Assume that orders were entered in that chronological order and that the network gives priority to the oldest orders. At the time specified for the crossing session, LVMH transacts at 51 euros on the Paris Bourse, its primary market.

1. What trades would take place on the crossing network?

2. Assume now that all the orders are AON (all or nothing), meaning that the whole block has to be traded at the same price. What trades would take place?

SOLUTION

1. One hundred thousand shares would be exchanged at 51 euros. Participant A would buy 100,000. Participants B and C would sell 50,000. Participant B's order has priority, so Participant C's order would not be executed entirely (20,000 shares remain unsold).

2. There is no way that the AON condition could be achieved for the three orders; so, no trade would take place.

---

[6] Participants also can specify various constraints on their orders.

crossed at prespecified times (once or a few times every day) at prices determined in the primary market for the security. The trade price is the mid-market quote, the midpoint between the bid and the ask, observed on the primary market at the prespecified time. POSIT® is a major crossing network in the United States; Instinet also provides some crossing at the close of the NYSE and Nasdaq. In Europe, E-Crossnet and POSIT provide crossing for European stocks.

Crossing networks present two advantages for large orders of institutional investors:

- *Low transaction costs.* The trade is executed at mid-market prices, so there is no market impact or bid–ask spread, even for large trades.

- *Anonymity.* The identity of the buyers and sellers, and the magnitude of their order is not revealed, so there is little exposure risk.

On the other hand, crossing networks have a distinct disadvantage:

- *No trading immediacy.* The trader must wait until the crossing session time to execute a trade, and the trade takes place only if there are offsetting orders entered by other participants. Only a small proportion of orders are executed at each crossing session. The order has to wait in the system, or needs to be worked through other market mechanisms.

Basically, crossing networks allow a substantial reduction in execution cost for large trades at the detriment of immediacy.

Cross-Border Alliances of Stock Exchanges   Fragmentation of national stock markets, especially the smaller ones, is a hindrance to international investors who often think in terms of regions rather than individual countries. Periodically, plans for cross-border mergers of national stock exchanges are drafted. But most of these projects collapse, in part because of the cultural heritage of different trading, legal, and regulatory systems, which makes it very difficult to harmonize trading systems. The canceled merger between the *London Stock Exchange* and the *Deutsche Boerse* is a vivid example. As of 2002, *Euronext* is the only successful merger. Paris, Amsterdam, Brussels, and Lisbon merged their trading platform using the French NSC electronic trading system. As we shall see later, stock markets also internationalize by listing shares of foreign companies. This is the route followed by U.S. stock exchanges (discussed in next section).

A related hindrance is the fragmentation of settlement systems. The multiplicity of national settlement systems adds to the cost of international investing. But a consolidation of settlement systems is taking place, especially in Europe. A common depository and counterparty platform has been developed around Euronext and Euroclear, the international securities clearing house. So, trades in several European stock markets, as well as international securities such as Eurobonds, use the same system, Clearnet. Another platform, Clearstream, has been created around the Deutsche Boerse and the other international securities clearing house, Cedel.

Some Statistics

Market Size

Relative national market capitalizations give some indication of the importance of each country for global investors. Market-capitalization weights are used in the commonly used global benchmarks; hence, market sizes guide global investment strategies.

Developed and emerging markets are usually classified in two different asset classes. Although they are somewhat arbitrary, and some countries have been moved from the status of emerging to developed in the recent past, these classifications are still widely used by investors.

Developed Markets   The U.S. stock exchanges are the largest exchanges in the world. It is worth noting that the U.S. capital market is very large compared with the U.S. economy. The U.S. stock market capitalization (cap) is much larger than the annual U.S. gross domestic product (GDP). Britain also has a market cap almost double its GDP, but the corresponding figure for France or Germany is below 80%. This difference between the United States and continental Europe has several explanations. Most U.S. firms prefer to go public, whereas in France, as well as in the rest of Europe, tradition calls for maintaining private ownership as much as possible. In many European countries, corporations are undercapitalized and rely heavily on bank financing. Germany is a typical example because banks finance corporations extensively, thereby reducing the need for outside equity capital. In Europe, banks tend to provide corporations with all financial services, assisting them in both their commercial needs and their long-term debt and equity financing. In contrast to banks in the United States, it is common for European banks to own shares of their client companies. U.S. companies, especially small- and medium-sized ones, tend to go public and raise capital in the marketplace, thereby increasing the public stock market cap. In other countries, many large firms are nationalized and, therefore, not listed on the capital markets. In France, for example, large portions of telecommunication, arms manufacturing, automobile, banking, and transportation industries are partly owned by the government. If countries like France, Italy, and Germany evolve along the U.S. model, their weights in a global index are likely to rise.

The market values of developed stock markets are given in Exhibit 5.1. Japan and the United Kingdom have the largest markets outside of the United States. The size of the world stock market grew steadily in the 1970s and 1980s and neared the $30 trillion mark at the end of 2000. It has multiplied by approximately 30 since the end of 1974. Currency movements induce changes in the total size and geographical breakdown of the world market. A drop in the value of the dollar reduces the market share of U.S. stocks; the dollar value of non-U.S. stocks increases by the amount of the dollar depreciation, assuming that the stocks' values in domestic currency do not change and that the dollar value of U.S. stocks stays constant. The

EXHIBIT 5.1

Market Sizes of Developed Markets

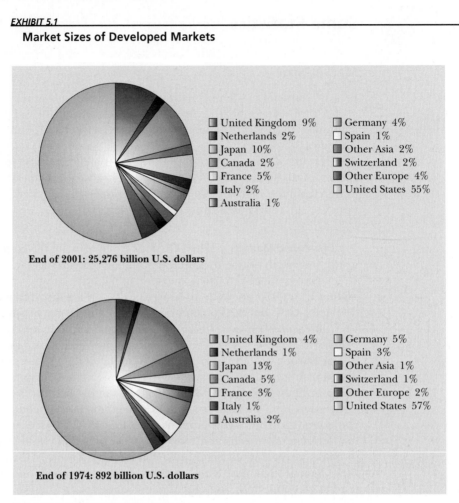

United Kingdom 9%   Germany 4%
Netherlands 2%   Spain 1%
Japan 10%   Other Asia 2%
Canada 2%   Switzerland 2%
France 5%   Other Europe 4%
Italy 2%   United States 55%
Australia 1%

End of 2001: 25,276 billion U.S. dollars

United Kingdom 4%   Germany 5%
Netherlands 1%   Spain 3%
Japan 13%   Other Asia 1%
Canada 5%   Switzerland 1%
France 3%   Other Europe 2%
Italy 1%   United States 57%
Australia 2%

End of 1974: 892 billion U.S. dollars

Source: Morgan Stanley Capital International.

share of U.S. markets has decreased from almost two-thirds of the world market cap in 1972 to only one-third by the early 1990s. It moved back up to over 50 percent in the early 2000s, partly because of a big drop in Asian markets. Meanwhile, the share of European markets grew from roughly 20 to 30 percent. Asia's importance increased dramatically from the 1980s through the mid 1990s. However, the lingering economic crisis in Japan, compounded by the 1997 crisis in southeastern Asia, drastically reduced Asia's importance in the world market cap.

The figure for Japan is somewhat inflated by the practice of cross-holding of stocks among publicly traded Japanese companies and financial institutions (*Mochiai*). A similar feature can be found in South Korea, where companies within large conglomerates (*chaebols*) are linked with extensive equity cross-holding. Index providers are trying to adjust the market cap weights used in the index. This is part of the so-called free-float adjustment, which attempts to eliminate the effects of cross-holdings, as illustrated in Example 5.4.

EXAMPLE 5.4 EXAMPLE OF ADJUSTMENT FOR CROSS-HOLDING

Three companies belong to a group and are listed on the stock exchange:

- Company A owns 30 percent of Company B.

- Company B owns 20 percent of Company C.

- Company C owns 10 percent of Company A.

Each company has a total market cap of 100 million.

You wish to adjust for cross-holding to reflect the weights of these companies in a market cap–weighted index. What adjustment would you make to reflect the free float?

SOLUTION

The apparent market cap of these three companies taken together is 300 million. But because of their cross-holding, there is some double counting. The usual free-float adjustment would be to retain only the portion that is not owned by other companies within the group. Hence, the adjusted market capitalization is:

$$90 + 70 + 80 = 240 \text{ million}$$

Emerging Markets   The 1980s saw the emergence and rapid growth of stock markets in many developing countries. In Africa, stock markets opened in Egypt, Morocco, and the Ivory Coast, but with limited growth. Growth has been somewhat faster in Latin America, especially in Brazil and Mexico. The most spectacular change, however, has been witnessed in Asia. Stock markets have grown rapidly in India, Indonesia, Malaysia, Thailand, South Korea, and Taiwan. The emerging market crisis of 1997 stopped that growth, but growth picked up again in 2002. Nevertheless, we see in Exhibit 5.2 that the total capitalization of emerging markets represents less than 10 percent of the world stock market cap. Taken together, all emerging markets have a market size somewhere between that of Great Britain and that of France or Germany.

Liquidity

Transaction volume gives indications on the liquidity of each market. In a liquid market, investors can be more active and design various arbitrage strategies. Some markets are large via their market cap, and hence their weight in a global index, but with little turnover. Illiquidity tends to imply higher transaction costs. Investors measuring performance relative to a global benchmark will tend to be more passive on such illiquid markets.

EXHIBIT 5.2

Market Sizes of Emerging Markets (as a % of the total value of US$1,790 billion, year-end 2001)	
Europe 5%	Taiwan 12%
Malaysia 7%	Thailand 2%
Mexico 8%	Peru 1%
Middle East 6%	South Korea 11%
India 6%	Indonesia 1%
Chile 3%	China 8%
Africa 10%	Brazil 11%
Philippines 3%	Other 5%
Argentina 1%	

Source: Morgan Stanley Capital International.

Exhibit 5.3 gives the turnover ratio of major markets computed as the ratio of the annual transaction volume to the market cap at year-end. This is a simple indicator of the liquidity on each market. Depending on market activity, these figures can vary widely from one year to the next, but it is apparent that some national markets are more active than others. The ranking of countries based on the volume of transactions differs slightly from that based on market cap. European markets tend to be more active than indicated by their relative market size, resulting in a higher turnover ratio.

In fact, the turnover ratio varies significantly over time. For example, the transaction volume in Japan soared in the late 1980s to surpass that of the NYSE, and the Japanese turnover ratio became a multiple of the U.S. ratio, but it dropped dramatically in the 1990s. Therefore, comparison of national market liquidity based on this variable could lead to different conclusions, depending on the years observed.

In addition, the transaction volume on some emerging markets is very large relative to their size. Transaction volumes in South Korea or Taiwan are sometimes larger than that of any developed market except the United States. But this is not the case for many other emerging markets that are quite illiquid.

Concentration

Another informative statistic is the degree of concentration of the market cap found in the major markets. It is important that investors know whether a national market is made up of a diversity of firms or concentrated in a few large firms. Institutional investors are reluctant to invest in small firms, fearing that they offer poor liquidity. Also, it is easier for the investor to track the performance of a market index, which is usually market cap weighted, if it is dominated by a few large issues. On the other

EXHIBIT 5.3

Annual Turnover Ratio on Major Stock Exchanges

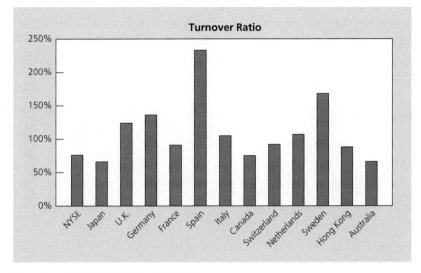

Source: Morgan Stanley Capital International, 2002.

hand, a market dominated by a few large firms provides fewer opportunities for risk diversification and active portfolio strategies.

As shown in Exhibit 5.4, the U.S. stock exchange is a diverse market in which the top 10 firms represent less than 20 percent of total market cap. In the United States, the largest firm represents less than 3 percent of the capitalization for the NYSE. At the other end of the spectrum, the top 10 Swiss multinational firms account for more than 70 percent of the Swiss stock exchange. Nokia is larger than the sum of all other Finnish firms.

Some Practical Aspects

A few practical aspects must be taken into account when investing abroad.

Tax Aspects

Taxes can add to the cost of international investment. Foreign investments may be taxed in two locations: the investor's country and the investment's country. Taxes are applied in any of three areas: transactions, capital gains, and income (dividends, etc.).

EXHIBIT 5.4

Share of the Ten Largest Listed Companies in the National Market Capitalization

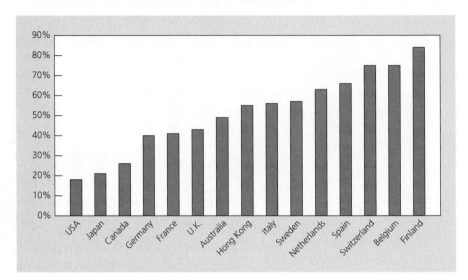

Source: Morgan Stanley Capital International, March 2002.

Some countries impose a tax on transactions. The United Kingdom has retained a stamp tax of 0.5 percent on purchases of domestic securities (but not on sales). Most countries have eliminated, or drastically reduced, such transaction taxes. In countries where brokers charge a commission rather than trade on net prices, a tax proportional to the commission is sometimes charged. For example, France levies a 19.6 percent VAT (value-added tax) on commissions (not on the transaction value), just as on any service. Market makers are usually exempted from these taxes when they trade for their own accounts.

Capital gains are normally taxed where the investor resides, regardless of the national origin of the investment. In other words, domestic and international investments are taxed the same way.

Income on foreign stocks is paid from the legal entity of one country to a resident of another country. This transaction often poses a conflict of jurisdiction, because both countries may want to impose a tax on that income. The international convention on taxing income is to make certain that taxes are paid by the investor in at least one country, which is why withholding taxes are levied on dividend payments. Because many investors are also taxed on income received in their country of residence, double taxation can result from this practice but is avoided through a network of international tax treaties. An investor receives a dividend net of withholding tax plus a tax credit from the foreign government. The investor's country of residence imposes its tax on the gross foreign dividends, but the amount of this tax is reduced by the withholding tax credit. In other words, the foreign tax credit is applied against the home taxes. Tax rules change frequently, but the typical withholding tax rate is 15 percent of dividends.

To a tax-free investor, such as a pension fund, this tax credit is worthless, because the investor does not pay taxes at home. In this case, the investor can reclaim the tax withheld in the foreign country. Reclaiming a withholding tax is often a lengthy process requiring at least a few months and even up to a couple of years. In a few countries, part of the withholding tax is kept by the country of origin. In other countries, tax-free foreign investors, especially public pension funds, can apply for a direct exemption from tax withholding.

EXAMPLE 5.5   *EXAMPLE OF TAX ADJUSTMENTS*

To illustrate these fiscal aspects, let's consider a U.S. investor who buys 100 shares of Heineken listed in Amsterdam for 40 euros. She goes through a U.S. broker, and the current exchange rate is one euro = 1.1 U.S. dollars. Her total cost is $4,400, or $44 per share of Heineken (40 times 1.1 $/€). Three months later, a gross dividend of €2 is paid (15 percent withholding tax), and she decides to sell the Heineken shares. Each share is now worth 38 euros, and the current exchange rate is $/€ = 1.2, because the euro has sharply risen against the dollar. The same exchange rate applied on the dividend payment date. What are the cash flows received in U.S. dollars?

SOLUTION

The cash flows are as follows:

Dividend Payment Minus Withholding Tax ($/€ = 1.2)

	Net Dividend	Tax Credit
In euros per share	1.70	0.30
In dollars per share	2.04	0.36
Net in dollars (100 shares)	204	36

Sale of Heineken Shares ($/€ = 1.2)

In euros per share	38
In dollars per share	45.6
Net in dollars (100 shares)	4560

Our investor has made a capital gain of $160 ($4,560 − $4,400), which will be taxed in the United States at the U.S. capital gains tax rate. She will also declare a total gross dividend of $240 as income, which will be taxed at her income tax rate. She can deduct from her income tax a tax credit of $36, however, thanks to the United States–Netherlands tax treaty.

Stock Market Indexes

Stock market indexes allow one to measure the average performance of a national market. One or several market indexes may track a national market at any given time. Historically, country stock indexes were computed by the local stock market, but global organizations have started to provide indexes for national markets around the world, as well as a series of global indexes.

Domestic Stock Indexes   Domestic investors usually prefer indexes that are calculated and published locally. Most of these are broadly based, market value–weighted indexes. Each company is assigned an index weight proportional to its market cap. Market value–weighted indexes are true market portfolio indexes in the sense that when the index portfolio is held by an investor, it truly represents movements in the market. This is not true of equal-weighted indexes, such as the U.S. Dow Jones 30 Industrial Average (DJIA) or the Japanese Nikkei 225 Stock Average. The DJIA adds up the stock price of 30 corporations. Each company is assigned an index weight proportional to its market price, when computing the index percentage price movement. For example, the return on a share with a price of $100 will have ten times more importance than the return on a share with a price of $10. So the weighting method is quite artificial. Not only is the DJIA narrowly based, but also its composition is somewhat arbitrary; for example, IBM was removed from the index in the 1970s because its price was too high compared with the other 29 corporations. Many stock exchanges have introduced indexes based on a small number of large stocks. There are two reasons for this trend toward narrow-based indexes. First, investors like to get instantaneous information and market movements by accessing Internet or information providers such as Reuters or Bloomberg. Meaningful market indicators must be computed using the most actively traded stocks, not those that trade infrequently. Second, exchanges have introduced derivatives (futures, options) on these stock indexes. Dealers in those derivative markets prefer to have an index that is based on a small number of actively traded stocks, because it makes it much easier to hedge their derivatives exposure in the cash stock market. Most stock indexes published do not include dividends, although some countries also report dividend-adjusted indexes.

Because some stocks are listed on several exchanges, some companies appear in different national indexes. For example, the S&P 500 used to include some very large non-U.S. companies.

Global Stock Indexes[7]   Morgan Stanley Capital International (MSCI) has published international market cap weighted indexes since 1970. They now publish country indexes for all developed as well as numerous emerging markets. They also publish a variety of regional and global indexes. The World index includes only developed markets, while the All Country World index includes both developed and emerging markets. Their index of non-U.S. stock markets has been extensively

---

[7] Up to date information can be found on the Web sites of the index providers: www.msci.com, www.ftse.com, www.spglobal.com, www.ssbgei.com, indexes.dowjones.com, and www.stoxx.com.

CONCEPTS IN ACTION   *S&P GOES ALL-AMERICAN*

Standard & Poor's said it will remove all seven non-U.S. companies from the large-cap S&P 500, the world's most widely benchmarked index, at the end of trading on July 19. It will replace them with seven U.S. corporations. On the out list: Royal Dutch/Shell, Unilever, Nortel, Alcan, Inco, Barrick Gold, and Placer Dome. S&P said foreign companies often cause tracking errors between the index and the markets they intend to track. . . . The newcomers are UPS, Goldman Sachs, Prudential, Principal Financial, as well as three tech companies—SunGard Data, Electronic Arts, and eBay. S&P, like *Business Week*, is owned by McGraw-Hill.

Source: Robin Ajello, *"S&P Goes All-American,"* reprinted from July 22, 2002 issue of *Business Week* by special permission, copyright 2002 by The McGraw-Hill Companies, Inc.

---

used as a benchmark of foreign equity portfolios by U.S. investors; it is called EAFE (Europe/Australasia/Far East). Besides market cap–weighted indexes, MSCI also publishes indexes with various weighting schemes (e.g., GDP weights) and with full currency hedging. Global industry indexes are also available.

FTSE, created as a joint venture of the *Financial Times* and the London Stock Exchange, has published international indexes since 1987. The most important international indexes are the World index, the Europe index, the Pacific Basin index, and the Europe and Pacific index. Country indexes are provided for developed and emerging markets, as well as numerous industrial and regional indexes. Global industry indexes are available.

Other series of global indexes are also available. Salomon Smith Barney publishes a series of global indexes that cover developed and emerging markets. There are country, region, and industry indexes. In 2000, Dow Jones started to publish a series of global indexes called the DJGI that covers developed and emerging markets. S&P publishes an S&P Global 1200 index of developed markets, as well as various subindexes, including the S&P 350 Europe index, intended to be the European counterpart of the S&P 500.

The introduction of the euro has created intensive competition among index suppliers. They all try to provide a European index that will be used as benchmark by global money managers. Besides, the well-established indexes of MSCI and FTSE, Dow Jones has launched a series of European indexes in collaboration with the French, German, and Swiss stock exchanges, which are named DJ Stoxx.

Emerging market indexes are available from the index providers mentioned previously. In the past the International Finance Corporation (IFC) of the World Bank published popular emerging market indexes. Standard and Poor's acquired its emerging market database and now performs the calculation of various S&P/IFC indexes. The Global index series (S&P/IFCG) is the broadest possible indicator of market movements, and the coverage exceeds 75 percent of local market capitalizations. Weights are adjusted for government and cross-holdings. The Investable index series (S&P/IFCI) is designed to represent the market that is legally and practically available to foreign investors. The Frontier index series tracks small and illiquid markets.

All these global indexes are widely used by international money managers for asset allocation decisions and performance measurements (benchmarks). They differ in terms of coverage and weights. Hence, these global indexes can have significant differences in performance. Besides deciding on which company and country should be included in the respective indexes, the provider must decide on the market-cap weights to be used. Because of cross-holding, government ownership, and/or regulations applying to foreign investors, the amount of market value available to foreign investors (the free float) can differ significantly from the market cap that can be obtained by multiplying the number of shares issued by their market price. Most indexes now perform an adjustment so that the weight of each security represents its free float.

Not all indexes are intended as investable benchmarks tracking an overall market. Specific European indexes have been launched, on which derivatives can be traded. They must comprise a small number of highly liquid stocks, so that market makers in the derivatives can easily hedge their exposure on the stock markets. The DJ Euro Stoxx 50 (50 leading Eurozone stocks) and the FTSE Eurotop 100 (100 leading European stocks) are European indexes on which futures, options, and ETFs are traded.

Which Index to Use?　　Local indexes are widely used by domestic investors. Private investors often prefer these indexes over country indexes of international providers, such as MSCI or FTSE, for several reasons:

- In most cases, the local indexes have been used for several decades.

- Local indexes are used for derivative contracts (futures, options) traded in that country.

- Local indexes are calculated immediately and are available at the same time as stock market quotations on all electronic price services.

- Local indexes are available every morning in all the newspapers throughout the world.

- The risk of error in prices and capital adjustment is possibly minimized in local indexes by the fact that all calculations are done locally, with excellent information available on the spot.

Institutional investors, on the other hand, prefer to use the MSCI, FTSE, or other international indexes for the following reasons:

- The pension funds do not need up-to-the-minute indexes.

- The indexes on all stock markets are available in a central location, whereas local indexes must be drawn from several locations.

- All international indexes are calculated in a single consistent manner, allowing for direct comparisons between markets.

- MSCI and FTSE provide global or regional indexes (World, Europe, EAFE), which international money managers need to measure overall performance.

- They also provide indexes cum-dividends.

The choice of index is important. In any given year, the performance between two indexes for the same stock market can differ by as much as several percentage points.

Information

The information available from different countries and companies varies in quality. Accounting standards differ across countries (see Chapter 6), but most developed countries are now enforcing accounting standards of increased quality. Under the pressure of international investors, companies are learning that they must report accurate information on their accounts and prospects in a timely fashion. The situation can be worse for smaller firms in countries where there is less tradition of information transparency, and it can become worrisome in some emerging markets.

In some emerging countries, the earnings forecasts announced by companies that become publicly listed are totally unverifiable. A notable case is China. The rapid move from a centrally planned economy to a partly capitalistic system means that the notion of accounting at the firm level is a new concept. State-owned companies have been listed on Chinese or foreign stock exchanges but have no tradition of having separate accounts, and therefore have problems trying to identify earnings to shareholders during a given time period. It is equally difficult to assess who is the legal owner of some of the assets of a Chinese firm; the state, the province, and the municipality all lay some claim on existing firms' assets, and legal property titles do not exist historically. Shanghai Petrochemical Co., for example, was the largest company to be introduced on the NYSE in 1993. Its value is clearly a function of its properties and equipment. A letter from America Appraisal Hong Kong Ltd., included in the 1993 listing prospectus, illustrates that reliable information on companies from emerging markets is sometimes difficult to get:

> We have relied to a considerable extent on information provided by you. . . . As all the properties are situated in the People's Republic of China, we have not searched the original documents to verify ownership. . . . All dimensions, measurements and areas are approximate. We have inspected the exterior and, when possible, the interior of all the properties valued. However, no structural survey has been made and we are therefore unable to report as to whether the properties are or not free of rot, infestation or any other structural defects.

Given the uncertainty about a company's information, it is not surprising that its valuation is a matter of highly subjective judgment. The uncertainty surrounding companies' information is damaging. Most emerging markets trade at low price–earnings ratios compared with developed markets with similar or lesser growth potential. Local authorities and the management of listed firms have come to realize that stricter standards must be applied to the timely release of reliable information. Many countries are adopting accounting standards that conform to the International Accounting Standards or U.S. generally accepted accounting principles (GAAP), but progress in their implementation can only be slow.

Execution Costs

The importance of execution costs, also referred to as *transaction costs,* is sometimes overlooked in portfolio management. These costs should be taken into account in active global investment strategies because execution costs vary among countries. Execution costs can reduce the expected return and diversification benefits of an international strategy. The difference in return between a paper portfolio and a managed portfolio can be significant. In theory, forecasted costs should be subtracted from expected return before implementing any active strategies. This is all the more important when investing in high-cost countries such as emerging countries. Portfolio managers must gain a good understanding of the determinants of execution costs and should develop some ability to measure them for trades worldwide.

A manager should try to get the best execution for each trade. *Best execution* refers to executing client transactions so that total cost is most favorable to the client under the particular circumstances at the time. Best execution is an objective even though it is difficult to quantify. Execution costs take many forms: some explicit and easily measurable, others implicit and more difficult to measure.

Components of Execution Costs

Costs can be listed in decreasing reliability of estimation, as described in the following three sections.

Commissions, Fees, and Taxes   Commissions paid to brokers are generally negotiated. They depend on the characteristics of the trade (market, liquidity of the stock, size of the order, etc.) and of the market mechanism used (see next section).

Some additional fees are generally paid to compensate for various services, including post-trade settlement costs. As discussed, some taxes are also levied in various countries.

The payment of commissions to brokers often allows access to the broker's research and other services. Therefore, some of the cost is an indirect way to obtain various services beyond direct trading execution. In theory, one should separate the direct dealing cost component and the cost of other services provided ("soft dollars").

All these costs are explicit and easily measurable, but getting the best execution is not equivalent to minimizing commissions and fees.

Market Impact   Executing a transaction will generally have an impact on the price of the security traded. Market impact can be defined as the difference between the actual execution price and the market price that would have prevailed had the manager not sought to trade the security. For example, an order to buy that is large relative to the normal transaction volume in that security will move the price up, at least temporarily. So, one must estimate the market impact of any trade.

In a price-driven system, the bid–ask spread is a major component of the market impact.[8] However, a bid–ask spread is generally quoted for a maximum number of shares that the market maker is willing to trade and is adjusted upward for large transactions; so, a large order will move quoted prices. When investing directly on an order-driven market, there is no bid–ask quote and the market impact has to be estimated from market data. Measuring the overall price impact is a difficult exercise because the price that would have prevailed if the transaction had not taken place, the benchmark price, is not observable. A traditional method to estimate this benchmark price is to compute the volume-weighted average price (VWAP) on the day of the transaction. The idea is that an average of the prices before and after the transaction is an unbiased estimate of the benchmark price. The VWAP method is further discussed below. Market impact is measured as the percentage difference between the execution price and this benchmark price. It must be stressed that the market impact is highly dependent on the order size, market liquidity for the security traded, and the speed of execution desired by the investor. Institutional investors often trade securities in order sizes which are a significant percentage, and even multiple, of the typical daily trading volume for that security. Hence, the market impact for institutional trades can be high, especially if the investor requires immediacy of trading.

Opportunity Cost   The costs mentioned in the preceding section are incurred on an executed trade. But there is also an opportunity cost in case of nonexecution. This opportunity cost can be defined as the loss (or gain) incurred as the result of delay in completion of, or failure to complete in full, a transaction following an initial decision to trade. Opportunity costs can be significant for investors using crossing networks or order-driven systems, in which the risk of nonexecution or partial execution is significant. On any market, it could take hours or days to execute a large trade, and the opportunity cost can be significant in case of an adverse market movement over that period, (for example a price rise in the case of a buy order). Because of this opportunity cost, an active manager is reluctant to complete a trade over a long time period. The information on which the manager bases his trading decision could be quickly reflected in market prices; that is, before the trade is completed. Furthermore there is a risk of information leakage, whereby the progressive price movement caused by the large order reveals that some trader possesses useful information; this can even be more pronounced if the trader's anonymity is not preserved. Anonymity is very important for large active fund managers. If it becomes known that a large active asset manager starts buying or selling some specific shares, other participants will immediately imitate on the assumption that the manager has some superior analysis or information or that the

---

[8] This is also the case when transacting on an order-driven market but asking the broker for a firm bid–ask quotation.

manager will continue buying or selling. The slower an order is completed, the higher the potential opportunity cost. But trading a large order with immediacy induces high market impact. So there is a trade-off between market impact and opportunity cost.

Estimation and Uses of Execution Costs

Deregulation and increased globalization of all stock markets has led to a global trend toward negotiated commissions. Market impact has also been reduced because of the improvement in trading mechanisms and liquidity on most markets. This does not alleviate the need for measurement of execution costs. Some surveys provide estimates of the average cost of a trade in various markets. Other methods, reviewed below, attempt to measure ex-post execution costs on a trade by trade basis. All these measures allow us to derive estimates of expected execution costs that can affect investment strategies.

Global Surveys   Several global surveys of execution costs are available. These give market averages for a typical trade in each country. Various studies come up with different estimates. Exhibit 5.5 reports some cost estimates for trading in the shares on major developed and emerging stock markets obtained from Barclays Global Investors. Market impact is measured at half the bid–ask spread plus price impact for a typical small transaction; the impact would be larger for a large transaction. Trading in non-U.S. securities tends to be somewhat more expensive than trading in U.S. securities. But trading in some European markets, notably France, the Netherlands, Spain, and Germany, tends to be cheaper than in the United States. The execution cost on U.K. securities is large on the buy side (0.76 percent) because of the stamp tax levied on purchases; it is much lower on sales (0.26 percent). Trading on emerging markets incurs large execution costs, often close to 1 percent; these costs can significantly affect the return on a portfolio invested in emerging markets.

Of course, the total execution cost is a function of the size of the transaction and the market depth. The average execution costs for buying a $10 million slice of an EAFE portfolio is estimated to be 0.36 percent by Barclays Global Investors (0.25 percent to sell). The same cost is 0.63 percent for a $1 billion slice (0.53 percent to sell). Execution costs for a large trade in a single stock can be considerably higher than the figures reported here for a diversified EAFE basket of stocks, for which the magnitude of a trade in each stock is rather small.

Detailed Measures: VWAP   As mentioned above, a traditional method to estimate the ex-post execution costs for a trade is to compute the volume-weighted average price (VWAP) on the day of the transaction. The difference between the actual trade price and this benchmark price is an indication of execution costs. The idea is that an average of the prices before and after the transaction is an unbiased estimate of the benchmark price.

EXHIBIT 5.5
Execution Costs in Basis Points

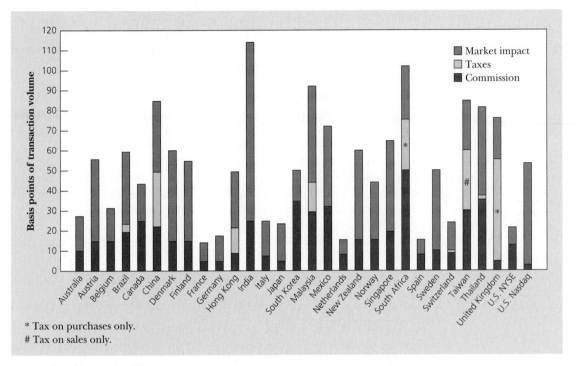

* Tax on purchases only.
# Tax on sales only.

Source: Barclays Global Investors, 2002.

Unfortunately, this method tends to understate the true market price impact of a trade that represents a significant proportion of the day's trading volume. Another criticism is that this method fails to reflect another hidden cost, namely opportunity cost. For example, suppose that a manager wishes to buy 100,000 shares of a stock upon the belief that its price will rise in the near future. An immediate purchase will result in a transaction price that will be significantly higher than the daily VWAP. Spreading the trade over ten days would result in daily transaction prices which will be closer to their daily VWAP. However if the expected price appreciation takes place very quickly, the manager will miss taking full advantage of the initial prediction. The opportunity cost is large and not reflected by the VWAP methodology.

The daily VWAP method has been adapted to measure the VWAP over longer time intervals to better reflect the impact of opportunity costs.

Detailed Measures: Implementation Shortfall A somewhat different approach to measure ex-post costs is the *implementation shortfall*. The implementation shortfall is the difference between the value of the executed portfolio (or share position) and the value of the same portfolio at the time the trading decision was made. This analysis does not require the use of market data on transaction prices and volumes over the period surrounding the executed transaction. The implementation shortfall measures the impact of the trade as well as the impact of intervening market events until the transaction is completed. While opportunity cost is captured, general market movements caused by other factors are also captured. This shortfall can be adjusted for general market movements by subtracting the return on some broad market index over the measurement period.

Using Expected Execution Costs   Estimates of ex-post execution costs can be used to judge whether best execution has been achieved. They also allow us to formulate expectations for execution costs on various types of prospective trades. Indeed, some sophisticated execution cost models have been developed.

Active international strategies should factor forecasted execution costs into their expected return estimates. For example, a manager who desires to sell German stocks and replace them with French stocks should estimate whether the expected return overweighs the execution costs incurred in the buy-and-sell transactions. More generally, execution costs are a drag on returns. To see how execution costs should be taken into account to calculate net expected returns, let's consider a strategy in which

- $E(R)$ is the annual expected return on a strategy before execution costs,

- execution costs are measured (in percentage) as the average cost of a round trip trade (purchase and sale) on the portfolio, and

- the annual turnover ratio is the percentage of the portfolio that is traded during the year; it is commonly measured as the lesser of purchases or sales for a year divided by the average market value of the portfolio during that year.

Then the annual expected return net of execution costs is measured as

Net expected return = $E(R)$ − Turnover ratio × Execution costs.

EXAMPLE 5.6   *EXAMPLE OF THE IMPACT OF EXECUTION COSTS*

An asset manager follows an active international asset allocation strategy. The average execution cost for a buy or a sell order is forecasted at 0.5 percent. On average, the manager turns the portfolio over 1.5 times a year. The annual expected return before transaction costs is 10%. What is the annual expected return net of execution costs?

SOLUTION

On the average, the portfolio is turned over 1.5 times. The average execution cost for a simultaneous purchase and sale of securities is 1 percent (0.5 percent for a buy and 0.5 percent for a sale). Hence, the net expected return is equal to

$$E(R) - \text{Turnover ratio} \times \text{Execution costs} = 10\% - 1.5 \times 1\% = 8.5\%$$

Clearly, the impact of execution costs on returns depends on the level of activity of the account and the markets in which the account is invested.

Some Approaches to Reducing Execution Costs

International investment strategies can be costly, especially for large portfolios. Several approaches can be used to reduce execution costs. Let's take the example of a tactical asset allocation approach, whereby a fund manager decides to reduce the exposure to a country or a region. This would require the sale of a large number of stocks from that region. Rather than trading stock by stock, the manager could engage in *program trading,* in which the manager offers simultaneously a basket of securities for sale. The manager would require a quote from the broker for the whole basket. For the other counterparty, such large trades are often deemed as less risky than a large trade for a single stock because it is clear that they are not motivated by useful information on a specific company; hence, the bid–ask spread quoted could be smaller. There is less risk for the counterparty making a firm quote.

When engaging in a large trade—that is, a trade size that is beyond the normal trade size for which dealers give a standard bid–ask spread, or one that will result in significant market impact—a manager can try to get the best execution through a variety of trading techniques:

- *Internal crossing:* The manager will attempt to cross the order with an opposite order for another client of the firm.
  — The *advantage* is that this is the trading method that minimizes costs.
  — The *disadvantage* is that few managers can use this technique because having offsetting orders among clients is rare. There is also a problem in setting the transaction price. One must be sure to determine the price that would have been obtained in the marketplace and not privilege one client at the expense of another. Internal crossing is mostly applied by very large asset management firms specialized in passive strategies, such as index funds. For example, it could be the case that one client wants to reduce its exposure to European stocks, while another is in the process of building a global portfolio, including European stocks. Active managers would have a difficult time justifying selling shares of one company for a client, based on some forecast or model, and at the same time buying shares of the same company for another client.

- *External crossing:* The manager sends the order to an electronic crossing network, as described above.
  — The *advantage* is that execution costs are very low and anonymity is assured.
  — The *disadvantage* is that it can take a very long time before an opposite order is entered on the crossing network and the trade is executed. Often orders have to be redirected to another trading venue. A large block is less

likely to be swiftly crossed than a small order, as it is unlikely that another party will happen to be interested in an opposite transaction of that magnitude. The speed of execution is a clear disadvantage of this technique which is exposed to opportunity cost.

- *Principal trade:* The manager trades through a dealer who guarantees full execution at a specified discount/premium to the prevailing price. The dealer acts as a principal because he commits to taking the opposite side of the order at a firm price.
  - The *advantage* is that trading immediacy is assured and opportunity cost minimized.
  - The *disadvantage* is the overall execution costs can be quite large. The principal broker commits some of its capital to complete the trade, often buying or selling shares on its own account. A principal dealer must maintain, and finance, an inventory of shares. Hence the dealer has to charge a "rent" for its capital, which increases execution costs. Anonymity cannot be assured, but this is not important as the trade is executed in full and immediately.

- *Agency trade:* The fund manager negotiates a competitive commission rate and selects a broker on the basis of his ability to reduce total execution costs. In turn the broker will "work" the order to try to get the best price for the manager. In a way, the search for best execution is delegated to the broker. The broker acts as an agent because he does not act as the counterparty on its own account but executes the order with another client.
  - The *advantage* is that the fund manager expects to achieve best execution by relying on the quality of the broker who is compensated by a commission. This often leads to a compromise between opportunity cost and market impact.
  - The potential *disdvantage* is that the commission paid could be too large for the quality of service provided. Also anonymity cannot be assured.

- *Use of dealer "indications of interest" (IOI):* Some other party might have a wish to engage in an opposite trade for a stock or basket of stocks. Polling IOIs from various dealers helps to identify possible pools of liquidity.
  - The *advantage* is that the fund manager can hope to achieve low execution costs by finding some opposite trading interest.
  - The *disadvantage* is that this search for liquidity among numerous dealers reveals publicly an interest in the security. Even if the anonymity of the investor is preserved, the trading interest is not.[9] It also slows trading speed. This technique is best suited for informationless trading by passive managers.

- *Use of futures:* There is an opportunity cost associated with the delay in execution of a large trade. The fund manager could use futures to monitor the po-

---

[9] Investors can ask for intentions of interest on a basket of securities to hide their interest in a specific security.

sition while the trade is progressively executed. For example, a manager whose tactical asset allocation decision is to reduce the French exposure on a large portfolio, because of the fear of a sudden drop in the French stock market, could immediately sell futures on the CAC, the French stock index. The manager will progressively sell the French stocks in the portfolio with low execution costs, while simultaneously reducing his position in futures.

— An *advantage* is the reduction in the opportunity cost component of execution costs.

— A *disadvantage* is the additional source of risk if the price of the security traded is not strongly correlated to that of the futures contract. Use of futures is well suited for building positions in diversified portfolios of stocks, with a high correlation between the price of the futures contract and that of the portfolio traded. But it is not well suited for trading in a single security, where the correlation with a stock index futures contract is not so large. So adding a futures position does little to eliminate the opportunity cost for that specific security while adding a new source of risk (the futures price volatility).

Several services, and asset management firms, provide models of expected execution costs. These can also be used as a benchmark when executing a trade. Looking at deviations from the forecasted cost model over a number of trades allows one to review the quality of execution of a broker and of various trading techniques. Choosing a venue to get best execution is basically searching for liquidity. It is a difficult task that depends on the type of trade and implies tradeoffs that depend on several parameters such as:

- *Desire for confidentiality:* An active manager looking for alphas (i.e., betting on the misvaluation of some securities) will be very sensitive to the confidentiality of trades, while a passive manager will be less sensitive.

- *Desire for urgency:* An active manager looking for alphas (i.e., betting on the misvaluation of some securities) will be very sensitive to the speed of transaction, while a passive manager will be a bit less sensitive.

- *Size of transaction:* The larger the transaction relative to the typical daily transaction volume, the higher the market impact.

Finally, fund managers often pay commissions to get additional services such as broker or third-party research (soft dollars). A detailed analysis of execution costs should unbundle these additional services, so that a broker charging a commission is not unduly penalized relative to other trading venues.

In the United Kingdom, the Myners report has prompted managers to focus on minimizing execution costs. A similar focus can be found in the United States. The need to invest in a sophisticated cost-reduction program[10] depends on the type of portfolio strategy followed. Passive index-linked strategies tend to incur

---

[10]Such a program is quite costly in terms of human resources, data management, and modeling.

lower execution costs than active stock-picking strategies because they trade on diversified baskets of securities. But execution cost is an important component of the performance of a manager attempting to closely track an index.[11] Saving a few basis points in execution costs is worth the effort, given the typical size of a passive portfolio. Also, index-linked basket trades are typically repetitive and more easily modeled.

On the other hand, in an active stock-picking strategy, trades are generally not repetitive. A pairwise trade, for example, buying an undervalued French oil company and selling an overvalued British one has unique characteristics. Such trades are not repetitive, and their costs are difficult to model *ex ante*. A focus on execution costs will usually mean finding the broker offering the best execution for this type of trade.

Investing in Foreign Shares Listed at Home

Investors need not go abroad to diversify internationally. We shall discuss several ways to accomplish this.

Global Shares and American Depositary Receipts

Some companies are listed on several stock markets around the world. Multinational firms, such as Royal Dutch/Shell or BP, are traded on more than a dozen markets.

Motivation for Multiple Listing   Foreign companies have a variety of reasons for being listed on several national stock markets, in spite of the additional costs involved:

- Multiple listing gives them more access to foreign ownership, allowing a better diversification of their capital and access to a larger amount of funds than is available from smaller domestic equity markets. For example, numerous firms combine an initial listing on the NYSE with a public offering of new shares in their home market.

- Diversified ownership in turn reduces the risk of a domestic takeover.

- Also, foreign listing raises the profile of a firm in foreign markets, which enables it to raise financing more easily both on the national level and abroad, and is good advertising for its product brands.

- Some companies from emerging countries, especially from remote countries, find multiple listing particularly attractive. Listing abroad allows access

---

[11]This is not only true for a purely indexed strategy, but also for any strategy that promises a small alpha while closely tracking a preassigned index (enhanced indexing).

to a wider capital base and increases the business visibility of the firm. Chinese companies provide a good illustration of this opportunity. Foreign listing is the way to raise new capital abroad. The advantage for non-Chinese investors is that it is easier, and sometimes cheaper, to buy shares on a well-known, developed market. The currency of quotation for shares listed in the United States is the dollar, dividends are paid in dollars, and information in English is provided.

A danger of foreign listing may be the increased volatility of the firm's stock due to a stronger response in foreign versus domestic markets to domestic economic news. Bad political and economic (domestic) news in the Scandinavian countries, for example, has frequently been followed by an immediate negative impact from shares cross-listed on foreign markets. Scandinavian shareholders display less volatile behavior than foreign investors for two reasons: They are not as shaken by bad domestic news, and they tend to keep their capital invested at home anyhow (home bias).

Foreign Listing and ADRs   The procedure for admitting foreign stocks to a local market varies; in some markets, the regulations are quite lenient. For example, in 1986 the Quebec Securities Act allowed a foreign company to list in Montreal simply by meeting the same regulatory requirements as those in the foreign company's jurisdiction. In other markets, foreign companies must abide by the same rules as domestic companies. For instance, non-U.S. companies wanting to be listed on U.S. stock exchanges must satisfy the requirements of both the exchange and the U.S. Securities and Exchange Commission. Although this SEC regulation offers some protection to the U.S. investor, it imposes substantial dual-listing costs on non-U.S. companies, which must produce frequent reports in English.

In the United States and a few other countries, trading takes place in negotiable certificates representing ownership of shares of the foreign company. In the U.S., trading is in Amercian Depositary Receipts (ADRs). Under this arrangement foreign shares are deposited with a U.S. bank, which in turn issues ADRs in the name of the foreign company. To avoid unusual share prices, ADRs may represent a combination of several foreign shares. For example, Japanese shares are often priced at only a few yen per share. They are therefore combined into lots of 100 or more so that their value is more like that of a typical U.S. share. Conversely, some ADRs represent a fraction of the original share. For example, the Nasdaq ADR of LVMH, the French luxury-goods firm, represents one-fifth of a French share.

The United States is the country of preference for foreign listing, with some 450 foreign companies traded on the NYSE and a similar number on the Nasdaq. The total turnover of foreign companies represents over 10% of the NYSE transaction volume. Foreign companies can be traded in several different ways in the United States.

An ADR program created without the company's involvement is usually called an *unsponsored* ADR. These over-the-counter (OTC) shares are traded through *pink sheets,* electronic bulletin boards, or an electronic trading system called PORTAL.

An ADR program created with the assistance of the foreign company is called a *sponsored* ADR. Sponsored ADRs are often classified at three levels:

- *Level I:* The company does not comply with SEC registration and reporting requirements, and the shares can be traded only on the OTC market (but not Nasdaq).

- *Level II:* The company registers with the SEC and complies with its reporting requirements. The shares can be listed on an official U.S. stock exchange (NYSE, ASE) or Nasdaq.

- *Level III:* The company's ADRs are traded on a U.S. stock exchange or Nasdaq and the company may raise capital in the United States through a public offering of the ADRs.

A nonregistered (Level I) company can also raise capital in the United States, but it must be done through a private placement under rule 144A. A drawback of this type of private placement is that only certain private investors and qualified institutional buyers (QIBs) can participate. The retail sector is excluded. Furthermore, liquidity of ADRs on the OTC market is not good. The cost of being registered with the SEC (Levels II and III) is the public reporting that must be performed. The foreign company must file a Form 20-F annually. If domestic statements using national accounting standards are presented as primary statements on Form 20-F, the company must provide a reconciliation of earnings and shareholder equity under domestic and U.S. GAAP. This implies that the company must supply all information necessary to comply with U.S. GAAP. Furthermore the stock exchanges require timely disclosure of various information, including quarterly accounting statements. Some national accounting practices can very easily be reconciled with U.S. practices. For example, the SEC considers that Canadian accounting practices are similar to U.S. practices and accepts Canadian statements: Canadian firms are not required to go through an ADR program; they can simply list their shares on a U.S. stock exchange. Many companies from Bermuda, the Cayman Islands, the Netherlands Antilles, Hong Kong, or Israel simply use the U.S. GAAP statements as their primary financial statements, so they do not even need to provide reconciliation data. At the other extreme, German and Swiss firms have been very reluctant to list shares in the United States because of the difficulty of reconciling U.S. and German or Swiss accounting practices and the detailed information that these firms are not accustomed to disclosing. German and Swiss have tended to smooth reported earnings by using various hidden reserves.

Some firms have issued Global Depositary Receipts (GDRs) that are simultaneously listed on several national markets. These GDRs give the firms access to a larger base to raise new capital. Several Japanese and Chinese firms have seized this opportunity.

When Daimler Benz merged with Chrysler, it decided to become listed on both the Deutsche Bourse and the NYSE. The *same* DaimlerChrysler share is traded on both exchanges, in euros in Frankfurt and in dollars in New York. This is exactly the same share, often called a "global share," that is traded on both exchanges (not an ADR), so an investor can buy shares in Frankfurt and sell them in New York. This would not be possible with an ADR that must go through a difficult conversion process. To make this dual trading possible, several legal and regulatory constraints have to be overcome, besides the accounting harmonization discussed previously. The NYSE has an ambitious program of listing the regular shares of many other foreign companies.

London is another market with trading of depositary receipts as well as very active trading of foreign stocks (SEAQ International). Foreign companies can list their shares and the listings can be in all major currencies. The motivation for trading in London is to reduce transaction costs by avoiding some taxes or high commissions charged on the home market and to benefit from the liquidity provided by highly professional market makers based in London. The reduction in cost brought by the automation of non-U.K. markets has reduced the attraction of London.

Valuation of ADRs   Multiple listing implies that the share values of a company are linked on several exchanges. One company should sell at the same share price all over the world, once adjustments for exchange rates and transactions costs have been made. Arbitrage among markets ensures that this is so. An important question is: What is the dominant force affecting the stock price of a multiple-listed company? In a dominant–satellite market relationship the home market is the dominant force, and the price in the foreign market (the satellite) simply adjusts to the home market price. This is clearly the case for many dual-listed stocks of which only a very small proportion of capitalization is traded abroad. For most ADRs, the price quoted by market makers is simply the home price of the share adjusted by the exchange rate. But, because the ADR market is less liquid, a large bid–ask spread is added. A fairly large discrepancy in prices between the home and foreign market can be observed because the arbitrage costs between the ADR and the original share can be sizable. The answer is less obvious, however, for a few large European companies that have a very active market in other countries (especially the United States). The volume of trading of a few European multinationals is sometimes bigger in New York and London than on their home market. This also applies to a few Latin American firms and to many of the GDRs.

The influence of time zones should also be noted. Because stock trading takes place at different times around the world, U.S. stocks listed on the Paris Bourse are traded before the opening of the U.S. markets. Their French prices reflect not only the previous close in New York and the current exchange rate, but also anticipation about the current day's new price, based on new information released following the U.S. close.

Advantages/Disadvantages   ADRs allow an easy and direct investment in some foreign firms. Although buying ADRs is an attractive alternative for retail investors, it is usually more costly than a direct purchase abroad for a large investor. On the other hand, some ADRs issued by companies from emerging countries tend to have larger trading volumes in New York than in their home markets, and the execution costs are lower in New York. Whereas the small investor may find it more convenient to trade in foreign shares listed on the home market, the large investor may often find the primary market of overseas companies to be more liquid and cheaper. In all cases, price levels, transaction costs, taxes, and administrative costs should be major determinants of whichever market the investor chooses.

Another disadvantage of ADRs is that only a limited number of companies have issued ADRs, and they represent only a small proportion of foreign market capitalization. They tend to be large companies in each country, so they do not offer full international diversification benefits.

EXAMPLE 5.7   EXAMPLE OF PRICE ARBITRAGE

DaimlerChrysler shares are listed in Frankfurt (XETRA) and on the NYSE. You are a German investor with a large portfolio of German and international stocks. You just bought 10,000 shares in Frankfurt at 51 euros per share. In addition, your broker charges a 0.25 percent commission. At the same time, a U.S. broker quotes DaimlerChrysler traded on the NYSE at 44.70–44.90 dollars, net of commissions. The exchange rate quoted in dollar per euro is 0.8800–0.8820 net. So you can buy one euro for 0.8820 dollar and sell one euro for 0.8800 dollar. Would it have been better to buy the shares in New York rather than in Frankfurt, knowing that these are the same global shares?

SOLUTION

Let's compute the euro purchase price of one share listed on the NYSE. You would buy the shares from the broker at 44.90 dollars. To pay for this purchase, you would need to exchange euros for dollars (sell euros, buy dollars) at the rate of 0.8800 dollar per euro. The net purchase cost per share in euros is

$$44.90/0.88 = 51.0227 \text{ euros}$$

The cost of purchasing shares directly in Frankfurt is the purchase price plus the 0.25 percent commission:

$$51 \times 1.0025 = 51.1275 \text{ euros}$$

You would have saved 0.1048 euro per share, or 1,048 euros for the 10,000 shares. Of course, you would end up with shares delivered in New York, but they could be held in custody with the rest of your U.S. stock portfolio.

Closed-End Country Funds

Closed-end country funds have been created for many countries, especially emerging countries.

Definition and Motivation   A closed-end fund is an investment vehicle that buys stocks in the market; in turn, shares of the closed-end fund are traded in the stock market at a price determined by supply and demand for that fund. The number of shares of the fund usually remains fixed and shares cannot be redeemed but are only traded in the stock market. The fund's market price can differ from the value of the assets held in its portfolio, which is called the *net asset value* (NAV). The *premium* on the fund is the difference between the fund market price and its NAV:

Fund market price = NAV + Premium

The premium is often expressed as a *percentage of the NAV* and is usually called a discount when negative. The situation is quite different for a portfolio directly entrusted to a portfolio manager or for an open-end fund, such as a mutual fund. There, the value of the portfolio or fund is, by definition, equal to the market value of the invested assets (the NAV). The advantage of a closed-end fund for the investment manager is that she does not have to worry about redemptions; once a closed-end fund is initially subscribed, the investment manager keeps the money under management. This vehicle is well suited to investing in emerging markets, because the manager does not face redemption demands and so the manager can invest it in the long term without liquidity concerns. The disadvantage for the closed-end shareholder is the uncertainty in the premium, as will be discussed later.

A *country fund* (e.g., the Korea Fund) is a closed-end fund whose assets consist primarily of stocks of the country for which the fund is named (e.g., stocks of Korean companies). Numerous country funds are listed in the United States, the United Kingdom, and major stock markets.

The motivation for investing in those country funds is twofold. First, they offer a simple way to access the local market and benefit from international diversification. For example, country funds invested in Italy, Spain, Australia, the United Kingdom, or Germany can be purchased in the United States. These funds invested in developed markets are of interest primarily to private investors, who find an easy way to hold a diversified portfolio of that country. Country funds are simply managed portfolios specializing in stocks of a specific country. The case for country funds investing in emerging markets is more compelling, because the alternative of investing directly in emerging markets is a more difficult process. Furthermore, some countries (e.g., Brazil, India, Korea, and Taiwan) traditionally restricted foreign investment. Country funds, approved by the local government, are a way to overcome foreign investment restrictions. So, foreign investment restriction is a second motivation for the creation and use of some of these country funds. The International Finance Corporation (IFC) of the World Bank has been instrumental in the launching of country funds in small emerging markets.

The Pricing of Country Funds   The price of a country fund is seldom equal to its NAV. Some funds trade at a substantial premium or discount from their NAV, which poses problems for investors. The change in market price of a country fund is equal to the change in NAV plus the change in the premium (discount). If the premium decreases or the discount widens, the return on the fund will be less than the return on underlying assets making up the portfolio.

Some country funds provide a unique way to invest in emerging countries with foreign investment restrictions. When these foreign investment restrictions are binding, one would expect the country fund to sell at a premium over its NAV; see Bonser-Neal et al. (1990) or Eun, Janakiramanan, and Senbet (1995). The premium should be equal to the amount that investors are willing to pay to circumvent the restriction. Indeed, funds invested in India, Korea, Taiwan, or Brazil have generally sold at a steep but volatile premium. Emerging countries are progressively liberalizing foreign access to their financial markets. When the lifting of a foreign investment restriction is announced, the premium on a local-country fund should drop, as local shares will be more widely available to foreign investors. This drop in premium is a risk associated with investing in these country funds. It can only be hoped that the local market will respond favorably to the prospect of attracting more foreign investors and that a rise in NAV will compensate for a drop in the fund's premium. The liberalization in Brazil and Korea has indeed led to large drops in the premium of closed-end funds invested in those countries.

EXAMPLE 5.8   EXAMPLE OF MOVEMENTS IN PREMIUM

Paf is an emerging country with severe foreign investment restrictions but an active stock market open mostly to local investors. The exchange rate of the pif, the local currency, with the U.S. dollar remains fixed at 1 Pif/$. A closed-end country fund, called *Paf Country Fund,* has been approved by Paf. Its net asset value is 100 dollars. It trades in New York with a premium of 30 percent.

1. Give some intuitive explanations for this positive premium.

2. Paf unexpectedly announces that it will lift all foreign investment restrictions, which has two effects. First, stock prices in Paf go up by 20 percent because of the expectation of massive foreign investment attracted by the growth opportunities in Paf. Second, the premium on the Paf Country Fund drops to zero. Is this scenario reasonable? What would be your total gain (loss) on the shares of Paf Country Fund?

SOLUTION

1. There is no alternative to investing in the closed-end fund for foreign investors. Foreign investors may find Paf shares attractive from a risk–return viewpoint so that they compete and bid up the price.

2. The scenario is reasonable. The net result can be calculated for 100 of original NAV. Before the lifting of restrictions, the fund was worth 130 for 100 of NAV. After the lifting of restrictions, the NAV moves up to 120 and the fund is now worth its NAV, or 120. The rate of return for the foreign investor is

$$\frac{120 - 130}{130} = -7.7\%$$

The volatility in the value of the premium can add volatility to that of the underlying assets. Historically, premiums on country funds have been very volatile. Johnson, Schneeweiss, and Dinning (1993) studied a sample of country funds listed in the United States and invested either in developed markets or in emerging markets. They measured the U.S. dollar volatilities of the fund, the fund's NAV, and the local underlying stock index (e.g., the Korean index for the Korean Fund). For emerging-country funds, the volatility of the fund was about 30 percent more than that of its NAV, and 10 percent more than that of the local stock index. This additional volatility might be a necessary cost to bear when few other alternatives are open. Because these markets are becoming much more accessible, the attraction of country funds is reduced. For developed-country funds, Johnson et al. (1993) found that the volatility of the fund was almost twice as large as that of its NAV or of the local stock index. To avoid the additional volatility of closed-end country funds invested in developed markets investors can buy open-end funds or buy a portfolio directly on the foreign market. These portfolios will always be valued at their NAV, without premium or discount. It can be argued that the large discount observed on many developed-country funds simply reflects large management fees[12] and the lack of liquidity of the market for the fund's shares.

Another interesting feature of the pricing of country closed-end funds listed in the United States is the fact that a fund's value is often strongly correlated with the U.S. stock market and reacts only slowly to changes in the fundamentals (i.e., changes in the NAV). Both phenomena are inconsistent with market efficiency. For example, a Korean fund is a portfolio of Korean stocks; its value should not be affected by movements in the U.S. stock market (beyond the normal correlation between Korea and the United States). Many behavioral finance explanations are provided, including over- and underreaction to news, investor demand, and investor "sentiment." Klibanoff, Lamont, and Wizman (1998) provide an interesting study that focuses on the "salience" of news. They show that, although the elasticity of the fund's price to news is less than one, it is much higher when the news appears on the front page of the *New York Times*. So, investors will react quickly only to salient news.

Advantages/Disadvantages   Closed-end funds allow investors access to a portfolio invested in some foreign region. The portfolio is generally better diversified than a collection of a few ADRs of that region.

The previous discussion of costs and volatility suggests, however, that buying closed-end funds is an inferior substitute for direct investment in foreign stock markets, even for most emerging markets.

Open-End Funds

An open-end mutual fund is publicly offered and its shares can be purchased and redeemed at the NAV of the assets owned by the fund. Although an open-end fund

---

[12]Indeed, Bekaert and Urias (1999) suggest that closed-end funds are not an attractive substitute for direct investment in foreign stock markets, even for most emerging markets.

is attractive from the shareholders' viewpoint, it would be risky for the fund manager if investors could redeem shares at a known NAV (which the manager might not be able to realize if he needs to liquidate assets to meet redemptions). Typically investors must announce their decision to buy/redeem their shares before the NAV is calculated. For example, investors must notify their decision before noon, and the NAV is calculated at the end of the day. For open-end funds invested in foreign shares, the lag between notification and determination of the NAV that will be used to execute the transaction can be a couple of days. A large bid-ask spreads on the fund's price can also be imposed. The efficiency improvements in many emerging markets have allowed managers to offer open-end funds on the most liquid markets. Open-end funds are now offered not only for individual countries but also for regions or international industries. Many of these funds take the form of index funds tracking an international index of developed or emerging market. Most new international open-end funds now take the form of ETFs.

Exchange Traded Funds

ETFs are funds that trade on a stock market like shares of any individual company. They can be traded at any time during market hours, and can be sold short or margined. But ETFs are shares of a portfolio, not of an individual company. ETFs are generally designed to closely track the performance of a specific index. ETFs on the indexes of several individual, developed stock markets, as well as on many international indexes, are listed on all major stock markets. ETFs on some emerging markets, or international emerging indexes, are also offered. So, they can be used for international diversification strategies. ETFs have been an exceptional commercial success in the early 2000s. ETFs are offered by the large asset management firms that specialize in indexing. Other financial institutions offer ETFs under their name by subcontracting with these specialists.

Definition and Motivation   An ETF is an open-end fund with special characteristics (see Gastineau, 2001). ETFs have a management cost advantage over traditional mutual funds because there is no shareholder accounting at the fund level. ETFs are traded like common stocks. A major feature is the redemption in-kind process. Creation/redemption units are created in large multiples of individual ETF shares, for example 50,000 shares. These units are available to exchange specialists (*authorized participants*) who will generally act as market makers for the individual shares. If an authorized participant decides to redeem ETF shares, it will do so by exchanging the redemption unit for a portfolio of stocks held by the fund and used to track the index. The fund publishes the portfolio that it is willing to accept for in-kind transactions. As opposed to traditional open-end funds, the in-kind redemption means that no capital gain will be realized in the fund's portfolio on redemption. If the redemption is in cash, a traditional fund may have to sell stocks held in the fund's portfolio. If their price has appreciated, the fund will realize a capital gain and the tax burden will have to be passed to all existing fund share-holders. This is not the case with ETFs. As in any open-end fund, though, individual ETF shareholders[13] can require in-cash redemption based on the NAV. Redemption in cash by individual ETF shareholders is discouraged in two ways:

- Redemption is based on the NAV computed one or a couple of days after the shareholder commits to redemption. So, the redemption value is unknown when the investor decides to redeem.

- A large fee is assessed on in-cash redemptions.

It is more advantageous for individual ETF shareholders to sell their shares on the market than to redeem them in cash. The sale can take place immediately based on observed share prices at a low cost. Arbitrage by authorized participants ensures that the listed price is close to the fund's NAV.[14] Authorized participants maintain a market in the ETF share by posting bid and ask prices with a narrow spread, or by entering buy-and-sell limit orders in an electronic order book. The transaction costs of ETFs can be estimated as the sum of the commission charged by the broker plus half this bid–ask spread.

International ETFs have distinguishing features. An ETF indexed on some less-liquid emerging market is bound to have high bid–ask spreads. Managing an ETF on a broad international index, such as EAFE, means holding stock from numerous countries with different custodial arrangements and time zones. Again, the bid–ask spreads are likely to be larger than for plain-vanilla ETFs. But the size of the ETF is an important factor influencing costs. The effect of non-overlapping time zones should be taken into account when comparing the ETF price with its NAV. Consider the example of an ETF on a Japanese stock index, traded in New York. During Wall Street opening hours, the Tokyo stock market is closed. The NAV available in the morning in the United States is based on the closing prices in Tokyo several hours before New York opens. Except for currency fluctuations, the NAV will remain unchanged as Tokyo is closed throughout the New York trading session. However, the ETF price will be affected by expectations about future stock prices in Tokyo, so it could differ significantly from the official NAV. This is not an inefficiency and there are no arbitrage opportunities, because the NAV is stale and does not correspond to current market pricing.

Advantages/Disadvantages ETFs are attractive to individual investors because they offer the benefits of international diversification with excellent liquidity at a low cost. They are also designed to be tax efficient. ETFs are useful in an inter-

---

[13]But authorized participants commit to redeem only in kind.

[14]The fund publishes an indicative intraday NAV every 15 seconds; it is available on major data providers, such as Bloomberg, Reuters, or Telekurs.

EXAMPLE 5.9   ETF PRICING

An ETF is indexed on a Japanese stock index and is listed in New York. Its NAV is computed based on closing prices in Tokyo. When it is 9 A.M. in New York, it is already 11 P.M. in Tokyo, on the same day. The NAV based on Tokyo closing prices is 10,000 yen. The exchange rate at 9 A.M. EST is 1 dollar = 100 yen.

1. What is the dollar NAV of this ETF at the opening of trading in New York?

2. When New York closes at 4 P.M. EST, Tokyo is still closed (6 A.M. local time), but the exchange rate is now 99 yen per dollar. What is the dollar NAV at closing time?

3. Bad international news hit after the Tokyo closing. European and U.S. stock markets dropped by 5 percent. Should the ETF price have remained at its NAV? Assuming that the Tokyo market is strongly correlated with the U.S. market (at least for this type of international news), give an estimate of the ETF price at the New York closing.

SOLUTION

1. The dollar NAV is $100 (= 10,000/100).

2. The closing dollar NAV is $101.01 (= 10,000/99)

3. The price of the ETF should reflect expectations that the Tokyo stock index will drop in reaction to the news, so its price should be below the NAV computed on past closing prices in Tokyo. If the markets are strongly correlated, we could estimate that Tokyo will also drop by 5 percent. Hence, we should have an estimated market value for the dollar NAV equal to

$$10{,}000 \times (1{-}0.05)/99 = \$95.96$$

This is an estimate of the current price of the ETF. It will trade at a 5 percent discount from its "official" NAV.

---

national portfolio strategy. They can be purchased in the home market while offering a diversified play on a foreign market or region. They are well designed to be used in active asset allocation. On the other hand, they usually are designed to match a benchmark and will not provide active return above that benchmark. To add active return, investors can combine them with the direct purchase of specific companies or ADRs.

For large institutional investors, the alternative is to invest directly in an indexed, or actively managed, international portfolio; the cost structure could be less and the tax situation equivalent or better.

Summary

- Stock exchanges throughout the world evolved from three models: private bourses, public bourses, and bankers' bourses.

- Trading procedures differ in an order-driven market and in a price-driven market. In a price-driven market, there are market makers who stand ready to buy or sell at posted prices (bid and ask prices). In an order-driven market, all buy-and-sell orders are entered in a central order book and a new order is immediately matched with the book of limit orders previously submitted. Each system presents advantages and risks for traders and customers.

- Electronic communication and crossing networks (ECNs) have developed alongside official stock exchanges. Electronic crossing networks match anonymously buy-and-sell orders submitted by institutional investors and broker-dealers at prespecified times and at prices determined in the primary market for the security. The trade is made at the midpoint between the bid and the ask prices of the primary market, so there is no market impact or bid–ask spread even for large orders. But there is also no trading immediacy.

- The relative market capitalization of national equity markets has changed dramatically over time. The share of the U.S. equity markets moved from two-thirds of the world market in 1972 to only one-third by the early 1990s, when Japan had about the same market size as the United States. In 2002, the U.S. equity market represented some 50 percent of the world market cap, followed by Europe (around 30 percent) and Japan (around 10 percent).

- Numerous stock indexes are available to track country and regional markets and measure performance. They can be domestic stock indexes computed locally, such as the U.S. Dow Jones Industrial Average or the Japanese Nikkei 225 stocks average. They can be global stock indexes computed by a global organization, such as MSCI, FTSE, DJ, or S&P.

- Many practical aspects must be taken into account in global equity investing: market concentration, liquidity, tax aspects, and transaction costs.

- Asset managers should try to get the best execution for each trade. Execution costs include several components: commissions and fees, market impact, and opportunity cost. Although commissions and fees are easy to measure, this is less true for market impact and opportunity cost. A transaction has an impact on the price of the security traded, so market impact can be a significant component of execution cost.

- To optimize global asset management, one should forecast the execution cost of trading in the various markets. Several global surveys of execution costs are available, but the actual cost depends on the transaction size and the market depth for the specific trade. Various trading techniques allow reduction of execution costs.

■ It is possible to get some of the benefits of international diversification by investing solely in securities or funds listed at home:

▪ Some companies have their shares traded on foreign exchanges; these are called ADRs in the United States. Unfortunately, the number of foreign-listed companies is small, and the price of these ADRs is sometimes unattractive. A few companies offer global shares listed and traded simultaneously in several stock markets.

▪ Some closed-end funds specialize in investing in foreign stock markets. The market price of these country funds often differs from their net asset value by a large premium (or discount). The uncertainty concerning this premium adds to investment risk.

▪ Exchange traded funds (ETFs) are special open-end funds that trade on a stock market like shares of individual companies. Their design has made them very successful. The most popular ETFs track some country or regional stock indexes.

Problems

1. Which of the following statements about stock markets is not true?
   I. Many of the stock markets are organized as private bourses.
   II. On most markets, stocks are traded on a cash basis, and transactions are settled within a two- to five-day period.
   III. The central electronic limit order book is the hub of those automated markets that are price-driven.
   IV. An auction market, such as the Paris Bourse, is also known as an order-driven market.

2. The central limit order book of Air Liquide, a French firm that trades on the Paris Bourse, is currently as follows:

Sell Orders		Buy Orders	
Quantity	Limit	Limit	Quantity
500	151	145	500
2,000	150	143	2,000
1,000	149	142	1,000
500	147	141	2,000
500	146	140	1,000

   a. Vincent Jacquet wishes to buy 1,500 shares and enters a market order to buy those shares. At what price will Jacquet buy the shares?
   b. Suppose Vincent Jacquet had instead wanted to sell 1,000 shares of Air Liquide that he already had in his investment portfolio. At what price will he sell those shares?

3. *Business Objects* trades on the Paris Bourse as ordinary shares and on the Nasdaq as American Depositary Receipts (ADRs). One ADR of *Business Objects* corresponds to one share on the Paris Bourse. Suppose the last transaction of *Business Objects* on the Paris Bourse was at €25. An investor then entered on the French electronic trading system a limit order to purchase *Business Objects* shares at €24. The ADR price quoted by a

Nasdaq dealer is $23.90–24.45. The exchange rate is $0.96/€. Suppose that some unfavorable information suddenly arrives that suggests that a lower price of *Business Objects* shares at €21 would be fair. Assuming that the exchange rate has not changed, discuss which parties stand to lose on the Paris Bourse and on Nasdaq?

4. It is often argued that automated order-driven trading systems must provide special arrangements for small trades (which are often market orders), as well as for block trades. Advance some explanations for this argument.

5. Which of the following statements about electronic communication and crossing networks (ECNs) is/are true?
   I. Electronic communication networks are order-driven systems, in which the limit order book plays a central role.
   II. Electronic crossing networks anonymously match buy-and-sell orders by a pool of participants, generally institutional investors and broker-dealers.
   III. In an ECN, a trade takes place only during a crossing session time and only if there are offsetting orders entered by other participants.

6. Consider a European electronic crossing network that runs six crosses daily, that is, the orders are matched six times a day. This network allows a participant to specify several constraints, such as price and minimum fill. Suppose that all the orders submitted to this network for the shares of Christian Dior are Good for Day (GFD); that is, any unfulfilled part of an order is automatically resubmitted to subsequent crossing sessions duing the day.
   a. The following orders are on the network for the shares of Christian Dior at the time of the first crossing session of the day. The most recent trading price of Christian Dior at the Paris Bourse is €37.
      - Participant A: a market order to buy 100,000 shares
      - Participant B: a market order to sell 50,000 shares
      - Participant C: a market order to sell 150,000 shares, with a minimum fill of 125,000 shares
      - Participant D: an order to buy 20,000 shares at €36

   Discuss what trades would take place on the crossing network and what orders would remain unfulfilled.

   b. The following new orders are submitted to the next crossing session. The most recent trading price of Christian Dior at the Paris Bourse is €38.
      - Participant E: a market order to buy 150,000 shares
      - Participant F: A market order to sell 50,000 shares

   Discuss what trades would take place on the crossing network in this crossing session and what orders would remain unfulfilled.

7. The U.S. stock market capitalization is larger relative to U.S. GDP than is the case in most European countries for all the following reasons *except:*
   a. A greater proportion of firms in Europe is nationalized.
   b. European banks cannot own shares of stock of their client firms.
   c. Many European companies rely heavily on bank financing.
   d. Privately held companies are a tradition in Europe.

8. Standard & Poor's (S&P) announced in 2001 that it was considering integrating free-float adjustments to its existing practices for the S&P Australian index. It said that it would use a measure called Investable Weight Factor (IWF) to reflect a company's free float. A full

free-floated company will have an IWF of 100 percent. For others, the IWF will be adjusted downward by subtracting the percentage of shares that are not freely available for trade. Now consider three Australian manufacturing companies: Alpha, Beta, and Gamma. Alpha owns 5 percent each of Beta and Gamma. Gamma owns 15 percent of Beta. Taking into account the cross-holdings, what will be the IWF of each company?

9. Four companies belong to a group and are listed on a stock exchange. The cross-holdings of these companies are as follows:
   - Company A owns 20 percent of Company B and 10 percent of Company C.
   - Company B owns 15 percent of Company C.
   - Company C owns 10 percent of Company A, 10 percent of Company B, and 5 percent of Company D.
   - Company D has no ownership in any of the other three companies.

   Each company has a market capitalization of $50 million. You wish to adjust for cross-holding in determining the weights of these companies in a free-float market capitalization–weighted index.
   a. What are the market capitalizations of each company after adjustment to reflect free float?
   b. What would be the total adjusted market cap of the four companies?

10. The shares of Volkswagen trade on the Frankfurt stock exchange. A U.S. investor purchased 1,000 shares of Volkswagen at €56.91 each, when the exchange rate was $/€ = 0.9790–0.9795. Three months later, the investor received a dividend of €0.50 per share, and the investor decided to sell the shares at the then prevailing price of €61.10 per share. The exchange rate was $/€ = 0.9810–0.9815. The dividend withholding tax rate in Germany is 15% and there is a tax treaty between the United States and Germany to avoid double taxation.
    a. How much did the U.S. investor receive in dividends in dollars, net of tax?
    b. What were the capital gains from the purchase and sale of Volkswagen shares?
    c. How would the dividend income be declared by the investor on a U.S. tax return, and what tax credit would he receive?

11. The shares of Microsoft were trading on Nasdaq on January 1 at $41. A Swedish investor purchased 100 shares of Microsoft at that price. The Swedish kroner to dollar exchange rate then was Skr/$ = 9.4173–9.4188. One year later, the investor received a dividend of $2 per share, and the investor then sold the shares at a price of $51 per share. The exchange rate at that time was Skr/$ = 9.8710–9.8750. The dividend withholding tax rate in the United States is 15 percent and there is a tax treaty between the United States and Sweden that allows the U.S. withholding tax to be used as a tax credit in Sweden. Suppose the Swedish investor is taxed at 50 percent on income and 15 percent on capital gains, and ignore any commissions on purchase and sale of shares.
    a. What is the gross rate of return on the investment, in dollars?
    b. What is the gross rate of return on the investment, in kroners?
    c. What is the rate of return on the investment, in kroners, net of taxes?

12. Which of the following statements best characterizes the taxation of returns on international investments in an investor's country and the country where the investment is made?
    a. Capital gains normally are taxed only by the country where the investment is made.
    b. Tax-exempt investors normally must pay taxes to the country where the investment is made.

    c. Investors in domestic common stock normally avoid double taxation on dividend income by receiving a tax credit for taxes paid to the country where the investment is made.

    d. The investor's country normally withholds taxes on dividends payments.

13. A U.S. institutional investor would like to purchase 10,000 shares of Lafarge. Lafarge is a French firm that trades on the Paris Bourse, the London stock exchange, and the NYSE as an ADR. At the NYSE, one depositary receipt is equivalent to one-fourth of a Lafarge share. The U.S. investor asks its brokers to quote net prices, without any commissions, in the three trading venues. There is no stamp tax in London on foreign shares listed there. The stock quotes are as follows:

New York:	$24.07–24.37
London:	£66.31–67.17
Paris:	€99.40–100.30

The exchange rate quotes from banks are as follows:

$/£ = 1.4575–1.4580

$/€ = 0.9691–0.9695

Compare the dollar costs of purchasing 10,000 shares, or its equivalent, in New York, London, and Paris.

14. The chief financial executive of a German firm is considering raising capital in the United States by cross-listing her firm on the NYSE as an ADR and having a public offering. However, the executive has some concerns about this. Discuss what you think some of these concerns might be.

15. A U.S. institutional investor would like to buy 10,000 shares of British polythene industries. This U.K. firm trades on the London stock exchange, but not on the NYSE or Nasdaq. A U.K.-based broker of the investor quotes the price as £3.45–3.60, with a commission of 0.10 percent of the transaction value. There is a 0.50 percent U.K. securities transaction tax on purchase. The exchange rate quoted by a bank is $/£ = 1.5005–1.5010. What would be the total cost in dollars?

16. A French institutional investor wishes to decrease its exposure to Taiwan. It is interested in selling 20,000 shares of a particular Taiwanese firm that is currently in its portfolio. This firm trades on the Taiwan Stock Exchange. A Taiwan-based broker quotes the Taiwan dollar (TW$) price of the shares of this firm as 150.35–150.75, with a commission of 0.10 percent of the transaction value. The Taiwan Stock Exchange charges a tax of 0.30 percent of the value traded from the seller. A bank is quoting the TW$ to € exchange rate as 32.8675–32.8800. How many euros will the French institutional investor receive on selling the shares?

17. Which of the following statements is/are true about stock indexes?

    I. Compared with the equal-weighted indexes, market value–weighted indexes are better representative of movements in the market.

    II. Many of the global indexes, such as those provided by MSCI (Morgan Stanley Capital International) and Standard and Poor's (S&P), are widely used by international money managers for asset allocation decisions and performance measurements.

    III. It is possible that, in any given year, the performance between two indexes for the same stock market can differ significantly, by as much as several percentage points.

18. In 1996, a group of securities called the World Equity Benchmark Shares (WEBS) started trading on the American Stock Exchange. WEBS for a country is a passively managed ETF indexed on the MSCI country benchmark index for that country. All else equal, what do you think would be the effect of the launch of WEBS for a country on the premium or discount of the closed-end country fund for that country?

19. Consider a closed-end country fund that trades in the United States. Suppose that country decides to impose restrictions on investments by foreigners in that country. All other things constant, what do you think would be the effect of these international investment restrictions on the price–net asset value ratio of the closed-end fund for that country?

20. A U.S. institutional investor with a large portfolio of U.S. and international stocks wants to add 20,000 shares of DaimlerChrysler to its portfolio. DaimlerChrysler trades as the same global share on several exchanges in the world. A U.S. broker quotes the NYSE price of DaimlerChrysler as $43.45–43.65, net of commissions. The institutional investor is also considering purchasing shares in Germany, where the offer price quoted for DaimlerChrysler's shares on the Frankfurt stock exchange (XETRA) is €44.95, with a 0.10 percent commission to be paid on the transaction value. Which of the two alternatives is better for the investor? How much would be the total saving by using the better of the two alternatives? The exchange rate is $/€ 0.9705–0.9710.

21. Consider a U.K. index fund that trades on a U.S. exchange. This fund is indexed on a British stock index based on several stocks that trade on the London stock exchange. The different time zones of the U.K. and the U.S. markets result in four distinct time periods in a 24-hour period: one, a six-hour time period prior to the U.S. open, when the market in London is open but the market in the United States is not. Two, a two-hour period between 9:30 A.M. and 11:30 A.M. in New York when both London and New York markets are open. Three, a 4.5 hour time period between 11:30 A.M. and 4:00 P.M. in New York when the New York market is open but the London market is not. And, four, the subsequent period when both markets are closed. For each of these time periods, discuss how British pound NAV and the U.S. dollar price of the fund would fluctuate.

Solutions

1. The central electronic limit order book is the hub of those automated markets that are order-driven (not price-driven.) Statement III, therefore, is not correct.

2. a. The market order will be executed against the best matching order(s). Accordingly, Vincent Jacquet will buy 500 shares at €146 each, 500 shares at €147 each, and the remaining 500 shares at €149 each.
   b. Again, the market order will be executed against the best matching order(s). Accordingly, Vincent Jacquet will sell 500 shares at €145 each and 500 shares at €143 each.

3. On the Paris Bourse, the investor who placed the limit order at €24 stands to lose. Informed market participants can sell the share to this investor at €24, although the share is truly worth only €21. In contrast, the dealer is exposed to lose on Nasdaq. The dealer quote is $23.90–24.45, which is equivalent to €24.90–25.47 at the prevailing ex-

change rate. Informed market participants can sell the share to the Nasdaq dealer at the bid price of $23.90, although the share is truly worth only €21 or $20.16.

4. Small orders are generally market orders (buy or sell at the best price available in the market). In an order-driven system without developed market making, the automated limit order book generally shows a huge spread between the lowest ask and the highest bid of the orders currently in the system. When a new market order reaches the system, it is unlikely that a matching opposing market order will reach the system at exactly the same time. So, the market order will be executed against the limit order book. Given the wide spread, this will generally imply a transaction at a price that is very different from that of the previous transaction. To avoid this problem, one could have a periodic auction system in which all small orders are stored for a while and an auction takes place infrequently. Another alternative is the "trading halt" used in Tokyo.

   Very large orders (such as block trades—trades of 10,000 shares or more) run a serious risk of being "picked off" on an order-driven system. A large limit order is likely to remain posted for a long time on the computer system. The client is exposed to the risk that someone gets some news about the company or the market before the client is able to revise the posted limit price on the order. Buyers or sellers of large blocks of shares do not wish to be exposed to such a risk. Hence, special procedures have been put into place. Generally, block trades take place off the automated system and are reported only after some accepted delay.

5. Each of the three statements about ECNs is true.

6. a.   There are not enough buy orders to meet the minimum fill requirement of Participant C, and his order would not be fulfilled. Participant A would buy 50,000 shares at €37 each, and Participant B would sell 50,000 shares at €37 each. Half of participant A's order would remain unfulfilled. Because the prevailing price is €37, Participant D's order to buy at €36 would remain unfulfilled. All unfulfilled orders of Participants A, C, and D would be resubmitted to the next crossing session because they are all GFD orders.
   b.   Taking into account the trading activity in the first crossing session and the new orders submitted to the next session, the following orders would be there for the next session:
      - Participant A: a market order to buy 50,000 shares
      - Participant C: a market order to sell 150,000 shares, with a minimum fill of 125,000 shares
      - Participant D: an order to buy 20,000 shares at €36
      - Participant E: a market order to buy 150,000 shares
      - Participant F: a market order to sell 50,000 shares

   In this session, the orders of participants A, C, E, and F would be completely filled. Participants A and E would buy 50,000 and 150,000 shares, respectively. Participants C and F would sell 150,000 and 50,000 shares, respectively. All the transactions would be at €38 per share. Participant D's order would still not be executed and would be resubmitted to the next crossing session later that day.

7. Unlike U.S. banks, it is common for European banks to own shares of their client banks. Accordingly, the answer is (b).

8. Because there are no cross-holdings by either Beta or Gamma in Alpha, IWF for Alpha = 100%. For Beta, IWF = 100 − 5 − 15 = 80%. For Gamma, IWF = 100 − 5 = 95%.

9. The apparent market capitalization of these four companies taken together is 50 million × 4 = 200 million. But because of their cross-holdings, there is some double counting. The usual free-float adjustment would be to retain only the portion that is not owned by other companies within the group.

   a. The adjusted market capitalization is as follows:
      - Company A: 50 × (1 − 0.10) = $45 million (because 10% of Company A is held by Company C.)
      - Company B: 50 × (1 − 0.20 − 0.10) = $35 million (because 20% of Company B is held by Company A and 10% of Company B is held by Company C.)
      - Company C: 50 × (1 − 0.10 − 0.15) = $37.5 million (because 10% of Company C is held by Company A and 15% of Company C is held by Company B.)
      - Company D: 50 × (1 − 0.05) = $47.5 million (because 5% of Company D is held by Company C.)

   b. From (a) above, the total adjusted market capitalization = 45 + 35 + 37.5 + 47.5 = $165 million. Because the unadjusted market capitalization of each company is the same, the total adjusted market cap can also be computed by subtracting the total cross-holdings from 200 million. The total cross-holdings are 50 × (0.20 + 0.10 + 0.15 + 0.10 + 0.10 + 0.05) = $35 million. Thus, the total adjusted market cap = 200 − 35 = $165 million.

10. a. Net dividend in euros, after deducting withholding tax = €0.50 per share × 1,000 shares × (1 − 0.15) = €425. So, the net dividend in dollars = €425 × $0.9810/€ = $416.93.

    b. The investor bought the shares for €56.91 per share × 1,000 shares = €56,910, or €56,910 × $0.9795/€ = $55,743.35.

       The investor sold the shares for €61.10 per share × 1,000 shares = €61,100, or €61,100 × $0.9810/€ = $59,939.1.

       Thus, capital gains = 59,939.1 − 55,743.35 = $4,195.75.

    c. The investor would need to declare the total dividends, that is, without deducting the withholding tax, as dividend income. So, the dividend income to be declared is €0.50 per share × 1,000 shares × $0.9810/€ = $490.50.

       Note that because of the tax treaty between the U.S. and Germany, however, the investor can deduct from income tax a tax credit for the dividends withheld in Germany; the tax credit is 490.50 − 416.93 = $73.57. (The tax credit can be computed alternatively as €0.50 per share × 1,000 shares × 0.15 × $0.9810/€ = $73.57.)

11. a. Initial investment = 41 × 100 = $4,100

       Gross dividend = 2 × 100 = $200

       Selling value = 51 × 100 = $5,100

       Gross return in dollars = (5,100 + 200 − 4,100)/4,100 = 0.2927, or 29.27 percent

    b. Initial investment = $4,100 × Skr9.4188/$ = Skr 38,617.08

       Gross dividend = $200 × Skr9.8710/$ = Skr 1,974.20

       Selling value = $5,100 × Skr9.8710/$ = Skr 50,342.10

       Gross return in kroners = (50,342.10 + 1,974.20 − 38,617.08)/38,617.08 = 0.3547, or 35.47 percent

c. Capital gains = Selling value − Initial investment = 50,342.10 − 38,617.08 = Skr 11,725.02

Capital gains tax = 0.15 × 11,725.02 = Skr 1,758.75

Though 15% of the dividend was withheld in the United States, income tax in Sweden would be levied on the gross dividend of Skr 1,974.20. So, income tax = 0.50 × 1,974.20 = Skr 987.10. The effect of the dividends withheld in the U.S. is exactly offset by the withholding tax credit. So, we could use the gross dividend (net of Swedish income taxes) in computing the net return. Accordingly, rate of return, in kroners, net of taxes = (Capital gains + Gross dividend − Capital gains tax − Income tax)/Initial investment = (11,725.02 + 1,974.20 − 1,758.75 − 987.10)/38,617.08 = 0.2836, or 28.36 percent.

12. The correct answer is (c): Investors in non-domestic common stock normally avoid double taxation on dividend income by receiving a tax credit for taxes paid to the country where the investment is made.

13. Cost in U.S. dollars per share = $24.37 × 4 = $97.48 (because one Lafarge ADR is equivalent to one-fourth of a Lafarge share.) Therefore,

Cost in U.S. dollars for 10,000 shares = $974,800

Cost of purchasing in London = £67.17 × $1.4580/£ × 10,000 = $979,338.60

Cost of purchasing in Paris = €100.30 × $0.9695/€ × 10,000 = $972,408.50

Thus, it is the cheapest to buy the shares in Paris.

14. The German firm is considering a Level III ADR program. Accordingly, it must satisfy the requirements of both the NYSE and the U.S. Securities and Exchange Commission (SEC). This could impose substantial dual-listing costs on the German firm. The SEC will require the German firm to file a Form 20-F annually. On this form, the firm will have to provide a reconciliation of earnings and shareholder equity under German and U.S. GAAP. This implies that the company will have to supply all information necessary to comply with U.S. GAAP. Furthermore, the NYSE will require timely disclosure of various information, including quarterly accounting statements.

Overall, the disclosure requirements may cause considerable concern, as German and U.S. accounting practices differ substantially. Also, German firms are not accustomed to disclosing as much information in Germany as is required in the United States. They are also not used to producing frequent reports in English. The firm may face another hurdle if it is accustomed to smoothening reported earnings by using various hidden reserves. Another concern that the German firm may have is that cross-listing may increase the volatility of its share prices. It may feel that the U.S. investors may be quicker in selling their shares of the German firm in response to bad news than would the German investors.

15. The cost in British pounds, including commission and transaction tax, would be £3.60/share × 10,000 shares × (1 + 0.0010 + 0.0050) = £36,216. So, the cost in dollars would be £36,216 × $1.5010£ = $54,360.22.

16. The receipt in TW$, after excluding commission and transaction tax, would be TW$150.35/share × 20,000 shares × (1 − 0.0010 − 0.0030) = TW$2,994,972. So, the receipt in euros would be TW$2,994,972 / TW$ 32.88/€ = €91,087.96.

17. Each of the three statements is true.

18. The creation of WEBS for a country creates an additional option for an investor seeking to invest in equities in that country. Having an additional method by which to participate in a foreign market is likely to cause the premium on an existing closed-end country fund to narrow if the fund is trading at a premium. Or, if the existing closed-end country fund is trading at a discount, the launching of WEBS for that country is likely to make it even less attractive, leading to a widening of the discount.

19. The announcement of foreign investment restrictions increases the importance of closed-end country funds for U.S. investors who want exposure to that country in their investment portfolios. Therefore, all other things constant, these restrictions are likely to increase the premium or decrease the discount on the country-fund's shares. That is, the price–net asset value ratio is likely to increase.

20. The cost of 20,000 shares in the United States is \$43.65 per share × 20,000 shares = \$873,000. The cost in Germany in euros, including a 0.10% commission, would be €44.95 × 20,000 shares × 1.0010 = €899,899. So, the cost in dollars is €899,899 × \$/€ 0.9710 = \$873,801.93. Thus, it is better to buy the shares traded on the NYSE, saving 873,801.93 − 873,000.00 = \$801.93.

21. During the six-hour time period when London is trading but the United States is not, the NAV of the fund in British pounds would be fluctuating in accordance with how the prices of the stocks in the index are changing. Because the U.S. market is closed, the most recent reported dollar price of the fund in the United States would not have changed. Then the U.S. market opens, and the fund's shares in the United States would open at a price based on the NAV in the United Kingdom at that time and the prevailing dollar-to-pound exchange rate. During the two-hour overlapping time period when both markets are open, the NAV in pounds would continue to change. The price of the fund in dollars would also be changing consistent with the changes in NAV and exchange rate. During the subsequent 4.5-hour time period when the New York market is open but the London market is not, the most recent reported NAV in pounds would remain the same. However, the price of the fund in the United States could change as the exchange rate changes and as new information comes in that affects investors' expectations about future stock prices in the United Kingdom. Then, the U.S. market closes, and during the time period when both markets are closed, the most recent reported U.S. prices and NAV in pounds also stay the same.

Bibliography

Bekaert G., and Urias, M. S. "Is There a Free Lunch in Emerging Market Equities?" *Journal of Portfolio Management,* 1999.

Bonser-Neal, C., Brauer, G., Neal, R., and Wheatley, S. "International Investment Restrictions and Closed-End Country Fund Prices," *Journal of Finance,* June 1990.

Conrad, J., Johnson, K. M., and Wahal, S. "Institutional Trading Costs and Alternative Trading Systems," *Journal of Financial Economics,* forthcoming.

Domowitz, I. "Liquidity, Transaction Costs and Reintermediation in Electronic Market," Penn State Working Paper, April 2001.

Eun, C., Janakiramanan, S., and Senbet, L.W. "The Design and Pricing of Country Funds under Market Segmentation," presented at the AFA annual meetings, January 1995.

Gastineau G. L., "Exchange-Traded Funds: An Introduction," *Journal of Portfolio Management,* Spring 2001.

Huang, R. "The Quality of ECN and Nasdaq Market Maker Quotes," *Journal of Finance,* 57 (3), June 2002.

Johnson, G., Schneeweiss, T., and Dinning, W. "Closed-End Country Funds: Exchange Rate and Investment Risk," *Financial Analysts Journal,* November-December 1993.

Klibanoff, P., Lamont, O., and Wizman, T. A. "Investor Reaction to Salient News in Closed-End Country Funds," *Journal of Finance,* 53(2), April 1998, pp. 673–699.

6

Equity: Concepts and Techniques

LEARNING OUTCOMES

After completing this chapter, you will be able to do the following:

- Discuss the major differences in national accounting standards, as well as between national standards and international accounting standards (IAS)

- Discuss off-balance-sheet assets and liabilities such as special purpose entities

- Discuss how to analyze the accounting treatment of employee stock option compensation

- Demonstrate how neoclassical growth theory and endogenous growth theory can be used to explain trends in economic growth

- Demonstrate how to conduct a global industry analysis by analyzing

- return potential and risk characteristics

- Demonstrate how to conduct global financial analysis, including DuPont analysis

- Discuss the role of market efficiency in individual stock valuation

- Discuss franchise value and the growth process

- Demonstrate how to analyze the effects of inflation for valuation purposes

- Discuss multifactor models as applied in the global context

Thomas R. Robinson, CPA, CFA, made significant contributions to the accounting material in this chapter.

Investing in foreign stocks poses at least two types of problems: First, the portfolio manager must gain sufficient familiarity with the operations, trading mechanisms, costs, and constraints of foreign markets. This issue was addressed in Chapter 5. Second, the portfolio manager's investment approach must be global; that is, his method of analyzing and selecting stocks should be part of an optimal worldwide investment strategy. The conceptual and technical aspects of this analysis are discussed in this chapter. Chapter 13 is devoted to designing a global international asset allocation strategy.

To structure their analysis of expected return and risk of stocks, investors must start from a view of the world. What are the worldwide factors affecting stock prices? In an open-economy world, companies should be valued relative to their global competitors; hence, global industry analysis is of primary importance. Before conducting such an analysis, it is important to understand the differences in national accounting standards that affect the raw information used. Then the important aspects of global industry analysis can be studied with data adjusted for comparability across countries. Global industry analysis of expected returns and risks leads naturally to a discussion of risk factor models used to structure global portfolios and manage their risk.

Approaching International Analysis

There is nothing unique to financial analysis in an international context. Analysts must already take foreign variables into account in evaluating domestic firms. After all, product markets in which many domestic industrial companies compete are international.

CONCEPTS IN ACTION   *TOYOTA ECLIPSES ITS U.S. RIVALS*

Japanese Carmaker Delivers Record Half-year Results with a 90% Surge in Profits

Toyota Motor yesterday reinforced the Japanese car industry's ranking as the most profitable in the world when it produced record half-year results.

The 90 percent jump in consolidated net profits to ¥553bn ($4.5bn) put it on track to top Ford's profits of $7.2bn in 1999, the record by any carmaker excluding one-off gains.

In the six months to September the world's third-biggest carmaker made more than the combined profits of its U.S. rivals, General Motors, Ford and Chrysler, part of the German-U.S. group DaimlerChrysler. Its automotive operating margins of 10.1 percent were more than five times the average of Detroit's big three.

The ability of Toyota and domestic competitors Nissan Motor and Honda Motor to make record profits while America's big three are struggling with restructuring plans reflects the popularity of their vehicles in the U.S., which has driven strong growth in sales.

"The biggest reason why Japanese have suddenly started to make supernormal profits is not what is going on in their domestic market but what is happening in their export markets," said Mark Little, motor industry analyst at Deutsche Bank.

American carmakers blame their loss of market share on the weakness of the yen against the dollar. Bill Ford, chairman of Ford, told shareholders this week: "It really, competitively, puts us at a disadvantage."

Even Europe's BMW, which operates exclusively in the high-margin luxury sector, cannot match the operating margins of the Japanese.

Unlike their U.S. counterparts, Japan's leading manufacturers have implemented cost-cutting measures while simultaneously increasing sales in their core markets—especially the U.S. . . .

All three carmakers have drawn attention to the fact that they increased sales without relying on discounts.

Toyota also reported rising sales in its three remaining markets. In Europe, where Toyota has struggled in the past, sales rose 21 percent to ¥746.2bn, while sales in Japan where it has a dominant market share of 42 percent, were up 9.5 percent at ¥5,388bn. Sales to the rest of the world rose 61.9 percent to ¥823bn.

It announced an interim dividend of ¥16 per share, an increase of ¥3 per share on the same period last year.

Source: Financial Times, October 31, 2002, p. 1.

Large domestic firms tend to export extensively and head a network of foreign subsidiaries. These companies must be analyzed as global firms, not purely domestic ones. In many sectors, the competition is fully global. The methods and data required to analyze international manufacturers are quite similar. In brief, research on a company should produce two pieces of information:

- *Expected return.* The expected return on an investment can be measured by a rate of return, including potential price appreciation, over some time period, or by some other quantified form of buy-or-sell recommendation.

- *Risk exposure.* Risk sensitivity, or risk exposure, measures how much a company's value responds to certain key factors, such as economic activity, energy costs, interest rates, currency volatility, and general market conditions. Risk analysis enables a manager or investment policy committee to simulate the performance of an investment in different scenarios. It also helps the manager to design more diversified portfolios.

The overall purpose of analysis is to find securities with superior expected returns, given current (or foreseeable) domestic and international risks.

Quantifying the analysis facilitates a consistent global approach to international investment. This is all the more desirable when the parameters that must be considered are numerous and their interrelationships are complex. Although qualitative analysis seems easier to conduct in some institutions than in others, it must be carefully structured so that it is consistent for every security, and provides an estimation of the reaction of security prices to various risk factors.

The Information Problem

Information on foreign firms is often difficult to obtain; once obtained, it is often difficult to interpret and analyze using domestic methods. It is no wonder, then, that comparisons of similar figures for foreign firms are often misleading.

In the United States, companies publish their quarterly earnings, which are publicly available within just a couple of weeks after the close of the quarter. The 10-K reports are particularly useful for trend analysis and intercompany comparisons. Moreover, these reports are available on computerized databases. In contrast, certain European and Far Eastern firms publish their earnings only once a year and with a considerable reporting time lag. French companies, for example, follow this pattern and don't actually publish their official earnings until two to six months after the end of their fiscal years. As a result, official earnings figures are outdated before they become public. To remedy this lack of information, most corporations with significant foreign ownership have begun announcing quarterly or semiannual earnings estimates a short time after the close of the quarter. This is true worldwide for large international corporations. These corporations also follow the American practice of issuing "warnings" as soon as some bad news is likely to affect earnings. The format and reliability of these announcements vary from firm to firm, but overall, they help investors to get better financial information more quickly. As do U.S. firms, British firms publish detailed financial information frequently. Similarly, Japanese firms have begun publishing U.S.-style financial statements, though sometimes only once a year.

Other problems arise from the language and presentation of the financial reports. Many reports are available only in a company's domestic language. Whereas multinational firms tend to publish both in their domestic language and in English, many smaller but nevertheless attractive firms do not. In general, financial reports vary widely from country to country in format, degree of detail, and reliability of the information disclosed. Therefore, additional information must sometimes be obtained directly from the company. Differences in national accounting standards are discussed later in this chapter.

As international investment has grown, brokers, banks, and information services have, fortunately, started to provide more financial data to meet investors' needs. In fact, today, many large international brokerage houses and banks provide analysts' guides covering companies from a large number of countries. The guides include information ranging from summary balance sheet and income statement information to growth forecasts, expected returns on equity investments, and risk measures, such as betas, which are discussed later. The reports are usually available in both the domestic language and English. Similarly, several data services, such as Bloomberg, Reuters, Thomson Financial, Factset, and Moody's, are extending their international coverage on companies and currently feature summary financial information on an increasing number of international corporations. Some financial firms, such as Thomson First Call, have specialized in collecting earnings forecasts from financial analysts worldwide. They provide a service giving the individual analyst's forecast for most large companies listed on the major stock exchanges of the world. They also calculate a consensus forecast, as well as various other global statistics.

Despite these developments, to get the most timely information possible, financial analysts may have to visit international corporations. This, of course, is a time-consuming and expensive process. Moreover, the information obtained is often not homogeneous across companies and countries. The next section reviews differences in international accounting standards.

A Vision of the World

A major challenge faced by all investment organizations is structuring their international research efforts. Their choice of method depends on what they believe are the major factors influencing stock returns. The objective of security analysis is to detect relative misvaluation, that is, investments that are preferable to other *comparable* investments. That is why sectoral analysis is so important. A financial analyst should be assigned the study of securities that belong to the same sector, that is, that are influenced by the *same* common factors and that can therefore be directly compared. The first task, though, is defining these sectors, or common factors. For example, one can reasonably claim that all dollar Eurobonds with fixed coupons belong to the same sector. Another sector would be French common stocks, which are all influenced by national factors. An alternative would be all high-technology companies across the world, which should be influenced by similar worldwide industrial factors. In a homogeneous sector, research should detect securities that are underpriced or overpriced relative to the others.

A first step for an organization to structure its global equity investment requires that it adhere to some vision of the world regarding the dominant factors affecting stock returns. Traditionally, investment organizations use one of three major approaches to international research, depending on their vision of the world:

- If a portfolio manager believes that the value of companies worldwide is affected primarily by global industrial factors, her research effort should be structured according to industrial sectors. This means that companies are valued relative to others within the same industry, for example, the chemical industry. Naturally, financial analysts who use this approach are specialists in particular industrial sectors.

- If a portfolio manager believes that all securities in a national stock market are influenced primarily by domestic factors, her research effort should be structured on a country-by-country basis. The most important investment decision in this approach is how to allocate assets among countries. Thereafter, securities are given a relative valuation within each national market.

- If a portfolio manager believes that some particular attributes of firms are valued worldwide, she will engage in *style* investing. For example, *value stocks* (corporations with a low stock market price compared with their book value) could be preferred to *growth stocks* (corporations with a high stock market price compared with their book value).

In general, an organization must structure its investment process based on some vision of the major common factors influencing stock returns worldwide.

Differences in National Accounting Standards

In this chapter, we develop a top-down approach to global equity investing. We examine country and industry analysis before moving to equity security analysis. Global industry financial analysis examines each company in the industry against the industry average. Plots of one financial ratio against another can show the relative location of individual companies within the industry. To carry out such analysis, we must first know something about the differences in national accounting standards so that we can adjust ratios to make them comparable. For example, discounted cash flow analysis (DCF) and compound annual growth rates (CAGR) in cash flows must be based on comparable data to be meaningful

In global industry financial analysis, the pattern is to contrast the financial ratios of individual firms against the same ratios for industry averages. The analyst will encounter and possibly need to adjust such ratios as: enterprise value (EV) to earnings before interest, taxes, depreciation, and amortization (EBIDTA), return on equity (ROE), and the book value multiple of price to book value per share (BV). In practice, one also sees such ratios as price to net asset value (NAV), EV to capital employed (CE), return on capital employed (ROCE), and value added margin. *Capital employed* is usually defined[1] as equity plus long-term debt. *Net asset value* is usually defined on a per-share basis as equity minus goodwill. *Value added margin* is ROCE minus the weighted average cost of capital (WACC).

With an understanding of differences in national accounting standards, the analyst will be prepared to evaluate companies from around the world within the context of global industry. After discussing these differences, we will return to global industry analysis.

---

[1] See Temple (2002) for definitions.

Today all companies compete globally. Capital markets of developed countries are well integrated, and international capital flows react quickly to any perceived mispricing. Hence, companies tend to be priced relative to their global competitors, and it is for this reason that this chapter focuses on global industry analysis.

Companies and investors have become more global. Mergers and acquisitions often occur on a global basis. Further, it is not unusual for a company to have its shares listed on multiple exchanges. Similarly, investors often seek to diversify their holdings and take advantage of opportunities across national borders. This globalization of financial markets creates challenges for investors, creditors, and other users of financial statements. Comparing financial statements of companies located in different countries is a difficult task. Different countries may employ different accounting principles, and even where the same accounting methods are used, currency, cultural, institutional, political, and tax differences can make between-country comparisons of accounting numbers hazardous and misleading.

For example, the treatment of depreciation and extraordinary items varies greatly among countries, such that net income of a company located in one country might be half that of a similarly performing company located in another country, even after adjustment for differences in currency. This disparity is partly the result of different national tax incentives and the creation of "secret" reserves (provisions) in certain countries. German and Swiss firms (among others), for example, have been known to stretch the definition of a liability; that is, they tend to overestimate contingent liabilities and future uncertainties when compared with other firms. The provisions for these liabilities reduce income in the current year, but increase income in later years when the provisions are reduced. This can have a smoothing impact on earnings and mask the underlying variability or riskiness of business operations.

Similarly, German and Swiss firms allow goodwill resulting from acquisitions to be deducted from equity immediately, bypassing the income statement and resulting in reporting the balance sheet based on book value, not on actual transaction prices. Similar idiosyncrasies often make comparisons of Japanese and U.S. earnings figures or accounting ratios meaningless. As a result, many large Japanese companies publish secondary financial statements in English that conform to the U.S. generally accepted accounting principles (GAAP). But even when we examine these statements, we find that financial ratios differ markedly between the two countries. For example, financial leverage is high in Japan compared with the United States, and coverage ratios are poor. But this does not necessarily mean that Japanese firms are more risky than their U.S. counterparts, only that the relationship between banks and their client corporations is different than in the United States.

With increasing globalization there has been a movement toward convergence of accounting standards internationally. In spite of this movement, there are still substantial differences in existing accounting standards that must be considered by investors.

Historical Setting

Each country follows a set of accounting principles that are usually prepared by the accounting profession and the national authorities. These sets of accounting principles are sometimes called national GAAP. Two distinct models can describe the preparation of these national accounting principles:

- In the Anglo-American model, accounting rules have historically been set in standards prepared by a well-established, influential accounting profession.

- In the Continental model, used by countries in Continental Europe and Japan, accounting rules have been set in a codified law system; governmental bodies write the law, and the accounting profession is less influential than in the Anglo-American model.

Anglo-American countries typically report financial statements intended to give a true and fair view of the firm's financial position. Hence, there can be large differences between accounting statements, the intent of which is to give a fair representation of the firm's financial position, and tax statements, the intent of which is to reflect the various tax provisions used to calculate the amount of income tax owed. Many other countries (France, Germany, Italy, and Japan, for example) have a tradition that the reported financial statements and earnings conform to the method used to determine taxable income. This implies that financial statements are geared to satisfy legal and tax provisions and may not give a true and fair view of the firm. This confusion between tax and book accounting is slowly disappearing under the pressure of international harmonization, as noted in the next section.

International Harmonization of Accounting Practices

Investors, creditors, and other users of financial statements have exerted pressure to harmonize national accounting principles. The *International Accounting Standards Committee (IASC)* was set up in 1973 by leading professional accounting organizations in nine countries: Australia, Canada, France, Germany, Japan, Mexico, the Netherlands, the United Kingdom and Ireland, and the United States. Over time, additional countries became members of the IASC. The IASC issued its first international accounting standard (IAS) in 1974, entitled Disclosure of Accounting Policies. In 2001, the IASC was renamed the *International Accounting Standards Board (IASB)*, and we will use this name hereafter.

Although the IASB is able to propose international accounting standards, it does not have the authority to require companies to follow these standards. Without a mechanism to compel companies to use IAS and enforce the standards, harmonization is not easily achievable. In 1995, the *International Organization of Securities Commissions (IOSCO)* stated that it would consider adopting the international accounting standards once the IASB had prepared a comprehensive set of standards covering all the major areas of importance to general business. IOSCO is an important organization whose members are the agencies regulating securities markets in all countries.[2] IOSCO's objectives are to promote high standards of regulation in or-

---

[2] One hundred seventy members as of 31 December 2001, according to IOSCO Annual Report 2001.

EXHIBIT 6.1

IOSCO Selected Standards for Cross-Border Listings	
IAS	**Description**
IAS 1	Presentation of Financial Statements (revised 1997)
IAS 2	Inventories (revised 1993)
IAS 4	Depreciation Accounting (reformatted 1994)
IAS 7	Cash Flow Statements (revised 1992)
IAS 8	Net Profit or Loss for the Period, Fundamental Errors and Changes in Accounting Policies (revised 1993)
IAS 10	Events after the Balance Sheet Date (revised 1999)
IAS 11	Construction Contracts (revised 1993)
IAS 12	Income Taxes (revised 1996)
IAS 14	Segment Reporting (revised 1997)
IAS 16	Property, Plant and Equipment (revised 1998)
IAS 17	Leases (revised 1997)
IAS 18	Revenue (revised 1993)
IAS 19	Employee Benefits (revised 1998)
IAS 20	Accounting for Government Grants and Disclosure of Governmental Assistance (reformatted 1994)
IAS 21	The Effects of Changes in Foreign Exchange Rates (revised 1993)
IAS 22	Business Combinations (revised 1998)
IAS 23	Borrowing Costs (revised 1993)
IAS 24	Related Party Disclosures (reformatted 1994)
IAS 27	Consolidated Financial Statements and Accounting for Investments in Subsidiaries (reformatted 1994)
IAS 28	Accounting for Investments in Associates (revised 1998)
IAS 29	Financial Reporting in Hyperinflationary Economies (reformatted 1994)
IAS 31	Financial Reporting of Interests in Joint Ventures (revised 1998)
IAS 32	Financial Instruments: Disclosure and Presentation (revised 1998)
IAS 33	Earnings Per Share (1997)
IAS 34	Interim Financial Reporting (1998)
IAS 35	Discontinuing Operations (1998)
IAS 36	Impairment of Assets (1998)
IAS 37	Provisions, Contingent Liabilities and Contingent Assets (1998)
IAS 38	Intangible Assets (1998)
IAS 39	Financial Instruments: Recognition and Measurement (1998)

Source: IASB Standards—Assessment Report, Report of the Technical Committee of the International Organization of Securities Commissions, May 2000.

der to maintain just, efficient, and sound markets. IOSCO has two important committees: The Emerging Markets Committee endeavors to promote the development and improvement of efficiency of emerging securities and futures markets. The Technical Committee is made up of sixteen agencies that currently regulate the world's larger, more developed and internationalized markets in fourteen countries:

Australia, France, Germany, Hong Kong, Italy, Japan, Mexico, the Netherlands, Canada, Spain, Sweden, Switzerland, the United Kingdom, and the United States.

"Multinational disclosure and accounting" is a major subject before this committee, and has led to the cooperation with the IASB. At the start of 1999, the IASB prepared a core set of standards and submitted them to IOSCO for review and endorsement. After deliberation, in May 2000 the Technical Committee of IOSCO recommended that IOSCO members use 30 selected IASB standards for cross-border listings and offerings by multinational companies. These 30 selected standards, referred to as IASB 2000 Standards by IOSCO, are listed in Exhibit 6.1. Due to concerns with some standards, the Technical Committee recommends that supplemental information be required for some standards in the form of reconciliations to national standards, additional disclosure, or specification of which alternative treatment in IAS must be used.

These two international organizations, one representative of the accounting profession (private sector) and the other of government regulators, play an important role in moving toward global harmonization of disclosure requirements and accounting practices. This is all the more important for multinational corporations that wish to raise capital globally. They need to be able to present their accounts in a single format, wherever they want to be listed or raise capital. Of particular importance is the attitude of the United States toward IAS. Convergence of the U.S. GAAP and IAS is a desirable but difficult goal. A topic under discussion is to allow foreign firms listed on a U.S. stock exchange to publish accounts according to IAS, rather than asking them to provide earnings statements calculated according to the U.S. GAAP.

The IASB also received the support of the *World Bank*. A large number of emerging countries, as well as Hong Kong, have adopted the IAS as a basis for their accounting standards. Corporations from many developed countries also use the IAS in their financial reporting. For example, most of the leading industrial companies in Switzerland voluntarily report their accounts according to international accounting standards.

In countries where accounting rules are governed by law, specific legislation is required to allow for the use of other accounting standards. The European Union (EU) is supporting the use of IAS. The harmonization of European accounting principles has come mostly through *Directives* published by the EU. These EU Directives are drafted by the EU Commission, and member states' parliaments must adapt the national law to conform to these Directives. The EU also issues *Regulations,* which have the force of law without requiring formal transposition into national legislation. In 2002, the EU issued a Regulation requiring listed companies to prepare their consolidated financial statements in accordance with IAS from 2005 onward.[3] The road to global cooperation is never easy, and it will be a long time before full harmonization of financial reporting is achieved.

---

[3] Regulation (EC) No. 1606/2002 of the European Parliament and of the Council of the European Union on the application of international accounting standards, 19 July 2002.

Differences in Global Standards

A complete presentation of International Accounting Standards is beyond the scope of this book. The full text of standards can be obtained from the International Accounting Standards Board (www.iasb.org.uk).[4] We focus here on areas of differences among IAS and various national GAAP. A group of international accounting firms prepared a comparison of IAS and national GAAP for 62 countries.[5] The study found that there remains a lack of convergence globally particularly with regard to the following:

- The recognition and measurement of
  - Financial assets and derivative financial instruments
  - Impairment losses
  - Provisions
  - Employee benefit liabilities
  - Income taxes
- Accounting for business combinations
- Disclosure of
  - Related party transactions
  - Segment information

Several inconsistencies in accounting standards require that the analyst take particular care in making cross-border comparisons. For example, one question to ask is whether all assets and/or liabilities are properly reflected on the balance sheet. If not, these off-balance-sheet assets and liabilities must be analyzed and appropriate adjustments made in any valuation exercise.

Business Combinations   Under IAS 22 the *purchase method* of accounting is generally used (recording acquired assets and liabilities at fair value at the acquisition date), although the *uniting of interest method* (recording acquired assets and liabilities at historical book value) is used when the acquirer cannot be identified (i.e., which one is the acquirer?). Until recently, the United States permitted use of the *pooling method* (substantially equivalent to uniting of interest) for many acquisitions. Now all new acquisitions in the United States must be accounted for by using

---

[4] Various summaries of IAS are also available. For example, *IAS In Your Pocket,* Deloitte Touche Tohmatsu, April 2002, and *GAAP Differences in Your Pocket: IAS and US GAAP,* Deloitte Touche Tohmatsu. Both are available at www.iasplus.com.

[5] *GAAP 2001: A Survey of National Accounting Rules Benchmarked against International Accounting Standards,* Anderson, BDO, Deloitte Touche Tohmatsu, Ernst & Young, Grant Thornton, KPMG, Pricewaterhouse-Coopers: Editor, Christopher W. Nobes. Available at www.ifad.net.

CONCEPTS IN ACTION   *RULES SET FOR BIG CHANGE*

Millions of Dollars of Debt Could Be Brought Back on to Companies' Balance Sheets

Among the many consequences of the collapse of Enron has been a new focus by regulators on how companies account for off-balance-sheet transactions.

Enron's swift demise raised questions over its complex web of off-balance-sheet transactions, leading the U.S.'s Financial Standards Accounting Board to consider new rules governing special purpose entities (SPEs). The changes could result in millions of dollars of debt being brought back on to corporate balance sheets, and represent a significant challenge for the rapidly developing structured finance market. SPEs are used for a wide range of financial transactions because they isolate assets from the financial fortunes of companies that own them.

SPEs can be organized in a variety of forms, such as trusts or corporations, but usually have no full-time employees or operating business. They can be used for different activities, including acquiring financial assets, property or equipment, and as a vehicle for raising funds from investors by issuing stock or other securities.

Depending on the type of SPE, its assets and liabilities may not appear in the financial statements of the entity that created it. . . .

Source: Jenny Wiggins, "Special Purpose Entities," *Financial Times*, October 7, 2002, p. 4.

---

the purchase method. Previous acquisitions under the pooling method continue to be reported by using the pooling method. Australia prohibits the pooling/uniting of interest method. In France, Germany, and Italy (at least until 2005), there is a more liberal use of uniting of interests than under IAS. Japan and Switzerland do not have specific rules related to the classification of business combinations.

Consolidation   In most countries, corporations publish financial statements that consolidate, to some extent, the accounts of their subsidiaries and affiliates. A full range of consolidation practices exists. In all countries, majority interests in domestic subsidiaries are typically consolidated. This is not always the case when dealing with foreign subsidiaries or with minority interests. In Italy and Japan, certain dissimilar subsidiaries can be excluded. In France, there is considerable leeway in the method used for consolidation. Japanese companies, like many German firms, tend to publish separately the (nonconsolidated) financial statements of the various companies belonging to the same group. This can be partly explained by the extent of cross-holdings in these countries. The perimeter of consolidation is often difficult to establish in Japan because of the extent of cross-holding. The practice of publishing (partly) nonconsolidated statements renders the valuation of a com-

---

CONCEPTS IN ACTION *ENRON COLLAPSE IS IAS WEAPON*

Enron's multibillion dollar collapse is set to become the weapon the global accounting standard-setter has been looking for in its battle to convince the US to adopt international accounting rules.

Sir David Tweedie, International Accounting Standards Board chairman, and Allan Cook, UK Accounting Standards Board technical director, have indicated Enron's collapse could not have happened under existing UK or global rules. UK standards are the closest in the world to international rules.

Tweedie is now likely to reapply pressure to US watchdog the Securities and Exchange Commission to allow American companies to use global rules. Both UK and global rules on off-balance sheet reporting, which brought Enron to its knees, are much tougher.

But FASB, the US standard setter, has consistently resisted attempts to push through an updated standard. Highlighting Enron's off-balance sheet reporting, Cook said: 'The IASB would probably have got it on the balance sheet. It's very tough.'

As if to show the US its determination, the IASB could issue an even tougher rule on off-balance-sheet reporting, or derecognition, as early as next year.

The ASB is compiling research into off-balance-sheet reporting to submit to the IASB in January.

Sir David Tweedie, IASB chairman, said: 'This wakes people up to the fact that accounting matters. They are looking across at us. The UK is well ahead of the rest of the world on this.'

A letter to the *Wall Street Journal* last week by Joe Berardino, chief executive of Andersen, Enron's auditor, also showed him in favour of a change in rules.

Source: Michelle Perry, "Enron collapse is IAS weapon," *Financial Director,* December 13, 2001.

---

pany a difficult exercise. IAS 27 imposes consolidation for all subsidiaries with uniform accounting policies. In addition to subsidiaries, there is also the question of nonoperating entities created to carry out a special purpose, such as leasing assets or securitizing receivables.

Under IAS 27, special purpose entities (SPEs) are consolidated if controlled. This is also the case in the United Kingdom. In the United States, SPEs are consolidated if certain criteria are met (or not met); this leaves considerable leeway. Germany, Spain, and Switzerland have no requirement regarding SPEs. France requires holding at least one share of an SPE to consolidate. The ability of firms to avoid consolidation of SPEs has often enabled them to keep large amounts of liabilities off the balance sheet to the detriment of investors and creditors alike. National standards setters, such as the U.S. Financial Accounting Standards Board, are reconsidering standards in this area.

Joint Ventures   Joint ventures are increasingly used in international business. Most European countries consolidate joint ventures using *proportional consolidation,* as provided under IAS. In this method, assets, liabilities, and earnings are consolidated line by line, proportional to the percentage of ownership in the subsidiary. U.K. and U.S. corporations use the *equity method*. A share of the subsidiary profits is consolidated on a one-line basis, proportional to the share of equity owned by the parent. The value of the investment in the subsidiary is adjusted to reflect the change in the subsidiary's equity. The two methods lead to marked differences in the corporation's balance sheet. IAS 31 states that the benchmark treatment should be proportional consolidation, although jointly controlled entities can alternatively be accounted for by using equity consolidation.

Goodwill   Goodwill can appear in various ways. Most commonly, goodwill is created when a company engages in an acquisition or merger at a market value different from the book value. Under IAS, goodwill is capitalized and amortized, usually over 20 years or less, and is subject to an impairment ("loss of value") test. In Switzerland and Germany, goodwill can be written off against equity immediately and does not affect the income statement. In the United Kingdom, goodwill need not be amortized. In the United States, until recently goodwill was capitalized as an asset and amortized. Now in the United States, goodwill and other intangibles without a determinable useful life are no longer amortized, but are subject to impairment tests.

Financial Leases   Financial leases are an indirect way to own an asset and provide the financing for it. In some countries, they are simply carried as off-balance-sheet items. In other countries, these leases are capitalized both as assets and liabilities. This was not common in countries in which accounting systems are driven by tax considerations (e.g., France, Germany, and Italy), but it is progressively implemented in most countries. IAS 17 requires capitalization of financial leases.

Asset Revaluation   Revaluation of assets is generally not permitted except when the market value declines, with the exception of financial assets discussed below. Investment properties can be revalued in Switzerland and Sweden. In Japan, land can be revalued. In Switzerland, Canada, and France, there is no requirement for recognizing impairment. Special laws have permitted periodic revaluation in France, Italy, and Spain in order to compensate for inflation, but the tax implications of these revaluations have sometimes been negative, making revaluation unpopular. Countries with higher inflation, such as Brazil, tend to have systems for automatic inflation indexing.

Provisions   A provision is an estimate of a likely future loss or expense. It appears as a liability on the balance sheet and is deducted from current reported earnings when initially taken. In many countries, such as the United States, United Kingdom, Italy, and Spain, provisions can be taken only for specific and likely future events. In Germany and Switzerland, generous provisions can be taken for all types of general risks. In the Netherlands, certain provisions can be made where there may not be a current obligation. In good times, German firms will build provisions to reduce earnings growth; in bad times, they will draw on these provisions to boost reported earnings. These provisions are called "hidden reserves" because they do not appear as equity reserves on the balance sheet, but rather as general liability (debt). However, they can be used to boost profits in bad times. IAS 37 supports a strong limitation on the creation of provisions, and when created, requires discounting. In the United States, provisions are not discounted.

Pensions   The accounting for pensions and retirement liabilities differs widely across countries, in part because of the national differences in pension systems. One difference is whether pension liabilities are accrued, that is, whether there is an actuarial evaluation of future pension expenses (and on what basis). Another difference is whether the pensions are funded off-balance sheets or whether pension assets and liabilities remain on a company's balance sheet. Some countries, for example, France and Italy, have primarily a national pay-as-you-go pension system, whereby current workers pay for the pensions of retired workers; companies contribute to pensions, but future pension liabilities are neither accrued nor funded, and current pension costs are expensed as incurred. In the United States, the Netherlands, Switzerland, the United Kingdom, and, to some extent, Japan, pensions are accrued and funded off-balance sheets; a separate entity, called a "pension fund," manages the pension assets and liabilities. In Germany or Spain, pensions are accrued but not funded, so pension liabilities do not appear on the company's balance sheet. The assumptions used to estimate accrued pension liabilities also vary among countries and firms.

Financial Assets and Derivatives   Under IAS and U.S. standards, trading and available-for-sale securities are recorded at fair value. Similarly, derivatives are reported at fair value, except certain hedging activities. In Switzerland, the United Kingdom, Spain, Canada, and Germany, trading securities, available-for-sale securities, and derivatives are not reported at fair value. Similarly, trading and derivative liabilities are not reported at fair value, and hedging treatment is applied more liberally.

Employee Stock Options   Employee stock options represent potential earnings dilution to existing shareholders. As a form of employee compensation, these stock options should be treated as expenses from an economic perspective. The fair value of this compensation paid to employees is treated as an expense, a deduction to pretax earnings recorded at the time the options are granted. The fair value is computed by using a standard option pricing model.

Currently IAS, as well as most national GAAP including the U.S. GAAP, does not require that an expense be recorded for the value of options granted to employees. In the United States, footnote disclosures are required, but recording of an expense is optional for most stock options. IAS requires some disclosures

---

EXAMPLE 6.1 *EMPLOYEE STOCK OPTIONS*

A company has 100,000 shares outstanding at $100 per share. To its senior management, the company granted employee stock options on 5,000 shares. The options can be exercised at a price of $105 any time during the next five years. For five years, the employees thus have the right but not the obligation to purchase shares at the $105 price, regardless of the prevailing market price of the stock. Using price volatility estimates for the stock, a standard Black–Scholes valuation model gives an estimated value of $20 per share option. Without expensing the options, the company's pretax earnings per share are reported as $1 million/100,000 = $10 per share. What would they have been if they had been expensed?

SOLUTION

The expense is $5000 \times \$20 = \$100,000$

The pretax income per share would be $(\$1,000,000 - \$100,000)/100,000 = \$9$ per share.

---

regarding options. In July 2000, the IASB in conjunction with some national standard-setters, issued a discussion paper proposing, among other things, that share based payments be expensed. The IASB added this project to their agenda and issued an exposure draft in November 2002. This matter is getting wide attention, and some U.S. firms have recently decided to voluntarily begin recording an expense for such stock options allocation.

CONCEPTS IN ACTION *SO MANY OPTIONS*

Have Accounting Regulators Chosen the Best Way of Expensing Share Options?

Several features of the wild bull market of the 1990s have since been branded as evil. Perhaps none more so than the billions of dollars of share options awarded to bosses and other employees. Once praised for their incentivizing power, share options are now blamed for encouraging bosses to do all manner of bad things to prop up their company's share price and so keep their lucrative options packages in the money, as the jargon has it. In this, it is now generally agreed, executives have been abetted by accounting standards that did not require the cost of awarding options to be treated as compensation and lopped off a company's reported profits.

This week, to right this wrong, the International Accounting Standards Board (IASB) unveiled proposals for expensing options, i.e., deducting their cost from a company's profits. In doing so, however, not only was the IASB declaring war on some powerful political opponents of expensing. It also took sides in a lively economic dispute.

Among economists, the debate is largely about how to value options and when to expense them, not about whether they should be expensed at all. (Only a few "renegades" disagree with expensing, declares Robert Merton, who won a Nobel prize in economics for his work on options pricing.) Economists mostly agree that options should be expensed using a so-called fair value method, one that broadly reflects what the options would cost to buy in the market, were they available.

In this, the economists agree with the IASB, which has chosen fair value accounting of options, ruling out several other methods. These include, for instance, intrinsic value: the difference between the market price of the underlying shares that the option confers the right to buy and the exercise price at which the underlying shares may be bought. If, when an option is issued, the exercise price equals the market price (and it often does), the intrinsic value is zero—which is nonsensical. Also ruled out is the minimum-value method, which is what somebody would willingly pay for an option if they knew that the firm's share price would be fixed for the life of the option. This ignores a big part of an option's value, namely the ability to cash in should the share price rise.

The IASB does not, though, specify exactly which method of fair value option pricing should be used. And here academics dispute vigorously. Mr. Merton helped to devise the Black–Scholes model for pricing options, named after Myron Scholes (who shared Mr. Merton's Nobel prize) and Fisher Black (who would have done, had he lived a little longer). The main alternative is what is called the binomial pricing model, developed by John Cox, Stephen Ross and Mark Rubinstein.

Both models were devised to price simple options traded on an exchange. So, as the IASB acknowledges, each needs to be modified to reflect several peculiarities of employee share options—such as longer lifespan or term (a typical executive option lasts ten years, against a few months to two years for an exchange-traded option), restrictions on when options may be exercised, and even the fact that they may not be sold. How these adjustments are made—and the IASB allows wide discretion—can make a big difference to the size of the expense.

The binomial method is much more complex than Black–Scholes, but if done properly, the price it produces is likely to be accurate more often. Of course, the very complexity may make it easier for the price to be manipulated by a company wanting to massage its profits. On the other hand, plenty of scope for creativity exists with the Black–Scholes method, even given the few simple assumptions that are used. These assumptions, in essence, are expected volatility (how much a share price is likely to fluctuate), term, the expected dividend yield, the risk-free interest rate, and the exercise price.

Some critics reckon that these vagaries of valuation undermine the entire case for expensing. Few economists agree, however. Whatever uncertainties there are in fair value option pricing, goes the argument, they are smaller than the uncertainty in the value of other items already routinely expensed, such as depreciation and pension fund gains or losses.

Ask Not Whether, but When

The biggest philosophical dispute among economists concerns when options should be expensed. The IASB wants it done once and for all from the date they are awarded to employees (in other words, the grant date). Mr. Scholes, the Nobel laureate, agrees. But others, such as Mr. Rubinstein, one of the creators of binomial pricing, do not. He argues for full expensing at the time options are exercised, i.e., when the holder trades in the options for underlying shares. Under this approach, options would still initially be expensed on the grant date; but in subsequent public filings this estimate would be adjusted to take into account changes in their value. Upon exercise, the company would take a final extraordinary gain or loss to match up with the option's actual value when exercised. Mr. Rubinstein argues that, under this method, there would be less incentive to manipulate option valuations, because any divergence from an option's final true value would, in the end, result in an extraordinary charge.

The issue boils down to this: is the granting of an option a once-only expense for the company, the equivalent of paying the employee in cash? Or is it a contingent liability, the potential cost of which to shareholders changes with the market price of the company's shares, and with the true cost becoming clear only when the option is either exercised or it expires? A once-only expense or a contingent liability: these are matters over which reasonable people can agree to differ. What is important is that share options are to be expensed at all.

The Effects of Accounting Principles on Earnings and Stock Prices

The same company using different national accounting standards could report different earnings. Some accounting standards are more conservative than others, in the sense that they lead to smaller reported earnings. Several comparative studies have attempted to measure the relative conservativeness of national standards. For example, Radebaugh and Gray (1997) conclude that U.S. accounting principles are significantly more conservative than U.K. accounting principles but significantly less conservative than Japanese and Continental European accounting principles. If the United States' earnings are arbitrarily scaled at 100, Japanese earnings would scale at 66, German earnings at 87, French earnings at 97, and British earnings at 125. Various studies come up with somewhat different adjustments, so these figures should be interpreted with some caution. Also, recent changes, particularly in the United States and Europe, will impact this assessment in the future.

These national accounting principles also affect the reported book value of equity. Speidell and Bavishi (1992) report the adjustment that should be made to the book value of foreign shareholders' equity if the U.S. GAAP were used. They find that the book value of equity would be increased by 41 percent in Germany and 14 percent in Japan, and would be reduced by 14 percent in the United Kingdom and 28 percent in France.

Price–earnings (P/E) ratios are of great interest to international investors, who tend to compare the P/E ratios of companies in the same industrial sector across the world. The P/E ratio divides the market price of a share by its current or estimated annual earnings. As of November 30, 1998, P/E ratios in the markets ranged from a low of 18.1 in Hong Kong to a high of 191.0 in Japan (at this time, the U.S. market P/E was 28.5).[6] Japanese companies have traditionally traded at very high P/E ratios in comparison with those of U.S. companies. For comparison purposes, these P/E ratios should be adjusted because of the accounting differences in reporting earnings. They also should be adjusted to reflect the fact that Japanese firms tend to report nonconsolidated statements despite the extent of cross-holding. For example, if Company A owns 20 percent of the shares of Company B, it will include in its own earnings only the dividend paid by Company B, not a proportion of Company B's earnings. In the P/E ratio of Company A, the stock price reflects the value of the holding of shares of Company B, but the earnings do not reflect the earnings of Company B. For all these reasons, French and Poterba (1991) claim that the average 1989 Japanese P/E ratio should be adjusted from 53.7 to 32.6. Other authors come up with an even bigger reduction in Japanese P/E ratios.

The Information Content of International Differences in GAAP

Investors request that companies disclose accurate information on a timely basis. The national GAAP dictates the format in which the information is disclosed. Investors would like companies to use accounting principles that provide the most informative presentation of the accounting numbers. It is difficult to tell whether an optimal accounting standard exists that would apply equally to all nations. The U.S. Securities and Exchange Commission (SEC) requests that all foreign firms listed on a public stock exchange in the United States, including Nasdaq, provide financial reports according to the U.S. GAAP (Form 10-K) or provide all necessary reconciliation information (Form 20-F). This is a controversial policy, as many foreign firms, especially medium-sized ones, do not wish to carry the burden and costs of presenting all their financial statements under two different accounting standards.

A major question for investors is determining which GAAP provides the best information. This is a difficult question to answer. Some insights can be gained by looking at the reaction of stock prices to earnings reported according to different national standards. Studies have focused on foreign firms that are dual-listed in the United States, which must also provide earnings statements calculated according to the U.S. GAAP. If the U.S. GAAP provides incremental information relative to the foreign GAAP, stock prices should show some reaction to the difference between the two reported earnings. Preliminary evidence seems to suggest that "the GAAP earnings adjustments add marginally to the ability of earnings to explain returns" (Pope and Rees, 1992, p. 190).

---

[6] Schieneman (2000).

Another approach has been to survey international money managers to see whether they find added value in obtaining financial statements under different national GAAP. Choi and Levich (1991) surveyed a variety of capital market participants (institutional investment managers, corporate issuers, and regulators) and found that roughly half of them feel that their capital market decisions are affected by accounting diversity. However, most of them find ways to cope with this diversity. Some translate all financial statements to a common, more familiar accounting framework; others have become familiarized with foreign accounting practices and adopt a local perspective when analyzing foreign statements; others simply do not use accounting numbers in their investment decisions. Bhushan and Lessard (1992) surveyed 49 U.S.-based international money managers. All of them regard accounting harmonization as a good thing but do not find that providing reconciled accounting information is crucial; they tend to focus on valuing firms within their own markets and stress the importance of the quality and timeliness of the information disclosed.

Indeed the quality and speed of information disclosure are of paramount importance to investors. Restating the same information in a different accounting standard does not address the issue of the quality of the information disclosed or the firm's future prospects. Investment managers deciding to include a specific stock in a portfolio need to do more than simply look at past accounting data.

Global Industry Analysis

The valuation of a common stock is usually conducted in several steps. A company belongs to a global industry and is based in a country. Hence, country and industry analysis is necessary. Companies compete against global players within their industry. Studying a company within its global industry is the primary approach to stock valuation.

With the knowledge that financial ratios from different international companies are difficult to compare, the analyst still faces the task of looking forward. What conditions in the industry prevail, and how are companies likely to compete in the future?

Within the framework of industrial organization, this section outlines the most important elements that should be looked at when conducting a company analysis in a global setting. Because a company is based in a country, we begin with a general introduction to country analysis to provide a starting point for the analysis of the company and industry.

Country Analysis

Companies tend to favor some countries in their business activities. They target some countries for their sales and base their production in only a few countries.

Hence, country analysis is of importance in studying a company. In each country, economists try to monitor a large number of economic, social, and political variables, such as

- anticipated real growth,

- monetary policy,

- fiscal policy (including fiscal incentives for investments),

- wage and employment rigidities,

- competitiveness,

- social and political situations, and

- investment climate.

In the long run, real economic growth is probably the major influence on a national stock market. Economists focus on economic growth at two horizons:

- Business cycle

- Long-term sustainable growth

What are favorable country conditions for equity investment? There can be favorable business cycle conditions as well as favorable long-term sustainable growth conditions. If the favorable conditions are a consensus view, however, they will already be priced in the equity markets. The analyst must find a way of discerning these conditions before others do.

A high long-term sustainable growth rate in gross domestic product (GDP) is favorable, because this translates into high long-term profits and stock returns. In creating GDP and productivity growth rate expectations, the analyst will undoubtedly examine the country's savings rate, investment rate, and total factor productivity (TFP). TFP measures the efficiency with which the economy converts capital and labor into goods and services. Increased investment rates due to technical progress will increase rates of return; but the savings and investment rates themselves must be closely analyzed. A country's investments reflect replacement and capacity expansion, and influences future productivity gains. If the ratio of investment to GDP is low, then the investments are largely replacement investments; whereas a high rate suggests that capacity expansion is under way.[7] Further, a positive correlation between investment rates and subsequent GDP growth rates cannot be taken for granted, because there are other factors to consider.

The main factors that interact with the country's investment rate to affect GDP growth are the rate of growth in employment, work hours, educational levels, technological improvement, business climate, political stability, and the public or private nature of the investment. A higher long-term growth in the work force will

---

[7] See Calverley (2003, p. 11)

lead to higher GDP growth just as a reduction in work hours will lead to less GDP growth. Increasing skills in the work force complement technological advances as they will both lead to higher GDP growth. A business climate of more privatization and reduced regulation is conducive to more investment. Attractive investment opportunities will also lead to more investment, although an increased propensity to invest can depress rates of return. Political stability will reduce the risk and hence increase the attractiveness of investments. Finally, private investments are more likely to be made with maximal return-on-invested capital as the objective and hence lead to higher GDP growth.

In the short term, business cycle conditions can be favorable for investments, but business cycle turning points are so difficult to predict that such predictions should only cause the analyst to make investment recommendations to slightly adjust portfolio. Business cycles represent a complex control system with many causes and interacting private and governmental decisions. For example, companies invest in plant and equipment and build inventories based on expected demand but face the reality that actual demand does not continuously meet expectations. Although an investor would benefit from buying stocks at the trough of a business cycle and bonds at the peak, such perfect market timing is virtually impossible, and one might better take the approach of ignoring the country's business cycle and concentrate rather on its long-term sustainable growth rate in GDP. Nevertheless, even limited prescient ability can lead to informed adjustments to portfolio holdings. Calverley (2003, pp. 15–19) classifies the business cycle stages and attractive investment opportunities as:

- *Recovery:* The economy picks up from its slowdown or recession. Good investments to have are the country's cyclical stocks and commodities, followed by riskier assets as the recovery takes hold.

- *Early Upswing:* Confidence is up and the economy is gaining some momentum. Good investments to have are the country's stocks and also commercial and residential property.

- *Late Upswing:* Boom mentality has taken hold. This is not usually a good time to buy the country's stocks. The country's commodity and property prices will also be peaking. This is the time to purchase the country's bonds (yields are high) and interest rate sensitive stocks.

- *Economy Slows or Goes into Recession:* The economy is declining. Good investments to have are the country's bonds, which will rally (because of a drop in market interest rates), and its interest rate sensitive stocks.

- *Recession:* Monetary policy will be eased but there will be a lag before recovery. Particularly toward the end of the recession, good investments to make are the country's stocks and commodities.

Inflation is generally associated with the late upswing, and deflation is possible in a recession. Inflation effects on equity valuation are analyzed later in this chapter.

CONCEPTS IN ACTION   *IRISH CENTRAL BANK SEES UNCERTAINTY, MODEST GROWTH AHEAD*

The Central Bank of Ireland said Thursday that a high degree of uncertainty and modest growth lie ahead for the Irish economy next year.

In its quarterly bulletin for autumn 2002, the bank sees gross national product growth of about 3.0% this year and 4.25% in 2003, which depends on whether the international economy picks up.

"This growth would be good by international standards and would be close to the medium-term sustainable rate for the economy," it said.

But, both the U.S. and U.K. economies, which take about four-fifths of Irish exports, are registering growth around 1.0%.

It is unlikely, therefore, that there will be an appreciable increase in Irish export demand in the short-run, the central bank said.

It said foreign direct investment is also likely to be adversely affected by the decline in stock markets and uncertainty regarding the true profitability of major multinationals.

The bank also cautioned the Irish government to ensure that the country's heady rate of inflation falls back as quickly as possible in-line with the rest of the euro zone.

Irish inflation, currently forecast at about 4.75% this year, continues to run above the European Central Bank's upper limit of 2.0% for euro-zone countries.

This, plus a stronger euro, has reduced Ireland's competitiveness and will subsequently impede employment growth in the future, the bank warned.

The European Union harmonized index of consumer prices, or HICP, forecasts Irish consumer price inflation to average about 4.25% next year owing to lower mortgage rates.

Adding more gloom to the central bank's report, Wednesday's data on third-quarter exchequer returns showed the Irish budget is back in the red for the first time since 1997.

The Irish government said it will now face a 2002 deficit of EUR750 million, compared with the EUR170 million surplus forecast nearly a year ago.

Many analysts, however, predict matters are even worse. Bloxham Stockbrokers forecasts a 2002 deficit of closer to EUR800 million, citing 20% annual growth in day-to-day spending in September.

Similarly, IIB Bank expects the government 2002 deficit to hit more than EUR1.0 billion owing to the government's high day-to-day spending.

Source: Quentin Fottrel, Dow Jones Newswires, October 3, 2002.

Business Cycle Synchronization   Stock market performance is clearly related to the business cycle and economic growth.[8] National business cycles are not fully synchronized. This lack of synchronization makes country analysis all the more important. For example, the United States witnessed a strong economic recovery in 1992, Britain started to enjoy strong economic growth in 1993, and the European continent only started to recover in 1995, but Japan's economy was still stagnant.

However, economies are becoming increasingly integrated. Growth of major economies is, in part, exported abroad. For example, growth in the United States can sustain the activity of an exporting European firm even if demand by European consumers is stagnant. But rigidities in a national economy can prevent it from quickly joining growth in a world business cycle. Studies of rigidities are important here.

What are the business cycle synchronization implications for equity valuation? Although national economies are becoming increasingly integrated with a world economy, there are so many economic variables involved that the chances of full synchronization are extremely remote. For example, within the European Union, tensions arise because governments are not free to pursue domestic and fiscal economic policies to deal with their own domestic business cycles. The experience of the 1990s and early 2000s is that the economies of Continental Europe, Japan, the United Kingdom, and the United States had markedly different GDP growth rates and entered various stages of the business cycle at different times. Recalling that any correlation less than unity supports diversification benefits, the lack of perfect business cycle synchronization is an a priori argument in favor of international diversification. If long-term GDP growth and business cycles were perfectly synchronized among countries, then one would expect a high degree of correlation between markets, especially in periods of crisis. In making investment asset-allocation decisions, one must always consider long-term expected returns, variances, and correlations. In the long term, international diversification will always be advantageous until national economies are expected to be perfectly synchronized around the world. It is difficult to imagine such a possibility. Expected returns and expected standard deviations will differ among countries with unsynchronized short-term business cycles and long-term GDP growth rates, even though investors may follow the crowd in their short term reactions to crises.

Further considerations in the divergence between countries come from a consideration of growth clubs. Baumol (1986) examined three convergence growth clubs (clubs converging to a similar steady state in terms of income per capita): western industrialized countries, centrally planned economies, and less developed countries. Regardless of the number of growth clubs, one can expect within-group convergence but inter-group divergence in TFP and income per capita. The degree of business cycle synchronicity also varies over time depending on the pattern of regional shocks and changes in economies' propagation mechanisms.

---

[8] See Canova and De Nicolo (1995). An analysis of the business cycle is provided in Reilly and Brown (2003).

Growth Theory   Growth theory is a branch of economics that examines the role of countries in value creation. The output of a country is measured by gross domestic product (GDP), and growth theory attempts to explain the rate of GDP growth in different countries. For two countries with equal risk, portfolio managers will want to overweight the country with sustainable expected long-term GDP growth. The inputs considered are labor, capital, and productivity. In addition to labor and capital, there are also human capital and natural resources. Increases in educational levels can lead to an increase in labor skills, and discoveries of natural resources can lead to resource-based growth. Two competing economic theories attempt to shed light on the sustainable long-term growth rate of a nation.

Neoclassical growth theory assumes that the marginal productivity of capital declines as more capital is added. This is the traditional case in economics with diminishing marginal returns to input factors. *Endogenous growth theory* assumes that the marginal productivity of capital does not necessarily decline as capital is added. Technological advances and improved education of the labor force can lead to efficiency gains. Any one firm faces diminishing returns, but endogenous growth theory assumes that externalities arise when a firm develops a new technology. Thus, one firm's technical breakthrough, begets another's breakthrough, perhaps through imitation. In this case, the marginal product of capital does not decline with increasing capital per capita.

In growth theory, *steady state* is defined as the condition of no change in capital per capita. This comes about when the savings rate times GDP per capita just matches the investment required to maintain the amount of capital per capita. The rate of growth in the population plus the yearly depreciation in equipment gives a replacement rate to be multiplied by the amount of capital per capita, and this multiplication yields the investment required to maintain the amount of capital per capita.

Neoclassical growth theory predicts that the long-term level of GDP depends on the country's savings rate, but the long-term growth rate in GDP does not depend on the savings rate. This is because a steady state is reached, and this steady state is reached, because additions to the capital stock provide smaller and smaller increases to GDP and consequently to savings (the savings rate times GDP). In the context of endogenous growth theory, steady state may never be reached, because the ability to avoid a decline in the marginal product of capital means there is no necessary decline in savings as capital is increased. Thus, endogenous growth theory predicts that the long-term growth rate in GDP depends on the savings rate.

Equity valuation implications are different for countries experiencing neoclassical versus endogenous growth. If a country is experiencing neoclassical growth and its savings rate increases, there would be an increase in dividends as the new level of GDP is reached, but not an increase in the dividend growth rate. For a country experiencing endogenous growth with cascading breakthroughs, however, there would be an increase in both dividends and the dividend growth rate.

In an open world economy, it is important to ascertain whether growth is caused by an increased mobilization of inputs or by efficiency gains. Input-driven growth is necessarily limited. For example, many developing countries have witnessed high growth rates because of capital flows from abroad, but face

> **CONCEPTS IN ACTION** *NEARLY 30 TRANSNATIONAL CORPORATIONS RICHER THAN MANY NATIONS, UN STUDY FINDS*
>
> Twenty-nine of the world's 100 largest economic entities are transnational corporations, according to a new list produced by the United Nations Conference on Trade and Development (UNCTAD) ranking both states and corporations.
>
> Exxon Mobile, with a "value added" worth of $63 billion, is bigger in economic size than Pakistan, while General Motors, worth $56 billion, outpaces both Peru and New Zealand, according to the list.
>
> UNCTAD also reports that Ford Motor and DaimlerChrysler, with value added of over $42 billion, are both larger than Nigeria, which is worth just $41 billion. Kuwait, at $38 billion, is outranked by General Electric. And Honda, Nissan and Toshiba all have more value than Syria.
>
> The rising importance of transnational corporations in the global economy is revealed in other statistics compiled by UNCTAD. The agency reports that the 100 largest companies accounted for 3.5 percent of global gross domestic product in 1990—a figure that jumped to 4.3 percent in 2000. There were 24 corporations in the 1990 combined top 100 list of companies and countries, compared with 29 in 2000.
>
> *Source:* UN News Centre, August 13, 2002.

diminishing returns in the absence of productivity gains. National sustainable growth rates require careful examination.

The Limitation of the Country Concept in Financial Analysis   The distinction between countries and companies is misleading in some respects. Both types of economic entities produce and market a portfolio of products. Indeed, some companies are bigger in economic size than some countries.

Many companies compete globally. The national location of their headquarters is not a determinant variable. Many multinational corporations realize most of their sales and profits in foreign countries. So, an analysis of the economic situation of the country of their headquarters is not of great importance. In Chapter 5, we showed that many national stock markets are dominated by a few multinationals. For example, Nokia market capitalization is larger than the sum of that of all other Finnish firms. The top ten Swiss multinational firms account for more than 70 percent of the Swiss stock exchange. But these companies do most of their business outside of their home country, so their valuation should be based on the global competition they face in their industry, not on the state of their home economy.

Industry Analysis: Return Expectation Elements

To achieve excess equity returns on a risk-adjusted basis, an investor must find companies that can earn return on equity (ROE) above the required rate of return and do this on a sustained basis. For this reason, global industry analysis centers on an examination of sources of growth and sustainability of competitive advantage. Growth must be distinguished from level. A high profit level may yield high current cash flows for valuation purposes, but there is also the question of how these cash flows will grow. Continued reinvestment opportunities in positive net present value investment opportunities will create growth. Curtailment of research and development expenditures may yield high current cash flows at the expense of future growth.

An analyst valuing a company within its global industry should study several key elements. Following are some important conceptual issues.

Demand Analysis   Value analysis begins with an examination of demand conditions. The concepts of complements and substitutes help, but demand analysis is quite complex. Usually, surveys of demand as well as explanatory regressions are used to try to estimate demand. Demand is the target for all capacity, location, inventory, and production decisions. Often, the analyst tries to find a leading indicator to help give some forecast of demand.

In the global context, *demand* means *worldwide demand*. One cannot simply define the automobile market as a domestic market. A starting point, then, is a set of forecasts of global and country-specific GDP figures. The analyst will want to estimate the sensitivity of sales to global and national GDP changes.

Country analysis is important for demand analysis, because most companies tend to focus on specific regions. Most European car manufacturers tend to sell and produce outside of Europe, but the European car market is their primary market. An increase in demand for cars in Europe will affect them more than it will affect Japanese car producers.

Value Creation   Sources of value come from using inputs to produce outputs in the value chain. The *value chain* is the set of transformations in moving from raw materials to product or service delivery. This chain can involve many companies and countries, some providing raw materials, some producing intermediate goods, some producing finished consumer goods, and some delivering finished goods to the consumer. From the point of view of an intermediate goods producer, basic raw materials are considered to be *upstream* in the value chain, and transformations closer to the consumer are considered *downstream*.

Within the value chain, each transformation adds value. Value chain analysis can be used to determine how much value is added at each step. Indeed, some countries have a value-added tax. The value added at each transformation stage is partly a function of four major factors:

- *The learning (experience) curve:* As companies produce more output, they gain experience, so that the cost per unit produced declines.

- *Economies of scale:* As a company expands, its fixed costs may be spread over a larger output, and average costs decline over a range of output.

- *Economies of scope:* As a company produces related products, experience and reputation with one product may spill over to another product.

- *Network externalities:* Some products and services gain value as more consumers use them, so that they are able to share something popular.

Equity valuation implications come from an analysis of the industry's value chain and each company's strategy to exploit current and future profit opportunities within the chain. For company managers, Christensen, Raynor, and Verlinden (2001) recommend a strategy of predicting profit migration within the industry's value chain. For example they break the computer industry down into value chain stages: equipment, materials, components, product design, assembly, operating system, application software, sales and distribution, and field service. In the early days of the computer industry, vertically integrated manufacturers delivered the entire value chain. The advent of the personal computer led to specialization within each stage and profits migrated to stages such as components and operating systems. For the analyst also, the strategy of predicting dividends and dividend growth rates must be based on profit migration in the value chain. The risk can be gauged from the degree of competition within the stage—the more the competition, the more the risk. The ability of companies to compete at each stage will be enhanced by their learning curve progress, economies of scale or scope, and network externalities.

Christensen et al. also point out that industries often evolve from vertical integration to disintegration. If an industry becomes too fragmented, however, consolidation pressures will come from resource bottlenecks as well as the continuing search for economies of scale. During the industry's life cycle, tension between disintegration and consolidation will require the company and the analyst to constantly monitor company positions in the profit migration cycle.

Industry Life Cycle   Traditionally, the industry life cycle is broken down into stages from pioneering development to decline. Of course, one must be careful in industry definition. If railroads were defined as an *industry,* we would see a global industry life cycle. Defining the industry as transportation provides a different picture. In any case, industry life cycles are normally categorized by rates of growth in sales. The stages of growth can clearly vary in length.

1. Pioneering development is the first stage and has a low but slowly increasing industry sales growth rate. Substantial development costs and acceptance by only early adopters can lead to low profit margins.

2. Rapid accelerating growth is the second stage, and the industry sales growth rate is still modest but is rapidly increasing. High profit margins are possible because firms from outside the new industry may face barriers to entering the newly established markets.

3. Mature growth is the third stage and has a high but more modestly increasing industry sales growth rate. The entry of competitors lowers profit margins, but the return on equity is high.

One would expect that somewhere in stage 2 or 3 the industry sales growth rate would move above the GDP growth rate in the economy.

4. Stabilization and market maturity is the fourth stage and has a high but only slowly increasing sales growth rate. The sales growth rate has not yet begun to decline, but increasing capacity and competition may cause returns on equity to decline to the level of average returns on equity in the economy.

5. Deceleration of growth and decline is the fifth stage with a decreasing sales growth rate. At this stage, the industry may experience overcapacity, and profit margins may be completely eroded.

One would expect that somewhere in stage 5, the industry sales growth rate would fall back to the GDP growth rate and then decline below it. (This cannot happen in stage 4 where the sales growth is still increasing.) The position of an industry in its life cycle should be judged on a global basis.

Competition Structure One of the first steps in analyzing an industry is the determination of the amount of industry concentration. If the industry is fragmented, many firms compete, and the theories of competition and product differentiation are most applicable. With more concentration and fewer firms in the industry, oligopolistic competition and game theories become more important. Finally, the case of one firm is the case in which the theory of monopoly applies.

In analyzing industry concentration, two methods are normally used. One method is the N firm concentration ratio: the combined market share of the largest N firms in the industry. For example, a market in which the three largest firms have a combined share of 80 percent would indicate largely oligopolistic competition. A related but more precise measure is the Herfindahl index, the sum of the squared market shares of the firms in the industry. Letting M_i be the market share of an individual firm, the index is $H = M_1^2 + M_2^2 + \ldots + M_N^2$.

If two firms have a 15 percent market share each and one has a 70 percent market share, $H = 0.15^2 + 0.15^2 + 0.7^2 = 0.535$.

The Herfindahl index has a value that is always smaller than one. A small index indicates a competitive industry with no dominant players. If all firms have an equal share, $H = N(1/N^2) = 1/N$, and the reciprocal of the index shows the number of firms in the industry. When the firms have unequal shares, the reciprocal of the index indicates the "equivalent" number of firms in the industry. Using our example above, we find that the market structure is equivalent to having 1.87 firms of the same size:

$$\frac{1}{H} = \frac{1}{(0.15^2 + 0.15^2 + 0.70^2)} = \frac{1}{0.535} = 1.87$$

One can classify the competition structure of the industry according to this ratio.

In practice, the equity analyst will see both the N firm concentration ratio and the Herfindahl index. The analyst is searching for indicators of the likely degree of cooperation versus competition within the industry. Although the balance between cooperation and competition is dynamic and changing, the higher the N firm concentration ratio and the higher the Herfindahl index, the less likely it is that there is cut-throat competition and the more likely it is that companies will cooperate.

The advantage of the N firm concentration ratio is that it provides an intuitive sense of industry competition. If the analyst knows that the seven largest firms have a combined share of less than 15%, he or she immediately knows that the industry is extremely fragmented and thus more risky because of competitive pressures and the likely lack of cooperation.

The Hefindahl index *(H)* has the advantage of greater discrimination because it reflects all firms in the industry and it gives greater weight to the companies with larger market shares. An H below 0.1 indicates an unconcentrated industry, an H of 0.1 to 0.18 indicates moderate concentration, and an H above 0.18 indicates high concentration. A high Herfindahl index can also indicate the presence of a market leader with a higher share than others, another indication of likely coordination as the leader might impose discipline on the industry.

Suppose the analyst is comparing two industries:

Market Shares in Industry A	Market Shares in Industry B
One firm has 45%	Four firms have 15% each
Three firms have 5% each	Four firms have 10% each
Ten firms have 4% each	
Four firm concentration ratio is 60%	Four firm concentration ratio is 60%
Herfindahl index is 0.23	Herfindahl index is 0.13

Even though the four firm concentration ratios are the same for both industries, the Herfindahl index indicates that industry A is highly concentrated, but industry B is only moderately concentrated.

Competitive Advantage   In his book, *The Competitive Advantage of Nations,*[9] Michael Porter used the notions of economic geography that different locations have different competitive advantages. National factors that can lead to a competitive advantage are

- factor conditions such as human capital, perhaps measured by years of schooling;

- demand conditions such as the size and growth of the domestic market;

- related supplier and support industries such as the computer software industry to support the hardware industry; and

- strategy, structure, and rivalry such as the corporate governance, management practices, and the financial climate.

---

[9] Porter (1990).

Competitive Strategies   A competitive strategy is a set of actions that a firm is taking to optimize its future competitive position. In *Competitive Advantage,*[10] Porter distinguishes three generic competitive strategies:

- *Cost leadership:* The firm seeks to be the low-cost producer in its industry.

- *Differentiation:* The firm seeks to provide product benefits that other firms do not provide.

- *Focus:* The firm targets a niche with either a cost or a benefit (differentiation) focus.

Equity valuation analysis in large part is analysis of the probability of success of company strategies. Analysts will consider the company's commitment to a strategy as well as the likely responses of its competitors. Is the company a tough competitor that is likely to survive a war of attrition? Is it likely that a Nash equilibrium will hold, in which each company adopts a strategy to leave itself with the best outcome regardless of the competitor's strategy and, by doing this, causes a reduction in the size of the total reward to both?

Co-opetition and the Value Net   *Co-opetition* refers to cooperation along the value chain and is an application of game theory. Brandenberger and Nalebuff[11] developed the concept of the value net as the set of participants involved in producing value along the value chain: the suppliers, customers, competitors, and firms producing complementary goods and services. Although these participants compete with each other, they can also cooperate to produce mutually beneficial outcomes. In this respect, co-opetition is an application of cooperative game theory.

In the context of equity valuation, co-opetition analysis is an important element of risk analysis. Cooperating participants in a good economy may become staunch competitors in a poor economy. If a company's abnormal profits depend on co-opetition, those profits are riskier than if they are the result of a purely competitive environment. In a good economy, a company may outsource some of its production to cooperating value net participants who may build capabilities based on lucrative long-term contracts. In a poor economy, however, no new contracts may be forthcoming.

Sector Rotation   Many commercial providers sell reports on the relative performance of industries or sectors over the business cycle, and sector rotation is a popular investment-timing strategy. Some investors put more weight on industries entering a profitable portion of their role in the business cycle. Certainly industries behave differently over the business cycle. Because consumer cyclical industries (durables and nondurables) correlate highly with the economy as a whole, these industries do well in the early and middle growth portion of the business

---

[10] Porter (1985).
[11] Brandenberger and Nalebuff (1996).

cycle. Defensive consumer staples (necessities) maintain their profitability during recessions. Nevertheless, a successful sector rotation strategy depends on an intensive analysis of the industry and faces many pitfalls. An upturn in the economy and the demand for industry products do not automatically mean an increase in profits, because factors such as the status of industry capacity, the competitive structure, the lead time to increase capacity, and the general supply/demand conditions in the industry also have an impact on profits.

Indicators of the various stages of the business cycle are complex. We have already seen that different sectors, for example cyclical sectors, will do well at various stages of the business cycle and that the five stages are:

- *Recovery:* The economy picks up from its slowdown or recession.

- *Early Upswing:* Confidence is up and the economy is gaining some momentum.

- *Late Upswing:* Boom mentality has taken hold.

- *Economy Slows or Goes into Recession:* The economy is declining.

- *Recession:* Monetary policy will be eased but there will be a lag before recovery.

Industry Analysis: Risk Elements

To achieve excess equity returns on a risk-adjusted basis, investors must be able to distinguish sources of risk in the investments they make. For example, an increase in ROE may be attributable solely to an increase in leverage (gearing). This increased leverage raises the financial risk and hence the required rate of return; the increased ROE then does not yield an excess risk-adjusted return. Although return expectations can be established by evaluating firm strategies within the industry, the analyst must always examine the risk that the strategy may be flawed or that assumptions about competition and co-opetition may hold only in a good economic environment. What seems to be an attractive strategy in good times, can turn into a very dangerous one in bad times. The risks can differ widely, not only between firms in the same industry, but also across industries. Some industries are more sensitive to technological change and the business cycle than are others. So, the outlined growth factors that affect return expectations should also be taken into account to assess industry risk.

Ultimately, firms that follow high-risk strategies in an industry that is also risky will have a higher ex ante stock market risk, and this should be incorporated in expected risk measures. Ex post, this stock market risk will eventually be measured by looking at volatility and covariance measures.

Market Competition   Microeconomics[12] examines the various types of competition in markets. The question is always to look at price versus average cost.

---

[12] See Besanko, Dranove, and Shanley (2000).

Particularly with oligopolies and monopolies, game theory helps to discern the likely success or failure of corporate strategies. Preservation of competitive position and competitive advantage often involves entry-deterring or exit-promoting strategies. *Limit pricing* is pricing below average cost to deter entry. Similarly, *holding excess capacity* can deter entry. *Predatory pricing* is pricing below average cost to drive others out of the industry. Any valuation of an individual company must examine the strategy contest in which companies in the industry are engaged. Risks are always present that the company's strategy will not sustain its competitive advantage.

Value Chain Competition   In producing goods and services of value, companies compete not just in markets, but also along the value chain. Suppliers can choose to compete rather than simply cooperate with the intermediate company. Labor, for example, may want some of the profit that a company is earning. In lean times, labor may make concessions, but in good times labor may want a larger share of the profits. Buyers may organize to wrest some of the profit from the company.

A major issue in value chain analysis is whether labor is unionized. Japanese automobile companies producing in the United States face lower production costs because of their ability to employ non-unionized workers. Union relations are a major factor in valuing airline companies worldwide.

Suppliers of commodity raw materials have less ability to squeeze profits out of a downstream company than do suppliers of differentiated intermediate products. Companies may manage their value chain competition by vertically integrating (buying upstream or downstream) or, for example, by including labor in their ownership structure.

Co-opetition risks are presented by the possibility that the company's supply may be held up or that its distributors may find other sources of products and services. Suppose a firm acts as a broker between producers and distributors and outsources its distribution services by selling long-term distribution contracts to producers, thus also keeping distributors happy. Because of the low fixed costs involved in brokering, this business strategy should make the firm less sensitive to recession than a distribution company with heavy fixed costs. But what if producers are unwilling to enter long-term distribution contracts during a recession?

In his book, Porter (1985) discussed five industry forces, as well as the generic competitive strategies mentioned earlier. Porter's so-called five forces analysis can be seen as an examination of the risks involved in the value chain. Oster (1999) provides a useful analysis of the five forces, and we show her insights as bulleted points below. In some cases, we slightly modify or extend them.

Rivalry Intensity   This is the degree of competition among companies in the industry. For example, airline competition is more intense now with more carriers and open skies agreements between countries than in the days of heavier regulation with fewer carriers limited to domestic companies. Coordination can make rivalry much less intense. The analyst must be alert for possible changes in coordination and rivalry intensity that are not yet reflected in equity prices.

- Intense rivalry among firms in an industry reduces average profitability.

- In an industry in which coordination yields excess profits (prices exceed marginal costs), there are market share incentives for individual companies to shade (slightly cut) prices as they weigh the benefits and costs of coordination versus shading.

- Large numbers of companies in a market reduce coordination opportunities.

- Rivalry is generally more intense when the major companies are all similarly sized, and no one large company can impose discipline on the industry.

- Generally, coordination is easier if companies in the market are similar. All gravitate to a mutually agreeable focal point, the solution that similar companies will naturally discern.

- Industries which have substantial specific (cannot be used for other purposes) assets exhibit high barriers to exit and intensified rivalry.

- Variability in demand creates more rivalry within an industry. For example, high fixed costs and cyclical demand creates capacity mismatches and price cutting from excess capacity.

Substitutes   This is the threat of products or services that are substitutes for the products or services of the industry. For example, teleconferencing is a substitute for travel. The analyst must be alert for possible changes in substitutes that are not yet reflected in equity prices.

- Substitute products constrain the ability of firms in the industry to raise their prices substantially.

- Industries without excess capacity or intense rivalry can present attractive investment opportunities; but substitute products can reduce the attraction by constraining the ability of firms in the industry to substantially raise their prices.

Buyer Power   This is the bargaining power of buyers of the producer's products or services. For example, car rental agencies have more bargaining power with automobile manufacturers than have individual consumers. The analyst must be alert for possible changes in buyer power that are not yet reflected in equity prices.

- The larger the number of buyers and the smaller their individual purchases, the less the bargaining power.

- Standardization of products increases buyer power because consumers can easily switch between suppliers.

- If buyers can integrate backwards, this increases their bargaining power because they would cut out the supplier if they choose to integrate.

- Greater buyer power makes an equity investment in the producer less attractive because of lower profit margins.

Supplier Power   This is the bargaining power of suppliers to the producers. For example, traditional aircraft manufacturers lost supplier power when niche players entered the market and began producing short-haul jets. The analyst must be alert for possible changes in supplier power that are not yet reflected in equity prices.

- The more suppliers there are for the industry, the less is the supplier power.

- Standardized raw materials (commodities) reduce supplier power because the supplier has no differentiation or quality advantage.

- If buyers can integrate backwards, this reduces supplier power because the buyer would cut out the supplier if it chooses to integrate.

- Greater supplier power makes an equity investment in the producer less attractive because of the possibility of a squeeze on profits.

New Entrants   This is the threat of new entrants into the industry. For example, a European consortium entered the aircraft manufacturing industry and has become a major company now competing globally. In addition, a Brazilian and a Canadian company have entered the short-haul aircraft market. The analyst must be alert for possible changes in new entrant threats that are not yet reflected in equity prices.

- The higher the payoffs the more likely will be the entry, all else equal.

- Barriers to entry are industry characteristics which reduce the rate of entry below that needed to remove excess profits.

- Expectations of incumbent reactions influence entry.

- Exit costs influence the rate of entry.

- All else equal, the larger the volume needed to reach minimal unit costs, the greater the difference between pre- and post-entry price (the increase in industry capacity would drive down prices), and thus the less likely entry is to occur.

- The steeper the cost curve, the less likely is entry at a smaller volume than the minimal unit cost volume.

- Long-term survival at a smaller than minimal unit cost volume requires an offsetting factor to permit a company to charge a price premium. Product differentiation and a monopoly in location are two possible offsets.

- Excess capacity deters entry by increasing the credibility of price cutting as an entry response by incumbents.

- Occasional actions that are unprofitable in the short run can increase a company's credibility for price cutting to deter entry, giving an entry deterring reputation as a tough incumbent.

- An incumbent contract to meet the price of any responsible rival can deter entry.

- Patents and licenses can prevent free entry from eliminating excess profits in an industry. They deter entry.

- Learning curve effects can deter entry unless new entrants can appropriate the experience of the incumbents. For example, Boeing learned about metal fatigue from the British experience of accidents with the Comet, the first commercial jet airliner.

- Pioneering brands can dominate the industry and deter entry when network externalities exist and when consumers find it costly to make product mistakes.

- High exit costs discourage entry. A primary determinant of high exit costs is asset specificity and the irreversibility of capital investments.

After presenting the insights above, Oster follows up with an excellent presentation of many related topics: strategic groups within industries, competition in global markets, issues of organizational structure and design, competitive advantage, corporate diversification, and the effect of rival behavior. Indeed, industry analysis is a complex subject as the analyst attempts to deduce the valuation implications of corporate strategies.

Government Participation   Governments subsidies to companies can seed companies in the early stages and can also give companies an unfair advantage in steady state. There is extra uncertainty for a company competing head to head with one subsidized by its home country. Governments also participate by supporting their domestic country stock prices in one way or another. This creates uncertainty about future policy in addition to the normal risk associated with cash flows.

Governments participate indirectly by their involvement in the social contract. In the United States, automobile companies bear the costs of defined benefit pension funds. Japanese automobile companies do not bear these costs because of government-sponsored pension schemes. Some European governments dealt with the possibility of increased unemployment by shortening the work week to keep employment spread out. Such government policy may make a European company less competitive.

Governments control competition. Open-skies laws allow foreign airlines to operate between domestic cities. Closed-skies laws in the past prevented Canadian carriers from operating between U.S. cities. Closed-skies laws have also been a factor in the Eurozone. Risks are presented by the uncertainty involved in trying to predict government policy.

Risks and Covariance   Investors care about stock market risk, that is, the uncertainty about future stock prices. Risk is usually viewed at two levels. The total risk of a company or an industry is the first level of risk, and it is usually measured by the standard deviation of stock returns of that company or industry. But part of this risk can be diversified away in a portfolio. So, the second level of risk is measured by the covariance with the aggregate economy, which tells how the returns of a company vary with global market indexes. Although this risk is usually measured by the beta from regressions of company returns against market returns, it is useful to note those beta changes over time as a function of business cycle conditions and shifting competition within the industry.

When analyzing an industry, the analyst is faced with a continuing challenge of determining diversifiable versus nondiversifiable risk. Because future cash flow and return covariance must be predicted in order to estimate the firm and industry's beta, simple reliance on past regressions is not sufficient. Part of the risk from a strategy failure or a change from co-opetition to competition may be firm-specific and diversifiable. At the same time, part of the risk may be nondiversifiable, because it involves fundamental shifts in industry structure.

In order to manage a global equity portfolio, the risk of a company is usually summarized by its exposure to various risk factors. The last section of this chapter is devoted to global risk factor models.

Global Industry Analysis in Practice: An Example

In the following analysis of the transportation and logistics industry, several global industry analysis factors are considered. Indeed, such analyses usually include a discussion of the competitive structure of the industry, the strategies of the players, and a comparative ratio analysis of companies within the industry.

CONCEPTS IN ACTION TRANSPORTATION AND LOGISTICS

Logistics remains a growth market. . . . the Asian logistics market should be a growth driver. For the individual logistics segments, we expect the following compound annual growth rates for the period 2002 to 2010: air freight: +5.9%; sea freight: +5.6%; overland transport: +3.3%; and value-added services/logistics outsourcing: 11%–12%.

Average 2003e price/earnings ratios of just below 10 and a price/book ratio of around 1.2 indicate attractive valuation levels for the sector. DCF and an economic profit analysis support this thesis. Higher valuation levels are strongly dependent on macroeconomic expectations. We will see ongoing dynamic changes in industry structures that are driven by positioning and repositioning questions. Related to this is the continuing consolidation process in the highly fragmented logistics market.

Attractive Sector Growth
Air freight: business is expected to grow until 2010 by 5.9% (CAGR)

In the period between 1981 and 2001, transport traffic in cross-border air freight increased at an average multiple of 2.5 times global GDP growth. In the last five years, the average multiple was much lower at 1.2 (3.4% p.a.[13]), because there were two slumps in a short period with the economic crisis in Asia and the terror-

---

[13]The abbreviation p.a. means per annum, or annually.

ist attacks in the U.S. It is noticeable that the growth trend has been slowing since the mid-1980s and that the top peaks have declined steadily since 1985.

For the period 2002 to 2010, 5.9% compound annual growth amounts to a multiple of 2.1. This is lower than the 1981–2001 average multiple. The declining growth trend in air freight traffic is extrapolated in the long-term projection and growth dips were perpetuated with a weaker annual growth dynamic. In the event of economic crisis and open hostilities, the multiples are expected to be sharply lower in the corresponding years.

Sea freight: expect a volume growth of 5.6% (CAGR)

That translates into an average multiple of 2.0 times global GDP. In the past, the growth of container handling has significantly exceeded GDP growth. This outperformance is due, on the one hand, to a rising use of containers in total sea freight tonnage—in eight years it has doubled from 5% to 10%—and, on the other, to more frequent turnover per container.

Land transport: up to 2010 overland transport in Europe is expected to increase by 3.3% p.a.

The reluctance of many companies to penetrate this market is understandable given the competitive pressure and especially the resources needed to create a Europe-wide network. Compared with sea and air freight as well as value-added services, historical growth is more modest: between 1970 and 1998, ton kilometers transported by road (in the EU) increased by an average of 4% per year with a falling trend.

Continental Europe still has ground to make up on outsourcing

In the field of value-added services (VAS), we expect further potential to catch up in outsourcing value-added services in Continental Europe. A comparison of the different outsourcing levels in the UK (currently 37%) and the states of Continental Europe (29%) suggests that the latter has a lot of ground to make up. We expect the overall European outsourcing ratio to come close to approaching the UK level by 2005. For the UK market, we project no significant increase in the outsourcing ratio.

Consolidation momentum driven by an extremely fragmented market

The logistics market is one of the most fragmented markets and the structure of the market will change over the coming years. Besides the search for economies of scale, resource bottlenecks are resulting in acquisition pressure. This relates to management, employees, warehousing capacities and other operating structures. In air freight, the 10 largest forwarding companies have a combined share of less than 40%. The seafreight market is even more fragmented: the seven largest transportation companies have a combined market share of less than 15%.

The most fragmented market is European overland transport. Danzas and Schenker are the leading providers, each with a market share of 2.2%. Apart from the French company Geodis (1.5%) and the unlisted Dachser (1.0%), the market shares of the other providers are less than one-tenth of a percent. In a market undergoing dynamic change, the big players and the innovative niche players are expected to win additional market share. The companies "stuck in the middle" will run into problems.

Furthermore, state-owned or formerly state-owned companies (Deutsche Post, TPG, SNCF, La Poste, Deutsche Bahn, etc.) are driving the consolidation process. They are looking into portfolio changes in order to improve their core business. We assume the sale of Stinnes will rekindle the consolidation pressure.

Trend towards consolidation accompanied by difficult questions of positioning

The consolidation trend and the following market pressure force companies to continuously monitor their positioning. Within the European sample, we think Exel is the strategy leader. But the UK company cannot rest on its laurels because some competitors are in close pursuit. When looking at the positioning of companies, there are four major issues:

- The high-volume players are attempting to achieve the optimal mix by filling in the network gaps and upgrading their portfolio of services;

- the outsourcing-driven business models are expanding their range of services in order to become more deeply involved in the customer's value chain within the framework of outsourcing;

- companies caught between these areas must take care not to be backed into a corner; and

- regional providers have little prospect of closing the gap to the big players; because they lack the financial strength to close the gap, they must rely on cooperation agreements or they will be purchased.

Valuation multiples in line with economic projections

The performance of logistics stocks hinges to a great extent on the market's expectations for the economy. Such a statement is underpinned by correlating the performance of our HVB logistics index (excluding postal service companies), HVB-Logidexx, with the economic indicator provided by the price of copper, which trades every day. The susceptibility of the individual companies to cyclical fluctuation should be assessed on the basis of their cost and contract-business structures, outsourcing focus, the cyclical resistance of the sector in general, as well as their diversification by segment, customer and regional breakdown.

A look at these parameters indicates that Tibbett & Britten and Kuehne & Nagel have defensive capabilities within this pan-European sampling, while

UK-based Exel is highly susceptible to cyclical fluctuation because of its exposure to the high tech and U.S. markets. We believe that a recovery by Exel is for the most part already factored into the price of its stock. We favor the stock of Tibbett & Britten and Kuehne & Nagel at present, both of which are likely to show more gains in market share.

A turnaround in the relative performance of the HVB-Logidexx and the Euro STOXX 50 index set in after September 11. Sentiment turned around: multiples of asset value—enterprise value/capital employed and price/book ratio—in some cases of well over one were exaggerated and did not correspond to either medium-term projections of earnings or forecast added-value margins. Upbeat guidance issued by Kuehne & Nagel, T&B and Stinnes, among others, resulted in the Logidexx's outperformance of the Euro STOXX.

Opinions differ at present over the logistics business. We still expect to see a macroeconomic turnaround in the second half of the year. The uptrend in cargo volume in both Asia and Europe, which has been gathering speed since April, underpins this view. The risk lies in the fact that the brightening picture in terms of cargo volume, driven partly by companies restocking, might be a mere flash in the pan.

First up in the clouds, then down in the dumps

D.Logistics and Thiel, Europe's former high flyers, have seen both their operating profits and stock prices plunge. This has had a negative impact on sentiment vis-à-vis the sector. The capital market is increasingly coming to the realization that the majority of their problems are specific to these companies. They proved incapable of adjusting their internal structures to the pace of acquisition. The assumption that their business models, which are focused on logistics outsourcing are resistant to cyclical fluctuation proved to be erroneous. What emerged was rather that customers are not prepared in tough times to enter into major contracts to outsource.

Adding value: looking at the margin alone is being too short-sighted

When looking at the returns on capital employed (2003), we find significant differences within the industry. Comparing Exel and Kuehne & Nagel makes it clear that looking at the margin alone does not provide guidance, because capital turnover can vary substantially due to the different business models. Kuehne & Nagel, for example, leads the ocean freight market but does not own a single vessel.

Compared with Exel, K&N's proportion of brokerage business is much greater, meaning that capital turnover on a low base of capital employed is substantially higher. A higher ROCE in particular reflects this. We think that Exel will grow at a stronger pace in the future and that it will boost its value driver of capital employed—without diluting its value-added margin—more quickly than K&N.

An attractive sector valuation

In our opinion, the European logistics stocks are favorably valued in fundamental terms. We would like to focus on the NAV multiples. We think Stinnes will be acquired without a valuation premium; one indication of this is the 2003 price/book ratio of 1.2x. On the basis of EV/capital employed, including goodwill, we calculate a multiple of 0.7x for the sample; even if all of the goodwill is subtracted, this value comes to 1.0x. A value of 1.0x means that the company will not create value in the future (value-added margin equals zero). But in fact, the value-added margins (ROCE minus WACC) are on average roughly three percentage points above the capital costs.

Things will remain exciting

Additional expected IPOs, such as that of Panalpina's, Deutsche Bahn's potential either full or partial access to the capital market, UPS' full war chest and Kuehne & Nagel's major scope for investment will keep the sector on the edge. Deregulation of postal markets, moreover, will provide a further source of conjecture, change and speculative appeal. A favorably priced growth market is just waiting for the economy to turn up.

Source: Markus Hesse and Christian Cohrs, *The Euromoney: International Equity Capital Markets Handbook* (Adrian Hornbrook: Colchester, Essex, U.K.), 2003, pp. 15–21. (For further information about *Euromoney Handbooks*, visit www.euromoney-yearbooks.com.)

Equity Analysis

Because it should be forward looking, equity analysis needs to be carried out within the context of the country and the industry. Reasonable prediction of cash flows and risk is required to provide useful inputs to the valuation process.

Industry Valuation or Country Valuation   A frequently asked question is whether a company should primarily be valued relative to the global industry to which it belongs or relative to other national companies listed on its home stock market. Indeed, many corporations are now very active abroad and, even at home, face worldwide competition. So, there are really two aspects to this question:

- Should the *financial analysis* of a company be conducted within its global industry?

- Do the stock prices of companies within the same global industry move together worldwide, so that the *relative valuation* of a company's equity should be conducted within the global industry rather than within its home stock market?

The answer to the first question is a clear yes. Prospective earnings of a company should be estimated taking into account the competition it is facing. In most cases, this competition is international as well as domestic. Most large corporations derive a significant amount of their cash flows from foreign sales and operations, so their competition is truly global.

The answer to the second question raised is less obvious. At a given point in time, different industries face different growth prospects, and that is true worldwide. Furthermore, different industries exhibit different sensitivities to unexpected changes in worldwide economic conditions. This implies that the stock market valuation should differ across industries. Some industries, such as "electronic components" or "health and personal care," have large P/E and P/BV ratios while other industries, such as "energy" and "materials," have low P/E and P/BV ratios. The major question related to the importance of industry factors in stock prices, however, is whether a company has more in common with other companies in the same global industry than with other companies in the same country. By "more in common," we mean that its stock price tends to move together with that of other companies, and to be influenced by similar events. Before presenting some empirical evidence on the relative importance of country and industry factor in stock pricing, let's stress some caveats:

- Any industry classification is open to questions. MSCI, S&P, FTSE, and Dow Jones produce global industry indexes with different industry classification systems. The number of industry groups identified differs. It is not easy to assign each company to a single industry group. Some industry activities are clearly identified (e.g., producing automobiles), but others are not so clear-cut. It is not unusual to see the same company assigned to different industry groups by different classification systems. Some large corporations have diversified activities that cut across industry groups. Standard and Poor's and Morgan Stanley Capital International have recently designed a common Global Industry Classification Standard (GICS). The GICS system consists of four levels of detail: 10 sectors, 23 industry groupings, 59 industries, and 122 subindustries. At the most specific level of detail, an individual company is assigned to a single GICS subindustry, according to the definition of its principal business activity determined by S&P and MSCI. The hierarchical nature of the GICS structure will automatically assign the company's industry, industry group, and sector. There are currently over 25,000 companies globally that have been classified.

- The answer could be industry-specific. Some industries are truly global (e.g., oil companies), while others are less so (e.g., leisure and tourism). However, competition is becoming global in most, if not all, industries. For example, travel agencies have become regional, if not global, through a wave of mergers and acquisitions. Supermarket chains now cover many continents, and many retailers capitalize on their brand names globally.

- The answer could be period-specific. There could be periods in which global industry factors dominate, and other periods in which national factors are more important (desynchronized business cycles).

- The answer could be company-specific. Some companies in an industry group have truly international activities with extensive global competition, while others are mostly domestic in all respects. Small Swiss commercial banks with offices located only in one province (canton) of Switzerland have little in common with large global banks (even Crédit Suisse or UBS).

- Even if industry factors dominate, two opposing forces could be at play.[14] A worldwide growth in the demand for goods produced could benefit all players within the industry. However, competition also means that if one major player is highly successful, it will be at the expense of other major players in the industry. For example, Japanese car manufacturers could grow by extensively exporting to the United States, but it will be at the expense of U.S. car manufacturers. The stock price of Nissan would therefore be negatively correlated with that of GM or Ford.

Despite these caveats, all empirical studies find that industry factors have grown in importance in stock price valuation.[15] Global industry factors tend now to dominate country factors, but country factors are still of significant importance. Companies should be valued relative to their industry, but country factors should not be neglected, particularly when conducting a risk analysis.

Two industry valuation approaches are traditionally used: ratio analysis and discounted cash flow models.

Global Financial Ratio Analysis   As already mentioned, global industry financial analysis examines each company in the industry against the industry average. One well-accepted approach to this type of analysis is the DuPont model. (It may be better to think of this as an *approach* of decomposing return ratios, but this approach is usually called the DuPont model.) The basic technique of the DuPont model is to explain ROE or return on assets (ROA) in terms of its contributing elements. For example, we will see that ROA can be explained in terms of net profit margin and asset turnover. The analysis begins with five contributing elements, and these elements appear in several variations, depending on what most interests the analyst. The five elements reflect the financial and operating portions of the income statement as linked to the assets on the balance sheet and the equity supporting those assets. In the analysis here, past performance is being examined. Because income is a flow earned over a period of time, but the balance sheet reflects a balance (stock) at only one point in time, economists would calculate the flow (e.g., net income) over an average (e.g., the average of beginning and ending assets). The typical decompostion of ROE is given by:

$$\frac{NI}{EBT} \times \frac{EBT}{EBIT} \times \frac{EBIT}{Sales} \times \frac{Sales}{Assets} \times \frac{Assets}{Equity} = \frac{NI}{Equity}$$

---

[14]See Griffin and Stulz (2001).
[15]See, for example, Cavaglia, Brightman, and Aked (2000) and Hopkins and Miller (2001).

where

NI   is net income

EBT   is earnings before taxes

NI/EBT   is one minus the tax rate, or the tax retention rate with a maximum value of 1.0 if there were no taxes (lower values imply higher tax burden)

EBIT   is earnings before interest and taxes, or operating income

EBT/EBIT   is interest burden, with a maximum value of 1.0 if there are no interest payments (lower values imply greater debt burden)

EBIT/Sales   is operating margin

Sales/Assets   is asset turnover ratio (a measure of efficiency in the use of assets)

Assets/Equity is   leverage (higher values imply greater use of debt)

NI/Equity is   return on equity (ROE)

The analyst would then compare each firm ratio with the comparable ratio for the industry. Does the firm have a higher operating margin than the industry's? If the company has a higher ROE than the industry ROE, is this higher-than-average ROE due to leverage, or is it due to more operations management-oriented ratios, such as operating margin or asset turnover?

Depending on the analyst's focus, the ratios can be combined in different ways. What is essential in DuPont analysis is the specification of the question of interest rather than the question of whether the model has five, three, or two factors.

One can collapse the first three ratios into the net profit margin (NI/sales) to leave

$$\text{ROE} = \text{Net profit margin} \times \text{Asset turnover} \times \text{Leverage}$$

One could also combine the first three ratios and include the fourth ratio to yield a return on assets breakdown:

$$\text{ROA} = \frac{\text{NI}}{\text{Assets}} = \text{Net profit margin} \times \text{Asset turnover}$$

Without combining the first three ratios, one could also have a four ratio ROA breakdown (tax retention rate × interest burden × operating margin × asset turnover). Also, one could explore a two-ratio ROE explanation by using ROA × leverage.

In all of this analysis, a global comparison of ratios of different companies in the same industry should take into account national valuation specificities. Due to national accounting differences detailed previously, earnings figures should sometimes be reconciled to make comparisons meaningful.

In global financial analysis, the methods of debt analysis can inform and supplement those of equity analysis. The following Concepts in Action feature (p. 282) provides a look at capital structure and industry analysis concerns resulting from debt burden and production capacity analysis.

EXAMPLE 6.2 *DUPONT ANALYSIS OF GENERAL MOTORS AND TOYOTA*

A comparison of Toyota Motor Corporation (NYSE: TM) with General Motors Corporation (NYSE: GM) reveals Toyota's superior net profit margin but inferior ROE as of late 2002. Is this a recent development? Has an ROE comparison been in General Motors' favor, historically, and how have differences in operating margin and other factors explained differences in ROE? In making an international comparison, differences in accounting must be considered. Toyota prepares its original financials according to Japanese GAAP. However, because Toyota trades on the NYSE as ADRs, Toyota also reports financial results according to U.S. GAAP, the basis for General Motors' accounting. Thus, the analyst's task is eased. Exhibit 6.2 presents a side-by-side DuPont analysis for General Motors and Toyota using Toyota's U.S. GAAP prepared financial results.

EXHIBIT 6.2

DuPont Analysis of ROE
GM and Toyota

	FY 1998 GM	FY 1998 TM	FY 1999 GM	FY 1999 TM	FY 2000 GM	FY 2000 TM	FY 2001 GM	FY 2001 TM	Average GM	Average TM
(1) NI/EBT	0.682	0.514	0.655	0.520	0.666	0.527	0.494	0.525	0.624	0.522
(2) EBT/EBIT	0.209	0.536	0.279	0.609	0.221	0.806	0.047	0.903	0.189	0.714
(3) EBIT/Sales	0.161	0.127	0.175	0.120	0.163	0.120	0.130	0.097	0.157	0.116
(4) Net profit margin = (1) × (2) × (3)	0.023	0.035	0.032	0.038	0.024	0.051	0.003	0. 046	0.019	0.043
(5) Sales/Assets	0.627	0.805	0.643	0.773	0.609	0.772	0.547	0.742	0.607	0.773
(6) Assets/Equity	17.18	2.380	13.31	2.379	10.04	2.405	16.44	2.658	14.24	2.456
(7) ROE = (4) × (5) × (6)	0.248	0.067	0.274	0.070	0.147	0.095	0.027	0.091	0.164	0.082

Source: Company reports, Thomson Financial, *The Value Line Investment Survey,* September 2002.

Note: Fiscal year end is 31 March (of the following calendar year) for Toyota, and 31 December for General Motors.

Exhibit 6.2 shows that in each year from 1998 through 2001, General Motors has had a higher operating margin than Toyota: Toyota's operating margin averaged 11.6 percent compared with 15.7 percent for General Motors, and was lower in each individual year. Despite General Motors' advantages in operating margin and generally lower tax rates, Toyota's much lower interest burden translated into a consistent advantage in net profit margin. Nevertheless, a raw comparison of ROE is dramatically in General Motors' favor. GM's average ROE was 16.4 percent, compared with 8.2 percent for Toyota. Toyota held the advantage in net profit margin and efficiency in the use of assets (as shown by a higher asset turnover ratio) but had consistently lower ROE. However, General Motors' highly levered its operating results using debt, while Toyota employed a conservative level of debt. General Motors' average assets–equity ratio was about 14.2 versus only about 2.5 for Toyota. Because of its leverage, the stream of returns to GM shareholders as reflected by ROE was much more volatile than for Toyota. What does this mean in practice? ROE must be evaluated in relation to risk. According to valuation theory, the benchmark for risk in evaluating a company's ROE would be the required rate of return on its equity. If the analyst were pursuing the implications of the differences in ROE on valuation, a next step would be to estimate these required rates of return.

CONCEPTS IN ACTION   *FORD AND GM'S BONDS LOOKING LESS ROADWORTHY*

Gyrations of the Carmakers' Securities Cause Concern

Corporate bond investors once thought of Ford and General Motors as bullet-proof. Their strong balance sheets and well-established positions in the automotive industry meant that their paper was eagerly snapped up by investors looking for safe, liquid investments. They were also active issuers of debt, making them easy credits to buy and sell.

But times have changed. Wearied by the unprecedented numbers of bond defaults and shocked by how quickly corporate creditworthiness can deteriorate, investors are re-evaluating how much they are prepared to invest in any one company.

"It used to be that a 2 percent position in Ford was fine," said Lee Crabbe, head of the corporate bond group at Credit Suisse Asset Management.

"Now a 2 percent position in any name isn't fine."

Meanwhile, concern has grown over the U.S. manufacturers' ability to compete with European rivals and to fund their pension liabilities.

More recently, worries have surfaced over the continuing strength of U.S. consumer demand. In July, Ford Credit's 10-year bonds started to diverge from those of similarly rated mid-investment grade companies. They have since widened some 300 basis points to trade at 570 basis points over U.S. Treasuries—in other words, like "junk" bonds.

General Motors Acceptance Corp's 10-year bonds have also widened and now trade at 455 basis points over Treasuries. Both companies recently had their long-term debt ratings lowered one notch by Standard & Poor's.

The widening in spreads does not reflect fears that the vehicle makers will go bankrupt—most investors say they believe Ford's fundamentals are sound. However, it does show that investors are no longer prepared simply to follow the index.

The vehicle manufacturers are among the largest issuers of debt in the U.S. corporate bond market, with Ford, GM and Daimler-Chrysler accounting for 6.5 percent of Lehman's Credit Index, or some $128bn in debt.

Ford, with $61bn in debt outstanding, has the biggest weighting in the index, accounting for 3 percent.

The group has issued an increasing amount of debt over the past decade to fund the growing activities of Ford Motor Credit, its financial services business.

In 1992 it sold about $12bn of debt in the U.S., but last year sold more than $40bn, according to Thomson Financial.

As the amount of debt Ford has issued has risen, so has its weight in market indices, which in turn has encouraged investors to buy its securities, because most investment funds gauge their performance against market indices.

This, however, leaves funds with a conundrum. Those that hold the bonds as spreads widen may take losses if the securities do not recover. Many investors were burnt earlier this year on investments in energy and telecommunications companies.

"Anything that smacks of excess capacity and a high debt burden has been a disaster this year," says Steven Zamsky, corporate bond strategist at Morgan Stanley.

However, funds that sell the vehicle makers' securities run the risk of missing a rally if the bonds tighten, and having their performance look bad in comparison with their peers.

Ford and GM's bonds have been extraordinarily volatile this year—in part because of increased activity by short sellers and hedge funds—so any rally could be quite substantial.

"When investors get nervous, they sell at any price," says Mark Kiesel, portfolio manager at bond fund Pimco. "But if the market bounces, they've lost both ways."

Source: Jenny Wiggins. "Ford and GM's Bonds Looking Less Roadworthy," *Financial Times,* Thursday, October 31, 2002, p. 15.

The Role of Market Efficiency in Individual Stock Valuation   The notion of an efficient market is central to finance theory and is important for valuing securities. Generally, the question in company analysis is whether a security is priced correctly, and if it is not, for how long will it be mispriced. In an efficient market, any new information would be immediately and fully reflected in prices. Because all current information is already impounded in the asset price, only news (unanticipated information) could cause a change in price in the future.

An efficient financial market quickly, if not instantaneously, discounts all available information. Any new information will immediately be used by some privileged investors, who will take positions to capitalize on it, thereby making the asset price adjust (almost) instantaneously to this piece of information. For example, a new balance of payments statistic would immediately be used by foreign exchange traders to buy or sell a currency until the foreign exchange rate reached a level considered consistent with the new information. Similarly, investors might use surprise information about a company, such as a new contract or changes in forecasted income, to reap a profit until the stock price reached a level consistent with the news. The adjustment in price would be so rapid it would not pay to buy information that has already been available to other investors. Hundreds of thousands of expert financial analysts and professional investors throughout the world search for information and make the world markets close to fully efficient.

In a perfectly efficient market, the typical investor could consider an asset price to reflect its true *fundamental value* at all times. The notion of fundamental value is somewhat philosophical; it means that at each point in time, each asset has an intrinsic value that all investors try to discover. Nevertheless, the analyst tries to find mispriced securities by choosing from a variety of valuation models and by carefully researching the inputs for the model. In this research, forecasting cash flows and risk is critical.

Valuation Models   Investors often rely on some form of a discounted cash flow analysis (DCF) for estimating the "intrinsic" value of a stock investment. This is simply a "present value" model, where the intrinsic value of an asset at time zero, P_0, is determined by the stream of cash flows it generates for the investor. This price is also called the "justified" price because it is the value that is "justified" by the forecasted cash flows. In a dividend discount model (DDM), the stock market price is set equal to the stream of forecasted dividends, D, discounted at the required rate of return, r:

$$P_0 = \frac{D_1}{1+r} + \frac{D_2}{(1+r)^2} + \frac{D_3}{(1+r)^3} \cdots \tag{6.1}$$

Financial analysts take great care in forecasting future earnings, and hence, dividends.

A simple version of the DDM assumes that dividends will grow indefinitely at a constant compounded annual growth rate (CAGR), g. Hence, Equation 6.1 becomes

$$P_0 = \frac{D_1}{1+r} + \frac{D_1(1+g)}{(1+r)^2} + \frac{D_1(1+g)^2}{(1+r)^3} \cdots$$

or

$$P_0 = \frac{D_1}{r-g} \tag{6.2}$$

Analysts forecast earnings, and a payout ratio is applied to transform earnings into dividends. Under the assumption of a constant earnings payout ratio, we find

$$P_0 = \frac{E_1(1-b)}{r-g} \tag{6.3}$$

where

P_0 is the justified or intrinsic price at time 0 (now)

E_1 is next year's earnings

b is the earnings retention ratio

$1 - b$ is the earnings payout ratio

r is the required rate of return on the stock

g is the growth rate of earnings

Note that Equation 6.3 requires that the growth rate g remain constant infinitely and that it must be less than the required rate of return r. Take the example of a German corporation whose next annual earnings are expected to be €20 per share, with a constant growth rate of 5 percent per year, and with a 50 percent payout ratio. Hence, the next-year dividend is expected to be €10. Let's further assume that the required rate of return for an investment in such a corporation is 10 percent, which can be decomposed into a 6 percent risk-free rate plus a 4 percent risk premium. Then the firm's value is equal to

$$P_0 = \frac{10}{0.10 - 0.05} = €200$$

The intrinsic price-to-earnings ratio (P/E) is defined as P_0/E_1. The intrinsic P/E of this corporation, using prospective earnings, is equal to

$$P/E = \frac{1 - b}{r - g} = \frac{0.50}{0.10 - 0.05} = 10$$

A drop in the risk-free interest rate would lead to an increase in the P/E and in the stock price. For example, if the risk-free rate drops to 5 percent, and everything else remains unchanged, a direct application of the formula indicates that the P/E will move up to 12.5 and the stock price to €250.

A more realistic DDM approach is to decompose the future in three phases. In the near future (e.g., the next two years), earnings are forecasted individually. In the second phase (e.g., years 3 to 5), a general growth rate of the company's earnings is estimated. In the final stage, the growth rate in earnings is assumed to revert to some sustainable growth rate[16]

A final step required by this approach is to estimate the normal rate of return required on such an investment. This rate is equal to the risk-free interest rate plus a risk premium that reflects the relevant risks of this investment. Relevant risks refer to risks that should be priced by the market.

Franchise Value and the Growth Process   Given the risk of the company's forecasted cash flows, the other key determinant of value is the growth rate in cash flows. The growth rate depends on relevant country GDP growth rates, industry growth rates, and the company's sustainable competitive advantage within the industry. Regardless of the valuation model used, some analysis of the

---

[16] A detailed analysis of the use of DDM in companies' valuation is provided in Stowe et al. (2002).

growth-rate input is useful. Using the DDM as a representative model, Leibowitz and Kogelman (2000) developed the *franchise value* method and separated the intrinsic P/E value of a corporation into a tangible P/E value (the no-growth or zero-earnings retention P/E value of existing business) and the franchise P/E value (derived from prospective new investments). The franchise P/E value is related to the *present value of growth opportunities* (PVGO) in the traditional break-down of intrinsic value into the no-growth value per share and the present value of growth opportunities. In that breakdown, the no-growth value per share is the value of the company if it were to distribute all its earnings in dividends, creating a perpetuity valued at E_1/r, where E_1 is next year's earnings and r is the required rate of return on the company's equity. Using the DDM and the company's actual payout ratio to generate an intrinsic value per share, P_0, the present value of growth opportunities must be the difference between intrinsic value and the no-growth value per share, $P_0 - E_1/r$.

The franchise value approach focuses on the intrinsic P/E rather than on the intrinsic value P_0; thus, the franchise value P/E is $PVGO/E_1$. In the franchise value approach, however, the franchise value P/E is further broken down into the *franchise factor* and the *growth factor*. The growth factor captures the present value of the opportunities for productive new investments, and the franchise factor is meant to capture the return levels associated with those new investments. The *Sales-Driven Franchise Value* has been developed to deal with multinational corporations that do business globally (see Leibowitz, 1997, 1998).

The separation of franchise P/E value into a franchise factor and a growth factor permits a direct examination of the response of the intrinsic P/E to ROE.[17] This factor helps an investor determine the response of the P/E to the ROE expected to be achieved by the company. It focuses on the sustainable growth rate of earnings per share. Earnings per share will grow from one period to the next because reinvested earnings will earn the rate of ROE. So the company's sustainable growth rate is equal to the retention rate (b) multiplied by ROE: $g = b \times \text{ROE}$. Substituting into Equation 6.3 the sustainable growth rate calculation for g, we get the intrinsic price:

$$P_0 = \frac{E_1(1 - b)}{r - b \times \text{ROE}}$$

and converting to an intrinsic P/E ratio,

$$\frac{P_0}{E_1} = \frac{(1 - b)}{r - b \times \text{ROE}}$$

---

[17]The model is derived here under the assumptions of a constant growth rate g, a constant earnings retention rate b, and a constant ROE. It can accommodate more complex assumptions about the pattern of growth.

Now, multiplying through by r/r yields

$$\frac{P_0}{E_1} = \frac{1}{r}\left[\frac{r(1-b)}{r - b \times \text{ROE}}\right]$$

$$= \frac{1}{r}\left[\frac{r - r \times b}{r - \text{ROE} \times b}\right]$$

and arbitrarily adding and subtracting $\text{ROE} \times b$ in the numerator,

$$\frac{P_0}{E_1} = \frac{1}{r}\left[\frac{r - r \times b + \text{ROE} \times b - \text{ROE} \times b}{r - \text{ROE} \times b}\right]$$

$$= \frac{1}{r}\left[\frac{r - \text{ROE} \times b + \text{ROE} \times b - r \times b}{r - \text{ROE} \times b}\right]$$

or

$$\frac{P_0}{E_1} = \frac{1}{r}\left[1 + \frac{b(\text{ROE} - r)}{r - \text{ROE} \times b}\right] \tag{6.4}$$

This P_0/E_1 equation is extremely useful because one can use it to examine the effects of different values of b and of the difference between ROE and r; that is, $\text{ROE} - r$. Two interesting results can be found. First, if $\text{ROE} = r$, the intrinsic P_0/E_1 equals $1/r$ regardless of b, the earnings retention ratio. Second, if $b = 0$, the intrinsic P_0/E_1 equals $1/r$ regardless of whether ROE is greater than r. These two results have an intuitive explanation.

- When the return on equity is exactly equal to the required rate of return ($\text{ROE} = r$), there is no *added* value in retaining earnings for additional investments, rather than distributing them to shareholders. A company with $\text{ROE} = r$ has no franchise value potential because its return on equity is just what the market requires, but no more.

- An earnings retention ratio of zero ($b = 0$) means that the company distributes all its earnings. So equity per share stays constant. There is no growth of equity and the stream of future earnings will be a perpetuity because the rate of return on equity (ROE) remains constant. The value of a share is given by discounting a perpetuity of E_1 at a rate r, hence the $P_0/E_1 = 1/r$ result. Of course, the total equity of the company could grow by issuing new shares, but there will be no growth of earnings per existing share. There is potential franchise value in the company with $\text{ROE} > r$, but because the company does not reinvest earnings at this superior rate of return, existing shareholders do not capture this potential.

In general, there is a franchise value created for existing shareholders, if the company can reinvest past earnings ($b > 0$) at a rate of return (ROE) higher than the market-required rate (r).

Examining equation (6.4) further, we return to the intrinsic value version of the equation. We can transform (6.4) by multiplying and dividing by ROE and replacing $b \times$ ROE by g:

$$\frac{P_0}{E_1} = \frac{1}{r}\left[1 + \frac{\text{ROE} \times b \times (\text{ROE} - r)}{\text{ROE} \times (r - \text{ROE} \times b)}\right] = \frac{1}{r} + \frac{g \times (\text{ROE} - r)}{r \times \text{ROE} \times (r - g)}$$

and simplify it as

$$\frac{P_0}{E_1} = \frac{1}{r} + \left(\frac{\text{ROE} - r}{\text{ROE} \times r}\right)\left(\frac{g}{r - g}\right)$$

$$\frac{P_0}{E_1} = \frac{1}{r} + \text{FF} \times \text{G} \qquad\qquad (6.5)$$

where the franchise factor is FF $= (\text{ROE} - r)/(\text{ROE} \times r)$ or $1/r - 1/\text{ROE}$, and the growth factor is G $= g/(r - g)$.

The growth factor is the ratio of the present value of future increases in the book value (BV) of equity to the current BV of equity. If the current BV of equity is B_0, then next year's increment to BV is gB_0. With a constant growth rate in BV increments, these increments can be treated as a growing perpetuity with a present value of $gB_0/(r - g)$. Because the present value of the BV increments is to be given as a ratio to the most recent BV, the growth factor is then given as $g/(r - g)$.

The franchise factor stems from the fact that a firm has a competitive advantage allowing it to generate a rate of return (ROE) greater than the rate of return normally required by investors for this type of risk (r). If the franchise factor is positive, it gives the rate of response of the intrinsic P_0/E_1 ratio to in the growth factor. The growth factor G will be high if the firm can sustain a growth rate that is high relative to r.

Consider a pharmaceutical firm with some attractive new drugs with large commercial interest. Its ROE will be high relative to the rate of return required by investors for pharmaceutical stocks. Hence, it has a large positive franchise factor FF. If it continues to make productive new investments (G positive), such a firm can continue to generate a return on equity well above the rate of return required by the stock market, and thus has a large positive franchise value. On the other hand, if the pharmaceutical company's sustainable growth rate is small because of a low earnings retention rate b, then G will be small and so will the franchise value, even though the franchise factor is large. For a firm with less franchise potential and ROE possibilities only equal to the company's required rate of return ($r =$ ROE) the franchise factor is zero and the intrinsic P_0/E_1 is simply $1/r$, regardless of the earnings retention ratio.

EXAMPLE 6.3   FRANCHISE VALUE

A company can generate an ROE of 15 percent and has an earnings retention ratio of 0.60. Next year's earnings are projected at $100 million. If the required rate of return for the company is 12 percent, what is the company's tangible P/E value, franchise factor, growth factor, and franchise P/E value?

SOLUTION

The company's tangible P/E value is $1/r = 1/0.12 = 8.33$.

The company's franchise factor is $1/r - 1/\text{ROE} = 1/0.12 - 1/0.15 = 1.67$.

Because the company's sustainable growth rate is $0.6 \times 0.15 = 0.09$, the company's growth factor is $g/(r - g) = 0.09/(0.12 - 0.09) = 3$.

The company's franchise P/E value is the franchise factor times the growth factor, $1.67 \times 3 = 5.01$.

Because its tangible P/E value is 8.33 and its franchise P/E value is 5.01, the company's intrinsic P/E is 13.34. Note that the intrinsic P/E calculated directly is $\text{P/E} = (1 - b)/(r - g) = 0.4/(0.12 - 0.09) = 13.33$. Thus, the franchise value method breaks this P/E into its basic components.

The Effects of Inflation on Stock Prices Because inflation rates vary around the world and over time, it is important to consider the effects of inflation on stock prices. To do this, we begin at the obvious place—earnings. After examining the effects of inflation on reported earnings, we discuss an inflation flow-through model.[18]

Because historical costs are used in accounting, inflation has a distorting effect on reported earnings. These effects show up primarily in replacement, inventories, and borrowing costs. Replacement must be made at inflated costs, but depreciation is recorded at historical cost—hence, reported earnings based on depreciation as an estimate of replacement costs gives an overstatement of earnings. Similarly, a first-in, first-out inventory accounting system leads to an understatement of inventory costs and an overstatement of reported earnings. Unlike replacement and inventory distortions, borrowing costs at historical rates cause an understatement of reported earnings. Inflation causes borrowing costs to increase, but nominal interest costs do not reflect the increase. Finally, capital gains taxes reflect an inflation tax, because the base for the capital gains tax is historical cost.

To analyze the effects of inflation on the valuation process, analysts try to determine what part of inflation flows through to a firm's earnings. A full-flow-through firm has earnings that fully reflect inflation. Thus, any inflation cost increases must be getting passed along to consumers.

In an inflationary environment, consider a firm that would otherwise have no growth in earnings, a zero earnings retention ratio and full-inflation flow-through. So, earnings only grow because of the inflation rate I, assumed constant over time. For example, we have

$$E_1 = E_0 \times (1 + I)$$

By discounting this stream of inflation-growing earnings at the required rate r, we find that the intrinsic value of such a firm would then be

$$P_0 = \frac{E_1}{r - I} = E_0 \left(\frac{1 + I}{r - I} \right) \tag{6.6}$$

---

[18]For example, see Leibowitz and Kogelman (2000).

where

P_0 is the intrinsic value

E_0 is the initial earnings level

I is the annual inflation rate

r is the nominal required rate of return

Let's now consider a company with a partial inflation flow-through of λ percent, so that earnings are only inflated at a rate λI:

$$E_1 = E_0(1 + \lambda I)$$

By discounting this stream of earnings at the nominal required rate r, we find

$$P_0 = E_0 \times \frac{1 + \lambda I}{r - \lambda I} \tag{6.7}$$

If we introduce the real required rate of return $\rho = r - I$, we get

$$P_0 = E_0 \times \frac{1 + \lambda I}{\rho + (1 - \lambda)I} = \frac{E_1}{\rho + (1 - \lambda)I}$$

The intrinsic P/E using prospective earnings is now equal to

$$P_0/E_1 = \frac{1}{\rho + (1 - \lambda)I} \tag{6.8}$$

From Equation 6.8 we can see that the higher the inflation flow-through rate, the higher the price of the company. Indeed, a company that cannot pass inflation through its earnings is penalized. Thus, the P/E ratio ranges from a high of $1/\rho$ to a low of $1/r$. For example, assume a real required rate of return of 6 percent and an inflation rate of 4 percent. Exhibit 6.3 shows the P/E of the company with different flow-through rates. With a full-flow-through rate ($\lambda = 100$ percent), the P/E is equal to P/E $= 1/\rho = 1/0.06 = 16.67$. The ratio drops to 12.5 if the company can only pass 50 percent of inflation through its earnings. If the company cannot pass through any

EXHIBIT 6.3

Inflation Effects on P/E

EXAMPLE 6.4   INFLATION

Consider two companies in the same line of business, but with mostly domestic operations. Company A is based in a country with no inflation. Company B is based in a country with a 4 percent inflation rate. There is no real growth in earnings for both companies. The real rate of return required by global investors for this type of stock investment is 6 percent. Company B can only pass 80 percent of inflation through its earnings. What should be the P/E of the two companies?

SOLUTION

The nominal required rate of return for Company A is equal to the real rate because there is no inflation: $r = \rho = 6\%$. Earnings are constant and the P/E is equal to

$$P/E(A) = 1/\rho = 1/0.06 = 16.67$$

There is a 4 percent inflation rate in the country of Company B. Its earnings will only be inflated at a rate of $\lambda I = 80\% \times 4\% = 3.2\%$. The P/E of company B will be

$$P/E(B) = \frac{1}{6\% + (20\%) \times 4\%} = \frac{1}{6.8\%} = 14.71$$

In the inflationary environment, Company B's earnings cannot grow as fast as inflation. Penalized by inflation and its inability to pass along inflation, Company B's P/E ratio is below that of Company A.

---

inflation ($\lambda = 0$), its earnings remain constant, and the P/E ratio is equal to P/E = $1/(\rho + I) = 1/r = 10$. The higher the inflation rate, the more negative the influence on the stock price if full inflation pass-through cannot be achieved.

This observation is important if we compare similar companies in different countries experiencing different inflation rates. A company operating in a high-inflation environment will be penalized if it cannot pass through inflation.

The Inflation-like Effects of Currency Movements on Stock Prices   A currency movement is a monetary variable that affects stock valuation in a fashion similar to the inflation variable. Just as some companies cannot fully pass inflation through their earnings, they cannot fully pass exchange rate movements either. Consider an importing firm faced with a sudden depreciation of the home currency. The products it imports suddenly become more expensive in terms of the home currency. If this price increase can be passed through to customers, earnings will not suffer from the currency adjustment. But this is often not the case. First, the price increase will tend to reduce demand for these imported products. Second, locally produced goods will become more attractive than imported goods, and some substitution will take place.

The currency exposure of individual companies was discussed in Chapter 4. Currency exposure depends on such factors as each particular company's production cycle, the competitive structure of its product market, and the company's financing structure.

Global Risk Factors in Security Returns

The analysis of an individual company can require a detailed review of various strategic risk elements that are difficult to quantify precisely. However, a portfolio manager needs to summarize the information on a large number of securities into a few statistics that help construct a portfolio and manage its risk. To structure a portfolio properly, a manager must have a clear understanding of the main factors influencing the return on a security and of the risk exposures of each security.

Global equilibrium pricing was discussed in Chapter 4. We showed that the risk premium of a security should be proportional to the covariance (or beta) of the security's return with the world market return; this is the world market risk of a security. In Chapter 13 we show how to use this theory to derive long-term expected returns for asset classes. However, the world market risk of a security is the result of the exposure to many sources of risk that can be detailed in factor models. Factor models allow a better understanding of the risks that affect stock returns in the short run and allow the risk management of a portfolio.

Risk-Factor Model: Industry and Country Factors

A factor model, where R is the rate of return on the security, may be written mathematically as

$$R = \alpha + \beta_1 f_1 + \beta_2 f_2 + \ldots + \beta_k f_k + \varepsilon \tag{6.9}$$

where

R is the rate of return on a security

α is a constant

$f_1 \ldots f_k$ are the k factors common to all securities

$\beta_1 \ldots \beta_k$ represent the sensitivity, or risk exposure, of this security to each factor

ε is a random term specific to this security

The ε is the source of idiosyncratic or diversifiable risk for the security, and $\beta_1 \ldots \beta_k$ represent the risk exposure of this security to each factor. The betas vary among securities. Some stocks may be highly sensitive to certain factors and much less sensitive to others, and vice versa.

A global risk-factor model would use industry and country as factors. The degree of granularity can be adapted; for example, one could use global sector factors, global industry factors, or regional industry factors. The geographical factors could be a list of regions (e.g., Europe) or of individual countries.

The factors are measured as the return on some index portfolio representative of the factor ("mimicking portfolios"). For example, the oil industry factor could be proxied by the return on a global stock index of oil firms. Various statistical techniques can be used to optimize the factor structure.

The determination of the risk-factor exposures can follow one of two techniques or a combination of the two:

- The exposure can be assessed a priori by using information on the company studied. This usually leads to a 0/1 exposure. For example, TotalFinaElf would have a unitary exposure to the oil industry factor and zero exposures to all other industry factors, because it is an oil company.

- The exposure can be estimated using a multiple regression approach. The exposures would then be the estimated betas in a time-series regression.

The question of currency should be addressed. A global risk-factor model can be written in some arbitrary currency (e.g., the U.S. dollar). It also can be written in currency-hedged terms. If companies are reacting differently to currency movements, currencies could be added as risk factors. For example, an exporting firm could be influenced negatively by an appreciation of its currency, while the reverse would be true for an importing firm. These currency exposures could be cancelled if the company adopts a currency-hedging policy in its business operations.

Other Risk Factors: Styles

Other factors influence the stock price behavior of companies worldwide. As mentioned, many researchers believe that the future performance of a stock also depends on other attributes of a company that have not been discussed so far. Among many others, three attributes have been researched extensively:

- *Value* stocks do not behave like *growth* stocks. A value stock is a company whose stock price is "cheap" in relation to its book value, or in relation to the cash flows it generates (low stock price compared with its earnings, cash flows, or dividends). A growth stock has the opposite attribute, implying that the stock price capitalizes growth in future earnings. This is known as the *value effect*.

- *Small* firms do not exhibit the same stock price behavior as *large* firms. The size of a firm is measured by its stock market capitalization. This is known as the *size effect*.

- In the short run, winners tend to repeat. In other words, stocks that have performed well (or badly) in the recent past, say in the past six months, will tend to be winners (or losers) in the next six months. This is known as the *momentum, success,* or *relative strength effect.*

The observation of these effects, or factors, has led to the development of *style investing,* in which portfolios are structured to favor some of these attributes (e.g., value stocks).

Risk-factor models often incorporate style factors in which the factors are proxied by some mimicking portfolio (e.g., long in value stocks and short in growth stocks). A security's exposure is either measured *a priori* by using some information on the company or by a regression technique, or by a combination of the two techniques.

Although this style approach has been extensively used in the United States, there is some practical difficulty in applying it in a global setting. This is best illustrated by looking at the size factor. An Austrian company that is regarded as "large" in Austria would be regarded as "medium-sized" in Europe and probably as "small" according to U.S. standards. To construct a global size factor, one must make assumptions on how to measure relative size. Different risk-factor models use different criteria.

Other Risk Factors: Macroeconomic

Factors are postulated *a priori* as sources of risk that are common to all companies. This clearly leads us to some macroeconomic variables that affect the economics of all firms, as well as the behavior of stock market participants who price those firms.

Selecting a set of *macroeconomic factors* is as much an art as a science. These factors must be logical choices, easy to interpret, robust over time, and able to explain a significant percentage of variation in stock returns. Some macroeconomic variables are logical candidates as factors but suffer from serious measurement error or long publication lags. For example, the evolution in industrial production is a logical candidate, but it is difficult to get timely, good-quality, reliable data. The technique is to use as factor proxies the returns on mimicking portfolios that are most strongly correlated with the economic variable.

Burmeister, Roll, and Ross (1994) propose a set of five factors.[19] These five factors, listed here, apply to domestic U.S. stocks:

- *Confidence factor* (f_1). This factor is measured by the difference in return on risky corporate bonds and on government bonds. The default-risk premium required by the market to compensate for the risk of default on corporate bonds is measured as the spread between the yields on risky corporate bonds

---

[19]Earlier, Chen, Roll, and Ross (1986) had identified four factors for the U.S. equity market as (1) growth rate in industrial production, (2) unexpected inflation, (3) slope of the yield curve (the difference between long- and short-term interest rates), and (4) changes in the attitude toward risk as proxied by changes in the pricing of default risk implicit in the difference between yields on Aaa and Baa corporate bonds.

and government bonds. A decrease in the default-risk spread will give a higher return on corporate bonds and implies an improvement in the investors' confidence level. Hence, confidence risk focuses on the willingness of investors to undertake risky investments. Most stocks have a positive exposure to the confidence factor ($\beta_1 > 0$), so their prices tend to rise when the confidence factor is positive ($f_1 > 0$). The underlying idea is that in periods when investors are becoming more sensitive to risks (less confident with $f_1 < 0$), they require a higher premium on risky corporate bonds, compared with government bonds. They also require a higher risk premium on risky stocks and will bid their prices down, inducing a negative stock-price movement.

- *Time horizon factor* (f_2). This factor is measured as the difference between the return on a 20-year government bond and a 1-month Treasury bill. A positive difference in return is caused by a decrease in the term spread (long minus short interest rates). This is a signal that investors require a lesser premium to hold long-term investments. Growth stocks are more exposed (higher β_2) to time horizon risk than income stocks. The underlying idea is to view the stock price as the discounted stream of its future cash flows. The present value of growth stocks is determined by the long-term prospects of growing earnings while current earnings are relatively weak (high P/E ratio). An increase in the market-required discount rate will penalize the price of growth stocks more than the price of value stocks.

- *Inflation factor* (f_3). This factor is measured as the difference between the actual inflation for a month and its expected value, computed the month before, using an econometric inflation model. An unexpected increase in inflation tends to be bad for most stocks ($\beta_3 < 0$), so they have a negative exposure to this inflation surprise ($f_3 > 0$). Luxury goods stocks tend to be most sensitive to inflation risk, whereas firms in the sectors of foods, cosmetics, or tires are less sensitive to inflation risk. Real estate holdings typically benefit from increased inflation.

- *Business-cycle factor* (f_4). This factor is measured by the monthly variation in a business activity index. Business-cycle risk comes from unanticipated changes in the level of real activity. The business-cycle factor is positive ($f_4 > 0$) when the expected real growth rate of the economy has increased. Most firms have a positive exposure to business-cycle risk ($\beta_4 > 0$). Retail stores are more exposed to business-cycle risk than are utility companies, because their business activity (sales) is much more sensitive to recession or expansion.

- *Market-timing factor* (f_5). This factor is measured by the part of the S&P 500 total return that is not explained by the first four factors. It captures the global movements in the market that are not explained by the four macroeconomic factors. The inclusion of this market-timing factor makes the capital asset pricing model (CAPM) a special case of this approach. If all relevant macroeconomic factors had been included, it would not be necessary to add this market-timing factor.

A common criticism of this approach is that the risk exposures (betas) have to be estimated statistically from past data and may not be stable over time. Even the factor proxies (mimicking portfolios) have to be constructed using statistical optimization, and the procedure could yield unstable proxies.

Practical Use of Factor Models

Risk-factor models are used in risk management and in selecting stocks. A major application is the analysis of the risk profile of portfolios. The exposure of the portfolio to the various factors is the weighted average of the exposures of the stocks making up the portfolio. A manager can estimate the risks taken and the exposure of the portfolio to the various sources of risk. If some specific stock index is assigned as a benchmark to measure performance, the manager can analyze the risks of deviations from the benchmark. This helps the manager identify and quantify the bets and risks that are taken in the portfolio.

Managers can also use factor models to tilt the portfolio along some factor bets. Assume, for example, that a manager believes that the economy is going to grow at a faster rate than generally forecasted, leading to some inflationary pressure. The manager will tend to increase the portfolio exposure to business risk but reduce its exposure to inflation risk. This could also lead the manager to take some industry bets and invest in small companies.

Summary

- The major differences in accounting standards around the world appear in the treatment of business combinations, consolidation of subsidiary and affiliate information, goodwill, financial leases, asset revaluation, provisions for likely future losses or expenses, pensions, financial assets and derivatives, and employee stock options.

- Off-balance-sheet assets and liabilities are those assets and liabilities not properly reflected in the balance sheet. Examples are special purpose entities and financial leases.

- From an economic perspective, employee stock option compensation should be treated as an expense, with the options valued by an option-pricing model.

- Neoclassical growth theory predicts that the long-term level of GDP depends on the country's savings rate, but the long-term growth rate in GDP does not depend on the savings rate. Endogenous growth theory predicts that the long-term growth rate in GDP depends on the savings rate.

- A global industry analysis should examine return potential evidenced by demand analysis, value creation, industry life cycle, competition structure, competitive advantage, competitive strategies, co-opetition and the value net, and sector rotation. The analysis also should examine risk elements evidenced by market competition, value chain competition, government participation, and cash flow covariance.

■ Global financial analysis involves comparing company ratios with global industry averages. In this context, DuPont analysis uses various combinations of the tax retention, debt burden, operating margin, asset turnover, and leverage ratios.

■ The role of market efficiency in individual asset valuation is to equate fundamental value with asset valuation so that the analyst searches for mispricing or market inefficiency.

■ Franchise value is the present value of growth opportunities divided by next year's earnings. The intrinsic P_0/E_1 ratio equals $1/r$ plus the franchise value, where r is the nominal required return on the stock. The franchise value is further divided into a franchise factor (FF) and a growth factor (G) to give $P_0/E_1 = 1/r + \text{FF} \times \text{G}$.

■ To analyze the effects of inflation for valuation purposes, the analyst must recognize the distorting effects of historical inventory and borrowing costs on reported earnings, as well as recognize the inflation tax reflected in capital gains taxes. Further, the analyst must estimate the degree of inflation flow-through, λ.

■ With earnings that are constant except for inflation, I as the inflation rate, r as the required nominal return on the stock, and ρ as the required real return on the stock, the P/E ratio can be estimated as $P_0/E_1 = 1/(\rho + (1 - \lambda)I)$.

■ Multifactor models can be used in the analysis of the risk profile of portfolios. The exposure of a portfolio to the various factors is the weighted average of the exposures of the stocks making up the portfolio.

Problems

1. Explain why a corporation can have a stock market price well above its accounting book value.

2. The accounting and fiscal standards of many countries allow corporations to build general provisions (or "hidden reserves") in anticipation of foreseen or unpredictable expenses. How would this practice affect the book value of a corporation and its ratio of market price to book value?

3. Discuss some of the reasons why the earnings of German firms tend to be understated, compared with the earnings of U.S. firms.

4. Consider a firm that has given stock options on 20,000 shares to its senior executives. These call options can be exercised at a price of $22 anytime during the next three years. The firm has a total of 500,000 shares outstanding, and the current price is $20 per share. The firm's net income before taxes is $2 million.
   a. What would be the firm's pretax earnings per share if the options are not expensed?

b. Under certain assumptions, the Black–Scholes model valued the options given by the firm to its executives at $4 per share option. What would be the firm's pretax earnings per share if the options are expensed accordingly?

c. Under somewhat different assumptions, the Black–Scholes model valued the options at $5.25 per share option. What would be the firm's pretax earnings per share if the options are expensed based on this valuation?

5. Japanese companies tend to belong to groups (*keiretsu*) and to hold shares of one another. Because these cross-holdings are minority interest, they tend not to be consolidated in published financial statements. To study the impact of this tradition on published earnings, consider the following simplified example:

Company A owns 10 percent of Company B; the initial investment was 10 million yen. Company B owns 20 percent of Company A; the initial investment was also 10 million yen. Both companies value their minority interests at historical cost. The annual net income of Company A was 10 million yen. The annual net income of Company B was 30 million yen. Assume that the two companies do not pay any dividends. The current stock market values are 200 million yen for Company A and 450 million yen for Company B.

a. Restate the earnings of the two companies, using the equity method of consolidation. Remember that the share of the minority-interest earning is consolidated on a one-line basis, proportionate to the share of equity owned by the parent.

b. Calculate the P/E ratios, based on nonconsolidated and consolidated earnings. How does the nonconsolidation of earnings affect the P/E ratios?

6. The annual revenues (in billion dollars) in financial year 2001 for the top five players in the global media and entertainment industry are given in the following table. The top five corporations in this industry include three U.S.-based corporations (AOL Time Warner, Walt Disney, and Viacom), one French corporation (Vivendi Universal), and one Australian corporation (News Corporation). The revenue indicated for Vivendi Universal does not include the revenue from its environmental business. Assume that the total worldwide revenue of all firms in this industry was $250 billion.

Company	Revenue
AOL Time Warner	38
Walt Disney	25
Vivendi Universal	25
Viacom	23
News Corporation	13

a. Compute the three-firm and five-firm concentration ratios.

b. Compute the three-firm and five-firm Herfindahl indexes.

c. Make a simplistic assumption that in addition to the five corporations mentioned in the table, there are 40 other companies in this industry with an equal share of the remaining market. Compute the Herfindahl index for the overall industry.

d. Suppose there were not 40, but only 10 other companies in the industry with an equal share of the remaining market. Compute the Herfindahl index for the overall industry.

e. Interpret your answers to parts (c) and (d) in terms of the competition structure of the industry.

7. News Corporation is headquartered in Australia, and its main activities include television entertainment, films, cable, and publishing.

   a. Collect any relevant information that you may need and discuss whether an analyst should do the valuation of News Corporation primarily relative to the global media and entertainment industry or relative to other companies based in Australia.

   b. One of the competitors of News Corporation is Vivendi Universal, a firm headquartered in France. Should an analyst be concerned in comparing financial ratios of News Corporation with those of Vivendi Universal?

8. You are given the following data about Walt Disney and News Corporation, two of the major corporations in the media and entertainment industry. The data are for the end of the financial year 1999, and are in US$ millions. Though News Corporation is based in Australia, it also trades on the NYSE and its data in the following table, like those for Walt Disney, is according to the U.S. GAAP.

	Walt Disney	**News Corporation**
Sales	23,402	14,395
EBIT	3,035	1,819
EBT	2,314	1,212
NI	1,300	719
Assets	43,679	35,681
Equity	20,975	16,374

   a. Compute the ROE for Walt Disney and News Corporation.

   b. Use the DuPont model to analyze the difference in ROE between the two companies, by identifying the elements that primarily cause this difference.

9. In the past 20 years, the best-performing stock markets have been found in countries with the highest economic growth rates. Should the current growth rate guide you in choosing stock markets if the world capital market is efficient?

10. Consider a French company that pays out 70 percent of its earnings. Its next annual earnings are expected to be €4 per share. The required return for the company is 12 percent. In the past, the company's compound annual growth rate (CAGR) has been 1.25 times the world's GDP growth rate. It is expected that the world's GDP growth rate will be 2.8 percent p.a. in the future. Assuming that the firm's earnings will continue to grow forever at 1.25 times the world's projected growth rate, compute the intrinsic value of the company's stock and its intrinsic P/E ratio.

11. Consider a company that pays out all its earnings. The required return for the firm is 13 percent.

   a. Compute the intrinsic P/E value of the company if its ROE is 15 percent.

   b. Compute the intrinsic P/E value of the company if its ROE is 20 percent.

   c. Discuss why your answers to parts (a) and (b) differ or do not differ from one another.

   d. Suppose that the company's ROE is 13 percent. Compute its intrinsic P/E value.

   e. Would the answer to part (d) change if the company retained half of its earnings instead of paying all of them out? Discuss why or why not.

12. Consider a firm with a ROE of 12 percent. The earnings next year are projected at $50 million, and the firm's earnings retention ratio is 0.70. The required return for the firm is 10 percent. Compute the following for the firm:

   i. Franchise factor

   ii. Growth factor

   iii. Franchise P/E value

    iv. Tangible P/E value

    v. Intrinsic P/E value

13. Consider a firm for which the nominal required rate of return is 8 percent. The rate of inflation is 3 percent. Compute the P/E ratio of the firm under the following situations:

    i. The firm has a full inflation flow-through.

    ii. The firm can pass only 40 percent of inflation through its earnings.

    iii. The firm cannot pass any inflation through its earnings.

    What pattern do you observe from your answers to items (i) through (iii)?

14. Company B and Company U are in the same line of business. Company B is based in Brazil, where inflation during the past few years has averaged about 9 percent. Company U is based in the United States, where the inflation during the past few years has averaged about 2.5 percent. The real rate of return required by global investors for investing in stocks such as B and U is 8 percent. Neither B nor U has any real growth in earnings, and both of them can only pass 60 percent of inflation through their earnings. What should be the P/E of the two companies? What can you say based on a comparison of the P/E for the two companies?

15. Omega, Inc., is based in Brazil, and most of its operations are domestic. During the period 1995–99, the firm has not had any real growth in earnings. The annual inflation in Brazil during this period is given in the following table:

Year	Inflation (%)
1995	22.0
1996	9.1
1997	4.3
1998	2.5
1999	8.4

Source: International Monetary Fund.

The real rate of return required by global investors for investing in stocks such as Omega, Inc., is 7 percent.

    a. Compute the P/E for Omega in each of the years if it can completely pass inflation through its earnings.

    b. Compute the P/E for Omega in each of the years if it can only pass 50 percent of inflation through its earnings.

    c. What conclusion can you draw about the effect of inflation on the stock price?

16. Consider a French company that exports French goods to the United States. What effect will a sudden appreciation of the euro relative to the dollar have on the P/E ratio of the French company? Discuss the effect under both the possibilities—the company being able to completely pass through the euro appreciation to its customers and the company being unable to completely pass through the euro appreciation to its customers.

17. Using the five macroeconomic factors described in the text, you outline the factor exposures of two stocks as follows:

Factor	Stock A	Stock B
Confidence	0.2	0.6
Time horizon	0.6	0.8
Inflation	−0.1	−0.5
Business cycle	4.0	2.0
Market timing	1.0	0.7

a. What would be the factor exposures of a portfolio invested half in stock A and half in stock B?

b. Contrary to general forecasts, you expect strong economic growth with a slight increase in inflation. Which stock should you overweigh in your portfolio?

18. Here is some return information on firms of various sizes and their price-to-book (value) ratios. Based on this information, what can you tell about the *size* and *value* style factors?

Stock	Size	P/BV	Return (%)
A	Huge	High	4
B	Huge	Low	6
C	Medium	High	9
D	Medium	Low	12
E	Small	High	13
F	Small	Low	15

19. You are analyzing whether the difference in returns on stocks of a particular country can be explained by two common factors, with a linear-factor model. Your candidates for the two factors are changes in interest rates and changes in the approval rating of the country's president, as measured by polls. The following table gives the interest rate, the percentage of people approving the president's performance, and the prices of three stocks (A, B, and C) for the past 10 periods.

Period	Interest Rate (%)	Approval (%)	Price of Stock A	B	C
1	7.3	47	22.57	24.43	25.02
2	5.2	52	19.90	12.53	13.81
3	5.5	51	15.46	17.42	19.17
4	7.2	49	21.62	24.70	23.24
5	5.4	68	14.51	16.43	18.79
6	5.2	49	12.16	11.56	14.66
7	7.5	72	25.54	24.73	28.68
8	7.6	45	25.83	28.12	21.47
9	5.3	47	13.04	14.71	16.43
10	5.1	67	11.18	12.44	12.50

Try to assess whether the two factors have an influence on stock returns. To do so, estimate the factor exposures for each of the three stocks by doing a time series regression for the return on each stock against the changes in the two factors.

20. You are a U.S. investor considering investing in Switzerland. The world market risk premium is estimated at 5 percent, the Swiss franc offers a 1 percent risk premium, and the current risk-free rates are equal to 4 percent in dollars and 3 percent in francs. In other words, you expect the Swiss franc to appreciate against the dollar by an amount equal to the interest rate differential plus the currency risk premium, or a total of 2 percent. You believe that the following equilibrium model (ICAPM) is appropriate for your investment analysis.

$$E(R_i) = R_f + \beta_1 \times RP_w + \beta_2 \times RP_{SFr}$$

where all returns are measured in dollars, RP_w is the risk premium on the world index, and RP_{SFr} is the risk premium on the Swiss franc. Your broker provides you with the following estimates and forecasted returns.

	Stock A	Stock B	Stock C	Stock D
Forecasted return (in francs)	0.08	0.09	0.11	0.07
World beta (β_1)	1	1	1.2	1.4
Dollar currency exposure (β_2)	1	0	0.5	−0.5

a. What should be the expected dollar returns on the four stocks, according to the ICAPM?

b. Which stocks would you recommend buying or selling?

Solutions

1. The book value represents mostly the historical value of the firm. Most assets and liabilities are carried at their historical cost, allowing for possible depreciation. The stock market price reflects the future earning power of the firm. If rapid growth in earnings is expected, the stock price could be well above the book value.

2. General provisions ("hidden reserves") appear as a liability, although they are in fact equity reserves. These provisions are "hidden" as a liability to allow the firm to use it in the future to smoothen earnings. Accordingly, the true book value is greater than the reported book value by the amount of these reserves. Thus, the practice of allowing corporations to build general provisions leads to an understatement of the reported book value, and an overstatement of the ratio of market price to book value.

3. Some of the reasons why German earnings are understated compared with U.S. earnings are as follows:
   - German firms take provisions quite generously, and they are deducted from the reported earnings when initially taken.
   - Reported earnings are tax earnings that are subject to many actions taken to reduce taxation.
   - Many German firms tend to publish separately the nonconsolidated financial statements of the various companies belonging to the same group.

4. a. Without expensing the options, the firm's pretax earnings per share are $2,000,000/500,000 = \$4$ per share.
   b. The expense due to the options is $20,000 \times \$4 = \$80,000$. The pretax income per share would be $(\$2,000,000 - \$80,000)/500,000 = \$3.84$ per share.
   c. The expense due to the options based on the different valuation is $20,000 \times \$5.25 = \$105,000$. The pretax income per share would be $(\$2,000,000 - \$105,000)/500,000 = \$3.79$ per share.

5. a. Consolidated earnings are as follows:

   Company A: 10 million + 10% of 30 million = 13 million

   Company B: 30 million + 20% of 10 million = 32 million

   b. The P/E ratios are as follows:

	Company A	**Company B**
Nonconsolidated	200/10 = 20	450/30 = 15
Consolidated	200/13 = 15.4	450/32 = 14.1

Due to nonconsolidation, the earnings are understated. Thus, the P/E ratios are overstated due to nonconsolidation. As seen here, the consolidation of earnings adjusts the P/E ratios downward.

6. Under the assumption that the total worldwide revenue of all firms in this industry was $250 billion, the market shares of the top five corporations are the following:

AOL Time Warner: $38 billion/$250 billion = 15.2%

Walt Disney: 25/250 = 10.0%

Vivendi Universal: 25/250 = 10.0%

Viacom: 23/250 = 9.2%

News Corporation: 13/250 = 5.2%

a. The three-firm concentration ratio is the combined market share of the largest three firms in the industry = 15.2 + 10 + 10 = 35.2%.
   The five-firm concentration ratio is the combined market share of the largest five firms in the industry = 15.2 + 10 + 10 + 9.2 + 5.2 = 49.6%.

b. The three-firm Herfindahl index is the sum of the squared market shares of the largest three firms in the industry = $0.152^2 + 0.10^2 + 0.10^2 = 0.043$, or 430 percent squared. The five-firm Herfindahl index is the sum of the squared market shares of the largest five firms in the industry = $0.152^2 + 0.10^2 + 0.10^2 + 0.092^2 + 0.052^2 = 0.054$.

c. The combined market share of the top five firms, as computed in part (a), is 49.6 percent. Therefore, the combined market share of the 40 other firms is $100 - 49.6 = 50.4\%$. Assuming that each of them has the same share, the share of each is $50.4/40 = 1.26\%$. So, the Herfindahl index for the industry, which is the sum of the squared market shares of all the firms in the industry, is $0.152^2 + 0.10^2 + 0.10^2 + 0.092^2 + 0.052^2 + 0.0126^2 + \ldots + 0.0126^2 = 0.054 + 40 \times 0.0126^2 = 0.0603$.

d. The combined market share of the 10 other firms is $100 - 49.6 = 50.4\%$. Assuming that each of them has the same share, the share of each is $50.4/10 = 5.04\%$. So, the Herfindahl index for the industry, which is the sum of the squared market shares of all the firms in the industry, is $0.152^2 + 0.10^2 + 0.10^2 + 0.092^2 + 0.052^2 + 0.0504^2 + \ldots + 0.0504^2 = 0.054 + 10 \times 0.0504^2 = 0.0794$.

e. There is greater competition in the scenario in part (c) than in part (d). The Herfindahl index in part (c) is smaller than that in part (d), reflecting a more competitive industry structure in part (c). Also, the reciprocal of the Herfindahl index is 16.6 in part (c) and 12.6 in part (d). Thus, the market structure in part (c) is equivalent to having 16.6 firms of the same size, and the market structure in part (d) is equivalent to having 12.6 firms of the same size. This reflects that the market structure in part (d) is relatively more oligopolistic, or less competitive, than in part (c).

7. a. Though News Corporation is based in Australia, it is really a global conglomerate, and a majority of its businesses are outside of Australia. About 77 percent of its revenues are in the United States, 15 percent in Europe, and only 8 percent in Australia and Asia together. Its major competitors include firms headquartered in

the United States and Vivendi Universal, a firm headquartered in France. In view of the global characteristics of News Corporation, its valuation should be done primarily relative to the global industry.

b. Due to differences in accounting standards and practices among countries, the analyst would be concerned if he were comparing ratios of News Corporation, computed as per Australian GAAP, with those of Vivendi Universal, computed as per French GAAP. However, both firms trade in the United States as registered ADRs and prepare statements as per U.S. GAAP. Therefore, the analyst could simply compare ratios computed based on these statements.

8. a. ROE = NI/Equity. So,

ROE for Walt Disney = 1,300/20,975 = 0.062

ROE for News Corporation = 719/16,374 = 0.044

Clearly, Walt Disney did better than News Corporation in terms of ROE.

b. One version of the DuPont model breaks down ROE into three contributing elements, as follows:

ROE = Net profit margin × Asset turnover × Leverage

where

Net profit margin = NI/Sales
Asset turnover = Sales/Assets
Leverage = Assets/Equity

The three contributing elements for both the companies are computed based on the data given in the problem, and are given in the following table:

	Walt Disney	**News Corp.**
Net profit margin	0.056	0.050
Asset turnover	0.536	0.403
Leverage	2.082	2.179

The numbers in the table indicate that the main reason Walt Disney did better than News Corporation is that it had a better asset turnover. That is, it utilized its assets more efficiently than did News Corporation. Walt Disney also had a higher net profit margin than did News Corporation. The only contributing element that is higher for News Corporation is leverage, implying that News Corporation levered its operating results using more debt than did Walt Disney.

To analyze why the net profit margin for Walt Disney is a little higher than that for News Corporation, the net profit margin is broken down as follows:

Net profit margin = NI/EBT × EBT/EBIT × EBIT/Sales

The breakdown of net profit margin is given in the following table:

	Walt Disney	**News Corp.**
NI/EBT	0.562	0.593
EBT/EBIT	0.762	0.666
EBIT/Sales	0.130	0.126

The data in the table suggest that the net profit margin for Walt Disney was higher than that for News Corporation because of a higher EBT/EBIT ratio (i.e., a lower debt burden, because a higher value of EBT/EBIT implies a lower debt burden.) This is not unexpected, because we saw in the breakdown earlier that Walt Disney had a lower leverage than did News Corporation.

9. In an efficient market, all available information is already incorporated in current stock prices. The fact that economic growth is currently higher in Country A than in Country B implies that current stock prices are already "higher" in A than in B. Only unanticipated news about future growth rates should affect future stock prices. Current growth rates can explain past performance of stock prices, but only differences in future growth rates from their current anticipated levels should guide your country selection. Hence, you should decide whether your own economic growth forecasts differ from those implicit in current stock prices.

10. The intrinsic value is given by:

$$P_0 = \frac{D_1}{r - g} = \frac{E_1(1 - b)}{r - g}$$

where

E_1 is next year's earnings = €4 per share

$1 - b$ is the earnings payout ratio = 0.70

r is the required rate of return on the stock = 0.12

g is the growth rate of earnings = $1.25 \times 2.8\% = 3.5\%$ or 0.035

So,

$$P_0 = 4 \times 0.70/(0.12 - 0.035) = €32.94 \text{ per share}$$

$$P_0/E_1 = 0.70/(0.12 - 0.035) = 8.24$$

11. a. Intrinsic P/E ratio $= \dfrac{P_0}{E_1} = \dfrac{1}{r}\left[1 + \dfrac{b(\text{ROE} - r)}{r - \text{ROE} \times b}\right]$. In this case, $b = 0$, because the company pays out all its earnings. So, $P_0/E_1 = 1/r = 1/0.13 = 7.69$.

b. Again, $P_0/E_1 = 1/r = 1/0.13 = 7.69$.

c. It is clear from the expression in part (a) that if $b = 0$, the intrinsic P/E value is independent of ROE. To further explore this, realize that the intrinsic P/E value can also be expressed as $P_0/E_1 = (1/r) + \text{FF} \times \text{G}$, where the franchise factor is FF = $(\text{ROE} - r)/(\text{ROE} \times r)$ or $1/r - 1/\text{ROE}$, and the growth factor is G = $g/(r - g)$. If $b = 0$, then $g = 0$, and therefore, the growth factor G = 0. Thus, regardless of how big the ROE—and consequently the franchise factor FF—is, the franchise value, FF $\times$ G, is zero, and the intrinsic P/E value is simply $1/r$.

d. Again, $P_0/E_1 = 1/r = 1/0.13 = 7.69$.

e. In part (d), ROE = r = 13%. It is clear from the expression in part (a) that if ROE = r, the intrinsic P/E value is independent of the retention ratio, b. To further explore this, let us again look at the expression for intrinsic P/E value discussed in part (c). If ROE = r, then the franchise factor FF = 0. Thus, regardless of how large the retention ratio—and consequently the growth factor G—is, the franchise value, FF $\times$ G, is zero, and the intrinsic P/E value is simply $1/r$.

12. i. Franchise factor $= 1/r - 1/\text{ROE} = 1/0.10 - 1/0.12 = 1.67$.
    ii. Growth factor $= g/(r - g) = (b \times \text{ROE})/(r - b \times \text{ROE}) = (0.70 \times 0.12)/(0.10 - 0.70 \times 0.12) = 5.25$.
    iii. Franchise P/E value $=$ Franchise factor $\times$ Growth factor $= 1.67 \times 5.25 = 8.77$.
    iv. Tangible P/E value $= 1/r = 1/0.10 = 10$.
    v. Intrinsic P/E value $=$ Franchise P/E value $+$ Tangible P/E value $= 8.77 + 10 = 18.77$. We can also verify that intrinsic P/E value $= (1 - b)/(r - g) = (1 - 0.70)/(0.10 - 0.70 \times 0.12) = 18.75$ (the slight difference is due to rounding).

13. The P/E is equal to

$$P_0/E_1 = \frac{1}{\rho + (1 - \lambda)I}$$

where

$I =$ rate of inflation $= 3\%$

$\rho =$ real required rate of return $= 8\% - 3\% = 5\%$

    i. $\lambda = 1$: $P_0/E_1 = 1/\rho = 1/0.05 = 20$.
    ii. $\lambda = 0.4$: $P_0/E_1 = 1/(0.05 + 0.60 \times 0.03) = 1/0.068 = 14.71$.
    iii. $\lambda = 0$: $P_0/E_1 = 1/(\rho + I) = 1/0.08 = 12.50$.

We observe that the higher the inflation flow-through rate, the higher the P/E ratio. In other words, the less a firm is able to pass inflation through its earnings, the more it is penalized.

14. For both Company B and Company U, $\lambda = 0.60$, or $1 - \lambda = 0.40$. Also, $\rho = 0.08$ for both.

$$P_0/E_1 \text{ for Company B} = \frac{1}{\rho + (1 - \lambda)I} = 1/(0.08 + 0.40 \times 0.09) = 8.62$$

$$P_0/E_1 \text{ for Company U} = \frac{1}{\rho + (1 - \lambda)I} = 1/(0.08 + 0.40 \times 0.025) = 11.11$$

P/E for Company B, which is subject to a higher inflation rate, is smaller than that for Company U. Thus, if full inflation pass-through cannot be achieved, then the higher the inflation rate, the more negative the influence on the stock price.

15. a. If the company can completely pass inflation through its earnings, $P/E = 1/\rho = 1/0.07 = 14.29$ in each of the years. Inflation has no effect on the P/E ratio, because the firm can completely pass inflation through its earnings.

    b. $P/E = \dfrac{1}{\rho + (1 - \lambda)I} = 1/(0.07 + 0.50 \times I)$

Year	Inflation (%)	P/E
1995	22.0	5.56
1996	9.1	8.66
1997	4.3	10.93
1998	2.5	12.12
1999	8.4	8.93

c. As mentioned in part (a), inflation has no effect on the P/E ratio if the firm can completely pass inflation through its earnings. However, if the firm cannot completely pass inflation through its earnings as in part (b), then the higher the inflation rate (e.g., in the year 1995), the more severe the influence on the stock price.

16. Due to the appreciation of the euro relative to the dollar, the French goods will become more expensive in terms of the dollar. If the French company is able to completely pass through this increase to its U.S.-based customers, its P/E ratio will not suffer. Regardless of the extent of the appreciation of the euro, the company's P/E ratio will be unaffected if it is able to completely pass the appreciation through to its customers. However, if the company is able to only partially pass the euro appreciation through to its U.S.-based customers, the P/E ratio will go down. The higher the euro appreciation, the more severe will be the decline in the P/E ratio.

17. a. Because the portfolio is equally invested in the two stocks, the factor exposures of the portfolio would be equally weighted averages of the factor exposures of the two stocks. So, the factor exposures of the portfolio would be as follows:

	Portfolio
Confidence	0.4
Time horizon	0.7
Inflation	−0.3
Business cycle	3.0
Market timing	0.85

b. The stocks have a positive exposure to business cycle and a negative exposure to inflation. Also, you expect strong economic growth and an increase in inflation. Therefore, you should overweigh the stock with a greater exposure to business cycle and a smaller exposure (in absolute terms) to inflation. Stock A satisfies both, and accordingly you should overweigh stock A.

18. It is clear by looking at the table that in each of the three size categories, the low price-to-book value stock (P/BV) outperforms the high P/BV stock. Thus, there seems to be a *value effect,* as the value firms seem to outperform the growth firms. That is, the value factor seems to be significant.

To clearly see the *size effect,* we rearrange the stocks in the two P/BV categories, as follows:

Stock	**Size**	**P/BV**	**Return (%)**
A	Huge	High	4
C	Medium	High	9
E	Small	High	13
B	Huge	Low	6
D	Medium	Low	12
F	Small	Low	15

In both P/BV categories, smaller firms outperform bigger firms. Thus, there seems to be a *size effect,* and the size factor seems to be significant.

19. We first compute the changes in the two factors and the returns on each stock. The following table has the numbers. Because we are computing the changes, we lose one observation.

Period	Change in Interest Rate	Change in Approval	Return on Stock A	B	C
2	−2.1	5	−0.12	−0.49	−0.45
3	0.3	−1	−0.22	0.39	0.39
4	1.7	−2	0.40	0.42	0.21
5	−1.8	19	−0.33	−0.33	−0.19
6	−0.2	−19	−0.16	−0.30	−0.22
7	2.3	23	1.10	1.14	0.96
8	0.1	−27	0.01	0.14	−0.25
9	−2.3	2	−0.50	−0.48	−0.23
10	−0.2	20	−0.14	−0.15	−0.24

We now estimate the following factor model for each of the three stocks, using the respective nine observations from the preceding table.

$$R_i = \alpha_i + \beta_{1i}f_1 + \beta_{2i}f_2 + \varepsilon_i$$

where

R_i is the rate of return on stock i

α_i is a constant

f_1 and f_2 are the two factors common to the three stocks (f_1 is the change in interest rate, and f_2 is the change in approval rating)

β_{1i} and β_{2i} are the risk exposures of stock i to each of the two factors

ε_i is a random term specific to stock i

The results of the estimation are as follows:

	Stock A	Stock B	Stock C
α	0.05	0.10	0.03
(*t*-statistic)	(0.56)	(1.31)	(0.36)
β_1	0.25***	0.31***	0.22***
(*t*-statistic)	(4.32)	(6.20)	(3.89)
β_2	0.01	0.01	0.01
(*t*-statistic)	(1.27)	(1.18)	(1.66)

***Statistically significant at the 99% level.

The values of β_1 are highly statistically significant, with a *p*-value of less than 0.01, for each of the three stocks. In contrast, none of the values of β_2 are statistically significant (each of the *p*-values is greater than 0.10). The magnitudes of β_1 are several times bigger than the magnitudes of β_2. Clearly, the first factor (change in interest rate) influences stock returns in this country, while the second factor (change in approval) does not.

20. a. $R_f = 4\%$, $RP_w = 5\%$, and $RP_{SFr} = 1\%$. So,

$$E(R_i) = 4\% + \beta_1 \times 5\% + \beta_2 \times 1\%$$

Accordingly,

$$E(R_A) = 4\% + 1 \times 5\% + 1 \times 1\% = 10\%$$

$$E(R_B) = 4\% + 1 \times 5\% + 0 \times 1\% = 9\%$$

$$E(R_C) = 4\% + 1.2 \times 5\% + 0.5 \times 1\% = 10.5\%$$

$$E(R_D) = 4\% + 1.4 \times 5\% - 0.5 \times 1\% = 10.5\%$$

b. Stocks that should be purchased are those with a forecasted return, higher than their theoretical expected return, given the stock's risk exposures. Because the forecasted returns given in the problem are the returns in Swiss francs, we need to convert them to dollar returns first. We expect the Swiss franc to appreciate relative to the dollar by 2 percent. Therefore, using a linear approximation, the dollar return is the return in Swiss francs + 2%. The following table summarizes the forecasted returns in francs and in dollars, and the theoretical expected returns in dollars (computed in part [a]).

	Stock A	Stock B	Stock C	Stock D
Forecasted return (in francs)	8%	9%	11%	7%
Forecasted return (in dollars)	10%	11%	13%	9%
Theoretical expected return (in dollars)	10%	9%	10.5%	10.5%

Looking at this table, we find that the broker forecasts superior returns for stocks B and C. Therefore, they should be bought. Conversely, stock D should be sold.

Bibliography

Baumol, W. "Productivity Growth, Convergence, and Welfare: What the Long-Run Data Show," *American Economic Review,* 76 (5) December, 1986, pp. 1072–1085.

Besanko, D., Dranove, D., and Shanley, M. *Economics of Strategy,* 2nd edition, New York: John Wiley & Sons, 2000.

Bhushan, R., and Lessard, D. R. "Coping with International Accounting Diversity: Fund Managers' Views on Disclosure, Reconciliation, and Harmonization," *Journal of International Financial Management and Accounting,* 4(2), 1992.

Brandenberger, A., and Nalebuff, B. *Co-opetition,* New York: Currency-Doubleday, 1996.

Burmeister, E., Roll, R., and Ross, S. "A Practitioner's Guide to Arbitrage Pricing Theory," in *A Practitioner's Guide to Factor Models,* Charlottesville, VA: The Research Foundation of the ICFA, 1994.

Calverley, J. *The Investor's Guide to Economic Fundamentals,* Chichester, West Sussex: Wiley, 2003.

Canova, F., and De Nicolo, G. "Stock Returns and Real Activity: A Structural Approach," *European Economic Review,* 39, 1995, pp. 981–1019.

Cavaglia, S., Brightman, C., and Aked, M. "On the Increasing Importance of Industry Factors," *Financial Analysts Journal,* 56(5), September/October 2000.

Chen, N., Roll, R., and Ross, S. "Economic Forces and the Stock Market," *Journal of Business,* September 1986.

Choi, F. D. S., and Levich, R. M. "International Accounting Diversity: Does It Affect Market Participants?" *Financial Analysts Journal,* July/August 1991.

Christensen, C., Raynor, M., and Verlinden, M. "Skate to Where the Money Will Be," *Harvard Business Review,* November 2001, pp. 72–81.

French, K. R., and Poterba, J. M. "Were Japanese Stock Prices Too High?" *Journal of Financial Economics,* October 1991.

Griffin, J. M., and Stulz, R. "International Competition and Exchange Rate Shocks: A Cross-Country Industry Analysis of Stock Returns," *Review of Financial Studies,* 14, 2001, pp. 215–241.

Hopkins, P., and Miller, H. *Country, Sector, and Company Factors in Global Portfolios,* Charlottesville, VA: The Research Foundation of AIMR, 2001.

Leibowitz, M. L. "Franchise Margins and the Sales-Driven Franchise Value," *Financial Analysts Journal,* 53(6), November/December 1997, pp. 43–53.

Leibowitz, M. L. "Franchise Valuation under Q-Type Competition," *Financial Analysts Journal,* 54(6), November/December 1998, pp. 62–74.

Leibowitz, M. L., and Kogelman, S. *Franchise Value and the Price/Earnings Ratio,* The Research Foundation of AIMR, 2000.

Oster, S. M. *Modern Competitive Analysis,* New York: Oxford University Press, 1999.

Pope, P. F., and Rees, W. P. "International Differences in GAAP and the Pricing of Earnings," *Journal of International Financial Management and Accounting,* 4(3), Autumn 1992.

Porter, M. E. *Competitive Advantage: Creating and Sustaining Superior Performance,* New York: Free Press, 1985.

Porter, M. E. *The Competitive Advantage of Nations,* New York: Free Press, 1990.

Radebaugh, L. H., and Gray, S. J. *International Accounting and Multinational Enterprises,* New York: John Wiley & Sons, 1997.

Reilly, F. K., and Brown, K. C. *Investment Analysis and Portfolio Management,* 7th edition, Orlando: Dryden Press, 2003.

Schieneman, G. S. "Cross-Border Financial Statement Analysis," in *Practical Issues in Equity Analysis,* AIMR, 2000, pp. 27–35.

Speidell, L. S., and Bavishi, V. B. "GAAP Arbitrage: Valuation Opportunities in International Accounting Standards," *Financial Analysts Journal,* November/December 1992.

Stowe, J., Robinson, T., Pinto, J., and McLeavey, D. *Analysis of Equity Investments: Valuation,* Charlottesville, Va: Association for Investment Management and Research, 2002.

Temple, P. *Magic Numbers,* New York: John Wiley & Sons, 2002.

7

Global Bond Investing

- Discuss the difference between domestic bonds, foreign bonds, and Eurobonds

- Describe the various stages of a Eurobond issue

- Describe the various ways to invest in bonds from emerging countries

- Describe a Brady bond

- Define bond quotation and day count conventions across the world

- Describe the basic valuation method for straight fixed-rate bonds

- Define a yield curve based on zero-coupon bonds

- Describe and contrast the various methods used to report a yield to maturity (simple yield, annual yield, semiannual yield)

- Define the duration, or interest sensitivity, of a bond

- Compute the expected excess return (risk premium) on a domestic bond as the sum of the yield spread over the cash rate plus the duration-adjusted expected yield movement

- Define the three components of the quality spread (expected loss component, credit-risk premium, liquidity premium)

- Compare yield curves in various currencies

- Define the implied forward exchange rate from yield curves in different currencies

- Conduct an exchange rate break-even analysis

- Explain the various sources of return and risk from an international bond

- Compute the return on a foreign-currency bond

- Compute the return on a foreign bond, hedged against currency risk

- Compute the expected excess return (risk premium) on a foreign-currency bond, hedged and not hedged against currency risk

- Recommend and justify whether to hedge a bond market investment

- Discuss the various stages of international bond portfolio management

- Describe and analyze a floating-rate note (FRN) and explain why an FRN is not always priced at par

- Describe the characteristics and valuation of straight FRNs, bull FRNs, bear FRNs, dual-currency bonds, and currency-option bonds, and the motivation for their issuance

Global bond investment is both technical and difficult because of the vast diversity of markets, instruments, and currencies offered. Terminology and conventions vary from one market to the next, as do trading methods and costs. For example, yields to maturity are computed on an annual basis on the Eurobond market but on a semiannual basis on the U.S. market. And the Japanese sometimes use a simple-interest method to calculate yield to maturity rather than the usual compound-interest method. Moreover, instruments vary in these markets from straight bonds and floating-rate notes denominated in various currencies to bonds with numerous, and often exotic, option clauses.

This chapter first presents some statistics on the various bond markets. It then outlines the major differences among markets and describes the Eurobond market. After a brief reminder on bond valuation, the chapter discusses multicurrency bond portfolio management. The last section reviews more exotic bonds, starting with floating-rate notes and ending with examples of structured notes found on the Eurobond market.

The Global Bond Market

The Various Segments

Debt certificates have been traded internationally for several centuries. Kings and emperors borrowed heavily to finance wars. Bankers from neutral countries assisted in arranging the necessary financing, thereby creating a market in debentures (bonds). The Rothschilds, for example, became famous for supporting the British war effort against Napoleon I through their European family network. As a matter of fact, organized trading in domestic and foreign debentures took place well before the start of any equity market.

Although debt financing has always been international in nature, there is still no unified international bond market. Instead, the global bond market is divided into three broad groups: *domestic bonds, foreign bonds,* and *Eurobonds.*

- Domestic bonds are issued locally by a domestic borrower and are usually denominated in the local currency.

- Foreign bonds are issued on a local market by a foreign borrower and are usually denominated in the local currency. Foreign bond issues and trading are under the supervision of local market authorities.

- Eurobonds are underwritten by a multinational syndicate of banks and are placed mainly in countries other than the one in whose currency the bond is denominated. These bonds are not traded on a specific national bond market.

Domestic bonds make up the bulk of a national bond market. Different issuers belong to different market segments: government, semi-government, and corporate. In many countries, local corporations and government agencies have issued asset-backed securities. These are debt securities backed by some assets typically used as collateral; for example, other loans such as mortgages.

Foreign bonds issued on national markets have existed for a long time. They often have colorful names, such as *Yankee* bonds (in the United States), *Samurai* bonds (in Japan), *Rembrandt* bonds (in the Netherlands), *Matador* bonds (in Spain), *Caravela* bonds (in Portugal), or *Bulldog* bonds (in the United Kingdom).

Because many non-U.S. firms have financing needs in U.S. dollars, they have a strong incentive to issue bonds in New York. But these bonds must satisfy the disclosure requirements of the U.S. Securities and Exchange Commission (SEC). This can be a costly process for non-U.S. corporations that use accounting standards different from U.S. GAAP. In 1963, the United States imposed an Interest Equalization Tax (IET) on foreign securities held by U.S. investors. The tax forced non-U.S. corporations to pay a higher interest rate in order to attract U.S. investors. A few years later, the Federal Reserve Board restricted the financing of foreign direct investment by U.S. corporations. These measures, taken to support the dollar, made the U.S. bond market less attractive to foreign borrowers and simultaneously created a need for offshore financing of U.S. corporate foreign activities. This led to the development of the Eurobond market in the early 1960s. Because of the Glass-Steagall Act, U.S. commercial banks were prevented from issuing and dealing in bonds. Such restrictions did not apply to their offshore activities, and foreign subsidiaries of U.S. commercial banks became very active on the Eurobond market. The repeal of the IET in 1974, the partial relaxation of the Glass-Steagall Act, as well as various measures to attract foreign borrowers and issuers on the U.S. domestic market, did not slow the growth of the Eurobond market. More important, the Eurobond market came to be recognized by borrowers and investors alike as an efficient, low-cost, and most innovative market.

In 1999, all bonds denominated in one of the former currencies of Euroland were translated into euros. For example, all French government bonds denominated in French francs became bonds denominated in euros, using the "legacy" exchange rate set on January 1, 1999. This denomination could create great confusion between "Eurobonds" and "bonds issued in euros." In other words, a French government bond issued in France is not a Eurobond, although it is a euro bond—that is, a bond denominated in euros. The name *Eurobond* comes from the historical fact that the banks placing the Eurobond are located in Europe. It is likely that the terminology will evolve to clear the confusion. The term *international bond* is often used in lieu of *Eurobond*.

Debt issued by companies and governments from emerging countries tend to be considered a separate segment of the market (discussion to follow). Floating-rate notes, issued in euros and dollars, are an important segment of the Eurobond market, where can also be found a variety of more complex bonds as we discuss later.

World Market Size

The world bond market comprises both the domestic bond markets and the international market. The size of the world bond market was estimated at around $37 trillion at the start of 2002. The world market capitalization of bonds is, therefore, somewhat higher than that of equity. Bonds denominated in dollars currently represent roughly half the value of all outstanding bonds. Yen bonds represent roughly 20 percent of the world bond market, and European currencies, 30 percent. Bonds denominated in euros amount to 20 percent of all bonds. Exhibit 7.1. gives the relative size of the domestic bond markets (total capitalization, $30 trillion). Note that the relative share of each currency market depends not only on new issues and repaid bonds, but also on exchange rate movements. Exhibit 7.2 details the Eurobond market (total capitalization around $7 trillion) by type of

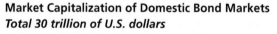

EXHIBIT 7.1

Market Capitalization of Domestic Bond Markets
Total 30 trillion of U.S. dollars

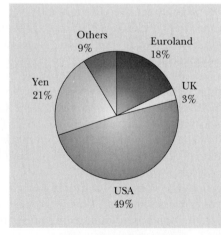

Source: Bank for International Settlements, 2002.

EXHIBIT 7.2

Market Capitalization of Eurobonds
Total 7 trillion of U.S. dollars.

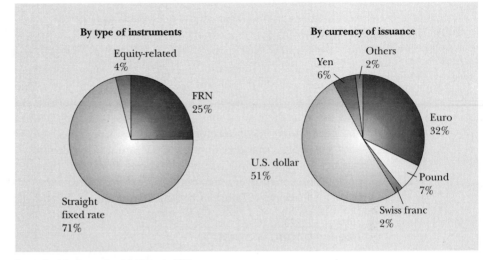

Source: Bank for International Settlements, 2002.

instruments and by currency of issuance. The major types of instruments are straight bonds with fixed coupons, floating-rate notes (FRNs) with a coupon indexed on a short-term interest rate, and bonds with some equity feature (e.g., convertibles). The major currencies of issuance are the dollar and the euro, followed by the pound, yen, and Swiss franc.

Bond Indexes

Bond indexes used to be less commonly available than stock indexes. However, total-return bond indexes serve many purposes and are increasingly used. A total-return index cumulates the price movement with accrued interest; it is a cumulative index of the total return on a bond portfolio.

These indexes are put to different uses:

- A bond index calculated daily for each bond market allows quick assessment of the direction and magnitude of movements in the market. Such an index must be based on a small but representative sample of actively traded bonds, because many bonds are not traded every day. A single actively traded bond, called a "benchmark" bond, is sometimes used. News services such as the Financial Times, Reuters, or Bloomberg publish daily quotes on benchmark bonds representative of each market.

- Total-return bond indexes are also required for measuring the performance of a bond portfolio in a domestic or multicurrency setting. This is usually done monthly or quarterly. One needs an exhaustive index covering all bonds in the market. Because many issues are not liquid and their prices may be old or out of line with the market, exhaustive market indexes tend to lag behind the interest rate movements, but they reflect the current valuation of a market portfolio.

Within a national market, the price movements of all fixed-rate bonds tend to be strongly correlated. This is because all bond prices are influenced by movements in the local interest rate. As for equity indexes, there are two major types of providers of bond indexes: domestic and global. In many countries, domestic providers calculate local bond indexes weekly, monthly, and sometimes daily. International investors find the indexes calculated by these institutions difficult to use because they differ in their construction methodology and calculation frequencies. Several global providers have developed consistent bond indexes for the major domestic and Eurobond markets. These are market capitalization–weighted indexes of various market segments and regions. Among those commonly used for performance measurements, one can cite the indexes computed by Salomon Smith Barney, J.P. Morgan, Lehman Brothers, Merrill Lynch, and Bloomberg/EFFAS.

The Eurobond Market

Of all the bond markets in the world, the Eurobond market is certainly an attractive one to the international investor. It avoids most national regulations and constraints and provides sophisticated instruments geared to various investment objectives. Because of the important role of Eurobonds in international investment, we will examine in some detail how they are issued and traded.

An example of such a Eurobond issue is presented in Exhibit 7.3. The tombstone advertises a bond issued by NKK, a Japanese company. An interesting feature of this bond is that it is a dual-currency bond: It is issued in yen (20 billion), with interest coupons fixed in yen (8 percent), but its principal repayment is fixed in U.S. dollars ($110,480,000). The underwriting syndicate is listed at the bottom of the tombstone.

In general, several points distinguish a Eurobond from a domestic bond, and some can be spotted on the tombstone in Exhibit 7.3:

- The underwriting syndicate is made up of banks from numerous countries.

- U.S. commercial banks can participate, as well as U.S. investment banks. This would not be the case for a domestic or foreign bond issued on the U.S. market.

- Underwriting banks tend to use subsidiaries established in London or a foreign country with a favorable tax situation. This can be easily recognized by the label appearing at the end of the banks' names listed on the tombstone: *Limited* (Britain or a British Isle), *SA* (usually Luxembourg), and *NV* (Netherlands or the Dutch Antilles). U.S. commercial banks must use a foreign subsidiary because of U.S. regulations.

EXHIBIT 7.3

Eurobond Tombstone

These securities have been sold outside the United States of America and Japan. This announcement appears as a matter of record only.

NEW ISSUE   22nd January, 1994

Nippon Kokan Kabushiki Kaisha

**8 per cent. Dual Currency
Yen/U.S. Dollar Bonds Due 2004**

Issue Price: 101 per cent. of the Issue Amount

Issue Amount:	¥20,000,000,000
Redemption Amount at Maturity:	U.S.$110,480,000

Nomura International Limited   Mitsubishi Trust & Banking Corporation
                                                                            (Europe) S.A.
Prudential-Bache Securities International   Yamaichi International (Europe) Limited

Bankers Trust International Limited   Crédit Lyonnais
Credit Suisse First Boston Limited   Dresdner Bank Aktiengesellschaft
EBC Amro Bank Limited   Fuji International Finance Limited
Generale Bank   Kleinwort, Benson Limited
Lloyds Merchant Bank Limited   Morgan Guaranty Ltd
Morgan Stanley International   Orion Royal Bank Limited
Swiss Bank Corporation International   Union Bank of Switzerland (Securities)
            Limited   Limited
                    S.G. Warburg & Co., Ltd.

- Corporate borrowers sometimes use a subsidiary incorporated in a country with a favorable tax and regulatory treatment. This is done to avoid double taxation or some stamp tax (as is the case in Switzerland). But the guarantee of the mother company is usually granted to the investor.

- The frequency of coupon payments is annual for fixed-rate Eurobonds, but it is semiannual for U.S. bonds.

The Issuing Syndicate   Eurobonds are sold in a multistage process. The issue is organized by an international bank called the *lead manager*. This bank invites several *comanagers* to form the *management group* (from 5 to 30 banks, usually). For large issues, there may be several lead managers. The managers prepare the issue, set the final conditions of the bond, and select the *underwriters* and *selling group*. One of the managers is appointed as the principal paying agent and fiscal agent. A large portion of the issue is directly subscribed by the management group.

The underwriters are invited to participate in the issue on the basis of their regional placement power. Their number varies from 30 to 300 and comprises international banks from all regions of the world. Together with the management group, the underwriters guarantee final placement of the bonds at a set price to the borrower.

The selling group is responsible for selling the bonds to the public and consists of managers, underwriters, and additional banks with a good selling base. Note that a participant may be, at the same time, manager, underwriter, and seller. Separate fees are paid to compensate for the various services. The total fee ranges from 1 percent to 2.5 percent. Unlike their U.S. counterparts, Eurobond underwriters are not obligated to maintain the bond's market price at or above the issue price until the syndicate is disbanded. This means that bonds are often placed at a price below the issue price. There is considerable price discrimination among clients, and selling members may pass along part of their fee to the final buyer of the bond.

The Timetable of a New Issue   Unlike national markets, the Eurobond market has neither *registration formalities* nor *waiting queues*. A new issue may be placed within three weeks. A typical timetable is depicted in Exhibit 7.4.

EXHIBIT 7.4

Timetable of a New Eurobond Issue

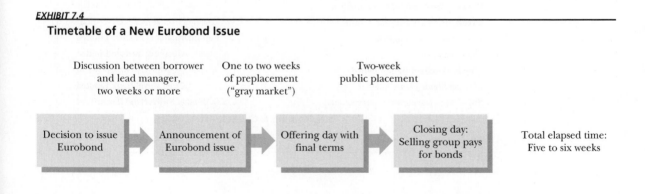

First, the lead manager gets together with the borrower to discuss the terms of the bond (amount, maturity, fixed or floating rate, and coupon). The terms generally remain provisional until the official offering date. During this period, the lead manager arranges the management syndicate and prepares various documents, one of which is a preliminary prospectus called, at this stage, a *red herring*. On the *announcement day*, the managers send e-mails or faxes describing the proposed bond issue and inviting banks to join the underwriting and selling groups. Potential underwriters are sent the preliminary prospectus. A week or two later, the final terms of the bond are set and the syndicate commits itself to the borrower. A final prospectus is printed, and the bonds are publicly offered on the *offering day*. At the end of a public placement period of about two weeks, the subscription is closed on the *closing day*, and the bonds are delivered in exchange for cash paid to the borrower. A *tombstone* is later published in international newspapers to advertise the successful issue and to list the participating banks.

After the closing day, the bonds can be publicly traded. However, bond trading actually takes place well before the closing day. A *gray* market for the bonds starts before the final terms have been set on the offering day; trading is contingent on the final issue price. That is, bonds are traded in the gray market at a premium or discount relative to the future price. For example, a quote of *less ¼* means that the bonds are exchanged at a price of 99.25 percent if the future issue price is set at 99.5 percent. This is a form of forward market for bonds that do not yet exist. The gray market is often used by members of the selling group to resell part of their bond allocation at a discount below the issue price, but possibly at a net profit if their fee is large enough.

Dealing in Eurobonds   The Eurobond secondary market is truly international and comprises an informal network of market makers and dealers. A market maker quotes a net price to a financial institution in the form of a bid–ask price. No commissions are charged. Although the Eurobond market has no physical location, most of the bonds are listed on the Luxembourg stock exchange to nominally satisfy the requirement of obtaining a public quotation at least once a year or quarter. However, very few transactions go through the exchange. Instead, Eurobond dealers created an around-the-clock market among financial institutions across the world, forming the *International Securities Market Association (ISMA)*, based in Zurich and London and formerly known as AIBD. The geographical composition of the ISMA shows the prominent role of London. But Swiss banks are large investors in the market and the second major force in ISMA.

All market makers and dealers in Eurobonds are part of the ISMA. The ISMA bears some similarities to the U.S. National Association of Securities Dealers (NASD). But, whereas NASD is under the supervision of the SEC, the ISMA is purely self-regulated and is subject to no government intervention.

Eurobond Clearing System   Let's assume that a Scottish investment manager wants to buy $100,000 worth of a specific Eurobond. The investment manager calls several market makers to get their best quotations and concludes the deal at the lowest price quoted. The trade is settled in three business days, and the transaction is cleared through one of the two major clearing systems, *Euroclear* or *Clearstream* (formerly known as *Cedel*). These clearing companies have now joined with major European bond and equity clearing systems.

Euroclear and Clearstream collect a transaction fee for each book entry, as well as a custody fee for holding the securities. The custody fees are a function of a client's transaction volume: If the member bank maintains a large bond turnover, the custodial fee is nil. Euroclear and Clearstream also provide security lending facilities.

Emerging Markets and Brady Bonds

Investors wishing to buy bonds issued by emerging countries have several alternatives:

- They can directly access the *domestic bond* markets of some emerging countries. These emerging markets have been growing, albeit in an erratic fashion. Various restrictions and liquidity problems reduce the amount available to foreign investors. Latin America dominates the fixed-income market of emerging countries, but some European and Asian markets, such as Turkey, Hungary, the Czech Republic, India, Indonesia, and the Philippines, are also worth mentioning. Most of the bonds traded on emerging markets are *not* investment grade, that is, rated Baa or above by Moody's or BBB or above by Standard & Poor's. This means that they are not eligible for many U.S. institutional investors. These instruments are generally denominated in the local currency and carry the exchange risk of that currency. On the other hand, local governments are less likely to default on these bonds, because they can always print more national currency.

- They can buy *foreign bonds* directly issued by some emerging country or corporation on a major national bond market. The bond is issued in the national currency of that market.

- They can buy *Eurobonds* issued by emerging countries. Latin American governments and firms represent the largest share of these new issues denominated in U.S. dollars and other major currencies. Major issuers come from Mexico, Argentina, Venezuela, and Brazil.

- They can buy *Brady bonds* on the international capital market. In 1990, the Brady plan allowed emerging countries to transform nonperforming debt into so-called Brady bonds, which are traded on the international bond market.

Brady Bonds: A Historical Perspective   In the 1980s, many developing countries were hit hard by the drop in commodity prices and other problems, and became unable or unwilling to service their loans from international banks. This led to an international debt crisis that threatened the international financial system. The emerging-country debt often took the form of bank loans, which are nontradable, as opposed to bonds. Although many emerging countries have not serviced their bank loans, leading to a negotiation to reschedule them, they have usually kept servicing their bond debt. The creditor banks formed the *Paris Club* to negotiate with emerging countries the rescheduling of their debts. A secondary market for nonperforming loans developed in which these loans traded at a steep discount from their par value. The principles of Brady plans, named after the U.S. Secretary of the Treasury, were implemented from 1990 to provide a satisfactory solution to this debt crisis.

To negotiate its Brady plan, the emerging country must initiate a credible economic reform program that receives approval and funding from the World Bank, the International Monetary Fund (IMF), and regional development banks, such as the Inter-American Development Bank, the African Development Bank, the Asian Development Bank, or the European Bank for Reconstruction and Development. Once the IMF and the World Bank have agreed that the economic reform plan will reduce the risk of new insolvency problems, these organizations provide funding, which can be used in part to provide collateral and guarantees in the debt rescheduling. One advantage for creditors is that they exchange commercial loans for tradable bonds. A Brady plan is basically a debt-reduction program whereby sovereign debt is repackaged into tradable Brady bonds, generally with collateral. Close to 20 countries have issued Brady bonds, including Argentina, Brazil, Bulgaria, Costa Rica, Nigeria, Poland, the Philippines, Uruguay, and Venezuela. These bonds are traded in the international capital market, with a total capitalization close to $100 billion.

International commercial banks, which were most active in lending to emerging countries, are the major market makers on the Brady bond market. The bid–ask spread on these bonds averages 25 basis points and is low relative to that of Eurobonds issued by emerging countries, because the issue size of Brady bonds can be very large and their market is quite active.

Characteristics of Brady Bonds   Brady bonds come with a large menu of options, which makes their analysis somewhat complicated. The basic idea is to replace existing government debt with Brady bonds, whose market value is less than the par value of the original debt, but that are more attractive than the original debt because of the guarantees provided and their tradability on the international bond market.

Types of Guarantees   Three types of guarantees can be put in place. These guarantees are not available on all types of Brady bonds.

- *Principal collateral.* The U.S. Treasury issues long-term (e.g., 30-year) zero-coupon bonds to collaterallize the principal of the Brady bond. The collateral is paid for by a combination of the IMF, the World Bank, and the emerging country. The value of the collateral increases with time (because of reinvested income) and reaches par at maturity of the Brady bond.

- *Rolling-interest guarantee.* The first semiannual coupons (generally three) are guaranteed by securities deposited in escrow with the New York Federal Reserve Bank, to protect the bondholder from interest suspension or default. If an interest payment is missed, the bondholder will receive that interest payment from the escrow account. If the interest payment is made by the emerging country, the interest collateral will be rolled forward to the next interest payments.

- *Value recovery rights.* Some bonds issued by Mexico and Venezuela have attached warrants linked to the price of oil. Investors can get extra interest payments if the oil export receipts of these countries increase over time.

Types of Bonds   Two major types of Brady bonds have been issued:

- *Par bonds.* PARs can be exchanged dollar for dollar for existing debt. Typically, these bonds have fixed coupons and a long-term maturity (30 years) and are repaid in full on the final maturity. In some cases, the coupon is stepped up progressively over the life of the bond. The debt reduction is obtained by setting a coupon rate on the par value of the bond well below the current market interest rate. In other words, the market value of the bond is well below its face value, because of the low coupon. These bonds are sometimes known as interest-reduction bonds. The difference between the par value of the bond and its market value at issue time can be regarded as the amount of debt forgiveness.

- *Discount bonds.* DISCs are exchanged at a discount to the par value of the existing debt but with a "market-rate" coupon. These bonds are sometimes known as principal-reduction bonds. Typically, these bonds have floating-rate coupons (LIBOR plus a market-determined spread) and a long maturity (20 years or more).

Other types of Brady bonds can be negotiated:

- *Front-loaded interest-reduction bonds.* FLIRBs have low initial coupons that step up to higher levels for a number of years, after which they pay a floating rate.

- *New-money bonds (NMBs) and debt-conversion bonds (DCBs).* These are generally issued together through the new-money option of the Brady plan. This option is designed to give debtholders incentives to invest additional capital in the emerging country. For every dollar of NMB subscribed, the investor can exchange existing debt for debt-conversion bonds in a ratio stated in the Brady plan (typically $5 of DCBs for each dollar of NMBs). The incentive is provided by making DCBs more attractive than the bonds available in other Brady options.

- *Past-due interest bonds.* PDIs are issued in exchange for unpaid past interest. In a way, they pay interest on interest.

This list is not exhaustive, and the option menu of a Brady plan can be quite varied.

Major Differences Among Bond Markets

A thorough technical knowledge of the various bond markets reduces investors' trading costs and enhances returns; it also helps investors to better understand the risks involved. Because bond markets are still rapidly developing, new types of instruments and issuing techniques appear throughout the world all the time. For this reason, the following description of these markets is bound to become partially outdated over time; it is meant to serve chiefly as a broad overview.

Types of Instruments

The variety of bonds offered to the international or even the domestic investor is amazing, because of the recent development of bonds with variable interest rates and complex optional clauses. Although the U.S. bond market is among the more innovative markets, the Eurobond market is surely the most creative of all. Investment bankers from many countries bring their expertise to this unregulated market. Each month, new instruments appear or disappear. The Eurobond market's major difference from domestic markets lies in its multicurrency nature. Many Eurobonds are designed to have cash flows in different currencies.

EXAMPLE 7.1   *SWISS FRANC JAPANESE CONVERTIBLE BOND*

Japanese firms, for example, have frequently issued Swiss franc–denominated bonds convertible into common shares of a Japanese company. This is a bond issued in Swiss francs, paying a fixed coupon in Swiss francs, and repaid in Swiss francs. But the bond can also be converted into shares of the Japanese issuing company. List various scenarios that would benefit a buyer of this bond.

SOLUTION

A Swiss investor can benefit from purchasing this bond in any one of three situations:

- A drop in the market interest rate on Swiss franc bonds (as on any straight Swiss franc bond)

- A rise in the price of the company's stock (because the bonds are convertible into stock)

- A rise in the yen relative to the franc (because the bond is convertible into a Japanese yen asset)

A non-Swiss investor would also benefit if the franc appreciates relative to the investor's currency.

Unfortunately, the reverse scenarios would lead to a loss.

In this chapter, we provide a refresher on the analysis of traditional bonds, such as straight fixed coupon bonds and floating-rate notes; we also analyze some of the more complex Eurobonds.

Quotations, Day Count, and Frequency of Coupons

Quotation Bonds are usually quoted on a price-plus-accrued-interest basis in percentage of face value.[1] This means that the price is quoted separately (as a percentage of the bond's nominal value) from the percentage coupon accrued from the last coupon date to the trade date. Accrued interest is computed linearly by multiplying the amount of coupon by the ratio of the time since the last coupon payment divided by the coupon period. It is also expressed in percentage of face value. The buyer pays (or the seller receives) both the quoted price of the bond and accrued interest. Thus, the price quoted is "clean" of coupon effect and allows meaningful comparisons between various bonds. This quoted price is often called a *clean* price. Hence the *full* price, P, is equal to the sum of the quoted, or clean price, Q, plus accrued interest, AI:

$$P = Q + AI \qquad (7.1)$$

Accrued interest is generally calculated as follows:

$$AI = \text{Coupon} \times \frac{\text{Days since last coupon date}}{\text{Days in coupon period}}$$

EXAMPLE 7.2   FULL PRICE AND CLEAN PRICE

The clean price of a Eurobond is quoted at $Q = 95\%$. The annual coupon is 6 percent, and we are exactly three months from the past coupon payment. What is the full price of the bond?

SOLUTION

$$P = Q + \text{accrued interest} = 95\% + 90/360 \times 6\% = 96.5\%$$

Coupon Frequency and Day Count Bonds differ internationally by the frequency of their coupon payments and in the way accrued interest is calculated. In the United States, straight bonds usually pay a semiannual coupon equal to half of the annual coupon reported. The day-count method used in accrued interest rate calculations for agency, municipal, corporate and foreign bonds assumes months of 30 days in a year of 360 days. In other words, the basic unit of time measurement is the month; it does not matter if a month is actually 28 or 31 days long. An in-

---

[1] Unfortunately, this method of quotation is not universal. Convertible bonds, some index-linked bonds, or FRNs in which the coupon is determined *ex post* (at the end of the coupon period) are quoted with coupons attached. Even some exceptions exist for straight bonds. For example, in the United Kingdom's *gilt* market, the market for U.K. government bonds, an *ex dividend* date, or *ex date*, is set roughly a month before the coupon payment when the bond trades without the next coupon payment. An investor who buys the bond after the *ex date* but before the payment date does not receive the coupon. Instead, it goes to the previous bondholder. Hence, the full price of the gilt (clean price plus accrued interest) still drops on the *ex date* as the security holder loses the right to the next coupon.

EXHIBIT 7.5

Coupon Characteristics of Major Bond Markets

Characteristic	United States	U.S. Treasuries	Canada
Usual frequency of coupon	Semiannual	Semiannual	Semiannual
Day count (month/year)	30/360	Actual/actual	Actual/365

Characteristic	Australia	United Kingdom	Switzerland
Usual frequency of coupon	Semiannual	Semiannual	Annual
Day count (month/year)	Actual/actual	Actual/actual	30/360

Characteristic	Germany	Netherlands	France
Usual frequency of coupon	Annual	Annual	Annual
Day count (month/year)	30/360	30/360	Actual/actual

Characteristic	Japan	Eurobonds	FRNs
Usual frequency of coupon	Semiannual	Annual	Quarter or semiannual
Day count (month/year)	Actual/365	30/360	Actual/360

vestor holding a bond for one month receives 30/360, or one-twelfth of the annual coupon (one-sixth of the semiannual coupon). This day-count convention is known as "30/360." The same method is used in Germany, Scandinavia, Switzerland, and the Netherlands. On the other hand, the day count for U.S. Treasury bonds is based on the actual number of days in a year of 365 or 366 days, so that an investor receives accrued interest proportional to the number of days the bond has been held. This day-count convention is known as "actual/actual." Many countries use this actual/actual convention. By contrast, Canada and Japan use a day count based on the actual number of days in a 365-day year (even in years of 366 days).

Straight Eurobonds usually pay an annual coupon and use the U.S. 30/360 day-count convention, regardless of their currency of denomination, so that a yen or pound Eurobond uses a 30-day month in a 360-day year. On the other hand, Euro-FRNs use actual days in a 360-day year, which is also the convention used for short-term deposits. This follows naturally from the fact that FRN coupons are indexed to short-term interest rates, which follow the "actual/360" day-count convention. Straight Eurobonds pay annual coupons, whereas FRNs pay quarterly or semiannual coupons. The coupon characteristics of the major bond markets are summarized in Exhibit 7.5.

Yield to Maturity   The issue of yields also needs to be addressed. Most financial institutions around the world calculate and publish yields to maturity (YTMs) on individual bonds. These calculations are detailed in the next section, but let's already stress that the methods used for this calculation vary among countries, so that yields are not directly comparable. Most Europeans, for instance, calculate an annual, and accurate, actuarial YTM using the ISMA-recommended formula. U.S.

(and often British) institutions publish a semiannual actuarial yield. For example, a U.S. bond issued at par with 6 percent coupons will pay a coupon of $3 semiannually per $100 of face value and is reported as having a semiannual YTM of 6 percent.

On the other hand, Europeans would quote this bond as having a 6.09 percent (annual) YTM because of the compounding of the two semiannual coupons. Common sense dictates that yields for all maturities and currencies be compared in an identical fashion. The tradition of using semiannual yields is understandably confusing for international investors.[2]

The situation is even worse in Japan, where financial institutions sometimes report YTM based on a simple-interest calculation. The following simple formula shows how this is done:

$$\text{Simple yield} = \frac{Coupon}{Current\ price} + \frac{(100 - Current\ price)}{Current\ price} \times \frac{1}{Years\ to\ maturity} \quad (7.2)$$

This simple yield is simply the immediate yield, measured by the coupon over the price, plus the future capital gain or loss amortized over the remaining maturity of the bond. This simple yield understates the true YTM for bonds priced over par and overstates the yield for bonds priced below par. The historical rationale for this approximate formula is the ease of calculation.

EXAMPLE 7.3   SIMPLE YIELD CALCULATION

A three-year bond has exactly three years till maturity, and the last coupon has just been paid. The coupon is annual and equal to 6 percent. The bond price is 95 percent. What is its simple yield?

SOLUTION

$$\text{Simple yield} = \frac{6}{95} + \frac{(100 - 95)}{95} \times \frac{1}{3} = 8.07\%$$

Legal and Fiscal Aspects

Bonds are issued in either *bearer* or *registered* forms. On the Eurobond market, as well as in many European countries, the bearer of a bond is assumed to be its legal owner. In the United States and many other countries, owners must be registered in the issuer's books. Bond registration allows for easier transfer of interest payments and amortization. Coupons are usually paid annually on markets in which bonds are issued in bearer form, reducing the cost associated with coupon payments. Eurobond coupons in all currencies are paid this way. Bearer bonds provide confidentiality of ownership, which is very important to some investors.

---

[2] The rationale for this method is that it is easy to calculate a yield for a bond issued at par with semiannual coupons. You just multiply the semiannual coupon by 2. However, the use of an annual actuarial yield (with compounding of semiannual yields) makes more sense and allows a direct comparison between instruments and markets.

The U.S. Securities Act is typical of government regulations designed to ensure that domestic investors are protected. The act requires that all public issues of securities be registered with the U.S. Securities and Exchange Commission (SEC). Any bond not registered with the SEC cannot be publicly offered to U.S. residents at the time of issue. SEC registration is imposed to ensure that accurate information on bond issues is publicly available. Bonds issued in foreign markets and Eurobonds do not meet this requirement, but Yankee bonds do, because they undergo a simplified SEC registration. No other bonds can be purchased by U.S. residents at the time of issue; they may be purchased only after they are seasoned (i.e., traded for some time). Sometimes it is difficult to know when an issue is seasoned; usually three months, but sometimes a longer period, such as nine months, is necessary. U.S. banks can participate in Eurobond-issuing syndicates only if they institute a procedure guaranteeing that U.S. investors cannot purchase the bonds. This can be difficult, because Eurobonds are issued in bearer form.

Fiscal considerations are important in international investment. Some countries impose withholding taxes on interest paid by their national borrowers. This means that a foreign investor is often taxed twice: once in the borrowing country (withholding tax) and again in the investor's home country through the usual income tax. Tax treaties help by allowing investors to claim the foreign withholding tax as a tax credit at home; nontaxable investors can also reclaim all or part of a withholding tax, but this is a lengthy and costly process. Avoiding double taxation, in fact, was a major impetus behind the development of the Eurobond market. And that is why today the official borrower on the Eurobond market is usually a subsidiary incorporated in a country with no withholding tax (e.g., the Netherlands Antilles). Of course, the parent company must fully guarantee the interest and principal payments on the bond. Nevertheless, the trend seems to be toward eliminating withholding taxes for foreign investors. To attract foreign investors in their government bonds, most countries eliminated withholding taxes on foreign investment in their domestic bond markets. The United States allowed domestic corporations to borrow directly from foreign investors on international markets without paying a 30 percent withholding tax. This removed the need to borrow through a subsidiary incorporated in the Netherlands Antilles or another tax-free base. Similar regulations already existed in other countries.

The repeal of withholding taxes promotes a greater integration of Eurobond and domestic markets, but not at the expense of the international market. The Eurobond market continues to grow despite the removal of these taxes on major national markets.

A Refresher on Bond Valuation

Bond portfolio management[3] requires the use of mathematical techniques. International bond management adds a new dimension to these techniques, namely, a multicurrency strategy. It also implies the analysis of a large variety of unusual bonds, floating-rate notes, currency option bonds, and other instruments.

---

[3] A detailed analysis can be found in Fabozzi (2000).

The following section could appear in any textbook that deals with domestic investment; as such, it is presented only briefly here. It is followed by a more detailed analysis of the techniques used in international portfolio management, especially the comparison of international yield curves, and an analysis of special bonds.

Zero-Coupon Bonds

It is useful to start the analysis with zero-coupon bonds, which are bonds that do not pay a coupon but pay only a fixed cash flow at their maturity.

Yield to Maturity: Zero-Coupon Bonds The theoretical value of a bond is determined by computing the present value of all future cash flows generated by the bond discounted at an appropriate interest rate. Conversely, we can calculate the internal rate of return, or *yield to maturity* (*YTM*), of a bond on the basis of its current market price and its promised payments.

For example, a bond that promises a payment of $C_1 = \$100$ one year from now, with a current market value of $P = \$90.91$, has a YTM r_1 given by

$$P = \frac{C_1}{(1 + r_1)} \quad \text{or} \quad 90.91 = \frac{100}{(1 + r_1)}$$

Hence,

$$r_1 = 10\%$$

Similarly, we can use the following formula to compute the YTM of zero-coupon bonds maturing in t years:

$$P = \frac{C_t}{(1 + r_t)^t} \tag{7.3}$$

where r_t is expressed as a yearly interest rate. The term $1/(1 + r_t)^t$ is the discount factor for year t. The YTM is defined as the interest rate at which P dollars should be invested today in order to realize C_t dollars t years from now.

For example, a two-year zero-coupon bond paying $C_2 = \$100$ two years from now and currently selling at a price $P = \$81.16$ has a YTM r_2 given by

$$81.16 = \frac{100}{(1 + r_2)^2}$$

Hence,

$$r_2 = 11\%$$

Finally, if the price is $P = 32.2$ and maturity $t = 10$ years, we have $r_{10} = 12\%$.

Prices and Yields All bonds of the same issuer (e.g., government bonds) with the same maturity and other contractual terms must have the same YTM; otherwise, an easy arbitrage would exist. If we know the market YTM for the relevant maturity, we can use Equation 7.3 to derive the price of the bond. For example, assume that the one-year market yield moves from 10 percent to 9 percent; then the price of the one-year zero-coupon bond should move from 90.91 percent to 91.74 percent as

$$P = \frac{C_1}{(1 + r_1)} = \frac{100}{1.09} = 91.74$$

We have an inverse relationship between the market yield and the bond price.

Yield Curves The YTMs of two zero-coupon bonds in the same currency but with different maturities are usually different. Graphing the YTMs on bonds with different maturities allows us to draw a yield curve. The yield curve shows the YTM computed on a given date as a function of the maturity of the bonds. It provides an estimate of the current term structure of interest rates. To be meaningful, a yield curve must be drawn from bonds with identical characteristics, except for their maturity.

The most important yield curve is derived from zero-coupon government bonds. This is a default-free yield curve. Different zero-coupon bonds are represented as points on the hypothetical yield curve in Exhibit 7.6. Although government bonds are seldom issued without coupons, a common technique for creating zero-coupon bonds is called "stripping." In many countries, the government lets bankers strip a government coupon bond: Each cash flow of a given government bond is transformed into a separate bond. So, there are as many zero-coupon bonds as there are coupon payments and final reimbursement. The government zero-coupon yield curve is derived from these strips.

A yield curve can also be calculated from the YTM on government coupon bonds. It is usually derived from bonds trading at, or around, par (100 percent) and is called the *par yield curve*. As discussed in the next section, the YTM of a coupon bond is really some average interest rate over the life of the bond, so it is preferable to rely on a zero-coupon yield curve for pricing of fixed-income securities. Other yield curves can be drawn for risky bonds—for example, those with an AA quality rating, or for bonds denominated in foreign currencies.

EXHIBIT 7.6

Example of Yield Curve

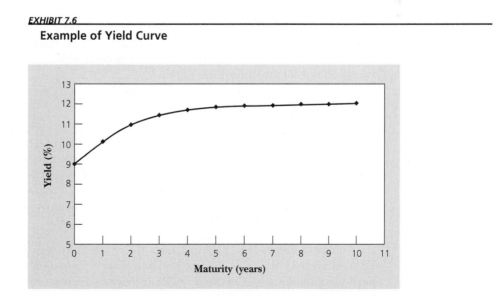

Bond with Coupons

Most bonds issued pay a periodic coupon.

Valuing a Bond with Coupons   The theoretical value of a coupon-paying bond is a little more difficult to assess. It may be considered the present value of a stream of cash flows consisting of each coupon payment and the principal reimbursement. Because the cash flows occur at different times, they should be discounted at the interest rate corresponding to their dates of payment. Accordingly, the coupon to be paid in one year should be discounted at the one-year interest rate on the yield curve. The coupon to be paid in two years should be discounted at the two-year rate, and so forth. In essence, then, a coupon-paying bond is a combination of zero-coupon bonds with different maturities. In general, we will call $C_1, C_2 \ldots, C_n$, the cash flows paid by the bond at times 1, 2, to n. The last cash flow will generally include a coupon and the principal reimbursement. We then have the pricing formula

$$P = \frac{C_1}{(1 + r_1)^1} + \frac{C_2}{(1 + r_2)^2} + \ldots + \frac{C_n}{(1 + r_n)^n} \qquad (7.4)$$

Yield to Maturity: Coupon Bonds   Portfolio managers dealing with a large number of bonds wish to obtain summary information on the yield promised by a bond on its entire life. They want some measure of the average YTM of the bond. The YTM of a coupon bond can still be defined as the internal rate of return, r, which equates the discounted stream of cash flows to the current bond market price. Keep in mind, however, that this is really an average yield provided by cash flows that take place at different times. For an annual coupon bond, the equation is as follows:

$$P = \frac{C_1}{(1 + r)^1} + \frac{C_2}{(1 + r)^2} + \ldots + \frac{C_n}{(1 + r)^n} \qquad (7.5)$$

where the same discount rate is applied to each cash flow.

In practice, coupons may be paid semiannually or quarterly, and a valuation may be made at any time during the coupon period. This calls for the more general valuation formula to determine YTM:

$$P = \frac{C_{t_1}}{(1 + r)^{t_1}} + \frac{C_{t_2}}{(1 + r)^{t_2}} + \ldots + \frac{C_{t_n}}{(1 + r)^{t_n}} \qquad (7.6)$$

where r is the annualized YTM, and t_1, t_2, to t_n are the exact dates on which the cash flows occur, expressed in number of years from the current date. Hence, these dates are usually fractional. For example, consider a bond with a semiannual coupon to be paid three months from now (one-fourth of a year); the next cash flow dates are $t_1 = 0.25$, $t_2 = 0.75$, etc. The cash flows include coupons and principal redemption. Again, P represents the total value of the bond, or *full price*.

European versus U.S. YTM   Equation 7.6 allows us to determine the annual YTM on a bond if we know its cash flows and observe its market value. This is the standard compounding, or actuarial, method that can be used whatever the frequency and dates of coupons. This method is used worldwide except in the United States, where the tradition is to calculate a YTM over a six-month period and multiply it by 2 to report an annualized yield. We call this annualized yield a U.S. YTM or bond-equivalent-basis YTM. Hence, the U.S. YTM or yield is a mixture of an internal rate of return calculation to obtain the semiannual yield, and of a multiplication to transform it into an annualized yield. Bond traders often refer to the *European, or ISMA,* method when they use the standard method described in Equation 7.6. They refer to the *U.S.* method when they use the U.S. convention.

This method for computing an annualized semiannual yield r' can be described by the formula

$$P = \frac{C_{t_1}}{(1 + r'/2)^{2t_1}} + \frac{C_{t_2}}{(1 + r'/2)^{2t_2}} + \ldots + \frac{C_{t_n}}{(1 + r'/2)^{2t_n}} \qquad (7.7)$$

where r' is the U.S. yield, and the cash flow dates are still expressed in number of years. The logic of Equation 7.7 is to use six months as the unit of time measurement. You can verify that it uses a semiannual yield $r'/2$ to discount the cash flows and that the exponents $(2t_1, 2t_2, \ldots, 2t_n)$ are the number of six-month periods from the valuation date. The difference between r' and r comes from the difference between compounding and linearizing semiannual yields to get annual yields. If a semiannual yield of 3 percent is found, the U.S. method will report a yield of $r' = 3 \times 2 = 6\%$, whereas the European method will report a yield of $(1.03) \times (1.03) - 1 = 6.09\%$. In general, we have

$$(1 + r) = (1 + r'/2)^2 \qquad (7.8)$$

EXAMPLE 7.4 *EUROPEAN AND U.S. YTMs*

A three-year bond has exactly three years till maturity, and the last coupon has just been paid. The coupon is annual and equal to 6 percent. The bond price is 95 percent. What are its European and U.S. YTMs?

SOLUTION

The European YTM is r, given by the formula

$$95 = \frac{6}{(1 + r)^1} + \frac{6}{(1 + r)^2} + \frac{106}{(1 + r)^3}$$

Using a spreadsheet, we find $r = 7.94\%$.

The U.S. YTM is r', given by the formula

$$95 = \frac{6}{(1 + r'/2)^2} + \frac{6}{(1 + r'/2)^4} + \frac{106}{(1 + r'/2)^6}$$

Hence, $r' = 7.79\%$. We verify that $1.0794 = (1 + 7.79\%/2)^2$.

Duration and Interest Rate Sensitivity

There is an inverse relationship between the price of a bond and changes in interest rates. As seen in Equation 7.3, if the bond's cash flows are fixed, the price is solely a function of the market yield. Practitioners usually define *interest rate sensitivity*, or *duration*, as the *approximate percentage price change for a 100 basis points (1 percentage point) change in market yield*. Mathematically, the duration D can be written as

$$\frac{\Delta P}{P} = -D \times \Delta r \tag{7.9}$$

where $\Delta P/P$ is the percentage price change induced by a small variation Δr in yield. The minus sign comes from the fact that bond prices drop when interest rates move up. For example, a bond with a duration of $D = 5$ would tend to decline by 5 basis points ($\Delta P/P = -5$) when yields go up by $\Delta r = 1$ basis point. Hence, duration is a measure of interest risk for a specific bond. The interest rate sensitivity or risk of a portfolio is the weighted average of the durations of individual bonds.

The Macaulay duration of a standard bond is its weighted-average maturity. This is a time-weighted average, with each date weighted by the present value of the cash flow paid by the bond on that date as a fraction of the bond's price. The price of a bond is a function of its yield to maturity, $P(r)$. By computing the first derivative of the bond price $P(r)$ relative to the yield r, it is easy to show that the interest rate sensitivity of a bond is simply its Macaulay duration divided by $1 + r$. Hence, some authors call it *modified duration*. We simply use the term *duration* and Equation 7.9 is for duration in this sense.[4] The longer the maturity of a bond, the larger its duration.

EXAMPLE 7.5   DURATION

You hold a government bond with a duration of 10. Its yield is 5 percent. You expect yields to move up by 10 basis points in the next few minutes. Give a rough estimate of your expected return.

SOLUTION

Given the very short horizon, the only component of return is the expected capital loss:

Return $= -10 \times 0.1 = -1\%$

Strictly speaking, the duration is a good approximation of the bond price reaction to interest rate movements only for small movements in the general level in

---

[4] The exact formula is $D = \dfrac{1}{(1 + r)} \times \dfrac{\sum \dfrac{t C_t}{(1 + r)^t}}{\sum \dfrac{C_t}{(1 + r)^t}} = \dfrac{1}{1 + r} \times [\textit{Macaulay Duration}].$

interest rates. In other words, it gives a good approximation for the percentage price movements only for small parallel shifts in the yield curve (yields for all maturities move together). For larger movements in yield, the *convexity* (or second derivative) can be introduced. Also note that the duration of a bond changes over time. To summarize, duration is a simple measure of the sensitivity of a bond, or a portfolio of bonds, to a change in interest rates. A more complete approach requires the full valuation of the bond under various interest rate scenarios.

The return on a bond is equal to the yield over the holding period plus any capital gain or losses due to movements in the market yield, $\Delta yield$. Using Equation 7.9, the bond return can be approximated as

$$Return = Yield - D \times (\Delta yield) \tag{7.10}$$

Over a short holding period, the risk-free rate is the short-term interest rate or cash rate. Hence, the return on a bond investment can be expressed as the sum of

- the cash rate,

- the spread of the bond yield over the cash rate, and

- the percentage capital gain/loss due to a movement in yield.

$$Return = Cash\ rate + (Yield - Cash\ rate) - D \times (\Delta yield) \tag{7.11}$$

The *expected* return on a bond is equal to the risk-free cash rate plus a *risk premium*:

$$E(return) = Cash\ rate + Risk\ premium \tag{7.12}$$

As seen from Equation 7.11, this risk premium is equal to the sum of

- the spread of the bond yield over the cash rate and

- the percentage gain/loss due to expected yield movements.

EXAMPLE 7.6   EXPECTED RETURN ON A DOMESTIC BOND

You hold a government bond with a duration of 10. Its yield is 5 percent, although the cash (one-year) rate is 2 percent. You expect yields to move up by 10 basis points over the year. Give a rough estimate of your expected return. What is the risk premium on this bond?

SOLUTION

The expected return on the year is the sum of the accrued interest plus the expected capital loss stated as a percent:

$$Return = 5\% - 10 \times 0.1 = 4\%$$

This is a rough estimate, because the duration is going to move down over the year as the bond's maturity shortens.

The risk premium is obtained by deducting the short-term interest rate:

$$Risk\ premium = 2\%$$

Credit Spreads

Credit risk is an additional source of risk for corporate bonds. The yield required by the market on a corporate issue is a function of the default risk of the bond: The greater the risk, the higher the yield the borrower must pay. This implies that the yield reflects a *credit spread,* or *quality spread,* over the default-free yield. The quality spread for a specific bond captures three components:

- An *expected loss* component. Investors expect that the bond will default with some probability. To compensate for that expected loss, the issuer must pay a spread above the default-free yield. If investors were risk-neutral, they would only require that the expected return on the corporate bond, taking into account the probability of default, be equal to the default-free yield.

- A *credit-risk premium.* Investors are risk-averse and cannot easily diversify the risk of default on bonds. Furthermore, when the economy is in recession, the financial situation of most corporations deteriorates simultaneously. This is, in part, systematic market risk (business cycle risk) as the stock market is also affected. So, investors require a risk premium to compensate for that risk, on top of the expected loss component.

- A *liquidity premium.* Each corporate bond is a bit different from another one, in part because each issuer has some distinctions in quality from other issuers. All domestic government bonds have the same credit quality within their domestic market (e.g., U.S. Treasury in the United States, British Gilts in the United Kingdom, or JGB in Japan); there is a vast amount issued and excellent trading liquidity. Because of the lack of liquidity on most corporate issues, investors require a compensation in the form of an additional yield, a liquidity premium. In practice, it is difficult to disentangle the liquidity premium and the credit-risk premium.

International rating agencies (Moody's, Standard & Poor's, Fitch) provide a credit rating for most debt issues traded worldwide. In some countries, local firms provide credit ratings for debt securities issued by domestic firms (e.g., Japan Credit Rating Agency in Japan or Dominion Bond Rating Service in Canada). These rating agencies play a crucial role in the pricing of debt securities. When a rating agency announces a revision in its rating of a company's debt, the prices of that company's securities are immediately affected and sometimes by a large amount.

On a specific bond market, one can draw yield curves for each credit rating; the credit spread typically increases with maturity. A top-quality issuer will generally not default immediately. It will first be downgraded one or serveral notches; reflecting an increase in the probability of default. So, in the short run, the credit spread will be affected by the probability of a change in the rating of the corporation. This is usually called *migration* probability; that is, the probability of moving from one credit rating to another. Rating agencies conduct migration studies and annually publish rating migration tables (also called rating transition tables) over some defined time horizons. The *n*-year migration table shows the percentage of issues with a given rating at the start of the year that migrated to another rating at the end of the *n* years. The information in a rating migration table can be used to infer the probability of default.

EXAMPLE 7.7   CREDIT SPREAD ESTIMATION

A one-year bond is issued by a corporation with a 1 percent probability of default by year end. In case of default, the investor will recover nothing. The one-year yield for default-free bonds is 5 percent. What yield should be required by investors on this corporate bond if they are risk-neutral? What should the credit spread be?

SOLUTION

Let's call y the yield and m the credit spread, so that $y = 5\% + m$. The bond is issued at 100 percent of par. If the bond defaults (1 percent probability), the investor gets nothing in a year. In case of no default (99 percent probability), the investor will get $(100 + y)$ percent. So, the yield should be set on the bond so that its expected payoff is equal to the expected payoff on a risk-free bond (105 percent):

$$105 = 99\% \times (100 + y) + 1\% \times 0$$

The yield is equal to $y = (105 - 99)/99 = 6.06\%$. The credit spread is equal to $m = 1.06\%$.

　　The spread is above 1 percent, the probability of default, for two reasons. First, the investor loses 105, not 100, in case of default, so the spread must offset both the lost principal and the lost interest. Second, the spread has to be a bit larger because it is paid on bonds only 99 percent of the time.

　　An investor who is risk-neutral, or who can diversify this risk by holding a large number of bonds issued by different corporations, would be satisfied with this 1.06 percent credit spread. But a risk-averse investor would usually add a risk premium on top, because risk of default tends to be correlated across firms (business cycle risk).

It should be noted that the expected loss on a bond is also affected by recovery rates. In case of default, the debt holder hopes to recover part of the loaned amount.

Multicurrency Approach

International Yield Curve Comparisons

A term structure of interest rates exists for each currency. Investors focus on the default-free yield curve for government bonds. YTMs generally differ across currencies. International interest rate differences are caused by a variety of factors, including differences in national monetary and fiscal policies and inflationary expectations. Furthermore, the interest rate differential for two currencies is not constant over the maturity spectrum.

　　Government yield curves in April 2001 for U.S. dollar, euro, yen, and British pound bonds are given in Exhibit 7.7. A major feature is that Japanese interest

EXHIBIT 7.7

Yield Curves in Different Currencies in 2001

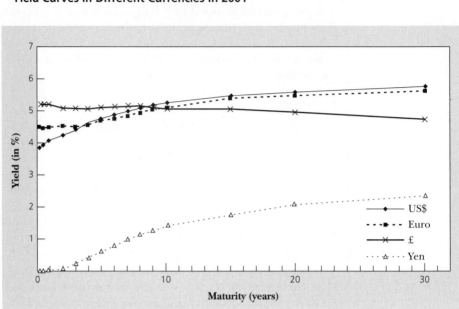

Source: Data from Bloomberg, 2001.

rates are well below those on other markets. For example, the one-year yield is close to zero in Japan (0.037 percent) and equal to 4.1 percent in the United States.

Clearly, the difference in yield curves between two currencies is caused by foreign exchange expectations. Otherwise, arbitrage would occur between bonds denominated in different currencies. This key relation between interest rate differentials and exchange rate expectations for a given maturity is the subject of our next discussion.

Implied Forward Exchange Rates and Break-Even Analysis   The purpose of this section is to introduce the analytical tools that can help a manager choose an optimal investment strategy, given a particular exchange rate and interest rate scenario. The main objective is to determine the implication for exchange rates of yield differentials on bonds denominated in different currencies but with similar maturities. In other words: How do we compare exchange rate movements and YTM differentials?

A higher yield in one currency is often compensated for, *ex post*, by a depreciation in this currency and, in turn, an offsetting currency loss on the bond. It is important to know how much currency movement will compensate for the yield differential. Let's first consider a one-year bond with an interest rate r_1 in domestic currency (e.g., US dollar) and r_1^* in foreign currency (e.g., yen). The current exchange rate is S, expressed as the foreign currency value of one unit of a domestic currency (e.g., 130 yen per dollar). One year from now, the exchange rate must move to a level F_1 in order to make the two investments identical (i.e., have the same total return). In Chapter 1, we called F_1 the forward exchange rate. It is expressed as follows:

$$F_1(1 + r_1) = S (1 + r_1^*) \tag{7.13}$$

The implied offsetting currency depreciation is given by

$$\frac{F_1 - S}{S} = \frac{r_1 - r_1^*}{(1 + r_1)}$$

As an illustration, assume that the dollar one-year yield is $r_1 = 4.10\%$, the yen one-year yield is $r_1^* = 0.037\%$, and the current exchange rate is $S = 130$ yen per dollar. From Equation 7.13 we see that the forward exchange rate should equal

$$F_1 = S \frac{(1 + r_1^*)}{(1 + r_1)} = 130 \frac{1.00037}{1.041} = 124.93$$

which is an implied depreciation of 3.90 percent for the dollar. Thus, a 3.90 percent depreciation of the dollar will exactly offset the yield advantage on the dollar bond relative to the yen bond. This is the *break-even* exchange rate. If the dollar is above 124.93 in a year, a dollar bond will have been a better investment; if it is below, a yen bond would have been a better investment.

Similarly, we can calculate implied forward exchange rates on two-year zero-coupon bonds, as well as on bonds of longer maturity. By comparing the yield curves in two currencies, we can derive the term structure of *implied forward exchange rates* and, therefore, of *implied currency appreciation or depreciation*. For zero-coupon bonds, the implied forward exchange rate for a *t*-year bond is given by

$$F_t = S \frac{(1 + r_t^*)^t}{(1 + r_t)^t} \tag{7.14}$$

The implied currency appreciation or depreciation over the *t*-year period is equal to $(F_t - S)/S$.

For example, the five-year yields given on Exhibit 7.7 are 4.793 percent in dollars and 0.622 percent in yen. The implied five-year forward exchange rate, or break-even rate, is equal to

$$F_5 = 130 \frac{(1.00622)^5}{(1.04793)^5} = 106.11$$

which amounts to an 18 percent depreciation of the dollar. These simple calculations assume that we use yield curves for zero-coupon bonds. The formulas are slightly more complicated if we use the par yield curves for coupon bonds, because we must assume that the coupons are reinvested each year or six-month period until final maturity.

Applications   The implied forward exchange rate is not a forecast but a break-even point. It provides investors with a yardstick against which to measure their own foreign exchange forecasts. In our hypothetical example, Japanese bond investments are clearly not attractive if we expect a stable dollar relative to the yen.

A more precise scenario analysis can be performed for individual bonds. Consider an investor from the United Kingdom who wants to buy bonds denominated in a foreign currency—say, the euro. Bonds are available on the market, with a variety of coupons and sinking fund provisions. To evaluate them, an investor should posit several scenarios for the British pound/euro exchange rate over time. Actuaries can compute the expected pound return for each bond, given these scenarios, by translating each bond payment at the expected exchange rate on the payment date. For example, a rapid euro appreciation over the next two years, followed by a period of stable exchange rate, would make high-coupon, short-term euro bonds very attractive.

Banks are interested in bonds for both lending and borrowing, and several banks in Europe prepare spreadsheets simulating a variety of interest rate and currency scenarios (i.e., one-time depreciation, trends, and combinations) and their influence on bond returns, taking duration into account. A final step is to engage in active currency hedging on bonds.

The Return and Risk on Foreign Bond Investments

The *return* from investing in a foreign bond has three components:

- During the investment period, the bondholder receives the foreign yield.

- A change in the foreign yield ($\Delta foreign\ yield$) induces a percentage capital gain/loss on the price of the bond.

- A currency movement induces a currency gain or loss on the position.[5]

$$Return = Foreign\ yield - D \times (\Delta foreign\ yield) + Percentage\ currency\ movement \quad (7.15)$$

The *risk* on a foreign bond investment has two major sources:

- *Interest rate risk*: the risk that the foreign yields will rise,

- *Currency risk*: the risk that the foreign currency will depreciate.

Of course, the two risks could be somewhat correlated, as discussed in Chapter 4. Furthermore, credit risk should also be taken into account for nongovernment bonds.

As for any investment, the expected return on a foreign bond is equal to the domestic cash rate plus a risk premium. This risk premium equals the sum of

- the spread of the foreign bond yield over the domestic cash rate,

- the percentage capital gain/loss due to an expected foreign yield movement, and

- the expected percentage currency movement.

---

[5] The percentage currency gain or loss also applies to the bond return in local currency, but this is a second-order effect.

EXAMPLE 7.8   RETURN ON A FOREIGN BOND

You are British and hold a U.S. Treasury bond with a full price of 100 and a duration of 10. Its yield is 5 percent. The next day, U.S. yields move up by 5 basis points and the dollar depreciates by 1 percent relative to the British pound. Give a rough estimate of your loss in British pounds.

SOLUTION

The dollar price of the bond should drop by

$$\frac{\Delta P}{P} = -D \times \Delta r = -10 \times 0.05\% = -0.5\%$$

On top of that, there will be a currency loss of 1 percent. So, the total loss in pounds is approximately equal to 1.5 percent.

Currency-Hedging Strategies

Foreign investments can be hedged against currency risk by selling forward currency contracts for an amount equal to the capital invested. Short-term forward contracts, typically up to a few months in maturity, are available for currency hedging. So, the currency hedge is periodically rolled over. By arbitrage (see Chapter 1), the percentage difference (discount or premium) of the forward rate with the current spot rate is equal to the interest rate differential between the two currencies. This is the differential between the two cash rates for the contract maturity. Hence, the return on the hedged bond will be

$$\textit{Hedged return} = \textit{Foreign yield} - D \times (\Delta \textit{foreign yield})$$
$$+ \textit{Domestic cash rate} - \textit{Foreign cash rate} \qquad (7.16)$$

So, the expected hedged return is simply equal to the investor's risk-free rate, the domestic cash rate, plus a risk premium equal to the sum of

- the spread of the foreign bond yield over the foreign cash rate, and

- the percentage gain/loss due to an expected foreign yield movement.

EXAMPLE 7.9   HEDGED RETURN ON A FOREIGN BOND

You are British and hold a U.S. Treasury bond with a full price of 100 and duration of 10. Its yield is 5 percent. The dollar cash rate is 2 percent, and the pound cash rate is 3 percent. You expect U.S. yields to move up by 10 basis points over the year. Give a rough estimate of your expected return if you decide to hedge the currency risk.

SOLUTION

The expected return on the year is equal to the U.S. dollar expected return plus the cash rate differential:

Expected return = 5% − (10 × 0.1) + 3% − 2% = 5%

The risk premium in pounds is equal to this expected return minus the British cash rate, or 5% − 3% = 2%. It is also equal to the risk premium on the same U.S. Treasury bond for a U.S. investor: expected return of 4 percent in dollars minus the U.S. cash rate of 2 percent. Hedging improves the expected return if you expect the dollar to appreciate by less than 1 percent. It also eliminates currency risk.

Note that this risk premium is exactly the same for a local (foreign) investor in that foreign bond. A local investor would use the foreign cash rate as risk-free rate, but the risk premium stated in Equation 7.12 would be identical. The foreign bond risk premium is just transferred domestically, and currency risk does not play a direct role anymore.

The decision to hedge depends on return and risk considerations. Hedging will turn out to improve return on a foreign bond if the percentage currency movement is less than the cash rate differential (domestic minus foreign); otherwise, hedging will not be advantageous *ex post*. In other words, if you expect the foreign exchange rate to move below the forward exchange rate, you should hedge; otherwise, you should not hedge. Hedging reduces currency risk, but interest and currency movements are somewhat correlated.

International Portfolio Strategies

Active management of international and global bond portfolios requires both a good technical knowledge of the various domestic and Eurobond markets and some ability to forecast interest rates and currencies. The *neutral*, or *normal*, position is dictated by the benchmark chosen for the portfolio. Assuming no forecasting ability, the portfolio will follow the benchmark weights in the major currencies and market segments; deviations from these weights are induced by specific forecasts.

International bond portfolio management includes several steps:

- Benchmark selection

- Bond market selection

- Sector selection/credit selection

- Currency management

- Duration/yield curve management

- Yield enhancement techniques

The choice of a benchmark is often imposed in the mandate set by the client, and it will clearly guide the structure of the portfolio.

Benchmark Selection　　The benchmark used is some bond index. The benchmark for bonds is open to more discussion than for equity. It depends in part on the investment objective; for example, do we want a global bond portfolio or an international one (e.g., ex-U.S. for a U.S. investor)? But even the logic of using market capitalization weights is open to debate. For equity, market cap weights represent the relative economic importance of corporations throughout the world. For bonds, market cap weights are influenced by the relative national budget deficits. For example, a country with chronic large budget deficits will see its government bonds have a relatively large weight in a global bond index. Do investors want to follow an investment policy favoring lax budget policy? Other questions influence the choice of benchmark:

- What types of issuers should be included? If corporates are included, do we put a threshold on their credit quality (e.g., no junk bonds)? Should we include debt from emerging countries? In other words, do we use a broad index or a narrow one?

- Do we include all countries/currencies, or do we restrict the benchmark to major ones (e.g., G7 countries)?

- Do we allow all maturities, or do we constrain the maturity of bonds included (e.g., only bonds with a long maturity)?

- Is the benchmark unhedged against currency risk, or is it hedged?

Benchmarks selected are usually some of the widely accepted bond indexes discussed. But index providers can also calculate "customized" or "normal" portfolios, as defined by a money manager or a specific client.

Bond Market Selection　　Managers will differ from national benchmark weights, and over- or underweight some markets based on interest rate and currency forecasts. More than for common stocks, the observation that all bonds issued in a given currency behave similarly tends to justify a top-down market/currency approach. For an international investor, the major differences in performance are caused by the selection of currency markets. All fixed-interest bond prices are influenced by changes in interest rates in the respective currencies, as well as the translation in the domestic currency. For example, the dollar performance of all British government bonds is influenced primarily by two factors: movements in British interest rates and movements in the pound/dollar exchange rate. In comparison, the difference in performance within a market segment is relatively small. When investing in international bonds, the volatility of the foreign exchange is often larger than the volatility of the bond market, measured in local currency. This has been observed repeatedly in empirical studies.

Hence, the overweighting of a market is both a bet on changes in local market yields and a bet on the currency. Such a decision must be based on sound economic analysis. Among economic fundamentals that bond managers follow for each country, one can cite the following:

- Monetary and fiscal policy

- Public spending

- Current and forecasted public indebtedness
- Inflationary pressures
- Balance of payments
- International comparison of the real yields
- National productivity and competitiveness
- Cyclical factors
- Political factors

Sector Selection/Credit Selection   In many countries and currencies, governments used to be the main issuers. Now, banks and corporations are increasingly borrowing on the bond markets. Within a given currency market (e.g., bonds issued in euros), there are also different segments grouping bonds issued by different types of issuers. Prices on different segments of the same currency market are not fully correlated. Besides the yield curve on government securities, different additional factors affect prices on each segment. The yields on each segment reflect a quality spread over government bonds. The quality spread is influenced by credit risk, liquidity, and possibly some specific institutional and tax aspects. Hence, bond managers tend to over or under weight some segments based on their forecast of these factors. Commonly used segments within a currency market are the following:

- Government securities
- Regional states and municipalities bonds
- Mortgage-backed and public-loan-backed bonds (e.g., the huge German *Pfandbrief* market)
- Investment-grade corporates
- Junk bonds
- Inflation indexed bonds
- Emerging-country debt

Currency Management   For default-free bonds, there are two main sources of unanticipated excess return: currency and duration-adjusted interest rate movements. The volatility of exchange rates tends to be higher than that of bond prices, so currency management is an important component of active global bond management. Exhibit 7.8 gives the volatility of major bond markets measured in U.S. dollar, in euro, and in local currency. For example, the British bond market has a volatility (annual standard deviation of returns) of 5.4 percent in pounds and 9.3 percent in dollars. The higher volatility for a U.S. investor stems from currency risk.

When investing in international bonds, the choice of a market often also implies the choice of a currency. If the manager forecasts a depreciation of a foreign currency, she can reduce the currency exposure by reducing the weight of that

EXHIBIT 7.8

Volatility of Bond Markets Measured in Local Currency, in U.S. Dollar, and in Euro *In % per year, January 1992–January 2002, Effas/Bloomberg Indexes*			
Bond Market	**In Local Currency**	**In Dollar**	**In Euro**
United States	4.8	4.8	10.6
Germany	3.7	10.4	3.7
United Kingdom	5.4	9.3	9.3
Japan	4.2	12.9	12.5

market relative to benchmark weights. Alternatively, the manager can retain the same market exposure and hedge the currency risk using forward contracts. Currency management requires a good understanding of the previously developed break-even analysis.

Duration/Yield Curve Management   In each currency market, the manager can adjust the duration of the portfolio according to a forecast about changes in the level of interest rates and deformations in the yield curve. The average duration in each market and segment provides an estimate of the portfolio's sensitivity to yield movements. If an increase in yields is expected in one market segment, the manager can trade bonds to reduce the duration of this segment. Another alternative is to retain the same bonds but to reduce the interest rate exposure through various derivatives, such as interest rate futures or swaps.

Yield Enhancement Techniques   Numerous techniques are proposed to add value to the performance of the basic strategy. Some specialized trading techniques are used to provide incremental returns with very little risk (e.g., securities lending). These techniques evolve over time and are too specialized to be described here.

Valuation techniques are used to detect the cheapest bonds to buy (undervalued) when the portfolio has to be rebalanced. Spread analysis is often used to assess the relative value of two securities with fairly similar characteristics. This spread analysis can even lead to an arbitrage between two bonds. The idea is very simple. Two bonds with close characteristics should trade at very similar prices and YTM. Each day, a manager computes the spread between the two bond prices and plots them. Because of market inefficiencies, the spread is likely to be high above (or below) its average, or "normal," value at some point in time. This is the time to arbitrage one bond against the other. This spread analysis is conducted in terms of YTM rather than in terms of prices. Other bond portfolio management techniques are more complex and involve instruments such as futures, swaps, or option contracts.

A typical way to enhance return on a bond portfolio is to add securities with higher promised yield, because of the borrower's credit risk. Investors can also obtain higher yields by investing in emerging-country bonds, for which the credit risk stems from the risk that a country will default on its debt servicing. Managers must be aware that the higher yield is a compensation for the risk of default. If this risk materializes, the realized yield on the bond investment can be very bad.

Other bonds have been designed as fairly complicated securities with uncertain cash flows, which offer some plays on interest rate, currencies, or other variables. Some of these more complicated bonds, often called "structured notes," are presented in the next section.

To summarize, the investment strategy is based on forecasted scenarios for interest rates, currencies, and quality spreads. Note that exchange rate movements are correlated, to some extent, with interest rate changes so that the two forecasts are not independent. Given the current portfolio, managers can simulate the effect of a scenario on the value of the portfolio. This simulation also suggests which securities to sell and buy, given the forecasted scenario. The three basic inputs are

- changes in the default-free yield curve for each currency,
- changes in quality spreads (e.g., changes in the spread between the domestic and Eurobond segments), and
- changes in exchange rates.

Yield enhancement techniques can help individual security selection.

Floating-Rate Notes and Structured Notes

Investment bankers bring domestic expertise from around the world to bear on the international market, and that is why the international market boasts so many sophisticated techniques. This sophistication is evident in the incredible diversity of bonds issued. We will start with plain-vanilla floating-rate notes (FRNs), which are an important segment of the Eurobond market, in euros, dollars, or pounds. We will then study some exotic bonds, involving some currency play, which have been frequently issued. They often take the form of a structured note. A *structured note* is a bond (note) issued with some unusual clause, often an option-like clause. These notes are bonds issued by a name of good credit standing and can therefore be purchased as investment-grade bonds by most institutional investors, even those that are prevented by regulations from dealing in options or futures. Another attraction for investors is that these structured notes offer some long-term options that are not publicly traded. Structured notes are designed for those specific investors wishing to take a bet on some forecasts such as interest rates and currencies. If their forecasts are correct, the yield on the note will be enhanced. In turn, the issuer seems to be basically taking the opposite bet. However, the bank structuring the note proposes to the issuer a hedging structure that will eliminate this risk. The idea is that the issuer should end up, after hedging, with a plain-vanilla bond (with fixed or floating-rate coupons) but at a total cost that is less than the prevailing market conditions for those bonds. To determine the "fair" price of the structured note, the investment bank constructs a replication portfolio using elementary securities (such as plain-vanilla FRNs, straight bonds, swaps, and options). The structured note can be issued at better conditions for the issuer, because it satisfies the needs of some investors. To summarize, structured notes are often used by institutional investors as a vehicle to make a bet within an investment-grade bond structure. On the other side, the issuer will hedge the bet and will end up with a plain-vanilla bond at a reduced all-in cost of funds because investors are willing to accept a lower yield to be able to bet.

Some structured notes offer interest rate plays (see discussion of *Bull* and *Bear* bonds that follows). Others offer currency play (see discussion of *dual-currency* bonds and *currency-option* that follows). Other structured notes offer a play on some other variables, such as equity or commodity prices. The list of bonds covered in this chapter is not exhaustive; some of them are discussed in the Problems section and on the web site at www.awlonline.com/solnik. For example, inflation-linked bonds can be found in many countries (e.g. the U.S., the U.K., and France). The coupons and principal of these bonds are indexed to the local inflation index (usually the local CPI). For example, U.S. treasury inflation protected securities (TIPS) pay a real yield fixed at time of issue. The principal value is adjusted for CPI on each semiannual coupon payment. So the nominal coupon, equal to the real yield times the CPI-adjusted principal, increases with inflation. At maturity, the CPI-adjusted principal is reimbursed. Inflation-linked bonds attract institutional investors wishing to get a risk-free yield to hedge their liabilities. As these bonds are mostly used by domestic investors to hedge their local-inflation risk, we will not detail them here. Many other types of complex bonds are periodically created.

Floating-Rate Notes (FRNs)

FRNs, or *floaters,* are a very active segment of the Eurobond market. This is explained by the fact that the interbank short-term lending/borrowing market, or *LIBOR* market, is primarily an international market, not a domestic market, even for the U.S. dollar. Because banks lend and borrow short term at a cost closely linked to LIBOR, it is natural that they use the international Eurobond market when they issue long-term bonds with a coupon indexed on LIBOR. FRNs represent a quarter of all Eurobonds, with issues in euros and dollars playing a dominant role. Major issuers are financial institutions.

Description　The clauses used in interest rate indexation are diverse, but plain-vanilla FRNs tend to dominate. FRNs are generally indexed to the London interbank offered rate (LIBOR), which is the short-term deposit rate on Eurocurrencies. This rate is called *EURIBOR,* for euros. The coupon on Eurobond FRNs is generally reset every semester or every quarter. The maturity of the LIBOR chosen as index usually matches the coupon period; for example, FRNs with semiannual coupons are indexed on the six-month LIBOR. The coupon to be paid is determined on the *reset date,* which usually coincides with the previous coupon date. On the reset date, the value of the index (say, the six-month LIBOR) is determined by looking at the quotations of a panel of major banks. The coupon to be paid the next period is then set equal to the LIBOR plus a spread that has been fixed at the time of issue. In other words, the coupon, C_t, that will be paid at time t is set at time $t - 1$ (the previous coupon date) equal to the LIBOR rate, i_{t-1}, plus a fixed spread, m_0:

$$C_t = i_{t-1} + m_0 \qquad (7.17)$$

All rates are annualized and quoted in percent. The spread is fixed when the bond is issued and generally remains fixed for the maturity of the bond. For top-quality issuers, the spread is very small, because some of them, such as banks, can easily borrow in the Eurocurrency short-term deposit market at LIBOR. LIBOR is already a short-term rate quoted for top-quality corporate borrowers; it is not a government rate such as the Treasury Bill rate. Some FRNs are issued with various mismatches that deviate from the plain-vanilla FRNs described earlier.

Motivation FRN prices behave quite differently from fixed-interest straight bond prices, which adjust to fluctuations in the market interest rate. The price of a straight bond must go down if the market interest rate goes up, in order to maintain a competitive YTM. By contrast, floaters have coupons that adjust to interest rates, so the coupons react to interest rate movements rather than the bond price. This means that FRNs exhibit great price stability when compared with straight bonds.

The motivation for an investor to buy FRNs is to avoid interest rate risk that could lead to a capital loss in case of a rise in interest rates. Investors have a long-term investment with little interest rate risk.

FRNs are generally issued by financial institutions with short-term lending activities. These institutions wish to have long-term resources but want to index the cost of their funds to their revenues. Because revenues on short-term loans are indexed on LIBOR, FRNs achieve this objective.

Valuing FRNs: No Default Risk From a theoretical viewpoint, we may ask why there is any price variability at all on floating-rate bonds. It turns out that there are several major reasons for this price variability. To study the pricing of FRNs, it is useful to look first at the case in which the borrower carries no default risk.

On Reset Date FRN coupons are periodically reset, or rolled over. The rollover may be annual, semiannual, or quarterly. This means that the coupon is fixed at the reset, or rollover, date for the coming period. The first question is to determine the theoretical price of the bond on the reset date, when the previous coupon has just been paid and the new coupon has just been fixed for the coming period. To disentangle the effects, it is useful to start the analysis by assuming that the borrower has, and will have, no default risk and that the index has been chosen as the relevant short-term interest rate for that borrower.[6] For example, assume that an FRN with annual reset[7] is issued by a major bank, which has to pay exactly LIBOR without any spread, in the absence of default risk:

$$C_t = i_{t-1}$$

Remember that all rates and prices are quoted in percent. Under this assumption of no default risk, we can show that the price of the bond should always be 100 percent on reset dates. The argument is recursive. There is a future date when we know the exact value of the bond: This is at maturity T. Right after the last coupon payment,

---

[6] To be precise, the assumption is that it is certain that the bank will retain its AAA credit rating forever and will therefore always be able to borrow at LIBOR.

[7] There is an annual coupon set at one-year LIBOR.

the bond will be reimbursed at 100 percent. Let's now move to the previous reset date $T - 1$. We know that the bond contract stipulates that the coupon C_T will be set equal to the one-year LIBOR observed at time $T - 1$. Of course, we do not know today (time 0) what this rate will be at $T - 1$, but we know that it will be exactly equal, by contractual obligation, to the market rate for a one-year instrument. Hence, a bond with a maturity of one year paying the one-year interest rate must have a price equal to its principal value. This is confirmed by discounting at time $T - 1$, the future cash flow received at time T:

$$P_{T-1} = \frac{100\% + C_T}{1 + i_{T-1}} = \frac{1 + i_{T-1}}{1 + i_{T-1}} = 100\%$$

Hence, we now know that the price one period before maturity must be equal to 100. We can apply the same reasoning to the price of the bond at time $T - 2$ and so on, until time 0. We have therefore shown that the bond price must be equal to 100 at each reset date.

EXAMPLE 7.10   VALUING FRNS BETWEEN RESET DATES

A company without default risk has issued a 10-year FRN at LIBOR. The coupon is paid and reset semiannually. It is certain that the issuer will never have default risk and will always be able to borrow at LIBOR. The FRN is issued on November 1, 2005, when the six-month LIBOR is at 5 percent. On May 1, 2006, the six-month LIBOR is at 5.5 percent.

1. What is the coupon paid on May 1, 2006, per $1,000 bond?

2. What is the new value of the coupon set on the bond?

3. On May 2, 2006, the six-month LIBOR has dropped to 5.4 percent. What is the new value of the FRN?

SOLUTION

1. The coupon paid on May 1 was set on November 1 at 5 percent or $25 per $1,000 bond. Remember that rates are quoted on an annual basis, but apply here to a semester period.

2. The coupon to be paid on November 1, 2006, is set at $27.5.

3. Neglecting that one day has passed, we discount the known future value of the bond on November 1, 2006, at the new six-month LIBOR of 5.4 percent:

$$P = \frac{1,000 + 27.5}{(1 + (5.4/2)\%)} = 1,000.49$$

To be exact, we should discount with a LIBOR for six months minus one day. To derive the quoted price, we should subtract one day of accrued interest from the full price.

Between Reset Dates   There is no reason, however, for the price to stay constant between reset dates. Once the coupon is fixed on a reset date, the bond tends to behave like a short-term fixed-coupon bond until the next reset date. FRN prices are more volatile just after the reset date, because that is when they have the longest fixed-coupon maturity. FRNs with a semiannual reset tend to be more volatile than FRNs with quarterly reset dates, but both should have stable prices on reset dates. This is illustrated in Exhibit 7.9 for the clean price of a Midland Bank FRN with a semiannual reset and maturing in May 1987. Prices on reset appear as a dot in the illustration. The period is chosen because 1979–80 was a period of high and extremely volatile interest rates; nevertheless, the FRN price is very close to 100 on reset dates (shown with dots on the graph). Note that in December 1980, six-month LIBOR climbed suddenly from 15 percent to over 20 percent, just after the coupon on the bond had been reset. This induced a 2 percent drop in the bond price. By contrast, the prices on reset dates are very stable.

Practitioners usually consider that the interest sensitivity to movements in the index interest rate is simply equal to the duration to the next reset date. The price of the FRN between reset dates can be estimated by assuming that it is worth 100 plus the reset coupon at the next coupon date, discounting by the LIBOR rate with maturity equal to the next reset date.

In practice, issuers carry some default risk, and a spread over LIBOR is required by the market. This can explain why the prices on reset dates observed on Exhibit 7.9 are not exactly equal to 100.

Valuing FRNs: Default Risk   Let's now assume that the issuer carries some default risk, justifying a credit spread as shown in Equation 7.17. The problem is that the credit spread paid by the FRN, m_0, is set at issuance and remains fixed over the whole maturity of the bond. On the other hand, the credit quality of the issuer could fluctuate over time (e.g., a change in its credit rating), or the risk premium required by the market for this type of borrower could be changed. The market-required spread at time t, m_t, is likely to be different from that at time of issuance, m_0. The market-required spread changes with the perception of credit risk.

Two observations have repeatedly been made on the FRN market:

- FRNs with long maturities tend to sell at a discount relative to those with a short maturity.

- Long-term FRN prices are more volatile than are short-term FRN prices.

Changes in the spread required by the marketplace explain these two observations.

The *first observation* can be explained by the fact that the default-risk premium tends to increase with time to maturity. A 20-year loan to a corporation, rated A, seems more risky than a 3-month loan to the same corporation. The coupon spread on an FRN is fixed over the life of the bond, whereas the market-required spread, which reflects the default-risk premium, tends to decrease as the bond nears maturity. Hence, bond prices, at least on reset dates, should progressively increase. This is observed in Exhibit 7.9. Of course, there is a survival bias, because defaulted bonds disappear from the comparison.

EXHIBIT 7.9

FRNs: The Stability of Reset Date Prices
Midland Bank, May 1987

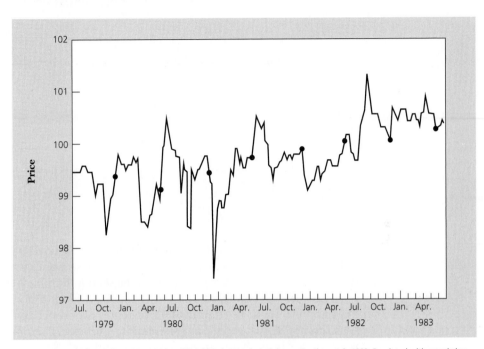

Source: J. Hanna and G. Pariente, *International Bond Market Analysis,* Salomon Brothers, July 1983. Reprinted with permission.

    The *second observation* can be explained by unexpected changes in the market-required spread. FRNs are "protected" against movements in LIBOR by their indexation clause, but they are sensitive to variations in the required spread, because they pay a spread that is fixed at issuance. Hence, the coupon of an FRN is not fully indexed to the market-required yield, because the interest rate component is indexed, but the spread is fixed over the life of the bond. The coupon paid is equal to LIBOR + m_0, while the market requires LIBOR + m_t. If the market-required spread changes over time, the FRN behaves partly like a fixed-coupon bond, precisely because of this feature. And we know that, technically, long-term bonds are more sensitive than are short-term bonds to changes in market yield. By contrast, short-term bonds are repaid sooner, and this drives their price close to par.

    This price volatility, induced by the fixity of the spread, is illustrated in Exhibit 7.10 for the price of a Midland Bank perpetual FRN, with semiannual reset at LIBOR plus 0.25 percent (a spread of 25 basis points). The price remained relatively stable until 1987, when an international debt crisis threatened the international financial system. Investors became afraid that banks had made too many bad loans, especially to many emerging countries, which stopped servicing their debts.

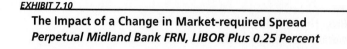

EXHIBIT 7.10

The Impact of a Change in Market-required Spread
Perpetual Midland Bank FRN, LIBOR Plus 0.25 Percent

Lenders shied away from the long-term debts of banks. The required spread for holding FRNs issued by banks increased by 100 basis points within a few weeks. This led to a huge drop in FRN prices, as can be seen in Exhibit 7.10.

FRNs cannot be valued as if they were fixed-coupon bonds. Their future cash flows are uncertain, because LIBOR fluctuates over time, and these uncertain cash flows cannot be discounted at risk-free interest rates. The modeling of default risk is a complex issue that requires many assumptions.[8] Nevertheless, practitioners often try to get an estimation of the impact of a change in spread on the FRN value by resorting to some approximate method. For example, they assume that LIBOR will remain at its current value until maturity ("freezing"). So, they discount the forecasted future cash flows, equal to a "frozen" LIBOR plus the original spread, m_0, at a discount rate equal to the "frozen" LIBOR plus the current market-required spread, m_t. A variant of this approach is to use forward LIBOR rates implied by the LIBOR yield curve, rather than the current LIBOR.

EXAMPLE 7.11   ESTIMATING THE VALUE OF A FRN WHEN THE REQUIRED SPREAD CHANGES

A perpetual bond is issued by a corporation rated A with an annual coupon set at yearly LIBOR plus a spread of 0.25 percent. Some time later, LIBOR is equal to 5 percent, and the market requires a spread of 0.5 percent for such an A corporation. Give an estimate of the bond value on the reset date using the "freezing" method.

---

[8] See a credit risk analysis in Sundaresan (1997), Duffee (1999), Duffie and Singleton (1999), and Collin-Dufresne, Goldstein, and Martin (2001).

SOLUTION

A perpetual bond pays a coupon forever. If the coupon were fixed at C, the bond could be valued as an annuity. The value of such an annuity, assuming a market-required yield of r, is given by

$$P = \sum_{t=1}^{\infty} \frac{C}{(1 + r)^t} = \frac{C}{r}$$

where C is the coupon rate and r is the current market-required rate.
    With the "freezing" method,

- the coupon is supposed to be fixed at $C = 5\% + 0.25\%$, and

- the market-required yield is supposed to be fixed at $r = 5\% + 0.5\%$.

Hence, an approximation of the value of this perpetual FRN is given by

$$P = \frac{5.25}{5.5} = 95.4545\%$$

We now turn to some structured notes involving interest rate or currency plays.

Bull FRN

Description   *Bull FRNs* are bonds that strongly benefit investors if interest rates drop. A typical example is a *reverse* (*inverse*) *floater,* whereby the coupon is set at a fixed rate minus LIBOR. Consider a five-year dollar FRN with a semiannual coupon set at 14 percent minus LIBOR. The coupon cannot be negative, so it has a minimum of 0 percent, which is attractive to investors if LIBOR moves over 14 percent.[9] At the time, the yield curve was around 7%.

Motivation   Let's consider an investor wishing to benefit markedly from a drop in market interest rates ("bullish" on interest rates). He can buy a bull bond. For a straight FRN, the coupon decreases if market interest rates drop and the bond price remains stable. For a straight (fixed-coupon) bond, the coupon remains fixed if market interest rates drop and the bond price increases, so this is an attractive investment. For a bull bond, the coupon increases if interest rates drop, and hence the bond price rises by much more than for a straight bond with fixed coupon, which is very attractive. The properties of various bonds are reproduced in Exhibit 7.11.

---

[9] In effect, the bull FRN includes a coupon of 14 percent minus LIBOR, as well as a 14 percent cap option on LIBOR (14 percent is the strike price of the cap; see the description of caps in Chapter 10). A cap option pays the difference between LIBOR and the strike of 14 percent, if LIBOR is above 14 percent on a coupon payment date. If LIBOR goes above 14 percent, this cap is activated and offsets the potentially negative coupon.

EXHIBIT 7.11

Characteristics of Bonds, Assuming a Drop in Market Interest Rates				
	Straight Bond	**Straight FRN**	**Bull FRN**	**Bear FRN**
Coupon	$\rightarrow$	$\downarrow$	$\uparrow$	$\downarrow\downarrow$
Price	$\uparrow$	$\rightarrow$	$\uparrow\uparrow$	$\downarrow$

Valuation   We have seen that straight bonds and FRNs proceed from two different pricing philosophies. So, it is useful to separate the cash flows of a bull bond in two different sets that can be easily priced.

The bull bond could be seen by investors as the sum of three plain-vanilla securities:

- two straight bonds with a 7 percent coupon,

- a short position in a plain-vanilla FRN at LIBOR flat, and

- a 14 percent cap option on LIBOR.

The reader can verify that the cash flows of this replicating portfolio exactly match those of the bull bond, including at time of redemption. It is straightforward to price the three plain-vanilla securities using quoted prices.

The issuer of a bull FRN seldom desires to retain such a coupon structure, but prefers to issue a straight fixed-coupon obligation or a plain-vanilla FRN. In turn, the issuer can hedge and transform this bull bond into a straight fixed-coupon bond by using interest rate swaps. For example, the bull FRN could be transformed into a fixed-coupon obligation by swapping for the face value of the bull FRN to pay floating and receive fixed.[10]

Of course, more volatile bull bonds can be created by introducing a higher multiple. For example, one could create a bond with a coupon set at 28% − 3 × LIBOR. This bull bond would be equivalent to four straight bonds at 7 percent minus three FRNs at LIBOR flat (plus three caps with a strike of 9.33 percent).

Bear FRN

Description   *Bear FRNs* are notes that benefit investors if interest rates rise. Plain-vanilla straight bonds or FRNs do not have that property. An example of a bear bond is a note with a coupon set at twice LIBOR minus 7 percent. Again, the coupon has a floor of 0 percent, which is attractive to the investor if LIBOR goes below 3.5 percent.

Motivation   The coupon of the bear bond will increase rapidly with a rise in LIBOR. We know that the price of a plain-vanilla FRN is stable, because its coupon increases parallel to LIBOR. So, the price of a bear bond will rise, because its coupon increases twice as fast as LIBOR.

---

[10] In addition, the issuer should buy a 14 percent cap option, but its cost is likely to be minimal, because the strike price of 14 percent is well above the current interest rate of 7 percent.

Valuation   Such a bond could be replicated by the investor as a portfolio long two plain-vanilla FRNs and short one straight bond with a coupon of 7 percent.[11]

Because the value of the plain-vanilla FRNs should stay at par on reset dates, even if LIBOR moves, the net result is that the portfolio should appreciate if market interest rates rise. In summary, this bear note could be seen by investors as the sum of

- two plain-vanilla FRNs at LIBOR flat,

- a short position in a straight bond (with a coupon of 7 percent), and

- two 3.5 percent floor options on LIBOR.

In turn, the issuer can hedge and transform this bear FRN into a plain-vanilla FRN by simultaneously entering into an interest rate swap to pay fixed and receive floating.[12]

Again, more volatile bear bonds can be created by increasing the multiple. For example, a bear bond could be issued with a coupon set at $4 \times \text{LIBOR} - 21\%$. This bear bond is equivalent to four FRNs at LIBOR flat minus three straight bonds at 7 percent (plus four floors with a strike price of 5.25 percent).

Dual-Currency Bonds

Description   A *dual-currency bond* is a bond issued with coupons in one currency and principal redemption in another. Exhibit 7.3 gave the tombstone of such a yen/dollar Eurobond. NKK, a Japanese corporation, issued a 10-year bond for 20 billion yen. During 10 years, it pays an annual coupon of 8 percent in yen, or 1.6 billion yen. Ten years later, it is redeemed in U.S. dollars for a total of 110,480,000 dollars. The redemption amount in dollars is set so that it is exactly equal to the issue amount using the spot exchange rate prevailing at time of issue, $S_0 = 181.02824$ yen per dollar. Based on historical accounting costs, the bond is thus reimbursed at par.

The fact that the bond is originally subscribed in yen, or dollars, or any other currency has no importance. A spot exchange rate transaction can be performed instantaneously at very little cost. What is important is that NKK takes on a series of future obligations in yen (coupons) and in dollars (redemption value). It is a dual-currency bond because future obligations are in two different currencies. Note that there is no option involved in dual-currency bonds, because all of their terms are fixed at issue.

Motivation   The motivation for all borrowers to issue any of these fancy bonds is to be able to end up borrowing money in their desired currency but at a lower cost than directly issuing straight bonds in that currency. For example NKK

---

[11] Furthermore, the investor gets two floor options with a strike price of 3.5 percent.

[12] The issuer should also buy two 3.5 percent floor options from the bank.

could swap,[13] at time of issue, the final bullet dollar payment to take place in 10 years into yen. Although, having to pay some 110 million dollars seems to carry a lot of currency risk for a Japanese issuer, it can be easily transformed into a pure yen liability. This can be done by selling forward, swapping, the redemption value of 110 million dollars for yen at a known 10-year forward exchange rate. Borrowers are not only Japanese corporations, but also non-Japanese entities, such as the U.S. Federal National Mortgage Association (Fannie Mae). Such U.S. issuers simply swap (or hedge on the forward exchange market), at time of issue, the stream of yen coupon payments for a stream of dollar coupon payments, ending up with a pure dollar liability. This type of bond will be attractive if the U.S. company ends up borrowing dollars at a cheaper rate than by issuing directly a U.S. dollar bond.

In the 1990s, many Swiss franc/U.S. dollar dual-currency bonds were issued at a time when Swiss franc yields were low and well below those on dollar bonds. These bonds were issued mostly by non-Swiss corporations.

The motivation of investors to buy these dual-currency bonds relies on institutional features and/or market conditions. We will illustrate those on the previously detailed NKK bond:

- Local investors (e.g., Japanese) are, in part, attracted to the issues by the opportunity for limited currency speculation, only on the principal, that they provided. Those who invested were betting on an appreciation of the dollar. This is a minor motivation, because it can easily be replicated by holding a portfolio of straight bonds issued in the two currencies.

- An institutional feature provided additional motivation, in the case of Japanese institutional investors. These bonds are attractive to Japanese investors because they are considered yen bonds for regulatory purposes, although they are dollar-linked. They allow institutional investors to increase the amount of fixed-income investments in higher yield currencies.

- On dual-currency bonds, the coupon is paid in a currency for which interest rates are low (e.g., yen or Swiss francs)[14] and reimbursed in a currency (dollar) with high interest rates. As we will see in the pricing section, dual-currency is a technique that allows investors to receive a higher coupon than would be received on a straight bond in that currency (e.g., yen). So, local investors (e.g., Japanese) are attracted to this type of bond because it announces a high coupon rate in that currency (e.g., yen). This is a major motivation for local retail or institutional investors looking for income.

The bond can be issued at attractive conditions to the issuer (below fair price) because it satisfies the need of a category of investors outlined previously. Issuers often do not wish to carry the currency risk implicit in those bonds. In the NKK example, the bank organizing the issue can offer the Japanese issuer the opportunity to swap the dollar exposure back into yen.

---

[13] A description of swaps is provided in Chapter 10.

[14] Of course, the yield curves in various currencies change over time, reducing or enhancing the attraction to use some currency pairs to construct those bonds.

Valuation   The value of a yen/dollar dual-currency bond can be broken down into two parts as follows:

- A stream of fixed coupon payments in yen: The current value of this stream of cash flow is obtained by *discounting at the yen yield curve.*

- A dollar zero-coupon bond for the final dollar principal repayment: The current value of this single cash flow is obtained by *discounting at the dollar yield* of the appropriate maturity.

Given the yield curve in the two currencies, this is a trivial valuation exercise, because there is no optional clause involved. Let's decide to value the dual-currency bond in yen. It is the sum of the present value of a yen bond corresponding to the stream of coupons and the present value of a zero-coupon dollar bond corresponding to the principal redemption. This latter dollar value can be transformed into yen at the current spot exchange rate.

A dual-currency bond is typically issued in two currencies with very different yield levels. The valuation formula ensures that the fair coupon rate on the dual-currency bond is set in between the two yield levels. For example, the NKK dual-currency bond pays an 8 percent coupon, while the yield on straight yen bonds is much lower. This is attractive to Japanese investors.

EXAMPLE 7.12   VALUING A DUAL-CURRENCY BOND

Let's consider the NKK bond described in Exhibit 7.3. It promises annual coupons of 8 percent on 20 billion yen and is redeemed in 10 years for $110.480 million. The current spot exchange rate is ¥181.02824 per dollar, so that $110.480 million is exactly equal to ¥20 billion. The yen yield curve is flat at 4 percent, and the dollar yield curve is flat at 12 percent.

a. What is the theoretical value of this dual-currency bond?

b. If the coupon on the bond was set at fair market conditions, what should be its exact value? (A bond is issued at fair market conditions if its coupon is set such that the issue price is equal to its theoretical market value).

SOLUTION

a. The NKK bond can be valued as the sum of a stream of yen cash flows and a zero-coupon dollar bond. The present value of this dollar zero-coupon bond is then translated into yen at the current spot exchange rate. The total market value in billion yen is V:

$$V = \frac{1.6}{(1.04)} + \frac{1.6}{(1.04)^2} + \ldots + \frac{1.6}{(1.04)^{10}}$$

$$+ \ 181.02824 \times \frac{\$110.48 \ million}{(1.12)^{10}} = ¥19.4169 \ billion$$

An alternative approach to derive the present value of the final dollar cash flow would be to first convert the dollar redemption value at the forward exchange rate, F, quoted today for a maturity of 10 years. This would yield a fixed amount of yen in 10 years. This amount would be discounted at the yen interest rate:

$$V = \frac{1.6}{(1.04)} + \frac{1.6}{(1.04)^2} + \ldots \frac{1.6}{(1.04)^{10}} + F \times \frac{\$110.48 \; million}{(1.04)^{10}}$$

The two alternatives would yield the same result if $F = S \times (1.04/1.12)^{10}$, which is indeed the theoretical value of the forward exchange rate.

The percentage price is obtained by dividing by the issue amount of 20 billion, obtaining a price, P, of 97.0845 percent.

$$P = \frac{8\%}{(1.04)} + \frac{8\%}{(1.04)^2} + \ldots + \frac{8\%}{(1.04)^{10}} + \frac{100\%}{(1.12)^{10}} = 97.0845\%$$

The bond has been issued below its fair value.

b. To be issued at fair market conditions, the coupon rate should have been set at x percent, such that

$$100\% = \frac{x\%}{(1.04)} + \frac{x\%}{(1.04)^2} + \ldots + \frac{x\%}{(1.04)^{10}} + \frac{100\%}{(1.12)^{10}}$$

or $x = 8.36\%$. This rate is in between the yen and dollar yields on straight bonds.

The dual-currency bond is attractive to some Japanese investors because it pays coupons in yen but has a large yield of 8 percent (compared with 4 percent for straight yen bonds). These investors are willing to buy this dual-currency bond below fair value.

At time of issue, investment bankers have to decide the fair coupon rate to set on this dual-currency bond, given current market conditions. Because, such bonds are particularly attractive to some categories of investors (see previous section), these investors are willing to subscribe to the bonds at conditions (coupon rate) that are below fair market conditions. This is typical of all of these complex bonds.

Currency-Option Bonds

Description   A *currency-option bond* is one for which the coupons and/or the principal can be paid in two or more currencies, as chosen by the bondholder. For example, a British company issues a five-year pound/euro bond. Each bond is issued at

£100 and is repaid £100 or €160. The annual coupon is £3, or €4.8. This particular option gives the bondholder the right to receive principal and interest payments in either pounds or euros, whichever is more advantageous to the investor. Both the coupon rate and the euro/pound exchange rate are fixed during the life of the bond. The exchange rate of 1.6 euros for a British pound was the market exchange rate at the time of issue. So, this currency-option bond is referred to as a 3 percent (the coupon rate) euro/pound bond. If the euro/pound exchange rate drops in future years (the pound depreciates), investors will naturally prefer to receive their interest payments in euros at that time. For example, if the pound depreciates to 1.2 euros, it is much more attractive to receive a coupon of €4.8 than £3. The €4.8 coupon is then equivalent to 4.8/1.2 = £4. If the same exchange rate holds at maturity, bondholders will ask to be reimbursed €160, which is equivalent to £133.33.

A currency-option bond benefits the investor who can always select the stronger currency. On the other hand, the interest rate set at issue is always lower than the yields paid on single-currency straight bonds denominated in *either* currency.[15] For example, the British company should have paid approximately 5 percent on a straight pound bond and 6 percent on a straight Eurobond. It should be obvious that the currency option bond must be issued at a coupon below the lowest of the two yields if the option clause is to be of any value. For example, suppose for a moment that the coupon on the currency-option bond were set at 5.5 percent. The currency-option bond, then, is always better than a straight pound bond paying 5 percent, because the bondholder can elect to always receive payments in pounds. Furthermore, the currency-option bond gives the option to receive payments in euros if the pound depreciates. Having a yield above that on straight bonds in pounds would be too good to be true.

Motivation   Investors select currency-option bonds because they offer a long-term currency play with limited risk. Retail investors can directly buy currency options on some options markets, but the maturity of these options is generally limited to a few months. Institutional investors are often prohibited from directly buying derivatives. On the other hand, currency-option bonds are usually issued by good-quality issuers and are therefore available to institutional investors who are attracted by the implicit currency play. Investors are willing to receive a lower yield in order to get the currency play.

Issuers pay a lower yield than on straight bonds but run currency risk. They might not wish to retain the currency exposure. For example, the British company might wish to issue a straight pound bond. The bank organizing the issue will then sell to the issuer a long-term currency option to exactly offset the currency exposure. If the sum of the low coupon paid on the currency-option bond and the cost of the option purchased from the bank is less than the coupon rate on a straight bond, the currency-option bond is an attractive low-cost alternative to a straight bond. As

---

[15] A call redemption clause usually protects the issuer against a large movement in one of the currencies.

with any complex bond, this alternative can only be made possible if a particular category of investors is attracted by the special features of the bond that they cannot access directly.

Valuation The value of such a currency-option bond can be broken down into two elements: the value of a straight 3 percent pound bond and the value of an option to swap a 3 percent pound bond for a 3 percent euro bond at a fixed exchange rate of 1.6 €/£. So, the value of this bond is the sum of the value of a

---

EXAMPLE 7.13 VALUING A CURRENCY-OPTION BOND

TATA issues a one-year euro/pound currency-option bond with a coupon rate of 3 percent. It is issued for £100, pays a coupon of either £3 or €4.8, and is redeemed for either £100 or €160, at the option of the bondholder. Of course, the bondholder will require payment in euros if the €/£ exchange rate is below 1.6 at maturity of the one-year bond. The current spot exchange rate is €1.6 per pound, and the one-year interest rates are 6 percent in euros and 5 percent in British pounds. A one-year put pound, with a strike price of 1.6 euros per pound, is quoted at £0.015. In other words, investors have to pay a premium of 0.015 pound to get the right to sell one pound at 1.6 euros.

a. What is the fair market value of this currency-option bond?

b. What should have been the fair coupon rate set on this currency-option bond according to market conditions? (A bond is issued at fair market conditions if its coupon is set such that the issue price is equal to its theoretical market value.)

SOLUTION

a. The currency-option bond can be replicated by a straight one-year pound bond redeemed at £100 with a 3 percent coupon plus an option to exchange £103 for €164.8. So, the value of this bond should be equal to the present value of a fixed £103 received in one year plus the value of the currency option:

$$V = \frac{103}{1.05} + 103 \times 0.015 = £99.64$$

The value of the bond is below par.

b. To be issued according to market conditions on the bond and options market, it should have been issued with a coupon rate of x percent, such that

$$\frac{100 \times (1 + x\%)}{1.05} + 100 \times (1 + x\%) \times 0.015 = £100$$

or $x = 3.37\%$

straight bond plus the value of currency options. Basically, the issuer is writing the currency options. Of course, the bond value could also be seen as the sum of a straight 3 percent bond in euros plus an option for a £/€ currency swap. The only difficulty in valuing such a bond is the theoretical valuation of the currency options.

Summary

- The global bond market comprises domestic bonds, foreign bonds, and Eurobonds.

- The Eurobond market is a dynamic international market without a physical market location.

- Debt from emerging countries can be purchased in many forms: domestic bonds issued in the emerging country, foreign bonds issued on a major bond market, Eurobonds, and Brady bonds.

- Bonds from emerging countries have often been restructured into Brady bonds to make them attractive to global investors.

- Bonds are quoted in the form of a clean price net of accrued interest. So, the full price (or value) of a bond is the sum of its clean price plus accrued interest. The day-count conventions to calculate accrued interest vary across markets and instruments.

- The yield curve based on zero-coupon government bonds is the central tool for valuing individual bonds in each currency.

- For each bond, it is common practice to report its yield to maturity (YTM), which is an average promised yield over the life of the bond. However, the convention used to calculate this YTM varies across markets. The simple yield used to be reported in Japan, and sometimes still is. Europeans tend to use an actuarial annual YTM, by discounting the bond cash flows at an annual rate. In the U.S., YTM is calculated by discounting the bond cash flows at a semiannual rate and multiplying the result by 2 to report an annualized rate.

- Practitioners usually define *interest rate sensitivity,* or *duration,* as the approximate percentage price change for a 100 basis points (1 percent) change in market yield. Duration provides a good approximation of the reaction of a bond price to small movements in market interest rates.

- The return on a domestic bond is the sum of the yield over the holding period plus any capital gain/loss caused by a movement in the market yield.

- The expected return on a domestic bond is the sum of the cash rate (the risk-free rate) plus a risk premium. This expected excess return, or risk premium, is the sum of the yield spread over the cash rate plus the duration-adjusted expected yield movement.

- Corporate bonds provide a yield equal to the yield on government bonds with similar duration plus a credit spread. This credit spread can be decomposed as the sum of an expected loss component, a credit-risk premium, and a liquidity premium.

- A multicurrency approach to bond management starts from a comparison of yield curves in each currency. Comparing the yield curves in two currencies allows one to calculate an implied forward exchange rate (or break-even exchange rate) between the two currencies. It is the future exchange rate that would make it equivalent, *ex post,* to invest in bonds of both currencies. The investor's forecast of future exchange rates has to be compared with this implied forward rate.

- The *return* from investing in a foreign bond has three components:
  - During the investment period, the bondholder receives the foreign yield.
  - A change in the foreign yield (Δ*foreign yield*) induces a percentage capital gain/loss on the price of the bond.
  - A currency movement induces a currency gain or loss on the position.

- The *risk* from investing in a foreign bond has two major components:
  - *Interest rate risk*: the risk that the foreign yield will rise
  - *Currency risk*: the risk that the foreign currency will depreciate

- The expected return on a foreign bond is equal to the domestic cash rate plus a risk premium. This risk premium equals the sum of
  - the spread of the foreign bond yield over the domestic cash rate,
  - the percentage capital gain/loss due to an expected foreign yield movement, and
  - the expected percentage currency movement.

- Currency hedging allows one to remove currency risk. The risk premium on a foreign bond hedged against currency risk is simply equal to its risk premium in its local currency.

- Global bond portfolio management includes several stages. First, a benchmark has to be chosen. Then, a bond manager tries to outperfom the benchmark by combining various strategies: bond market selection, sector selection/credit selection, currency management, duration/yield curve management, and yield enhancement techniques.

- Because currency is a major source of return and risk in global bond management, special attention should be devoted to the currency dimension.

- FRNs are a major segment of the Eurobond market. Their valuation proceeds from a logic that is quite different from that of straight fixed-rate bonds. In the absence of default risk, an FRN should be priced at par on the reset dates. In between reset dates, its value could fluctuate slightly in case of a movement in market interest rates, because the coupon is fixed until the next reset date. In the presence of default risk, the value of an FRN can move if the market-required credit spread becomes different from the spread that has been set at time of issue.

- Various complex bonds, often called "structured notes," are issued on the international market. A *structured note* is a bond (note) issued with some unusual clause, often an option-like clause. These notes are bonds issued by a name of good credit standing and can therefore be purchased as investment-grade bonds by most institutional investors, even those that are prevented by regulations from dealing in options or futures. Structured notes are designed for specific investors wishing to take a bet on some forecasts. If the forecasts are correct, the yield on the note will be enhanced.

- The issuer will usually hedge the unusual risks (bets) of a structured note and end up with a plain-vanilla bond at a low all-in cost.

- Some bonds offer plays on interest rates (bull and bear FRNs). Others offer play on currencies (dual-currency bond, currency-option bond).

Problems

1. Which of the following is the most appropriate term for the bonds issued in the United States by a European corporation and denominated in U.S. dollars?
   a. Domestic bonds
   b. Foreign bonds
   c. Eurobonds
   d. European bonds

2. Which of the following statements about the global bond market are true?
   I. Bonds issued in the United States by a non-U.S. corporation must satisfy the disclosure requirements of the U.S. Securities and Exchange Commission.
   II. Two bond indexes of the same market tend to be highly correlated, even if their composition is somewhat different.
   III. It is not necessary that a bond be denominated in euros for it to be termed a *Eurobond*.

3. An international bank had loaned money to an emerging country a few years ago. Because of the nonpayment of interest due on this loan, the bank is now negotiating with the borrower to exchange the loan for Brady bonds. The Brady bonds that would be issued would be either par bonds or discount bonds, with the same time to maturity.
   a. Would both types of bonds, par and discount, provide debt reduction to the emerging country?
   b. Would both types of bonds, par and discount, have a lower coupon amount than the original?
   c. Of the two types of bonds being considered, which one would have a lower coupon amount?

4. Consider a newly issued dollar/yen dual-currency bond. This bond is issued in yen. The coupons are paid in yen and the principal will be repaid in dollars. The market price of this bond is quoted in yen. Discuss what would happen to the market price of this dual-currency bond if the following happens:
   a. The market interest rate on yen bonds drops significantly.
   b. The dollar drops in value relative to the yen.
   c. The market interest rate on dollar bonds drops significantly.

5. A European corporation has issued bonds with a par value of SFr 1,000 and an annual coupon of 5 percent. The last coupon on these bonds was paid four months ago, and their current clean price is 90 percent.
   a. If these bonds are Eurobonds, what is their full price?
   b. Would your answer to part (a) be different if the bonds were not Eurobonds, but were issued in the Swiss domestic bond market?

6. a. Compute the yield to maturity (YTM) of a zero-coupon bond with nine years to maturity and currently selling at 45 percent.
   b. Compute the YTM of a perpetual bond with an annual coupon of €6 and currently selling at €108.

7. a. Consider a bond issued at par. The annual coupon is 8 percent and frequency of coupon is semiannual. How would the YTM of this bond be reported in most of the European markets?
   b. The market price of a two-year bond with annual coupon is 103 percent of its nominal value. The annual coupon to be paid in exactly one year is 6 percent. Compute its
      i. YTM (European way), and
      ii. YTM (U.S. way).

8. Bonds A and B are two straight yen-denominated Eurobonds, with the same maturity of four years and the same YTM of 9 percent. Bond A has an annual coupon of 11 percent and is accordingly priced at 106.48 percent. Bond B has an annual coupon of 7 percent and is accordingly priced at 93.52 percent.
   a. Compute the simple yield for each of these bonds, as reported sometimes by financial institutions in Japan.
   b. What does your answer to part (a) indicate about the potential biases in using the simple yield?

9. You hold a bond with nine years until maturity, a YTM of 4 percent, and a duration of 7.5. The cash (one-year) rate is 2.5 percent.
   a. In the next few minutes, you expect the market yield to go up by five basis points. What is the bond's expected percentage price change, and your expected return, over the next few minutes?
   b. Over the next year, you expect the market yield to go down by 30 basis points. For this period, estimate
      i. the bond's expected price change,
      ii. your expected return, and
      iii. the bond's risk premium.

10. a. Discuss the statement that it is easy to estimate the credit spread of a corporate bond because it could be done by simply comparing the bond's YTM with that of a Treasury bond that has identical cash flows.
    b. There is a 0.5 percent probability of default by the year-end on a one-year bond issued at par by a particular corporation. If the corporation defaults, the investor will get nothing. Assuming that a default-free bond exists with identical cash flows and liquidity, and the one-year yield on this bond is 4 percent, what yield should be required by risk-neutral investors on the corporate bond? What should the credit spread be?

11. An investor is considering investing in one-year zero-coupon bonds. She is thinking of investing in either a British-pound-denominated bond with a yield of 5.2 percent, or a euro-denominated bond with a yield of 4.5 percent. The current exchange rate is €1.5408/£.

   a. What exchange rate one year later is the break-even exchange rate, which would make the pound bond and the Eurobond investments equally good?

   b. Which investment would have turned out to be better if the actual exchange rate one year later is €1.4120/£?

12. A French investor has purchased bonds denominated in Swiss francs that have been issued by a Swiss corporation with a mediocre credit rating. Which of the following is a source of risk for this investment?

   a. Interest rate risk on Swiss francs
   b. Currency risk
   c. Credit risk
   d. a and b only
   e. a, b, and c.

13. A Swiss investor has purchased a U.S. Treasury bond priced at 100. Its yield is 4.5 percent, and the investor expects the U.S. yields to move down by 15 basis points over the year. The duration of the bond is 6. The Swiss franc cash rate is 1 percent and the dollar cash rate is 2 percent. The one-year forward exchange rate is SFr1.4600/$.

   a. The Swiss investor has come up with his own model to forecast the SFr/$ exchange rate one year ahead. This model forecasts the one-year ahead exchange rate to be SFr1.3500/$. Based on this forecast, should the Swiss investor hedge the currency risk of his investment using a forward contract?

   b. If the Swiss investor decides to hedge using a forward contract, give a rough estimate of his expected return.

   c. Verify for the hedged investment that the risk premium in Swiss francs is the same as the risk premium on the same U.S. Treasury bond for a U.S. investor.

14. In determining the composition of an international bond portfolio, the decision regarding the weights of different national markets/currencies is more critical than the decision regarding the weights of different bonds within a national market/currency. Discuss why you agree or disagree with this statement.

15. A company without default risk has issued a perpetual Eurodollar FRN at LIBOR. The coupon is paid and reset semiannually. It is certain that the issuer will never have default risk, and will always be able to borrow at LIBOR. The FRN is issued on March 1, 2002, when the six-month LIBOR is at 5 percent. The Eurodollar yield curve on September 1, 2002, and December 1, 2002, is as follows:

	September 1, 2002 (%)	December 1, 2002 (%)
One month	4.25	4.00
Three months	4.50	4.25
Six months	4.75	4.50
Twelve months	5.00	4.75

   a. What is the coupon paid on September 1, 2002, per $1,000 FRN?

b. What is the new value of the coupon set on the FRN on September 1, 2002?

c. What is the new value of the FRN on December 1, 2002?

16. A company rated A has issued a perpetual Eurodollar FRN. The FRN has a semiannual coupon set at six-month LIBOR plus a spread of 0.5 percent. Six months later, LIBOR is equal to 6 percent, and the market-required spread for an A-rated corporation has moved up to 1 percent. Give an estimate of the value of the FRN on the reset date using the "freezing" method.

17. The yield curves on the dollar and yen are flat at 7 percent and 3 percent per year, respectively. An investment banker is considering issuing a dollar/yen dual-currency bond for ¥150 million. This bond would pay the coupons in yen, and the principal would be repaid in dollars. The bond will make a principal payment of $1.36 million in two years, with interest paid in years 1 and 2. The spot exchange rate is ¥110.29/$.

a. What should the coupon rate be if the bond is issued at fair market conditions—that is, if the issue price is equal to its theoretical market value?

b. If the actual coupon rate is 6 percent, compute the percentage price.

18. The current dollar yield curve on the Eurobond market is flat at 6.5 percent for AAA-rated borrowers. A French company of AA standing can issue straight and plain FRN dollar Eurobonds at the following conditions:

▪ Bond A: Straight bond. Five-year straight-dollar Eurobond with a semiannual coupon of 6.75 percent.

▪ Bond B: Plain FRN. Five-year dollar FRN with a semiannual coupon set at LIBOR plus 0.25 percent and a cap of 13 percent. The cap means that the coupon rate is limited at 13 percent, even if the LIBOR passes 12.75 percent.

An investment banker proposes to the French company the option of issuing bull and/or bear FRNs at the following conditions:

▪ Bond C: Bull FRN. Five-year FRN with a semiannual coupon set at 12.75 percent − LIBOR.

▪ Bond D: Bear FRN. Five-year FRN with a semiannual coupon set at $2 \times$ LIBOR − 6.5%.

The coupons on the bull and bear FRNs cannot be negative. The coupon on the bear FRN is set with a cap of 19 percent.

Assume that LIBOR can never be below 3.25 percent or above 12.75 percent.

a. By comparing the net coupon per bond for the following combination to that of a straight Eurobond, show that it would be more attractive to the French company to issue the bull and/or bear FRNs than the straight Eurobond.

i. Issue 2 bull FRNs + 1 bear FRN.

ii. Issue 1 plain FRN (bond B) + 1 bull FRN.

b. By comparing the net coupon per bond for the combination of 1 straight bond (bond A) + 1 bear FRN, show that it would be more attractive to the French company to issue the bull and/or bear FRNs than the plain FRN.

19. An investment banker is considering the issue of a one-year Australian dollar/U.S. dollar currency-option bond. The currency option bond is to be issued in A$ (A$1,000), and the interest and principal are to be repaid in A$ or US$ at the option of the bondholder. The principal repaid would be either A$1,000 or US$549.45. The current spot exchange rate is A$1.82/US$. The current one-year market interest rates are 8 percent

in A$ and 5 percent in US$. A one-year put option on the A$, with a strike price of A$1.82/US$, is quoted at 2 U.S. cents; this is an option to sell one A$ for 1/US$1.82.

   a. What should be the fair coupon rate set on this currency-option bond, according to market conditions?

   b. What is the value of the bond if it is issued at a coupon of 3.4 percent?

20. A French bank offers an investment product ("guaranteed bond with stock market participation") that has been extremely successful with European retail investors. This is a two-year bond with a zero coupon. However, there is an attractive clause at maturity. The bondholder will get full principal payment plus the percentage capital appreciation on the French CAC stock index between the date of issuance and maturity, if this capital appreciation is positive. So, a bondholder investing 100 will get, at maturity, either 100 (if the CAC index went down over the two years) or 100 plus the percentage gain of the index (if the CAC index went up over the two years).

   a. Assume that the stock market is expected to go up by 20 percent over the two years. What is the expected annual yield on the bond?

   b. At time of issue, the euro yield curve was flat at 6 percent. A two-year at-the-money call on the CAC index was quoted at 11 percent of the index value. What was the fair value of the bond at issuance?

Solutions

1. Bonds issued in the United States by a European corporation and denominated in U.S. dollars would be classified as foreign bonds. The correct answer, accordingly, is (b).

2. Each of the three statements is true.

3. a. Both types of bonds would provide some debt reduction for emerging countries. The amount of debt reduction would be visible immediately in the case of a discount bond. From then on, the emerging country would pay a market interest rate on the reduced principal. In the case of a par bond, though the redemption value would remain unchanged, the debt reduction would be obtained through a coupon rate reset well below the market rate.

   b. Both types of bonds would pay a lower coupon amount than the original. The coupon amount would be reduced for a discount bond because the market rate would be applied to a smaller principal. The interest payment would be reduced for a par bond because a below-market rate would be applied to the original principal.

   c. The final redemption value would be much greater for a par bond than for a discount bond. As a compensation for this, the coupon payments would be lower for the par bonds than for the discount bonds.

4. The market price of these bonds is a sum of (1) the present value of the coupons in yen, with the discounting done based on the yen interest rate; and (2) the present value of the principal, converted to yen based on the spot exchange rate, with the discounting done based on the dollar interest rate.

   a. If the market interest rate on yen bonds drops significantly—that is, if the yen interest rate drops—the present value of the coupons should increase. Thus, the market price should increase.

   b. If the dollar drops in value relative to the yen—that is, the yen/dollar exchange rate drops—the principal in dollars converts to a lower yen amount. Thus, the market price should decrease.

c. If the market interest rate on dollar bonds drops significantly—that is, if the dollar interest rate drops—the present value of the principal should increase. Thus, the market price should increase.

5. a. Full price = Clean price + Accrued interest.
Clean price = 90%.
Because straight Eurobonds denominated in any currency use the U.S. "30/360" day-count convention, accrued interest = $120/360 \times 5\% = 1.67\%$. So, full price = $90\% + 1.67\% = 91.67\%$ of the par value of SFr 1,000 = SFr 916.70.
b. Because the Swiss bond market also follows the U.S. "30/360" day-count convention, the answer won't be different.

6. a. Because it is a zero-coupon bond, the YTM, r, is calculated simply as follows:

$$45 = \frac{100}{(1 + r)^9}$$

So, $1 + r = 1.0928$, r = 0.0928, or 9.28%.
b. Because it is a perpetual bond, the YTM, r, is calculated simply as follows:

$$108 = \frac{6}{r}$$

So, $r = 0.0556$, or 5.56%.

7. a. In most European markets, the actual YTM would be reported after taking into account that the coupon frequency is semiannual. Thus, in most European markets, the YTM reported would be an annual YTM of $(1 + 0.08/2)^2 - 1 = 0.0816$, or 8.16%.
b. i. $103 = \dfrac{6}{1 + r} + \dfrac{106}{(1 + r)^2}$, r is the yield (European way).

So, $r = 4.40\%$.

ii. $103 = \dfrac{6}{\left(1 + \dfrac{r'}{2}\right)^2} + \dfrac{106}{\left(1 + \dfrac{r'}{2}\right)^4}$

Or, $\left(1 + \dfrac{r'}{2}\right)^2 = 1 + r$, r' is the yield (U.S. way).

So, $r' = 4.35\%$.

8. a. Simple yield = $\dfrac{Coupon}{Current\ price} + \dfrac{(100 - Current\ price)}{Current\ price} \times \dfrac{1}{Years\ to\ maturity}$

Simple yield for bond A = $\dfrac{11}{106.48} + \dfrac{(100 - 106.48)}{106.48} \times \dfrac{1}{4} = 8.81\%$

Simple yield for bond B = $\dfrac{7}{93.52} + \dfrac{(100 - 93.52)}{93.52} \times \dfrac{1}{4} = 9.22\%$

b. For bond A, which is selling above par, the simple yield of 8.81 percent is less than the actual YTM of 9 percent. On the other hand, for bond B, which is selling below par, the simple yield of 9.22 percent is more than the actual YTM of 9 percent. Thus, the simple yield understates the true yield for a bond priced over par and overstates it for a bond priced under par.

9. a. Expected price change $= -7.5 \times 0.05\% = -0.375\%$. Given that the time horizon is just the next few minutes, this is also the expected return over the next few minutes.

    b. i.   Expected price change $= -7.5 \times -0.30\% = 2.25\%$.

        ii. Because the time horizon is one year, the estimated expected return $= 4 + 2.25 = 6.25\%$.

        iii. Risk premium $= 6.25 - 2.5 = 3.75\%$.

10. a. In theory, because Treasury bonds entail no default risk, a corporate bond's credit spread could be measured by comparing its YTM with that of a Treasury bond that has identical cash flows. However, the problem is that such a Treasury bond will rarely exist. Moreover, the comparison would not take into account liquidity differences between the Treasury bond and the corporate bond.

    b. Let y be the yield on the corporate bond. There are two possibilities at year-end. One, the corporation defaults (0.5 percent chance), and the investor gets nothing. Two, the corporation does not default (99.5 percent chance), and the investor gets $(100 + y)\%$. Equating the expected payoff on the corporate bond to that on the identical default-free bond, we have

    $$104 = 0.005 \times 0 + 0.995 \times (100 + y)$$

    So, $y = 4.52\%$.

    Let m be the credit spread on the corporate bond. Then, $y = 4\% + m$. So, $m = 0.52\%$.

11. a. The breakeven exchange rate is the forward rate, which can be computed using the interest rate parity relation. Because the exchange rate is given in €/£ terms, the appropriate expression for the interest rate parity relation is $F = S(1 + r_{\text{€}})/(1 + r_{\text{£}})$ (that is, $r_{\text{€}}$ is a part of the numerator and $r_{\text{£}}$ is a part of the denominator.) Accordingly, the break-even rate is

    $$F = 1.5408 \left(\frac{1 + 0.045}{1 + 0.052} \right) = 1.5305$$

    b. Because the euro appreciated more relative to the pound than what the break-even rate implied, the euro investment would have turned out to be better. Of course, this is in hindsight.

12. If the interest rate on Swiss francs increases, the bond price will go down. Also, a depreciation of the Swiss franc relative to the euro is undesirable for the French investor. Finally, the bonds are corporate bonds with a credit risk. Thus, the correct answer is (e).

13. a. Because the model indicates that the Swiss franc will become stronger relative to the U.S. dollar than as indicated by the forward rate, the investor would be better off hedging the currency risk. If he doesn't hedge, he expects to receive SFr135 for every US$100 that he gets one year later. If he hedges using a forward contract, he will receive SFr146 for every US$100 that he gets one year later.

    b. Hedged return $=$ foreign yield $- D \times \Delta$foreign yield $+$ Domestic cash rate $-$ Foreign cash rate $= 4.5\% - 6 \times (-0.15\%) + 1\% - 2\% = 4.4\%$.

    c. Risk premium in Swiss franc $=$ Expected hedged return to the Swiss investor $-$ Swiss franc cash rate $= 4.4\% - 1\% = 3.4\%$.

    Risk premium for the U.S. investor $=$ Expected return to the U.S. investor $-$ Dollar cash rate $= [4.5\% - 6 \times (-0.15\%)] - 2\% = 3.4\%$.

14. The statement is correct. First, within a particular market, the prices of different straight bonds are highly correlated, because they all tend to move up or down when the interest rate in that market moves down or up. However, the prices of bonds in different markets need not be highly correlated, because the interest rates may move in different directions in different markets. Second, the bonds in a particular market are denominated in the same currency. Thus, all bonds within the market are influenced similarly by the exchange rate movements of their currency relative to the domestic currency of the investor. However, currency movements across different markets would be different.

15. a. The coupon paid on September 1 is based on the rate set on March 1, which is 5 percent. Because the coupon is semiannual, the coupon paid is 5% of $1,000/2 = $25.
    b. As per the yield curve on September 1, the six-month rate is 4.75 percent. Thus, the new value of the coupon set on September 1 is 4.75% of $1,000/2 = $23.75.
    c. On December 1, three months have elapsed since September 1, and three months are remaining until the next reset date of March 1, 2003. We know that on this next reset date three months later, the bond will be worth 100 percent. Then it will pay a coupon of 2.375 percent (as set on September 1). The three-month rate on December 1 is 4.25 percent. Hence the present value of the FRN on December 1 is

$$V = \frac{1{,}000 + 23.75}{1 + 4.25\%/4} = \$1{,}012.99$$

If the bond is quoted as a clean price plus accrued interest, the accrued interest on December 1 is equal to 1.1875 percent (or three months of a coupon of 4.75 percent), or $11.875. Hence, the clean price would be

$$P_c = 1{,}012.99 - 11.875 = \$1{,}001.12, \text{ or } 100.11\%$$

16. Under the "freezing" method, the LIBOR is assumed to stay forever at 6 percent. Under this assumption, the FRN has an annual fixed coupon of 6.5 percent ("frozen" LIBOR + original spread). So, the semiannual coupon is 3.25 percent. The annual market-required yield is $6 + 1 = 7\%$. So, the semiannual yield is 3.50 percent. Because the value of a perpetual bond is given by $P = C/r$, the new value of the FRN should be

$$P = 3.25/3.50 = 0.9286, \text{ or } 92.86\%$$

17. a. Let x be the coupon rate. The fair interest rate x on the bond should be found by equating the present yen value of all cash flows to the issue value of ¥150 million. The cash flows are as follows:
    - Coupons in years 1 and 2, of ¥150 x million. The discount rate for these would be the yen yield.
    - Principal repayment at maturity of $1.36 million. The discount rate for this would be the dollar yield. The dollar present value of this zero-coupon dollar bond is then translated into yen using the spot exchange rate of ¥110.29/$.

    So, to get the fair interest rate, we have in million yen,

$$150 = \frac{150x}{1.03} + \frac{150x}{1.03^2} + \frac{\$1.36}{1.07^2} \times (110.29)$$

$$x = 6.62\%$$

b. Because the coupon is 6 percent and the face value is 100 percent of the issue value, the percentage price can be computed as follows:

$$P = \frac{6\%}{(1.03)} + \frac{6\%}{(1.03)^2} + \frac{100\%}{(1.07)^2} = 98.82\%$$

18. a.i. The net coupon for the combination of three bonds is

$$2(12.75\% - \text{LIBOR}) + 2 \times \text{LIBOR} - 6.5\% = 19\%$$

or 6.333 percent per bond compared with 6.75 percent on a straight bond. Thus, the net coupon per bond is lower for the combination.

a.ii. The net coupon for the combination of two bonds is

$$\text{LIBOR} + 0.25\% + 12.75\% - \text{LIBOR} = 13\%$$

or 6.5 percent per bond compared with 6.75 percent on a straight bond. Thus, the net coupon per bond is lower for the combination.

b. The net coupon for the combination of the two bonds is

$$6.75\% + 2 \times \text{LIBOR} - 6.50\% = 2 \times \text{LIBOR} + 0.25\%$$

or LIBOR + 1/8% per bond compared with LIBOR + 1/4% on the plain FRN.

19. a. The currency-option bond can be replicated by a straight one-year A\$ bond redeemed at A\$1,000 with an x percent coupon plus an option to exchange A\$1,000 $(1 + x)$ for US\$1,000$(1 + x)/1.82$. The value of the option is 2 U.S. cents per A\$, which is A\$0.0364, based on the exchange rate of A\$1.82/US\$. To be issued according to market conditions on the bond and options market, the coupon rate x percent of the currency-option bond should be such that the issue price of this bond is equal to the present value of a fixed A\$1,000$(1 + x)$ received in one year plus the present value of the currency option:

$$1,000 = \frac{1,000 \times (1 + x\%)}{1.08} + 1,000 \times (1 + x\%) \times 0.0364$$

So, $x = 0.03915$, or 3.915%.

b. The value of the currency-option bond is the sum of the present value of a straight one-year A\$ bond redeemed at A\$1,000 with a 3.4 percent coupon plus the value of the put option on the A\$.

$$V = \frac{1,000 \times (1 + 0.034)}{1.08} + 1,000 \times (1 + 0.034) \times 0.0364 = \text{A}\$995.05$$

20. a. The final payment will be 120. So, the expected yield, r, is given in the following equation:

$$100 = \frac{120}{(1 + r)^2}$$

Hence, $r = 9.54\%$.

b. The bond can be decomposed as the sum of a zero-coupon bond plus a two-year at-the-money call on the CAC index. The present value of this guaranteed bond is equal to

$$P = \frac{100}{1.06^2} + 11 = 100\%$$

So, the bond is fairly valued.

Bibliography

Collin-Dufresne, P., Goldstein, R. S., and Martin, J. S. "The Determinants of Credit Spread Changes," *Journal of Finance,* December 2001.

Duffee, G. R. "Estimating the Price of Default Risk," *Review of Financial Studies,* 12, 1999, pp. 197–226.

Duffie D., and Singleton, K. J. "Modelling Term Structures of Defaultable Bonds," *Review of Financial Studies,* 12, 1999, pp. 687–720.

Fabozzi, F. J. *Fixed Income Analysis for the Chartered Financial Analyst Program,* New Hope, PA: Frank J. Fabozzi Associates, 2000.

Sundaresan, S. M. *Fixed Income Markets and their Derivatives,* Mason, OH: Thomson: Southwestern, 1997.

8

Alternative Investments

LEARNING OUTCOMES

After completing this chapter, you will be able to do the following:

- Discuss the general features of alternative investments and distinguish between alternative assets and alternative strategies

- Distinguish between an open-end and a closed-end fund and between a load and a no-load fund

- Explain how the net asset value of a fund is calculated

- Explain the nature of various fees charged by mutual funds

- Distinguish between style, sector, index, global, and stable value strategies in equity investment

- Distinguish between exchange traded funds (ETFs), traditional mutual funds, and closed-end funds

- Explain the advantages and risks of ETFs

- Discuss the characteristics of real estate as an investable asset class

- Describe the various approaches to the valuation of real estate

- Calculate the net operating income from a real estate investment

- Calculate the value of a property under the cost, sales comparison, and income approaches

- Calculate the after-tax cash flow, net present value, and yield of a real estate investment

- Outline the various stages in venture capital investing

- Discuss venture capital investment characteristics as well as the challenges to venture performance measurement

- Calculate the net present value of a venture capital project given its possible payoffs and its conditional failure probabilities

- Discuss the descriptive accuracy of the term *hedge fund* and define hedge fund in terms of objectives, legal structure, and fee structure

---

Jot Yau, CFA, made contributions to the exchange traded and hedge funds sections of this chapter.

- Calculate the return of a hedge fund, given an absolute return scenario and the fund's fee structure

- Discuss the various types of hedge funds

- Discuss the benefits and drawbacks to fund of funds investing

- Discuss the leverage and unique risks of hedge funds

- Discuss the performance of hedge funds and the biases present in hedge fund performance measurement

- Identify the possible presence of survivorship bias in a hedge fund data base

- Explain how the legal environment affects the valuation of closely held companies

- Discuss alternative valuation methods for closely held companies; and distinguish between the bases for

- the discounts and premiums for these companies

- Discuss distressed securities investing and the similarities between venture capital investing and distressed securities investing

- Discuss the role of commodities as a vehicle for investing in production and consumption

- Explain the role of commodity trading advisors (CTAs) and the role of managed futures in commodity investing

- Discuss the sources of return on a collateralized commodity futures position

- Discuss the motivation for investing in commodities, commodity derivatives, and commodity-linked securities

- Explain how to manage risk for managed futures

Alternative investments complement stocks, bonds, and other traditional financial instruments traded on international financial markets. There is a large variety of alternative investments, and the list evolves over time. Both alternative assets (such as real estate) and alternative strategies (hedge funds) are classified as alternative investments. Alternative investments generally have lower liquidity, sell in less efficient markets, and require a longer time horizon than publicly traded stocks and bonds. Sharpe, Alexander, and Bailey (1999) provide a nice summary of the common features of alternative investments:

- Illiquidity

- Difficulty in determining current market values

- Limited historical risk and return data

- Extensive investment analysis required

When present, liquidity can make alternative investments, such as real estate, attractive; but are there cases in which the general illiquidity of alternative investments can be attractive? Alternative investments beckon investors to areas of the market where alpha[1] is more likely to be found than in more liquid and efficient markets. Illiquidity, limited information, and less efficiency do not suit all investors, but can be attractive features to those looking for likely places to add value through investment expertise.

Terhaar, Staub, and Singer (2003) discuss two additional features of alternative investments:

- A liquidity premium compensates the investor for the investor's inability to continuously rebalance the alternative investments in the portfolio.

- A segmentation premium compensates investors for the risk of alternative assets that, by nature, are generally not priced in a fully integrated global market.

It is difficult to give a broad characterization of alternative investments, but they are often equity investments in some nonpublicly traded asset. In some cases, however, they may look more like an investment strategy than an asset class. Whatever the nature of alternative investments, specialized intermediaries often link the investor to the investments. Whether the investor invests directly or through an intermediary, he must know the investment's characteristics. In the case of investing through an intermediary, he must make sure that the incentive structure for any intermediary suits his investor needs.

Finally, alternative investments can be characterized as raising unique legal and tax considerations. A financial advisor would coordinate with an attorney and a tax accountant before recommending any specific real estate investment. Also, many forms of alternative investments involve special legal structures that avoid some taxes (exchange traded funds) or avoid some regulations (hedge funds).

Investment Companies

Investment companies are financial intermediaries that earn fees to pool and invest investors' funds, giving the investors rights to a proportional share of the pooled fund performance. Both managed and unmanaged companies pool investor funds in this manner. Unmanaged investment companies (unit investment trusts in the United States) hold a fixed portfolio of investments (often tax exempt) for the life of the company and usually stand ready to redeem the investor's shares at market value. Managed investment companies are classified according to whether or not they stand ready to redeem investor shares. Open-end investment companies (mutual funds) offer this redemption feature, but closed-end funds do not. Closed-end investment companies issue shares that are then traded in the secondary markets.

---

[1] *Alpha* is risk-adjusted return in excess of the required rate of return, but, more colloquially, stands for positive excess risk-adjusted return, the goal of active managers.

Valuing Investment Company Shares

The basis for valuing investment company shares is net asset value (NAV). NAV is the per-share value of the investment company's assets minus its liabilities. Liabilities may come from fees owed to investment managers, for example. Share value equals NAV for unmanaged and open-end investment companies because they stand ready to redeem their shares at NAV. The price of a closed-end investment company's shares is determined in the secondary markets in which they trade, and, consequently, can be at a premium or discount to NAV.

Fund Management Fees

Investment companies charge fees, some as one-time charges and some as annual charges. By setting an initial selling price above the NAV, the unmanaged company charges a fee for the effort of setting up the fund. For managed funds, loads are simply sales commissions charged at purchase (front-end) as a percentage of the investment. A redemption fee (back-end load) is a charge to exit the fund. Redemption fees discourage quick trading turnover and are often set up so that the fees decline the longer the shares are held (in this case, the fees are sometimes called contingent deferred sales charges). Loads and redemption fees provide sales incentives but not portfolio management performance incentives.

Annual charges are composed of operating expenses including management fees, administrative expenses, and continuing distribution fees (12b-1 fees in the U.S.). The ratio of operating expenses to average assets is often referred to as the fund's "expense ratio." Distribution fees are fees paid back to the party that arranged the initial sale of the shares and are thus another type of sales incentive fee. Only management fees can be considered a portfolio management incentive fee. Example 8.1 is an illustration of the effects of investment company fees on fund performance.

Investment Strategies

Investment companies primarily invest in equity. Investment strategies can be characterized as style, sector, index, global, or stable value strategies. Style strategies focus on the underlying characteristics common to certain investments. Growth is a different style than value, and large capitalization investing is a different style than small stock investing. A growth strategy may focus on high price-to-earnings stocks, and a value strategy on low price-to-earnings stocks. Clearly, there are many styles.[2] A sector investment fund focuses on a particular industry. An index fund tracks an index. In the simplest implementation, the fund owns the securities in the index in exactly the same proportion as the market value weights of those securities in the index. A global fund includes securities from around the world and might keep portfolio weights similar to world market capitalization weights. An international

---

[2] See, for example, Richard Bernstein, *Style Investing*, Wiley, 1995, and Richard Michaud, *Investment Styles, Market Anomalies, and Global Stock Selection*, The Research Foundation of AIMR, 1999.

EXAMPLE 8.1   *INVESTMENT COMPANY FEES: EFFECTS ON PERFORMANCE*

An investor is considering the purchase of TriGroup International Equity Fund (TRIEF) for her portfolio. Like many U.S.-based mutual funds today, TRIEF has more than one class of shares. Although all classes hold the same portfolio of securities, each class has a different expense structure. This particular mutual fund has three classes of shares, A, B, and C. The expenses of these classes are summarized in the following table:

Expense Comparison for Three Classes of TRIEF

	Class A	Class B*	Class C
Sales charge (load) on purchases	3%	None	None
Deferred sales charge (load) on redemptions	None	5% in the first year, declining by 1 percentage point each year thereafter	1% for the initial two years
Annual expenses:			
Distribution fee	0.25%	0.50%	0.50%
Management fee	0.75%	0.75%	0.75%
Other expenses	0.25%	0.25%	0.25%
	1.25%	1.50%	1.50%

*Class B shares automatically convert to Class A shares 72 months (6 years) after purchase, reducing future annual expenses.

The time horizon associated with the investor's objective in purchasing TRIEF is six years. She expects equity investments with risk characteristics similar to TRIEF to earn 8 percent per year, and she decides to make her selection of fund share class based on an assumed 8 percent return each year, gross of any of the expenses given in the preceding table.

A. Based on only the information provided here, determine the class of shares that is most appropriate for this investor. Assume that expense percentages given will be constant at the given values. Assume that the deferred sales charges are computed on the basis of NAV.

B. Suppose that, as a result of an unforeseen liquidity need, the investor needs to liquidate her investment at the end of the first year. Assume an 8 percent rate of return has been earned. Determine the relative performance of the three fund classes, and interpret the results.

C. Based on your answers to A and B, discuss the appropriateness of these share classes as it relates to an investor's time horizon; for example, a one-, six- and ten-year horizon.

SOLUTION

A. To address this question, we compute the terminal value of $1 invested at the end of year 6. The share class with the highest terminal value, net of all expenses, would be the most appropriate for this investor, as all classes are based on the same portfolio and thus have the same portfolio risk characteristics.

Class A. $1 \times (1 - 0.03) = \$0.97$ is the amount available for investment at $t = 0$, after paying the front-end sales charge. Because this amount grows at 8 percent for six years, reduced by annual expenses of 0.0125, the terminal value per \$1 invested after six years is $\$0.97 \times 1.08^6 \times (1 - 0.0125)^6 = \$1.4274$.

Class B. After six years, \$1 invested grows to $\$1 \times 1.08^6 \times (1 - 0.015)^6 = \$1.4493$. According to the table, the deferred sales charge disappears after year 5; therefore, the terminal value is \$1.4493.

Class C. After six years, \$1 invested grows to $\$1 \times 1.08^6 \times (1 - 0.015)^6 = \$1.4493$. There is no deferred sales charge in the sixth year, so \$1.4493 is the terminal value.

In summary, the ranking by terminal value after six years is Class B and Class C (\$1.4493), followed by Class A (\$1.4274). Class B or Class C appears to be the most appropriate for this investor with a six-year horizon.

B. For Class A shares, the terminal value per \$1 invested is $\$0.97 \times 1.08 \times (1 - 0.0125) = \$1.0345$. For Class B shares, it is $\$1 \times 1.08 \times (1 - 0.015) \times (1 - 0.05) = \$1.0106$, reflecting a 5 percent redemption charge; for Class C shares, it is $\$1 \times 1.08 \times (1 - 0.015) \times (1 - 0.01) = \$1.0532$, reflecting a 1 percent redemption charge. Thus, the ranking is Class C (\$1.0532), Class A (\$1.0345), and Class B (\$1.0106).

C. Although Class B is appropriate given a six-year investment horizon, it is a costly choice if the fund shares need to be liquidated soon after investment. That eventuality would need to be assessed by the investor we are discussing. Class B, like Class A, is more attractive the longer the holding period, in general. Because Class C has higher annual expenses than Class A and Class B (after six years), it becomes less attractive the longer the holding period, in general.

After 10 years Class B shares would return $\$1 \times 1.08^{10} \times (1 - 0.015)^6 \times (1 - 0.0125)^4 = \$1.8750$, reflecting conversion to Class A after six years. Class C would return $\$1 \times 1.08^{10} \times (1 - 0.0150)^{10} = \$1.8561$. Class A shares would return the smallest amount, $\$0.97 \times 1.08^{10} \times (1 - 0.0125)^{10} = \$1.8466$. Though Class A underperforms Class C for a ten-year investment horizon, one could verify that Class A outperforms Class C for an investment horizon of 13 years or more. Also, in practice, the sales charge for Class A shares may be lower for purchases over certain sizes, making them more attractive in such comparisons.

fund is one that does not include the home country's securities, whereas a global fund includes the securities from the home country. A stable value fund invests in securities such as short-term fixed income instruments and guaranteed investment contracts which are guaranteed by the issuing insurance company and pay principal and a set rate of interest.

Exchange Traded Funds

Exchange traded funds (ETFs) are index-based investment products that allow investors to buy or sell exposure to an index through a single financial instrument. ETFs are funds that trade on a stock market like shares of any individual companies. Gastineau (2001) gives a good introduction to ETFs. They can be traded at any time during market hours, can be sold short or margined. But they are shares of a portfolio, not of an individual company. They represent shares of ownership in either open-end funds or unit investment trusts that hold portfolios of stocks or bonds in custody, which are designed to track the price and yield performance of their underlying indexes—broad market, sector/industry, single country/region (multiple countries), or fixed income. Although many investors regard ETFs simply as a form of diversified equity investment, their novelty and legal specificity suggested their inclusion in this chapter.

Recent Developments of ETFs ETFs first appeared as TIP 35 (Toronto Index Participation Fund) in Canada in 1989, and appeared in the United States in 1993 with the introduction of Standard & Poor's 500 (S&P 500) Depositary Receipts. The first Asian ETF, the Hong Kong Tracker Fund, was launched in 1999. The first ETF launched in Europe, Euro STOXX 50, did not appear until 2000. Japan did not trade ETFs until 2001, when eight were listed. Their popularity has grown so quickly that they have become one of the most successful financial products of the decade.

According to Merrill Lynch (2002), there were 102 ETFs listed in the United States as of June 2002, 14 in Canada, 106 in Europe, and approximately 24 in Asia, including Japan—a total of 246.[3] Total global assets under management approached $130 billion, 75 percent of which are invested in U.S.-listed products. Although ETFs had a slow trading start in the United States, the trading volume of ETFs has grown rapidly in the last few years. According to Goldman Sachs (2002), the total shares outstanding for U.S. ETFs amounts to 1.9 million shares, with total assets of $92 billion, while average daily trading volume reached $7.0 billion, or 146.6 million shares per day, in mid-2002. ETFs based on international indexes have shown a strong growth and now represent almost 10 percent of total U.S.-listed ETF assets. The latest additions to the universe of ETFs are fixed-income ETFs, which started trading in July 2002 on the American Stock Exchange.

In Europe, the first ETF was launched by Merrill Lynch in April 2000 to track the Euro STOXX 50, which is the most actively replicated index in Europe. Listings of multiple ETFs on the same underlying index are common in Europe. In general, ETFs traded in Europe fall into four categories: single-country ETFs, regional ETFs

---

[3] Complete listings of ETFs can be found at www.indexfunds.com.

based mostly on some pan-European or Eurozone indexes, European-sector ETFs, and global ETFs. The most popular ETFs are based on Euro STOXX 50, CAC 40, and the DAX. Although assets under management ($8 billion in mid-2002) and average daily volumes are still small compared with U.S. figures, the growth in terms of volume and number of outstanding products has been impressive. The daily trading volume grew from $6 million in the third quarter of 2000 to over $250 million in the first quarter of 2002 (Mussavian and Hirsch, 2002).

In Asia, the growth in ETFs comes primarily from Japan. Merrill Lynch (2002) estimates that the total assets under management in Asian ETFs were in excess of $13.9 billion in mid-2002.

ETF Structure   The usual ETF structure adopted worldwide is that of open-end funds with special characteristics, such as the "in-kind" process for creation and redemption of shares described subsequently (see Gastineau, 2001). Details of the legal structure vary depending on the country where the ETF is incorporated. In the United States, ETFs have adopted three different legal structures:

- *Managed investment companies:* Managed investment companies are open-ended investment companies registered under the Investment Company Act of 1940. They offer the most flexible ETF structure. The index can be tracked using various techniques, such as holding only a sample of the underlying securities in the index, lending of securities, and trading in derivatives. Dividends paid on the securities can be immediately reinvested in the fund. Sector SPDRs, iShares, and WEBS use this legal structure.

- *Unit investment trusts:* Unit investment trusts (UITs) are also registered investment companies, but they operate under more constraints, because they do not have a manager per se (but trustees). UITs are required to be fully invested in all underlying securities forming the index and must hold dividends received on securities in cash until the ETF pays a dividend to shareholders. This could result in a slight cash drag on performance. UITs are not permitted to lend securities and do not generally use derivatives. S&P 500 SPDR, Midcap 400 SPDR and NASDAQ-100 QQQ use this legal structure.

- *Grantor trusts:* Grantor trusts are not registered investment companies. Accordingly, owning a grantor trust is substantially similar to holding a basket of securities. A grantor trust often takes the form of an American Depositary Receipt (ADR) and trades as such. Because a grantor trust is fully invested in the basket of securities, no investment discretion is exercised by the trust. This is basically an unmanaged (and unregistered) investment company with a limited life. The trust passes all dividends on the underlying securities to shareholders as soon as practicable. Securities lending and use of derivatives are generally not practiced. HOLDRs use this legal structure. Grantor trusts are a structure that allows investors to indirectly own an unmanaged basket of stocks rather than tracking an index, and some do not classify them as ETFs.

We will now introduce the unique "in-kind" creation and redemption process used by open-end and UIT ETFs. This in-kind process is a major distinguishing feature of ETFs. Creation/redemption units are created in large multiples of individual ETF shares, for example, 50,000 shares. These units are available to exchange specialists (*authorized participants* or *creation agents*) that are authorized by the fund and who will generally act as market makers on the individual ETF shares. The fund publishes the index tracking portfolio that it is willing to accept for in-kind transactions. When there is excess demand for ETF shares, an authorized participant will create a *creation unit* (a large block of ETF shares) by depositing with the trustee of the fund the specified portfolio of stocks used to track the index. In return, the authorized participant will receive ETF shares that can be sold to investors on the stock market. The redemption process is the same but in reverse. If there is an excess number of ETF shares sold by investors, an authorized participant will decide to redeem ETF shares; it will do so by exchanging with the fund a *redemption unit* (a large block of ETF shares) for a portfolio of stocks held by the fund and used to track the index. Exhibit 8.1 depicts the ETF structure and the creation/redemption process.

As opposed to traditional open-end funds, the in-kind redemption means that no capital gain will be realized in the fund's portfolio on redemption. If the redemption were in cash, the fund would have to sell stocks held in the fund's portfolio. If their price had appreciated, the fund would realize a capital gain, and the tax burden would have to be passed to all existing fund shareholders. This is not the case with ETFs. This in-kind transfer for redemptions does not create a tax burden for the remaining ETF shareholders under current U.S. tax law, unlike the capital gains distributions on traditional mutual fund shareholders that could result from the sale of securities to meet redemption demand.[4] As in any open-end fund, individual ETF shareholders[5] can require in-cash redemption based on the NAV. Redemption in cash by individual ETF shareholders is discouraged in two ways:

- Redemption is based on the NAV computed a couple of days after the shareholder commits to redemption. So, the redemption value is unknown when the investor decides to redeem. This is a common feature of mutual funds.

- A large fee is assessed on in-cash redemptions.

It is more advantageous for individual shareholders to sell their shares on the market than to redeem them in cash. Arbitrage[6] by authorized participants ensures that the listed price is close to the fund's NAV, and the sale can take place

---

[4] As pointed out by Chamberlain and Jordan (2002), there are situations in which capital gains distributions are generated for the ETF, such as capital gains resulting from selling securities directly to the capital markets due to an index reconstitution. Thus, zero capital gains distributions are not guaranteed.

[5] But authorized participants commit to redeem only in kind.

[6] ETFs usually publish an indicative intraday NAV every 15 seconds that is available from major data providers.

EXHIBIT 8.1

Creation/Redemption Process of Exchange Traded Funds

immediately based on observed share prices and at a low transaction cost. Authorized participants maintain a market in the ETF share by posting bid-and-ask prices with a narrow spread, or by entering in an electronic order book buy-and-sell limit orders, which play the same role. The transaction cost of ETFs can be estimated as the sum of the commission charged by the broker plus half this bid–ask spread.

In comparing the ETF structure presented in Exhibit 8.1 with that of the traditional mutual fund structure, it is clear that market makers in the ETF structure play an instrumental role in the creation and redemption process. In the traditional mutual fund structure, an increase in demand for the shares of the mutual fund is met by the mutual fund, which simply issues new shares to the investor, and the fund manager will take the cash to the capital markets and buy securities appropriate to the fund's objective. When the customer wants to sell the mutual fund shares, the fund manager may need to raise cash by selling securities back to the capital markets. In contrast, when a customer wants to buy ETF shares, the order is not directed to the fund but to the market makers on the exchange. The market maker will exchange ETF shares for cash with the customer (via broker/dealer) and, when necessary, replenish the supply of ETFs through the creation process outlined earlier.

Advantages/Disadvantages of ETFs   ETFs are used by a wide spectrum of investors, both individual and institutional, in a wide variety of investment strategies. This is because ETFs have the following advantages:

- Diversification can be obtained easily with a single ETF transaction. With equity-oriented ETFs, investors can gain instant exposure to different market capitalizations, style (value or growth), sector or industries, countries or geographic regions. With fixed income ETFs, they can gain exposure to different maturity segments and bond market sectors. Thus, ETFs provide a convenient way to diversify.

- Although ETFs represent interests in a portfolio of securities, they trade similarly to a stock on an organized exchange. For example, ETFs can be sold short and also bought on margin.

- ETFs trade throughout the whole trading day at market prices that are updated continuously, rather than only trading once a day at closing market prices, as do the traditional open-end mutual funds.

- For many ETFs, there exist futures and options contracts on the same index, which is convenient for risk management.

- Portfolio holdings of ETFs are transparent. The ETF sponsor publishes the constituents of the fund on a daily basis. This should closely resemble the constituents of the underlying index. This is in contrast to other funds, for which the manager publishes only the list of assets in the fund from time to time.

- ETFs are cost effective. There are no load fees. Moreover, because the ETFs are passively managed, the expense ratio (which includes management fee for open-end funds, trustee fee for UITs, and custody fee for HOLDRs) can be kept low relative to actively managed funds. The expense ratio is comparable to that of an index mutual fund. For example, management fee can be as low as 8 basis points for the most successful U.S. ETFs, and up to 90 basis points for sector and international products (Mussavian and Hirsch, 2002). ETFs have a cost advantage over traditional mutual funds because there is no shareholder accounting at the fund level.

- ETFs have an advantage over closed-end index funds because their structure can prevent a significant premium/discount. Although supply and demand determine the market price of an ETF just like any other security, arbitrage helps keep the traded price of an ETF much more in line with its underlying value. By simultaneously buying (or selling) the ETF basket of securities and selling (or buying) the ETF shares in the secondary market, and creating (or redeeming) ETF shares to be delivered against the sale, market makers can capture the price discrepancy and make an arbitrage profit. Thus, UIT and open-end ETFs have the capability to avoid trading at large premiums and discounts to the NAVs. This is in contrast to closed-end index funds, which offer a fixed supply of shares, and as demand changes, they frequently trade at appreciable discounts from—and sometimes premiums to—their NAVs.

- The exposure to capital gains distribution taxes is lower than for traditional funds, so the consequences of other shareholders' redemptions are limited. As mentioned, capital gains resulting from in-kind transfer for redemptions do not create a tax burden for the remaining ETF shareholders. For this reason, capital gains tax liability is expected to be lower for ETF shareholders than for mutual fund shareholders.

- Dividends are reinvested immediately for open-end ETFs (but not for UIT ETFs), whereas for index mutual funds, timing of dividend reinvestment varies.

However, ETFs are not necessarily the most efficient alternative for investing in a market segment.

- In many countries, actively traded ETFs track a narrow-based market index, including only stocks with large market capitalization. So, no ETF is available for mid or low market-cap stocks. This is not the case in the United States, where a variety of ETF products trade actively.

- Many investors do not require the intraday trading opportunity provided by ETFs, because they have a long investment horizon.

- Some ETFs do not have large trading volumes and the bid–ask spread can be quite large. For example, some U.S. ETFs based on some sector indexes or on some foreign indexes (e.g., emerging markets) do not trade actively, and directly investing in a managed fund can be a less costly alternative, especially for large investors. Sector and international ETFs have an expense ratio that can be substantial (close to 1 percent) compared with that of a managed portfolio.

- For large institutional investors, the alternative to international ETFs is to invest directly in an indexed, or actively managed, international portfolio; the costs could be less, and the tax situation equivalent or better.

Types of ETFs   ETFs can be grouped by investment category, based on their investment target (broad domestic market index, style, sector/industry, country or region). For a given investment target, ETFs can be created based on different indexes of the same market, as well as by different sponsors. The number of ETFs keeps growing, and the diversity of investment targets increases, although all ETFs launched are not successful. We only cite some notable examples under each of the following categories:

- *Broad domestic market index:* In many countries, the most active ETFs are those launched on the major local stock index. Hong Kong Tracker Fund was the first ETF listed in Asia and the largest ever IPO in Asia excluding Japan. In Japan, Nikkei 225 and TOPIX ETFs have amassed significant assets under management, and there are several competing sponsors offering ETFs on the same indexes. In Europe, ETFs based on the French CAC 40 index and the German DAX 30 index are, by far, the most actively traded. In the United States, there are many market indexes followed by investors, so there are many competing ETFs; the most notable examples in this category include S&P 500 Depositary Receipts (SPDRs or "spiders"), Nasdaq-100 Index Tracking Stock (QQQs or "cubes"), and Diamonds Trust Series (DIAs or "diamonds"). There are also ETFs based on very broad U.S. market indexes, such as the Russell 1000, Russell 3000, or Wilshire 5000 indexes. It is fair to say that ETFs based on local market indexes now exist in most countries, including in many emerging countries.

- *Style:* Some ETFs track a specific investment style. This type of ETF is mostly found in the United States, because investors from other countries are less accustomed to style investing. ETFs exist on growth and value indexes developed by S&P/BARRA and Russell. Investors can also find ETFs specialized by market capitalization (large, mid, and small cap).

- *Sector or industry:* Some ETFs track a sector index or invest in baskets of stocks from specific industry sectors, including consumer, cyclicals, energy, financial, heath care, industrials, insurance, materials, media, staples, technology, telecommunications, transportation, and utilities. Sector and industry ETFs can be found in the United States, Europe, and Japan. Many European funds track pan-European or global-sector indexes. In the United States, industry HOLDRs offer a series of investment portfolios that are based not on an index, but on a basket of 20 to 50 companies in the same industry.

- *Country or region (multiple countries):* A fast-growing segment of the ETF market is funds tracking foreign-country indexes and regional indexes. In the United States, iShares are indexed to several developed and emerging equity markets, as well as to international indexes such as MSCI Europe and EAFE. Fresco introduced on the NYSE an ETF indexed on the Euro STOXX 50 index of the major 50 stocks of the Eurozone. Country and regional ETFs have also been launched in Europe and Japan. Again, several sponsors are competing for products on the same international indexes.

- *Fixed income:* This category is the latest addition to the universe of ETFs, and mostly in the United States. They have had limited success so far.

As stressed in Chapter 5, international ETFs have distinguishing features. An ETF indexed on some less-liquid emerging market is bound to have high bid–ask spreads. Managing an ETF on a broad international index means holding stocks from numerous countries with different custodial arrangement and time zones. Again, the bid–ask spreads are bound to be larger than for plain-vanilla ETFs. But the size (assets under management) of the ETF is an important factor influencing costs. The effect of non-overlapping time zones should be taken into account when comparing the ETF price and its NAV. Take the example of an ETF on a Japanese stock index, traded in New York. During Wall Street opening hours, the Tokyo stock market is closed. The NAV available in the morning in America is based on the closing prices in Tokyo several hours before New York opened. Except for currency fluctuations, the NAV will remain unchanged because Tokyo is closed throughout the New York trading session. However, the ETF price will be affected by expectations about future stock prices in Tokyo, so it could differ significantly from the official NAV. This is not an inefficiency and there are no arbitrage opportunities, because the NAV is stale and does not correspond to current market pricing.

Risks in ETFs   Listed next are the major risks faced by ETFs. They, however, do not affect all ETFs to the same extent. For example, market risk, trading risk, and tracking error risk affect all ETFs, while sector risk, currency risk, and country risk may affect sector and country ETFs. Likewise, derivatives risk affects only those funds that employ derivatives in their investment strategies. In addition, different ETFs may face risks that are unique to the fund (not discussed in this chapter).

- *Market risk:* ETF shareholders are subject to risks similar to those of holders of other diversified portfolios. The NAV of the ETF will change with changes in the market index tracked by the fund.

- *Asset class/sector risk:* Some ETFs invest in some market segment. The returns from the type of securities in which an ETF invests may underperform returns from the general securities markets or different asset classes. For example, the performance of a sector ETF may be susceptible to any single economic, market, political, or regulatory occurrence. Thus, a sector ETF also may be adversely affected by the performance of that specific sector or group of industries on which it is based. This risk is directly implied by the investment strategy offered by the fund.

- *Trading risk:* Although an ETF is designed to make it likely that it will trade close to its NAV, impediments to the securities markets may result in trading prices that differ, sometimes significantly, from NAV. Moreover, there is no assurance that an active trading market will always exist for the ETF on the exchange, so the bid–ask spread can be large for some ETFs. The overall depth and liquidity of the secondary market also may fluctuate.

- *Tracking error risk:* Although ETFs are designed to provide investment results that generally correspond to the price and yield performance of their respective underlying indexes, the funds/trusts may not be able to exactly replicate the performance of the indexes because of fund/trust expenses and other factors. Tracking risk comes from trading risk (the ETF market price deviates from its NAV), but also from the fact that the ETF NAV differs from the index value.

- *Derivatives risk:* ETFs that invest in index futures contracts and other derivatives to track an index are subject to additional risks that accrue to derivatives, for example, counterparty credit risk and higher leverage.

- *Currency risk and country risk:* ETFs that are based on international indexes may involve risk of capital loss from unfavorable fluctuations in currency values or from economic and political instability in other nations. ETFs invested in emerging markets bear greater risk of market shutdown and of the imposition of capital controls than those typically found in a developed market. Country risk also includes the risk of expropriation. It could be that foreign investors are discriminated against, so that the return of an ETF will significantly underperform the local market index return achieved by a local investor.

Applications of ETFs   ETFs can be used in a wide variety of investment strategies. Following are some suggested popular applications:

- *Implementing asset allocation:* ETFs can be used to effect asset allocation among baskets of stocks and bonds at either the strategic or the tactical level.

- *Diversifying sector/industry exposure:* ETFs on broad market indexes can be used to diversify away the sector- or industry-specific event risks borne in an otherwise undiversified portfolio. Such ETF exposure is a natural complement to an investment strategy of holding only a few attractive stocks.

- *Gaining exposure to international markets:* Money managers can quickly and easily purchase ETFs for instant and extensive international exposure to a single country or multiple countries within a geographic region, compared with the expense and difficulty of assembling a portfolio of foreign securities.

- *Equitizing cash:* By investing in ETFs, money managers can put idle cash to work temporarily while determining where to invest for the longer term. For example, a fund manager using the Nikkei 225 as its benchmark could invest cash inflows into one of the ETFs tied to this benchmark before he decides which stocks to buy. This can minimize cash drag or benchmark risk. It is a convenient alternative to buying futures contract on the market index.

- *Managing cash flows:* Investment managers can take advantage of ETFs' liquidity during periods of cash inflows and outflows. A portfolio manager can establish a position in an ETF that corresponds to the portfolio's benchmark or investment strategy, investing inflows into the ETF and liquidating the position as needed to meet redemptions or invest in specific stocks or bonds.

- *Completing overall investment strategy:* Fund or money managers can use ETFs to quickly establish or increase exposure to an industry or sector to "fill holes" in an overall investment strategy.

- *Bridging transitions in fund management:* Pension plan assets can often lie dormant during times of investment manager appointments, replacements, or shifts. Institutions can use ETFs as a cost-effective method to keep assets invested in the interim.

- *Managing portfolio risk:* Because ETFs can be sold short in a declining equity market (or rising interest rate market for fixed-income ETFs), portfolio managers can use ETFs to hedge overall portfolio risk or sector/industry exposure.

- *Applying relative value, long/short strategies:* Institutions can take advantage of ETF features to apply long/short strategies aimed at increasing returns. For example, an institution can establish a long position in a broad market, country, sector, or bond index expected to outperform while shorting an index expected to underperform. Doubling the size of the long position versus the short position can leverage the total position. Market makers can use ETFs to exploit price discrepancies between ETFs, the underlying index, the futures, and/or options.

Real Estate

Real estate is usually considered to be buildings and buildable land, including offices, industrial warehouses, multifamily buildings, and retail space. Real estate is a form of tangible asset, one that can be touched and seen, as opposed to financial claims that are recorded as pieces of paper. Other forms of tangible assets are available for investment purposes. These include natural resources, timber, containers, artwork, and many others. We will focus on real estate, which is, by far, the most common form of investment in tangible assets.

Real estate as an investment has several unique characteristics as well as several characteristics common to other types of investments. Even the definition of real estate isolates it as a unique investment. Real estate is an immovable asset—land (earth surface) and the permanently attached improvements to it. Graaskamp defines real estate as artificially delineated space with a fourth dimension of time referenced to a fixed point on the face of the earth.[7] This astrophysical definition stresses the idea that ownership rights to earth areas can be divided up not only in the three dimensions of space, but also in a time dimension, as well as divided up among investors. One plot of land with its building can be divided into above ground (e.g., buildings) and below ground (e.g., minerals), into areas within the building (e.g., rooms), and into periods of time (timesharing). Different investors can own the different divisions. Many classifications can be adopted for real estate. Real estate can be classified by usage (office space, multifamily housing, retail space) and location. It can also be classified into four quadrants by form of ownership, public or private, and by form of financing, debt or equity.[8] Clearly, it is not possible to adopt a simple classification of real estate, because this asset class covers so many different investment products.

Real estate is an important investment category. In many countries, domestic real estate is a common investment vehicle for pension funds and life insurance companies. It is not uncommon to have private European investors owning and renting directly a few real estate units, such as houses, condominium apartments, or parking spaces. But there are some obstacles for institutions and individuals

---

[7] Jarchow (1991), p. 42.
[8] See, for example, Hudson-Wilson (2001).

wishing to invest in foreign real estate. First, it is difficult to monitor properties located abroad. Second, taxes, paperwork, and unforeseen risks may make foreign real estate investment impractical on a large scale, although investments can be made through specialized managers in the countries of interest. To be sure, private deals can be arranged for special projects, but these are well beyond the scope of this book. There is, however, a definite trend toward the development of negotiable forms for real property interest. In many countries, pooled funds have been created with the specific purpose of real estate investment. Mortgage-backed Eurobonds are rapidly growing in popularity. Many institutional investors, especially in Europe, have started to invest in international real estate. The time may not be too far off when real estate will be a normal component of international investment strategies.

Forms of Real Estate Investment

There are several forms of real estate investment: free and clear equity, leveraged equity, mortgages, and aggregation vehicles.

Free and Clear Equity   "Free and clear equity," sometimes called "fee simple," refers to full ownership rights for an indefinite period of time, giving the owner the right, for example, to lease the property to tenants and resell the property at will. This is straightforward purchase of some real estate property.

Leveraged Equity   Leveraged equity refers to the same ownership rights but subject to debt (a promissory note) and a pledge (mortgage) to hand over real estate ownership rights if the loan terms are not met. A mortgage is a pledge of real estate ownership rights to another party as security for debt owed to that party. Thus, leveraged equity involves equity ownership plus a debt and a requirement to transfer ownership of the equity in case of default on the debt. The debt and the mortgage are usually packaged together into a mortgage loan.

Mortgages   Mortgages (or more precisely, mortgage loans) themselves are another real estate investment vehicle, representing a type of debt investment. Investing in a mortgage provides the investor with a stream of bondlike payments. These payments include net interest, net of mortgage servicing fees, and a scheduled repayment of principal. This is a form of real estate investment because the creditor may end up owning the property being mortgaged. Mortgage loans often include a clause of early repayment (at a cost) at the option of the debtor. So, the debtholder may also receive excess principal repayments, called mortgage prepayments. These prepayments produce uncertainty in the amount and timing of mortgage cash flows.

To diversify risks, a typical investor does not invest in one mortgage, but in securities issued against a pool of mortgages. An intermediary buys a pool of mortgages and then issues securities backed by the mortgages, but with the securities passing through the net mortgage payments to the investors.

Aggregation Vehicles   Aggregation vehicles aggregate investors and serve the purpose of giving investors collective access to real estate investments. *Real estate limited partnerships (RELPs)* allow investors (the limited partners) to participate in real estate projects while preserving limited liability (the initial investment) and leaving management to the general partners who are real estate experts. *Commingled funds* are pools of capital created largely by like-minded institutional investors organized together by an intermediary to invest chiefly in real estate investment projects. The investors share in the investment rewards according to the amount of capital they invest. Commingled funds can be either open or closed end. Closed-end funds have a set termination date, typically allow no new investors after initiation of the fund, and typically buy and hold a real estate portfolio for the life of the fund, with no reinvestment as sales occur. By contrast, open-end funds have indefinite lives, accept new investors, and revise their real estate portfolios over time. Finally, *real estate investment trusts (REITs)* are a type of closed-end investment company. They issue shares that are traded on a stock market, and they invest in various types of real estate. Thus, they aggregate individual investors and provide them easy access to real estate and diversification within real estate. Of course, the risk and return characteristics of REITs depend on the type of investment they make. Mortgage REITs, which invest primarily in mortgages, are more akin to a bond investment, while equity REITs, which invest primarily in commercial or residential properties using leverage, are more akin to an investment in leveraged equity real estate. The shares of REITs trade freely on the stock market, so they are liquid investments, but their share price can trade at a discount (or premium) to the NAV of the properties in their portfolio.

Valuation Approaches

Real estate assets are quite different from securities traded on a financial market: "Because the real estate market is not an auction market offering divisible shares in every property, and information flows in the market are complex, these features place a premium on investment judgment. Managers who want to own some of IBM simply buy some shares. Managers who want to participate in the returns on, say, a $300 million office building, must take a significant position in the property."[9] Following are some characteristics of real estate as an investable asset class:

- Properties are immovable, basically indivisible, and unique assets, as contrasted to fungible (perfectly interchangeable) and divisible assets such as currencies. Though unique, even art is movable and thus not as unique as real estate.

- Properties are only approximately comparable to other properties.

- Properties are generally illiquid, due to their immobility and indivisibility.

- There is no national, or international, auction market for properties. Hence, the "market" value of a given property is difficult to assess.

---

[9] Firstenberg, Ross, and Zisler (1988).

- Transaction costs and management fees for real estate investments are high.

- Real estate markets suffer inefficiencies because of the nature of real estate itself and because information is not freely available.

Valuation of real estate focuses on intrinsic value just as does the valuation of any asset. In real estate, the term *appraisal* is used for the process of estimating the market and the investment value of the property. The market value estimate is independent of the particular investor, but the investment value depends on the particular use that the investor plans for the property.

To estimate a property's value, a real estate appraiser generally uses one of three approaches or a combination of the approaches. The approaches are the cost approach, the sales comparison approach, and the income approach. An investor can further take into account her specific tax situation to value the property using a discounted after-tax cash flow approach. These four approaches are used worldwide.

The Cost Approach   The cost approach is analogous to the use of replacement cost of total assets in the calculation of Tobin's Q for equity valuation. What would it cost to replace the building in its present form? Of course, an estimate of the land value must be added to the building replacement cost estimate. The replacement cost approach is relatively easy to implement because it is based on current construction costs, but it suffers from severe limitations. First, an appraisal of the land value is required and that is not always an easy task. Second, the market value of an existing property could differ markedly from its construction cost. An office building could be very valuable because it has some prestigious and stable tenants that pay high rents, not because of the value of the construction. Conversely, an office building in poor condition, with a large vacancy rate and in a bad neighborhood, could be worth much less than its replacement cost.

The Sales Comparison Approach   The sales comparison approach is similar to the "price multiple comparables" approach in equity valuation. Market value is estimated relative to a benchmark value. The benchmark value may be the market price of a similar property, or the average or median value of the market prices of similar properties, in transactions made near the time of the appraisal. The benchmark-based estimate needs to be adjusted for changing market conditions, the possibility that the benchmark itself is mispriced, and the unique features of the property relative to the benchmark. Properties with comparable characteristics might not have traded recently.

One formal variation of the sales comparison approach is the method of *hedonic price estimation*. In this method, the major characteristics of a property that can affect its value are identified. The characteristics of a residential property that are relevant to its value can be the age of the building, its size, its location, its vacancy rate, its amenities, and so on. Individual properties are given a quantitative rating for each of the characteristics. For example, location could be ranked from 1 (very bad) to

10 (very good). The sales price for all recent transactions of the properties in the benchmark are then regressed on their characteristics ratings. This is a regression in which there is one observation for each transaction. The dependent (left-hand side) variable is the transaction price, and the independent (right-hand side) variables are the ratings for each of the characteristics. The estimated slope coefficients are the valuation of each characteristic in the transaction price. The result is a benchmark monetary value associated with each characteristic's rating. It is then possible to estimate the selling price of a specific property by taking into account its rating on each feature. Although this has become a standard technique in residential property appraisal, it has also been applied to income producing property.[10]

EXAMPLE 8.2   *SALES COMPARISON APPROACH: HEDONIC PRICE MODEL*

A real estate company has prepared a simple hedonic model to value houses in a specific area. A summary list of the house's characteristics that can affect pricing are:

- the number of main rooms,
- the surface area of the garden,
- the presence of a swimming pool, and
- the distance to a shopping center.

A statistical analysis of a large number of recent transactions in the area allowed the company to estimate the following slope coefficients:

Characteristics	Units	Slope Coefficient in Pounds per Unit
Number of rooms	Number	20,000
Surface area of the garden	Square feet	5
Swimming pool	0 or 1	20,000
Distance to shopping center	In miles	−10,000

A typical house in the area has five main rooms, a garden of 10,000 square feet, a swimming pool, and a distance of one mile to the nearest shopping center. The transaction price for a typical house was £160,000.

You wish to value a house that has seven rooms, a garden of 10,000 square feet, a swimming pool, and a distance of two miles to the nearest shopping center. What is the appraisal value based on this sales comparison approach of hedonic price estimation?

---

[10]See Söderberg (2002), pp. 157–180.

> **SOLUTION**
>
> The appraised value is given by the equation
>
> Value $= 20{,}000 \times$ (# Rooms) $+ 5 \times$ (Garden surface) $+ 20{,}000$
>
> $\times$ (Pool) $- 10{,}000 \times$ (Distance to shopping center)
>
> $= 20{,}000 \times 7 + 5 \times 10{,}000 + 20{,}000 \times 1 - 10{,}000 \times 2$
>
> $= £190{,}000$
>
> This specific house has an appraised value of £190,000. Compared to the typical house in the area, it has two more rooms but is one mile farther from the nearest shopping center.

The Income Approach The income approach to real estate valuation values property using a perpetuity discount type of model. The perpetuity is the annual net operating income (NOI). This perpetual stream is discounted at a market required rate of return (the market capitalization or cap rate). NOI is gross potential income minus expenses, which include estimated vacancy and collection losses, insurance, taxes, utilities, and repairs and maintenance. Technically, the market cap rate is the rate used by the market in recent transactions to capitalize future income into a present market value. For a constant and perpetual stream of annual NOI, we have

$$\text{Appraisal price} = \frac{\text{NOI}}{\text{Market cap rate}}$$

And the market cap rate is calculated on the benchmark transactions as

$$\text{Market cap rate} = \frac{\text{Benchmark NOI}}{\text{Benchmark transaction price}}$$

Benchmark may refer to a single comparable property or the median or mean of several comparable properties, with any appropriate adjustments.

It must be stressed that the income approach makes the simplifying assumption of a constant and perpetual amount of annual income. The income approach can also be adjusted for the special cases of a constant growth rate in rentals or a constant growth rate in rentals coupled with long-term leases. Valuation with a constant growth rate in rentals parallels the constant growth dividend discount model. Inflation could make NOI grow at the inflation rate over time. As long as inflation can be passed through, it will not affect valuation, because the market cap rate also incorporates the inflation rate. In the long-term lease case, the growth in rentals is not fully reflected in the NOI growth rate. The rent remains fixed over the term of the lease, while costs grow at the inflation rate. This is analogous to the inflation pass-through question raised in equity valuation (see Chapter 6). If expected inflation will cause operating expenses to rise, how much of the inflation can the owner pass through to the tenants? Longer lease terms delay the pass-through. Another limitation of this approach is that all calculations are performed before tax.

EXAMPLE 8.3   THE INCOME APPROACH

An investor wants to evaluate an apartment complex using the income approach. Recent sales in the area consist of an office building and an apartment complex. He gathers the following data on the apartment complex, as well as on recent sales in the area. All income items are on an annual basis. According to the income approach, what is the value of the apartment complex?

	Apartment Investment under Consideration	Office Building Recently Sold	Apartment Complex Recently Sold
Gross potential rental income	$120,000		
Estimated vacancy and collection losses	6%		
Insurance and taxes	$10,000		
Utilities	$7,000		
Repairs and maintenance	$12,000		
Depreciation	$14,000		
Interest on proposed financing	$11,000		
Net operating income		$300,000	$60,000
Sales price		$2,000,000	$500,000

SOLUTION

The NOI for the apartment complex is gross potential rental income minus estimated vacancy and collection costs minus insurance and taxes minus utilities minus repairs and maintenance.

   NOI = 120,000 − 0.06 × 120,000 − 10,000 − 7,000 − 12,000 = 83,800

The other apartment complex is the comparable property, and that has a capitalization rate of

   NOI/(Transaction price) = 60,000/500,000 = 0.12

Applying this cap rate to the apartment complex under consideration gives an appraisal price of

   NOI/(Cap rate) = 83,800/0.12 = $698,333

Note that we do not use the financing costs to determine the NOI, because we wish to appraise the value of the property independently of its financing. Neither do we subtract depreciation. The implicit assumption is that repairs and maintenance will allow the investor to keep the building in good condition forever.

The Discounted After-Tax Cash Flow Approach   Supplementing the cost, sales comparison, and income approach used for market value appraisals, the discounted after-tax cash flow approach is a check on investment valuation. If the investor can deduct depreciation and any interest payments from NOI, then the investor's after-tax cash flows depend on the investor's marginal tax rate. Hence, the value of a property for a specific investor depends on the investor's marginal tax rate. Once these cash flows and after-tax proceeds from future property disposition are estimated, the net present value of the property to an equity investor is obtained as the present value of the cash flows, discounted at the investor's required rate of return on equity, minus the amount of equity required to make the investment.

For an equity investment to be worthwhile, its expected net present value must be positive. Alternatively, the investment's yield (internal rate of return) should exceed the investor's required rate of return.

EXAMPLE 8.4   *THE DISCOUNTED CASH FLOW APPROACH*

An analyst is assigned the task of evaluating a real estate investment project. The purchase price is $700,000, which is financed 20 percent by equity and 80 percent by a mortgage loan at a 10 percent pretax interest rate. According to the applicable country's tax rules, the interest on real estate financing for this project is tax deductible. The mortgage loan has a long maturity and level annual payments of $59,404. This includes interest payments on the remaining principal at a 10 percent interest rate and a variable principal repayment that steps up with time. The analyst calculated NOI in the first year to be $83,800. NOI is expected to grow at a rate of 5 percent every year.

The analyst faces the following valuation tasks: determining the first year's after-tax cash flow, determining interim after-tax cash flows, determining the final year's after-tax cash flow, and calculating two measures of the project's profitability, the investment's net present value (NPV) and the investment's yield (internal rate of return).

i. Determine the first year's after-tax cash flow, using the following data:

Net operating income (NOI) for first year	$83,800
Straight-line depreciation	18,700
Mortgage payment	59,404
Purchase price	700,000
80% financing at a 10% interest rate	
NOI growth rate	5%
Marginal income tax rate	31%

ii. Determine the second year's after-tax cash flow, using the preceding table and with a growth rate of 5% in NOI.

iii. The property is sold at the end of the fifth year. Determine the after-tax cash flow for that property sale year, using the following data (the after-tax cash flow without property sale has been calculated as previously).

After-tax cash flow without property sale	$33,546
Straight-line depreciation	18,700
Mortgage payment	59,404
Cumulative mortgage principal repayments by end of fifth year	20,783
Purchase price	700,000
80% financing at 10% interest rate	

NOI growth factor	5%
Marginal income tax rate	31%
Capital gains tax rate	20%
Forecasted sales price	$875,000
Property sales expense as a percentage of sales price	6%

Use the information below to answer Parts iv and v.

The following data summarize the after-tax cash flows for all five years of the project's life (the table includes the results we have calculated previously for years 1, 2, and 5, as well as results for years 3 and 4):

Year	1	2	3	4	5
Cash flow	21,575	24,361	27,280	30,339	273,629

The analyst now turns to evaluating whether the project should be undertaken. She estimates the required rate of return for an equity investment in projects of similar risk as 16 percent. The purchase price for the property is $700,000. The financing plan calls for 80 percent debt financing, so the equity investment is only $140,000. The investor's cost of equity for projects with this level of risk is 16 percent, but a sensitivity analysis on cost of equity helps provide some perspective for the analyst. She decides to conduct a sensitivity analysis, calculating the present value of the year 1 to year 5 after-tax cash flows using a range of discount rates other than 16 percent; the results appear in the following table:

Discount Rate	Present Value
0.10	$250,867
0.14	$216,161
0.18	$187,637
0.22	$164,012
0.26	$144,303
0.30	$127,747
0.34	$113,750

iv. Determine the real estate project's NPV, using the analyst's required rate of return, and make a purchase recommendation based only on this analysis.

v. Determine an approximate yield for the real estate project, and make a purchase recommendation based only on this analysis.

SOLUTION TO i

Because interest is tax deductible here, calculate the first year's interest, and then calculate after-tax net income. The amount borrowed is $560,000 = 700,000 \times 0.8$. The first year's interest at 10 percent is then $56,000 = 0.1 \times $560,000. After-tax net income is then ($83,800 - $18,700 - $56,000) \times (1 - 0.31) = $6,279.

To get after-tax cash flow from after-tax net income, depreciation must be added and the principal repayment component of the $59,404 mortgage payment must be subtracted. The principal repayment is the mortgage payment minus the interest payment, or $3,404 = $59,404 - $56,000. Thus, the after-tax cash flow is $21,575 = $6,279 + $18,700 - $3,404.

SOLUTION TO ii

First we calculate the new NOI, equal to $87,990 = $83,800 \times (1.05)$.

Second, we calculate after-tax net income. We need to calculate the second year's interest payment on the mortgage balance after the first year's payment. This mortgage balance is the original principal balance minus the first year's principal repayment, or $556,596. The interest on this balance is then $55,660. After-tax net income is then ($87,990 - $18,700 - $55,660) \times (1 - 0.31) = $9,405.

Third, the second year's principal repayment is the mortgage payment minus the interest payment, or $3,744 = $59,404 - $55,660.

Finally, then calculate the second year's after-tax cash flow, which equals the second year's after-tax net income plus depreciation minus the principal repayment, or $24,361 = $9,405 + $18,700 - $3,744.

SOLUTION TO iii

The after-tax cash flow for the property sale year is equal to the sum of the after-tax cash flow without the property sale plus the after-tax cash flow from the property sale. When a property is sold, the outstanding mortgage principal balance (the outstanding mortgage, for short) must be paid to the lender. In the following calculations, we incorporate that effect into the after-tax cash flow from the property sale.

To begin, we calculate the capital gains on the sale of the property. To do that, first determine the ending book value as the original purchase price minus five years' worth of depreciation, or $606,500 = $700,000 - 5 \times $18,700$. The net sale price is equal to the forecasted sale price, $875,000, minus sales expenses of 6 percent, or $52,500. Capital gains taxes are paid on the difference between the net sales price and the book value, or a difference of $216,000 = ($875,000 − $52,500) − $606,500. The capital gains taxes are then $43,200 = 0.2 × $216,000. The after-tax cash flow from the property sale is then the net sales price minus the outstanding mortgage minus the capital gains taxes. The outstanding mortgage is the original mortgage minus five years' worth of principal repayments, or $539,217 = $560,000 − $20,783. Thus the after-tax cash flow from the property sale is $240,083 = ($875,000 − $52,500) − $539,217 − $43,200. The after-tax cash flow for the property sale year is then $273,629 = $33,546 + $240,083.

SOLUTION TO iv

At a cost of equity of 16 percent, the present value of the cash flow is $201,215 = $21,575/1.16 + $24,361/1.16^2 + $27,280/1.16^3 + $30,339/1.16^4 + $273,629/1.16^5. The investment requires equity of $140,000 = 0.2 × $700,000. Thus, the NPV is $61,215 = $201,215 − $140,000. The analyst recommends this investment because it has a positive NPV.

SOLUTION TO v

We can address the question using the results of the analyst's sensitivity analysis. The yield or internal rate of return is the discount rate that makes the project's NPV equal to zero. The yield must be between 26 percent and 30 percent because discounting at 26 percent gives a present value ($144,303) that is larger than the initial investment (of $140,000), or a positive NPV, while discounting at 30 percent gives a present value ($127,747) that is smaller than the initial investment, or a negative NPV. Consequently, the project's yield must lie between 26 percent and 30 percent. Actually, the internal rate of return of this project is slightly below 27 percent. The analyst recommends the investment because the investment's yield exceeds the investor's required rate of return (16 percent).

Real Estate in a Portfolio Context

Some real estate indexes have been developed to attempt to measure the average return on real estate investment. Good-quality indexes with a long-term historical record exist in the United States and United Kingdom, but they are more recent or even nonexistent in other countries.

Real estate returns consist of income and capital gain or loss. The income on a property can usually be measured in a straightforward fashion. The value appreciation is more difficult to assess. The most common method is to use changes in *appraised* value. Appraisal of each property is conducted by specialists fairly infrequently (typically once a year). Appraisals are generally based on the approaches discussed previously. In practice, appraisal prices exhibit remarkable inertia. The value of a real estate portfolio is further smoothed because properties are appraised infrequently, so their prices remain constant between appraisals.

Following are the major U.S. real estate indexes, based on appraisal values:

- The *Frank Russell Company (FRC)* and the *National Council of Real Estate Investment Fiduciaries (NCREIF)* indexes. These are quarterly indexes, starting in 1978 and broken down by regions and property types.

- The *Commingled Real Estate Equity Fund (CREF)* index, published by Evaluation Associates. This is a quarterly index of major tax-exempt funds, starting in 1969.

Another method of measuring price appreciation is to use a reference to REITs. The total return on a REIT is made up of the income paid to shareholders, as well as of the stock market appreciation of the REIT share price. Various REIT indexes are used to proxy the average total return on real estate investments. They are easier to construct, because they are simply some weighted average of market-traded shares. The major REIT indexes are as follows:

- The *National Association of Real Estate Investment Trusts (NAREIT)*, a monthly equal-weighted index of some one hundred REITs, starting in 1972.

- REIT indexes published by various institutions, for example, Wilshire or Goldman Sachs.

The two types of indexes provide very different performance and risk characteristics, which have been studied by Firstenberg, Ross, and Zisler (1988), Goetzmann and Ibbotson (1990), and Gyourko and Keim (1993). Appraisal-based indexes are much less volatile than REIT indexes. For example, Goetzman and Ibbotson found that a REIT index had an annual standard deviation of 15.4 percent, comparable to that of the S&P 500 index, but six times larger than that of the CREF index, of 2.6 percent. Furthermore, appraisal-based indexes and REIT indexes have very little correlation. Appraisal-based indexes exhibit persistent returns (returns are correlated over time), showing the inertia in appraisals. REIT indexes are strongly correlated with the rest of the stock market.

In summary, real estate returns can be calculated using either appraisal indexes or REIT indexes. Appraisals do not provide continuous price data and they do not provide market prices but only market price estimates. REIT indexes provide continuous market prices of REITs but not of the underlying real estate. Thus, they reflect the amount of leverage used in the REITs. Therefore neither approach to calculating returns is entirely satisfactory. In any case, the issue in investment is one of forecasting returns, standard deviations, and correlations. For example, in analyzing a particular real estate project, an investor would supplement cash flow forecasts and discounted cash flow analysis with considerations of how the project's cash flows will covary with his existing portfolio. An individual investor will not receive diversification benefits from a real estate project whose returns are highly correlated with his own business employment income.

A few studies have looked at real estate from a global viewpoint. These studies examine the proposed portfolio benefits of real estate, risk reduction (through diversification) and inflation protection. Eichholtz (1996) looked at the diversification benefits of real estate shares quoted in many countries. He found that international diversification strongly reduces the risk of a real estate portfolio. However, Mull and Soenen (1997) showed that REITs are strongly correlated with other U.S. stocks, so that foreign investors who buy U.S. REITs do not gain much diversification benefit, beyond the U.S. stock market exposure. Liu, Hartzell, and Hoesli (1997) looked at real estate securities traded on seven national stock markets and concluded that their correlation with inflation is low, so they do not provide a good hedge against inflation. Quan and Titman (1997) studied commercial real estate values in 17 countries, where property values and rents are calculated using an appraisal-based approach. Commercial real estate prices and stock prices are both affected by the general level of economic activity, so they should be strongly correlated. Pooling their international data, Quan and Titman did find that the relation between stock returns and changes in real estate values is very strong.

Although research studies have not provided overwhelming evidence to support the risk reduction and inflation protection benefits of real estate, such studies are always limited by the use of either appraisal indexes or REIT indexes. Judgment is needed in assessing the impact of real estate on a portfolio. First, what are the projected cash flows and what are the predicted covariances of the cash flows with the current portfolio? Second, what are the inflation pass-through characteristics of the real estate investment?

Private Equity: Venture Capital

Venture capital is one of the main categories of private equity investing. Private equity investments are equity investments that are not traded on exchanges. Venture capital investments are private equity investments in business ventures from idea stage through expansion of a company already producing and selling a product and through preparation for exit from the investment via buyout or initial public offering. Venture capital investing may be done at stages along the way, but eventual exit is a primary consideration. By its very nature, such investing requires a horizon of several years and the willingness to accept several failures for every success in the venture capital portfolio: The possibly enormous return on the winning venture must compensate for many likely failed ventures.

Institutional and individual investors usually invest in private equity through limited partnerships. Limited partnerships allow investors (the limited partners) to participate in a portfolio of venture capital projects while preserving limited liability (the initial investment) and leaving management to the general partners who are private equity experts. Typically, the general partners are associated with a firm that specializes in private equity or with the private equity department of a financial institution. Funds of funds are also offered that pool investments in several ventures.

As stock markets continue to offer weak returns, foreign investors have poured money into US real estate at a fast pace this year, attracted by superior yields and the transparency and liquidity of the market.

Jacques Gordon, international director of investment strategy and research for LaSalle Investment Management, said US real estate has always been attractive to foreign money, but the magnitude of the sums incoming has been particularly noteworthy this year.

Much of the attraction is based on the higher yields from US properties, which average between 7 and 8 per cent compared with 4 to 5 per cent in Europe.

Real Capital Analytics, a real estate monitoring group, estimates foreign investors will have acquired nearly $9bn of US commercial property by the end of 2002, double the $4.5bn seen in 2001.

Overseas money is largely being spent on office space in metropolitan areas such as New York and Washington. Foreigners bought $6.7bn of office properties, representing 16 per cent of total office investments in the US in 2002. German-based Jamestown Immobilien is just about to close a $745m deal to buy the Axa Financial Center on Sixth Avenue in New York.

Of greatest interest to foreigners have been "trophy" buildings in the central business districts of big cities. That heightened interest has boosted property prices to new records, despite rising vacancies and falling rents.

This discrepancy in the fundamentals is raising concerns for the future profitability of current investments, especially in light of continuing weakness in the US economy. "There is a disconnect between the price of commercial real estate and if there is a renewed recession that disconnect cannot persist," said Hugh Kelly, professor of real estate at New York University.

But Mr Gordon said that although record prices are being paid for office properties, he sees limited risk to the downside, given that the amounts being paid are only about 10 per cent higher than previous records.

"Although record amounts are being paid, it is not anything like the tech frenzy we saw in the stock market. [The record prices] do not trouble me in the sense that there's a bubble about to burst," Mr Gordon said.

Interest in the US market has been heaviest from Germany, accounting for 51 per cent of total foreign capital in US real estate this year. Germans invested $4.9bn in US property in 2002 compared with just $2.7bn a year earlier.

The main reason for the increased interest is that money is flowing at an unprecedented rate into German open-ended and closed-end funds, and analysts say investing large sums in high-profile buildings in the US is an easy way to invest the funds quickly and efficiently.

Markus Derkum of Jamestown, a real estate investment company that raises money in Germany for investments in the US, says weak stock-market performance already saw German investors turning to US real estate in 2001. He said the terrorist attacks in the World Trade Center and the Pentagon in September only caused a minor blip on the flow.

"We thought nobody would touch US real estate any more, especially the international capital. We were wrong," he said.

In 2001, foreign acquisitions in apartment, industrial and retail properties totaled $1bn and that is set to jump to $2.2bn this year.

Non-German European investors account for about 22 per cent of the foreign interest in the US, and Middle Eastern investors, Israeli and Arab, account for about 14 per cent. Canadians invested 8 per cent of total foreign investment and Australians, with 5 per cent, have this year emerged as a significant new source of capital, particularly in the retail sector.

Source: Global Investing, Zarina Rijnen, *Financial Times,* 10 December 2002.

Stages of Venture Capital Investing

Schilit (1996) provides a good review of the various stages of venture capital investing. Several rounds of financing take place, and these can be characterized by where they occur in the development of the venture itself. Here, Schilit's classification review is adapted and blended with other common industry terminology.[11] Each stage of financing is matched by investments, so that aggregate investment activity is often reported by the amount in different stage funds.

1. *Seed-stage* financing is capital provided for a business idea. The capital generally supports product development and market research.

2. *Early-stage* financing is capital provided for companies moving into operation and before commercial manufacturing and sales have occurred.

   - *Start-up* is capital provided for companies just moving into operation but without any commercial product or service sales. The capital generally supports product development and initial marketing.

   - *First-stage* financing is capital provided to initiate commercial manufacturing and sales.

3. *Formative-stage* financing includes seed stage and early stage.

4. *Later-stage* financing is capital provided after commercial manufacturing and sales have begun but before any initial public offering.

   - *Second-stage* financing refers to capital used for initial expansion of a company already producing and selling a product but perhaps not yet profitably.

---

[11]See, for example, Thomson Venture Economics, the National Venture Capital Association (in the United States), the European Venture Capital Association, and the British Venture Capital Association.

- *Third-stage* financing is capital provided for major expansion, such as physical plant expansion, product improvement, or a major marketing campaign.

- *Mezzanine* (bridge) financing is capital provided to prepare for the step of going public and represents the bridge between the expanding company and the initial public offering (IPO).

Expansion-stage financing includes second and third stage. *Balanced-stage* financing is a term used to refer to all the stages, seed through mezzanine.

Investment Characteristics

Venture capital investing has several characteristics, some of which are common to alternative investing in general, but many of which are unique:

- *Illiquidity:* Venture capital investments do not provide an easy or short-term path for cashing out. Liquidation or divestment of each venture within a

---

CONCEPTS IN ACTION *VENTURE CAPITAL INVESTMENTS CONTINUE TO DECLINE IN Q3 2002: ECONOMIC REALITIES RETURN INVESTING TO PRE-1998 LEVELS*

Stage of Development

Expansion stage companies continue to receive the most venture capital, receiving 56% of all capital invested and 55% of the number of deals in the third quarter. At the same time, investors continued to fund earlier stage companies. In Q3, companies in the "formative" stages of development (early stage and startup/seed) received similar levels as last quarter, 23% of dollars invested and 30% of the number of deals. This stability in earlier stage investing indicates venture capital firms continue to take longer-term views.

Later stage investing became more dominant in the third quarter, representing 20% of the dollars invested and 15% of the number of deals compared to 13% of the dollars invested and 9% of the number of deals in Q2. This increase in later stage deals demonstrates that venture capitalists have remained committed to their existing portfolio companies and continue to finance their development during this difficult economic period.

According to Jesse Reyes, vice president at Thomson Venture Economics, "Venture funds that focus on later stage deals are finding fewer traditional later stage opportunities—that is, deals a couple of years from exit—because the time to exit has lengthened. As a result, VCs are finding that the only new investments that fit their focus are expansion stage deals that require even more time to mature before exit is a possibility."

Source: PricewaterhouseCoopers, Venture Economics, National Venture Capital Association MoneyTree™ Survey.

portfolio is dependent on the success of the fund manager in creating a buy-out or initial public offering (IPO) opportunity. One particular risk is that inexperienced venture fund managers will "grandstand" and bring ventures to the market too early, especially when the IPO market is good. Conversely, a poor IPO market may mean that otherwise successful ventures may afford no immediate path to liquidity.

- *Long-term commitment required:* Venture capital requires a long-term commitment because of the time lag to liquidity. If the average investor is averse to illiquidity, this will create a liquidity risk premium on venture capital. Thus, an investor with a longer than average time horizon can expect to profit from this liquidity risk premium. It is not surprising that university endowments (with their long horizons) have sought venture capital vehicles.

- *Difficulty in determining current market values:* Because there is no continuous trading of the investments within a venture fund portfolio, there is no objective way of determining the current market value of the portfolio. This poses a problem for reporting the market value exposure of the current venture capital portion of an investor's portfolio.

- *Limited historical risk and return data:* Because there is no continuous market in venture capital, historical risk and return data have limitations.

- *Limited information:* Because entrepreneurs operate in previously uncharted territory, there is little information on which to base estimates of cash flows or the probability of success of their ventures

- *Entrepreneurial/management mismatches:* Although surely profit motivated, some entrepreneurs may be more wedded to the success of their favorite idea than to the financial success of the venture. During the early life of a firm, there are also two major problems that may arise. First, the entrepreneur may not be a good manager, so the existence or creation of a good management team is critical. Second, rapid growth produces a change in the type of managerial expertise required, so that entrepreneurs/managers who can succeed with small ventures need the ability to adapt to the different demands of larger companies, or the investors must be in a position to replace them.

- *Fund manager incentive mismatches:* Fund managers may be rewarded by size of their fund rather than by performance of their fund. Investors interested in performance must look for fund managers whose incentives are aligned with theirs.

- *Lack of knowledge of how many competitors exist:* Because entrepreneurs operate in uncharted territory, there is often little way for them or for analysts to know how many other entrepreneurs are developing substitute ideas or products at the same time. Thus, competitive analysis for venture capital investments is even more difficult than for investments in established companies in established industries.

- *Vintage cycles:* Some years are better than others. Both entry and exit are factors here. If too many entrepreneurial firms enter at the prompt of increased venture capital availability, the economics of perfect competition will prevail and returns will be weak. On the exit side, poor financial market conditions can cause venture capital to dry up, and perhaps some firms that could be successful will not find the financing needed for their success. Thus, some years provide better firm planting and growing conditions than others.

- *Extensive operations analysis and advice may be required:* More than financial engineering skill is required of fund managers. Venture capital investments require extensive investment analysis, but they also require extensive operating management experience. Thus, a venture capital manager who can add value will be the one who has both financial and operating experience, and knowledge of the emerging industry in which the entrepreneur is operating. The venture capital manager must be able to act as both a financial and an operations management consultant to the venture. Reflecting David Swensen's philosophy[12] at the Yale Endowment, the investor is well advised to choose a fund manager who knows the business and can add value.

Types of Liquidation/Divestment[13]

Exit strategies are critical for venture capital investing. The main types of liquidation/divestment are trade sales, initial public offerings (IPOs) followed by the sale of quoted equity, and write-offs. Trade sales are sales or mergers of the private company for cash or stock of the acquirer. An IPO is the initial issuance of shares registered for public trading. Shares are distributed to the private equity investors who can sell them in the marketplace only after the expiration of a lock-up period. (In rare cases, a sale or merger of the private company follows the IPO.) Write-offs are voluntary liquidations that may or may not produce any proceeds. In addition to the main types of liquidation, there are also cases of bankruptcy as well as the situation in which the founder/entrepreneur buys out the outside venture capital investors and takes the company back to a privately held company without institutional shareholders.

Participating in a venture capital fund, investors get distributions of public stock or cash from realized venture capital investments. The fund may require additional investments (drawdowns) from limited partners and may make cash or share distributions at random times during the life of the fund. Investors might also be able to sell their interests if they can find a buyer. Also, at the end of the fund's life, there are often illiquid, barely alive companies (living dead) that are transferred to a liquidating vehicle with minimal fees. A very few funds have an evergreen type of structure, which rolls old fund investments into a new fund that has new cash commitments.

In the following box, note that divestment by flotation and sale of quoted equity together constitute the second main exit mechanism (exit via a public market).

---

[12]See pages 17 and 18 in Lerner (2000).
[13]This section has benefited from correspondence with Dean Takahashi.

CONCEPTS IN ACTION   *EUROPEAN DIVESTMENT REPORTED THROUGH THE THIRD QUARTER OF 2002*

Excluding write-offs, the highest amount divested at cost this year was in quarter three. A total of €1.5bn was divested at cost in Q3, up from €1.3bn in Q2 and just over €1bn in Q1. A total of 502 companies were divested in Q3, down from the 774 divested in Q2. Trade sales remained the most significant route to exit and accounted for 28.8% of total divestment at cost (€434m), a 5% decrease in amount on the previous quarter. At €342m, write-offs remained significant in Q3, but fell by 18% on the previous quarter. IPOs as an exit were still a rare option, but the slow trickle of activity (2 companies divested through IPO in Q3) showed that some practitioners still managed to use the IPO, even in the prevailing difficult climate. Between Q1 and Q3 of 2002, a total of €3.9bn was divested at cost.

	Q3 2002				
	Amount at Cost (€m)	%	No of Divestments	%	No of Co.s
Divestment by Trade Sale	433.6	28.8	118	17.5	81
Divestment by Flotation (IPO)	5.1	0.3	6	0.9	2
Sale of Quoted Equity	62.0	4.1	99	14.7	58
Divestment by Write-Off	342.0	22.7	194	28.8	177
Other	664.7	44.1	257	38.1	184
Total	**1,507.5**	**100.0**	**674**	**100.0**	**502**

Source: Reprinted with permission from European Venture Capital & Private Equity Association, Thomson Economics and PricewaterhouseCoopers.

(Quarterly Activity Indicator, Q3 2002).

Valuation and Performance Measurement

In the venture capital area, valuation and performance measurement is a difficult exercise. This is true at the level of a single venture project, but also at the level of an investment in a venture capital fund.

Valuation and Project Risk   Valuing a prospective venture capital project is a challenging task. Although some valuation methods can be applied, quantifying future cash flows is difficult. Investing in a particular venture capital project is motivated by an anticipated large payoff at time of exit. But many projects will fail along the way. In addition to the normal risk of equity investments, the particular risk of venture capital stems from the increased uncertainty created by possibly inexperienced entrepreneurs with innovative products or product ideas and uncertain time to success, even if successful. Some of the unique risks of venture capital projects come from their investment characteristics, as described. Of course, the risk of a portfolio of venture capital investments is less than the risk of any individual venture project, because of risk diversification.

So, there are three main parameters that enter into valuing a venture capital project:

- An assessment of the expected payoff at time of exit, if the venture is successful;
- An assessment of the time it will take to exit the venture successfully; and
- An assessment of the probability of failure.

This is illustrated in Example 8.5.

EXAMPLE 8.5   VENTURE CAPITAL VALUATION AND RISK

An investor estimates that investing $1 million in a particular venture capital project will pay $16 million at the end of seven years if it succeeds; however, she realizes that the project may fail at any time between now and the end of seven years. The investor is considering an equity investment in the project and her cost of equity for a project with this level of risk is 18 percent. In the following table are the investor's estimates of some probabilities of failure for the project. First, 0.25 is the probability of failure in year 1. For year 2, 0.25 is the probability that the project fails in the second year, given that it has survived through year 1. For year 3, 0.20 is the probability that the project fails, given that it has survived through year 2, and so forth.

Year	1	2	3	4	5	6	7
Failure probability	0.25	0.22	0.20	0.20	0.20	0.20	0.20

i. Determine the probability that the project survives to the end of the seventh year.

ii. Determine the expected NPV of the project.

iii. Make a recommendation.

SOLUTION

i. The probability that the project survives to the end of the first year is $(1 - 0.25) = 1$ minus the probability of failure in the first year; the probability that it survives the end of second year is the product of the probability it survives the first year times the probability it survives the second year, or $(1 - 0.25) (1 - 0.22)$. Using this pattern, the probability that the firm survives to end of the seventh year is $(1 - 0.25) (1 - 0.22) (1 - 0.20)^5 = (0.75) (0.78) (0.80)^5 = 0.192$ or 19.2%.

ii. The NPV of the project, given that it survives to the end of the seventh year and thus earns $16 million, equals $4.02 million $= -\$1$ million $+ \$16$ million$/1.18^7$. The NPV of project given that it fails is $-\$1$ million. Thus, the project's expected NPV is a probability-weighted average of

> these two amounts, or $(0.192)(\$4.02 \text{ million}) + (0.808)(-\$1 \text{ million})$
> $= -\$36,160$.
>
> iii. Based on its negative NPV, the recommendation is to decline the investment.

The payoff structure of actual projects is generally more complex than that of Example 8.5. Practitioners may use a multiple-scenario approach to valuation. In this approach, payoffs are simulated under each scenario (from optimistic to pessimistic) and weighted by the probability of occurrence of the scenario.

Performance Measurement   Investors in a venture capital fund need to evaluate the performance of their investment, not only at time of liquidation, but also during the life of their investment. This is usually done by calculating an internal rate of return based on cash flows since inception and the end-of-period valuation of the unliquidated remaining holdings (residual value or net asset value). The European Venture Capital Association (www.evca.com), the British Venture Capital Association (www.bvca.co.uk), and AIMR have valuation guidelines bearing on this.

There are several challenges to performance measurement in the venture capital area. Lerner (2000) points these out in a discussion of future directions for an endowment fund:

- The difficulty in determining precise valuations. Venture capital funds do not have market prices to value their holdings, so they use some arbitrary technique to value their portfolios of ongoing projects. For example, some managers apply an average internal rate of return to the historical investment costs of their ongoing projects. Of course, the actual exit value is used at the time of exit of a project, or a zero value is used if a project failed.

- The lack of meaningful benchmarks against which fund manager and investment success can be measured.

- The long-term nature of any reliable performance feedback in the venture capital asset class.

Hedge Funds and Absolute Return Strategies

The early 1990s saw the explosive development of *hedge funds*. Even though the attraction of these funds was tempered by many huge losses suffered in 1994 and 1998, the hedge fund industry continued to prosper. The number of global hedge funds, estimated to be 1,373 in 1988 grew to an estimated 7,000 at the end of 2001. The assets under management of hedge funds grew from $42 billion in 1988 to $311 billion in 1998, and to about $600 billion by the end of 2001.[14] The asset base of U.S. and non-U.S. hedge funds are of the same order of magnitude.

---

[14]The source for this is Van Hedge Fund Advisors International at www.vanhedge.com, accessed on 12 December 2002.

CONCEPTS IN ACTION   *LOSSES IN PRIVATE EQUITY BUSINESS REACH $10bn*

Financial services companies' private equity operations have lost more than $10bn in total since the bear market in technology began in 2000, according to their financial reports.

Many institutions—including Deutsche Bank, which has lost $1.7bn, and GE Capital Services, which has taken a $592m hit to earnings—are planning to leave the business, while those that remain are radically changing their practices.

The banks with the largest private equity operations, JP Morgan Chase and Credit Suisse First Boston—both of which have assets of more than $20bn in their groups—remain committed to their business.

But JP Morgan, which has lost at least $1.8bn during the downturn, will have a much reduced presence in the market.

In a memo last week, Bill Harrison, chief executive, reiterated his support for the private equity group, but also set a multi-year target of halving private equity exposure to 10 percent of common equity from 20 percent.

He also noted that the private equity group would have to seek more outside money to support their efforts. The bank recently launched a private equity fund with $1.7bn of outside money, but that fell well short of the initial $5bn target.

JP Morgan also intends to sell its interests in other people's private equity partnerships. Both JP Morgan and CSFB, among others, bought into the idea of investing in buyout funds to cement their growing relationships with buyout firms, which are important Wall Street clients.

But the fall in some funds injected unwanted volatility into banks' income statements and bankers now acknowledge those positions were less useful in attracting buyout business.

Banks have reacted to those losses by turning to the secondary and securitization markets in an effort to find an exit. JP Morgan sold more than $1bn of partnerships 18 months ago and CSFB is in the process of concluding a $100m sale.

Deutsche Bank plans to securitize its investments in other private equity partnerships, as well as allowing its own group to launch a management buyout.

Many firms have found it difficult to divest their private equity exposures, however.

Secondary private equity funds have raised billions of dollars to buy unwanted private equity partnerships.

But after a year when the average buyout fund declined 11 percent in value and the average venture capital fund has fallen 27 percent, according to Thomson Venture Economics, secondary funds are cautious about what they will pay for other people's portfolios.

Source: Robert Clow, *Financial Times: Companies & Markets,* 13 December 2002, p. 19.

Although individual investors have been the traditional client bases of hedge funds, institutional investors, especially endowments and foundations, have started to invest en masse. We start this section by a description of the different types of hedge funds available, including funds of funds. A discussion of the leverage and unique risk characteristics of hedge funds will complete this description. Hedge funds follow strategies that promise a large absolute return, and deserve a close investigation of the actual performance and risk of those strategies. We therefore present the case for investing in hedge funds in some detail, but also provide the caveats.

CONCEPTS IN ACTION   ENDOWMENTS, FOUNDATIONS MOVE MORE TO HEDGE FUNDS

WILTON, Conn.—Endowments and foundations increased their allocations to hedge funds in the year ended June 30, a Commonfund report shows.

Among those that altered their asset allocations during the year, hedge fund exposure rose to 35% of the average alternatives portfolio from 22%.

Increased use of hedge funds helped boost alternative investments to 15% of total assets as of June 30, from 11% a year earlier among the funds that changed their asset allocations.

Of the 97 endowments and foundations surveyed, 29% reported changes in the asset allocation in the previous year.

The $197 million University of Connecticut foundation in Storrs is among those hiking hedge fund exposure. The foundation doubled its hedge fund allocation to 10% of total assets following an asset allocation study by Wilshire Associates, Santa Monica, Calif.

"We've been adding diversification," said Kevin Edwards, director of treasury services.

Of those institutions that made changes, the average allocation to domestic equities dropped three percentage points to 47%; the average allocation to international equities dropped one point to 10%.

John Griswold, executive director of Commonfund Institute, said while he's pleased endowments and foundations largely "are sticking to their guns" on asset allocation, he expects more shifts soon.

"This fall, there will be meetings of committees with a lot of concern," he said.

This is the second consecutive year that endowments and foundations showed negative returns. The average return was −5.4% for the year ended June 30 and −3% for the previous one-year period. For the year ended June 30, 2000, the average return was 13.2%.

The smaller the fund, the worse the return, the survey shows. Respondents with assets between $51 million and $100 million reported an average return of −7.4%, while those assets between $101 million and $500 million reported an average −6.1% return.

By contrast, funds with more than $1 billion in assets returned an average −3.4% for the year ended June 30.

The findings are from the interim edition of Commonfund's benchmark study, an annual survey of higher-education endowments and foundations. The interim study covers 97 endowments and foundations that were surveyed through an Internet questionnaire. The final results of the study will be released in 2003.

Source: Mike Kennedy, *Pensions & Investments,* 30 September 2002, p. 33. Reprinted with permission, *Pensions & Investments,* September 30, 2002. Copyright Crain Communications Inc.

Definition

Objective   It is difficult to provide a general definition of hedge funds. The original concept of a hedge fund was to offer plays *against* the markets, using short-selling, futures, and other derivative products. Today, funds using the "hedge fund" appellation follow all kinds of strategies and cannot be considered a homogeneous asset class. Some funds are highly leveraged; others are not. Some engage in hedging activities, and others do not. Some focus on making macroeconomic bets on commodities, currencies, interest rates, and so on. Some are mostly "technical" funds trying to take advantage of the mispricing of some securities within their market. Futures funds belong to the world of hedge funds. In fact, the common denominator of hedge funds is not their investment strategy but the *search for absolute returns*.

Money management has progressively moved toward a focus on performance *relative to preassigned benchmarks*. An institutional money manager's performance is generally evaluated relative to some market index that is assigned as a mandate. In turn, these benchmarks guide (some would say "unduly constrain") the money manager's investment policy. The risk of deviating from the performance of the benchmark has become huge, given all of the publicity surrounding relative performance in a very competitive money management industry. The development of hedge funds can be seen as a reaction against this trend, with the search for absolute return in all directions. In practice, this means that hedge funds might have more appropriately been termed *isolation* funds. They generally try to isolate specific bets for the purpose of generating alpha. One can infer the particular bet from each hedge fund position. Hedge fund managers seek freedom to achieve high absolute returns and wish to be rewarded for their performance. These objectives are apparent in the legal organization and the fee structure of hedge funds. These two aspects are probably the only uniform characteristics of hedge funds.

Legal Structure   Hedge funds are typically set up as a *limited partnership*, as a limited liability corporation (in the United States), or as an *offshore corporation*. These legal structures allow the fund manager to take short and long positions in any asset, to use all kinds of derivatives, and to leverage the fund without restrictions. Hedge funds based in the United States most often take the form of a limited partnership organized under section 3(c)(1) of the Investment Company Act, thereby gaining exemption from most U.S. Securities and Exchange Commission (SEC) regulations. The fund is limited to no more than 1,009 partners, who must be "accredited investors,"[15] and is prohibited from advertising. Some U.S. hedge funds are organized under section 3(c)(7) of the Investment Company Act, and are also exempt from most SEC regulations. In that case, the fund is limited to no more than 500 investors, who must be "qualified purchasers,"[16] and is prohibited from advertising. Given the small number of partners, a minimum investment is typically more than $200,000. Institutional investors can become partners. U.S. hedge funds are typically incorporated in a "fund-friendly" state, such as Delaware. *Offshore funds* have also proved to be an attractive legal structure. These are incorporated in locations such as the British Virgin Islands, Cayman Islands, Bermuda, or other locations attractive from a fiscal and legal point of view. A hedge fund might consider using "feeders" (vehicles that have an ownership interest in the hedge fund) that enable the hedge fund to solicit funds from investors in every imaginable tax and legal domain—one feeder for ordinary U.S. investors; another for tax-free pensions; another for Japanese who want their profits hedged in yen; still another for European institutions, which invest only in shares that are listed on an exchange (i.e., a dummy listing on the Irish Stock Exchange). These feeders don't keep the money; they are used as paper conduits that channel the money to a central fund, typically a Cayman Islands partnership.

Fee Structure   The manager is compensated through a *base* management fee based on the value of assets under management (at one time as much as 2 to 3 percent, now more typically 1 percent of the asset base) plus an *incentive fee* proportional to the realized profits (ranging from 15 percent to 30 percent, typically 20 percent of total profits).[17] The base fee is paid whatever the performance of the fund. The incentive fee cannot be negative, so a negative return on the funds implies a zero incentive fee. The incentive fee is sometimes applied to profits measured above a risk-free rate applied to the assets. In other words, the hedge fund return has to be greater than the risk-free rate before the incentive fee is activated. The fee structure sometimes includes a "high water mark" stating that following a year in which the fund declined in value, the hedge fund would first have to recover those losses before any incentive fee would be paid. Example 8.6 shows the effect of a hedge fund's fee structure on its net return.

Classification

Hedge funds have become quite global, as evidenced by the wide array of global investments used by these hedge funds and the international diversity of their client

---

[15]An accredited investor under the Securities and Exchange Act is an individual with a net worth in excess of $1 million or an annual income in excess of $200,000; or an entity with total assets of $5 million or more.

[16]A qualified purchaser (or qualified investor) is an individual with at least $5 million in investments or an entity with at least $25 million in investments.

[17]Besides the management and incentive fees that almost all hedge funds charge their clients, hedge funds may charge other fees, such as surrender fees, ticket charges, and financing fees.

EXAMPLE 8.6   HEDGE FUND FEE

A hedge fund has an annual fee of 1 percent base management fee plus a 20 percent incentive fee applied to profits above the risk-free rate, taken to be the Treasury Bill rate. Hence the incentive fee is applied to annual profits after deduction of the Treasury bill rate applied to the amount of assets under management at the start of the year. The gross return during the year is 40 percent. What is the net return (the return after fees) for an investor, if the risk-free rate is 5 percent?

SOLUTION

$$\text{Fee} = 1\% + 20\% \times (40\% - 5\%) = 8\%$$

$$\text{Net return} = 40\% - 8\% = 32\%$$

---

base. Some classifications of hedge funds by investment strategy is provided in the media and by hedge funds databases. These classifications are somewhat arbitrary, exhibit a large degree of overlap, and differ extensively across sources. Following is one possible classification system:

- *Long/short funds* are the traditional types of hedge funds, taking short and long bets in common stocks. They vary their short and long exposures according to forecasts, use leverage, and now operate on numerous markets throughout the world. These funds often maintain net positive or negative market exposures; so they are not necessarily market-neutral. In fact, a subgroup within this category is funds that have a systematic short bias, known as dedicated short funds, or short-seller funds. Long/short funds represent a large amount of hedge fund assets.

- *Market-neutral funds* are a form of long/short funds that attempt to be hedged against a general market movement. They take bets on valuation differences of individual securities within some market segment. This could involve simultaneous long and short positions in closely related securities with a zero net exposure to the market itself. A market-neutral long-short portfolio is constructed so that the total value of the positions held long equals the total value of the positions sold short (dollar neutrality) and so that the total sensitivity of the long positions equals and offsets the total sensitivity of the short positions (beta neutrality). The long position would be in stocks considered undervalued, and the short position would be in stocks considered overvalued. Leverage is generally used, so that the investment in the long position (or the short position) is a multiple of the hedge fund equity. Another alternative is to use derivatives to hedge market risk. For example, a manager could buy some bond deemed to be underpriced with a simultaneous short position in bond futures or other fixed-income derivatives.

This type of fund is sometimes called a fixed-income arbitrage fund. Other types of arbitrage make use of complex securities with option-like clauses, such as convertibles, warrants, or collateralized mortgage obligations (CMOs). Among the various techniques used by market-neutral funds are

- equity long/short,
- fixed-income hedging,
- pairs trading,
- warrant arbitrage,
- mortgage arbitrage,
- convertible bond arbitrage,
- closed-end fund arbitrage, and
- statistical arbitrage.

It must be stressed that despite their labels ("arbitrage," "neutral"), these funds are not riskless because hedges can never be perfect. Loss can be incurred if the model used is imperfect, and can be high because hedge funds tend to be highly leveraged.

EXAMPLE 8.7   LONG/SHORT MARKET-NEUTRAL STRATEGY

A hedge fund has a capital of $10 million and invests in a market-neutral long/short strategy on the British equity market. Shares can be borrowed from a primary broker with a cash margin deposit equal to 18 percent of the value of the shares. No additional costs are charged to borrow the shares. The hedge fund has drawn up a list of shares regarded as undervalued (list A) and a list of shares regarded as overvalued (list B). The hedge fund expects that shares in list A will outperform the British index by 5 percent over the year, while shares in list B will underperform the British index by 5 percent over the year. The hedge fund wishes to retain a cash cushion of $1 million for unforeseen events. What specific investment actions would you suggest?

SOLUTION

The hedge fund would sell short shares from list B and use the proceeds to buy shares from list A for an equal amount such that the overall beta of the portfolio with respect to the market equals zero. Some capital needs to be invested in the margin deposit. The hedge funds could take long/short positions for $50 million:

- Keep $1 million in cash.
- Deposit $9 million in margin.

- Borrow $50 million of Shares B from a broker, and sell those shares short.

- Use the sale proceeds to buy $50 million worth of shares A.

The positions in shares A and B are established so that the portfolio's beta is zero. Also, note that the invested assets of $50 million equals $9 million divided by 0.18. The ratio of invested assets to equity capital is roughly 5:1.

If expectations materialize, the return for investors in the hedge fund will be high. The long/short portfolio of shares should have a gain over the year of 10 percent on $50 million, whatever the movement in the general market index. This $5 million gain will translate into an annual return before fees of 50 percent on the invested capital of $10 million. This calculation does not take into account the return on invested cash ($1 million) and assumes that the dividends on long positions will offset dividends on short positions.

- *Global macro funds* take bets on the direction of a market, a currency, an interest rate, a commodity, or any macroeconomic variable. These funds tend to be highly leveraged and make extensive use of derivatives. There are many subgroups in this category, including the following:

  - *Futures funds* (or *managed futures funds*) are commodity pools that include commodity trading advisor funds (CTAs). They take bets on directional moves in the positions they hold (long and short) in a single asset class, such as currency, fixed income, or commodities and tend to use many actively traded futures contracts.

  - *Emerging-market funds* primarily take bets on all types of securities in emerging markets. The securities markets in these economies are typically less efficient and less liquid than those in developed markets. There typically is not an organized lending market for securities, so it is difficult to sell short most issues. Emerging market investments tend to be fairly volatile and greatly influenced by economic and political factors.

- *Event-driven funds* take bets on some event specific to a company or a security. Typically the events are special situations or opportunities to capitalize on price fluctuations. These include the following, among others:

  - *Distressed securities funds:* The manager invests in the debt and/or equity of companies having financial difficulty. Such companies are generally in bankruptcy reorganization or are emerging from reorganization or appear likely to declare bankruptcy in the near future. Because of their distressed situations, the manager can buy such companies' securities at deeply discounted prices. The manager stands to make money should the company successfully reorganize and return to profitability. The manager may take short positions in companies whose situations he believes will worsen, rather than improve, in the short term.

- *Risk arbitrage in mergers and acquisitions:* Before the effective date of a merger, the stock of the acquired company will typically sell at a discount to its acquisition value as officially announced. A hedge fund manager simultaneously buys stock in a company being acquired and sells stock in its acquirers. Even though a merger has been accepted by the board of directors of the two companies, there is always a chance that the merger will not go through, possibly because of objections by regulatory authorities. This is a reason for the existence of the discount. If the takeover falls through, fund managers can be left with large losses.

EXAMPLE 8.8   MERGER RISK ARBITRAGE AND LONG/SHORT MARKET-NEUTRAL STRATEGY

A merger has been announced between a French company A and a German company B. A will acquire B by offering one share of A for two shares of B. Shares of B were trading in a €15 to €20 range prior to the merger announcement. Shares of B currently trade at €24, while shares of A trade at €50. The merger has been approved by both boards of directors but is awaiting ratification by all shareholders (which is extremely likely) and approval by the EU commission (there is a slight risk of non-approval because the combined company has a large European market share in some products). How could a hedge fund take advantage of the situation? What are the risks?

SOLUTION

The hedge fund should construct a hedged position whereby it buys two shares of B for every share of A that it sells short. Because the proceeds of the short sale of one share of A (€50) can be used to buy two shares of B (€48), the position can be highly leveraged. Of course, the cost of securities lending and margin deposit should also be taken into account. When the merger is completed, the hedge fund will make a profit of approximately two euros for each share of A.

The risk is that the merger will fall through. If it does, the stock price of B will drop sharply, because it was to be acquired at a price well above its premerger market value. If the stock price of A also falls, it should be by less than for B, resulting in an overall loss. The stock price of A might also rise, adding to the loss related to the position in B. That would mean a sizable loss for the hedge fund.

Funds of Funds

Funds of funds (FOF) have been created to allow easier access to small investors, but also to institutional investors. An FOF is open to investors and, in turn, invests in a selection of hedge funds. If an FOF has a large client base, it can invest large sums of money in each hedge fund. With their attractive benefits, FOF have grown rapidly and now compose more than a quarter of all hedge fund assets (McCrary [2002]). An FOF provides investors with several benefits:

- *Retailing:* Typically, a single hedge fund requires an investment of one to several hundred thousand dollars or euros. For the same amount, an investor can get exposure to a large number of hedge funds.

- *Access:* FOF managers may be able to offer investments in successful hedge funds that are closed to individual investors because the maximum number of investors has been reached. As long-time investors, they may have "old" money invested with funds that have been closed to new investment. They are also privileged clients that will have priority in buying shares of individual investors who cash out from the hedge fund for personal reasons.

- *Diversification:* An FOF allows investors to diversify the risk of a single hedge fund. The good performance of a single hedge fund could be due to specific market conditions prevailing in the past. An FOF can diversify across several types of hedge funds that may have good performance in different market conditions.

- *Expertise:* The manager of the FOF is supposed to have expertise in finding reliable and good-quality hedge funds in a world where information on the investment strategies of hedge funds is difficult to obtain. Selecting the right hedge fund and strategy requires a large database and intimate knowledge of strategies, and their advantages and potential pitfalls.

- *Due diligence process:* The due diligence (both at the outset and ongoing) that has to be performed by an institutional investor when selecting a hedge fund is highly specialized and time consuming, given the secretive nature of hedge funds and their complex investment strategies. An FOF may be better equipped to perform this due diligence than is a typical institutional investor.

However, there are drawbacks with an FOF:

- *Fee:* The fee charged by its manager is in addition to that charged by each hedge fund. The total fee can be quite hefty.

- *Performance:* Individual hedge funds are mostly selected by the FOF on the basis of past performance, which in practice often gives little indication of future performance. Biases of the existing databases on hedge funds used by FOFs in their selection process are described subsequently. There is little evidence of persistence in the performance delivered by FOFs.

- *Diversification is a two-edged sword:* Blending a high expected return hedge fund with many others for risk reduction purposes means that the overall FOF expected return will be lowered by this diversification. But the fees paid are still very high.

Leverage and Unique Risks of Hedge Funds

Prior to discussing the performance of hedge funds, we review the use of leverage by hedge funds and the unique risks for hedge funds. Some people regard the use of leverage as one of the main sources of risk for hedge funds, while others maintain that proper use of leverage with appropriate risk management benefits hedge fund investors. In addition, risks that are unique to hedge funds may make hedge funds look unduly risky. Thus, we can usefully discuss hedge funds' risks prior to presenting their historical track record.

Use of Leverage   One of the common characteristics of hedge funds is their use of leverage as part of their trading strategy, although some hedge funds do not use leverage at all.[18] For certain strategies (such as arbitrage strategies), leverage is essential because the arbitrage return is so small that leverage is needed for amplifying the profit. However, leverage is a double-edged sword that also magnifies losses on the downside. In this traditional sense, leveraged investments are more aggressive than those without leverage, and to some people, this may mean high risk.

Leverage in hedge funds often runs from 2:1 to 10:1 (depending on the type of assets held and strategies used) and can run higher than 100:1 (e.g., at one point in time, a well known hedge fund, Long Term Capital Managment or LTCM, had leverage that stood over 500:1 [Lhabitant, 2002]). Thus, some hedge funds may specifically limit the leverage they will employ in the limited partnership agreement so that hedge fund managers are legally bound by that limit. Within the limit, however, hedge fund managers have considerable flexibility.

In general, hedge fund managers can create leverage in trading by:

- borrowing external funds to invest more or sell short more than the equity capital they put in,

- borrowing through a brokerage margin account, and

- using financial instruments and derivatives that require posting margins (typically a fraction of the full value of the position) in lieu of trading in the cash securities that require full payment.

Unique Risks for Hedge Funds   In addition to market and trading risks in different markets, hedge funds face the following unique risks:

- *Liquidity risk:* The liquidity risk is common to all investors who trade in illiquid or thin markets. However, the lack of liquidity under extreme market conditions can cause irreversible damage to hedge funds whose strategies rely on the presence of liquidity in specific markets. For example, the demise of LTCM was attributed to the unexpected absence of normal liquidity.

---

[18]According to survey results, more than 70 percent of hedge funds use leverage to some degree (McCrary, 2002; Van Hedge Fund Advisors International, 2002).

- *Pricing risk:* Hedge funds often invest in complex securities traded over-the-counter. Pricing securities that trade infrequently is a difficult task, especially in periods of high volatility. Broker-dealers tend to adopt an extremely conservative pricing policy to protect themselves in periods of high volatility. The marking-to-market (margin calls) of positions based on these prices can create severe cash needs for hedge funds, even if the funds do not try to liquidate their positions. For example, it is widely believed that the cash drain of marking-to-market positions based on brokers' conservative pricing of derivatives compounded the problems of LTCM. A similar problem arose for Askin Capital's market-neutral funds (see Concepts in Action on page 418). Pricing risk compounds liquidity risk.

- *Counterparty credit risk:* Because hedge funds deal with broker-dealers in most transactions—from buying securities on margin to mortgage trading—counterparty credit risk can arise from many sources. Thus, hedge funds face significant counterparty risk.

- *Settlement risk:* Settlement risk refers to the failure to deliver the specified security or money by one of the parties to the transaction on the settlement day.

- *Short squeeze risk:* A short squeeze arises when short sellers must buy in their positions at rising prices, for example because owners of the borrowed stock demand their shares back. Because some hedge fund strategies require short selling (e.g., long/short strategies), this risk can affect fund performance significantly.

- *Financing squeeze:* If a hedge fund has reached or is near its borrowing capacity, its ability to borrow cash is constrained. Margin calls and marking position to market might result in a cash need for the fund. This risk puts the hedge fund in a vulnerable position when it is forced to reduce the levered positions, say, in an illiquid market at substantial losses, in order to stop the leverage from rising. If the hedge fund were able to borrow more cash, these substantial losses could be avoided.

The Case for Hedge Funds

The case for investing in hedge funds is based on their historical track record and managerial talent. Hedge funds use their track record to support the claim of superior returns, with low risk and low correlation with conventional investments.

Track Record   Because of their heterogeneity, it is impossible to talk about the performance of hedge funds as an asset class. Some indexes of hedge fund performance are available from consultants or fund managers. They are constructed from a database on hedge funds.[19] Among the many indexes, one can list CISDM

---

[19]For a description of hedge fund indexes, see McCarthy and Spurgin (1998), Amenc and Martellini (2002), and Lhabitant (2002).

CONCEPTS IN ACTION   *THE COLLAPSE OF ASKIN'S GRANITE MARKET-NEUTRAL FUNDS AND PRICING PROBLEMS*

The Askin Capital debacle carries with it some sobering lessons for any pension sponsor who invests in specialized corners of the OTC markets.

It does not seem plausible that the collective brainpower brought to bear on David Askin's adventure in high-yield investing could have produced such costly errors. But in piecing together the story from dozens of interviews with investors, money managers, consultants, broker-dealers, and Wall Street risk control specialists, a cautionary tale emerges for plan sponsors in an era of increasingly arcane, specialized investment strategies.

Foremost is a simple lesson about the perils of markets that grow up around esoteric financial instruments like the ones Askin held. Combining illiquid securities—the ones Askin held were priced by very few dealers—with leverage is extremely risky.

The limited liquidity available for esoteric CMO tranches permitted the development of a pricing pattern peculiar to a few OTC markets. Traders call it "free finesse," a term credited to former junk bond king Michael Milken. It means that when a few dealers—some 13 sell esoteric CMOs—are pricing securities for a small group of buyers and extending full financing, price levels achieve an artificial buoyancy.

In such a setting, disasters can happen easily. Askin was trying to make as much money as possible for himself and his investors. Dealers who were eager to deal and extend credit a short time before, in March suddenly demanded repayment from Askin's highly leveraged funds—leaving the end investor in the lurch. An intimate circle of over-the-counter buyers and sellers, which seemed small and comfortable weeks before, suddenly turned into pitiless adversaries.

Another lesson is the importance of knowing how specific money managers value portfolios. Askin's holdings were so highly structured that some bonds had taken as long as a week to create. With this degree of complexity, first, investors were unable to create shadow portfolios; then, changes to a few elements of the formula resulted in large shifts in prices.

Askin could and did argue with dealers about pricing—until he finally took matters into his own hands. By late December, Askin reportedly was using his own "internal manager marks" to price his portfolio.

Such situations are a danger not only to highly sophisticated institutional investors like the ones who bet on Askin Capital's three hedge funds, but to any fund sponsors who invest in specialized corners of the OTC markets. Despite the complexities of Askin's "market neutral" strategy, the crisis that enveloped his funds—an interest rate shift, sparking a turnaround in expectations for mortgages—is all too familiar in the burgeoning CMO market.

Source: Jinny St Goar, *Pension Sponsor,* June 1994.

(by the Center for International Securities and Derivatives Markets at the University of Massachusetts), a successor of indexes by Zurich Capital Management and MAR (Managed Account Reports); CSFB/Tremont (by Credit Suisse First Boston and Tremont, a company producing the TASS database); VAN (by Van Hedge Funds Advisor International); Henessee (by Henessee Group); EACM 100 (Evaluation Associates Capital Market); HFR (by Hedge Fund Research); and Carr/Barclays for CTAs. These indexes are also broken down in subindexes for various classifications of hedge funds. Some indexes are equal-weighted, while others are weighted by the assets under management for each fund. Some are audited, but others are not. The criteria for inclusion vary; in many cases, all that is required is that the hedge fund volunteers to be included in the database used for the index construction. Any index only includes a (small) number of the existing hedge funds. For any month, the performance reported by the various indexes varies widely. For example, Amenc and Martellini (2002) indicate that Zurich Capital Management reported a 20.48 percent return on long/short strategies in February 2000, while EACM reported a −1.56 percent return in the same month.

However, the study of performance and risk of all of these hedge fund indexes yields a strong case for investing in hedge funds:

- Hedge funds tend to have a net return (after fees) that is higher than equity markets and bond markets. For example, Exhibit 8.2 reports the average U.S. hedge fund net returns for various indexes over the period January 1996 to

EXHIBIT 8.2

Net Return and Risk of Hedge Funds and Conventional Investments January 1996 to September 2002, Annualized

	HFR Fund Weighted Composite	HFR Fund of Funds	EACM 100	CSFB/ Tremont	S&P 500	Lehman Government/ Corporate Bond Index
Annualized Return	10.92%	8.29%	9.96%	11.55%	5.86%	7.24%
Standard Deviation	8.59%	7.00%	4.93%	9.34%	17.49%	3.99%
Sharpe Ratio	0.74	0.54	1.10	0.75	0.08	0.68
Correlation with HFR Fund Weighted Composite	1.00	0.91	0.88	0.77	0.73	−0.11
Correlation with HFR Fund of Funds	0.91	1.00	0.94	0.91	0.56	−0.04
Correlation with EACM 100	0.88	0.94	1.00	0.88	0.52	0.01
Correlation with CSFB/ Tremont	0.77	0.91	0.88	1.00	0.51	0.13
Correlation with S&P 500	0.73	0.56	0.52	0.51	1.00	−0.04
Correlation with Lehman Government/Corporate Bond Index	−0.11	−0.04	0.01	0.13	−0.04	1.00

Source: CISDM, University of Massachusetts at Amherst, Winter 2002.

September 2002, as calculated by CISDM. The mean annual return for U.S. hedge funds is 10.92 percent based on the HFR Fund Weighted Composite index, compared with 5.86 percent for the S&P 500, and 7.24 percent for the Lehman Brothers government/corporate bond index.

- Hedge funds tend to have lower risk (measured by the volatility of return or standard deviation) than equity investments. Their investment strategies appear to provide more stable return than traditional equity investments. This is shown on Exhibit 8.2.

- The Sharpe ratio is the reward-to-risk ratio measured as the mean return in excess of the risk-free rate and divided by the standard deviation. Services that follow hedge funds frequently report this metric which may not be appropriate, however, when returns have option-like characteristics as discussed later. Over the period 1996–2002, the Sharpe ratio of hedge funds (represented by all indexes) was higher than that of equity investments and that of bonds (except for the HFR fund of funds index).

- The correlation of hedge funds with conventional investments is generally low, though still positive. In periods of bear equity markets, hedge funds tend to produce returns that are positive (or less negative than equity). Note, however, in Exhibit 8.2, that the correlation of major fund indexes with the S&P 500 is still positive and fairly large over the period 1996–2002. Exhibit 8.3 reports the correlations of hedge fund subindexes (including a CTA subindex) with the S&P 500 index and the Lehman Brothers government/corporate bond index over the same 1996–2002 period. Although some correlations with the S&P 500 are low, especially for market-neutral funds (only 0.15), the

EXHIBIT 8.3

Correlation of Hedge Fund Subindexes with S&P 500 Index and Lehman Government/Corporate Bond Index
January 1996 to September 2002

Hedge Fund Subindex	Correlation with S&P 500	Correlation with Lehman Government/ Corporate Bond Index
HFR Convertible Arbitrage	0.35	−0.08
HFR Equity Hedged	0.70	−0.08
HFR Fixed Income Arbitrage	−0.13	−0.12
HFR Emerging Markets	0.61	−0.20
HFR Event Driven	0.66	−0.14
HFR Merger Arbitrage	0.52	−0.15
HFR Equity Market Neutral	0.15	0.18
HFR Macro	0.40	0.21
CISDM CTA Dollar Weighted	−0.11	0.45

Source: CISDM, University of Massachusetts at Amherst, Winter 2002.

correlation for equity hedge funds is a fairly large 0.70. The correlations of hedge fund subindexes with the bond markets are low and mostly negative, with the CTA dollar-weighted index being the highest at 0.45.

Talent The fee structure and flexibility of hedge funds attract talented fund managers. Someone having an outstanding investment idea can apply it in a hedge fund with few constraints. The investment idea can be leveraged to generate high returns for investors and for the manager. So, the search for an attractive hedge fund is based on its track record and also on the perceived talent of the manager to generate superior performance.

Caveats

Investors should exercise caution when using the historical track record of hedge funds in reaching asset allocation decisions. The hedge fund industry does not adhere to rigorous performance presentation standards. Biases in historical performance data can make it difficult to interpret hedge fund performance; past winners may also not repeat.

Biases The performance data from hedge fund databases and indexes suffer from serious biases that are listed here. Both performance and risk measures are affected.

- *Self-selection bias:* Hedge fund managers decide themselves whether they want to be included in a database. Managers that have funds with an unimpressive track record will not wish to have that information exposed.

- *Instant history bias:* When a hedge fund enters a database, it brings with it its track record. Because only hedge funds with good track records enter the database, this creates a positive bias in past performance in the database, as stressed by Fung and Hsieh (2002).

- *Survivorship bias: Return:* In the investment industry, unsuccessful funds and managers tend to disappear over time. Only successful ones search for new clients and present their track records. This creates a survivor bias. This problem is acute with hedge funds because they often do not have to comply with performance presentation standards. It is not uncommon to see hedge fund managers present the track records of only their successful funds, omitting those that have been closed. If a fund begins to perform poorly, perhaps even starting to go out of business, it may stop reporting its performance entirely, thus inflating the reported average performance of hedge funds. Hedge fund indexes and databases may only include funds that have survived. Funds with bad performance disappear and are removed from the database that is used by investors to select among existing funds. Some data bases are now available that may be free from survivorship bias as defunct hedge funds are left in the data base; however, funds that simply stop reporting still pose a problem.

- *Survivorship bias: Risk:* Biases also affect risk measures. A similar survivorship bias applies to risk measures. Investors shy away from high risk, as well as from negative returns. Hedge funds that exhibited highly volatile returns in the past tend to disappear. Only strategies that have experienced low volatility in the past survive. So, reported volatility of existing funds will tend to be low. There is no guarantee that the same strategy will also be low risk in the future. Examples abound of hedge funds that were regarded as low risk but lost all of their capital.

- *Smoothed pricing: Infrequently traded assets:* Some assets trade infrequently. This is the case for many alternative assets that are not exchange-traded, such as real estate or private equity. This is also the case for illiquid exchange-traded securities or OTC instruments often used by hedge funds. Because prices used are often not up-to-date market prices, but estimates of fair value, their volatility is reduced (smoothing effect). The infrequent nature of price updates for alternative investments, induces a significant downward bias to the

---

EXAMPLE 8.9   BIASES IN REPORTED PERFORMANCE

A manager without any expertise has decided to launch five long/short hedge funds with some seed money. The investment strategies of the five funds are quite different. Actually, the investment strategy of fund A is just the opposite of that of fund E. After a couple of years, some have performed well and some badly, as could be expected by pure chance. The annualized gross returns on the five funds are listed in the following table. All have an annualized standard deviation of 10 percent and the annual risk-free rate is 3 percent. The manager decides to close funds A, B, and C and to enter funds D and E in a well-known hedge fund database. The marketing pitch of the manager is that the funds have superior performance (Sharpe ratio of 1.7 and 2.7). What do you think?

Fund Name	Mean Annual Return	Standard Deviation	Sharpe Ratio
Fund A	−30%	10%	−3.3
Fund B	−20%	10%	−2.3
Fund C	0%	10%	−0.3
Fund D	+20%	10%	1.7
Fund E	+30%	10%	2.7

SOLUTION

The performance on the funds is purely random. But only the good-performing funds are included in the hedge fund database. The performance reported for a selection of funds is misleading. There is obvious survivorship and self-selection bias. Similarly, the performance of the hedge fund index is biased upward and misleading.

measured risk of the assets. In addition, correlations of alternative investment returns with conventional equity and fixed income returns, and correlations among the alternative investments, are often artificially low simply because of the smoothing effect and the absence of market-observable returns. The bias can be very large,[20] so the true risk is much larger than the reported estimates.

- *Option-like investment strategies:* Traditional risk measures used in performance appraisal assume that portfolio returns are drawn from normal or, at least, symmetric, distributions. Many investment strategies followed by hedge funds have some option-like features that violate these distributional assumptions. For example, hedge funds following so-called arbitrage strategies will generally make a small profit when asset prices converge to their estimated fair value, but they run the risk of a huge loss if their arbitrage model fails. Standard deviation or traditional value at risk (VaR) measures understate the true risk of losses, and the Sharpe ratio can be an inappropriate performance measure.

- *Fee structure and gaming:* It is also important to remember the high fees charged by hedge funds: Typically a fixed fee of 1 percent plus an incentive fee of 20 percent of the total return, if positive. This compensation structure is option-like. Clearly, fund managers are paid to take risks. One can argue that they have strong incentives to take a huge amount of risk if their recent performance has been bad. However, one can also argue that because of the high water mark provision, hedge fund managers may not want to ruin their chance to stage a comeback by taking more risk as their performance diminishes. In either case, past risk measures may be misleading for forecasting future performance and risk for a fund that has performed badly in the recent past.

Persistence of Performance   Because of various biases, judging the average performance of the hedge fund industry by using the indexes discussed can be difficult. To appraise individual hedge funds, investors should look at their persistence of performance. Before a specific hedge fund is purchased, investors should judge whether their good track record will persist in the future. A similar attitude must be adopted when considering an FOF.[21]

Talented hedge fund managers can exploit market inefficiencies that cannot be exploited by conventional asset managers and/or design innovative investment strategies that may yield excellent returns. But, again, two caveats are in order. First, the size of the hedge fund industry is huge (some $600 billion by the end of 2001), and the

---

[20]See, for example, Asness, Krail, and Liew (2001).

[21]In a study that may come as a surprise to proponents of hedge funds, Brown, Goetzmann, and Ibbotson (1999) found "no evidence of performance persistence in raw returns or risk-adjusted returns, even when we break funds down according to their returns-based style classification." They conclude that "the hedge fund arena provides no evidence that past performance forecasts future performance." It's important to note, however, that this study covers a relatively short time period and that determining accurate and comparable performance figures in the hedge fund arena is extremely complex.

leverage used means that the industry is a very large player in capital markets. But the existence of pricing inefficiencies, for which many managers search, is necessarily limited. Thus there is a very large pool of capital chasing after what is likely to be a limited supply of pricing inefficiencies. Second, any successful strategy will quickly be imitated by many other investors, thereby reducing its future profitability.

To summarize, investors need to exercise great caution in interpreting the reported performance of hedge funds; the risks in hedge fund investments are easily underestimated.

Closely Held Companies and Inactively Traded Securities

Investments in closely held companies and inactively traded securities require analysis of legal, financial, and ownership considerations with account taken of the effects of illiquidity. Closely held companies are those that are not publicly traded. Inactively traded securities are securities of companies that are infrequently traded; they generally do not trade on major exchanges. Illiquidity, limited information availability, and minority ownership issues are common to such companies.

Legal Environment

Closely held companies may be organized in various legal forms, such as special tax-advantaged corporations (subchapter S corporations in the United States), regular corporations, general partnerships, limited partnerships, and sole proprietorships. These forms have tax implications, as well as ownership differences, for the investor. Ownership is a bundle of rights, and these rights differ, depending on the business form. Because valuations can be required to provide evidence in litigation—for example, minority shareholder claims—much case law defines terms such as *intrinsic value, fundamental value,* and *fair value.* These definitions may vary in different jurisdictions. Even what is judged as evidence for a valuation can vary. There has long been a tension between the theory of value as based on projected cash flows and the acceptance of the *hard* evidence of recent cash flows. In a real sense, then, valuation of closely held and inactively traded securities requires extensive knowledge of the law and the purposes of the valuation.[22]

Valuation Alternatives

The basic types of valuation are the cost approach, the comparables approach, and the income approach.

The Cost Approach   This approach attempts to determine what it would cost to replace the company's assets in their present form.

---

[22]See Pratt, Reilly, and Schweihs (1996) for an extensive treatment of the analysis and appraisal of closely held companies.

The Comparables Approach   In the company comparison approach, market value is estimated relative to a benchmark value. The benchmark value may be the market price of a similar but actively traded company, or the average or median value of the market prices of similar companies, in transactions made near the time of the appraisal. The benchmark-based estimate needs to be adjusted for changing market conditions, the possibility that the benchmark itself is mispriced, and the unique features of the company relative to the benchmark. Companies with comparable characteristics might not have traded recently.

The Income Approach   For business valuation, Pratt, Reilly, and Schweihs (1996) essentially define the income approach as one of appropriately discounting any anticipated future economic income stream.

Bases for Discounts/Premiums

Because closely held companies and inactively traded securities are illiquid, some discount must be made for that illiquidity. For infrequently traded stocks, share prices should reflect a liquidity discount compensating investors for illiquidity in the market for the shares. Shares of closely held companies lack a public market (lack marketability) and so their valuation should reflect a marketability discount to account for the extra return investors should require on those shares. In addition to a discount for lack of marketability for a closely held company, the analyst may also need to apply a discount for minority interest, or a premium for control. The minority interest discount is applied if the interest will not be able to influence corporate strategy and other business decisions. To estimate a marketability discount, minority discount, or control premium, the analyst must carefully define the amount or base to which the discount or premium should be applied.

To estimate a marketability discount for a closely held company, the analyst identifies a publicly traded comparable company with a liquid market. The comparable's market value of equity is the base to which the marketability discount is applied.

To estimate a minority interest discount for a company, the base is an estimate of that company's value of equity inclusive of the value arising from ownership of all rights of control. To estimate a control premium, the base is an estimate of that company's value of equity not reflecting control (the value of equity from a minority shareholder perspective).

Distressed Securities/Bankruptcies

Distressed securities are securities of companies that have filed or are close to filing for bankruptcy court protection, or that are seeking out-of-court debt restructuring to avoid bankruptcy.[23] The legal framework of bankruptcy proceedings differs across countries. In the United States, two types of bankruptcy protection are

---

[23]See Tremont Advisers, 2002.

available: protection for liquidation (called Chapter 7) and protection for reorganization (called Chapter 11). Valuation of such securities requires legal, operational, and financial analysis.

To understand distressed securities, one must appreciate the inherent divergence of interests between the stockholders and bondholders of a company. Stockholders own the successful company, but bondholders have a prior claim to the assets of the bankrupt company. In reorganizations, bondholders' prior claim can allow them to negotiate for ownership in the postbankruptcy company, thus diluting the original shareholders' claims. Investing in distressed securities, then, usually means investing in distressed company bonds with a view toward equity ownership in the eventually reconstituted company. In this regard, such investments have characteristics somewhat similar to those of venture capital investing. For example, they are illiquid and require a long horizon, as well as intense investor participation in guiding the venture to a successful outcome. Another similarity, though, is the possibility of mispricing. Hooke (1998) reports on the disappointment of some traditional distressed-securities investors that these investments are attracting attention and efficient prices; but he suggests that business volatility and high leverage will guarantee many problem companies with inevitable value discrepancies (mispricing).

Distressed-security investing may be viewed as the ultimate in value investing. A distressed company with low enterprise value (EV) to earnings before interest, taxes, depreciation, and amortization (EBITDA) will attract the attention of an investor looking for positive, postrestructuring cash flows. The primary question for any distressed security is the question of the distress source. Is the company operationally sound but financially hampered by too much gearing (leverage), or is the company weak operationally? If the company is weak operationally, is it a candidate to be turned around by cost cutting and improvement in the business cycle or else by new management and/or a new competitive strategy? Distressed-security investing requires intense industry analysis, as well as analysis of business strategies and of the management team that will conduct the restructuring.

Commodity Markets and Commodity Derivatives

Commodities present an unusual investment alternative. Investing in commodities complements the investment opportunities offered by shares of corporations that extensively use those commodities in their production process. Investing directly in agricultural products and other commodities gives the investor a share in the

---

CONCEPTS IN ACTION   UAL STRATEGY CHIEF OUTLINES PLANS

Competitive costs, services for range of customers will form basis of revival

The business plan that UAL Corp.'s United Airlines hopes will be the foundation for its emergence from bankruptcy-court protection features competitive costs and a suite of discrete air-service products designed to make the airline "relevant" to as many customers as possible.

In a message to employees, Doug Hacker, UAL's new executive vice president of strategy, said the company intends to develop a "mainline" jet service that has the lowest costs among its peers. United will court international travelers through increased reliance on its airline partners in the Star Alliance, he said.

To serve small domestic cities, United intends to continue to build up small-jet flights offered by its regional affiliates. And to cater to leisure fliers, it expects to operate a separate airline that offers "a low-cost, no-frills" product in markets dominated by leisure customers and low-cost competition, Mr. Hacker said.

Lenders set conditions

UAL, the world's second-largest carrier, filed for protection from its creditors Monday in U.S. Bankruptcy Court in Chicago. As part of its filing, the company said it arranged $1.5 billion in interim financing to help it operate while under court protection. The lenders, who next week will extend an initial $800 million of that funding, insist that the airline meet strict financial benchmarks if it is to receive the balance.

Mr. Hacker, who served for several years as UAL's chief financial officer before leaving to head a United subsidiary, on Wednesday was named to the new post as strategy chief. Yesterday, he presented an overview of United's business plan to leaders of the carrier's union. In a telephone message to employees, he noted that the terms of the interim bankruptcy financing require lower labor costs "under very tight time frames."

In discussions with union leaders yesterday, it wasn't clear whether the company spelled out specific savings targets. A United spokesman last night declined to discuss details on the business plan or the savings targets.

Possible low-fare product

"We want to make the United brand relevant to as many customers as we can," Mr. Hacker told employees. "We'll do that through a family of products that meets customers' different needs."

Glenn Tilton, UAL's chairman and chief executive, has hinted in recent days that United would revive a product similar to its low-fare shuttle service that operated in the Western U.S. in the late 1990s to help the carrier fight off competition from Southwest Airlines. Mr. Tilton also hinted in employee meetings the past few days in the airline's hubs that UAL may seek government aid to facilitate its exit from Chapter 11.

The Air Transportation Stabilization Board, whose refusal to grant government-loan backing forced the airline into bankruptcy, has indicated it would consider a revised application from United for loan guarantees to back up financing to help the airline emerge from reorganization.

Source: Susan Carey, *Wall Street Journal*, 13 December 2002, p. A2.

commodity components of the country's production and consumption. Money managers and average investors, however, usually prefer commodity derivatives (financial instruments that derive their value from the value of the underlying commodity) rather than commodities themselves. The average investor does not want to store grains, cattle, crude oil, or metals. A common investment objective is to purchase indirectly those real assets that should provide a good hedge against inflation risk. There are several indirect ways to invest in commodities:

- Futures contracts: A commodity futures contract is a standardized, exchange-traded agreement between two parties in which the buyer agrees to buy a commodity from the seller at a future date at a price agreed upon today.

- Bonds indexed on some commodity price.

- Stocks of companies producing the commodity.

Investing in commodity futures is the most common strategy. Commodity trading advisers (CTAs) offer *managed futures funds* that take positions in exchange-traded derivatives on commodities and financials.[24]

Commodity Futures

Futures contracts are the easiest and cheapest way to invest in commodities. Commodities can be grouped into three major categories:

- *Agricultural products,* including fibers (wool, cotton), grains (wheat, corn, soybeans), food (coffee, cocoa, orange juice), and livestock (cattle, hogs, pork bellies). These are often called soft commodities by professionals.

- *Energy,* including crude oil, heating oil, and natural gas

- *Metals,* such as copper, aluminum, gold, silver, and platinum

Numerous commodity indexes have been developed. Some traditional indexes are broadly based, with a global economic perspective; they aim to track the evolution of input prices. Other indexes have been developed as *investable* indexes. They are based on the most liquid commodity futures contracts, so they can easily be replicated by taking positions in individual commodities. For example, the Goldman Sachs Commodity Index (GSCI) is a world-production weighted index of 26 commodities with liquid futures contracts. Futures contracts on the GSCI trade in Chicago. The composition and weights of the various commodity indexes differ widely, and so do their performances.

Motivation and Investment Vehicles

Commodities are sometimes treated as an asset class because they represent a direct participation in the real economy. The motivation for investing in commodities ranges from the diversification benefits achievable by a passive investor to the

---

[24]See Jaeger (2002) p. 18.

speculative profits sought by an *active* investor. The design of the investment vehicle used reflects these different motivations.

Passive Investment   A passive investor would buy commodities for their risk-diversification benefits. When inflation accelerates, commodity prices go up, whereas bond and stock prices tend to go down. A passive investor would typically invest through a collateralized position in a futures contract. Many banks and money managers offer collateralized futures funds based on one of the investable commodity indexes. A collateralized position in futures is a portfolio in which an investor takes a long position in futures for a given amount of underlying value and simultaneously invests the same amount in government securities, such as Treasury bills. The various investable indexes and collateralized futures indexes are published both in excess-return and in total-return form. The indexes reported assume that the *total return* on the index is continuously reinvested. The *excess return* is the return above the risk-free rate. The total return is the risk-free rate plus the excess return.

EXAMPLE 8.10   *COLLATERALIZED FUTURES*

Assume that the futures price is currently $100. If $100 million is added to the fund, the manager will take a long position in the futures contract for $100 million of underlying value and simultaneously buy $100 million worth of Treasury bills (part of this will be deposited as margin). If the futures price drops to $95 the next day, the futures position will be marked to market, and the manager will have to sell $5 million of the Treasury bills to cover the loss. Conversely, if the futures price rises to $105, the manager will receive a marked-to-market profit of $5 million, which will be invested in additional Treasury bills. Discuss the sources of total return from such an investment.

SOLUTION

The total return on the collateralized futures position comes from the change in futures price and the interest income on the Treasury bills.

Generally, the volatility of commodity futures is higher than that of domestic or international equity, but commodities have a negative correlation with stock and bond returns and a desirable positive correlation with inflation. Nevertheless, the excellent long-term performance of some commodity indexes requires a word of caution. The commodities and weights selected to enter indexes reflect a selection bias when they include data from time periods prior to the initiation of the index, which biases any back-calculated performance.

Active Investment

Besides making inflation bets, another motivation for investing in commodities is that they provide good performance in periods of economic growth. In periods of rapid economic growth, commodities are in strong demand to satisfy production needs, and their prices go up. Because of productivity gains, the prices of finished goods are unlikely to rise as fast as those of raw materials. This suggests an active management strategy in which specific commodities are bought and sold at various times. Managed futures are proposed by a large number of institutions.

As with any investments, the return–risk characteristics of managed futures must be analyzed carefully. Schneeweis (2002) discusses the proposed attraction of managed futures: the possibility of positive returns in months when the market does well and in the months when it does poorly. Jaeger (2002) proposes several principles for the risk management of managed futures portfolios:

- Diversification

- Liquidity monitoring, because diversification into a larger universe of contracts can include illiquid contracts

- Volatility dependent allocation where the weight of the different contracts in the portfolio is determined by their historical or implied volatility

- Quantitative risk management techniques such as value at risk (VaR) and stress tests

- Risk budgeting on various aggregation levels to detect undesired risk concentrations

- Limits on leverage

- Use of derivatives to hedge any unwanted currency risk

- Care in model selection with respect to data mining, in and out of sample performance, and adequate performance adjustments for risk

The Example of Gold

Gold has always played a special role in investments. It is a commodity traded worldwide, but more important, it has been regarded by many Europeans and Asians as the ultimate store of value. It is considered an international monetary asset that offers protection in case of a major disruption. Furthermore, central banks and most non-U.S. investors regard gold as a monetary asset because it has been the core of domestic and international monetary systems for many centuries. This section focuses on gold investment because of the historical importance of gold in investment strategies, and as an example of a real asset investment. Of course, precious stones, stamps, or paintings could also be profitable long-term investments, but they usually require high transaction costs; moreover, each stone or painting is in a sense unique, which reduces its marketability. Gold is offered in a wide variety of investment vehicles that can be used in passive or active strategies. Gold-linked investments include gold bullion, coins, bonds, mining equity, futures, and options on gold and on mining equity or bonds.

The Motivation for Investing in Gold   The traditional role of gold as the ultimate hedge and store of value is well known. For centuries, Europeans and Asians alike have regarded gold as the best possible protection against inflation and social, political, or economic crises because it can easily be traded worldwide at any time, and its real value increases during crises. Europeans and others who have suffered revolutions, invasions, and periods of hyperinflation need no correlation coefficients to be convinced of this attractive portfolio hedge characteristic. For example, gold kept its real value during the U.S. stock market crash from 1929 to 1932 and the London Stock Exchange collapse in equity and bonds from 1973 to 1975. Furthermore, the central role gold has played in domestic and international monetary systems for thousands of years makes it, in part, a monetary asset with exceptional liquidity. Other real assets, such as diamonds or stamps, do not have this characteristic.

In general, gold often allows investors to diversify against the kinds of risks that affect all stock markets simultaneously. For example, in 1973 and 1974, the price of bullion tripled when stock markets worldwide dropped dramatically during the oil crisis; the NYSE dropped approximately 50 percent.

A theoretical comment is in order here. In modern portfolio theory, a small or negative beta implies that the expected return on gold should be small. For example, a negative beta caused by a negative correlation between gold and the market portfolio implies that in the capital asset pricing model (CAPM) framework, the expected return on gold should be less than the risk-free interest rate. Indeed, it can be claimed that we should expect a modest long-term performance in gold and a greater return on the other assets in the portfolio; however, gold assets will reduce the risk of the portfolio in the event of adverse economic conditions. The question for a prudent portfolio manager, then, is whether these hedge benefits are worth the implicit cost she must pay in the form of a smaller expected long-term return for a small part of the portfolio.

Gold Price Determinants　　The following material is intended to indicate the kind of information and methods that analysts and investment managers use to analyze real asset investments. Commodities other than gold could also serve as examples.

Gold is a tangible international asset in limited supply. Gold can be extracted at a cost but cannot be produced artificially. Although gold is immune to the effects of weather, water, and oxygen, it suffers from human habits. The tradition of hiding gold treasures in the ground is consistent with the observation that gold is the ultimate physical store of value during major disruptions such as civil unrest, coup d'état, and war. During World War II, most Europeans dug a hole in their gardens or cellars to hide their gold holdings. Part of this hidden gold is never recovered if the owner dies. Most of the gold used in dentistry also disappears with the owner. Despite these losses, the stock of gold keeps slowly increasing with the amount extracted.

In a sense, the price of gold should be easy to forecast: The product is well defined. The supply sources are well identified, and reserves can be reasonably estimated. The major demands are clearly identified: carat jewelry, industrial needs, coins, and investment.

Supply and demand clearly determine the price of gold. It is therefore necessary to study the various components of supply and demand to forecast the price of gold. A different model may be required for each component. For example,

Western mine production is affected by technological considerations, South African extraction policy, and political situations in sensitive countries. Russia's gold sales depend on their need for hard currencies. Official sales may also be induced by monetary and balance of payments problems. Industrial demand depends on technological innovation and the discovery of cheaper substitutes. Jewelry demand is sensitive to short-term gold price movements, as well as fashion; the investment motivation is often present in jewelry purchases. Investment demand for bullion and coins is a component of the total demand affecting gold price but is also determined by expectations of future price movements.

So, although gold is a single, well-identified, extensively researched product, its analysis and valuation is not a simple exercise. This difficulty may add another dimension to gold's mystical attraction.

Commodity-Linked Securities

Holding commodities provides no income, so the sole return to the owner is through price increase. Investors can also select securities that are linked to some commodity prices and also provide some income. This can be an attractive alternative for investors who wish to, or must, hold financial investments rather than real assets. The two major types of commodity-linked securities are bonds and equity. The indexation clause is explicit for commodity-linked bonds but implicit for equity. Again, we focus on the example of gold.

Commodity-Linked Bonds   There are many examples of commodity-linked bonds in the world capital markets.[25] In periods of high inflation, governments have often been forced to offer loans with coupons or principal indexed to either the price of a specific good or a global inflation index. Inflation-indexed gilts became popular in the United Kingdom during the 1980s. The capital and coupons of these bonds are indexed to British retail prices.

In 1997, the U.S. Treasury started to offer Inflation-Indexed Securities, also known as Treasury Inflation Protected Securities (TIPS).[26] The first such security was a 10-year bond, issued with a real yield of 3.45 percent. The principal value is adjusted for changes in the consumer price index (CPI) on each semiannual coupon payment date. So, the nominal coupon, equal to the real yield times the CPI-adjusted principal, increases with inflation. At maturity, the CPI-adjusted principal is reimbursed. In the United States, some government agencies, municipalities, and corporations have also issued inflation-indexed bonds. Often, the inflation adjustment to the principal is paid out immediately rather than at final maturity. This structure has been adopted because seeing their nominal credit exposure on nongovernment issues accumulate automatically over time worried investors.

---

[25]Jacquillat and Roll (1979) provide an empirical analysis of the benefits of commodity-linked bonds. Schwartz (1982) provides a theoretical model for an index-linked bond with an option to repay the bond at face value or at an index-linked price. Such a model was tested on a silver-linked bond issued by Sunshine Mining in Brauer and Ravichandran (1986). An interesting analysis of oil-linked securities is provided by Gibson and Schwartz (1990).

[26]McFall Lamm (1998) and Anderson and Moore (1998) provide an analysis of TIPS.

Several countries have issued inflation-indexed bonds, and corporations and governments have issued bonds indexed to a variety of specific prices, such as oil prices. Gold bonds, and bonds with warrants on gold, have been an attractive alternative to holding gold ingots.

Commodity-Linked Equity   The value of some companies is directly affected by commodity prices. This is clearly the case with the so-called *energy companies*. For example, companies in the oil and gas industries are affected by the evolution of oil prices. The link between commodity prices and stock prices is more evident for small, undiversified companies that specialize in one type of activity, for example, oil and gas exploration and production. However, large oil companies tend to be quite diversified across activities and the link between commodity prices and stock prices is weaker. An integrated exploration, production, and refining company will be less affected by oil price increases than a company operating in only one of the industry segments.

Gold mining companies are another example of commodity-linked equity. Gold mining shares differ from commodity-linked bonds in that the indexation clause is not fixed by contract but depends on mining economics. In fact, the mining industry is probably the simplest activity to describe in a valuation model. The economics of mining can be described by a simple discounted cash flow model. The principal relationship in the model is the cost structure of the mine as measured by the ratio of costs to revenues. The cost to remove an ounce or a gram of gold from so-called storage and refine it depends on several factors: technology, wage rates, power rates, and the grade and depth of the mine. Revenues depend on the world price of gold. Any movement in the market price of gold will directly affect the cash flows of a mine and therefore its market value; the higher the ratio of costs to revenues, the more sensitive will be the cash flows to gold price movements. However, note that the correlation between gold mine share prices and the price of gold is far from perfect. Gold mine values are influenced by factors other than gold prices; for example, social and political factors have strongly affected South African share prices over time.

Summary

- Alternative investments usually involve illiquidity, difficulty in the determination of current market values, limited historical risk and return data, the requirement for extensive investment analysis, a liquidity risk premium, and a segmentation risk premium. Alternative assets are assets not traded on exchanges. Alternative strategies are strategies that mostly use traded assets for the purpose of isolating bets and generating alpha.

- An open-end fund stands ready to redeem investor shares at market value, but a closed-end fund does not. A load fund has sales commission charges, and a no-load fund does not. Sales fees may also appear in annual distribution fees.

- The net asset value of a fund is calculated as the per-share value of the investment company's assets minus liabilities.

- Mutual funds may charge several different fees: Loads and redemption fees provide sales incentives; distribution and operating fees are annual fees; the part of the operating fee that is allocated to the fund manager can be considered an investment performance incentive.

- An exchange traded fund (ETF) is a special type of fund that tracks some market index but that is traded on a stock market as any common share.

- A mutual fund's purchases and sales of stocks held in the fund lead to taxable gains at the level of the fund, but this is not the case for an ETF because of its in-kind creation and redemption process.

- The advantages of ETFs are diversification; trading similarly to a stock; management of their risk augmented by futures and options contracts on them; transparency; cost effectiveness; avoidance of significant premiums or discounts to NAV; tax savings from payment of in-kind redemption; and immediate dividend reinvestment for open-end ETFs. The disadvantages are only a narrow-based market index tracked in some countries; intraday trading opportunity is not important for long-horizon investors; large bid–ask spreads on some ETFs; and possibly better cost structures and tax advantages to direct index investing for large institutions.

- Some characteristics of real estate as an investable asset class are that each property is immovable, basically indivisible, and unique; not directly comparable to other properties; illiquid; and bought and sold intermittently in a generally local marketplace, with high transaction costs and market inefficiencies.

- The main approaches to real estate valuation are the cost approach, the sales comparison approach, the income approach, and the discounted after-tax cash flow approach.

- The net operating income from a real estate investment is gross potential income minus expenses, which include estimated vacancy and collection costs, insurance, taxes, utilities, and repairs and maintenance.

- The value of a property can be calculated as the cost to replace the building in its present form in the cost approach; an adjusted value from a benchmark of comparable sales in the sales comparison approach; or a hedonic price estimate from a regression model in the sales comparison approach; and capitalized net operating income in the income approach.

- The net present value of a property to an equity investor is obtained as the present value of the after tax cash flows, discounted at the investor's required rate of return on equity, minus the amount of equity required to make the investment.

- Venture capital investing is done in many stages from seed through mezzanine.

- Venture capital investment characteristics include illiquidity; long-term commitment required; difficulty in determining current market values; limited historical risk and return data; limited information; entrepreneurial/management mismatches; fund manager incentive mismatches; lack of knowledge of how many competitors exist; vintage cycles; and the requirement for extensive operations analysis and advice. The challenges to venture capital performance measurement are the difficulty in determining precise valuations, the lack of meaningful benchmarks, and the long-term nature of any performance feedback.

- The expected net present value of a venture capital project with a single, terminal payoff and a single, initial investment can be calculated, given its possible payoff and its conditional failure probabilities, as the present value of the expected payoff minus the required initial investment.

- The term *hedge fund* is not fully descriptive, because the hedged position is generally designed to isolate a bet rather than to reduce risk. Hedge funds can be defined as funds that seek absolute returns; have a legal structure avoiding some government regulations; and have option-like fees, including a base management fee and an incentive fee proportional to realized profits.

- The net performance of a hedge fund can be calculated by subtracting its fees from its gross performance.

- Hedge funds can be classified in a variety of ways. One classification of hedge funds comprises the categories: long/short, market neutral, global macro, and event driven.

- The advantages of fund of funds investing are availability to the small investor, access to funds closed to new investors, diversification, managerial expertise, and a due diligence process. The disadvantages to fund of funds investing are high fees, little evidence of persistent performance, and the absolute return loss through diversification.

- High leverage is often present in hedge funds as part of the trading strategy and is an essential part of some strategies in which the arbitrage return is so small that leverage is needed to amplify the profit. The unique risks of hedge funds are liquidity risk, pricing risk, counterparty credit risk, settlement risk, short squeeze risk, and financing squeeze risk.

- In terms of performance, hedge funds are generally viewed as having a net return higher than available for equity or bond investments, lower standard deviation of return than equity investments, a Sharpe ratio that is comparable to bonds and higher than that of equity investments, and a low correlation with conventional investments. The biases present in hedge fund performance reporting include self-selection bias, instant history bias, survivorship bias on return, survivorship bias on risk, smoothed pricing on infrequently traded assets, option-like investment strategies, and fee structure–induced gaming.

- For closely held companies and inactively traded securities, a discount is used for lack of liquidity, lack of marketability, and for a minority interest, but a control premium is added for controlling ownership. The base for the marketability discount is the market value of equity for a comparable publicly traded company.

- Distressed-securities investing usually means investing in distressed company bonds with a view to equity ownership in the eventually reconstituted company. Such investments are similar to venture capital investments because they are illiquid; they require a long investment horizon; they require intense investor participation/consulting; and they offer the possibility of alpha because of mispricing.

- As a vehicle for investing in production and consumption, commodities complement the investment opportunities offered by shares of corporations that extensively use these as raw materials in their production processes. Investing directly in agricultural products and other commodities gives the investor exposure to the commodity components of the country's production and consumption.

- Commodity trading advisors (CTAs) offer managed futures funds that take positions in exchange traded derivatives on commodities and financials.

- The return on a collateralized futures position comes from the change in the futures price plus the interest income on risk-free government securities.

- The motivation for investing in commodities, commodity derivatives, and commodity-linked securities is that they may have negative correlation with stock and bond returns and a desirable positive correlation with inflation. In the case of commodity-linked securities, the investor can receive some income rather than depending solely on commodity price changes.

- The risk of managed futures can be managed through diversification, liquidity monitoring, volatility dependent allocation, quantitative techniques such as VaR, risk budgeting on various aggregation levels, limits on leverage, use of derivatives, and care in model selection.

Problems

Use the following information for Problems 1 and 2: Global Leveraged Equity Fund (GLEF) has three classes of shares, each holding the same portfolio of securities but having a different expense structure. The following table summarizes the expenses of these classes of shares.

Expense Comparison for Four Classes of GLEF

	Class A	Class B*	Class C
Sales charge (load) on purchases	5%	None	None
Deferred sales charge (load) on redemptions	None	4% in the first year, declining by 1% each year thereafter	1% for the initial 2 years only
Annual expenses:			
Distribution fee	0.25%	0.50%	0.50%
Management fee	0.50%	0.50%	0.50%
Other expenses	0.50%	0.50%	0.50%
	1.25%	1.50%	1.50%

*Class B shares automatically convert to Class A shares 72 months (6 years) after purchase.

Assume that expense percentages given will be constant at the given values. Assume that the deferred sales charges are computed on the basis of NAV.

An investor is considering the purchase of GLEF shares. The investor expects equity investments with risk characteristics similar to GLEF to earn 9 percent per year. He decides to make his selection of fund share class based on an assumed 9 percent return each year, gross of any of the expenses given in the preceding table.

1. Decide which class of shares of GLEF is best for the investor if he plans to liquidate his investment toward the end of
   a. Year 1
   b. Year 3
   c. Year 5
   d. Year 15

2. You have analyzed the relative performance of different classes of GLEF shares for liquidation in several years. Specifically, you have looked at liquidation in years 1, 3, 5, and 15. Your results are as follows. (The > symbol implies that the class preceding the sign performs better than the class following and the = symbol implies equal performance of the two classes.)
   - Liquidation in year 1: Class C > Class B > Class A
   - Liquidation in year 3: Class C > Class B > Class A
   - Liquidation in year 5: Class B = Class C > Class A
   - Liquidation in year 15: Class B > Class C > Class A

   Provide an intuitive explanation for the pattern of relative performance that you observe.

3. Using the price data for several houses recently sold in a particular area, a real estate firm has identified the main characteristics that affect the prices of houses in that area. The characteristics identified include the living area, the number of bathrooms, whether the house has a fireplace, and how old the house is. The estimated slope coefficient for each of these characteristics and the constant term are as follows:

Characteristic	Units	Coefficient in Euros per Unit
Intercept	—	140,000
Living area	Square meters	210
Number of bathrooms	Number	10,000
Fireplace	0 or 1	15,000
Age of the house	Years	−6,000

Use these above estimates to value a five-year-old house with a living area of 500 square meters, three bathrooms, and a fireplace.

4. A real estate firm is evaluating an office building, using the income approach. The real estate firm has compiled the following information for the office building. All information is on an annual basis.

Gross potential rental income	$350,000
Estimated vacancy and collection losses*	4%
Insurance and taxes	$26,000
Utilities	$18,000
Repairs and maintenance	$23,000
Depreciation	$40,000
Interest on proposed financing	$18,000

*As a percentage of gross potential rental income

There have been two recent sales of office buildings in the area. The first building had a net operating income of $500,000 and was sold at $4 million. The second building had a net operating income of $225,000 and was sold at $1.6 million.

a. Compute the net operating income for the office building to be valued.

b. Use the income approach to compute the appraisal price of the office building.

5. An analyst is evaluating a real estate investment project using the discounted cash flow approach. The purchase price is $3 million, which is financed 15 percent by equity and 85 percent by a mortgage loan. It is expected that the property will be sold in five years. The analyst has estimated the following after-tax cash flows during the first four years of the five-year life of the real estate investment project.

Year	1	2	3	4
Cash flow	$60,000	$75,000	$91,000	$108,000

For the fifth year, that is, the year when the property would be sold by the investor, the after-tax cash flow without the property sale is estimated to be $126,000 and the after-tax cash flow from the property sale is estimated to be $710,000.

Compute the NPV of this project. State whether the investor should undertake the project. The investor's cost of equity for projects with level of risk comparable to this real estate investment project is 18 percent.

6. An investment firm is evaluating a real estate investment project, using the discounted cash flow approach. The purchase price is $1.5 million, which is financed 20 percent by equity and 80 percent by a mortgage loan at a 9 percent pre-tax interest rate. The mortgage loan has a long maturity and constant annual payments of $120,000. This includes interest payments on the remaining principal at a 9 percent interest rate and a variable principal repayment that steps up with time. The net operating income (NOI) in the first year is estimated to be $170,000. NOI is expected to grow at a rate of 4 percent every year. The interest on real estate financing for the project is tax deductible. The marginal income tax rate for the investment firm is 30 percent. Using straight-line depreciation, the annual depreciation of the property is $37,500.

a. Compute the after-tax cash flows in years 1, 2, and 3 of the project.

b. It is expected that the property will be sold at the end of three years. The projected sale price is $1.72 million. The property's sales expenses are 6.5 percent of the sale price. The capital gains tax rate is 20 percent. Compute the after-tax cash flow from the property sale in year 3.

c. The investor's cost of equity for projects with level of risk comparable to this real estate investment project is 19 percent. Recommend whether to invest in the project or not, based on the NPV of the project.

7. Would you suggest using real estate appraisal-based indexes in a global portfolio optimization?

8. Suppose the estimated correlation matrix of the Wilshire 5000 U.S. stock index and two real estate indexes, the Federal Russell Company index (FRC) and the National Association of Real Estate Investment Trusts (NAREIT) is as follows:

	Wilshire 5000	NAREIT	FRC
Wilshire 5000	1.00	0.79	0.18
NAREIT	0.79	1.00	0.02
FRC	0.18	0.02	1.00

Based on this above matrix, compare the expected price behavior of the two real estate indexes.

9. An investor is evaluating a venture capital project that will require an investment of $1.4 million. The investor estimates that she will be able to exit the venture successfully in eight years. She also estimates that there is an 80 percent chance that the venture will not survive until the end of the eighth year. If the venture does survive until then, she expects to exit the project then, and it is equally likely that the payoff at the time of exit will be either $25 million or $35 million. The investor is considering an equity investment in the project, and her cost of equity for a project with similar risk is 20 percent.
   a. Compute the net present value of the venture capital project.
   b. Recommend whether to accept or reject the project.

10. VenCap, Inc. is a venture capital financier. It estimates that investing €4.5 million in a particular venture capital project can return €60 million at the end of six years if it succeeds; however, it realizes that the project may fail at any time between now and the end of six years. The following table has VenCap's estimates of probabilities of failure for the project. First, 0.28 is the probability of failure in year 1. The probability that the project fails in the second year, given that it has survived through year 1, is 0.25. The probability that the project fails in the third year, given that it has survived through year 2, is 0.22; and so forth. VenCap is considering an equity investment in the project, and its cost of equity for a project with this level of risk is 22 percent.

Year	1	2	3	4	5	6
Failure probability	0.28	0.25	0.22	0.18	0.18	0.10

Compute the expected net present value of the venture capital project and recommend whether VenCap should accept or reject the project.

11. Consider a hedge fund that has an annual fee structure of 1.5 percent base management fee plus a 15 percent incentive fee applied to profits above the risk-free rate. If the risk-free rate is 5.5 percent, compute the net percentage return for an investor if the gross return during the year is
   a. 35%
   b. 5%
   c. −6%

12. A hedge fund currently has assets of $2 billion. The annual fee structure of this fund consists of a fixed fee of 1 percent of portfolio assets plus a 20 percent incentive fee. The fund applies the incentive fee to the gross return each year in excess of the portfolio's previous high watermark, which is the maximum portfolio value since the inception of the fund. The maximum value the fund has achieved so far since its inception was a little more than a year ago when its value was $2.1 billion. Compute the fee that the manager would earn in dollars if the return on the fund this year turns out to be
   a. 29%
   b. 4.5%
   c. −1.8%

13. Consider a hedge fund whose annual fee structure has a fixed fee and an incentive fee with a high watermark provision. The fund manager earns an incentive fee only if the fund is above the high watermark of the maximum portfolio value since the inception

of the fund. Discuss the positive and negative implications of the high watermark provision for the investors of the hedge fund.

14. A hedge fund has compiled a list of French firms that it believes will outperform the overall French stock market by 7 percent over the year. It also has compiled a list of French firms that it believes will underperform the overall French stock market by 7 percent. The hedge fund wants to invest in a market-neutral long/short strategy on the French stock market. It has a capital of €25 million for this purpose. However, it would like to retain a cash cushion of €1 million for unforeseen events. The hedge fund can borrow shares from a primary broker with a cash margin deposit equal to 20 percent of the value of the shares. No additional costs are charged to borrow the shares.
    a. Outline the strategy for the hedge fund.
    b. Compute the return on the hedge fund's capital of €25 million if the returns on both lists of stocks are as expected. Ignore the return on invested cash of €1 million, and assume that dividends on the long stocks will offset dividends on the short stocks.

15. The shares of an Italian firm have been trading earlier around €6. Recently, a Spanish firm entered into talks with the Italian firm to acquire it. The Spanish firm offered two of its shares for every three shares of the Italian firm. The boards of directors of both firms have approved the merger, and ratification by shareholders is expected soon. The shares of the Spanish firm are currently trading at €12.50, and the shares of the Italian firm are trading at €8.
    a. Should the shares of the Italian firm trade at a discount? Explain.
    b. What position do you think a hedge fund that specializes in risk arbitrage in mergers and acquisitions will take in the two firms? Assume that the hedge fund's position will involve 250,000 shares of the Italian firm.
    c. It turns out that the European Union commission does not approve the merger because it fears that the merged firm will have a monopolistic position in its industry. After this announcement, the shares of the Italian firm fell to €6.10 each. The shares of the Spanish firm are still trading at €12.50 each. Discuss the consequences for the hedge fund. Ignore the cost of securities lending and margins deposit.

16. Global group manages hedge funds, and has three hedge funds invested in the stock market of a particular emerging country. These three hedge funds have very different investment strategies. As expected, the 2000 returns on the three funds were quite different. Over the year 2000, an index based on the overall stock market of the emerging country went up by 20 percent. Here are the performances of the three funds before management fees set at 15 percent of gross profits:

Fund	Gross Return
A	50%
B	20%
C	−10%

At year end, most clients had left fund C, and Global group closed this fund. At the start of 2001, Global group launched an aggressive publicity campaign among portfolio managers, stressing the remarkable return on fund A. If potential clients asked whether the firm had other hedge funds invested in the particular emerging market, it mentioned the only other fund, fund B, and claimed that the group's average gross performance during 2000 was 35 percent.

a. Compare the average gross return and the average net return on the three hedge funds with the percentage increase in the stock market index.

b. Comment on the publicity campaign launched by Global group.

17. An analyst is examining the performance of hedge funds. He looks at the 90 hedge funds that are in existence today, and notes that the average annual return on these funds during the last 10 years is 25.17 percent. The standard deviation of these returns is 17.43 percent and the Sharpe ratio is 1.15. The analyst also observes that the average of the annual returns on a stock market index during the last 10 years is 14.83 percent. The standard deviation of these returns is 11.87 percent and the Sharpe ratio is 0.81. The analyst concludes that the hedge funds have substantially outperformed the stock market index. Discuss why the comparison by the analyst could be misleading.

18. Consider the four major commodities traded on a commodity futures exchange today (year 10). The following table lists the average annualized price movements from year 1 to year 10, as well as the production volumes, expressed in the local currency unit, today (year 10) and ten years ago (year 1).

Commodity	Average Return	Annual Production	
		Year 1	Year 10
A	20%	10	50
B	20%	5	20
C	−10%	50	10
D	0%	35	20

The futures exchange has now decided to create a commodity index based on the four commodities, with weights equal to their current relative importance in economic production. These indexes are back-calculated till year 1 using today's weights.

a. Would such an index give unbiased indications over the past 10 years?

b. What suggestions do you have regarding weights that can be used to back-calculate the indexes?

19. The beta of gold relative to the market portfolio is −0.3. The risk-free rate is 7 percent, and the market risk premium is 4 percent.

a. What is the expected return on gold based on the capital asset pricing model (CAPM)?

b. Give an intuitive explanation for the magnitude of the expected return on gold.

Solutions

1. Let us compute the terminal value of $1 invested. The share class with the highest terminal value net of all expenses would be the most appropriate, because all classes are based on the same portfolio and thus have the same portfolio risk characteristics.

a. Class A. $1 × (1 − 0.05) = $0.95 is the amount available for investment at $t = 0$, after paying the front-end sales charge. Because this amount grows at 9 percent per year, reduced by annual expenses of 0.0125, the terminal value per $1 invested after 1 year is $0.95 × 1.09 × (1 − 0.0125) = $1.0226.

Class B. Ignoring any deferred sales charge, after 1 year, $1 invested grows to $1 × 1.09 × (1 − 0.015) = $1.0737. According to the table, the deferred sales charge would be 4 percent; therefore, the terminal value is $1.0737 × 0.96 = $1.0308.

Class C. Ignoring any deferred sales charge, after 1 year, $1 invested grows to $1 $\times$ 1.09 $\times$ (1 − 0.015) = $1.0737. According to the table, the deferred sales charge would be 1 percent; therefore, the terminal value is $1.0737 $\times$ 0.99 = $1.063.

Class C is the best.

b. Class A. The terminal value per $1 invested after three years is $0.95 $\times$ 1.09^3 $\times$ $(1 − 0.0125)^3$ = $1.1847.

Class B. Ignoring any deferred sales charge, after three years, $1 invested grows to $1 $\times$ 1.09^3 $\times$ $(1 − 0.015)^3$ = $1.2376. The deferred sales charge would be 2 percent; therefore, the terminal value is $1.2376 $\times$ 0.98 = $1.2128.

Class C. There would be no deferred sales charge. Thus, after three years, $1 invested grows to $1 $\times$ 1.09^3 $\times$ $(1 − 0.015)^3$ = $1.2376.

Class C is the best.

c. Class A. The terminal value per $1 invested after five years is $0.95 $\times$ 1.09^5 $\times$ $(1 − 0.0125)^5$ = $1.3726.

Class B. There would be no deferred sales charge. So, the terminal value per $1 invested after five years is $1 $\times$ 1.09^5 $\times$ $(1 − 0.015)^5$ = $1.4266.

Class C. There would be no deferred sales charge. So, the terminal value per $1 invested after 5 years is $1 $\times$ 1.09^5 $\times$ $(1 − 0.015)^5$ = $1.4266.

Classes B and C are the best.

d. Class A. The terminal value per $1 invested after 15 years is $0.95 $\times$ 1.09^{15} $\times$ $(1 − 0.0125)^{15}$ = $2.8653.

Class B. There would be no deferred sales charge. So, the terminal value per $1 invested after 15 years is $1 $\times$ 1.09^{15} $\times$ $(1 − 0.015)^6$ $\times$ $(1 − 0.0125)^9$ = $2.9706.

Class C. There would be no deferred sales charge. So, the terminal value per $1 invested after 15 years is $1 $\times$ 1.09^{15} $\times$ $(1 − 0.015)^{15}$ = $2.9036.

Class B is the best.

2. Class A performs quite poorly unless the investment horizon is very long. The reason is the high sales charge of 5 percent on purchases. Even though the annual expenses for class A are low, that is not enough to offset the high sales charge on purchases until a very long investment horizon. One could verify that Class A outperforms Class C for an investment horizon of 21 years or more.

Class B performs worse than Class C at very short-term horizons because of its higher deferred sales charges. However, after its deferred sales charges disappear, the relative performance of Class B starts improving. After six years, Class B shares convert to Class A with its lower annual expenses. At longer horizons, Class B starts to outperform Class C due to its annual expenses, which are lower than that of Class C.

Class C performs well at shorter investment horizons because it has no initial sales charge and it has a low deferred sales charge.

3. The estimated model is

House value in euros = 140,000 + (210 $\times$ Living area) + (10,000 $\times$ Number of bathrooms) + (15,000 $\times$ Fireplace) − (6,000 $\times$ Age)

So, the value of the specific house is

140,000 + (210 $\times$ 500) + (10,000 $\times$ 3) + (15,000 $\times$ 1) − (6,000 $\times$ 5) = €260,000

4. a. The net operating income for the office building is gross potential rental income minus estimated vacancy and collection costs minus insurance and taxes minus utilities minus repairs and maintenance.

$$\text{NOI} = 350{,}000 - 0.04 \times 350{,}000 - 26{,}000 - 18{,}000 - 23{,}000 = \$269{,}000$$

b. The capitalization rate of the first office building recently sold in the area is

$$\text{NOI}/(\text{Transaction price}) = 500{,}000/4{,}000{,}000 = 0.125$$

The capitalization rate of the second office building recently sold in the area is

$$\text{NOI}/(\text{Transaction price}) = 225{,}000/1{,}600{,}000 = 0.141$$

The average of the two capitalization rates is 0.133.

Applying this capitalization rate to the office building under consideration, which has an NOI of \$269,000, gives an appraisal value of:

$$\text{NOI}/(\text{Capitalization rate}) = 269{,}000/0.133 = \$2{,}022{,}556$$

5. The after-tax cash flow for the property sale year is \$126,000 + \$710,000 = \$836,000. At a cost of equity of 18 percent, the present value of the after-tax cash flows in years 1 through 5 is as follows.

$$\$60{,}000/1.18 + \$75{,}000/1.18^2 + \$91{,}000/1.18^3 + \$108{,}000/1.18^4$$
$$+ \$836{,}000/1.18^5 = \$581{,}225$$

The investment requires equity of $0.15 \times \$3{,}000{,}000 = \$450{,}000$. Thus, the NPV = \$581,225 − \$450,000 = \$131,225. The recommendation based on NPV would be to accept the project, because the NPV is positive.

6. a. The amount borrowed is 80 percent of \$1.5 million, which is \$1.2 million. The first year's interest = 9% of \$1.2 million = \$108,000. So,

After-tax net income in year 1 = (NOI − Depreciation − Interest) × (1 − Marginal tax rate) = (\$170,000 − \$37,500 − \$108,000) × (1 − 0.30) = \$17,150

After-tax cash flow = After-tax net income + Depreciation − Principal repayment

And,

Principal repayment = Mortgage payment − Interest = \$120,000 − \$108,000 = \$12,000

So,

After-tax cash flow in year 1 = \$17,150 + \$37,500 − \$12,000 = \$42,650

New NOI in year 2 = 1.04 × \$170,000 = \$176,800. We need to calculate the second year's interest payment on the mortgage balance after the first year's payment. This mortgage balance is the original principal balance minus the first year's principal repayment, or \$1,200,000 − \$12,000 = \$1,188,000. The interest on this balance is \$106,920. So,

After-tax net income = (\$176,800 − \$37,500 − \$106,920) × (1 − 0.30) = \$22,666

Principal repayment = \$120,000 − \$106,920 = \$13,080

So,

After-tax cash flow in year 2 = \$22,666 + \$37,500 − \$13,080 = \$47,086

New NOI in year 3 = 1.04 × \$176,800 = \$183,872. We need to calculate the third year's interest payment on the mortgage balance after the second year's payment. This mortgage balance is the original principal balance minus the first two years' principal repayments, or $\$1,200,000 - \$12,000 - \$13,080 = \$1,174,920$. The interest on this balance is $\$105,743$. So,

After-tax net income $= \$183,872 - \$37,500 - \$105,743) \times (1 - 0.30) = \$28,440$

Principal repayment $= \$120,000 - \$105,743 = \$14,257$

So,

After-tax cash flow in year 3 $= \$28,440 + \$37,500 - \$14,257 = \$51,683$

b. Ending book value = Original purchase price − Total depreciation during three years = $\$1,500,000 - 3 \times \$37,500 = \$1,387,500$.

The net sale price $= \$1,720,000 \times (1 - 0.065) = \$1,608,200$

Capital gains tax $= 0.20 \times (\$1,608,200 - \$1,387,500) = \$44,140$

After-tax cash flow from property sale = Net sales price − Outstanding mortgage − Capital gains tax

And,

Outstanding mortgage = Original mortgage − Three years' worth of principal repayments,

or

$\$1,200,000 - (\$12,000 + \$13,080 + \$14,257) = \$1,160,663$

So,

After-tax cash flow from the property sale $= \$1,608,200 - \$1,160,663 - \$44,140 = \$403,397$

c. The total after-tax cash flow for the property sale year is $\$51,683 + \$403,397 = \$455,080$. At a cost of equity of 19 percent, the present value of the after-tax cash flows in years 1 through 3 is as follows:

$\$42,650/1.19 + \$47,086/1.19^2 + \$455,080/1.19^3 = \$339,142$

The investment requires equity of $0.20 \times \$1,500,000 = \$300,000$. Thus, the NPV = $\$339,142 - \$300,000 = \$39,142$. The recommendation based on NPV would be to accept the project, because the NPV is positive.

7. No, one would not suggest using real estate appraisal–based indexes in a global portfolio optimization. Real estate appraisal values are a smoothed series. One of the reasons for this smoothness is that the appraisals are done quite infrequently. Another reason is that the appraised values typically show relatively few changes. Due to these two reasons, an appraisal-based index understates volatility. This spuriously low volatility would inflate the attractiveness of real estate.

8. Clearly, the two real estate indexes have very different price behaviors. Their correlation is almost null. As expected, the NAREIT *index* exhibits a strong correlation with U.S. stocks because the REIT share prices are strongly influenced by the stock market. In contrast, the FRC index, which is much less volatile, is not highly correlated with the stock market.

9. a. There are three possibilities.
   - Project does not survive until the end of the eighth year
   - Project survives and the investor exits with a payoff of $25 million
   - Project survives and the investor exits with a payoff of $35 million

   There is an 80 percent chance that the project will not survive until the end of the eighth year. That is, there is a 20 percent chance that the project will survive, and the investor will exit the project then. If the project survives, it is equally likely that the payoff at the time of exit will be either $25 million or $35 million.

The project's NPV is the present value of the expected payoffs minus the required initial investment of $1.4 million.

$$\text{NPV} = 0.8 \times \$0 + 0.2 \times [(0.5 \times \$25 \text{ million} + 0.5 \times \$35 \text{ million})/1.2^8]$$
$$- \$1.4 \text{ million} = -\$0.004592 \text{ million or } -\$4,592$$

b. Because the expected NPV of the project is negative, the project should be rejected.

10. The probability that the venture capital project survives to the end of the first year is $(1 - 0.28)$, 1 minus the probability of failure in the first year; the probability that it survives to the end of second year is the product of the probability it survives the first year times the probability it survives the second year, or $(1 - 0.28)(1 - 0.25)$. So, the probability that the project survives to end of the sixth year is $(1 - 0.28)(1 - 0.25)(1 - 0.22)$ $(1 - 0.18)(1 - 0.18)(1 - 0.10) = (0.72)(0.75)(0.78)(0.82)(0.82)(0.90) = 0.255$, or 25.5%. The probability that the project fails is $1 - 0.255 = 0.745$, or 74.5%.

The net present value of the project, if it survives to the end of the sixth year and thus earns €60 million, is $-€4.5 \text{ million} + €60 \text{ million}/1.22^6 = €13.70 \text{ million}$. The net present value of the project if it fails is $-€4.5$ million. Thus, the project's expected NPV is a probability-weighted average of these two amounts, or $(0.255)(€13.70 \text{ million})$ $+ (0.745)(-€4.5 \text{ million}) = €141,000$.

Based on the project's positive net present value, VenCap should accept the investment.

11. a. Fee $= 1.5\% + 15\% \times (35\% - 5.5\%) = 1.5\% + 4.425\% = 5.925\%$.

Net return $= 35\% - 5.925\% = 29.1\%$

b. Because the gross return is less than the risk-free rate, the incentive fee is zero. The only fee incurred is the base management fee of 1.5 percent.

Net return $= 5\% - 1.5\% = 3.5\%$

c. Again, the incentive fee is zero.

Net return $= -6\% - 1.5\% = -7.5\%$

12. a. Fixed fee $= 1\%$ of $2 billion $= \$20$ million.
If the return is 29 percent, new value of the fund would be $2 billion $\times 1.29 = \$2.58$ billion. This new value would be $2.58 billion $- \$2.1$ billion $= \$0.48$ billion above the high watermark. So, the incentive fee $= 20\% \times \$0.48$ billion $= \$0.096$ billion, or $96 million.

Total fee $= \$20$ million $+ \$96$ million $= \$116$ million

b. Fixed fee $= 1\%$ of $2 billion $= \$20$ million.
If the return is 4.5 percent, new value of the fund would be $2 billion $\times 1.045 = \$2.09$ billion. Because this new value is below the high watermark of $2.1 billion, no incentive fee would be earned.

Total fee $= \$20$ million

c. Fixed fee $= 1\%$ of $2 billion $= \$20$ million.
If the return is -1.8%, no incentive fee would be earned.

Total fee $= \$20$ million

13. Clearly, high watermark provision has the positive implication for the investors that they would have to pay the manager an incentive fee only when they make a profit. Further, the hedge fund manager would need to make up any earlier losses before becoming eligible for the incentive fee payment. However, a negative implication is that the option-like characteristic of the high watermark provision (the incentive fee being zero everywhere below the benchmark and increasing above the benchmark) may induce risk-taking behavior when the fund is below the high watermark. The manager may take more risky positions when the fund is below the high watermark in order to get to above the high watermark and earn an incentive fee. The worst case for the manager is a zero incentive fee, regardless of how far below the benchmark the fund turns out to be. Another negative implication is that the incentive fees, if the fund exceeds the high watermark, are set quite high (typically at 20 percent), which reduces long-run asset growth.

14. a. The hedge fund would sell short the overvalued shares and use the proceeds to buy the undervalued shares. The fund has €25 million − €1 million = €24 million to be used toward cash margin deposit. Because the cash margin deposit requirement is 20 percent, the fund could take long and short positions totalling €24 million/0.20 = €120 million. So, the fund would do the following:
    - Keep €1 million in cash
    - Deposit €24 million in a margin account
    - Borrow €120 million of overvalued stocks from a broker
    - Sell the overvalued stocks for €120 million
    - Use the sale proceeds to purchase undervalued stocks for €120 million

    b. If the performances of both lists of stocks are as expected, there would be a gain of 7 percent on the long position of €120 million and a gain of 7 percent on the short position of €120 million. So, the total gain would be 7% × €120 million × 2 = €16.8 million. Ignoring the return on invested cash of €1 million, and assuming that dividends on the long stocks will offset dividends on the short stocks, this translates to an annual return of (€16.8 million/€25 million) × 100 = 67.2%. The return is so high when the expectations are realized, because the position is highly levered.

15. a. The Spanish firm will give two of its shares, which are worth €25, for three of the Italian firm's shares, which are worth €24. Thus, the shares of the Italian firm are trading at a discount. The reason for the discount is that there is a possibility that the merger may not go through. If the merger does not go through, the shares of the Italian firm are likely to fall back to the premerger announcement level. An investor currently buying shares of the Italian firm is taking the risk that the merger will indeed occur.

    b. The hedge fund will take a hedged position by selling two shares of the Spanish firm short for every three shares of the Italian firm that it buys. So, the hedge fund will buy 250,000 shares of the Italian firm by selling (2/3) × 250,000 = 166,666.67, that is, 166,667 shares of the Spanish firm. The proceeds from the short sale are 166,667 × €12.50 = €2,083,338, which is €83,338 more than the cost of buying the shares of the Italian firm, which is 250,000 × €8 = €2,000,000.

    c. Because the merger did not go through and the stock price of the Italian firm fell, the hedge fund incurs a substantial loss. The loss is 250,000 × (€8 − €6.10) = €475,000.

16. a. Net return on fund A = 50% × (1 − 0.15) = 42.5%

Net return on fund B = 20% × (1 − 0.15) = 17%

Net return on fund C = − 10%

So, average net return = (42.5% + 17% − 10%)/3 = 16.5%

Average gross return = (50% + 20% − 10%)/3 = 20%

Thus, the average gross return on the three hedge funds is the same as the percentage increase in the stock market index, and the average net return is lower.

b. The publicity campaign launched by Global group illustrates the problem of survivorship bias in performance measure of hedge funds. Although the average gross return on the three hedge funds is the same as the percentage increase in the stock market index, the performance reported by Global group seems much better because it is based on only the funds that survive. That is, the average performance reported by Global group is inflated.

17. The measurement of the performance of the hedge funds suffers from survivorship bias. The 90 hedge funds that the analyst has examined include only those funds that have survived during the last 10 years. Thus, any poorly performing funds that have been discontinued due to low return or high volatility, or both, have been excluded. Accordingly, the average return on hedge funds has been overstated, while the volatility has been understated. Consequently, the Sharpe ratio for the hedge funds has been overstated. Furthermore, the Sharpe ratio may be a misleading measure of risk-adjusted performance for hedge funds because of the optionality in their investment strategies.

18. a. The construction of the index is okay in year 10 but not in the earlier years. By using today's weights in construction of the index in earlier years, the exchange is overweighing those commodities that have become important over the period, and have simultaneously gone up in price.

b. For each year, use the relative economic importance of the commodities in that year as the weights for that year. That is, use year 1 weights for the index calculated in year 1, and so on.

19. a. The expected return on gold, as theoretically derived by the CAPM, is

$$E(R_{gold}) = 7\% + \beta_{gold} \times 4\%$$
$$= 7\% - 0.3 \, (4\%) = 5.8\%$$

b. Given its negative beta, gold is likely to perform well when the overall market performs poorly. Thus, our investment in gold is likely to offset some of the loss on the rest of the portfolio. Investors should be willing to accept an overall lower expected return on gold because, in periods of financial distress, gold tends to do well.

Bibliography

Amenc, N., and Martellini, L. "The Brave New World of Hedge Fund Indices," Working paper, Marshall School of Business at the University of Southern California, October 19, 2002.

Anderson, R., and Moore, B. "The Update Files: U.S. Inflation-Indexed Bonds," *Investment Policy,* May/June 1998.

Asness, C., Krail, R., and Liew, J. "Do Hedge Funds Hedge?" *Journal of Portfolio Management,* Fall 2001.

Brauer, G. A., and Ravichandran, R. "How Sweet Is Silver?" *Journal of Portfolio Management,* Summer 1986.

Brown, S. J., Goetzmann, W. N., and Ibbotson, R. G. "Off-Shore Hedge Funds, Survival and Performance: 1989–1995," *Journal of Business,* 72(1), 1999, pp. 91–118.

Chamberlain, M., and Jordan, J. "An Introduction to Exchange-Traded Funds," Barclays Global Investors Services, 2002.

Eichholtz, P. M. A. "Does International Diversification Work Better for Real Estate Than for Stocks and Bonds?" *Financial Analysts Journal,* January/February 1996.

Firstenberg, P. M., Ross, S. A., and Zisler, R. C. "Real Estate: The Whole Story," *Journal of Portfolio Management,* Spring 1988.

Fung W., and Hsieh, D. A., "Hedge-Fund Benchmarks: Information Content and Biases," *Financial Analysts Journal,* January/February 2002.

Gastineau, G. L., "Exchange-Traded Funds: An Introduction," *Journal of Portfolio Management,* Spring 2001.

Gibson, R., and Schwartz, E. "Stochastic Convenience Yield and the Pricing of Oil Contingent Claims," *Journal of Finance,* July 1990.

Goetzmann, W. N., and Ibbotson, R. G. "The Performance of Real Estate as an Asset Class," *Journal of Applied Corporate Finance,* Fall 1990.

Goldman Sachs, *Index and Derivatives Perspective,* NY: Goldman Sachs, 2002.

Gyourko, J., and Keim, D. B. "Risk and Return in Real Estate: Evidence from a Real Estate Index," *Financial Analysts Journal,* September/October, 1993.

Hooke, J. C. *Security Analysis on Wall Street,* New York: John Wiley & Sons, 1998.

Hudson-Wilson, S. "Why Real Estate?" *Journal of Portfolio Management,* 28(1), Fall 2001.

Jacquillat, B., and Roll, R. "French Index-Linked Bonds for U.S. Investors?" *Journal of Portfolio Management,* Spring 1979.

Jaeger, L. *Managing Risk in Alternative Investment Strategies,* London: Prentice Hall, 2002.

Jarchow, S. P. *Graaskamp on Real Estate,* Washington, DC: Urban Land Institute, 1991.

Lerner, J. *Venture Capital and Private Equity,* New York: John Wiley & Sons, 2000.

Lhabitant, F. *Hedge Funds: Myths and Limits,* New York: John Wiley & Sons, 2002.

Liu, C., Hartzell, D. J., and Hoesli, M. "International Evidence on Real Estate Securities as an Inflation Hedge," *Real Estate Economics,* 25(2), Summer 1997, pp. 193–233.

McCarthy, D., and Spurgin, R. "A Review of Hedge Fund Performance Benchmarks," *Journal of Alternative Investments,* Summer 1998, pp. 18–28.

McCrary, S. A. *How to Create & Manage a Hedge Fund: A Professional's Guide.* New York: John Wiley & Sons, 2002.

McFall Lamm Jr., R. "Asset Allocation Implications of Inflation Protection Securities," *Journal of Portfolio Management,* Summer 1998.

Merrill Lynch, *Global ETF Guide,* London: Merrill Lynch, July 2002.

Mull, S. R., and Soenen, L. A. "U.S. REITs as an Asset Class in International Investment Portfolios," *Financial Analysts Journal,* March/April 1997.

Mussavian, M., and Hirsch, J. "European Exchange-Traded Funds: An Overview," *Journal of Alternative Investments,* 5(2), Fall 2002, pp. 63–77.

Pratt, S. P., Reilly, R. F., and Schweihs, R. P. *Valuing a Business,* 3rd ed., Chicago: Irwin, 1996.

Quan, D. C., and Titman, S. "Commercial Real Estate Prices and Stock Market Returns: An International Analysis," *Financial Analysts Journal,* May/June 1997.

Schilit, W. K. "Venture Catalysts or Vulture Capitalists?" *Journal of Investing,* Fall 1996.

Schneeweis, T. "Managed Futures," in D. R. Jobman, Ed., *The Handbook of Alternative Investments,* New York: John Wiley & Sons, 2002.

Schwartz, E. "The Pricing of Commodity-Linked Bonds," *Journal of Finance,* May 1982.

Sharpe, W. F., Alexander, G. J., and Bailey, J. V. *Investments,* 6th ed., Upper Saddle River, NJ: Prentice-Hall, 1999.

Söderberg, B. "A Note on the Hedonic Model Specification for Income Properties," in K. Wang and M. L. Wolverton, Eds., *Real Estate Valuation Theory,* Boston: Kluwer Academic, 2002.

Tremont Advisers. "Distressed Securities," in D. R. Jobman, Ed., *The Handbook of Alternative Investments,* New York: John Wiley & Sons, 2002.

Terhaar, K., Staub, R., and Singer, B. "The Appropriate Policy Allocation for Alternative Investments," *Journal of Portfolio Management,* Spring 2003.

Van Hedge Fund Advisors International, www. vanhedge.com, 2002.

9

The Case for International Diversification

- Discuss the reasons that investors should consider constructing global portfolios

- Compare the relative size of the U.S. market with other global stock and bond markets

- Discuss the changes in risk that occur when investors add international securities to their portfolios and calculate the expected return and standard deviation for a two-asset portfolio containing a domestic asset and a foreign asset

- Demonstrate how changes in currency exchange rates can affect the returns that investors earn on foreign security investments

- Demonstrate how changes in currency exchange rates can affect the risk that investors bear on foreign security investments

- Explain the effect of international diversification on the efficient frontier by comparing a frontier that includes foreign investments with one that does not

- Discuss the factors that cause equity market correlations across countries to be relatively low

- Discuss the factors that cause bond market correlations across countries to be relatively low

- Discuss the influence of time differences between countries on the correlation of daily returns

- Discuss the reasons for an increased Sharpe ratio with international investing and explain why this increase could be simultaneously true for investors of different countries

- Illustrate the potential risk–return impact of adding bonds to a global asset allocation

- Discuss patterns of global equity returns and global market correlations for different market environments

- Discuss the reasons that currency risk may only slightly magnify the volatility of foreign currency–denominated investments

- Explain the increasing correlation argument against international diversification and discuss the factors leading to increased correlations

- Evaluate the implication of non-normal return distributions and changes in volatility for the usual case in favor of global risk diversification

- Explain the country-specific outperformance argument against international diversification

- Discuss the barriers to international investing

- Discuss the pitfalls in estimating correlations during volatile periods

- Explain why international performance opportunities have increased over time

- Distinguish between global investing and international diversification

- Discuss the potential benefits of investing in emerging markets

- Evaluate the historical performance of emerging equity markets

- Discuss the return volatility, return correlation, and expected return characteristics that result from including emerging-market securities in a portfolio

- Discuss the importance of currency issues in emerging-market investing

- Describe the concept of "investability" in emerging markets

- Discuss the segmentation versus integration characteristics of emerging markets

International portfolio investment has long been a tradition in many European countries, but it is a more recent practice in North America.[1] There is now a strong trend toward international diversification in all countries, however, especially among U.S. institutional investors, such as corporate and public pension funds. In the early 1970s, U.S. pension funds basically held no foreign assets; the percentage of foreign assets approached 15 percent of total assets by 2000. British institutional investors hold more than 25 percent of their assets in non-British securities. Some Dutch pension funds have more than half of their assets invested abroad. Recently, private investors have joined the trend toward global investment.

Indeed, the mere size of foreign markets justifies international diversification, even for U.S. investors. At the end of 2001, the world stock market capitalization was around $25 trillion. The U.S. stock market accounted for roughly half of the

---

[1] The terminology varies across countries. Americans use the word *international* to refer to non-American investments and *global* to refer to American plus non-American investments. Other English-speaking nationals tend to use the word *foreign* to refer to nondomestic investments and *international* to refer to domestic plus foreign investments. We use the American terminology.

EXHIBIT 9.1

Stock Market Capitalization
Developed Markets

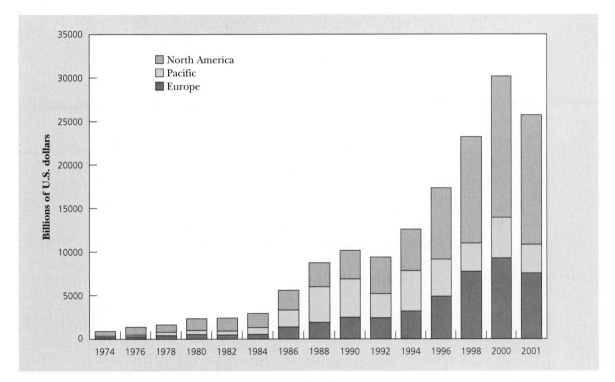

world market. The growth of the world stock market since the early 1970s has been remarkable. In 1974, the New York Stock Exchange was the only significant market in the world, representing 60 percent of a world market capitalization of less than a trillion dollars.[2] As shown in Exhibit 9.1, the size of the world market multiplied by a factor of 30 in the next 25 years, and the share of U.S. equity moved from 60 percent to less than 30 percent in 1988, and back to 50 percent by the end of 2000. The Pacific region, which made up a big third of the world stock market in the early 1990s, shrank to 15 percent at the end of 2001. Exhibit 9.1 covers only developed markets; the share of the Asian markets would be somewhat increased if emerging markets were included. Europe makes up one-third of the world market. The Bank for International Settlements estimated the world market capitalization of publicly issued bonds to be around $37 trillion at the end of 2001. U.S. dollar bonds accounted for roughly 50 percent of the world bond market, while yen

---

[2] At that time, Solnik (1974) presented the case for international diversification to U.S. pension plans that had zero overseas investments.

bonds accounted for somewhat less than 20 percent and bonds denominated in European currencies accounted for some 30 percent.

In a fully efficient, integrated, global capital market, buying the world market portfolio would be the natural passive strategy. In theory, an American investor should hold half of the portfolio in international securities. But, even if one does not believe in a perfect, integrated world market, the case for diversifying in international securities is strong. The basic argument in favor of international diversification is that foreign investments allow investors to reduce the total risk of the portfolio, while offering additional profit potential. By expanding the investment opportunity set, international diversification helps to improve the risk-adjusted performance of a portfolio.

Domestic securities tend to move up and down together because they are similarly affected by domestic conditions, such as monetary announcements, movements in interest rates, budget deficits, and national growth. This creates a definite positive correlation among nearly all stocks traded in the same national equity market. The correlation applies equally to bonds; bond prices on the same national market are very strongly correlated. Investors have searched for methods to spread their risks and diversify away the national market risk. In their variety, foreign capital markets provide good potential for diversification beyond domestic instruments and markets.

This chapter presents the advantages and disadvantages of international investing. It focuses on equity investments but also refers to bond investments. The first section presents the traditional case for international diversification. However, this case has been criticized recently because of an increase in international correlations, especially in periods of high market volatility. The second section reviews these criticisms. The third section revisits the benefits of a global approach in light of the recent changes in the global economic landscape. The last section presents the case for investing in emerging markets.

The Traditional Case for International Diversification

There are two motivations for global investment. All else being equal, a low international correlation allows reduction of the volatility, or total risk, of a global portfolio. A low international correlation also provides profit opportunities for an active investor: Because markets do not move up or down together, an expert investor can hope to adjust the international asset allocation of the global portfolio toward markets with superior expected returns. This should lead to a superior risk-adjusted performance. On the other hand, barriers to international investments also exist. Hence, we will discuss risk reduction through attractive correlations, superior expected returns, and trends in barriers.

Risk Reduction through Attractive Correlations

The objective of risk diversification is to reduce the total risk of a portfolio. Of course, one hopes simultaneously to achieve high expected returns, as discussed in the next section. The total risk of most stock markets is larger than that of the U.S.

market when the dollar is used as the base currency. In part, this is caused by currency risk, which adds to the risk of a foreign investment, even though the volatility of national markets is often comparable when measured in their local currency.[3] Nevertheless, the addition of more risky foreign assets to a purely domestic portfolio still reduces its total risk as long as the correlation of the foreign assets with the domestic market is not large. This can be shown mathematically.

Let's consider a portfolio partly invested in domestic assets (e.g., a U.S. stock index for a U.S. investor) and partly invested in foreign assets (e.g., a French stock index). The proportions invested in each asset class is denoted w_d for domestic assets and w_f for foreign assets; they sum to 100 percent. The returns are denoted R_p for the portfolio, R_d for the domestic assets, and R_f for the foreign assets. All returns are measured in the base currency (e.g., the U.S. dollar for a U.S. investor). So, the return on foreign assets is subject to currency risk. The domestic and foreign assets have standard deviations denoted σ_d and σ_f, respectively. The total risk of the portfolio is its standard deviation σ_p. The correlation between the two asset classes is denoted $\rho_{d,f}$. Remember that the variance of the portfolio is the square of its standard deviation, and that the covariance between the two asset classes is given by

$$cov_{d,f} = \rho_{d,f}\,\sigma_d\sigma_f$$

First note that the expected return on the portfolio is simply equal to the average expected return on the two asset classes:

$$E(R_p) = w_d\,E(R_d) + w_f\,E(R_f) \tag{9.1}$$

A well-known mathematical result is that the variance of the portfolio is equal to

$$\sigma_p^2 = w_d^2\,\sigma_d^2 + w_f^2\,\sigma_f^2 + 2\,w_d\,w_f\,cov_{d,f}$$

or

$$\sigma_p^2 = w_d^2\,\sigma_d^2 + w_f^2\,\sigma_f^2 + 2\,w_d\,w_f\,\rho_{d,f}\,\sigma_d\sigma_f$$

The standard deviation is simply equal to the square root:

$$\sigma_p = (w_d^2\,\sigma_d^2 + w_f^2\,\sigma_f^2 + 2\,w_d\,w_f\,\rho_{d,f}\,\sigma_d\sigma_f)^{1/2} \tag{9.2}$$

The portfolio's total risk (σ_p) will always be *less* than the average of the two standard deviations: $w_d\,\sigma_d + w_f\sigma_f$. The only case in which it will be equal is when the correlation[4] is exactly equal to 1.0 (perfect correlation between the two assets). Otherwise diversification benefits will show, and the lower the correlation, the bigger the risk reduction.

---

[3] Similarly, the volatility of the U.S. stock market would look larger than that of the French stock market when returns are measured in euros.

[4] A correlation coefficient between two random variables lies between +1.0 and −1.0. A coefficient of 1.0 means that the two markets go up and down in identical cycles, whereas a coefficient of −1.0 means that they are exactly countercyclical. For more details, see DeFusco, McLeavey, Pinto, and Runkle (2001).

EXAMPLE 9.1   INTERNATIONAL RISK DIVERSIFICATION BENEFITS

Assume that the domestic and foreign assets have standard deviations of $\sigma_d = 15\%$ and $\sigma_f = 17\%$, respectively, with a correlation of $\rho_{d,f} = 0.4$.

1. What is the standard deviation of a portfolio equally invested in domestic and foreign assets?

2. What is the standard deviation of a portfolio with a 40 percent investment in the foreign asset?

3. What is the standard deviation of a portfolio equally invested in domestic and foreign assets if the correlation is 0.5? What if the correlation is 0.8?

SOLUTIONS

1. The variance of the total portfolio equally invested ($w_d = w_f = 50\%$) in both assets, σ_p^2, is given by

$$\sigma_p^2 = 0.5^2 [\sigma_d^2 + \sigma_f^2 + (2 \, \rho_{df} \sigma_d \sigma_f)]$$
$$\sigma_p^2 = 0.5^2 [\, 225 + 289 + (2 \times 0.4 \times 255)] = 179.5$$

Hence, the standard deviation σ_p is given by $\sqrt{179.5}$, or 13.4 percent which is significantly less than that of the domestic asset. Since one can diversify in several foreign markets, the total risk of the portfolio could be further reduced.

2. The risk reduction depends on the percentage invested in each asset. A portfolio invested 60 percent in the domestic asset and 40 percent in the foreign asset has a variance given by

$$\sigma_p^2 = (0.6^2 \times \sigma_d^2) + (0.4^2 \times \sigma_f^2) + (2 \times 0.4 \times 0.6 \times \rho_{d,f} \sigma_d \sigma_f) = 176.2$$

The standard deviation is $\sigma_p = 13.27$ percent, and this is the lowest risk portfolio.

3. The risk reduction also depends on the level of correlation. If the correlation is 0.5 instead of 0.4, the risk of the portfolio equally invested becomes $\sigma_p = 13.87\%$. If the correlation is 0.8, the risk of the portfolio equally invested becomes $\sigma_p = 15.18\%$. The risk of the portfolio increases with the level of correlation.

Currency Considerations   The return and risk of an asset depend on the currency used. For example, the return and risk of a French asset will be different if measured in the euro or in the dollar. The dollar value of the asset is equal to its euro value multiplied by the exchange rate (number of dollars per euro):

$$V^\$ = V \times S$$

where V and $V^\$$ are, respectively, the values in the local currency (euro) and in the dollar, and S is the exchange rate (number of dollars per euro). The rate of return in dollars from time 0 to time 1 is given by

$$r^\$ = \frac{V_1^\$ - V_0^\$}{V_0^\$} = \frac{V_1 S_1 - V_0 S_0}{V_0 S_0} = \frac{V_1 - V_0}{V_0} + \frac{S_1 - S_0}{S_0} + \frac{V_1 - V_0}{V_0} \times \frac{S_1 - S_0}{S_0}$$

$$r^\$ = r + s + (r \times s)$$

where r is the return in local currency, $r^\$$ is the return in dollars, and s is the percentage exchange rate movement.[5]

For example, if the return on a French asset is 5 percent in euros and the euro appreciates by 1 percent, the return in dollar is 6.05 percent. This is slightly different from the sum of the euro return and of the currency movement, because the currency appreciation applies not only to the original capital, but also to the capital gain. This cross-product is equal to $5\% \times 1\% = 0.05\%$.

It is easy to compare the risks of an asset measured in different currencies. To simplify notations, it is usually assumed that the cross-product $r \times s$ is small relative to r and s and can be ignored for risk calculations. Hence, the variance of the dollar return is simply equal to the variance of the sum of the local currency return and of the exchange rate movement:

$$var(r^\$) = var\,(r + s) = var(r) + var(s) + 2\,cov(r,s)$$

or

$$\sigma_f^2 = \sigma^2 + \sigma_s^2 + 2\,\rho\sigma\sigma_s$$

where, σ_f^2 is the variance of the foreign asset measured in dollars, σ^2 is its variance in local currency, σ_s^2 is the variance of the exchange rate (number of dollars per local currency), and ρ is the correlation between the asset return, in local currency, and the exchange rate movement. As the correlation is never greater than 1.0, the asset and currency risks are not additive, and we have

$$\sigma_f \le \sigma + \sigma_s$$

The difference between σ_f and σ is called the contribution of currency risk.

EXAMPLE 9.2   CURRENCY RISK CONTRIBUTION

Suppose that we have a foreign investment with the following characteristics

$$\sigma = 15.5\%, \qquad \sigma_s = 7\% \quad \text{and} \quad \rho = 0$$

What is the risk in domestic currency and the contribution of currency risk?

SOLUTION

We have:

$$\sigma_f^2 = \sigma^2 + \sigma_s^2 + 0 = (15.5)^2 + (7.0)^2 = 289.25$$

Hence the standard deviation σ_f is given by $\sqrt{289.25}$, or 17 percent. Note that this number is well below the sum of the risk of the asset measured in the local currency ($\sigma = 15.5\%$) and the risk of the currency ($\sigma_s = 7\%$). Currency risk only increases the asset risk from 15.5 percent in the local currency to 17 percent in domestic currency. Hence the difference between σ_f and σ is the contribution of currency risk, here $\sigma_f - \sigma = 1.5\%$.

---

[5] If a dividend or coupon is paid in period 1, it will be included in V_1.

In this chapter, we assume that we measure all returns and risk in the currency of the investor, namely the U.S. dollar. The issue of currency hedging is discussed in other chapters.

Efficient Portfolios   A portfolio is mean–variance efficient if it has the highest level of expected return for a given level of risk.[6] The set of all efficient portfolios is called the *efficient frontier*.

EXAMPLE 9.3   RISK-RETURN TRADEOFF OF INTERNATIONALLY DIVERSIFIED PORTFOLIOS

Assume that the domestic and foreign assets have standard deviations of $\sigma_d = 15\%$ and $\sigma_f = 17\%$, respectively, with a correlation of $\rho_{d, f} = 0.4$. The expected returns of the domestic and foreign assets are equal, respectively, to $E(R_d) = 10\%$ and $E(R_f) = 12\%$. Draw the set of all portfolios combining these two assets with positive weights in a risk-return graph.

SOLUTION

We can use equations 9.1 and 9.2 to derive the set of portfolios invested in various proportions in the two assets. Their representation in a risk-return graph is given in Exhibit 9.2, in which D and F represent the domestic and foreign assets respectively.

EXHIBIT 9.2

Risk–Return Trade-off of Internationally Diversified Portfolios

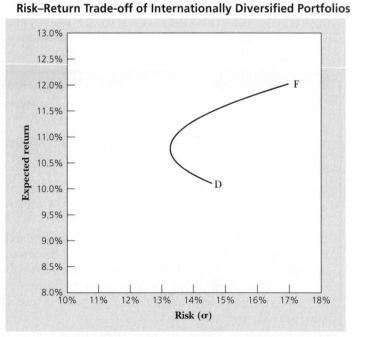

---

[6] See DeFusco, McLeavey, Pinto, and Runkle (2001).

EXHIBIT 9.3

Risk–Return Trade-off of Internationally Diversified versus Domestic-Only Portfolios

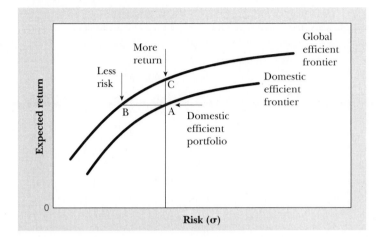

Of course, one can invest in many different domestic and international assets. Combining all domestic stocks in an efficient mean–variance fashion, we derive the domestic efficient frontier represented in Exhibit 9.3. Combining all domestic and international stocks in an efficient mean-variance fashion, we derive the global mean–variance-efficient frontier represented on the same exhibit. The global efficient frontier is to the left of the domestic efficient frontier, showing the increased return opportunities and risk diversification benefits brought by the enlarged investment universe. For example, portfolio A is on the domestic efficient frontier. Portfolio B on the global efficient frontier has the same return but less risk than portfolio A; portfolio C on the global efficient frontier has the same risk but more return than portfolio A.

A prerequisite for this argument is that the various capital markets of the world have somewhat independent price behaviors. If the Paris Bourse and the London Stock Exchange moved in parallel with the U.S. market, diversification opportunities would not exist. So, we start by an empirical investigation of the level of international correlation.

The correlations between various stock and bond markets are systematically monitored by major international money managers. Although the correlation coefficients between markets vary over time, they are always far from unity. For the portfolio manager, this means that there is ample room for successful risk diversification. Following is a discussion of some recently estimated correlations, as illustration. Correlation estimates change somewhat over time, and the issue of stability in the correlation is discussed in the next sections of this chapter.

Equity   Exhibit 9.4 gives the correlations across selected national stock markets with returns measured in two different currencies over the 10-year period January 1992 to January 2002. The bottom left part of the matrix gives the correlation

EXHIBIT 9.4

Correlation of Stock Markets, January 1992–January 2002
Monthly Returns in U.S. Dollars (bottom left) and Currency Hedged (top right)

	USA	Canada	U.K.	France	Germany	Italy	Switz.	Japan	Hong Kong	Europe	EAFE	World	S&P/ IFCG
USA	1.00	0.69	0.63	0.58	0.59	0.34	0.60	0.39	0.51	0.69	0.63	0.86	0.56
Canada	0.70	1.00	0.58	0.63	0.59	0.42	0.53	0.39	0.58	0.67	0.66	0.76	0.63
U.K.	0.66	0.54	1.00	0.74	0.62	0.49	0.69	0.30	0.53	0.74	0.63	0.71	0.56
France	0.58	0.59	0.72	1.00	0.82	0.64	0.68	0.36	0.40	0.74	0.63	0.67	0.54
Germany	0.61	0.59	0.61	0.77	1.00	0.61	0.63	0.34	0.44	0.70	0.56	0.63	0.56
Italy	0.32	0.41	0.34	0.50	0.48	1.00	0.45	0.31	0.23	0.48	0.44	0.44	0.40
Switzerland	0.51	0.42	0.61	0.58	0.50	0.25	1.00	0.30	0.43	0.65	0.55	0.63	0.52
Japan	0.40	0.42	0.44	0.39	0.31	0.27	0.36	1.00	0.17	0.40	0.69	0.62	0.35
Hong Kong	0.51	0.60	0.48	0.40	0.44	0.22	0.37	0.24	1.00	0.49	0.50	0.56	0.70
Europe	0.69	0.65	0.88	0.90	0.84	0.56	0.72	0.45	0.49	1.00	0.87	0.87	0.55
EAFE	0.63	0.65	0.78	0.77	0.70	0.53	0.65	0.79	0.50	0.87	1.00	0.93	0.56
World	0.86	0.76	0.80	0.76	0.72	0.48	0.64	0.69	0.56	0.87	0.93	1.00	0.62
S&P/IFCG	0.56	0.66	0.46	0.48	0.49	0.35	0.36	0.32	0.69	0.55	0.56	0.62	1.00

when all returns are measured in U.S. dollars. The top right part of the matrix gives the correlation when the foreign investments are fully hedged against currency risk; in other words, the foreign currency is assumed to be sold forward for an amount equal to that of the foreign stock investment. Let's first examine the correlations when no currency hedging is undertaken (U.S. dollar returns).

For example, Exhibit 9.4 indicates that the correlation between the French and U.S. stock markets is 0.58. The square of this correlation coefficient, usually called R^2, indicates the percentage of common variance between the two markets. Here only 34 percent ($R^2 = 0.58^2$) of stock-price movements are common to the French and U.S. markets.[7] Note that, on the average, the common variance between the U.S. and other markets is less than 30 percent (average R of 0.54). The correlation with Canada is, of course, quite strong (0.70), because the two economies are closely linked. Other groups of countries are also highly correlated, indicating strong regional links. Germany and France tend to have high correlations because their economies are interrelated. Conversely, Japan shows little correlation with European or U.S. markets. This result confirms that the Japanese business cycle has been somewhat disconnected from the rest of the world.

The last four rows and columns in Exhibit 9.4 give the correlation of each national market with four international indexes. The first three indexes are computed in U.S. dollar terms by Morgan Stanley Capital International for developed

---

[7] An R^2 of 34 percent may be interpreted as follows: 34 percent of the French stock-price movements are the result of influences shared with the U.S. stock market. In other words, 66 percent of the price movements are independent of U.S. market influences.

equity markets. The world index is a market capitalization–weighted index of all the major stock markets of the world. The Europe, Australasia, and Far East (EAFE) index is the non-American world index and is made up of stock markets from those parts of the world. The Europe index is made up of stock markets from Western Europe. The S&P/IFCG composite index is a U.S. dollar market cap–weighted index of emerging stock markets computed initially by the IFC (International Finance Corporation of the World Bank) and now by S&P. The correlation of the U.S. market with the EAFE index is only 0.63. Therefore, the overall common variance between U.S. and non-U.S. stock indexes is 40 percent ($R^2 = 0.63^2 = 40\%$). This implies that any well-diversified portfolio of non-U.S. stocks provides an attractive risk-diversification vehicle for a domestic U.S. portfolio. The same conclusion—that foreign stocks provide attractive risk-diversification benefits to a domestic stock portfolio—holds true from any other national viewpoint.

The correlation of the U.S. stock market with the world index is much larger ($R^2 = 0.86^2 = 74\%$) than it is for the EAFE index. But this should not be surprising, because the U.S. market accounts for a significant share of the world market.

In general, the low correlation across countries offers risk-diversification and return enhancement opportunities. It allows naive investors to spread risk, because some foreign markets are likely to go up when others go down. This also provides opportunities for expert international investors to time the markets by buying those markets that they expect to go up and neglecting the bearish ones.

The degree of independence of a stock market is directly linked to the independence of a nation's economy and governmental policies. To some extent, common world factors affect expected cash flows of all firms and therefore their stock prices. However, purely national or regional factors seem to play an important role in asset prices, leading to sizable differences in the degrees of independence among markets. It is clear that constraints and regulations imposed by national governments, technological specialization, independent fiscal and monetary policies, and cultural and sociological differences all contribute to the degree of a capital market's independence. On the other hand, when there are closer economic and governmental policies, as among the euro countries, one observes more commonality in capital market behavior. In any case, the covariation between markets is still far from unity, leaving ample opportunities for risk diversification.

The last row/column of Exhibit 9.4 reports the correlation with a diversified index of emerging markets. Emerging markets present a positive but rather low correlation with developed markets; the correlation with the world index of developed markets is around 0.6.

Let's now examine the correlation across stock markets when full currency hedging is undertaken. The correlation coefficients in the top right part of the matrix are very similar to those in the bottom left part. For example, the correlation between the U.S. and French markets remains the same; the correlation between the U.S. and Italian markets increases slightly to 0.34; but some other correlations are slightly smaller such as the correlation between the Hong Kong and Japanese markets (0.17 versus 0.24). There is little difference between stock market correlations when we look at hedged and unhedged returns.

EXHIBIT 9.5

Correlation of Bond Markets, January 1992–January 2002
Monthly Returns in U.S. Dollars (bottom left) and Currency Hedged (top right)

	USA	Canada	U.K.	France	Germany	Italy	Switz.	Nether.	Japan	U.S. Equity
USA	1.00	0.64	0.51	0.49	0.55	0.33	0.37	0.57	0.23	0.19
Canada	0.49	1.00	0.47	0.37	0.36	0.28	0.23	0.38	0.16	0.26
U.K.	0.49	0.30	1.00	0.68	0.74	0.50	0.51	0.75	0.05	0.19
France	0.38	0.11	0.61	1.00	0.85	0.71	0.63	0.83	0.09	0.09
Germany	0.40	0.13	0.62	0.92	1.00	0.58	0.68	0.94	0.25	0.07
Italy	0.27	0.23	0.54	0.61	0.53	1.00	0.34	0.57	0.08	0.21
Switzerland	0.32	0.05	0.50	0.88	0.89	0.43	1.00	0.71	0.24	−0.05
Netherlands	0.40	0.14	0.59	0.96	0.96	0.55	0.90	1.00	0.24	0.12
Japan	0.17	0.06	0.23	0.42	0.46	0.12	0.50	0.48	1.00	−0.09
U.S. Equity	0.19	0.41	0.17	−0.01	0.00	0.08	−0.14	0.01	0.11	1.00

Bonds   Similar conclusions can be reached for bonds, as can be seen in Exhibit 9.5, which is presented in a fashion similar to that of Exhibit 9.4. Let's first look at the correlation of the various bond markets when returns are all expressed in U.S. dollars (the bottom left part of the exhibit). For example, the correlation of U.S. dollar returns of U.S. and French bonds is only 0.38, or an average percentage of common variance of less than 15 percent (the square of 0.38). The correlation of U.S. bonds with every foreign bond market is below 0.50. Canadian dollar bonds are most strongly correlated with U.S. dollar bonds. In general, long-term return variations are not highly correlated across countries.

Regional blocs do appear. European bond markets tend to be quite correlated. This is especially true of countries from the Eurozone, because a common currency was progressively introduced over the period under study. The Eurozone bond markets now exhibit a correlation close to 1.0 for government bonds.

The general observation is that national monetary/budget policies are not fully synchronized. For example, the growing U.S. budget deficit in the mid-1980s, associated with high U.S. interest rates and a rapid weakening of the dollar, was not matched in other countries. The relative independence of national monetary/budget policies, influencing both currency and interest rate movements, leads to a surprisingly low correlation of U.S. dollar returns on the U.S. and foreign bond markets. Hence, foreign bonds allow investors to diversify the risks associated with domestic monetary/budget policies.

Finally, the last asset class in Exhibit 9.5 is U.S. equity. The correlation of foreign bonds with the U.S. stock market is quite small. This is not surprising, given the independence between U.S. and foreign national economic and monetary policies. Foreign bonds offer excellent diversification benefits to a U.S. stock portfolio manager.

EXHIBIT 9.6

Stock Exchange Trade Hours in GMT and EST Clocks

Let us now examine the correlation across bond markets when full currency hedging is undertaken. The correlation coefficients in the top-right part of the matrix are somewhat different from the U.S. dollar correlations. This is because there exists a correlation between currency movements and bond yield movements (and hence bond returns), as discussed in Chapter 4. For example, some countries practice a "leaning against the wind" policy, whereby they raise their interest rates to defend their currencies. So the correlation of two national bond markets would be different if we look at hedged returns or at currency-adjusted returns.

Leads and Lags   So far, we have talked about the contemporaneous correlation across markets taking place when an event or factor affects two or more markets simultaneously. Some investigators have attempted to find leads or lags between markets. For example, they studied whether a bear market in February on Wall Street would lead to a drop in prices on other national markets in March. No evidence of a systematic delayed reaction of one national market to another has ever been found, except for daily returns, as outlined later. The existence of such simple market inefficiencies is, indeed, unlikely, because it would be easy to exploit them to make an abnormal profit.

One must take into account the time differences around the world, however, before assessing whether a given national market leads or lags other markets. The stock exchanges in New York and Tokyo are not open at the same time. If important news hits New York prices on a Tuesday, it will affect Tokyo prices on Wednesday. If important news hits London prices on a Tuesday, it will affect New York prices the same day, because New York generally lags London by five hours. Indeed, when it is Tuesday noon in New York, it is already Tuesday 17:00 (or 5 P.M.) local time in London and Wednesday 02:00 (or 2 A.M.) in Tokyo.[8] The opening and closing times of the three major stock markets are depicted in Exhibit 9.6, in which

---

[8] Europe and America, but not Asia, change time during the summer (daylight savings time in the United States), but not on the same date. Hence, the time difference between Europe and the United States generally increases by one hour during a few weeks in the year.

the trading hours are indicated using both the universal GMT (Greenwich Mean Time) and the American EST (Eastern Standard Time). It can be seen that New York and Tokyo official trading hours never overlap. London and New York trading hours generally overlap for two hours. If the markets are efficient, international news should affect all markets around the globe simultaneously, with markets closed at that hour reflecting the news immediately on opening. For example, if important news is revealed after noon EST, it can be impounded in Japanese and British stock prices only the next day; because of the time differences involved, we should not be surprised to find a lagging correlation of Tokyo and London with New York when returns are measured from closing price to closing price. This lagged correlation can be explained by the difference in time zones, not by some international market inefficiency that could be exploited to make a profit. This effect gets drastically reduced when looking at correlation of longer-period return, for example, monthly returns.

Portfolio Return Performance

We have devoted so much attention to the risk-reduction benefits of international investment because risk diversification is the most established and frequently invoked argument in favor of foreign investment, justifying foreign investment even to the naive investor. However, risk reduction is not the sole motive for international investment. Indeed, mere risk reduction could more easily be achieved by simply investing part of one's assets in domestic risk-free bills. Unfortunately, although the inclusion of risk-free bills lowers the portfolio risk, it also lowers expected return. In the traditional framework of the capital asset pricing model (CAPM), the expected return on a security is equal to the risk-free rate plus a risk premium. In an efficient market, reducing the risk level of a portfolio by adding less-risky investments implies reducing its expected return. International diversification, however, implies no reduction in expected return. Such diversification lowers risk by eliminating nonsystematic volatility without sacrificing expected return. A traditional way to evaluate a portfolio's risk-adjusted performance is to evaluate its Sharpe ratio. This is the ratio of the return on a portfolio, in excess of the risk-free rate, divided by its standard deviation. Money managers attempt to maximize this Sharpe ratio, which gives the excess return per unit of risk. Global investing should increase the Sharpe ratio because of the reduction in risk. Investing in foreign assets allows a reduction in portfolio risk (the denominator of the Sharpe ratio), without necessarily sacrificing expected return (the numerator of the Sharpe ratio). Both domestic and foreign investors can see their Sharpe ratio increase if they diversify away from purely local assets. As long as the expected returns on domestic and foreign assets are comparable, both types of investors would benefit from international risk reduction compared to a portfolio of purely local assets. The second argument for an increase in the Sharpe ratio is that more profitable investments are possible in an enlarged investment universe. Higher expected returns may arise from faster-growing economies and firms located around the world, or simply from currency gains. These advantages can be obtained by optimizing the global asset allocation.

EXAMPLE 9.4   INTERNATIONAL DIVERSIFICATION AND THE SHARPE RATIO

Assume that the domestic and foreign assets have standard deviations of $\sigma_d = 15\%$ and $\sigma_f = 17\%$, respectively, with a correlation of $\rho_{d,f} = 0.4$. The risk-free rate is equal to 4% in both countries.

1. The expected returns of the domestic and foreign assets are both equal to 10 percent, $E(R_d) = E(R_f) = 10\%$. Calculate the Sharpe ratios for the domestic asset, the foreign asset, and an internationally diversified portfolio equally invested in the domestic and foreign assets. What do you conclude?

2. Assume now that the expected return on the foreign asset is higher than on the domestic asset, $E(R_d) = 10\%$ but $E(R_f) = 12\%$. Calculate the Sharpe ratio for an internationally diversified portfolio equally invested in the domestic and foreign assets, and compare your findings to those in question 1.

SOLUTION

1. The domestic asset has an expected return of 10 percent a standard deviation of 15 percent. For this asset,

$$\text{Sharpe ratio} = \frac{E(R) - \text{risk-free rate}}{\sigma} = \frac{10\% - 4\%}{15\%} = 0.4$$

The foreign asset has a Sharpe ratio of $\dfrac{10\% - 4\%}{17\%} = 0.353$

   A portfolio equally invested in the domestic and foreign asset has an expected return of 10 percent and a standard deviation σ_p given by:

$$\sigma_p^2 = 0.5^2[\sigma_d^2 + \sigma_f^2 + (2\,\rho_{d,f}\,\sigma_d\,\sigma_f)]$$

$$\sigma_p^2 = 0.5^2\,[225 + 289 + (2 \times 0.4 \times 255)] = 179.5$$

Hence, the standard deviation σ_p is given by $\sqrt{179.5}$, or 13.4 percent. The Sharpe ratio of the portfolio is equal to:

$$\text{Sharpe ratio} = \frac{E(R_p) - \text{risk-free rate}}{\sigma_p} = \frac{10\% - 4\%}{13.4\%} = 0.448$$

The foreign asset has a lesser Sharpe ratio than the domestic asset because it has the same expected return but a larger standard deviation. However, the equally weighted portfolio benefits from risk diversification and a lower standard deviation. Hence its Sharpe ratio is better than the ratios of both the domestic and the foreign assets.

2. A portfolio equally invested in the domestic and foreign asset has now an expected return of 11 percent ($0.5 \times 10\% + 0.5 \times 12\% = 11\%$). Hence the Sharpe ratio is equal to $(11\% - 4\%)/13.4\% = 0.522$. The portfolio's Sharpe ratio is now better than that of the domestic asset (0.4), both because of risk-diversification benefits and because of the superior expected return of the foreign asset [new Sharpe ratio of $(12\% - 4\%)/17\% = 0.471$].

EXHIBIT 9.7

Efficient Frontier for Stocks (U.S. dollar, 1980–1990)

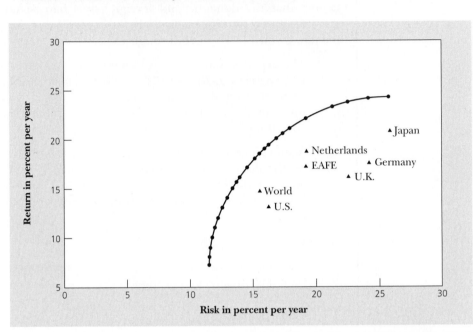

An Ex Post Example   It is easy to derive the global asset allocation that would have been optimal from a risk–return viewpoint over some past period, but the results depend on the period selected. To illustrate such an analysis, Exhibit 9.7 shows optimal global stock allocations for different risk levels and for a U.S. investor, as reported by Odier and Solnik (1993). This is the efficient frontier based on returns for the period 1980–1990. No investment constraints other than no short selling are applied; results do not reflect any currency hedging. The mean annual return is given on the Y axis, and the asset volatility (standard deviation) is given on the X axis. Each asset or portfolio is represented by one point on the graph (a few selected markets are plotted on the graph). The U.S. stock market has a risk of 16.2 percent and an annualized total return of 13.3 percent. Other stock markets are more volatile, partly because of currency risk. By combining the various national stock markets, we get diversified portfolios whose returns and risks can be calculated, because we know the returns and covariances of all the assets. Investors select asset allocations that lie on the efficient frontier depicted in Exhibit 9.7. The best achievable risk–return trade-offs—the optimal asset allocations—lie on the efficient frontier.

As Exhibit 9.7 shows, international diversification of a pure U.S. stock portfolio would greatly enhance returns without a large increase in risk. A global stock port-

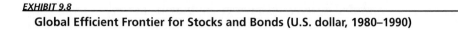

EXHIBIT 9.8

Global Efficient Frontier for Stocks and Bonds (U.S. dollar, 1980–1990)

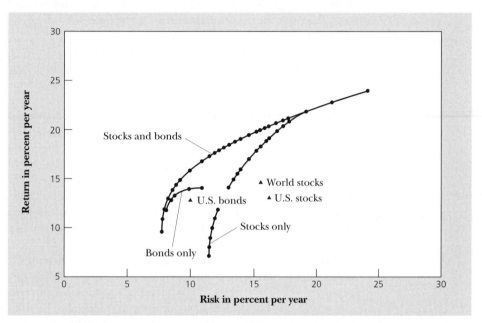

Source: P. Odier and B. Solnik. Adapted from "Lessons for International Asset Allocation,"*Financial Analysts Journal,* March/April 1993. Copyright 1993, Association for Investment Management and Research. Reproduced and republished from *Financial Analysts Journal* with permission from the Association for Investment Management and Research. All rights reserved.

folio with the same risk level as the purely U.S. stock portfolio (16.2 percent per year) would achieve an annualized total return above 19 percent, compared with 13.3 percent for the U.S. portfolio.

Can bonds help improve the risk-adjusted performance of globally diversified portfolios? The question here is not whether investors should prefer portfolios made up solely of bonds or solely of stocks, but whether bonds should be added to a stock portfolio in a global investment strategy. Exhibit 9.8 gives the efficient frontier for a global asset allocation allowing for bonds and stocks, foreign and domestic. To keep the exhibit readable, we did not plot individual bond and stock markets, but only the U.S. bond and stock indexes, as well as the world stock index. Their relative positions are consistent with theory. U.S. bonds have a lower risk and a lower return. Over the long run, riskier stock investments are compensated by a risk premium. The global asset allocations on the efficient frontier strongly dominate U.S. investments. The global efficient asset allocation with a return equal to that of the U.S. stock market (13.3 percent per year) has a risk equal to only half that of the U.S. stock market. Conversely, a global efficient allocation with the same risk as the U.S. stock market outperforms the U.S. stock market by 8 percent per year. Similarly, any domestic U.S. stock/bond strategy is strongly dominated by a global stock/bond strategy. A domestic portfolio of U.S. stocks and bonds tends to have half the return of that on a global efficient allocation with the same risk level. Adding foreign bonds in a global asset allocation can be attractive from a risk–return viewpoint because of their low correlation with domestic bond and stock investments as outlined previously.

Exhibit 9.8 also shows the global efficient frontier for stocks only (same as Exhibit 9.7), as well as the efficient international frontier for bonds only. Clearly, stocks offer a strong contribution to a bond portfolio in terms of risk–return trade-off; the bond-only efficient frontier is also dominated by a global strategy.

Exhibit 9.9 shows the efficient frontier for Japanese, German, and British investors. All calculations are performed in the respective national currencies. Conclusions similar to those developed earlier can be reached when we take the viewpoint of investors from different countries of the world. The benefits of global investing can hold from all national viewpoints simultaneously. The expanded investment universe (from domestic to global) offers potentials for risk diversification and return improvement, hence an improvement in the Sharpe ratio for all investors.

The potential profits are large, but optimizing them requires some forecasting skills. A major question is how much of the potential can be achieved through superior management skills. Even if only 20 percent of the profits could be reaped, global-asset allocation would seem to be very valuable in risk–return terms. It is, of course, quite difficult to know in advance what these optimal asset allocations will be. Therefore, all we can conclude is that the opportunities for increased risk-adjusted returns are sizable and that the performance gap between optimal global asset allocations and a simple world index fund is potentially quite wide. Whether any money manager has sufficient expertise to realize most, or even part, of this performance differential is yet another question.

Different Market Environments   It is important to stress that the expected benefits of global investing in terms of risk and return of a portfolio are different. Because of the low (less than 1.0) correlation across different national assets, the volatility of a portfolio is *less* than the average volatility of its components. Risks get partly diversified away. This international risk reduction appears from any currency viewpoint. However, the return on a diversified portfolio is exactly *equal* to the average return of its components. By definition, the return on the world index is the average return of all national markets. In other words, some countries will outperform the world index, whereas others will underperform the world index. Although international diversification has looked attractive from 1980 to 1990 from both a risk and a return viewpoint for a U.S. investor, this is not the case for a Japanese investor, whose national stock market had higher returns than the world index. Over that decade, Japanese investors benefited only from the risk reduction provided by a passive global portfolio, such as the world index. Again, this illustrates the mathematics of the world index, whose return is exactly the weighted average of its components. It is unlikely that any single market will under- or overperform the other markets in all time periods. Hence, passive global diversification is

EXHIBIT 9.9

Global Efficient Frontiers for Non-U.S. Investors

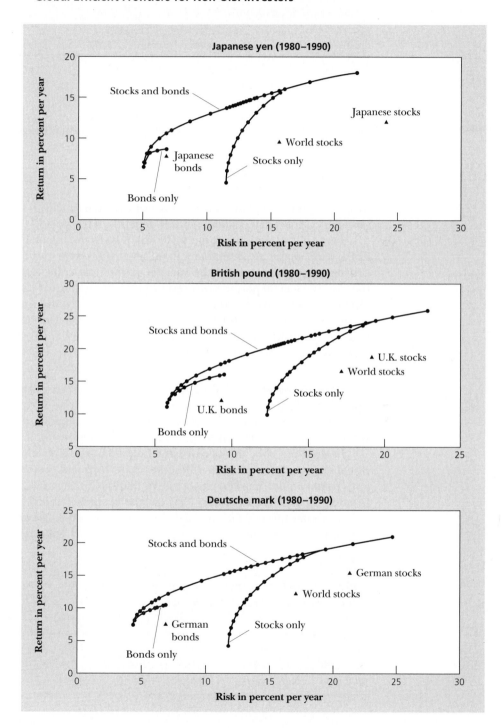

EXHIBIT 9.10

Mean Return and Correlation of Selected Markets with the U.S. Equity Market
Five-Year Periods from 1971 to 2000, in U.S. Dollars

5-Year Period	Mean Return (in % per year)				Correlation with U.S.		
	U.S.	Japan	Europe	EAFE	Japan	Europe	EAFE
1971–1975	1.4	22.1	5.5	9.8	0.40	0.61	0.59
1976–1980	12.3	20.7	12.2	17.0	0.12	0.28	0.36
1981–1985	15.0	19.3	16.3	16.8	0.32	0.49	0.46
1986–1990	12.7	20.6	18.2	18.7	0.25	0.64	0.44
1991–1995	16.9	5.6	12.9	10.1	0.22	0.65	0.47
1996–2000	18.4	−4.6	16.0	7.6	0.48	0.62	0.66

wise in terms of risk, but it does not provide a "free lunch" in terms of return. Similarly the *ex post* optimal allocation will depend on the period under study.

This is illustrated in Exhibit 9.10, which gives the mean annual return (in U.S. dollars) on major stock markets in successive five-year periods. Exhibit 9.10 also provides the correlation of the various markets with the U.S. stock market. Note that the 1990–2000 period saw a reversal of perfomance for Japanese investors. The Japanese stock market strongly underperformed the world index. International diversification was very attractive for Japanese investors. The fact that national stock markets have different long-term performances is not surprising and could justify an active asset allocation strategy.

Forward-Looking Optimization   Although *ex post* exercises yield some interesting general lessons, portfolio management needs to be forward looking. An adequate global asset allocation should be based on market forecasts, not on past returns. Several factors can help formulate expectations.

In the long run, the performance of stock markets can be explained by national economic factors. The difference in performance between the U.S., Europe, and Japan equity markets reported in Exhibit 9.10 is largely the result of differences in real growth rates. This can be seen in Exhibit 9.11, which gives the mean annual growth rate in GDP for successive 10-year periods for the United States, Japan, Europe, and the average of all OECD countries. For example, real

EXHIBIT 9.11

Real Growth Rate (GDP Growth) of Selected Regions
Ten-Year Periods from 1971 to 2000

GDP Growth	USA	Japan	Europe	OECD
1971–1980	2.76%	4.51%	2.95%	3.13%
1981–1990	2.48%	4.15%	2.34%	2.71%
1991–2000	3.40%	1.30%	2.50%	2.30%

growth was much higher in Japan than in the United States in the 1970s and 1980s, and much lower in the 1990s. The stock markets' performance followed the same pattern.

Economic flexibility is also an important factor in investment performance, which may explain differences between past and future performances among emerging countries. Wage and employment rigidity is bad for the national economy. In countries such as France, Canada, and Sweden, corporations have a difficult time adjusting to slowing activity; on the other hand, they do not take full advantage of growth opportunities, because they are reluctant to hire new employees, whom they cannot fire if activity slows.

Economic forecasting is a useful exercise, but it should be stressed that scenarios that are widely expected to take place should already be impounded in current asset prices. For example, if a Country X is widely expected to experience higher economic growth than other countries, it should be reflected in higher stock prices in country X. If future growth develops according to expectations, there is no reason to have higher future returns for stocks of Country X. So, investors forecasting economic growth rates must take into account the market consensus about future growth rates.

It should be stressed that there is no guarantee that the past will repeat itself. Indeed, over any given period, one national market is bound to outperform the other, and if an investor had perfect foresight, the best strategy would be to invest solely in the top-performing market, or even in the top-performing security in that market. But because of the great uncertainty of forecasts, it is always better to spread risk in the fund by diversifying globally across markets with comparable expected returns. This ensures a favorable risk–return trade-off or, in the jargon of theory, higher risk-adjusted expected returns. If managers believe that they have some relative forecasting ability, they will engage in active investment strategies that reap the benefits of international risk diversification while focusing on preferred markets. For example, a U.S. investor may concentrate on U.S. and European stocks if she is bullish on those markets and may avoid Japan for political or currency reasons.

Some emerging economies offer attractive investment opportunities. The local risks (volatility, liquidity, political environment) are higher, as illustrated by numerous crises, but the expected profit is large. Furthermore, those risks get partly diversified away in a global portfolio. Hence, emerging markets and alternative investments can have a positive contribution in terms of risk–return trade-offs.

Currency Risk Not a Barrier to International Investment

Currency fluctuations affect both the total return and the volatility of any foreign currency–denominated investment. From time to time, in fact, the effects of currency fluctuations on the investment return may exceed that of capital gain or income, especially over short periods of time. Empirical studies indicate that currency risk, as measured by the standard deviation of the exchange rate movement, is smaller than the risk of the corresponding stock market (roughly half). On the other hand, currency risk is often larger than the risk (in local currency) of the corresponding bond market (roughly twice). In a global portfolio, the depreciation of one currency is often offset by the appreciation of another. Indeed, several points are worth mentioning regarding currency risk.

First, market and currency risks are not additive. This would be true only if the two were perfectly correlated. In fact, there is only a weak, and sometimes negative, correlation between currency and market movements. This point was stressed in the previous section. In Example 9.2, the exchange rate standard deviation is 7 percent compared with a local-currency standard deviation of 15.5 percent for the foreign stock. However, the contribution of currency risk to total risk is only 1.5 percentage points. So, currency risk only adds some 10 percent (1.5 percent as a fraction of 15.5 percent) to the risk of a foreign asset. This is a typical figure.

The correlation between changes in the exchange rate and the asset price is an important element in assessing the contribution of currency risk. The lower the correlation, the smaller the contribution of currency risk to total risk.

Second, the exchange risk of an investment may be hedged for major currencies by selling futures or forward currency contracts, buying put currency options, or even borrowing foreign currency to finance the investment. So, currency risk can easily be eliminated in international investment strategies. But currencies can also provide some attractive profit opportunities.

Third, the contribution of currency risk should be measured for the total portfolio rather than for individual markets or securities, because part of that risk gets diversified away by the mix of currencies represented in the portfolio. As stressed by Jorion (1989), the contribution of currency risk to the total risk of a portfolio that includes only a small proportion of foreign assets (say, 5 percent) is insignificant. The contribution of currency risk is larger if one holds the world market portfolio and, hence, a large share of foreign assets. Actually holding some foreign-currency assets can provide some diversification to domestic fiscal and monetary risks. A lax domestic monetary policy can be bad for domestic asset prices and lead to a home-currency depreciation. Foreign currencies help diversify that risk.

Fourth, the contribution of currency risk decreases with the length of the investment horizon. As shown in Chapters 2 and 3, exchange rates tend to revert to fundamentals over the long run (mean reversion). Hence, an investor with a long time horizon should care less about currency risk than should an investor who is concerned about monthly fluctuations in the portfolio's value. Froot (1993) shows that currency risk can disappear over very long term horizons (over one or several decades).

The Case Against International Diversification

Several impediments to international portfolio investing are often mentioned. First, the case for international diversification presented earlier has been attacked on the basis that it strongly overstates the risk benefits of international investing. Second, skeptics also look at the historical performance of their domestic market relative to other foreign markets. Third, there are numerous physical barriers to international investing.

Increase in Correlations

It is often argued that the benefits of international diversification are overstated because markets tend to be more synchronized than suggested previously. There is no reason for the correlation between two equity markets to remain constant over a long period of time. Indeed, it has been observed that international correlations have trended upward over the past decade. It has also been observed that international correlation increases in periods of high market volatility.

Correlations Have Increased over Time   Economies and financial markets are becoming increasingly integrated, leading to an increase in international correlation of asset prices. Economic and financial globalization observed at the turn of the millennium can be witnessed in many areas.

- Capital markets are being deregulated and opened to foreign players. Markets that used to be segmented are moving toward global integration.

- Capital mobility has increased, especially among developed countries. International capital flows have dramatically increased since the 1950s. The success of international investing means that foreign institutional investors, such as pension funds, are now major players on most domestic markets.

- National economies are opening up to free trade, in part under the pressure of the World Trade Organization and of regional agreements such as NAFTA, ASEAN, and the European Union. Hence, national economies are becoming more synchronized.

- As the economic environment becomes global, corporations become increasingly global in their operations. They achieve this global strategy through increased exports, international organic growth, and foreign acquisitions. A simple indicator is provided by the amount of cross-border mergers and acquisitions (M&As) shown in Exhibit 9.12. The amount of cross-border M&As has risen dramatically from 1991 to 2000, both in dollar amount and in percentage of world GDP. Cross-border M&As were few in the early nineties, but they have become an increasing proportion of total M&As. While the economic slowdown of the early 2000s has slowed down M&As, the share of cross-border M&As among total M&As is still on the rise.

As corporations become more global, it is not surprising to see the correlation between their stock prices increase. The legal nationality of a corporation becomes less important. As a firm competes globally and derives a significant part of its cash flows from abroad, its value is affected by global factors, not primarily by the location of its headquarters. Hence, it is not surprising to find that country factors become less important and that the correlation among national stock markets tends to increase.

EXHIBIT 9.12

Value of Cross-Border M&A and Its Share in World GDP (1991–2000)

Source: Data from KPMG, Computasoft Research limited/CommScan, UNCTAD.

International correlations move over time, as can be seen on Exhibit 9.10. Correlation is high in periods when global shocks affect all countries (e.g., the oil shock of the early 1970s) and lower in other periods. However, Exhibit 9.10 suggests that the correlation between the U.S. and other stock markets has been trending upward since 1975.

Goetzmann, Li, and Rouwenhorst (2001) examined the correlation structure of the major world equity markets from the late 19th century until the end of 2000. They found that correlations varied considerably through time, with peaks in the late 19th century, the Great Depression, and the late 20th century. They concluded that the current diversification benefits to global investing were relatively low compared with the rest of capital market history, because correlation was at a high point.

Correlation Increases When Markets Are Volatile A major criticism addressed to the mean–variance framework used to present the case for international diversification is that it assumes "normality." In statistical terms, all returns are supposed to have a "joint multivariate normal distribution." In real life, returns are not exactly drawn from normal probability tables with constant correlations across assets. Three deviations from market "normality" are most often mentioned:

- Distributions of returns tend to have fat tails (leptokurtic distribution). In other words, the occurrence of large positive or negative returns is more frequent than expected under normal distributions.[9]

---

[9] See, for example, Longin (1996).

- Market volatility varies over time, but volatility is "contagious." In other words, high volatility in the U.S. stock market tends to be associated with high volatility in foreign stock markets, as well as in other financial markets (bond, currency).

- The correlation across markets increases dramatically in periods of high volatility, for example, during major market events such as the October 1987 crash.

The fact that there are fat tails or that volatility tends to move up or down together on all markets is not a direct attack on global risk diversification. It simply says that a static mean–variance analysis is a simplified view of the world and that more sophisticated quantitative methods could be used; but it does not negate the advantage of international risk reduction. Correlation moves over time[10] for obvious reasons. There are tranquil periods during which domestic factors dominate and markets are not strongly correlated across countries. There are times during which global shocks affect simultaneously all economies, and business cycles move in sync. The oil shock of 1974 provides an example, as shown in Exhibit 9.10, and the correlation measured from 1971 to 1975 was much higher than in the next five years. The correlation estimated over a long period of time is simply an average over these various market cycles. For reasons mentioned previously, correlation of developed stock markets tends to increase slowly over time. But what is really troubling is that correlation seems to increase dramatically in periods of crises, so that the benefits of international risk diversification disappear when they are most needed. This phenomenon is sometimes referred to as "correlation breakdown."

If all markets crash when your domestic market is crashing, there is little risk benefit to be internationally diversified. While it might be beneficial in "normal" times, it becomes useless in the exceptional times when there is a huge loss on domestic investments. And remember, that fat tails mean that the occurrence of such crashes is more frequent than expected under "normality."

This concept is illustrated in Exhibit 9.13, which is reproduced from Bookstaber (1997). In one day of October 1987, the U.S. stock market crashed by some 20 percent, or about 20 times its historical daily standard deviation. The British, Japanese, and German markets dropped between 8 and 15 times their normal standard deviations. Other bond and currency market indicators also witnessed large declines.

Implications of such "correlation breakdowns" extend well beyond international portfolio diversification. If they occur, correlation breakdowns would render very inefficient any hedging operations based on correlations, or betas, estimated over long-term historical data.

---

[10]Longin and Solnik (1995) studied the eight major stock markets from 1960 to 1990, using a GARCH methodology. They rejected the hypothesis that correlation is constant and found a modest but significant increase in international correlation over this 30-year period. Goetzmann, Li, and Rouwenhorst (2001) studied the correlation of the stock markets of France, Germany, the United Kingdom, and the United States from 1870 to 2000. They split the data into six periods based on historical events such as world wars. They found that the correlation structure differed significantly among many of the six time periods.

EXHIBIT 9.13
1987 U.S. Stock Market Crash
One-Day Movement in Units of "Normal" Daily Standard Deviations

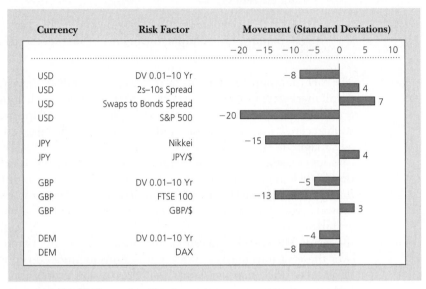

Currency	Risk Factor	Movement (Standard Deviations)
USD	DV 0.01–10 Yr	−8
USD	2s–10s Spread	4
USD	Swaps to Bonds Spread	7
USD	S&P 500	−20
JPY	Nikkei	−15
JPY	JPY/$	4
GBP	DV 0.01–10 Yr	−5
GBP	FTSE 100	−13
GBP	GBP/$	3
DEM	DV 0.01–10 Yr	−4
DEM	DAX	−8

Source: Bookstaber (1997).

Past Performance Is a Good Indicator of Future Performance

Another criticism of international investing is country-specific, as it is typically formulated by investors whose markets have enjoyed a prolonged period of good performance. Skeptics point to the fact that, in recent periods, their domestic markets have generated greater returns than most other markets, and hence, that there is no need for international investments in the future. As can be seen on Exhibit 9.10, the Japanese equity market had a superb performance relative to the rest of the world in the 1970s and 1980s. International investing was not in favor in Japan in 1990. A similar attitude has been adopted recently in the United States: U.S. equity yielded greater returns than overseas equity markets, especially Japan, in the 1990s and early 2000s. After a few years of poor performance of their foreign investments relative to domestic equities, U.S. investors were less inclined toward international investing.[11]

Simply extrapolating past performance to forecast future expected returns is questionable. It is unlikely that one country will always outperform all others. Just as one domestic sector is unlikely to continually outperform all other domestic sectors. It could be that one economy is deemed to be more efficient than others, but

---

[11]See, for example, Joel Chernoff, "International Investments May Not Decrease Risk after All," *Pensions & Investments,* January 7, 2002.

this should be reflected in higher equity prices. Let's assume, for example, that the U.S. economy is indeed more flexible and competitive than all others in the foreseeable future. In a global context, in which foreign investors extensively invest in the United States and vice versa, this forecast should be discounted today in higher U.S. equity prices. If investors share the vision that the U.S. economy will be superior to other economies forever, that forecast should be reflected immediately into higher U.S. stock prices today, not by higher future returns forever. Future outperformance of U.S. stocks must be caused by "surprise," the unexpected news that the U.S. economy is doing even better than expected. To justify continuing outperformance in the future, we must go from positive surprise to positive surprise.

Barriers to International Investments

The relative size of foreign capital markets would justify extensive foreign investment by investors of any nationality. Empirical studies build a strong case for international diversification. However, international investment, although rapidly growing, is still not widespread in several countries and is certainly far from what it should be according to the world market portfolio weights. This conservative behavior may be explained by the prevalence of potential barriers to foreign investment.

Familiarity with Foreign Markets   Culture differences are a major impediment to foreign investment. Investors are often unfamiliar with foreign cultures and markets. They feel uneasy about the way business is done in other countries: the trading procedures, the way reports are presented, different languages, different time zones, and so on. Many investors, especially Americans, feel more comfortable investing in domestic corporations. In turn, these local corporations provide some international exposure through their exports, foreign subsidiaries, or acquisitions of foreign corporations. Foreign markets and corporations are perceived as more risky simply because they are unfamiliar.

Political Risk   Some countries run the risk of being politically unstable. Many emerging markets have periodically suffered from political, economic, or monetary crises that badly affected the value of local investments. For example, a currency crisis could curtail the dollar value of local investments. Simply looking at a statistical measure of risk based on recent-past stock-price behavior can be misleading and underestimate the risk of a crisis. A statistician would say that the distribution of return on such investments is not "normal" and that the standard deviation of return is not a good proxy of the risk borne.

Market Efficiency   A first question in market efficiency is that of *liquidity*. Some markets are very small; others have many issues traded in large volume. Of course, some issues on the major markets, as well as some of the smaller national markets, trade on little volume. Large institutional investors may wish to be careful and invest only a small part of their portfolios in these small-capitalization, less-liquid shares. Indeed, it may be difficult to get out of some national markets on a large scale. An excellent performance on a local index may not translate into a similarly good performance on a specific portfolio because of the share price drop when liquidating the portfolio. Another liquidity risk is the imposition of capital controls on foreign portfolio investments. Such capital control prevents the sale of a portfolio of foreign assets and the repatriation of proceeds. This has never happened on any of the major capital markets of the world; the cost of such a political decision would be very high for any government, because it would reduce its borrowing capacity on the international capital market. However, it is a definite risk for investments in many emerging countries. Such capital controls may be imposed in an extreme financial or political crisis, and international money managers need to carefully monitor a few high-risk countries.

In some countries, corporations do not provide timely and reliable *information* on their activity and prospects. Foreign investors tend to avoid such corporations. The rapid growth in international investing has put intense pressure on these corporations to live up to the transparency that is the norm in major developed markets.

Another issue in market efficiency is *price manipulation* and *insider trading.* If foreign markets were too affected by these problems, a manager would probably not run the risk of investing in these markets to benefit the domestic speculators. Many studies have established that all major stock markets are nearly efficient in the usual sense. Some countries, however, have historically been quite lax in terms of price manipulation, insider trading, and corporate governance. In some countries, majority stockholders can take advantage of their controlling interest to the detriment of minority stockholders.[12] The globalization of financial markets leads to a rapid improvement in national regulations to control this type of behavior. Some U.S. pension plans, notably CalPERS, have been very active in inciting corporations worldwide to improve their corporate governance.

Regulations   In some countries, regulations constrain the amount of foreign investment that can be undertaken by local investors. For example, institutional investors are sometimes constrained on the proportion of foreign assets they can hold in their portfolios. Such quotas can be found in some European countries and even among U.S. public pension plans.

Some countries limit the amount of foreign ownership in their national corporations. This is typically the case for emerging countries, which tend to limit foreign ownership to a maximum percentage of the capital of each firm. This is also the case for some developed countries. For example, Swiss corporations tend to issue special shares to foreign owners, and these shares trade at a premium over those available solely to Swiss nationals. Again, the trend is toward progressive removal of these constraints. For example, the European Union prohibits any ownership discrimination among its members. Such constraints are rarely found for bond investments. All governments are happy to have foreign investors subscribe to their

---

[12]See, for example, the case of Italy in Zingales (1994).

bond issues, financing their budget deficit. Conversely, they often force their national institutional investors to hold domestic bonds. This limits the scope of international investing by these institutional investors.

Transaction Costs   The transaction costs of international investments can be higher than those of domestic investments. It is difficult to calculate the average transaction cost on a typical trade. A first component of transaction costs is the brokerage commission, and it varies in the way it is charged (fixed or negotiable commission, variable schedule, or part of the bid–ask spread). However, brokerage commissions on stocks tend to be low in the United States (typically 0.10 percent for large transactions) and higher in foreign countries (ranging from 0.10 percent to 1.0 percent). In a few countries, commissions are fixed, and a stamp tax applies. However, the deregulation of capital markets is lowering these commissions worldwide. A large component of transaction costs is the price impact of a trade. For example, a large buy order will raise the price. This is a function of the size of the order. Liquidity can be limited on many national stock markets, inducing high transaction costs. However, this effect is present in any country. For example, transaction costs on the Nasdaq can be large, because of the limited liquidity on most issues. Some estimates of the overall transaction costs on the major stock markets are provided in Chapter 5.

It is even more difficult to quote a so-called average commission for bonds. On most of the major bond markets (including the Eurobond market), prices are quoted net, so that the commissions have to be inferred from the bid–ask spread, which depends on the volume of transactions on a specific bond. In general, commissions on bonds tend to be very low on all markets.

Custody costs tend to add to the costs of international investments. Custody costs tend to be higher for international investments because, here, investors engage in a two-level custodial arrangement, in which a master custodian deals with a network of subcustodians in every country. Higher costs are also incurred because of the necessity of a multicurrency system of accounting, reporting, and cash flow collection. Some countries have a very inexpensive and efficient centralized custodial system with a single clearinghouse, and local costs tend to be less than in the United States. However, the need for the international network may raise the annual cost to more than 0.10 percent of assets.

Management fees charged by international money managers tend to be higher than those charged by domestic money managers. This is justified by the higher costs borne by the money managers in terms of

- international database subscriptions,
- data collection,
- research,
- the international accounting system, and
- communication costs (international telephone, computer links, and travel).

Management fees for foreign portfolios typically run a few basis points higher than fees on similar domestic portfolios. Some investors believe that they can limit costs by simply buying foreign firms listed on their domestic markets (called American Depositary Receipts, or ADRs, in the United States; see Chapter 5). Although this may be a practical alternative for the private investor, it is a questionable strategy for larger investors. A growing number of companies have multiple listings, but these companies tend to be large multinational firms that provide fewer foreign diversification benefits than a typical foreign firm. Also, the foreign share price of a corporation (e.g., the U.S. dollar ADR price of a French firm) is often determined by its domestic market price adjusted by the exchange rate. When a large order to buy an ADR is received, brokers will generally arbitrage between the prices in New York and the local market. This means that on most ADRs, the execution will be made at a high price compared with the local price (adjusted for the exchange rate). The commission seems low, but the market impact on the price tends to be high. It is often in the best interest of a large customer to deal on the primary market, where there is the largest transaction volume for the shares. However, there are significant exceptions. Several Dutch and British companies have a very large transaction volume on U.S. markets.

Taxes   Withholding taxes exist on most stock markets. The country where a corporation is headquartered generally withholds an income tax on the dividends paid by the corporation. This tax can usually be reclaimed after several months; this time lag creates an opportunity cost. In a very few cases, part of the tax is completely lost, according to the tax treaty between the two countries. Alternatively, a taxable investor may claim this amount as a tax credit in his home country, but this is not possible for a nontaxable investor, such as a pension plan. However, the withholding tax (generally 15 percent) applies only to the dividend yield. For a yield of 2 percent, a total loss of withholding tax on common stocks would imply a 0.30 percent reduction in performance. There are also a few countries (e.g., Australia and France) where investors benefit from some tax credit for the tax that the local corporation has paid on its profits distributed as dividends. This tax credit is usually not available to nonresidents. Withholding taxes have been progressively eliminated on bonds.

Currency Risk   As discussed, currency risk can be a major cause of the higher volatility of foreign assets, but is often overstated. Furthermore, it is a risk that need not be borne, because it can be hedged with derivatives. Nevertheless, currency hedging leads to additional administrative and trading costs.

Conclusions   Altogether, foreign investment may not seem more costly for a resident from a high-cost country, such as Switzerland, but it is clearly more expensive for a U.S. resident. For a U.S. investor, a ballpark estimate of the increase in total costs (management fee, taxes, commissions, custody) is on the order of 0.10 percent to 0.50 percent for stocks[13] and 0 percent to 0.20 percent for bonds. The

---

[13]See Chapter 5 for more details.

difference would be less for a passively managed fund. These figures are still small compared with the risk–return advantage of foreign investment, as presented in the first part of this chapter. However, they could explain why an investor would want to overweigh the domestic component of the portfolio compared with the world market portfolio weights. Information and transaction costs, differential taxes, and sometimes political or transfer risk give a comparative advantage to the domestic investor on the home market. This does not imply that foreign investment should be avoided altogether.

The Case for International Diversification Revisited

Many of the barriers to global investing are disappearing because of the market liberalization induced by global investors. For example, on many days, trading by foreign investors on European equity markets dominates trading by local investors. The global equity landscape has changed dramatically in past decades. Some of the attacks on global diversification are faulty because they are based on poor statistical analysis. More importantly, the scope of international investing has changed, and investors should adapt accordingly.

Pitfalls in Estimating Correlation During Volatile Periods

In the presence of positive correlation between two markets, one would expect that a large market drop (rise) in one country be associated with a large market drop (rise) in the other country, even if the correlation remains constant. The question is whether the simultaneous movements are so large that they indicate that correlation is truly increasing in crisis periods. Before concluding on the basis of casual observations, we need to address some econometric issues in correlation estimation. The correlation coefficient is a complex parameter whose statistical properties are not well understood. The conclusion of a correlation breakdown is derived by estimating the correlation in periods of high volatility of returns. This is called "conditioning" correlation on high volatility. Unfortunately, many authors have shown that this is a biased sampling estimate of the true correlation.[14] An example can illustrate this argument. Suppose that two markets have a constant joint-normal distribution of returns with a constant correlation of 0.50. Let's now estimate what would be the sampling correlation if we focus only on volatile observations. For example, suppose that we split the sample in two fractiles (50 percent) based on the absolute return of one market. The first sample is made of "small" returns, the second of "large" returns (positive or negative). Under the assumption of normality with constant correlation, the estimated conditional correlation of small returns is 0.21 and the conditional correlation of large returns is 0.62, even though the true correlation is constant and equal to 0.50. This result

---

[14]See Boyer, Gibson, and Loretan (1999); Loretan and English (2000); and Forbes and Rigobon (2002).

can easily be replicated by a simulation on a spreadsheet. If we only focus on the 5 percent most volatile observations, the estimated correlation jumps to 0.81. Still, the true market correlation has not changed. So, the apparent shift in correlation is spurious.

Loretan and English (2000) use a correct statistical procedure to study the correlation of equities, bonds, and foreign exchange during various periods of market turbulence. They conclude that "a significant portion of shifts of correlations over time—including those that occurred in the fall of 1998—may reflect nothing more than the predictable effect of differences in sample volatilities on measured correlation, rather than breaks in the data-generating process for asset returns." In other words, the apparent observation that correlation increases in periods of market turbulence is simply an observation that market volatility has increased, but the true correlation remains constant. Forbes and Rigobon (2002) also study numerous crisis periods, including the October 1987 stock market crash. They conclude that "tests for contagion based on cross-market correlation coefficient are problematic due to the bias introduced by changing volatility in market returns (i.e. heteroskedasticity)." They propose an adjustment for this heteroskedasticity bias and find that correlation does not increase significantly in periods of crisis. To summarize, the conclusion that correlation increases in periods of crisis seems to be simply a statistical bias due to faulty econometrics.

Previous results are based on the volatility of asset returns, with no distinction made between bear and bull markets. Longin and Solnik (2001) find that measured correlations behave as expected under the theory of constant correlation in the presence of large positive shocks, but tend to increase in the presence of large negative shocks. So, there still is some evidence that the international correlation of equity markets increases in periods of market distress, but the evidence is not as strong as suggested by some practitioners. Simply graphing the conditional correlation estimated over moving windows of 52 weeks or 200 days can be very misleading, because correlation estimates are biased upward or downward, depending on the volatility of market returns. This bias begs for correction. In reality, the true correlation is much more stable than implied by a casual visual inspection of the graph. Furthermore, Ang and Bekaert (2002) introduce an asset allocation model with different correlation regimes (normal and volatile periods), and they show that the existence of increased correlation in bear markets has only a small influence on the optimal global asset allocation.

To compute a correlation coefficient, one resorts to a time-series estimation over a rather long period, assuming that the distribution of returns stays the same over the estimation period. Overlapping data have been used to study the changes in correlations; this is a poor method to study changes in correlation over time. An alternative is to look at the cross-sectional dispersion of country market returns at any given point of time. If the markets move quite independently, there should be a large dispersion of returns across national markets in any given day, week, or month. Conversely, if the markets move together, all returns should be closely bunched together. Solnik and Roulet (2000) suggest the cross-sectional standard deviation of returns as a simple measure of dispersion to study the correlation of markets.

Expanded Investment Universe and Performance Opportunities

International correlation among developed equity markets is expected to increase over time for reasons outlined earlier. Economies and markets are becoming increasingly integrated, as corporations pursue global strategies. However, the secular increase can only be slow. In some periods, global factors dominate, but should not to be confused with a secular trend. The rise and demise of the technology, media, and telecommunications (TMT) sector in late 1990s was a worldwide phenomenon. Business cycles are increasingly synchronized, but there still exist vast regional and national differences. To take the late 1990s as an example, most of Asia was in a prolonged recession while the United States was booming. Even within the European Union, the economic performance differs widely among countries. The three leading economies, France, Germany, and the United Kingdom, demonstrated big differences in the timing and intensity of their economic growth.

As major markets become intertwined, new investment opportunities emerge. In the early 1960s, there were only a couple of developed equity markets in the world. Countries like France, Germany, or Japan could be regarded as risky taken in isolation, but they provided diversification benefits to a U.S. or British investor. At the time, they had all the characteristics of emerging markets. Markets in Italy, Spain, Scandinavia, or Hong Kong progressively emerged a few years later. Many national stock markets, which were viewed as "outlandish" 30 years ago, have become "mainstream." But new markets are emerging. Associated with the slow increase in correlation of developed markets is the expansion of the investment universe. This is a natural evolutionary process. As stressed by Goetzmann, Li, and Rouwenhorst (2001), periods of globalization imply both an increase in correlation among developed markets and the emergence of new markets. The investment opportunity set enlarges, thereby offering additional international diversification benefits.

The question of global investing also should be put in a broader context. Although stock markets have become more mature and integrated, the investment universe has greatly expanded beyond equity. The case for global diversification now applies to a wide range of asset classes beyond foreign stock markets. These include emerging stock markets, foreign bonds, and alternative investments such as high-yield bonds, currency, global real estate, private equity, and various arbitrage strategies.

Global Investing Rather Than International Diversification

In the 1990s, the traditional approach to international diversification was based on the premise that country factors were the dominant factors affecting all stocks of a country. Investors were diversifying across country factors, and each stock was assigned to a country based on the location of its headquarters. The investment process was to adopt a two-step process:

- First, decide on a country allocation.

- Second, select securities within countries.

EXHIBIT 9.14

Average Correlation of Countries and of Industries

Source: UBS Global Asset Management.

Today we can observe that companies compete in global industries and have extensive foreign operations. This simple process breaks down in a world where the nationality of a firm becomes fuzzy and industries cut across countries.

Global Industry Factors With increased globalization, industry factors are growing in importance, while country factors see their influence reduced. Numerous studies[15] show that industry factors have a growing influence on stock returns relative to country-specific factors. For example, Exhibit 9.14 displays the pure factor return correlation that considers the country and industry effects independent of each other. The lower the correlation, the larger the risk benefit diversification. In the early 1990s, countries were less correlated than industries, and country diversification brought great risk diversification benefits. It is clear that there is still benefit from country diversification in the 2000s, but that the benefits from industry diversification, in the form of declining correlation, have become prominent. Increasingly, corporations are focusing on their core business in world-wide fashion, rather than spreading domestically across many business lines. For example, Ford, DaimlerChrysler, Renault, and Toyota belong to the same car manufacturing industry and are, to some extent, affected by the same industry factor. All of them have activities in many countries. For example, Daimler Benz, a German firm, ac-

---

[15]See Cavaglia Brightman and Aked (2000), Baca, Garbe and Weiss (2000), and Gérard, Hillion and de Roon (2002).

quired Chrysler, an American firm, while Renault, a French firm, linked with Nissan, a Japanese firm. Ford has many subsidiaries and brand names worldwide.

Regional and Country Factors   But regional factors are still present. When car sales are buoyant in France, there is a much bigger impact on Renault than on Ford. Diermeier and Solnik (2001) showed that the stock valuation of corporations reflect the geograpical distribution of their activities. For example, a corporation like DaimlerChrysler, which has extensive activities in Germany and in the United States is strongly influenced by both country factors. So, the picture is quite complex because from a market valuation perspective, we cannot simply use the location of the corporation's headquarters to define its nationality. When we talk about country factors, we should take into account the geographical distribution of activities. The more international the corporation is, the less it is sensitive to purely domestic country factors.

EXAMPLE 9.5   COUNTRY AND INDUSTRY EXPOSURES

Ford and Honda are two companies in the car manufacturing industry, deriving, respectively, 19% and 9% of their revenues in Europe. Lehman and Nomura are two companies in the financial services industry, deriving, respectively, 7% and 42% of their revenues in Europe.

You are bullish about the European economy and neutral about the Japanese and American economies. You are bullish about the financial services industry. Which stock would you overweight in your portfolio?

SOLUTION

You should overweight Nomura. It is a Japanese company but with extensive operations in Europe (42% of revenues) which will enable it to capitalize on European economic growth. Lehman is also in the financial services industry but has small operations in Europe.

Why Still Diversify Internationally?   Even if industry factors have become increasingly important and corporations are becoming more international, it would be wrong to assume that investing purely at home is a wise strategy from a risk viewpoint. A question sometimes asked is, "Since domestic companies are engaging in international activities, why not simply gain the risk diversification benefits in my portfolio by simply holding domestic companies?" This is because country factors still have a significant influence, and because a purely domestic portfolio is poorly diversified. Let us take the example of a Swiss investor who only holds Swiss equity. The portfolio is, to some extent international, but it carries a lot of specific, or idiosyncratic, risk. First some industries are not present among Swiss corporations. Second, it is still very exposed to the risk of the Swiss country factor. Third, such an investment strategy makes the implicit bet that a Swiss firm is the best firm worldwide in each industry. Although Swissair might have been considered the best airline by some Swiss investors, its bankruptcy in 2001 showed that this was a risky, undiversified bet. This argument would carry to investors from other countries, such as the United States. Why favor, *a priori,* Ford or GM rather than BMW or Peugeot? Although the riskiness of a purely domestic strategy seems obvious if we take the viewpoint of a small country like Switzerland, the conceptual argument extends to large countries like the U.S.

Global Investing   In a way, the investment world is more complex than it was years ago with segmented national equity markets. It will probably be years from now before we have a single, fully integrated, global equity market. In this light, the analysis of the individual firm and its diversity becomes more critical. To some extent, the analysis should still be country-specific: Country factors are still significant and many firms are still primarily domestic in their activities. It must also be industry-specific and firm-specific.

Globalization gives more importance to industries and individual companies and less to countries. It implies that investors should be more global in their investment approach, from research to portfolio construction. Even for a purely domestic portfolio, analysts must research the global product market of the domestic companies and their international competition. In global portfolio construction, a cross-country, cross-industry approach is required to capture the full-risk benefits of international diversification, and this is rarely practiced. More fundamentally, it seems increasingly harder to justify a "nationalistic" approach to equity investment, with a separation of domestic versus foreign investments. In a world where financial markets have become very integrated across borders and where corporations pursue global strategies, investment managers should respond with truly global financial analysis and portfolio construction. Industries cut across national boundaries, and factors that affect stock pricing are global. The question is no longer, "Should I put 20% of my assets abroad?" but rather, "How can I afford not to be global in all aspects of my investment management approach?"

The Case for Emerging Markets

The Basic Case

Emerging economies offer attractive investment opportunities. The local risks (volatility, liquidity, and political risk) are higher, as illustrated by numerous crises, but the expected profit is large. Exhibit 9.15 plots the value of the MSCI indexes of developed stock markets ("World") and of emerging stock markets ("Emerging") over the period December 1987 to August 2002. Although the higher volatility of emerging markets is apparent, they also had a significantly larger return over the long run. Both indexes are based at 100 at the end of 1987. Although the higher volatility of emerging markets is apparent, they also had a significantly larger return over the

EXHIBIT 9.15

Performance of World Developed Markets and Emerging Markets

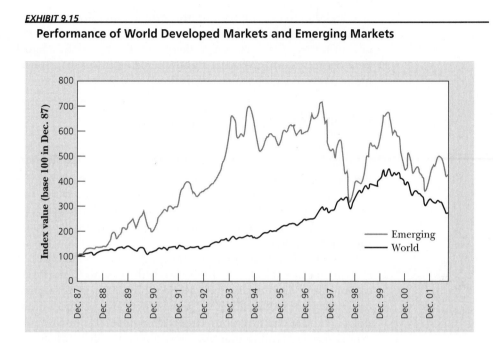

long run. While most emerging markets were still in their infancy, they had an excellent performance in the early 1980s. As shown in Exhibit 9.15, the excellent performance continued until the mid-1990s. The Emerging index rose from 100 in December 1987 to approximately 700 in September 1994, while the World index rose to only 180. In late 1994, Mexico suffered a severe financial crisis that partly spread to other equity markets in Latin America: The Emerging index dropped to 520 within six months (loss of 25%), but quickly recovered and reached a new peak in July 1997 at some 720. In 1997, Russia defaulted on some of its debt and several emerging Asian countries got into severe currency and economic troubles: The Emerging index dropped to 320 by August 1998 (a yearly loss of some 50%). By March 2000, the Emerging index was up again around 680 (a gain of over 200%). But emerging markets followed the world bear market of the early 2000s and dropped again to reach approximately 430 in August 2002, as opposed to 275 for developed markets. From 1987 to August 2002, the geometric mean returns are 3.9% per year for the World index and 8.4% per year for the Emerging index; but the volatility (annualized standard deviation) is 14.4% for the World index and 24% for the Emerging index.

Emerging markets also present a positive but moderate correlation with developed markets (see Exhibit 9.4); the correlation with the world index of developed markets is around 0.6. Because of the low correlation[16] between emerging and

---

[16]The correlation, however, is still generally positive. One should not be surprised to find that in some periods when developed markets drop, emerging markets also drop and by a large amount, because of their high volatility. This happened in 2000. In other periods, an appreciation of emerging markets can offset a loss in developed markets.

developed markets, the risks of investing in emerging markets get partly diversified away in a global portfolio. Hence, emerging markets can have a positive contribution in terms of risk–return trade-offs. Let's review the main factors affecting expected returns and risks that should be taken into account when including emerging markets in a global asset allocation.

Volatility, Correlations, and Currency Risk

Volatility   The volatility of emerging markets is much larger than that of developed markets (see Bekaert, Erb, Harvey, and Viskanta [1998]). Furthermore, the distribution of returns is not symmetric, and the probability of a shock (a large price movement) is higher than would be the case if the distribution of returns were normal. This finding implies that the standard deviation is not a sufficient measure of market risk. Investment risk in emerging economies often comes from the possibility of a crisis.

The development of many emerging markets stems from the winds of political reform and liberalization. This is clearly the case in Central Europe since the fall of communism. This is also the case in China with its economic reforms. Problems can easily materialize, however. Some emerging countries do not have a fully stable political and social situation. The explosive social transformation brought about by rapid, and sometimes anarchic, economic growth can lead to serious imbalances, causing social and political unrest. For example, some Chinese cities have industrialized very rapidly, while rural regions became more aware of their poverty.

The infrastructure can limit growth. Thailand and China, for example, have stretched the limit of their existing road infrastructures. Education structures are often insufficient to train a large number of workers and managers in modern international techniques. Multilateral development banks have made education a priority, but improvements are very slow, as local teachers must first be trained but are then tempted to leave the education system after their training. The quality of goods produced may be below international standards because of a lack of training and quality standards different from those required in developed countries.

Corruption is a rampant problem everywhere but may be more so in some emerging countries. Family ownership tends to favor family and friends at the detriment of other stockholders, especially foreign ones. Links between politicians and companies' managers sometimes go beyond what would be in the best interest of stockholders. The banking sector is sometimes poorly regulated, unsupervised, undercapitalized for the lending risks assumed, and lacking in the sophistication required by modern financial operations.

Correlation   International correlation tends to increase in periods of crises, and emerging markets are subject to periodic large crises. Patel and Sankar (1998) find that crises on emerging markets tend to be more prolonged than crises on developed markets, and tend to spread to all emerging markets in the region. It is often the case, however, that a crisis affecting one emerging country does not spread to other emerging countries, especially outside of its region. This is the case when the crisis is caused primarily by domestic political problems; many examples can be found in the recent past. An emerging market boom or crisis does not necessarily spread to developed markets, explaining the rather low correlation between developed and emerging markets. Spread depends on whether the factors creating the boom or crisis are primarily local or global.

Currency Risk   Another observation is the correlation between stock and currency returns. Developed markets sometimes exhibit a negative correlation with the value of their currencies. Namely, the local stock market tends to appreciate when the value of the local currency depreciates; the argument is based on an improvement in the international competitiveness of the local firms. This is not the case for emerging stock markets. Both the stock market and the currency are affected by the state of the economy. In periods of crisis, both drop significantly. For example, the Korean won lost more than 50 percent of its value in 1997, and the Seoul stock market also dropped. Both went up significantly in 1998, when the Korean situation showed some encouraging signs. Numerous similar examples could be found in Asia or Latin America. This positive correlation means that foreign investors suffer doubly from currency risk in emerging markets.

Portfolio Return Performance

Emerging markets have a vocation to become developed markets. To emerge, an equity market has to move from an embryonic stage to that of a truly active market attracting international investors. If successful, the market will grow, become more mature, and reach the stage of becoming a developed market. This process should lead to high returns. Clearly, a major argument for investing in emerging economies is their prospective economic growth. Portfolio managers want to find countries that will exhibit in the future the type of growth witnessed by Japan between the 1960s and the 1980s. Most analysts expect emerging economies to grow at a higher rate than developed nations, given the liberalization of international trade. Arguments frequently mentioned are lower labor costs, lower level of unionization and social rigidities, delocalization of production by high-cost developed countries, and rapid growth in domestic demand. The arrival of foreign capital helps those countries develop at a rapid pace and to compete on the world goods market. The transition to a more democratic political system with less corruption, more efficient regulation of the financial industry and other sectors, promotion of free enterprise, and application of the rule of law should strongly benefit local stock markets. Some specific factors could also affect the local stock markets. For example, pension funds have recently been created in many Latin American countries and are likely to invest heavily in their local stock markets. Many countries are pursuing an active program of privatization, and more local firms are attracted by the financing potential of stock markets. Under pressure from international investors, emerging markets are becoming more efficient, providing more rigorous research on companies and progressively applying stricter standards of market supervision. Accounting standards that conform with international accounting standards (IAS) have been adopted in many countries and are progressively implemented. Most of these markets have automated their trading and settlement procedures, using computer software tested on developed markets. High returns can be expected in emerging economies that are successful in achieving this transition.

Investability of Emerging Markets

Foreign investors face restrictions when investing on many emerging markets. Although many emerging countries are very liberal toward foreign capital, investability is somewhat restricted in other countries. Restrictions can take many forms:

- *Foreign ownership* can be limited to a maximum percentage of the equity capital of companies listed on the emerging market. This limit can be zero for "strategic" companies, and a fixed percentage for all other companies.[17]

- *Free float* is often small because the local government is the primary owner of many companies. Even though the total market cap of a company looks large, the float available to foreign or domestic private investing is limited.

- *Repatriation of income or capital* can be somewhat constrained. Such capital flows have been liberalized in most emerging countries, but controls are periodically applied in periods of severe crisis. For example, this happened in Malaysia during the 1997 crisis.

- *Discriminatory taxes* are sometimes applied to foreign investors, although this is becoming exceptional.

- *Foreign currency* restrictions are sometimes applied. For example, China applied a dual-currency system for residents and for foreign investors.

- *Authorized investors* are the only investors allowed to invest in some emerging countries (e.g., India and Taiwan). These authorized foreign investors are typically institutional investors, not private ones.

The pace of liberalization of emerging markets is rapid, and investability regulations are undergoing continual change. However, there is always the risk of an imposition of constraints in periods of crisis.

Another major problem with investing in emerging market is the lack of *liquidity*. Any sizable transaction can have a very large price impact. So, there could be a significant performance difference between a "paper" portfolio, such as a passive index, and an actual portfolio.

Providers of emerging-market stock indexes have tried to reflect the investability of markets by constructing "investable" or "free" indexes. In building global emerging-market indexes, foreign ownership restrictions, and free float strongly affect the weight of a given emerging country in the index.

---

[17]Similar restrictions apply, to a much smaller extent, in developed markets. For example, American companies in the defense or transportation industries have foreign ownership constraints.

Segmentation versus Integration Issue

In integrated markets, assets with identical risk should command identical return, regardless of location. In segmented markets, the expected returns on similar assets from different countries should not be related. In practice, emerging markets are somewhat segmented from the international market. Segmented asset pricing is attractive to the global investor. It implies that assets are mispriced relative to their "international" value. Harvey (1995) and Erb, Harvey, and Viskanta (1998) found evidence to reject the hypothesis that emerging stock markets are priced as if they were integrated in the world market. Returns on local companies are strongly influenced by domestic variables rather than by global variables, and domestic risk is priced, not global risks. As emerging markets are increasingly liberalized, this conclusion is likely to change. In a segmented market pricing expected asset return should be proportional to local risks. The local volatility is much higher than the contribution of the asset to the world market risk (its beta), which is what should matter in integrated asset pricing. So, expected returns in segmented markets should also be higher.

Despite all the problems of emerging economies, which create higher investment risks, emerging stock markets are an attractive asset allocation opportunity. Again, the idea is that investors should be willing to buy emerging markets, which are inherently very volatile, because some of them are likely to produce very high returns. Altogether, the contribution of emerging markets to the total risk of the global portfolio is not very large, because of their low correlation with developed markets.

Summary

- International investing reduces risk because the correlations between country markets are less than 1.0. For a two-asset portfolio of domestic and foreign assets, the expected portfolio return is the weighted average of the domestic expected return and the foreign expected return. The standard deviation is the square root of the quantity: the weight squared times the variance of the domestic asset plus the weight squared times the variance of the foreign asset plus twice the product of the weights times the correlation times the standard deviations of the two assets.

- The domestic rate of return on a foreign asset is the rate of return of that asset in the foreign currency plus the rate of return on the exchange rate plus the product of the rate of return in the foreign currency times the rate of return on the exchange rate. The variance of the domestic rate of return is approximately the variance of the local return plus the variance of the exchange rate return plus twice the covariance of the local return and exchange rate return.

- International diversification provides an efficient frontier that dominates the domestic-only efficient frontier because the domestic-only frontier is more constrained.

- The factors causing equity market correlations across countries to be relatively low are the independence of different nations' economies and government policies, technological specialization, independent fiscal and monetary policies, and cultural and sociological differences.

- The factors causing bond market correlations across countries to be relatively low are the differences in national monetary and budgetary policies.

- No evidence has been found of a systematic delayed reaction of one national market to another, except for daily returns as a result of time differences around the world.

- An increased Sharpe ratio from international investing is possible because of risk reduction and the increase in profitable investment opportunities in an enlarged investment universe.

- Currency risk may only slightly magnify the volatility of foreign currency-denominated investments, because market and currency risks are not additive; exchange risk can be hedged; the contribution of currency risk should be measured for the total portfolio; and the contribution of currency risk decreases with the time horizon. Currency risk is relatively more important for bond investments than equity investments.

- The increase in correlations between national markets reduces diversification benefits. This increase is due to such factors as deregulation, capital mobility, free trade, and the globalization of corporations.

- The country-specific argument against international diversification arises during periods when the domestic market does better than most other markets, leading some to say that there is no need for international investments in the future because the domestic market is outperforming.

- The potential physical barriers to international investing include lack of familiarity with foreign markets, political risk, lack of market efficiency, regulations, transaction costs, taxes, and currency risks.

- The pitfall in estimating correlations during volatile periods is that correlations conditioned on part of a sample are biased. The apparent observation that correlation increases in periods of market turbulence can simply be an observation that market turbulence has increased but the true correlation has remained constant.

- International performance opportunities have increased over time because many markets are moving from the emerging to the developing category.

- International diversification refers to diversifying internationally because correlations between country markets are less than 1.0. As the industry factor becomes more important relative to the country factor, global investing refers to investing in the best companies, wherever they are located in the world, and recognizing that these companies will also be investing worldwide.

■ Compared with developed markets, emerging markets exhibit higher volatility than developed markets, with asymmetric return distributions and increasing international correlations in times of crises, but they also exhibit higher return opportunities because of the early growth stages of their economies.

■ In contrast to developed economies, emerging markets exhibit positive correlations between the local stock market and the currency; that is, when they do poorly, both the local stock market and the currency do poorly together.

■ The investability in emerging markets is constrained by various regulations and liquidity problems.

■ Emerging markets tend to be somewhat segmented, and mispricing is evident.

Problems

1. The estimated volatility of a domestic asset is $\sigma_d = 15\%$ (annualized standard deviation of returns). A foreign asset has a volatility of $\sigma_f = 18\%$, and a correlation of $\rho = 0.5$ with the domestic asset. What is the volatility of a portfolio invested 80 percent in the domestic asset and 20 percent in the foreign asset?

2. You are given the expected return and standard deviation of asset 1 and asset 2:

$$E(R_1) = 10\%, \sigma_1 = 10\%$$

$$E(R_2) = 14\%, \sigma_2 = 16\%$$

The correlation between the two assets is $\rho = 0.2$.
   a. Calculate the expected return and risk of portfolios invested in the following proportions:

Asset 1	Asset 2
100%	0%
80%	20%
60%	40%
50%	50%
40%	60%
20%	80%
0%	100%

   b. Use the expected return and risk calculations for all the portfolios to plot an expected return–risk graph.

3. Consider the following information on the expected return and risk of two assets:

$$E(R_1) = 10\%, \sigma_1 = 14\%$$

$$E(R_2) = 16\%, \sigma_2 = 16\%$$

   a. Calculate the expected return and risk of portfolios invested in the following proportions listed. Assume a correlation of $\rho = 0.5$.

Asset 1	Asset 2
100%	0%
80%	20%
60%	40%
50%	50%
40%	60%
20%	80%
0%	100%

Use the expected return and risk calculations for all the portfolios to plot the efficient frontier.

b. Repeat part (a), assuming $\rho = -1$, $\rho = 0$, and $\rho = +1$.

c. Looking at the four graphs you have just drawn for parts (a) and (b), what do you conclude about the importance of correlation in risk reduction?

4. The standard deviation of a foreign asset in local currency is $\sigma = 8.5\%$, and the standard deviation of the exchange rate is $\sigma_s = 5.5\%$.

a. If the correlation between the asset return, in local currency, and the exchange rate movement is $\rho = 0$, calculate the amount of risk that can be attributed to currency risk.

b. If the correlation between the asset return, in local currency, and the exchange rate movement is $\rho = 0.25$, calculate the amount of risk that can be attributed to currency risk.

c. If the correlation between the asset return, in local currency, and the exchange rate movement is $\rho = -0.45$, calculate the amount of risk that can be attributed to currency risk.

d. What is the impact of the level of correlation between the asset return in local currency and the exchange rate movement on the risk of a foreign asset measured in dollars?

5. Assume that the domestic volatility (standard deviation) of the German stock market (in euros) is 18.2 percent. The volatility of the euro against the U.S. dollar is 11.7 percent.

a. What would the dollar volatility of the German stock market be for a U.S. investor if the correlation between the stock market returns and exchange rate movements were zero?

b. Suppose the dollar volatility of the German stock market is 20.4 percent. What can you conclude about the correlation between German stock market movements and exchange rate movements?

6. Assume that the domestic volatility (standard deviation) of the German bond market (in euros) is 5.5 percent. The volatility of the euro against the U.S. dollar is 11.7 percent.

a. What would the dollar volatility of the German market be for a U.S. investor if the correlation between the bond market returns and exchange rate movements were zero?

b. Suppose the dollar volatility of the German bond market is 13.6 percent. What can you conclude about the correlation between German bond market movements and exchange rate movements? What might explain this correlation?

7. Indicate whether the following statement is correct, and explain your reasoning: "The best diversification vehicle is an asset with high volatility and low correlation with the portfolio."

8. a. Exhibit 9.4 provides correlations of stock markets (currency hedged). Which markets are most correlated, and which are the least correlated with Germany? Provide some explanations for the differences in correlations.

   b. Once again, consider the correlations in Exhibit 9.4. Which markets are most correlated, and which are the least correlated with the United States? Provide some explanations for the differences in correlations.

9. Consider the correlations (in U.S. dollars) of worldwide bond markets presented in Exhibit 9.5. Explain the reasons for the correlations observed between the United States and other countries, and indicate the motivations for diversifying a U.S. dollar bond portfolio into foreign-currency bonds.

10. Explain whether there are any benefits to adding bonds to a stock portfolio in a global investment strategy.

11. What factors can be used to explain differences in the long-run performance of equity markets of different countries?

12. Is currency risk a barrier to international investment?

13. It is often claimed that financial markets are becoming increasingly integrated worldwide. Advance some reasons for this trend.

14. Studies of international financial markets have documented a phenomenon referred to as "correlation breakdown." Explain what is meant by this term. What are the implications of correlation breakdown for global portfolio strategy?

15. Despite strong arguments in favor of international diversification, international portfolio investment is still not widespread in many countries. One reason for this is the presence of barriers to international investment. List and explain the various barriers to international investment.

16. The traditional approach to global investing was a two-step procedure, in which the first decision was country allocation and the second decision was to select industries and stocks within countries. Is this approach still valid, or have changes in international markets called this two-step approach into question?

17. Risk in developed financial markets is typically measured by the standard deviation of returns. Is the standard deviation a sufficient measure of risk in emerging markets? Explain your answer.

18. Emerging markets are often perceived to be very risky investment propositions. Provide some arguments in favor of investing in emerging markets.

19. TMP has been experiencing increasing demand from its institutional clients for information and assistance related to international investments. Recognizing that this is an area of growing importance, the firm has hired an experienced analyst/portfolio manager specializing in international equities and market strategies. Her first assignment is to represent TMP before a client company's investment committee to discuss the possibility of changing their present "U.S. securities-only" investment approach to one including international investments. She is told that the committee wants a presentation that fully and objectively examines the basic, substantive considerations on which the committee should focus attention, including both theory and evidence. The company's

pension plan has no legal or other barriers to adoption of an international approach, and no non-U.S. liabilities currently exist.

   a. Identify and briefly discuss three reasons for adding international securities to the pension portfolio and three problems associated with such an approach.

   b. Assume that the committee has adopted a policy to include international securities in its pension portfolio. Identify and briefly discuss three additional policy-level investment decisions the committee must make before management selection and actual implementation can begin.

20. The HFS Trustees have solicited input from three consultants concerning the risks and rewards of an allocation to international equities. Two of them strongly favor such action, while the third consultant commented as follows:

> The risk reduction benefits of international investing have been significantly overstated. Recent studies relating to the cross-country correlation structure of equity returns during different market phases cast serious doubt on the ability of international investing to reduce risk, especially in situations in which risk reduction is needed the most.

   a. Describe the behavior of the cross-country equity return correlations to which the consultant is referring. Explain how that behavior may diminish the ability of international investing to reduce risk in the short run.

   b. Assume the consultant's assertion is correct. Explain why it might still be more efficient on a risk/reward basis to invest internationally rather than only domestically in the long run.

Solutions

1. The domestic and foreign assets have annualized standard deviations of return of $\sigma_d = 15\%$ and $\sigma_f = 18\%$, respectively, with a correlation of $\rho = 0.5$. The variance (σ_p) of the portfolio invested 80 percent in the domestic asset and 20 percent in the foreign asset is

$$\sigma_p^2 = (0.8^2 \times \sigma_d^2) + (0.2^2 \times \sigma_f^2) + (2 \times 0.8 \times 0.2 \times \rho \times \sigma_d \times \sigma_f)$$

$$\sigma_p^2 = (0.8^2 \times 15^2) + (0.2^2 \times 18^2) + (2 \times 0.8 \times 0.2 \times 0.5 \times 18 \times 15) = 200.16$$

$$\sigma_p = \sqrt{200.16}, \text{ or } 14.15\%$$

2. a. For each portfolio, expected return is calculated using Equation 9.1, and portfolio standard deviation is calculated using Equation 9.2. Expected returns and standard deviations for the portfolios are listed in the following table.

Invested in Asset 1	Invested in Asset 2	Portfolio Expected Return	Portfolio Risk
100%	0%	10.00%	10.00%
80%	20%	10.80%	9.19%
60%	40%	11.60%	9.61%
50%	50%	12.00%	10.25%
40%	60%	12.40%	11.11%
20%	80%	13.20%	13.34%
0%	100%	14.00%	16.00%

b. The plot of the portfolios on a risk–return graph is provided here:

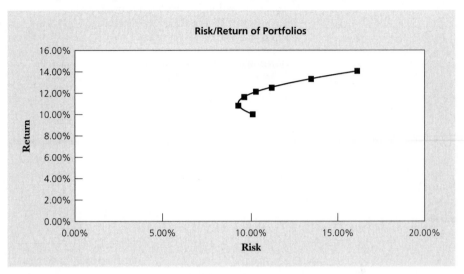

3. a. For each portfolio, expected return is calculated using Equation 9.1, and portfolio standard deviation is calculated using Equation 9.2. Expected returns and standard deviations for the portfolios are listed in the following table.

When $\rho = 0.5$:

Invested in Asset 1	Invested in Asset 2	Portfolio Expected Return	Portfolio Risk
100%	0%	10.00%	14.00%
80%	20%	11.20%	13.10%
60%	40%	12.40%	12.86%
50%	50%	13.00%	13.00%
40%	60%	13.60%	13.31%
20%	80%	14.80%	14.41%
0%	100%	16.00%	16.00%

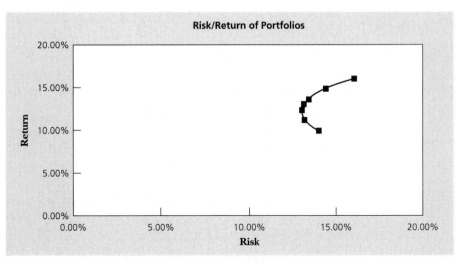

b. For each portfolio, expected return is calculated using Equation 9.1, and portfolio standard deviation is calculated using Equation 9.2. Expected returns and standard deviations for the portfolios are listed in the following tables for various correlations. When $\rho = -1.0$:

Invested in Asset 1	Invested in Asset 2	Portfolio Expected Return	Portfolio Risk
100%	0%	10.00%	14.00%
80%	20%	11.20%	8.00%
60%	40%	12.40%	2.00%
50%	50%	13.00%	1.00%
40%	60%	13.60%	4.00%
20%	80%	14.80%	10.00%
0%	100%	16.00%	16.00%

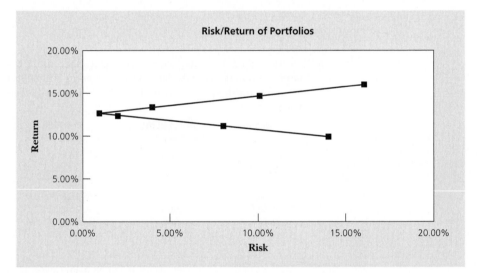

When $\rho = 0$:

Invested in Asset 1	Invested in Asset 2	Portfolio Expected Return	Portfolio Risk
100%	0%	10.00%	14.00%
80%	20%	11.20%	11.65%
60%	40%	12.40%	10.56%
50%	50%	13.00%	10.63%
40%	60%	13.60%	11.11%
20%	80%	14.80%	13.10%
0%	100%	16.00%	16.00%

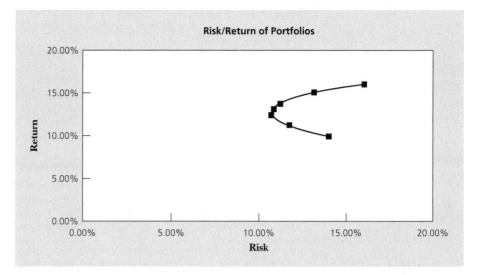

When ρ = 1.0:

Invested in Asset 1	Invested in Asset 2	Portfolio Expected Return	Portfolio Risk
100%	0%	10.00%	14.00%
80%	20%	11.20%	14.40%
60%	40%	12.40%	14.80%
50%	50%	13.00%	15.00%
40%	60%	13.60%	15.20%
20%	80%	14.80%	15.60%
0%	100%	16.00%	16.00%

    c. The graphs for parts (a) and (b) illustrate that, holding all else constant, lower correlations translate into lower levels of portfolio risk, without sacrificing expected return.

4. a. $\sigma_f^2 = \sigma^2 + \sigma_s^2 + 2\rho\sigma\sigma_s = (8.5)^2 + (5.5)^2 + 2(0)(8.5)(5.5) = 102.5$
    $\sigma_f = 10.12\%$
    Contribution of currency risk $= 10.12 - 8.5 = 1.62\%$
  b. $\sigma_f^2 = \sigma^2 + \sigma_s^2 + 2\rho\sigma\sigma_s = (8.5)^2 + (5.5)^2 + 2(0.25)(8.5)(2.5) = 125.9$
    $\sigma_f = 11.22\%$
    Contribution of currency risk $= 11.22 - 8.5 = 2.72\%$
  c. $\sigma_f^2 = \sigma^2 + \sigma_s^2 + 2\rho\sigma\sigma_s = (8.5)^2 + (5.5)^2 + 2(-0.45)(8.5)(5.5) = 60.4$
    $\sigma_f = 7.77\%$
    Contribution of currency risk $= 7.77 - 8.5 = -0.73\%$
  d. When the correlation between the asset return, in local currency, and the exchange rate movement is low enough, currency risk may actually reduce the asset risk measured in dollars. However, in cases in which the correlation is zero or positive, asset risk in dollars is higher than asset risk in local currency because of currency risk.

5. a. If the correlation between stock market returns and exchange rate movements were equal to zero, the dollar volatility of the German stock market would be
    $\sigma_f^2 = \sigma^2 + \sigma_s^2 + 2\rho\sigma\sigma_s = (18.2)^2 + (11.7)^2 + 2(0)(18.2)(11.7) = 468.13$
    $\sigma_f = 21.64\%$
  b. Because the actual dollar volatility is only 20.4 percent, we conclude that the correlation between stock market returns and exchange rate movements is negative.

6. a. If the correlation between bond market returns and exchange rate movements were equal to zero, the dollar volatility of the German bond market would be
    $\sigma_f^2 = \sigma^2 + \sigma_s^2 + 2\rho\sigma\sigma_s = (5.5)^2 + (11.7)^2 + 2(0)(5.5)(11.7) = 167.14$
    $\sigma_f = 12.93\%$
  b. Because the actual dollar volatility is 13.6 percent, we conclude that the correlation between bond market returns and exchange rate movements is positive. When the euro gets weaker, U.S. investors lose on the exchange rate and also on bond market returns measured in euros. This can be explained by the idea that a weak currency usually goes with rising interest rates (and negative bond market return).

7. The best diversification vehicle is an asset whose value gets significantly higher when the rest of the portfolio's value is low, and thereby partially offsets the loss of other assets. The best vehicle is an asset with a negative correlation (so it goes up when the portfolio goes down) and high volatility (large upswings when the portfolio goes down). Thus the statement is correct.

8. a. The markets that are highly correlated (currency-hedged) with Germany are the European countries and, in particular, the French market (0.82) and the Swiss market (0.63). Both Switzerland and France are countries bordering Germany, and their economies are highly dependent on the German economy. Besides, Swiss companies are mostly multinationals that are very active on the German market. Although France has more economic power and autonomy than Switzerland, tight links have been developed through the EU between the two countries, and they are significant contributors to each other's economy.
       Hong Kong (0.44) and Japan (0.34) have relatively low correlations. This reflects the fact that these are markets with loose links to the German economy.
  b. The markets that are highly correlated (currency-hedged) with the United States are the Canadian market (0.69), the British market (0.63), and the Swiss market (0.60).

Canada is obviously highly dependent on the U.S. economy. Switzerland is a small economic power with very active multinational groups on the U.S. market. The U.K. economy is very open to international investments. It has a great number of banks, insurance companies, and other financial institutions investing on the U.S. market, which explains the high correlation.

Italy (0.34) and Japan (0.39) have low correlations with the United States. Italy is a South European-oriented economy with a weaker link to the U.S. economy. Its development is explained by local factors such as integration into Europe. Japan has traditionally been less correlated with the United States, in part because of the importance of regional factors.

9. A review of the correlations in Exhibit 9.5 indicates that correlations of the U.S bond market with foreign bond markets are below 0.50, when measured in dollar terms. These low correlations can be attributed to the fact that national monetary/budget policies are not fully synchronized. The conclusions reached regarding the risk-reducing benefits of low correlations in global equity markets also apply to global bond markets. Foreign bonds are therefore a good vehicle of diversification and can significantly reduce the volatility of the portfolio. This makes foreign bonds attractive to a U.S. investor, despite foreign exchange risk.

10. Exhibit 9.5 indicates that correlation of the U.S. equity market with global bond markets is quite low, suggesting that adding bonds from foreign countries can reduce overall global portfolio risk. Thus, from the viewpoint of a U.S. investor, Exhibit 9.5 provides strong justification for including global bonds in a global portfolio strategy. In addition, empirical research shows that a portfolio of global stocks and bonds dominates U.S. stock/bond portfolios.

11. In general, over the long run, the performance of stock markets is closely tied to national economic factors. For example, in the case of Japan, real average annual GDP growth was 4.51 percent from 1971 to 1980, and 4.15 percent from 1981 to 1990 (see Exhibit 9.11). These real GDP growth rates dominated growth rates for the United States, Europe, and the Organization for Economic Cooperation and Development for the same periods. This is reflected in stock market performance numbers presented in Exhibit 9.10. For the period from 1971 to 1990, the average annual mean return for Japanese stocks was 20.68 percent, much higher than stock returns in the United States and Europe. From 1991 to 2000, it was the United States that had the highest real GDP growth rates and best-performing stock market.

Economic flexibility is another important factor. Countries such as France, Canada, and Sweden suffer from wage and employment rigidities not typically faced in many emerging countries. This economic flexibility is likely to reflect itself in stock market performance in the long run, in which emerging countries are expected to do well.

12. Currency fluctuations have an impact on the total return and volatility of foreign currency–denominated investments. However, there are at least four reasons why currency risk is not a barrier to international investment:
   - Market and currency risks are not additive. This is because the correlation between currency and market movements is quite weak and sometimes negative. Consequently, the contribution of currency risk to the risk of a foreign investment is quite small.
   - Currency risk can be hedged away by selling currency futures or forward contracts.

- If foreign assets represent a small portion of the portfolio, then the contribution of currency risk is insignificant (Jorion, 1989). Also, if the portfolio consists of multiple currencies, some portion of the risk is diversified away.
- Currency risk decreases with the length of the investment horizon.

13. There is no doubt that financial markets are becoming increasingly interconnected worldwide. Some of the reasons for this are as follows:
    - *Free trade.* Because of the World Trade Organization (WTO) and as a result of regional agreements such as NAFTA, ASEAN, and the EU, national economies are opening up to free trade. This has caused national economies to become more integrated.
    - *International capital flows.* The amount of foreign investment is growing rapidly on all national markets. Profit opportunities across markets are being arbitraged away.
    - *Capital market deregulation.* Deregulation has opened markets to foreign investors, and markets that used to be segmented are becoming more integrated.
    - *Corporations are becoming more global.* As corporations become more global, they derive significant portions of their income from overseas, and thus valuations are impacted more by global factors and less by country factors. This has caused stock-price correlations to increase, because corporate valuations are determined by a similar set of factors.

14. *Correlation breakdown* is a reference to the finding that during periods of crisis, when market volatility is high, correlations across markets increase dramatically. This phenomenon has been documented during major market events, such as the October 1987 crash and the Asian markets crisis of 1997.

    The increase in correlations across international financial markets during periods of crisis is problematic because one of the primary reasons for diversifying overseas is risk reduction due to low correlations. It appears, however, that correlations rise at the worst possible time, causing the benefits of international diversification to disappear when they are most needed. Further exacerbating the situation is the finding that distributions of returns tend to have fat tails rather than being normal. Fat tails imply that the occurrence of market crashes is likely to be more frequent than under "normality." This, in turn, suggests that periods of high correlations are more likely to occur.

15. There are a number of barriers to international investment, including the following:
    - *Familiarity with foreign markets.* Many investors are not familiar with business customs overseas and are therefore inclined to invest in domestic companies.
    - *Political risk.* This is a major concern, especially in emerging markets in which political and economic instability have had a debilitating impact on security prices in local-currency and dollar terms.
    - *Market efficiency.* Liquidity risk is a major concern for investors venturing overseas because it limits the ability of large investors to change asset allocations without signaling their actions to the rest of the market. Capital controls are another source of liquidity risk because such controls limit the repatriation of funds to the home country. In many countries, market efficiency is limited by the fact that companies do not provide accurate and timely information. Price manipulation and insider trading also limit market efficiency and benefit local investors at the expense of foreign investors.
    - *Regulations.* Certain countries have regulations that inhibit foreign investment by limiting the amount of overseas investment by local investors. Other countries limit

the amount of foreign ownership in domestic firms. These regulations generally limit the scope of international investment.

- *Transactions costs.* Transactions costs tend to be higher for international investments relative to domestic investments. The higher transactions costs for international investments are due to higher brokerage commissions and market impact, custody costs, and higher portfolio management fees.
- *Taxes.* Taxes have a relatively small impact on the international investment decision. Withholding taxes on dividends are typically reclaimed after a few months, but this represents an opportunity cost because funds are tied up.
- *Currency risk.* Although currency risk can be hedged, it does lead to additional administrative and trading costs and thus adds to the overall cost of international investment.

16. In the past, pure country return correlations were much lower than pure industry return correlations. Exhibit 9.14 shows that country correlations were lower than industry correlations between 1993 and 1999. Thus, for this period, the two-step procedure of first determining country allocations and then industry allocations within each country was justified. However, Exhibit 9.14 also shows that since mid-2000, industry correlations have been lower than country correlations. This means that while diversification across countries is still important, diversification across industries has become more important for risk-diversification purposes. In addition, when you consider that many corporations now operate globally while still remaining focused in their core businesses, it becomes difficult to determine the level of exposure to country factors. In this global environment, industries cut across countries. Thus, a better approach to global portfolio selection, one that can capture full benefits of international risk diversification, is a cross-industry, cross-country approach.

17. The distribution of returns in emerging markets is not symmetric. This calls into question the applicability of the standard deviation as a measure of risk, because the standard deviation is appropriate only if returns are normal. Investment risk in emerging markets must take the following into account:
- *Political and social stability.* The development of many emerging markets is tied to political and economic reforms. However, economic growth can result in serious imbalances that lead to political and social upheavals. Thus, political risk must be taken into account when measuring risk in emerging markets.
- *Infrastructure.* Inadequate physical infrastructure can limit economic growth no matter how great the potential. The same can be said of educational systems. That is, existing educational systems may be insufficient to train large numbers of workers and managers. Thus, in general, infrastructure can be a limiting factor and thus a source of risk in emerging markets.
- *Correlation.* Studies have shown that emerging markets are subject to periodic, prolonged crises that tend to spread to all other emerging markets in the region. Another issue that complicates the picture is the finding that for emerging markets, local stock markets changes and exchange rate movements display positive correlations, meaning that foreign investors suffer more from currency risk in emerging markets.

18. Although it is true that local risks in emerging markets are high because of volatility, liquidity, and political risk, correlations between emerging markets and developed markets are low. The low correlations mean that some of the higher risk in emerging markets can be diversified away in a global portfolio. Thus, the contribution of emerging markets to the total risk of a global portfolio is not likely to be very large.

Expected returns in emerging markets are higher because the economies of emerging markets are expected to grow at a higher rate than developed markets. Emerging market economies are expected to grow at a higher rate because of lower labor costs, lower levels of unionization, and rapid growth in domestic demand. In addition, the introduction of pension funds and the trend to privatization have benefitted local emerging stock markets.

Another factor that favors emerging-market investment is research that indicates emerging markets are somewhat segmented from international markets. Segmented markets imply that assets are mispriced and may offer portfolio managers investment opportunities at attractive valuations.

19. a. Arguments in favor of adding international securities include the following:
    1. Benefits gained from broader diversification, including economic, political and/or geographic sources
    2. Expected higher returns at the same or lower (if properly diversified) level of portfolio risk
    3. Advantages accruing from improved correlation and covariance relationships across the portfolio's exposures
    4. Improved asset allocation flexibility, including the ability to match or hedge non-U.S. liabilities
    5. Wider range of industry and company choices for portfolio construction purposes
    6. Wider range of managers through whom to implement investment decisions
    7. Diversification benefits realizable despite the absence of non-U.S. pension liabilities

    At the same time, there are a number of potential problems associated with moving away from a domestic-securities-only orientation:
    1. Possible higher costs, including those for custody, transactions, and management fees
    2. Possible reduced liquidity, especially when transacting in size
    3. Possible unsatisfactory levels of information availability, reliability, scope, timelessness, and understandability
    4. Risks associated with currency management, convertibility, and regulations/controls
    5. Risks associated with possible instability/volatility in both markets and governments
    6. Possible tax consequences or complications
    7. Recognition that EAFE underperformed in the 1990s

    b. A policy decision to include international securities in an investment portfolio is a necessary first step to actualization. However, certain other policy-level decisions must be made prior to implementation. That set of decisions would include the following:
    1. What portion of the portfolio shall be invested internationally; and in what equity and fixed-income proportions?
    2. Shall all or a portion of the currency risk be hedged, or not?
    3. Shall management of the portfolio be active or passive?
    4. Shall the market exposures be country/marketwide (top-down) or company/industry-specific (bottom-up)?
    5. By what benchmarks shall results be judged?

6. How will manager style be incorporated into the process?
7. How will the process reflect the important differences in risk between developed non-U.S. markets and emerging markets?

Until decisions on these additional policy-level issues have been made, implementation of the basic decision to invest internationally cannot begin.

20. a. The consultant is alluding to the behavior of cross-country equity return correlations during different market phases, as reported in various research studies. Specifically, the consultant is referring to the fact that correlations in down markets tend to be significantly higher than correlations in up markets. In other words, equity markets appear to be correlated more when they are falling than when they are rising.

b. Although cross-country equity return correlations can vary significantly in the short run, they remain surprisingly low when measured over long periods of time. This implies that, from a policy standpoint, international investing still offers the potential to construct more efficient portfolios, in a risk–return trade-off sense, than ones constructed using domestic assets only. This is so because global investing has the potential to reduce risk without sacrificing returns, even with adverse short-run outcomes.

Bibliography

Ang, A., and Bekaert, G. "International Asset Allocation with Regime Shifts," *Review of Financial Studies,* 15(4), Winter 2002.

Baca, S., Garbe, B., and Weiss, R. "The Rise of Sector Effects in Major Equity Markets," *Financial Analysts Journal,* 56(5), September/October 2000.

Bekaert, G., Erb, C. B., Harvey, C. R., and Viskanta, T. E. "Distributional Characteristics of Emerging Market Returns and Asset Allocation," *Journal of Portfolio Management,* Winter 1998.

Bookstaber, R. "Global Risk Management: Are We Missing the Point?" *Journal of Portfolio Management,* Spring 1997.

Boyer, B., Gibson, M. S., and Loretan, M. "Pitfalls in Tests for Changes in Correlations," Working Paper 597R, Federal Reserve Board, International Finance Division, 1999.

Cavaglia, S., Brightman, C., and Aked, M. "On the Increasing Importance of Industry Factors," *Financial Analysts Journal,* 56(5), September/October 2000.

DeFusco, R. A., McLeavey, D., Pinto, R., and Runkle, D. *Quantitative Methods for Investment Analysis,* Charlottesville, VA: AIMR, 2001.

Diermeier, J., and Solnik, B., "Global Pricing of Equity," *Financial Analysts Journal,* July/August 2001.

Erb, C. B., Harvey, C. R., and Viskanta, T. E. *Country Risk in Global Financial Management,* Charlottesville, VA: The Research Foundation of the IFCA, 1998.

Forbes, K., and Rigobon, R. "No Contagion, Only Interdependence: Measuring Stock Market Co-movements," *Journal of Finance,* October 2002.

Froot, K. A. "Currency Hedging over Long Horizons," NBER Working Paper #4355, May 1993.

Gérard, B., Hillion, P., and de Roon, F. "International Portfolio Diversification: Industrial Structure, Country and Currency Effects Revisited," Working Paper, 2002.

Goetzmann, W., Li, L., and Rouwenhorst, G. "Long-Term Global Market Correlation," Working Paper, 2001.

Harvey, C. R. "Predictable Risk and Return in Emerging Markets," *Review of Financial Studies,* 8(3), Fall 1995.

Jorion, P. "Asset Allocation with Hedged and Unhedged Foreign Stocks and Bonds," *Journal of Portfolio Management,* Summer 1989.

Longin, F., "The Asymptotic Distribution of Extreme Stock Market Returns," *Journal of Business,* 63, 1996.

Longin, F., and Solnik, B. "Is the International Correlation of Equity Returns Constant: 1960–1990?" *Journal of International Money and Finance,* February 1995.

Longin, F., and Solnik, B. "Extreme Correlation of International Equity Returns," *Journal of Finance,* April 2001.

Loretan, M., and English, W. B. "Evaluation 'Correlation Breakdowns' during Periods of Market Volatility," in *International Financial Markets and the Implications for Monetary and Financial Stability,* Bank for International Settlements, Switzerland, 2000.

Odier, P., and Solnik, B. "Lessons for International Asset Allocation," *Financial Analysts Journal,* March/April 1993.

Patel, S. A., and Sankar, A. "Crises in Developed and Emerging Stock Markets," *Financial Analysts Journal,* November/December 1998.

Solnik, B. "Why Not Diversify Internationally Rather Than Domestically?" *Financial Analysts Journal,* July/August 1974.

Solnik, B., and Roulet, J. "Dispersion as Cross-Sectional Correlation," *Financial Analysts Journal,* January/February 2000.

Zingales, L. "The Value of the Voting Right: A Study of the Milan Stock Exchange Experience," *Review of Financial Studies,* 7, 1994.

10

Derivatives

Investments based on some underlying asset are often known as derivatives. The capital invested is less than the price of the underlying asset, offering financial leverage and allowing investors to multiply the rate of return on the underlying asset. Because of this leverage, derivatives may be used either to take better advantage of a specific profit opportunity or to hedge a portfolio against a specific risk.

Derivatives can be traded on an organized exchange, which is usually the case for futures and options. Other types of derivatives exist in the form of private contracts between two parties, such as forwards and swaps. Once signed, these

507

contracts are not easily traded. This chapter presents a review of major derivatives (forwards and futures, swaps, options) and focuses on their use in investment management. The coverage of each derivative type is structured along the following sequence: a discussion of some basic principles, a review of the different instruments, an analysis of valuation of this derivative type, and a discussion of its use in investment management. The next chapter is devoted to currency risk management, and we will use concepts from this chapter on derivatives.

Forward and Futures

Forward contracts have existed for many centuries. They are simply a commitment to buy or sell goods at a future date and price specified at time of contracting.

The Principles of a Forward and a Futures Contract

Definition   In both a *forward* contract and a *futures* contract, all terms of a goods exchange are arranged on one day, but the physical delivery takes place at a later date (delivery date). More precisely, a forward or futures contract is a commitment to purchase or deliver a specified quantity of the underlying asset on a designated date in the future for a price determined competitively when the contract is transacted. A forward contract is a private agreement between two parties, and nothing happens between the contracting date and the delivery date. On the other hand, a futures contract is traded on an organized exchange, and the mechanics are a bit complex.

Let's consider the British pound futures traded on the Chicago Mercantile Exchange (CME). Contracts on the exchange specify delivery of 62,500 British pounds; all futures prices traded in the United States are quoted in dollars per unit of the second currency, in this case dollars per pound. On February 18, an investor could have bought a futures contract for delivery next March at a price of $1.6350 per pound. This means that the buyer of the futures contract was obliged to buy 62,500 pounds in March from the seller of the contract, who likewise was obliged to sell to the buyer. Exchanges offer contracts with different delivery months: On the CME, currency futures are traded with delivery months in March, June, September, and December.

A futures contract is simply a commitment to buy or sell. There is no money exchanged when the contract is signed. To ensure that each party fulfills its commitment, therefore, some form of deposit is required. This is called the *margin*. The exchanges set a minimum margin for each contract. In fact, two types of margins are required: When the client first enters a contract, an *initial margin* must be posted. The initial margin on the British pound contract was $1,080 for one 62,500 pounds contract. The *maintenance margin* is the minimum level below which the margin is not allowed to fall once losses on the contract value have been taken into account. The maintenance margin was $800 for the British pound contract. The maintenance margin is typically 70 percent to 80 percent of the initial margin, but is often equal to the initial margin on non-U.S. futures exchanges. Margins are usually deposited in the form of cash, but brokers often allow large customers to use interest-bearing securities, such as Treasury bills, as deposits. In that case, there is no opportunity cost associated with a futures contract investment, because the margin position continues earning interest.

Futures prices fluctuate every day and even every instant. Therefore, all contract positions are *marked to market* at the end of every day. If net price movements induce a gain on the position from the previous day, the customer immediately receives cash in the amount of this gain. Conversely, if there is a loss, the customer must cover the loss. As soon as a customer's account falls below the maintenance margin, the customer receives a margin call to reconstitute the initial margin. If this is not done immediately, the broker will close the position on the market. The following example illustrates how this works.

Assume that an investor buys a March contract in British pounds at $1.6350 per pound on February 18 and puts up an initial cash margin of $1,080. The maintenance margin is $800. The next day, the futures price drops to $1.6250, and the position is marked to market. The investor loses $0.0100 per pound, or $625 per contract. This amount is debited from the investor's cash position, which is reduced to $455, which is less than the maintenance margin. The investor receives a margin call for $625 to reconstitute the initial margin to $1,080. Investors receive a margin call only when their margin falls below the maintenance margin, but then they must deposit cash to reconstitute the initial margin (not the maintenance margin). The next day, the futures price rises to $1.6400 per pound, and the investor's cash account is credited $937.50 [(1.6400 − 1.6250) × 62,500]. The cash account now has a balance of $2,017.5, and the investor may draw up to $937.50 from the account. An investor short in the futures contract has the opposite cash flows.

Margins are set by the exchange, subject to periodic revision. The margin is determined by looking at the risk of a given contract. However, the risk on a portfolio of futures position is not equal to the sum of the risks on each position. For example, an investor who is long in a March contract and short in a June contract should not be required to post twice the initial margin on a single contract. The CME developed a margin system known as SPAN (Standard Portfolio Analysis of Risk®), which has been progressively adopted by most major exchanges throughout the world. SPAN calculates margin requirements on the basis of overall portfolio risk.

The procedure of marking to market implies that all potential profits and losses are immediately realized. This is a major difference between futures and forward contracts. In effect, futures contracts are canceled every day and replaced by new contracts with a delivery price equal to the new futures price, that is, the settlement price at the end of the day.

Market Organization: Futures versus Forward Contracts   Like futures contracts, forward contracts are made in advance of delivery. But a forward contract is a private agreement between two parties made "over-the-counter" (OTC). A forward contract cannot be resold, because there is no secondary market for it. For the same reason, forward contracts cannot be marked to market, and the investor has to wait for the delivery date to realize the profit or loss on the position. The margin is set initially and usually never revised. This could lead to fairly large initial margins, in order to cover default risk over the life of the contract. In practice, the margin is often set at zero for good-quality parties.

Futures contracts have succeeded because they are standardized. A clearinghouse handles the two sides of a transaction. For any transaction, two contracts are written: one between the buyer and the clearinghouse and one between the clearinghouse and the seller. Through this procedure, all contracts are standardized in terms of a specific counterparty, as well as size and delivery date. To cancel a position, the investor simply has to reverse the trades by selling contracts previously bought or buying back contracts previously sold. This creates a highly liquid market in standardized contracts. Forward contracts do not offer the same liquidity, because all contracts are different in terms of size, delivery date, and name of the other contracting party. Even if a reverse trade were possible in the forward market (and it would require an identical amount and delivery date), the investor would have to carry both contracts until the delivery date, because both are private commitments with two different parties. The reverse trade locks in the profit (or loss) on the initial contract, but this profit (or loss) will be realized only on the delivery date. Of course, the contract could also be renegotiated with the original counterparty with some side payment reflecting current market conditions, but this is usually a costly process because the counterparty does not have to oblige. Exhibit 10.1 summarizes the major differences between the two types of markets.

It should be stressed that, contrary to forward contracts, futures contracts are seldom used to take physical delivery. These contracts are used to hedge, or take advantage of, price movements rather than to delay the sale or purchase of goods. Most investors reverse their position in the futures market before the contract expires.

Futures contracts have become successful relative to forward contracts because their various mechanisms (marking to market, and the clearinghouse as the counterparty on each contract) basically eliminate default risk. Developed forward markets have prospered only for contracts in which the volume of transactions is large and involves market participants of top credit quality. This is the case for forward

EXHIBIT 10.1

Major Differences between Forward and Futures Contracts

Forward Contracts	Futures Contracts
1. Customized contracts in terms of size and delivery dates.	1. Standardized contracts in terms of size and delivery dates.
2. Private contracts between two parties.	2. Standardized contract between a customer and a clearinghouse.
3. Difficult to reverse a contract.	3. Contract may be freely traded on the market.
4. Profit or loss on a position is realized only on the delivery date.	4. All contracts are marked to market; profits and losses are realized immediately.
5. Margins are set once, on the day of the initial transaction.	5. Margins must be maintained to reflect price movements.

oil transactions, in which oil companies are active players. This is also the case for the interbank forward exchange rate market described in Chapter 1. The forward currency market is a wholesale market in which huge positions are taken at extremely low transaction costs. The futures currency market is more of a retail market, although arbitrage between the two markets aligns prices.

The Different Instruments

Currencies   The interbank foreign exchange market is usually considered the largest market for forward and futures transactions in currencies. This forward market is closely linked to that of Eurocurrency deposits because of the technical relationship between forward exchange rates and interest rate differentials between two currencies. It is also very large and efficient and boasts minimal transaction costs for normal transactions (several millions). Moreover, the market is open around the clock, with participants throughout the world.

As mentioned, forward contracts are not standardized, and there is no organized secondary market. Forward contracts are usually negotiated on the interbank market with maturities of 1, 2, 3, 6, or 12 months. Because the length of the contracts rather than the delivery date is fixed, each day, a new contract is traded on the market. For example, someone buying a 1-month contract on June 2 with maturity July 1 cannot resell it on June 6, because 1-month contracts traded on this day expire on July 5.

To assist a customer, a bank may propose a forward contract tailored to the customer's needs and charge a large commission for this service, because the bank cannot take an exactly offsetting position in the interbank market. Thus, a bank could propose on June 6 a forward contract with a maturity of 25 days expiring on July 1. The *currency swaps* described later in this chapter are also a form of forward exchange rate contract. They involve swapping at a fixed exchange rate a series of cash flows denominated in one currency for a series of cash flows denominated in another currency. This swap may be regarded as a package, or strip, of forward currency contracts where the payments on the contracts are matched to the cash flow dates of the swap. This currency swap market allows for long-term currency hedging. The forward and futures markets cover contracts ranging from one month to several months, whereas swaps extend this range to 10 years.

The CME actively trades futures contracts in many currencies. The CME also offers cross rate contracts not involving the U.S. dollar, for example a euro/British pound contract.[1] As shown in Exhibit 10.2, all prices are expressed in U.S. dollars per unit of foreign currency. An investor could have bought, on February 18, a Swiss franc contract with a March delivery wherein he would agree to buy 125,000 Swiss francs in March for a price of 0.7049 dollars per Swiss franc (latest price). If the Swiss franc appreciates and goes above 0.7049 dollars by March, the buyer will make a profit; if the Swiss franc depreciates, the buyer will take a loss.

---

[1] However, quotations and costs reflect the lower liquidity of these cross-rate contracts.

<u>EXHIBIT 10.2</u>

Quotations for Currency Futures, February 18

■ JAPANESE YEN FUTURES (CME) Yen 12.5m per Yen 100

	Open	Latest	Change	High	Low	Est. vol.	Open Int.
Mar	0.8425	0.8364	−0.0059	0.8473	0.8361	40,254	69,382
Jun	0.8560	0.8467	−0.0057	0.8560	0.8462	273	5,239
Sep	—	0.8629	—	—	—	4	1,494

■ STERLING FUTURES (CME) £62,500 per £

	Open	Latest	Change	High	Low	Est. vol.	Open Int.
Mar	1.6350	1.6320	−0.0020	1.6378	1.6316	5,283	54,485
Jun	1.6330	1.6316	−0.0018	1.6348	1.6310	42	1,884
Sep	—	1.6330	−0.0006	1.6340	1.6330	26	230

■ SWISS FRANC FUTURES (CME) SFr125,000 per SFr

	Open	Latest	Change	High	Low	Est. vol.	Open Int.
Mar	0.7060	0.7049	+0.0001	0.7080	0.7041	7,880	55,689
Jun	0.7108	0.7115	+0.0001	0.7118	0.7108	89	530
Sep	—	0.7184	+0.0005	0.7184	—	3	269

Source: Financial Times, February 19, 1999.

The currency futures quotations shown in Exhibit 10.2 illustrate the type of information available in the international financial press. For example, note the futures prices for the Swiss franc contracts. The size of the contract is 125,000 Swiss francs. All contract prices are given per unit of goods traded, that is, one Swiss franc. The March contract opened at 0.7060 dollars per Swiss franc and closed, or settled, at 0.7049. The *high* and *low* prices of the day were 0.7080 and 0.7041 dollars. The *change* gives the price change from the settlement price on the previous day. The settlement price is also the price used for the marking-to-market procedure. Someone who had bought one March Swiss franc contract at the close of February 17 at 0.7048 would have gained $12.50 on February 18 (SFr125,000 × $0.0001/SFr). Someone who had sold one contract on February 17 would have lost $12.50 on February 18. The *estimated volume* is the number of contracts traded during that day, and the *open interest* is the number of contracts outstanding.

The advantage of currency futures is that the investor may transact in small amounts for reasonable transaction costs. Moreover, the market is very liquid. An investor may engage in active currency exposure management, because clearing procedures permit covering positions at any time by reverse transactions in the futures contracts. In addition, the procedure of marking to market allows an investor to realize a profit or a loss immediately rather than having to wait until delivery. On the CME, there is physical delivery of currency at expiration of the contract. But reverse trades are often made to cancel the position before the delivery date.

Commodities   There has always been a need for futures markets in commodities with volatile spot prices. Farmers and harvest buyers have long used futures markets to hedge price risks arising from climatic conditions. A large variety of commodities are now traded on futures markets throughout the world: perishable goods, such as soybeans or live cattle; metals, such as copper, silver, and gold; energy sources, such as oil. For each commodity, the quality and quantity of the product traded are precisely specified, as are the locations and conditions of delivery. Some contracts on commodity indexes are also traded (Goldman Sachs Commodity Index futures on the CME).

Interest Rate Futures   The most actively traded futures contracts in the world are interest rate futures,[2] such as Eurodollar or U.S. Treasury bonds contracts. Commercial banks and money managers use these futures to hedge their interest rate exposure, that is, to protect their portfolios of loans, investments, or borrowing against adverse movements in interest rates. Speculators use them as leveraged investments, based on their forecasts of movements in interest rates.

Organized markets for interest rate futures exist for instruments in several currencies. All countries with an active bond market have developed a futures market for long-term bonds and short-term paper. Active U.S. dollar markets exist in three-month U.S. Treasury bills, in Eurodollar deposits (3-month LIBOR), and in Treasury bonds for long-term rates. Other futures contracts have been introduced for certificates of deposit (CDs), Fed funds, 5- and 10-year Treasury bonds, municipal bonds, and inflation-linked bonds. Similarly, all national futures markets offer, at least, a contract on their three-month interest rate and long-term government bond. The introduction of the euro led a consolidation among European futures exchanges, with the domination of EUREX (Germany–Switzerland) and Euronext-LIFFE (United Kingdom, France, Netherlands, and Belgium).

Short-Term Deposits   The quotation method used for these contracts is difficult to understand but tends to be similar among countries. Quotations for Euribor[3] interest rate futures are given in Exhibit 10.3. Contracts on short-term instruments are quoted at a discount from one hundred percent. At delivery, the contract price equals 100 percent minus the interest rate of the underlying instrument. For example, three-month Euribor contracts are denominated in units of €1 million; the price is quoted in points of 100 percent. For this reason, the March contract in Exhibit 10.3 is quoted at 96.980 percent (settlement price) on the Euronext-LIFFE. The price of 96.98 percent is linked to a forward interest rate on three-month Euribor deposits of 3.02 percent (100 − 96.98). If the three-month interest rate at delivery is less than 3.02 percent, the buyer of the contract at 96.98 percent will make a profit.

This quotation method is drawn from the Treasury bill market. However, further calculations are required to derive the profit or loss on such a futures position, because the interest rates for three-month instruments are quoted on an annualized basis. The true interest (not annualized) paid on a three-month instrument is

---

[2] *Interest rate swaps* are described later in this chapter. They are akin to periodic interest rate forward contracts. As mentioned, they may be considered long-term packages of forward contracts.

[3] Euribor (euro interbank offered rate) is the short-term interest rate in euros on the international market. It is equivalent to the LIBOR (London interbank offered rate) for the U.S. dollar.

EXHIBIT 10.3

Quotations for Interest Rate Futures, February 18

■ **THREE-MONTH EURIBOR FUTURES (LIFFE) €1m, 100 − rate**

	Open	Sett Price	Change	High	Low	Est. Vol.	Open Int.
Mar	96.985	96.980	−0.005	96.995	96.960	38,244	146,771
Jun	97.085	97.085	+0.005	97.100	97.070	29,048	134,205
Sep	97.115	97.115	+0.005	97.130	97.095	19,978	91,904
Dec	96.870	96.850	—	96.870	96.845	6,087	86,886

■ **NOTIONAL U.K. GILT FUTURES (LIFFE) £100,000 100ths of 100%**

	Open	Latest	Change	High	Low	Est. Vol.	Open Int.
Mar	117.27	116.98	−0.07	117.40	116.82	45,227	89,090
Jun	118.17	118.00	—	118.39	117.95	2,581	6,963

Source: Financial Times, February 19, 1999.

equal to the annualized rate divided by four. Therefore, the profit or loss on one unit of a Euribor contract (or any other three-month financial contract) equals the futures price variation divided by four. The total gain or loss on one three-month contract is therefore equal to

$$\text{Gain (loss)} = \left(\frac{\text{Futures price variation}}{4}\right) \times \text{Size of contract} \qquad (10.1)$$

Assume that in March the Euribor interest rate drops to 2 percent on the delivery date. The futures price will be 98 percent on that date. The profit to the buyer of one contract is

$$\text{Gain} = \left(\frac{98\% - 96.98\%}{4}\right) \times €1 \text{ million} = €2,550$$

The same quotation technique is used for Treasury bills and other short-term interest rate contracts.

Bonds   The quotation method for contracts on long-term instruments is quite different. The contract is usually defined in reference to a theoretical bond of well-defined characteristics, usually called a *notional bond*. For example, the British bond contract traded on the Euronext-LIFFE is defined in reference to a long-term gilt (U.K. government bond) with a 7 percent (notional) yield. The notional bond is a theoretical bond, which does not exist in real life. Contract specifications, including delivery conditions, are a bit technical and are detailed in Exhibit 10.4. For the purpose of most investors, it is sufficient to know that bond futures contracts are based on a specific bond.

Exhibit 10.3 also shows the quotations for futures contracts on U.K. gilts. The contract size is £100,000 of par value (or nominal value) of the bond. Quotations are expressed in hundredths of 100 percent, that is, in points and basis points. The quotation is in percentage of the par value of the bond. For example, the March

EXHIBIT 10.4

Bond Contracts Specifications (*U.S. Illustration in Italics*)

The **notional bond** is a theoretical bond, which does not exist in real life and is assumed to be "refreshed" every day, that is, priced as a newly issued bond (without accrued interest). Its main feature is its **notional yield,** the coupon rate on the bond.

Because the notional bond does not exist, we need to specify which bond can be delivered at maturity of the contract in lieu of the notional bond, and what are the conditions of delivery. If the seller of a contract wants to physically deliver a bond, the seller can do so with any bond belonging to a list of bonds published by the exchange.

For example, the U.S. Treasury bond contracts traded on the Chicago Board of Trade are defined in reference to a notional Treasury bond with a 6 percent notional yield. The contract is to deliver 100,000 U.S. dollars of par value of any U.S. Treasury bond that has a minimum life of 15 years and is noncallable over that period.

However, the futures price quoted applies strictly to the notional *6 percent coupon* bond. The price received by the seller of the futures contract who delivers a specific bond at maturity of the contract is equal to the settlement price of the notional bond futures adjusted by a **conversion factor** that takes into account the different characteristics in terms of coupon and maturity of the bond delivered (for example, a high-coupon security is worth more than a comparable low-coupon bond). The conversion factor equals the theoretical price of the delivered bond obtained by discounting its cash flows at the notional yield, on the maturity date of the futures contract. Note that bonds with coupons in excess of the notional yield have conversion factors greater than one (i.e., 100 percent). Bonds with coupons below the notional yield have conversion factors less than one. Actually, bonds are quoted on the basis of their clean price. So, the total present value of a bond (PV) is equal to its clean price quoted plus the accrued interest, which is equal to the proportion of the coupon accrued since the last payment date. Hence, the conversion factor[4] for each deliverable bond is calculated for the maturity date of the contract and is equal to the present value of the bond (discounted at the notional yield) minus accrued interest. For a given deliverable bond B, we have

$$\text{Conversion factor}_B = PV_B \ (\text{@ Notional yield}) - \text{Accrued interest}_B$$

On delivery date, the seller of the futures contract selects a bond to deliver, and delivers a quantity of par value of this delivered bond equal to the contract size (*$100,000 of par value for U.S. contracts*). The buyer of the futures contract will receive this quantity of delivered bonds and pay an **invoice** price equal to the futures settlement price times the contract size times the conversion factor of this specific delivered bond. Furthermore, the invoice paid by the buyer is adjusted for accrued interest on the delivered bond.

---

[4] Each futures exchange publishes a list of all deliverable bonds and a list of their conversion factors calculated on the maturity date of each available futures contract.

> Invoice = (Futures price × Conversion factor$_B$ + Accrued interest$_B$)
>   × Contract size
>
> At each point in time, some bonds will be cheaper to deliver than others; their market price is low compared to the invoice price received on delivery. Futures prices tend to correlate most closely with the price of the **cheapest-to-deliver** security. This is because the seller of the futures contract, who decides on the bond to be physically delivered at maturity, will naturally select the cheapest to deliver.[5]

contract of U.K. gilts settled at 116.98 percent on February 18. The change from the previous day's settlement price was −0.07 percent.

The gain or loss[6] is simply equal to the futures price variation, in percent, times the size of the contract:

$$\text{Gain (loss)} = (\text{Futures price variation}) \times \text{Size of contract} \tag{10.2}$$

In this illustration, the loss taken by the holder of one U.K. gilt contract from the previous trading day is equal to

$$\text{Gain} = -0.07\% \times £100{,}000 = -£70$$

Stock Futures   Futures are traded on stock indexes and on single stocks.

Stock Index Futures   Stock index contracts are linked to a published stock index. The contract size is a multiple of the index. For example, the dollar size of the S&P 500 contracts traded on the CME is $250 times the S&P 500 index. The gain (loss) on a stock index futures is calculated by applying the multiple to the futures price variation:

$$\text{Gain (loss)} = \text{Futures price variation} \times \text{Contract value multiple} \tag{10.3}$$

A characteristic of stock index futures is that the underlying asset, the stock index, does not exist physically as a financial asset. As a result, all final settlements take place in cash rather than by delivery of a good or security. On the delivery date, the buyer of a stock index contract receives the difference between the calculated value

---

[5] The design of these bond futures contracts may seem unduly complicated. An alternative would have been to write a contract on a single benchmark bond. Because the market capitalization of any single bond is rather small, this creates liquidity problems and opens up the possibility of price manipulation. By increasing the number of deliverable bonds, this market manipulation becomes very difficult. Assume for a moment that the yield curve is flat and equal to the notional yield, for example, 6 percent for U.S. bonds. Then it can be easily verified that the futures price will be 100 percent and that all bonds will be equally desirable for delivery because their quoted clean price is simply equal to their conversion factor. This is not the case when the yield curve is not flat at 6 percent, but the contract mechanism ensures that other bonds will replace the cheapest-to-deliver bond if its price is manipulated.

[6] Because of the inverse relationship between the long-term interest rate and the market price of a bond, the buyer of a bond contract gains if the interest rate drops (the bond price rises) and loses if the interest rate rises.

> **EXAMPLE 10.1   STOCK INDEX CONTRACT**
>
> The December futures contract of the Australian ASX index quotes at 4,050. The multiple is 25 Australian dollars (A$). The next day, this contract quotes at 4,070. What is the gain for an investor long in one contract?
>
> **SOLUTION**
>
> The gain in Australian dollars for the holder of one contract is equal to
>
> $$\text{Gain} = (4{,}070 - 4{,}050) \times \text{A\$25} = \text{A\$500}$$

of the index and the previous futures price. The procedure works as if the contract were marked to market on the last day, with the final futures price replaced by the stock index value. The cash delivery procedure avoids most of the transaction costs involved in buying and selling a large number of stocks.

Numerous stock index contracts are available in the United States and all major countries. These indexes are sometimes broadly based, as is the S&P 500, to allow for broad participation in the market. They are useful to manage the risk of well-diversified portfolios. More often, these indexes are based on a small number of actively traded stocks. For example, the Euro STOXX 50 contract traded on Eurex tracks the most active European stocks. A narrowly based index has two advantages. First, it is based on stocks that trade frequently, so it gives better indications on instantaneous movements in the market. Second, it allows derivatives professionals to hedge their futures positions with opposite transactions in the cash market more easily and cheaply, hence providing good liquidity to the futures market.

Single-Stock Futures   Futures contracts on a single stock are traded in several countries. This is a convenient way to buy a stock on margin or short sell it. Euronext-LIFFE has a joint venture with Nasdaq to trade single-stock futures on European and American stocks. OneChicago (a joint venture of the Chicago Board of Trade, Chicago Mercantile Exchange, and the Chicago Board of Options Exchange) started trading U.S. single-stock futures in late 2002. The contract is usually for 100 shares of the underlying stocks.

Forward and Futures Valuation

Valuation models for forward and futures[7] attempt to explain the difference between the current spot price, S, and the futures price, F, quoted today for delivery at a future date.

---

[7] Theoretical prices for forwards are easier to derive than for futures, because there are no intermediate cash flows until expiration of the contract caused by the marking-to-market procedure. But the usual practice, adopted in this chapter, is to value futures as if they were forwards with the full profit or loss realized at expiration. As discussed later, the theoretical difference between the two prices is sufficiently small to be ignored in practice.

CONCEPTS IN ACTION COMPETITION HEATS UP
AMONG DERIVATIVES EXCHANGES

Volatility in underlying equity markets has led to a rise in the need to hedge risks

Derivatives exchanges have had a fantastic year, with volumes traded on their platforms growing sharply in fixed income and equity derivatives.

The main reason for the growth is increased need by investors to hedge risks. Market volatility, in equity and fixed-income markets, remains at all-time highs because of uncertainty about economic growth and concerns about war.

The equity derivatives business overall—which includes over-the-counter trading at banks and exchange-traded derivatives—is believed to have shrunk, but the share captured by exchanges has grown as investors have sought out the security they provide.

"Equity derivatives are the main growth area for the derivatives exchanges," says Hugh Freedberg, chief executive of Euronext-liffe, the derivatives exchanges owned by Euronext.

The main driver of this boom is growing volatility in the underlying equity markets over the past five years, according to Mr. Freedberg.

Individual equity options are by far the most popular instruments among equity derivatives and this is the main battleground between the exchanges. Euronext-liffe says the volume of single equity options increased by 64 percent in the first eight months of the year.

"The attraction of single stock options is that they are standardized products traded electronically with no credit or counterparty risk," says Mr. Freedberg.

"Investors are increasingly aware of how effective stock options can be in volatile markets. This market has enormous potential," he says.

Equity derivatives are largely used by institutions such as pension funds, hedge funds and large proprietary traders but retail investors are showing increasing appetite for the products. The Netherlands has a highly developed retail market in single stock futures. "The Netherlands is a role model that other countries should try to emulate," says Mr. Freedberg.

European exchanges have also been fast developing options and futures on different stock indices that allow investors to hedge their exposure to certain sectors and countries.

Far more controversial are single stock futures, a derivative product on individual companies. Euronext-liffe has staked its reputation on single stock futures. It has a joint venture with Nasdaq in the United States to trade these products.

Its biggest rival, Eurex, has so far shunned single stock futures, saying equity options are far more effective instruments for hedging. "We simply don't see any demand for single stock futures, whereas the demand for equity options is enormous," says Rudolf Ferscha, chief executive of Eurex.

Eurex also sees stock options as the cornerstone of its expansion policy.

While Euronext-liffe sees its strength in the combination of different European exchanges that share the same trading platform, Eurex believes the key to success is not in the size of the operation, but in value-added pan-European products traded on the derivatives exchange.

The main example of this strategy is Eurostoxx-50 futures contracts which has increased in terms of turnover by 162 percent year on year, according to Mr. Ferscha. "We believe this product adds value to the chain."

"The pan-European index field is wide open to competition between the various exchanges and this [competition] will continue to intensify," he says.

The potential for equity derivatives is also recognized by exchanges dominant in the cash markets. The London Stock Exchange, for example, has ambitions to capture some of this market share.

While the battle for market share among exchanges in Europe is firmly on the equities side, the focus in the United States is still very much on whether electronic trading will replace the traditional pits. In Europe, this battle was fought out several years ago, with electronic trading winning the day. But in Chicago, pit traders survive.

From the users' point of view, this continues to keep the costs of trading U.S. derivatives higher than European ones. Supporters of the pits argue that they have more liquidity, but detractors say Europe's exchanges have higher volumes. Industry figures estimate the costs of trading in Europe to be a quarter of those in the U.S.

Richard Berliand, in charge of all of JP Morgan's exchange traded derivatives business, says costs are becoming increasingly important because the margins in derivatives are shrinking. "How the U.S. exchanges make the transition to new technologies will be extremely important for the market in the next year," he said.

Source: Arkady Ostrovosky and Aline van Duyn, "Exchanges," *Financial Times,* Monday, October 7, 2002, p. 4.

Profit and Loss at Expiration   At expiration, the futures price converges to the spot price. Hence, the payoff structure is very simple: For each increase of one cent in the spot price at expiration, there will be an additional one cent profit for the buyer of the futures. The profit and loss structure of a forward or futures that is held until expiration is shown in Exhibit 10.5. F is the futures price per unit of underlying asset at time of contracting and the profit at expiration depends on the asset spot price at expiration. Exhibits 10.5a and b show the profit structures for long and short positions in the futures. The link between profit on the futures and the spot price at delivery is a straight line of slope 1. The slope is -1 for the seller of a futures. This feature makes it easy to derive an arbitrage value for the futures.

EXHIBIT 10.5

Profits and Losses from Buying ("Long") and Selling ("Short") a Futures

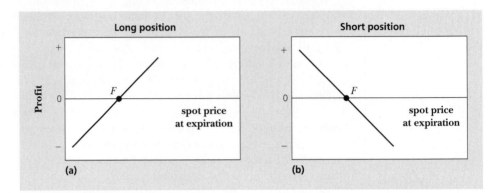

The Basis   A futures price equals the spot price at delivery, though not during the life of the contract. The difference between the two prices is called the *basis:*

$$\text{Basis} = \text{Futures price} - \text{Spot price} = F - S \qquad (10.4)$$

The basis is often expressed as a percentage of the spot price (discount or premium).

$$\text{Percentage basis} = \frac{F - S}{S} \qquad (10.4')$$

Futures valuation models determine a theoretical value for the basis. The bases for perishable goods depend on complex factors that are often difficult to forecast, including harvesting cycles and expected crop sizes. But the bases for financial contracts, such as currencies, interest rates, stock indexes, and gold, depend on much simpler factors.

The theoretical value of the basis is constrained by the existence of profitable riskless *arbitrage* between the futures and the spot markets for the asset. Arbitrage takes place to eliminate this profit opportunity. Hence, an arbitrage value of the futures is determined within transaction costs.

This arbitrage is often referred to as a *cash and carry,* and the basis is sometimes referred to, in percentage of the spot price, as the cost of carry of the arbitrage. We will take the example of a currency futures.

Currency Futures   A futures pricing argument was developed in Chapter 1. It has been shown that the futures exchange rate cannot differ from the spot exchange rate adjusted by the interest rate differential in the two currencies.

Let's suppose that the current spot exchange rate, S, is €/$ = 0.80, that the U.S. dollar one-year interest rate is $r_\$ = 10\%$, and that the euro one-year interest rate is $r_\text{€} = 14\%$. Then the one-year futures rate, F, has to be equal to 0.82909. To illustrate again how the arbitrage works, let's suppose for a moment that the futures rate is only €/$ = 0.81. Then the following (riskless) arbitrage would be possible:

Borrow $1 and transfer it into euros on the spot market:	€ 0.800
Invest the euros for a year at 14 percent with an income of	<u>€ 0.112</u>
	€ 0.912
Sell a futures contract to repatriate enough of these euros	
to cover the dollars borrowed plus the financing cost, that is,	
$1.10. At delivery, $1.10 will be obtained for € 0.81 × 1.10	<u>− € 0.891</u>
The € net profit is	€ 0.021

This is a certain profit, with no invested capital. Arbitrage will take place until this profit opportunity disappears and the futures rate is such that

$$F = S\,(1 + r_{€})/(1 + r_{\$}) \tag{10.5}$$

or

$$(F - S)/S = (r_{€} - r_{\$})/(1 + r_{\$})$$

In the example, the futures rate must be equal to €0.82909/$. The cost of carry, in percentage of the spot rate, $(F - S)/S$, is linked to the interest differential.[8] Of course, bid-and-ask quotes on the spot and interest rates should be used, as in Chapter 1, to derive theoretical bid-and-ask quotes for the currency futures.

Other Futures Contracts   A similar arbitrage reasoning holds for other contracts. If the futures price is too high relative to the current spot price, the following arbitrage can be undertaken:

- Borrow money to buy spot.

- Simultaneously sell the futures.

- While carrying the spot asset, some income might be received.

- At maturity of the futures contract, use the spot to deliver on the futures contract.

The reverse arbitrage will be done if the futures price is too low relative to the spot price.

At equilibrium, the percentage basis should be equal to the carrying cost. For example, the percentage basis (cost of carry) of a stock index futures should be linked to the differential between the interest rate involved in financing the spot purchase of shares and the dividends received on the shares held (but not on the futures).

Calculations are a bit more difficult for a futures contract on bonds. The spot position taken in the arbitrage should involve the cheapest-to-deliver bond and use

---

[8] The contract is quoted in dollars, and the percentage basis is equal to the present value of the interest rate differential.

its conversion factor. The calculation for a futures contract on a short-term interest rate is also a bit more difficult.

Futures and Forward The pricing relations just described should hold more exactly for forward than for futures contracts because forward contracts have a fixed margin that is not revised over the life of the contract. So far, we have assumed that the initial margin was deposited in the form of interest-bearing securities, so that there was no financing cost for this margin. However, futures contracts are marked to market, so that any loss on the futures position must be paid for and financed. This financing cost is uncertain because it depends on the future price variation. Also, the interest rate used to finance this margin may vary over time. It has been shown that futures and forward prices should be equal if the interest rates are constant over the life of the contract. If interest rates are uncertain, the correlation of interest rate and asset price movements will induce a theoretical difference between forward and futures prices, but the impact will be quite small for contracts that last only a few weeks.[9]

Other futures contract quirks affect futures pricing. For example, many contracts traded in the United States can be delivered within a few days before expiration, so that the exact maturity of the contract is uncertain. Bond contracts traded on the Chicago Board of Trade have an implied put option, or *wild card play*. The seller may choose to deliver securities on any day during the delivery month. The invoice price is based on the futures settlement price at the close of trading (around 2:00 P.M.). But the seller has until 8:00 P.M. the same day to decide whether to deliver, during which time the bonds continue to be traded in the cash market. If bond prices drop sharply between 2:00 and 8:00 P.M., the seller may buy cheap bonds in the cash market, bonds that can be used to deliver at the settlement price fixed at 2:00 P.M. Of course, this option held by the seller affects futures pricing[10] and lowers the value of the futures contract.

Use of Forward and Futures

Forward and futures contracts can be used to speculate on the underlying asset because of their leverage. But their major use in investment management is hedging.

Speculation The leverage provided by futures contracts allows investors to capitalize on some market forecast without much capital investment. This can be achieved by buying or selling futures, depending on the direction of the forecast. For example, someone who believes that the stock market will drop can sell stock index futures.

---

[9] Cornell and Reiganum (1981) studied the relation between futures and forward exchange rates and found no significant differences. Most authors conclude that forward and futures prices should be empirically very close.

[10] See Fleming and Whaley (1994).

Someone who believes that the Swiss franc will rise in value against the dollar could buy Swiss franc futures. Although the rate of return on the invested capital (the margin) can be large, so can the loss if the forecast is proved wrong. Remember that the profit/loss structure outlined in Exhibit 10.5 is symmetric. Prudence, as well as regulations, usually prevents institutional investors from engaging in outright speculation.

Hedging: Basic Principles   Leveraged securities allow hedging of specific risks with minimal capital investment. It is customary to distinguish between two types of hedge:

- *Long hedge:* A long or anticipatory hedge generally involves buying futures contracts in anticipation of a spot purchase.

- *Short hedge:* A short hedge involves selling futures contracts to cover the risk on a position in the spot market. This is the most common use of hedging in investment management and is the focus of this section.

EXAMPLE 10.2   *A LONG HEDGE*

A British asset manager manages a global portfolio and has decided to increase the asset allocation in Japanese equity by 1 billion yen. The manager is very bullish on the Japanese economy. It will take a week to transfer the money to Japan and build the portfolio of Japanese shares. The manager believes there is a good chance that the Japanese stock market will rise quickly. What should the manager do?

SOLUTION

Immediately buy futures contracts on the Nikkei index for a value of 1 billion yen. In addition to the few days required for the cash transfer, it may take a few more days to get best execution prices on the desired Japanese shares. The position in Japanese shares is progressively built on the Japanese stock market. As Japanese shares are purchased, the futures exposure should be accordingly reduced.

Hedging the risk of an individual asset is easy if futures contracts on that specific asset exist. However, futures contracts do not exist for every asset, so somewhat imperfect hedging strategies have to be designed. This problem is all the more important in portfolios with an international asset allocation and numerous sources of risk.

As an illustration, let's consider a Swiss manager worried about the British bond part of her portfolio. The manager might fear an increase in British interest rates, while forecasting a strong British pound relative to the Swiss franc. This would lead the manager to selectively hedge against the British interest rate risk, while retaining the British pound currency exposure. Similarly, the manager might be bullish on a few Australian mining companies, while fearing an adverse movement in both the general level of Australian stock prices and the value of the Australian dollar.

Two major questions must be answered when hedging a specified source of risk:

- Which contract should I use?

- What amount should I hedge?

The answer to the first question is fairly straightforward. The motivation is to reduce, at least temporarily, the exposure to some market risk that could negatively affect a portfolio. The source of risk will dictate the use of some specific stock market index, interest rate, or currency contract.[11] The answer to the second question requires a more detailed study of the optimal hedge ratio to be used.

Currency risk management is addressed in Chapter 11; here, we focus on the hedging approach to a single national market (equity or fixed income).

The Simple Approach: Unitary Hedge Ratio A hedge ratio is the ratio of the size of the (short) position taken in futures contract to the size of the exposure (the value of the portfolio to be hedged).

$$\text{Hedge ratio} = \frac{\text{Number of contracts} \times \text{Size} \times \text{Spot price}}{\text{Market value of asset position}} = \frac{N \times \text{Size} \times S}{V} \quad (10.6)$$

For example, take a portfolio invested in Australian stocks worth A\$1 million. The ASX index is 4,000 and the futures contract has a multiple of A\$25 and trades at 4,050. If you sell $N = 10$ contracts, the hedge ratio is equal to

$$h = \frac{10 \times 25 \times 4,000}{1,000,000} = 1$$

Note that to be consistent, both the asset and the futures positions are valued at current market value, using spot prices, not futures prices.[12]

The simplest approach to hedging is to use a hedge ratio of 1. In the preceding example, the Australian portfolio is worth 1 million, or 250 stock indexes, and we sell 10 futures contracts ($10 \times 25 = 250$).[13]

Conversely, we can use Equation 10.6 to derive the number of contracts to be sold if we know the hedge ratio that we want to implement:

$$N = h \times \frac{V}{\text{Size} \times S} \quad (10.6')$$

For example, if we decide to hedge only 50 percent of the portfolio ($h = 0.5$), we can compute that we need to sell $N = 5$ contracts.

Minimum-Variance Hedge Ratio Because of cross-hedge and basis risks (discussion follows), it is usually impossible to build a perfect hedge. One objective is

---

[11] If the investor is bearish on a specific security in the portfolio, the only reasonable action is to directly sell that security.

[12] See Hull (2002).

[13] If an investor is worried about currency risk on a foreign investment, the simple strategy is to sell the foreign currency forward, for an amount equal to that of the portfolio market value.

to search for minimum variability in the value of the hedged portfolio. Investors usually care about the rate of return on their investments and the variance thereof. It is easy to show the rate of return on a portfolio hedged, R_H, is equal to the rate of return on the original portfolio (unhedged), R, minus h times the percentage change in the futures price, R_F:

$$R_H = R - h \times R_F \tag{10.7}$$

So, if investors decide to hedge, they would like to set the hedge ratio h to minimize the variance of the return on the hedged portfolio. The optimal hedge ratio h^*, which minimizes the variance of R_H, is equal to the covariance of the asset, or portfolio, return to be hedged with the return on the futures, divided by the variance of the return on the futures (see the derivation in Exhibit 10.6):

$$h^* = \frac{\text{cov}(R, R_F)}{\sigma_F^2} \tag{10.8}$$

<u>EXHIBIT 10.6</u>

Derivation of the Minimum-Variance Hedge Ratio

Assuming you select a specific hedge ratio h, the return on the hedged position is given by Equation 10.7:

$$R_H = R - h \times R_F$$

The rates of return on the portfolio, R, and on the future, R_F, are uncertain, so the return on the hedged portfolio, R_H, is also uncertain. An investor trying to minimize the volatility of the hedged portfolio will try to minimize the standard deviation of R_H (or, equivalently, its variance). Let's call σ, σ_F, and σ_H the standard deviations of the original portfolio (unhedged), of the futures, and of the hedged portfolio, respectively. Because the hedge ratio is a fixed parameter, we know that the return on the hedged portfolio is simply the sum of two random variables, R and $-h \times R_F$. Hence its variance is given by

$$\sigma_H^2 = \sigma^2 + h^2 \times \sigma_F^2 - 2 \times h \times \text{cov}(R, R_F)$$

The objective is to choose an optimal hedge ratio, h^*, that minimizes the variance of the hedged portfolio σ_H^2 (or, equivalently, its standard deviation σ_H). The risks of the original portfolio and of the futures are known, and the hedge ratio is the decision variable. The optimum is obtained by setting to zero the derivative of the variance of the hedged portfolio:

$$\frac{d\sigma_H^2}{dh} = 2 \times h \times \sigma_F^2 - 2 \times \text{cov}(R, R_F) = 0$$

Hence,

$$h^* = \frac{\text{cov}(R, R_F)}{\sigma_F^2}$$

This optimal hedge ratio is sometimes called the *regression hedge ratio* because it can be estimated as the slope coefficient of the regression of the asset, or portfolio, return on the futures return:

$$R = \alpha + h^* R_F + \epsilon$$

where

R is the return on the asset or portfolio

R_F is the return on the futures

α is a constant term

ϵ is an error term because the relation between R and R_F is not perfect

---

EXAMPLE 10.3   MINIMUM VARIANCE HEDGE

Let's consider a portfolio of small Australian stocks with a value of A\$1 million. This portfolio of small stocks is much more volatile than the market. It tends to amplify the movement in the Australian market index by 50 percent. In other words, its beta relative to the market is equal to 1.5, the slope of the regression of the portfolio return on the market index return. The current ASX stock index is 4,000, and the futures quotes at 4,050 with a multiple of A\$25.

1. What is the optimal hedge ratio?

2. How many futures contracts should you sell?

SOLUTION

1. The minimum-variance optimal hedge ratio is equal to 1.5. Whenever the market drops by X percent, the portfolio tends to drop by 1.5X percent. If the value of the portfolio is A\$1 million, the manager should sell A\$1.5 million worth of stock index futures.

2. Using Equation 10.6', we find that we should sell:

$$N = h^* \times \frac{V}{\text{Size} \times S} = 1.5 \times \frac{1,000,000}{25 \times 4,000} = 15 \text{ contracts}$$

Hedge Ratio for Bonds   Interest rate risk affects all bond portfolios, but we know the mathematical relation between a movement in the general yield level and the value of a bond portfolio. Chapter 7 introduced the concept of duration or interest rate sensitivity. The approximate percentage price change of the portfolio is equal to the duration times the change in market yield (in percent). Mathematically, this can be written as

$$\frac{\Delta P}{P} = -D_p \times \Delta r$$

where

> P is the average price of the bond portfolio (i.e., the market value divided by the par value)
>
> ΔP is a small change in P
>
> D_P is the duration (or interest rate sensitivity) of the portfolio
>
> Δr is a small change in market yield

Then it can be shown[14] that the optimal hedging policy that reduces the impact of an up-movement Δr in yields is such that the hedge ratio would be

$$h^* = \frac{P \times D_p}{F \times D_F} \tag{10.9}$$

where D_F is the duration of the cheapest-to-deliver bond for the futures contract. The intuition is that one should adjust the hedge ratio to reflect the difference in interest rate sensitivity (duration) between the portfolio and the futures price. If the portfolio has a duration of 5 and the futures has a duration of 10, one should adopt a hedge ratio of roughly 50 percent.

An Imperfect Hedge   A hedge is seldom perfect for at least two reasons:

- Basis risk

- Correlation, or cross-hedge, risk

The portfolio's value depends on the spot price, while hedging is done using futures whose price differs from the spot price by the basis. The basis varies over time in a somewhat unpredictable manner. For example, interest rates, which are part of the cost of carry, vary over time. To reduce basis risk, one should select contracts' maturity to match the investment horizon over which risk is to be managed.

The chance of matching a futures contract to a specific portfolio of bonds or stocks is slim. A cross-hedge has to be constructed in order to hedge the volatility of specific securities in a portfolio, so a hedge is often built with a contract that is only partly correlated with the portfolio to be hedged. This induces correlation, or cross-hedge, risk. For example, a portfolio invested only in shares of a specific industry would be hedged by contracts on the general stock index. But the evolution of the value of a specific industry and that of the stock market as a whole are not similar. Various techniques attempt to determine an optimal hedge ratio, but correlation risk remains.

The Pros and Cons of Hedging   Futures allow a manager to monitor the market risk exposures of a portfolio. If a manager temporarily fears an adverse movement in

---

[14] The futures price follows price movements in the cheapest-to-deliver bond, so it has the same duration as that bond: $\Delta F/F = -D_F \times \Delta r$. Equation 10.9 is derived by equating the "dollar" capital loss on the portfolio and the "dollar" gain on the futures position for any small movement in the interest rate Δr.

some market (equity, interest rate, or currency), he can sell the proper amount of futures and buy them back after fears have materialized or disappeared. This is much less costly, in terms of transaction costs, than first selling the securities and then buying them back. It could also be that the manager likes the specific securities held in the portfolio but fears a drop in the overall market. Selling futures on the market allows the manager to capture the excess performance (alpha) on the portfolio.

However, hedging could turn out to be painful if the market goes up contrary to expectations, because futures have a symmetric profit/loss structure. Assume that a manager has temporarily hedged a well-diversified portfolio of French stocks by selling futures on the CAC index. Contrary to expectations, the French stock market goes up by 10 percent, so that the capital gain on the portfolio is offset by an equivalent loss on the futures position. That is a cash loss because of the marking-to-market procedure. The client who focuses on that visible loss might be very upset with the manager, although it might have been a wise *ex ante* risk management decision. Psychologically, it would have been less visible to reduce the French risk exposure by simply selling stocks, despite higher transaction costs. Those psychological considerations are often a factor in a manager–client relationship. This could also lead managers to manage their market risks by using contracts with asymmetric profit/loss structures such as options.

Swaps

Futures are short-term contracts with a maturity rarely exceeding a few months. Risk often extends well past such a short time horizon, however. This is especially the case when dealing with interest rate and currency risks. In dealing with longer term exposures, investors frequently rely on swaps. Swaps are used extensively by banks to manage risk exposure on their assets and liabilities. Some other types of corporations also use swaps extensively. In investment management, swaps are used in the construction of structured products and in dynamic arbitrage strategies, such as the strategies followed by numerous hedge funds.

The Principles of a Swap

Definition   A *swap* is a contract whereby the two parties agree to a periodic exchange of cash flows. On each payment date, only a net payment is made (the obligations of the two parties are netted). A swap resembles a back-to-back loan arrangement but is packaged into a single contract, as opposed to two separate loans.[15] On each swap payment date, the two cash flows are netted and a payment is made by the party owing money. In swap jargon, each side of the swap is called a *leg*. For example, an interest rate swap in euros could have a 5.10 percent fixed interest

---

[15] In currency back-to-back loans, each party lends money to the other party for the same initial amount but in different currencies and at respective market interest rates.

rate as one leg, and six-month Euribor, the euro floating interest rate, as the other leg. A swap is simply a contract stating the formula to be used to compute the net amount paid or received on each payment date. A swap must be studied independently of any initial borrowing or lending operation that motivates it. An important point to remember is that swaps appear off-balance-sheet. They are simply commitments to make future payments. A swap can be regarded as a long-term package of periodic forward contracts.

Market Organization   The swap market is an OTC market in which major commercial and investment banks participate. They belong to the International Swaps and Derivatives Association (ISDA). Typically, an investor wishing to arrange a swap will call one or several banks specialized as swap dealers and providing swap rate quotes. The quotes are the interest rates on the swap.[16] Dealers quote a bid–ask spread because the investor does not indicate the side she wishes to take. For example, a five-year interest rate swap in euros could be quoted as 5.10 to 5.15 percent fixed against Euribor, meaning that the dealer is willing to pay 5.10 percent and receive Euribor, or receive 5.15 percent and pay Euribor.

As for any forward contract, there is no organized secondary swap market. This can be a problem, because swaps are long-term contracts. An investor wishing to get out of a swap has three alternatives:

- *Agree on a voluntary termination with the original counterparty.* This popular agreement is simple and implies only a lump-sum payment to reflect the changes in market conditions, but it requires the agreement of the other party.

- *Write a mirror swap with the original counterparty.* A swap is reversed by writing an opposite swap contract with the same maturity and amount but at current market conditions. The difference between a mirror swap and a termination is that the settlement is paid over the remaining maturity of the swap, and some credit risk remains on the differential interest rate payment.

- *Write a reverse swap in the market with another counterparty.* This is the easiest deal to arrange but has two drawbacks. First, it is difficult and expensive to find a swap that exactly offsets the previous one in all its terms. Second, engaging in another swap doubles credit risk.

The Different Instruments

Historically, three major types of swaps were offered in the marketplace: currency swaps, interest rate swaps, and currency–interest rate swaps. Recently, many other types of swaps have been successfully offered.

---

[16] Swap dealers use different conventions to quote interest rates (linear, actuarial, etc.), so it is important to clarify the conventions used when a quote is made.

Currency Swaps   A *currency swap* is a contract to exchange streams of fixed cash flows denominated in two different currencies. A typical currency swap can be illustrated by using the following example. An investor enters in a five-year swap with a bank to receive yen and pay dollar, for 100 million dollars. In this swap, $100 million and ¥10 billion are the principal amounts (called notional principals), because the spot exchange rate is ¥100/$. The fixed interest rates are 2 percent on the yen leg and 6 percent on the dollar leg, and payments are annual; these are the current market conditions in each currency. Each year, the investor will receive ¥200 million (the annual interest of 2 percent on the Japanese yen principal of ¥10 billion) minus $6 million (the annual interest of 6 percent on the U.S. dollar principal of $100 million) valued at the then-current spot ¥/$ exchange rate. When this amount is negative, the investor will pay it. After five years, the principal amounts of ¥10 billion and $100 million valued at the then-current spot ¥/$ exchange rate are netted and the net amount owed is paid.

Currency swaps may involve an exchange of principal at initiation of the swap when one of the parties has an actual need for the principal amount in a particular currency. However, we will consider the case where such a need is absent. Because the swap is designed to have the same principal value in yen and dollars at the time of contracting (¥10 billion equals $100 million at the spot exchange rate of ¥/$ = 100), there is no initial payment between the two parties. Future swap payments depend on the evolution of the ¥/$ exchange rate, S_t. On each of the first four swap payment dates t, the investor will receive in millions of yen,

$$200 - (S_t \times 6)$$

or in millions of dollars,

$$(200/S_t) - 6$$

If this figure is positive, the investor will receive this amount from the bank; if this figure is negative, the investor will have to pay it.

On the fifth payment date, the investor will receive the balance of the last interest and principal, or in million yen,

$$10{,}200 - (S_5 \times 106)$$

To motivate the type of swap just illustrated, suppose that a European company had issued an international bond in yen a few years ago, with five years remaining on its maturity. The company is now worried that the yen will strongly appreciate against all currencies. By entering the previously discussed swap to receive yen and pay dollars, the company is basically transforming its yen liability into a dollar liability.

Interest Rate Swaps   An *interest rate swap* is a contract to exchange streams of cash flows in the same currency but based on two different interest rates. The most common interest rate swaps are U.S. dollar swaps involving a fixed interest rate and a floating rate. The floating-rate index used is generally the six-month London interbank offer rate (LIBOR). As on a floating-rate note, the floating-rate leg is generally reset on a date that precedes the payment date, with a lead equal to the maturity of the floating interest rate. For example, the six-month LIBOR is preset six months before the next swap payment date. Interest rate swaps in euros are generally indexed on Euribor.

The uncertainty over the future swap payments on date t stems from the evolution of the floating rate. Interest rate swaps do not involve exchange of principal, because the same amount and currency are involved on both legs of the swap.

EXAMPLE 10.4   SWAP PAYMENT

An investor has entered a three-year interest rate swap for €1 million, receiving fixed at 5.10 percent and paying six-month Euribor. Payments are semiannual, and interest rates are computed linearly (i.e., the semiannual rate is obtained by dividing the annualized rate by 2). At some later reset date, the six-month Euribor is at 4 percent. What is the payment six months later (i.e., on the following payment date)?

SOLUTION

The investor receives a payment of

$$\text{Payment} = \left(\frac{5.1\% - 4\%}{2}\right) \times 1{,}000{,}000 = 5{,}500 \text{ euros}$$

Currency–Interest Rate Swaps   A *currency–interest rate swap* is a contract to exchange streams of cash flows in two different currencies, one with a fixed interest rate and the other with a floating interest rate. For example, an investor could decide to swap a five-year yen obligation with a fixed interest rate of 2 percent into a five-year dollar obligation at the six-month LIBOR plus 0.25 percent. Future swap payments are uncertain because of the evolution of both the exchange rates and the floating interest rate.

Other Swaps   Swaps are often customized products. Banks quote swap rates for generic, or plain-vanilla, swaps, but customers often require some specific features on their swaps to match some specific characteristics of their existing liabilities or assets. Furthermore, exotic swaps are being marketed. Swaps are often part of a more complex package of securities offered to a customer as a way to reduce its financing costs, speculate, or manage an interest rate or currency position. This package is tailor-made to take advantage of some specific aspect of the market environment, such as supply/demand imbalance and tax or regulation considerations.

Some interest rate swaps involve two floating rates; these are often referred to as *basis swaps*. A typical example is the exchange of a LIBOR-indexed obligation for a Treasury bill rate-indexed obligation. This basis swap is known as a Treasury–Eurodollar spread (TED spread swap). Another example is the exchange of obligations indexed on the one-month and the six-month LIBOR. A *forward swap* begins at some specified future date, but with the binding terms set in advance. An *amor-*

tizing swap has a regular fixed or floating coupon on one leg, and a zero coupon on the other leg. Hence, the counterparties exchange a future stream of coupons for a large lump sum. Amortizing swaps can be designed to have this lump sum paid at contracting, or to have it paid at maturity. A *total return swap* has a regular fixed or floating coupon on one leg, and the total return on some asset on the other leg. An *equity swap* is an exchange of a fixed or floating coupon against the return on some equity index. This is a form of total return swap. An equity swap is sometimes used to invest in a foreign stock market without making the necessary transactions in the cash market.

Credit derivatives have been the fastest-growing segment of the swap market. A *default swap* (or *credit swap*) is an exchange of a fixed or floating coupon against the payment of a loss caused by default on a specific loan or bond. For example, an institutional investor could be holding some corporate bonds of doubtful quality. The investor could then enter a default swap with a payment of a fixed coupon on one leg, and the receipt of an amount equal to the default loss on the corporates, if any. Credit derivatives, such as default swaps, have been very successful, and their design is sometimes quite complex.

CONCEPTS IN ACTION   *INDUSTRY FLOURISHES IN BEAR MARKET TURMOIL*

Sector is booming and is consistently profitable amid investor uncertainty and risk aversion

It can fairly be said, in the depths of this bear market, that if the derivatives industry did not exist, it would by now have been invented. It is the one area of the international capital markets where activity continues to expand exponentially, and remains a consistent source of profit now that mergers and acquisitions activity—and the primary markets for stocks and bonds—have slowed to a trickle.

According to the International Swaps and Derivatives Association, the entire sector is booming. Its mid-year survey for 2002 showed the volume outstanding of interest rate and currency derivatives had reached $82,700bn, a rise of 20 percent in six months. Equity derivatives, which ISDA measured for the first time, reached $2,300bn, although market participants say over-the-counter (OTC) equity derivatives business is slowing while activity in exchange-traded products such as index futures is rising. Trading of exchange-listed derivatives is growing faster than that of OTC products for the first time in a decade, as investors in all asset classes become more aware of—and concerned about—counterparty risk. According to Huw van Steenis, financial services analyst at Morgan Stanley: "There is a fundamental change in the approach that European institutions, particularly insurance companies, are taking to risk management, with derivatives being used far more frequently."

Once again, however, the fastest-growing segment of the market is credit derivatives. The volume of outstanding contracts increased 35 percent in the first six months of this year to $1,600bn, according to ISDA. In the mid-1990s, the market did not exist. It is forecast to continue growing. The British Bankers' Association believes credit derivatives will reach $1,952bn by the end of this year and $4,800bn by the end of 2004.

This growth reflects investor reaction to the bear market, which is marked by volatile share prices, profound uncertainty about fundamental economic and corporate trends and an acute case of risk aversion among investors.

"Risk management is at the forefront of investors' minds," says Bill Winters, co-head of JP Morgan Chase's global derivatives business. Robert Pickel, ISDA's chief executive adds: "It's not an accident that the credit derivatives market is growing so fast. It is an important part of users' ability to manage risk."

Observers say that while banks are still by far the biggest users of derivatives products, corporations are also emerging as significant market participants, as are investment fund managers seeking specific investment goals. Still, a notable feature of the market as it is developing today is a greater concentration among a smaller number of participating banks.

This is one of the main differences between the current market volatility and previous bouts of turmoil. During the Asian, Russian and Long-Term Capital Management crises in the late 1990s, some banks lost large amounts of money. Not all of it was lost through direct exposure to derivatives trades, but money was made and lost through exposure to risk and volatility.

Derivatives allowed the exposure to be increased without putting up large amounts of extra capital. When volatility increased, money was lost, both by banks' proprietary trading desks and by investors such as hedge funds, which take large strategic positions.

After some of their peers incurred large losses during these events, many banks decided this approach to the derivatives market was too risky. Now, they approach it as a business where money is made through trading large volumes and by moving risk between investors and between products.

According to Yassine Bouhara, managing director of global equity derivatives at Deutsche Bank, repackaging risk is a vital part of managing the derivatives business at a bank. "It is not just bringing together a buyer and a seller of a particular type of risk—for example, finding someone who wants to reduce exposure to a company and someone who wants to increase it."

Instead, he says, risk is taken on by the bank and then redistributed, for example, through the issuing of bonds with attached warrants on particular companies to retail investors.

Source: Aline van Duyn and Vincent Boland, *Financial Times Special Report: Derivatives: Instruments, Exchanges, Legal Issues, Bright Spots and Weak Links,* Monday, October 7, 2002, pp. 1–2.

Swaps Valuation

We now turn to the important question of the value of a swap contract. At the time of contracting, the two parties agree on the terms of the swap. The value of the swap at the time of contracting is zero. However, as market conditions change over time, so does the value of the swap. Swaps are treated as off-balance-sheet items, but this does not mean they should not be valued periodically to reflect current market value. This is true for nonfinancial corporations publishing annual or quarterly accounting reports. Financial institutions, and portfolio managers, need to value their derivatives position frequently, ideally daily.

The financial profession uses standard methods to value a swap. We will first assume that there is no credit (default) risk for either party to the swap. Later, we will introduce credit risk.

Valuation in the Absence of Credit Risk   Let's take the example of the five-year yen/dollar swap introduced earlier. At the time of issue, interest rates in the two currencies (6 percent in dollar and 2 percent in yen) are set at prevailing market conditions, so that there is no actual exchange of money. In our example, $100 million is worth ¥10 billion at the current exchange rate, and no money need be exchanged to enter into this swap agreement. The market value of this currency swap is zero on the contracting day. However, the market value of this swap will change because of movements in interest rates and in the spot exchange rate. The question is: How should we value a swap in the secondary market? For example, assume that the corporation entered this swap contract to pay dollars and receive yen and wants to sell it a year later. How should we price this swap?

Two approaches can be used:

- Value a currency swap as a package of long-term forward currency contracts.

- Value a swap as a portfolio of two bonds.

A currency swap can be broken down into a series of forward currency contracts for each cash flow. In our example, the swap can be treated, at time of contracting, as a package of five forward contracts with maturity from one to five years, as depicted in Exhibit 10.7. We can price the swap as a sum of forward currency prices. In other words, we can unbundle the package of forward currency contracts.

There are two problems with this approach, however. First, it is not obvious that a fixed bundle of contracts would be priced exactly as the sum of its components, because markets are incomplete and unbundling a package of contracts is difficult. Second, forward contracts are not frequently traded for long-term maturities, so forward currency rates have to be inferred from interest rate yield curves, as discussed in Chapter 7. As a matter of fact, it is more common to derive forward currency prices from swap prices rather than the reverse.

Currency swaps can be treated as a portfolio of two bonds, short in one currency and long in the other. Basically, the swap is treated as a back-to-back loan, and each leg of the swap is valued separately. The value of this hedged portfolio changes if interest rates in either of the two currencies move or if the spot exchange rate moves. Let's denote $P_1(r_\$)$ and $P_2(r_¥)$ as the respective values of the dollar and yen bonds, given the current market interest rates, $r_\$$ and $r_¥$, on bonds in the two currencies. Then the yen value of the swap, given the spot exchange rate, S, expressed as yen per dollar, is

EXHIBIT 10.7

Valuing a Currency Swap as a Package of Forward Currency Contracts (in millions)

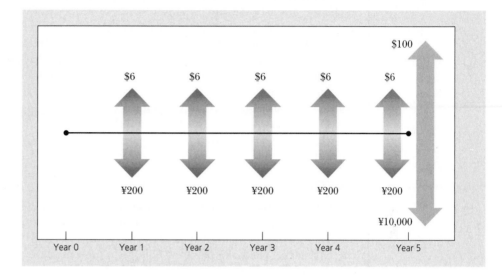

$$\text{Swap value} = P_2(r_¥) - S \times P_1(r_\$) \tag{10.10}$$

This is the value of a swap to pay dollars and receive yen. The dollar value of the swap is simply deducted from the yen value of the swap by dividing by the spot exchange rate, S. The value of the swap for the other party, which agreed to pay yen and receive dollars, is exactly the opposite of that computed in Equation 10.10. Example 10.5 that follows illustrates the valuation of a currency swap as a portfolio of two bonds.

The only practical problem with this approach is determining the relevant market interest rates used on both legs of the swap. For each cash flow on the fixed-rate leg, we should use a zero-coupon term structure. The practice in the finance profession is to derive a zero-coupon structure from the current swap rates quotations and use it to price outstanding swaps. This term structure is usually called *zero swap rates.*

Interest rate swaps can be valued likewise using a portfolio of a fixed-rate bond and a floating-rate bond. The floating-rate leg is assumed to have a market value that remains set at par on the reset date (see Chapter 7). The fixed-rate leg is valued as described earlier, using the current zero swap rates. The same applies to a mixed currency–interest rate swap.

Valuation in the Presence of Credit Risk   The swap quotations should differ for a party with credit risk. For example, a AAA bank quoting swap rates to an A customer is likely to increase the bid–ask spread on the swap rates. Typically, the credit quality spread for an A party would be from one to five basis points on either side.

EXAMPLE 10.5   VALUATION OF A CURRENCY SWAP

One hundred million U.S. dollars are swapped against 10 billion yen. The spot exchange rate is ¥/$=100; the interest rates on dollars and yen are 6 percent and 2 percent, respectively. The maturity of the contract is five years, and interest coupons are swapped once a year. At time of contracting, the two interest rates were equal to the market yield to maturity on five-year bonds in dollars (6 percent) and yen (2 percent). Assume that a year later, the yield curves in dollars and yen are flat and that interest rates have dropped to 5 percent on U.S. dollar bonds and 1 percent on yen bonds. The spot exchange rate has dropped to ¥/$= 90. A swap payment of ¥340 million has just been made (200 − 90 × 6). What is the new value of the swap for the party that agreed to receive yen and pay dollars?

SOLUTION

We value the two bonds implied in the swap separately. The dollar bond was worth $100 million (its par value) when the swap was contracted with a dollar interest rate of 6 percent. A year later, the bond is worth $103.55 million at the current market yield of 5 percent. This is the present value of a stream of yearly coupons of $6 million and a principal of $100 million repaid in four years, discounted at 5 percent:

$$P_1 = \frac{6}{(1.05)} + \frac{6}{(1.05)^2} + \frac{6}{(1.05)^3} + \frac{106}{(1.05)^4} = 103.55$$

Similarly, the yen bond was worth ¥10 billion (its par value) when the swap was contracted, with a yen interest rate of 2 percent. A year later, the bond is worth ¥10,390 million at the current market yield of 1 percent. This is the present value of four yearly coupons of ¥200 million and a principal of ¥10 billion repaid in four years, discounted at 1 percent. The yen value of the swap (to pay dollars and receive yen) is equal to

Swap value (in million yen) = 10,390 − 90 × 103.55

= ¥1,071 million, or $11.9 million

For the other party, the swap now has a value of −¥1,071 million.

A quality spread of a few basis points may seem small as compensation for the risk of default on a swap.[17] However, the potential losses on swaps, especially interest rate swaps, are much smaller than for a loan. The default risk does not apply to

---

[17] Duffie and Huang (1996) studied the quality spread that should be paid by a risky party (e.g., rated A or Baa) over the AAA rate on a bond issuance and on a swap, as a function of its credit quality. They found that if a quality spread of 100 basis points is required on a bond, it should only be around 1 basis point on an interest rate swap of similar maturity.

the principal and interest payments, but only to the differential in interest payments in the case of an interest rate swap. The default risk also applies to the differential in principal repayment in the case of a currency swap, so the quality spread should be somewhat higher. Further, note that the default of a risky customer will affect the bank (the other party) only if the interest rate and currency movements are such that the customer is in a position to owe money to the bank. If the market conditions are such that the swap has a negative value for the bank, the default of the customer will not imply an additional loss for the bank.

Swap contracts specify how the swap will be terminated in case of bankruptcy of one of the parties. These termination clauses can vary across swaps and market participants. The most common clause is the "full two-way payments" option proposed in the ISDA master agreement. Under this clause, a party is deemed to default on the swap if it becomes insolvent on its debt. All outstanding swaps are "netted," and the settlement is based on the replacement values of the outstanding swaps. In other words, the net market value of the swap position between the two parties is computed using standard methods and quotes from major swap dealers.

Use of Swaps

As usual in finance, the major motivations for using swaps are return and risk. Companies use swaps to reduce their financing costs (return motivation). They also use swaps to manage their long-term exposure to currency and interest rate risks, especially when they are faced with risks to existing assets and liabilities. For example, if a U.S. corporation borrowed in Swiss francs two years ago and is concerned about an anticipated strong appreciation of the Swiss franc, a U.S. dollar/Swiss franc swap can be used to transform the Swiss franc liability into a U.S. dollar liability.

Cost Benefits of Swaps   The usual argument for the use of swaps in new borrowing is cost savings. The main motivation in the early stage of the market was to take advantage of borrowing cost differentials between two markets to raise funds cheaply. It must be stressed that, by itself, the swap does not provide a cost benefit, but it does provide a bridge across several financing markets. Given competition, swaps are priced at fair value, but they allow the transfer of some cost advantage obtained by borrowing in one market to another market.

Simple Cost-Financing Advantage   The motivation for a classic currency swap can be illustrated in the following hypothetical example. A supranational borrower (say, the World Bank) can tap the U.S. dollar market on favorable terms but would prefer to borrow Swiss francs because of the low interest rate in that market and because it needs to diversify its financing currencies. Supranational borrowers, such as the World Bank, the EU, or the European Investment Bank, are not favorites of Swiss investors, who prefer nonstate borrowers. Alternatively, a large U.S. corporation can borrow on very attractive terms in the foreign Swiss franc market but needs dollars. Each party is better off borrowing in the market in which it holds a comparative advantage and then entering a swap with a bank to obtain the desired structure of cash flows. For example, the supranational borrower issues a bond in the U.S. dollar market and swaps the proceeds for the low-interest-rate Swiss francs. Conversely, the U.S. corporation issues a Swiss franc bond and swaps the francs for dollars. Each party is bound to benefit from this swap by obtaining funds more cheaply than if it had directly accessed its desired currency market.

The idea is to use financing on a specific market in which a borrower has a *comparative advantage* and to transfer that advantage to another market or currency by making a swap at prevailing market conditions. The swap helps only as a bridge across markets. However, these cost savings based on the comparative advantage of some companies in some market segments are a form of market inefficiency. Financial arbitrage, such as a swap, exploits these market inefficiencies. As the volume of swaps increases, these simple inefficiencies are bound to disappear; they are arbitraged away.

More Complex Engineering   Many swap dealers believe that the growth of the market depends on the ability to identify and exploit new arbitrage opportunities as they develop in world markets. Many of these temporary or persistent arbitrage opportunities are caused by the regulatory and fiscal environment. For example, some domestic firms have access to subsidized lending (some government agency subsidizes part of the interest cost) at home but wish to borrow foreign currencies to finance their foreign operations. Example 10.6 illustrates some financial engineering that could be done in response to a particular regulatory and fiscal environment.

Swaps are similarly used in complex investment strategies to take advantage of some excess risk-adjusted return (alpha) in one market and transfer it to another market. This comparative advantage transfer is sometimes referred to as *alpha transfer.*

A Word of Caution   Swaps are often offered as part of a package that replicates an existing security at a cost advantage. However, investors must be careful to verify that this synthetic replication is indeed perfect, and that the apparent cost benefits are not simply due to higher assumed risks. Let's take the example of a synthetic fixed-rate loan in euros sold to a corporate customer by a bank. The customer wishes to borrow fixed-rate euros for 10 years. This can be done by issuing a bond at a yield of 7 percent. Instead, the bank suggests borrowing short-term, by issuing six-month commercial paper (CP) and entering an interest rate swap in euros to receive floating and pay fixed. The CP is supposed to be rolled over every six months. The corporation can currently borrow through CP at Euribor + 1/2% and enter a 10-year swap paying a fixed 6 percent and receiving Euribor. If the corporation rolls over its CP every six months, it recreates with the swap the economic position of borrowing fixed. The net annual cost to the corporation is 6.5 percent [6% − Euribor + Euribor + 1/2 %] compared with 7% on a fixed-rate bond. The cost benefit appears to be 50 basis points. However, the synthetic position is not exactly equal to the fixed-rate bond. If the corporation's credit quality deteriorates over time, its short-term borrowing costs will increase, as the quality spread over Euribor could move from 0.5 percent to 1 percent or more. Actually, if the corporation experiences severe financial problems, it could even face a situation in which it cannot issue more CP. This is called *rollover risk.* If the corporation borrows fixed at 7 percent, it knows that the rate will remain fixed whatever its future credit quality.

EXAMPLE 10.6   SOME COMPLEX ENGINEERING

An interesting example can be found in the yen market, in which Japanese regulatory pressure is strongly felt. In the 1990s, three Japanese regulatory and fiscal situations could have led to an interesting packaging of securities:

1. The Ministry of Finance limited the amount of foreign currency (non-yen) bonds held by Japanese institutions, such as pension funds and insurance companies.

2. A dual-currency bond issued in yen, with interest payments in yen but principal repayment in a foreign currency, qualified as a yen bond for purposes of the yen limit imposed by the Ministry of Finance. This was attractive to Japanese institutions as a legal way to invest in foreign currency assets.

3. Zero-coupon bonds were taxed as non-income-generating assets. At maturity, the difference between the nominal value and the purchase price of the bond was taxed as capital gain, at a lower tax rate than income. Zero-coupon bonds were attractive to taxable Japanese investors.

In response to this regulatory and fiscal environment, a corporation wanting to borrow U.S. dollars could instead have engaged in the following operations:

- Issued a five-year dual-currency bond[18] with a 4 percent interest coupon in yen and principal repayment in dollars (Bond A). The repayment value would have been $100 million U.S., and the issue amount would have been 10 billion yen. The spot exchange rate was 100 yen/dollar.

- Issued a five-year zero-coupon yen bond with the same maturity as the dual-currency bond and a nominal value of 10 billion yen (Bond B). There would be no interest payment, simply a principal repayment of 10 billion yen in five years.

- Entered into an agreement to swap a five-year yen fixed-rate obligation of 10 billion yen, with an annual interest rate of 4 percent (400 million yen), for a fixed-rate dollar obligation. This is a yen/dollar currency swap where the corporation receives yen and pays dollars. The dollar leg has a principal of $100 million and a coupon $c\%$ set at the conditions prevailing in the swap market. So, the dollar leg has a coupon of $c\% \times \$100$ million = C million dollars.

1. What is the currency exposure and the resulting position for the corporation?

2. What is the motivation of the corporation for entering into this complex package?

---

[18] See a description of dual-currency bonds in Chapter 7.

SOLUTION

1. Let's look at the economic position taken. The combination of the zero-coupon and dual-currency loan is equivalent to a straight yen bond, with a principal of 10 billion yen and annual coupons of 400 million yen, plus a U.S. dollar zero-coupon bond with a nominal value of $100 million. The reasoning is simple if we look at the cash flows by currency, as shown in Exhibit 10.8. The corporation ends up with a pure dollar exposure by swapping the yen obligation of 10 billion yen for a U.S. dollar obligation.

2. The motivation is to reduce the borrowing cost in dollars. The issue of the two bonds would capitalize on a regulatory and a fiscal attraction to Japanese investors, and therefore could be done on attractive (low-cost) terms. But the final product for the corporation would be a U.S. dollar loan, at a cheaper cost than a straight U.S. dollar loan, because the cost benefit is transferred from Japanese yen to U.S. dollars.

EXHIBIT 10.8

Cash Flows

	Payments (in millions)	
	Yen	**Dollar**
Before swap (dual currency and yen bonds)		
Year 1: Interest	400[A]	0
Year 2: Interest	400[A]	0
Year 3: Interest	400[A]	0
Year 4: Interest	400[A]	0
Year 5: Interest	400[A]	0
Year 5: Principal	10,000[B]	100[A]
After swap (dual currency and yen bonds plus swap)		
Year 1: Interest	0	C
Year 2: Interest	0	C
Year 3: Interest	0	C
Year 4: Interest	0	C
Year 5: Interest	0	C
Year 5: Principal	0	100+100

[A]Cash flow from Bond A.
[B]Cash flow from Bond B.

To summarize, investors should exercise caution when faced with large cost benefits on fairly simple synthetic packages.

Risk Management   Interest rate swaps can be used to alter the exposure of a portfolio of assets or liabilities to interest rate movements. Swaps are all the more useful when assets or liabilities cannot be traded, as is the case for bank loans.

Risk management using swaps requires several steps:

1. Identify the source of uncertainty that could induce losses.

2. Measure the amount of exposure to this risk.

3. Identify the type of swaps that could best be used to hedge the risk.

4. Decide on the amount of hedging that should be undertaken. It is useful to start from the risk-minimizing hedge and to deviate from this neutral position as a function of expectations and risk aversion.

EXAMPLE 10.7   RISK MANAGEMENT WITH SWAPS

Let's consider a small British bank that provided a loan in euros to a top-quality customer that had to finance an acquisition in Germany. The amount of the loan is €50 million, with a fixed annual coupon of 7 percent and three years remaining. The British bank finances this euro fixed-rate loan by rolling over short-term borrowing on the Eurocurrency market. This bank is mostly domestic, and this loan and its associated euro floating-rate borrowing are the only asset and liability in euros appearing on the bank's balance sheet. The current six-month rate on Euribor is 6 percent, and the bank fears a rise in euro interest rates that would affect short- and long-term rates in a similar fashion. This interest rate increase is specific to the Eurozone, and no particular movements in the exchange rates are predicted.

How could this bank use interest rate swaps to hedge the risk that the euro interest rate will rise?

SOLUTION

The following analysis of this simple example could be performed:

1. The source of risk is a movement in the general level of euro interest rates. This can be seen in two ways. In terms of annual cash flows, the rise in interest rates will increase the financing costs (floating) of the bank without a corresponding increase in its interest income (fixed). However, the overall impact on the bank is best measured by looking at the change in market value of its assets and liabilities. A rise in euro interest rates should not affect the value of the floating-rate borrowing; however, the value of the fixed-rate loan would drop as market yields increase. A rise in euro interest rates would hurt the bank; a drop in euro interest rates would benefit the bank.

2. The amount at risk is €50 million, the market value of the exposed asset.

3. A euro interest rate swap is a good hedge against this risk. The bank should enter into a swap to pay fixed and receive floating.

4. The risk-minimizing strategy would be to swap €50 million. If the bank is very sure of its rate prediction, it could enter a swap for a larger amount. This would be equivalent to "speculating" on this prediction.

For the same reasons that swaps can be used to hedge risks on existing positions, they can also be used to take speculative bets on interest and exchange rates. Corporations have often used swaps as investment vehicles. They regard swaps as highly leveraged long-term contracts that help them capitalize on predictions about exchange rate or interest rate movements. Although swaps are off-balance-sheet contracts, their risks should be clearly accounted for.

Options

Forward, futures, and swap contracts have a symmetric profit-and-loss structure. Options are very different contracts.

Introduction to Options

Definition   In general, an option gives the buyer the right, but not the obligation, to buy or sell an asset, and the option seller must respond accordingly. Many types of option contracts exist in the financial world. The two major types of contracts traded on organized options exchanges are *calls* and *puts*.

A *call* gives the buyer of the option contract the right to buy a specified number of units of an *underlying asset* at a specified price, called the *exercise price* or *strike price*, on or before a specified date, called the *expiration date* or *strike date*. A *put* gives the buyer of the option contract the right to sell a specified number of units of an underlying asset at a specified price on or before a specified date. In all cases, the seller of the option contract, the *writer,* is subject to the buyer's decision to exercise or not, and the buyer exercises the option only if it is profitable to her. The buyer of a call benefits if the price of the asset is above the strike price at expiration. The buyer of a put benefits if the asset price is below the strike price at expiration.

The buyer of an option acquires something of value. A buyer can make a profit, potentially large, if the asset price moves in the right direction. A buyer will let the option expire worthless if the asset price moves in the wrong direction. Such an attractive profit-and-loss structure has a price: This is the option price, or *premium,* that has to be paid to purchase the option. This premium is received by the seller of the option.

The complete definition of an option must clearly specify how the option can be exercised. A *European-type* option can be exercised only on the expiration date. An *American-type* option can be exercised at any time until the expiration date. American options are used on most of the organized options exchanges in the world. Both types of options can be freely traded at any time until expiration.

Market Organization   The organization of the market for listed, or traded, options is somewhat similar to that of the futures market. An options clearing corporation, or clearinghouse, plays a central role. All option contracts are represented by bookkeeping entries on the computers of the clearinghouse corporation. As soon as a buyer and a seller of a particular contract decide to trade, the clearinghouse corporation steps in and breaks the deal down into two option contracts: one between the buyer and the clearinghouse corporation acting as seller, and the other between the seller and the clearinghouse corporation acting as buyer. This procedure completely standardizes the contracts. It allows an investor to close a position by simply selling out the options held, while a seller may buy options to close a previous position. If a buyer decides to exercise an option, the clearing-house corporation randomly selects a seller of the option and issues an exercise notice. Selling an option entails a sizable risk. Hence, selling an option (naked sale) requires depositing a *margin.*[19]

In most cases, investors offset their positions by making a reverse trade before the expiration date. Option buyers usually find it more profitable to resell an option on the market than to exercise it. There are times, however, when exercising an option is more profitable; this can be the case for a call option on a stock, when a large dividend is about to be paid on the underlying stock. Listed options markets can be found all over the world.

There is also an OTC market with banks writing European-type currency options tailored to the specific needs of commercial customers. This interbank market has developed successfully for interest rate and currency options.

The Different Instruments

Currency Options   Markets in currency options have developed to cope with the volatility of exchange rates. Currency options are now traded on markets throughout the world. Three types of currency options contracts are negotiated:

1. *Over-the-counter currency options* are not tradable and can be exercised only at maturity; that is, they are European-type options.[20] Commercial customers often turn to a bank when they need a large amount of options of this type for a specific date. For example, a German car exporter may expect a payment of $20 million, three months from now, to be transferred into euros. Listed options do not offer this specific expiration date, and the amount involved may be too large for the volume of transactions on the options exchange. Moreover, a commercial exporter would not be interested in the possibility of early exercise or sale of the options, anyway. Once the bank has written the option, it uses forward contracts or listed currency options to actively hedge the position it has created. Options are also written for longer terms (over two years) than the maturity available on the exchange-listed options.

2. *Spot currency options* are traded on some exchanges. When a currency option is exercised, foreign currency must be physically delivered to a bank account, usually in the country in whose currency the delivery is made. The Philadelphia stock exchange trades option contracts on currencies.

3. Other listed currency options are *options on currency futures* contracts. For example, the CME trades options on its own currency futures.[21]

---

[19] The seller of a call can deposit as collateral the asset on which the option is written (covered sale).

[20] European-type options are generally used in OTC markets because they are simpler. But any type of option can be negotiated in such a customized market.

[21] The price of an option on spot and futures exchange rates may differ slightly. Technical differences are also important. For example, spot currency options on the Philadelphia stock exchange and futures currency options on the CME do not expire on the same day of the month.

To offer more flexibility, options exchange also offers the possibility of writing some customized options in terms of expiration date, amount, and option type.

Currency options are quoted in several ways. Interbank currency options are basically traded in the fashion desired by the investor. Typically, U.S. options are quoted in terms of U.S. dollars per unit of foreign currency. The quotations from various options markets are published in slightly different formats, but they all include the same information. For example, Exhibit 10.9 reports quotes for £/$ options. The contract size is £31,250, and the option prices are expressed in U.S. cents per pound. The first column gives the strike price (the dollar value of one pound) and the next columns give the option premium (in U.S. cents per pound) for different expiration months of calls and puts. The call British pound April 1.620 quoted in Philadelphia is an option contract giving the right to buy 31,250 pounds at a strike price of 1.620 dollars per British pound on or before April. At the time (February 18), the spot exchange rate was 1.633 dollars per British pound, and the premium was 2.63 cents per British pound. If the British pound had gone up, the price of the option would have increased and the holder of the call would have profited. An investor could also have bought a British pound put, which would have given the investor the right to sell 31,250 British pounds at a fixed strike price. For example, the put British pound April 1.620 was worth 1.32 cents per British pound. If the British pound had depreciated (i.e., if its value had gone down in terms of U.S. dollars), the holder of the put would have profited.

Stock Options   Trading in listed options started with options on individual common stocks. Markets have developed throughout the world to the point at which options are now traded on all major stocks. In most countries, the national stock exchange or an associated options exchange trades options on domestic companies listed on the stock exchange.

Stock options are usually protected against capital adjustments, such as splits or stock rights, but not against dividend payments. This is why it can be more profitable to exercise a call option just before a dividend is paid than to keep it and lose the dividend.

Options on stock indexes have also developed in most countries. They can be options on the stock index or on the stock index futures contract. All settlement

---

EXHIBIT 10.9

Currency Options Quotations: February 18

■ *PHILADELPHIA Sterling OPTIONS £31,250 (cents per pound)*

Strike Price	CALLS			PUTS		
	Mar	**Apr**	**May**	**Mar**	**Apr**	**May**
1.620	2.01	2.63	3.11	0.63	1.32	1.77
1.630	1.38	2.10	2.56	0.97	1.75	2.21
1.640	0.94	1.67	2.13	1.44	2.22	2.69

Previous day's vol., Calls–Puts 422. Prev. day's open int., Calls 1553 Puts 19,754

Source: Financial Times, February 19, 1999.

procedures require cash rather than physical delivery of an index. The cash settlement is based on the calculated value of the index at the time of expiration.

Interest Rate Options   Listed options are traded on the interest rate futures contracts (bonds, and short-term deposits) described previously. Options use the same convention as futures. For example, a put on Euribor with a strike of 97 percent and the exercise month June is quoted on February 19 at 0.10 percent. The underlying asset is a three-month Euribor futures contract with a nominal value of €1 million and delivery in June. Following the futures convention, the premium on one option contract is 0.10 percent of €1 million divided by four, or €250. This gives the investor the right to sell one Euribor futures contract in June at a price of 97 percent (i.e., to borrow in June for three months at a 3 percent interest rate). If Euribor futures quote at 96 percent on expiration, the put option contract will be worth 1 percent times €1 million divided by four, or €2,500.

Also, some interest rate options are traded OTC. Example 10.8 shows an interest rate call option (cap) based on LIBOR. Typically, OTC options such as caps and floors (a type of interest rate put) are longer-term options on short-term interest rates.

EXAMPLE 10.8   *CAP*

Consider a five-year 6 percent cap on the three-month LIBOR for $1 million. The current LIBOR is 5 percent, and the yearly cap premium is an annualized 0.5 percent paid quarterly. You buy such a cap. What would be the quarterly payment on the cap if

1. LIBOR stays below 6 percent, the strike price?

2. LIBOR moves up to 8 percent?

SOLUTION

1. If LIBOR stays below 6 percent over the next five years, the cap option will be useless. Each quarter in which LIBOR is below 6 percent, you will have to pay the premuim of 0.5 percent annualized, hence a payment of

$$\$1,000,000 \times \left(\frac{0.5\%}{4} \right) = \$1,250$$

2. If LIBOR is equal to 8 percent on a quarterly payment date, you will receive the difference between LIBOR and the strike rate of 6 percent, minus the premium payment of 0.5%:

$$\$1,000,000 \times \left(\frac{8\% - 6\% - 0.5\%}{4} \right) = \$3,750$$

A cap can benefit a borrower who has a LIBOR-indexed loan. For a 0.5 percent premium payment, the cap buyer gains protection from a LIBOR-based interest cost increase because a rise in LIBOR above the strike rate yields an offsetting gain on the cap.

The basic contract in an interest rate *cap option* is an agreement between the buyer and the seller of the option, stating that if a chosen rate, such as the three-month LIBOR, is above the agreed-on strike price at prespecified dates in the future, the seller will reimburse the buyer for the additional interest cost until the next specified date. A floor option has the reverse characteristics. A five-year cap on the three-month LIBOR can be broken down into a series of 19 European options with quarterly strike dates. The option premium may be paid in the form of a single front-end price (e.g., 2 percent of the amount specified in the option) or a yearly cost paid up regularly (e.g., 0.5 percent per year).

Option Valuation

Profit and Loss at Expiration　The profit-and-loss structure of an option that is held until expiration is shown in Exhibit 10.10 The strike price, *K,* is assumed to equal the spot price at the time of contracting. The profit at expiration depends on the spot price at expiration.

Exhibits 10.10a and b show the profit structures for long and short positions in an underlying asset. This illustrates the profit structure for buying and selling futures. We see from the diagram that the profit structures on these two positions exactly mirror each other. This stems from the fact that for any dollar increase in the spot price of the asset, the buyer of futures earns a dollar profit and the seller loses a dollar.

The profit structures for options must take premiums into account. The buyer and the writer of a call option have opposite profit opportunities at expiration. The maximum loss for an option buyer is limited to the premium, although the profit may be quite large. The reverse holds true for the option writer, which is why Exhibits 10.10c and d also are mirror images of each other. Another way of saying this is that the risk structure of options is asymmetric when compared with a direct investment in the spot or futures market. That is, though the option buyer risks losing the premium, the seller of that same option bears the risk of an almost unlimited loss.

Valuation Models　Option premiums fluctuate so rapidly as a function of price movements in underlying assets that computerized models are necessary to properly value them. To understand how options are valued, recall both the parameters that determine option premiums and the famous valuation formula proposed by Black and Scholes (1973).[22]

Most options traded in the world are American options in the sense that they can be exercised any time before expiration, which means that premiums must at least equal the profit an investor could obtain by immediately exercising the option. *Intrinsic value* is the value of an option that is immediately exercised. A rational option buyer would never exercise a call when the underlying asset price is below the strike price, because he would lose money. Such an option is said to be *out of the money,* and its intrinsic value is zero. When an asset price is above the strike

---

[22] See also Hull (2002) and Kolb (2001).

EXHIBIT 10.10

Profits and Losses from Various Positions

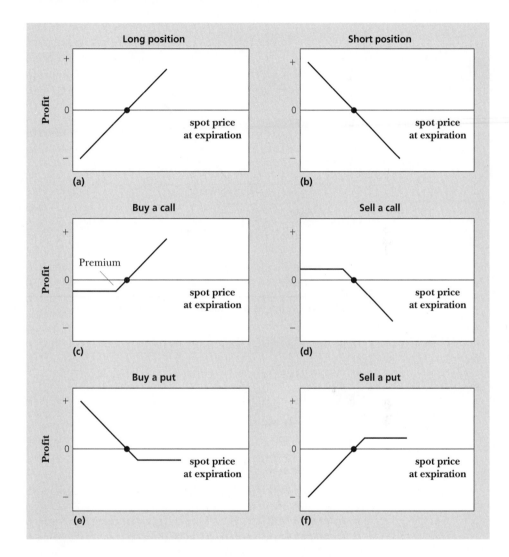

price, the call is said to be *in the money,* and its intrinsic value is the difference be-tween the asset price and the strike price. The intrinsic value of a call as a function of asset price is shown in Exhibit 10.11.

An option will generally sell above its intrinsic value; the difference between an option's market value and its intrinsic value is called its *time value.* At any time be-fore expiration, call option premiums vary with the underlying asset prices along a curve similar to that shown in Exhibit 10.12 *(dashed line).* For very low values of the asset price relative to the strike price, the intrinsic value is zero and the time value of the option is close to zero, because the probability that the option will ever be

EXHIBIT 10.11

Call Option Intrinsic Value as a Function of Asset Price

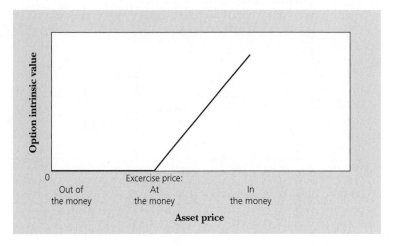

EXHIBIT 10.12

Call Option Value as a Function of Asset Price

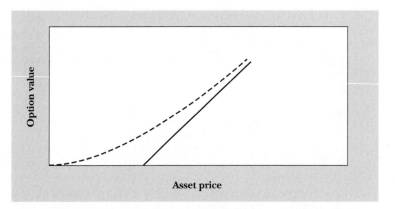

exercised is almost zero. For very high asset prices relative to the strike price, the option premium is almost equal to the option's intrinsic value. The option is almost sure to be exercised at expiration, because it is unlikely that the asset price will ever drop below the strike price; therefore, the time value of the option is close to zero and the premium approaches the intrinsic value. When the asset price is close to the strike price *(at the money)*, the time value of the option is largest. Note that the slope of a tangent to the curve shown in Exhibit 10.12 gives the instantaneous reaction of the option premium to a change in the asset price. This slope is usually called *delta* (δ).

As shown by Black and Scholes (1973), option values depend on just four variables. The influence of each of these variables on call and put options can be described as follows:

Volatility: The value of a call or put increases with the volatility of the underlying asset because options are perfectly protected against downside risk. The buyer can never lose more than the premium paid. Yet, simultaneously, the buyer may potentially realize large gains on the upside. The more volatile the asset, the larger the expected gain on the option and, hence, the larger its premium.

Asset price relative to strike price: The value of an option depends critically on its strike price, relative to its current asset price. The lower the asset price relative to the strike price, the lower the premium for a call (the higher for a put).

Interest rate: The value of a call (put) is an increasing (decreasing) function of the *domestic* interest rate. Buying a call enables an investor to lay claim to an asset, although making a much smaller capital investment than required to buy the asset outright. A call reduces the opportunity or financing cost for claiming an asset. In the case of a currency option, buying a call rather than the currency itself deprives the buyer of the foreign interest rate paid on the foreign currency. Hence, the value of a currency call is a decreasing function of the *foreign interest rate*. The reverse is true for a currency put.

Time to expiration: The value of an option is an increasing function of the time to expiration. Take the example of a call. The opportunity for the underlying asset price to far exceed the strike price increases with time to expiration. Of course, there is also an increased opportunity for a large adverse price movement, but once again, the call holder's loss is always limited to the premium paid.

All the determinants of option premiums, except volatility of the underlying asset, can be measured precisely. Hence, options premiums are directly related to the *anticipated* volatility, that is, the volatility expected to prevail until expiration. Therefore, traders often express options prices in terms of implicit volatility. From these four parameters, a valuation model for options can be constructed. Analytical valuation models have been derived for European-type options, which cannot be exercised until expiration. They offer an operational approximation for American-type options, which can be exercised at any time; this is the case for a majority of options traded in the world. The most famous valuation model was developed by Black and Scholes and is currently used on options markets worldwide. It is a fairly complex mathematical formula which is explained in derivatives textbooks such as Hull (2002), Chance (2003), and Kolb (2001).

Use of Options

Options can be put to several uses. Selling (writing) options allows an investor to pocket income if the option expires worthless, but the risks are huge if the price of the underlying asset moves in an unfavorable direction. *Covered call writing* is the sale of a call option written on assets held in the portfolio; but the risk is that the assets will have to be delivered if the option is exercised. Hence, selling options is a strategy left to specialized investors. Some strategies involve dynamic trading based on sophisticated valuation models and are again reserved for specialists. In traditional portfolio management, options are mainly used either to invest in a specific security or market, while limiting the downside risk potential, or for temporarily insuring some types of portfolio risk. In both cases, investment managers only buy options—they do not sell them. Options are also used in constructing some structured notes designed for the specific need of some investors, mostly institutional.

Speculation with Limited Risk   The buyer of an option can take a position in the underlying asset with a limited downside risk, namely the option premium. For example, the call British pound April 1.620 quoted in Exhibit 10.9 gives the right to buy 31,250 pounds at a strike price of 1.620 dollars per British pound, and the option premium is 2.63 cents per British pound. An investor could speculate on an appreciation of the pound against the dollar by buying one contract on 31,250 pounds and paying $0.0263 \times 31,250 = 821.875$ dollars. If the pound rises to $1.800 by April, the investor will make a profit equal to the difference between the spot and the strike price, minus the option premium. This will be a profit per contract of

$$31{,}250 \times (1.800 - 1.620 - 0.0263) = 4{,}803.125 \text{ dollars}$$

This is less than the pound appreciation because of the cost of the call premium. But if the pound drops in value by April, the investor will only lose the premium that she paid initially.

Insurance   Options provide a unique tool with which to insure portfolios. Insurance means that a portfolio is protected against a negative performance while it retains its positive performance potential. By contrast, hedging with futures removes both negative and positive performance potentials. The case of insuring against currency risks is detailed in Chapter 11. Example 10.9 illustrates how to insure an equity portfolio against market risk.

Structured Notes   A *structured note* is a bond issued with some unusual option-like clause.[23] These notes are bonds issued by a name of good credit standing and can therefore be purchased as investment-grade bonds by most institutional investors, even those that are prevented by regulations from dealing in derivatives. Another attraction for investors is that these structured notes offer some long-term options that are not publicly traded. Structured notes with equity participation are in strong demand in many countries, especially in Europe, where they are sometimes called *guaranteed notes*.

Guaranteed notes with equity participation are bonds having guaranteed redemption of capital and a minimum coupon; in addition, some participation in the price movement of a selected index is offered if this price movement is positive. For

---

[23] Some other examples of structured notes offered to international investors are discussed in Chapter 7.

EXAMPLE 10.9   *INSURING AGAINST MARKET RISK*

A portfolio manager has an allocation of €4 million to French equity. The French portfolio is well diversified and tracks the local CAC stock index. The manager believes that the French market offers excellent returns prospects. However, the manager is worried that French elections taking place next month (April) could lead to a severe market correction. Although the probability of such an outcome is quite small, the manager wishes to insure against it. The current value of the CAC index is 4,000. Futures on the CAC with maturity in June also trade at 4,000. Put options with maturity in June trade as follows:

Strike Price	Premium (€ per unit of index)
3,900	30
4,000	100

CAC options and futures have a multiple of €10 times the index. Thus, the total premium for one put with exercise price €3900 is 30 × €10 = €300, for example. The manager hesitates between selling 100 futures contracts, buying 100 puts with a strike of 3,900, or buying 100 puts with a strike of 4,000.

1. Calculate the outcome of each strategy if the CAC is equal to 3,500, 4,000, or 4,500 at expiration of the contracts in June.

2. Recommend a strategy to the portfolio manager.

SOLUTION

1. The value of the portfolio under the various strategies is given below:

Value of CAC at expiration	Initial Portfolio (No Futures or Options)	Portfolio Hedged with Futures	Portfolio Insured with Puts 3,900	Portfolio Insured with Puts 4,000
3,500	3,500,000	4,000,000	3,870,000	3,900,000
4,000	4,000,000	4,000,000	3,970,000	3,900,000
4,500	4,500,000	4,000,000	4,470,000	4,400,000

2. Hedging with futures provides the best protection in case of a drop in the market, but it deprives the manager of any profit potential. Buying puts provides protection in case of a market drop while keeping most of the upside potential (the put premium is deducted from the portfolio value). Given the manager's expectations, buying puts is a natural strategy. Out-of-the-money puts are cheaper, so they are more attractive in case of an up-movement, but offer less protection in case of a down-movement. To get the best downside protection while retaining upside potential, the portfolio manager should buy 100 puts with a strike price of 4,000.

example, let's consider a two-year note that guarantees the initial capital (redemption at 100 percent) plus an annual coupon of 3 percent and offers a 50 percent participation rate in the percentage price appreciation in the Japanese Nikkei index over the two years. At time of issue, the yield curve was flat at 8 percent. The 50 percent participation rate works as follows: If the stock index goes up by x percent, the investor will get 50 percent of x. For example, if the Nikkei stock index goes up by 30 percent from the time of issue to the time of redemption, the option will yield a profit of 15 percent and the bond will be redeemed for 115 percent. The participation rate is, in effect, the percentage of a call option on the index obtained by the investor. In summary, the structured note can be viewed by investors as the sum of

- a straight bond with a coupon of 3 percent,
- plus 50 percent of an at-the-money call option on the Nikkei.

All of these bonds can be analyzed as the sum of a straight bond with a low coupon plus an option play.

EXAMPLE 10.10   GUARANTEED NOTE

Consider the guaranteed note on the Nikkei described previously.

1. Value the call option implicit in the bond.

2. Assume that you offer a similar bond but with a coupon set at zero. What is the equity participation that you could offer?

SOLUTION

1. The present value of the straight bond is

$$P = \frac{3}{1.08} + \frac{103}{(1.08)^2} = 91.08\%$$

Because the bond is issued at 100 percent, the implicit value of 50 percent of a call option on the Nikkei is therefore equal to

$$100 - 91.08\% = 8.92\%$$

and the implicit value of 100 percent of one call option on the Nikkei index is equal to

$$2 \times (100 - 91.08) = 17.84\%$$

2. There is clearly a negative relation between the amount of the guaranteed coupon and the participation rate that can be offered in the option. For example, a structured note with a zero coupon will leave more money to invest in the call option:

$$P = \frac{0}{1.08} + \frac{100}{(1.08)^2} = 85.73\%$$

The difference between the redemption value and the current market value of the zero-coupon bond ($14.27\% = 100 - 85.73$) can be invested by the issuer in call options. The remaining question is to determine the number of call options that can be purchased with this amount. The number of call options that can be purchased is equal to the participation rate that is set in the structured note. In the example, one call option on the Nikkei index is worth 17.84, and 14.27 is available to invest in options. Hence, this allows a participation rate of

$$14.27/17.84 = 80\%$$

instead of 50 percent, as above.

CONCEPTS IN ACTION   *PLAYING YOUR CARDS RIGHT*

The market offers derivative instruments for all types of tactical plays

Strategies for derivatives fall into three basic camps: speculative trades which attempt to produce large profits from small stakes, defensive trades which protect an existing investment through hedging, and income generation strategies which exploit the volatility of underlying assets.

It is probably fair to say that the first type holds the greatest attraction for private investors. Speculative trades can quickly magic huge rewards from small stakes, so long as the market is correctly judged. Mistakes, however, are punished with hefty losses, which with some instruments can be greater than the initial deposit.

For example, on September 20 I purchased a number of January 420p call options in life insurer Aviva on the Liffe. These allow the holder the chance to buy Aviva stock at that fixed price at any time until January 15, when they expire. I bought them for 22p each when the underlying stock was trading at 346p, and on October 7 sold half of them for 51p each when the Aviva shares had risen to 419p.

My profit was 132 percent in seven days. If I had merely backed my judgment by buying and then selling the shares, the gain would have been 21 percent because capital outlay over which the price improvement was divided would be so much greater.

I could have just as easily used a spread bet. Assuming a 10 percent initial margin, I would have deposited 35p per share and borrowed the rest, 311p, from the broker. After seven days I would have closed out my position at 419p, returned the borrowed 311p and kept 108p, more than trebling my stake.

The result from a contract for difference (CFD)[24] would have been similar. (All examples here ignore commission and spread costs.)

---

[24] Note from the authors: A contract for difference is a contract between an investor and a broker. The investor will receive (or pay) the difference between the price of the underlying share when it closed the contract and its price when it opened it. It is frequently used in the United Kingdom. It is a non-traded single stock futures contract.

However, this is only half the story. If Aviva had announced a surprise rights issue and the shares had fallen to say 280p, my maximum loss with the traded options would be its cost, 22p.

A spread bet or CFD would, however, be at a 66p deficit to the purchase price of 346p, and an investor would either have to deposit extra funds to keep the position open or close it at a loss and make up that deficit. Many spread–bet and CFD brokers offer accounts with stop-loss limits built in, to close out positions before losses become too large.

Covered warrants, which are being launched on the London Stock Exchange, provide similar possibilities to options, with profits heavily geared to a small stake and the maximum loss being known at the outset.

Universal stock futures, which are Liffe's standardized futures contracts on the shares of individual companies, can be used like spread bets and like them have fixed expiry dates.

Derivatives make it simple to construct defensive strategies. By adopting derivative positions opposite to those being protected, they neutralize investment risk. Losses on the underlying investment are offset by profits on the derivates, and vice-versa.

For example, life insurers have been exposed to relentless selling pressure as the value of those investments has fallen.

Many of them have been reluctant to ditch whole portfolios of shares especially at low prices, so have instead hedged those positions in recent months by the purchase of put options and short selling of index futures.

Derivatives can help us hold open positions which for tax and other reasons we are unable or unwilling to close. Let us say an employee of Marks & Spencer has Save As You Earn share options which become due in January, but believes that the price by then will be lower than now.

He or she cannot sell actual shares they do not yet have, but could hedge that position until the shares come due by shorting M&S shares, that is selling them more cheaply through a CFD, spread bet or, when available, a covered put warrant.

If the shares are down 30p by January, the 30p per share profit on buying back the CFD to close the short position will offset the 30p notional loss on the actual shares.

In practice, hedging comes down to choosing the right moment to act, and keeping overheads low. Using put options—which give the right to a given security at an agreed price before a known expiry—to hedge a long position can be highly cost effective, because the put offsets any deterioration in the price of the underlying security, but on upside movements the maximum loss is the option's cost.

So, for example, if you own shares in a risky company that will double in value if it succeeds in getting a refinancing, but will go bankrupt if it fails, a put option (if it can be secured for less than the cost of a share) or a put covered warrant would be more cost effective than a short spread bet, CFD or universal stock future which merely freezes your investment returns on either outcome.

> Income strategies are only available on traded options. By granting rights to others to buy certain of your shares at prices you think high (writing calls), or sell shares to you at prices you judge low (writing puts), you get paid returns which not only compensate for the difference between the agreed price and the actual share price, but an extra premium which covers the potential of this right to acquire value.
>
> *Source:* Nick Louth, "Strategies for Derivatives," *FT Money Guide,* October 26/27, 2002, p. 8.

Summary

- Derivatives offer high financial leverage and liquidity. Major derivative contracts are futures and forward contracts, swaps, and options.

- Futures contracts are standardized in terms of size and delivery dates. They may be freely traded on the market. They are marked to market every day so that profits and losses are immediately realized.

- Forward contracts are private contracts between two parties. They are customized in terms of size and delivery date and have to be held until delivery. The margin is set once and never revised.

- Futures contracts have a symmetrical payoff structure.

- Futures prices are usually broken down into the spot, or cash, price of the asset plus a basis. The basis is referred to as a discount, or premium, for currency or stock index contracts.

- The major question in futures valuation is how to determine the theoretical value of the basis. This is usually done using an arbitrage argument taking offsetting positions in the spot and futures or forward markets. The cost of carrying this arbitrage puts limits on the basis. In all cases, the basis tends to reflect the financing cost of holding a cash position minus the income lost, if any, in holding a futures position. Various technical aspects render the valuation of bond futures more difficult.

- Futures and forward contracts are used to hedge assets or portfolios of assets against price risk. Several types of hedges can be designed. Two major decisions are the contracts to be used and the amount of hedging. Because few futures contracts exist, investors must often engage in cross-hedging by using contracts that are close, but not identical, to the assets to be hedged. The aim is to use contracts whose futures price most closely correlates with that of the type of risk to be hedged

- Perfect hedges can seldom be created because of basis risk (unexpected fluctuations in the basis) and cross-hedge risk (imperfect correlation between the asset and the contract). Hedging strategies range from a simple approach using a unitary hedge ratio to a minimum-variance optimization approach.

- Swaps are long-term periodic forward contracts.

- Currency swaps involve the exchange of obligations in two currencies. Interest rate swaps involve the exchange of two obligations in the same currency: one with a fixed interest rate, the other with a floating rate. Currency–interest rate swaps involve the exchange of a fixed interest rate in one currency for a floating interest rate in another currency.

- Swaps are used to transfer a comparative advantage enjoyed in one market to another market. They are often part of a complex financing or investment package. Swaps also are used to manage a company's long-term exposure to currency and interest rate risk.

- Swaps are generally valued as a portfolio of two bonds. Credit risk on a swap involves smaller potential losses than on a bond. This explains why the quality spread (the difference between the swap rate for parties with and without credit risk) amounts to only a few basis points.

- Options, like futures, are leveraged instruments but have an attractive asymmetric risk–return characteristic. Calls and puts are the major types of options traded on organized exchanges.

- Exchange traded options are written on all types of financial instruments, including commodities, currencies, individual stocks, stock indexes, fixed-income instruments, and interest rates. Options exist on spot asset prices as well as on futures contracts.

- The valuation of options is somewhat complex. Analytical valuation models have been derived for European-type options, which cannot be exercised until expiration. They offer an operational approximation for American-type options, which can be exercised at any time up to and including the expiration date—the case for a majority of options traded in the world.

- Options can be used to invest in a specific security or market, while limiting the downside risk potential. They are also used to "insure" an existing portfolio. For example, buying a put on an asset (or portfolio) allows the reduction, or elimination, of loss in case of a drop in value of the asset. In-the-money options offer better protection than out-of-the-money options, but at a higher cost.

- Options are also used in constructing some structured notes designed for the specific need of some investors, mostly institutional.

Problems

1. In Chicago, the size of a yen futures contract is 12.5 million yen. The initial margin is $2,025, and the maintenance margin is $1,500. You decide to buy ten contracts, with maturity in June, at the current market futures price of $0.01056/¥. The contract expires on the second-to-last business day before the third Wednesday of the delivery month (expiration date: June 17). Today is April 1, and the spot exchange rate is

$0.01041/¥. Indicate the cash flows on your position if the following prices are subsequently observed. (Assume that spot and futures prices stay equal to the previous quotes on the dates that are not indicated in the following table.)

	April 1	April 2	April 3	April 4	June 16	June 17
Spot $/¥	0.01041	0.01039	0.01000	0.01150	0.01150	0.01100
Futures $/¥	0.01056	0.01054	0.01013	0.01160	0.01151	0.01100

2. Eurodollar futures contracts are traded on the Chicago Mercantile Exchange with a size of $1 million. The initial margin is $540, and the maintenance margin is $400. You are the treasurer of a corporation, and we are at April 1. You know that you will have to pay cash for some goods worth $10 million that will be delivered on June 17. In turn, you will sell those goods with a profit, but you will not receive payment until September 17. Hence, you know that on June 17, you will have to borrow $10 million for three months. Today is April 1, and the current 3-month LIBOR is 6.25 percent. On the Chicago Mercantile Exchange, the Eurodollar futures contract with June delivery is quoted at 93.280 percent. The contract expires on the second business day before the third Wednesday of the delivery month (expiration date: June 17).
   a. What is the forward interest rate implicit in the Eurodollar futures quotation (93.280 percent) on April 1? Why is it higher than the current three-month Eurodollar rate (6.25 percent)?
   b. What position would you take in futures contracts to lock in a three-month borrowing rate for June 17?
   c. On June 17, the Eurodollar futures contract quotes at 91 percent, while the current Eurodollar rate in London is 9 percent. You unwind your position on that date. Describe the cash flows involved.

3. Consider a currency trader based in Germany. The current spot exchange rate is €1.1 per $1. The risk-free rate in the United States is 5 percent per year, and the euro risk-free rate is 8 percent per year. The current forward price on a one-year contract is €1.15 per $1.
   a. Calculate the arbitrage-free forward price.
   b. Based on the current forward price of €1.15 per $1, indicate how the trader can earn a risk-free arbitrage profit.

4. Consider a currency trader based in the United States. The current spot rate is $0.90 per euro. The risk-free rate in the United States is 7 percent, and the euro risk-free rate is 5 percent. The current forward price on a one-year contract is $0.85 per euro.
   a. Calculate the arbitrage-free forward price.
   b. Based on the current forward price of $0.85 per euro, indicate how the trader can earn a risk-free arbitrage profit.

5. A pension fund manager expects a cash inflow of $250 million in two weeks. He wishes to avoid missing a significant increase in equity prices over the next two weeks. Assume that the beta of the portfolio under management is 1.1. A stock index futures contract is quoted at 1225 and has a multiplier of 250. The current stock index is also 1225.
   a. Indicate whether the pension fund manager should undertake a long hedge or a short hedge.
   b. How many contracts should be bought or sold?

6. Consider a portfolio manager who wishes to reduce the allocation to equities in his portfolio by $500 million. The manager is concerned that equity prices may drop quickly. Assume that the beta of the portfolio under management is 0.90. A stock index futures contract is quoted at 1052 and has a multiplier of 250. The current stock index stands at 1050.
   a. Indicate how the portfolio manager can reduce the exposure to equities by using stock index futures.
   b. How many contracts should be bought or sold?

7. A U.S. company has issued floating-rate notes with a maturity of 10 years, an interest rate of six-month LIBOR plus 25 basis points, and total face value of $10 million. The company now believes that interest rates will rise and wishes to protect itself against this by entering into an interest rate swap. A dealer provides a quote on a 10-year swap whereby the company will pay a fixed rate 5 percent and receive six-month LIBOR. Interest is paid semiannually. Assume the current LIBOR rate is 4 percent. Indicate how the company can use a swap to convert the debt to a fixed rate. Calculate the first net payment and indicate which party makes the payment. Assume that all payments are semiannual and made on the basis of 180/360.

8. Consider a bank that is currently lending $25 million at an interest rate of six-month LIBOR plus 65 basis points. The loan maturity is two years and calls for semiannual payments. The bank expects interest rates to fall and wishes to hedge against this by entering into an interest rate swap. A dealer provides the following quotes on swaps:
   a. The bank will pay a fixed rate of 5.05 percent and receive six-month LIBOR.
   b. The bank will receive a fixed payment of 5.25 percent and pay a floating rate of LIBOR plus 25 basis points.
   Indicate which swap the bank should choose. How might the swap hedge the bank against a decline in interest rates? Assume that all payments are semiannual and made on the basis of 180/360.

9. Suppose a U.S. company enters into a currency swap with a counterparty in which the U.S. company pays a fixed rate of 5 percent in euros and the counterparty pays a fixed rate of 6 percent in dollars. The notional principals are $50 million and €45 million. The spot exchange rate is €0.90 per dollar. Payments are made semiannually on the basis of 30 days per month and 360 days per year.
   a. Calculate the initial exchange of payments that takes place at the beginning of the swap if the parties have no immediate need for each other's currency.
   b. Indicate how to calculate the semiannual payments.
   c. Indicate how to calculate the final exchange of payments that takes place at the end of the swap.
   d. Indicate a scenario in which the U.S. company might wish to enter into this currency swap.

10. Suppose a British company enters into a currency swap with a counterparty in which the counterparty pays a fixed rate of 6.5 percent in dollars and the British company pays a fixed rate of 5.5 percent in pounds. The notional principals are £25 million and $41.25 million. The spot exchange rate is $1.65 per pound. Payments are made annually and the parties have no immediate need for each other's currency.
   a. Calculate the initial exchange of payments that takes place at the beginning of the swap.

b. Indicate how to calculate the annual payments.
c. Indicate a scenario in which the British company might wish to enter into this currency swap.

11. Four years ago, a Swiss firm entered into a currency swap of 100 million U.S. dollars for 150 million Swiss francs, with a maturity of seven years. The swap fixed rates are 8 percent in dollars and 4 percent in francs, and swap payments are annual. The Swiss firm contracted to pay dollars and receive francs. The market conditions for zero swap rates (i.e., rates to be used to discount the two legs of the swap) are now (exactly four years later) as follows:

Spot exchange rate: 1.5 Swiss francs/U.S. dollar

The current structure of zero swap rates:

Maturity (years)	U.S. Dollar (% annual)	Swiss Franc (% annual)
1	9	5
2	9.5	5.75
3	10	6
4	10.25	6.25
5	10.75	6.5
6	11	7
7	11.5	7.5

a. Calculate the swap payments at the end of the fourth year (i.e., today).
b. Right after this payment, what is the market value of the swap to the Swiss firm?

12. A French corporation plans to invest in Thailand to develop a local subsidiary to promote its French products. The creation of this subsidiary should help boost its exports from France. The Thai baht is pegged to a basket of currencies dominated by the U.S. dollar, so borrowing in U.S. dollars would reduce the currency risk on this investment. The corporation needs to borrow $20 million for five years. A bank has proposed a five-year dollar loan at 7.75 percent. The French government wishes to support this type of foreign investment helping French exports. A French government agency can subsidize a 1.50 percent improvement in euro interest costs. In other words, the corporation can get a five-year, €22 million loan at 7.5 percent instead of the current market rate of 9 percent. The current spot exchange rate is €1.1 per dollar. A bank offers to write a currency swap for a principal of $20 million, whereby the corporation would pay dollars at 7.75 percent and receive euros at 9 percent. What could the corporation do to obtain a loan in dollars, its desired currency position, while capturing the French interest rate subsidy? What is the cost saving compared with directly borrowing in dollars?

13. Susan Fairfax is President of Reston. She realizes that her $10 million holding of Reston stock presents a problem in terms of diversification and specific risk for her total portfolio of $12 million ($10 million in Reston stock plus a $2 million savings portfolio). A major brokerage firm has reviewed her situation and proposed an equity swap having the following features:

Term:	3 years
Notional principal:	$10 million
Settlement frequency:	Annual, commencing at end of year 1

Fairfax pays to broker: Total return on Reston stock

Broker pays to Fairfax: Total return on S&P 500 stock index

Ignore the tax consequences of the swap transaction and assume Fairfax plans to renew the contract at the expiration of its three-year term.

  a. Justify advising Fairfax to enter into the swap, including in your response

     i. a description of the swap's effect on Fairfax's total portfolio and

     ii. two reasons why use of such a swap may be superior to an alternative strategy of selling a portion of her Reston stock.

  b. Explain one risk to be encountered by Fairfax under each of the three following scenarios, assuming that she enters the swap at the beginning of year 1. Your answer must cite a different risk for each scenario.

     i. At the end of year 1, Reston stock has significantly outperformed the S&P 500 index.

     ii. At the end of year 1, Reston stock has significantly underperformed the S&P 500.

     iii. At the end of year 3, Fairfax wants to negotiate a new three-year swap on the same terms as the original agreement, adjusted for the new market value of her Reston holding.

14. a. Calculate the payoff at expiration for a call option on the euro in which the underlying is at $0.90 at expiration, the options are on 62,500 euros, and the exercise price is

     i. $0.75

     ii. $0.95

  b. Calculate the payoff at expiration for a put option on the euro in which the underlying is at $0.90 at expiration, the options are on 62,500 euros, and the exercise price is

     i. $0.75

     ii. $0.95

15. An American investor believes that the dollar will depreciate and buys one call option on the euro at an exercise price of $1.10 per euro. The option premium is $0.01 per euro, or $625 per contract of 62,500 euros (Philadelphia).

  a. For what range of exchange rates should the investor exercise the call option at expiration?

  b. For what range of exchange rates will the investor realize a net profit, taking the original cost into account?

  c. If the investor had purchased a put with the same exercise price and premium, instead of a call, how would you answer the previous two questions?

16. You are currently borrowing $10 million at six-month LIBOR + 50 basis points. The LIBOR is at 4 percent. You expect to borrow this amount for five years but are worried that LIBOR will rise in the future. You can buy a 6 percent cap on six-month LIBOR over the next five years with an annual cost of 0.5 percent (paid semiannually). Describe the evolution of your borrowing costs under various interest rate scenarios.

17. A lender makes a loan of $5 million that carries an interest rate of six-month LIBOR + 125 basis points and matures in two years. The lender is worried about a decline in the LIBOR rate and in order to hedge against this risk decides to purchase a 5 percent floor on six-month LIBOR over the next two years. The annual floor premium is 0.75 percent

(paid semiannually). Indicate the annualized lending rates if LIBOR rates are above and below 5 percent.

18. You hold a diversified portfolio of German stocks with a value of €50 million. You are getting worried about the outcome of the next elections and wish to hedge your German stock market risk. However, you like the companies that you hold and believe that the German stock market will do well in the long run. Transaction costs are too high to sell the stocks now and buy them back in a few weeks. Instead, you decide to use DAX futures or options to temporarily protect the value of your portfolio. Current market quotations are as follows:

DAX index value:	Spot, 5,000
	June futures, 5,000
DAX call June 5,000:	62
DAX put June 5,000:	60
DAX put June 4,950:	30
DAX put June 4,900:	10

The standard contract size is €25 times the index for futures and €5 times the index for options.
a. What would you do to hedge your portfolio with futures?
b. What would you do to insure your portfolio with options?
c. Calculate the results of the four protection strategies: selling June futures, buying puts June 5000, buying puts June 4,950, and buying puts June 4,900. Look at the value of your portfolio, assuming that it follows the movements in the market exactly. Assume that the DAX index in June is equal to 4,800, 4,900, 5,000, 5,100, and 5,200, successively.

19. Consider a U.S. portfolio manager holding a portfolio of French stocks. The market value of the portfolio is €20 million, with a beta of 1.2 relative to the CAC index. In November, the spot value of the CAC index is 4,000, and the price of a futures contract on the CAC index for December delivery is 4,000. The dividend yield, euro interest rates, and dollar interest rates are all equal to 4 percent (flat yield curves).
a. The portfolio manager fears a drop in the French stock market (but not the euro). The size of CAC index futures contracts is €10 times the CAC index. There are futures contracts quoted with December delivery. How many contracts should he buy or sell to hedge the French stock market risk?
b. Puts on the CAC index with December expiration and a strike price of 4,000 sell for 50. Assume the standard contract size for the index options is €10 times the CAC index. How many puts should he buy or sell to insure the portfolio? Compare the results of this insurance with the hedge suggested previously. Assume that the CAC index in December is equal to 3,800, 4,000, and 4,200, successively.
c. Suppose the manager fears a depreciation of the euro relative to the U.S. dollar. Will the previously mentioned strategies protect against this depreciation?

20. You are an investment banker considering the issuance of a guaranteed note with stock index participation for a client. The current yield curve is flat at 8 percent for all maturities. Two-year at-the-money calls trade at 17.84 percent of the index value; three-year

at-the-money calls trade at 20 percent of the index value. You are hesitant about the terms to set in the structured note. You know that if you guarantee a higher coupon rate, the level of participation in the stock appreciation will be less.

a. Your supervisor asks you to compute the "fair" participation rate that would be feasible for various guaranteed coupon rates and maturities. Based on the current market conditions (as described), estimate the participation rates that are feasible with a maturity of two or three years, and a coupon rate of 0, 1, 2, 3, 5, and 7 percent.

b. Explain the relationship between the amount of the guaranteed coupon and the participation rate that can be offered.

Solutions

1. Following are the results for 10 contracts, in dollars:

	April 1	April 2	April 3	April 4	June 16	June 17
Gain/loss	0	−2,500	−51,250	183,750	−11,250	−63,750
Margin *before* cash flow	0	17,750	−33,500	204,000	9,000	−43,500
Cash flow from investor	20,250	0	53,750	−183,750	11,250	43,500
Margin *after* cash flow	20,250	17,750	20,250	20,250	20,250	0

- On April 2, you lose $2,500 = (12,500,000)(10)(0.01054 − 0.01056)$. Your margin is reduced to $17,750, but you remain above the maintenance margin of $(10)(1,500) = $15,000$. No cash addition is needed.
- On April 3, you lose another $51,250 = (12,500,000)(10)(0.01013 − 0.01054)$. You must get the margin back to the initial level of $20,250 and transfer $53,750 to your margin account.
- On April 4, you gain $183,750 = (12,500,000)(10)(0.01160 − 0.01013)$. You can withdraw exactly this amount, keeping the margin at $20,250.
- On June 16, you lose $11,250 = (12,500,000)(10)(0.01151 − 0.01160)$ and must transfer this amount to reconstitute the initial margin.
- On June 17, you lose $63,750 = (12,500,000)(10)(0.01100 − 0.01151)$, and the contracts expire. You must add $43,500 to your initial margin and close the position.

The total gain is $55,000. This does not include any financing cost of the margin.

2. a. The implicit interest rate is $100 − 93.28 = 6.72\%$. This is a forward interest rate. It suggests that the term structure of interest rate is upward sloping (long-term rates higher than short-term rates).

b. Your position will be to borrow (i.e., *sell* debt paper). Your risk exposure here is that interest rates will rise, and that the price of the Eurodollar contract will fall. To hedge interest rate risk, you need to *sell forward* debt paper. Therefore, to lock in the borrowing rate, you should sell 10 Eurodollar contracts.

c. There would have been various marking-to-market gains and losses from April 1 to June 17. The net result, neglecting financing costs (or profits) on the margin, is a gain of $(10)(1,000,000)(0.9328 − 0.91)/4 = $57,000$. This gain offsets your increased borrowing costs.

3. a. In order to prevent any arbitrage opportunities, the forward price F should be $F = €1.1(1.08)/(1.05) = €1.13143/\$$.

b. If the trader invested €1 at the euro risk-free rate, he would have $1(1.08) = €1.08$ at the end of one year. Alternatively, he could convert €1 to U.S. dollars, invest at the U.S. risk-free rate, and use a forward contract to lock in the rate at which U.S. dollars are converted back to euros. In this scenario:
- One euro would be worth $1/1.1 = \$0.90909$.
- Invest this for one year and receive $= 0.90909(1.05) = \$0.95454$.
- Use the short forward contract to sell dollars for euros at €1.15 per dollar $= 1.15(0.95454) = €1.09772$.

Because this option yields more than investing at the euro interest rate, there is an arbitrage opportunity. To earn this arbitrage profit, you would borrow €1 at an interest rate of 8 percent. Convert to U.S. dollars at the spot exchange rate and invest at the U.S. risk-free rate and then use a forward contract to convert dollars back to euros. The arbitrage profit per euro is €1.09772 − €1.08 = €0.01772.

4. a. To prevent any arbitrage opportunities, the forward price F should be $F = \$0.90(1.07)/(1.05) = \$0.91714$ per euro.
   b. If the trader invested \$1 at the U.S. risk-free rate, at the end of one year he would have $1(1.07) = \$1.07$. Alternatively, he could convert \$1 to euros, invest at the euro risk-free rate, and use a forward contract to lock in the rate at which euros are converted back to dollars. In this scenario:
   - One dollar would be worth $1/0.90 = €1.1111$.
   - Invest this for one year and receive $1.1111(1.05) = €1.16667$.
   - Use a forward contract to sell euros for dollars at \$0.85 per euro, receiving $1.16667(0.85) = \$0.99167$ per euro.

   Because this option yields less than investing at the U.S. interest rate, there is an arbitrage opportunity. To earn this arbitrage profit, you would borrow $€1/0.9 = €1.1111$ at an interest rate of 5 percent. Convert to 1 U.S. dollar and invest at the U.S. risk-free rate and then use a forward contract to convert a portion of the dollar proceeds to euros to repay the loan plus interest.
   - One dollar invested at the risk-free rate $= 1(1.07) = \$1.07$.
   - The repayment of the euro loan $= 1.1111(1.05) = €1.16667$.
   - Using the forward contract, you would convert $\$0.99167 = (1.16667)(0.85)$ to euros.

   The arbitrage profit per dollar $= \$1.07 − \$0.99167 = \$0.07833$.

5. a. A long hedge would be appropriate here. Because the objective is to lock in the price at which the manager can purchase shares at a future date, buying a futures contract is the appropriate hedge transaction.
   b. The number of futures contracts $= N = 1.1 × [250,000,000/(1225 × 250)] = 897.96$, or 898 contracts long.

6. a. A short hedge would be appropriate here. Because the objective is to lock in the price at which the manager can effectively sell a portion of the portfolio, selling a futures contract is the appropriate hedge transaction.
   b. The number of futures contracts $= N = 0.90 × [500,000,000/(1050 × 250)] = 1714.29$, or 1714 contracts short.

7. The company can enter into a swap to pay a fixed rate of 5 percent and receive a floating rate of LIBOR. Remember that the floating payment is based on LIBOR in arrears and is therefore known now. It will be reset after six months on the settlement date.

$$\text{Interest payment on the floating rate note} = \$10,000,000 \times (0.04 + 0.0025)$$
$$\times (180/360) = \$212,500$$

The first swap payment is calculated as the difference between

$$\text{Swap fixed payment} = \$10,000,000(0.05)(180/360) = \$250,000$$

and

$$\text{Swap floating receipt} = \$10,000,000(0.04)(180/360) = \$200,000$$

The first net swap payment is \$50,000 paid by the company to the counterparty.

$$\text{The overall cash payment made by the company} = \$212,500 + \$50,000$$
$$= \$262,500$$

Thus, the company has converted its floating rate to a fixed rate of 5.25 percent per year.

8. Because the risk exposure faced by the bank is a decline in interest rates, the bank should enter into the swap to receive a fixed rate of 5.25 percent and pay a floating rate of $\text{LIBOR}_{t-1} + 0.0025$. Clearly, the bank should choose swap (b).

 The bank receives $\text{LIBOR} + 0.65\%$ on the loan. On the swap, the bank receives the difference between 5.25 percent and $\text{LIBOR} + 0.25\%$. The net result is that the bank receives a fixed interest rate of 5.65 percent:

$$\text{LIBOR} + 0.65\% + (5.25 - \text{LIBOR} - 0.25\%) = 5.65\%$$

This can be confirmed by looking at the semiannual payments:
1. Interest received on the loan $= \$25,000,000(\text{LIBOR}_{t-1} + 0.0065)(180/360)$
2. Swap floating payment $= \$25,000,000(\text{LIBOR}_{t-1} + 0.0025)(180/360)$
 Swap fixed receipt $= \$25,000,000(0.0525)(180/360) = \$656,250$
 The overall cash payment received by the bank $= \$25,000,000[0.0525$
 $+ (\text{LIBOR}_{t-1} + 0.0065) - (\text{LIBOR}_{t-1} + 0.0025)](180/360)$
 $= \$25,000,000(0.0565)(180/360) = \$706,250$

Thus, the bank has converted its floating rate to a fixed rate of 5.65 percent per year. The interest payment received by the bank is \$706,250.

9. a. There is no payment at the beginning of the swap; the notional principals are equal in value.
 b. The semiannual payments are calculated as the difference between the following:

 The U.S. company owes the counterparty €1,125,000
$$= €45,000,000(0.05)(180/360)$$
 The counterparty owes the U.S. company \$1,500,000
$$= \$50,000,000(0.06)(180/360)$$

 c. The payments at the end of the swap are calculated as the difference between the value of the notional principals and the difference between the last semiannual payments, valued at the then-current spot exchange rate.
 d. This currency swap might suit a U.S. company that has a customer based in Germany (or anywhere in the Eurozone). The supply contract may involve semiannual shipments for which the U.S. company will receive €1,125,000. The currency swap will

ensure that the U.S. company is hedged against declines in the value of the euro, in which case the company will be receiving a lower dollar price for supplies.

10. a. There is no payment at the beginning of the swap; the notional principals are equal in value.

    b. The annual payments are calculated as the difference between the following:

    The counterparty owes the British company $2,681,250 = $41,250,000 × 0.065
    The British company owes the counterparty £1,375,000 = £25,000,000 × 0.055

    c. This currency swap might suit a British company that has a supplier based in the United States. The supply contract may involve annual shipments for which the British company will have to pay $2,681,250. The currency swap will ensure that the British company is hedged against declines in the value of the pound, in which case the company will be paying a higher price in pounds for supplies from the United States.

11. a. Each year, the Swiss firm receives Swiss francs and pays dollars. Given the interest rates as of the inception of the swap contract (8 percent in dollars and 4 percent in Swiss francs), the net payment for year 4 is the balance of
    - receipt of SFr6,000,000 = SFr150,000,000 × 0.04, and
    - payment of $8,000,000 = $100,000,000 × 0.08

    Net cash flow = 6 − (1.5 × 8) = −SFr6 million, or −$4 million

    This is a net payment of SFr6 million by the Swiss firm.

    b. Right after the fourth payment, the market value of the swap, V, is

    $$V = P_{SFr} - \text{spot SFr/\$} \times P_\$$$

    where

    P_{SFr} is the value of a SFr150 million three-year bond with an SFr6 million annual coupon
    $P_\$$ is the value of a $100 million three-year bond with an $8 million annual coupon

    $$V = \frac{6}{1.05} + \frac{6}{(1.0575)^2} + \frac{156}{(1.06)^3} - 1.5\left[\frac{8}{1.09} + \frac{8}{(1.095)^2} + \frac{108}{(1.1)^3}\right]$$
    $$= -\text{SFr}0.67 \text{ million, or } -\$0.447 \text{ million}$$

12. The French corporation could borrow directly 20 million dollars at 7.75 percent, with annual interest rate payments of $1,550,000. Instead, the French corporation should
    - borrow €22 million at the subsidized rate of 7.5 percent. The interest payment will be €1,650,000.
    - swap euros for dollars. The corporation would swap €22 million (equal to $20 million), agreeing to pay 7.75 percent on dollars and receive 9 percent on euros. Thus, the annual swap interest cash flows are

    Corporation will pay = 0.0775 × $20,000,000 = $1,550,000

    and

    Corporation will receive = 0.09 × €22,000,000 = €1,980,000

with a final cash flow including the principal exchange of €22 million for $20 million. Note that this is a currency swap involving the exchange of notional principals at initiation and swap maturity.

Effectively, the corporation will end up borrowing 20 million in dollars at 7.75 percent (annual interest of $1,550,000) and make an annual 1.5 percent cost saving in euros (annual cost saving of €330,000). This is illustrated in the following table, which gives the payments (negative sign) and receipts (positive sign) of the French corporation:

	Year 1	Year 2	Year 3	Year 4	Year 5	Year 5
	Interest	Interest	Interest	Interest	Interest	Principal
Loan in €	−€1,650,000	−€1,650,000	−€1,650,000	−€1,650,000	−€1,650,000	−€22,000,000
Swap						
▪ € leg	+€1,980,000	+€1,980,000	+€1,980,000	+€1,980,000	+€1,980,000	+€22,000,000
▪ $ leg	−$1,550,000	−$1,550,000	−$1,550,000	−$1,550,000	−$1,550,000	−$20,000,000
Net Cash Flow						
▪ €	+€330,000	+€330,000	+€330,000	+€330,000	+€330,000	0
▪ $	−$1,550,000	−$1,550,000	−$1,550,000	−$1,550,000	−$1,550,000	−$20,000,000

13. a. The swap is an appropriate and cost-effective tool for controlling risk in Fairfax's portfolio.
   i. Reston Industries represents a disproportionately large portion of Fairfax's total portfolio. As a consequence, the portfolio is nondiversified and exposed to a high level of specific risk. Entering into the swap has the desired effect of diversifying Fairfax's portfolio, replacing its exposure to the performance of Reston stock with an equivalent exposure to the performance of the S&P 500 index. Specific risk in the portfolio is substantially reduced.
   ii. As a strategy for hedging Fairfax's exposure to Reston, the swap is potentially superior to an equivalent buy–sell strategy in the underlying securities:
      ▪ The swap allows Fairfax to reduce her exposure to Reston stock without being taxed on capital gains on the sale of Reston stocks.
      ▪ The swap avoids the transactions costs of buying and selling in the cash market.
      ▪ The swap can be implemented quickly in a simple transaction, avoiding the risk of being exposed to Reston's performance during a transitional period of buying and selling in the cash market.
      ▪ Fairfax may be restricted or inhibited from selling her Reston holdings because of regulatory issues (e.g., stock registration) or internal corporate considerations (e.g., her position as president).
   b. i. Personal liquidity and cash flow risk: Because Reston has outperformed the S&P 500 index, Fairfax must pay her broker the difference.
      ii. Counterparty risk: Because Reston has underperformed the S&P 500, Fairfax should receive a payment from her broker. The broker could default, resulting in the swap's failure as a hedge.
      iii. Rollover risk: Fairfax is unhedged against her Reston holding until she can enter into a new swap. There is no guarantee of being able to replicate the original swap terms at a reasonable cost.

14. a. Price of euro at expiration = $0.90
   i. Call payoff, $K = 0.75$: $\text{Max}(0, 0.90 - 0.75) \times 62,500 = \$9,375$
   ii. Call payoff, $K = 0.95$: $\text{Max}(0, 0.90 - 0.95) \times 62,500 = 0$.

b. Price of euro at expiration = $0.90
    i. Put payoff, $K = 0.75$: Max(0, 0.75 − 0.90) × 62,500 = 0
    ii. Put payoff, $K = 0.95$: Max(0, 0.95 − 0.90) × 62,500 = $3,125

15. a. If the exchange rate at expiration is greater than the exercise price, the call option is in-the-money and should be exercised. Therefore, an investor should exercise the call if the $/€ spot exchange rate is above $1.10 at expiration.

    b. The investor will realize a net profit if the exchange rate movement covers his initial investment. Therefore, the $/€ spot exchange rate must be above $1.11. This does not take into account the financing cost of the purchase of the call.

    c. In the case of put options, the option is in-the-money when the price at expiration is less than the exercise price. Therefore, the investor would exercise the put if the $/€ spot exchange rate were below $1.10 on the last day of the option, and would make a net profit if the $/€ rate moved below $1.09.

16. Let's study the net cash flow on each semiannual payment date:

If LIBOR ≤ 6%

The cap is worthless.
The annualized borrowing cost = interest rate on loan + premium paid for the option = LIBOR + 0.5% + 0.5% = LIBOR + 1%
The dollar cost = (LIBOR + 1%)($10,000,000)

If LIBOR > 6%

The cap pays the option holder the difference between LIBOR and 6 percent.
The annualized borrowing cost = interest rate on loan + premium paid for the option − (LIBOR − 6%) = LIBOR + 0.5% + 0.5% + 6% − LIBOR = 7%
The dollar cost = (7%)($10,000,000) = $700,000

Thus, the interest rate cap ensures that borrowing costs are never higher than 7 percent per year.

17. Let's study the net cash flow on each semiannual payment date:

If LIBOR ≥ 5%

The floor is worthless.
The annualized lending rate = interest rate on loan − premium paid for the option = LIBOR + 1.25% − 0.75% = LIBOR + 0.5%
The dollar amount of interest received = (LIBOR + 0.5%)($5,000,000)

If LIBOR < 5%

The floor pays the option holder the difference between 5 percent and LIBOR.
The annualized lending rate = interest rate on loan − premium paid for the option + 5% − LIBOR = LIBOR + 1.25% − 0.75% + 5% − LIBOR = 5.5%
The dollar amount of interest received = (5.5%)($5,000,000) = $275,000

Thus, the interest rate floor ensures that the lending rate never falls below 5.5 percent per year.

18. a. Because you are long on the underlying (the German stock portfolio), a short futures position would be an appropriate hedge. You should sell DAX futures. Assuming that the portfolio moves in line with the stock index, the hedge ratio is equal to 1. Hence, you would sell:

$$\frac{50,000,000}{(5,000)(25)} = 400 \text{ contracts}$$

b. Buy DAX puts. The put options allow you to lock in the rate at which you can sell and thus provide a hedge against falling equity values.

$$\frac{50,000,000}{(5,000)(5)} = 2,000 \text{ contracts}$$

The cost for June 5,000 puts is $(2000)(5)(60) = €600,000$.

c. When we hedge with futures, we will be using 400 contracts; when we hedge with options, we will be using 2,000 contracts, because the contracts' sizes are different. The simulated results at maturity are given in the following table. We basically assume that the portfolio is equal to 10,000 times the DAX index. We also assume a zero interest rate; otherwise, we would have to reflect the fact that the payment of option premiums precedes the expiration date.

Sample calculations when DAX index is at 4,800:

- *Unhedged position:* We assume that the portfolio rises or falls by the same percentage as the index. The DAX has declined by 4 percent: $(4,800 - 5,000)/5,000 = -4\%$. Thus, the new portfolio value is $50,000,000(1 - 0.04) = €48,000,000$.
- *Hedged with futures:* Because we have a short futures position, the 4 percent decline in the portfolio value is offset by a 4 percent rise in the value of your short futures position. Thus, the value of the overall position remains at €50,000,000.
- *Insured with June 5,000 puts:* The gain on the put position $= (5,000 - 4,800) - 60 = 140$. For 2,000 contracts, the gain $= (140)(2,000)(5) = €1,400,000$. Thus, the overall value of the portfolio with the long put is $48,000,000 + 1,400,000 = €49,400,000$.
- *Insured with June 4,950 puts:* The gain on the put position $= (4,950 - 4,800) - 30 = 120$. For 2,000 contracts, the gain $= (120)(2,000)(5) = €1,200,000$. Thus, the overall value of the portfolio with the long put is $48,000,000 + 1,200,000 = €49,200,000$.
- *Insured with June 4,900 puts:* The gain on the put position $= (4,900 - 4,800) - 10 = 90$. For 2,000 contracts, the gain $= (90)(2,000)(5) = €900,000$. Thus, the overall value of the portfolio with the long put is $48,000,000 + 900,000 = €48,900,000$.

Value of the Portfolio at Maturity (in € million)

			Insured with Puts		
DAX Index	**Unhedged**	**Hedged with Futures**	**June 5,000**	**June 4,950**	**June 4,900**
4,800	48.00	50.00	49.40	49.20	48.90
4,900	49.00	50.00	49.40	49.20	48.90
5,000	50.00	50.00	49.40	49.70	49.90
5,100	51.00	50.00	50.40	50.70	50.90
5,200	52.00	50.00	51.40	51.70	51.90

19. a. Because the beta of the portfolio is 1.2, the hedge ratio should be equal to 1.2. Because you are long the underlying (the portfolio), a short futures position will afford a hedge against declines in share values. The number of contracts to be sold is

$$1.2\left(\frac{20,000,000}{(4,000)(10)}\right) = 600$$

   b. The manager should buy 600 put contracts. The cost is €10 × 50 × 600 = €300,000. If the CAC index goes above 4,000 in December, the put option will expire worthless and the manager is out the premium paid of €300,000. If the index falls below 4,000, the gain on the put position will offset declines in portfolio value. Assuming that the portfolio exactly follows the CAC index with a beta of 1.2, we can simulate the result of the strategies in December.

   Sample calculations when CAC index is at 4,200 in December (5 percent rise in the index):

   - *Unhedged position:* The portfolio rises or falls by (1.2)(the percentage change in the index). The CAC has risen by 5% = (4,200 − 4,000)/4,000. The portfolio rises by 6% = (1.2)(0.05). Thus, the new portfolio value is 20,000,000(1 + 0.06) = €21,200,000, a gain of €1,200,000.
   - *Hedged with futures:* Because we have a short futures position of 600 contracts, there is a loss on the futures position equal to €10 × (4,000 − 4,200) × 600 = −€1,200,000. The 6 percent rise in the portfolio value is offset by a 6 percent loss of your short futures position. Thus, the value of the overall position remains at €20,000,000.
   - *Insured with December 4,000 puts:* The put option expires worthless, so the only loss on the put is the premium paid. For 600 contracts the loss = −10 × 50 × 600 = −€300,000. Thus, the overall value of the portfolio with the long put is 21,200,000 − 300,000 = €20,900,000.

Value of the Portfolio in December (in € million)

CAC Index	Unhedged	Hedged with Futures	Insured with Puts
3,800	18.8	20.0	19.7
4,000	20.0	20.0	19.7
4,200	21.2	20.0	20.9

   c. No. CAC futures or options cannot protect against a depreciation of the euro. You would have to use currency futures or option on the euro to hedge against a depreciation in the euro.

20. a. The guaranteed note can be decomposed as the sum of a straight bond with a coupon C plus p times a call option on the index (p is the participation rate). For a two-year note, we have

$$100 = \frac{C}{1.08} + \frac{C}{1.08^2} + \frac{100}{1.08^2} + p \times 17.84$$

   Hence,

$$p = \frac{14.266 - 1.7833 \times C}{17.84}$$

For a three-year note, we have

$$100 = \frac{C}{1.08} + \frac{C}{1.08^2} + \frac{C}{1.08^3} + \frac{100}{1.08^3} + p \times 20$$

Hence,

$$p = \frac{20.617 - 2.5771 \times C}{20}$$

Sample calculations at a 2 percent coupon rate:
- For the two-year bond, $p = [14.266 - (1.7833)(100)(0.02)]/17.84 = 59.97\%$
- For the three-year bond, $p = [20.617 - (2.5771)(100)(0.02)]/20 = 77.31\%$

The following table gives the fair participation rates for various coupon rates:

Coupon Rate	p (2-Year Bond)	p (3-Year Bond)
0%	79.97%	103.08%
1%	69.97%	90.20%
2%	59.97%	77.31%
3%	49.98%	64.43%
5%	29.99%	38.66%
7%	9.99%	12.89%

b. There is a negative relationship between the coupon rate and participation rates that can be offered in the option. This is because a higher coupon rate leaves less to be invested in the call option.

Bibliography

Black, F., and Scholes, M. "The Pricing of Options and Corporate Liabilities," *Journal of Political Economy*, May/June 1973.

Chance, D. *Analysis of Derivatives for the CFA® Program*, Charlottesville, VA: AIMR, 2003.

Cornell, B., and Reiganum, M. "Forward and Futures Prices: Evidence from the Foreign Exchange Market," *Journal of Finance*, December 1981.

Duffie, D., and Huang, M. "Swap Rates and Credit Quality," *Journal of Finance*, 51(3), July 1996.

Fleming, J., and Whaley, R. E. "The Value of the Wildcard Option," *Journal of Finance*, March 1994.

Hull, J. C. *Fundamentals of Futures and Options Markets*, 4th ed., Upper Saddle River, NJ: Prentice Hall, 2002.

Kolb, R. W. *Futures, Options and Swaps*, 3rd ed., Malden, MA: Blackwell, 2001.

11

Currency Risk Management

LEARNING OUTCOMES

After completing this chapter, you will be able to do the following:

- Demonstrate how to protect a portfolio against currency risks

- Demonstrate how to hedge the current value of a foreign investment

- Discuss the difference between translation and economic risk

- Discuss the factors to consider in hedging the future value of a foreign investment

- Discuss how to hedge multicurrency portfolios

- Discuss how to insure a portfolio against currency risks using currency options

- Discuss dynamic hedging strategies with currency options

- Calculate the future value of a portfolio under several alternative strategies, including no hedging, hedging with futures, and insuring with options with different strike prices

- Discuss methods to reduce currency exposure and to take positions in foreign markets without incurring excessive exchange rate risk and without using currency futures, forwards, or options as hedging vehicles

The traditional international investment strategy is first to decide on an international asset allocation. An allocation breaks down a portfolio by both asset class (short-term deposit, bond, equity, sectors) and country or currency of investment (U.S. dollar, British pound, euro). The resulting allocation can be used to form a matrix of currencies and asset classes. Ten percent of a typical portfolio's value may be allocated to Japanese stocks, 5 percent to Eurobonds, and so forth. Specific bonds and stocks are selected using the various techniques discussed in previous chapters. Once

571

a portfolio is structured, it must be managed according to changes in expectations. For example, periodic revisions of the forecasted earnings of specific companies can lead to equity arbitrage within a portfolio. More common revisions in expectations, however, are the result of macroeconomic variables. News about economic growth or changes in interest rates may cause a manager to alter his asset allocation, at least temporarily. But frequent reallocation can lead to heavy transaction costs, especially on bonds and some illiquid foreign stocks.

Derivative instruments, such as options and futures, are used domestically to hedge risks. They protect a manager from being forced to arbitrage or liquidate a large part of her portfolio. For example, interest rate futures or options may be used to hedge a long-term bond portfolio if fears about a rise in interest rates materialize. Similarly, a domestic manager who is heavily invested in bonds but suddenly becomes bullish on the stock market can immediately act on his expectation by buying stock index futures or options and thereafter slowly switching his portfolio from bonds to stocks. This technique reduces transactions costs, gives the manager time to select the best stocks, and locks in potential profits on the anticipated rise in the stock market. Moreover, if, after a few days, the manager changes his mind about how well the stock market will perform, he needs only close his futures and options position and stick with the initial portfolio allocation. These and other short-term risk management techniques are used extensively by portfolio managers when the use of derivative instruments are allowed. The use of financial futures and options in controlling portfolio risk is described in textbooks that deal with domestic investment. The most important area of risk management in international investment is currency risk. This chapter is therefore devoted to currency risk management.

Most portfolio managers are often confronted with practical problems such as these:

- A U.S. investor is bullish about her portfolio of Australian stocks but is concerned that the Australian dollar may drop sharply in the wake of local elections. On the other hand, the Australian dollar may appreciate strongly as a result of these elections.

- A Japanese investor holds British gilts. He expects the long-term U.K. interest rate to drop, which in turn would cause a depreciation of the pound that will offset the capital gain on the bond in pound terms.

- A Canadian investor would like to buy KLM stock because she is bullish about the Dutch airline, but she is concerned that the euro may depreciate.

- A British investor specializes in forecasting monetary variables, such as interest and exchange rates. Which strategies should he choose to capitalize on his forecasts?

This chapter is intended to assist the reader in better handling these kinds of situations. The issue of whether to systematically hedge currency risk is addressed in Chapter 4.

Hedging with Futures or Forward Currency Contracts

Either *futures* or *forward* currency contracts may be used to hedge a portfolio. They differ in several ways, as outlined in Chapter 10. Futures are exchange-traded contracts while forwards are over-the-counter (OTC) contracts. Currency forwards are sometimes referred to as *currency swaps*. Portfolio managers tend to primarily use forward contracts in currency hedging. But forward and futures contracts allow a manager to take the same economic position. Therefore, in this chapter, the generic term *futures* will denote both futures and forward (or swap) contracts.

The Basic Approach: Hedging the Principal

Hedging with futures is very simple. An investor takes a position with a foreign exchange contract that offsets the currency exposure associated with the principal being hedged. In other words, a citizen of Country A who wants to hedge a portfolio of assets denominated in currency B would sell a futures contract to exchange currency B for currency A. The size of the contract would equal the market value ("principal") of the assets to be hedged. For example, a U.S. investor with £1 million invested in British gilts (treasury bonds) would sell futures for £1 million worth of dollars. The direction of a foreign exchange rate contract is often confusing because it involves the exchange rates of two currencies.

On the Chicago Mercantile Exchange (CME), investors can buy and sell contracts of £62,500 wherein the futures price is expressed in dollars per pound. The same size contract is also found on the London International Financial Futures Exchange (LIFFE). Let us assume that on September 12, a U.S. investor can buy or sell futures with delivery in December for 1.95 dollars per pound; the spot exchange rate is 2.00 dollars per pound. In order to hedge her £1 million principal, the investor must sell a total of 16 contracts. Now let us assume that a few weeks later, the futures and spot exchange rates drop to \$1.85 and \$1.90, respectively, whereas the pound value of the British assets rises to 1,010,000. The hedge is undertaken at time 0, and we study the rate of return on the portfolio from time 0 to a future time t. We introduce the following notation:

V_t The value of the portfolio of foreign assets to hedge, measured in foreign currency at time t (e.g., £1 million)

V_t^* The value of the portfolio of foreign assets measured in domestic currency (e.g., \$2 million)

S_t The spot exchange rate: domestic currency value of one unit of foreign currency quoted at time t (e.g., \$2.00/£)

F_t The futures exchange rate: domestic currency value of one unit of foreign currency quoted at time t (e.g., \$1.95/£)

R The rate of return of the portfolio measured in foreign currency terms, $(V_t - V_0)/V_0$

R^* The rate of return of the portfolio measured in domestic currency terms, $(V_t^* - V_0^*)/V_0^*$

s The percentage movement in the exchange rate, $(S_t - S_0)/S_0$

In this example, the pound value of the British assets appreciates by 1 percent and the pound exchange rate drops by 5 percent, causing a loss in the dollar value on the portfolio of 4.05 percent. In absolute dollar terms, this loss in portfolio value is $81,000:

$$V_t^* - V_0^* = V_t S_t - V_0 S_0 \tag{11.1}$$

Hence, $\$1,919,000 - \$2,000,000 = (£1,010,000 \times \$1.90/£) - (£1,000,000 \times \$2.00/£) = -\$81,000$. On the other hand, the realized gain on the futures contract sale is $100,000, as follows:

$$V_0(-F_t + F_0) = \text{Realized gain} \tag{11.2}$$

Hence, $£1,000,000 \times (\$1.95/£ - \$1.85/£) = \$100,000$. Therefore, the net profit on the hedged position is $19,000:

$$\text{Profit} = V_t S_t - V_0 S_0 - V_0 (F_t - F_0) \tag{11.3}$$

Hence, Profit $= -\$81,000 + \$100,000 = \$19,000$. The rate of return in dollars on the hedged position, R_H, can be found by dividing the profit in Equation 11.3 by the original portfolio value $V_0 S_0$. We find

$$R_H = \frac{V_t S_t - V_0 S_0}{V_0 S_0} - \frac{F_t - F_0}{S_0} = R^* - R_F \tag{11.4}$$

where R_F is the futures price movement as a percentage of the spot rate $(F_t - F_0)/S_0$. In the example, we find

$$\text{Hedged return} = R_H = \frac{19,000}{2,000,000} = 0.95\%$$

This position is almost perfectly hedged, because the 1 percent return on the British asset is transformed into a 0.95 percent return in U.S. dollars, despite the drop in value of the British pound. The slight difference between the two numbers is explained by the fact that the investor hedged only the principal (£1 million), not the unexpected return on the British investment (equal here to 1 percent). The 5 percent drop in sterling value applied to this 1 percent return exactly equals $1\% \times 5\% = 0.05\%$.

EXHIBIT 11.1

Relationships between Portfolio Value and Rate of Return

	Period 0	Period t	Rate of Return (%)
Portfolio value (in pounds), V	1,000,000	1,010,000	1.00
Portfolio value (in dollars), V^*	2,000,000	1,919,000	−4.05
Exchange rate ($/pound), S	2.00	1.90	−5.00
Futures rate ($/pound), F	1.95	1.85	−5.00

The exact relationship between dollar and pound returns on the foreign portfolio is as follows:

$$R^* = R + s(1 + R) \tag{11.5}$$

Hence, $R^* = 1\% - 5(1.01)\% = -4.05\%$

The currency contribution, $R^* - R$, is equal to exchange rate variation plus the cross-product sR (equal here to 0.05 percent). When the value of the portfolio in foreign currency fluctuates widely, the difference can become significant over long periods. This implies that the amount of currency hedging should be adjusted periodically to reflect movements in the value of the position to be hedged. A portfolio manager could decide to hedge the expected future value of the portfolio rather than its current (principal) value. This could be risky if expectations do not materialize; and therefore this approach is only applied for fixed-income securities to hedge both the principal value and the yield to be accrued. Still, periodic adjustment of the currency hedge would be required to cover unexpected capital gains or losses on the price of the fixed-income securities.

The hedge result could also be affected by the basis; that is, the difference between the futures and the spot prices. Basis risk is discussed on page 580.

EXAMPLE 11.1   HEDGED PORTFOLIO

You are French and own a portfolio of U.S. stocks worth $1 million. The current spot and one-month forward exchange rates are €1/$. Interest rates are equal in both countries. You are worried that the results of U.S. elections could lead to a strong depreciation of the dollar and you decide to sell forward $1 million to hedge currency risk. A week later, your U.S. stock portfolio has gone up to $1.02 million, and the spot and forward exchange rates are now €0.95/$. Analyze the return on your hedged portfolio.

SOLUTION

The U.S. stock portfolio went up by 2 percent, but the dollar lost 5 percent relative to the euro. If the portfolio had not been hedged, its return in euros would have been

$$\frac{1{,}020{,}000 \times 0.95 - 1{,}000{,}000 \times 1}{1{,}000{,}000 \times 1} = -3.1\%$$

As per Equation 11.3, your profit on the hedge portfolio in euros is

$$\begin{aligned} \text{Profit} &= 1{,}020{,}000 \times 0.95 - 1{,}000{,}000 \times 1 - 1{,}000{,}000 \times (0.95 - 1) \\ &= 19{,}000 \end{aligned}$$

The rate of return on the hedged portfolio in euros is equal to 19,000/ 1,000,000 = 1.9%, which is very close to the 2 percent portfolio rate of return in dollars. The difference comes from the fact that the dollar capital gain on the U.S. portfolio (2 percent) was not hedged and suffered the 5 percent currency loss.

We could also directly apply Equation 11.4:

$$R^* - R_F = -3.1\% + 5\% = 1.9\%$$

Minimum-Variance Hedge Ratio

The objective of a currency hedge is to minimize the exposure to exchange rate movement. If the foreign investment were simply a foreign currency deposit—a fixed amount of local currency—it would be sufficient to sell forward an equivalent amount of foreign currency to eliminate currency risk. However, a problem appears when the foreign currency value of a foreign investment reacts *systematically* to an exchange rate movement. For example, a drop in the value of the British pound could lead to an increase in the value of a British company (measured in pounds). This is because this pound depreciation will increase the pound value of cash flows received from abroad, as well as make the company's products more attractive abroad. Another example is provided by bonds issued in a country that has an exchange rate target. A depreciation in its domestic currency will lead the country to raise its interest rates, pushing local bond prices down. In both cases, there is a covariance[1] between the asset return measured in local currency and the exchange rate movements. The covariance between asset returns and movements in the local currency value is negative in the first case and positive in the second case.

One objective is to search for minimum variability in the value of the hedged portfolio. Investors usually care about the rate of return on their investment and the variance thereof. So, if they decide to hedge, investors would like to set the hedge ratio h to minimize the variance of the return on the hedged portfolio. Although the hedge ratio was defined in Chapter 10, it bears repeating that it is the ratio of the size of the short futures position in foreign currency to the size of the currency exposure (value of the portfolio in foreign currency). For example, the hedge ratio is one if an investor has a portfolio of British gilts worth 1 million pounds and decides to sell forward 1 million pounds in futures currency contracts. It is easy to show that the rate of return on a hedged portfolio, R_H, is equal to the rate of return on the original portfolio (unhedged), R^*, minus h times the percentage change on the futures price, R_F:

$$R_H = R^* - h \times R_F \tag{11.6}$$

As shown in Chapter 10, the optimal hedge ratio h^*, which minimizes the variance of R_H, is equal to the covariance of the portfolio return to be hedged with the return on the futures, divided by the variance of the return on the futures

$$h^* = \frac{\text{cov}(R^*, R_F)}{\sigma_F^2} \tag{11.7}$$

This optimal hedge ratio is sometimes called the *regression hedge ratio* because it can be estimated as the slope coefficient of the regression of the asset, or portfolio, return on the futures return:

$$R^* = a + h R_F \tag{11.8}$$

where R^* is the return on the asset or portfolio, R_F is the return on the futures, and a is a constant term.

---

[1] Remember that the covariance between two variables is equal to the correlation times the product of the standard deviations of the two variables.

EXAMPLE 11.2   PORTFOLIO WITH A FIFTY PERCENT HEDGE RATIO

You are French and own a portfolio of U.S. stocks worth $1 million. The current spot and one-month forward exchange rates are €1/$. Interest rates are equal in both countries. You are worried that the results of U.S. elections could lead to a strong depreciation of the dollar and decide to hedge 50 percent of the portfolio value against currency risk ($h = 0.5$). A week later, your U.S. stock portfolio has gone up to $1.01 million, and the spot and forward exchange rates are now €0.95/$. Analyze the return on your hedged portfolio.

SOLUTION

The U.S. stock portfolio went up by 1 percent, but the dollar lost 5 percent relative to the euro. If the portfolio had not been hedged, its return in euros would have been

$$R^* = \frac{1{,}010{,}000 \times 0.95 - 1{,}000{,}000 \times 1}{1{,}000{,}000 \times 1} = -4.05\%$$

According to Equation 11.6, the return on your 50 percent-hedged portfolio is

$$R_H = R^* - h \times R_F = -4.05\% - 0.5 \times (-5\%) = -1.55\%$$

To get a better understanding of this minimum-variance hedge ratio, it is useful to substitute the value of R^* given in Equation 11.5 into Equation 11.6. From now on, we will further assume that the cross-product term of Equation 11.5 is small and will drop it.[2] We find

$$R_H = R + s - hR_F \tag{11.9}$$

The futures exchange rate differs from the spot exchange rate by a "basis" equal to the interest rate differential (see Chapters 1 and 10). Let's first assume that the basis is zero (interest rates equal in the two currencies) and remains so over time. Hence, the futures exchange rate is equal to the spot exchange rate. Then the rate of return on a futures contract, $R_F = (F_t - F_0)/S_0$, is equal to the spot exchange rate movement, $s = (S_t - S_0)/S_0$. Equation 11.9 can now be written as follows:

$$R_H = R + s(1 - h) \tag{11.10}$$

and the minimum-variance hedge ratio is equal to

$$h^* = \frac{\mathrm{cov}(R^*, R_F)}{\sigma_F^2} = \frac{\mathrm{cov}(R + s, s)}{\sigma_s^2} = 1 + \frac{\mathrm{cov}(R, s)}{\sigma_s^2} \tag{11.11}$$

---

[2] This assumes very frequent adjustment of the currency hedge to follow movements in the value of the portfolio.

where σ_s^2 is the variance of the exchange rate movement. Equation 11.11 shows the minimum-variance hedge ratio as the sum of two components, h_1 and h_2, linked to different aspects of currency risk:

- Translation risk $(h_1 = 1)$

- Economic risk $\left(h_2 = \dfrac{\text{cov}(R,\,s)}{\sigma_s^2} \right)$

Translation Risk   *Translation risk* comes from the translation of the value of the asset from the foreign currency to the domestic currency. It would be present even if the foreign currency value of the asset were constant (e.g., a deposit in foreign currency). The hedge ratio of translation risk is 1.

This is usually taken to mean that a currency hedge should achieve on a foreign asset the same rate of return in domestic currency as can be achieved on the foreign market in foreign currency terms. For example, a U.S. investor would try to achieve a dollar rate of return on a British gilts portfolio equal to what he could have achieved in terms of pounds. Creating a perfect currency hedge is equivalent to nullifying a currency movement and translating a foreign rate of return directly into a similar domestic rate of return. Considering only translation risk, the optimal amount to hedge is determined by finding the value of h such that the hedged return in domestic currency terms, R_H, closely tracks the return in foreign currency terms, R.

Equation 11.10 can be written as

$$R_H - R = s(1 - h) \tag{11.12}$$

To minimize the variance of $R_H - R$, we must obviously set a hedge ratio of 1. This is basically the strategy of "hedging the principal" outlined previously.

Economic Risk   *Economic risk* comes when the foreign currency value of a foreign investment reacts systematically to an exchange rate movement. This is in addition to translation risk. Let's take again the example of a country that has an exchange rate target. A depreciation in its local currency will lead the country to raise its interest rates, pushing local bond prices down. So, there is a positive covariance between bond returns, measured in local currency, and the exchange rate movement. An investor from abroad will lose twice from the foreign currency depreciation. First, the percentage translation loss will be equal to the percentage depreciation of the foreign currency. Second, the value of the investment measured in foreign currency itself will drop.

The hedge ratio required to minimize this economic risk can be estimated by $\text{cov}(R,\,s)/\sigma_s^2$. This is the slope that we would get on a regression of the foreign currency return of the asset on the exchange rate movement.

Hedging Total Currency Risk   If an investor worries about the total influence of a foreign exchange rate depreciation on her portfolio value, measured in domestic currency, she should hedge both translation and economic currency risk. In this approach, the objective is to minimize the overall influence of an exchange rate movement, whether direct or indirect, on the asset return in domestic currency. The objective is not to try to minimize the tracking error between R_H and R (translation risk).

Most portfolio managers only care about translation risk, so they adopt a unitary hedge ratio if they try to minimize the impact of currency risk. From a portfolio accounting standpoint, currency loss is simply stated as the difference in return when measured in domestic and foreign currencies, $R^* - R$. So, minimizing accounting currency losses is an objective choice. Also, the sensitivity of an asset value to an exchange rate movement has to be estimated from some economic model and/or from historical data. Even though estimates might be imprecise and unstable, hedging only translation risk might not be optimal from an economic viewpoint.

In practice, stock returns and currency movements are quite independent. If a foreign asset's returns are uncorrelated with short-term currency movements, a hedge ratio of 1 is a reasonable strategy.

EXAMPLE 11.3   *PORTFOLIO WITH MINIMUM-VARIANCE HEDGE RATIO*

You are French and own a portfolio of U.S. stocks worth $1 million. The current spot and one-month forward exchange rates are €1/$. Interest rates are equal in both countries. You are worried that the results of U.S. elections could lead to a strong depreciation of the dollar. You have observed that U.S. stocks tend to react favorably to a depreciation of the dollar. A broker tells you that a regression of U.S. stock returns on the €/$ percentage exchange rate movements has a slope of −0.20. In other words, U.S. stocks tend to go up by 1 percent when the dollar depreciates by 5 percent.

a. Discuss what your currency hedge ratio should be.

b. A week later, your U.S. stock portfolio has gone up to $1.01 million and the spot and forward exchange rates are now €0.95/$. Analyze the return on your hedged portfolio.

SOLUTION

a.

- To hedge only translation risk would require a hedge ratio of 1 (100 percent).

- To hedge economic risk would require an additional hedge ratio of −20 percent.

The minimum-variance hedge ratio reflecting both translation and economic risk should therefore be 80 percent.

b. Let's now study the return on the optimally hedged portfolio under the proposed scenario. Using Equation 11.10, we find that the return on the hedged portfolio is equal to 0 percent (remember that we neglected the cross-product term). So, we have removed the overall impact of the currency movement. But we do not track the rate of return in foreign currency.

Optimal Hedge Ratio

Note that the minimum-variance hedge, as described, is not necessarily optimal in a risk–return framework:

- Portfolio managers can have expectations about currency movements. In Chapters 2 and 3, we reviewed factors that affect exchange rates and discussed forecasting models. Expected currency returns could suggest deviation from a pure risk-minimizing strategy.

- Transaction costs can affect hedging strategies.

- Futures and spot exchange rates differ by a basis. Changes in the basis can affect hedging strategies, which creates *basis risk.*

- Futures and spot exchange rates differ by a basis. Over time, the percentage movement in the futures and in the spot exchange rate will differ by this basis. In the long run, the return on the hedged portfolio will differ from the portfolio return achieved in foreign currency by the basis, even with a hedge ratio of 1.

These last two aspects are now addressed.

Basis Risk   Forward (or swap) and futures exchange rates are directly determined by two factors: the spot exchange rate and the interest rate differential between two currencies. The forward discount, or the premium—which is the percentage difference between the forward and the spot exchange rates—equals the interest rate differential for the same maturity as the forward contract. In futures jargon, we say that the basis equals the interest rate differential. If we express the exchange rate as the dollar value of one pound (e.g., $/£ = 2.00) and call $r_\$$ and $r_\pounds$ the interest rates in dollars and pounds, respectively, with the same maturity as the futures contract, the relation known as interest rate parity is

$$\frac{F}{S} = \frac{1 + r_\$}{1 + r_\pounds} \quad \text{and} \quad \frac{F - S}{S} = \frac{r_\$ - r_\pounds}{1 + r_\pounds} \tag{11.13}$$

Note that the interest rates in equation 11.13 are period rates, not annualized. They equal the annualized rates multiplied by the number of days until maturity and divided by 360 days. Because interest rate parity is the result of arbitrage on very liquid markets, it technically holds at every instant (see Chapters 1 and 2). Changes in the basis have an impact on the quality of the currency hedge. Although currency risk is removed by hedging, some additional risk is taken in the form of basis risk. But this basis risk is quite small.

The correlation between futures and spot exchange rates is a function of the futures contract term. Futures prices for contracts near maturity closely follow spot exchange rates because at that point the interest rate differential is a small component of the futures price. To illustrate, consider the futures price of British pound contracts with 1, 3, and 12 months left until delivery. The spot exchange rate is currently $2.00 per pound, and the interest rates and the calculated values for the fu-

EXHIBIT 11.2

Importance of Interest Rate Differentials to Futures Prices

	Maturity		
	One Month	**Three Months**	**Twelve Months**
Pound interest rate (%)	14	13.5	13
Dollar interest rate (%)	10	10	10
Futures price (dollars per pound)	1.993	1.983	1.947
Interest rate component (dollars)	−0.007	−0.017	−0.053
Spot rate: £1 = $2.00.			

tures are as given in Exhibit 11.2. The 1-month futures price should equal $2.00 plus the 1-month interest rate differential applied to the spot rate. The interest rate differential for 1 month equals the annualized rate differential of −4 percent multiplied by 30 days and divided by 360 days, or divided by 12:

$$F = S + S\frac{r_\$ - r_£}{1 + r_£} = 2.00 - 2.00 \frac{\frac{4}{12}\%}{1 + \frac{14}{12}\%}$$

Hence, $F = 1.993$.

We see, then, that even though the interest rate differential is very large, its effect on the one-month futures price is minimal, because the spot exchange rate is the driving force behind short-term forward exchange rate movements. This is less true for long-term contracts. More specifically, a reduction of 1 percentage point (100 basis points) in the interest rate differential causes a futures price movement of approximately 0.25 percentage point (3/12) for the three-month contract and 1 percentage point (12/12) for the one-year contract, as compared with 0.08 percentage point (1/12) for the one-month contract. So, basis risk is very small compared with the currency risk that is being hedged.

Another factor that can affect the quality of the hedge is that movement in the interest rate differential (basis) could be correlated with movement in the spot exchange rate itself.

Expected Hedged Return and the Basis We have so far focused on minimizing risk. A hedge ratio of 1 will minimize transaction risk. But in the long run, the return on the hedged portfolio will differ from the portfolio return achieved in foreign currency by the interest rate differential, even with a hedge ratio of 1. Although we can minimize, or even eliminate, the variance of $R_H - R$, it is impossible to set them equal. This is because we can only hedge with futures contracts with a price F different from S. Over time, the percentage movement in the futures price used in the hedge, R_F, will differ from the percentage movement in the spot exchange rate, s, which affects the portfolio by the interest rate differential.

Hedging Strategies

A major decision in selecting a currency hedge, whether it be with a forward (or swap) contract or with a futures contract, is the choice of contract terms. Short-term contracts track the behavior of the spot exchange rates better, have greater trading volume, and offer more liquidity than long-term contracts. On the other hand, short-term contracts must be rolled over if a hedge is to be maintained for a period longer than the initial contract. For long-term hedges, a manager can choose from three basic contract terms:

1. Short-term contracts, which must be rolled over at maturity

2. Contracts with a matching maturity, that is, contracts that match the expected period for which the hedge is to be maintained

3. Long-term contracts with a maturity extending beyond the hedging period

Contracts for any of the three terms may be closed by taking an offsetting position on the delivery date. This avoids actual physical delivery of a currency. Exhibit 11.3 depicts three such hedging strategies for an expected hedge period of six months. The results of the strategy depend on the evolution of interest rates and, hence, of the basis. Any contract maturity different from six months implies basis risk.

Another consideration in choosing a hedging strategy is transaction costs. Rolling over short-term contracts generates more commissions because of the larger number of transactions involved. Also, the number of futures contracts used in order to reflect changes in the market value of the hedged portfolio should be adjusted frequently to reflect changes in the asset value.

Longer hedges can be built using currency swaps, which can be arranged with horizons of up to a dozen years. However, currency swaps are used primarily by corporations in the currency management of their assets and liabilities. Portfolio managers usually take a shorter horizon.

Hedging Multiple Currencies

Cross-hedges are sometimes used for closely linked currencies. For example, a U.S. investor could use euro futures to hedge the currency risk in Swiss stocks, because the Swiss franc and the euro are highly correlated. Futures and forward currency contracts are actively traded only for the major currencies. International portfolios are often invested in assets in Hong Kong, Norway, Sweden, Singapore, and other countries where futures contracts in the local currency are sometimes not actively traded. In these cases, investors must try to find contracts on other currencies that are closely correlated with the investment currencies.

Some investment managers fear the depreciation of only one or two currencies in their portfolios and therefore hedge currency risk selectively. Other managers fear that their domestic currency will appreciate relative to all foreign currencies. For example, the strong U.S. dollar appreciation in the early 2000s was realized

EXHIBIT 11.3

Three Hedging Strategies for an Expected Hedge Period of Six Months

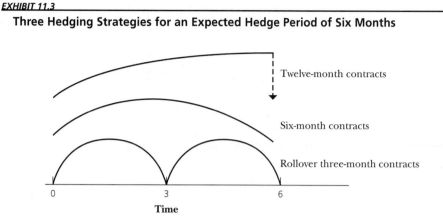

against all currencies. This domestic currency appreciation induced a negative currency contribution to the U.S. dollar return on all foreign portfolios. An overall currency hedge on their foreign investments would have drastically improved their performance by nullifying the negative currency contribution to the total dollar performance of non-U.S. portfolios.

Systematic currency hedging also reduces the total volatility of the portfolio, as noted in Chapter 9. A complete foreign currency hedge can be achieved by hedging the investments in each foreign currency. This is not feasible for many currencies, however, and is very cumbersome administratively. Also, it is not necessary to hedge each currency component in a multicurrency portfolio. In a portfolio with assets in many currencies, the residual risk of each currency is partly diversified away. Optimization techniques can be used to construct a hedge with futures contracts in only a few currencies (e.g., yen, euro, and sterling). Although the residual risk of individual currencies is not fully hedged, the portfolio is well protected against a general appreciation of the home currency.[3] Another alternative is to use contracts on a basket of currencies as offered by some banks.

The stability of the estimated hedge ratios is crucial in establishing effective hedging strategies, especially when cross-hedging is involved. Empirical studies indicate that hedges using futures contracts in the same currency as the asset to be hedged are very effective but that the optimal hedge ratios in cross-hedges that involve different currencies are somewhat unstable over time.[4]

---

[3] For an empirical examination of the multicurrency betas of international portfolios, see Adler and Simon (1986).

[4] See Eaker and Grant (1987), Dale (1981), and Grammatikos and Saunders (1983). The importance of basis risk (movements in interest rate differential) for determining the risk-minimizing hedge ratio has been illustrated by Briys and Solnik (1992). Kroner and Sultan (1993) derive risk-minimizing dynamic hedging strategies if the distribution of returns changes over time and follows some GARCH process.

In practice, a diversified international portfolio can be hedged using only the futures contracts available in a few currencies by following this procedure:

- Select the most independent major currencies with futures contracts available. For an American investor, these may be the yen, the euro, and the pound. For a Swiss investor, these may be the yen, the euro, the pound, and the U.S. dollar.

- Calculate the hedge ratios jointly by running a multiple regression of the domestic currency returns of the portfolio (U.S. dollar return for a U.S. investor) on the futures returns in the selected currencies. With the example of three currencies, we have:

$$R^* = a + h_1 R_{F1} + h_2 R_{F2} + h_3 R_{F3} + \text{error term} \qquad (11.14)$$

- Use the estimates of the regression coefficients h_1, h_2, and h_3 as the hedge ratios in each currency. Because the spot currency movement is the major component of futures volatility, the hedge ratios obtained would be fairly close if we used currency movements in the regression instead of futures return.

Of course, this procedure requires historical data on the portfolio and will work well only if the estimated regression coefficients are stable over time.

Insuring and Hedging with Options

Two approaches are used for reducing currency risk exposure with options. The traditional method exploits the asymmetric risk–return characteristic of an option, so that it is used as an *insurance* vehicle. The second approach takes into account the dynamics of the relationship between the option premium and the underlying exchange rate. This second approach is closer to a *hedging* strategy.

Insuring with Options

Many investors focus on the characteristics of options at expiration. Currency options are purchased in amounts equal to the principal to be hedged. It is not trivial to determine which options to use (calls or puts), because they involve the rate of exchange between two currencies. Consider a U.S. investor with £1 million of British assets. Let us assume that on the Philadelphia Stock Exchange he buys British pound puts for December with a strike price of 200 U.S. cents per pound. The contract size is £12,500. A British pound put gives him the right, but not the obligation, to sell British pounds at a fixed exercise (or strike) price with payment in dollars. Similarly, a British pound call gives him the right to buy British pounds with U.S. dollars. Note that a call to buy British pounds with U.S. dollars is equivalent to a put to sell U.S. dollars for British pounds. Options markets in some countries sometimes offer reverse contracts, so that investors must be sure they understand the position they are taking. In all cases, however, a good hedge implies buying options (puts or calls), not selling or writing them.

Suppose the spot exchange rate is $2.00 per pound. The strike price for the December put is 200 cents per pound (or 2 dollars per pound), and the premium is 6 cents per pound. The investor must buy puts for £1 million or 80 contracts. In this traditional approach, puts are treated as insurance devices. If the pound drops below $2.00 at expiration, a profit will be made on the put that exactly offsets the currency loss on the portfolio. If the pound drops to $1.90, the gain on the puts at expiration is

$$80 \times 12,500 \times (2.00 - 1.90) = \$100,000$$

The advantage of buying options rather than futures is that options simply expire if the pound appreciates rather than depreciates. For example, if the British pound moves up to $2.20, the futures contract will generate a loss of $200,000, nullifying the currency gain on the portfolio of assets. This does not happen with options that simply expire. Of course, investors must pay a price for this asymmetric risk structure, namely, the premium, which is the cost of having this insurance.

Note that the cost of the premium prevents a perfect hedge. In the previous example, the net profit on the put purchase equals the gain at expiration minus the premium. If we call V_0 the number of pounds, P_0 the premium per £, and K the strike (or exercise) price, the net dollar profit on the put at the time of exercise t is

$$\text{Net dollar profit} = V_0(K - S_t) - V_0P_0 \quad \text{when } K > S_t \tag{11.15}$$

$$= -V_0P_0 \quad \text{otherwise}$$

That is, when $K > S_t$, we have net dollar profit = £ quantity $\times$ (Exercise price $-$ Spot price) $-$ £ quantity $\times$ premium per pound, but the investor loses the premium otherwise.

Hence, if the pound drops to $1.90, the net dollar profit is

$$£1,000,000 \times (\$2.00/£ - \$1.90/£) - £1,000,000 \times \$0.06/£ = \$40,000$$

This profit does not cover the currency loss on the portfolio (equal to roughly $100,000), because the option premium cost $60,000. An alternative solution is to buy out-of-the-money puts with a lower exercise price and a lower premium. But with those, exchange rates would have to move that much more before a profit could be made on the options. In general, what is gained in terms of a lower premium is lost in terms of a lower strike price for the put option.

In fact, this approach does not allow for a good currency hedge except when variations in the spot exchange rate swamp the cost of the premium. Instead, this approach uses options as insurance contracts, and the premium is regarded as a sunk cost. Note, however, that options are usually resold on the market rather than left to expire; when the option is resold, part of the initial insurance premium is recovered. On the other hand, the approach still exploits the greatest advantage of options, namely, that an option can be allowed to expire if the currency moves in a favorable direction. Options protect a portfolio in case of adverse currency movements, as do currency futures, and maintain its performance potential in case of favorable currency movements, whereas futures hedge in both directions. The price of this asymmetric advantage is the insurance cost implicit in the time value of the option. To summarize, using options allows us to insure a portfolio against currency losses, rather than hedge it, and the option premium is the insurance cost.

EXAMPLE 11.4   INSURING WITH OPTIONS

You are an American investor holding a portfolio of European assets worth €1 million. The current spot exchange rate is $1 = 1 euro but you fear a depreciation of the euro in the short term. The three-month forward exchange rate is $0.9960 = 1 euro. You are quoted the option premiums for calls euro and puts euro with a three-month maturity. These are options to buy (call) or sell (put) one euro at the dollar exercise price mentioned for each option. The contract size on the CME is €125,000. The quotations are as follows:

Euro Options (All Prices in U.S. Cents per Euro)

Strike	Call Euro	Put Euro
105	0.50	6.50
100	2.10	3.00
95	6.40	0.50

You decide to use options to insure your portfolio.

    a. Should you buy (or sell) calls (or puts)? What quantity?

    b. You decide to buy at-the-money puts, puts 100 (strike price of 100 U.S. cents) for €1 million. Suppose that you can borrow the necessary amount of dollars to buy these puts at a zero interest rate. Calculate the result at maturity of your strategy, assuming that the euro value of your portfolio remains at €1 million.

    c. You have the choice of three different strike prices. What is the relative advantage of each option? What is the advantage relative to hedging, using forward currency contracts.

SOLUTION

    a. To insure you need to buy options. Here, you want to be able to translate euros at a fixed exchange rate, so you should buy euro puts for €1 million, or eight contracts.

    b. You buy at-the-money puts on €1 million. The cost (premium) is equal to

$$€1,000,000 \times \$0.03/€ = \$30,000$$

If the euro rises in value, the put will expire worthless. If the euro depreciates, the gain on the option (per euro) will be equal to the difference between $1 and the spot exchange rate at maturity (in dollar per euro). For example, if the spot exchange rate is $0.90 = 1 euro, the gain on the puts will be

$$€1,000,000 \times (\$1/€ - \$0.90/€) = \$100,000$$

But the original portfolio is now only worth $900,000 (€1,000,000 × 0.90). The net result is a dollar portfolio value equal to

$$\$900,000 - \$30,000 + \$100,000 = \$970,000$$

The simulation of the dollar value of the position for a different value of the exchange rate at maturity is given in the first column of the following table. The portfolio is insured for down movements in the euro and benefits from up movements. But the cost of the insurance premium has to be deducted in all cases.

Exchange Rate at Maturity (U.S. Cents per Euro)	Using Puts 100	Using Puts 105	Using Puts 95	Hedging with Forward
110	1,070,000	1,035,000	1,095,000	996,000
105	1,020,000	985,000	1,045,000	996,000
100	970,000	985,000	995,000	996,000
95	970,000	985,000	945,000	996,000
90	970,000	985,000	945,000	996,000

c. The preceding table simulates the results of using the various options as well as the forward. An "expensive" option (in-the-money, put 105) gives better downside protection at the expense of a lesser profit potential in case of an appreciation of the euro. A "cheap" option (out-of-the-money, put 95) provides less downside protection but a larger profit potential. Using forward contracts freezes the value of the portfolio at 996,000 dollars. You are well protected on the downside, but cannot benefit from an appreciation of the euro. You will decide on the strategy, depending on your scenario for the euro exchange rate. If a depreciation of the euro seems very likely, you will hedge; if a depreciation seems very unlikely, you will buy out-of-the-money options, which are the cheapest. The other two strategies lie in between.

Dynamic Hedging with Options

Listed options are traded continually, and positions are usually closed by reselling the option in the market instead of exercising it. The profit is therefore completely dependent on market valuation. The dynamic approach to currency option hedging recognizes this fact and is based on the relationship between changes in option premiums and changes in exchange rates.

The definition of a full currency option hedge is simple and similar to the one given previously. A full hedge is a position in which every dollar loss from currency movement on a portfolio of foreign assets is covered by a dollar gain in the value of the options position.

We know that an option premium is related to the underlying exchange rate, but in a complex manner. Exhibit 11.4 shows the relationship we usually observe for a put. Beginning with a specific exchange rate, say, $/£ = 2.00, a put premium can go up or down in response to changes in the exchange rate. The slope of the curve at point A denotes the elasticity of the premium in response to any movements in the dollar exchange rate. In Exhibit 11.4, the premium is equal to 6 cents when the exchange rate is 200 U.S. cents per pound, and the slope of the tangent at point A equals -0.5. This slope is usually called delta (δ).

In this example, a good hedge would be achieved by buying two pound puts for every pound of British assets. One pound put is defined here as a put option on one unit of British currency. One contract includes several pound puts, depending on the contract size. If the pound depreciated by 1 U.S. cent, each put would go up by approximately 0.5 cents, offsetting the currency loss on the portfolio. In general, if n pound put options are purchased, the gain on the options position is

$$\text{Options gain} = n(P_t - P_0) \tag{11.16}$$

EXHIBIT 11.4

Value of Pound Puts in Relation to the Exchange Rate

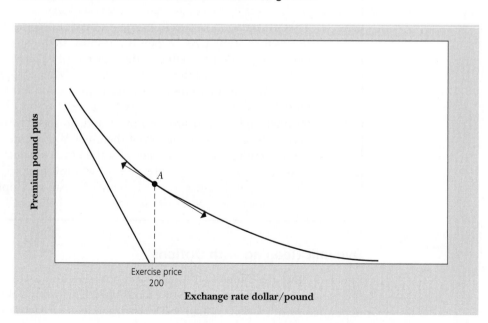

where P_t is the put value at time t, and P_0 is the put value at time zero. For small movements in the exchange rate,

$$P_t - P_0 = \delta(S_t - S_0) \tag{11.17}$$

Hence, the gain on the options position is:

$$\text{Options gain} = n(P_t - P_0) = n \times \delta \times (S_t - S_0) \tag{11.18}$$

Assuming that the value of the portfolio in foreign currency remains constant at V_0, the gain (loss if negative) on the portfolio in domestic currency is equal to

$$\text{Portfolio gain} = V_0 \times (S_t - S_0) \tag{11.19}$$

A good currency hedge is obtained by holding $n = -V_0/\delta$ options. The hedge ratio is equal to $-1/\delta$. The profit on the options position offsets the currency loss on the portfolio. In the example, the hedge ratio is equal to two as $\delta = -0.5$. One should buy two pound puts for every pound of portfolio value.

We must emphasize that δ and the hedge ratio vary with the exchange rate, so that the number of options held must be adjusted continually. This strategy is called the *delta hedge*.

Let's illustrate a delta hedge on the previous example. If the pound depreciates, options protect the portfolio, but its δ changes. For example, the slope δ could move to -0.8 if the pound drops to \$1.95. Then the hedge ratio should be equal to $1/0.8 = 1.25$. To avoid overhedging, the investor must either sell some puts or switch to options with a lower exercise price (and lower δ); in both cases, a profit will be realized. If the pound later reverses its downward trend, the puts will become worthless; however, most of the profit will have been realized previously and saved.

Transaction costs make continuous rebalancing impractical and expensive. In reality, a good hedge can be achieved only with periodic revisions in the options position, that is, when there is a significant movement in the exchange rate. Between revisions, options offer their usual asymmetric insurance within the general hedging strategy. This strategy may be regarded as a mixed hedging insurance strategy.

Implementing such a strategy requires a good understanding of option valuation and the precise estimation of the hedge ratio. As with futures, the strategy should take into account the expected return on the foreign portfolio, as well as its correlation with exchange rate movements.

Hedging Strategies

Hedging strategies with options can be more sophisticated than those with forwards or futures for two reasons: The hedge ratio of options fluctuates, but is constant for futures; and an investor can play with several maturities and exercise prices with options only.

A hedging strategy can combine futures and options.[5] Futures markets are very liquid and have low transaction costs. Options offer the advantage of an asymmetric

---

[5] For a detailed description of currency options strategies, see the "Currency Options Strategy Manual" by the Chicago Mercantile Exchange, as well as various brochures prepared by options exchanges.

risk structure but have higher costs, in terms of both the fair price for this insurance risk structure and their transaction costs.

If a hedging decision is necessary because an investor faces an increasing volatility in exchange rates and doesn't have a clear view of the direction of change, currency options are a natural strategy. In the scenario described at the beginning of this chapter, Australian elections created uncertainties about the future of the Australian dollar. In that case, options would have allowed the investor to hedge a drop in the Australian dollar while maintaining the opportunity to profit in case it rose.

Where the direction of a currency movement is clearly forecasted, currency futures provide a cheaper hedge. In setting the hedge, however, investors should take into account the expected return on the portfolio and its correlation with currency movements.

Other Methods for Managing Currency Exposure

Many methods are used to reduce currency exposure and to take positions in foreign markets without incurring excessive exchange risk. First, an investor can rearrange a portfolio so as to increase its risk level in a foreign market without increasing its currency exposure. For stocks, this means buying equities with higher betas (relative to the market index) and selling those with lower betas. This makes the portfolio more sensitive to local market movements without increasing its sensitivity to currency fluctuations. For bonds, this means adjusting the duration of the foreign portfolio to increase the portfolio's sensitivity to foreign interest rates without increasing its currency exposure.

An international portfolio manager who wants to invest in countries where the currency is expected to weaken has a few choices. She can buy common stock outright and hedge the exchange risk with currency futures or options, or buy options on the stock. For example, a U.S. investor may want to buy call options on the British firm ABC rather than ABC shares. The reason is simple: If ABC stock goes up by the same percentage as the British pound drops, the dollar value of a direct investment in ABC stock will remain unchanged. On the other hand, options on ABC will yield both a pound profit and a dollar profit. With options, currency fluctuations affect mostly the translation of the profit into dollars, not the principal. The price quotations given in Exhibit 11.5 illustrate how this strategy works.

The dollar profit of buying one share of ABC is zero because the currency loss on the principal offsets the capital gain in pounds. If the investor had instead purchased an option, the profit per share would have been $36 (= $52.50 − $16.50) despite the currency loss. Also, note that the initial investment in options is only $16.50 compared with $300 for shares. The difference could have been invested in U.S. cash instruments. Because the initial foreign currency investment in an option is very small, the currency impact is always limited compared with a direct investment in the asset.

A similar approach can be used to invest in an entire foreign market rather than only specific securities. This is done by buying stock index futures or options. Like any futures, stock index futures limit an investor's foreign currency exposure to the

<u>EXHIBIT 11.5</u>

Price Quotations on ABC Shares

	Prices December 1	Prices January 15	Price Variation (%)
Dollars per pound	1.50	1.25	
Pounds per dollar	0.667	0.800	+20
ABC stock (in pounds)	200	240	+20
ABC stock (in dollars)	300	300	0
ABC February 200 options (in pounds)	11.0	42	
ABC February 200 options (in dollars)	16.5	52.5	

margin. Any realized profit can be repatriated immediately in the domestic currency. For example, a Swiss investor who is bullish on the U.S. stock market, but not on the U.S. dollar, can buy Standard & Poor 500 index futures. In addition, hedging the margin deposited in dollars against currency risk would provide the Swiss investor with complete currency protection. Stock index options can likewise be used.

EXAMPLE 11.5 *BUYING STOCK INDEX FUTURES*

A European portfolio manager wishes to increases her exposure to Japanese stocks by €10 million, without taking much foreign exchange risk. Futures contracts are available on the TOPIX index. Each contract is for ¥1,000 times the index. The current futures price of the TOPIX index is 1,000, and the spot exchange rate is ¥100 per euro. What strategy could she adopt using those contracts?

SOLUTION

She would buy TOPIX futures contracts to gain an overall exposure in the Japanese stock market corresponding to €10 million, or ¥1 billion at the current exchange rate. The number of contracts N to be bought is determined as follows:

$$N = \frac{¥1,000,000,000}{\text{Multiplier} \times \text{Index value}} = \frac{¥1,000,000,000}{¥1,000 \times 1,000} = 1,000 \text{ contracts}$$

The futures contracts are not exposed to currency risk. However, she also has to deposit a margin in yen that can be hedged against currency risk.

A similar strategy applies to bond investments. For example, a U.S. investor who is bullish on interest rates in the United Kingdom can buy gilt futures on the LIFFE rather than bonds, and thereby simultaneously hedge against exchange risk. Other alternatives include buying bond warrants.

Futures and options on foreign assets reduce currency exposure as long as an investor does not already own the assets in question. In addition, costs involved in taking such positions are less than those for actually buying foreign assets and hedging them with currency futures or options. On the other hand, if the assets are already part of a portfolio, more conventional methods of currency hedging are probably better, especially for assets that will remain in the portfolio for a long time.

Investors also should be aware of the currency impact on an investment strategy involving different types of instruments whose currency exposures are not identical. As an illustration, let's consider the following strategy. An American investor buys Australian natural resource companies stock for A$1 million and sells stock index futures for the same amount to hedge the Australian stock market risk. The beta of this portfolio relative to the Australian market is assumed to be 1. The motivation for this strategy is the belief that natural resource stocks are undervalued relative to the Australian market. The American investor believes that the portfolio will generate a positive alpha ("alpha strategy"). Such a position, which is long in stocks and short in futures, is not exposed to Australian stock market risk; however, it does require an Australian dollar net investment, and is therefore exposed to the risk of the Australian dollar. A depreciation of the Australian dollar would induce a currency loss in the stock position that would not be offset by a currency gain on the stock index futures.[6] This is illustrated in Example 11.6.

EXAMPLE 11.6   CURRENCY RISK FOR ALPHA STRATEGIES

On September 1, an American investor buys Australian natural resource companies stock for A$1 million and sells ASX stock index futures (December maturity) for the same amount to hedge the Australian stock market risk. The ASX contract has a multiplier of A$25. The current ASX futures price is 2,000. The investor sells 20 contracts.

The Australian dollar drops from 1.0 U.S. dollar on September 1 to 0.90 U.S. dollar on October 1. In the same period, the ASX index and the ASX futures price drop by 10 percent (in A$), while the portfolio only loses 7 percent (in A$). What is the profit or loss on this alpha strategy in Australian dollars and in U.S. dollars if the investor does not engage in currency hedging?

SOLUTION

Calculations are detailed in the following table (the margin deposit is neglected here). The investor would have realized a gain of A$30,000 corresponding to the 3 percent return difference between the portfolio and the market (alpha). If the US$/A$ exchange rate had remained stable at 1, this would have translated into a US$30,000 profit. Instead, the 10 percent depreciation of the Australian dollar induced a loss of 73,000 U.S. dollars. To reduce the impact of currency movements, the investor should have hedged the stock portfolio against currency risk.

---

[6] As a matter of fact, there will even be an additional small currency loss in the initial margin deposited for the futures contracts.

	Futures Market	**Stock Market**
September 1	Sell 20 December ASX futures	Buy natural resource stocks;
(US$/A$ = 1)	at 2,000	cost = A$1,000,000,
		US$1,000,000
October 1	*Market declines 10%, but natural resource stocks decline 7%*	
(US$/A$ = 0.9)	Buy 20 December ASX futures	Sell natural resource stocks;
	at 1,800	proceeds = A$930,000,
		US$837,000
	Profit on futures = A$100,000,	Loss on stocks = A$70,000,
	US$90,000	US$163,000
	Net loss on trade = US$73,000	

Several investment vehicles and strategies may be used either to take advantage of or to hedge against monetary factors. Many of these strategies have been discussed before, so we already know that they usually involve a combination of investments in money, capital, and speculative markets. For example, a British investor expecting a weak U.S. dollar and falling U.S. interest rates could buy long-term U.S. bonds, or zero coupons, to maximize the sensitivity of her portfolio to U.S. interest rate movements and, at the same time, to hedge against exchange risk with currency futures or options. A matrix of alternative investments in the U.S. dollar fixed-income markets is given in Exhibit 11.6 on page 594. Each quadrant represents a specific scenario concerning U.S. interest rates and the U.S. dollar. Group I, for example, represents a set of strategies designed to capitalize on a strong U.S. dollar and falling dollar interest rates.

The purpose in outlining strategies is to help an investor to take advantage of his specific forecasts with respect to interest rates and currencies. Of course, the actual performance of these strategies depends on the accuracy of the investor's forecasts. A similar strategy matrix can be designed for nondollar investments, although the absence of speculative markets in some currencies sometimes limits the range of strategies an investor can choose.

Currency Overlay

International portfolios are managed under diverse investment policy statements set by clients. The approach to currency management is specified in the investment policy statement. The various approaches can be categorized in three broad models:

1. *Balanced mandate:* Some clients, especially private clients, delegate to the investment manager responsibility for all aspects of international portfolio management:

   - The asset allocation of the international portfolio
   - The selection of individual securities
   - Currency management

EXHIBIT 11.6

A Strategy Matrix of Alternative Investments in the U.S. Dollar Fixed-Income Markets

Dollar
strength

Group I

A. Long-maturity bonds
B. Long-maturity mortgage-related securities
C. CATS
D. Zero-coupon bonds
E. Money market plus bond options/futures/
   warrants
F. Bond warrants
G. Financial options—bull strategies
H. Financial futures—bull strategies
I. Currency options—$ bull strategies
J. Currency futures—$ bull strategies
   Government yield curve arbitrage—
   bull strategies

Group II

A. Money market
B. Eurodollar FRNs
C. Repurchase agreements
D. "Cash and carry"
E. Hedged nondollar money market
F. Short-maturity bonds
G. Financial options—bear strategies
H. Financial futures—bear strategies
   Government yield curve arbitrage—
   bear strategies
   Currency options—$ bull strategies
   Currency futures—$ bull strategies

Falling
dollar
interest
rates

Rising
dollar
interest
rates

Group IV

A. Hedged long-maturity bonds
B. GNMA forward plus base-currency
   money market
C. Reverse repos (overnight) plus base-
   currency money market
D. Government yield curve arbitrage—
   bull strategies
   CATS
   Zero-coupon bonds
   Bond warrants
   Financial options—bull strategies
   Financial futures—bull strategies
   Currency options—$ bear strategies
   Currency futures—$ bear strategies

Group III

A. Hedged money market
B. Hedged Eurodollar FRNs
C. Reverse repos to maturity plus base-
   currency money market (for loss-
   constrained portfolios)
D. Currency options—$ bear strategies
E. Currency futures—$ bear strategies
F. Government yield curve arbitrage—
   bear strategies
   Financial options—bear strategies
   Financial futures—bear strategies

Dollar
weakness

Securities/strategies are generally listed with the more traditional, or less risky, at the top of each group; the more highly leveraged, or risky, are toward the bottom of the list. In some instances, the same instruments/strategies appear in more than one quadrant. In such cases, they appear only with a code letter in that quadrant where they are especially appropriate. They appear without a code letter in the other quadrants.

Source: J. Hanna and P. Niculescu. "The Currency and Interest Rate Strategy Matrix: An Investment Tool for Multicurrency Investors," Bond Market Research, Salomon Brothers Inc., September 1982. Reprinted with permission.

Of course, guidelines, and possibly a benchmark, guide the construction of the international portfolio. For example, assigning an unhedged benchmark will make no-currency-hedging the neutral decision of the investment manager in the absence of specific currency forecasts. On the opposite, the neutral position will be to fully hedge investments against currency risks if a fully hedged benchmark is assigned. Taking into account forecasts on markets and currencies, the investment manager will optimize simultaneously the asset allocation and the currency hedging decisions.

2. *Currency overlay:* Some clients delegate the currency management of the international portfolio to a specialized manager, called the *currency overlay* manager. This is based on the assumption that the primary manager of the international assets does not have the currency expertise of the currency overlay specialist. The composition of the portfolio is periodically transferred to the currency overlay manager, who decides on the positions taken in currencies and manages currency risk. In the currency overlay approach, currencies are regarded as financial prices that require the expertise of a specialist; in that sense, currencies can be regarded as an asset class. However, currency management is still part of the overall management process of the whole international portfolio.

3. *Currency as a separate asset allocation:* An extreme approach to currency overlay is to treat currencies as a totally separate asset class. So, the manager of the international portfolio is assumed to be passive in currency terms, but a specific sum is allocated to a separate account with active management of currencies. The management of that allocation is done independently of the rest of the portfolio. It is a pure currency play, with a benchmark usually set as an absolute return.

Jorion (1994) proposed a mean-variance analysis of currency overlay. He found that currency overlays are suboptimal. It is better to optimize simultaneously the asset allocation and the currency hedging decision (as in the "balanced mandate approach") rather than adopting a two-step currency overlay approach in which the asset allocation is optimized first (without taking currencies into consideration) and currency hedging is optimized second, assuming the asset allocation as given (currency overlay). But if the correlation between currency movements and asset returns is small, the difference between the two approaches will be small in terms of risk optimization.

Summary

- Currency futures, forward, and option contracts are used primarily to protect a portfolio against currency risks. Managers adapt their hedging strategies to their expectations of an asset's performance in foreign currency and of exchange rate movements.

- The basic approach to the use of currency futures contracts is to hedge the foreign currency value of the foreign asset. Managers would sell short currencies in the amount of an asset's value. Ideally, investors should hedge the future value of an investment, taking into account the expected price change and income.

- The hedge ratio is the ratio of the size of the short futures position in foreign currency to the value of the portfolio in foreign currency.

- The covariance between the asset return and the exchange rate movement should be considered. A minimum-variance hedge sets a hedge ratio that minimizes both translation risk and economic risk. Translation risk comes from the fact that the principal value of a foreign asset is translated at the exchange rate, so that a movement in the exchange rate affects the domestic currency value of the asset. Economic risk comes from the fact that the foreign currency value of a foreign asset can be influenced by a movement in the exchange rate.

- The interest rate differential is the forward basis, the percentage difference between the futures and the spot exchange rates. Basis risk affects the quality of currency hedging.

- Because a currency hedge must use futures (or forward) exchange rates, not spot exchange rates, the return on the hedged asset will differ over time from the return on the asset measured in foreign currency by the interest rate differential.

- Hedging strategies for multicurrency portfolios usually involve the use of futures in the major currencies. The instability of the estimated hedge ratios reduces the effectiveness of hedging strategies.

- Currency options are used for their asymmetric risk–return characteristics. They provide insurance against adverse currency movements while retaining the profit potential in case of a favorable currency movement. There is a cost associated with this attractive insurance characteristic. More dynamic hedging strategies can also be implemented using currency options. They require option valuation models to estimate the hedge ratio.

- Other methods can be used to manage the currency exposure of international portfolios. Leveraged instruments on foreign assets, such as futures and options, have little currency exposure, because the capital invested in foreign currency is very small compared with the value of the underlying asset. The impact of a currency movement on a combined position of several assets and contracts should be studied carefully.

- A currency overlay approach is sometimes used in international investment management. Some clients delegate the currency management of the international portfolio to a specialized manager, called the *currency overlay* manager. This is based on the assumption that the primary manager of the international assets does not have the currency expertise of the currency overlay specialist.

The composition of the portfolio is periodically transferred to the currency overlay manager, who decides on the positions taken in currencies and manages currency risk.

Problems

1. An American investor holds a portfolio of Japanese stocks worth ¥160 million. The spot exchange rate is ¥158/$, and the three-month forward exchange rate is ¥160/$. The investor fears that the Japanese yen will depreciate in the next month but wants to keep the Japanese stocks. What position can the investor take based on three-month forward exchange rate contracts? List all the factors that will make the hedge imperfect.

2. Consider a German portfolio manager who holds a portfolio of U.S. stocks currently worth $5 million. In order to hedge against a potential depreciation of the dollar, the portfolio manager proposes to sell December futures contracts on the dollar that currently trade at €1.02/$ and expire in two months. The spot exchange rate is currently €0.974/$. A month later, the value of the U.S. portfolio is $5,150,000, and the spot exchange rate is €1.1/$, while the futures exchange rate is €1.15/$.
   a. Evaluate the effectiveness of the hedge by comparing the fully hedged portfolio return with the unhedged portfolio return.
   b. Calculate the return on the portfolio, assuming a 50 percent hedge ratio.

3. Consider a U.S. portfolio manager who holds a portfolio of French stocks currently worth €10 million. In order to hedge against a potential depreciation of the euro, the portfolio manager proposes to sell December futures contracts on the euro that currently trade at $1/€ and expire in two months. The spot exchange rate is currently $1.1/€. A month later, the value of the French portfolio is €10,050,000 and the spot exchange rate is $1.05/€, while the futures exchange rate is $0.95/€.
   a. Evaluate the effectiveness of the hedge by comparing the fully hedged portfolio return with the unhedged portfolio return.
   b. Calculate the return on the portfolio, assuming a 35 percent hedge ratio.

4. A Dutch investor holds a portfolio of Japanese stocks worth ¥160 million. The current three-month dollar/euro forward exchange rate is $1.2/€, and the current three-month ¥/$ forward exchange rate is ¥160/$. Explain how the Dutch investor could hedge the ¥/€ exchange risk, using ¥/$ and $/€ forward contracts.

5. You are a U.S. investor and currently have a portfolio worth €100 million in German bonds. The current spot exchange rate is €2/$. The current one-year market interest rates are 6 percent in the euro area and 10 percent in the U.S. One-year currency options are quoted with a strike price of $0.50/€; a call on euros is quoted at $0.01 per euro, and a put on euros is quoted at $0.012 per euro. You are worried that inflation in euro area will cause a drop in the euro. You consider using forward contracts or options to hedge the currency risk.
   a. What is the one-year forward exchange rate €/$?
   b. Calculate the dollar value of your portfolio, assuming that its euro value stays at €100 million; use €/$ spot exchange rates equal in one year to 1.6, 1.8, 2, 2.2, and 2.4. First consider a currency forward hedge, then a currency option insurance.
   c. What could make your forward hedge imperfect?

6. You are a Swiss investor who has $10 million in short-term dollar deposits. You are worried that the dollar will drop relative to the Swiss franc in the next month. You care only about the Swiss franc value of your assets. Currency options exist that would guarantee that the $10 million would be worth a minimum amount of Swiss francs in one month (in March), if the dollar dropped, but would benefit from a dollar appreciation. The March forward exchange rate is $0.7389/SFr (or SFr1.3534/$). The quotes for Swiss franc currency options in Chicago are as follows:

March SF Options (all prices in US$ per SFr)

Strike	Call SFr	Put SFr
0.73	0.0243	0.0154

   a. What minimum portfolio value in SFr can you *guarantee* for March, using these options? Make the simplifying assumption that all interest rates are equal to zero and that you can buy exactly the desired number of SFr options. You must use some of the $10 million to get the options.
   b. What would be the difference if you used forward contracts?

7. You are an American investor who holds a portfolio of French stocks. The market value of the portfolio is €20 million, with a beta of 1.2 relative to the CAC index. In November, the spot value of the CAC index is 4,000. The exchange rate is $1.1/€. The dividend yield, euro interest rates, and dollar interest rates are all equal to 4 percent (flat yield curves).
   a. You fear a drop in the French stock market (but not the euro). The size of CAC index contracts is €10 times the CAC index. There are futures contracts quoted with March delivery. How many contracts should you buy or sell to hedge the French stock market risk?
   b. You are optimistic about the French stock market (different scenario from item [a]) but fear a depreciation of the euro. How many euros should you sell forward?
   c. You have the following quotes in Chicago on euro options, maturity March. Should you buy or sell calls or puts to insure against currency risk? What is the premium?

March Euro Options (all prices in US$ per euro)

Strike	Call Euro	Put Euro
1.10	0.021	0.02

   d. Calculate the result of your strategies (unhedged, hedged with March forward, insured with March options), assuming that your French stock portfolio is still worth €20 million in March. Simulate for different values of the spot $/€ in March, namely, €1 = $1, $1.1, $1.2.

8. The spot exchange rate is 10 Mexican pesos (MXP) per U.S. dollar. Today is November 4. The three-month interest rates are 12 percent in pesos and 8 percent in dollars. A Mexican peso call traded in Chicago with a strike price of $0.10 per peso has a premium of $0.005. The peso call gives the right to buy one peso for a strike price of $0.10. A Mexican peso put traded in Chicago with a strike price of $0.10 per peso has a premium of $0.0062. The size of the option contract is MXP 500,000. Both calls and puts can be exercised on February 4 (in three months).
   a. What is the three-month forward exchange rate MXP/$?

b. You are Mexican and will receive $1 million U.S. on February 4. Should you buy or sell pesos forward to hedge your future dollar cash flow? How many pesos will you get on February 4 if you hedge?

c. Should you buy or sell peso calls or puts to insure your cash flow? Assuming that you have some cash available to buy the options, how many option contracts should you buy? Calculate the resulting peso cash flows on February 4 for spot exchange rates of 8, 9, 9.5, 10, 10.5, 11, and MXP12/$.

9. A U.S. investor is attracted by the high yield on British bonds but is worried about a British pound depreciation. The currency market data are as follows:

	United States	United Kingdom
Bond yield (%)	7	12
Three-month interest rate (%)	6	8
Spot exchange rate, $/£ = 2		

A bond dealer has repeatedly suggested that the investor purchase hedged foreign bonds. This strategy can be described as the purchase of foreign currency bonds (here, British pound bonds) with simultaneous hedging in the short-term forward or futures currency market. The currency hedge is rolled over when the forward or futures contract expires.

a. What is the current three-month forward exchange rate ($/£)?

b. Assuming a £1 million investment in British bonds, how would you determine the exact hedge ratio necessary to minimize the currency influence?

c. When will this strategy be successful (compared with a direct investment in U.S. bonds)?

10. Futures and forward currency contracts are not readily available for all currencies. However, many currencies are closely linked. For example, many European countries, which are not part of the euro, attempt to maintain a close link with the euro.

An American investor has a portfolio of Danish stocks that she wishes to hedge against currency risks. No futures contracts are traded on the Danish kroner, so she decides to use euro futures contracts traded in Chicago, because both countries belong to the European Union. Here are some quotes:

Value of the portfolio	DKK 100 million
Spot exchange rates	DKK6.6/$
	$1.10/€
Futures price (contract of €125,000)	$1.11/€

How many euro contracts should the U.S. investor trade?

11. Consider a U.S. investor who owns a portfolio of Japanese securities worth ¥160 million. In order to hedge currency risk, he considers buying currency puts on yen instead of selling futures contracts. In Philadelphia, a yen put with a strike price of $0.62 per 100 yen and three-month maturity is worth $0.007 per 100 yen (0.007 cents per yen). The current exchange rate is ¥158/$.

Assume that three months later the portfolio is still worth ¥160 million. Compare the results of the following two currency-hedging strategies for values of the exchange rate three months later of ¥140/$, ¥150/$, ¥158/$, ¥170/$, and ¥180/$. In the first strategy, the investor sells ¥160 million forward; in the second strategy, he buys yen puts for ¥160 million.

12. On October 1, a Swiss investor decides to hedge a U.S. portfolio worth $10 million against exchange risk, using Swiss franc call options. The spot exchange rate is SFr2.5/$ or $0.40/SFr. The Swiss investor can buy November Swiss francs calls with a strike price of $0.40/SFr at a premium of $0.01 per Swiss franc. The size of one contract is SFr62,500. The delta of the option is estimated at 0.5.
    a. Reflecting this delta, how many Swiss franc calls should the investor buy to *hedge* (not insure) the U.S. portfolio against the SFr/$ currency risk (*dynamic* or *delta* hedge)?
        A few days later, the U.S. dollar has dropped to SFr2.439/$, or $0.41/SFr, and the dollar value of the portfolio has remained unchanged at $10 million. The November 40 Swiss franc call is now worth $0.016 per Swiss franc and has a delta estimated at 0.7.
    b. What is the result of the hedge?
    c. How should the hedge be adjusted?

13. You are a French investor holding a portfolio of U.S. stocks worth $10 million. You wish to engage in a dynamic hedge of the $/€ exchange risk by buying € calls. On April 1, a June 100 € call is quoted at $0.02 per euro. This gives you the right to buy one euro for $1 in June. The delta of this call is equal to 0.5. The spot exchange rate is $1/€. The size of an option contract is €125,000.
    a. How many € calls should you buy to get a good dynamic hedge?
        A few days later, your portfolio is still worth $10 million. The dollar, however, has dropped to $1.1/€. The call is now worth $0.11, and its delta is equal to 0.9.
    b. What is the result, in euros, of your strategy?
    c. Has the hedge resulted in a net gain or loss?
    d. What should you do to rebalance your hedge?

14. Why is a purchase of a futures contract or an option on a foreign asset not exposed to much currency risk?   Take the following example for a U.S. investor on the British stock market:

	November	December
FTSE 100 index	6,000	6,100
FTSE 100 December futures	6,030	6,100
FTSE Call December 6,050	20	50
$/£ spot rate	2.00	1.80

The FTSE 100 is an index of the top one hundred British stocks. One FTSE futures contract has a multiplier of £10. The margin deposit is £1,500 per contract. FTSE options have a contract size of £10 times the index. What is the dollar amount of currency loss per index unit if the U.S. investor had bought
    a. the index in the form of stocks (e.g., £6,000 worth of an FTSE index fund)?
    b. a December futures on FTSE?
    c. a December 6,050 FTSE call?

15. The current yield curve is much lower in the United States than in Great Britain. You read in the newspaper that it is unattractive for a U.S. investor to hedge currency risk on

British assets. The same journal states that British investors should hedge the currency risk on their U.S. investments. What do you think?

16. Salomon Brothers proposes to investors a contract called "Range Forward Contract." Here is an example of such a U.S. dollar/British pound contract:

    The contract has a size of £100,000 and a maturity of three months. At maturity, the investor will purchase the pounds at a price that is a function of the spot exchange rate.
    - If the spot exchange rate at maturity is less than $1.352/£, the investor will pay $1.352 to get one pound.
    - If the spot exchange rate at maturity is between $1.352/£ and $1.470/£, the investor will pay the current spot exchange rate to get one pound.
    - If the spot exchange rate at maturity is more than $1.470/£, the investor will pay $1.470 to get one pound.

    Assume that you are a British exporter who will receive $10 million in three months that will have to be transferred into British pounds at the time. Currently, the spot and forward exchange rates are $1.4200/£ and $1.4085/£, respectively.
    a. Explain why such a Range Forward Contract could be attractive if you fear a depreciation of the dollar during the three months.
    b. Explain why Salomon Brothers can sell such a contract at a very low price.

17. You are a British exporter who knows in December that you will receive $15 million in three months (March). The current spot exchange rate is $1.5/£, and the March forward exchange rate is also $1.5/£. Calls on the British pound are quoted by your bank for the exact amount that you desire, as follows:

    March Sterling Options (all prices in $ per £)

Strike	Call £
1.50	0.03
1.55	0.015
1.60	0.005

    Calculate the £ value of the $15 million received in three months, assuming that the $/£ spot exchange rate in March is equal to 1.3, 1.4, 1.5, 1.6, 1.7, and 1.8. Perform this calculation under five different scenarios about your hedging decision in December:
    - You do nothing.
    - You hedge with forward contracts.
    - You insure with calls 150.
    - You insure with calls 155.
    - You insure with calls 160.

    Put all of these figures in a table, and discuss the relative advantages of the various strategies.

18. Consider a U.S. portfolio manager who invests £5,000,000 in shares of a U.K. company. In order to hedge the stock market risk, he sells FTSE stock index futures that expire in three months. The current price of the FTSE stock index futures contract is 4,098 with a multiplier of £10. The current exchange rate is $1.58/£. One month later, the investment in the U.K. company is worth £5,022,000. The FTSE stock index futures price is now 4,200 and the exchange rate is $1.65/£.
    a. Calculate the number of futures contracts that the portfolio manager must sell.
    b. Calculate the profit-or-loss in dollar terms and pound terms.

19. Consider a French portfolio manager who invests $10,000,000 in shares of a U.S. company. In order to hedge the stock market risk, he sells S&P 500 stock index futures that expire in three months. The current price of the S&P 500 stock index futures contract is 902 with a multiplier of $250. The current exchange rate is €1.2/$. One month later, the investment in the U.S. company is worth $10,050,000. The S&P 500 stock index futures price is now 890, and the exchange rate is €0.98/$.
    a. Calculate the number of futures contracts that the portfolio manager must sell.
    b. Calculate the profit-or-loss in euro terms and dollar terms.

20. The HFS Trustees have decided to invest in international equity markets and have hired Jacob Hind, a specialist manager, to implement this decision. He has recommended that an unhedged equities position be taken in Japan, providing the following comment and data to support his views:

    Appreciation of a foreign currency increases the returns to a U.S. dollar investor. Because appreciation of the yen from 100¥/$ to 98¥/$ is expected, the Japanese stock position should not be hedged.

Market Rates and Hind's Expectations	United States	Japan
Spot rate (direct quote)	n/a	100
Hind's 12-month currency forecast	n/a	98
One-year Eurocurrency rate (% per annum)	6.00	0.80
Hind's 1-year inflation forecast (% per annum)	3.00	0.50

Assume that the investment horizon is one year and that there are no costs associated with currency hedging. State and justify whether Hind's recommendation should be followed. Show any calculations.

Solutions

1. To lock in the rate at which yen can be converted into U.S. dollars, the investor should enter into a contract to sell ¥160 million forward at a forward exchange rate of ¥/$ = 160. The hedge will be imperfect for the following reasons:
    - If the price of the Japanese stocks changes. For example, if the value of the portfolio suddenly goes up to ¥180 million, the investor will have underhedged ¥20 million. To remain fully hedged, the investor should continually adjust the amount hedged.
    - Another reason for an imperfect hedge is the possibility of a change in the forward basis caused by a change in interest rate differential.

2. a. The return on the unhedged portfolio in dollar terms is

    $$\frac{5,150,000 - 5,000,000}{5,000,000} = 0.03 = 3.0\%$$

    The return on the unhedged portfolio in euro terms is

    $$\frac{(5,150,000)(1.1) - (5,000,000)(0.974)}{(5,000,000)(0.974)} = 0.1632 = 16.32\%$$

The return on the hedged portfolio in euro terms is determined as follows:

The portfolio profit in euros $= (5,150,000)(1.1) - (5,000,000)(0.974) = €5,665,000$
$$- €4,870,000 = €795,000$$

The loss on the futures contract in euros $= (5,000,000)(1.02 - 1.15) = -€650,000$

The net profit on the hedged position $= €795,000 - €650,000 = €145,000$

The return on the hedged portfolio in euros $= €145,000/€4,870,000 = 0.0298$
$$= 2.98\%$$

This indicates that the position is almost perfectly hedged because a return of 3 percent in dollars has been transformed into a return of 2.98 percent in euros.

b. The return on a portfolio with a hedge ratio of 0.5 is calculated as follows:

Profit in euros $= (0.5)(-€650,000) + €795,000 = €470,000$

Return on partially hedged portfolio $= €470,000/€4,870,000 = 0.0965 = 9.65\%$

3. a. The return on the on the unhedged portfolio in euros is

$$\frac{10,050,000 - 10,000,000}{10,000,000} = 0.005 = 0.5\%$$

The return on the unhedged portfolio in dollar terms is

$$\frac{(10,050,000)(1.05) - (10,000,000)(1.1)}{(10,000,000)(1.1)} = -0.0407 = -4.07\%$$

The return on the hedged portfolio in dollar terms is determined as follows:

The portfolio loss in dollars $= (10,050,000)(1.05) - (10,000,000)(1.1) = \$10,552,500$
$$- \$11,000,000 = -\$447,500$$

The gain on the futures contract in dollars $= (10,000,000)(1 - 0.95) = \$500,000$

The net profit on the hedged position $= \$500,000 - \$447,500 = \$52,500$

The return on the hedged portfolio in dollars $= \$52,500/\$11,000,000 = 0.0048$
$$= 0.48\%$$

This indicates that the position is almost perfectly hedged because a return of 0.5 percent in euros has been transformed into a return of 0.48 percent in dollars.

b. The return on a portfolio with a hedge ratio of 0.35 is calculated as follows:

Profit in dollars $= (0.35)(\$500,000) - \$447,500 = -\$272,500$

Return on partially hedged portfolio $= -\$272,500/\$11,000,000$
$$= -0.0248$$
$$= -2.48\%$$

4. The investor should sell ¥160 million forward against euros, a transaction that combines two forward operations:
- Sell ¥160 million for \$ 1 million ($\$1,000,000 = ¥160,000,000/¥160/\$$)
- Sell \$1 million for € 833,333 $= \$1,000,000/\$1.20/€$

5. a. The one-year forward exchange rate is

$$F = (2)\left[\frac{1.06}{1.10}\right] = €1.9273/\$$$

b. Calculated portfolio values are summarized in the following table. To illustrate the calculations, assume an exchange rate of €1.6 per $ one year from now.
- The value of the unhedged portfolio at the end of one year is

€100,000,000(1/1.6) = $62,500,000

- To hedge using forward contracts, you would sell euros forward at €1.9273 per dollar. The value of the portfolio hedged with the currency forward contract is calculated as follows:

The profit on the portfolio in dollar terms is

€100,000,000(1/1.6 − 1/2.0) = $12,500,000

The profit on the forward contract in dollars terms is

€100,000,000(1/1.9273 − 1/1.6) = −$10,613,941.78

The overall profit on the hedged portfolio is

12,500,000 − 10,613,941.78 = $1,886,058.22

Thus, the value of the portfolio is

$50,000,000 + $1,886,058.22 = $51,886,058.22, or $51.89 million rounded

- To insure using options you will need to buy puts on the euro. Because the premium is paid in dollars, there is no exchange risk on the option premium. Assuming that the premium is financed at a dollar interest rate of 0 percent, you would buy €100 million worth of puts on the euro at a cost of

Premium = ($0.012 per euro) (€100,000,000) = $1,200,000

The profit on the put is calculated as follows:

If Strike price > Current price, Profit = (Strike price − Current price) × Quantity
If Strike price ≤ Current price, Profit = 0
The strike price is $0.50/€ and the current price is €1.6/$ = $0.625/€. Because 0.5 is less than 0.625, the profit is zero.

The currency gain = €100,000,000(1/1.6 − 1/2.0) = $12,500,000

The net profit on the position = $12,500,000 − $1,200,000 = $11,300,000

The value of the portfolio = $50,000,000 + $11,300,000 = $61,300,000

Portfolio Value (in $ million)

Exchange Rate (€/$)	Unhedged Value	Hedged Value	Insured Value
1.6	62.50	51.89	61.30
1.8	55.56	51.89	54.36
2.0	50.00	51.89	48.80
2.2	45.45	51.89	48.80
2.4	41.67	51.89	48.80

c. Basis risk, transactions costs, and cross-hedge risk.

6. a. As a Swiss investor with dollar investments, you would want to buy puts to sell the U.S dollar ($) for Swiss Francs (SFr). Puts on the $ are not available. However, puts on the $ are equivalent to calls to buy SFr for $. Therefore, you should buy calls on the

SFr to insure the SFr value of the portfolio. Because the option premium is paid in dollars while you care about SFr, the purchase of the call will reduce the dollar currency exposure. Hence, the quantity of calls purchased should reflect this reduction in currency risk. To determine the exact amount of calls to be bought, we will start the reasoning by looking at how we can insure 1 SFr. The option will be needed when the value of the SFr goes above $0.73. When the call is exercised, the total dollar cost to buy one SFr is

$$0.73 + 0.0243 = \$0.7543$$

Because you have $10 million, you can buy

$$\frac{10,000,000}{0.7543} = \text{SFr } 13,257,325$$

Note that the dollar cost of the premium paid is

$$\frac{(0.0243)(10,000,000)}{0.7543} = \$322,153$$

b. If you hedge using forward currency contracts, the portfolio will have a fixed SFr value of

$$\frac{10,000,000}{0.7389} = \text{SFr } 13,533,631$$

This looks better than the insured SFr13,257,325, but the disadvantage is that the hedged value will remain fixed, even if the dollar appreciates against the SFr.

7. a. To protect against a decline in share value, you should sell futures. You should sell 600 contracts:

$$\frac{20,000,000 \times 1.2}{10 \times 4,000} = 600$$

b. To hedge against a decline in the euro, you should sell €20 million forward. Because the euro and dollar interest rates are equal, the forward rate is equal to the spot rate, $1.10/€.

c. If you worry about a € depreciation, you should buy puts on the € worth €20 million. The cost is

Premium = ($0.02 per €)(€20 million) = $400,000

d. Assuming that the investor can get this amount from some other sources, that is, borrow at a zero-dollar interest rate (this is a dollar investment not exposed to currency risk), we get the final dollar simulated portfolio values in the following table. To illustrate, the calculations are explained, assuming an exchange rate of $1.0 per € in March.

  ▪ The value of the unhedged portfolio at the end of March is

€20,000,000(1) = $20,000,000

- To hedge using forward contracts, you would sell euros forward at $1.1 per €. The value of the portfolio hedged with the currency forward contract is calculated as follows:

The profit on the portfolio in dollar terms is

€20,000,000(1 − 1.1) = −$2,000,000

The profit on the forward contract in dollars terms is

€20,000,000(1.1 − 1) = $2,000,000

The overall profit on the hedged portfolio is $0

Thus, the value of the portfolio is $22,000,000 + $0 = $22,000,000

- To insure using options, you will need to buy puts on the euro. You would buy €20 million worth of puts on the euro at a cost of

Premium = ($0.02 per euro) (€20,000,000) = $400,000

The profit on the put is calculated as follows:

If Strike price > Current price, Profit = (Strike price − Current price) × Quantity

If Strike price ≤ Current price, Profit = 0

Because $1.10 > $1, Profit = (1.1 − 1)(€20,000,000) = $2,000,000

The currency gain = €20,000,000(1 − 1.1) = −$2,000,000

The net profit on the position = −$400,000

The value of the portfolio = $22,000,000 − $400,000 = $21,600,000

Portfolio Value (in $ million)

Exchange Rate ($/€)	Unhedged	Hedged	Insured
1.00	20	22	21.6
1.10	22	22	21.6
1.20	24	22	23.6

8. a. The three-month forward rate (MXP/$) is

$$F = (10)\left[\frac{1 + \dfrac{0.12}{4}}{1 + \dfrac{0.08}{4}}\right] = (10)\left[\frac{1.03}{1.02}\right] = 10.0980$$

b. Buy Mexican pesos forward against U.S. dollars. You would sell $1 million forward and get MXP 10.0980 million on February 4.

c. You would want to buy a put to sell $ for MXP. This is equivalent to buying a call to buy MXP for $. Thus, you should buy MXP calls to insure the U.S. dollar cash flow. If you have cash available, you should buy 20 contracts:

$$N = \frac{\$1,000,000}{(\$0.10/MXP)(MXP500,000)} = 20$$

at a cost of

Premium = (20)(500,000)(0.005) = $50,000, or MXP500,000

Assuming that the call premiums can be financed by borrowing MXP at a zero interest rate, the resulting cash flows at different exchange rates are shown in the following table.

When the exchange rate is below the strike price of MXP10/$, the option is exercised; for example, when the exchange rate is MXP8/$ the cash flow is

$$(\$1,000,000)(10) - MXP500,000 = MXP9,500,000$$

When the exchange rate is above MXP10/$, the option expires; for example, when the exchange rate is MXP12/$, the cash flow is

$$(\$1,000,000)(12) - MXP500,000 = MXP11,500,000$$

Exchange Rate MXP/$	MXP Cash Flow (in MXP million)
8.0	9.5
9.0	9.5
9.5	9.5
10.0	9.5
10.5	10
11.0	10.5
12.0	11.5

9. a. The three-month forward exchange rate is

$$F = (2)\left[\frac{1 + \dfrac{0.06}{4}}{1 + \dfrac{0.08}{4}}\right] = \$1.9902 \text{ per } \pounds$$

b. The optimal hedge ratio is determined by regressing the dollar returns of the British bonds on returns on the exchange rate. The result is strongly dependent on the correlation between the British interest rates and the pound value. In practice, the proposed strategy uses a hedge ratio of 1. This would be optimal if there were no correlation between interest rate and exchange rate movements.

c. Assume that the American investor buys £1 million of British bonds and sells forward £1 million for U.S. dollars.

If the various interest rates stay constant over the year and the currency hedge is rolled over every three months, the hedged British bonds will yield 12 percent minus 2 percent (the hedge's cost, i.e., the short-term interest rate differential) or an approximate total of 10 percent. This yield will be realized no matter what happens to the currency. Therefore, the performance is better than that of a direct investment in U.S. bonds, which would yield only 7 percent. If long-term interest rates move, this advantageous yield differential (10 percent instead of 7 percent) could be offset by a capital loss on the British bond position.

Illustrative Calculations

Initial investment = £1,000,000 or $2,000,000

Value after three months = (£1,000,000)(1 + 0.12/4) = £1,030,000

Hedged value in $ = (£1,030,000)(1.9902) = $2,049,906

Three month return = ($2,049,906/$2,000,000) − 1 = 0.025

Annualized return on hedged investment = (4)(0.025) = 0.10, or 10%

10. She would use € futures as a proxy for Danish kroner futures because the two exchange rates, €/$ and DKK/$, tend to move together. Denmark is part of the EU, but has not adopted the euro. However, Denmark attempts to maintain a stable exchange rate with the euro.

    At the current spot exchange rate, the Danish stock portfolio is worth

$$\left[\frac{\text{DKK}100,000,000}{(\$1.10/€)(\text{DKK}6.6/\$)}\right] = €13,774,105$$

Therefore, the American investor should sell €13.774 million of futures contracts against dollars. In Chicago, the € futures contracts have a size of €125,000, so the investor should sell

$$110 \text{ contracts} \approx 13,774,105/125,000$$

In practice, the proposed strategy uses a hedge ratio of 1. This would be optimal if there were no correlation between interest rate and exchange rate movements.

11. The following table provides the value of the portfolio in dollars at various exchange rates for the two hedging strategies, as well as the unhedged value. The calculations are explained for an exchange rate of ¥180/$ or $0.005556/¥.

    1. Unhedged portfolio value:

$$\frac{¥160,000,000}{¥180/\$} = \$888,888.89$$

    2. Hedged portfolio value, sale of yen futures at ¥160/$:

$$\frac{¥160,000,000}{¥160/\$} = \$1,000,000$$

    3. Insured portfolio value, purchase of yen puts at $0.007 per 100 yen: To insure using options you will need to buy puts on the yen. You would buy ¥160 million puts on the yen at a cost of

    Premium = ($0.00007 per yen)(¥160,000,000) = $11,200

    The profit on the put is calculated as follows:

    If Strike price > Current price, Profit = (Strike price − Current price) × Quantity
    If Strike price ≤ Current price, Profit = 0

    Because $0.0062 > $0.005556, profit = ($0.0062 − $0.005556)(¥160,000,000) = $103,111[7]

$$\text{The currency gain} = \frac{¥160,000,000}{¥180/\$} - \frac{¥160,000,000}{¥158/\$} = -\$123,769$$

    The net profit on the position = $103,111 − $11,200 − $123,769 = −$31,858

$$\text{The value of the portfolio} = \frac{¥160,000,000}{¥158/\$} - \$31,858 = \$980,800$$

---

[7] The result of 103,111 is obtained with the exact exchange rate of 1/180, rather than the approximation of 0.005556.

The following table summarizes the portfolio's final dollar value as a function of the spot exchange rate:

Value of the Portfolio (in $ million)

¥/$ Exchange Rate	140	150	158	170	180
Unhedged portfolio	1.143	1.067	1.013	0.941	0.889
Futures sale	1	1	1	1	1
Puts purchase	1.132	1.056	1.002	0.981	0.981

12. a. The Swiss investor wishes to use options as a delta-hedging device; therefore, the delta of the option should be taken into account.

   The portfolio is worth $10 million, or SFr25 million at the spot exchange rate of SFr2.5/$. Ignoring the correlation of the U.S. stock market with the SFr/$ exchange rate, which is very small anyway, he should buy SFr call contracts as shown below (remember this is equivalent to buying puts on the $):

$$\frac{25,000,000}{(62,500)(\delta)} = \frac{25,000,000}{(62,500)(0.5)} = 800 \text{ contracts}$$

   This would require payment of a premium of

   $(800)(62,500)(0.01) = \$500,000$, or $(500,000)(2.50 \text{ SFr}/\$) = \text{SFr}1,250,000$

   b. A few days later, the Swiss investor lost on his portfolio an amount of

   $(\$10,000,000)(\text{SFr}2.939/\$ - \text{SFr}2.5/\$) = -\text{SFr}610,000$

   But he gained on the option position, because his options are now worth

   $(800)(62,500)(0.016) = \$800,000$, or $(\$800,000)(\text{SFr}2.439/\$) = \text{SFr }1,951,200$

   hence a gain on the options of

   $1,951,200 - 1,250,000 = \text{SFr}701,200$

   The net gain is equal to SFr91,200 = 701,200 - 610,000. The portfolio has been overhedged because the delta of the option has increased with the appreciation of the SFr.

   c. In a dynamic strategy, the Swiss investor could sell part of his option contracts to adjust to the new delta. The investor now needs only 557 contracts, as shown:
   - New SFr value of the portfolio: SFr24,390,000 = ($10,000,000)(2.439SFr/$)
   - Contracts needed for a delta hedge:

$$\frac{24,390,000}{(62,500)(0.70)} = 557.5 \text{ contracts}$$

13. a. To have a good dynamic hedge, you should buy 160 call contracts on the euro:

$$\frac{10,000,000}{(125,000)(0.5)} = 160 \text{ contracts}$$

   The € value of the option position is

   $(\$0.02/€)(160)(€125,000)(€1/\$) = €400,000$

   b. The portfolio value shows a loss in euros of

   $(\$10,000,000)/(\$1.1/€) - (\$10,000,000)(€1/\$) = -€909,091$

The option position value is

$$(\$0.11/\text{€})(160)(\text{€}125{,}000)/(\$1.1/\text{€}) = \text{€}2{,}000{,}000$$

Hence, a gain on the option position of €1,600,000 = €2,000,000 − €400,000. The net gain is equal to €690,909 = €1,600,000 − €909,091.

c. This net gain is due to the fact that the delta increased to 0.9, but the hedge was not rebalanced dynamically.

d. We can reduce the number of option contracts to

$$\frac{9{,}090{,}909}{(125{,}000)(0.9)} = 81 \text{ contracts}$$

where €9,090,909 is the current portfolio value = ($10,000,000)/($1.1/€).

14. This question can be answered by calculating the impact of the depreciation of the pound in the three strategies for an equivalent claim of one FTSE index.

In a direct investment in the British stock market (e.g., index fund), we must invest £6,000 to get one unit of index. In a future purchase, we only have to deposit £1,500/10 = £150 per unit of index because one futures contract is for the index times 10. In the call purchase, we only invest £20 per unit of index.

a. Direct investment in the FTSE index: You invest £6,000, or (£6000)($2/£) = $12,000. The £ profit is equal to

£6,100 − £6,000 = £100

But converted into dollars, this gives a loss of

$$(£6{,}100)(\$1.8/£) − (£6{,}000)(\$2/£) = −\$1020$$

b. December futures on the FTSE index: You invest £150 per unit of index, or $300 = (£150)($2/£). The contract is marked-to-market, so by December you realize a profit of = £6,100 − £6,030 = £70. The final value is therefore £220 (£150 + £70), or $396 = (£220)($1.8/£). The net dollar profit is equal to

$396 − $300 = $96

c. December 6050 FTSE call option: You invest £20 per unit of index or $40. The final value is £50, or $90 at the spot exchange rate of $1.8/£. The net dollar profit is equal to

$90 − $40 = $50

15. An American investor hedging the British pound risk has to "pay" the interest rate differential (British minus U.S. interest rate), while a British investor hedging the U.S. dollar risk "receives" it. It seems to be the reason why the journal suggests that Americans should *not* hedge their British investments, but that British should hedge their U.S. investments.

If the interest rate differential simply reflects the expected depreciation of the pound relative to the dollar, there is no *expected* "cost" of hedging in the sense intended by the journal. Furthermore, short-term currency swings can be very large relative to the interest rate differential, so risk should also be considered. To hedge currency *risk* could turn out to be a good decision, even if you have to "pay" an interest rate differential.

The journal could also be suggesting that a currency with a higher interest rate tends to appreciate. Even if this statement is true on the average, exchange rates are very volatile. A currency hedge still allows the reduction of the risk of a loss.

16. a. Traditional ways for the exporter to hedge against a decline in the value of the dollar would be to (i) buy puts on the dollar or, equivalently, (ii) buy calls on the pound. The Range Forward Contract ensures that the exporter will not pay more than $1.470/£, even if the dollar depreciates strongly relative to the pound. Typically the range forward insurance costs nothing. On the other hand, a traditional call on the pound is costly in that it involves payment of a call premium. The same applies to put options on the pound. The disadvantage of the range forward is that the exporter will not fully benefit from an appreciation of the dollar. In the case of options, the exporter can allow the option to expire worthless if the dollar appreciates. With a range forward contract, the exporter will benefit up to an exchange rate of $1.352/£, but not beyond that rate. So, the exporter sacrifices some profit potential to get "free" insurance.

    b. This contract is the sum of
       - a call pound, giving the exporter the right to buy pounds at $1.470/£; and
       - a put pound, giving Salomon Brothers the right to sell pounds at $1.352/£.

    In other words, the exporter buys a call with a strike of $1.470/£ and sells a put with a strike of $1.352/£. The fair value of the Range Forward Contract should be the difference between the call premium and the put premium. The fair value should be much smaller than that of the call alone. Typically, the strike prices are chosen so that the option costs nothing.

17. Again, assume that we buy the calls by borrowing pounds at a zero interest rate. For example, to "insure" with $1.50 strike calls on the £, we need to buy calls on £10 million. The cost is $300,000, which we finance with £200,000, given the spot exchange rate.

    The following table provides portfolio values at various exchange rates. To explain, portfolio values are calculated at an exchange rate of $1.7/£.

    1. Unhedged portfolio value:

       $15,000,000/$1.7 per pound = £8,823,529

    2. Hedged portfolio value, using forward contract $1.5 per pound:

       $15,000,000/$1.5 per pound = £10,000,000

    3. Insured portfolio, using March 1.50 calls: Once again, remember that you can insure using a put to sell $ for £, or buying a call to buy £ using $. The call option will be exercised if Current price > Strike price. Otherwise, it will expire worthless, and you lose only the option premium:

    $$\text{Option premium} = \frac{15,000,000}{1.5}(0.03) = \$300,000 \quad \text{or}$$

    £200,000 = $300,000/1.5

Current price = $1.7/£ and the Strike price = $1.5/£. The option is exercised because it allows the exporter to buy pounds at a cheaper rate:

$$\text{Profit on call} = \frac{15,000,000}{1.5} - \frac{15,000,000}{1.7} = £1,176,471$$

The dollar depreciation leads to a currency loss:

$$= \frac{15,000,000}{1.7} - \frac{15,000,000}{1.5} = -£1,176,471$$

The net profit on the position $= £1,176,471 - £1,176,471 - £200,000 = -£200,000$

The portfolio value $= £10,000,000 - £200,000 = £9,800,000$

Rounded Portfolio Value (in £ thousand):

Exchange Rate ($/£)	Unhedged	Hedged	Insured with Call (150)	Insured with Call (155)	Insured with Call (160)
1.3	11,538	10,000	11,338	11,438	11,505
1.4	10,714	10,000	10,514	10,614	10,681
1.5	10,000	10,000	9,800	9,900	9,967
1.6	9,375	10,000	9,800	9,577	9,342
1.7	8,824	10,000	9,800	9,577	9,342
1.8	8,333	10,000	9,800	9,577	9,342

- Hedging with forward contracts allows to the exporter to eliminate the risk of a decline in the dollar. However, it also means that the British exporter will not benefit if the dollar appreciates.
- Options allow the exporter to "insure" rather then "hedge." In other words, a floor is set on the total amount of pounds that the exporter will receive. If the dollar is "strong," the exporter will benefit. However, an insurance has a cost that has to be borne in all cases (i.e., the premium paid to purchase the option).
- An *expensive* option (in-the-money; in this case, the $1.50 call) provides better protection in the case of a "weak" dollar, but reduces the profit potential in case of a "strong" dollar.
- A *cheap* option (the out-of-the-money $1.60 call) provides less protection in case of a "weak" dollar, but only slightly reduces the profit potential in case of a "strong" dollar.

The choice between the following five alternatives depends on the expectations and risk aversion of the exporter. We can rank them in decreasing order of protection against a drop in the dollar (e.g., from $1.50 to $1.70 per pound), as follows:

1. Hedge—Portfolio value £10,000,000
2. Call 150—Portfolio value £9,800,000
3. Call 155—Portfolio value £9,577,000
4. Call 160—Portfolio value £9,342,000
5. No Hedge—Portfolio value £8,824,000

18. a. The manager would have to sell

$$\frac{5,000,000}{(4098)(10)} = 122 \text{ contracts}$$

b. The profit on the investment in the U.K. company:

In pounds $= 5,022,000 - 5,000,000 = £22,000$

In dollars $= (5,022,000)(1.65) - (5,000,000)(1.58) = \$386,300$

The loss on the futures contract:

In pounds = $(122)(10)(4098 - 4200) = -£124,440$

In dollars = $(124,440)(1.65) = -\$205,326$

The net profit or loss on the position:

In pounds = £22,000 − £124,440 = −£102,440

In dollars = \$386,300 − \$205,326 = \$180,974

19. a. The manager would have to sell

$$\frac{10,000,000}{(902)(250)} = 44 \text{ contracts}$$

   b. The profit on the investment in the U.S. company:

In dollars = 10,050,000 − 10,000,000 = \$50,000

In euros = $(10,050,000)(0.98) - (10,000,000)(1.2) = -€2,151,000$

The profit on the futures contract:

In dollars = $(44)(250)[902 - 890] = \$132,000$

In euros = $(132,000)(0.98) = €129,360$

The net profit or loss on the position:

In dollars = \$50,000 + \$132,000 = \$182,000

In euros = €129,360 − €2,151,000 = −€2,021,640

Notice that, in this case, the currency losses on the depreciation of the euro swamped the dollar gains on the stock and futures positions.

20. Appreciation of a foreign currency will, indeed, increase the dollar returns that accrue to a U.S. investor. However, the amount of the expected appreciation must be compared with the forward premium or discount on that currency in order to determine whether or not hedging should be undertaken.

   In the present example, the yen is forecast to appreciate from 100 to 98 (2 percent). However, the forward premium on the yen, as given by the differential in one-year Eurocurrency rates, suggests an appreciation of over 5 percent:

Forward premium = $[(1.06)/(1.008)] -1 = 5.16\%$

Or, using interest rate parity, the implied forward rate for the yen is

$$(100)\left[\frac{1.008}{1.06}\right] = ¥95.09/\$$$

Thus, the manager's strategy to leave the yen unhedged is not appropriate. The manager should hedge, because, by doing so, a higher rate of yen appreciation can be locked in. Given the one-year Eurocurrency rate differentials, the yen position should be left unhedged only if the yen is forecast to appreciate to an exchange rate of less than 95.09 yen per U.S. dollar.

Bibliography

Adler, M., and Simon, D. "Exchange Rate Surprises in International Portfolios," *Journal of Portfolio Management,* Winter 1986.

Briys, E., and Solnik, B. "Optimal Currency Hedge Ratios and Interest Rate Risk," *Journal of International Money and Finance,* December 1992.

Dale, C. "The Hedging Effectiveness of Currency Futures Markets," *Journal of Futures Markets,* Spring 1981.

Eaker, M., and Grant, D. "Cross-Hedging Foreign Currency Risks," *Journal of International Money and Finance,* March 1987.

Grammatikos, T., and Saunders, A. "Stability and the Hedging Performance of Foreign Currency Futures," *Journal of Futures Markets,* Fall 1983.

Hanna, J., and Niculescu, P. "The Currency and Interest Rate Strategy Matrix: An Investment Tool for Multicurrency Investors," Bond Market Research, Salomon Brothers, September 1982.

Jorion, P. "Mean/Variance Analysis of Currency Overlays," *Financial Analysts Journal,* May–June 1994.

Kroner, K. F., and Sultan, J. "Time-Varying Distributions and Dynamic Hedging with Foreign Currency Futures," *Journal of Financial and Quantitative Analysis,* December 1993.

12

Global Performance Evaluation

■ **LEARNING OUTCOMES** ■

After completing this chapter, you will be able to do the following:

- Explain the three steps of global performance evaluation: measurement, attribution, and appraisal

- Calculate, explain, and contrast the following measures for computing a rate of return: money-weighted return and time-weighted return

- Explain why time-weighted returns should be used in performance evaluation and discuss the problems that arise when approximate methods are used

- Calculate and explain the effect of currency movements on the portfolio rate of return calculated in its base currency

- Explain the decomposition of portfolio return into yield, capital gains in local currency, and currency contribution, and calculate those components of portfolio return

- Explain the purpose of global performance attribution and calculate the contribution of market allocation, currency allocation, and security selection

- Interpret the results of performance attribution for a global portfolio

- Calculate and discuss total risk and tracking error for a portfolio

- Calculate and interpret the Sharpe ratio and the information ratio for a portfolio

- Explain how risk budgeting is used in global performance evaluation

- Discuss the various biases that may affect performance appraisal

- Discuss the characteristics of different global and international benchmarks used in performance evaluation

The management of a global portfolio is a complex task with numerous parameters to take into account. The portfolio's performance and risk can be attributed to many management decisions, including the choice of instruments, markets, currencies, and individual securities. This book has shown the wide variety of institutional features, investment techniques, and concepts that a capable international money manager must master. Given this complexity, a detailed and frequent evaluation of the performance and risk of global portfolios is required, for both the investment manager and the client. A money management firm typically has several portfolio managers with responsibility for a large number of accounts under diverse mandates. It is of the utmost importance for the firm to perform an in-house assessment of the performance of each account and manager, of the risks and bets taken, and of the areas in which expertise, or lack of expertise, has been demonstrated. Performance must be attributed to the various investment decisions of the manager. From an external viewpoint, clients wish to compare the performance of competing money managers and judge their investment skills; this requires that performance on managed accounts be analyzed in a comparable fashion and that proper risk adjustment be performed. This chapter deals with the principles, mathematics, and implementation of performance evaluation in a global context.

The first section of this chapter details the principles and objectives of global performance evaluation (GPE). Because performance evaluation can be quite complex in a global environment, a good understanding of the basic return measurement concepts is required, and some words of caution are in order. The second section details performance attribution in multicurrency, multiasset portfolios: The return relative to a benchmark is attributed to the major investment decisions. The final step of a GPE is to analyze investment skills. Performance appraisal, discussed in the third section, requires one to consider the risks taken to determine whether the manager has a true ability to add value. The final section deals with some implementation issues and discusses various performance standards, especially Global Investment Performance Standards™ (GIPS®).

The Basics

Principles and Objectives

GPE can be separated into three components:

- Performance measurement

- Performance attribution

- Performance appraisal

Clients (individual investors, plan sponsors) and investment managers focus on different aspects of this process. GPE can be conducted by the investment manager using a proprietary system or some specialized software. It is also performed by consultants offering a GPE service. The latter service also allows one to compare performance with that of a universe of investment managers.

Performance Measurement   The core of GPE is to calculate rates of return on the portfolio and its various segments. Performance is then measured by comparing these returns with those on preassigned benchmarks. Performance is a return relative to that of a benchmark. In a global context, it is important to be able to measure the return on various portfolio segments (e.g., "European equity," "yen bonds"), both in the local currency of the investment and in the base currency of the investor. This is an added complexity compared with the performance measurement of domestic portfolios. *Performance measurement* is the GPE component by which returns are calculated over a measurement period for the overall portfolio and various segments.

Performance measurement should not be confused with accounting valuation. Multicurrency accounting systems keep track, on a daily basis, of all transactions, including forward commitments, and provide a valuation of the account based on current market prices from around the world and computed in one *base currency* (also called *reference currency*). The base currency is the currency chosen by the investor to value the portfolio; for example, a British pension fund would use the British pound as base currency. Every item, including stocks, bonds, alternative investments, derivatives, and, of course, cash, is included in an accounting valuation.

GPE systems measure the return on a portfolio and various portfolio segments over a short *measurement period,* usually on a monthly basis but sometimes daily. These returns are then compounded over longer *performance evaluation periods* (a quarter, a year, or several years). A huge amount of valuation and transaction information is synthesized into a few return figures. So, the way rates of returns are calculated to synthesize the information is of great importance (as we discuss later). The quality of data is an important issue that will affect the method used and the reliability of the results. Using short measurement periods (ideally, daily) allows one to generate more precise performance numbers but also better risk estimates.

At the end of the measurement process, one should be able to answer questions such as these three:

- What is the total return on the portfolio over a specific period, and its performance relative to a benchmark?

- What are the total returns on each segment of the portfolio, in local and base currencies, and the performance relative to their benchmarks?

- What is the volatility of the portfolio and its tracking error?

The major focus of performance measurement is to perform correct calculations of return.

Performance Attribution   Managers and clients need to understand how the total performance was reached. *Performance attribution* is the GPE component by which the total portfolio performance is attributed to major investment decisions taken by the manager. For example, a manager is assigned the MSCI World index as benchmark for a global equity portfolio with the British pound as base currency. A country allocation different from that of the index could result in currency gains or losses, as well as market gains or losses relative to the index. Even with the same country weights, the manager could decide to favor some industries or investment styles worldwide; this decision could again result in superior return.

To quantify performance attribution, detailed calculations need to be performed, as illustrated in next section. In particular, we need to account for exchange rate translation, a source of complexity in performance attribution. One should also try to attribute the total risk of the portfolio to major investment decisions, and again currency risk could be of importance.

At the end of the performance attribution process, one should be able to answer questions such as

(a) What is the breakdown of the return in terms of capital gains, currency fluctuations, and income?

(b) To what extent are returns explained by asset allocation, country weighting, industry weighting, investment style selection, currency selection and hedging, or individual security selection?

(c) How is the total risk of the portfolio explained by the major investment decisions outlined in question (b)?

Performance Appraisal Clients wish to know if their managers possess true investment skill. *Performance appraisal* is the GPE component by which some judgment is formulated on the investment manager's skills. It requires one to look at performance over longer horizons, taking into account the risks borne. Risk-adjusted measures are used.

The choice of benchmarks used to appraise performance is important, and again the multicurrency environment makes it a more difficult issue (e.g., should benchmarks be currency-hedged?). At the end of the performance appraisal process, one should be able to answer questions such as

- Has the manager provided a good risk-adjusted performance over some long-run horizon?

- How does the manager compare with a peer group (i.e., a universe of managers with similar investment objectives)?

- Is the performance due to luck, higher risks taken, or true investment skill?

- Is there evidence of unusual expertise and added value in a particular market (e.g., Japanese stocks or British bonds) or dimension (industry, style, currency overlay, etc.)?

The goal of GPE is ambitious and the conclusions drawn are of significant importance. Unfortunately, technical and conceptual problems arise, due in part to the quality of the data used as inputs to the analysis. These problems are present to some extent in a domestic performance evaluation, but they are magnified in an international setting, in which a detailed GPE requires the calculation of rates of return on various segments and in different currencies. The method used to calculate a rate of return is of significance.

Calculating a Rate of Return

The rate of return[1] is typically calculated on a short *measurement period* (say, one month) and then compounded over a performance period (say, one year). The first, and somewhat unexpected, problem encountered in performance evaluation is the method to be used in calculating a basic rate of return on a portfolio or on a portfolio segment for a specific measurement period.

The rate of return over a measurement period is easy to calculate if there are no cash flows in or out of the portfolio. Its return, r, is simply equal to the change in value over the period ($V_1 - V_0$) divided by the initial value V_0:

$$r = \frac{V_1 - V_0}{V_0} \quad \text{or} \tag{12.1}$$

$$1 + r = \frac{V_1}{V_0}$$

The rate of return is not annualized but applies to the measurement period.

However, let's now assume that a cash flow, C_t, took place on day t during the period.[2] Then the calculation of the rate of return is less obvious. The problem is that the capital invested has changed over the period, so a simple formula such as Equation 12.1 cannot be used.

There are two very different approaches to calculating a rate of return in the presence of interim cash flow:

- The *money-weighted return*[3] (MWR) concept captures the return on the *average invested capital*. It is a measure of the net enrichment of the client, taking cash flows into account.

- The *time-weighted return* (TWR) concept captures the return *per dollar invested* (or per unit of base currency).[4] It is a measure of the performance of the manager independently of the cash flows to the portfolio. In other words, the TWR measures the performance that would have been realized had the same capital been under management during the whole period. It allows meaningful comparisons with a passive index or with other managers.

---

[1] It must be stressed that rates of return discussed in this chapter are not annualized. They are the return over the period considered.

[2] We use the convention that a positive cash flow is an addition to the portfolio and that a negative cash flow is a withdrawal from the portfolio (a reduction in invested capital). This convention is changed from previous editions of this book.

[3] It is often called *dollar-weighted return* in the United States.

[4] The traditional label *time-weighted* sometimes leads to confusion. It simply means that only time matters in calculating the rate of return, but not the amount of invested capital.

We now detail the various methods, exact or approximate, to measure the MWR and TWR and illustrate them in simple examples.

EXAMPLE 12.1   SIMPLE PORTFOLIO: RATE OF RETURN

Consider a "simple portfolio" with a single cash flow during the measurement period. For simplicity, the measurement period is supposed to be one year.[5] The details on the portfolio are as follows:

- Value at start of the year is $V_0 = 100$

- Cash withdrawal on day t is $C_t = -50$

- The cash outflow takes place 30 days after the start of the period, or at $t = 30/365 = 0.082$ year

- Value on day t, before the cash flow, is $V_t = 95$

- Final value at year end is $V_1 = 60$

What would be the rate of return using Equation 12.1?

SOLUTION

If Equation 12.1 were applied directly, we would find a rate of return of $(60 - 100)/100 = -40\%$, which is clearly incorrect.

Money-Weighted Return   Financiers are accustomed to using discounting to calculate the rate of return on an investment with multiple cash flows. This MWR is sometimes called an *internal rate of return*. It is the discount rate that sets the present value of future cash flows (including the portfolio final value) equal to the initial investment (the start-of-period value).

The MWR can be calculated for any measurement period. The time index t of a cash flow C_t is expressed as a fraction of the length of the measurement period. It is simply the number of days from the start of the period, divided by the number of days in the period:

$$t = \frac{\text{Number of days since start of period}}{\text{Total number of days in measurement period}}$$

So t starts from zero at the start of the measurement period and moves to one at the end of the measurement period. In general, the MWR is the value of r in the following equation:

$$V_0 = \sum_t \frac{-C_t}{(1+r)^t} + \frac{V_1}{(1+r)^1} \tag{12.2}$$

The cash flows C_t enter with a negative sign because of the convention that a positive C_t is a contribution made by the client to the portfolio, while a negative C_t is a cash flow withdrawn by the client.

---

[5] In practice, it is typically one month as shown in another example.

> ### EXAMPLE 12.2   SIMPLE PORTFOLIO: MONEY-WEIGHTED RETURN
>
> What is the MWR of the "simple portfolio" in Example 12.1?
>
> **SOLUTION**
>
> In the example, the internal rate of return is the value of r in the following equation:
>
> $$100 = \frac{50}{(1 + r)^{30/365}} + \frac{60}{1 + r}$$
>
> Thus, the MWR is equal to
>
> $$r = \text{MWR} = 18.37\%$$

Again, the MWR is *not* annualized; it is the average return over the measured period, taking into account the amount of capital invested. Its calculation does not require one to value the portfolio at the time of cash flows. Computers can easily calculate an internal rate of return; it can also be done on a spreadsheet. With to-day's computing power, this is a trivial task. However, the calculation can yield multiple answers when there are negative and positive cash flows, and it is sensitive to measurement errors and the exact dating of cash flows. For ease of calculation, some approximations to MWR were developed.

Approximation to the MWR: Dietz Method   A linear approximation to the MWR can be obtained by calculating a simple ratio as proposed by Dietz. This is an "accounting" measure of the return on the average invested capital and is obtained by dividing the profit on the portfolio by the average capital invested during the period:

$$\text{MWR}_1 = \frac{\text{Profit}}{\text{Average invested capital}} \tag{12.3}$$

Everyone agrees on the profit over the period: It is the change in value of the portfolio minus the net cash flow (sum of all cash flows). The only question remaining is how to compute the "average invested capital." This is obtained by weighting each cash flow by the amount of time it is held in the portfolio. In general, each cash flow taking place at time t has a weight in the average capital equal to $1 - t$. Hence the formula[6] is

---

[6] It can be easily verified that this is just the linear approximation to the internal rate of return. Simply multiply both sides of Equation 12.2 by $1 + r$ and replace $(1 + r)^{1-t}$ by its first-order linear expansion $1 + r(1 - t)$. Then Equation 12.2 becomes

$$V_0 (1 + r) = - \sum_t C_t(1 + r(1 - t)) + V_1 \quad \text{or} \quad r = \frac{V_1 - V_0 - \sum_t C_t}{V_0 + \sum_t (1 - t) C_t}$$

which is identical to Equation 12.4. The first-order approximation works well for small values of r.

$$\text{MWR}_1 = \frac{\text{Profit}}{\text{Average invested capital}} = \frac{V_1 - V_0 - \sum_t C_t}{V_0 + \sum_t (1 - t) C_t} \qquad (12.4)$$

Generally, the Dietz method gives a reasonable approximation to the MWR for short measurement periods (up to one month).

A further crude approximation could be performed. Rather than keeping track of the timing of the cash flows, one assumes arbitrarily that the net cash flow takes place at the middle of the period. Then, the average invested capital is simply equal to the starting capital plus 50 percent of the net cash flow. The resulting rate of return is

$$\text{MWR}_2 = \frac{\text{Profit}}{\text{Average invested capital}} = \frac{V_1 - V_0 - \sum_t C_t}{V_0 + \frac{1}{2} \sum_t C_t}$$

This formula, sometimes called the "original" Dietz method, can provide a poor approximation of the MWR. Given today's data processing capabilities, it is a trivial task to keep track of the timing of cash flows and calculate their weighted average. Use of the original Dietz method is hard to justify any longer.

EXAMPLE 12.3   SIMPLE PORTFOLIO: APPROXIMATIONS TO THE MWR

Calculate an approximation to the MWR of the "simple portfolio," using the Dietz method.

SOLUTION

In Example 12.1, a cash flow of 50 was removed after 30 days, so that it was not available for investment during 335 days of the one-year measurement period. Hence, this approximation to the MWR yields a rate of

$$\text{MWR}_1 = \frac{\text{Profit}}{\text{Average invested capital}} = \frac{60 - 100 + 50}{100 - \dfrac{365 - 30}{365} \times 50} = \frac{10}{54.11} = 18.48\%$$

The difference with the correct MWR is 0.11% over a year. The "original" Dietz method yields an approximate MWR of

$$\text{MWR}_2 = \frac{\text{Profit}}{\text{Average invested capital}} = \frac{60 - 100 + 50}{100 - \dfrac{1}{2} \times 50} = \frac{10}{75} = 13.33\%$$

Although MWR_1 is close to MWR (18.48% instead of 18.37%), MWR_2 is very different (13.33%).

Time-Weighted Return   By contrast with the MWR methods, the time-weighted rate of return (TWR) is the performance per dollar invested (or per unit of base currency) and is calculated independently of the cash flows to or from the portfolio.

In other words, the TWR measures the performance that would have been realized had the same capital been under management over the whole period. This method is necessary for comparing performance among managers or with a passive benchmark. The TWR is obtained by calculating the rate of return between each cash flow date and chain-linking those rates over the total measurement period. As mentioned, the rate of return over a period without cash flows suffers no controversy, and the TWR simply compounds the rates of return per unit of base currency. Calculating a TWR with interim cash flows requires the valuation of a portfolio each time a cash flow takes place. Basically, a daily valuation is required. Let's call V_t the value of the portfolio just before the cash flow takes place. In the presence of a single cash flow, C_t, during the measurement period, we need to calculate the rate of return from the start of the measurement period until the cash flow takes place, and then from the date of the cash flow till the end of the period.

The rate of return for the first subperiod, from zero to t, is given by r_t.

$$1 + r_t = \frac{V_t}{V_0}$$

where the value of the portfolio just before the cash flow takes place is V_t.

The rate of return for the second subperiod, from t to 1, is given by r_{t+1}:

$$1 + r_{t+1} = \frac{V_1}{(V_t + C_t)}$$

where the value of the portfolio just after the cash flow is $V_t + C_t$.

The total TWR[7] over the measurement period, r, is obtained by chain-linking:

$$(1 + r) = (1 + r_t)(1 + r_{t+1}) = \frac{V_t}{V_0} \times \frac{V_1}{(V_t + C_t)} \tag{12.5}$$

If there are more cash flows during the measurement period, we need to calculate a rate of return between each cash flow date and chain-link them as done here.

The MWR is useful for measuring the return of invested capital: It gives an assessment of the *client's* net enrichment over the measurement period. However, everyone agrees that the TWR is the preferred method for measuring and comparing the performance of money managers. To evaluate the *manager's* ability, the comparison should be independent of the cash movements imposed by clients. Benchmarks or peer groups are not affected by the same cash flows. The TWR must be used for performance evaluation.

---

[7] Remember that the rates of return are not annualized.

EXAMPLE 12.4   SIMPLE PORTFOLIO: TIME-WEIGHTED RETURN

Calculate the TWR of the "simple portfolio." Contrast the result with the MWR found in Example 12.2.

SOLUTION

In the example, the portfolio was worth 95 at the time cash was withdrawn, so the TWR is equal to 26.67%, as shown here:

rates of return

$$1 + r_t = \frac{95}{100} \qquad\qquad r_t = -5\%$$

$$1 + r_{t+1} = \frac{60}{45} \qquad\qquad r_{t+1} = 33.33\%$$

$$1 + r = 0.95 \times 1.3333 = 1.2667 \qquad r = \text{TWR} = 26.67\%$$

Clearly the various methods of calculating a rate of return yield very different results: from 13.33% to 26.67%. In the example, the client withdrew some funds just before a bull market, so the invested capital was smaller in the bull market than in the bear market. This is why the MWR is less than the TWR in the example.

Returns over Long Horizons: A Word of Caution   Once rates of return are calculated over a measurement period, they are geometrically chain-linked[8] over longer performance periods (a quarter, one or several years). For example, the quarterly return can be calculated from three monthly returns, using the formula

$$r_q = (1 + r_1) \times (1 + r_2) \times (1 + r_3) - 1 \tag{12.6}$$

where r_q is the portfolio quarterly return, and r_1, r_2, and r_3 are the monthly returns in months 1, 2, and 3.

An exact TWR cannot be calculated for a portfolio or its various segments unless the portfolio is valued at the date of any addition or withdrawal of funds. With a high level of cash flow activity, this may be costly. A compromise that has been tried is to calculate MWRs over measurement periods of one month, and to chain-link them over a longer performance period. One must be aware, however, that a discrepancy in a monthly return (between the calculated MWR and the true TWR) will subsist permanently in the chain-linked performance.[9] There is no technical reason to expect the discrepancy to be offset in the next month. In a world in which clients increasingly focus on alphas relative to passive benchmarks, the magnitude of the potential discrepancy between an MWR and a true TWR over a month has signifi-

---

[8] A *geometric* average uses compounding of rates of return. This is different from an *arithmetic* average, which uses a simple summation of rates of return.

[9] Further, if an approximation to the MWR is used, such as the original Dietz method, there is an additional source of error.

cant importance. To avoid serious distortions, one should revalue the portfolio on each large cash flow (as recommended by GIPS). The shorter the measurement period used for an MWR, the smaller the discrepancy. And reliable daily valuation should be the goal of any asset management firm.

To conduct a detailed GPE, one should calculate the return for the various segments of the portfolio. This allows one to judge the contribution of various investment decisions to total performance. In the international context, the problems associated with using monthly MWR figures are compounded by the multicurrency and multimarket nature of performance measurement. In a detailed international analysis of the performance of each national segment, shifting funds between markets creates the same cash flow problem. Because these internal cash flows are frequent, the portfolio should be valued frequently. Time differences and lags in reporting of international transactions can introduce various statistical problems with daily valuation. But using monthly MWR for the various segments leads to the same problem discussed previously. An illustration is given in Example 12.5.

EXAMPLE 12.5   VALUING STOCK SELECTION ABILITY ON A JAPANESE EQUITY PORTFOLIO

Consider a £10 million fund that is restricted to a 10 percent investment in Japan. One hundred million yen (£1 million) is invested in the Japanese stock market and managed by a local money manager. The British fund's trustee wants to evaluate the manager's security selection skill in this market. Assuming a fixed exchange rate (i.e., ¥100/£rate), we will consider the following scenario. The Japanese manager invests ¥100 million in the Japanese stock index, via an index fund, thereby exactly tracking the index. After two weeks, the index rises from 100 to 130, and the fund's trustee asks the manager to transfer ¥30 million to a falling market (such as the U.K. market) in order to keep within the 10 percent limitation on Japanese investment and rebalance the asset allocation to its desired target. Over the next two weeks, the Japanese index loses 30 percent of its value (falling to 91), so that by the end of the month, the Japanese portfolio is down to ¥70 million. The MWR approximation, using the Dietz method, and the TWR of the portfolio are indicated in Exhibit 12.1. If a consultant performed a GPE using the Dietz method, what would be his conclusion regarding the security selection ability of the manager in Japan? Would his conclusion be correct?

EXHIBIT 12.1

TWR and Dietz Approximation to MWR for a Hypothetical Japanese Portfolio

	Day				
	0	**15**	**30**	**TWR %**	**MRW %**
Index	100	130	91	—	—
Portfolio before transfer	100	130			
Portfolio after transfer		100	70	−9	0

SOLUTION

The TWR on the Japanese portfolio is −9 percent; that is the performance of the Japanese index, which was perfectly tracked and fell from 100 to 91. The MWR computed by the consultant will be 0 percent (a net profit equal to zero, divided by some average capital), wrongly implying that the manager outperformed the Japanese market and has great skills in Japanese stock selection. In fact, the manager precisely tracked the Japanese market and no more.

The importance of exact computations cannot be overstressed. Astute stock selection is supposed to be a significant contribution made by a manager. This is computed as a residual, subtracting the currency and market effects from the overall performance of the portfolio's segments. Unfortunately, this residual is also the repository for a variety of errors arising from poor data, incorrect calculations and approximations, and transaction costs.

Frequent calculation of return is also needed to estimate operational risk measures, especially on a global portfolio. A few years of monthly data (the usual practice is five years) are required to obtain statistically significant estimates of an overall fund's volatility, and this assumes stationary currency and market returns over that period, as well as a constant risk objective on the part of the manager. These assumptions are risky (especially for currencies) in light of the marked instability that many financial markets have displayed over time.

Performance Attribution In Global Performance Evaluation

The exact measurement of returns is an important task in a domestic as well as global performance evaluation. Performance attribution is more difficult in a GPE because a portfolio can be invested in many different national markets and because prices are quoted in different currencies on these markets.

To conduct a detailed global performance attribution, a portfolio is broken down into various segments according to type of asset and currency. Each homogeneous segment (say, Japanese stocks) is valued separately in its local currency as well as in the base currency of the portfolio. Thus, Japanese stocks are valued in yen as well as in the investor's base currency.

In Example 12.6, we introduce a "simple portfolio B" that will be followed throughout the chapter.

EXAMPLE 12.6   SIMPLE PORTFOLIO B: TOTAL RETURN

An American investor has invested $100,000 in an international equity portfolio (which we will call "simple portfolio B") made up of Asian and European stocks. On December 31, the portfolio is invested in four hundred Sony shares listed in Tokyo, and one hundred BMW shares listed in Frankfurt. She wants to beat some international index used as benchmark. This index has an equal weight in the Japanese stock index and in the European stock index. She uses the U.S. dollar as the base currency. All necessary data are given in Exhibit 12.2. There were no cash flows in the portfolio, nor were any dividends paid. What is the total return on "simple portfolio B" in dollars, and how does it compare with the benchmark return?

SOLUTION

On March 31, her portfolio has gained 3.13 percent, while the benchmark has lost 1.53 percent in dollars. Of course, she will want to know why her portfolio had such a good performance over the quarter.

EXHIBIT 12.2

Simple Portfolio B: Composition and Market Data

Portfolio	Number of Shares	Price (in local currency)		Portfolio Value on Dec. 31		Portfolio Value on Mar. 31	
		Dec. 31	Mar. 31	Local Currency	Dollar	Local Currency	Dollar
Japanese Stocks							
Sony	400	10,000	11,000	4,000,000	40,000	4,400,000	41,905
European Stocks							
BMW	100	600	600	60,000	60,000	60,000	61,224
Total					100,000		103,129

Market Data	Dec. 31	Mar. 31					
Benchmark ($)	100	98.47					
Japanese index (¥)	100	105					
European index (€)	100	95					
Yen/dollar	100	105					
Euro/dollar	1	0.98					

The Mathematics of Multicurrency Returns

The basic unit of measurement is the rate of return on each segment before any cash movement between segments. To avoid a notational crisis, all time indexes are indicated with superscripts, and specific portfolio segments are indicated with subscripts. We now present the rate of return calculations for a specific segment, both in its local currency and in the investor's base currency.

Return in Local Currency　If we call V_j the value of one segment j, in local currency, the rate of return in local currency for period t is given by

$$r_j = \frac{V_j^t - V_j^{t-1} + D_j^t}{V_j^{t-1}} = \frac{V_j^t - V_j^{t-1}}{V_j^{t-1}} + \frac{D_j^t}{V_j^{t-1}} = p_j + d_j \qquad (12.7)$$

where

D_j is the amount of dividends or coupons *paid* during the period

p_j is the capital gain (price appreciation) in percent

d_j is the yield in percent

Further precision is needed for fixed-income segments. In most countries, as well as on the Eurobond market, accrued interest, A, is computed and quoted separately from the quoted price of a bond, P. An investor must pay both the price and accrued interest to the seller. Therefore, the total *value* of the bond is $V = P + A$. The rate of return on the bond segment is given by

$$r_j = \frac{V_j^t - V_j^{t-1} + D_j^t}{V_j^{t-1}} = \frac{P_j^t - P_j^{t-1}}{P_j^{t-1} + A_j^{t-1}} + \frac{A_j^t - A_j^{t-1} + D_j^t}{P_j^{t-1} + A_j^{t-1}} = p_j + d_j \qquad (12.8)$$

Return in Base Currency   The base currency rate of return is easily derived by translating all prices[10] into the base currency 0 at exchange rate S_j:

$$r_{j0} = \frac{V_j^t S_j^t + D_j^t S_j^t - V_j^{t-1} S_j^{t-1}}{V_j^{t-1} S_j^{t-1}}$$

where r_{j0} is the segment return in base currency 0, while r_j is the segment return in its local currency and s_j is the number of units of currency 0 per unit of currency j. After some algebraic reshuffling, this may be written as

$$r_{j0} = p_j + d_j + s_j(1 + p_j + d_j), \text{ or}$$

$$r_{j0} \quad = \quad p_j \quad + \quad d_j \quad + \quad c_j \qquad (12.9)$$

Total return in base currency	=	Capital gain component	+	Yield component	+	Currency component

where s_j denotes the percentage exchange rate movement, and c_j denotes the influence of the exchange rate movement on the estimated return in the base currency. Note that the currency component, c_j, is equal to zero if the exchange rate movement s_j, is zero. If s_j is not zero, c_j differs slightly from s_j because of the cross-product terms.

The compounding of currency and market movements on a foreign security is illustrated in Exhibit 12.3. The value of a foreign investment is represented as a rectangle, where the horizontal axis represents the exchange rate, and the vertical axis represents the value of the investment in local currency. As an illustration, consider a U.S. investor holding £10,000 of British assets with an exchange rate of $/£ = 2. The dollar value of the assets is represented by area A, or $20,000. Later, the British assets have gone up by 10 percent to £11,000, and the pound has appreciated by 5 percent to $/£ = 2.10. The total dollar value is now £23,100, or a gain of 15.5 percent. The dollar gain, if the currency had not moved, is represented by area B (10 percent of initial value). Because of the currency movement, this gain is transformed to a total gain of

---

[10] For simplicity, assume that the dividend is paid at the exchange rate prevailing at the end of the period.

EXHIBIT 12.3
Market and Currency Gains

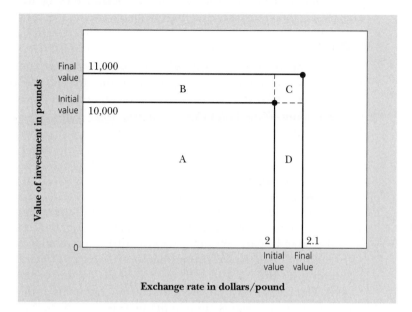

15.5 percent, equal to the sum of areas B, C, and D. Area C plus D is the currency component of the total return. Note that it can be seen as a pure exchange rate movement (area D) and a cross-currency market term (area C). It is equal to the exchange rate movement applied to the final pound value of the investment, not its initial value.

Total Return Decomposition

The first objective of GPE is to decompose the portfolio's total return, measured in base currency, into the three main sources of return:

- Capital gain (in local currency)
- Yield
- Currency

The total return is simply the weighted average of the returns on all segments. Over period t, the total portfolio's return r is computed in the base currency as follows:

$$r = \sum_j w_j r_{j0} = \sum_j w_j(p_j + d_j + c_j)$$

where w_j represents the percentage of segment j in the total portfolio at the start of the period. The various sources of return may be regrouped into three components:

$$r = \underset{\substack{\text{Capital gain} \\ \text{component}}}{\sum_j w_j p_j} + \underset{\substack{\text{Yield} \\ \text{component}}}{\sum_j w_j d_j} + \underset{\substack{\text{Currency} \\ \text{component}}}{\sum_j w_j c_j} \qquad (12.10)$$

EXAMPLE 12.7   *SIMPLE PORTFOLIO B: TOTAL RETURN DECOMPOSITION*

Let's now return to "simple portfolio B." Decompose the total return into capital gain, yield, and currency components.

SOLUTION

There is no yield, so we will focus on the other components of return. The Japanese shares went up by 10 percent in the first quarter (from ¥10,000 per share to ¥11,000). The rate of return in yen on the Japanese equity segment is 10 percent (from ¥4 million to ¥4.4 million). When translated into dollars, the rate of return of the Japanese equity segment becomes 4.76 percent (from $40,000 to $41,905). The difference between 4.76 percent and 10 percent is due to the currency contribution (−5.24 percent), caused by a drop in the value of the yen relative to the dollar. Note that this figure is not exactly equal to the percentage currency loss on the yen, which dropped from ¥100 = $1 to ¥100 = $0.9524. As mentioned, the currency contribution is equal to the currency loss applied to the original investment plus the capital gain.

These results are reproduced in the first four columns of Exhibit 12.4. The first column gives the weights in the portfolio, as of December 31. The second column gives the rates of return in the base currency (dollar), for each segment. The last line gives the weighted average return for the total portfolio, using the portfolio weights given in the first column. Note that the weighted average return in dollars is indeed 3.13 percent, which is consistent with the total portfolio appreciation reported in Exhibit 12.2. The third and fourth columns give the return in local currency and the currency contribution for each segment, as well as for the total portfolio (by taking the weighted average for each segment). For example, the total currency contribution of −0.87 percent is equal to the currency contribution for Japanese equity (−5.24 percent) multiplied by the weight of Japanese equity in the total portfolio (40 percent), plus the currency contribution of European equity (2.04 percent) multiplied by the weight of European equity in the total portfolio (60 percent).

In the end, the total portfolio return of 3.13 percent can be decomposed as a nice capital gain in local currency of 4.00 percent, minus a currency loss of −0.87 percent. Note that columns 3 and 4 add up to column 2. Columns 5–7 are discussed in the next example.

EXHIBIT 12.4

Simple Portfolio B: Total Return Decomposition

	(1) Portfolio Weights	(2) Rate of Return in $	(3) Capital Gain in Local Currency	(4) Currency Contribution	(5) Market Index	(6) Security Selection	(7) Currency Contribution
Japanese Stocks	40%	4.76%	10.00%	−5.24%	5.00%	5.00%	−5.24%
European Stocks	60%	2.04%	0.00%	2.04%	−5.00%	5.00%	2.04%
Total Portfolio	**100%**	**3.13%**	**4.00%**	**−0.87%**	**−1.00%**	**5.00%**	**−0.87%**

Performance Attribution

A manager's relative performance may be measured by making several comparisons. The basic idea is to provide a comparison with some passive benchmarks for all major investment decisions. Active management decisions will induce deviations from the benchmarks' returns. Some of the many management decisions that are commonly analyzed are discussed next.

Security Selection   A manager's security selection ability is determined by isolating the local market return of the various segments. Let's call I_j the return, in local currency, of the market index corresponding to segment j (e.g., the Tokyo Stock Exchange index). Remember that market indexes are usually price-only indexes (do not reflect dividends). Assuming a portfolio has market-index-average risk, the return derived from security selection is simply $p_j - I_j$. The rate of return on segment j (Japanese stocks) may be broken down into the following components:

$$r_{j0} = I_j + (p_j - I_j) + d_j + c_j$$

The total portfolio return may be written as

$$r = \underbrace{\sum w_j I_j}_{\substack{\text{Market} \\ \text{return} \\ \text{component}}} + \underbrace{\sum w_j (p_j - I_j)}_{\substack{\text{Security} \\ \text{selection} \\ \text{contribution}}} + \underbrace{\sum w_j d_j}_{\substack{\text{Yield} \\ \text{component}}} + \underbrace{\sum w_j c_j}_{\substack{\text{Currency} \\ \text{component}}} \qquad (12.11)$$

The first term on the right-hand side of Equation 12.11 measures the performance that would have been achieved had the manager invested in a local market index instead of individual securities. This contribution is calculated net of currency movements, which are picked up by the last term in the formula. The second term measures the contribution made by the manager's individual security selection. It is simply the weighted average of the security selection on each segment.

EXAMPLE 12.8   SIMPLE PORTFOLIO B: SECURITY SELECTION

Calculate the overall contribution of security selection to the performance of "simple portfolio B."

SOLUTION

These calculations are given in the last columns of Exhibit 12.4. Column 5 is the market index return component and column 6 is the contribution of security selection. The return on the Japanese index is 5 percent in yen, while the Japanese segment of the portfolio returns 10 percent in yen. Hence, the contribution of security selection is 5 percent. So columns 5 and 6 simply add up to column 3. The currency contribution columns 4 and 7 are identical. To derive information at the total portfolio level, we take the weighted average of the figures reported for the various segments, using the portfolio weights reported in column 1. Hence, the market return component is a negative 1 percent; if the investor had passively allocated 40 percent of her portfolio to the Japanese stock

> index and 60 percent to the European stock index, she would have taken a capital loss of -1 percent. However, superior security selection ($+5$ percent) led to an actual capital gain, in local currency, of $+4$ percent.

Asset Allocation   Another step in performance attribution is to study the performance of the total portfolio relative to that of a global benchmark. This comparison is usually made with respect to the return I^* on an international index, such as the MSCI, Europe/Australasia/Far East index (EAFE), or the World index. The objective is to assess the portfolio manager's ability as measured by the difference in return, $r - I^*$.

To do this, additional notations are required. Let's call I_{j0} the return on market index j, translated into base currency 0. We have

$$I_{j0} = I_j + C_j$$

where C_j is the currency component of the index return in base currency, that is, $C_j = s_j(1 + I_j)$. Let's call w_j^* the weight of market j in the international benchmark chosen as a standard. In base currency, the return on this international index equals

$$I^* = \sum w_j^* I_{j0}$$

Equation 12.11 may be rewritten and transformed into Equation 12.12 by simultaneously adding $\sum w_j^* I_{j0}$ and subtracting $\sum w_j^* I_{j0} = \sum w_j^*(I_j + C_j)$:

$$r = \sum w_j^* I_{j0} + \sum (w_j - w_j^*)I_j + \sum (w_j c_j - w_j^* C_j) + \sum w_j d_j + \sum w_j(p_j - I_j) \quad (12.12)$$

International benchmark return I^*	+	Market allocation contribution	+	Currency allocation contribution[11]	+	Yield component	+	Security selection contribution

This breakdown allows us to estimate the contribution to total performance of any deviation from the standard asset allocation, $w_j - w_j^*$.

The word *contribution* in this context indicates performance relative to a selected benchmark; the word *component* refers to a breakdown of the portfolio's total return. Equation 12.12 states that a manager's relative performance, $r - I^*$, can be attributed to the following three factors (after allowing for the yield on the portfolio):

1. *An asset allocation different from that of the index.* This factor is a source of positive performance for the manager who overweighs ($w_j > w_j^*$) the best-performing markets and underweighs the poorest-performing markets.

2. *A currency allocation different from that of the index.* This factor is a source of positive performance for the manager who overweighs ($w_j > w_j^*$) the best-performing currencies and underweighs the poorest-performing currencies. So, it is possible for a manager to have chosen his markets very effectively (resulting in a positive market allocation contribution) but be penalized by ad-

---

[11] Remember that c_j and C_j are close to s_j, the exchange rate movement, so that the currency allocation contribution is close to $\sum (w_j - w_j^*)s_j$.

verse currency movements (resulting in a negative currency allocation contribution). The market allocation and currency allocation contributions are sometimes combined into a single allocation contribution.

3. *Superior security selection*

This breakdown of relative performance is the simplest of many possibilities. GPE services use a variety of similar approaches and employ graphics in presenting their results.

EXAMPLE 12.9   SIMPLE PORTFOLIO B: GLOBAL PERFORMANCE ATTRIBUTION

Perform a global performance attribution for "simple portfolio B."

SOLUTION

The benchmark has equal weights (0.50) in Europe and Japan, while the investor allocated weights of 0.60 to Europe and 0.40 to Japan. The total dollar return on the benchmark index is −1.53 percent. The dollar return on the Japanese index is calculated by simply dividing the index by the yen/dollar exchange rate. Hence, the dollar return on the Japanese market equals 0 percent (constant index in dollars), while the yen return is equal to 5 percent. The currency contribution on the index is −5 percent. Similarly, the European index return is −3.06 percent in dollars, −5 percent in euros, and the currency contribution is +1.94 percent. Let's now study the impact of the allocation decision to overweight Europe compared with the benchmark (0.60 instead of 0.50). This resulted in a negative deviation from the benchmark, because the European index lost 5 percent. The underweighting in Japan was also an unfortunate decision, because the Japanese market went up in yen terms. The net market allocation contribution is equal to

Market allocation contribution = 0.10 × (−5%) − 0.10 × (+5%) = −1%

Performing a similar calculation for the currency allocation contribution, we find a net contribution of 0.66 percent. Hence, the asset allocation deviation relative to the benchmark led to a negative performance on the markets and a positive performance on the currencies.

A direct application of Equation 12.12 gives the following performance attribution for "simple portfolio B":

Benchmark return	−1.53%
Market allocation contribution	−1.00%
Currency allocation contribution	0.66%
Yield component	0.00%
Security selection contribution	5.00%
Portfolio return	3.13%

These figures allow us to conduct a global performance attribution. The portfolio had a great return (+3.13 percent) compared with the benchmark (−1.53 percent). However, the added value of 4.66 percent does not come from the asset allocation decision. The decision to overweight Europe relative to Japan led to a loss on the markets (−1 percent) and a gain on the currencies (0.66 percent). The major contributor to the performance is the individual stock selection on each market (+5 percent). The excellent selection of securities explains the superior performance of "simple portfolio B."

Market Timing   Asset allocation varies over time, so that over a given performance period, *market timing* makes a contribution, due to the time variation in weights, w_j. Moreover, the contribution made by market timing can be further broken down and measured for each segment (e.g., Japanese equity).

Industry and Sectors   We presented a GPE in which performance is attributed to country allocation. Equity managers often focus on the global industry allocation, across countries. Hence, another line of analysis is to attribute performance to the industry weighting chosen by the manager. Attribution along global industry lines is gaining in importance.

Factors and Styles   Performance within a segment can further be attributed to the choice of investment style (see Sharpe, 1992). For example, a manager could favor value stocks over growth stocks in his European portfolio. Differences in portfolio return can be explained by the relative allocation between value and growth stocks. Hence, performance would not be attributed along country lines, but along style lines. This investment style approach is less common outside of the United States. Various factors are sometimes favored by investment managers using factor models such as Barra (Barr, Rosenberg, & Associates). Once a manager takes investment positions on various factors within a national market segment, a GPE system can analyze how much of the performance relative to the national market index, or globally, can be attributed to each factor bet.

Risk Decomposition   Just as the total rate of return is decomposed into its main contributors, the total risk of a portfolio can be decomposed along the same lines. The counterpart of *performance attribution* in the return dimension is called *risk allocation* (or *risk budgeting*) in the risk dimension. This is discussed in the performance appraisal section of the chapter, after risk measures are introduced.

An Example of Output

Graphic displays of performance attribution are proposed by most external GPE services. These services collect information on a large number of portfolios with comparable investment mandates. Exhibit 12.5 presents the comparison of the performance of a specific portfolio with that of a universe of managers with a similar mandate (non–North American equity). The performance attribution is presented

EXHIBIT 12.5

Analysis of Performance: Non–North American Equity Return in U.S. Dollars: One year ending September 1994 (in percent)

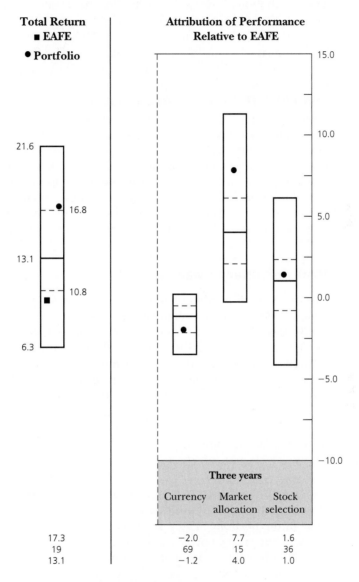

	Currency	Market allocation	Stock selection	
17.3	−2.0	7.7	1.6	Your portfolio (●)
19	69	15	36	Percentile rank
13.1	−1.2	4.0	1.0	Universe median

Source: InterSec Research Corp., Stamford, CT. Reprinted with permission.

here for one year. The left part of the exhibit gives the total return on the fund, the MSCI EAFE index, and a universe of 117 portfolios. The return of the studied portfolio is represented by a dot; that of the EAFE index is represented by a square. The distribution of the same statistics for the universe of managed funds surrounds the dot. For example, the return on the portfolio is 17.3 percent over the year, whereas the EAFE index went up by only 10.0 percent. The median of the universe had a return of about 13.1 percent *(full line)*. The first quartile of the distribution (top 25 percent of the universe) is around 16.8 percent *(dashed line),* whereas the third quartile (bottom 25 percent of the universe) is around 10.8 percent *(other dashed line)*. The best manager had a return of 21.6 percent; the worst one had a return of 6.3 percent. The portfolio ranked quite high in the universe; on a percentile scale of 0 to 100, its rank is 19. The performance relative to the EAFE index is attributed in the right part of Exhibit 12.5. The relative performance of the portfolio is 7.3 percent (a return of 17.3 percent minus the return on the EAFE index of 10.0 percent). This can be decomposed into a market allocation contribution of 7.7 percent, a currency allocation contribution of -2.0 percent, and a stock selection contribution of 1.6 percent. The manager ranked high in the universe on asset allocation and stock selection but poorly on currency allocation.

More on Currency Management

Part of the total portfolio could be hedged against currency risk. This is usually done by *selling forward* foreign currencies against the base currency. As mentioned in Chapters 1 and 2, a forward currency *purchase* is equivalent to being long in foreign cash (receiving the foreign short-term interest rate R_j) and short in the domestic, or base-currency, cash (paying the domestic short-term interest rate R_0). A forward currency sale is just the reverse position. Using the linear approximation,[12] the forward purchase of currency j has a pure-currency component c_j^f equal to the percentage exchange rate movement s_j (change in the domestic currency value of one unit of foreign currency) plus the interest rate differential (foreign minus domestic):

$$c_j^f = s_j + R_j - R_0$$

Assume that a portfolio is hedged for a proportion of w_j^f in currency j. This means that the forward position in currency j represents $-w_j^f$ percent of the total value of the portfolio. There is a negative sign because we are *selling* forward contracts on currency j, not *buying* them.

With the above hedging, the decomposition of return can be written as:

$$r = \sum_j w_j p_j + \sum_j w_j d_j + \sum_j w_j c_j - \sum_j w_j^f c_j^f \qquad (12.13)$$

Remember that both c_j^f and c_j are close to the movement in exchange rate s_j. Hence, the contribution of currency j is fully hedged when $w_j^f = w_j$. Note however, that the

---

[12] See Chapters 1 and 2.

return on the forward currency hedge differs from the exchange rate movement by the interest rate differential, as stressed by Ankrim and Hensel (1994) and Singer and Karnosky (1995).

From Quarterly to Multi-Year Performance

The return of a portfolio has been decomposed in Equations 12.11 and 12.12 in a *linearly additive* fashion. This is common industry practice. The linearity has been achieved by assigning all cross-product terms to a specific effect.[13] For example, the product of the percentage capital appreciation and the currency movement has been assigned to the currency component. This cross-product of two returns is generally a smaller term. For example, if both returns are equal to 1 percent, their cross-product will be only 0.01 percent.

The simple mathematical formulas shown in Equations 12.11 and 12.12 break down when there are movements between portfolio segments during a period. Adjusting for these cash movements (i.e., changes in w_j over time) is not easy. The linearity of the decomposition of total time-weighted return, as well as the linear attribution of the performance, are not preserved in the compounding of successive periods. A multiperiod extension of Equation 12.12 with changing weights would prevent us from deriving simple breakdowns of performance, such that each component could easily be identified. Only approximations can be used. Four quarterly performance attributions do not add up, or compound, easily into a yearly performance attribution, even when time-weighted returns are used.[14]

To summarize, we can get good indications on the attribution of performance, but one must realize that the numbers obtained are not, and can never be, more than good indicators.

Performance Appraisal in Global Performance Evaluation

The final stage of GPE is to appraise the investment skills of a manager. Because short-term results can be due to chance, rather than skills, a long horizon must be used. Performance may result from the level of risk taken by the manager, rather than from true investment skill. So, performance should be appraised after adjusting for risk.

---

[13] This is sometimes justified by saying that the linear decomposition of returns would be exact (i.e., not imply any cross-product terms) if continuously compounded returns were used. This statement is incorrect, as all students of continuous-time finance and of Ito's lemma learn.

[14] Methods to improve on performance attribution over long periods are discussed in Karnosky and Singer (1994), Singer, Gonzalo and Lederman (1998) and Spaulding (2002).

Risk

The final calculation step in GPE is to analyze the risks borne by the portfolio. The most common approach to global investment involves two steps.

- *First,* the investor decides on an asset allocation across various asset classes (domestic equity, European equity, international bonds, emerging markets, etc.) based on expected returns and risks for the various asset classes. At this level, risk measures are calculated on *absolute* returns (i.e., not returns in relation to a benchmark).

- *Second,* an actively managed portfolio is constructed for each asset class, and a benchmark is assigned. Within each asset class, the risk of the portfolio is measured *relative* to this benchmark.

In practice, two types of risk measures are widely used.

Total or Absolute Risk: Standard Deviation The risk of the total portfolio is measured by the standard deviation of total returns over time. It is sometimes called *absolute risk,* because it does not value risk relative to a benchmark. If the standard deviation is calculated over T periods, the standard deviation σ_{tot} is given by

$$\sigma_{tot} = \sqrt{\frac{1}{T-1} \sum_{t=1}^{T} (r_t - \bar{r})^2} \qquad (12.14)$$

The standard deviation is usually annualized[15] and expressed in percent per year. In other words, if the standard deviation is computed with monthly returns, the result is multiplied by $\sqrt{12}$.

If a global benchmark is assigned to the total portfolio, the standard deviation of the total portfolio and of the global benchmark can be compared. A regression of total portfolio returns on the benchmark returns allows one to calculate the beta of the portfolio relative to the benchmark.

The total risk of a portfolio is not the only relevant measure of risk. Investors who are interested primarily in diversification typically spread their assets among several funds. Pension funds, for example, invest abroad partly to diversify their domestic holdings. Calculating the correlation of an international portfolio to a domestic benchmark reveals whether the benefits of diversification have been achieved. A low correlation means that there are great international diversification benefits.[16]

Other risk measures, such as VaR (Value at Risk), are closely linked to the standard deviation.

Relative Risk: Tracking Error Investors measure how closely their portfolio, or segment of a portfolio, tracks a benchmark. Active managers take positions to beat

---

[15] The standard deviation computed on monthly (or daily) returns is annualized by multiplying by the square root of the number of months (or days) in a year.

[16] Some services compute betas rather than correlation coefficients to derive the same type of information. (A beta coefficient is equal to the correlation coefficient times the ratio of the standard deviation of the portfolio over that of the market index.)

a benchmark, but they also assume risks because they deviate from the benchmark. The *tracking error* is the standard deviation of returns in excess of the benchmark's returns. For any period t, the excess return in relation to a benchmark is given by

$$er_t = r_t - I_t$$

And the tracking error is

$$\sigma_{er} = \sqrt{\frac{1}{T-1} \sum_{t=1}^{T} (er_t - \overline{er})^2} \qquad (12.15)$$

The tracking error is usually annualized and expressed in percent per year. Tracking error is sometimes called *active risk*. In the hope of positive performance, an active manager will deviate from the passive benchmark, thereby taking active risk. The tracking error quantifies this active risk. Example 12.10 illustrates tracking error for the "simple portfolio B."

Risk estimates are often unstable over time because they are derived from a mixture of many types of assets and sources of uncertainty. Currency markets are particularly prone to periods of calm followed by periods of extreme volatility. Portfolios that are low risk during one period can experience a larger standard deviation, or beta, during the next period. That is why an analysis of both past and present risk exposures is necessary. Again, frequent return data are required to obtain statistically significant risk estimates. Further insights can be gained by a detailed risk decomposition, as discussed in the next section.

Risk-Adjusted Performance

In a domestic setting, performance measurement services often attempt to rank managers on their risk-adjusted performance. It seems attractive to derive a single number, taking into account both performance and risk.

Sharpe Ratio The usual approach to risk-adjusted performance measurement is to calculate a *reward* (mean excess return over the risk-free rate) *to variability* (standard deviation of returns) ratio. This measure, introduced by Sharpe, is known as the *Sharpe ratio,*[17] which is both simple and intuitive. Let's note $\overline{r}$, the *ex post* mean return on the portfolio; R_0, the risk-free interest rate; and σ_{tot}, the total risk of the portfolio, where all variables have been annualized. Then, the Sharpe ratio is equal to

$$\text{Sharpe ratio} = \frac{\overline{r} - R_0}{\sigma_{tot}} \qquad (12.16)$$

This reward-to-variability measure is intuitive, because it measures the return in excess of the risk-free rate (risk premium) per unit of risk taken.

---

[17] Sharpe (1994) extends the definition to include a Sharpe ratio relative to any benchmark.

However, the Sharpe ratio should be used only for the investor's global portfolio. A portfolio whose objective is to be invested in foreign assets to diversify risk of the domestic assets cannot be evaluated separately from the total portfolio. The standard deviation of the foreign portfolio will get partly diversified away in the global portfolio. The pertinent measure of risk of a portfolio of foreign assets should be its *contribution* to the risk of the global portfolio of the client (see Jorion and Kirsten, 1991). Other methods are the ratio of mean excess return to the market risk (β) (the Treynor ratio) and the Jensen measure.[18] Unfortunately, the application of these methods poses some problems, as outlined by Roll (1978), in a domestic context. The problems are even worse in an international context, in which investors disagree on what constitutes the "passive" world market portfolio, and these methods are seldom used.

EXAMPLE 12.10   SIMPLE PORTFOLIO B: TOTAL RISK AND TRACKING ERROR

In "simple portfolio B," the investor is interested to know the tracking error of the Japanese (European) segment of her portfolio relative to the Japanese (European) stock index. These calculations are performed in the local currency, yen or euro. She also wants to know the tracking error of the total portfolio relative to the benchmark, in dollars. Finally, she wants to know how the total risk of her portfolio compares with that of the benchmark. Annualized risk estimates for the simple portfolio are reported in Exhibit 12.6. Standard deviations are calculated using daily returns, and then annualized. Comment on these figures.

SOLUTION

The tracking errors are very large, which is not surprising, because this portfolio is very poorly diversified. The total risk is much higher than that of the benchmark (24 percent compared with 20 percent). The information ratio reported in Exhibit 12.6 is discussed in the next section on risk-adjusted performance.

EXHIBIT 12.6

Tracking Error and Total Risk of Simple Portfolio B

Portfolio Segment	Total Risk (% per year)	Tracking Error to Relevant Benchmark (% per year)	Information Ratio (annualized)
Japanese stocks		6%	3.33
European stocks		8%	2.50
Total portfolio	24%	7%	2.66
Benchmark	20%	0	0

The Sharpe ratio focuses on the total risk of the portfolio (uncertainty of absolute returns). But a manager who is assigned a benchmark will measure the risk of deviations from the benchmark's return.

---

[18] See Reilly and Brown (2003).

Information Ratio   When an investor measures performance relative to benchmarks, the *information ratio* is used.[19] The information ratio, IR, is defined as the ratio of the excess return from the benchmark, divided by the tracking error relative to the benchmark:

$$\text{IR} = \frac{er}{\sigma_{er}} \tag{12.17}$$

where *er* is the excess return over the benchmark for some observed period (often called *alpha*), and the tracking error σ_{er} is defined in Equation 12.15. A manager attempting to "beat" a benchmark takes some active bets and therefore incurs tracking error. The information ratio measures whether the excess return generated (often called *alpha*) is large relative to the tracking error incurred. Grinold and Kahn (1995) assert that an IR of 0.50 is "good," and that an IR of 1.0 is "exceptional." In practice, very few managers achieve an IR of 0.5 over a long period of time, so an IR of 0.2 or 0.3 realized over a few years is regarded as excellent by the profession.

**EXAMPLE 12.11   SIMPLE PORTFOLIO B:
INFORMATION RATIOS AND SHARPE RATIO**

Analyze the information ratio for the "simple portfolio B" and calculate its Sharpe ratio.

SOLUTION

Performance is measured over a very short period of time (one quarter), so it is hard to conclude whether the good performance is the result of luck or of some true stock selection expertise. The Japanese stocks outperformed the Japanese benchmark by 5 percent over the quarter, an annualized 20 percent rate.[20] This leads to a 3.33 information ratio (20/6). The various information ratios are reported in Exhibit 12.6; they are all good. We can also compute the Sharpe ratio for the total portfolio. The risk-free dollar interest rate is 10 percent. Hence, for this portfolio of non-U.S. stocks

$$\text{Sharpe ratio} = \frac{3.13 \times 4 - 10}{24} = 0.105$$

Again, because this "simple portfolio B" of non-U.S. stocks is only part of the global portfolio of our investor, it is somewhat unfair to compare the *ex post* risk premium realized to the total risk of that simple portfolio. The total risk (24 percent) looks very high, but it would get partly diversified away in the global portfolio of the investor that also includes U.S. stocks. So, the risk contribution of that simple portfolio is smaller than 24 percent, while the realized excess return is unquestionable.

---

[19] A good discussion of the information ratio can be found in Grinold and Kahn (1995) and Goodwin (1998).

[20] For illustration purposes, we use a simple arithmetic average to calculate the annualized mean return. In practice, returns should be compounded (geometric average).

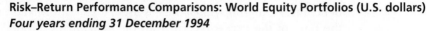

EXHIBIT 12.7

Risk–Return Performance Comparisons: World Equity Portfolios (U.S. dollars)
Four years ending 31 December 1994

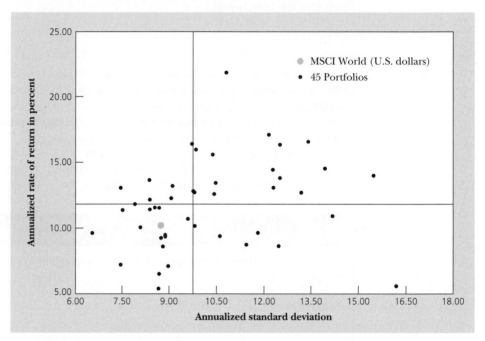

Source: Frank Russell Company. Reprinted with permission.

If risk is a complex, multidimensional notion, no single reward-to-risk ratio can be used, and we are left with a more qualitative discussion of the risk–return trade-off. GPE services display risk–return performance comparisons for the universe of managers they evaluate. An example for World equity portfolios is reproduced in Exhibit 12.7. Each point in the exhibit is one managed portfolio from a universe of 45 portfolios with a global equity mandate. The annualized rate of return over four years is given on the *y*-axis. The annualized standard deviation is given on the *x*-axis. The large dot represents the MSCI World index, which is a natural benchmark. The median return (about 12 percent) and risk (about 9.75 percent) of the universe are represented by a straight line. The best portfolios should lie in the upper-left quadrant of this graph (more return and less risk).

Risk Allocation and Budgeting

Just as the total portfolio performance can be attributed to the various investment decisions *(performance attribution)*, the total risk can be decomposed into the various risk exposures taken by the manager *(risk allocation)*. This leads to a better understanding of the total risk borne.

In GPE, a client will judge in which areas their investment managers have skills; i.e., they can add value relative to a passive benchmark. Based on the performance appraisal, the client will then decide to allocate more active risk to those managers. This process is called *risk budgeting*. In other words, the client will allow some managers to have a large tracking error, because they expect to add value in their segment, but will allow some other managers to have only a small tracking error. For example, a pension plan could assign a 4 percent tracking error to a European equity manager and to a currency overlay manager, but a minimal tracking error to an Asian equity manager.

So, the total risk (standard deviation) of a portfolio is the result of decisions at two levels:

- The *absolute risk allocation* to each asset class: This is a traditional asset allocation approach, wherein the risk on each asset class is measured using passive benchmarks. The risk of active managers who deviate from their benchmarks is not introduced at this level.

- The *active risk allocation* of managers in each asset class: This is the risk budgeted to generate alphas relative to each benchmark.

Such a risk decomposition can be quite complex in a global portfolio, because risks are correlated and, hence, not additive. The currency risk dimension is always an important element in GPE.

Because the investment policy statement usually contains risk objectives and constraints, it is important that a GPE be able to provide a consistent risk analysis at the various levels of the investment process, from the strategic allocation to the appraisal of each manager.

CONCEPTS IN ACTION   RISK BUDGETING AT ABP[21]

Risk budgeting needs to be understood

There must be a "specific and conscious decision to allocate financial risk. Without that decision, no pension fund can beat the benchmark and get the return which we all seek," says Thijs Coenen at ABP.

"Risk is key to investment. In our view the risk allocation process is the most important assumption when examining investment strategy," he adds. "As one implements such a strategy one is developing risk allocation too. Consequently we try to develop a top-down process on financial risk, not exactly a novel approach among managers. However, we also believe it is vitally important to budget risk in practice, not just in theory."

Coenen believes it is vital to decide what level of risk a fund can stand, inside a liability framework. This involves total risk, but also levels of active risk. "To maximise income it is important to allocate the total risk budget to active risk segments, and to do so efficiently," he says. "That active risk may be a sector bet or a country bet."

Source: Investment & Pensions Europe, *2001 Awards Supplement,* December 2001, p. 23.

---

[21] ABP is the largest Dutch pension plan, with assets on the order of € 150 billion.

Some Potential Biases in Return and Risk

GPE is used by a client, in part, to evaluate and select managers on the basis of their historical track records. However, it is difficult to separate expertise from luck. Past performance is not necessarily a good indicator of future performance, and switching from one manager to the next is a costly process. It is important not to overestimate the statistical significance of performance comparisons to prevent inefficient churning of the portfolio and management changes based on insignificant information.

Performance appraisal requires that both return and risk measures be unbiased. Performance standards such as GIPS (see the implementation section of the chapter) attempt to ensure the reliability of the data presented, but it is hard to differentiate between past performance due to luck or to true investment skills that will lead to superior performance in the future. Furthermore, several problems can introduce severe biases in performance appraisal. This is typically the case for some asset classes, such as alternative investments or hedge funds. Past return-and-risk figures can be biased estimates of the future for a variety of reasons:

- Infrequently traded assets

- Option-like investment strategies

- Survivor bias: risk

- Survivor bias: return

Following are discussions of some of these problems, with an illustration of hedge funds performance appraisal.

Infrequently Traded Assets　　Some assets trade infrequently. This is the case for many alternative assets that are not exchange traded, such as real estate or private equity. This is also the case for illiquid exchange traded securities or over-the-counter instruments often used by hedge funds. Because prices used are not up-to-date market prices, they tend to be smoothed over time.[22] For example, the appraisal process used in real estate introduces a smoothing of returns, because properties are appraised only infrequently. The internal rate of return methodology used in private equity also introduces a smoothing of returns. The infrequent nature of price updates in the alternative asset world induces a significant downward bias to the measured risk of the assets. In addition, correlations of alternative investment returns with conventional equity and fixed income returns, and among the alternatives, are often close to zero or even negative, because of the smoothing effect and the absence of market-observable returns. The bias can be large,[23] so that the true risk can be larger than the reported estimates.

---

[22] See, for example, Terhaar, Staub, and Singer (2003).

[23] See, for example, Asness, Krail, and Liew (2001).

Option-like Investment Strategies   Risk measures used in performance appraisal assume that portfolio returns are normally distributed. Many investment strategies followed by hedge funds have some option-like features that violate the normality assumption. For example, hedge funds following so-called arbitrage strategies will generally make a "small" profit when asset prices converge to their arbitrage value, but they run the risk of a huge loss if their arbitrage model fails. Standard deviation or traditional VaR measures understate the true risk of losses.

Survivor Bias: Performance   In the investment industry, unsuccessful funds and managers tend to disappear over time. Only successful ones search for new clients and present their track record. This creates a survivor bias. This problem is acute with hedge funds that often do not have to comply with performance presentation standards. It is not uncommon to see hedge fund managers present only the track records of their successful funds, forgetting those that have been closed. Many studies show that survivor bias can be of large magnitude.[24]

To illustrate the concept of survivor bias, let's take a hypothetical example of a world in which no managers have any investment skill; that is, the markets are fully efficient and any outperformance is purely due to luck. At the end of any period, there will still be hedge fund managers and funds who will report, by luck, a good performance *ex post*. They will survive, and the others will disappear. All existing funds will tend to report excellent track records, and the average[25] past performance of the group of all existing funds will be positive. But the question is whether those surviving managers will deliver a superior performance in the future.

Survivor Bias: Risk   A similar survivor bias applies to risk measures. Investors shy away from high risk, as well as from negative performance. Hedge funds that exhibited large downside shocks in the past tend to disappear. So, the average reported risk of existing funds will tend to be lower than had all funds been included in the calculation. But there is no guarantee that the same strategy will also be low risk in the future. Examples abound of hedge funds that were regarded as low risk but lost all of their capital.

Implementation

In-house performance measurement is useful in determining the strengths and weaknesses of an investment organization. This is even more important in a global than in a domestic setting because of the larger number of factors influencing

---

[24] See Brown, Goetzmann, and Ibbotson (1999).

[25] There is also a self-selection bias in the publicly available databases and indexes of alternative investment funds. Managers choose to be included in these databases only if they have had a good past performance and their good-performance history for the previous years is instantly incorporated in the database. See Fung and Hsieh (2002).

return and risk. The development of a GPE system requires some sophisticated information technology, given the enormous mass of data that must be summarized into a few performance figures. The diversity of instruments, quotation, time zones, trading techniques, and information sources, renders the analysis susceptible to errors. However, a good investment organization should be able to master this issue.

Once an investment organization is able to generate reliable and detailed return-and-risk numbers, two issues have to be addressed:

- What are the benchmarks used to evaluate performance?

- What are the standards used for performance presentation?

More on Global Benchmarks

Manager Universes and Customized Benchmarks   The traditional approach to evaluate the performance of an asset manager has been to compare the return on the managed fund with that of peers (other managers). This process is referred to as *peer group* or *manager universe* comparison. Managers are compared even if the investment policies followed in the portfolio are widely different. A criticism often voiced is that this approach "mixes apples and oranges." This peer group approach is understandable if the client delegates to the manager the task of setting the investment policy of the fund and its strategic, or long-term, allocation. A comparison of returns of managers with balanced mandates is meaningful.

However, most institutional investors have now taken the responsibility of setting the investment policy of their overall fund. They translate this investment policy into benchmarks and assign a customized benchmark to each of their managers. The performance of an asset manager should be judged relative to the customized benchmark that has been assigned to them, not relative to the universe of all managers. Some individual investors also set benchmarks in their investment policy statement.

Comparison with benchmarks has become the rule for the U.S. pension fund industry. Other types of clients, however, such as foundations and endowment funds, still resort to comparisons with manager universes. In the early 1990s, peer group comparison was the dominant method used to evaluate the performance of U.K. pension scheme managers. But a majority of British pension schemes moved to comparison with customized benchmarks during the 1990s. For example, the Unilever Superannuation Fund made the move to scheme-specific benchmarks in 1996, as described in the following Concepts in Action feature.

Choosing benchmarks in a global setting is not an easy task, especially if the benchmark spans several countries/currency (e.g., "European equity" or "non-dollar bonds"). Important issues in constructing customized international benchmarks are

- individual country/market weights;

- countries, industries, and styles; and

- currency hedging.

CONCEPTS IN ACTION   *LESSONS FROM THE UNILEVER/MERRILL CASE*

. . . a peer group benchmark arrangement conflates the two big tasks facing the stewards of our pension assets: setting long-term policy on the one hand, and implementing it on the other.

The original objectives of the Unilever scheme called for Merrill and its other managers to "maximise long-term returns subject to an acceptable level of risk normally associated with a balanced approach to fund management". This really was a 'managers know best' approach. By contrast, the new benchmark had a target rate of return of the benchmark plus 1%, as measured over three years, and a downside risk tolerance of -3%, as measured over any trailing four calendar quarter period. Effectively, the more precise wording of the new objectives, and the specification of a benchmark portfolio, reflected the greater responsibility taken by the client for setting the scheme's investment policy. Indeed, the Pension Act of 1995 seems to demand that trustees, not managers, take on this responsibility.

Source: Extract from Mark Tapley, "Lessons from the Unilever/Merril case", *IPE*, May 2002, p. 36.

Individual Country/Market Weights   Standard international equity indexes are weighted by market capitalization. Some clients prefer equity indexes whose national allocation is based on different sets of weights—for example, relative national gross domestic products (GDP). This gives each country a weight proportional to its economic importance in world production, rather than the size of its financial market. The problem with international indexes based on GDP weights is that they are difficult and costly to track in a managed portfolio. GDP figures are adjusted only every few months, whereas stock market prices move continuously; hence, the portfolio must be continuously rebalanced to adjust to GDP weights. This can be costly in terms of transaction costs. Replicating a GDP-weighted benchmark is not practically feasible because rebalancing would be needed whenever country weights differ from market-capitalization weights.

National bond markets have market capitalizations that depend on the budget deficit of the country. Governments that run large budget deficits must issue more bonds to finance the deficits. It is unclear why the country/currency allocation should favor lax fiscal/budget policies. Again, the choice of national weights is an important investment policy decision.

Countries, Industries, and Style   The traditional approach to international equity investing has been a top-down country allocation. So, it was natural to assign to managers country or regional benchmarks. However, many believe that industry factors have grown to be more important than country factors. Hence, it could be natural to assign benchmarks that favor global or regional industry allocation rather than country allocation. Similarly, many believe that investment styles are important in explaining differences in global portfolio returns. So, it could be natural to assign benchmarks along investment styles. For example, an asset manager that specializes in value stocks could be assigned an international value benchmark, allowing the manager to invest internationally in value stocks.

Global industry and style approaches are different ways to slice global portfolios. Hence, global benchmarks could be customized along country/regional lines but also along global industry lines or global style lines.

Currency Hedging   Publicly available market indexes are generally not hedged against currency movements. But a client could decide to assign to an asset manager a customized benchmark that is fully hedged against currency risk. This is because the client does not wish to take on any currency risk, or because the client decides to delegate currency management to a separate currency-overlay manager. Some clients even decide to apply to the benchmark an arbitrary hedge ratio, between zero and 100 percent; it is not uncommon to see pension plans assigning international benchmarks that are 50 percent hedged against currency risk.

It should be noted that a fully hedged benchmark does not mean that the asset manager can neglect the currency dimension. This is because the value of corporations is influenced, in a different way, by currency movements (see Chapter 4).

Global Investment Performance Standards and Other Performance Presentation Standards

Some countries have adopted performance presentation standards that apply to global portfolios. In the United States, various regulations apply to different types of portfolios. Mutual funds have to follow rules mandated by the Securities and Exchange Commission (SEC). Corporate pension funds apply the Employee Retirement Income Security Act (ERISA). Public pension funds follow regulations set by federal or local governments. These performance presentation regulations are not very restrictive and provide little guidance for internationally diversified portfolios.

The Association for Investment Management and Research (AIMR®) implemented Performance Presentation Standards (AIMR-PPS®) for North American asset managers in the late 1980s. Subsequently, AIMR developed the Global Investment Performance Standards (GIPS®), which are voluntary guidelines for the ethical presentation of investment performance.[26] AIMR believes that the establishment and acceptance in all countries of performance presentation standards based on GIPS are vital steps in facilitating the availability of comparable investment performance history on a global basis. Global standardization of performance reporting guidelines allow investors to compare investment firms on a global level and allow these investment firms to compete for business on an equal footing with investment firms in other countries. GIPS are a set of detailed, ethical

---

[26] The U.S. AIMR-PPS were simultaneously amended to bring the standards into close harmony with the GIPS.

principles intended to promote full disclosure and fair representation by investment managers in reporting their investment results to existing and prospective clients. A secondary objective is to ensure uniformity in reporting so that results are directly comparable among investment managers. To this end, some performance presentation aspects are mandatory, whereas others are only recommended. AIMR standards carefully detail the calculation and presentation of historical records of performance by base currency.

Clearly, prospective and existing clients of investment management firms benefit from a global standard, by having a greater degree of confidence in the performance numbers presented by investment management firms. Performance standards, uniform in all countries, are required so that clients can readily compare investment performance among firms. GIPS have become the standards for presenting performance to institutional clients worldwide. This can be explained by the recognized quality of GIPS, the fast-growing number of CFA® charterholders in all countries, and the pressures of global competition in asset management. An investment manager that presents historical performance figures that are not GIPS compliant is at a clear competitive disadvantage.

The concept of composites is central to AIMR presentation standards. All portfolios managed by an investment firm must enter the composites. A *composite* is an aggregation of a number of portfolios into a single group that is representative of a particular investment objective or strategy. The composite return is the asset-weighted average of the performance results of all the portfolios in the composite. The idea is that an investment firm cannot present to existing or prospective clients a track record that is based only on a few selected accounts. Composites therefore ensure that prospective clients have a fair and complete representation of a manager's past performance record. Each composite must comprise portfolios or asset classes representing a similar strategy or investment objective. For each composite, the firm must select a benchmark that reflects the investment strategy of the composite, and the benchmark return must be presented for the same period for which the composite return is presented. Time-weighted rates of return, adjusted for cash flows, are required.[27] Investment firms must meet all the requirements set forth in GIPS to claim compliance. GIPS also detail the verification procedures that a third-party verifier must follow to establish that an investment firm claiming compliance with GIPS has adhered to the standards.

As mentioned, AIMR strongly encourages all countries to adopt GIPS as their performance presentation standards. Where existing laws, regulations, or industry standards already impose performance presentation standards, investment firms are strongly encouraged to meet both sets of requirements and to disclose any possible conflicts. For example, British actuaries have set rules for U.K. pension funds. The National Association of Pension Funds (NAPF) has established British standards requiring that performance be calculated by an outside service. This British industry practice of relying on outside services to calculate and present historical

---

[27] The authoritative statement of the GIPS, and associated guidelines, can be found on the AIMR web site (www.aimr.org).

performance makes the aggregation into a composite more difficult if different outside services are used for different portfolios. A diversity of outside services is the rule for large investment firms, with many clients requesting that performance be calculated by their preferred actuarial service. However, a U.K. version of GIPS has now been adopted by the NAPF. Industry practices in continental Europe lag behind Anglo-American standards. Only recently has the focus been on performance among Europeans, partly because of institutional investors' extensive reliance on in-house portfolio management. But national performance presentation standards are likely to be formulated in the near future, given the development of pension funds and the internationalization of competition among investment managers.

Japan used to rely extensively on book-value accounting of performance. In other words, unrealized profits or losses were not included in the calculation of the total rate of return. Deregulation and competition are progressively pushing Japan toward the Anglo-American approach to performance measurement. In all countries, GIPS are increasingly used on a voluntary basis.

Summary

- Global performance evaluation is conducted in three steps: measurement, attribution, and appraisal.

- The rate of return on a portfolio or on one of its segments can be measured using various methods to account for cash flows. Money-weighted rates measure the return on the average invested capital, whereas time-weighted rates measure the return per unit of invested currency. The time-weighted rate should be used for performance evaluation.

- Global performance evaluation is important to understanding how performance has been achieved. A good performance evaluation relies on the quality and availability of data, and the problems are magnified in the international context. Frequent cash flows among the various portfolio segments are a major problem, and calculation of the performance of each segment (e.g., Japanese equity) requires the valuation of segments on each cash flow date.

- In a global setting, the investment rate of return should be decomposed into the return made in local currency (capital gain/loss plus yield) and the currency return component (from the local currency to the base currency of the account).

- In active management, superior performance can result from any of the major investment decisions: asset allocation, currency allocation, market timing, and security selection on each market. The total performance should therefore be broken down and attributed to the various management decisions (performance attribution).

■ The realized performance should be appraised in light of the risk assumed. Risk is measured in absolute terms *(total or absolute risk)* but also relative to some benchmarks *(tracking error)*. Each measure gives useful, but different, information. Because risk reduction is an important motivation for international investing, the contribution to the risk of the overall fund of an investor could be considered when studying the absolute risk of an international portfolio. Risk-adjusted return can be measured on absolute risk *(Sharpe ratio)* or relative risk *(information ratio)*. Just as the total portfolio returns can be attributed to the various investment decisions *(performance attribution)*, the total risk can be decomposed into the various risk exposures taken by the manager *(risk allocation)*.

■ Performance is measured relative to some benchmarks. In a global setting, the choice of benchmarks is an important decision that reflects investment policy; many alternatives are available.

■ Global standardization of performance reporting guidelines allows investors to compare investment firms on a global level and allows investment managers to compete globally. Performance presentation standards are a set of detailed, ethical principles intended to promote full disclosure and fair representation by investment managers in reporting their investment results to existing and prospective clients. GIPS are a set of standards developed by the AIMR that are widely adopted worldwide by managers of institutional assets.

Problems

1. A client invested €100 at the start of the month. Assume that the manager tracks an assigned benchmark index. After 20 days, the portfolio gained 10 percent (value = €110), as did the index, and the client added an extra €50 (total portfolio value = €160). From day 20 to day 30, the portfolio, and the index, lost 9.09 percent—the final portfolio value is €160 × (1 − 0.0909) = €145.46. What are the rates of returns using the various methods outlined in the text? Which rate should you use to evaluate the performance of the manager relative to its benchmark?

2. You are managing a portfolio worth $200 at the start of the period. After one month, the value of the portfolio is up to $220, and the client, who needs cash, withdraws $40. Two months later, the portfolio is still worth $180. Give various measures of the return on the portfolio over the three-month period.

3. You own a portfolio of British assets worth £100,000 on January 1. The portfolio is worth £90,000 on January 10, and you withdraw £20,000. On January 20, the value of your portfolio has gone up to £90,000, and you add £50,000. On January 31, your portfolio is worth £145,000. Compute the rate of return in January, using the methods proposed in this text.

4. An American pension fund wants to invest $1 million in foreign equity. Its board of trustees must decide whether to invest in a commingled index fund tracking the EAFE index or to give the money to an active manager. The board learns that this active manager turns the portfolios over about twice a year. Given the small size of the account, the transaction costs are likely to be an average of 1.5 percent of each transaction's value. The active manager charges 0.75 percent in annual management fees, and the indexer charges 0.25 percent. By how much should the active manager outperform the index to cover the extra costs in the form of fees and transaction costs on the annual turnover?

5. You are a French investor holding some U.S. bonds. Over the month, the value of your bond portfolio goes from $1 million to $1.05 million. The exchange rates move from €1 per dollar to €1.02 per dollar.
   a. What is your rate of return in dollars?
   b. What is your rate of return in euros?
   c. Is the difference exactly equal to the percentage movement in the exchange rate? If not, why?

6. You own a portfolio of Swedish and American stocks. Their respective benchmarks are the OMX and S&P 500 indexes, and the Swedish and American portfolios are closely matched to their benchmarks in risk. There have been no movements during the year (cash flows, sales or purchase, dividends paid). Valuation and performance analysis is done in Swedish kronor (SKr). Here are the valuations at the start and the end of the year:

	January 1	December 31
Swedish stocks	SKr600,000	SKr660,000
U.S. stocks	SKr600,000	SKr702,000
Total	SKr1,200,000	SKr1,362,000
Exchange rate	SKr6/$	SKr5.4/$
OMX index	100	120
S&P index	100	125

   a. What is the total return on the portfolio?
   b. Decompose this return into capital gain, yield, and currency contribution.
   c. What is the contribution of security selection?

7. An American investor has invested $100,000 in a global equity portfolio made up of U.S., Asian, and European stocks. On December 31, the portfolio is invested in 500 IBM shares listed in New York, 200 Sony shares listed in Tokyo, and 50 BMW shares listed in Frankfurt. He wants to beat the World index used as benchmark. This index has a 50 percent weight in the U.S. stock index, a 25 percent weight in the Japanese stock index, and a 25 percent weight in the European stock index. The country components of the portfolio have average risk relative to their respective country indexes. He uses the U.S. dollar as base currency. On March 31, his portfolio has gained 4.065 percent, while the World index gained only 0.735 percent in dollars. He wishes to understand why his portfolio had such a good performance over the quarter. All necessary data are given in the following tables. There were no cash flows in the portfolio, nor any dividends paid.
   a. Decompose the total return on the portfolio into capital gains (in local currency) and currency contribution.
   b. What is the contribution of security selection?
   c. Attribute the performance relative to the benchmark (World index) to the various investment decisions.

Global Equity Portfolio: Composition and Market Data

Portfolio	Number of Shares	Price (in local currency) Dec. 31	Price (in local currency) Mar. 31	Portfolio Value on Dec. 31 Local Currency	Portfolio Value on Dec. 31 Dollar	Portfolio Value on Mar. 31 Local Currency	Portfolio Value on Mar. 31 Dollar
U.S. stocks							
IBM	500	100	105	50,000	50,000	52,500	52,500
Japanese stocks							
Sony	200	10,000	11,000	2,000,000	20,000	2,200,000	20,952
European stocks							
BMW	50	600	600	30,000	30,000	30,000	30,612
Total					100,000		104,065

Market Data	Dec. 31	Mar. 31
World index ($)	100	100.735
U.S. index ($)	100	103
Japanese index (¥)	100	105
European index (€)	100	95
Yen/dollar	100	105
Euro/dollar	1	0.98

8. A U.S. pension plan hired two international firms to manage the non-U.S. equity portion of its total portfolio. Each firm was free to own stocks in any country market included in the MSCI Europe, Australasia, and Far East index (EAFE), and free to use any form of dollar and/or nondollar cash or bonds as an equity substitute or reserve. After three years had elapsed, the records of the managers and the EAFE index were as shown in the following table:

Summary: Contributions to Return

	Currency	Country Selection	Stock Selection	Cash/Bond Allocation	Total Return Recorded
Manager A	−9.0%	19.7%	3.1%	0.6%	14.4%
Manager B	−7.4	14.2	6.0	2.8	15.6
Composite of A&B	−8.2	16.9	4.5	1.7	15.0
EAFE index	−12.9	19.9	—	—	7.0

"Country selection" is the local-currency return that would have been achieved if the portfolio were invested in country indexes rather than specific stocks. You are a member of the plan sponsor's pension committee, which will soon meet with the plan's consultant to review manager performance. In preparation for this meeting, you go through the following analysis:

a. Briefly describe the strengths and weaknesses of each manager, relative to the EAFE index data.

b. Briefly explain the meaning of the data in the Currency column.

9. Your discussion with a client has turned to the measurement of investment performance, particularly with respect to international portfolios.

Performance and Attribution Data: Annualized Returns for Five Years Ended 12/31/94

International Manager/Index	Total Return	Country/Security Selection	Currency Return
Manager A	−6.0%	2.0%	−8.0%
Manager B	−2.0	−1.0	−1.0
EAFE index	−5.0	0.2	−5.2

a. Assume that the data in this table for Manager A and Manager B accurately reflect their investment skills and that both managers actively manage currency exposure. Briefly describe one strength and one weakness for each manager.

b. Recommend and justify a strategy that would enable the fund to take advantage of the strength of each of the two managers while minimizing their weaknesses.

10. A U.S. portfolio manager has a global equity portfolio with investments in the United States, United Kingdom, and France. The local currency values of the equity investments on December 31, 2000, and December 31, 2001, are shown in the following table. The performance of the portfolio manager is measured against the World index, which has 60 percent weight in the U.S. stock index, a 20 percent weight in the U.K. stock index, and a 20 percent weight in the French stock index. Assume that no dividends were paid and there were no cash flows in the portfolio during the year. The base currency is the U.S. dollar. The country components of the portfolio have average risk relative to their respective country indexes. Use the information provided in the following tables to answer the questions asked.

Country	Dec. 31 2000 Local Currency Value	Dec. 31, 2001 Local Currency Value
United States	$50,000,000	$55,000,000
United Kingdom	£20,000,000	£20,500,000
France	€25,000,000	€32,000,000

Market Data	Dec. 31, 2000	Dec. 31, 2001
World index ($)	780	834.622
U.S. index ($)	760	829
U.K. index (£)	1,090	1,148
France index (€)	950	1,009
Pounds per dollar	0.65	0.62
Euros per dollar	1.1	1.2

a. Calculate the local currency return and dollar return on the portfolio for the period December 31, 2000, to December 31, 2001.

b. Decompose the total return on the portfolio into the following components:
   - Capital gains in local currency
   - Currency contribution

c. Decompose the total return on the portfolio into the following components:
   - Market component
   - Security selection contribution
   - Currency component

d. Carry out a global performance evaluation for the portfolio relative to the World index. Make sure the global performance attribution identifies the following components:
   - Benchmark return
   - Market allocation

- Currency allocation
- Security selection

11. A U.S. pension fund has a domestic portfolio with an expected return of 10 percent and a standard deviation of 12 percent. It also invests in a foreign equity fund that has an expected dollar return of 11 percent and a dollar standard deviation of 20 percent. The correlation of the foreign and U.S. portfolio is 0.2. The current dollar interest rate is 8 percent. Would you say that the foreign equity portfolio is attractive from a risk–return viewpoint?

12. Consider a U.S. pension fund with the following performance:

	Percentage Total Portfolio (%)	Total Dollar Return (%)	Standard Deviation of Return (%)	Correlation with U.S. Stock Index
U.S. equity	90	10	15	0.99
Foreign equity	10	11	20	−0.10

Is the risk–return performance of the foreign portfolio attractive?

13. You are provided with annual rates of return for a portfolio and relevant benchmark index for the years 1996 to 2000. Calculate the tracking error for the portfolio.

Year	Portfolio Return	Benchmark Return
1996	12%	14%
1997	14%	10%
1998	20%	12%
1999	14%	16%
2000	16%	13%

14. You are provided with annual return, standard deviation of returns, and tracking error to the relevant benchmark for three portfolios. Calculate the Sharpe ratio and information ratio for the three portfolios and rank them according to each measure.

Portfolio	Return	Standard Deviation	Tracking Error
1	13.50%	19.00%	6.50%
2	16.25%	24.00%	8.00%
3	17.00%	23.00%	7.00%
Benchmark	13.00%	20.00%	
Risk-free	5.00%		

15. The SOL group specializes in hedge funds invested in the U.S. stock market. Over the year 1999, the U.S. stock market index went up by 20 percent. The SOL group had three hedge funds with very different investment strategies and with roughly the same size at the start of 1999. As expected, the 1999 returns on the three funds were quite different. Here are the performances of the three funds before and after management fees set at 20 percent of gross profits:

Fund	Gross Return	Net Return
SOL A	50%	40%
SOL B	20%	16%
SOL C	−10%	−10%

One can observe that the average gross performance of the three funds is exactly equal to the performance on the U.S. stock index. At year end, most clients had left the third fund, and SOL C was closed. At the start of 2000, the SOL group launched an aggressive publicity campaign among portfolio managers, stressing the remarkable return on SOL A. If potential clients asked whether the SOL group had other hedge funds invested in the United States, the SOL group mentioned the only other fund, SOL B, and claimed that their average gross performance during 1999 was 35 percent. What do you think of this publicity campaign?

16. Investment markets are highly competitive and professional investors now dominate the marketplace. What should the average performance of all investors be, compared with market indexes? If international investment managers, as a group, beat some national market index, what does it tell us about the performance of local investment managers? Would you reach the opposite conclusion if international managers underperform, as a group, relative to some local market index?

17. A client has given you $100 million to invest abroad in an equity GDP-indexed fund. There are only two foreign countries, A and B, and their GDPs are currently equal to $100 billion each. Their respective stock market capitalizations are $150 and $100 billion. The performance of the fund is compared monthly with the GDP-weighted index. Assume that exchange rates remain fixed and that there are no new listings on the stock markets, so that national market capitalizations go up and down in line with movements in the national stock indexes. Here are the stock market indexes and the published GDPs for the next six months:

Month	GDP-A	GDP-B	Index A	Index B
0	100	100	100	100
1	100	100	95	110
2	100	100	100	100
3	102	101	100	120
4	102	101	105	125
5	102	101	110	135

a. Calculate the values at the end of each month of the two international indexes: GDP-weighted index and market capitalization–weighted index. In both cases, use the international weights (GDP and market cap) that are valid at the start of the month.
b. Assume that you build a portfolio using two national index funds. What operation should you do each month to track the GDP-weighted index?

18. a. Explain how total portfolio risk can be decomposed into various risk exposures, and indicate why risk decomposition can be a complex exercise.
b. Explain what is meant by the term *risk budgeting*.

19. List and explain three factors that introduce potential biases in performance and risk measurement of portfolios.

20. Mr. Smith is a foreign investor who has an account with a small Luxembourg bank. He does not pay taxes on his account. He gave a complete management mandate to the

bank and wants to judge the performance of the manager. He is using the U.S. dollar as his base currency.

a. He is looking at the two most recent valuation monthly reports, which are given in Exhibit A, and wonders how to compute the performance. He reads in the financial press that the Morgan Stanley Capital International (MSCI) World index has risen by 2 percent this month (in U.S. dollars). Basically, he would like to answer the following questions:

   i. What is the total return on his portfolio?

   ii. What are the sources of this return; that is, how much is due to capital appreciation, yield, and currency movements?

   iii. How good is the manager in selecting securities on the various markets?

You must give him precise, quantified information that will help him to answer these questions. (First, compute the return for each segment of the portfolio and its components, that is, price, yield, and currency; then combine these returns to answer the last two queries.)

b. Mr. Smith is aware that cash flows, as well as movements among the various segments of his portfolio, may obscure his analysis. He tries to compute the performance during the next month where the manager has been more active.

He wants to make sure he understands how a valuation report is constructed before doing his analysis. He gets the following information to prepare his own version of the valuation report:

Cash flow. Mr. Smith added $10,000 to his account.

Transactions. The manager sold the 500 Exxon. The total proceeds of the sale, net of commissions, were $20,000. He bought 400 Pernod-Ricard on the Paris bourse for a total cost of $30,860.

Income received. A semiannual coupon was paid on the EIB bond for a total receipt of $575. AMAX dividends were $357.

Market Prices on February 28

AMAX	24	Dollar/yen	0.0047
Hitachi	880	Dollar/euro	1.05
TDK	6,000	U.S. stock index	103
Club Méditerranée	85	Japan stock index	97
Pernon-Ricard	72	France stock index	110
Government 6% 92	92	Yen bond index	101
(accrued interest, 1.55%)		World index	104
EIB 8.5% 93	98		
(accrued interest, 0.62%)			

Mr. Smith has no indication of the exact day of the transactions, and it would be too complicated to break down the month into subperiods, anyway. He therefore decides to make the assumption that every transaction or cash flow occurred just before the end of the month and at the month-end exchange rate. To help him, you should

   i. establish a new valuation report (see Exhibit A),

   ii. discuss the methodology for adjusting for cash movements, and

   iii. analyze the manager's performance.

EXHIBIT A

Account Valuation Reports (explanation)

The valuation report is set up following a standard method:

- Column 1 describes the security and its quotation currency.
- Column 2 gives either the number of securities for common stocks or the nominal invested for fixed income.
- Column 3 gives the market price in local currency. For bonds, this is given in percentage of the nominal (par) value.
- The accrued interest is given in column 4 as the percentage of the nominal (par) value. Usually, a yen bond with a coupon of, say, 8% will bear an interest of 8/365% per day. This is cumulated in the accrued interest column until the coupon is paid (semiannual, here).
- Column 5 gives the capital amount in base currency (here, U.S. dollars). It is the market price (column 3), multiplied by the column 2 value, multiplied by the exchange rate.
- Column 6 gives the amount of accrued interest in base currency. It is the accrued interest in percentage (column 4), multiplied by the column 2 value, multiplied by the exchange rate.
- Columns 7 and 8 give subtotals in capital and percentage.

Account Valuation for Mr. Smith, December 31

(1) Description of Security	(2) Number of Securities or Nominal	(3) Market Price (local cur.)	(4) Accrued Interest (%)	(5) Capital Amount ($)	(6) Accrued Interest ($)	(7) Sub-total ($)	(8) Sub-total (%)
Equity							
United States (in $)							
AMAX	1,000	24.50		24,500			
Exxon	500	37.25		18,625		43,125	29.8
Japan (in yen)							
Hitachi	10,000	800		34,320			
TDK	1,000	6,500		27,885		62,205	43.0
France (in euros)							
Club Med	200	77		18,326		18,326	12.7
Bonds							
Yen							
Govt. 6% 92	2,000,000	91.0%	0.52%	7,807	45		
EIB 8.5% 93	3,000,000	98.5%	3.47%	12,677	447	20,976	14.5
Cash							
U.S. dollars	0			0	0	0	0
Total				144,140	492	144,632	100

Exchange rates:
  Yen = 0.00429 dollars
  Euro = 1.19 dollars

Market indexes (price only):
  U.S. stocks = 100   Yen bonds = 100
  Japanese stocks = 100   World index = 100
  French stocks = 100

EXHIBIT A (CONTINUED)

Account Valuation for Mr. Smith, January 30

(1) Description of Security	(2) Number of Securities or Nominal	(3) Market Price (local cur.)	(4) Accrued Interest (%)	(5) Capital Amount ($)	(6) Accrued Interest ($)	(7) Sub-total ($)	(8) Sub-total (%)
Equity							
United States (in $)							
AMAX	1,000	23.50		23,500			
Exxon	500	38.00		19,000		42,500	28.8
Japan (in yen)							
Hitachi	10,000	820		36,900			
TDK	1,000	6,100		27,450		64,350	43.5
France (in euros)							
Club Med	200	87		19,140		19,140	12.9
Bonds							
Yen							
Govt. 6% 92	2,000,000	90.0%	1.04%	8,100	94		
EIB 8.5% 93	3,000,000	96.9%	4.16%	13,081	562	21,837	14.8
Cash							
U.S. dollars	0			0	0	0	0
Total				**147,171**	**656**	**147,827**	**100**

Exchange rates:
  Yen = 0.0045 dollars
  Euro = 1.10 dollars

Market indexes (price only):
  U.S. stocks = 102.5   Yen bonds = 99
  Japanese stocks = 98   World index = 102
  French stocks = 108

Solutions

1. ▪ The return on the index is zero, as is the properly calculated TWR of the portfolio:

$$1 + \text{TWR} = \frac{110}{100} \times \frac{145.46}{160} = 1$$

$$\text{TWR} = 0\%$$

▪ The MWR, using an Excel spreadsheet, is an internal rate of return of -3.89 percent:

$$\text{MWR} = -3.89\%$$

▪ The Dietz method gives an approximation to the MWR of

$$\text{MWR}_1 = \frac{\text{Profit}}{\text{Average invested capital}} = \frac{145.46 - 100 - 50}{100 + \dfrac{10}{30} \times 50} = \frac{-4.54}{116.67} = -3.90\%$$

- The "original" Dietz method gives an approximation to the MWR of

$$\text{MWR}_2 = \frac{\text{Profit}}{\text{Average invested capital}} = \frac{145.46 - 100 - 50}{100 + 0.5 \times 50} = \frac{-4.54}{125} = -3.63\%$$

Note that the "original" Dietz method gives a poor approximation of the true MWR (the difference is 26 bp). The Dietz method is much closer (a difference of 1 bp). *Much more importantly*, the MWR is very different from the TWR, which is equal to 0 percent. All three MWRs give the false indication that the manager underperformed the index by more than 300 bp. Indeed, the manager exactly tracked the index.

2. We compute the quarterly return (not annualized):

- MWR = IRR = 11.51%, with $200 = \dfrac{40}{(1 + \text{MWR})^{1/3}} + \dfrac{180}{(1 + \text{MWR})}$

- $\text{MWR}_1 = \dfrac{180 - 200 + 40}{200 - 2/3 \times 40} = \dfrac{20}{173.33} = 11.54\%$

- $\text{MWR}_2 = \dfrac{180 - 200 + 40}{200 - 1/2 \times 40} = \dfrac{20}{180} = 11.11\%$

- TWR = 10%, as $1 + \text{TWR} = (1 + 10\%) \times (1 + 0\%) = 1.1$

3. We compute the monthly return (not annualized):

- MWR = IRR = 14.58%, with $100 = \dfrac{20}{(1 + \text{MWR})^{1/3}}$

$$- \frac{50}{(1 + \text{MWR})^{2/3}} + \frac{145}{(1 + \text{MWR})}$$

- $\text{MWR}_1 = \dfrac{15}{100 + K_t} = 14.52\%$

  where $K_t = -\left(\dfrac{30 - 10}{30} \times 20\right) + \left(\dfrac{30 - 20}{30} \times 50\right) = 3.33$

- $\text{MWR}_2 = \dfrac{145 - 100 + 20 - 50}{100 + 1/2 \times 30} = \dfrac{15}{115} = 13.04\%$

- TWR = 19.85%, as $1 + \text{TWR} = \dfrac{90}{100} \times \dfrac{90}{70} \times \dfrac{145}{140} = 1.1985$

4. For the active manager, a portfolio turnover of twice a year implies transactions costs of $(4)(0.015) = 0.06$. Thus, transactions costs and fees amount to $6\% + 0.75\% = 6.75\%$.

   For the passive manager, the fees amount to 0.25%. Thus, the active manager must outperform the indexer, gross of costs, by at least $6.75\% - 0.25\% = 6.50\%$.

5. a. The return in dollars is $5\% = (1,050,000 - 1,000,000)/1,000,000$.

   b. The value of the portfolio moves from €1,000,000 = $1,000,000(€1/$) to €1,071,000 = $1,050,000 \times (€1.02/$).

   The return in euros is $7.1\% = (1,071,000 - 1,000,000)/1,000,000$.

   c. The difference is equal to 2.1 percent, while the exchange rate went up by 2 percent. The currency contribution is 2.1 percent because the exchange rate gain applies not only to the initial invested dollar capital (100 percent), but also to the dollar capital gain (5 percent). So, the currency contribution is equal to $2\% \times 1.05 = 2.1\%$.

6. a. The total return on the portfolio, measured in SKr is equal to

$$\frac{1,362,000}{1,200,000} - 1 = 0.135 \text{ or } 13.5\%$$

b. The *capital gain* amounts to
   - $660,000 - 600,000 = \text{SKr}60,000$ on the Swedish stocks, or 10%.
   - $702,000/5.40 - 600,000/6 = \$130,000 - \$100,000 = \$30,000$ on the U.S. stocks.

If we use the SKr6/\$ exchange rate, this is $(30,000)(6) = \text{SKr}180,000$

The total capital gain is SKr240,000, or 20% = $240,000/1,200,000$

Also note that:

- The dollar return on U.S. stocks is 30% = $30,000/100,000$.
- The SKr return on U.S. stocks is 17% = $102,000/600,000$.
- The SKr return on Swedish stocks is 10% = $60,000/600,000$.

The capital gain is in local currency = $(0.5)(0.30) + (0.5)(0.10) = 0.20 = 20\%$

The *currency contribution* can be calculated as follows:

Currency contribution of U.S. investment = SKr return on U.S. stocks

$$- \text{ dollar return on U.S stocks}$$

$$= 17\% - 30\% = -13\%$$

Portfolio currency contribution = portfolio weight U.S. stocks

$$\times \text{ currency contribution}$$

$$= (0.5)(-0.13) = -0.065 = -6.5\%$$

The *total return* can be decomposed as follows:

13.5% = Capital gain + Yield + Currency contribution = $20\% + 0\% - 6.5\%$

c. If the same amounts had been invested respectively in the OMX index and in the S&P index, returns would have been the following:
   - 20% on the Swedish index.
   - 25% on the U.S. index.
   - Portfolio-weighted market return in local currency = $(0.5)(0.20) + (0.5)(0.25) = 0.225 = 22.5\%$.

   We would have obtained 22.5 percent in local currency while our realized capital gain was only 20 percent.
   - Portfolio return in local currency = $(0.5)(0.10) + (0.5)(0.30) = 0.20 = 20\%$.
   - Hence, *security selection* contributed negatively for −2.5 percent because of a poor selection on the Swedish market: The Swedish portfolio only achieved a 10 percent return, while the OMX index showed a 20 percent growth. On the other hand, our U.S. stocks had a return of 30 percent in dollars, compared with 25 percent on the S&P index.

   Hence the capital gain itself can be broken down into market (22.5 percent) and security selection (−2.5 percent).

7. Calculations are summarized in the following table:

Global Equity Portfolio: Total Return Decomposition

	(1) Portfolio Weights	(2) Rate of Return in $	(3) Capital Gain in Local Currency	(4) Currency Contribution	(5) Market Index	(6) Security Selection	(7) Currency Contribution
U.S. stocks	50%	5.000%	5.000%	0.000%	3.000%	2.000%	0. 000%
Japan stocks	20%	4.762%	10.000%	−5.238%	5.000%	5.000%	−5.238%
Europe stocks	30%	2.041%	0.000%	2.041%	−5.000%	5.000%	2.041%
Total portfolio	**100%**	**4.065%**	**4.50%**	**−0.435%**	**1.00%**	**3.50%**	**−0.435%**

a. Total return of the portfolio: $4.065\% = (0.5)(0.05) + (0.2)(0.04762) + (0.3)(0.02041)$

Capital gain in local currency on U.S. shares: $(52,500 − 50,000)/50,000 = 5\%$

Currency contribution on U.S. shares: 0%

Capital gain in local currency on Japanese shares: $(2,200,000 − 2,000,000)/2,000,000 = 10\%$

Capital gain in U.S. dollars on Japanese shares: $(20,952 − 20,000)/20,000 = 4.76\%$

Currency contribution on Japanese shares: $4.76\% − 10\% = − 5.24\%$

Capital gain in local currency on European shares: $(30,000 − 30,000)/30,000 = 0\%$

Capital gain in U.S. dollars on European shares: $(30,612 − 30,000)/30,000 = 2.04\%$

Currency contribution on European shares: 2.04%

Return in local currency $= 4.50\% = (0.5)(0.05) + (0.2)(0.10) + (0.3)(0.0)$

Currency contribution $= −0.435\% = (0.5)(0.0) + (0.2)(−0.0524) + (0.3)(0.0204)$

We verify that $4.065\% = 4.5\% − 0.435\%$

b. The return in local currency of 4.50 percent can be decomposed as the weighted average of the index returns (1%) and the contribution of security selection.

Return on the U.S. stock index: $(103 − 100)/100 = 3\%$

Contribution of security selection on the U.S. stock: $5\% − 3\% = 2\%$

Return on the Japanese stock index: $(105 − 100)/100 = 5\%$

Contribution of security selection on the Japanese stock: $10\% − 5\% = 5\%$

Return on the European stock index: $(95 − 100)/100 = − 5\%$

Contribution of security selection on the European stock: $0\% − (− 5\%) = 5\%$

Net contribution of security selection: $= 3.50\% = (0.5)(0.02)$
$$+ (0.2)(0.05) + (0.3)(0.05)$$

c. We now focus on the performance relative to the benchmark (World index). The portfolio was overweighted in Europe (30 percent instead of 25 percent) and underweighted in Japan (20 percent instead of 25 percent). This is unfortunate, because Europe went down and Japan up. Using the formula in the text, we can attribute the performance relative to the World index, as done in the following table. The World index had a return of 0.735 percent in dollars. The performance of the portfolio is good: $4.065 - 0.735 = 3.33\%$. It is explained as follows:

Benchmark return	0.735%
Market allocation	−0.500%
Currency allocation	0.330%
Security selection	3.500%
Portfolio return	4.065%

Calculations of benchmark return and security selection have already been explained.

The market allocation = $(0)(0.03) + (-0.05)(0.05) + (0.05)(-0.05) = -0.5\%$

The currency allocation = $-0.435\% - (-0.765\%) = 0.33\%$

-0.435% is the currency contribution calculation shown in part (a).

$-0.765\% = (0.25)(-0.05) + (0.25)(0.0194)$

where

0.25 is the weight of Japan in the World index

−0.05 is dollar return on the Japan index minus the yen return on the index

0.25 is the weight of Europe in the World index

0.0194 is the dollar return on the Europe index minus the euro return on the index

The following table summarizes the solution.

Global Equity Portfolio: Performance Attribution

	Portfolio Weights	World Index Weights	Index Return in Local Currency	World Index Return in $	Market Allocation Contribution	Currency Allocation Contribution	Security Selection
U.S. stocks	50%	50%	3.00%	1.500%	0.000%	0.000%	2.000%
Japan stocks	20%	25%	5.00%	0.000%	−0.250%	0.202%	5.000%
European stocks	30%	25%	−5.00%	−0.765%	−0.250%	0.128%	5.000%
Total portfolio				**0.735%**	**−0.500%**	**0.330%**	**3.500%**

8. a. Overall, both managers added value by mitigating the currency effects present in the Index. Both exhibited an ability to "pick stocks" in the markets they chose to be in (Manager B in particular). Manager B used his opportunities *not* to be in stocks quite effectively (via the cash/bond contribution to return), but neither of them matched the passive index in picking the country markets in which to be invested (Manager B in particular).

	Manager A	**Manager B**
Strengths	Currency management	Currency management
		Stock selection
		Use of cash/bond flexibility
Weaknesses	Country selection (to a limited degree)	Country selection

b. The column reveals the effect on performance of adjustment for movements in the U.S. dollar relative to local currencies and, therefore, the currency effect on the portfolio. Currency gains/losses arise from translating changes in currency exchange rates versus the U.S. dollar over the measuring period (three years in this case) into U.S. dollars for the U.S. pension plan. The Index mix lost 12.9 percent to the dollar, reducing what would otherwise have been a very favorable return from the various country markets of 19.9 percent to a net return of only 7.0 percent.

9. a. The following briefly describes one strength and one weakness of each manager.

1. Manager A

Strength: Although Manager A's one-year total return was slightly below the EAFE index return (−6.0 percent versus −5.0 percent, respectively), this manager apparently has some country/security return expertise. This large local market return advantage of 2.0 percent exceeds the 0.2 percent return for the EAFE index.

Weakness: Manager A has an obvious weakness in the currency management area. This manager experienced a marked currency return shortfall compared with the EAFE index of −8.0 percent versus −5.2 percent, respectively.

2. Manager B

Strength: Manager B's total return slightly exceeded that of the index, with a marked positive increment apparent in the currency return. Manager B had a −1.0 percent currency return versus a −5.2 percent currency return on the EAFE index. Based on this outcome, Manager B's strength appears to be some expertise in the currency selection area.

Weakness: Manager B had a marked shortfall in local market return. Manager B's country/security return was −1.0 percent versus 0.2 percent on the EAFE index. Therefore, Manager B appears to be weak in security/market selection ability.

b. The following strategies would enable the Fund to take advantage of the strengths of the two managers and simultaneously minimize their weaknesses.

1. *Recommendation:* One strategy would be to direct Manager A to make no currency bets relative to the EAFE Index and to direct Manager B to make only currency decisions, and no active country or security selection bets.

Justification: This strategy would mitigate Manager A's weakness by hedging all currency exposures into index-like weights. This would allow capture of Manager A's country and stock selection skills while avoiding losses from poor currency management. This strategy would also mitigate Manager B's weakness, leaving an index-like portfolio construct and capitalizing on the apparent skill in currency management.

2. *Recommendation:* Another strategy would be to combine the portfolios of Manager A and Manager B, with Manager A making country exposure and security selection decisions and Manager B managing the currency exposures created by Manager A's decisions (providing a type of currency overlay).

Justification: This recommendation would capture the strengths of both Manager A and Manager B and would minimize their collective weaknesses.

10. a. The local currency returns are shown in the following table:

Country	Dec. 31, 2000	Dec. 31, 2001	Return (%)
United States	$50,000,000	$55,000,000	10.0%
United Kingdom	£20,000,000	£20,500,000	2.5%
France	€25,000,000	€32,000,000	28.0%

For example, the local currency return for the French portion of the portfolio is

$$\frac{32,000,000 - 25,000,000}{25,000,000} = 0.28 = 28\%$$

The dollar returns and portfolio weights are shown in the following table:

Country	Dec. 31, 2000	Dec. 31, 2001	Return	Weight
United States	$50,000,000	$55,000,000	10.0%	48.31%
United Kingdom	$30,769,231	$33,064,516	7.46%	29.73%
France	$22,727,273	$26,666,667	17.33%	21.96%
Total portfolio	**$103,496,504**	**$114,731,183**	**10.855 %**	**100.0%**

To explain the calculations, the United Kingdom will be used as an illustration. First the pound values of the U.K. portion of the portfolio must be converted to dollars:

For Dec. 31, 2000, dollar value = $30,769,231 = £20,000,000/£0.65 per $

For Dec. 31, 2001, dollar value = $33,064,516 = £20,500,000/£0.62 per $

The dollar return for the U.K. portion of the portfolio is

$$\frac{33,064,516 - 30,769,231}{30,769,231} = 0.0746 = 7.46\%$$

The portfolio weight for the United Kingdom = 0.2973 = $30,769,231/$103,496,504
The portfolio return = 0.10855 = (0.4831)(0.10) + (0.2973)(0.0746) + (0.2196)(0.1733)

b. The total portfolio return decomposition table is shown here:

Country	Dollar Return	Capital Gain (local currency)	Currency Contribution
U.S.	10.0%	10.0%	0.0%
U.K.	7.46%	2.5%	4.96%
France	17.33%	28.0%	−10.667%
Total portfolio	**10.855%**	**11.723%**	**−0.868%**

The total portfolio return in U.S. dollars = 10.855%. This can be decomposed into the capital gain of 11.723% in local currency, and the currency contribution of −0.868%.

The capital gain in local currency = 0.11723 = (0.4831)(0.10)

$$+ (0.2973)(0.025) + (0.2196)(0.28)$$

The currency contribution for the United States is 0%.

The currency contribution for the United Kingdom $= 0.0496 = 0.0746 - 0.025$
$$= 4.96\%$$

The currency contribution for France $= -0.10667 = 0.17333 - 0.28 = -10.667\%$

The overall currency contribution $= -0.00868$
$$= (0.4831)(0.0) + (0.2973)(0.0496)$$
$$+ (0.2196)(-0.10667)$$
$$= -0.868\%$$

c. The total portfolio return decomposition table is shown here:

Country	Dollar Return	Currency Contribution	Market Index	Security Selection
United States	10.0%	0.0%	9.079%	0.92%
United Kingdom	7.46%	4.96%	5.321%	-2.82%
France	17.33%	-10.667%	6.211%	21.79%
Total portfolio	**10.855%**	**-0.868%**	**7.332%**	**4.391%**

The dollar returns and currency contributions are the same as in part (b) above.

The total portfolio return in U.S. dollars $= 10.855\%$. This can be decomposed into the currency contribution, plus the market return, plus security selection $= -0.00868 + 0.07332 + 0.04391$

The currency contribution for the United States is 0%.

The currency contribution for the United Kingdom $= 0.0496 = 0.0746 - 0.025$
$$= 4.96\%$$

The currency contribution for France $= -0.10667 = 0.17333 - 0.28 = -10.667\%$

The overall currency contribution $= -0.00868$
$$= (0.4831)(0.0) + (0.2973)(0.0496)$$
$$+ (0.2196)(-0.10667)$$
$$= -0.868\%$$

The market return for the United States $= 0.09079 = (829 - 760)/760 = 9.079\%$

The market return for the United Kingdom $= 0.05321 = (1148 - 1090)/1,090$
$$= 5.321\%$$

The market return for France $= 0.06211 = (1009 - 950)/950 = 6.211\%$

The overall market return contribution $= 0.07332$
$$= (0.4831)(0.09079) + (0.2973)(0.05321)$$
$$+ (0.2196)(0.06211)$$
$$= 7.332\%$$

The security selection contribution for each country is calculated by subtracting the market return from the local-currency capital gain.

Security selection for the United States $= 0.0092 = 0.10 - 0.0908 = 0.92\%$

Security selection for the United Kingdom $= -0.0282 = 0.025 - 0.0532 = -2.82\%$

Security selection for France $= 0.2179 = 0.28 - 0.0621 = 21.79\%$

The overall security selection contribution $= 0.04391$
$$= (0.4831)(0.0092)$$
$$+ (0.2973)(-0.0282)$$
$$+ (0.2196)(0.2179)$$
$$= 4.391\%.$$

d. The following table indicates the global performance attribution:

Benchmark return	7.003%
Market allocation	−0.422%
Currency allocation	−0.117%
Security selection	4.391%
Total return	10.855%

$$\text{Benchmark return} = \frac{834.622 - 780}{780} = 0.07003 = 7.003\%$$

$$\text{Market allocation} = (-0.1169)(0.09079) + (0.0973)(0.05321) + (0.0196)(0.06211)$$

$$= -0.00422 = -0.422\%$$

Data are obtained from the following table (Index Return Breakdown).

Index Return Breakdown

Country	Under/Over Weight*	Dollar Return	Capital Gain (local currency)	Currency Contribution
United States index	−11.69%	9.079%	9.079%	0.0%
United Kingdom index	9.73%	10.417%	5.321%	5.096%
France index	1.96%	−2.64%	6.211%	−8.851%

*The portfolio weight minus the index weight.

The currency allocation = −0.00868 − (−0.00751) = −0.00117 = −0.117%
−0.00868 is the overall currency contribution, the calculation for this is shown above in part c.
−0.00751 is the currency contribution for the world market index:
$$-0.007508 = (.60)(0.0) + (0.20)(0.05096) + (0.20)(-0.08851)$$

The security selection contribution is 4.391 percent and has been shown in part (c).

11. Yes. The return on foreign assets looks small relative to its volatility. But the risk that counts is the contribution to the risk of the total portfolio. Here are some return-and-risk characteristics for global portfolios with increasing proportions of foreign assets.

% U.S.	% Foreign	Return (%)	Volatility (%)
100	0	10.00	12.00
95	5	10.05	11.64
90	10	10.10	11.37
85	15	10.15	11.19
80	20	10.20	11.11
75	25	10.25	11.14
70	30	10.30	11.26
65	35	10.35	11.48
60	40	10.40	11.78
55	45	10.45	12.18
50	50	10.50	12.65

A portfolio invested 20 percent in foreign fund increases the return from 10.0 percent to 10.2 percent and reduces the volatility from 12.0 percent to 11.1 percent. Portfolio risk is calculated using the following formula:

$$\sigma_p^2 = x^2\sigma_d^2 + (1-x)^2 \sigma_f^2 + 2x(1-x)\rho\,\sigma_d\sigma_f$$

Portfolio return is calculated using the following formula:

$$R_p = R_d(x) + R_f(1-x)$$

where

σ_p is the risk of the portfolio

σ_d is the risk of domestic stocks

σ_f is the risk of foreign stocks

ρ is the correlation between domestic and foreign stocks

x is the proportion of the portfolio invested in domestic stocks.

12. Yes. The risk counts is the contribution of the foreign assets to the total risk of the global portfolio. In the proposed example, foreign stocks have a larger standard deviation (20 percent) than U.S. stocks (15 percent). However, let's calculate the standard deviation of the diversified portfolio made up of 90 percent domestic stocks and 10 percent foreign stocks. We have

$$\sigma_p^2 = x^2\sigma_d^2 + (1-x)^2 \sigma_f^2 + 2x(1-x)\rho\,\sigma_d\sigma_f$$

where

σ_p is the risk of the portfolio

σ_d is the risk of domestic stocks

σ_f is the risk of foreign stocks

ρ is the correlation between domestic and foreign stocks

x is the proportion of the portfolio invested in domestic stocks.

Here, we will take $\rho = -0.10$, because the U.S. portfolio is very strongly correlated with the U.S. stock index.

$$\sigma_p^2 = (0.9^2)(15^2) + (0.1^2)(20^2) + 2(0.9)(0.1)(-0.1)(15)(20)$$
$$\sigma_p^2 = 182.25 + 4 - 5.4 = 180.85$$
$$\sigma_p = 13.45\%$$

Thus, the addition of foreign equity allows us both to increase the return (here, $R_p = (0.9)(10) + (0.1)(11) = 10.1$ percent) and reduce the risk of a domestic portfolio.

13.

Year	Portfolio Return	Benchmark Return	Excess Return	Squared Deviation
1996	12%	14%	−2.0%	0.18%
1997	14%	10%	4.0%	0.03%
1998	20%	12%	8.0%	0.34%
1999	14%	16%	−2.0%	0.18%
2000	16%	13%	3.0%	0.01%

The squared deviation column is the squared deviation of the excess return for each period from the mean excess return of 2.20 percent.

$$\text{Tracking error} = \sqrt{\frac{0.0073}{4}} = 0.0427, \text{ or } 4.3\%$$

14. Sharpe ratio calculations:

$$\text{Portfolio } 1 = \frac{0.135 - 0.05}{0.19} = 0.4474 = 44.74\%. \text{ Rank } 3$$

$$\text{Portfolio } 2 = \frac{0.1625 - 0.05}{0.24} = 0.4688 = 46.88\%. \text{ Rank } 2$$

$$\text{Portfolio } 3 = \frac{0.17 - 0.05}{0.23} = 0.5217 = 52.17\%. \text{ Rank } 1$$

Information ratio calculations:

$$\text{Portfolio } 1 = \frac{0.135 - 0.13}{0.065} = 0.08. \text{ Rank } 3$$

$$\text{Portfolio } 2 = \frac{0.1625 - 0.13}{0.08} = 0.41. \text{ Rank } 2$$

$$\text{Portfolio } 3 = \frac{0.17 - 0.13}{0.07} = 0.57. \text{ Rank } 1$$

15. This publicity campaign is misleading because of survivor bias. Only the funds that survive, because of their good performance, are included in the track record.

16. The average performance should be that of the market index minus costs (transaction costs, management fees).

If international investors, as a group, beat some national index, it must be that local investors, as a group, underperform the index.

No. Because of costs, both international and local investors can, as a group, underperform the local index.

17. a. To calculate the indexes, we proceed in four steps:
  - Calculate the return of month *t* for each market as the difference between the ending and beginning values of the index, divided by the beginning value of the index.
  - Calculate the weights of the country indexes at the start of the month.
  - Calculate the return on the global index.
  - Chain-link the global index value.

For the GDP-weighted index in period 1

$\text{Index}_{\text{GDP}} = 100$ at beginning of period

$$\text{Weight}_{\text{GDPA}} = \frac{100}{100 + 100} = 0.5 \qquad \text{Weight}_{\text{GDPB}} = \frac{100}{100 + 100} = 0.5$$

$$\text{Return}_{\text{A}} = -5\% \qquad \qquad \text{Return}_{\text{B}} = 10\%$$

$$\text{Return}_{\text{GDP}} = 2.5\%$$

$$\text{Index}_{\text{GDP}} = 102.5 \text{ at end of period}$$

For the capitalization-weighted index:

$$\text{Weight}_{\text{CAPA}} = \frac{1.5 \times 100}{1.5 \times 100 + 100} = 0.6 \qquad \text{Weight}_{\text{CAPB}} = \frac{100}{1.5 \times 100 + 100} = 0.4$$

The country index returns are given in the following table:

Month	Index$_A$	Index$_B$	Return$_A$	Return$_B$
0	100	100		
1	95	110	−0.05	0.1
2	100	100	0.0526	−0.0909
3	100	120	0	0.2
4	105	125	0.05	0.0417
5	110	135	0.0476	0.08

For example, for month 1:

$$\text{Return}_A = \frac{95}{100} - 1 = -0.05$$

$$\text{Return}_B = \frac{110}{100} - 1 = 0.10$$

$$\text{CAP}_A = (1 - 0.05)(150) = 142.5$$

$$\text{CAP}_B = (1 + 0.10)(100) = 110$$

Month	GDP$_A$	GDP$_B$	CAP$_A$	CAP$_B$
0	100	100	150	100
1	100	100	142.5	110
2	100	100	150	100
3	102	101	150	120
4	102	101	157.5	125
5	102	101	165	135

For example, for month 1:

Month	Weight$_{\text{GDPA}}$	Weight$_{\text{GDPB}}$	Weight$_{\text{CAPA}}$	Weight$_{\text{CAPB}}$
0	0.5000	0.5000	0.6000	0.4000
1	0.5000	0.5000	0.5644	0.4356
2	0.5000	0.5000	0.6000	0.4000
3	0.5025	0.4975	0.5556	0.4444
4	0.5025	0.4975	0.5575	0.4425
5	0.5025	0.4975	0.5500	0.4500

For example, for month 1:

$$\text{Weight}_{\text{GDPA}} = \frac{100}{100 + 100} = 0.50$$

$$\text{Weight}_{\text{GDPB}} = \frac{100}{100 + 100} = 0.50$$

$$\text{Weight}_{\text{CAPA}} = \frac{142.5}{142.5 + 110} = 0.5644$$

$$\text{Weight}_{\text{CAPB}} = \frac{110}{142.5 + 110} = 0.4356$$

Month	Return$_{\text{GDP}}$	Index$_{\text{GDP}}$	Return$_{\text{CAP}}$	Index$_{\text{CAP}}$
0	—	100	—	100
1	0.0250	102.5	0.01	101
2	−0.0191	100.5383	−0.0099	100
3	0.1	110.5921	0.08	108
4	0.0459	115.6632	0.0463	113
5	0.0637	123.0344	0.0619	120

For example, for month 1:

$$\text{Return}_{\text{GDP}} = (0.50)(-0.05) + (0.50)(0.10) = 0.025$$

$$\text{Index}_{\text{GDP}} = (100)(1 + 0.025) = 102.5$$

$$\text{Return}_{\text{CAP}} = (0.6)(-0.05) + (0.4)(0.10) = 0.01$$

$$\text{Index}_{\text{CAP}} = (100)(1 + 0.01) = 101$$

b. At the end of each month, we must rebalance the portfolio tracking the GDP-weighted index. For example, at the end of month 1, the shares of Market B have gone up in value and we must sell some of them to get back to a 50-50 breakdown.

18. a. The total risk of a portfolio can be decomposed into
   - absolute risk on each asset class without regard to risk of active managers, and
   - active risk allocation of managers of each asset class.
   Risk decomposition is complicated by the fact that risks in a global portfolio are correlated. Currency risk is another dimension that adds further complications.
   b. *Risk budgeting* refers to the process by which a client allocates the amount of risk it is willing to assign to different asset classes or portfolio managers. Some portfolio managers are allowed to have large tracking errors, because they can provide specific added value for the segment of the portfolios they manage. On the other hand, portfolio managers of some segments may only be allowed to have small tracking errors, because they are judged not to be able to add value relative to the benchmark.

19. The following factors can introduce potential biases in the measurement of portfolio risk and performance:
   - Infrequently traded assets in the portfolio
   - Option-like investment strategies
   - Survivor bias

Infrequently traded assets do not have up-to-date market prices; consequently, their prices tend to be smoothed over time. This introduces a downward bias in risk measures for these assets. In addition, the correlations of returns of these infrequently traded assets with conventional asset returns can be very low because of the smoothing effect. In a portfolio context, the net effect is that the calculated risk measure will underestimate true risk.

Traditional risk measures, such as standard deviation, assume that returns are normally distributed. The assumption of normality is also usually made when using value at risk (VaR) in asset management. However, some investment strategies, for example, option-like strategies, can result in return distributions that are highly nonnormal. Thus, the validity of such measures of risk as the standard deviation is questionable.

Survivor bias impacts performance measurement and risk measurement. Survivor bias means that, over time, unsuccessful managers disappear. Thus, taking as an example of hedge funds, the existing or surviving funds will report good track records. However, there is no guarantee that the surviving managers will deliver superior performance in future years. Similarly, from a risk perspective, funds that experienced high levels of risk in the past may have disappeared, leaving behind funds with low volatility. There is no guarantee, however, that funds with low volatility will display low volatility in the future.

20. a. The results are given in the following table:

Performance Decomposition (in %), January

	Weights	Total Return	Yield	Currency Gain	Capital Gain	Market Index	Security Selection
U.S. stocks	29.8	−1.45	0.00	0.00	−1.45	2.50	−3.95
Japan stocks	43.0	3.45	0.00	4.83	−1.38	−2.00	0.62
France stocks	12.7	4.44	0.00	−8.55	12.99	8.00	4.99
Japan bonds	14.5	4.10	0.64	4.86	−1.39	−1.00	−0.39
Total	**100**	**2.21**	**0.09**	**1.70**	**0.42**	**0.76**	**−0.34**

The total return is 2.21 percent, decomposed as

Capital gain	0.42%
Yield	0.09%
Currency gain	1.70%

He did better than the World index. The market index returns were, respectively, 2.5 percent, −2 percent, 8 percent, and −1 percent. If the manager had invested with the same proportions in market indexes, instead of individual securities, he would have obtained +0.76 percent in local currency. So, his security selection gave him $0.42 - 0.76 = -0.34\%$. He underperformed the indexes for U.S. stocks and yen bonds, but outperformed for French and Japanese stocks.

By way of illustration, a set of calculations is shown for Japanese stocks.

$$\text{Total return in dollars} = \frac{64,350 - 62,205}{62,205} = 3.45\%$$

$$\text{Capital gain in yen (\%)} = \frac{(8,200,00 + 6,100,000) - (8,000,000 + 6,500,000)}{(8,000,000 + 6,500,000)}$$

$$= -1.38\%$$

Currency contribution = $0.0345 - (-0.0138) = 4.83\%$

The market index return = $\dfrac{98 - 100}{100} = -2.0\%$

Security selection contribution is equal to the local currency capital gain minus the market index return = $-0.0138 - (-0.02) = 0.0062 = 0.62\%$.

The totals are calculated by applying portfolio weights to the component returns; for example, the total dollar return is 2.21 percent, calculated as follows:

$$(0.298)(-0.0145) + (0.43)(0.0345) + (0.127)(0.044) + (0.145)(0.041) = 0.0221$$

b. The following table gives the valuation report at the end of February.

Number of Securities or Nominal	Description	Market Price	Accrued Interest in %	Amount in $	Accrued Interest in $	Subtotal in $	Sub total in %
	Equity						
	U.S.A.						
1,000	AMAX	24		24,000		24,000	14.6%
	Japan						
10,000	Hitachi	880		41,360			
1,000	TDK	6,000		28,200		69,560	42.3%
	France						
200	Club Med	85		17,850			
400	Pernod	72		30,240		48,090	29.2%
	Bonds						
	Yen						
2,000,000	Govt 6% 92	92%	1.55%	8,648	146		
3,000,000	EIB 8.5% 93	98%	0.62%	13,818	88	22,700	13.8%
	Cash						
	U.S. dollars			72		72	0.1%
	Total			**164,188**	**234**	**164,422**	**100%**

Exchange rates:
Yen = 0.0047 dollars
Euro = 1.05 dollars

Market indexes:
U.S.A. stocks	103
Japanese stocks	97
French stocks	110
Japanese bonds	101
World index	104

By way of explanation, consider the valuation numbers for the Japanese Government bond:

The nominal (face) yen value is ¥2,000,000.

The market price is 92 percent of face value.

The accrued interest is 1.55 percent.

The market price in dollars is $(0.92)(2,000,000)(0.0047) = \$8,648$.

The accrued interest in dollars is $(0.0155)(2,000,000)(0.0047) = \$145.7$, or \$146.

The following table gives the return computations for the account over February. For convenience, we assumed that all cash flows took place at the end of the month.

Otherwise, we would have to adjust the mean capital invested and take account of the currency rate at the time of each cash flow. The same calculation would yield slightly different results if the cash flows were assumed to take place at the start of the month or at the middle of the month.

Performance Decomposition (in %), February

	Weights	Total Return	Yield	Currency Gain	Capital Gain	Market Index	Security Selection
U.S. stocks	28.8	4.37	0.84	0.00	3.53	0.49	3.04
Japan stocks	43.5	8.10	0.00	4.60	3.50	−1.02	4.52
French stocks	12.9	−9.98	0.00	−4.29	−5.69	1.85	−7.54
Japan bonds	14.8	6.59	0.54	4.54	1.51	2.02	−0.51
Total	**100%**	**4.46**	**0.32**	**2.12**	**2.02**	**0.23**	**1.79**

Bibliography

AIMR. *Global Investment Performance Standards,* Charlottesville, VA: Author, 1999.

Ankrim, E. M., and Hensel, C. R. "Multicurrency Performance Attribution," *Financial Analysts Journal,* March/April 1994.

Asness, C., Krail, R., and Liew, J. "Do Hedge Funds Hedge?" *Journal of Portfolio Management,* Fall 2001.

Brown, S. J., Goetzmann, W. N., and Ibbotson, R. G. "Offshore Hedge Funds: Survival and Performance." 1989–95, *Journal of Business* 72, 1999.

Fung W., and Hsieh, D. A., "Hedge-Fund Benchmarks: Information Content and Biases," *Financial Analysts Journal,* January/February 2002.

Goodwin, T. H. "The Information Ratio," *Financial Analysts Journal,* July/August 1998.

Grinold, R. C., and Kahn, R. N. *Active Portfolio Management,* Chicago: Irwin, 1995.

Jorion, P., and Kirsten, G. "The Right Way to Measure International Performance," *Investing,* Spring 1991.

Karnosky, D. S., and Singer, B. D. *Global Asset Management and Performance Attribution,* Charlottesville, VA: The Research Foundation of the IFCA, 1994.

Reilly, F., and Brown, K. *Investment Analysis and Portfolio Management,* 7th ed., Orlando: South-Western, 2003.

Roll, R. "Ambiguity When Performance Is Measured by the Securities Market Line," *Journal of Finance,* September 1978.

Sharpe, W. F. "Asset Allocation: Management Style and Performance Measurement," *Journal of Portfolio Management,* Winter 1992.

Sharpe, W. F. " The Sharpe Ratio," *Journal of Portfolio Management,* Fall 1994.

Singer, B. D., Gonzalo, M., and Lederman, M. "Multi-period Attribution: Residual and Compounding," *Journal of Portfolio Management,* Fall 1998.

Singer, B. D., and Karnosky, D. S. "The General Framework for Global Investment Management and Performance Attribution," *Journal of Portfolio Management,* Winter 1995.

Spaulding, D. "Is Linking Attribution Effects as Hard as it Looks?" *Journal of Performance Measurement*, Spring 2002.

Terhaar, K., Staub, R., and Singer, B. "Asset Allocation: The Alternatives Approach," *Journal of Portfolio Management*, Spring 2003.

Structuring the Global Investment Process

Bruno Solnik
Dennis McLeavey
Victoria Rati
Jan Squires

LEARNING OUTCOMES

After completing this chapter, you will be able to do the following:

- Discuss the functions of and relationships among the major participants in the global investment industry

- Discuss the components of a formal investment policy statement

- Discuss the role of capital market expectations in strategic and tactical asset allocation

- Evaluate the appropriateness of an investment policy statement for a global investor

- Interpret capital market data and capital market expectations in the context of strategic asset allocation for a global investor

- Compare and contrast the major choices—active/passive, top-down/bottom-up, style, global/specialized, currency, quantitative/subjective—available to a global investor in structuring the global investment decision-making process

- Evaluate the appropriateness, in terms of implementing the investment policy statement and strategic or tactical asset allocation, of fund/manager choices available to a global investor

- Discuss the important issues—particularly scope, weights, and currency allocation—in choosing a global benchmark for strategic asset allocation

- Compare and contrast alternative approaches to hedging currency risk in strategic asset allocation

- Discuss the determinants of effective global tactical asset allocation

- Compare and contrast strategic and tactical asset allocation in the global context

- Describe and evaluate the components of the global asset allocation process

- Design an appropriate strategic asset allocation for a global investor

- Interpret capital market data and capital market expectations in the context of tactical asset allocation for a global investor

- Design an appropriate tactical asset allocation for a global investor

- Evaluate the implications of a portfolio performance analysis for a global investor

- Summarize the primary issues that must be addressed by an investor contemplating global investment

An investment organization that is planning to offer global investment products to its clients first needs the information on institutions and techniques provided earlier in this book. Then the manager needs to properly structure its entire global investment decision process, from research to management and control. Among the many global investment organizations in the world today, there are a great variety of approaches to structuring the global investment process. Different approaches reflect different investment philosophies and strategies.

The chapter is organized as follows. It starts with a brief tour of the global investing industry. A global investment philosophy has to be chosen and proposed to the clients. The various approaches are reviewed in the second section. The rest of the chapter discusses the various steps of the global portfolio management process. The clients' objectives, constraints, and requirements are specified in an investment policy statement; the investment policy statement presented in the third section forms the basis for the strategic asset allocation. Capital market expectations have to be formulated and will be used to determine the asset allocation. This crucial step in a world with many equity, debt, and currency markets is discussed in the fourth section.

Some important issues in terms of global asset allocation are then discussed. Strategic asset allocation and tactical asset allocation are usually viewed as two different steps of the asset allocation process. The chapter concludes with an example of how to structure and quantify the global investment process. A case study serves as a review and application of the principles outlined in the chapter.

A Tour of the Global Investment Industry

Readers unfamiliar with the global investment scene often ask for a brief presentation of the major players. Such a description quickly becomes outdated, because the investment management industry changes rapidly. Nevertheless, let's take a quick tour. There are several types of participants in the global investment arena: investors (private or institutional), investment managers, brokers, consultants, and custodians. Some players belong to several categories.

Investors

Private Investors   Investors belong to two broad categories: private and institutional. The term *private investor* usually refers to an individual or small group of individuals, such as those represented by a family trust. Private investors have many ways to invest globally. They can buy foreign shares listed on their domestic markets. They can also buy, through a broker, foreign shares not listed domestically. They can buy mutual funds that diversify across multiple international markets or funds that invest only in specific markets. Finally, they can have their money managed by investment professionals; high-net-worth individuals are a clientele actively sought by many investment management firms. Whether a private or institutional investor, one must prepare, with the manager, a policy statement outlining the investment goals and the risks that can be taken. This is all the more important in global investing, in which the investment universe is enormous, as are the potential returns, costs, and risks.

The tax treatment of domestic and foreign investments is sometimes different. Furthermore, the tax situation of investors differs across countries. Even within the European Union, each country has retained specific tax codes for its domestic individual investors. This poses a challenge to investment managers and advisors who wish to serve clients in many countries.

The financial assets of high-net-worth individuals (HNWIs) are huge and present an attractive market for investment professionals. Exhibit 13.1 provides a worldwide estimate of the number and financial assets of individuals with a financial wealth above $1 million. Merrill Lynch/Cap Gemini Ernst & Young[1] estimate that there are some 7.1 million HNWIs with a total financial assets in excess of $26 trillion. Europe and North America represent the largest share of the worldwide market.

The investment behavior of individual investors is somewhat different from that of institutional investors described in sections to follow. Individuals tend to invest relatively more in nontradable assets such as real estate, hedge funds, or structured products. But there are also marked differences in the profile and behavior of HNWIs across regions. Merrill Lynch/Cap Gemini Ernst & Young contrast the

---

[1] Merrill Lynch/Cap Gemini Ernst & Young, "World Wealth Report," 2002.

EXHIBIT 13.1

High-Net-Worth Individuals Worldwide
Number and financial assets of individuals with a financial wealth above $1 million, 2001

Region	Number of Individuals (in million)	Financial Assets (in trillion dollars)
Africa	0.06	0.6
Middle East	0.29	1.0
Latin America	0.28	3.5
Asia Pacific	1.73	5.1
Europe	2.54	8.4
North America	2.22	7.6
Total	*7.1*	*26.2*

Source: Merrill Lynch/Cap Gemini Ernst & Young, "World Wealth Report," 2002.

differences between European and American HNWIs. Key differences are summarized in Exhibit 13.2.

Institutional Investors: Mutual Funds   The term *institutional investor* is generally used to describe an organization that invests on behalf of others, such as a mutual fund, pension fund, or charitable organization. A variety of institutional investors exist. *Mutual funds* pool money from investors and invest it in financial assets to achieve a stated investment objective. Mutual funds are offered to the pub-

EXHIBIT 13.2

Key Differences between American and European HNWIs

	North America	Europe
Cultural aspects	Capital market-led, with a strong equity culture	Banking-led, protecting capital from war, hyperinflation, and high taxation
Wealth sources	Highly entrepreneurial, emphasis on technology and finance	Inheritance and multiple sectors, including retailing and manufacturing
Demographics	Average HNWI age 55–57: • Distributed down through younger age bands • Increasing female component	Average HNWI age 59–62: • High concentration in upper age bands • Fewer women
Investment manager	Tend toward one principal provider of investment services	Use multiple providers and a less integrated approach
Investment preference	Domestically focused equity culture, mainly in onshore vehicles	More balanced across asset classes, stronger offshore flavor.
Performance measurement	Focus on short-term performance relative to benchmarks (market indexes)	Focus on medium-term return relative to inflation and local interest rate

Source: Merrill Lynch/Cap Gemini Ernst & Young, "World Wealth Report," 2002.

lic, which can buy them at a listed price reflecting the market value of the assets owned by the mutual fund. Mutual funds are called *unit trusts* in the United Kingdom or *Sociétés d'Investissement à Capital Variable (SICAV)* in France, Belgium, and Luxembourg. The mutual fund industry is growing rapidly worldwide. Its growth in Europe has been spectacular, especially in countries that do not have a pension fund system. Mutual funds established in one country often cannot be marketed in other countries. The European Directive on the *Undertaking for Collective Investments in Transferable Securities (UCITS)* allows the establishment of funds that can be marketed across Europe from a single domicile or launch base, without having to request special administrative authorization in each individual European country. Many of the cross-border UCITS are Luxembourg-domiciled. Luxembourg is the second largest domicile[2] for investment funds, after the United States.

International mutual funds listed domestically provide an efficient alternative to the direct purchase of foreign shares. Buying a country fund or a regional fund (e.g., European equity) allows participation in some markets in a risk-diversified and cost-efficient way. Exchange traded funds (ETFs) have grown in popularity worldwide. ETFs are funds that trade on a stock market like shares of any individual companies. They can be traded at any time during market hours, and can be sold short or margined. But they are shares of a portfolio, not of an individual company. ETFs are generally designed to closely track the performance of a specific index. ETFs on the indexes of several individual developed stock markets, as well as on many international indexes, are listed on many national stock markets.[3] In turn, mutual funds are institutional investors, because they invest large amounts of money that is not their own. Investment management of an international mutual fund is done internally or is delegated to a specialized foreign asset manager.

Determining the performance of a mutual fund is relatively straightforward, because the share prices of mutual funds are published daily in the financial press and are available on the Internet. Some services, such as S&P Micropal and Morningstar, specialize in comparing the performance of mutual funds by investment objective, not only in the United States, but also in many other countries. An estimate of mutual fund assets for major countries is given in Exhibit 13.3. This exhibit provides estimates of institutional assets by category and countries at the end of 2001.[4]

Institutional Investors: Pension Funds Retirement provisions are diverse throughout the world, and even within each country. Basically, two very different

---

[2] This can be explained by the existence of efficient administrative fund services, appropriate regulatory and legal framework, and low taxes.

[3] A major feature of ETFs is the redemption in-kind process. See Chapters 6 and 8.

[4] Estimates from different sources for pension and insurance assets can vary widely. This can be explained by differences in classification, valuation, and double counting. It is hard to estimate pension assets in countries in which pension funds do not have a separate legal structure; figures for Japan pension assets vary widely according to classification. It would be misleading to sum all the institutional assets reported in Exhibit 13.3 as pension funds and insurance companies often hold some mutual funds shares.

philosophies can be found. Many countries have a pay-as-you-go system: Active workers pay for the pensions of retired workers. Workers, and their employers, do not contribute to the future pensions of the employees; they do not "capitalize" their contributions. Rather, these contributions are immediately paid to the current retirees. Except for some minimal technical reserves, there is no money to be invested, because it is immediately disbursed. This system can be found in France, Italy, and most of Continental Europe.

In the Anglo-American system, workers, and their employers, contribute to a pension fund, which capitalizes all contributions and pays them back at the time of retirement. In this case, pension funds are considered as long-term institutional investors. This pension fund model can be found in countries such as the United Kingdom, the United States, Canada, the Netherlands, and Denmark. Many countries, such as Switzerland, Japan, and several Latin American countries, are moving to this pension fund system. The transition is difficult because it implies that active workers have to pay for current retirees and for their own future pensions. In general, a basic social security (pay-as-you-go) system tends to coexist with supplementary pension funds (sometimes called "second pillar"). The size of these pension funds is impressive, as shown on Exhibit 13.3.

The investment approach of pension funds is greatly affected by the way future benefits are planned. There are basically two types and a combination thereof. A *defined benefit* pension plan (DB) promises to pay beneficiaries a defined income after retirement. This benefit depends on factors such as the workers' salary and

EXHIBIT 13.3

Institutional Assets for Selected Countries
(2001, billions of dollars)

Country	Pensions	Insurance	Mutual Funds
United States	7,010	2,645	6,970
Japan	2,235	1,523	466
United Kingdom	1,200	1,113	363
France	65	684	705
Germany	294	596	211
Netherlands	384	202	83
Italy	250	170	356
Ireland	45	33	189
Switzerland	318	238	75
Sweden	213	na	65
Luxembourg	1	na	750
Australia	272	na	334
Canada	350	na	268

Source: OECD, Fédération Européenne des Fonds et Sociétés d'Investissement (FEFSI), 2002. International Financial Services London (IFSL), Investments & Pensions Europe.

years of service. The contributions are set based on an actuarial rate of return assumption. The contributions, capitalized at this actuarial rate, should be equal to the promised benefits. If the investment performance of the pension assets is insufficient, over time, to meet this assumption, the employer may have to increase its contribution to cover the shortfall. Therefore, the corporation carries the risk of the pension plan. This leads to investment policies that focus on both meeting the return objective over the long term, while reducing the risk of a major shortfall in the near term. Defined benefit plans in the United States tend to prefer investing in stocks to increase the likelihood of meeting the return objective over the long term. This is not the case in all countries, however, because some prefer to invest in bonds to reduce the risk of not meeting the promised payments in the near term.

Defined contribution pension plans (DCs) are increasingly favored worldwide. In a defined contribution plan, the amount of contributions paid is set, usually as a percentage of wages, but future benefits are not fixed. If the rate of return on invested assets is high, large benefits will be paid at time of retirement. If the rate of return on invested assets is low, smaller benefits will be paid at time of retirement. Given the long time horizon of invested assets, defined contribution plans can afford to take more risks than defined benefits plans, and choose an asset allocation that will yield potentially higher long-term returns for a long-term participant in the plan. Pension reforms in many countries have pushed employers to move from DB to DC plans. This is the case for Canada, the Netherlands, and the United Kingdom,[5] which were home to developed DB markets. In some countries, DC provisions retain some regulatory minimum guaranteed rate of return.

For either type of plan, a board makes the selection of a long-term asset allocation. Investment management is either delegated to external managers or done in-house, or a combination of both. The selection of investment managers is a lengthy process, often assisted by consultants. External managers are given a mandate, detailed in an investment brief. For example, one manager could be selected to manage a portfolio invested in emerging stock markets. The mandate will state the investment objective (e.g., outperform the S&P/IFC composite index) and provide guidelines on the type of investments that are acceptable and the amount of risk that can be taken.

In a traditional pension fund, all contributions are pooled and the total money is managed collectively. A recent trend is to give more investment decision power to each employee. This is found in many countries. For example, the United States allows employees to put their contributions into a type of DC plan known as 401(k) plan. The plan sponsor offers a range of asset allocations and investment products from which each employee can select. Hence, external investment managers have to pass two selection hurdles: the plan sponsor and the individual investors. Pension reforms in many countries follow the U.S. model and give employees flexibility in asset allocation.

---

[5] For example, U.K. regulation FRS17 makes DB provisions potentially more costly for employers and has lead U.K. pension plans to move to DC provisions.

Institutional Investors: Endowments and Foundations   These institutional investors accumulate the contributions made to charitable and educational institutions. For example, the Nobel Foundation manages the former estate of Alfred Nobel and uses income to pay the annual Nobel prizes. Some university endowments are quite large; for example, Harvard University's endowment is well over $10 billion. Endowments and foundations typically set a target spending rate, which is the percentage of the assets that is spent as current income each year. For example, endowment income contributes some 20 percent of Harvard's budget, and the annual spending rate has been around 4 percent to 5 percent in the past 10 years. Endowment and foundation funds are concerned about total return, because both capital gains and income on the assets can be used to meet budgetary needs. Actually, endowments and foundations tend to have great investment freedom, because they operate under few regulatory constraints. As a result, their return objective tends to focus on total return over the long run. Their investment policies are often the most aggressive among institutional investors, with many having extensive global and alternative investments.

Institutional Investors: Insurance Companies   Life insurance companies are major institutional investors. They collect premiums on life insurance, which are invested until claims are paid. Insurance companies are heavily regulated in each country and state in which they operate. They tend to adopt conservative investment policies, focusing on fixed-income assets, in order to assure their claim-paying ability. Global asset allocation is often limited by regulatory constraints. Property and casualty insurance companies operate under a different regulatory framework that is somewhat more permissive in all countries. The investment policy of any insurance company depends on its surplus. Loosely speaking, the surplus is the difference between the total value of the invested assets and the expected claim payments. Although the assets matching the expected claim payments are typically invested in domestic bonds, the surplus can be invested in riskier assets, including global investments. Exhibit 13.3 gives some estimates of invested assets of insurance companies in major countries.

Investment Managers

Investment managers form a diverse group. It is hard to offer a single classification of asset managers. They range from the asset management department of banks to independent asset management boutiques specializing in offering specific investment products. Some asset managers offer a diversified menu of products (they are mostly like a supermarket) and basically charge a fee based on the assets under management, while others offer only a specialized product promising high investment performance and may charge fees linked to their performance. Some asset managers cater to retail clients as well as institutional clients, while others, sometimes less known by the public, only serve the needs of one type of client, such as a pension fund. Others, such as hedge funds, are a highly specialized type of asset manager. Many asset managers are now offering global investment capabilities, either directly or through joint ventures with foreign partners. U.S. asset managers that offer global investment management to U.S. pension funds can easily offer a similar product to British, Dutch, or Swiss pension funds. So, the competition among managers has truly become global.

Mergers and acquisitions are taking place so rapidly in the global investment management world that any description of the industry is quickly outdated. For example, Wells Fargo, the leading U.S. passive manager in the 1980s, merged its asset management activity with that of Nikko, a leading Japanese broker, to form a major global investment manager. This firm was purchased a few years later by Barclays, a major British bank, was integrated as Barclays Global Investors; and is a leading passive manager worldwide. Merrill Lynch, a leading U.S. brokerage house and investment bank, acquired Mercury Asset Management, a leading British asset manager, in 1998. UBS acquired, over time, GAM, O'Connor, Brinson Partners, and Paine Webber in the United States; RT Capital Management in Canada; Phillips & Drew in the United Kingdom; and many smaller managers. Allianz acquired, over time, Dresdner bank and AGF in Europe; RCM, Nicholas Applegate, Oppenheimer Capital, and PIMCO in the United States; and many smaller asset management firms. The same could be said of leading global players such as Deutsche Bank or AXA. Five European, four American, and one Japanese investment managers compose the top 10 worldwide investment managers ranked by total assets under management (AUM) in 2002.[6] UBS leads the way with about $1.5 trillion, followed by Allianz Group and Fidelity Investments with about $1 trillion. Only one U.S. manager (Fidelity) is among the top five. The largest asset managers outside of the United States are the huge global banks (UBS, Crédit Suisse, Deutsche Bank, Barclays) and insurance companies (Kampo, AXA, Allianz), which can make use of their global presence and their retail base. However, companies that only offer asset management services are also major players. This is typically the case in the United States. It was the case in the United Kingdom, but global players have purchased many independent investment managers. The different investment approaches used by asset managers are discussed later in the chapter.

Brokers

Stockbrokers have traditionally played an important role in asset management, both in terms of implementing security trades and in research of companies and markets. They have a large staff of financial analysts that covers companies domestically, and sometimes worldwide. This financial analysis is called "sell side," because brokers use this research to sell trading ideas to investors ("buy side" analysts work for investment managers and institutional investors). In many countries, the standards of professional conduct are lax compared with those in the United States or the United Kingdom. However, all CFA® charterholders and CFA candidates must follow the AIMR® Code of Ethics and Standards of Professional

---

[6] *Global Investment Review,* Watson Wyatt, 2003.

Conduct, wherever they work and invest. Many brokers also act as investment banks, but the independence of sell-side analysts must be maintained.

Major global brokers have offices in all major financial centers and cover most markets in the world. Other brokers specialize in some niches (e.g., European small-cap stocks). Bond brokers provide extensive research on interest rates, exchange rates, and company and country risk. The research efforts at these brokerage houses have moved in two directions. As a result of their excellent research capabilities, brokers moved successfully into investment banking. Financial analysts extended their approach to cover mergers and acquisitions, as well as corporate finance. Others applied their research expertise and knowledge of the financial markets to asset management. Asset management is a low-margin business compared with investment banking, but profits are much more stable. Brokers in Japan have always offered asset management, and it is now a major priority for the big U.S. brokerage houses, which are marketing their asset management skills in Europe and Asia.

Consultants and Advisers

Consultants and advisers provide several types of advice and play a major role in the asset management industry. Although they are better known for their work with the pension fund market, they are also employed by other investors, such as insurance companies, endowments, foundations, and HNWIs. Independent consulting firms have traditionally advised U.S. pension funds, while actuaries played a similar role in the United Kingdom. For many years, consultants played no role in most other countries, but this changed dramatically in the late 1990s.

Consultants can help with all the actuarial calculations of the pension plan obligations, such as liabilities to plan members and technical reserves. These calculations depend on many factors, such as the age structure of the plan members, retirement patterns, the plan's benefits formula, and so on. Although these actuarial calculations are often performed in-house in the United States and other countries, the United Kingdom traditionally requires the intervention of external actuaries. Consultants also focus on services such as recommending asset allocation, selecting investment managers, and monitoring performance, and may give tax and legal advice.

Major consultants measure the performance of a large number of managers with different mandates. Hence, they maintain a large database that allows them to compare the performance of a universe of managers. But probably the most sensitive role of consultants, which has spread throughout Europe and the United States, is their assistance in the process of selecting, hiring, and firing external managers. Some commentators state that pension fund sponsors are relieved to share their fiduciary responsibilities with consultants who have a worldwide reputation and are used by numerous other pension funds. When looking for an external manager, a pension fund typically prepares a request for proposal (RFP) or request for information (RFI), which specifies the type of manager sought. The consultant organizes the selection process by sending out the RFP or RFI in the form of a questionnaire to be completed by prospective managers. Based on the responses and the consultant's own research on the managers, a short list is established, and managers on this list make a presentation to the pension fund, detailing their case. The board of the pension fund decides, with the consultant's advice, which manager(s) will be selected. It should be noted that the arrangement between pension plan sponsors and consultants varies considerably. Some plan sponsors delegate much of the decision-making process regarding manager hiring and firing to the consultant, while others prefer to make the decision themselves and use the consultant in an advisory role. Many consulting firms advise only domestic institutional clients. But there are several large consultants, such as Frank Russell, Watson Wyatt, Towers Perrin, and William Mercer, with a global presence.

A new trend for pension consultants is to go one step further and offer multi-manager funds. The consultant does not manage money directly, but creates a fund of selected managers. This approach has caused some controversy over a potential conflict of interest in the advisory capacity.

Individual investors are also in need of professional advice for the management of personal or family assets. As discussed earlier, the taxable environment of private investors poses a challenge, and tax systems vary markedly across countries, even within the same region. For example, the tax environment is different for each country in the European Union. Hence, advisers tend to be domestic rather than global players, but they may be part of a global network.

Custodians

Securities owned by investors are deposited with a custodian, which often uses a global network of subcustodians. Given the complexities of global investing due to national differences in taxation, trading, and settlement procedures, an efficient and reliable custodian is a necessity. Accurate information from around the world should be gathered rapidly. Automated trade notification is necessary. Computer-to-computer links with the subcustodians, clearing services, and the manager should be set up. Income collection should be swift and correctly reported. Tax recovery should be automated and carefully checked with each government. Securities-lending facilities should be available in most markets. Finally, a cash management system in many currencies should be implemented. Cost and reliability are two important features of custodial services.

Information technology is an important component of custodial services. With the high development costs of such software, many banks have sold their custodial activities, and further consolidation is expected in the future, because economies of scale can be significant in this business. Leading names in global custody are JP Morgan, State Street Bank, Mellon Group, Bank of New York, Northern Trust, UBS, and Citibank. Although economies of scale have led to a global consolidation of custodial services (e.g., Deutsche Bank sold its custodial services to State Street in 2002), there are still many subcustodial banks with regional capabilities.

Global Investment Philosophies

Global investment has grown rapidly among institutional investors of all nationalities. Investment managers worldwide can no longer treat foreign investments as an exotic, minor consideration, and they must now have a clear view of how to approach global investing. An investment management organization must make certain major choices in structuring its global decision process, based on several factors:

- Its view of the world regarding security price behavior

- Its strengths, in terms of research and management

- Cost aspects

- Its location and prospective domestic/global marketing strategy

Similarly, investors will select managers based on the same factors plus their ability to control currency risks. These important choices are discussed in the following sections in terms of investment philosophy and strategy from the viewpoint of a fund manager. But individual or institutional investors face exactly the same choices when deciding on their approach to global investing and their selection of fund managers. The global approach to equity is more complex than to bonds. So, some of the points discussed next are primarily relevant for equity portfolio management.

The Passive Approach

A fund managed according to a passive approach simply attempts to reproduce a market index of securities. This type of fund is often called an *index fund*. The sole purpose of an index fund is to exactly track the return on a selected market index, to capitalize on its long-term performance while keeping all costs at a minimum. The passive approach is an extension of modern portfolio theory, which claims that the market portfolio should be efficient. In the United States, the domestic index fund approach is supported by extensive empirical evidence of the efficiency of the stock market. A similar domestic index fund approach has developed in the United Kingdom and, more recently, in other European countries and Japan. Large pension funds have moved extensively to indexing their domestic assets.

The trend toward global indexing is strongly felt among institutional investors. The basic argument supporting the passive indexing approach is that the alternative, an active strategy, requires above-average ability in forecasting markets, currencies, and security valuation. Forecasting is never easy; moreover, it entails higher commissions and costs. With a passive strategy, the fund can achieve the full benefits of global risk diversification without incurring these high costs.

Various indexing methods can be used:

- *Full replication:* All securities in the index are bought, with proper weighting. This method is impossible globally, given the huge number of securities involved.

- *Stratified sampling:* This approach tracks the index by holding a representative sample of securities. The securities are grouped according to various criteria (country, firm's size, industry, yield), and the index fund sample attempts to replicate the characteristics of the index across the various criteria.

- *Optimization sampling:* This is a sampling method using factor models to minimize the tracking error of the index. It is a sophisticated statistical method based on a large number of factors, or firm attributes, and using optimization techniques based on historical relationships.

- *Synthetic replication:* A stock index can be replicated by using a futures contract on the index plus a cash position. The fair pricing of the futures ensures that the index is closely tracked, and that transaction costs are low. For some investors, legal aspects regarding the use of derivatives constrain the implementation of this approach on a global scale. Another problem is that futures contracts tend to be written on indexes based on a subset of the broad market, while natural market benchmarks are broadly based indexes. Stock index swaps are also used.

Although indexing does reduce costs, perfect tracking of a global index is not feasible. For example, whenever a dividend is paid in one currency—say, the Australian dollar—it should be reinvested simultaneously in all global securities with proper weights, which is an impossible task. Indexing requires superior computer, administrative, and trading technology, but does result in large economies of scale. As the quality of the indexer shows up quickly, and objectively, in the form of a low tracking error, only the best indexers are likely to capture a large market share of this management style. A remaining issue, discussed later, is the choice of the global benchmark to be passively tracked.

The Active Approach

In an active strategy, investors place bets on the various factors that affect securities' behaviors. A benchmark is often imposed in the mandate set by the client, and it will clearly guide the structure of the portfolio. Active deviations from the benchmark can lead to superior performance. Of course, the strategy itself depends on the investor's view of the world. Active decisions of a portfolio manager show up at various levels:

- *Regional/country allocation:* This is the choice of national markets and currencies. The manager can select long-term weights that differ from those of market indexes, such as the EAFE index. This long-term allocation is often called *strategic allocation*. Periodic, temporary revisions in the weights can be justified by changes in market expectations or risk estimates. This is often called *tactical asset allocation*. These decisions also are discussed later in the chapter.

- *Sector/industry selection:* The globalization of the economy pushes some managers to allocate funds across worldwide industries, rather than countries.

This is more commonly done when managing a portfolio within integrated regions such as Continental Europe.

- *Style selection:* Some managers believe that companies with similar attributes tend to have similar stock price behavior. Common style decisions are value versus growth stocks, or small versus large firms.

- *Security selection:* To achieve a given asset allocation, managers can engage in active selection of securities within each asset class and conduct pair arbitrage between two similar securities.

- *Market timing:* Managers can resort to market timing to temporarily increase or reduce the exposure in one or more markets or currencies. This is a short-term trading tactic (as opposed to long-run strategies for allocating assets) that often involves the use of derivatives.

- *Currency hedging:* Managers can actively manage their currency position.

A few additional dimensions can be found in the active management of global debt securities (see Chapter 7):

- *Sector selection/credit selection:* Managers can deviate from a bond benchmark by overweighting some market sectors or investing in higher credit risk, such as low-credit-rating bonds and emerging debt. This leads to an increase in yield but also in credit risk.

- *Duration/yield curve management:* In each currency market, the manager can adjust the duration of the portfolio according to forecasts about changes in the level of interest rates and shapes of the yield curve.

- *Yield enhancement techniques:* Numerous techniques are proposed to add value to the performance of the basic strategy; these include security lending, using swaps and other derivatives, investing in complex bonds, and doing pairs arbitrage.

A manager can be active in some dimensions and not in others. For example, active asset allocation management can be achieved using national index funds for each market. Conversely, a manager could follow a fixed asset allocation, using active security selection within each market.

The risk diversification argument is usually at the heart of the rationale of both active and passive global money managers. In the quickly changing global environment, active money managers must be able to evaluate and control the risk of their portfolios as rapidly as possible. Taking active bets on markets, currencies, or securities could result in portfolios that turn out to be quite risky and do not provide the global risk diversification benefits so widely claimed.

Following is a review of major choices to be made in active global asset management; it focuses primarily on equity, because the management of portfolios of debt securities is more technical and has already been addressed in Chapter 7.

Balanced or Specialized

Investment managers for private clients have traditionally been balanced money managers. For example, a European bank advising a private client will suggest both the global asset allocation and the selection of each security for the portfolio; it will advise on all aspects of private wealth management. The asset allocation covers all asset classes: equity, debt securities, alternative investments, and cash.

Even for pension assets, the tradition in Europe is to retain a single balanced manager (or, at most, a few). For example, U.K. pension funds traditionally retained one British investment management firm to oversee all of their assets and decide on asset allocation. The investment policy statement tended to be quite loose, with objective statements such as "maximize long-term returns subject to an acceptable level of risk normally associated with a balanced approach to fund management."[7]

By contrast, American pension plans tend to hire managers that specialize in particular investment areas, such as Japanese stocks, European growth stocks, or emerging market debt. The trend toward specialized global management is based on the hypothesis that no manager is an expert on all markets, although some can be superior on one or a few markets. So, the client decides first on the asset class segmentation. Large institutional investors would have a fine segmentation going down to the level of regions or country (e.g., European equity or Japanese equity), but most individual clients would segment the investment universe in only a few asset classes (e.g., domestic equity, international equity, bonds, cash, real estate, other investments). The allocation decision is made by the client, based on advice from consultants and advisers. Then the client selects one or several specialized managers for each asset class. It is not unusual to find institutional investors with the bulk of their global portfolio in passive, well-diversified funds and the remainder invested in a few active funds in specialized areas. European pension funds are also moving toward specialized management. U.K. funds are following the trend set by U.S. funds, which tend to make the asset allocation at the fund level and retain specialized managers for each asset class. This is quite a revolution in Britain, where a few balanced managers historically dominated the asset management market.

For a client, the central question in the specialized approach is to know how to decide on asset allocation. Because asset allocation is potentially the most profitable and important investment management decision, it seems a bit odd to deprive asset managers of this important opportunity to add value. This is especially true in equity management when listed companies compete globally and stock markets are increasingly correlated. To study European equity, one must compare European firms with their U.S. and Asian competitors. If an equity manager is expert on European equity, she should (must) also be expert on global equity. So, there is a recent trend to move from specialized equity mandates back to balanced international (foreign) or global equity mandates. Indeed, a combination of balanced and specialized management could be useful. Performance attribution, as

---

[7] Extract from Mark Tapley, "Lessons from the Unilever/Merrill Case," *IPE,* May 2002, p. 36.

reviewed in Chapter 12, could help assess whether a manager adds value in a balanced mandate by asset and currency allocation decisions or only by security selection on some specific asset classes.

Industry or Country Approach

Asset managers should structure their investment processes along the major factors affecting security prices:

- If a manager believes that the nationality of a company is a major factor affecting the return and risk on the company's stock, then the global portfolio should be structured primarily according to country or region. The allocation to countries/regions would be a major investment decision. Then stocks would be selected within countries.

- If a manager believes that the industry or sector in which a company operates is a major factor affecting its return and risk, then the global portfolio should be structured primarily according to industry or sector. The allocation to industry/sector would be a major investment decision. Then stocks would be selected within global industries.

- If a manager believes that the major factors affecting the return and risk on the company's stock are specific to that company (quality of management, cost structure relative to competition, prospects for its products, etc.), the manager should rely primarily on company analysis.

Top-Down or Bottom-Up

Domestically, portfolio managers use either a top-down or a bottom-up approach or combination to the investment process. The same is true globally.

- *Top-down approach:* The manager using a top-down approach first allocates his assets across asset classes and then selects individual securities to satisfy that allocation. The most important decision in this approach is the choice of markets and currencies. In other words, the global money manager must choose from among several markets (stocks, bonds, or cash) as well as a variety of currencies. Once these choices have been made, the manager selects the best securities available in each market. In global equity portfolios, a manager following the country approach decides on the percentage allocated to the various countries and then selects the best stocks in each market; a manager following the industry approach decides on the percentage allocated to the various global industries and then selects the best stocks in each industry.

- *Bottom-up approach:* The manager using this approach studies the fundamentals of many individual stocks, from which she selects the best securities (regardless of their national origin or currency denomination) to build a portfolio. For example, a manager may be bullish on car manufacturers and buy shares in all of them (GM, Toyota, Volkswagen, Peugeot, and others); or the manager may buy shares in only the best oil company in the world, regardless of its national origin. The product of this approach is a portfolio with a market and currency allocation that is more or less the random result of the securities selected. Implicit in this approach is the manager's greater concern with risk exposure in various sectors than with either market or currency risk exposure.

- *Top-down/bottom-up approach:* Some investment organizations attempt to combine a top-down with a bottom-up approach, but this is not easy to achieve. The rationale for combining the two is often one of risk control. For example, a top-down manager may choose to limit exposure to a particular country when the bottom-up manager would indicate otherwise. The entire investment decision process has to be consistent, and sophisticated risk management tools are needed. A manager would typically base his security selection on worldwide company analysis. Factor models are used to control the exposure to countries and industries. Pair trades between companies in the same industry (but different countries) or in the same country (but different industries) allow the manager to satisfy risk objectives in terms of geographic and sector/industry allocation, while taking advantage of superior company analysis.

EXAMPLE 13.1   *PAIR TRADES*

You own a well-diversified global portfolio mimicking the World index. You wish to retain the same regional and industry exposure as the World index. You believe that TotalFina Elf, a French oil company is undervalued (much lower P/E) relative to ExxonMobil. You also believe that BMW is overpriced relative to General Motors. You own $100,000 of ExxonMobil shares and $120,000 of BMW shares. What could you do?

SOLUTION

- I would sell the shares of ExxonMobil in my portfolio and buy TotalFina Elf shares for $100,000.

- I would sell $100,000 of my BMW shares and buy $100,000 of General Motors shares.

The net result will leave unchanged my asset allocation to European and American stocks. It will also leave unchanged my global industry allocation.

Style Management

In previous chapters, we talked about style managers who construct portfolios based on some attributes of companies. This approach has been extended to global investing. Common style decisions are value versus growth stocks, or small versus large firms. In the 1980s and early 1990s, a simple strategy that favored small and value stocks yielded above-average returns in the United States. The simplest global extension was to choose stocks based on the firm's size and its price-to-book ratio. However, style analysis does not extend globally in a simple manner; see Michaud (1999). For example, a firm of a given size may look small in the United States and rather big in France. Similarly, a given style indicator, such as the price-to-book ratio, which works well in identifying a value factor in one country, may not work in another country, in part due to accounting differences. To define a value stock, managers resort to different indicators in different countries. Careful analysis is required to derive style factors that would apply to companies in all countries. Furthermore, a given style factor is not necessarily synchronized across countries. For example, value stocks could underperform growth stocks in France, while the reverse could simultaneously be true in Germany. Finally, no style can systematically outperform others forever. This was amply demonstrated by the poor relative performance of small stocks and value stocks in the late 1990s. This does not mean that active style management cannot achieve superior performance. Style rotation strategies can add value if the manager can forecast when a given style will become favored by market participants (or lose favor).

Currency

Some managers treat currencies only as residual variables; their currency breakdowns are determined by the countries, industries, and securities they select for their portfolios. They generally consider currency risk a necessary evil and argue that currency movements are impossible to predict and wash out in the long run anyway, because it is the real economic variables that ultimately determine a portfolio's performance.

Other managers fully hedge their foreign portfolios or decide on a permanent hedge ratio based on an historical estimate. This strategy is based on some of the theories outlined in Chapter 4 or on the belief that foreign currency risk premiums are small or unpredictable and, hence, that investors are not compensated for carrying foreign exchange risk. Others adopt a passive, uniform currency-hedging strategy with a fixed hedge ratio different from 100 percent (e.g., 50 percent).

Still other managers take a proactive approach to currency forecasting. They try to minimize the contribution currency makes to total risk, and cash in on opportunities created by currency movements.

At the extreme end of the spectrum is a new breed of global money managers, called *currency-overlay managers*. These currency-overlay managers actively manage the currency exposure of a portfolio and often resort to currency options and forward or futures contracts for selective hedging and speculation. Currency-overlay managers do not manage the portfolio itself. The client transfers the composition of the portfolio managed by another party on a daily basis. This other party makes no currency-hedging decisions, only manages the assets. The currency-overlay managers take currency positions on the portfolio using currency derivatives.

Naturally, the approach an investment manager takes toward currencies leads to very different portfolio strategies. The question of currency hedging is raised again later in this chapter.

Quantitative or Subjective

Whether a manager employs a quantitative or subjective decision-making process, a great deal of information is required before portfolios are constructed. Quantification of the investment process is very helpful in global investment management because of the large number of parameters and decision variables involved. Quantification can be applied to various models or aids used in the global investment process, including

- econometric or technical forecasting models of markets and currencies;
- global asset allocation optimizers;
- dividend-discount models, factor models, duration models, or option valuation models (for quantitative assessment of individual securities);
- risk management models; and
- performance and risk analysis.

Managers who favor the subjective approach argue that the global environment is too complex to permit formal quantification. They think that models based on past data are not helpful because constant changes in the global environment distort such models. Quantitative managers also believe that the global environment is complex, but eventually come to the opposite conclusion. Models are used to extract from past data some useful lessons for the future. An advantage of a purely quantitative approach is that it is highly disciplined and therefore avoids some emotional reactions that can lead to poor decisions and impaired performance.

Many managers rely on subjective judgment, but make use of some quantitative models in their portfolio management process. Others tend to follow models, but inject some judgment as they think appropriate.

The Investment Policy Statement

An investment policy statement (IPS) is the cornerstone of the portfolio management process. The IPS is prepared by the advisor and the client, and serves as the governing document for the portfolio manager and for all investment decision making. The IPS is extensively discussed in Maginn and Tuttle (2005),[8] and we summarize only its main features and stress aspects that should be taken into account when investing globally. The case study at the end of this chapter details the preparation of such a document.

IPSs vary in terms of content, especially between private and institutional clients. IPSs for private clients often reflect a balanced mandate to manage the whole wealth. But an IPS could be more specialized and target specific asset classes.

[8] See Chapter 1, "The Portfolio Management Process and the Investment Policy Statement," and Chapter 4, "Managing Individual Investor Portfolios," in John Maginn and Donald Tuttle (forthcoming 2005).

For example, an investor could give a mandate to manage international assets and prepare an IPS accordingly. A well-constructed policy statement typically includes a summary of the various elements:

1. *Client description and purpose:* The IPS starts with a brief description of the client and the purpose of the establishment of the investment policy statement. It could detail the duties and investment responsibilities of the various parties involved.

2. *Return and risk objectives:* Establishing objectives for return and risk is an important step for individual as well as institutional clients. One must be sure that investment goals, especially the return objective, are attainable within the client's risk tolerance. Some institutional investors set quantified objectives. For example, a British pension plan could set as an objective for a manager to outperform the World equity index, ex-U.K, by 3 percent per year, with a maximum annual tracking error of 4 percent. Return is measured as total return from income and capital appreciation, which is specified as real or nominal, and as pre-tax or after-tax. Investors have stated return desires that may or may not be realistic. Nevertheless, the adviser and the client also must determine the investor's required return, the return that must be achieved on average. The required return is necessary, as contrasted with the stated return, which may be more in the nature of a hope. The return objective must be set to achieve the investor's required return balanced with the investor's risk tolerance. Risk tolerance is the capacity to accept risk, but risk aversion is the inability and unwillingness to take risk. Risk tolerance is a function both of the investor's ability and his willingness to take risk. An investor may have more willingness to take risk than he has ability to accept the consequences of large losses. Ability is a function of such characteristics as income needs and asset base, as well as liquidity requirements and time horizon.

3. *Constraints:* All economic and operational constraints on the investment portfolio should be identified in the investment policy statement. Portfolio constraints generally fall into one of five categories:

   - Liquidity requirements stem from liquidity events when the investor must make specific cash payments higher than normal, long-term net cash flows. An example of a liquidity event is the planned purchase of a house in one year. Even though stocks are liquid, their future price is uncertain. The liquidity requirement constrains asset allocation because the portfolio should include risk-free government securities targeted to supply the cash required.[9] As a practical matter, the presence of both liquidity risk (the need to sell less marketable assets) and price risk (the risk of fluctuations in market prices) means that the investor must anticipate liquidity requirements by holding some proportion of assets that are *both* liquid and relatively low-risk. Without such assets, the investor may well be forced to sell other assets in an unfavor-

---

[9] Of course, an alternative to holding government securities is to maintain the long stock position and short the appropriate number of stock futures contracts.

able market environment, endangering the portfolio's ability to meet critical return and risk objectives.

- Time horizon is the period associated with the investor's objectives. Long-term horizons are generally considered to be those over 10 years, but many investor horizons are multistage horizons, mixtures of short- and long-term objective horizons. A long-term retirement objective and a short-term college financing objective would produce a multistage time horizon. Because different investments are appropriate for different horizons, the investor's time horizon constrains asset allocation.

- Tax concerns constrain asset allocation decisions because taxable investors must look for after-tax returns in their taxable portfolios, as well as plan for tax payments on retirement distributions in their tax-deferred portfolios.

- Legal and regulatory factors constrain asset allocation because they may rule out certain investments. In some countries, pension funds are limited to certain asset classes. Legal and regulatory factors are constraints external to the investor and imposed by others.

- Unique circumstances constrain asset allocation. They include constraining factors other than liquidity requirements, time horizon, tax concerns, and legal and regulatory factors. These "other" constraints are internal to the investor and limit his choice of investments or asset classes. Investor preferences, investment knowledge, staff, and capabilities are examples of unique circumstances.

4. *Asset allocation considerations:* The IPS can state some asset allocation objectives and constraints that have to be followed by the manager. These can be varied, and a few examples are listed. In particular, the investment policy statement could

- give a global balanced mandate to the manager giving its "best effort" to satisfy the risk/return investment goals of the client;

- set a specific benchmark for the manager, which is often the case with institutional clients who use several specialized managers;

- list the asset classes that can be considered, thereby excluding various types of investments (e.g., derivatives, emerging markets, shares of "unethical" firms, etc.);

- set constraints on the allocation to be followed at all times. For example, the IPS could state that no more than 40 percent of the portfolio should be allocated to international investments and that the foreign currency exposure should not exceed 20 percent of the portfolio; and

- outline the investment philosophy to be followed by the manager.

Some investment policy statements include the strategic asset allocation to be used in the portfolio, but we maintain a distinction between the IPS and the determination of the strategic asset allocation. This asset allocation process is addressed in the section on global asset allocation.

5. ***Schedule for review and monitoring:*** Feedback and control of the portfolio are essential in reaching investment goals. The investment policy statement can include a schedule for review of the investment performance and of the IPS itself. *Performance evaluation* is a critical step in the review of the portfolio and is discussed in Chapter 12. The client should be provided with rates of return for the portfolio on a periodic basis (*performance measurement*), but that is not sufficient. *Performance attribution* allows us to understand the sources of performance. So many factors can affect the performance of a global portfolio that global performance attribution is crucial in understanding why and how the portfolio performed as it did. Finally, *performance appraisal,* typically conducted over a long period of time, should enable the client to judge whether the manager is doing a good job. The IPS should detail the performance information that will be provided to the client to form a judgment. The conclusions of the investment performance evaluation are used as feedback to revise the portfolio.

The IPS also could include monitoring and rebalancing guidelines. Because of price movements, the composition of the portfolio will progressively deviate from the strategic asset allocation. Rebalancing the portfolio entails transaction costs, and some guidelines have to be established regarding rebalancing. More generally, changes in capital market expectations, or in the client's investment objectives and constraints, would dictate revisions in the portfolio.

Capital Market Expectations

Capital market expectations are expectations about the future distributions of returns to asset classes, including expected returns, volatility of returns, and correlation of returns. Formulating capital market expectations is potentially the most rewarding part of global asset management, but it is also the most difficult. The formulation process is usually decomposed into three steps:

- Defining asset classes

- Formulating long-term expectations used in strategic asset allocation

- Formulating shorter-term expectations used in tactical asset allocation

Defining Asset Classes

An asset class is a set of "homogeneous" securities, those whose prices are affected by a common factor. The segmentation of asset classes is usually based on various criteria:

- Asset type (e.g., debt, equity, real estate)

- Geography (e.g., domestic vs. international, or regional breakdown)

- Sector (e.g., technology stocks, energy stocks, intermediate bonds, high yield bonds, etc.)

- Style (e.g., growth vs. value stocks)

The segmentation and its number of categories depend on the size of the portfolio and the characteristics of the investor. An institutional investor with a long horizon can include private equity and other illiquid alternative investments, but this would not be the case for an elderly individual investor with little wealth. Individual investors tend to consider few asset classes, and a typical breakdown could include domestic equity, international equity, domestic bonds, international bonds, domestic real estate, and cash. A large institutional investor usually considers a more detailed breakdown, which could include American equity, European equity, Asian equity, emerging-market equity, investment-grade domestic bonds, high-yield domestic bonds, international bonds, inflation-linked bonds, emerging-market debt, and so on.

Long-Term Capital Market Expectations: Historical Returns

Long-term capital market expectations, perhaps over the next 5 or 10 years, are now used to determine the strategic asset allocation of a portfolio. Several approaches are used. As suggested in Maginn and Tuttle (2005),[10] two basic approaches are used to formulate long-term expectations: historical returns and forward-looking returns.

Historical records for mean returns, volatility, and correlation can simply be projected to repeat in the future. For example, Exhibit 13.4 reports the record for a sample of countries based on a century of data. Let's look at the U.S. experience. The average nominal return on equity was 10.3 percent, and the average real return was 7.1 percent (10.3 percent minus the average inflation rate of 3.2 percent). The average risk-free rate was 4.3 percent, so that the risk premium of U.S. stocks was an average 6 percent (average equity return of 10.3 percent minus 4.3 percent). The equity risk premium for other countries ranged from 3.4 percent in Denmark to 8 percent in France. These *ex post* equity risk premiums are very large.[11] There are many limitations in using past returns to directly formulate expectations on future returns.

Economic conditions in the past, especially the distant past, may not be relevant for the future. A market that has done exceptionally well (or poorly) in the past because of some specific events (e.g., liberalization of the economy) may not do so in the future, because that specific event will not repeat. The exceptional equity risk premium in the 20th century (6 percent for U.S. stocks) was caused by two factors:

---

[10] See Chapter 4, "Managing Individual Investor Portfolios," and Chapter 5, "Managing Institutional Investor Portfolios," in John Maginn and Donald Tuttle (forthcoming 2005).

[11] In risk theory, an *ex ante* risk premium of 6 percent would require a huge risk aversion on the part of investors; this is usually referred to as the *equity premium puzzle*. See Campbell and Viceira (2002).

EXHIBIT 13.4

Stocks, Bonds, Bills, Inflation: The Global Record (1900–2000)
(Nominal returns in local currency in %; means calculated using geometric mean)

Country	Equity		Bonds		Bills		Inflation	
	Mean Annual Return	Standard Deviation	Mean Annual Return	Standard Deviation	Mean Annual Return	Standard Deviation	Mean Annual Return	Standard Deviation
Australia	11.9	18.2	5.7	13.0	4.5	4.2	4.0	5.5
Canada	9.7	16.8	4.9	9.0	4.9	3.7	3.1	4.9
Denmark	10.4	22.6	7.0	10.6	7.0	4.5	4.1	6.6
France	12.3	24.7	6.9	8.8	4.3	2.3	8.0	14.6
Germany	9.9	36.4	2.8	13.6	4.6	3.4	5.2	15.8
Italy	12.1	34.4	6.7	9.1	4.7	3.3	9.2	36.8
Japan	13.1	30.5	6.1	15.1	5.5	1.9	7.7	40.4
Netherlands	9.1	22.7	4.1	7.6	3.7	2.4	3.0	5.0
Sweden	12.2	23.7	6.1	9.2	5.8	3.1	3.7	6.8
United Kingdom	10.2	21.9	5.4	12.6	5.1	3.9	4.1	6.9
United States	10.3	20.0	4.7	8.1	4.3	2.8	3.2	5.0

Source: Dimson, Marsh, and Staunton (2002).

- Earnings per share grew steadily.

- Valuation multiples, such as the price/earnings ratio, grew dramatically over time.

Stock prices went up in part because of real growth, but more importantly, because valuation multiples rose impressively until 2000. To expect a similar equity risk premium in the future, an analyst must make the assumption that valuation multiples will keep rising to unprecedented levels.[12]

Another problem is the quality of past data. For example, many countries in Exhibit 13.4 had fixed income markets that were controlled by their local governments until the 1980s. This is typically the case for Continental Europe. Bond yields and cash rates were not market rates but rates regulated by the governments so that they could borrow cheaply. Various capital and currency controls, as well as regulations of institutional investors, forced local investors to purchase fixed-income securities with low returns. This is an explanation for the negative historical real yields in many countries, as shown on Exhibit 13.4. Fixed-income markets are now open worldwide.

Problems also arise when looking at historical volatility and correlation. Correlation across equity and bond markets in the past is likely to change over time because of market integration worldwide. The problem in using unadjusted historical estimates of volatility and correlation is even more acute for alternative

---

[12] An interesting discussion is provided by Arnott and Bernstein (2002).

investments. Some assets trade infrequently. This is the case for many alternative assets that are not exchange traded, such as real estate or private equity. This is also the case for illiquid exchange traded securities or over-the-counter instruments often used by hedge funds. Because prices used are not up-to-date market prices, they tend to be smoothed over time.[13] For example, the appraisal process used in real estate introduces a smoothing of returns, as properties are only appraised infrequently. The internal rate of return methodology used in private equity also introduces a smoothing of returns. The infrequent nature of price updates in the alternative asset world induces a significant downward bias to the measured risk of the assets. In addition, correlations between alternative investment returns and conventional equity and fixed-income returns, and among the alternative asset returns themselves, are often close to zero because of the smoothing effect and the absence of market-observable returns. The bias can be large, so that the true risk is larger than the reported estimates. Traditional indexes of hedge funds returns also suffer from a serious survivorship bias (only good-performing hedge funds are included in the database) that biases historical return measures for this asset class.[14]

Long-Term Capital Market Expectations: Forward-Looking Returns

Although the past can be useful to forecast the future, simply extrapolating past return-and-risk measures is not sufficient. A useful approach is to derive long-term estimates that would be consistent with market equilibrium. In an integrated world financial market, expected returns should reflect the risks borne by investors. Although short-term events could create attractive investment opportunities in the short run, long-term capital market expectations that are consistent with market equilibrium are useful to guide investment strategy. An interesting approach has been developed by Singer and Terhaar (1997) and Terhaar, Staub, and Singer (2003). It uses the international capital asset pricing model (CAPM)[15] as an anchor but takes into account market imperfections, such as segmentation and illiquidity. The approach can be summarized in three steps:

- Calculate an updated covariance matrix[16] (volatility and correlation of asset classes).

- Infer expected returns for each asset class, using the CAPM.

- Adjust expected returns for possible market segmentation and illiquidity.

The historical covariance matrix serves as the starting point, but it is adjusted to reflect some of the biases mentioned previously for infrequently traded assets and

---

[13] See Terhaar, Staub, and Singer (2003).

[14] See Asness, Krail, and Liew (2001).

[15] See Chapter 4.

[16] Remember that the covariance between two assets is equal to the product of the standard deviation (volatility) of the two assets times their correlation. So, the covariance matrix contains all risk information on asset classes.

is updated to be forward-looking. A multifactor updating approach ensures consistency of the updated matrix.

The expected return on an asset class is equal to the risk-free rate plus a risk premium. The CAPM states that the risk premium on any asset class should be proportional to its beta with the world market portfolio:

$$RP_i = \beta_{iM} RP_M \tag{13.1}$$

where:

RP_i is the risk premium for asset class i

β_{iM} is the beta of asset class i

RP_M is the risk premium on the world market portfolio

We assume that the risk premium on any currency is equal to zero. This assumption could be relaxed if one assumes that a specific currency is undervalued and will revert to its fundamental purchasing power parity (PPP) value in the long run (see Chapter 2).

Plotting the risk premiums versus the betas would result in all the points lying on a straight line. Equation 13.1 can be rewritten by replacing β_{iM} by its value

$$\beta_{iM} = \rho_{iM} \frac{\sigma_i}{\sigma_M}$$

$$RP_i = \rho_{iM} \frac{\sigma_i}{\sigma_M} RP_M = \rho_{iM} \sigma_i \frac{RP_M}{\sigma_M} \tag{13.2}$$

or

$$\frac{RP_i}{\sigma_i} = \rho_{iM} \frac{RP_M}{\sigma_M} \tag{13.3}$$

where σ_i and σ_M are the standard deviations of returns of asset class i and of the market portfolio, and ρ_{iM} is the correlation of returns between asset class i and the market portfolio.

Equation 13.3 simply states that the expected reward-to-risk ratio (RP_i/σ_i), the Sharpe ratio of an asset class, is simply equal to the Sharpe ratio of the market portfolio times the correlation of the asset class with the market portfolio. The lower the correlation, the lower the Sharpe ratio of an asset class. In a fully integrated world, the risk premium on an asset reflects the risk-diversification property of the asset. An asset with a correlation of 0.50 with the market portfolio should have a Sharpe ratio equal to half that of the market. This is because half of the volatility of asset i can be diversified away and therefore should not be rewarded by a risk premium.

However, world financial markets are not fully integrated, and equilibrium pricing of some asset classes (e.g., emerging equity markets or private equity) should reflect their partial segmentation from the world market. To illustrate, let's consider an asset class, called "emerging market," that is fully segmented. The international CAPM does not hold for this asset class. Local investors cannot invest abroad, and they dominate the local market. They will require a high risk premium on this asset class, because its total risk cannot be diversified away in a global portfolio. The risk premium is set in isolation by local investors, reflecting the total risk (σ_i) of the segmented asset class without regard to its diversification ability. If the market were integrated in the world market, global investors would set a lower risk premium (higher price), reflecting the fact that part of the risk of this asset class can be diversified away in a global portfolio (correlation less than 1).

EXAMPLE 13.2 RISK PREMIUM

Suppose all investors in the world have similar risk aversion and require a Sharpe ratio of 0.2 on their diversified portfolios. The world market portfolio has a volatility of 20 percent. The emerging-market asset has a volatility of 30 percent and a correlation of 0.5 with the world market portfolio. The beta of the emerging market asset class is $0.5 \times 30\%/20\% = 0.75$.

   A. What is the equilibrium risk premium for the market portfolio?

   B. Assuming full integration, what is the equilibrium risk premium for the emerging market?

   C. Assuming full segmentation, what is the equilibrium risk premium for the emerging market?

SOLUTION

   A. The equilibrium Sharpe ratio required for a well-diversified portfolio is 0.2 percent. Hence, the risk premium on the world market portfolio is 4 percent:

   $$0.2 = \frac{RP_M}{\sigma_M} = \frac{RP_M}{20\%}, \ RP_M = 4\%$$

   B. If we assume full integration, the CAPM tells us what should be the Sharpe ratio for the emerging market:

   $$\frac{RP_i}{\sigma_i} = \rho_{iM}\frac{RP_M}{\sigma_M} = 0.5 \times \frac{4\%}{20\%} = 0.10$$

   Hence, $RP_i = 0.10 \times \sigma_i = 3\%$. This is also equal to beta times the risk premium on the world market: $0.75 \times 4\% = 3\%$.

   C. If we assume full segmentation, the CAPM does not hold, and the emerging market is priced locally, reflecting its total volatility. Local investors search for a Sharpe ratio of 0.20 for a diversified portfolio, so

   $$\frac{RP_i}{\sigma_i} = 0.20$$

   Hence, $RP_i = 0.2 \times \sigma_i = 6\%$.

EXHIBIT 13.5

The Reward for Risk from Conventional and Alternative Investments

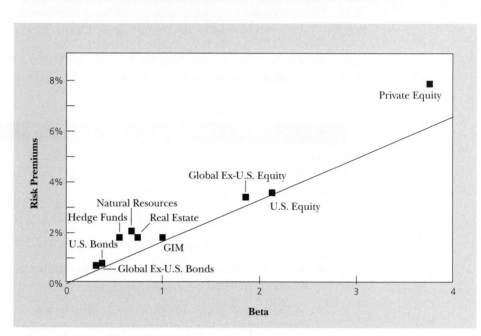

Source: Terhaar, Staub, and Singer (2003).

In a way, global investors can take advantage of segmented markets. In practice, some markets are partly segmented, so the equilibrium risk premium on these assets should be somewhat higher than what is dictated by a fully integrated CAPM, but less than under full segmentation.

Exhibit 13.5 shows the result of such a calculation performed by UBS Global Asset Management for conventional and alternative investments. Plotting the integrated risk premiums versus the betas would result in all the points lying on a straight line in an integrated CAPM. Because of partial segmentation and illiquidity, some asset classes lie above the integrated market line. For example, "private equity" lies well above the integrated market line. The beta of the world market portfolio (GIM, or Global Investable Market, in Exhibit 13.5) is equal to 1. The world market portfolio includes all investable assets, such as fixed-income assets, equity, and alternative investments. The beta of U.S. equity relative to the world market portfolio is approximately equal to 2, and U.S. equity lies on the integrated market line, because there is no segmentation premium. The world market portfolio lies a bit above the integrated market line because it includes assets that suffer from some segmentation.

To hold illiquid assets, investors are required to be compensated. This takes the form of an illiquidity premium to be added to the risk premium dictated by the CAPM, which assumes liquid markets. Although the expected return on an illiquid

EXHIBIT 13.6

Excess Returns of Conventional and Alternative Investments		
	Risk Premium (including segmentation)	**Excess Return** (Risk Premium + Illiquidity Premium)
GIM	1.84%	1.97%
U.S. equity	3.59	3.59
Ex-U.S. equity	3.42	3.42
U.S. bonds	0.80	0.80
Ex-U.S. bonds	0.75	0.75
Private equity	7.88	9.92
Real estate	1.82	3.06
Natural resources	2.07	3.88
Hedge funds	1.82	2.57

Source: Terhaar, Staub, and Singer (2003).

asset can therefore look high, such an asset has the unpleasant characteristic that any sale of a sizable order cannot be achieved quickly except at a significant price discount. Estimating the premium that is required by market participants to compensate for the illiquidity of an asset class is a difficult task. Terhaar, Staub, and Singer (2003) calculate illiquidity premiums for a full array of asset classes. Their estimates for major asset classes[17] are reproduced in Exhibit 13.6. The first column gives the risk premium as presented in Exhibit 13.5. The second column gives the total expected excess return, including the illiquidity premium. Let's take the example of natural resources: The integrated risk premium is equal to 1.12 percent (the point on the integrated market line with a beta of 0.68; see Exhibit 13.5). Because of market segmentation, the risk premium of natural resources rises to 2.07 percent as shown in Exhibits 13.5 and 13.6. An additional illiquidity premium of 1.81 percent raises the total expected excess return to 3.88 percent.

These equilibrium expected returns are used to "guide" the formulation of long-term capital market expectations. Additional forward-looking factors could be considered to adjust those expectations, but one should ensure that the long-term risk-and-return assumptions are consistent.

Short-Term Capital Market Expectations

The definition of *short term* varies according to the investor. *Long term* typically refers to ten years or more. *Short term* typically refers to less than a year or a few years. Changes in market environment and valuations could suggest that some assets are under- or overvalued. This can happen when investors have become very optimistic on some asset class and asset prices have risen well above their perceived intrinsic

---

[17] They estimate the illiquidity premium for detailed asset classes and aggregate them for the major asset classes reported here.

values. The opposite can occur when pessimism prevails. Many forecasting and valuation techniques are used, from subjective to quantitative. Some have been reviewed in previous chapters. For example, Chapters 2 and 3 suggested approaches to forecasting currency movements. Chapter 6 dealt with equity valuation. Short-term capital market expectations will suggest (temporary) tactical deviations from the strategic asset allocation, as discussed in the following section.

Global Asset Allocation: From Strategic to Tactical

The most important global investment decision is the selection of an asset allocation. The first step for a global investor is to decide on a *strategic asset allocation* (*SAA*), or the structure of the portfolio for the long term. This is based on long-term capital market expectations. The process of periodically adjusting asset allocation to reflect changes in the market environment is referred to as *tactical asset allocation* (*TAA*).

Strategic Asset Allocation

The SAA is derived by conducting an asset allocation optimization using long-term capital market expectations. For portfolio management with *individual clients,* the objectives and constraints indicated in the investment policy statement play a big role in the optimization. In *institutional* investment management, the SAA often takes the form of an investable benchmark that is assigned as an objective by the sponsor to the manager(s). Because the performance of the portfolio is measured against this benchmark, it provides a strong guide to the manager's investment strategy. The question that remains is the choice of the proper global benchmark. Three important issues are the

- scope of the benchmark,

- set of weights chosen, and

- attitude toward currency risk.

Scope of Global Benchmark   A truly global investor should include all asset classes, domestic and foreign, in the global benchmark. This global benchmark could then be broken down into various sub-benchmarks that can be assigned to different investment managers. In practice, many investors treat domestic and foreign investments as different asset classes. For example, a Dutch investor could decide to invest 50 percent of its assets out of the Netherlands, with half invested in foreign stocks and half invested in foreign bonds. Then the Dutch investor could assign the MSCI or S&P world index to the foreign equity manager and the Salomon Smith Barney or J.P. Morgan world bond index to the foreign bond manager. These global indexes should then be calculated by excluding the Netherlands from the indexes. Note that the global asset allocation will be strongly biased toward Dutch assets, because 50 percent of the assets are invested domestically, so the natural benchmark for the total assets of the fund will not be a market capitalization–weighted world index. Further note that within equity, the distinction is often made between investments in developed and emerging markets, which are usually treated as different asset classes.

Weights in the Global Benchmark   A whole range of approaches is used to determine the benchmark weights. The simplest, most common approach is to use a *published global market index*. The weights are proportional to the relative market capitalizations (caps). A market cap–weighted index is a natural implication of the theory. It can be easily replicated in a passive strategy, because the weights change in line with price movements in the portfolio. This type of global index is widely published and commonly used by institutional investors worldwide. Hence, the performance can easily be compared across funds and managers.

Some investors are using *GDP country weights* instead of market-cap country weights. The idea is interesting, because it gives each country a weight proportional to its economic strength. But implementing this approach is not easy and is fairly costly in a passive portfolio that must be rebalanced each time a new GDP figure is published or revised in any country. The same problem occurs when a given stock market goes up or down, while the GDP weights stay constant.

The inclusion of bonds and alternative investments in a variety of currencies makes the concept of a world market portfolio very difficult to measure and implement. UBS Global Asset management calculates an index of the total investable capital market. This index includes equity, bonds, and other assets. Its size and breakdown, as of the end of 2001, is given in Exhibit 13.7.

Investors seldom consider the world market portfolio of all assets as a practical global investment strategy. Most investors exhibit a strong home bias in their investment strategy. This is often justified by the fact that foreign investments are regarded as more risky and costly because of lack of information/familiarity, currency risk, transaction costs, and differential tax treatments. A large investor will therefore treat each asset class separately, for example, assigning separate benchmarks for domestic equity, international equity, domestic bonds, and so on. This leaves open the question of the strategic global asset allocation across all asset classes. Different investor groups should follow different core strategies that reflect their situations and comparative advantages in terms of costs, taxes, and risks. This leads private and institutional investors to select a *customized* global strategic asset allocation. This allocation is then translated into a customized benchmark combining indexes for each asset class. Studies by Blake, Lehmann, and Timmermann (1999) and Brinson, Singer, and Beebower (1991) show that the asset allocation decision is a major determinant of returns on U.K. and U.S. pension plans. So, the weights chosen are of great importance for performance. Optimization techniques are often used, based on long-term capital market expectations and on characteristics and constraints of the investor (see next section).

Institutional investors face constraints in the form of various regulations that they must follow. But deviating from the peer group also poses a "business" risk. For example, a pension sponsor that decides to have a much greater international

EXHIBIT 13.7
_____

Total Investable Capital Market
Total U.S. $64.1 trillion, Dec. 31, 2001

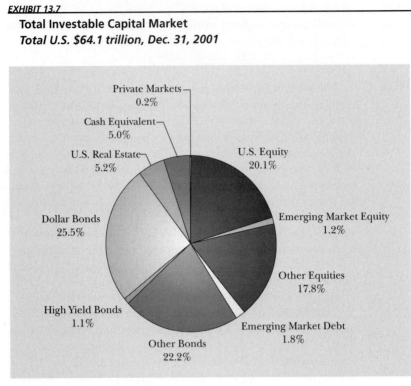

Source: UBS Global Asset Management

allocation than its peers is under severe pressure in times when international investments underperform domestic investments. So, the current asset allocation of
peers is also a form of benchmark. Exhibit 13.8 reports some average asset allocations of pension funds in various countries.[18] The asset allocation of British and
Dutch pension funds is much more global than that of U.S., German, and Swiss
pension funds. Pension funds in some small countries have a majority of their investments abroad. The equity allocation also differs markedly, with British funds
typically investing some 70 percent of their assets in stocks, while French funds typically invest 10 percent. All of these numbers are for an "average" pension fund,
vary greatly across funds, and change over time. Nevertheless, the obvious picture is
that institutional investors do not follow a uniform investment strategy across the
world.

Currency Allocation in the Benchmark   Should foreign investments be systematically hedged against currency risks? This question has led to an extensive contro-

_____

[18] Such estimates vary, depending on the types of pension plans (corporate, public) included in the average and the weighting system used. See also Griffin (1998).

EXHIBIT 13.8

Typical Asset Allocation of Pension Funds by Country of Residence (in %)

Country	Domestic Equity	Foreign Equity	Domestic Bonds	Foreign Bonds	Real Estate	Cash/Other
Belgium	10	43	15	18	4	10
Denmark	17	21	50	3	6	3
France	5	8	27	25	2	33
Germany	10	16	39[a]	—	6	19
Ireland	19	52	8	12	6	3
Italy	6	1	37	10	45	1
Netherlands	15	29	30	18	5	3
Spain	11	25	32	11	1	20
Sweden	24	16	41	13	4	2
Switzerland	20	11	27	10	11	21[b]
United Kingdom	46	25	17	3	6	3
Australia	42	16	19	3	5	15
Japan	38	19	31	8	1	3
United States	48	11	34	1	2	4

a. Includes Eurozone bonds.
b. Includes mortgages.

Source: Investments & Pensions Europe and UBS Global Asset Management, 2002.

versy (already addressed in Chapters 4 and 9). The international CAPM provides useful insights on risk management. The basic conclusion from theoretical research is that the optimal portfolio is the world market portfolio *partly hedged* against currency risk (see Chapter 4). Partly hedged means that all foreign assets are optimally hedged when the market is in equilibrium. We can objectively observe the world market portfolio; we can use world market caps as weights for the benchmark. Although investment managers may disagree as to the exact benchmark to use, all of these portfolios approximate the investable world portfolio and are observable. The problem is identifying the optimal hedge ratios, because theory tells us that optimal hedge ratios are a function of the asset to be hedged, and depend on unobservable parameters such as relative preferences of different nationals, risk aversions, and the net foreign investment position of each country. The existence of currency risk premiums is central to the determination of optimal hedge ratios. Exchange rates, like interest rates and stock prices, are financial prices, and risk premiums are justified. Unfortunately, these currency risk premiums cannot be measured directly and are likely to be unstable over time. So, *pragmatic shortcuts* are necessary:

- A first pragmatic possibility is *full hedging*. The motivation for a full-hedging policy is based on the assumption that we cannot tell whether currency risk premiums are positive or negative; hence, the sole objective is to minimize the risk. Therefore, we hedge 100 percent and use a fully hedged or unit-hedge benchmark as the strategic benchmark.[19] Full hedging is simply focusing on minimizing the volatility of the foreign part of the portfolio. This simple approach has been severely attacked from several angles:

- First, theory tells us that currency risk premiums should exist if some countries are net foreign investors (e.g., Japan) or exhibit more risk aversion than others (see Chapter 4).

- Second, even if we were doing only a passive, risk-minimization hedge and only cared about risk, not about expected return, we would take into account the correlation between the currency risk and the asset risk. In the presence of correlation between currency and market risk, we should use "regression" hedges, which will generally not equal one because of the correlation between asset returns and currency movements.

- Third, the relevant measure of risk should not be the volatility of the foreign assets taken in isolation, but their contribution to the total risk of the global portfolio (domestic and foreign). Indeed, currencies provide an element of monetary risk diversification for the domestic portfolio. As long as the proportion of foreign assets in the total portfolio is small (e.g., less than 10 percent), the contribution of currency risk is minimal and not worth the trouble and costs of engaging in systematic currency hedging (see Nesbitt, 1991, and Jorion, 1989).

- A second pragmatic alternative often proposed is *no hedging*. This approach refutes the assumption that full currency hedging reduces the volatility of return on foreign assets. The question raised is the investor's time horizon. A pension fund has a long-term objective and should not be concerned with short-horizon risk, such as monthly or quarterly volatility. Given the structure of its liabilities, a pension fund should instead focus on the risk that a sufficient return will not be realized over a long horizon, for example, 5 or 10 years. Froot (1993) shows, theoretically and empirically, that the risk-minimizing currency hedge is a function of the investment horizon. With a horizon of 5 years, foreign stocks display a greater return volatility when hedged than unhedged. The reason for this finding is the mean reversion in exchange rates. Over the short run, currency returns are explained mostly by changes in the real exchange rate. In the very long run, the purchasing powers of two currencies tend toward parity, and exchange rate trends are explained mostly by the inflation differential between the two currencies. Another motivation for this approach is that systematic currency hedging can be a costly process. Whether a fund trustee or an investment manager, whose jobs are at stake in

---

[19] Many practitioners use Pérold and Schulman (1988) as a justification for unit-hedge ratio (100 percent hedge). Actually, Pérold and Schulman do consider the case of a zero-currency risk premium, but they advocate taking into account the correlation between currency and market risk to determine the "full" hedge ratio.

the short run, will feel comfortable with measuring performance and risk solely on such a long horizon is another question. Also, significant deviations from purchasing power parity persist in the long run.

- A third pragmatic shortcut is to use *universal hedge ratios* (or arbitrary hedge ratios). Black (1990) came up with a 0.75 hedge ratio and Gastineau (1995) suggested a 0.50 hedge ratio. As mentioned in Chapter 4, Black had to make many extreme assumptions to derive his universal hedge ratio.[20] For example, all countries should have exactly the same amount of investment abroad (no net foreign investment) and no inflation. Also, he postulated that all investors should have an identical risk aversion, and so on. Even if the principle that each investor should use exactly the same hedge ratio for every single asset were to be accepted, the exact value of the universal hedge ratio is still arbitrary because it is based on a forecast of the future return and volatility of the world market portfolio. If investors are to make so many "arbitrary" assumptions in order to derive a universal hedge ratio of, say, 0.75, why not simply assume the result at the start? In a sense, Gastineau's "Why bother?" approach is cleaner. He *assumes* that 0.50 is the best. Why 0.50? Because it is halfway between 0 and 1, neither of which is appropriate.

To summarize, the extent of strategic currency hedging remains an open theoretical and empirical question. Because hedge ratios differ across assets and currencies, depending on unobservable foreign asset positions, utility functions, individual risk aversion, and inflation, there is no simple practical solution and no theoretically unquestionable benchmark for the currency allocation, and there never will be. In the absence of a natural benchmark dictated by theory or systematic empirical observation, investors have taken different routes. Some use different currency-hedging strategies for different asset classes. For example, they could keep their foreign stock benchmark unhedged while fully hedging their foreign bond benchmark, because currency risk is relatively more important for bonds than for stocks. Currency-hedged global indexes are now available for both stocks and bonds from the major index providers, so performance of fully hedged portfolios can easily be assessed.

Tactical Asset Allocation

Active managers adjust their asset allocations periodically, typically monthly but sometimes more often, to reflect changes in the market environment. This is called dynamic or *tactical asset allocation* (TAA). TAA is the process of deciding which *asset classes* are attractively or unattractively priced, and making short-term departures from the long-term policy by buying more of the attractive markets and reducing the holding of unattractive markets. Through this process, the aim is to add value by achieving a higher return than the return that would be achieved by simply holding the portfolio defined by the long-term policy. Adjustments made are *conditional* on some new information. So, deviations from the SAA are based on short-term

---

[20] For a criticism of this model, see Adler and Solnik (1990) and Adler and Prasad (1992).

developments and reflect forecasts on market trends in the next few months. This is typically the case when it is perceived that investors have become too optimistic (pessimistic) on some asset class, pushing asset prices very high (low) relative to fundamentals. How to exploit these forecasts depends on the investment philosophy chosen by the investment manager (see a discussion of various philosophies in a previous section).

Some managers use a systematic quantitative approach to TAA, in which adjustments strictly follow some *disciplined* risk–return optimization process. A set of variables is used to evaluate the relative attractiveness of markets, namely their risk premium. Typical variables used are the level of the dividend yield, the level of the interest rate, the spread between long-term yields and cash rates, and so on.[21] The holdings of an equity market with a low dividend yield (relative to its historical average) would be adjusted downward on the premise that the market is overpriced and will soon revert to normality. Rebalancing is done automatically in a disciplined fashion to prevent emotions or fads from influencing the TAA.

Other managers base their revision on various models of currencies, interest rates, and equity markets to determine the fundamental value (or fair value) of various asset classes (i.e., their fair price). TAA decisions are taken if market prices come to deviate significantly from their fundamental value. While many of the inputs are quantitative, the TAA decisions are not automatic and take into account the current market environment. Efforts are made to understand why those discrepancies have arisen. Some of these discrepancies could be explained by theories grounded in behavioral finance. Finding that an asset class is overvalued will not be useful in TAA unless the market corrects the discrepancy fairly quickly. Other managers simply use a subjective assessment of changes in the current market environment.

Global Asset Allocation: Structuring and Quantifying the Process

The process described, with its separation between strategic and tactical asset allocations, is common among *institutional* investors, such as pension funds. *Private* investors make less use of benchmarks and tend to state their investment objectives in a less formal manner. They sometimes seem to care more about absolute returns than about deviations from a prespecified benchmark. This does not mean that the

---

[21] There is some evidence that the direction of worldwide stock and bond prices can be predicted to some extent by using a set of information variables. See, for example, Harvey (1991); Bekaert and Hodrick (1992); Solnik (1993a, 1993b); Ferson and Harvey (1994a, 1994b); Emanuelli and Pearson (1994); Harvey (1995); Kahn, Roulet, and Tajbakhsh (1996), and Jensen, Mercer, and Johnson (1996). This does not necessarily imply that these markets are inefficient; this predictability could also be explained by a time variation in risk premiums justified by a change in the socioeconomic environment. In statistical jargon, the strategic asset allocation could be based on long-term, unconditional risk premiums; the tactical asset allocation could be based on conditional risk premiums. A review of TAA can be found in Goodsall (1998).

investment process should not be structured. We will discuss an adaptable global investment process.

Apart from the obvious technical and practical problems inherent in investing abroad, the key issue in global investing is how to structure the *asset allocation* process. Essential to this decision process are a variety of uncertain forecasts concerning exchange rates, interest rates, and stock market patterns. The task is further complicated by the fact that many of these variables are, to varying degrees, interdependent in the global context. For example, all the major stock markets are linked, but some are more closely linked than others, depending on the integration of the underlying economies. Global industry factors cut across borders. Similarly, a change in the interest rate of one currency will affect the exchange rates and interest rates of other currencies, but not to the same degree. Domestic asset allocation is simplified by the fact that an investor chooses from a limited variety of assets, namely cash, bonds, common stocks, and possibly alternative assets. In the global context, however, these choices are multiplied by the number of countries and currencies available, which can, in and of themselves, present certain practical problems. For example, an investor may be bullish on the Japanese stock market but not on the yen. The complexity of the global scene, which involves so many interactions, makes quantification all the more useful and calls for computer technology. Any added value should be transferred immediately and efficiently to all accounts, even if they have diverse objectives and constraints as stated in their investment policy statement.

This section describes a quantified system or process for portfolio management based on a top-down approach that is currently used by several global money management firms. Because it is internally consistent, it avoids the pitfalls sometimes found in the bottom-up approach. The purpose of this system is to ensure the most efficient use of existing expertise within an organization and a rapid implementation of new investment ideas in all accounts. The system must therefore be structured along the lines of the major common factors affecting a security's price behavior. A different model of the world capital market would lead to a different system. We will discuss here a *balanced* approach centered along a *country investment philosophy;* but an investment philosophy focusing on worldwide industry factors, or both country and industry factors, could also be considered.

Our portfolio management system has four major stages: research and market analysis, asset allocation optimization, portfolio construction, and performance and risk control. The attraction of the system lies not in its components, but in the way it integrates the four stages, with the aid of computers, to benefit money managers and their clients. The idea is not to generate more reliable forecasts, but to use currently available forecasts better. That requires capitalizing most efficiently on the existing expertise within an organization. A diagram of this system is shown in Exhibit 13.9.

Research and Market Analysis

To cope with the complexity and rapid changes of the global environment, a manager must have the technological tools to analyze and interpret large streams of data. Ideally, everyone involved in the investment decision process—analysts,

EXHIBIT 13.9

An Integrated Investment Process

Real-time database updating

Research Department

Various qualitative inputs

Macroeconomic and company models

Historical risk and return study

Evaluation of individual securities

Forecasts and risk estimates for markets and currencies

Investment Policy Committee

Qualitative evaluation

Asset allocation optimizer

Optimal asset allocation for aggressive and defensive strategies and various types of accounts

Managers

Management assistance

- Financial data on manager's screen
- Account structure and computed divergence from stated objectives and updated asset allocation policy
- Revision suggestions by account and aggregated by manager
- Various models and administrative programs

Performance Evaluation and Control

Global performance analysis

- Study of performance and risk by account and manager
- Study of performance of analysts
- Study of performance of the investment policy

Monitoring and periodic adjustments

investment committee members, and managers—should operate with a common electronic platform (the "platform") that allows a free flow of data and research findings between decision makers.

To monitor markets, a large global database with online connections to major outside databank services is necessary. The database available on the platform should contain price histories on markets and individual securities, as well as economic statistical data. Ideally, the data should cover several previous years and be updated daily. All research reports and recommendations produced by research analysts should be available instantly on the platform. Another major use of the platform is the development and revision of forecasts on currencies, interest rates, commodity prices, and national stock indexes. The manager should then translate these forecasts into estimates of total returns in particular base currencies. Similarly, risk parameters for markets and securities should be available on the platform and frequently updated.

Asset Allocation Optimization

The Principles The objective of any investment strategy is to achieve a superior performance for a given level of risk. This can be done through subjective discussion among the members of an investment strategy committee or by using formal optimization models. Given the investment philosophy selected in this example, an investment strategy should aim to achieve an efficient asset allocation by regions/country (or currency) and type of investment (stocks, bonds, money markets). Toward this end, a mean-variance quadratic program is often used to merge the forecasts and risk estimates generated by an investment organization. Providing it is optimal, the resulting asset allocation will outperform a passive strategy only to the extent that the organization's forecasts reflect superior expertise in one or more markets, such as stocks, bonds, or currency. Also, the allocation must conform to the objectives and constraints set in the investment policy statement of the various accounts managed by an organization. Some accounts permit only equity investment; others impose restrictions on selling short; and still others do not permit investment in specific asset classes. Plainly, constraints such as these will affect the potential return on an account, as will the choice of risk level or any other limitation.

Unless currency risk is systematically hedged, optimal asset allocations will differ according to the client's base currency. In theory, managers should care about real returns, not nominal returns. They should consider the returns calculated in the currency of the investor and adjusted by the appropriate inflation rate. Nevertheless, because the volatility of inflation rates is very small compared with that of most asset returns or currency movements, the use of real or nominal returns would not make much difference in the results of the optimization procedure.[22]

---

[22] Some institutional investors take the structure of their liabilities into account to determine the appropriate investment strategy. The risk of the assets is measured relative to that of the liabilities rather than in absolute terms. But the modeling of the liabilities is a difficult task. This process is called asset/liability management (ALM).

The optimization can be conducted on absolute returns. It also can be conducted relative to a prespecified benchmark, with return and risk being measured in deviation from the benchmark. This is the case when an SAA is first determined (the benchmark) and tactical revisions are considered based on the current market environment. The SAA is optimized based on long-term capital market expectations when the IPS is drafted. The SAA can be periodically revised (e.g., once a year) following the same process. Tactical deviations from this SAA can be implemented more frequently based on an optimization using short-term capital market expectations and taking transaction costs into account.

Mean-Variance Optimization   The optimal asset allocation can be derived using a mean-variance optimizer, as reviewed in DeFusco et al. (2001). Mathematically, the optimizer minimizes risk for various levels of expected returns. Capital market expectations are used to derive the expected return-and-risk parameters of the various asset classes. Taxes borne by the client should be taken into account in the capital market expectations. Investment constraints stated in the IPS are entered as linear constraints in the optimization. The optimizer yields an efficient frontier, a set of optimal asset allocations for different risk levels.

The computer programs employed should be interactive so that an investment committee can simulate several capital market expectation scenarios and thereby determine the most appropriate investment strategy. They should also allow the investment committee to check the sensitivity of the optimal asset allocation against a variety of other projected scenarios. Under the same capital market expectation scenario, optimal asset allocations for different risk levels can be calculated. The composition of the portfolio on the efficient frontier is quite sensitive to small changes in forecasted returns.[23] The inclusion of transaction costs and various statistical techniques can alleviate this problem.

Ultimately, the quality of inputs is what counts. Bad forecasts will not generate superior performance, no matter which optimization method is used. However, any forecasting ability will best be exploited through such an approach.

Limitations of Mean-Variance Optimization   Mean-variance optimization assumes that return distributions are normal. This is only approximately true in real life. Rather than minimizing the variance of the portfolio, another approach is to set a specific loss level (shortfall) and to build a portfolio that minimizes the probability of losing more than this set value. This is often known as minimizing *shortfall risk* or *downside risk* (see Harlow, 1991). Alternatively, managers can set a given loss probability and attempt to minimize the loss amount for that probability. The value at risk (VaR) methodology usually takes this approach. Note that downside risk management reduces to mean-variance analysis if the return distribution is normal. Results can be somewhat different otherwise. The downside risk approach does have some problems (see Sortino and Forsey, 1996). It does not have the simplicity of the mean-variance approach when optimizing an asset allocation. The variance

---

[23] See Michaud (1989, 1998).

of a portfolio can easily be derived from the variance and covariances (or correlations) of the individual assets by a straightforward formula. This is not the case for the downside risk of a portfolio. Furthermore, the main criticism of the mean-variance optimization is that it is very sensitive to changes in the inputs. The same criticism applies to downside risk optimization. In using an asset allocation optimization model, we only hope to have a model that captures enough of the risk–return trade-offs to add value in setting the asset allocation. The mean-variance approach, in part because it is quite simple and easy to understand intuitively, accomplishes this objective.

Various methods have been proposed to improve the mean-variance approach. Black and Litterman (1992) propose starting with a "neutral" view of the asset allocation. This neutral view is obtained by assuming that the world market is in equilibrium. Knowing the world market caps and the observed covariance matrix, we can infer the expected returns on all assets that would be consistent with market equilibrium. This is sometimes called *inverse optimization,* because we start from the portfolio weights (their observed market cap) and infer the expected returns that would make an investor optimally hold these assets in market-cap proportions. If an investor has no particular views about asset returns, she can use this set of "neutral" returns derived from market equilibrium. If an investor has some views about the relative performance of assets, she can adjust the "neutral" returns accordingly using a Bayesian updating methodology. The basic idea is to combine global equilibrium with investors' views.

In a similar spirit, Grinold (1999) proposes looking at deviations from a benchmark. The idea is to start from a benchmark set of expected returns, which are consistent with market equilibrium. These are called *unconditional* returns. An investor who has some special information would update those expected returns *conditional* on the special information. Grinold shows that, using this approach, the mean-variance optimization and scenario-based optimization (such as downside risk optimization) yield similar results.

Portfolio Construction

Active security selection in each market is a natural complement to active market selection. A research department should maintain on the platform an *active list* of individual securities in each market. This regularly updated list should provide a manager with an analyst's recommendation, possibly in the form of an expected return in local currency, as well as major risk characteristics of the security, including sensitivities to various factors and, for bonds, actuarial yields and a measure for duration. The manager can then use this active securities list to construct the portfolio according to the asset allocation strategy of a specific client. Multifactor risk models are necessary to control the active risks taken in security selection.

Managers of a large number of medium-sized accounts find that rebalancing those accounts to reflect even modest alterations in the client's investment policy or the firm's strategy is extremely time consuming and unduly repetitive. Reacting to a major policy or strategy change takes even longer. To cope with this problem, a manager should first value each portfolio in the asset allocation format. Next, each manager should modify the new investment strategy so that it reflects client IPS guidelines for his major classes of accounts. The extent of this modification will depend on the type of client, base currency, and size of the account. Total transaction costs and taxes (e.g., on realized capital gains) must be taken into account. Any deviations of the current asset allocation appear on the manager's screen. Drawing on the active securities list, a computer program will make sell-and-buy recommendations for stocks and bonds that would enable the account to satisfy the new asset allocation guideline. The manager can either validate the proposed transactions on the screen or make his own decisions. The market orders and attendant paperwork required for implementing the validated transactions can be generated automatically by the computer.

More quantitatively oriented managers would probably make extensive use of the models described elsewhere in this book. They could adjust the sensitivity of the portfolio to specific market factors in each cell of the asset allocation; for example, a manager who is bullish on interest rates in Britain could select sterling bonds with a long duration to increase the sensitivity to a drop in sterling bond yields. Futures and options can be used to react to sudden threats of a large market movement in some currency or asset classes. At this level, fine-tuning of the risk management of the portfolio should come into play.

Performance and Risk Control

The final step in the investment process is to monitor the performance and risk of individual portfolios. A common problem is that all money managers are very outspoken about global risk diversification, but many do not use a structured allocation process to achieve it. This problem is all the more serious for managers with active strategies, who tend to concentrate on a few currencies and markets and are therefore vulnerable to the high risk associated with those currencies and markets.

Performance control should be driven by an organization's daily accounting system. As mentioned in Chapter 12, the objective is to be able to answer the following questions about a portfolio and, in doing so, to assess the effectiveness of its manager:

- What is the total return on the fund over a specific period?

- What is the breakdown of the return in terms of capital gains, currency fluctuations, and income?

- To what extent is the performance explained by asset allocation, market timing, currency selection, or individual security selection?

- How does the overall return compare with that of certain benchmarks?

- Is there evidence of particular expertise in various asset classes and markets?

- Has the risk-diversification objective been achieved?

- How aggressive is the manager's strategy? How does this compare with the goals of the client?

The characteristics and use of an account review of a global performance analysis (GPA) system were discussed in Chapter 12. It should be stressed that the performance of a research department should also be studied to pinpoint the areas of expertise. This can be done by constructing mock portfolios based on analyst recommendations for each country and comparing the subsequent returns with those on the corresponding national indexes.

Summary

- There are several types of participants in the global investment arena: investors (private or institutional), investment managers, brokers, consultants and advisers, and custodians. Some players belong to several categories.

- Major choices in terms of investment philosophy and strategy must be made by an investment organization firm structuring its global investment process. These choices are based on a view of the global behavior of security prices. A major question is how active a global strategy should be. In an active strategy, a manager can decide on (1) global asset allocation by type of asset and currency, (2) security selection, and (3) market timing. An active manager can also selectively hedge certain types of risks, such as currency risk. Another question is whether the major emphasis should be on market analysis (top-down approach) or on security analysis (bottom-up approach). Yet another important question is whether the focus should be on regional/country factors or on global factors that cut across countries, such as industry factors. These and other choices dictate how the investment process should be structured.

- The client's objectives, constraints, and requirements are then specified in an investment policy statement (IPS); the investment policy statement forms the basis for the strategic asset allocation.

- Capital market expectations are expectations about the future distributions of returns to asset classes, including expected returns, volatility of returns, and correlation of returns. Formulating capital market expectations is potentially the most rewarding part of global asset management, but it is also the most difficult. The formulation process is usually decomposed into three steps:
  - Defining asset classes
  - Formulating long-term expectations used in strategic asset allocation
  - Formulating shorter-term expectations used in tactical asset allocation

- The most important global investment decision is the selection of an asset allocation. The first step for a global investor is to decide on a *strategic asset allocation,* or the structure of the portfolio for the long term. This is based on long-term capital market expectations. The process of periodically adjusting asset allocation to reflect changes in the market environment is referred to as *tactical asset allocation.*

- The strategic asset allocation is formalized through one or several benchmarks set as guidelines to investment managers. Important questions that must be resolved concern:
  - the scope of the global benchmark,
  - the weights in the global benchmark, and
  - the attitude toward currency risk and hence the currency allocation in the global benchmark.

- Structuring and quantifying the investment process is a difficult task because of the large number of parameters involved. A disciplined and efficient approach calls for a partly quantified, integrated system. The objective is to make optimal use of all expertise and to control risk.

John Bouderi: Case Study A

Background

When John Bouderi was a young child, his parents emigrated to Australia from Europe. The Bouderis started a business, called Bestbuilt, producing and selling custom-built fine household furniture.

When his parents retired, John took responsibility for the business. On his parents' deaths, he became the sole owner. Bestbuilt was very successful under John's leadership and grew substantially.

March

John retired at age 60 in March, selling the business and receiving net proceeds after tax of $1,500,000. (Because John is Australian, the dollar symbol in this case refers to Australian dollars.) John is looking forward to a long retirement, because his parents lived a relatively healthy life to an old age. He expects to do the same.

John's wife died 10 years ago. He has two children, both now in their late 20s and self-sufficient. Although John has no grandchildren now, he hopes for them some day and would like to provide a financial legacy for them. John desires a comfortable retirement and is determined that this objective not be jeopardized by poor investment decisions. He has developed an understanding of investments, gained primarily from years of personal study and observing markets and has begun to develop and implement his own investment strategy.

Given his long time horizon, he initially decided to invest $600,000 in direct purchase of Australian equities. Although he understood the benefits of global investing, he limited his initial investments to Australian issues, such as AMP, ANZ, and Westpac. This was due partially to his familiarity with the companies, but also because he felt that the Australian market had shown strong performance. John also was concerned about investment costs and decided to be a "buy and hold" investor with respect to the Australian equities.

The $900,000 remaining was added to an existing money market account, bringing the total money market balance to $1,000,000. The account currently yields 5 percent and will be used to cover his living expenses while awaiting further investment.

July

Australian and global equity markets have declined, and John is concerned about his initial investment decisions. He is devoting more time than expected to increasing his investment knowledge and monitoring his holdings. Despite his long-term perspective, the fact that the Australian equity market and his equity portfolio declined by 5 percent in the last quarter causes him to wonder whether his strategy should be refined.

He has learned that investing in a number of different "asset classes" can increase diversification and reduce risk, and that international investments can be helpful in this regard, particularly because the Australian equity market is dominated by a few large companies in three or four industries. He now doubts whether placing such a large portion of his assets into Australian equities was sound. Because of his parents' European background and because of some magazine articles he has been reading, he likes the idea of investing in U.S. and European equities. He believes that Australian equity already provides him some exposure to Asia because of its proximity and extensive trading links; but he also plans to investigate more direct Asian investments at some stage in the future.

John has decided that professional investment management should be considered, because he understands that such management can potentially add value above the additional cost and can use strategies designed to protect investments when share prices decline. To discuss his situation, he will be meeting with Leigh Brennan, CFA, a financial adviser from one of the major investment firms in Sydney.

Financial Circumstances

The first several meetings between John and Brennan were devoted to evaluating his current financial circumstances in detail. John provided the following information on his financial situation.

Assets

Residence: Sydney, Australia. Market value	$1,000,000
Domestic equity portfolio:	570,000
Money market account:	1,000,000
Total:	$2,570,000
Estimated after-tax annual income desired:	$ 90,000

Immediate Plans

1. Take a family vacation in Europe: estimated cost $50,000
2. Sell existing home and purchase smaller retirement home for approximately 520,000.
3. Place net cash proceeds from home transactions in investment portfolio
4. Establish a trust for grandchildren with initial contribution of $100,000

   Expected investable assets after completion of immediate plans: $1,900,000
   (= $2,570,000 − 50,000 − 520,000 − 100,000)

Liabilities

John has fully paid off his old home and has no mortgage or any other loans outstanding.

Objectives and Constraints

Brennan next conducted several interviews to determine John's investment goals and to identify any constraints that may limit John's achieving those goals.

Desired Return

John desires to lead a comfortable retirement, with an income that keeps pace with inflation. He prefers steady returns consistent with a modest level of risk and desires a return from equity investments of 10 percent annually before tax. For his overall portfolio, he decides that 7 to 8 percent annually before tax would be acceptable.

Required Return

Brennan believes that John's required return is in excess of 9 percent, given total investment assets, liquidity needs, time horizon, and inflation protection needs. John finally agrees with Brennan's figure, but he is concerned about the level of risk a higher return target will bring to the portfolio.

Risk Tolerance

John's personal investing style suggests he is prudent, diligent, and methodical. This is consistent with the approach he took in running his business. Despite his recent experience in the equity market, he still believes that it is necessary to take calculated risks to realize appropriate rewards.

In their final discussion about risk tolerance, John indicates his willingness to accept a possible 10 percent decline in the value of his portfolio in any one year in order to achieve his objectives. Brennan also introduces the concepts of ability and willingness to take risk. She discusses the idea that ability to take risk is determined by such factors as wealth position, annual spending requirements, and inflation expectations. John realizes that the two concepts may be substantially different but is unsure how to combine them to understand his own risk position.

Time Horizon

Based on the family history of longevity and John's current good health, Brennan determines that John can be expected to experience another 20 years of active retirement.

Liquidity

Apart from funding the trip to Europe and establishment of the trust, John has no unusual liquidity requirements.

Tax Issues

All income earned by John, regardless of source, is assumed to be taxed at a 15 percent annual rate.

Legal and Regulatory Issues

Neither John nor Brennan has identified any material legal or regulatory issues facing John, including the establishment of the trust.

Unique Circumstances

- The anticipated exchange of homes within the next year will increase the size of John's portfolio substantially.

- $100,000 to set up a trust for his future grandchildren. This trust would establish an investment account to manage the funds on behalf of the future beneficiaries. A share of the funds would be available to each grandchild at the age of 21 years. Should there be no grandchildren, the funds would be available to his children for their retirement. He may add to this trust in later years. These assets would be held separately from those of Bouderi and once the trust is established, they are no longer part of his portfolio.

Subsequently, Brennan prepared an initial investment policy statement for John Bouderi's review. After several discussions and further fact finding by Brennan, the following investment policy statement was approved by Bouderi.

INVESTMENT POLICY STATEMENT   *JOHN BOUDERI*

Summary

This investment policy statement outlines the goals and objectives of John Bouderi (the client) and the long-term investment strategy that is proper for the achievement of his financial goals. These goals include providing a retirement income and meeting several near-term spending plans.

To fund his retirement, John sold his share of the family business. The investment returns from this portfolio are his sole means of support.

In order to achieve a comfortable retirement, this statement will outline the return-and-risk objectives, acceptable asset classes for inclusion in the portfolio, portfolio strategies, and any constraints on achieving these goals.

Objectives

Return Requirement
A return requirement of 9.6 percent is established.

A total return of 4.7 percent after inflation, taxes and investment expenses is required to meet the anticipated annual spending needs of $90,000 in current dollars. Taking into account expected annual inflation of 3 percent and a tax rate of 15 percent gives a required nominal total return of 9.1 percent on an annualized basis, before expenses. The return requirement of 9.6 percent reflects an initial estimate of annual transaction costs and investment management expenses of 50 basis points.

Such a return is expected to meet after-tax income needs in real terms over an extended time horizon. A return of approximately 1 percent in excess of this amount is desirable to provide modest long-term growth, but is not required.

Risk Tolerance

The risk tolerance of the client is best described as average to slightly below average. To meet the return requirement, it is understood that risk must be taken. Although a fluctuation in portfolio value is expected, the portfolio should be constructed to minimize the likelihood that the portfolio declines by more than 10 percent in any one year. The achievement of a stable portfolio with predictable returns is a highly desired outcome.

Constraints

Time Horizon

John has a two-stage time horizon:

- The next year, defined by several substantial liquidity events, outlined below.

- The remainder of his retirement period, expected to be at least 20 years.

Liquidity

The following liquidity events are expected to occur in the next year:

- $50,000 outflow for a European trip

- $100,000 outflow for a trust for future grandchildren

- $480,000 net inflow from sale and purchase of homes

No liquidity events past the next year are known to exist, apart from meeting annual spending requirements.

Tax Issues

The client faces a maximum tax rate of 15 percent on all income, regardless of the source. He has no outstanding tax liabilities or unresolved issues with the taxing authorities.

Legal and Regulatory Issues

The client faces no material legal or regulatory constraints; his desire to establish a trust for his grandchildren is not expected to present any unusual problems or concerns.

Unique Circumstances

- The timing of establishing the trusts for John's grandchildren, though material, is largely indeterminate.

- The anticipated exchange of homes, though material, is largely indeterminate.

Acceptable Investments

In order to meet the return objective the following asset classes have been identified as acceptable within the framework of a diversified portfolio:

- Australian Equities

- Debt instruments of the Australian Government

- Debt instruments of Australian Corporations

- Equity investments in the United States

- Equity investments in Europe

- Money market instruments

Both active and passive strategies may be employed. It is understood that active strategies may employ higher risk in order to exceed a benchmark return and that results may not meet expectations.

It is understood that investments outside Australia add currency risk to the portfolio. Hedging strategies designed to mitigate this risk are acceptable.

Frequency of Review

This investment policy statement and the resulting strategic asset allocation should be reviewed periodically to ensure it remains appropriate to the client's needs and circumstances, or sooner if a material event occurs. Material events would include, but not be limited to, the following:

- The exchange of homes, resulting in net proceeds substantially different than the anticipated $480,000 inflow

- John's health deteriorating markedly

The client further understands the importance of his understanding the investment strategies adopted and the role his ability and willingness to tolerate risk will play in meeting his objectives.

In a subsequent interview after John had agreed with Brennan on the final version of the investment policy statement, Brennan reviewed his current investment portfolio asset allocation in Exhibit 13A.1.

Brennan and John then discussed her concerns about his current portfolio, as well as some general investing ideas that John might consider. They note that the Australian equity market has underperformed the U.S. and European markets over the past 10 or 20 years, in part due to a strong appreciation of foreign currency. The long-term performance when measured in local currency has been offset by

<u>EXHIBIT 13A.1</u>

Current Asset Allocation

Asset Class	Asset Allocation (%)	Dollar Asset Allocation ($)
Domestic equity	36	570,000
European equity		
U.S. equity		
Government bonds		
Corporate bonds		
Money market	64	1,000,000
Total	100	1,570,000

the Australian dollar depreciation. Brennan reminds John that his initial equity investments are based solely on Australian equities. The Australian economy and stock market have done reasonably well in the past few years, compared with the rest of the world, but there are several reasons to believe this trend will not continue. The liberalization/deregulation of the Australian economy in recent years provided a strong impetus for growth. The benefits of this have largely been realized. The Australian dollar has been undervalued, making Australian exports very competitive and foreign imports expensive, which gave a further boost to the local economy. Although a plus for Australian growth (and the equity market) in the past, the currency factor is now a risk for the future. Strong Australian dollar appreciation will harm local firms. This suggests diversifying abroad but hedging currency risk.

Brennan continues:

Diversification is an important consideration for you. Our economy is relatively small from a worldview. Australia's weighting in the MSCI World is approximately 2 percent, meaning that most investment opportunities lie outside of Australia. The Australian equity market is dominated by a few large companies and does not offer the ability to broadly diversify across industries. Approximately a dozen companies make up more than half of the Australian market capitalization. The financial industry dominates the market with six of the top ten companies being banks. The economy is also well known for its exposure to the mining industry. A severe downturn in the natural resource industry could significantly impair your returns, because it would likely impact not only that sector of the economy, but also large Australian banks with credit exposure to it. Although there are a few other large companies, such as NewsCorp (media), Telstra (telecom) and BHP (natural resources), many important industries/sectors are absent or have a minimal presence. A global approach to investment could solve this diversification problem, because it will allow you to focus on important sectors that are not represented in Australia, such as automobile, luxury goods, and the defense industry.

Brennan then discussed her own opinions as well as some capital market expectation data developed by her firm. She observes that the Australian economy has emerged from a recession and is experiencing a solid recovery. The outlook for the next one to three years is for continued economic recovery with moderately positive economic growth. Firm economists have been forecasting real domestic economic growth of approximately 3 percent annually.

Although the economy has been experiencing a neutral or steady monetary policy over the past year, Brennan expects monetary policy to tighten over the next one to three years as economic growth accelerates. She believes the official interest rate and short-term interest rates may increase by 0.5 percent by the end of the next year. Thereafter, increases in the official rate may accelerate.

Australia's central bank has a stated inflation objective of a maximum rate of inflation of 2 to 3 percent annually. This objective has been in place since the 1990s and has been consistently achieved. Brennan expects inflation of 2 1/2 to 3 percent over the next three years.

Part of her firm's capital market expectations analysis is based on long-term historical data, such as shown in Exhibit 13A.2, which shows the annualized average return for the U.S., European, and Australian equity markets over the 20 years prior to 2001. The return is broken down into capital gain in local currency, yield, and local currency appreciation against the Australian dollar. All returns are expressed in percent per year. Brennan used the historical data as part of her forecasting analysis of equilibrium returns in the capital markets.

Foreign equity strongly benefited from the depreciation of the Australian dollar, but she believes that this scenario will not repeat and the Australian dollar will appreciate over the long run.

Another part of her firm's analysis included some forward-looking assessment of the various economies and currencies. The firm came up with capital market expectations for the various asset classes, as shown in exhibit 13A.3. In recent years, the Australian equity market had become less volatile than U.S. and European equity markets, and Brennan believes that this will continue, given the industry structure of shares listed in Sydney.

Brennan believed that the risk associated with foreign currencies was high. The volatility of the foreign exchange rates was significant. Furthermore, the Australian dollar appeared undervalued. Brennan realized that the past real depreciation of

EXHIBIT 13A.2

Long-Term Historical Returns (20 years to end-2001)				
	Annual Return (%)	Capital Gain (%)	Dividend Yield (%)	Currency Gain (%)	Total Risk (%)
Australia	14.3	9.8	4.5	0	18.7
United States	19.8	11.6	3.5	4.7	17.3
Europe	19.8	11.0	4.0	4.7	17.1

EXHIBIT 13A.3
Capital Market Expectations

Asset Class	Expected Return	Standard Deviation
Domestic equity	11%	15%
European equity	14	21
U.S. equity	12	19
Government bonds	6	7
Corporate bonds	7	9
Money market	5	2

the Australian dollar can be estimated by comparing its actual value with its purchasing power value.[24] A final part of her firm's analysis informed Brennan's opinion that the Australian dollar was undervalued and that the undervaluation will get corrected in the long run at a rate of 2 to 3 percent per year. She confirmed her conclusion by reviewing a report prepared by her firm and based on some IMF data. An excerpt from the report indicated:

Exhibit 13A.4 provides data on the A$/US$ exchange rate and the consumer price indexes in the U.S. and Australia in 1981 and 2001.

Assuming that the Australian dollar was fairly priced relative to the U.S. dollar in 1981, its 2001 value dictated by purchasing power parity (PPP) can be calculated by adjusting by the inflation differential between the U.S. and Australia:

$$\text{PPP value of US\$ per A\$ in } 2001 = 1.1279 \times \frac{116.2}{64.6} \times \frac{44.4}{114.8} = 0.7847$$

The theoretical PPP value of the Australian dollar is US$0.7847, while the actual spot exchange rate at the end of 2001 was US$0.5106, or a 35 percent undervaluation.

The real effective exchange rate given in Exhibit 13A.4 is an index number that takes the weighted average exchange rate of the Australian dollar with all currencies, adjusted for relative movements in national prices. Although it should have remained constant according to PPP, the real effective exchange rate has depreciated from 136.8 to 91.1, a depreciation of about 33 percent.

EXHIBIT 13A.4
Calculation of the Undervaluation of the Australian Dollar over the Past Twenty-One Years (to end-2001)

Period	1981	2001
1. End of period exchange rate (US$ per A$)	1.1279	0.5106
2. CPI Australia	44.4	114.8
3. CPI U.S.	64.6	116.2
4. PPP value of US$ per A$	1.1279	0.7847
5. Effective real exchange index (source IMF) of A$	136.8	91.1

---

[24] Brennan had carefully read Chapter 2 of this book.

Brennan knows that the possibility of a strong Australian dollar raises the question of hedging the currency risk of the non-Australian investments. She is curious to get John's reaction to the capital market expectations and exchange rate data she has presented.

John Bouderi's Reaction

John finds the projected returns from outside Australia compelling but is concerned about the increased volatility of European and U.S. markets. Brennan explains the benefits of adding asset classes with a low correlation to the Australian market. To support her position, she provides the following table of historical correlation information (Exhibit 13A.5), along with the expected correlations developed by the research department of her firm.

John concurs with Brennan's rationale for global investing from a diversification standpoint, but he understands that this will add a new risk to his portfolio due to currency fluctuations. He has read of investors who have lost substantial sums speculating on currency movements and wonders whether currency hedging is worth the expense or risk. He expresses doubts about hedging: "I am familiar with currency fluctuations because Bestbuilt buys many of its supplies from Asian firms. Some years it would hurt us, some years it would help, but in the long run it seemed to balance out. Isn't the same true with global investing?"

Brennan replies that fine-tuned risk management is an important component of global asset management. If currency fluctuations induce pure risk without return compensation, it makes sense to hedge to avoid excessive volatility in portfolio returns. Currency-hedging transaction costs are low. Furthermore, an appreciation of the Australian dollar is likely, and that will induce a currency loss on foreign investments. Although it is true that currency fluctuations tend to balance out in the long run, it may take many, many years before that happens; and we start from a point at which the Australian dollar seems really low. Something like a 50 percent hedging strategy would be a reasonable middle-of-the-road position, given current market expectations and the fact that there is currently no forward premium to pay.

EXHIBIT 13A.5

Historical and Expected Correlations of Australian Stock Index with U.S. and Europe Indexes

Period	United States	Europe
30 years to end-2001	0.34	0.34
20 years to end-2001	0.28	0.31
10 years to end-2001	0.36	0.45
5 years to end-2001	0.43	0.43
Expected (Brennan)	0.50	0.45

Assignment: Create a strategic asset allocation that you think Brennan should recommend.

Assignment: Create an appropriate currency hedging strategy for Bouderi, and explain how to implement it.

Leigh Brennan: Solution A

Brennan prepared the following solution to the problem of strategic asset allocation and hedging for John Bouderi and examines it with him.

As we have discussed, your portfolio should be more broadly diversified by adding equity investments from Europe and the United States. Although your portfolio will continue to have a bias toward the Australian economy, the risks will be lessened, because approximately one-half of your equity investments will now be outside Australia.

You have suggested that you are willing to move away from a strict buy-and-hold strategy toward a more active value-oriented approach. This is particularly appropriate for financial and natural resource companies, where we might be able to exploit inefficiencies in the Australian equity market.

The American and European portfolios should be invested mostly in Australian-domiciled mutual funds in a well-diversified approach. This should enable you to capture the returns of these markets while minimizing investment costs, but we will use active strategies when we think we can uncover some undervalued stocks.

Brennan had analyzed possible asset allocations using her firm's optimization model. She selected the asset allocation shown in Exhibit 13A.6. She chose a mix close to the efficient frontier and meeting all of John's objectives, following the liquidity events.

EXHIBIT 13A.6

Recommended Strategic Asset Allocation

Asset Class	Proposed Asset Allocation	Proposed Dollar Asset Allocation	Expected Return	Standard Deviation
Domestic equity	30%	$570,000	11%	15%
European equity	15	285,000	14	21
U.S. equity	15	285,000	12	19
Government bonds	12	228,000	6	7
Corporate bonds	25	475,000	7	9
Money market	3	57,000	5	2
Total	100%	$1,900,000*	9.82%	8%

* Includes proceeds of $480,000 from the home transactions and $150,000 expenses for trip to Europe and the trust.

Given her capital market expectations, Brennan believed that foreign currency hedging was in order. She reviews her thinking:

> Interest rates in Australia, Europe, and the United States are comparable, so that the forward discount/premium is equal to zero. Hence, currency hedging will exactly offset the loss that could be caused by a future depreciation of foreign currencies against the Australian dollar, without having to pay a forward premium. Of course, any potential foreign currency gain would also be eliminated. Full hedging would be a natural strategy, given expectations. But it can take a very long time before currencies revert to their PPP value. Furthermore, having some foreign currency exposure in the portfolio could provide some risk-diversification elements in case of a sudden surge of inflation in Australia. Also, you seem reluctant to do any hedging. A 50 percent hedge ratio seems a reasonable middle-of-the-road strategy and could be easily implemented with foreign currency forward contracts.

John agrees, and Brennan explains the details. To minimize transaction costs, the hedge will consist of buying a one-year maturity forward contract for Australian dollars equal to half the amount initially invested in U.S. dollars and euros (selling forward U.S. dollars and euros). The hedge amount will be rebalanced yearly. Brennan realized that this static hedging policy would mean that the hedge ratio would diverge from 50 percent as the value of foreign equity moves up or down. All expected returns provided in Exhibit 13A.6 reflect this hedging strategy.

John Bouderi: Case Study B

One year has passed, and Brennan met with John Bouderi for a scheduled review of his investment policy statement and a review of his portfolio's performance for the year. Brennan began by asking John about his European vacation. John thoroughly enjoyed the family get-together. Moving into a review of the investment policy statement, Brennan ascertained that John still held the same views about risk and return and had basically the same time horizon, tax concerns, legal and regulatory factors, and unique circumstances. The liquidity events had taken place. The trust for the grandchildren had been set up and the home sale and new home purchase had been accomplished. The forecasted cash flow requirements for the liquidity events were accurate. Brennan and John then agreed on a slightly revised investment policy statement to reflect the lack of a liquidity requirement of any significance.

Brennan then moved on to discuss portfolio performance for the year. She had prepared an informal presentation and several performance reports. Based on her experience with John's reaction to quarterly performance reports, she knew that John was finding it difficult to understand the sources of international equity performance, although he had become much more willing to accept hedging after all the reading he had done about it. At their meeting the previous year to set up the strategic asset allocation, Brennan and John had agreed on an unhedged benchmark for the international equity portion of the portfolio. The passive benchmark had a 60 percent weight in the U.S. index and a 40 percent weight in the European index. Brennan had encouraged John to follow performance against this benchmark.

Global Performance Evaluation

John's portfolio had appreciated by 11 percent before taxes and inflation. Brennan gave John several reports, including the performance report shown below. John wanted to compare the performance of the unhedged portfolio with the unhedged benchmark and then reflect on the impact of currency hedging. The Australian dollar had appreciated over the year against most currencies by approximately 5 percent. After reviewing the document, John felt happy with the performance of his international portfolio.

PERFORMANCE REPORT FOR INTERNATIONAL PORTFOLIO

Your international equity portfolio rose from $570,000 to $630,285 (a gain of $60,285 or 10.58%). An additional gain of $14,492 came from the forward currency contracts in which we sold forward US$79,800 and €79,800 for $285,000 forward. So, the total value of the international portfolio is $644,777, or a total return of 13.12 percent in Australian dollars. Net of currency hedging the return was 10.58 percent, which is only 0.09 percent below the return on your unhedged benchmark (10.67 percent). All data and calculations are reported in the tables herein.

The performance of your *unhedged* international equity portfolio relative to the benchmark is explained by two factors:

- Your U.S. equity investments had exactly the same return as the U.S. index component of the benchmark, namely 12 percent in Australian dollars. But your European equity investments overperformed the European equity index by 0.47% = 9.15% − 8.68%. Because European equity accounted for 50 percent of your international investments, the contribution of security selection to total return is a positive 0.24% = 50% × 0.47%.

- Your asset allocation was more heavily weighted toward European equity (50 percent weight) than the benchmark (40 percent weight). Because European equity underperformed U.S. equity, this made your international portfolio underperform the benchmark. The contribution to performance of the asset allocation decision is −0.33 percent.

Hence,[25]

---

[25]Let's denote R, R_{US}, and R_{EU} as the returns on the portfolio and on the U.S. and European segments; I, I_{US}, and I_{EU} the returns on the benchmark and on the U.S. and European indexes; and SS_{EU} the security selection return on European equity. We have

$$R - I = 0.5\,R_{US} + 0.5\,R_{EU} - (0.6\,I_{US} + 0.4\,I_{EU}) = 0.5\,I_{US} + 0.5\,(I_{EU} + SS_{EU}) - (0.6\,I_{US} + 0.4\,I_{EU})$$
$$= (0.5 - 0.6)\,I_{US} + (0.5 - 0.4)\,I_{EU} + 0.5\,SS_{EU} = -0.33\% + 0.24\%$$

Portfolio return = Benchmark return + Asset allocation + Security selection
   10.58%   =   10.67%   −   0.33%   +   0.24%

The currency hedge that you applied contributed an additional 2.54 percent to your performance. You sold forward US$79,800 (countervalue $142,500), that is, half of your U.S. dollar exposure. You did this at a forward rate[26] of US$0.56 per A$, or A$1.7857 per US$ (equal to 1/0.56). The exchange rate has now moved to US$0.59 per A$, or $1.6949 per US$ (equal to 1/0.59). So, you can buy back the US$79,800 for $135,254, with a gain of $7,246 = 142,500 − 135,254. A similar gain is made on the forward euro sale, and the total gain is $14,492. Hence, hedging has given an additional return of 2.54% = 14,492/570,000.

   The total return on the international equity portfolio is 13.12 percent, well above your benchmark return of 10.67 percent.

Index	July Previous	July Current In Local Currency	July Current In A$	Return in A$
United States	100	118	112	12.00%
Europe	100	114.50	108.68	8.68%
Benchmark	100	116.25	110.67	10.67%
US$ per A$	0.56	0.59		
EUR per A$	0.56	0.59		

Explanatory note: All indexes are based at 100 in July 2002. Weights in the benchmark are 60 percent U.S. and 40 percent Europe.

Segment	July Previous In Local Currency	July Previous In A$	July Current In Local Currency	July Current In A$	Return in Local Currency	Return in A$	Contribution to Portfolio Return
U.S. stocks	159,600	285,000	188,328	319,200	18%	12%	6.00%
Europe stocks	159,600	285,000	183,540	311,085	15%	9.15%	4.58%
Currency futures		0		14,492			2.54%
Total		570,000		644,777			13.12%

Explanatory note: All local currency values are converted at the exchange rates given above. Starting weights in the portfolio are 50 percent U.S. stocks and 50 percent European stocks.

Revisions in Capital Market Expectations

Several significant events have subsequently taken place including the enactment in much of Europe of a series of tax incentives designed to encourage capital spending, particularly in the construction of new plants and equipment. The

---

[26]The forward rate is equal to the spot rate, because interest rates are equal in the three countries.

United States, Mexico, and Canada saw this as a potential long-term competitive threat and enacted similar legislation.

During the spring of the next year, a severe disruption occurred in world energy supplies. Forecasts placed the earliest date for normal demand–supply conditions to return at three years into the future.

This led to a slowdown in spending among European and U.S. consumers, who were faced with higher energy prices, but had surprisingly little impact on capital spending in either region. This began to have an inflationary impact on metals and mining prices due to higher energy costs associated with running equipment, transportation, and higher demand. The metals industry found it surprisingly easy to pass on higher costs. Most experts expected a period of strong pricing power for the metals and mining industry that could continue for the next three years.

Based on these events, Brennan's firm developed the forecasts in Exhibit 13A.7 for the Australian, U.S., and European markets.

EXHIBIT 13A.7

Revised Capital Market Expectations		
Asset Class	**Expected Annual Return for Next Three Years**	**Expected Long-Term Annual Return**
Australian equity	14%	11%
European equity	9	14
U.S. equity	8	12
Government bonds	5	6
Corporate bonds	6	7
Money market	3	5

Brennan states,

We foresee a period of strong growth for the Australian economy, due primarily to the strong presence of the mining and metals industries in our country. Despite the worldwide slowdown of consumer spending, we expect capital spending for new plants and equipment to continue strong for at least the next two years. By that time, energy production should begin to return to normal, and our preliminary estimate calls for a rebound in consumer spending. Such a rebound would create additional demand for the purchase of durable consumer goods, which should further benefit our natural resources and metals industries.

Another specific factor could favorably affect the Australian economy. In the past couple of years, domestic growth has been curtailed by the extreme droughts that we experienced. We have been blessed by rain so far this year, and the prediction for the end of the year is good. Faster economic growth at home could put some pressure on the Australian dollar. Also, interest rates are currently lower in Australia than abroad (the Australian dollar cash rate is 3 percent compared with 5 percent on the U.S. dollar and on the euro). There could be capital outflow to take advantage of this interest rate differential, and this would push the Australian dollar lower, at least in the short run.

Assignment: Develop a tactical asset allocation for John Bouderi, and develop an appropriate hedging policy for this allocation.

Leigh Brennan: Solution B

Brennan prepared the following solution to the problem of tactical asset allocation and hedging for Bouderi, and discussed it with him.

Tactical Asset Allocation

Although I believe the asset allocation we developed is appropriate for the long-term, I believe that we should adjust your portfolio to take advantage of recent favorable developments for our economy. In my firm, we do not believe that the capital markets have fully accounted for the favorable impact these developments will have on the Australian economy and corporate earnings.

Based on our revised view of world markets for the short term, and your current portfolio value, we performed the optimization calculation again. Given the relatively short time period involved, we did not change the risk or correlation assessments for the various markets. The actual volatility and correlation will obviously have an impact on your final return.

We believe that currency hedging should be eliminated in the proposed tactical allocation. Our short-term view of the Australian dollar is that it will remain stable or weaken slightly. A forward premium of 2 percent (the interest rate differential) must currently be paid in currency hedging. This premium is not expected be offset by a corresponding appreciation of the Australian dollar (depreciation of foreign currencies). Furthermore, your foreign currency exposure has been reduced to 20 percent of the overall portfolio, so hedging that small component would not materially lower the overall risk of your portfolio. See Exhibit 13A.8.

If we leave your asset allocation unchanged, we estimate the return will fall from 9.8 percent to 8.9 percent, which is below your required return. We estimate that, by making these changes, your return will increase to approximately 10.3 percent, a substantial improvement, with only slightly higher portfolio volatility.

EXHIBIT 13A.8

Tactical Asset Allocation

Asset Class	Proposed Asset Allocation	Expected Return	Standard Deviation
Domestic equity	50%	14%	15%
European equity	10	9	21
U.S. equity	10	8	19
Government bonds	12	5	7
Corporate bonds	15	6	9
Money market	3	3	2
Total	100%	10.29%	8.7%

Bibliography

Adler, M., and Prasad, B. "On Universal Currency Hedges," *Journal of Financial and Quantitative Analysis,* February 1992.

Adler, M., and Solnik, B. Letter to the Editor, "The Individuality of 'Universal' Hedging," *Financial Analysts Journal,* May/June 1990.

Ambachtsheer, K. P., and Ezra, D. D. *Pension Fund Excellence,* New York: John Wiley & Sons, 1998.

Arnott, R. D., and Bernstein, P. L., "What Risk Premium is 'Normal'?" *Financial Analysts Journal,* March/April 2002.

Asness, C., Krail, R., and Liew, J. "Do Hedge Funds Hedge?" *Journal of Portfolio Management,* Fall 2001.

Bekaert, G., and Hodrick, R. J. "Characterizing Predictable Components in Excess Returns on Equity and Foreign Exchange Markets," *Journal of Finance,* June 1992.

Black, F. "Equilibrium Exchange Rate Hedging," *Journal of Finance,* July 1990.

Black, F., and Litterman, R. "Global Portfolio Optimization," *Financial Analysts Journal,* September/October 1992.

Blake, D., Lehmann, B., and Timmermann, A. "Asset Allocation Dynamics and Pension Fund Performance," *Journal of Business* 9, 1999.

Brinson, G., Brian P., Singer, D., and Beebower, Gilbert L. "Determinants of Portfolio Performance II: An Update," *Financial Analysts Journal* 47(3), 1991.

Campbell, J. Y., and Viceira, L. M. *Strategic Asset Allocation: Portfolio Choice for Long-Term Investors.* Oxford: Oxford University Press, 2002.

DeFusco, R. A., McLeavey, D., Pinto, R., and Runkle, D. *Quantitative Methods for Investment Analysis,* Charlottesville VA: AIMR, 2001.

Dimson, E., Marsh, P., and Stauton, M. *Triumphs of the Optimists: 101 Years of Global Investment Returns,* Princeton, NJ: Princeton University Press, 2002.

Emanuelli, J. F., and Pearson, R. G. "Using Earnings Estimates for Global Asset Allocation," *Financial Analysts Journal,* March/April 1994.

Ferson, W. E., and Harvey, C. R. "An Exploratory Investigation of the Fundamental Determinants of National Equity Returns," in J. A. Frankel, ed., *The Internationalization of Equity Markets,* Chicago: NBER–University of Chicago Press, 1994a.

———. "Sources of Risk and Expected Returns in Global Equity Markets," *Journal of Banking and Finance,* September 1994b.

Froot, K. A. "Currency Hedging over Long Horizons," NBER Working Paper No. 4355, May 1993.

Gastineau, G. L. "The Currency Hedging Decision: A Search for Synthesis in Asset Allocation," *Financial Analysts Journal,* May/June 1995.

Goodsall, W. A. R. "Tactical Asset Allocation," *Asset Allocation in a Changing World,* ICFA Continuing Education, vol. 7, Charlottesville, VA: AIMR, 1998.

Griffin, M. W. "A Global Perspective on Pension Fund Asset Allocation," *Financial Analysts Journal,* March/April 1998.

Grinold, R. C. "Mean-Variance Optimization and Scenario-Based Approaches to Portfolio Selection," *Journal of Portfolio Management*, 25(2), Winter 1999.

Harlow, W. V. "Asset Allocation in a Downside Risk Framework," *Financial Analysts Journal*, September/October 1991.

Harvey, C. R. "Predictable Risk and Returns in Emerging Markets," *Review of Financial Studies*, 8(3), Fall 1995.

———. "The World Price of Covariance Risk," *Journal of Finance*, March 1991.

Jensen, G. R., Mercer, J. M., and Johnson, R. R. "Business Conditions, Monetary Policy, and Expected Security Returns," *Journal of Financial Economics*, 40(2), February 1996.

Jorion, P. "Asset Allocation with Hedged and Unhedged Foreign Stocks and Bonds," *Journal of Portfolio Management*, Summer 1989.

Kahn, R. N., Roulet, J., and Tajbakhsh, S. "Three Steps to Global Asset Allocation," *Journal of Portfolio Management*, Fall 1996.

Maginn, J., and Tuttle, D. *Portfolio Management*, Charlottesville, VA; AIMR (forthcoming 2005).

Michaud, R. O. *Efficient Asset Management*, Boston: Harvard Business School Press, 1998.

———. *Investment Styles, Market Anomalies, and Global Stock Selection*, Charlottesville VA: The Research Foundation of the ICFA, 1999.

———. "The Markowitz Optimization Enigma: Is Optimized Optimal?" *Financial Analysts Journal*, January/February 1989.

Nesbitt, S. L. "Currency Hedging Rules for Plan Sponsors," *Financial Analysts Journal*, March/April 1991.

Pérold, A., and Schulman, E. "The Free Lunch in Currency Hedging: Implications for Investment Policies and Performance Standards," *Financial Analysts Journal*, May/June 1988.

Singer, B., and Terhaar, K. *Economic Foundations of Capital Market Returns*, Charlottesville, VA: Research Foundation of the Institute of Chartered Financial Analyst, 1997.

Solnik, B. "Currency Hedging and Siegel's Paradox: On Black's Universal Hedging Rule," *Review of International Economics*, June 1993.

———. "The Performance of International Asset Allocation Using Conditioning Information," *Journal of Empirical Finance*, March 1993a.

———. *Predictable Time-Varying Components of International Asset Returns*, Charlottesville, VA: The Research Foundation of Chartered Financial Analysts, 1993b.

Sortino, F. A., and Forsey, H. J. "On the Use and Misuse of Downside Risk," *Journal of Portfolio Management*, Winter 1996.

Terhaar, K., Staub, R., and Singer, B. "Asset Allocation: The Alternatives Approach," *Journal of Portfolio Management*, Spring 2003.

Watson Wyatt Worldwide, "The World's Largest Asset Managers," *Global Investment Review*, 2003 issue; www.watsonwyatt.com.

Glossary

Accrued interest Interest earned but not yet due and payable. This is equal to the next coupon to be paid on a bond multiplied by the time elapsed since the last payment date and divided by the total coupon period. Exact conventions differ across bond markets.

Actuarial yield The total yield on a bond, obtained by setting the bond's current market value equal to the discounted cash flows promised by the bond. Also called *yield to maturity*.

Agency trade A trade in which a broker acts as an agent only, not taking a position on the opposite side of the trade.

AIMR The Association for Investment Management and Research (AIMR®) awards the CFA® certification and sets professional standards that must be applied by its members worldwide.

American Depositary Receipt (ADR) A certificate of ownership issued by a U.S. bank to promote local trading in a foreign stock. The U.S. bank holds the foreign shares and issues ADRs against them.

American terms With reference to U.S. dollar exchange rate quotations, the U.S. dollar price of a unit of another currency.

American-type option An option that can be exercised at any time before expiration.

Amortizing swap An interest rate swap with a decreasing notional principal amount.

Arbitrage The simultaneous purchase of an undervalued asset or portfolio and sale of an overvalued but equivalent asset or portfolio, in order to obtain a riskless profit on the price differential. Taking advantage of a market inefficiency in a risk-free manner.

Arbitrage approach A common approach used to value derivative securities, based on an arbitrage strategy involving the underlying securities.

Ask price The price at which a market maker is willing to sell a security (also called *offer price*).

Asset allocation Dividing of investment funds among several asset classes to achieve diversification.

At-the-money option An option for which the strike (or exercise) price is close to (at) the current market price of the underlying asset.

Back office Settlement and related processes.

Back-to-back Transactions in which a loan is made in one currency against a loan in another currency.

Balance of payments   A record of all financial flows crossing the borders of a country during a given time period (a quarter or a year).

Balance of trade   See *Trade balance.*

Basis   The difference between the futures (or forward) price of an asset and its spot (or cash) price. The basis can be expressed as a value or as a percentage of the spot price.

Basis point   One hundredth of 1 percent (0.01%).

Basis risk   The risk that arises from fluctuation in the basis.

Basis swap   An interest rate swap involving two floating rates.

Bearer security   A negotiable security. All cash flows paid on the security are remitted to its bearer. No register of ownership is kept by the issuing company.

Benchmark   A standard measurement used to evaluate the performance of a portfolio. The benchmark may be some passive index or the aggregate performance on a universe of comparable portfolios (see *Composite*).

Benchmark bond   A bond representative of current market conditions and used for performance comparison.

Beta (β)   A statistical measure of market risk on a portfolio; traditionally used to estimate the elasticity of a stock portfolio's return relative to the market index.

Bid–ask spread   The difference between the quoted ask and the bid prices.

Bid price   The price at which a market maker is willing to buy a security.

Bilateral arbitrage   With reference to currencies, an arbitrage involving two currencies only.

Black-Scholes or Black-Scholes-Merton formula   A standard option pricing formula derived by F. Black and M. Scholes and also by R. Merton.

Bond   A long-term debt security with contractual obligations regarding interest payments and redemption.

Book value   The accounting value of a firm.

Bottom-up investing   With respect to investment approaches, a focus on selecting individual securities with whatever allocation of money to asset classes, countries, or industry securities results.

Bourse   A French term often used to refer to a stock market.

Brady bonds   Bonds issued by emerging countries under a debt-reduction plan named after Mr. Brady, former U.S. Secretary of the Treasury.

Break-even exchange rate   The future exchange rate such that the return in two bond markets would be even for a given maturity. Also called *implied forward exchange rate.*

Bretton Woods   The site of a 1944 conference that led to the establishment of a semifixed exchange rate system.

Broker   An agent who executes orders to buy or sell securities on behalf of a client in exchange for a commission.

Bull floating-rate note   A floating-rate note whose coupon increases if interest rates drop; an inverse floater.

Call auction   See *Fixing.*

Call option   A contract giving the right to buy an asset at a specific price on or before a specified date.

Cap   A contract on an interest rate, whereby at periodic payment dates, the writer of the cap pays the difference between the market interest rate and a specified cap rate if, and only if, this difference is positive. This is equivalent to a stream of call options on the interest rate.

Capital account   A component of the balance of payments that reflects unrequited (or unilateral) transfers corresponding to capital flows entailing no compensation (in the form of goods, services, or assets). Examples include investment capital given (without future repayment) in favor of poor countries, debt forgiveness, and expropriation losses.

Capital asset pricing model (CAPM)   An equilibrium theory that relates the expected return of an asset to its market risk (see *Beta*).

Cash-and-carry arbitrage   An arbitrage strategy with a simultaneous spot purchase and forward sale of an asset. The reverse transaction (borrowing the asset, selling it spot, and buying it forward) is known as a reverse cash and carry, or as a carry-and-cash arbitrage. These arbitrages lead to a relation between spot and forward, or futures, prices of the same asset.

Cash settlement   A procedure for settling futures contracts in which the cash difference between the futures price and the spot price is paid instead of physical delivery.

Clean price   The price of a bond obtained as the total price of the bond minus accrued interest. Most bonds are traded on the basis of their clean price.

Clearinghouse   An organization that settles and guarantees trades in some financial markets.

Closed-end fund   An investment company with a fixed number of shares. New shares cannot be issued and the old shares cannot be redeemed. Shares are traded in the marketplace, and their value may differ from the underlying net asset value of the fund.

Collar   A combination of a cap and a floor.

Composite   A universe of portfolios with similar investment objectives.

Conditional expected value   Expected value of a variable conditional on some available information set. The expected value changes over time with changes in the information set.

Conditional variance   Variance of a variable conditional on some available information set.

Consumer Price Index (CPI)   A price index defined on a basket of goods consumed.

Contract for difference (CFD)   A contract between an investor and a broker in which the investor receives (or pays) the difference between the price of the underlying share when the contract is closed and the price when the contract was opened.

Convexity   A measure of the change in duration with respect to changes in interest rates.

Cost of carry   The cost associated with holding some asset, including financing, storage, and insurance costs. Any yield received on the asset is treated as a negative carrying cost.

Covered option   An option position that is offset by an equal and opposite position in the underlying security.

Cross-rate   The exchange rate between two currencies, derived from their exchange rates with a third currency.

Currency exposure   The sensitivity of the asset return, measured in the investor's domestic currency, to a movement in the exchange rate.

Currency-option bond   A bond in which the coupons and/or the principal may be paid in more than one currency, at the option of the bondholder.

Currency overlay In currency risk management, the delegation of the management of currency risk in an international portfolio to a currency specialist.

Currency swap A contract to exchange streams of fixed cash flows denominated in two different currencies.

Current account A component of the balance of payments covering all current transactions that take place in the normal business of the residents of a country, such as exports and imports, services, income, and current transfers.

Dealer An agent that buys and sells securities as a principal (for its own account) rather than as a broker for clients. A dealer may function, at different times, as a broker or as a dealer. Sometimes called a *market maker*.

Default risk The risk that an issuer will be unable to make interest and principal payments on time.

Delta (δ) Ratio of change in the option price to a small change in the price of the underlying asset. Also equal to the derivative of the option price with respect to the asset price.

Delta hedge A dynamic hedging strategy using options with continuous adjustment of the number of options used, as a function of the delta of the option.

Derivatives Securities bearing a contractual relation to some underlying asset or rate. Options, futures, forward, and swap contracts, as well as many forms of bonds, are derivative securities.

Devaluation Deliberate downward adjustment of a currency against its fixed parity.

Direct exchange rate The amount of local or domestic currency required to purchase one unit of foreign currency.

Dual-currency bond A bond with coupons fixed in one currency and principal repayment fixed in another currency.

Duration A measure of an option-free bond's average maturity. Specifically, the weighted average maturity of all future cash flows paid by a security, in which the weights are the present value of these cash flows as a fraction of the bond's price. More importantly, a measure of a bond's price sensitivity to interest rate movements (see *Modified duration*).

EAFE index A stock index for Europe, Australia, and the Far East published by Morgan Stanley Capital International.

Early stage With reference to venture capital financing, the stage associated with moving into operation and before commercial manufacturing and sales have occurred. Includes the start-up and first stages.

Earnings multiplier See *Price–earnings ratio*.

Economic risk As used in currency risk management, the risk that arises when the foreign currency value of a foreign investment reacts systematically to an exchange rate movement.

Efficient frontier The set of all efficient portfolios for various levels of risk.

Efficient market A market in which any relevant information is immediately impounded in asset prices.

Efficient portfolio A portfolio that provides the best expected return for a given level of risk.

Electronic communications networks Order-driven trading systems in which the book of limit orders plays a central role.

Electronic crossing networks Order-driven trading systems in which market orders are anonymously matched at prespecified times at prices determined in the primary market for the system.

Endogenous growth theory A theory of economic growth that does not assume that the marginal productivity of capital declines as capital is added.

Euribor Interbank offer rate for short-term deposits in euros. Euribor is determined by an association of European banks.

Euro The common currency of many European countries.

Eurobond A bond underwritten by a multinational syndicate of banks and placed mainly in countries other than the country of the issuer; sometimes called an *international bond.*

Eurocurrency market Interbank market for short-term borrowing and lending in a currency outside of its home country. For example, borrowing and lending of U.S. dollars outside the United States. Thus, it is an offshore market escaping national regulations. This is the largest money market for several major currencies.

Eurodollar market The U.S. dollar segment of the Eurocurrency market.

European Monetary System A formal arrangement linking some, but not all, of the currencies of the EU.

European terms With reference to U.S. dollar exchange rate quotations, the price of a U.S. dollar in terms of another currency.

European Union (EU) A formal association of European countries founded by the Treaty of Rome in 1957. Formerly known as the EEC.

European-type option An option that can be exercised only at expiration.

Exchange traded funds (ETFs) A type of mutual fund traded like other shares on a stock market, having special characteristics particularly related to redemption, and generally designed to closely track the performance of a specified stock market index.

Ex-dividend A synonym for "without dividend." The buyer of a security ex-dividend does not receive the next dividend.

Exercise price See *Strike price.*

Expected return The rate of return that an investor expects to get on an investment.

Expiry The expiration date of a derivative security.

Face value The amount paid on a bond at redemption and traditionally printed on the bond certificate. This face value excludes the final coupon payment. Sometimes referred to as *par value.*

Fair value The theoretical value of a security based on current market conditions. The fair value is the value such that no arbitrage opportunities exist.

Financial account A component of the balance of payments covering investments by residents abroad and investments by nonresidents in the home country. Examples include direct investment made by companies, portfolio investments in equity and bonds, and other investments and liabilities.

Fixed exchange rate regime A system in which the exchange rate between two currencies remains fixed at a preset level, known as official parity.

Fixing A method for determining the market price of a security by finding the price that balances buyers and sellers. A fixing takes place periodically each day at defined times. Sometimes called a *call auction.*

Flexible exchange rate system   A system in which exchange rates are determined by supply and demand.

Floating-rate note (FRN)   Bond issued with variable quarterly or semiannual interest rate payments, generally linked to LIBOR.

Floor   A contract on an interest rate, whereby the writer of the floor periodically pays the difference between a specified floor rate and the market interest rate if, and only if, this difference is positive. This is equivalent to a stream of put options on the interest rate.

Foreign bond   A bond issued by a foreign company on the local market and in the local currency (e.g., Yankee bonds in the United States, Bulldog bonds in the United Kingdom, or Samurai bonds in Japan).

Foreign currency risk premium   The expected movement in the (direct) exchange rate minus the interest rate differential (domestic risk-free rate minus foreign risk-free rate).

Foreign exchange   The purchase (sale) of a currency against the sale (purchase) of another.

Foreign exchange controls   Various forms of government-imposed controls on the purchase (sale) of foreign currencies by residents or on the purchase (sale) of local currency by nonresidents.

Foreign exchange expectation   A relation that states that the forward exchange rate, quoted at time 0 for delivery at time 1, is equal to the expected value of the spot exchange rate at time 1. When stated relative to the current spot exchange rate, the relation states that the forward discount (premium) is equal to the expected exchange rate movement.

Foreign exchange parity   A foreign exchange rate of two currencies that is officially fixed by international agreement.

Forex   Foreign exchange.

Formative stage   With respect to venture capital financing, the seed and early stages.

Forward contract   A customized contract to buy (sell) an asset at a specified date and a specified price (forward price). No payment takes place until maturity.

Forward discount or premium   Refers to the percentage difference between the forward exchange rate and the spot exchange rate (premium if positive, discount if negative).

Forward rate agreement (FRA)   An agreement between two parties that will apply to a future notional loan or deposit.

Franchise value   In P/E ratio analysis, the present value of growth opportunities divided by next year's expected earnings.

Full price (or dirty price)   The total price of a bond, including accrued interest.

Futures contract   A standardized contract to buy (sell) an asset at a specified date and a specified price (futures price). The contract is traded on an organized exchange, and the potential gain/loss is realized each day (marking to market).

Generic   See *Plain-vanilla.*

Gilt (or Gilt-edged)   A U.K. government bond.

Global Investment Perfomance Standards™ (GIPS®)   A global industry standard for the ethical presentation of investment performance results promulgated by the Association for Investment Management and Research.

Gold standard   An international monetary system in which the parity of a currency is fixed in terms of its gold content.

Gray market   A forward market for newly issued bonds before the final terms on the bond are set.

Gross domestic product (GDP)   Total value of a country's output produced by residents within the country's physical borders.

Gross national product (GNP)   Total value of a country's output produced by residents both within the country's physical borders and abroad.

Group of Seven (G-7)   The seven countries (Canada, France, Germany, Italy, Japan, the United Kingdom, and the United States) that meet periodically to enhance cooperative action on international economic matters. [The Group of Eight (G-8) includes Russia.]

Hedge fund   A type of investment vehicle often set up as a limited partnership, limited liability corporation, or offshore corporation to be exempt from most governmental regulation.

Hedge ratio   The percentage of the position in an asset that is hedged with derivatives.

Hedging   The process of reducing the uncertainty of the future value of a portfolio by taking positions in various derivatives (e.g., forward and futures contracts).

Herfindahl index   A measure of industry concentration equal to the sum of the squared market shares of the firms in the industry.

Implementation shortfall   With respect to execution costs, the difference between the value of the executed portfolio or share position and the value of the same portfolio at the time the trading decision was made.

Implied forward exchange rate   See *Break-even exchange rate.*

Implied volatility   The volatility of an asset that is implicit in the current market price of an option (using a standard Black-Scholes-Merton formula).

In-the-money option   An option that has a positive value if exercised immediately. For example, a call when the strike price is below the current price of the underlying asset, or a put when the strike price is above the current price of the underlying asset.

Index-linked bond   A bond whose interest rate payments and/or redemption value are contractually linked to some specified index (e.g., a commodity price).

Indirect exchange rate   The amount of foreign currency required to purchase one unit of domestic currency.

Information ratio   The ratio of excess return over the benchmark to tracking error relative to the benchmark.

Initial margin   The amount that an investor must deposit to open a position in futures and some other derivatives; also used to refer to the initial equity required when a stock is purchased using borrowed money.

Insuring   The process of setting a minimum level for the future value of a portfolio by taking positions in various derivatives (e.g., options).

Interest rate parity   An arbitrage process that ensures that the forward discount or premium equals the interest rate differential between two currencies.

Interest rate swap   A contract to exchange streams of fixed-interest-rate for floating-interest-rate cash flows denominated in the same currency.

Internal Rate of Return (IRR)   The discount rate that equates the present value of a future stream of cash flows to the initial investment.

International CAPM   An equilibrium theory that relates the expected return of an asset to its world market and foreign exchange risks.

International Fisher relation   The assertion that the interest rate differential between two countries should equal the expected inflation rate differential over the term of the interest rates.

International Monetary Fund (IMF)   An organization set up in 1944 to promote exchange rate stability and to assist member countries facing economic difficulties.

International Securities Market Association (ISMA)   An association formed in 1969 to establish uniform trading procedures in the international bond markets. Formerly named AIBD.

International Swaps and Derivatives Association (ISDA)   An association of swap dealers formed in 1985 to promote uniform practices in the writing, trading, and settlement procedures of swaps and other derivatives.

Intrinsic value   The value that would be obtained on an option if it were to be exercised immediately.

Investment company   A firm that issues (sells) shares, and uses the proceeds to invest in various financial instruments or other assets.

Later stage   With respect to venture capital financing, the stage after commercial manufacturing and sales have begun. Later-stage financing includes second-stage, third-stage, and mezzanine financing.

Lead manager   The bank in charge of organizing a syndicated bank credit or a bond issue.

Leverage   The relation between the value of the asset position and the amount of equity invested.

LIBMEAN   The average of LIBID and LIBOR.

Limit order   An order to buy or sell a security at a specific price or better (lower for a buy order and higher for a sell order).

Limit pricing   Pricing below average cost to deter entry into an industry.

Local currency (foreign currency) exposure   The sensitivity of the asset return, measured in the asset's local currency, to a movement in the exchange rate.

London Interbank Bid (LIBID)   The rate quoted to a top-quality lender on the London interbank market.

London InterBank Offer Rate (LIBOR)   The rate at which international banks lend on the Eurocurrency market. This is the rate quoted to a top-quality borrower. The most common maturities are one month, three months, and six months. There is a LIBOR for the U.S. dollar and a few other major currencies. LIBOR is determined by the British Banking Association in London. See also *Euribor*.

Long hedge   A hedge involving the purchase of forward or futures contracts in anticipation of a spot purchase. Also known as anticipatory hedge.

Maintenance margin   The minimum margin that an investor must keep on deposit in a margin account at all times.

Margin deposit   The amount of cash or securities that must be deposited as guarantee on a futures position. The margin is a returnable deposit.

Market impact   With reference to execution costs, the difference between the actual execution price and the market price that would have prevailed had the manager not sought to trade the security.

Market maker   An institution or individual quoting firm bid and ask prices for a security and standing ready to buy or sell the security at those quoted prices. Also called a *dealer*.

Market order   An order to buy (sell) immediately at the best obtainable price.

Marking to market   Procedure whereby potential profits and losses on a futures position are realized daily. The daily futures price variation is debited (credited) in cash to the loser (winner) at the end of the day.

Mezzanine financing   With respect to venture capital financing, capital provided to prepare for the step of going public. Also known as bridge financing.

Minimum-variance hedge ratio   The hedge ratio that is expected to minimize the variance of the rate of return on the hedged portfolio.

Modified duration   Measure of a bond's price sensitivity to interest rate movements. Equal to the duration of a bond divided by one plus its yield to maturity.

Money-weighted return   A rate of return measure corresponding to the internal rate of return; captures a return on average invested capital.

Mutual fund   An open-end investment company. Also called unit trust in the United Kingdom and some other countries.

Neoclassical growth theory   A theory of economic growth that assumes that the marginal productivity of capital declines as more capital is added.

Net asset value   The market value of the assets owned by a fund.

Offer price   The price at which a market maker is willing to sell a security (also called *ask price*).

Official reserves   The amount of reserves owned by the central bank of a government in the form of gold, Special Drawing Rights, and foreign cash or marketable securities.

Open-end fund   An investment company that continuously offers to sell new shares, or redeem them, at prices based on the market value of the assets owned by the fund (net asset value).

Open interest   The total number of futures or option contracts that have not been closed out by offset or fulfilled delivery.

Opportunity cost   With reference to execution costs, the loss (or gain) incurred as the result of failure or delay in the execution of a trade, or failure to complete a trade in full.

Option premium   The price of an option.

Order-driven market   A market without active market makers in which buy-and-sell orders directly confront each other; an auction market.

Out-of-the-money option   An option that has no value if exercised immediately. For example, a call when the strike price is above the current price of the underlying asset, or a put when the strike price is below the current price of the underlying asset.

Overnight   A deal from today to the next business day.

Over-the-counter (OTC)   A market for securities made up of dealers. It is not an organized exchange, and trading usually takes place by telephone or other electronic means.

Par value   The principal amount repaid at maturity of a bond. Also called *face value*.

Par yield curve The yield curve drawn for government coupon bonds of different maturities that trade at, or around, par.

Pegged exchange rate regime A system in which a country's exchange rate in relation to a major currency is set at a target value (the peg) but allowed to fluctuate within a small band around the target.

Performance appraisal The assessment of an investment record for evidence of investment skill.

Performance attribution The attribution of investment performance to specific investment decisions (such as asset allocation and country weighting).

Perpetual bond A bond with no stated maturity.

Pip The smallest incremental move an exchange rate can make, i.e., the last decimal place in a quote.

Plain-vanilla Refers to a security, especially a bond or a swap, issued with standard features. Sometimes called *generic*.

Point One percent (1%).

Predatory pricing Pricing below average cost to drive competitors out of the industry.

Present value The current worth of a future cash flow. Obtained by discounting the future cash flow at the market-required rate of return.

Price-driven market A market in which dealers (market makers) adjust their quotes continuously to reflect supply and demand; also known as a dealer market.

Price–earnings ratio (P/E ratio) The ratio of the stock market price to the earnings per share. Sometimes called *earnings multiplier*.

Principal trade A trade through a broker who guarantees full execution at specified discount/premium to the prevailing price.

Purchasing power parity (PPP) A theory stating that the exchange rate between two currencies will exactly reflect the purchasing power of the two currencies.

Put–call parity The theoretical relation between a put and a call option with the same underlying strike price, asset, and expiration.

Put option A contract giving the right to sell an asset at a specified price, on or before a specified date.

Quanto An option in which the foreign exchange risk in the underlying asset has been removed.

Random walk theory A theory stating that all current information is reflected in current security prices and that future price movements are random because they are caused by unexpected news.

Rating evaluation Performed by a credit rating agency, such as Moody's or Standard & Poor's, to assign a rating to an issue's investment quality.

Real exchange rate The exchange rate adjusted by the inflation differential between the two countries.

Real foreign currency risk The risk that real prices of consumption goods might not be identical in different countries. Also known as real exchange rate risk, or purchasing power risk.

Real interest rate The interest rate adjusted by the inflation rate of the country.

Risk allocation   The decomposition of the risk of a portfolio into the various risk exposures taken by a manager.

Risk aversion   Describes the fact that investors want to minimize risk for the same level of expected return. To take more risk, they require compensation by a risk premium.

Risk budgeting   In a portfolio management context, the setting of risk limits for individual managers.

Risk premium   The difference between the expected return on an asset and the risk-free interest rate.

Seed stage   With reference to venture capital financing, the stage associated with product development and market research.

Settlement price   The official closing price of a futures contract set by the clearinghouse at the end of the day and used for marking to market.

Sharpe ratio   The ratio of mean excess return (return minus the risk-free rate) to standard deviation of returns (or excess returns).

Short hedge   A hedge involving the sale of forward or futures contracts to cover the risk of a long position in the spot market.

Short sale   The sale of a security not owned by the seller at the time of trade.

Sinking fund   Bond provision that requires the bond to be paid off progressively rather than in full at maturity.

Sovereign risk   The risk that a government may default on its debt.

Special Drawing Right (SDR)   An artificial official reserve asset held on the books of the IMF.

Spot price   Current market price of an asset. Also called cash price.

Spread   Difference between the ask and the bid quotations. Also refers to a mark-up paid by a given borrower over the market interest rate paid by a top-quality borrower.

Standard deviation of return   A common measure of risk, often calculated using a time series of returns observed over the past. Equal to the square root of the variance.

Straight bond   Refers to a plain-vanilla bond with fixed coupon payments and without any optional clauses.

Strategic asset allocation   The allocation to the major investment asset classes that is determined to be appropriate, given the investor's long-run investment objectives and constraints.

Strike price   Price at which an option can be exercised (same as exercise price).

Structured note   A bond or note issued with some unusual, often option-like, clause.

Swap   A contract whereby two parties agree to a periodic exchange of cash flows. In certain types of swaps, only the net difference between the amounts owed is exchanged on each payment date.

Swaption   An option to enter into a swap contract at a later date.

Tactical asset allocation   Short-term adjustments to the long-term asset allocation to reflect views on the current relative attractiveness of asset classes.

Tap   Procedure by which a borrower can keep issuing additional amounts of an old bond at its current market value. This procedure is used for bond issues, notably by the British and French governments, as well as for some short-term debt instruments.

Technical analysis   A forecasting method for asset prices based solely on information about past prices.

Term structure   See *Yield curve.*

Time-weighted return   A rate of return measure that captures the rate of return per unit of currency initially invested.

Tombstone (or **Tumbstone**)   Advertisement that states the borrower's name, gives the conditions of an issue, and lists the various banks taking part in the issue.

Top-down   With respect to investment approaches, the allocation of money first to categories such as asset classes, countries, or industry followed by the selection of individual securities within category.

Trade balance   The balance of a country's exports and imports; part of the current account.

Tranche   Refers to a portion of an issue that is designed for a specific category of investors. French for "slice."

Translation risk   Risk arising from the translation of the value of an asset or flow from a foreign currency to the domestic currency.

Triangular arbitrage   With respect to currencies, an arbitrage involving three currencies only.

Uncovered interest rate parity   The assertion that expected currency depreciation should offset the interest differential between two countries over the term of the interest rate.

Underlying   Refers to a security on which a derivative contract is written.

Unitary hedge ratio   A hedge ratio equal to 1.

Value at risk (VaR)   A money measure of the minimum loss that is expected over a given period of time with a given probability.

Value chain   The set of transformations to move from raw material to product or service delivery.

Variation margin   Profits or losses on open positions in futures and option contracts that are paid or collected daily.

Volatility   A measure of the uncertainty about the future price of an asset. Typically measured by the standard deviation of returns on the asset.

Wholesale Price Index (WPI)   A price index defined on a basket of goods produced.

Withholding tax   A tax levied by the country of source on income paid.

World Bank   A supranational organization of several institutions designed to assist developing countries. The International Bank for Reconstruction and Development (IBRD) and the International Finance Corporation (IFC) are the more important members of the World Bank group.

Writer of an option   A term used for the person or institution selling an option and therefore granting the right to exercise it to the buyer of the option.

Yield curve   A curve showing the relationship between yield (interest rate) and maturity for a set of similar securities. For example, the yield curve can be drawn for U.S. Treasuries or for LIBOR. Typically, different yield curves are drawn for zero-coupon bonds (zero-coupon yield curve) and for coupon bonds quoted at par (par yield curve).

Yield to maturity   The total yield on a bond obtained by equating the bond's current market value to the discounted cash flows promised by the bond. Also called *actuarial yield*.

Zero-coupon bond   A bond paying no coupons until final redemption. Such bonds trade at a discount to their face value so that the price differential (face value minus market price) ultimately provides a return to the investor commensurate with current interest rates.

Index

Page numbers followed by n refer to footnotes.

Absolute PPP, 46, 59
Absolute risk, 638
Accounting
    equity method of, 250
    performance measurement vs., 617
    pooling method of, 247
    purchase method of, 247, 248
    uniting of interest method of, 247
Accounting standards. *See also* Generally accepted accounting principles (GAAP); International Accounting Standards (AIS)
    earnings and stock prices and, 254–255
    global, 247–253
    historical setting for, 243–244
    international differences in GAAP and, 255–256
    international harmonization of, 244–246
    national, 242–243
    overview of, 205–206
Acquisitions, 414
Active approach, 689–690
Adler, M., 153n, 158, 181, 583n, 613, 711n, 736
Advisers, 686–687
Agency trades, 212
Aggregation vehicles, 388
AIMR-PPS®, 648
Aked, M., 279n, 309, 484n, 505
Alexander, G. J., 143n, 183, 372, 449
Allen, H., 117n, 129
Allsopp, Christopher, 99
Alpha, 372–373, 641
Alpha transfer, 538
Alternative investments
    closely held companies and inactively traded securities as, 424–425
    commodities as, 426, 428–433
    distressed securities as, 425–427
    exchange traded funds as, 377–386
    features of, 372–373
    hedge funds as, 406, 408–424
    real estate as, 386–391
    venture capital as, 398, 400–406
Ambachtsheer, K. P., 736
Amenc, N., 417n, 447

American Depositary Receipts (ADR)
    advantages and disadvantages of, 217–218
    foreign listing and, 215–216
    grantor trusts as, 378
    value of, 217
American terms, 4
American-type options, 542
Amortizing swaps, 531–532
Amsterdam Bourse, 186
Anderson, R., 432n, 448
Ang, A., 482, 505
Angel, J. J., 127, 135n
Anglo-American model of accounting principles, 244
Ankrim, E. M., 637, 674
Annaert, J., 89
Annualized forward premium, 15
APB, 643
Arbitrage
    bilateral, 10–12
    cross-rates and, 7–10
    explanation of, 7
    interest rate parity and, 100
    risk, 414
    triangular, 7, 12–14
ARCH models, 113, 134
ARIMA process, 132–133
Arnott, R., 89, 118n, 127, 700n, 736
Artificial intelligence, 135–136
Artificial neural networks (ANN), 136
Askin, David, 418
Askin Capital, 417, 418
Ask price, 5
Asness, C., 423n, 448, 644n, 674, 701n, 736
Asset allocation. *See also* International diversification
    insurance companies and, 684
    investment policy statement and, 697–698
    optimizing global, 464, 466–468, 715–719
    performance attribution and, 632–633
    specialized approach and, 691
    strategic, 706–711
    structuring and quantifying, 712–719
    tactical, 711–712
Asset/liability management (ALM), 715n

Asset market approach
    challenges of, 76–77
    exchange rate dynamics and, 72–76
    explanation of, 70–71
    interest rates and, 71–72
Asset pricing. *See also* Capital asset-pricing model (CAPM)
    asset returns and exchange rate movements and, 146–147
    currency hedging and, 158–161
    domestic CAPM and, 143–149
    estimating currency exposures and, 161–169
    international CAPM and, 150–157
    market imperfections and segmentation and, 157–158
    tests of ICAPM and, 169–170
Assets
    accounting standards for, 251
    classes of, 698–699
    reevaluation of, 250
    return on, 279–280
Association for Investment Management and Research (AIMR), 648, 649, 685
Auction markets, 189
Autoregressive integrated moving average (ARIMA) estimations, 113

Baca, S., 484n, 505
Back-end load, 374
Bailey, Jeffrey V., 143n, 183, 372, 449
Baillie, R. T., 110, 114n, 127
Balanced approach, 691
Balance of payments
    exchange rate determination and, 62–70
    explanation of, 34–45, 92
    of France, 37
    of Japan, 37
    of United Kingdom, 37
Bankers' bourses, 187
Bank of England, 114–115, 117
Base currency
    explanation of, 617
    rate of return in, 628–629
Basis risk, 580–581
Basis swaps, 531

Baumol, W., 309
Bavishi, V. B., 254, 310
Bear FRNs, 352–353
Beebower, Gilbert L., 707, 736
Bekaert, G., 105n, 111n, 114n, 127, 132n,
    170, 181, 234, 482, 488, 505, 712, 736
Benchmarks
  comparison with, 646–648
  currency allocation in, 708–711
  scope of global, 706–707
  weights in global, 707–708
Bentsen, Lloyd, 115
Bernstein, P. L., 700n, 736
Bernstein, Richard, 374n
Besanko, D., 268n, 309
Best execution, 206. *See also* Execution costs
Beta, 144, 145
Bhushan, R., 256, 309
Bid-ask spread
  cross-rate calculations with, 7–10
  execution costs and, 207
  explanation of, 5–6, 14–15
  triangular arbitrage and, 12–14
Bid price, 5
Big Mac Index, 57–59
Bilateral arbitrage, 10–12
Bilson, I., 118n, 127
Black, F., 158n, 182, 546, 549, 570, 711, 717,
    736
Blake, D., 707, 736
Boland, Vincent, 533n
Bollerslev, T., 110, 127, 134n
Bond futures, 514–516, 522
Bond indexes, 315–316
Bond markets
  correlation across, 462–463
  international diversification and, 467–468
  size of, 314–315
  transaction costs in, 479
Bonds
  bear FRN, 352–353
  Brady, 320–322
  bull FRNs, 351–352
  commodity-linked, 432–433
  coupon characteristics of, 324–325
  with coupons, 330–331
  credit spreads for, 334–335
  currency exposure of, 168
  currency-hedging strategies for, 339–340
  currency-option, 356–358
  debt-conversion, 322
  discount, 322
  domestic, 313
  dual-currency, 353–356
  duration and interest rate sensitivity of,
    332–333
  Eurobond, 316–320, 325
  floating-rate notes, 344–350
  foreign, 313
  front-loaded interest-reduction, 322
  hedge ratio for, 526–527
  historical background of, 312
  international portfolio strategies for,
    340–344
  international yield curve comparisons for,
    335–338
  issued by emerging countries, 320
  legal and fiscal aspects of, 326–327
  new-money, 322
  notational, 514, 515

overview of, 313–314
par, 322
past-due interest, 322
quotations for, 6–7, 324
return and risk on foreign, 338–339
types of, 6–7, 313, 323
yields for, 325–326
zero-coupon, 328–329
Bonser-Neal, C., 220, 234
Bookstaber, R., 475, 505
Bottom-up approach, 692–693
Bouhara, Yassine, 533
Box, G. E., 127, 132
Boyer, B., 481n, 505
Brady bonds
  characteristics of, 321–322
  explanation of, 320
  historical background of, 320–321
Brandenberger, A., 267, 309
Branson, W. H., 182
Brauer, G., 234, 432n, 448
Break-even exchange rates, 337
Bretton Woods system, 95, 114
Brian, P., 736
Brightman, C., 279n, 309, 484n, 505
Brinson, G., 707, 736
British Venture Capital Association, 406
Briys, E., 583n, 614
Brokers, 685–686
Brown, K., 183, 310, 640n, 645n, 674
Brown, S. J., 423n, 448, 674
Brunner, K., 128
Bull FRNs, 351–352
Burmeister, E., 294, 309
Business cycle, 258, 260
Business-cycle factor, 295
Buyer power, 270

CAC 40 index, 377, 382
Call auction system, 189, 190
Calls, 542, 543n, 549
CalPERS, 478
Calverley, J., 258, 309
Campbell, John Y., 699n, 736
Canova, F., 309
Capital account, 35n, 64
Capital asset-pricing model (CAPM). *See also*
    Asset pricing; International CAPM
  assumptions of, 143–144, 464
  extended to international context, 147–149
  international, 150–160, 169–170
  intuition and, 145
  risk-pricing relation and, 144–145
  separation theorem and, 144
Capital market expectations
  asset classes and, 698–699
  explanation of, 698
  long-term, 699–705
  short-term, 705–706
CAPM. *See* Capital-asset pricing model
    (CAPM)
Carey, Susan, 427n
Case studies, 720–735
Cassel, G., 89
Cavaglia, S., 105n, 127, 279n, 309, 484n, 505
Central Bank of Ireland, 259
Central banks, 114–116
Chamberlain, M., 379n, 448
Chance, D., 549, 570
Chaos theory, 113, 134–135

Chaotic systems, 135
Chartism analysis, 112–114
Chen, N., 309
Chernoff, Joel, 476n
Cheung, Y-W., 102n, 127
Chicago Board of Trade, 522
Chicago Mercantile Exchange (CME), 508,
    509, 511, 543, 573
Choi, F.D.S., 256, 310
Chou, R. Y., 127, 134n
Christensen, C., 264, 310
Closed-end country funds
  advantages and disadvantages of, 221
  explanation of, 218–219
  pricing of, 219–221
Closely held companies, 424–425
Clow, Robert, 407n
Coenen, Thijs, 643
Collin-Dufresne, P., 370
Commingled funds, 388
Commingled Real Estate Equity Fund
    (CREF), 397
Commodities
  explanation of, 426, 428
  future contracts for, 428
  gold as, 430–432
  motivation for investing in, 428–430
Commodity-linked bonds, 432–433
Commodity-linked equity, 433
Competition
  along value chain, 269
  among companies in industry, 269–270
  market, 268–269
Competitive advantage, 266
Competitive strategies, 267
Composites, 649
Compound annual growth rates (CAGR),
    242
Confidence factor, 294–295
Conrad, J., 234
Consolidation, accounting standards for,
    248–249
Constant compounded annual growth rate
    (CAGR), 284
Consultants, 686–687
Continental model of accounting principles,
    244
Contract for difference (CFD), 553–554
Conversion factor, 515
Cook, Allan, 249
Cooper, I., 169, 182
Co-opetition, 267, 269
Cornell, B., 522n, 570
Cost approach, to real estate valuation,
    389
Counterparty credit risk, 417
Country analysis
  business cycle synchronization and, 260
  explanation of, 256–258
  growth theory and, 261–262
  industry valuation vs., 277–279
  limitation of country concept and, 262
Country approach, 692
Country funds, closed-end, 218–221
Covered call writing, 549–550
Credit spread, 334–335
Crièe system, 189
Cross-hedges, 582
Crossing, 211–212
Crossover of moving averages, 113

Cross-rates
  calculation of, 7–10
  explanation of, 7
  principles applied to, 5–6
  principles of, 5–6
Cumby, R. E., 90
Currencies. *See also* Exchange rates; Foreign
    exchange markets
  abbreviations for, 4
  appreciation and depreciation of, 38–40
  base, 617
  forward and future transactions in, 511–512
  investment approach toward, 694
  movement in, 291–292
  rate of return in base, 628–629
  rate of return in local, 627–628
  strengthening and weakening of, 3
  token-based, 93–95
Currency boards, 96
Currency exposure
  of bonds, 168
  economic vs. accounting, 168
  estimation of, 161–162
  explanation of, 162–163
  of individual companies, 163–165
  of national economies and equity markets,
    166–167
Currency futures, 511–512, 520–521
Currency hedge funds, 115–117
Currency hedging
  explanation of, 158–159, 648
  strategies for, 339–340, 582–584
  use of, 690
Currency-interest rate swaps, 531
Currency-option bonds
  explanation of, 356–358
  value of, 358–359
Currency options, 543–544
Currency overlay, 595
Currency-overlay managers, 694
Currency risk
  for alpha strategies, 593
  in emerging markets, 489
  explanation of, 471–472, 480
  international diversification and, 455–457
Currency risk management
  currency exposure management and,
    590–592
  currency overlay and, 592–595
  hedging with futures or forward currency
    contracts and, 573–584, 636
  insuring and hedging with options and,
    584–590
Currency risk premium, 709
Currency swaps, 511, 530, 534, 536
Current account, 34–35, 63–64
Current account deficit
  effects of, 36–37
  explanation of, 35
  financial account surplus and, 35–36
  sustainability of large, 37–38
Custodians, 687
Custody costs, 479

DaimlerChrysler, 216
Dale, C., 583n, 614
Data mining, 136–137
Data snooping, 137
DAX 30 index, 377, 382
Debt-conversion bonds (DCBs), 322

De Ceuster, M., 89
Decomposition
  risk, 634, 643
  total return, 629, 630, 637
Default swaps, 532
Defined benefit pension plans (DBs),
    682–683
Defined contribution pension plans (DCs),
    683
DeFusco, R. A., 455n, 505, 716, 736
Delta, 548
Delta hedge, 589
Demand analysis, 263
De Nicolo, G., 309
Derivatives.
  accounting standards for, 251
  explanation of, 507–508, 572
  forward and futures as, 508–528
  options as, 542–553
  strategies for, 553–555
  swaps as, 528–542
Derkum, Markus, 399–400
de Roon, F., 484n, 506
De Santis, G., 169, 170, 182
Deterministic models, 134–135
Deutsche Bank, 407, 687
Deutsche Boerse, 190, 194
Diamonds Trust Series, 383
Diermeier, J., 182, 485, 505
Dietz method, 621–622, 624n
Dimson, E., 736
Dinning. W., 221, 235
Direct exchange rate, 4
Direct quotes, 4
Disclosure of Accounting Policies
    (International Accounting Standards
    Committee), 244
Discount bonds (DISCs), 322
Discounted after-tax cash flow approach,
    393–396
Discounted cash flow analysis (DCF), 242,
    284
Distressed securities, 425–426
Distressed securities funds, 413
Distribution fees, 374
Diversification. *See* International diversification
Divestment, venture capital, 403, 404
Dividend discount model (DDM), 284–286
DJGI, 203
Dollar
  cross-rates with, 8–9
  fall in, 67–68
  quotation for exchange rate for, 16
Dollar-weighted return. *See* Money-weighted
    return (MWR)
Domestic bonds, 313, 320. *See also* Bonds
Domestic capital asset-pricing model. *See*
    Capital asset-pricing model (CAPM)
Domestic currency (DC)
  explanation of, 4, 5
  interest rate parity and, 16–18, 20
  to measure asset returns, 146–147
Dominguez, K. M., 110n, 114n, 127
Domowitz, I., 191, 234
Dornbusch, R., 90
Dow Jones Industrial Average (DJIA), 202
Dranove, D., 268n, 309
Dual-currency bonds
  explanation of, 353–354
  value of, 355–356

Duffee, G. M., 350n, 370, 536n
Duffie, D., 570
Dumas, B., 106n, 127, 153n, 158, 169, 181
DuPont model, 279
Duration, for bonds, 332–333, 343

EAFE index, 203, 461, 636, 689
Eaker, M., 583n, 614
Earnings statements, 240, 254–255
East Indies Trading Company, 186
Econometric model, 111–112
Economic growth
  currency appreciation and depreciation
    and, 40
  stock market performance and, 260
Economic risk, 578
E-Crossnet, 194
Efficient frontier
  for bonds, 467, 468
  explanation of, 458
  for non-U.S. investors, 468, 469
  for stocks, 466, 468
Efficient markets
  asset pricing in, 143 (*See also* Asset
    pricing)
  explanation of, 140–143
  forward exchange rates and, 108–110
  liquidity and, 477–478
  price manipulation and insider trading
    and, 478
  stock valuation and, 283–284
Eichholtz, P.M.A., 398, 448
Electronic communication networks,
    (ECNs), 193
Electronic crossing networks (ECNs),
    193–194
Elton, E., 143n, 182
Emanuelli, J. F., 712, 736
Emerging index, 487
Emerging-market funds, 413
Emerging markets
  bonds issued by, 320
  correlation in, 488–489
  currency risk in, 489
  explanation of, 197, 198
  investability of, 490
  overview of, 486–488
  portfolio return performance in, 489–490
  segmentation in, 491
  volatility in, 486, 488
Employee Retirement Income Security Act
    (ERISA), 648
Employee stock options, 251–254
Endogenous growth theory, 261
Endowments, 684
Energy companies, 433
Engle, R., 127, 134n
English, W. B., 481n, 482, 506
Enron Corporation, 248, 249
Equities markets. *See also* Emerging markets
  concentration of, 198–199
  developed, 195–197
  efficient, 108–110, 140–143
  emerging, 197, 198
  historical differences in, 186–187
  integrated, 141–142
  international diversification and, 452–454
  liquidity of, 197–198
  segmented, 141–143, 157–158, 170
  size of, 195–198

Equity
  commodity-linked, 433
  correlation estimates and, 459–461
  free and clear, 387
  leveraged, 387
  return over, 280, 286–288
Equity analysis
  effect of inflation on stock prices and,
    289–291
  franchise value and growth process and,
    286–288
  global financial ratio analysis and,
    279–281
  industry valuation or country valuation and,
    277–279
  inflation-like effects of currency movements
    on stock prices and, 291–292
  market efficiency in individual stock valua-
    tion and, 283–284
  valuation models and, 284–286
Equity premium puzzle, 699n
Equity swaps, 532
Equity valuation
  competition structure and, 265–266
  competitive advantage and, 266
  competitive strategies and, 267
  co-opetition and value net and, 267
  demand analysis and, 263
  industry life cycle and, 264–265
  overview of, 262–263
  sector rotation and, 267–268
  value creation and, 263–264
Erb, C. B., 488, 491, 505
Errunza, V., 158n, 182
Eun, C., 158n, 182, 220, 235
EUREX, 513
Euribor, 513, 514
Euro
  background of, 97–98
  bonds denominated in, 313–314
  cross-rates with, 8–9
  European stability and growth pact and,
    98–99
  issues related to, 93–95
  value of, 3
Eurobonds
  clearing system for, 319–320
  coupons for, 325
  dealing in, 319
  domestic vs., 316, 318
  example of, 317
  explanation of, 313, 314
  issued by emerging countries, 320
  issue of, 318–319
  legal and fiscal aspects of, 326, 327
  market for, 314–316
Euronext, 194
Euronext-LIFFE, 513, 514, 517–519
European Central Bank (ECB), 97–98
European Commission, 98
European terms, 5
European-type options, 542, 543n
European Union (EU)
  accounting standards and, 246
  explanation of, 97–98
European Venture Capital Association,
    406
Euro STOXX 50, 377
Evans, M. D., 111n, 127
Event-driven funds, 413–414

Exchange rate determination
  asset market approach and, 70–77
  balance of payments approach and, 62–70
  fundamental value based on absolute PPP
    and, 59
  fundamental value based on relative PPP
    and, 59–62
  purchasing power parity and, 56–59, 72,
    101–105
Exchange rate forecasting
  central bank intervention and, 114–115
  econometric approach to, 111–112
  explanation of, 107–108
  rational and efficient markets and, 108–111
  statistical models used in, 130–137
  technical analysis and, 112–114
  use and performance of, 115–118
Exchange rates. *See also* Foreign exchange ex-
    pectations; Foreign exchange forecast-
    ing; Foreign exchange markets
  asset market approach and, 72–76
  asset returns and movement of, 146–147
  break-even, 337
  direct, 4, 147–148
  explanation of, 16
  fiscal policy and, 41
  fixed, 42–43
  flexible, 42
  floating, 96–97, 115
  forward, 14–21, 44, 52, 108
  historical background of, 92–99
  implied forward, 336–337
  indirect, 4
  jumps in, 110, 131–132
  monetary policy and, 40–41
  overview of, 32
  pegged, 43–44, 95–96
  spot, 14–15, 44
Exchange traded funds (ETFs)
  advantages and disadvantages of, 223–224,
    380–382
  applications of, 385–386
  explanation of, 222–223, 377, 681
  recent developments of, 377–378
  risks in, 384–385
  structure of, 378–380
  types of, 382–384
Execution costs
  approaches to reducing, 211–214
  components of, 206–208
  estimation and uses of, 208–211
  of international investments, 479–480
  overview of, 206
Exercise price, 542. *See also* Strike price
Expense ratio, 374
Expert systems, 135–136
Expiration date, 542
External crossing, 211–212
Ezra, D. D., 736

Fabozzi, F. J., 327n, 370
Fama, E., 110n, 127, 170, 182
Federal National Mortgage Association, 354
Federal Reserve Board, 313
Ferson, W. E., 170, 182, 712, 736
Filter rule, 113
Financial account, 35, 64–65
Financial analysis. *See* International analysis
Financial leases, 250
Financing squeeze, 417

Firstenberg, P. M., 388n, 397, 448
Fischer, S., 90
Fisher, Irving, 48, 49, 71, 94
Five forces analysis, 269
Fixed exchange rates, 42–43
Fleming, J., 522n, 570
Flexible exchange rates, 42
Floating exchange rates
  background of, 96–97
  central banks and, 115
Floating-rate notes (FRNs)
  bear, 352–353
  bull, 351–352
  default risk and, 348–351
  explanation of, 344–346
  no default risk and, 346–348
Forbes, K., 481n, 505
Ford Motor Company, 282–283
Foreign bonds. *See also* Bonds
  explanation of, 313
  issued by emerging countries, 320
  return and risk from investing in, 338, 339
Foreign currency (FC)
  explanation of, 4, 5
  interest rate parity and, 16–18, 20
  to measure asset returns, 146–147
  restrictions placed on, 490
Foreign currency risk premiums
  domestic CAPM and, 151–152
  international CAPM and, 154–156, 160
Foreign exchange expectations
  explanation of, 45, 52–53, 105–106
  practical implications of, 106–107
Foreign exchange forecasting
  central bank intervention and, 114–115
  econometric approach to, 111–112
  explanation of, 107–108
  rational and efficient markets and, 108–111
  statistical models used in, 130–137
  technical analysis and, 112–114
  use and performance of, 115–118
Foreign exchange markets. *See also* Exchange
    rates
  asset market approach and, 70–77
  balance of payments and, 34–35, 62–70
  basic principles of, 3–5
  bid-ask quotations and spreads and, 5–7
  cross-rates and, 7–10
  current account deficits and, 35–38
  economic performance and, 40
  efficiency of, 108–111
  exchange rate regimes and, 42–44
  explanation of, 5
  fiscal policy and, 41
  foreign exchange expectation and, 52–54
  forward quotes and, 14–21
  fundamental value based on absolute PPP
    and, 59
  fundamental value based on relative PPP
    and, 59–62
  inflation and, 38–39
  interest rate parity and, 45
  International Fisher relation and, 48–50
  international parity relations and global as-
    set management and, 55
  monetary policy and, 40–41
  overview of, 3
  purchasing power parity and, 46–48, 56–59
  quotations and, 3–7
  real interest rates and, 39

supply and demand and, 33–34
uncovered interest rate parity and, 50–51
Forex convention, 3–4
Forsey, H. J., 717, 737
Forward contracts
  explanation of, 508–509
  futures vs., 509–511
  markets for, 511
  use of, 522–528
  value of, 517, 519–522
Forward exchange rates
  explanation of, 14–21, 44, 108
  foreign exchange expectation and, 52
  interest rate parity and, 16–21
  market efficiency and, 108–110
  quotes for, 14–16
Forward swaps, 531
Fottrel, Quentin, 259n
Foundations, 684
401(k) plans, 683
Fractal models, 135
Franchise factor, 286
Franchise value
  example of, 288–289
  explanation of, 285–288
Frankel, J. A., 100n, 110n, 127, 128
Frank Russell Company (FRC) index, 397
Free and clear equity, 387
Free float, 490
French, K., 169, 170, 182, 310
Front-end load, 374
Front-loaded interest-reduction bonds
  (FLIRBs), 322
Froot, K. A., 110n, 127, 505, 710, 736
FTSE, 203, 204
Full replication, 688
Fundamental value
  based on purchasing price parity, 59–62
  explanation of, 141
Funds of funds (FOF), 414–415
Fung, W., 421, 448, 645n, 674
Futures
  bond, 514–516
  commodity, 512–513
  currency, 511–512, 520–521
  explanation of, 508–509
  forward contracts vs., 509–511
  hedging with, 573–575
  interest rate, 513–517
  markets for, 511–517
  opportunity costs and, 212–213
  stock, 516–517
  use of, 522–528
  value of, 517, 519–522
Futures funds, 413

GAAP. *See* Generally accepted accounting
  principles (GAAP)
Galler, M., 128
Garbe, B., 484n, 505
GARCH, 111, 133–134, 475n, 583n
GDP country weights, 707
Generally accepted accounting principles
  (GAAP). *See also* Accounting standards;
  International Accounting Standards
  (IAS)
  convergence of IAS and, 246, 247
  differences between IAS and various na-
  tional, 246–253

earnings and stock prices and, 254–255
explanation of, 206, 216, 244
information content of international differ-
  ences in, 255–256
General Motors Corporation, 281–283
Geometric average, 624n
Gérard, B., 169, 170, 182, 484n, 506
Gibson, M. S., 481n, 505
Gibson, R., 432n, 448
Glass-Steagall Act, 313
Glen, J., 118n, 128
Global Depository Receipts (GDRs), 216,
  217
Global financial ratio analysis, 279–281
Global investment industry
  brokers in, 685–686
  consultants and advisers in, 686–687
  custodians in, 687
  investment managers in, 684–685
  investors in, 679–684
Global Investment Performance Standards
  (GIPS), 644, 648–650
Global investments
  active approach to, 689–690
  balanced or specialized, 691–692
  currency approach to, 694
  industry or country approach to, 692
  passive approach to, 688–689
  philosophy of, 688
  quantitative or subjective approach to, 695
  style management approach to, 693–694
  top-down or bottom-down approach,
  692–693
Global macro funds, 413
Global performance evaluation (GPE)
  implementation of, 625, 645–650
  performance appraisal in, 618–619,
  637–645
  performance attribution in, 617–618,
  626–637
  performance measurement in, 617,
  619–626
  principles and objectives of, 616–619
Goetzmann, W., 397, 423n, 448, 474, 475n,
  483, 506, 645n, 674
Gold
  motivation for investing in, 430–431
  price determinants for, 431–432
Gold mining companies, 433
Gold standard
  abandonment of, 94–95
  explanation of, 42–43, 95
  historical background of, 92–93
Goldstein, R. S., 370
Gonzalo, M., 637n, 674
Goodhart, C.A.E., 115n, 128
Goodsall, W.A.R., 712n, 736
Goodwill, 250
Goodwin, T. H., 641n, 674
Gordon, Jacques, 399
Government regulation, 478–479
Grammatikos, T., 583n, 614
Grant, D., 583n, 614
Grantor trusts, 378
Grauer, F., 182
Gray, S., 114n, 127, 132n, 254, 310
Griffin, J. M., 279n, 310
Griffin, M. W., 708, 736
Grinold, R. C., 641, 674, 717, 737
Griswold, John, 408

Gross domestic product (GDP)
  business cycles and, 260
  country analysis and, 257, 258
  current account deficit and, 37–38
  growth theory and, 261
  industry sales growth rate and, 265
  international indexes based on, 647
Grossman, G., 101n, 102n, 128
Growth factor, 286
Growth theory, 261–262
Gruber, M., 143n, 182
Guaranteed products, 550
Gyourko, J., 397, 448

Hacker, Doug, 427
Hanna, J., 594n, 614
Harlow, W. V., 716, 737
Hartzell, D. J., 398, 448
Harvey, C. R., 170, 181, 182, 488, 491, 505,
  506, 712, 736, 737
Heckman, C. R., 182
Hedge funds
  background of, 406, 408
  biases related to, 421–423
  classification of, 410–414
  fee structure for, 410
  funds of funds, 414–415
  legal structure of, 409–410
  leverage and, 416
  objectives of, 409
  persistence of performance of, 423–424
  risks for, 416–417
  track record of, 417, 419421
Hedge ratios
  application of, 158–159
  for bonds, 526–527
  explanation of, 153
  minimum-variance, 524–526, 576–579
  optimal, 580–581
  regression, 154n
  unitary, 524–526
  universal, 711
Hedging
  advantages and disadvantages of, 527–528
  currency, 158–159, 339–340, 648
  explanation of, 523–524
  with futures or forward currency contracts,
  573–584
  imperfect, 527
  long, 523
  with options, 587–589
  regression, 526
  short, 523
  strategies for, 339–340, 589–590
  volatility and, 518–519
Hedonic price estimation, 389–391
Hensel, C. R., 637, 674
Herfindahl index, 265–266
Hietla, P. T., 158n, 183
High-net-worth individuals (HNWIs),
  679–680
Hillion, P., 484n, 506
Hirsch, J., 449
Hodrick, R. J., 105n, 111n, 127, 128, 712, 736
Hoesli, M., 398, 448
HOLDRs, 378, 381, 383
Hong Kong Tracker Fund, 377, 382
Hooke, Jeffrey C., 448
Hopkins, P., 279n, 310
Hsieh, D. A., 421n, 448, 645n, 674

Huang, M., 536n, 570
Huang, R., 235
Hudson-Wilson, Susan, 386n, 448
Huizanga, J., 111n, 128
Hull, J. C., 524n, 549, 570

IAS. *See* International Accounting Standards (IAS)
Ibbotson, R. G., 397, 423n, 448, 645n, 674
IBM, 202
ICAPM. *See* International CAPM
Illiquidity premium, 704–705
Implementation shortfall, 208–209
Implied forward exchange rates
  application of, 337–338
  explanation of, 336–337
Income approach, to real estate valuation, 391–392
Index funds, 688–689
Index of market momentum, 113
Indications of interest, 212
Indirect exchange rate, 4
Indirect quotes, 4
Industry analysis
  country analysis and, 256–262
  overview of, 256
  return expectation elements and, 262–268
  risk elements and, 268–273
Industry approach, 692
Industry concentration, 265–266
Industry life cycle, 264–265
Industry valuation, 277–279
Inflation, 289–291
Inflation factor, 295
Inflation-Indexes Securities, 432
Inflation rate differentials
  exchange rate movement and, 53
  explanation of, 44–45
  international Fisher relation and, 48–50
Inflation rates
  currency appreciation and depreciation and, 39
  explanation of, 44–45
  measurement of, 60
Information
  forecasting and variables related to, 133
  international analysis and access to, 240–241, 255–256
Information ratio, 641–642
Initial margin, 508
Initial public offerings (IPOs), 402, 403
In-kind redemption, 222, 378, 379
Insider trading, 478
Institutional investors
  endowments and foundations as, 684
  insurance companies as, 684
  mutual funds as, 680–681
  pension funds as, 681–683
Insurance companies, 684
Integrated markets, 141–142
Interest Equalization Tax (IET), 313
Interest rate differentials
  explanation of, 44, 51, 55, 100
  forward discount and, 53
  relations to, 53–54
Interest rate futures, 513–517
Interest rate options, 545–546
Interest rate parity (IRP)
  example of, 45–46, 151
  explanation of, 16–21, 45, 54, 100

international CAPM and, 150
  uncovered, 45, 50–51
Interest rates
  asset market approach and, 71–72
  currency appreciation and depreciation and, 39
  explanation of, 44
  international Fisher relation and, 48–50
Interest rate sensitivity, 332–333
Interest rate swaps, 513n, 530–531, 535, 540
Internal crossing, 211
International Accounting Standards Board (IASB)
  core standards of, 246
  function of, 244, 246, 247
International Accounting Standards Committee (IASC), 244
International Accounting Standards (IAS)
  asset revaluation and, 250
  business combinations and, 247–248
  consolidation and, 248–249
  differences between various national GAAP and, 246–253
  in emerging markets, 489–490
  employee stock options and, 251–253
  explanation of, 206, 244
  financial assets and derivatives and, 251
  financial leases and, 250
  goodwill and, 250
  joint ventures and, 250
  pensions and, 251
  provisions and, 250–251
  United States and, 246
International analysis
  information issues and, 240–241, 255–256
  overview of, 238–240
  vision of world and, 241–242
International CAPM
  capital market expectations and, 701–702, 704
  currency hedge ratios and, 158, 159
  currency hedging and, 158, 159
  explanation of, 150, 158
  foreign currency risk premiums and, 152, 154–156, 160
  investment horizon and, 160
  risk-pricing relation and, 153–154
  separation theorem and, 152–153
  tests of, 169–170
International diversification
  case against, 472–481
  case for, 481–486
  currency risk and, 471–472
  emerging markets and, 486–491
  global industry factors and, 484–485
  global investing vs., 483–484
  overview of, 452–454
  portfolio return performance and, 464–471
  regional and country factors and, 485
  risk reduction and, 454–464
International Finance Corporation (IFC), 203, 461
International Fisher relation
  example of, 50
  exchange rate and, 100–101
  explanation of, 45, 48–50
International Monetary Fund (IMF), 95
International monetary system
  euro and, 97–99
  floating exchange rates and, 96–97

gold standard and, 92–93
  interest rate parity and, 100
  international Fisher relation and, 100–101
  pegged exchange rates and, 95–97
  purchasing power parity and, 101–105
International Organization of Securities Commissions (IOSCO), 244–246
International Securities Market Association (ISMA), 319
International Swaps and Derivatives Association (ISDA), 529, 532
In the money, 547
Intrinsic value, 546, 547
Inverse optimization, 717
Investment companies
  explanation of, 373
  fees charged by, 374–376
  net asset value of, 373–374
  strategies of, 374
Investment Company Act, 378, 409–410
Investment industry. *See* Global investment industry
Investment managers, 684–685
Investment policy statement (IPS)
  elements of, 696–698
  explanation of, 695–696
Investors
  institutional, 680–684
  private, 679–680
iShares, 378, 383

Jacquillat, B., 432n, 448
Jaeger, Lars, 428n, 448
Janakiramanan, S., 158n, 182, 220, 235
Jarchow, Stephen P., 386n, 448
J-curve effect, 66, 166, 167
Jenkins, G. M., 127, 132
Jensen, G. R., 712, 737
Jensen measures, 640
Jobman, Darrell R., 449
Johnson, G., 221, 235
Johnson, K. M., 234
Johnson, R. R., 712, 737
Joint ventures, 250
Jordan, J., 379n, 448
Jorion, P., 118n, 128, 132n, 159n, 183, 506, 595, 614, 640, 674, 710, 737
Jumps, 110, 131–132

Kahn, R. N., 641, 674, 712, 737
Kaminsky, G., 105n, 128
Kaplanis, E., 169, 182
Karnosky, D. S., 637, 674
Keim, D. B., 397, 448
Kennedy, Mike, 409n
Keyes, John Maynard, 94
Kirsten, G., 640, 674
Klibanoff, P., 235
Kogelman, S., 289n, 310
Kolb, R. W., 549, 570
Kothari, S. P., 170, 183
Krail, R., 423n, 448, 644n, 674, 701n, 736
Kroner, K. F., 127, 134n, 583n, 614
Krugman, P., 90
Kryzanowski, L., 128

Lai, K. S., 102n, 127
Lamont, O., 235
Leahy, M. P., 115n, 128
Lederman, M., 637n, 674

Leg, 528
Legacy rates, 97
Lehmann, B., 707, 736
Leibowitz, M. L., 286, 289n, 310
Lerner, Josh, 406, 448
Lessard, D. R., 256, 309
Leverage, 416
Leveraged equity, 387
Levich, R. M., 118n, 128, 256, 310
Lewis, K., 111n, 114n, 127, 128
Lhabitant, F., 417n, 448
Li, L., 474, 475n, 483, 506
LIBOR rate, 345–353, 530–531, 545, 546
Liew, J., 423n, 448, 644n, 674, 701n, 736
Life insurance companies, 684
Limited liability corporations, 409
Limited partnerships, 409
Liquidity
 market, 197–198
 market efficiency and, 477–478
Liquidity risk, 416
Litterman, R., 717, 736
Litzenberger, R., 182
Liu, C., 398, 448
Liu, P. C., 105n, 128
Loads, 374
Logistics, 273–277
London International Financial Futures
    Exchange (LIFFE), 573
London Stock Exchange, 194, 203
Long hedge, 523
Longin, F., 474n, 475n, 482, 506
Long-run moving average (LRMA), 112–113
Long/short funds, 411–413
Long Term Capital Management (LTCM),
    416, 417
Loretan, M., 481n, 482, 505, 506
Losq, E., 158n, 182
Lothian, J., 101n, 102n, 128
Louth, Nick, 555n
Lucas, R., 183
Lyons, R. K., 118n, 128

MacArthur, M. A., 100n, 128
Macaulay duration of bonds, 332
Macroeconomic factors, 294–296
Maddala, G. S., 105n, 128
Maginn, J., 695, 699n, 737
Magnus, George, 67
Maintenance margin, 508
Managed futures funds, 413, 428
Managed investment companies, 378
Management fees, 479–480
Manager universe comparison, 646
Margins, 508–509, 543
Mark, N., 102n, 129
Market analysis, 713, 715
Market competition, 268–269
Market efficiency. *See* Efficient markets
Market equilibrium, 143
Market impact, 207, 208
Market makers, 188–189
Market-neutral funds, 411–412
Market risk, 145
Markets. *See also* Emerging markets; Equities
    markets; Foreign exchange markets
 concentration of, 198–199
 correlations in volatile, 474–476, 481–483
 developed, 195–197
 efficient, 108–110, 140–143

emerging, 197, 198
 historical differences in, 186–187
 integrated, 141–142
 liquidity of, 197–198
 segmented, 141–143, 157–158, 170
 size of, 195–198
Market timing, 634, 690
Market-timing risk, 295
Marsh, P., 736
Martellini, L., 417n, 447
Martin, J. S., 370
Mathur, I., 115n, 118n, 129
McCarthy, D., 417n, 448
McCrary, S. A., 416n, 449
McFall Lamm, R., Jr., 432n, 449
McKibbin, Warwick, 99
McLeavey, D., 310, 455n, 505, 736
Mean-variance optimization, 716–717
Medsker, L., 129
Meese, R., 111n, 129
Meltzer, A., 128
Mercer, J. M., 712, 737
Mergers, 414
Merrill Lynch, 377, 378
Michaud, R., 374n, 737
Midcap 400 SPDR, 378
Migration probability, 334
Miller, H., 279n, 310
Minimum-variance hedge ratio, 524–526,
    576–579
Model mining, 137
Moments
 explanation of, 130
 statistical models with constant, 131–132
 time-varying, 132–134
Momentum models, 113
Monetary policy, 40–41
Monetary system. *See* International monetary
    system
Money, 3
Money market, 71–72
Money-weighted return (MWR)
 approximation to, 621–622
 explanation of, 619–621
 over long horizons, 624, 625
Moore, B., 432n, 448
Morgan Stanley Capital International
    (MSCI), 202–203, 460
Morningstar, 681
Mortgages, 387
Moving-average models, 112–113
MSCI Europe. Australasia and Far East
    (EAFE) index, 203, 461, 636, 689
MSCI World Index, 642
Mull, S. R., 398, 449
Murphy, J. J., 129
Mussavian, M., 449
Mutual funds, 680–681
Myners report, 213

Nalebuff, B., 267, 309
Napoleon I, 187
Nasdaq, 189, 479
NASDAQ-100 QQQ, 378
National Association of Pension Funds
    (NAPF), 649, 650
National Association of Real Estate
    Investment Trusts (NAREIT), 397
National Association of Securities Dealers
    (NASD), 319

National Council of Real Estate Investments
    Fiduciaries (NCREIF) index, 397
Neal, R., 234
Neely, C. J., 114n, 118n, 129
Neoclassical growth theory, 261
Nesbitt, S. L., 710, 737
Net asset value (NAV)
 of closed-end country funds, 219–221
 of exchange traded funds, 379, 381, 383,
    384
 explanation of, 219
 of investment companies, 373–374
Net errors and omissions, 35n
Net operating income (NOI), 391, 392
Neural networks, 136
New-money bonds (NMBs), 322
New York Stock Exchange (NYSE), 188n,
    190n, 191, 198, 215, 453
N firm concentration ratio, 265–266
Niculescu, P., 594n, 614
Nikkei 225, 382
Nikkei Stock Average, 202
Nobel, Alfred, 684
Nobel Foundation, 684
Nokia, 199
Nominal exchange rates, 147, 148
Normal distribution, 131
Notional bonds, 514, 515
Notional yield, 515

Obstfeld, M., 90
Odier, P., 466, 506
Offer, 5
Official parity, 42
Official reserve account, 35, 65–66
Offshore corporations, 409
Offshore funds, 410
One-Chicago, 517
Open-end funds, 221–222
Operating fees, 374
Opportunity costs
 explanation of, 207–208
 futures and, 212–213
Optimization sampling, 689
Options
 American-type, 542
 currency, 543–544
 dynamic hedging with, 587–589
 European-type, 542
 explanation of, 542
 insuring with, 584–587
 interest rate, 545–546
 market organization for, 542–543
 stock, 544–545
 use of, 549–552
 value of, 546–549
Order-driven markets
 benefits and drawbacks of, 191–193
 explanation of, 189–190
Oster, S. M., 269, 310
Osterberg, W. P., 114n, 127
Out of the money, 546
Overall balance, 35
Overshooting, 76
Over-the-counter currency options, 543
Over-the-counter (OTC) market
 forward contracts and, 509
 options and, 543, 545
 swaps and, 529

Par bonds, 322
Paris Bourse, 187, 217
Parity
  explanation of, 42, 45
  interest rate, 16–21, 45–46
  official, 42
  purchasing power, 46–48
Parity relations
  explanation of, 91
  global asset management and international, 55–56
Passive approach, 688–689
Past-due interest bonds (PDIs), 322
Patel, S. A., 488, 506
Pearson, R. G., 712, 736
Peer group comparison, 646
Pegged exchange rates
  background of, 95–96
  explanation of, 43–44
Pension Act of 1995, 647
Pension funds
  accounting standards for, 251
  approaches to managing, 691
  asset allocation of, 708, 709
  benchmark use by, 646, 647
  defined benefit, 682–683
  defined contribution, 683
  explanation of, 681–682
  external managers for, 686–687
  regulations for, 648, 649
Performance appraisal
  biases in, 644–645
  explanation of, 618–619, 637, 698
  risk-adjusted, 639–642
  risk allocation and budgeting and, 642–643
  risk and, 538–639
Performance attribution
  asset allocation and, 632–633
  currency management and, 636
  example of, 633–634
  explanation of, 617–618, 698
  industry and sectors and, 634
  market timing and, 634
  multicurrency returns and, 626–630
  presentations for, 634–636
  quarterly to multiannual performance and, 637
  risk decomposition and, 634
  security selection and, 631
Performance evaluation, 698. *See also* Global performance evaluation (GPE)
Performance measurement, 617. *See also* Rate of return
Pérold, A., 710n, 737
Perpetuity, 391
Perry, Michelle, 249
Peruga, R., 105n, 128
Peters, E., 129, 135n
Pickel, Robert, 533
Pink sheets, 215
Pinto, J., 310, 455n, 505, 736
Poisson distributions, 132
Pope, P. F., 310
PORTAL, 215
Porter, M. E., 266, 267n, 269, 310
Portfolios
  beta of, 145
  efficient, 458–459
  emerging markets and, 489–490
  return performance of, 464–471

  total risk of, 454–456
  variance of, 455
POSIT®, 194
Poterba, J., 169, 182, 310
PPP. *See* Purchasing power parity (PPP)
Prasad, B., 711n, 736
Pratt, Shannon P., 424n, 425, 449
Present value of growth opportunities (PVGO), 286
Price-driven markets
  benefits and drawbacks of, 191–193
  execution costs and, 207
  explanation of, 189–190
Price-earnings (P/E) ratios
  explanation of, 255
  intrinsic, 285, 286
Price manipulation, 478
Pricing. *See* Asset pricing; Capital asset-pricing model (CAPM)
Pricing risk, 417
Principal trade, 212
Pring, M. J., 129
Private investors, 679–680
Program trading, 211
Provisions, accounting standards for, 250–251
Purchasing power parity (PPP)
  absolute, 46, 59
  exchange rate determination and, 56–59, 72, 101–105
  explanation of, 45, 46, 50, 51
  gold standard and, 93
  relative, 47–48, 59–62
Puts, 542, 549

Quality spread, 334
Quan, D. C., 398, 449
Quantification, 695
Quebec Securities Act, 215

Radebaugh, L. H., 254, 310
Rate of return
  money-weighted, 619–622
  over long horizons, 624–626
  time-weighted, 619, 623, 624
Ratio analysis, 279–281
Ravichandran, R., 432n, 448
Raynor, M., 264, 310
Real estate indexes, 396–397
Real estate investments
  foreign interest in, 399–400
  forms of, 387–388
  overview of, 386–387
  in portfolio context, 396–398
  valuation of, 388–396
Real estate investment trusts (REITs), 388, 397
Real estate limited partnerships (RELPs), 388
Real exchange rates, 147–148
Real interest rates
  currency appreciation and depreciation and, 39
  international Fisher relation and, 48–50
Redemption fees, 374
Rees, W. P., 310
Reference currency, 617
Regression hedge, 526
Regression hedge ratios, 154n
Reiganum, M., 522n, 570

Reilly, F., 183, 310, 640n, 674
Reilly, Robert F., 424n, 425, 449
Relative PPP
  explanation of, 47–48
  fundamental value based on, 59–62
Research, 713, 715
Residual risk, 145
Return on assets (ROA), 279–280
Return over equity (ROE), 280, 286–288
Reward-to-variability measure, 639
Rigobon, R., 481n, 505
Rijnen, Zarina, 400n
Risk
  absolute, 638
  buyer power and, 270
  credit, 334–335, 535–537
  currency, 471–472
  default, 534–535
  economic, 578
  government participation and, 272
  hedging total currency, 578–579
  levels of, 272–273
  market, 145, 551
  market competition and, 268–269
  new entrants and, 271–272
  in performance appraisal, 644–645
  residual, 145
  rivalry intensity and, 269–270
  rollover, 538, 540
  specific, 145
  substitutes and, 270
  supplier power and, 271
  translation, 578
  types of, 268
  value chain competition and, 269
Risk allocation, 634, 642–643
Risk arbitrage, 414
Risk budgeting, 634, 643
Risk-factor models
  industry and country, 292–293
  macroeconomic, 294–296
  practical use of, 296
  styles, 293–294
Risk premium, 106, 110, 149, 703
Risk-pricing relation
  domestic CAPM and, 144–145
  international CAPM and, 153–154
Risk reduction
  with swaps, 540–542
  through attractive correlations, 454–464
Rivalry intensity, 269–270
Roach, Stephen, 68
Robinson, T., 310
Robinson, Thomas R., 237n
Rogoff, K., 90, 101n, 102n, 111n, 128–129
Roll, R., 145, 183, 294, 309, 432n, 448, 640, 674
Rollover risk, 538, 540
Root mean squared error (RMSE), 117
Rosenberg, M., 129
Ross, S., 294, 309, 388n, 397, 448
Roulet, J., 482, 506, 712, 737
Rouwenhorst, G., 474, 475n, 483, 506
Runkle, D., 455n, 505, 736
Russell 1000, 383
Russell 3000, 383

Sales comparison approach, to real estate valuation, 389–390
Sales-driven franchise value, 286

Salomon Smith Barney, 203
S&P Depositary Receipts, 377, 383
S&P Global 1200 index, 203
S&P/IFCG composite index, 461
S&P/IFC indexes, 203–204, 683
S&P Micropal, 681
S&P 500 SPDR, 378
Sankar, A., 488, 506
Sargent, Thomas, 93, 95
Saunders, A., 583n, 614
Schieneman, G. S., 310
Schilit, W. Keith, 400, 449
Schneeweiss, Thomas, 221, 235, 449
Scholes, M., 546, 549, 570
Schroder, Gerhard, 98
Schulman, E., 710, 737
Schwartz, E., 432n, 448, 449
Schweihs, Robert P., 424n, 425, 449
SEAQ International, 217
Sector rotation, 267–268
Sector SPDRs, 378
Securities and Exchange Commission (SEC)
  bonds and, 313, 327
  Investment Company Act and, 410
  requirements of, 215, 216, 648
Security market line, 145
Segmented markets
  asset pricing and, 157–158, 170
  emerging economies and, 491
  explanation of, 141–143
  risk premium, 702–703
Senbet, L. W., 220, 235
Separation theorem
  domestic CAPM and, 144
  international CAPM and, 152–153
Sercu, P., 158, 183
SETS (Stock Exchange Electronic Trading
  Service), 191
Settlement risk, 417
Shanghai Petrochemical Co., 205
Shanken, J., 170, 183
Shanley, M., 268n, 309
Sharpe, William F., 143n, 183, 372, 449, 639,
  674
Sharpe ratio
  explanation of, 420, 639–640, 702
  international diversification and, 464, 465
Short hedge, 523
Short-run moving average (SRMA), 112, 113
Short squeeze risk, 417
Simon, D., 583n, 613
Singer, B., 637, 644n, 674, 675
Singer, Brian, 373, 449, 701, 704n, 737
Singer, D., 707, 736
Single-stock futures, 517, 518
Singleton, K., 350n, 370
Sloan, R. G., 170, 183
Sociétés d'Investissement á Capital Variable
  (SICAV), 681
Söderberg, Bo, 390n, 449
Soenen, L. A., 398, 449
Solnik, B., 106n, 118n, 127, 129, 133n, 158,
  169, 182, 183, 466, 475n, 482, 485,
  505–506, 583n, 614, 711n, 712, 736, 737
Sortino, F. A., 717, 737
SPAN, 509
Spaulding, D., 637n, 675
SPDRs, 378
Specialized approach, 691–692
Special purpose entities (SPEs), 248, 249

Specific risk, 145
Speculation
  forward and futures contracts, 522–523
  options and, 550
Speidell, L. S., 254, 310
Sponsored ADR, 216
Spot currency options, 543
Spot exchange rates
  explanation of, 14–15
  forward exchange rates and, 108–110
Spreads, 6
Spurgin, R., 417n, 448
Squires, Jan R., 186n
Stapleton, R. C., 158n, 183
Startz, R., 90
Staub, R., 373, 449, 644n, 675, 701n, 704n,
  737
Stauton, M., 736
Steady state, in growth theory, 261
Stock exchanges
  automation in, 189–194
  bank, 187
  cross-border alliances of, 194
  historical background of, 186–187
  private, 187
  public, 187
  size of, 195–197
  trading procedures in, 188–189
Stock futures, 516–517
Stock indexes
  domestic, 202
  explanation of, 202
  global, 202–204
  use of, 204–205
Stock index futures, 516–517, 590–591
Stock market crash of 1987, 475, 476
Stock markets. *See also* Equities markets
  correlation across, 459–461, 463–464
  economic growth and performance of, 260
  emerging, 486–487
  international diversification and, 452–454,
    466–471
  risk of, 454–455
Stock options, 544–545
Stocks
  effects of inflation on, 289–291
  growth, 293
  inflation-like effects of currency movements
    on, 291–292
  value, 293
Stock valuation
  models for, 284–286
  role of market efficiency in, 283–284
Stowe, J., 310
Strange, B., 118n, 129
Strategic asset allocation (SAA), 689,
  706–711, 716
Stratified sampling, 689
Strengthening of currency, 3
Strike date, 542
Strike price, 542, 549
Structured notes, 344–345, 550, 552
Stulz, R., 183, 279n, 310
Style management, 693–694
Subjective analysis, 111, 112
Subrahmanyam, M. G., 158n, 183
Substitute products, 270
Sultan, J., 583n, 614
Summers, Lawrence, 115
Sundaresan, S. M., 350n, 370

Swaps
  amortizing, 531–532
  basis, 531
  currency, 511, 530, 534, 536
  currency-interest rate, 531
  customized, 531–532
  default, 532
  equity, 532
  explanation of, 528–529
  forward, 531
  interest rate, 513n, 530–531, 535, 540
  market organization for, 529
  total return, 532
  use of, 537–542
  value of, 533–537
Synthetic replication, 689
Szakmary, A. C., 115n, 118n, 129

Tactical asset allocation (TAA), 689, 706,
  711–712
Tajbakhsh, S., 712, 737
Takahashi, Dean, 403n
Tapley, Mark, 647, 691
Taxes
  discriminatory, 490
  international investment and, 199–201, 480
Taylor, M., 101n, 102n, 117n, 128, 129
Technical analysis
  computer models in, 113
  of exchange rates, 112–114
  forecast performance and, 115–118
Temple, P., 242, 310
10-K reports, 240
Terhaar, K., 373, 449, 644n, 675, 701n, 704n,
  737
Tesar, L., 169, 183
Thaler, R. H., 128
Thomas, L., 118n, 128
Thomson First Call, 241
Tilton, Glenn, 427
Time horizon factor, 295
Time value, 547
Time varying expected return, 132–133
Time-weighted return (TWR)
  example of, 624
  explanation of, 619, 623
  over long horizons, 624, 625
Timmermann, A., 707, 736
TIP 35 (Toronto Index Participation Fund),
  377
Titman, S., 398, 449
Tokyo Stock Exchange, 192
Top-down approach, 692
Top-down/bottom-up approach, 693
TOPIX, 382
Total factor productivity (TFP), 262
Total return swaps, 532
Toyota Motor Corporation, 281–282
Tracking error, 638–639
Trading techniques, 211–214
Transaction costs. *See* Execution costs
Translation risk, 578
Treasury-Eurodollar spread (TED spread
  swap), 531
Treasury Inflation Protected Securities
  (TIPS), 432
Treynor measures, 640
Triangular arbitrage, 7, 12–14
Trippi, R., 129
Turban, E., 129

Tuttle, D., 695, 699n, 737
Tweedie, Sir David, 249

UAL Corp., 426–427
Uncovered interest rate parity, 45, 50–51
Undertaking for Collective Investments in
    Transferable Securities (UCITS), 681
Unilever Superannuation Fund, 646, 647
Unitary hedge ratio, 524–526
United Nations Conference on Trade and
    Development (UNCTAD), 262
Unit investment trusts (UITs), 378, 381,
    382
Unit trusts, 681
Unsponsored ADR, 215
Upstairs trading, 191
Urias, M. S., 234
U.S. Securities Act, 327

Value chain
  competition along, 269
  explanation of, 263–264
van Duyn, Aline, 533n
van Steenis, Huw, 532
Variance, 130–131
Velde, François, 93, 95n
Venture capital funds, 403, 405
Venture capital investments
  characteristics of, 401–403
  explanation of, 398

liquidation/divestment procedures for, 403,
    404
performance measurement for, 405,
    406
stages of, 400–401
value of, 404–406
Verlinden, M., 264, 310
Verschoor, W. F., 105n, 127
Viceira, Luis M., 699n, 736
Vines, David, 99
Viskanta, T. E., 488, 491, 505
Volatility
  correlation in markets experiencing,
      474–476, 481–483
  derivatives and, 518–519
  in emerging markets, 486, 488
  explanation of, 130
  option, 549
Volume-weighted average price (VWAP),
    207–209

Wahal, S., 234
Wang, Ko, 449
Wave-and-cycle models, 113
Weakening of currency, 3
WEBS, 378
Weiss, R., 484n, 505
Weller, P. A., 114n, 118n, 129
Werner, L., 169, 183
Whaley, R. E., 522n, 570

Wheatley, S., 234
Wiggins, Jenny, 248, 283n
Wilshire 500, 383
Winters, Bill, 533
Wizman, T. A., 235
Wolff, C. P., 105n, 127
Wolverton, Marvin L., 449
World Bank, 203
Wright, D. W., 128

XETRA, 190

Yield curve
  for bonds, 329, 334, 343
  international comparisons of, 335–338
Yield to maturity (YTMs)
  annual vs. semiannual, 330–331
  for coupon bonds, 330–331
  explanation of, 325–326
  portfolio management and, 343
  for zero-coupon bonds, 328–329
Young, Philip J., 186

Zaraba, 190
Zero-coupon bonds
  explanation of, 328–329
  implied forward exchange rate for, 337
Zero swap rates, 535
Zingales, L., 478n, 506
Zisler, R. C., 388n, 397, 448